Property of the Half blood

Springer Texts in Business and Economics

For further volumes:
http://www.springer.com/series/10099

Victor J. Tremblay • Carol Horton Tremblay

New Perspectives on Industrial Organization

With Contributions from Behavioral Economics and Game Theory

 Springer

Victor J. Tremblay
Department of Economics
Oregon State University
Corvallis, Oregon, USA

Carol Horton Tremblay
Department of Economics
Oregon State University
Corvallis, Oregon, USA

ISBN 978-1-4614-3240-1   ISBN 978-1-4614-3241-8 (eBook)
DOI 10.1007/978-1-4614-3241-8
Springer New York Heidelberg Dordrecht London

Library of Congress Control Number: 2012937657

Printed on acid-free paper

Springer is part of Springer Science+Business Media (www.springer.com)

Preface

Industrial organization explains how large corporations affect the utility of consumers and the profit of competitors. With few industries characterized by perfect competition or monopoly in today's world, most of the attention of industrial organization economists is focused on imperfectly competitive markets. When competition is limited, strategic play becomes central. A firm's profits will be affected by another firm's actions, unlike when there are no rivals as in monopoly or when there are many rivals as in perfect competition. To analyze strategic interactions among firms, the field of industrial organization turned to game theory. In the last several decades, the field has been transformed by contributions from game theory and more recently by behavioral economics.

Behavioral economics has an important role to play in studying imperfectly competitive markets. Lack of competition opens the door for the exercise of behavioral weaknesses on the part of managers, such as overconfidence, and for the exploitation of behavioral tendencies of consumers, such as cognitive dissonance and impulsivity. Although the contributions of game theory and behavioral economics have given us a better understanding of how real world markets work, most of the recent advances deriving from behavioral economics are concentrated in academic journals. Thus, our reason for writing *New Perspectives in Industrial Organization* is to synthesize this material into a single book.

Our overall philosophy is to bring information from different approaches to the study of industrial organization. We cover a wide range of research methods as well as topics. To understand the theoretical foundations of industrial organization requires knowledge of consumer, producer, and game theory. To get a grasp on deviations from theoretical predictions, we draw on psychological insights and experimental evidence from behavioral economics. We also incorporate empirical evidence from the application of statistics and econometrics techniques to data, and we present case studies. Ultimately, the goal is to combine theory, models, and evidence to gain a better understanding of imperfectly competitive markets and the rationale for public policy intervention.

Regarding mathematics, we recognize that many students may be unprepared in calculus. At the same time, we feel that many problems in economics cannot be thoroughly understood without the use of calculus. After all, marginal analysis and calculus are inherently linked. To make industrial organization accessible to students who do not know or feel comfortable with calculus, we take a three-pronged approach. We provide an appendix which contains the basic calculus that is needed for the book; couch all optimization results as cases where marginal benefit = marginal cost; and use only simple linear and quadratic functions. In our experience with this approach, students who have not had calculus have been able to understand the material. Appendix A also covers other math and basic econometrics tools.

The book is organized as follows. Part I provides an introduction to the field, a review of background material, and foundational information on game theory and behavioral economics. In Part II, we discuss nonstrategic issues related to market structure, including the markets of perfect competition, monopoly, and monopolistic competition, and product differentiation. Part III reviews the classic (static and dynamic) models of oligopoly theory and the estimation of market power. Part IV analyzes a myriad of business strategies, such as product design, price discrimination, advertising, research and development, and mergers. Part V summarizes our findings and investigates policy issues related to antitrust and economic regulation. It also contains several case studies, which illustrate how the knowledge found in this book enables us to better understand the real world.

We owe a large debt to many industrial organization scholars. Especially influential in terms of theory were the works of Cournot (1838), Bertrand (1883), Stackelberg (1934), Nash (1950), Stigler (1968), and Tirole (1988). We learned a great deal about empirical methods in industrial organization from Iwata (1974), Applebaum (1979, 1982), Bresnahan (1989), Gasmi et al. (1992), Slade (1995), Genesove and Mullin (1998), Corts (1999), and Perloff et al. (2007). The following studies about behavioral economics were especially beneficial: Simon (1955), Tversky and Kahneman (1981), Kahneman (2003), Akerlof and Kranton (2000, 2005), Glaeser (2004), Lo (2004), Camerer et al. (2005), Ellison (2006), McFadden (2006), and McClure et al. (2004a, b, 2007). Much of what we know about antitrust and regulation derives from Asch (1983, 1988), Viscusi et al. (2005), Sherman (2008), and Kwoka and White (2009). Finally, Scherer and Ross (1990) taught us about the facts and institutions that are most relevant to industrial organization. We apologize to those authors whose contributions we have omitted.

A number of colleagues and friends have been most helpful. First, we would like to thank our former professors, Yeon-Koo Che, Ray Deneckere, Greg Duncan, Bill Hallagan, Fred Inaba, Larry Samuelson, and Stan Smith. We would also like to thank Kenneth Elzinga for his valuable help throughout our careers. Colleagues and students who have been especially helpful with various parts of the book include

Jan Boone, Yang-Ming Chang, Rolf Färe, Stephen Farr, Roger Frantz, Philip Gayle, Avi Goldfarb, Jay Gokhale, Shawna Grosskopf, Lynn Hunnicutt, Kosin Isariya-wongse, Natsuko Iwasaki, Patty Jackson, Ed King, Terry King, James Konow, Yasushi Kudo, Mervin Kurniawan, Scott Logan, Jason Mann, Carlos Martins-Filho, Megan McCullough, Lacy Moore, Steve Polasky, Marc Rysman, Barry Seldon, Andrew Stivers, Ben Stoddard, Dan Stone, Jarod Thompson, Larry White, Michael Vardanyan, Thomas Williams, and Wenfeng Yan. We are also grateful to our editor, Jon Gurstelle, for his faith in us and in the project.

We would like to thank Mark Tremblay for graphing the figures and providing answers to the review questions. Lastly, we owe special thanks to our family and friends for their support. It goes without saying that any remaining errors are our own.

Corvallis, Oregon, USA   Victor J. Tremblay
                                                               Carol Horton Tremblay

Contents

List of Figures

Part I
Introductory and Review Material

Chapter 1
Introduction

The field of industrial organization encompasses a host of intriguing questions. Why do cell phone companies charge a fixed fee for a given number of minutes and a high price for each additional minute? Why do firms produce a vast number of brands? If advertising persuades consumers to buy something, are they better off? If two large firms merge, is society better or worse off? What if one of the firms is failing? These are just a few of the questions that are addressed in the book.

Even before taking a course in principles of microeconomics, most people realize that monopolies (i.e., markets with one firm) tend to charge higher prices than firms in competitive markets with many firms. That is, if we had a magic wand and could instantly change a competitive industry into one with a single seller, most people would predict an increase in price. In *Politics and Ethics*, Aristotle wrote about the problem of the high price associated with monopoly, which is frequently called an "unjust price." What is less understood is what happens between the limiting cases of monopoly and perfect competition, when markets are imperfectly competitive and have just a few sellers. Yet, most markets are imperfectly competitive.

Industrial organization, which is sometimes called industrial economics, analyzes the theory and empirical evidence of imperfectly competitive markets.[1] In this book, we emphasize three main topics. First, we are interested in studying the forces that shape market structure and the reasons why some industries have many producers while others have just a few.

Second, we analyze how markets function and the economic consequences of imperfect competition. Unlike competitive and monopoly markets, strategic behavior typically plays a key role in imperfect competition. Our understanding of firm strategy benefits from both game theory and behavioral economics. Game theory provides a rigorous foundation for studying the strategic actions of rational players. Behavioral economics provides insights from psychology and evidence from experiments to show that some consumers suffer from cognitive weaknesses and have

---

[1] Schmalensee (1988) provides an excellent overview of the field.

V.J. Tremblay and C.H. Tremblay, *New Perspectives on Industrial Organization*,
Springer Texts in Business and Economics, DOI 10.1007/978-1-4614-3241-8_1,
© Springer Science+Business Media New York 2012

preferences that are more complicated than traditional consumer theory would suggest. Contributions from behavioral economics help us to identify many of the marketing tactics that are used by firms to exploit these consumer traits.

Finally, we are interested in public policy towards business, especially with problems related to market power resulting from imperfect competition. Understanding how markets are structured and the economic consequences of imperfect competition will allow us to better evaluate the merits of antitrust and regulatory policy.

In this chapter, we provide a brief introduction to the field of industrial organization. We review its origins and discuss how behavioral economics is contributing to the field. Next, we outline policy issues that motivate much of the theoretical and empirical research in industrial organization. We also discuss the connections among theoretical ideas, economic models, and reality. Finally, we outline the topics and approaches used in the book.

1.1   The Origins and Methods of Industrial Organization

The field of industrial organization has been influenced by developments in other branches of economics and by various schools of thought. The theoretical underpinnings of the field derive from microeconomics, which provides the foundation for consumer theory, producer theory, and game theory. Industrial organization differs from microeconomic theory in that it puts greater emphasis on real-world markets, institutional arrangements, and empirical evidence. Our understanding of the real world has also been enhanced by behavioral economics, a relatively new field of economics that will be described more fully in the next section.

Before discussing the origins of industrial organization, it is important to emphasize that the field benefits from both theoretical analysis and empirical studies of real markets. Problems arise, however, when there is a disconnect between the two, a concern raised by Barbra Wootton over 70 years ago. According to Wootton (1938), 5), "What is lacking [in economics] is any effective means of communication between abstract theory and concrete application." Part of the problem is that it takes very different intellectual gifts to be successful in theoretical and applied research. This was clearly understood by Joseph Schumpeter (1954), 815) who said:

> There are such things as historical and theoretical temperaments. That is to say, there are types of minds that take delight in all the colors of historical processes and of individual cultural patterns. There are other types that prefer a neat theorem to everything else. We have use for both. But they are not made to appreciate one another.

On this issue, Shubik (1980, 21) argues that "it has been the tendency of these groups to work almost as though the other did not exist."

We will see that this tension has influenced the development of the field. Theoretical economists constructed precise models to describe imperfectly competitive markets. On the other hand, early empirical and institutional economists rejected theory and studied the real world to gain an understanding of such markets. Both approaches are valuable, and we strive to reach a balance between the two. As Leamer (2007, 4587) points out, we run into problems in our research when we take "theory too seriously" and when we fail to take "theory seriously enough."[2]

1.1.1   Early Theoretical Foundations

Although the ancients clearly understood the high price associated with monopolies, modern economic thought began with Adam Smith's publication of *The Wealth of Nations* in 1776, which discussed the benefits of competition and the costs of monopoly.[3] Formal models of competition and monopoly were not developed until the nineteenth century, however, and did not become widely disseminated until Alfred Marshall published *Principles of Economics* in 1890. His book was a major success because it was so accessible, emphasizing graphical over more advanced mathematical modeling techniques. Although monopoly and competitive models provide a clear picture of the polar extremes of market structure, they have one obvious limitation. Most real markets have just a few firms, differentiated products, and consumers and producers with limited information. These are qualities not found in perfectly competitive and simple monopoly models.

In the early 1930s, Chamberlin (1933) and Robinson (1933) developed models of imperfect competition.[4] Chamberlin's model of monopolistic competition gained immediate acceptance because it was simple and filled the gap between perfect competition and monopoly by allowing competing firms to produce differentiated products. The model has elements of both monopoly and perfect competition. Like monopoly, each firm has a monopoly over the sale of its particular brand and faces a negatively sloped demand function. Like perfect competition, there are no entry barriers and the market consists of many competitors, albeit competitors who sell differentiated products. The major drawback with the model is that with many competitors, strategic interaction is rendered nonexistent. That is, each firm is so small that the action of one firm has an insignificant effect on the profits and behavior of competing firms.

---

[2] This is consistent with his earlier work where Leamer (1996) argued that to do good research in economics, we must do three things. First, we must address relevant policy and scientific questions. Second, we need to develop theories that shed light on the question and help organize the data analysis. Finally, we need to use data that are consistent with theory and help answer the question at hand. See Varian (1997) for a discussion of the social value of economic theory.

[3] For a discussion of monopoly theory prior to Adam Smith, see De Roover (1951).

[4] For a discussion of the similarities and differences in their models, see Bellant (2004).

Strategic interaction can be critical in oligopoly markets, imperfectly competitive markets with just a few sellers. In this setting, the actions of one firm affect the behavior and profits of other firms. The first formal models were analyzed long before the model of monopolistic competition. Cournot (1838) developed a static duopoly model, an oligopoly model with just two firms that compete by simultaneously choosing output, and Bertrand (1883) developed a static duopoly model where two firms simultaneously choose price.[5] Although these models allowed for strategic interaction, they were essentially ignored by industrial organization economists until the second half of the twentieth century.

Part of the problem with Cournot's work in particular was that it was highly abstract and technical for its time. Bertrand (1883, 74) commented that Cournot's "ideas disappear under the abundance of mathematical symbols." Bertrand also criticized Cournot for making the unrealistic assumption that firms compete in output, when most real firms compete in price. Fisher (1898, 133) provided a more favorable review of Cournot's model and the use of mathematics in economics, stating that Cournot's work was ignored because "[i]t was too far in advance of the times." Today, the study of the Cournot and Bertrand models is the starting point for investigation of oligopoly theory.

Another early criticism of oligopoly theory is that it predicts that almost anything can happen. At one pole is the cartel model which predicts monopoly pricing. At the other is the simple Bertrand model that produces competitive pricing. The Cournot model produces an equilibrium price that is in between these extremes. We will see that game theory addresses this criticism by showing how the rules of the game (i.e., the institutional setting and the legal and market constraints) better align theoretical models with reality.

1.1.2   Institutional and Empirical Traditions

In the first half of the twentieth century, many economists were critical of the formal models of imperfect competition. Not only could these models produce any outcome from cartel to perfect competition,[6] critics argued that the formal models were overly abstract and had little connection to the real world. In response, economists from the "institutional school" used inductive analysis to study the effect of legal, social, public, and private institutions on the evolution of real-world markets. A notable example is the work by Clark (1927), who synthesized the economics of industry concentration with legal and political factors to study the role of government regulation.

---

[5] In addition, von Stackelberg (1934) developed a dynamic version of the Cournot model.

[6] This can be seen in Bowley's (1924) "conjectural variation" model of oligopoly that is summarized in Hicks (1935).

At the same time, empirical economists also contributed to the development of the field. They conducted case studies to investigate the pricing behavior and economic performance of large corporations and manufacturing industries. For example, Ripley (1907, 1916) analyzed growing industrial concentration in the USA, particularly in the salt, steel, and leather industries. Means (1935a, b) made a valuable contribution to our understanding of price movements in individual industries. He found that prices in concentrated markets were relatively sticky and did not follow the laws of demand and supply. In the backdrop of the Great Depression, Means raised the concern that the failure of prices in oligopoly markets to fall during an economic downturn would exacerbate a recession.[7]

1.1.3 The Structure–Conduct–Performance Paradigm

The field of industrial organization began to take shape in the 1930s with the work of Edward Mason (1939) and others at Harvard. This work produced what is now called the **structure–conduct–performance (SCP) paradigm**.[8] Because this paradigm has had such an influence on the field, we discuss it in some detail.

Mason's goal was to develop a model that would allow one to assess the economic performance of real-world markets. In essence, he tried to synthesize the best of theory and institutionalism in a way that was empirically applicable to real markets. Mason's efforts led to a taxonomy of fundamental market attributes. The general categories of market attributes are their basic conditions, structure, conduct, and performance. These categories and several key elements in each are summarized in Table 1.1.

Basic conditions refer to the demand and cost conditions of the market. They include the price elasticity of demand and the nature of technology, factors that are generally fixed for a considerable length of time. Market structure describes characteristics that identify departures from perfect competition. These include the number and size distribution of firms, the degree of entry and exit barriers, and whether or not products are differentiated. Conduct identifies the key choice variables of firms, including price/output, advertising, and product design.

A crucial goal in industrial organization is to evaluate whether or not a market performs well from society's perspective. Important performance elements include static and dynamic efficiency, macroeconomic stability, and equity. By equity we mean that which is just, fair, and impartial. Questions of equity are normative, which involve issues of "what ought to be." In contrast, positive questions involve issues of "what is." An example of a normative economic question is: Should we regulate

---

[7] This conclusion was later questioned by Stigler and Kindahl (1973) and Carlton (1979, 1986).

[8] Discussion of the evolution of the structure–conduct–performance paradigm borrows from Grether (1970) and Phillips and Stevenson (1974). A paradigm refers to a theoretical or accepted framework within a discipline at a given time.

Table 1.1 Taxonomy
of market attributes: basic
conditions, structure,
conduct, and performance

Basic conditions	
Demand	*Cost*
Price elasticity of demand	Technology
Substitutes and complements	Input prices
Cyclical character	Value/weight ratio
Market structure	
Number and size of firms	Entry and exit barriers
Product differentiation	Vertical integration
Conglomerateness	
Conduct	
Pricing behavior	Advertising
Product design	Research and
Mergers	development
Performance	
Static efficiency	Equity
Dynamic efficiency	Macroeconomic stability

electricity rates? An example of a positive economic question is: What is the most efficient way to regulate electricity rates?

Although equity concerns are sometimes thought to be outside the domain of economics because they require value judgments, equity is still important. As a society, we want firms to behave in a socially responsible manner and refrain from deceptive and unfair business practices. We may also deem it unfair if producers earn excessively high economic profits, especially if excess profits predominately benefit the wealthy. In the end, we want markets to be efficient, stable, and equitable. Unfortunately, we frequently cannot attain more of one without giving up some of another. With regard to efficiency and equity, this is the well-known efficiency–equity trade-off.[9]

Development of the SCP paradigm produced two outcomes. First, it categorized the principle characteristics of markets, making market classifications and comparisons more scientific. Second, the simplest version of the paradigm postulated the testable hypothesis that causality runs from structure to conduct to performance. It was thought that high concentration facilitated collusion and poor economic performance (as reflected in high profits). Although there is little support for this simple version of the hypothesis today, the classification of key SCP elements remains useful.

In spite of its limitations, many scholars favored the SCP paradigm over purely theoretical models because of its empirical applicability. First, data could be used to identify the important distinctions in structure, conduct, and performance of different

---

[9] The classic work on the efficiency–equity trade-off is Okun (1975, 120), who said that "the conflict between equity and economic efficiency is inescapable." We will see in Chap. 19 that this is more of a trade-off between efficiency and equality than efficiency and equity. For a less pessimistic view, see Blank (2002).

industries. This led to a number of studies that examined the facts relating to a particular industry. Second, the SCP paradigm resulted in a slew of empirical studies using a cross section of data from different manufacturing industries to determine the influence of market structure and conduct on industry performance.[10] Many of these early studies found a weak but positive correlation between concentration and industry profits, evidence that was thought to support the hypothesis that high concentration is a cause of high profits and is, therefore, inefficient.

The SCP evidence led to a shift in public policy. A growing confidence that markets with fewer firms will be inefficient led to strict enforcement of the antitrust laws in the 1950s and 1960s. It also provided theoretical support for the structural standards that are found in the 1968 Merger Guidelines of the Department of Justice.

1.1.4   Competing Paradigms and Public Policy

The SCP paradigm and empirical evidence did not go unchallenged. In the 1960s, economists associated with the Chicago School of economic thought began to question both the theory and the empirical evidence in support of the SCP paradigm.[11] The Chicago School perspective is based on several tenets. First, the perfectly competitive model generally provides a good approximation of how markets in the real world operate.[12] Second, competition is desirable because it rewards success and eliminates inefficiency. Third, monopoly power is possible, but unless it is supported by government, dynamic market forces make it short lived. Fourth, even if a market fails to produce a socially optimal outcome, there is no guarantee that government action can improve things.

Although the Chicago School is frequently thought to support a conservative, free market (i.e., laissez faire) economics agenda, this is not quite right.[13] For instance,

---

[10] For a review of 46 studies that used data from 1936 to 1970, see Weiss (1974). For more recent reviews, see Schmalensee (1989), Scherer and Ross (1990), Carlton and Perloff (2005), Waldman and Jensen (2006), and Perloff et al. (2007).

[11] The Chicago School is associated with the Department of Economics at the University of Chicago. However, not all members of the department adhere to the tenets of the Chicago School, and not all Chicago economists are at the University of Chicago. Leading Chicago economists include Milton Friedman, George Stigler, and Gary Becker, all Nobel Prize winners. For a more complete discussion of the Chicago School and its critics, see Reder (1982), Van Overtveldt (2007), Pitofsky (2008), Crane (2009), and Wright (2009).

[12] According to Reder (1982, 12), when dealing with an applied problem Chicago School economists "have a strong tendency to assume that, in the absence of sufficient evidence to the contrary, one may treat observed prices and quantities as good approximations to their long-run competitive equilibrium values."

[13] The Austrian School is more closely associated with a faith in free markets and limited government. Like Chicago, it places greater emphasis on dynamic efficiency, but unlike Chicago it has less faith in mathematical modeling and empirical analysis. For more information about the Austrian School, see The Ludwig von Mises Institute at http://mises.org.etexts.austrian.asp.

followers of the Chicago School favor antitrust legislation that makes collusion and
large horizontal mergers illegal. At the same time, their work raised concerns with
government policy. The most important of these are that government agents need not
pursue socially desirable goals, that government intervention is costly, and that
government policies can produce unintended consequences.[14] Thus, government
intervention may be desirable but only if the social benefits outweigh the social
costs (Demsetz 1969). It is more accurate to characterize members of the Chicago
School as skeptics of the political process than as conservatives (Reder 1982, 31).[15]

It is from this vantage point that Chicago School economists questioned the SCP
paradigm and its supporting evidence. They scrutinized every aspect of the paradigm
and empirical evidence, including data limitations, sample selection, the static nature
of the model, and the argument that causality runs from structure to performance.[16]

Demsetz' (1973) **superior efficiency hypothesis** provided a credible alternative
interpretation of the empirical evidence that concentration is positively correlated
with industry profits.[17] According to Demsetz (1973, 3), markets are dynamic, and
successful firms with lower costs or better products will earn higher profits or
economic rents and capture a larger share of the market. This will cause both
industry concentration and profits to increase. Thus, the positive correlation between
concentration and profits is due to the superior efficiency of larger corporations, not
collusion. In other words, causality runs from performance to structure, rather than
from structure to performance as predicted by the SCP paradigm.

These conflicting hypotheses led to divergent policy recommendations.
While the SCP paradigm favors deconcentration policies, the superior efficiency
hypothesis does not. In the words of Demsetz (1973, 3), "[t]o destroy such power
[through antitrust enforcement] ... may very well remove the incentive for progress." That is, dynamic efficiency requires that we refrain from penalizing successful
firms that monopolize a market because such a policy may reduce the incentive to
invest in innovations that produce monopoly power but still benefit society overall.
Of course, these differing views are not mutually exclusive. That is, excess profits
could be due to both monopoly power and the superiority of leading firms.

---

[14] Regarding monopoly power, for example, Demsetz (in Goldschmidt et al. 1974, 238) states that
"If we could surgically cut out this monopoly power without bearing the costs of frequently
penalizing efficiency and competition, I would say, 'I am for it.' I just don't believe it is possible to
do that. The costs of trying would greatly exceed the potential benefits."

[15] The great recession or financial crisis of 2008–2009 has led to greater scrutiny of the market
system and of the Chicago position. For instance, a recent series of papers in Pitofsky (2008)
presents evidence that the Chicago School "overshot the mark" in the area of antitrust. Furthermore, Posner (2009), a Chicago economist and legal scholar, argues uncharacteristically that the
recent crisis is due to insufficient government involvement in financial markets.

[16] For a review of these criticisms and the evidence, see Stigler (1968), Goldschmidt et al. (1974),
and Scherer (1980, Chap. 9).

[17] Others who have expressed similar views include Brozen (1971) and McGee (1971). Alternatively, Mancke (1974) argued that this strategic advantage can be driven by luck rather than
superiority.

According to Bresnahan and Schmalensee (1987, 373), by the end of the 1970s "the critics [of the SCP paradigm] generally prevailed." It became clear that market structure need not reliably predict performance. In addition, concerns with causality and data limitations virtually eliminated empirical research that used inter-industry data to investigate the relationship between structure and performance. As a result, the status of the SCP paradigm was greatly diminished.[18] Nevertheless, the classification of structure, conduct, and performance elements still provides a useful taxonomy of variables that are important in industrial organization.

1.1.5   Game Theory and the New Theoretical Industrial Organization

Although contributions from the SCP and Chicago traditions have been valuable, arguably the foremost contribution has been the application of game theory to industrial organization problems. Game theory developed into an influential modeling tool with John Nash's (1950) discovery of the solution concept to noncooperative games, known as the Nash equilibrium.[19] Game theory became invaluable as a tool for analyzing strategic problems that occur in all of the social sciences. Although it was not until the 1970s that game theory made its way into industrial organization, today virtually every theoretical model in the field builds from the Nash equilibrium concept.

In a game-theoretic setting, the Nash equilibrium identifies the actions that each rational player will pursue to maximize the player's payoff (i.e., utility or profit). This requires that each player choose a best response to the actions of all other players in the game. The Nash equilibrium is reached when each player behaves optimally, assuming that all other players behave optimally as well. Once there, players cannot improve their payoffs by changing their behavior. It may seem obvious that fully rational players would behave this way, but of course many good ideas are obvious once they are revealed. Nevertheless, Nash's contribution goes beyond the idea. He also proved that all games that meet certain conditions have at least one Nash equilibrium. Thus, he is known for both the idea and its existence proof.

---

[18] For example, in his overview of the field, Schmalensee (1988) gave little attention to the SCP paradigm. In addition, in a 1996 survey of industrial organization economics, Aiginger et al. (1998) found that those surveyed did not expect the SCP paradigm to be revived. Caves (2007) provides a less pessimistic view, however.

[19] This won him the Nobel Prize in economics. You may know John Nash from the Russell Crowe movie, *A Beautiful Mind*. In true Hollywood fashion, in the movie Nash gains inspiration for his contribution to game theory from a bar scene where he and his friends discuss their strategy for meeting women. In reality, his idea came to him in an economics class in international trade. For a more accurate picture of Nash's life, see Nasar (1998). Nash won the Nobel Prize in 1994, along with two other game theorists, John Harsayni and Reinhard Selten, who refined the Nash equilibrium concept to solve games with imperfect information and dynamic settings.

As we stated previously, analysis of the Cournot and Bertrand models is the starting point for the study of oligopoly theory. Each of these models represents a Nash equilibrium to an oligopoly game that has a different set of characteristics. In the classic Cournot model, there are two firms that produce homogeneous goods (e.g., spring water) and compete by simultaneously choosing output. The only difference between the Cournot and Bertrand models is that firms compete by setting price instead of output in the Bertrand model. A significant outcome of these models is that they show how a simple change in the rules of the game can have a dramatic effect on the Nash equilibrium. In the Cournot model, the equilibrium price is between the monopoly and perfectly competitive price, while in the Bertrand model it equals the perfectly competitive price.

There are several reasons why game theory is essential to theoretical research in industrial organization. First, it provides a clear picture of how fully rational players will behave in a strategic setting. Second, it provides a set of tools that allow us to make more realistic modeling assumptions concerning the rules of the game (i.e., goals, market conditions, laws, and social norms). Game theory informs us of what can and cannot happen, conditional on a given set of assumptions. When assessing the validity of a model, the game-theoretic approach directs attention to the realism of assumptions as well as the predictive power of the model (Fudenberg and Tirole 1987).[20] In other words, game theory clarifies how the outcome in an imperfectly competitive market depends on the key features of the legal, institutional, and market setting. Thus, modern models address concerns raised by critics that early theoretical models of imperfect competition (1) were based on overly simple assumptions and (2) could prove that almost anything can happen. Finally, game theory is especially useful to policy analysis, as it can give us a better understanding of the economic consequences of an institutional change.

1.1.6   New Empirical Industrial Organization

While game theory changed the way we study theoretical industrial organization, the empirical tradition continues to be influential. New empirical research in industrial organization uses a structural framework in which empirical models derive directly from theoretical models.[21] New studies also benefit from better data sets and econometric techniques.

---

[20] We have purposefully avoided the debate about whether a model should be judged by the realism of its assumptions or the accuracy of its predictions. We may choose a simplifying assumption in order to build a model that is tractable but would want to avoid assumptions that are clearly false. Differing positions can be found in Friedman (1953) and Nagel (1963). For a discussion of the debate, see Boland (1979) and Martin (2007a, b).

[21] For a discussion of the use of structural methods in industrial organization, see Nevo and Whinston (2010).

Beginning in the 1970s, empirical scholars began to abandon inter-industry data sets, reverting back to case studies. According to Einav and Nevo (2006, 86), "In the last 25 years, [industrial organization] studies have increasingly focused on single industries, using a combination of economic theory and statistics to analyze interaction between firms." This work has produced more accurate estimates of market power and the economic consequences of events such as a merger or change in the economic or legal environment. Unfortunately, it is frequently difficult to obtain sufficient data to test some of the finer predictions of game-theoretic models.

In response, a recent and promising line of research has emerged where the unit of study has moved from the industry or firm to the brand. For instance, the widespread use of price scanners and supermarket discount cards has enabled scholars to create detailed data sets that link market conditions to data on price, promotional activity, consumer characteristics, and consumer demand for particular products. These new sources of data have allowed for better controls of some of the relevant game theory characteristics and have improved the quality of empirical research in the field. Another response has been the use of experimental methods to analyze industrial organization questions (Plott 2007).

1.2 Behavioral Economics and Industrial Organization

The field of behavioral economics began with pioneering studies by Simon (1955) and Kahneman and Tversky (1979), which use concepts and evidence from psychology to gain a better understanding of human behavior. Early studies were based on experimental evidence, and more recent work uses neuroscience methods, where brain scans provide insight into how people make decisions. This has produced a promising new subfield of behavioral economics called neuroeconomics.

Two important conclusions emerge from behavioral economics research. First, consumer preferences are generally more complicated than simple theory presumes. For example, some people suffer from loss aversion, which occurs when a person places much greater weight on the loss of $x than a gain of $x (measured in the absolute value of the change in utility). Second, due to cognitive limitations, people sometimes make mistakes. You may make a mistake when calculating which brand of cornflakes is cheaper per ounce when a 1.25 pound box of brand X sells for $4.99 and a 21 ounce box of brand Y sells for $5.09. Many people also have problems with overconfidence and time inconsistency. In the case of dieting, it may be rational to begin a diet tomorrow, but once tomorrow arrives procrastination sets in and the starting date is postponed for another day.

The cognitive weaknesses of consumers can have a dramatic effect on market outcomes. For instance, online dating sites use a special pricing scheme to exploit consumers who are biased in favor of the default option. A contract for a 6 month subscription might include one of the following defaults. When the

6 month subscription period is over, service for another 6 months (1) continues automatically unless the subscriber takes action (i.e., actively cancels service by phone or e-mail) or (2) continues only if the subscriber takes action (i.e., actively renews service by phone or e-mail). Because some subscribers who do not wish to continue the service will fail to actively cancel their subscription, choosing a default that automatically continues service transfers revenues from consumers to producers. Successful companies are well aware of such flaws and exploit them to earn greater profit.

Given this growing body of evidence, economists have begun to enrich traditional economic theory by incorporating insights from behavioral economics. One of our goals is to do just that. We will summarize some of the flaws revealed by behavioral economics and show how companies develop strategies to exploit those flaws.

1.3   Public Policy and Industrial Organization

A crucial goal in any field of economics is to gain a sufficient understanding of the economy to provide enlightened policy recommendations. This involves evaluating the effectiveness of new and current policies by assessing their benefits and costs. A socially desirable policy will produce positive net social benefits (total benefits minus total costs).

The process of identifying potentially beneficial laws and regulations has three steps. First, we need to uncover areas of potential market failure—situations where markets may fail to allocate resources in socially optimal ways. Second, we need to identify the most effective policy that will correct the problem.[22] Stopping here would lead to what Demsetz (1969) calls the "nirvana" approach to public policy analysis. This approach can produce undesirable policies because it ignores the fact that the implementation of a policy can be expensive and produce unintended consequences. Thus, the third and final step requires a comparative institution approach where we evaluate a real market outcome with a real policy-corrected outcome. We would then choose the option that is most socially desirable. When the cost of government action is excessively high, the free market outcome would be optimal even with its imperfections. Nevertheless, we begin our discussion using the nirvana approach and reserve discussion of the cost of government policy to Chap. 20.

In industrial organization, a central policy interest relates competition and efficiency. When inadequate competition leads to market power, price exceeds marginal cost and markets are statically inefficient. In a dynamic world, competition for market dominance causes firms to make investments that are designed to

---

[22] Frequently, there are many equally effective policies. In that case, we would select the lowest cost policy.

Table 1.2 Major antitrust statutes in the USA

Sherman Act (1890): The Sherman Act has two important provisions.

Section 1: "Every contract, combination in the form of trust or otherwise, or conspiracy, in restraint of trade or commerce among several states, or with foreign nations, is declared to be illegal."

Section 2: "Every person who shall monopolize, or attempt to monopolize, or combine or conspire with any other person or persons, to monopolize any part of the trade or commerce ... shall be deemed guilty of a felony."

Clayton Act (1914): The Clayton Act addresses four specific business practices.

Section 2: Price discrimination is illegal where the effect may be "to substantially lessen competition or tend to create a monopoly." The provision does allow for price differences that reflect differences in costs and when it meets the low price of a competitor.[a]

Section 3: Market restrictions such as exclusive-dealing contracts and tying contracts are illegal where the effect is "to substantially lessen competition or tend to create a monopoly."

Section 7: Mergers are illegal where the effect may be "to substantially lessen competition or tend to create a monopoly." Section 7 had a loophole that allowed mergers by asset acquisition. The loophole was later eliminated in the *Celler–Kefauver Act (1950)*.

Section 8: Interlocking directories of corporations larger than a certain threshold are prohibited.[b]

Under the Clayton Act, injured parties can recover treble damages.

Federal Trade Commission Act (1914): This Act established the Federal Trade Commission (FTC) that was charged, along with the Department of Justice (DOJ), with interpreting and enforcing the antitrust laws. Section 5 states that "the Commission is hereby empowered and directed to prevent persons, partnerships, or corporations ... from using unfair methods of competition in commerce."

Hart–Scott–Rodino Act (1976): The Hart–Scott–Rodino Act required firms of a minimum size to notify the DOJ and the FTC of their intention to merge. In most cases the government works with the firms involved to reach a negotiated settlement.

[a]The Robinson–Patman Act (1936) amended Section 2 and gave greater protection to small retailers who were battling the growing chain-store movement in the USA.
[b]This means that large corporations in the same industry cannot be controlled by a common board of directors.

give them a competitive advantage over their competitors. When this behavior leads to market power alone, it is socially harmful. If it produces lower costs and better products, however, it can be dynamically efficient and socially desirable.

Two forms of policy address anticompetitive concerns, antitrust legislation and government regulation of business.[23] The antitrust laws are designed to foster a competitive economy, and the major antitrust statutes are listed in Table 1.2. The first major piece of legislation is the Sherman Act (1890), followed by the Clayton Act (1914), the Federal Trade Commission Act (1914) and the Hart–Scott–Rodino Act (1976).

These laws address issues related to market structure and firm conduct. Section 2 of the Sherman Act and Section 7 of the Clayton Act address structural issues.

---

[23] A third policy would be for the government to nationalize an industry to form a public enterprise. Although this is how we operate the postal, water, and sewer services, it is less common and is not addressed here.

Firms guilty of monopolization are in violation of Section 2 of the Sherman Act
and can be broken up into smaller enterprises, directly affecting market structure.
When a merger is successfully challenged under Section 7 of the Clayton Act,
industry concentration is kept from rising. Other sections of the Sherman and
Clayton Acts address issues of anticompetitive practices. For example, Section 1
of the Sherman Act makes collusive activity illegal.

In some cases, legislation gives a government agency discretionary power to
regulate business. "Social regulation" is established to protect the environment and
the welfare of consumers and workers. For instance, the Food and Drug Administration is responsible for regulating the safety of food and drugs. The Occupational
Safety and Health Administration is responsible for the safety and health of
workers. In this book, we are primarily concerned with "economic regulation,"
which involves price/output regulation that is designed to address market failure
due to market power. Today, this typically involves the regulation of natural
monopolies where industry production costs are minimized when there is only
one firm. In these industries, regulatory agencies may be established to promote
static and dynamic efficiency.

1.4 Economic Theory, Models, and Mathematics

1.4.1 Theory, Models, and Reality

Although the words theory and model are sometimes used interchangeably, there
are useful distinctions between them.[24] Theories embody a set of ideas and insights
about an aspect of the economy and how it functions. They describe a broad
conceptual approach. Examples include consumer theory, producer theory,
and game theory. Theories represent abstract ideas that are distinct from reality.
Economic models sit in the middle, connecting theory to reality. Historical facts
may describe an economic event, but facts alone cannot explain why an event
occurred. Theories and models are used to provide explanations of economic events
and predict how we might change the course of events.

A model is a formal representation of a part of a theory and is used to explain
and make predictions about some aspect of the economy. Models are more
specific than theories and are reductionist by definition. That is, they are designed
to make sense of reality by reducing complex relationships to their fundamental
elements. A road map can be helpful even though it excludes some of the details
of a city. In the same way, an economic model can be useful in analyzing the
market for cell phones, even though it ignores some of the details of the market.

---

[24] Our discussion of the distinction between a theory and a model borrows from Leijonhufvud
(1997), Morgon (2002), Sutton (2002), and Goldfarb and Ratner (2008).

In economics, we frequently use simplifying assumptions to produce tractable models of complex economic phenomena. To capture every aspect of reality would produce a model that is unmanageable or hyperfactual.[25] At the same time, a model that oversimplifies will be unrealistic and of little use in explaining or predicting reality. The art of good economic modeling is to reach the proper balance and avoid oversimplifying and overfactualizing.

Describing models as bridges between theory and reality enables us to classify them in a meaningful way. Models that are closely connected to theory are more general and abstract; they are typically called purely theoretical or abstract models. Models that are more realistic and empirical (i.e., based on data and observation) are typically called applied models. One example is an econometric model that uses data to address a concrete economic issue.

Consider an example from consumer demand theory. General models of consumer choice tells us that consumer demand for a particular good will depend on prices, income, consumer preferences, and a variety of other social and institutional factors. Given this general theory, we might use a reductionist model to gain insights into the relationships of a handful of key variables. In this case, we are implicitly invoking the *ceteris paribus* assumption where all other variables are taken to be held fixed and are ignored.

A purely theoretical model might assume that a rational consumer has a demand function (D) for a particular good that depends only on the price of the good (p), the price of a substitute good (p_s), and consumer income (m). The demand function could be described generally as $D(p, p_s, m)$, meaning that demand is a function of p, p_s, and m. From this model, one can show that the effect of a price change can be decomposed into two parts: the substitution effect and the income effect. This is a purely abstract or theoretical result, as it is not connected to any real market. The model becomes more concrete as we give it more structure. If we assume that demand is linear, then $D = a - b_1 \cdot p + b_2 \cdot p_s + b_3 \cdot m$, where a, b_1, b_2, and b_3 are constants. With appropriate data from a particular market and a proper estimation technique, we can estimate the parameters of the model to produce an even more specific specification, such as $D = 12 - 4p + 3p_s + 2m$.

In industrial organization we are interested in different types of models. Theoretical models are abstract but can be used to address real world problems. Cournot's oligopoly model is one example. Empirical models are applied and employ real world data to estimate parameters and test important hypotheses. For example, an empirical model might be used to test whether real firms in a particular industry behave as Cournot or Bertrand competitors.

Another characteristic of a model is its degree of formality. A less formal model might rely on geometry and graphs to connect theory with reality. More formal models utilize advanced mathematical techniques. The use of advanced

---

[25] For example, Stigler (1949, 319) states that "... the role of description is to particularize, while the role of theory is to generalize—to disregard an infinite number of differences and capture the important common element in different phenomena."

mathematics allows us to analyze more complex models such as those that have a greater number of dimensions. With geometry, it is difficult to graph a three-dimensional problem and impossible to describe one that has ten dimensions. More advanced mathematics overcomes this limitation. This comes at a cost, though, as mathematics is a difficult subject.

1.4.2 Modeling and Mathematics

Most of the formal analysis in this book relies on geometry and algebra. In some cases, however, calculus is useful. We realize that many undergraduate textbooks avoid calculus, but we think that this is a mistake because calculus makes some forms of analysis much easier.[26] Furthermore, we implicitly use calculus all of the time in applied microeconomics courses: marginal cost is the first derivative of the total cost function, and a firm's profit maximizing level of output is found by setting the first derivative of the profit equation equal to zero. Some books avoid calculus by replacing the symbol for small change, d (or ∂), with the symbol for change, Δ. But this does not eliminate the underlying calculus; it is just a way of avoiding the term "derivative." Other books relegate calculus to footnotes, but this can disrupt the flow of the analysis.

Our applications in the book that rely on calculus require more intuition than technical skill. That is, our goal is to understand how a change in one variable affects another variable. Wherever reasonable, we will use linear functions, where the slope of the line informs us of the change in the dependent variable (y) due to a change in the independent variable (x), as in Figs. 1.1 and 1.2. Occasionally we will use smooth functions that are hill or bowl shaped (i.e., quadratic functions), as in Fig. 1.3. In this case, the slope of a tangent line to the curve represents the change in y with respect to a "small" change in x (dy/dx). Maximum and minimum values of functions such as these occur where the tangent to the curve is horizontal (i.e., it has a 0 slope) (Figs. 1.1–1.3).

The Mathematics and Econometrics Appendix at the end of the book describes the math and statistical tools that are used in the book. In mathematics, these include a review of graphs, areas of rectangles and right triangles, linear and quadratic equations, slopes of tangents to curves, and derivatives of linear and quadratic equations. The regression section covers basic distribution functions, regression analysis, hypothesis testing, and methods to evaluate regression estimates.

---

[26] Even though mathematics is difficult for most of us, according to Weintraub (2002) the use of mathematics in economics is the most important development in the field of economics in the twentieth century.

Fig. 1.1 The relationship between x and y when y is a constant

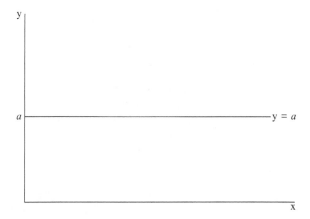

Fig. 1.2 The relationship between x and y when y is a positively sloped linear function

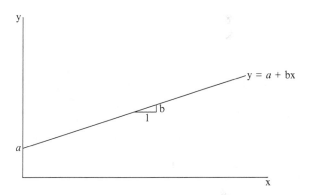

Fig. 1.3 The relationship between x and y when $y = 12x - x^2$

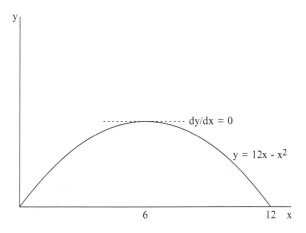

1.5 Approach of the Book

In this book, we strive to present a balanced view of the field of industrial organization. First, we address fundamental questions in the field, including:

• Why do some markets have many producers, while others have just a few?
• What forces foster competition and enhance economic efficiency?
• Why do firms advertise and how does advertising affect social welfare?
• What factors encourage technological progress?
• To what extent have our antitrust laws and government regulations been socially beneficial?

Second, we develop the classic theories and models used to address these questions. By bridging the gap between abstract theory and the real world, these models provide a better understanding of how imperfectly competitive markets work. Third, data and empirical evidence are presented to further understanding of real markets. Finally, we provide an eclectic set of evidence and points of view that do not represent any one particular school of thought. Both the theoretical models and the empirical evidence are used to enlighten policy analysis.

Ultimately, we want to know whether or not imperfectly competitive markets perform well from society's perspective. Society's performance goals are (static and dynamic) efficiency, macroeconomic stability, and equity. As with other books, we devote most of our attention to issues of static and dynamic efficiency. Ethical corporate behavior is also important, especially to policy analysis, and we discuss this topic at the end of the book. Of course, macroeconomic stability is desirable too, but like most books in industrial organization we leave this topic to others.[27] We also devote relatively little time to market imperfections that are directly associated with externalities, public goods, and risk and uncertainty.

Whenever possible, we will use the scientific method to analyze the economic problems associated with imperfectly competitive markets. The goal is to (1) tackle important questions, (2) use models to address these questions by constructing clear conjectures or hypothetical explanations (i.e., hypotheses), (3) report on empirical evidence that tests these hypotheses, and (4) interpret and draw conclusions about the results.[28] With this method, reliable answers are more likely to emerge over time.

Of course, there are limitations with the scientific method when applied to the social sciences where value judgments come into play, experiments can be too costly to perform, and data are inadequate to perform a proper hypothesis test. Nevertheless, a leading American physicist Lisa Randall (2011, 20) makes a strong case for using the scientific method to address public policy questions.

---

[27] For discussion of the relationship between industrial organization and macro stability, especially as it applies to administered or sticky prices, see Carlton (1979, 1986) and Scherer and Ross (1990).

[28] This also involves publishing the results and retesting hypotheses to assure their validity. For further discussion, see Wilson (1952).

Public policy is more complicated than clean and controlled [scientific] experiments, but considering the large and serious issues we face—in the economy, in the environment, in our health and well-being—it's our responsibility to push reason as far as we can. Far from being isolating, a rational, scientific way of thinking could be unifying. Evaluating alternative strategies; reading data, when available, . . . about the relative effectiveness of various policies; and understanding uncertainties—all features of the scientific method—can help us find the right way forward.

Part I of the book provides a review of the economic tools that we use throughout the book. Chapter 2 discusses demand and cost theory. Chapter 3 summarizes the relevant tools of game theory, and Chap. 4 outlines many contributions from behavioral economics. For most readers, some of this will be review material.

In Part II, we discuss nonstrategic issues that are relevant in industrial organization. In Chaps. 5 and 6, we review the competitive and monopoly models, the static benchmarks of policy analysis. In Chap. 7, we describe different types of product differentiation and discuss how product differentiation affects firm demand and costs. In Chap. 8, we present the theory of market structure.

Game theory is used extensively in Part III, where we discuss oligopoly theory and market power. The most abstract analysis is found in Chaps. 10 and 11, where we review the traditional static and dynamic models of oligopoly, such as the Cournot, Bertrand, and Stackelberg models. We connect theory to reality in most other chapters by including empirical evidence and case studies where relevant, such as Chap. 9 where we discuss cartels and in Chap. 12 where we discuss empirical studies of market power.

Part IV is the most eclectic, as it uses models that build from game theory and benefit from behavioral economics. It also presents empirical evidence and discusses real-world examples to illustrate a variety of marketing strategies that are used by firms. Primary topics in this section include product design (Chap. 13), advertising and other marketing practices (Chaps. 14–16), technological change (Chap. 17), and mergers (Chap. 18).

A review of overall market performance, case study analysis, and policy issues are discussed in Part V. Chapter 19 summarizes the evidence regarding the efficiency, equity, and corporate responsibility in imperfectly competitive markets. Antitrust and regulation policies are discussed in Chap. 20. Industry and firm case studies are found in Chap. 21.

Rather than provide an encyclopedic review of the evidence, in most cases we focus on seminal and relatively recent studies. Throughout the book, concrete examples of firm behavior and industry performance derive from the major sectors of the US economy, including manufacturing, transportation, and wholesale–retail (see Table 1.3). The choice of case studies reflects our tastes and is driven by historical significance, strategic importance, and policy relevance. These include the antitrust litigation of cartel activity in the steel industry from the past and the continued cartel activity in the petroleum industry. Strategic behavior becomes vivid when reviewing the marketing battles between Coke and Pepsi in the soft drink industry. The economic consequences of rising concentration and negative externalities can be seen in the market for alcoholic beverages, particularly in the

Table 1.3 Percent of gross domestic product (GDP) by major sector of the economy

| | Share of GDP by sector (%) | |
Sector	1982	2003
Agriculture, forestry, and fisheries	2.8	1.0
Utilities	–	1.9
Transportation	3.5	2.8
Construction	4.0	4.4
Health care and social assistance	–	6.8
Finance and insurance services	4.2	7.9
Real estate	11.8	12.4
Government	–	12.7
Manufacturing	20.5	12.7
Wholesale and retail trade	16.0	13.1

Sources: Scherer and Ross (1990, 58) and the US Department of Commerce, Bureau of Economic Analysis at http://www.bea.gov, accessed May 20, 2011.

brewing industry. Finally, the effect of deregulation has been most dramatic in the airline industry. Discussion of these and other industries can be found throughout the book, as well as in Chap. 21.

A significant departure from other books in industrial organization is the incorporation of evidence from behavioral economics. We review behavioral economics in Chap. 4 and later show how firms exploit common cognitive errors made by consumers. We also show how managerial overconfidence and bias can affect firm behavior to the detriment of stockholders. Contributions from behavioral economics are employed most frequently in Part IV, where we discuss the non-price–output marketing practices of firms, and in Chap. 20, where we discuss policy prescriptions. We believe that this approach enhances our understanding of the field of industrial organization.

1.6   Summary

1. The field of **industrial organization** is the study of imperfectly competitive markets. In this field, we analyze why some markets have many competitors, while others have just a few. We investigate the strategic behavior of firms and the economic performance of imperfectly competitive markets. Poor economic performance can justify antitrust and regulatory policy.
2. A crucial goal in industrial organization is to evaluate whether or not a market performs well from society's perspective. Economic performance elements include static and dynamic efficiency, macroeconomic stability, and equity. Most of our discussion will involve positive economics, that is, the study of what is. The study of equity issues will also be important. It requires value judgments, making it the purview of normative economics—the study of what ought to be.

3. The origins of the field trace back to the theoretical development of duopoly models of Cournot and Bertrand in the nineteenth century. Other noteworthy contributions include the development of the monopolistically competitive model in the 1930s by Chamberlin and the institutional and empirical traditions of the early twentieth century. The field began to take shape in the late 1930s with the development of the **structure–conduct–performance (SCP) paradigm**, which categorizes the principle characteristics of markets. The simplest version of the paradigm predicted that performance depends on conduct, and conduct depends on market structure. Work by Chicago and other economists have successfully shown that causality is not so simple. Demsetz' (1973) **superior efficiency hypothesis** states that firm success will lead to higher concentration and better economic performance. Thus, the SCP paradigm no longer plays a prominent role in industrial organization analysis. Nevertheless, the taxonomy of important elements of structure, conduct, and performance is still useful today.

4. Since the 1970s, **game theory** has transformed how we think about industrial organization issues. It provides a method for analyzing how fully rational players will behave in a strategic setting. It also allows us to develop models with considerable institutional reality, enabling us to better understand how institutional changes will affect firm behavior and market performance.

5. **Behavioral economics** is a relatively new field that brings insights from psychology and experimental evidence to enhance our understanding of consumer and manager decision making. One point is that consumers suffer from cognitive limitations. These insights influence research in industrial organization, as they provide economic motivation for the strategic actions taken by firms that clearly exploit these limitations.

6. Both abstract theory and concrete empirical work in industrial organization provide a knowledge base for evaluating public policy regarding large corporations. In particular, we are interested in investigating the justification and application of economic regulation and the antitrust laws.

7. It can be useful to view theory, models, and reality as separate entities. Theories represent a set of ideas regarding how the economy functions. Models are designed to connect theory to reality. Models are naturally reductionist, reducing a description of a particular aspect of the economy to its core elements. Models that are more closely connected to theory are called purely theoretical or abstract models. Those that are realistic and empirical are called applied models. Modern industrial organization makes use of game theory and behavioral economics to develop both abstract and empirical models of firms and industries.

8. Most abstract models in this book are described using graphs and algebra. Where appropriate, calculus is used. Calculus enables us to analyze a model in greater depth, to discuss a wider set of models, and to work with problems involving more than three variables. Most of our examples use linear or quadratic functional forms, making calculus derivations relatively easy. The Mathematics and Econometrics Appendix provides the tools needed to understand the book.

Chapter 2
Demand, Technology, and the Theory of the Firm

One of our goals is to understand the forces that influence firm behavior. The principal constraints derive from consumers (demand), nature (technology), and competitors.[1] Demand derives from consumers who strive to maximize their utility or satisfaction within their budget and other constraints. When tastes are under the full control of consumers, firms take market demand as given. That is, demand is exogenously determined. This is the basis of consumer sovereignty—consumer preferences determine what firms produce.

With at least some consumers, however, preferences are less insular and more flexible. Some people care what others think, inducing them to purchase a particular style of clothing because it is accepted by their peers. When this becomes a dominant feature of a market, a firm may invest marketing dollars to manipulate consumer demand in ways that benefit the firm. In this case, there is a certain amount of producer sovereignty—firms influence demand by manipulating consumer preferences. That is, demand is endogenous to the firm, at least to a certain extent.

Similarly, technology has both exogenous and endogenous qualities. The laws of physics place limits on technology, which defines the set of feasible production opportunities and determines the maximum amount of output that can be produced from a given quantity of inputs. For instance, there is an upper limit on the efficiency of your gas furnace at creating heat (100%). Although this is a technological bound, a firm may invest in a research effort to improve the efficiency of its heater from 95 to 97%. Thus, technology is given until someone comes up with a better way of doing things, which is a technological change.

In this chapter, we consider demand and technological constraints. Once basic demand and technological conditions are reviewed, we discuss the theory of the firm and the complex goals and aims of a firm. Constraints imposed by competitors will be considered when we discuss firm strategy later in the book.

---

[1] Legal constraints are also important and are taken as given until the end of the book.

V.J. Tremblay and C.H. Tremblay, *New Perspectives on Industrial Organization*,
Springer Texts in Business and Economics, DOI 10.1007/978-1-4614-3241-8_2,
© Springer Science+Business Media New York 2012

2.1 The Short Run and the Long Run

Before discussing demand and technological conditions, we first must be clear about the time in which an economic agent has to make adjustments. On the demand side, consumers will respond relatively quickly to a fall in the price of apples, but it may take a considerable amount of time for consumer demand to respond to a drop in the price of an expensive sports car. For some consumers, it will take time to find financing for the car. Others may have just purchased a new car, making it impractical or uneconomic for them to purchase another car for years to come. We will see that the time period in question will be particularly important when discussing the demand for a durable good like an automobile.

On the production side, we normally divide up time into two periods: the short run and the long run. In the short run, some inputs are variable and others are fixed. If we assume just two inputs, labor and capital (i.e., plant and equipment), labor is the variable input and capital is the fixed input. The short run is a period that is too short for the firm to change the size of its plant in response to a change in demand. Thus, capital is predetermined at its current level in the short run. In the long run, all inputs are variable. In this case, the firm has sufficient time to adjust the level of all of its inputs in response to a change in demand.[2] In short-run analysis, this distinction allows us to divide costs into variable costs (payments to variable inputs) and fixed costs (payments to fixed inputs).

The length of time required for capital to be variable depends on the industry and type of capital being used. The time it takes to expand the size of a fast-food restaurant may be less than a year, while it may take several years to expand the size of a steel mill. Thus, the time period identified as the short run differs by industry.

The nature of technology is also related to time. Many firms spend large sums of money on research and development to come up with a better technology, one that will lower production costs. In some cases, this can take a considerable amount of time, but in others inspiration and application can be rather quick. The point is that a technological change will alter the nature of technology, as described by the firm's cost function.

In this book, we will focus on the long run. We are interested in investigating policies that address social concerns with imperfectly competitive markets, and new laws and regulations generally address long-run economic problems. Development and implementation of a new policy takes a considerable amount of time, making it infeasible for policy to address short-run or transitory market imperfections.

---

[2] There is also the very short run, a period when all inputs are fixed. In this case, the firm cannot adjust its production level in response to a change in demand.

2.2   Consumer Theory and Demand[3]

Consumer preferences are extraordinarily diverse and complex. Most people like ice cream, but some prefer vanilla while others prefer chocolate. One person likes to snowboard, and another likes to ski. One chooses a clothing style because it is "cool," while another does not care about fashion. And even for a simple product like coffee, consider the variety and complexity of drink orders placed at Starbucks. These are just a few examples of differing preferences across individuals.

Consumer demand depends not only on these complicated preferences but also on constraints. We cannot afford to buy an unlimited amount of goods and services.[4] In economics, we focus on the consumer's budget constraint, but individuals face other kinds of constraints as well. Time available for searching and consuming goods is limited. A diamond ring and a Hawaii vacation may cost the same, but the vacation uses up much more time to enjoy than the ring. We are also bound by laws, social mores, and religious doctrines. The job of explaining how people seek to fulfill their needs and wants in line with their complicated preferences while subject to multiple constraints is a tall order to say the least. We take a first step towards that challenge by starting with the introductory model of demand. We review this simple model first and then turn to more complicated cases.

2.2.1   The Introductory Model of Consumer Choice

The introductory model of consumer choice assumes that an individual's utility (happiness or satisfaction) depends on the consumption of goods and services.[5] It also assumes a single constraint, the budget constraint. If there are only two goods, we can represent an individual's utility function as $U = U(q_1, q_2, t)$ where q_1 is the quantity of good 1, q_2 is the quantity of good 2, and t represents tastes. The taste parameter, t, identifies the desires and characteristics of a particular consumer.

Consumer i will demand the amounts of goods that generate the highest level of utility within the consumer's budget. That is, consumer i will choose q_1 and q_2 to maximize $U_i(q_1, q_2, t_i)$ given that total spending equals income (that is, $p_1q_1 + p_2q_2 = m$ where p_1 = price of good 1, p_2 = price of good 2, and m = consumer i's income). At a particular point in time, p_1, p_2, m, and t are given or predetermined. Demand

---

[3] You can learn more about the details of consumer theory from any introductory or intermediate microeconomics textbook, such as Frank and Bernanke (2008), Mankiw (2011), Bernheim and Whinston (2008), Pindyck and Rubenfield (2009), and Varian (2010). For more advanced treatments, see Nicholson and Snyder (2012), Varian (1992), and Mas-Colell et al. (1995).

[4] Throughout the book, we frequently use product or good to mean goods and services.

[5] Of course, economists know that happiness depends on more than just the consumption of goods. Examples include nontangibles such as health, friendships, familial relationships, and beliefs. We focus on the utility of goods because the realm of economics is the production and allocation of goods. For further discussion on the economics of happiness, see Bruni and Porta (2007).

Fig. 2.1 An individual
consumer's demand
curve (d_i)

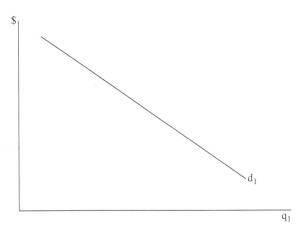

depends on these givens or parameters in the utility function and the budget constraint.
Specifically, consumer i's demand function for good 1 (d_1) derives from the constrained
optimization process and can be written as

$$q_1 = d_1(p_1, p_2, m_i, t_i). \tag{2.1}$$

In other words, demand originates from the consumer's underlying preferences and
budget parameters.

The demand curve graphs the relationship between quantity demanded (on the
horizontal axis) and price (on the vertical axis) for given levels of income, price of
good 2, and tastes (see Fig. 2.1). The assumption that factors other than p_1 are given
or held constant is known as the *ceteris paribus* assumption (as discussed in
Chap. 1). It allows us to focus on the price-quantity relationship separate from
other factors which affect demand. Later we will allow other factors to change, but
first we start with this simplifying assumption.

Figure 2.1 depicts a negative relationship between price and quantity demanded.
That a consumer would prefer to buy less when price goes up is somewhat intuitive.
The slope of demand derives from substitution and income effects. Consider Allison's
demand for cake. If the price of cake increases, Allison substitutes ice cream or another
dessert for cake (the substitution effect). This diminishes her consumption of cake.
Further, the higher price of cake diminishes her purchasing power, which also reduces
her consumption of cake (assuming cake is a normal good). The magnitude of these
combined effects determines the steepness of the demand curve.[6] This negative
relationship between price and quantity demanded is called the **law of demand**.

---

[6] With an inferior good, the income effect works against the substitution effect, making for a
steeper demand curve. In theory, a super inferior good, called a Giffen good, results in a positively
sloped demand. We ignore the possibility of a Giffen good. For further discussion of normal,
inferior, and Giffen goods, see Bernheim and Whinston (2008), Pindyck and Rubenfield (2009),
and Varian (2010).

Fig. 2.2 A change
in consumer demand

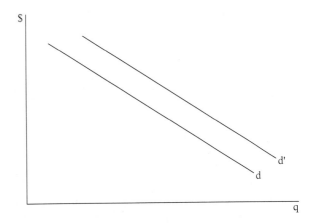

Notice in (2.1) that quantity is on the left-hand side of the equality and its price on the right hand-side. The graph of the demand curve, though, has price on the y-axis and quantity on the x-axis, which is inconsistent with the usual way of graphing functions in mathematics. The reversal of axes was started by Marshall (1890), a convention that has continued to this day. The equation that is consistent with the convention in mathematics, ignoring all variables except p_1 and q_1, is $p_1 = d_1(q_1)$ or $p_1 = p_1(q_1)$. This is known as the "inverse demand function." In this case, p_1 represents the maximum price the consumer is willing to pay for q_1, which is called the demand (or reservation) price. The distinction becomes important in solving for specific demand models later in the book. Nevertheless, keep in mind that the inverse demand function and the demand function represent the same relationship between price and quantity. To illustrate, the inverse demand function $p_1(q_1) = a - b \cdot q_1$ has a corresponding demand equal to $q_1(p_1) = (a - p_1)/b$. With either specification, the demand curve has the following qualities: (1) the price intercept is a, (2) the quantity intercept is a/b, and (3) the slope $(\partial p_1/\partial q_1)$ is b.[7]

All other demand determinants (p_2, m, and t) are known as demand shifters. If there is a change in any of the demand shifters, the demand curve changes location. A demand shifter that increases (decreases) demand will cause the demand curve to shift to the right (left). An increase in demand means that quantity demanded is greater at any given price. In Fig. 2.2, a shift from d to d' represents an increase in demand, and a shift from d' to d represents a decrease in demand. The effect of p_2 on the demand curve depends on whether good 2 is a substitute or complement to good 1. If the goods are **substitutes**, an increase in the price of good 2 would cause people to switch to good 1, increasing demand for good 1 (shifting demand to the right). Coke and Pepsi are examples of substitute goods. Goods that are **complements** are consumed together, such as cameras and batteries or lattes and scones. If good 1 and good 2 are complements, an increase in the price of

---

[7] Throughout the book, we will frequently replace d with ∂ to remind us that there are many other variables in the model that are implicitly assumed to be held fixed.

good 2 (e.g., cameras) will reduce demand for good 2 and therefore reduce the demand for good 1 (batteries).

Changes in a consumer's income also affect demand. When higher income generates greater demand for a good, the good is said to be a **normal good**. Most goods are normal goods. When higher income leads to a reduction in demand, the good is an **inferior good**. For some people, instant Macaroni 'n Cheese or noodle soups are inferior goods. In college you might buy a lot of these products because they are cheap, but as you graduate and earn more you may not eat them as frequently. For inferior goods, an increase in income results in decreased demand, shifting the demand curve to the left. Finally, when the demand for a product is unaffected by income, the product is an **income-neutral good**, and the demand curve does not shift.

Changes in tastes will also shift the demand curve.[8] For instance, if a product becomes fashionable, people who like to be in style will demand more of the good, shifting the demand curve to the right. Some people might demand less of a product that is no longer popular, causing demand to fall.

2.2.2 Market Demand

So far, we have looked at an individual consumer's demand for a product, but we are also interested in aggregate or market demand. **Market demand** identifies the determinants of quantity demanded for all consumers, *ceteris paribus*. To construct the aggregate demand curve, we simply sum up the demands of each consumer.

Like individual demand curves, the market demand curve has a negative slope. Since the aggregate demand curve derives from individual demand curves, it depends upon all of the factors in individual consumer demands: prices and the income and tastes of each consumer. For simplicity, t is used to capture taste effects for all consumers and average income (m) is used to capture income effects. This is accurate if the distribution of income remains unchanged. In this case, the market demand for good 1 is

$$Q_1 = D_1(p_1, p_2, m, t). \tag{2.2}$$

[8] It is common in economics to assume that tastes are fixed and to look for changes in relative prices and income to explain changes in consumer behavior. In the words of Stigler and Becker (1977, 76), "tastes neither change capriciously nor differ importantly between people." From this perspective, changes in education, experience, and learning-by-doing may influence consumer behavior by changing their consumption capital or the shadow or full price of purchasing a commodity. Regarding fashion, Karni and Schmeidler (1990) show how the fluctuating demand for fashion goods can result from changes in a commodity's "social attributes" rather than changes in tastes. Bikhchandani et al. (1992) show how demand fluctuations can derive from informational imperfections. We are sympathetic to this viewpoint but continue to use the taste moniker because it simplifies the discussion.

To distinguish the individual from the market, we use capital Q to represent market output and capital D to represent market demand. Changes the demand shifters (prices of complements and substitutes, income, and tastes) shift the market demand curve in the same way as with individual demand curves. Demand shifts right with an increase in demand and shifts left with a decrease in demand. There are situations when we will want to focus only on the relationship between price and quantity. In that case, we will write demand as $Q(p)$ and inverse demand as $p(Q)$. This implicitly assumes that all other relevant variables are held constant.

2.2.3   Demand Elasticities

At times, we want to know how much market demand responds to a change in a demand determinant, such as price or income. A measure of the responsiveness of demand (Q) to a change in its price (p) is the **price elasticity of demand**. It is defined as the percentage change in quantity demanded divided by the percentage change in price. For large changes it is defined as $(\Delta Q/Q)/(\Delta p/p)$. At times, we are interested in the effect on demand of a small change in price, which requires the use of calculus. In this case, the price elasticity of demand equals[9]

$$\epsilon \equiv \frac{\partial Q}{\partial p}\frac{p}{Q}. \tag{2.3}$$

Because demand is negatively sloped (i.e., $\partial Q/\partial p < 0$), the convention is to convert the price elasticity of demand to a positive value, a convention we adopt here. To avoid confusion with notation, we refer to the price elasticity of demand as $\eta = -\epsilon$. Normally, the price elasticity of demand is used to identify the absolute value of the percentage change in quantity demanded in response to a 1% change in price.[10] If $\eta = 2$, for example, this means that a 1% increase in price will lead to a 2% decrease in quantity demanded. When $\eta > 1$, demand is said to be elastic or relatively responsive to a price change. If $\eta = 1$, demand is said to be unit elastic. When $\eta < 1$, demand is said to be inelastic or relatively unresponsive to a price change.

Consider the example of a linear inverse demand function, $p = a - bQ$, where a and b are positive constants. In this case, $\partial Q/\partial p = -1/b$, and the price elasticity is

---

[9] The percentage change in Q is $\partial Q/Q$ and the percentage change in p is $\partial p/p$. Thus, $=(\partial Q/Q)/(\partial p/p) = (\partial Q/\partial p)(p/Q)$.

[10] Percentage changes are used because they are invariant to how output and price are measured. Across industries, it would be difficult to compare changes in gallons of milk with units of cars. Across countries, it would be difficult to compare price changes in dollars versus Euros.

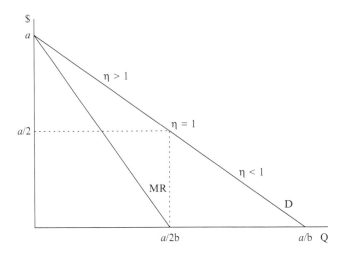

Fig. 2.3 Market demand, marginal revenue, and price elasticity

$$\eta = \frac{1}{b}\frac{p}{Q} = \frac{1}{b}\frac{a - bQ}{Q} = \frac{a}{bQ} - 1. \tag{2.4}$$

For a linear demand function, the elasticity varies along the demand curve. For the example where $p = a - bQ$, demand is unit elastic when $Q = a/(2b)$, is elastic when $Q < a/(2b)$, and is inelastic when $Q > a/(2b)$. This is illustrated in Fig. 2.3. Notice that the unit elastic point is halfway between the origin and the point where demand crosses the quantity axis. In general, the demand function is relatively more inelastic for necessities and for products that have few substitutes.

We are also interested in analyzing the effect of a change in consumer income on demand. We capture this effect with the **income elasticity of demand** (η_m), which measures the percentage change in quantity demanded resulting from a 1% change in income:

$$\eta_m \equiv \frac{\partial Q}{\partial m}\frac{m}{Q}. \tag{2.5}$$

As an example, if $\eta_m = 1.5$, a 1% increase in income results in a 1.5% increase in quantity demanded. As implied by the discussion above, a positive value of the income elasticity indicates that the good is a normal good, a negative value indicates that the good is inferior, and a zero value indicates that income has no effect on demand.

Another useful elasticity measure is the **cross-price elasticity of demand** between products i and j (η_{ij}). This measures the percentage change in the demand for good i resulting from a unit change in the price of good j:

$$\eta_{ij} \equiv \frac{\partial Q_i}{\partial p_j}\frac{p_j}{Q_i}. \tag{2.6}$$

The cross-price elasticity identifies when two goods are substitutes or complements. The cross-price elasticity is positive for substitute goods, negative for complement goods, and zero for unrelated goods. Estimating the cross-price elasticity of demand is useful for a firm producing multiple brands. For instance, Kellogg's produces Cornflakes and Special K (as well as a number of other brands of cereal). If Kellogg's is considering lowering the price of Cornflakes, the cross-price elasticity of demand would indicate the potential negative impact on the demand for Special K. Kellogg's can then judge the overall impact on revenues from a price reduction of Cornflakes. The cross-price elasticity is also useful to antitrust authorities in defining a market, the group of goods that constitute reasonably close substitutes.

2.2.4   Total Revenue, Marginal Revenue, Average Revenue, and Price Elasticity

Total, average, and marginal revenue are key concepts in economics. **Total revenue (TR)** or the total dollar value of sales equals price multiplied by quantity sold. Total revenue can be calculated for a firm or for the industry as a whole. **Average revenue (AR)** is the revenue per unit of output, and **marginal revenue (MR)** is the change in total revenue associated with a small change in output. For the industry as a whole, where total output is Q,

$$\text{TR} \equiv p(Q) \cdot Q, \tag{2.7}$$

$$\text{AR} \equiv \frac{\text{TR}}{Q} = p, \tag{2.8}$$

$$\text{MR} \equiv \frac{\partial \text{TR}}{\partial Q}. \tag{2.9}$$

Because AR equals price, the average revenue function is the same as the inverse demand function in the market. Along with (2.7), we can say that $\text{TR} = \text{AR} \cdot Q$.

From these definitions, we can derive a relationship between average revenue and marginal revenue. Given that $\text{TR} = \text{AR} \cdot Q$, marginal revenue can be written as

$$\text{MR} = \frac{\partial \text{TR}}{\partial Q} = \frac{\partial \text{AR}}{\partial Q} Q + \text{AR}. \tag{2.10}$$

Note that $\partial AR/\partial Q$ is the slope of the AR function. If $\partial AR/\partial Q > 0$, then MR $>$ AR; if $\partial AR/\partial Q < 0$ then MR $<$ AR; and if $\partial AR/\partial Q = 0$, then MR $=$ AR.[11] Because the slope of demand is negative, $\partial AR/\partial Q$ is always less than 0, and MR is always less than AR.

Next, we derive the relationship between marginal revenue and the price elasticity of demand. That is,[12]

$$MR = \frac{\partial TR}{\partial Q} = \frac{\partial [p(Q)Q]}{\partial Q},$$

$$MR = p + \frac{\partial p}{\partial Q}Q,$$

$$MR = p\left(1 + \frac{\partial p}{\partial Q}\frac{Q}{p}\right),$$

$$MR = p\left(1 - \frac{1}{\eta}\right). \tag{2.11}$$

Alternatively, by solving for η, (2.11) becomes

$$\eta = \frac{p}{p - MR}. \tag{2.12}$$

This tells us that if MR $= 0$, $\eta = 1$; if MR > 0, $\eta > 1$; and if MR < 0, $\eta < 1$.

As a simple example, consider the following linear inverse demand function, $p(Q) = a - bQ$, which is the same as the average revenue function in the market. Total revenue is

$$TR = p(Q) \cdot Q = aQ - bQ^2, \tag{2.13}$$

and marginal revenue is

$$MR = \frac{\partial TR}{\partial Q} = a - 2bQ. \tag{2.14}$$

The slope of the marginal revenue function is $-2b$, implying that it is twice as steep as the inverse demand function. As we saw above in (2.4), the price elasticity of demand in this linear case is

---

[11] This relationship holds for the average and marginal of any function, whether it be a revenue, production, or cost function. That is, the average is falling when marginal is below the average, the average is rising when the marginal is above the average, and the average is constant when the marginal equals the average.

[12] This is an application of the product rule, as discussed in the Mathematics and Econometrics Appendix at the end of the book. That is, if $y = wz$ where $w = f(x)$ and $z = g(x)$, then $dy/dx = w(dz/dx) + z(dw/dx)$. The derivative of the product of two functions equals the first function times the derivative of the second function plus the second function times the derivative of the first function.

Fig. 2.4 The total
revenue curve

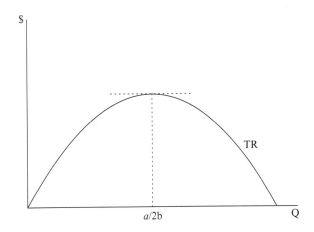

$$\eta = \frac{1}{b}\frac{p}{Q} = \frac{1}{b}\frac{a-bQ}{Q} = \frac{a}{bQ} - 1. \qquad (2.15)$$

Notice that a market with these qualities has several interesting features:

- Total revenue reaches a maximum when MR $= 0$, where $Q = a/(2b)$. At this output level, demand is unit elastic ($\eta = 1$).[13]
- When $Q < a/(2b)$, MR > 0 and demand is elastic ($\eta > 1$). In the elastic region of demand, a decrease in price (increase in output) causes total revenue to increase.
- When $Q > a/(2b)$, MR < 0 and demand is inelastic ($\eta < 1$). In the inelastic region of demand, a decrease in price (increase in output) causes total revenue to decrease.

These relationships are illustrated in Figs. 2.3 and 2.4. As a final point, because MR is the change in TR with respect to a small change in Q, TR is also the area under the MR curve for a given value of Q.[14]

In the next section, we extend the introductory demand model. We elaborate on the role of tastes and preferences when they are allowed to vary and depend upon a complex set of phenomena. The constructs of nonfunctional demand and behavioral economics allow us to accommodate varying tastes and preferences in the utility and demand equations.

2.2.5   Nonfunctional Demand and Behavioral Economics

The demand function discussed above corresponds to what Leibenstein (1950) called **functional demand**. With functional demand, a consumer purchases a

---

[13] We find Q that maximizes TR by taking its derivative (which is MR) and setting it to 0. Geometrically, the maximum or minimum occurs where the slope of a tangent line to a curve equals zero. Because TR is concave from below, TR reaches a maximum when MR $= 0$.

[14] That is, adding up all of the marginals gives us the total. In calculus, this is the integral of the marginal revenue function.

product based only on its intrinsic characteristics. We extend the model by allowing for nonfunctional motives of demand. This will enable us to better understand some of the marketing strategies used by real firms in the marketplace. **Nonfunctional** demand is motivated by qualities other than a product's inherent characteristics.

One source of nonfunctional demand occurs when utility functions are interdependent. An example of interdependence is the **bandwagon effect**, sometimes called a network effect, in which a consumer's demand for a good increases as more and more consumers purchase it. For example, your utility of contracting with a wireless phone company increases as more of your friends and relatives contract with the same company. The bandwagon effect can also occur when a person simply wants to feel a part of a particular group. Fads and fashion trends are types of bandwagon effects. The presence of bandwagon effects can cause market demand to be more elastic, because a drop in the price that causes more consumers to purchase the good will induce still more consumers to jump on the bandwagon and purchase the good as well.

Another example of interdependent utility is the **snob effect** which is the opposite of the bandwagon effect. A snob effect is present when someone enjoys being different from the crowd. Because a snob will experience greater utility when market demand is low, the demand curve with a snob effect will be less elastic than for the functional demand curve, *ceteris paribus*.

A third example is the **Veblen or conspicuous consumption effect** in which people purchase a good simply to impress others. Goods that are expensive and that have the quality that their consumption is readily observed by others are liable to have this conspicuous effect. Veblen effects are more likely to be present with a Rolls Royce automobile than with generic aspirin. The presence of Veblen effects causes demand to become more inelastic, as a higher price adds to the prestige factor and keeps demand from falling appreciably. Like a Giffen good, the Veblen effect could produce a positively sloped demand, at least in theory for a certain region of demand, when it dominates functional motives of demand.[15]

Leibenstein discussed two other types of nonfunctional demand: speculative and irrational. With the speculative motive, a consumer purchases a good only as an investment in the hope that the price will go up. Irrational demand stems from whims or sudden urges, a topic of behavioral economics.

Behavioral economics melds evidence from psychology and economics to provide a more accurate picture of consumer preferences. The evidence shows that consumers are not always fully rational. For instance, individuals tend to be overconfident, starting businesses that have a lower probability of success than they anticipate. People also make mistakes in optimizing when addressing complex problems. If you have money to invest, would you buy bonds, stocks, property, leave your money in the bank, or some combination? If you decide on stocks, which stocks would you buy and how many shares? It would be very difficult to choose the portfolio that maximizes utility within a budget. In addition to complexity,

---

[15] Anti-Veblen effects are also possible in which some consumers prefer goods that are inconspicuous.

consumers can make mistakes when they operate on "autopilot," making routine choices automatically without thinking about them. As discussed in the next chapter, operating on autopilot works well much of the time but can lead to serious errors when economic conditions change.

We can augment the utility function by adding a set of variables, $\underline{z}$, to control for errors and nonfunctional motives for demand. This set of variables also includes other taste and preference factors, which we identified as t in the introductory model discussed above. We underline z to imply that it is a vector, i.e., it represents more than just one variable. A consumer's utility function then becomes $U = U(q_1, q_2, \underline{z})$ and the demand function for good 1 can be written: $q_1 = d_1(p_1, p_2, m, \underline{z})$.

2.3 Technology and Costs[16]

The nature of technology also imposes a constraint on firm production. By **technology** we mean the entire body of knowledge concerning the methods used to bring inputs together to produce goods and services. This body of knowledge identifies the set of feasible production plans that are **technically efficient**, that is, the firm is not wasting inputs. This can be thought of in two different ways: (1) a firm is using the fewest inputs to produce a given output and (2) a firm is producing the maximum output from a given set of inputs.[17] Thus, a change in technology means that we add to technological knowledge, making inputs more productive in producing output.

One way to describe a given technology is with a production function. If just two inputs, labor (L) and physical capital (K),[18] are used to produce total output (q), the production function can be written as

$$q = q(L, K, T), \tag{2.16}$$

where T represents the level of technology. The production function identifies the maximum output that can be produced for this technology from a given quantity of inputs. It is sometimes called the *frontier production function*, because it represents the maximum level of output for a given quantity of inputs and technology. From production theory, the average product of input x (AP_x) is defined as q/x and the marginal product (MP_x) is defined as $\partial q/\partial x$, where x equals L or K.

To provide a concrete example, consider a Cobb–Douglas production function of the following form: $q = \alpha \cdot L^{1/2} \cdot K^{1/2}$. This functional form has just one

---

[16] You can learn more about the details of production and cost theory from any introductory or intermediate microeconomics textbook, such as Mankiw (2011), Bernheim and Whinston (2008), Pindyck and Rubenfield (2009), and Varian (2010). For more advanced treatments, see Nicholson and Snyder (2012), Varian (1992), and Mas-Colell et al. (1995).

[17] Technical and other types of efficiency are discussed in Chap. 5.

[18] This is different from financial capital, which is money used to make investments. In this simple model, other inputs such as raw materials are assumed to be included in capital.

parameter, α, which increases with a technological change. Regarding labor productivity, $AP_L = \alpha \cdot L^{-1/2} \cdot K^{1/2}$ and $MP_L = (\frac{1}{2})\alpha \cdot L^{-1/2} \cdot K^{1/2}$. If $L = 9$, $K = 16$, and $\alpha = 1$, then $q = 12$, $AP_L = 1.33$, and $MP_L = 0.67$. In this model, a technological change will cause α to increase, which increases total, average, and marginal productivity. For example, if α were to increase to 1.25, then $q = 15$, $AP_L = 1.67$, and $MP_L = 0.83$.

Duality theory demonstrates that a cost function contains the same economically relevant information about technology as a production function (Varian 1992). Thus, because many of the issues of interest in this book relate directly to costs, we will generally focus on cost functions rather than production functions. By costs we mean economic costs, which include the opportunity cost of all inputs used by the firm, whereas accounting costs typically mean historic costs (what a factor originally cost rather than its cost if purchased today).

A cost function is defined as the minimum expenditure of producing a given output for a given technology and is sometimes referred to as a *frontier cost function*. In our model with two inputs where w_L is the price of labor and w_K is the price (or rental rate) of capital, the long-run **total cost function** (TC) is given by[19]

$$TC = TC(w_L, w_k, q, T). \tag{2.17}$$

Costs increase with an increase in output and input prices, and costs decrease with a technological change, *ceteris paribus*. When a firm operates on its cost function, it is both technically and economically efficient. **Economic efficiency** means that the firm chooses the cost minimizing combination of inputs to produce a given output. If the firm were inefficient, it would produce a given output at a higher cost than the minimum identified by the cost function.

From the long-run total cost function, we can derive the average and marginal cost functions. The long-run **average cost** is $AC = TC/q$, and the long-run **marginal cost** is $MC = \partial TC / \partial q$.[20] In many cases, we will assume a U-shaped AC curve, as depicted in Fig. 2.5. It illustrates two important scale concepts: economies of scale and diseconomies of scale. The cost function exhibits **economics of scale** when long-run average cost falls as output increases. There are many reasons why this may occur. For example, a large firm may have less demand fluctuation than a smaller firm, enabling the larger enterprise to hold a smaller proportion of its sales as inventories. The presence of set-up costs that do not vary with output can also produce a declining average cost function. For instance, if a publisher pays an author $10,000 to write a book and the average cost of printing and distributing the book is constant, then average total cost falls with production.

---

[19] This solves the following long-run problem where all inputs are variable: minimize total expenditures, $w_L \cdot L + w_K \cdot K$, with respect to L and K given the production function. For further discussion, see Varian (2010, Chap. 20).

[20] In future chapters, we will usually be discussing long-run phenomena and will refer to long-run average cost as AC and long run marginal cost as MC.

Fig. 2.5 The long-run average and marginal cost curves

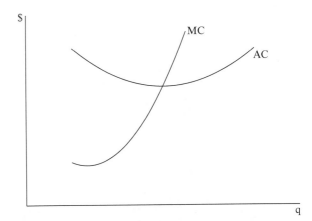

Another principle reason for economies of scale is associated with gains from specialization. Adam Smith's (1776) discussion of a British pin factory provides the most striking historical example:

> ...One man draws out the wire, another straights it, a third cuts it, a fourth points it, a fifth grinds it at the top for receiving, the head; to make the head requires two or three distinct operations; to put it on is a peculiar business, to whiten the pins is another; it is even a trade by itself to put them into the paper; and the important business of making a pin is, in this manner, divided into about eighteen distinct operations ... I have seen a small manufactory of this kind where ten men only were employed ... [who] could make among them upwards of forty-eight thousand pins in a day. Each person ... might be considered as making four thousand eight hundred pins in a day. But if they had all wrought separately and independently ... they certainly could not each of them have made twenty, perhaps not one pin in a day ...

This illustrates how the specialization of labor can produce economies of scale.

Of course, average costs cannot decline forever. At some point, long-run average cost must begin to rise. When this occurs, the cost function exhibits **diseconomies of scale**. Organization rather than technological considerations causes scale diseconomies. Management costs may eventually rise disproportionately with size. When surveyed, most people indicate that they would prefer to work for a larger organization if they were lazy and less productive than the average worker. When the cost of supervising a larger number of employees rises sufficiently with firm size, a larger enterprise will have a larger set-up (managerial) cost per unit of production. We will talk more about costs such as these subsequently.

In reality, long-run cost functions may be constant over a particular range of output. This is depicted between x and y in Fig. 2.6. When the long-run average cost function remains unchanged for an increase in output (i.e., region $x - y$), the cost function exhibits **constant returns to scale**.[21] The notion of replication explains why this segment is flat. Once all scale economies have been exploited,

---

[21] Note that because AC reaches a minimum between x and y, MC equals AC from x to y.

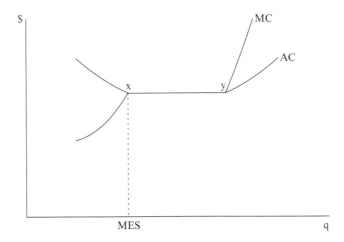

Fig. 2.6 The long-run average and marginal cost curves when there are constant returns to scale over a range of output

replicating what has been done before assures that long-run average costs remain constant. The minimum level of production needed to take advantage of all economies of scale is a useful concept in industrial organization and is given a special name, **minimum efficient scale** (MES).

In many cases, we will assume a simple U-shaped AC. One way to describe such a technology is to assume that AC is a parabola. As an example, assume that it is

$$\text{AC} = \frac{100 - 20q + q^2 + 40\alpha}{4\alpha}, \qquad (2.18)$$

where $\alpha > 0$ is a parameter which indicates how fast the parabola will open up. A larger α means that AC is flatter, implying that technology is approaching constant returns to scale.[22] In this example, MC is

$$\text{MC} = \frac{100 - 40q + 3q^2 + 40\alpha}{4\alpha}. \qquad (2.19)$$

Notice that at $q = 10$, AC reaches a minimum and equals MC (AC = MC = 10). AC and MC are described in Fig. 2.7 for two different technologies, one

---

[22] More generally, we can write this as AC $= [(q - x_1) + 4\alpha y_1]/4\alpha$, where (x_1, y_1) is the vertex of the parabola (where it reaches a maximum or a minimum). When $\alpha > 0$, the parabola is concave from above (i.e., it opens up from above), as in (2.18). When $\alpha < 0$, the parabola is concave from below (i.e., it opens up from below). We can also describe a parabola that opens up from the left or right by reversing x_1 and y_1 and reversing AC and q in the equation above. In this case, the parabola opens to the right when $\alpha > 0$ and opens to the left when $\alpha < 0$. In both cases, the parabola opens up faster with a larger value of α.

Fig. 2.7 Curvature of long-run average cost curves

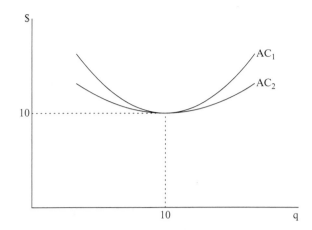

where $\alpha = 1$ (AC$_1$) and the other where $\alpha = 2$ (AC$_2$). In the limit, as α approaches infinity, both AC and MC approach horizontal lines at the value 10; technology exhibits constant returns to scale for all values of output.

There are occasions when we will assume a technology that exhibits constant returns to scale. This simplification can be useful in oligopoly models where strategic interaction complicates the analysis. In this case, long-run total, average, and marginal cost functions are linear:

$$\text{TC} = c \cdot q, \tag{2.20}$$

$$\text{AC} = \frac{\text{TC}}{q} = c, \tag{2.21}$$

$$\text{MC} = \frac{\partial \text{TC}}{\partial q} = c. \tag{2.22}$$

Notice that AC = MC = c, a constant value regardless of output level. The cost functions for this model are graphed in Fig. 2.8. Note that this cost function exhibits constant returns to scale for all values of output.

As we said previously, a technological change will cause a decrease in costs, *ceteris paribus*. Recall from our discussion of the production function that a technological change increases the total, average, and marginal product. The firm can use fewer inputs to produce a given output, enabling total, average, and marginal costs to fall with a technological change.[23]

---

[23] To illustrate, in our two input example, total cost equals $w_L \cdot L + w_K \cdot K$. AC = TC/$q$ = $w_L \cdot L/q + w_K \cdot K/q = w_L/\text{AP}_L + w_K/\text{AP}_K$. MC = $\partial \text{TC}/\partial q = w_L \cdot \partial L/\partial q + w_K \cdot \partial K/\partial q = w_L/\text{MP}_L + w_K/\text{MP}_K$. Because a technological change increases the average and marginal product of each input, AC and MC fall with a technological change.

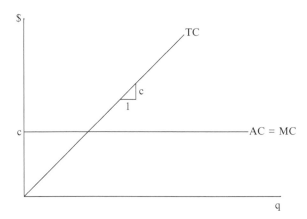

Fig. 2.8 Linear total, average, and marginal cost curves

Although most of our attention will be devoted to the technologies described above, there is another cost structure that will be useful when discussing investments that affect entry. An entrant may face an initial set-up cost, which is called a **quasi-fixed cost** (F).[24] These are costs that must be paid before any output can be produced. Traditional fixed costs are associated with fixed inputs that are present in the short run but not the long run, whereas quasi-fixed costs inputs do exist in the long run. Assuming a linear total cost function when there are set-up costs, $TC = c \cdot q + F$ and $MC = c$. Average cost is nonlinear, however: $AC = c + F/q$. Thus, average cost declines with output.

When we consider the cost of entering a market, it will be important to identify the portion of F that is a sunk cost. A **sunk cost** is an expenditure that cannot be recovered once it is made. To illustrate, a firm may buy a factory with a market value of $10 million and spend $2 million on an advertising campaign. Both are fixed costs. If the firm goes out of business, the money spent on advertising is entirely sunk. On the other hand, if the market value of the plant is $9, only $1 million of the $10 million spent on the plant is sunk.

The cost function is more complex for firms that produce multiple products, a common feature in the real world. For example, General Electric provides financial services and produces electrical equipment. General Mills produces over 30 different types of breakfast cereal. When this occurs, we use a multiproduct cost function to describe technology. To illustrate this idea, consider the case with just two goods, 1 and 2. The total cost of producing both goods would depend upon the quantity produced of both goods, the price of inputs, and the state of technology:

$$TC = TC(w_L, w_k, q_1, q_2, T). \tag{2.23}$$

---

[24] For further discussion of variable, fixed, and quasi-fixed costs, see Varian (2010, Chap. 20).

An important motive for multiproduct production is the presence of **economies of scope** (Baumol et al. 1982). In our two good example, there are economies of scope if joint production by a single firm is cheaper than production by two separate firms. Ignoring other variables, scope economies exist if

$$TC(q_1 = x, q_2 = y) < TC(q_1 = x, q_2 = 0) + TC(q_1 = 0, q_2 = y), \qquad (2.24)$$

where x and y are positive constants.

Economies of scope can arise for a variety of reasons. One is the presence of complementarities in production. For example, hides are a by-product of beef production, and beef is a by-product of hide production. Clearly, separate production would be cost ineffective, with the beef producer throwing hides away and the hides producer throwing beef away. Economies of scope can also result when production of different products share a common input. In the railroad industry, for instance, the sharing of a common railroad track makes the joint offering of passenger and freight services cost effective for a single firm.

2.4   The Theory of the Firm

To this point, we have referred rather loosely to the concept of a firm. Firms are complex and multifaceted enterprises, making it difficult to provide a simple explanation of the goals and nature of a firm. As a result, most theories focus on a few key elements. In this section, we discuss the motives of the firm and the most important forces that shape its boundaries.[25]

In the USA, there are two basic types of business enterprises, **unincorporated firms**, which include single proprietorships (single owner) and partnerships (multiple owners), and **corporations**. The primary distinction between them is the degree of owner liability if the firm goes out of business. In an unincorporated business, owners are liable for all the firm's debts, which may exceed the amount of money that owners have invested in the firm. In a corporation, stockholders (owners) risk only the amount of money they have invested in the firm. This limited liability makes it easier for an incorporated firm to raise the financial capital needed to build a large business enterprise. In 2008, only 18% of businesses were corporations, but they accounted for 81% of total US sales.[26]

---

[25] For a more complete discussion of the theory of the firm, see Tirole (1988), Shughart (1990), Hay and Morris (1991), and Greer (1992).

[26] This information is available at http://www.census.gov/compendia/statab/2012/tables/12s0744.pdf, accessed November 22, 2011.

2.4.1 Firm Motives

In the simple neoclassical approach, the firm is considered a "black box" or institution that transforms inputs into outputs to maximize profits. In this case, profits mean economic profits, not accounting profits. Economic profits equal total revenue minus economic costs.[27] Profit maximization requires cost minimization, so the neoclassical firm is always technically and economically efficient. What takes place within the black box is assumed to be efficient and is ignored. Assuming that profit maximization is the goal of the firm simplifies the analysis of both firms and markets alike. But how realistic is this assumption?

There are two main concerns with the profit maximization assumption. First, it presumes a static world in which a decision today affects current but not future profits. When this is true, the firm can ignore the future when making a decision today, but this would be untrue in some markets. As an example, cigarette companies have been known to give away free cigarettes. Setting price to zero is not profit maximizing in a static market, but it may be wealth maximizing in a dynamic market. That is, giving away cigarettes today will lead to greater consumer addiction and enable the firm to charge a higher price tomorrow. Thus, the firm must weigh the gain tomorrow against the loss today of giving away cigarettes. In dynamic markets such as this, firms are more likely to utilize the dynamic version of profit maximization—maximization of the value of the firm.

From a financial perspective, the fundamental value of an asset such as the security (stock) of a firm equals the present value of the stream of its expected future returns (profits).[28] Analysis of such problems is complicated by the fact that $1 received a year from today is not valued the same as a $1 received today. For most of us, including financial planners, $1 received in the future is worth less and must be discounted to obtain its present value (i.e., its value today).

The discount factor (D) is used to convert future dollars to their present value. It is defined as the current or present value of $1 received next period. At one extreme, when D equals 1, there is no discounting: $1 received next period is worth $1 today. At the other extreme, when D equals 0, the future does not matter at all: $1 received next period is worth nothing today. Thus, D ranges from 0 to 1, with a higher D implying that a greater value is placed on the future. For example, if $D = 0.9$, then

---

[27] Accounting profits equal total revenue minus accounting costs, which ignore the opportunity cost of the resources supplied by company owners. Thus, zero economic profit means that the firm would stay in business, because all input suppliers are paid their opportunity costs and owners earn a normal rate of return on their financial investments. Zero economic profit corresponds to a positive accounting profit that would earn the firm a normal rate of return. For further discussion of the distinctions between accounting profit and economic profit, see Frank and Bernanke (2008), Pindyck and Rubenfield (2009), or Varian (2010).

[28] According to Fama (1965), the market value of a security will equal its fundamental value in an efficient market. This is called the efficient market hypothesis. Nevertheless, market frictions may cause market values to deviate from fundamental values, and they may take time to converge (Farmer and Lo, 1999; Lo, 2004; Malkiel, 2011).

$1 received in period 1 is worth 90¢ in period 0. To get the present value of $1 received in period 2, we must multiply $1 by D twice (or by D^2), which equals 81¢. Similarly, the present value of receiving $1 three periods from now is D^3, and so on.

Given this information about discounting, it is now rather easy to define the fundamental value of a firm. Consider the simple case where a firm is expected to earn the same profit (π) in each period, t, from $t = 0$ (this period), 1, 2, 3, ..., ∞. In this case, the value of the firm (V) is

$$V(\pi, \infty) = D^0\pi + D^1\pi + D^2\pi + \cdots + D^\infty\pi,$$
$$= \pi(D^0 + D^1 + D^2 + \cdots + D^\infty). \qquad (2.25)$$

Although it may appear that the value of the firm is infinite, this is not the case. As we prove in Appendix 2.A,

$$V(\pi, \infty) = \frac{\pi}{1 - D}. \qquad (2.26)$$

In our example where $D = 0.9$ and $\pi = \$1$, $V = \$10$. That is, the present value of receiving $1 every period starting today is $10.

The assumption that the goal is to maximize the value of the firm is essentially the dynamic version of profit maximization. The model allows the firm to give up profit today when it can gain sufficient profit tomorrow. If no such investment opportunities across periods exist, static profit maximization in each period is equivalent to the maximization of the fundamental value of the firm.

The second concern with assuming that the goal of a firm is to maximize profit (or value) is that most large corporations are run by managers, not owners (stockholders). Owners may want managers to maximize profit, but managers are more likely to be concerned with their own utility, which may depend on income, prestige, and other psychological factors. This creates a conflict of interest, which can be costly to rectify given that it can be expensive for owners to monitor the effort and behavior of managers. Thus, managers may get away with pursuing goals other than profit maximization. This is called a **principle–agent problem**, which exists when the principle's (owner's) welfare depends on the actions of the agent (manager), and their goals are not aligned (Jensen and Meckling, 1976; Fama and Jensen, 1983).

The principle–agent problem is especially difficult for large corporations with many stockholders. First, it may be difficult to manage and observe manager effort in a large enterprise. After all, this is why owners hire managers in the first place. Second, when ownership is dispersed over many stockholders, each of whom owns a small fraction of the company's stock, it would not be cost effective for any one stockholder to closely monitor manager behavior. Consequentially, managers have substantial discretion. In theory, unprofitable conduct can be corrected for managers who are income maximizers. In this case, owners would simply tie manager salaries to profits. This is a type of incentive-compatible contract, because it aligns the interests of managers with owners. In practice, such contracts may make it difficult to hire good managers who are risk averse and want to avoid wide swings in income associated with profit variation that is caused by exogenous shocks.

Incentive compatibility is even more problematic when managers have uneconomic motivations. Marris (1964) argues that managers have three dominant motives: income, status, and power. Managers who are more interested in status than income may emphasize unprofitable growth over profits if this behavior places them on the cover of a business magazine, for example. In this case, tying manager income to profits will fail to encourage profit-maximizing behavior.

Of course, managers do not have unlimited discretion. In addition to incentive-compatible contracts, market forces also encourage managers to pursue profit maximizing goals. Competition in product markets will pressure a manager to maximize profits; otherwise the firm will eventually go out of business. In the long run, survivors will evolve and must be profit maximizers (Alchian 1950). Even when insulated from competition, pressure to generate profits still persists. First, underperforming managers can be fired by the company's board of directors who monitor management performance and represent the interests of shareholders. Second, there is a labor market for managers, and those who are better at maximizing profits will be more mobile and will command higher salaries. Third, there is a market for corporate control, where firms with successful management teams buy firms with unsuccessful ones and replace underperforming managers with those who have goals that are more in line with profit maximization.[29]

Given the compelling arguments on both sides, we will not always use the profit maximization assumption. For the most part, we will assume profit maximization, because it simplifies the analysis and because profits certainly have a role to play in business. When managerial and behavioral motives are likely to provide better explanations of actual firm behavior, especially regarding merger activity in Chap. 18, we relax the profit maximization assumption in favor of other motives.

2.4.2   The Boundaries of the Firm

In this section, we discuss the reasons why firms exist and the forces that shape the size and boundaries of a firm. Economic activity can be coordinated through markets, where price movements guide production, or within firms, where managers make production decisions. At issue is the extent to which a firm should perform its own production and service tasks or purchase them in the market from outside suppliers. If we stick with the profit maximization assumption, then a firm will exist and increase or decrease its size if it is profitable to do so.

There are many advantages and disadvantages of setting up a firm to produce output. In terms of production costs, the presence of scale economies provides one reason why a firm may expand its scale of operation. This is referred to as **horizontal growth**. A merger between two firms within the same industry, such as McDonald's

---

[29] See Chap. 13 for a more complete discussion of the market for corporate control.

and Burger King, is called a horizontal merger. Economies of scope provide another reason for firm growth. In this case, the firm may expand into related markets, such as passenger and freight rail service, or into unrelated markets, such as beef and hides. Expansion into unrelated markets is called **conglomerate growth**.

Coase (1937) was the first to state that firms emerge for more than purely technological reasons. He argued that one advantage of organizing production within a firm rather than through markets is that the firm reduces the number of market transactions. Thus, transaction costs are lower as the firm expands its scale and scope of operation. **Transaction costs** are those expenses that are associated with trading (and are in addition to the price itself). Besides price, a cabinet manufacturer that transacts with an independent lumber supplier must negotiate the type of wood and the delivery date of each order. These transaction costs can be substantially reduced if the cabinet manufacturer buys the lumber supplier. When a wholesaler grows by purchasing an input supplier or a retail distributor, this is called **vertical growth**.

Of course, there are forces that limit firm size as well. Otherwise, the most cost-efficient structure would be to have just one firm, call it the super firm (or government), that produces everything. Regarding vertical growth, Grossman and Hart (1986) point out that when a manufacturer buys an input supplier, the merger reduces the input supplier's flexibility and control, which may lead to inefficiencies. Second, when there are substantial scale economies at the input supply level, a scale-efficient input supplier may be too large to be profitably owned by a single wholesaler.

The size of the firm is also limited by managerial capacity, as organization and monitoring costs may increase with the complexity and number of tasks found in larger and larger enterprises. Alchian and Demsetz (1972) illustrate how this can be a problem when the firm is viewed as an institution that captures the benefits of team production. The role of the manager or coach is to monitor workers to ensure adequate performance. The case below provides an historical example where workers actually hired an overseer (manager) to perform the task of monitor.

> On the Yangtze River in China, there is a section of fast water over which boats are pulled upstream by a team of coolies [unskilled workers] prodded by an overseer using a whip. On one such passage an American lady, horrified at the sight of the overseer whipping the men as they strained at their harnesses, demanded that something be done about the brutality. She was quickly informed by the captain that nothing could be done: Those men own the right to draw boats over this stretch of water and they have hired the overseer and given him his duties. (McManus 1975, 341)

If shirking of one's duties among team members grows with firm size, managerial costs will increase with the size of the firm.[30]

---

[30] Alchian and Demsetz' view also explains why football and track coaches behave differently. It is more difficult to identify shirking (i.e., less that 100% effort) of an offensive lineman on a football team than of a sprinter on a track team. Thus, coaches spend more time monitoring performance and promoting team spirit that is designed to minimizing shirking in football than in track.

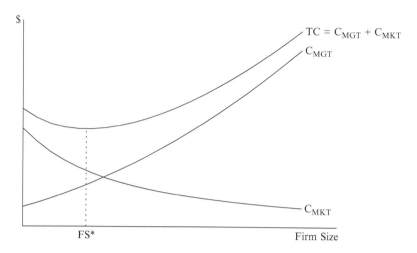

Fig. 2.9 Cost-minimizing firm with market (C_{MKT}) and management (C_{MGT}) costs

We can summarize the influence of these factors on cost-minimizing firm size by dividing costs into two groups. The first consists of those that decline with firm size, such as transaction costs. These are the costs associated with using the market instead of the firm. We call this the cost of using the market (C_{MKT}). The second increases with firm size, as is true with managerial costs. We call this the cost of managing a firm (C_{MGT}). These costs are illustrated in Fig. 2.9. If they represent all relevant costs, the firm size that minimizes total costs ($C_{MKT} + C_{MGT}$) is FS^*.[31]

At the same time, firm size is not driven by cost considerations alone. Strategic reasons can also influence the size and growth of a firm. For example, a horizontal merger between McDonald's and Burger King may be profitable only because it raises price by reducing competition. In addition, a firm that would like to charge different prices to distributors in different geographic markets may buy up its distributors in the low price market, eliminating the possibility of arbitrage between low and high priced distributors. **Arbitrage** is the purchase and almost immediate sale of a security or commodity to profit from price discrepancies. In this case, the firm is engaging in price discrimination by charging a high price to distributors in region H and a low price in region L. Without the merger, type-L distributors could make a profit by selling to H-type distributors, and the firm would be unable to charge a high price to H-types. The merger would eliminate such trading.

Analysis of the constraints imposed by competing firms is a key theme throughout the book. In the next chapter, we lay out the basics of game theory, which is used to identify firm strategy and the constraints imposed by rival firms.

---

[31] Notice that unlike most problems in economics, the solution does not occur where the two curves intersect.

2.5 Summary

1. The production process is generally divided up into two periods, the short run and the long run. In the short run, some inputs are variable and others are fixed. In the long run, all inputs are variable. In this book, we focus on long-run economic problems.

2. Demand is derived from the individual's pursuit of utility maximization, while facing budget and other constraints. The **law of demand** holds that consumers will demand less of a good when its price increases, *ceteris paribus*.

3. The factors that shift the demand curve are those that affect utility or the budget constraint: prices of substitute and complementary goods, tastes, and income.

4. If the price of good 1 increases and the quantity demanded of good 2 rises, the goods are **substitutes**. Chevy and Ford trucks are examples of substitute goods. **Complements** are goods that are used together. If the price of good 1 increases, the quantity demanded of good 2 will fall if goods 1 and 2 are complements. Cell phones and cell phone batteries are examples of complements.

5. If an increase in income leads to an increase in demand, the good is a **normal good**. If an increase in income decreases demand, the good is **inferior**. And if an increase in income has no effect on demand, the good is **income-neutral**.

6. **Market demand** is the horizontal sum of the demand curves for all of the individuals in the market. It depends on the number of consumers, as well as prices of related goods, income, and tastes.

7. The **price elasticity of demand** (η) measures the responsiveness of quantity demanded to a change in price. If it exceeds 1, demand is elastic; if it equals 1, demand is of unitary elasticity; and if it is less than 1, demand is inelastic.

8. The **income elasticity of demand** (η_m) measures the responsiveness of demand to a change in income. The sign determines whether a good is normal, inferior, or income-neutral.

9. The **cross-price elasticity of demand** for goods 1 and 2 (η_{12}) indicates the responsiveness of the demand for good 1 to a change in the price of good 2. A positive value indicates the goods are substitutes; a negative value indicates they are complements; and a zero value means that they are unrelated.

10. **Total revenue** (TR) is price times the quantity sold of a good. **Marginal revenue** (MR) is the change in total revenue associated with a small change in quantity sold. **Average revenue** (AR) is the revenue per unit and is total revenue divided by quantity sold. By definition, average revenue equals the price, and total revenue equals average revenue times quantity sold.

11. For a linear demand curve, the MR curve lies below and is twice as steep as the demand curve. The relationship between MR and the price elasticity of demand (η) is: $MR = p(1 - 1/\eta)$; $\eta = p/(p - MR)$. When $MR > 0$, $\eta > 1$; when $MR = 0$, $\eta = 1$; when $MR < 0$, $\eta < 1$.

12. **Functional demand** derives from the inherent characteristics of a commodity and from actually using or consuming the good. **Nonfunctional demand** refers to a part of demand that is not due to the intrinsic qualities of a good. The speculative motive is one example, which occurs when a consumer buys a good as an

investment in the hope that it will go up in value. Other non-functional motives are bandwagon, snob, and Veblen effects. **Bandwagon effects** occur when a person desires a good because others do. **Snob effects** occur when a person desires a good because others do not—he or she does not want to buy goods that are popular. **Veblen effects** (conspicuous consumption) occur when a person wants to show off his or her wealth by buying prestigious and expensive goods.

13. **Behavioral economics** integrates evidence from psychology into economics. It informs us that people make particular kinds of mistakes when they make choices, such as being overconfident. People might also make mistakes because choices are too complex.

14. The production function specifies how output depends on inputs and technology. The total cost function relates total cost to the quantity of output, input prices, and technology.

15. The **total cost function** is derived by minimizing costs for a specific technology (represented by the production function). **Average cost** or unit cost is total cost divided by quantity produced. **Marginal cost** is the change in total cost associated with a small change in quantity produced.

16. There may be regions of output under which long-run average cost declines, is constant, or increases as output increases. When average cost is falling, marginal cost is below average cost. When average cost is constant or reaches a minimum, marginal cost equals average cost. When average cost is rising, marginal cost is above average cost. **Economies of scale** arise when long-run average costs decline as output increases. Gains from specialization provide one reason for economies of scale. **Constant returns to scale** means that average cost is constant when output changes. Efficient replication in the absence of managerial constraints predicts constant returns to scale. **Diseconomies of scale** occur when long-run average costs rise with additional units of output and may arise because of increasing organization and monitoring costs associated with large enterprises. The minimum level of production needed to take advantage of all economies of scale is called **minimum efficient scale**.

17. **Quasi-fixed costs** are set-up costs that must be paid before output can be produced. There are no fixed costs in the long run, but quasi-fixed costs do exist in the long run.

18. A fixed cost is an expenditure that is associated with fixed inputs and unaffected by the level of production. A **sunk cost** is an expenditure that cannot be recovered once it is made.

19. Many firms in the real world are multiproduct producers, companies that produce a variety of different products. A technological motive for multiproduct production is the presence of **economies of scope**, which exists when joint production is cheaper than separate production.

20. There are two basic types of business enterprises: **unincorporated firms**, which include single proprietorships (single owner) and partnerships (multiple owners), and **corporations**. In an unincorporated business, owners are liable for all the firm's debts, which may exceed the amount of money owners

have invested in the firm. In a corporation, stockholders risk only the amount of money they have invested in the firm.

21. The common, neoclassical assumption is that firms behave as profit maximizers. In dynamic markets, however, investments today increase revenues tomorrow but not today. In this case, the dynamic equivalent of profit maximization is maximization of the value of the firm. Another problem with profit maximization arises in large corporations where managers and owners are different individuals and their goals are not aligned. This creates a **principle–agent problem**: the principle's (owner's) welfare depends on the behavior of the agent (manager) but their goals are not the same. In this case, managerial goals may be pursued rather than profit maximization.

22. If we assume that firms are profit (wealth) maximizers, then a firm will exist and adjust its size if it is profitable to do so. The presence of high transaction costs associated with using the market and substantial scale and scope economies will lead to larger firms. The cost of managing a larger and larger enterprise limits firm size. These include the cost of organizing a complex enterprise and the cost of monitoring employees. Strategic considerations can also influence firm size.

23. A firm can expand its size through horizontal, vertical, and conglomerate growth. **Horizontal growth** refers to an increase in the scale of operation of a firm. One example is when a cabinet manufacturer increases its capacity to produce kitchen cabinets. **Vertical growth** means that a manufacturer expands along its stream of production, such as a manufacturer that starts producing its own inputs and distributing its final products to customers. **Conglomerate growth** refers to an increase in the scope of operation of a firm. One example is if a cabinet manufacturer expanded into the fast-food industry.

24. **Arbitrage** is the purchase and almost immediate sale of a security or commodity to profit from price discrepancies across markets.

2.6   Review Questions

1. Show how an increase in the number of consumers will affect the market demand for a good or service.

2. What is the difference between the snob effect and conspicuous consumption?

3. Suppose that goods 1 and 2 are substitutes, and that the price of good 2 falls. How would demand for good 1 be affected? Illustrate graphically.

4. If income falls and demand for a good decreases, is the good normal, inferior, or income-neutral?

5. The income elasticity of a good is 0.

   A. Interpret the value of the income elasticity.
   B. Is the good normal or inferior?

6. A firm sells two brands of a good, x and y. The firm is considering raising the price of brand y. The cross-price elasticity is -0.5.

   A. Interpret the value of the cross-price elasticity.
   B. State whether the two brands are substitutes, complements, or unrelated.

7. Consider a market with the following inverse demand function, $p = a - 2bQ$, where a and b are positive constants.

   A. Write down the TR function and the MR function.
   B. Graph the demand curve and the MR curve.
   C. What is the value of MR when the price elasticity of demand (η) equals 1?
   D. What is the maximum value of TR, and what is the value of η when TR reaches a maximum?

8. In the 1940s and 1950s, tattoos were popular, but then tattoos fell out of favor until the first decade of the twenty-first century.

   A. Did the functional demand for tattoos change from 1950 to 1970? From 1970 to 2010?
   B. Is the demand for tattoos influenced by speculative, snob, bandwagon, or conspicuous consumption effects?

9. Fill in the appropriate numbers in the empty cells in the table below.

Q	Total cost	Average cost	Marginal cost
0	70	–	–
1	200	200	130
2	320		
3		153.3	139.9

10. A technological change improves the efficiency of the production of a good. How do you expect that this will affect a firm's long-run average and marginal costs?

11. How do you think that the development and use of the Internet affects transaction costs for the firm? Do you think that it would affect the optimal firm size associated with transaction costs? If so, how?

12. Every day, a clothing design firm needs workers who sew. It could contract out these services to tailor shops or hire tailors and conduct the business of sewing in house. Compare the relative firm versus market costs for this problem for two firms: Firm 1 sells low-cost dresses, and firm 2 sells high cost, designer dresses. Which business is more likely to use the market and which is more likely to have tailors within the firm?

13. Why might a firm engage in horizontal, vertical, and conglomerate growth?

Appendix A: A Review of Present Value and Discounting[32]

In general, people value assets differently when they are received today versus sometime in the future. When children are given the option of receiving a candy bar now or tomorrow, most want it now. The candy dilemma exhibits a fundamental principle about human behavior—a given asset is generally valued more when received today than in the future. There are many reasons why preferences may exhibit this quality. There is always the risk that we may not be here tomorrow. In addition, most people are impatient. As a person becomes more impatient, he or she will place a higher value on the present.

Given these tendencies, we need to adjust the value of a given asset when received in different periods of time. One way to see how we might account for time differences is to look at how an asset grows in value over time. Given that people place a higher value on current dollars, they must receive some compensation to induce them to loan it to others. Assuming that this rate equals r, the annual rate of return on an investment, then an investment of $\$x$ will be worth $\$y_1$ in 1 year (or period one) according to the following formula:

$$\text{Value of } x \text{ in 1 Year}: y_1 = x(1+r). \tag{A.1}$$

Ignoring risk and assuming that all assets earn a rate of r per year, we can work backwards and determine today's value of any asset worth y_1 in 1 year. This is called the present value (PV) of asset y_1 that is received 1 year from now. It simply equals x and is calculated as follows:

$$\text{PV}(y_1): x = y_1/(1+r) = y_1 \cdot D, \tag{A.2}$$

where $D \equiv 1/(1+r)$ is defined as the discount factor, the rate at which a payment next year must be discounted to give us its present value.[33] In other words, D represents the present value of $\$1$ received next year.

You can get a better feel for the discount factor by considering extreme values of D. When $D = 1$, there is no discounting. In this case, $\$1$ received next period is worth $\$1$ today. When $D = 0$, future dollars are worthless today (i.e., there is no tomorrow). If $D = 0.95$, then $\$1$ received next period is worth 95¢ today. Thus, D will range from 0 to 1, which can be written as $D \in [0, 1]$.

To determine the PV of asset y_2 when it is received 2 years from now, we must discount it twice. Discounting it one time gives the present value of the asset 1 year from now. Discounting it again gives the present value of the asset today. Thus,

$$\text{PV}(y_2) = y_2 \cdot D \cdot D = y_2 \cdot D^2 = y_2/(1+r)^2. \tag{A.3}$$

---

[32] For a more detailed discussion, see Chiang (1984, 280–281; 462–464) and Simon and Blume (1994, 97–99).

[33] Alternatively, $r \equiv (1 - D)/D$.

More generally, an asset received t years from now is

$$PV(y_t) = y_t \cdot D^t = y_t/(1+r)^t. \tag{A.4}$$

In some problems in finance and economics, it is useful to identify the PV of a stream of payoffs that will be received in every period from today (period 0) to infinity. Assuming the payoff (π) is the same in each period,

$$PV(\pi, \infty) = \pi/(1+r)^0 + \pi/(1+r)^1 + \pi/(1+r)^2 + \pi/(1+r)^3 + \cdots$$
$$+ \pi/(1+r)^\infty,$$
$$= \pi \cdot \left[1 + D^1 + D^2 + D^3 + \cdots + D^\infty\right]. \tag{A.5}$$

This can be simplified as follows. First, we define

$$\alpha_0 \equiv \left[1 + D^1 + D^2 + D^3 + \cdots + D^\infty\right], \tag{A.6}$$

$$\alpha_1 \equiv \left[D^1 + D^2 + D^3 + \cdots + D^\infty\right] = \alpha_0 \cdot D. \tag{A.7}$$

Substituting (A.6) into (A.5) yields

$$PV(\pi, \infty) = \pi \cdot \alpha_0. \tag{A.8}$$

Note that $\alpha_0 - \alpha_1 = 1$ or that $\alpha_0 - \alpha_0 \cdot D = 1$ by substitution. Thus,

$$\alpha_0 = 1/(1 - D). \tag{A.9}$$

Substituting (A.9) into (A.8) yields

$$PV(\pi, \infty) = \pi/(1 - D). \tag{A.10}$$

Equation (A.10) makes it easy to calculate the present value of a payoff stream that is received each period from today to infinity. For example, if $\pi = \$100$ and $D = 0.9$ (i.e., $r = 1/9$), then $PV(\pi = 100, \infty) = \$1,000$.

Chapter 3
Introductory Game Theory and Economic Information

Strategic decisions are an integral part of our daily lives. Game theory provides a foundation for analyzing strategy, and as such, is a vitally important subject. At work, you may need to decide whether it is worth it to put in extra hours to earn a bigger bonus than your colleagues. Strategic decisions are especially common in competitive games, such as chess, tennis, football, and the TV show Survivor. These are considered games because strategic interaction is important to success. That is, to decide your best course of action, you must consider how others are likely to behave. Two examples make this point clear.

First, consider the dollar auction developed by Shubik (1971). A dollar bill is put up for auction. The auction has two rules: (1) The highest bidder pays the amount bid and receives the dollar. (2) The second highest bidder gets nothing but also pays the amount bid. How would you behave in such an auction? In classroom experiments, students frequently bid more than a dollar. The reason for this is that if you have bid 90¢ and another student has bid a dollar, you have an incentive to raise your bid to $1.01. If you do not raise your bid you will be out 90¢, and if you win you are out only 1¢. Once you have mastered the material in this chapter, you should be able to figure out the best way to play the dollar auction game.

The second example involves the game of tennis. When returning Mark's serve in a tennis game, you might consider hitting the ball crosscourt or down the line, a decision that will be based on the side of the court that you believe Mark will not cover. Likewise, Mark wants to cover the side of the court where he expects you to hit the ball. Clearly, your success depends on Mark's action as well as your own.

These examples pose rather deep strategic problems for each player. When returning Mark's serve, Mark is thinking about what you will do, and you are thinking about what Mark will do. So you will want to anticipate what Mark thinks you will do. Mark will do the same and try to anticipate what you think he will do. But knowing this, you will want to anticipate what Mark thinks that you think that

V.J. Tremblay and C.H. Tremblay, *New Perspectives on Industrial Organization*,
Springer Texts in Business and Economics, DOI 10.1007/978-1-4614-3241-8_3,
© Springer Science+Business Media New York 2012

Mark will do. This thought process, which can go on forever, is called **infinite regress**. If you really want to win the game, solving this strategic dilemma appears quite daunting. Remarkably, game theory provides tools that help solve infinite regress problems.

Before we begin our formal discussion, it is important to realize that a game is a social phenomenon where strategy is vital. Strategy is not an issue in the physical sciences. The planets do not orbit around the sun to meet a particular goal, and an asteroid cannot change its course to avoid hitting a planet. Strategic interaction is not possible in physics but instead is the purview of the social sciences, as well as with card, board, and sports games. Strategy is a cornerstone of economics and business, where firms engage in strategic rivalry for profit. Thomas Watson, founder of IBM, is quoted as saying, "Business is a game, the greatest game in the world if you know how to play it." Game theory also contributes to political science, where political candidates develop strategies to gain voter support, and to psychology, where children choose different bargaining strategies to stay up just one hour later. Game theory has even been used in biology to explain animal behavior.

Of course, not all social settings produce games. A track meet is social, with many athletes from competing teams, but a 50 meter race is not a game. Individual runners do not anticipate and react to the actions of other runners. If the goal is to win the race, runners simply run as fast as they can to the finish line.

In a strategic game the actions of one player influences the performance or payoff of other players. This excludes games of pure chance (i.e., playing a slot machine) or pure skill (i.e., a 50 meter race). Successful play of a strategic game involves the choice of an appropriate strategy, as well as luck and skill. To be successful at tennis, you must be fit and be able to serve and hit the ball accurately. In poker, it is difficult to win if you are always dealt a weak hand. In both cases, choosing a better strategy will always improve your chances of success.

In this chapter, we review the basic concepts of *non*cooperative game theory.[1] In this type of game, contracts and cooperation among players are not allowed. This characterizes the US business environment where cooperation among competitors is a violation of antitrust laws. Cooperative behavior may still occur when firms form a secret cartel, a topic we take up in Chap. 9.

We begin by describing the basic characteristics of static and dynamic games. We then identify methods to determine the optimal strategy for each player. Finally, we discuss how information plays a role in game theory and how it affects the final outcome or equilibrium in a game. At the beginning of each section, we focus on games outside the economic arena. Knowledge of these games will then serve as a starting point for economic and business applications that are discussed at the end of each section in this chapter and throughout the book.

---

[1] For a more complete discussion of game theory as applied to economics, see Gibbons (1992), Watson (2002), Dixit and Skeath (2004), Rasmusen (2007), and Harrington (2009).

3.1 Describing a Game

As we have already said, our focus here is on games that are strategic in nature. Formally, a game is a description of a strategic setting that identifies a set of rules that describe player motives, actions, and payoffs. Game theory provides a set of tools that allows us to identify optimal play and equilibrium outcomes in a strategic situation. This requires a formal treatment that is mathematically precise.

To keep things as simple as possible, we begin with a discussion of introductory game theoretic models. The introductory models are built from simplifying, sometimes unrealistic, assumptions. Consequently, they can produce unreasonable predictions. Nevertheless, they are still useful as launching points for more realistic but more complex models. In addition, this approach helps us to organize our thoughts about how to make strategic decisions. Finally, it provides a prescription for optimal play given the assumptions of the game. Once we have mastered these introductory models, we will discuss models with more realistic assumptions and more advanced methods.

A key feature of introductory game theory is that players are assumed to behave rationally. In economics, this means that as a player:

1. You are aware of your preferences (i.e., objectives) and constraints.
2. You choose actions that are consistent with your goals given your constraints and the behavior of others.

Note that we are refraining from making value judgments about people's preferences. Some people like broccoli, while others do not; some people prefer to be cruel, while others prefer to be kind. At this point, preferences are taken as given. Because all players are assumed to be fully rational, we can think of introductory game theory as the study of rational behavior in strategic settings where players make flawless calculations in determining the actions that best serve their interests.

Of course, economists know that real people make mistakes and are not always rational. We introduce more realistic assumptions in the next chapter where we discuss contributions from behavioral economics. One case is bounded rationality which holds that people make errors because they have limited information and cognitive ability. **Behavioral game theory** incorporates behavioral features into game theory.[2] We devote much of Parts III, IV, and V of the book to analyzing how the integration of ideas from behavioral economics and game theory provides us with a better understanding of industrial organization issues.

Simple games assume that the objective of each player is to maximize his or her payoff. Payoffs accrue at the end of the game. How they are measured depends on the type of game being played. For example, payoffs of a professional tennis tournament are dollar awards. Generally, we assume that firms maximize profits and individuals maximize utility. Exceptions will be obvious from the context of the game. As indicated above, a defining feature of a strategic setting is that a player's payoff depends on his or her own actions and the actions of the other players in the game.

---

[2] For those interested in behavioral game theory, see Camerer (1997) and Ellison (2006).

To use game theory to predict a strategic outcome, we must first identify each player's strategy. A **strategy** defines a player's contingency plan or decision rule. In other words, it identifies a player's optimal action in every possible circumstance. To illustrate, assume that you are playing a tennis game against Mark. When returning Mark's serve, your possible actions are to hit the ball crosscourt and down the line. Mark has two options, to move over and defend a crosscourt shot or move over to defend a down-the-line shot. Here, your strategy is the following rule: hit the ball down the line if you expect Mark to defend a crosscourt shot and hit a crosscourt shot if you expect Mark to defend a down-the-line shot. This is a strategy, because it defines your optimal action in response to any expected action that Mark takes.

A second important characteristic of a game is the **timing of play**. In a **static game**, each player makes a move simultaneously. A classic example is a game called "matching pennies," where two players (1 and 2) each have a penny and must decide whether to reveal it heads up or tails up. If the pennies match (i.e., both are heads or tails), then player 1 wins both pennies. If they do not match (i.e., one is a head and the other is a tail), then player 2 wins both pennies. If the rules of the game require that they must reveal their choices simultaneously and without previous discussion, the game is static or a simultaneous move game.

If the order of play is sequential, the game is called a **dynamic game**. A classic example of a dynamic game is the "bank robber game." In this game, a bank robber goes up to a teller and says, "give me $10,000 or I'll blow up the bank." The teller then responds by either giving the robber the money or refusing to give. Finally, the robber must decide to walk out of the bank or blow it up. When defining the rules of a dynamic game, we must indicate which player moves first, second, third, and so on. Establishing a time line is essential in a dynamic game.

Lastly, it is important to identify the information that each player has at each stage of the game. In game theory, this is called a player's **information set**. There are four basic types of information that we will use in this chapter.[3]

1. **Complete information**: This means that each player knows the payoff or objective function of all players in the game. When a player does not know the payoff of one or more competitors, information is said to be incomplete.
2. **Perfect information**: This concept is associated with dynamic games and implies that each player knows the history of previous actions in the game. If the history of play is unknown, information is said to be imperfect.
3. **Common knowledge**: Information is common knowledge if it is known by all players in the game; each player knows that all players know that all players know this, and so forth in infinite regress.

---

[3] There are also games of uncertainty, where nature plays a role in the game. For example, nature may decide whether a player (firm or worker) has a high or low level of productivity. For further discussion, see Rasmusen (2007).

4. **Symmetric information**: Information is symmetric when each player has the same set of information. When one player has more information than another player, information is asymmetric.

We will see that the type of information that players have can affect the outcome of a game.

One thing to note is that information can affect how we characterize a game as being static or dynamic. Players need not make decisions simultaneously in a static game. All that is required is that they make their decisions without knowing the choices of other players. In the matching pennies problem, player 1 may make a choice first but does not reveal that choice until player 2 has made a choice. In essence, you can think of this as a dynamic game where player 1 makes a decision in the first period, and player 2 makes a decision in the second period but without knowing player 1's choice. Although we normally call this a static game, we can also think of it as a dynamic game of imperfect information where player 2 does not know the history of play. We will address this issue later in the chapter.

To summarize, the characteristics described above identify what we normally call the "rules of the game." They are:

1. The players.
2. Each player's possible actions.
3. The timing of play.
4. The payoff function for each player.
5. The information available to each player.

To demonstrate, consider the game of chess. In a chess game, the rules identify (1) two players; (2) the legal moves of each piece; (3) the sequential order of play; (4) player goals, which normally is that a win is preferred to a draw and a draw is preferred to a loss (5) information that is perfect and complete, which is common knowledge.

We will begin our formal discussion with static games and then discuss dynamic games. To help you think more generally, we begin discussion in each section with noneconomic applications. Our goal will be to look for outcomes that meet two conditions. First, each player is behaving optimally, that is, choosing actions that meet his or her goals given their constraints. Second, the outcome is an equilibrium, which means that no player has an incentive to change once the equilibrium is reached. Thus, both optimization and equilibrium conditions are used to identify the rational outcome of a game.

3.2   Static Games of Complete Information

In a static game, the time dimension is irrelevant because players reveal their decisions at the same point in time. In this section we begin our discussion of simple games with two players and two courses of actions. This makes it easier to identify the strategy or optimal course of action for fully rational players. To solve

Fig. 3.1 Payoff matrix
for the right–left game

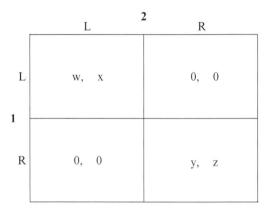

more realistic games that have many players and a continuum of actions requires the use of calculus. We discuss problems such as these at the end of the section and throughout the book.

3.2.1   Fundamental Types of Static Games

We first consider a class of games called **coordination games** (or cooperation games) in which players benefit from cooperating. Consider a game with two players (1 and 2) who must choose between two possible actions: move left (L) or move right (R). You can think of this as a problem where you are in a foreign land and must choose between driving your vehicle on the right and the left side of the road. This decision is made simultaneously, players cannot communicate before making a move, and the game is played only once. Payoffs, which will be defined subsequently, are common knowledge (i.e., information is complete). We call this the "Right–Left game."

Static games such as these are normally described with a **payoff matrix** (sometimes called a game matrix, game box, or game table). The box in Fig. 3.1 is the payoff matrix for the Right–Left game, where R and L identify the possible actions, and w, x, y, and z identify the payoffs. The payoff matrix identifies payoffs for each player given all possible actions. The numbers in the upper left-hand corner of the payoff matrix correspond to payoffs to each player when they both choose L, with the first value (w) representing the payoff to player 1 and the second value (x) representing the payoff to player 2. If one chooses L and the other chooses R, they each earn 0. If they both choose R, player 1 receives y and player 2 receives z. Notice that the payoff matrix describes all of the relevant features of the static game: players, actions, and payoffs. Game theorists call this representation the **normal form** or strategic form of a game.

In the Right–Left game, it might be reasonable to assume that the payoffs to each player are positive and the same for symmetric play. Such an example is illustrated

Fig. 3.2 Payoff matrix
for the right–left game

		2	
		L	R
1	L	1, 1	0, 0
	R	0, 0	1, 1

in Fig. 3.2, where $w = x = y = z = 1$. In other words, we are all better off if everyone drives on the right-hand or the left-hand side of the road. These outcomes are sometimes called win–win, because both players benefit by coordinating. A game with this structure is called a **coordination game** because communication before playing the game leads to a better outcome. Without communication, it is difficult to determine what the players will do. At this point, all we can say is that if player i (1 or 2) believes that player j (the other player) will choose R (L), then player i should choose R (L).

Another type of coordination game is a **Pareto coordination game**. In this case, one outcome clearly stands out as a better one for both players. An example of a Pareto coordination game is provided in Fig. 3.3. Players 1 and 2 have two choices, A and B. They are better off by matching their behavior, but the best outcome is for both to choose action A. This is a unique Pareto outcome because it maximizes joint payoffs,[4] and the game is coordination game because the players are better off with pregame communication.

In Pareto coordination games, you might think that there is an obvious course of action. Wouldn't the high payoffs from both choosing action A induce them to each make this choice? Schelling (1960) thought so, calling this a psychologically prominent **focal point** that can help resolve coordination problems when communication is impossible. To test this idea, Schelling asked a group of his students the following question: If you are told to meet a stranger in New York City tomorrow but you do not know the time or place and you cannot communicate with this person, what would you do? The most common answer was noon at Grand Central Station, a time and a location that are natural focal points.

---

[4] This is similar to the concept of Pareto optimality, which is reached when there is no way to make one person better off without making someone else worse off. Generally, Pareto optimality applies to everyone in society, while a Pareto outcome in a coordination game applies only to the players in the game. For a review of the concept of Pareto optimality, see Frank and Bernanke (2008), Bernheim and Whinston (2008), Pindyck and Rubenfield (2009), or Varian (2010).

Fig. 3.3 Payoff matrix for
the Pareto-coordination game

		2	
		A	B
1	A	2, 2	0, 0
	B	0, 0	1, 1

Given the presence of a focal point, it might appear to be irrational for a player to choose action B in the Pareto coordination game described in Fig. 3.3. It would be rational for player 1 to choose B, however, if player 1 believes that player 2 will choose B. If you play this game with your 5-year-old brother and know that he prefers the letter B to A in every game he plays, it would be rational to choose B. Beliefs can be critical in determining behavior in a game theoretic setting. To be successful, you must be able to put yourself in the shoes (or mind) of your opponent.

Historical events can also cause us to get stuck in a non-Pareto outcome. The classic example is the widespread use of the standard QWERTY computer (typewriter) keyboard.[5] QWERTY refers to the sequence of letters that begin on the left side of the second row from the top of the keyboard. The QWERTY keyboard was developed in the 1870s, when the keys were placed in this location in order to slow down typing speeds. The problem was that early typewriters were mechanical and would jam if the typist typed too fast. Of course, this is not a problem with electronic keyboards linked to computers today. Although more efficient keyboard configurations exist, such as the Dvorak Simplified Keyboard, we all use QWERTY because we believe that others will continue to use QWERTY. If you were the only one to switch, you would not be able to effectively use other computers and other people would be unable to use your computer.

The last example of a coordination game that we present here is the classic "dating game." In this game, Chris and Pat are dating and decide to have dinner at Chris's apartment. Chris will make dinner, which will consist of a main course of meat or fish. Pat will bring wine, either red or white. Because of poor communication, a final decision was not made about the main course or choice of wine. In addition, further communication is impossible (e.g., all cell phone towers are inoperative). Their payoffs are described in the matrix in Fig. 3.4, where (1) Chris most prefers meat and red wine; (2) Pat most prefers fish and white wine; and (3)

---

[5] This example derives from David (1985). For an alternative viewpoint, see Liebowitz and Margolis (1990).

Fig. 3.4 Payoff matrix
for the dating game

		Pat	
		Red	White
Chris	Meat	3, 1	0, 0
	Fish	0, 0	1, 3

neither like meat with white wine or fish with red wine. The dating game clearly highlights the infinite regress problem. Chris loves Pat and may decide to prepare a fish dish. But because Pat loves Chris, Chris may fear that Pat will bring red wine. Of course, Pat is thinking along the same lines. To avoid the appearance of being uncaring of the other person, Chris may make a fish dish and Pat may bring red wine, leaving them with a ruined dinner.[6] The moral of this story is that good communication makes for a better dinner (and relationship).

The next class of games that we wish to discuss are **competitive games**. Any game where there is a winner and a loser, as in chess, tennis, and baseball, is a competitive game. The simplest example of a competitive game is the matching pennies game. Recall that player 1 wins if the pennies match, and player 2 wins if they do not match. Figure 3.5 displays the payoff matrix for this game. Notice that the winner receives a payoff of 1 (cent) and the loser gives up 1 (cent). A game with this structure is called a **zero-sum game**, because the sum of payoffs to all players equals 0. This structure captures the payoffs of most board and sports games.

Not all competitive games are zero sum. One example is the following war game. Assume there are two neighboring countries (1 and 2), and they must decide to behave aggressively (Hawk behavior) or peacefully (Dove behavior). Payoffs are described in Fig. 3.6. In this game, each wants its neighbor to be a dove. If they are both doves, they each receive a payoff of 2. However, with a neighboring dove, it pays to be a hawk and earn a payoff of 3. Unfortunately, disaster strikes if they are both hawks, earning them −1 each. This is a coordination game, because peace talks that avoid a Hawk–Hawk outcome are the key to success.

The last and most prominent type of game in social science is the **prisoners' dilemma**. In this game, two co-conspirator suspects (1 and 2) are arrested by the police.

---

[6] Of course, you might think that this enables Chris and Pat to avoid being disappointed with each other and actually leads to the highest payoff. This possibility is ruled out by their payoffs, which leaves them both with 0, as compared to a payoff of (3, 1) or (1, 3). In other words, they each really dislike the meat–white and fish–red outcome.

Fig. 3.5 Payoff matrix for
the matching pennies game

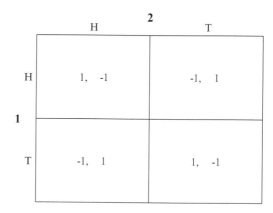

Fig. 3.6 Payoff matrix
for the war game

The police have limited evidence, so they place the suspects in separate rooms
for interrogation. Each suspect can choose to testify against the other (Confess)
or remain silent (Not Confess). Actions and options are as follows:

1. If suspect 1 (2) confesses and suspect 2 (1) does not, then suspect 1 (2) goes free
   and suspect 2 (1) receives a 20-year sentence.
2. If both confess, then each receives a 10-year sentence.
3. If neither confesses, each receives a 1-year sentence on a lesser charge due to a
   lack of evidence on the more serious charge.

The suspects cannot communicate and their decisions are made simultaneously.
Figure 3.7 provides the payoff matrix for this game.

Notice that this is a Pareto coordination game. The sum of the number of years
spent in jail is clearly lowest if neither confesses (2 versus 20 years). In addition, if a
player chooses Confess, this decision imposes a negative externality on the
other player. For example, if suspect 2 chooses Not, suspect 1 receives 1 year less
prison time by choosing Confess but this causes suspect 2 to receive 19 years more

Fig. 3.7 Payoff matrix
for the prisoners' dilemma

		2	
		Not	Confess
1	Not	-1, -1	-20, 0
	Confess	0, -20	-10, -10

prison time. If suspect 2 chooses Confess, suspect 1 receives 10 years less prison time by choosing Confess but this causes suspect 2 to receive 10 more years in prison. Thus, communication/cooperation clearly helps the criminals at the expense of law enforcement. The question is how will rational criminals behave if communication is impossible? If you were one of the suspects, how would you play the game? These questions are answered in the next section.

3.2.2   Static Game Equilibria

There are three types of equilibrium concepts to static games that we address here: a dominant-strategy equilibrium, an iterated-dominant strategy equilibrium, and a Nash equilibrium.

3.2.2.1   Dominant-Strategy and Iterated Dominant-Strategy Equilibria

The easiest way to think about a dominant strategy is to start with a discussion of a dominated strategy. Assume that S and S' are feasible strategies. Strategy S' is a **strictly dominated strategy** if there is some feasible strategy that always earns a strictly higher payoff.[7] Conversely, strategy S is a **strictly dominant strategy** if it earns a strictly higher payoff than could be earned from playing any other feasible strategy.

The prisoners' dilemma provides an example, because each player has a dominated and a dominant strategy. From Fig. 3.7, notice that player 1's strategy (or contingency plan) is the following:

• Play Confess if player 2 plays Not. That is, player 1 earns -1 from choosing Not and earns 0 from choosing Confess.

---

[7] It is weakly dominated if there exists a feasible strategy that earns a payoff that is at least as high.

- Play Confess if player 2 plays Confess. That is, player 1 earns -20 from choosing Not and earns -10 from choosing Confess.

Thus, Not is a dominated strategy because player 1 can always do better by playing Confess. With just two options, this makes Confess a dominant strategy. One thing to notice is that if the elimination of all dominated strategies leaves just one strategy remaining, it must be a dominant strategy.

Another thing to notice is that this is a **symmetric game**. If we switch player identities, each player's strategic options and payoffs remain the same. As a result, player 2 has the same dominated and dominant strategies as player 1. Not is a dominated strategy for both players, and Confess is a dominant strategy for both players.

In this game, we would expect rational players to play their dominant strategy. That is, we expect them to play a game according to the following behavioral or game theory (GT) rules[8]:

GT Rule 1. Never play a dominated strategy.
GT Rule 2. If you have a dominant strategy, always play it.

Applying these rules means that we expect each suspect to confess and spend 10 years in prison.[9] This Confess–Confess outcome is called a **dominant-strategy equilibrium**. One problem is that it is not the Pareto solution, as the joint time spent in prison is minimized when both players choose Not. If they could cooperate by making a binding agreement, which violates the rules of this simple game, it would require that they both choose Not. Without such an agreement, if one player chooses Not it is always in the interest of the other player to defect and choose Confess. Thus, each player has a strong incentive to choose Not.

The reason that the prisoners' dilemma game is so important is that its payoff structure can be found in many games that are played in the social sciences. In political science it represents the problem faced by two political candidates. Both are better off from refraining from using negative advertising campaigns, but the dominant strategy is to utilize them. In sports, the same argument applies to performance enhancing drugs that have negative long-term consequences. All athletes are better off if no one takes them, but any one athlete gains a competitive advantage unless everyone takes them. Thus, the dominant strategy is for each athlete to use the drugs.

In economics, the prisoners' dilemma problem explains why cartel agreements are unstable. If competitive firms could agree to set the monopoly price, their profits would rise. We will see later in the chapter that each firm can increase its

---

[8] The game theory rules listed in this chapter borrow from Dixit and Nalebuff (1991).

[9] Of course, real criminals know this and may agree beforehand never to squeal when caught by the police. With organized crime, for example, a crime syndicate may threaten to harm the family members of squealers and make this a dynamic game. These possibilities are ruled out here, and this game is simply meant to serve as a thought-provoking example.

Fig. 3.8 Payoff matrix
for the dominant-submissive
pig game

		Small Pig	
		Push	Not
Big Pig	Push	4, 2	2, 3
	Not	6, -1	0, 0

profits even further by undercutting the price of its competitors. The dominant strategy is to behave competitively. Thus, in most countries cartels face two obstacles: (1) each firm has an incentive to cheat on the cartel agreement by behaving more competitively and (2) cartels are illegal.

If all games had a dominant-strategy equilibrium, our discussion of game theory would be complete. Unfortunately, this is not the case. Consider an example of real animal behavior in a game played by a dominant (big) pig and a submissive (small) pig. In an experiment conducted by Baldwin and Meese (1979), a large pig and a small pig were placed in a pen. At one end of the pen was a button that when pushed dispensed food in a trough at the other end of the pen. Possible actions for each pig are (1) to push the button (Push) and (2) not push the button and wait at the trough for the food to be dispensed (Not). The payoff matrix is described in Fig. 3.8. The payoffs imply:

- If they both push the button, the big pig gets most of the food. The big pig earns a payoff of 4 and the small pig earns 2.
- If neither pig pushes the button, they each earn 0.
- If the small pig pushes the button and the big pig does not, then the big pig gets all of the food. This earns the big pig 6 and the small pig -1. A payoff of -1 reflects the fact that pushing the button requires energy and does not earn the small pig any food.
- If the big pig pushes the button and the small pig does not, then the big pig earns 2 and the small pig earns 3.

The question is how would you expect the big pig to behave if fully rational?

There are several things to notice in the dominant–submissive pig game. First, the big pig does not have a dominated or dominant strategy. Thus, a dominant-strategy equilibrium does not exist. Second, the small pig does have a dominant strategy—it is always better off choosing Not. This fact should make it easy to see how the big pig should behave. Because Push is a dominated strategy for the small pig, a small pig will always play Not. Given this, the best course of action for the

Fig. 3.9 A game with
an iterated-dominant
equilibrium

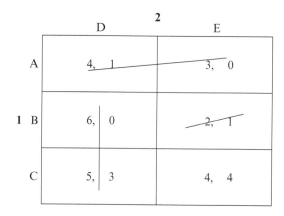

big pig is to Push.[10] Thus, if pigs are rational we would expect the following to be the equilibrium: big pig chooses Push and small pig chooses Not. Eventually, this is exactly how the pigs behaved.[11]

Does this mean that pigs are rational? Yes, if we mean by rational that their behavior is consistent with their own best interest. As with people, it can take time for animals to identify their optimal play. Clearly the small pig will learn quickly that playing Push reduces its welfare. Similarly, the big pig will learn quickly that choosing Not is suboptimal. The only way they can both gain is for the big pig to choose Push and the small pig to choose Not. Trial and error may bring them to this outcome, especially if survival is at stake.

The rational outcome of the dominant–submissive pig game has a special name. The Push–Not[12] outcome is an example of an **iterated-dominant equilibrium**. In situations such as these, rational players would behave according to the following rule:

GT Rule 3. Eliminate dominated strategies and continue successively until all dominated strategies are eliminated.

Iterated dominance is a bit more complicated when players face more than two strategic choices. Consider the game that is described in Fig. 3.9. In this case, player 1 has three options: A, B, and C; player 2 has two options: D and E. This game has one iterated-dominant equilibrium: player 1 chooses C and player 2 chooses E. This is derived as follows.

---

[10] The dominant pig earns 2 by choosing Push and earns 0 by choosing Not.

[11] The lag is probably due to the fact that pigs have incomplete information, cannot talk, and it takes time to learn the payoffs from each possible course of action. These are called evolutionary games, which are described by Samuelson (1997).

[12] Where the first term, Push, represents player 1's (the big pig's) strategy and the second, Not, represents player 2's (the small pig's) strategy.

1. For player 1, A is dominated by C, so action A can be eliminated from the payoff matrix.
2. Given that action A is eliminated, D is dominated by E for player 2. Thus, action D is eliminated.
3. For player 1, this leaves options B and C, and C dominates B.

Thus, the iterated-dominant equilibrium C–E.

There are several problems with this approach to determining how rational players will play a game. First, the process can be complex, especially when there are many players and strategic options. Second, the order of iteration may matter. That is, if we start by eliminating player 1's dominated strategy, we may get a different answer than if we begin by eliminating player 2's dominated strategy. Finally, there may be more than one choice left. That is, there may not be a dominant-strategy or an iterated-dominant equilibrium. For example, neither player has a dominated (or dominant) strategy in the coordination games found in Figs. 3.1–3.4 or in the competitive and war games in Figs. 3.5–3.6. What will rational players do in cases such as these?

3.2.2.2 The Nash Equilibrium

Fortunately, John Nash (1950) discovered a solution to such problems, one that has revolutionized game theory and won him the Nobel prize in economics in 1994.[13] Nash's development, what is now called a Nash equilibrium, is so general that it encompasses many special cases introduced long before Nash. The earliest is that of Cournot (1838), who derived a Nash equilibrium for a duopoly model where firms compete in output. The Nash equilibrium is sometimes called a Cournot–Nash equilibrium, but we will follow the convention of most game theorists and call it a Nash equilibrium.

We begin with a formal description of a Nash equilibrium for a static game with two players (1 and 2). Players have a closed and bounded set of feasible strategic options. [14] The payoff for player i is defined as $\pi_i(S_i, S_j)$, where subscript i stands for player 1 or 2, subscript j stands for the other player, S_i is player i's feasible strategy, and S_j is player j's feasible strategy.

---

[13] Nash won the prize with two other economists: Reinhard Selten (1965) who applied Nash's concept to dynamic games and John Harsanyi (1967, 1968a, 1968b) who incorporated imperfect information into game theory. You can learn more about Nash's contributions to game theory and his life struggles with mental illness by reading Nasar's (1998) book, *A Beautiful Mind*. The movie with the same title is based on the book but is a Hollywood rendition that is not very accurate. In true Hollywood fashion, in the movie Nash gains inspiration for his game theory ideas from a bar scene where he and his friends discuss strategies for meeting women. In reality, his ideas came to him in an economics class in international trade.

[14] A set is closed if it contains all of its boundary points, and it is bounded if the distance between any two points in the set is less than infinity.

A strategy profile $\mathcal{S}_1^*$ and $\mathcal{S}_2^*$ constitutes a **Nash Equilibrium** for a normal form game if for every $i = 1, 2$,

$$\pi_i\left(\mathcal{S}_i^*, \, \mathcal{S}_j^*\right) \geq \pi_i\left(\mathcal{S}_i', \, \mathcal{S}_j^*\right)$$

for all feasible values of $\mathcal{S}_i'$.[15]

Because the Nash equilibrium concept will be used throughout the book, we abbreviate it by NE.

This concept is less obvious than a dominant-strategy equilibrium or an iterated-dominant equilibrium and, therefore, deserves further discussion. At a NE:

- Player i chooses $\mathcal{S}_i$ to maximize his or her payoff ($\mathcal{S}_i^*$). To be a NE, each player behaves optimally assuming that all other players behave optimally. Thus, a NE is said to produce a **mutual best reply**: Given $\mathcal{S}_2^*$, player 1 does what is best by playing $\mathcal{S}_1^*$; given $\mathcal{S}_1^*$, player 2 does what is best by playing $\mathcal{S}_2^*$.
- The NE is an equilibrium because neither player has an incentive to deviate or make a change once a NE is reached.

This illustrates that a NE has qualities of both an optimum and an equilibrium. Each player behaves optimally, a condition that must hold simultaneously for every player in the game, and no player has an incentive to change. These qualities help us know when we have found a NE: a NE is reached when players have achieved a mutual best reply and when no player has an incentive to deviate.

It may be helpful to compare the strategies and concepts of a NE with those of a dominant-strategy equilibrium. At a NE, my strategy is best for me assuming that you are doing what is best for you. At a dominant-strategy equilibrium, my dominant strategy is always best regardless of the feasible action that you take. In equilibrium, these respective statements hold for all players. It turns out that every dominant-strategy equilibrium is a NE. For an outcome to be a dominant-strategy equilibrium, it must be the best outcome for every player regardless of the choices made by other players. There is no incentive for any player to deviate. Thus, it must be a NE. However, a NE need not be a dominant-strategy equilibrium, which we will see subsequently.

Because the definition does not tell us how players get to a NE, the best way to identify one is by example. To begin, consider the prisoners' dilemma in Fig. 3.7. It has a unique dominant-strategy equilibrium, Confess–Confess. We know that this is a NE for two reasons. First, Confess–Confess is a mutual best reply: if player 2 chooses Confess, the best option or reply for player 1 is to Confess; if player 1

---

[15] The greater than or equal to sign is important to Nash's proof that at least one Nash equilibrium will exist in static games with a finite number of players and the strategy space that meets certain regularity conditions (i.e., it is nonempty, convex, closed, and bounded). For further discussion and a more advanced treatment, see Mas-Colell et al. (1995) and Rasmusen (2007).

chooses Confess, player 2's best reply is Confess. Second, neither player has an incentive to deviate from the Confess–Confess outcome.

It is also true that an iterated-dominant equilibrium is a NE. In the dominant–submissive example in Fig. 3.8, Push–Not is the iterated-dominant equilibrium and the NE. Notice that it is a mutual best reply, and neither pig has an incentive to deviate.

The beauty of Nash's concept is that even without dominance, a NE will always exist in games with a finite number of players and a strategy space that meets certain regularity conditions. For example, the coordination games in Figs. 3.1–3.4 each have two NE: the strategy pairs in the upper-left and in the lower-right corners of each payoff matrix. Consider the dating game in Fig. 3.4. Meat–Red is a NE, because neither Chris nor Pat has an incentive to deviate. Fish–White is also a NE, because neither player has an incentive to deviate. The war game in Fig. 3.6 also has two NE, Hawk–Dove and Dove–Hawk. Of course, each player is better off if the other player is a dove and is worse off if the other player is a hawk. Each of these games has a NE even though none of them has a dominant-strategy equilibrium.

The only game that we have discussed so far that does not appear to have a NE is the matching pennies game in Fig. 3.5. That is, the Heads–Heads outcome is not a NE, because player 2 would prefer to switch from Heads to Tails when player 1 plays Heads. Similarly, Heads–Tails is not a NE, because player 1 would prefer to switch to Tails; Tails–Heads is not a NE, because player 1 would prefer to switch to Heads; Tails–Tails is not a NE, because player 2 would prefer to switch to Tails.

Fortunately, Nash (1950) was able to prove that at least one NE will always exist, even in games such as the matching pennies game, but one NE may be in what is called a mixed strategy. A **pure strategy** is a decision rule that does not involve randomizing. In the matching pennies game, pure strategies are Heads and Tails. When players develop a decision rule that does involve randomizing, they are playing a **mixed strategy**. For instance, a player could use the following decision rule: play Heads with a probability of ¼ and Tails with a probability of ¾. In other words, a mixed strategy is defined in terms of a probability rather than a certain course of action.

Playing a mixed strategy is especially important in competitive games where it pays to behave unpredictably or to outguess your opponent. A pitcher in baseball must decide whether to throw a fastball or a curveball. Should the pitcher throw in the following order—2 fastballs, 1 curveball, 2 fastballs, 1 curveball, etc.? Batters have an easier time hitting a ball if they know when it is a fastball and when it is a curveball. Thus, to keep hitters off balance, it pays for pitchers to behave unpredictably by throwing a curveball in a random order, with probability 1/3 perhaps. Similarly, it pays the hitter to try to outguess the pitcher. The same logic applies in other sports and card games. In football, the offense must decide on a run or a pass play. To always run on first down is easier to defend than running the ball 80% of the time. Similarly, in a poker game it is optimal to be unpredictable when deciding whether or not to bluff.

The same argument applies to the matching pennies game. If you are player 1 and are playing with your little brother who likes heads over tails in any game he plays, then you should always play heads. As your brother gets older, he will begin

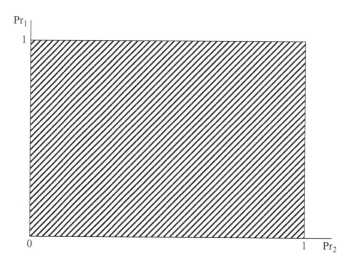

Fig. 3.10 The mixed-strategy probability space for players 1 and 2

to realize his mistake and will change his behavior if he is rational. This interpretation implies that the game will be repeated, which it need not be. All that matters is that you do not want the other player to know what your action will be. One way to assure this is to make your choice in a completely random fashion.[16]

Several steps are involved in finding a mixed-strategy NE to a game like the matching pennies game. First, we must define possible mixed strategies. Assume that player 1 believes that pr_2 is the probability that player 2 will play heads, and assume that player 2 believes that pr_1 is the probability that player 1 will play heads. Because probabilities are bounded from 0 to 1, the feasible mixed-strategy space is identified by the shaded box in Fig. 3.10. Notice that this set of possible probabilities is closed and bounded.

Next, we need to identify each player's best-reply function (or best-reply correspondence in this case). A **best-reply function** (or best-response function) identifies a player's strategy or best course of action in response to all possible actions of other players. Consider the best reply for player 1 who wins by matching Heads–Heads or Tails–Tails. To maximize the likelihood of winning the game, player 1 will:

- Play Heads ($pr_1 = 1$) if player 1 believes that player 2 will play Heads with $pr_2 > \frac{1}{2}$.
- Play Tails ($pr_1 = 1$) if player 1 believes that player 2 will play Heads with $pr_2 < \frac{1}{2}$.

---

[16] It turns out that for most people, this is difficult to do. To get around this problem, you could decide to use the second hand on your watch to determine your action. If the second hand is between 1 and 30, choose heads; if it is between 31 and 60, choose tails.

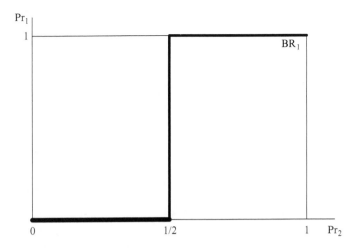

Fig. 3.11 Player 1's best reply in matching pennies game (pr_i = probability that player i chooses heads)

- Be indifferent between playing Heads or Tails if player 1 believes that player 2 will play Heads with $pr_2 = \frac{1}{2}$.

This defines player 1's strategy, because it identifies an optimal response to every possible action of player 2. Player 1's best reply (BR_1) is the thick, dark line drawn in Fig. 3.11. It shows that when player 2 is more likely to play Heads, player 1 should play Heads; when player 2 is more likely to play Tails, player 1 should play Tails; when there is a 50–50 chance that player 2 will play Heads, player 1 is indifferent between any value of pr_1 from 0 to 1.

What is the best reply for player 2? Because the game is symmetric, the process parallels that of player 1. That is, player 2 will choose Tails if player 2 believes that player 1 will play Heads with $pr_1 > \frac{1}{2}$, will choose Heads if player 2 believes that player 1 will play Heads with $pr_1 < \frac{1}{2}$, and will be indifferent between choosing Heads or Tails if player 2 believes that player 1 will play Heads with $pr_1 = \frac{1}{2}$. The best replies for players 1 and 2 (BR_2) are graphed in Fig. 3.12. As you might have expected, the mixed-strategy NE occurs where the best replies intersect at $pr_1^* = pr_2^* = \frac{1}{2}$. This is consistent with the way children in the 1930s actually played the game: two children simultaneously tossed their pennies against a wall. It also demonstrates that the matching pennies game has a single mixed-strategy NE and no pure-strategy NE.

We now turn to a more formal method of solving a mixed-strategy NE. We illustrate this method using the matching pennies game by comparing the expected payoff from playing Heads versus Tails. Player 1 is assumed to believe that player 2 will play a mixed strategy by choosing Heads with probability pr_2 and

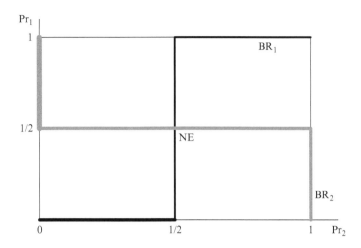

Fig. 3.12 Best replies and the Nash equilibrium in matching pennies game (pr_i = probability that player i chooses heads)

Tails with probability $1 - pr_2$. Player 1's expected payoff from playing Heads $(E\pi_{1H})$ is[17]

$$E\pi_{1H} = pr_2(1) + (1 - pr_2)(-1) = 2pr_2 - 1. \tag{3.1}$$

The first set of terms between the equal signs is the probability that player 2 chooses Heads (pr_2) times the payoff from the Heads–Heads outcome (1); the second set of terms is the probability that player 2 chooses Tails ($1 - pr_2$) times the payoff from the Heads–Tails outcome (−1). Player 1's expected payoff from playing Tails $(E\pi_{1T})$ is

$$E\pi_{1T} = pr_2(-1) + (1 - pr_2)(1) = 1 - 2pr_2. \tag{3.2}$$

The first set of terms between the equal signs is the probability that player 2 chooses Heads times the payoff from the Tails–Heads outcome (−1); the second set of terms is the probability that player 2 chooses Tails times the payoff from the Tails–Tails outcome (1).

From information about expected payoffs in (3.1) and (3.2), we can identify player 1's best reply. Player 1's best reply is:

- Play Heads ($pr_1 = 1$) if $E\pi_{1H} > E\pi_{1T}$, which implies that $(2pr_2 - 1) > (1 - 2pr_2)$ or $pr_2 > \frac{1}{2}$.

---

[17] This is called the expected value of a risky event, where the expected value is the weighted average of the return associated with each possible outcome and the weights are the probabilities of each respective outcome. In this case, there are two possible returns: 1 (associated with the H–H outcome that has a probability of pr_2) and −1 (associated with the H–T outcome that has a probability of $1 - pr_2$).

- Play Tails ($pr_1 = 0$) if $E\pi_{1H} < E\pi_{1T}$, which implies that $(2pr_2 - 1) < (1 - 2pr_2)$ or $pr_2 < \frac{1}{2}$.
- Play either Heads or Tails ($0 \leq pr_1 \leq 1$) if $E\pi_{1H} = E\pi_{1T}$, which implies that $(2pr_2 - 1) = (1 - 2pr_2)$ or $pr_2 = \frac{1}{2}$.

Notice that this is identical to the rule derived from our informal discussion above.

We continue by deriving the best reply for player 2. In this case, we assume that player 2 believes that player 1 will play a mixed strategy and play Heads with probability pr_1 and play Tails with probability $1 - pr_1$. Player 2's expected payoff from playing Heads ($E\pi_{2H}$) is

$$E\pi_{2H} = pr_1(-1) + (1 - pr_1)(1) = 1 - 2pr_1. \tag{3.3}$$

Player 2's expected payoff from playing Tails ($E\pi_{2T}$) is

$$E\pi_{2T} = pr_1(1) + (1 - pr_1)(-1) = 2pr_1 - 1. \tag{3.4}$$

From (3.3) and (3.4), Player 2's best reply is:

- Play Heads ($pr_2 = 1$) if $E\pi_{2H} > E\pi_{2T}$, which implies that $(1 - 2pr_1) > (2pr_1 - 1)$ or $pr_1 < \frac{1}{2}$.
- Play Tails ($pr_2 = 0$) if $E\pi_{2H} < E\pi_{2T}$, which implies that $(1 - 2pr_1) < (2pr_1 - 1)$ or $pr_1 > \frac{1}{2}$.
- Play either Heads or Tails ($0 \leq pr_2 \leq 1$) if $E\pi_{2H} = E\pi_{2T}$, which implies that $(1 - 2pr_1) = (2pr_1 - 1)$ or $pr_1 = \frac{1}{2}$.

Again, this is identical to our informal rule discussion above and produced a NE where $pr_1{}^* = pr_2{}^* = \frac{1}{2}$. This is a NE strategy because neither player has an incentive to deviate. If, for example, player 1 decides to play H more than half the time, then player 2 will gain at the expense of player 1.

The approach of constructing best replies from expected payoffs is quite general and can identify both pure-strategy and mixed-strategy NE. Two basic structures stand out. The first can be seen from the Pareto-coordination game described in Fig. 3.3. This game has two pure-strategy NE, A–A and B–B. We calculate the best reply for each player following the procedure above and graph them in Fig. 3.13, where pr_i is the probability that player i chooses A. For player 1, BR_1 indicates that player 1 should play A (B) if player 2 has a high probability of playing A (B). The same strategy applies to player 2. Notice that there are three NE in this game, which occur where the best replies intersect. Point x corresponds to the pure-strategy NE of A–A (where $pr_1{}^* = pr_2{}^* = 1$). Point y corresponds to the pure-strategy NE of B–B (where $pr_1{}^* = pr_2{}^* = 0$). Finally, point z corresponds to the mixed-strategy NE of $pr_1{}^* = pr_2{}^* = 1/3$.

The Pareto-coordination game produces two notable implications. First, a game can have both a pure-strategy and mixed-strategy NE. Second, a pure-strategy is just a mixed-strategy where the probability of action is 1. At point x in Fig. 3.13,

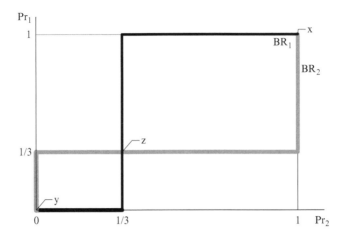

Fig. 3.13 Best replies and the Nash equilibrium for the Pareto-coordination game (pr_i = probability that player i chooses heads)

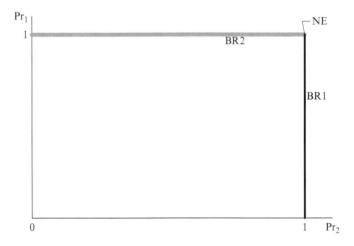

Fig. 3.14 Best replies and the Nash equilibrium in the prisoners' dilemma (pr_i = probability that player i chooses heads)

the probability that each player chooses A is 1. At point y, the probability that each player chooses B is 1.

The second structure of interest involves games with dominant-strategy equilibria. For the prisoners' dilemma described in Fig. 3.7, for example, the best replies are quite simple. In this game, let pr_i equal the probability that player i confesses. Because it is always optimal to choose Confess in this game, the best replies are linear, and a single NE occurs where $pr_1^* = pr_2^* = 1$. Following the procedure outlined above produces the best replies depicted in Fig. 3.14. No matter what the other player does, the optimal strategy is to always play Confess (i.e., $pr_i^* = 1$).

The last issue we need to address in this section is how to solve problems when players have a continuum rather than a finite set of economic choices. To make this concrete, consider two lemonade stands (1 and 2) that are competing for customers by simultaneously choosing the profit-maximizing price. Let price be a continuous variable, such that there are an infinite number of potential prices that the owner could choose.[18] This makes it impossible to represent all possible actions with a payoff matrix.

Fortunately, we have a method of finding the NE when the choice variable is continuous. To solve such problems is a bit more complex, as it requires the use of calculus. To keep things as simple as possible, we consider only pure-strategy NE and assume simple quadratic profit equations for each stand. Profit equations are also symmetric, which enables us to represent profits for stand i, where i represents stand 1 or 2 and j represents the other stand. The profit (π) function for stand i is $\pi_i(p_i, p_j) = ap_i - p_i^2 + p_i p_j$, where a is a positive constant that represents the strength of consumer demand. A higher a implies a higher level of demand. This game is played only once, decisions are made simultaneously, and information is complete. In other words, the rules of the game are:

1. Players: lemonade stand owners 1 and 2.
2. Strategic variable: price.
3. Timing: decisions are made simultaneously.
4. Payoff Function: $\pi_i(p_i, p_j) = ap_i - p_i^2 + p_i p_j$.
5. Information: complete.

NE prices and profit levels for this game are derived in two steps. First, we must find each stand's best-reply function, which identifies stand i's profit maximizing price (p_i^{BR}) for all feasible values of p_j. This defines the stand's strategy or contingency plan and is simply firm i's first-order condition of profit maximization,[19] where we take the first derivative of the firm's profit with respect to p_i and set it to 0. The first derivative identifies the slope of the tangent to the profit equation, which must equal 0 when profits are maximized. We obtain p_i^{BR} by solving this first-order condition for p_i. Second, we must derive the prices that constitute a mutual best reply where the best-reply functions simultaneously hold, which produces NE prices.

To illustrate, we take the first derivative of each stand's profit equation and set it to 0. The first-order conditions are

$$\frac{\partial \pi_1}{\partial p_1} = a - 2p_1 + p_2 = 0, \tag{3.5}$$

---

[18] This does not appear to be correct, because the smallest change in price is 1¢. Nevertheless, the owner could make infinitesimally small changes in quantity, giving the owner an infinite number of possible prices per ounce. We also assume product differentiation, an issue we discuss in later chapters.

[19] A maximum is reached because the profit equation is concave. If it were convex, this procedure would produce the price that minimizes profit. See the Mathematics and Econometrics Appendix at the end of the book for further discussion.

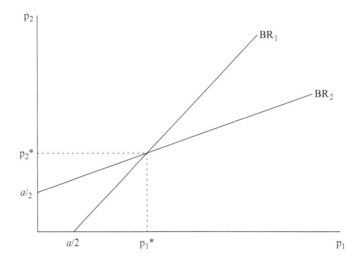

Fig. 3.15 Best-reply functions for lemonade stands 1 and 2

$$\frac{\partial \pi_2}{\partial p_2} = a - 2p_2 + p_1 = 0. \tag{3.6}$$

You can see that these equations are symmetric: once you have one equation, you can obtain the other equation by replacing subscript 1 with 2 and replacing subscript 2 with 1. We obtain the best-reply functions by solving the first-order conditions for p_2 (we solve for p_2 because we want to graph them with p_2 on the vertical axis). They are

$$BR_1 : p_2 = -a + 2p_1, \tag{3.7}$$

$$BR_2 : p_2 = \frac{a + p_1}{2}. \tag{3.8}$$

Each best-reply function specifies the profit maximizing p_i for all values of p_j. For example, (3.8) tells us that if stand 1 chooses a price of 2, the profit maximizing price for stand 2 equals $(1 + a/2)$. Notice that these are linear functions. BR_1 has a p_2-intercept of $-a$ and a slope of 2; BR_2 has a p_2-intercept of $a/2$ and a slope of ½. Their positive slopes mean that the best reply to an increase in p_j is to increase p_i. We graph these best-reply functions in Fig. 3.15.

For a NE, we must have mutual best replies. Graphically, this occurs where the best-reply functions intersect. To obtain a more precise solution, we solve (3.7) and (3.8) simultaneously for p_1 and p_2. Substituting these prices into each stand's profit equation yields NE profits. NE prices (p_i^*) and profits (π_i^*) are

$$p_1^* = p_2^* = a,$$
$$\pi_1^* = \pi_2^* = a^2. \tag{3.9}$$

Because this is a symmetric game, equilibrium values are identical. Even though this model is rather simple, it yields reasonable predictions: NE prices and profits increase with an increase in consumer demand (i.e., an increase in a).[20]

In summary, there are several rules to follow when trying to determine how fully rational players will behave in a static game. First, they will never play a dominated strategy and will always play a dominant strategy. Second, they will always play a dominant strategy. Third, if a dominant-strategy equilibrium does not exist, they will look for an iterated-dominant equilibrium. Finally, if these fail to identify an equilibrium, they will follow the fourth rule:

GT Rule 4. If a dominant-strategy or iterated-dominant equilibrium does not exist, look for a Nash equilibrium where there are mutual best replies and no player has an incentive to deviate.

Nash (1950) has shown that all static games such as those discussed in this chapter will have at least one NE, perhaps in mixed strategies.

There are several ways of motivating a NE. First, for coordination games a NE could be the result of preplay communication, which helps solve coordination problems. Second, a NE could result from learning or trial and error. This leads to social norms, such as driving a car on the right side of the road in the USA and on the left side in Japan. Third, when there is a focal point, it can lead us to a NE. Finally, you can think of it as a prescription for optimal play or the consequence of rational introspection when you believe that others in the game are fully rational. This will be especially true when there is a unique NE. The point is that in addition to shedding light on firm behavior, knowledge of game theory can make us all more effective players in the game of life.

Nash's contribution has transformed the study of industrial organization, as it provides a framework for analyzing the rational behavior of oligopoly firms. Later in the book, we will learn how to derive a NE in more complex games where firms compete in a variety of choice variables, including output, price, and advertising. We will also see that firms use mixed strategies. For instance, your local grocery store does not put all of its grocery items on sale every Tuesday, because this would induce most consumers to shop only on Tuesdays. Instead, the store behaves unpredictably by putting different items on sale each week. In the next section, we will see how Nash's work is used and extended to study dynamic games.

3.3 Dynamic Games of Complete and Perfect Information

Many games in business are dynamic or sequential in nature. For example, General Motors and Ford have been competing against each other for more than a century. When General Motors introduces a successful new model design this period, we

---

[20] This is comparative static analysis, which we discuss in Chap. 5 and in the Mathematics and Econometrics Appendix.

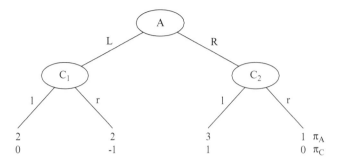

Fig. 3.16 Dynamic game between Allison (A) and Christopher (C) with choices left and right

would expect Ford to respond with a new model design next period. This, in turn, will lead to a counter response by General Motors.

The first step to understanding a dynamic game is to clearly define all of its relevant characteristics in what is called its **extensive form**. Recall from Sect. 3.1 that this requires that we identify the players, their possible actions, their payoffs, the information available to each player, and the timing of play. Unlike static games, the order of play or the time line is crucial and must be clearly defined in a dynamic game. Initially, we investigate games with two players, two courses of action, and information that is complete and perfect. That is, each player knows the rules of the game and the history of play. Once these models are mastered, we analyze a dynamic version of the lemonade stand problem, where there are an infinite number of possible actions. Issues of incomplete and imperfect information are discussed in the subsequent section.

3.3.1 Dynamic Games of Complete and Perfect Information

The extensive form of a dynamic game is described by a **game tree** (sometimes called a decision tree or tree diagram). We develop a game tree by example. Assume a simple game between Allison (A) and Christopher (C), where Allison moves first and Christopher moves second. Allison's only strategic actions are Left (L) and Right (R), and Christopher's are left (*l*) and right (*r*). The game tree and payoffs are pictured in Fig. 3.16, which shows:

1. Nodes: Each of the circled letters (A, C_1, and C_2) in Fig. 3.16 is a **decision node**. It identifies a point where each player must make a decision. The top node at A is the **initial node**. The initial node is where the game begins and identifies the player who moves first. The very bottom of the lowest branches of the game is called a **terminal node**. This is where the game ends. There are four terminal nodes in this game, which are the end points of the line segments just above the numbers at the bottom of the tree.
2. Timing: The initial node is where the game starts and indicates the player who moves first, which is A in this example. The next player down the tree moves second, which is C, etc.

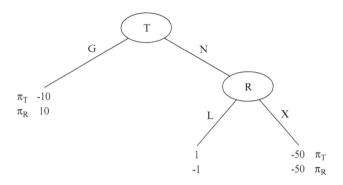

Fig. 3.17 Bank robber game

3. Actions: Each branch at a decision node identifies a course of action for that player. For example, Allison's decision node at the top of the tree splits into two branches: the left branch is marked L, indicating her choice of Left, and the right branch is marked R, indicating her choice of Right.
4. Payoffs: Below each terminal node are the payoffs for each player (labeled π_A, π_C). For example, if A chooses L and B chooses l, A earns a payoff of 2 and C earns a payoff of 0 ($\pi_A = 2$, $\pi_C = 0$).

Information is perfect (i.e., the history of play is common knowledge) and complete (i.e., the payoffs of all players are common knowledge).

To solve this type of game, we might simply determine all NE. Unfortunately, not all NE in dynamic games are reasonable. Consider the "bank robber game" described earlier. In this game, a bank robber enters the bank and tells a bank teller, "give me $10,000 or I'll blow up the bank." In the first stage of the game, the teller (T) has two options, to give the money (G) or not give (N). In the second stage, if the teller gives the money, the robber (R) takes the money and runs. If the teller says no, the robber can leave (L) or use explosives to blow up the bank (Explode, X). This game is diagramed in Fig. 3.17. If the teller gives the money, notice that the payoff to the robber is equal to minus the loss to the teller (i.e., the teller feels bad for the bank). If the teller says no and the robber leaves, the robber is embarrassed and earns −1, while the teller gains 1 (i.e., the teller is proud to have saved the bank money). The robber's decision to Explode is bad for both the teller and robber.

There are two NE to the bank robber game:

1. NE_1, the N–L outcome: It is a NE because (1) the robber has no incentive to deviate, as the robber's payoff would fall from −1 to −50 by switching to Explode; (2) the teller has no incentive to give, as the teller's payoff would fall from 1 to −10 by switching to give.
2. NE_2, the G(x) outcome: This outcome is based on the teller's belief that the robber will Explode if the teller chooses not to give, a belief that is denoted by (x). It is a NE because (1) the robber has no incentive to deviate, as the robber's payoff would fall from 10 to −50 by switching to Explode; (2) the teller has no incentive to deviate, as the teller's payoff would fall from −10 to −50 based on the x belief.

Although NE_1 seems reasonable, there is a problem with NE_2. It is based on the teller's belief that the robber will Explode if the teller does not give up the money. This is clearly a <u>false belief</u> because once the teller chooses not to give, the rational response from the robber is to leave. Because the teller knows the robber's rational response, given the assumption of complete information, one would not expect a fully rational teller to give. In such a setting, the robber's threat to blow up the bank is sometimes called "cheap talk" because it is not a **credible threat**: it is never rational for the robber to follow through with the threat. Thus, a fully rational and informed teller should never give up the money.

You might question this outcome, arguing that in the real world the teller would always give the money to the robber. There are two reasons why the predictions of the model may not coincide with reality. First, the teller will not have complete information about the robber's payoffs. If the teller believes that the robber is irrational and places a low value on life, the teller may believe that the robber's payoff from Explode is 0 instead of –50. In this case, the only NE is to give up the money. That is, the threat to Explode is now credible. This illustrates what is called the "rationality of irrationality": it pays the robber to appear to be irrational in order to make the teller believe that the robber will blow up the bank if the teller does not give up the money. That is why movies about bank robber gangs often have at least one robber who is or appears to be irrational or unpredictable.

The second reason why the predictions of the bank robber model may be incorrect is that there is always the chance that the bomb will go off unexpectedly. If this probability is high enough, it would be optimal for the teller to give up the money to get the robber and the bomb out of the bank as soon as possible. Thus, a high degree of rationality, complete information, and a very low probability of making a mistake are needed for the predictions of the bank robber model to be reasonable, simplifications that are normally invalid in the real world.[21]

3.3.1.1 Sequential Rationality and Subgame-Perfect Nash Equilibrium

Is there a way to solve dynamic games that rule out noncredible threats? Fortunately, Selten (1965) came up with a refinement of Nash's concept that did just that. Returning to the bank robber game with fully informed and rational players, NE_2 assumes that the teller holds false beliefs. But we would expect a fully rational player to hold correct beliefs. Selten's analysis requires a special type of rationality, called **sequential rationality**, where players make optimal actions at every decision node on the tree. To obtain an equilibrium that is sequentially rational, we use **backwards induction** (i.e., dynamic programming techniques): we start at the

---

[21] The first issue is addressed in perfect Bayesian models, which deal with how players form beliefs and behave when faced with imperfect information. The second problem where there is a chance that one or more players make errors is addressed in trembling hand models (Selten 1975).

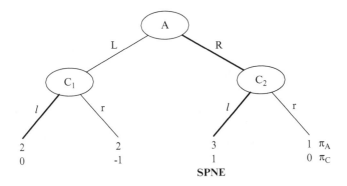

Fig. 3.18 SPNE of Allison–Christopher dynamic game

decision nodes at the bottom of the tree and rule out or crop off all branches that will never be played by rational players. This process eliminates all NE that are based on noncredible threats. The NE that remains is called **subgame-perfect Nash equilibrium** (SPNE).[22] More formally, a strategy profile or outcome is a SPNE if it induces a NE in every subgame, where a subgame is a self-contained part of a game that can itself be played as a game.

The notion of a SPNE can be better understood by an example. Return to Allison and Christopher's game, with the game tree reproduced in Fig. 3.18. It has 3 subgames: the first two are the decision nodes for Christopher, circled C_1 and C_2, and their corresponding terminal nodes. The third is the entire game itself.[23] Backwards induction requires that we first find the NE to all subgames at the bottom of the tree. At C_1, Christopher's optimal choice is l (Christopher earns 0 by choosing l and earns –1 by choosing r), which we identify with a thicker branch. This means that the r branch will not be played and is therefore cropped off (cropped off branches include all thinner branches). At C_2, Christopher's optimal action is l (Christopher earns 1 by choosing l and earns 0 by choosing r). Now, we move up the tree to the next decision node at A. Because the players are fully rational, we assume that Allison can look forward and reason back. In other words, she can forecast which branches will be optimal and which will be cropped off at the next stage of the game. Allison knows that Christopher will choose l if Allison chooses L and will choose l if Allison chooses R. Because Allison can expect to earn 2 by choosing L and 3 by choosing R, Allison will choose R. Thus, R–l is the SPNE.

To verify that the SPNE will rule out NE based on noncredible threats, we return to the bank robber game. In this game, there are only 2 subgames: the subgame around the decision node R and the entire game itself. Using backwards induction,

---

[22] Problems in this section have a unique SPNE. Unfortunately, some dynamic games will have more than one SPNE. See the Mathematics and Econometrics Appendix for further discussion of dynamic programming techniques.

[23] The first two are called proper subgames to distinguish them from the entire game itself.

at the robber's decision node (labeled R) the robber will earn -1 by leaving the bank (L) and earn -50 from Explode (X). Thus, the robber will choose to leave, which crops off the Explode branch. Given that the teller can look forward and reason back, the teller will earn -10 from giving up the money (G) and earn 1 from not giving the money (N). Thus, the only SPNE to this game is N–L. The NE based on the noncredible threat of Explode is eliminated and not a SPNE.

In the final example in this section, we convert the game between lemonade stands in the previous section to a dynamic problem. All characteristics of the game are the same except that stand 1 sets price in the first period and stand 2 sets price in the second period. The rules of the game are summarized below.

1. Players: lemonade stands 1 and 2.
2. Strategic variable: price.
3. Timing: Stand 1 sets price in period I and stand 2 sets price in period II.
4. Payoff Function: $\pi_i(p_i, p_j) = ap_i - p_i^2 + p_i p_j$.
5. Information: complete and perfect.

To identify the SPNE to this game, we use backwards induction. That is, we solve the stage II problem first. In stage II, stand 2 maximizes profits by choosing a price that is consistent with its first-order condition, (3.6), and its best-reply function, (3.8). The owner of stand 1 is assumed to be fully rational, meaning that the owner can look forward to identify stand 2's best-reply function. Stand 1 will then maximize its profit given firm 2's best-reply function: $p_2^{BR} = (a + p_1)/2$. This means that stand 1 substitutes p_2^{BR} into its profit equation to give

$$\pi_1\left(p_1, p_2^{BR}\right) = ap_1 - p_1^2 + p_1 p_2^{BR} = \frac{3ap_1 - p_1^2}{2}. \tag{3.10}$$

Next, stand 1 maximizes its profit in (3.10) with respect to p_1, which gives its first-order condition.

$$\frac{\partial \pi_1}{\partial p_1} = \frac{3a}{2} - p_1 = 0. \tag{3.11}$$

Solving this for p_1 gives the NE price for stand 1. Plugging this into firm 2's best reply gives the NE price for stand 2. Substituting NE prices into the profit equations yields NE profits. These are listed below:

$$p_1^* = \frac{6a}{4} > p_2^* = \frac{5a}{4},$$

$$\pi_1^* = \frac{18a^2}{16} < \pi_2^* = \frac{25a^2}{16}. \tag{3.12}$$

Two interesting results emerge. First, the stand that moves second has a strategic advantage (i.e., it earns higher profits). This is called a second mover advantage.

We will see in subsequent chapters that in some circumstances it pays to move second and in others it pays to move first in dynamic games. Second, even though firms are identical, the solution is asymmetric because players move at different points in time. The purpose of discussing the lemonade stand problem is to show how converting the game from static to dynamic can change the outcome. In addition, the lemonade stage game shows how calculus can be used to obtain the NE and SPNE when action variables are continuous rather than discrete.

In summary, to derive a SPNE, we use backwards induction as follows.

1. Identify the NE at the last stage of the game and eliminate all other choices that are nonoptimal (i.e., crop off all remaining branches that will never be played).
2. Do the same thing for the second to last stage of the game. That is, identify the NE at this stage and eliminate all other choice options.
3. Continue doing this backwards up the stages of the game until you reach the initial node. Optimal play at this stage determines all SPNE.

The backwards induction technique provides a simple game theoretic rule for optimal play in a dynamic game:

GT Rule 5. In a dynamic game, look forward and reason back to obtain the SPNE.

This rule guarantees optimal play at each decision node, meaning that players are sequentially rational. By assuring a NE in every subgame, all equilibria based on a noncredible threat are eliminated.

3.3.1.2 Classic Examples and Experimental Evidence

It is difficult to test whether individuals and firms behave optimally in games played in the real world. As a result, most evidence derives from experiments, not all of which are consistent with the predictions of introductory game theory models. Listed below are several classic examples.

The first is the **ultimatum game** (Guth et al. 1982), which is second to the prisoners' dilemma in importance in game theory. The ultimatum game consists of two players (1 and 2) and two periods. In the first period, player 1 makes an offer to player 2, which splits the total pie or payoff of $1 between them. That is, player 1 is free to make any offer: keep 0¢ and give 100¢ to player 2, 1¢–99¢, 2¢–98¢,..., or 100¢–0¢. Player 2 has two choices. Player 2 can accept, and the dollar is split as offered by player 1. Alternatively, player 2 can reject the offer. In this case, each player receives nothing. What would be the SPNE to the ultimatum game? The answer is for player 1 to propose 99¢–1¢ and for player 2 to accept.[24] By accepting, player 2 receives 1¢, compared to receiving 0¢ if player 2 rejected

---

[24] Actually, most game theorists assume it to be 100¢ − 0¢. This makes player 2 indifferent between accepting and rejecting. When indifferent, participants are assumed to play the game or accept the offer. In more complex games, this can simplify the mathematical analysis.

the offer. Player 1 knows this, so will make the smallest offer possible to motivate player 2 to accept, thus the 99¢–1¢ offer.

The 99¢–1¢ split rarely happens in experiments. For example, Roth et al. (1991) conducted ultimatum game experiments in four countries (Israel, Japan, Slovenia, and USA), which produced results that are representative of those found in other studies.[25] They found that the SPNE was reached only about 1% of the time. Most offers were between 40 and 50% of the total pie. Offers below 30% were rejected about 75% of the time. In addition, the results are remarkably similar across countries.

Comparable results are obtained from an extreme variant of the ultimatum game, called the **dictator game** (Kahneman et al. 1986). In this case, player 1 is a dictator, and player 2 must accept the offer from player 1. In this case, the SPNE is for the dictator to give nothing to player 2. In their survey of numerous experimental studies, however, Levitt and List (2007) indicate that money is passed from the dictator to player 2 in more than 60% of trials, and the mean transfer is approximately 20% of the total pie.

The final game that we discuss in this section is the **trust game** (Berg et al. 1995). Here, the pie grows in size over time, and the players take turns deciding how much to give to the other player. To illustrate, consider two players (1 and 2) and two periods. In the first period, player 1 must decide how much of $1 to give to player 2. All of the money passed to player 2 doubles in value. In the second period, player 2 is a dictator and decides how much to give back to player 1. For instance, if player 1 gives $1 to player 2, the size of the pie increases to $2. Player 2 then dictates how much of the $2 will be given back to player 1.

To determine the SPNE to the trust game, we use backwards induction. Solving player 2's problem first, the optimal strategy is to give nothing to player 1. Next, we solve player 1's problem. Because player 1 can look forward and reason back, player 1 knows that player 2 will give nothing back in the second period. The best response is then for player 1 to give player 2 nothing in the first stage of the game. Thus, the SPNE is for player 1 to keep the $1, leaving nothing for player 2.[26] As is true with the previous cases, this is not how individuals play the game in an experimental setting. Levitt and List's (2007) survey shows that the average transfer from player 1 is 50% of the initial pie, and the average transfer back from player 2 is almost 50% of the amount transferred to player 2.

Some social scientists conclude that these results undermine that validity of game theory and suggest that people are much more altruistic or socially generous than introductory game theory models suggest. This is not a fair assessment for two reasons. First, more advanced (and complex) economic models account for

---

[25] For a survey of the evidence, see Levitt and List (2007).

[26] But, you might ask why player 2 does not make the following offer to player 1: "give me the $1 and I promise to give back $1.01 and make us both better off." Because a legal contract is not enforceable in this game, player 2's promise is not credible and would not be believed by player 1. Thus, the optimal strategy is for player 1 to give nothing in the first stage of the game.

altruism.[27] Second, recent experimental evidence shows that people may not be as altruistic as earlier evidence suggests. In one study, List (2007) modified the dictator game to create the **taking game**, which allows the dictator to take up to $1 from player 2 as well as to give up to $1 to player 2. In this case, only 10% of dictators gave anything to player 2 and more than 60% took money from player 2. The point of his study was to show how the results are sensitive to the rules of the game. By simply changing the "action" set, most altruistic dictators were converted into thieves.

Levitt and List (2007) and Levitt and Dubner (2009) identify several reasons why experimental evidence can be rather fragile. These include the following:

1. **Money v. Utility**: Payoffs in the above games are measured in money, not utility. Fully rational people will maximize their utility, not dollar payoffs. Thus, it is not surprising that behavior is influenced by moral considerations, fairness, and emotion, as well as money.
2. **Scrutiny**: The scrutiny of experimental subjects in the social sciences can change their behavior. For instance, subjects may behave in a way that they think will gain approval from the experimenter or others playing the game. This is not a problem with experiments in the physical sciences.
3. **Stakes**: Most experiments involve payoffs with very small payouts. Games in business are played for much larger stakes. The evidence shows that as the size of the money involved increases, players behave more in line with the predictions of game theory. In the ultimatum game, for example, player 2 may reject on offer of 1¢ when the size of the pie is $1, but is more likely to accept an offer of $1 million when the size of the pie is $100 million.
4. **Artificial Restrictions of the Action Set**: Compared to real market games, the choice set faced by players is overly restrictive in experimental settings.

What this means is that when using human subjects, lab results may be different from real world results. Thus, caution is warranted when performing experiments and interpreting experimental evidence in the social sciences.

3.4 Repeated Games

One way to make our introductory models more realistic is to assume that the game is played more than one time. After all, we might expect experienced players to make fewer errors and behave more rationally than inexperienced players. Further, repeated games are quite common. As we said previously, General Motors and Ford have been competing against each other year after year for over a century. This is called a repeated game in which a particular game, called a stage game, is played

---

[27] Altruism has been an important part of economics research for centuries, going back at least as far as Adam Smith (1776). For a recent example, see Levitt and List (2007).

Fig. 3.19 GM-Ford game in
Soft (S) versus Tough (T)
competition

		Ford	
		S	T
GM	S	5, 5	-1, 10
	T	10, -1	0, 0

over and over again at different stages or periods in time. The rules of the basic
stage game remain unchanged over time, and the history of play is known to all
players. We consider repeated games that continue for a finite number of stages and
then for an infinite number of stages.

To make our discussion more concrete, we consider an economics problem
where General Motors (GM) and Ford (F) compete by simultaneously choosing
between tough (T) and soft (S) competition. The companies have complete information. Payoffs are described in Fig. 3.19 and have the same payoff structure as a
prisoners' dilemma. The Pareto outcome that maximizes joint payoffs occurs when
GM and Ford cooperate on S–S. Before considering a repeated game, we begin by
analyzing the outcome in a single period stage game. If GM and Ford were allowed
to cooperate and form a cartel, they would choose S–S. If cooperation were
effectively stopped, the NE (and dominant strategy equilibrium) would result
with both players choosing tough competition (T–T). The question is: will the
equilibrium change if the game is played more than once?

You might think that repetition would enable firms to behave more cooperatively.
To investigate this issue, we begin with a **finitely repeated game**. In this example,
GM and Ford compete in 3 periods or stages (I, II, and III). To keep things simple, we
ignore discounting. That is, $1 received a year from now is worth $1 today. We will
relax this assumption when we talk about games that have more stages. Notice that if
GM and Ford choose S in each of the 3 stage games, they will each earn a total payoff
of 15 (5 in each period). In contrast, if they choose a NE strategy (T–T) in each
period, they each earn a total payoff of 0 (0 in each period). One strategy that each
firm might try is to choose S if the firm's competitor chose S in the previous period
and choose T if the competitor chose T in the previous period. This is called a **tit-for-
tat strategy**, which appears promising if they both start out with S in the first period.

Unfortunately, this logic does not hold up in the last period of play. In the last
stage (stage III), it pays GM to choose T, because this will earn GM a payoff of 10
instead of 5 and there is no next period for Ford to retaliate. Of course, if the
strategic planners at Ford are fully rational, they will understand this too. Given

sequential rationality, both firms will see what is to come and will want to choose T in stage II of the game.[28] Similarly, this will induce them to choose T in stage I of the game. Thus, the game unravels, and the only fully rational outcome is for each player to choose T in each period.

In essence, what we have done is found another way of describing a SPNE to the GM–Ford game. That is, in a finitely repeated game, the SPNE is the NE in each stage game. Using backwards induction, we would solve the stage III problem first, which produces NE strategies of T–T. Moving back to stage II, the NE is again T–T. In stage I, it is again T–T. Once we know the NE in a stage game, it is easy to solve for the SPNE in finitely repeated games: play NE strategies in every stage game. However, experimental evidence shows that players in repeated games frequently cooperate. It turns out that cooperation is more likely if players believe that the game will be played many more times.

We now consider a game that does not have a predetermined end point: an **infinitely repeated game**, sometimes called a supergame, in which the stage game is played for an infinite number of periods.[29] To solve such games, we need to be able to discount future payoffs to their present value. As we saw in Chap. 2, the discount factor (D) equals the present value of $1 that is received in the next period, with $0 \leq D \leq 1$. For example, if $D = 0.95$, then $1 received next period is worth 95¢ today. Similarly, the present value of receiving $1 two periods from now is D^2, three periods from now is D^3, and so on. Finally, we also know that the present value of receiving $x each period out to infinity equals $x/(1 - D)$. For example, if you received $1 every year forever and $D = 0.95$, the present value of the income stream is $20.[30]

In an infinitely repeated game, we cannot use backwards induction to find the SPNE because there is no last period in which to start. Thus, we must be a bit creative to find a SPNE in an infinitely repeated game. One obvious solution is for each firm to play its NE strategy at each stage of the game. By definition, this is a SPNE. However, it turns out that certain strategies can support an outcome that produces a higher payoff.

A trigger strategy is one example that is commonly used in industrial organization to support a more cooperative solution in infinitely repeated games. Returning to our GM–Ford game, a **trigger strategy** is defined as follows:

- A player cooperates in the current period if its competitor cooperated in the previous period. In the GM–Ford example, the cooperative strategy is S.

---

[28] This will earn Ford a total payoff of 15 = (5 + 10 + 0) instead of 10 = (5 + 5 + 0).

[29] You might ask why we would make this assumption when no game can be played forever. Many companies plan to survive well into the future, regardless of the management team running the company. We can get dramatically different results when we assume an infinitely repeated game. You will also find that solving such games will be easier than you may think.

[30] In other words, $\sum_{t=1}^{\infty} D^t \cdot 1 = 0.95 + 0.9025 + 0.8574 + 0.8145 + \cdots = 20$.

• If a competitor did not cooperate in the previous period, the player plays its NE strategy forever after.[31] In the GM–Ford example, the NE strategy is T.

To determine if a trigger strategy will support cooperation, we must compare the payoff from cooperating with the payoff from not cooperating. In this game, if a firm cooperates forever, its payoff is $5/(1 - D)$. If it defects and does not cooperate, its payoff is 10 today and reverts to NE payoffs forever after, which is 0. Therefore, the firm will cooperate if the following condition holds:

$$\frac{5}{1 - D} \geq 10 + 0. \tag{3.13}$$

For the inequality to hold, it must be true that $D \geq \frac{1}{2}$ (i.e., $r \leq 1.0$, where r is the rate of time preference). To illustrate, if there were no tomorrow or the future did not matter, then $D = 0$. In this case, it would clearly pay the firm to defect from cooperation (i.e., the payoff from cooperation is 5 and the payoff from defection is 10). However, cooperation is optimal when $D \geq \frac{1}{2}$, implying that the rate of time preference (or interest rate on your investment) is less than 100%, which is reasonable in most economic environments.

Later in the book we will see that the cutoff for D will not always be this low. Nevertheless, Friedman (1971) proved that as long as D is sufficiently high, a trigger strategy will support cooperation. Thus, the cooperative outcome can be a SPNE, especially when it is unclear when the game will end.

3.5   Bargaining and Fair Allocations

Bargaining is a common occurrence in everyday life. Within a family, children may bargain over the division of the last piece of pie. Consumers bargain with salespersons over the price of a new car. Large corporations bargain with labor unions over worker salaries. Our goal in this section is to study the rational bargaining process and the extent to which bargaining leads to a "fair" outcome.

To demonstrate how value judgments influence an assessment of fairness, consider a problem facing two siblings, Allison and Christopher, who are bargaining over the division of the last piece of pie. One rule that may result in a fair division is to allow one child to divide the pie in two and the other child to choose between the two slices. This is likely to lead to a 50/50 split, but is this a fair allocation? One could make a case that a fair allocation would give a bigger slice to the larger, older, or better behaved child. Alternatively, Varian (1974) defines a fair

---

[31] This is sometimes called a "grim strategy," because the players can never get back to the cooperative equilibrium once one player fails to cooperate.

distribution as one in which there is no envy. By this definition, the 50/50 split of pie is fair. Neither Allison nor Christopher is envious of the other's piece of pie. But with different circumstances an unequal split can also be fair. What if the choices are two chocolate cookies and one vanilla cookie? If Allison loves chocolate and Christopher is allergic to chocolate, giving Allison the two chocolate cookies and Christopher the vanilla cookie is fair by Varian's definition.

This example shows how complex it can be to come up with a fair distribution of pie or other economic good. In the case of Allison and Christopher, to identify a fair allocation requires an understanding of their personal characteristics (e.g., preferences, age, behavior, and allergies) and the relative importance we place on these characteristics. In our analysis below, we assume that society deems a 50/50 split as fair and equitable. Our goal is to see how bargaining can lead to an equal distribution of the pie or economic surplus, which is viewed as socially desirable here. We discuss other notions of equity in Chap. 19.

Rubenstein (1982) addressed the bargaining problem, where players are allowed to make alternative offers. Assume that Allison (A) and Christopher (C) are bargaining over the division of 12 oz of ice cream. The game is dynamic—Allison makes the first offer, and Christopher can accept or make a counteroffer. In response to Christopher's counteroffer, Allison can accept or counteroffer, etc. Negotiation is over once an offer is accepted. To make the game more realistic, we add discounting, which means that there is some loss due to continued negotiation. In this case, the ice cream is on a plate in the hot sun, and a longer negotiation period means that more of the ice cream melts onto the ground. Information is perfect and complete, which means that both siblings know how much ice cream remains at each point in time, and they recall all previous offers and counteroffers. The question we wish to address is how the outcome will change as we increase the number of bargaining periods.

We begin by assuming that there is just one period because the ice cream is melted away by the second period. That is, player A makes an offer of a division of the ice cream, and C can accept or reject. If accepted, they take their respective amounts of ice cream. If rejected, they each receive nothing.[32] Each player is assumed to want to maximize his or her share of ice cream, and neither is affected by other motives. Notice that this is a simple ultimatum game, where the SPNE is a division of 99/1%. To simplify the analysis, however, we assume that the SPNE is 100–0%.[33] Player C is then indifferent between accepting and rejecting the offer. We assume that an indifferent player always accepts the offer, which simplifies the discussion without noticeably affecting the outcome. If we define equity to mean equality, this is an extremely inequitable distribution.

---

[32] C's decision to reject may take so long that the ice cream has melted away, or C may toss the ice cream on the ground in disgust with the offer.

[33] It would be more precise to assume a split of $(100 - \varepsilon)$ and ε percent, where ε is infinitesimally small, but this notation is rather cumbersome.

Next, we consider the two-period case. Details about timing and discounting in this two-period game are as follows:

- In period I, there are 12 oz of ice cream to divide up between A and C. Player A makes an offer to player C. If C accepts the offer, the game is over. If C rejects the offer, we move to period II.
- In period II, there are 6 oz of ice cream to divide up between A and C. Player C makes an offer to player A. If A accepts the offer, the game is over. If A rejects the offer, the game is over and each player receives nothing. The ice cream is completely melted away by the third period.

To solve this game, we use backwards induction. In the last period, this is a simple ultimatum game and C will offer A the following division (0, 6), where the first number is the amount of ice going to player A and the second number the amount of ice cream going to player C. Because player A is indifferent between accepting and rejecting, A accepts (by assumption). In the first stage of the game, player A can look forward and anticipate the offer C will make. So, player A will want to offer C just enough to make him accept. That will be the following division (6, 6). Because C receives the same by accepting or rejecting, C is assumed to accept. This means that bargaining will not extend beyond the first period and that the SPNE is an equal division of (6, 6). Thus, by simply extending the length of the bargaining period, we get an equal distribution.

To further investigate the bargaining problem, we consider a three-period model. Timing and discounting are as follows:

- In period I, there are 12 oz of ice cream to divide up between A and C. Player A makes an offer to player C. If C accepts the offer, the game is over. If C rejects the offer, we move to period II.
- In period II, there are 8 oz of ice cream to divide up between A and C. Player C makes an offer to player A. If A accepts the offer, the game is over. If A rejects the offer, we move to period III.
- In period III, there are 4 oz of ice cream to divide up between A and C. Player A makes an offer to player C. If C accepts the offer, the game is over. If C rejects the offer, the game is over and each player receives nothing. The ice cream is completely melted away by the fourth period.

Again, using backwards induction we begin with the last period. This is a simple ultimatum game in period III. Player A will offer (4, 0), and C will accept. In period II, player C can look forward and see the outcome in period III. Thus, C will offer (4, 4), and player A will accept. In period I, player A can look forward and see what will happen in later periods. This will induce her to offer just enough to get player C to accept, which is (8, 4). This 2/3–1/3 split is the SPNE. Although this is not as equitable as the two-period case, it is much better than the single-period case.

Can you anticipate what the SPNE will be in the four-period case? Rubinstein (1982) proved that the t-period bargaining game has four interesting properties:

1. Bargaining never extends beyond the first round; a settlement is reached immediately.[34]
2. For an even number of bargaining periods, the SPNE is an equal division (½, ½).
3. The split is unequal with an odd number of bargaining periods. In general, the fractional splits are $(t + 1)/(2t)$ for player A and $1 - (t + 1)/(2t)$ for player C, where t is the number of periods.
4. As t approaches infinity, the SPNE with an odd number of periods approaches (½, ½). You could interpret this as giving the players no bargaining deadline, which is common in many business negotiations, or that there is very gradual decay of the pie (melting of the ice cream).

The main conclusion is that bargaining can yield a equal distribution of an economic surplus when players have sufficient time to bargain back and forth.

3.6 Games with Incomplete, Asymmetric, and Imperfect Information

Another way to make introductory game theory models more realistic is to assume that some or all players do not have complete or perfect information. We present only a cursory discussion of these models due to their complexity.[35]

We begin with imperfect information. Recall that this means that one or more players do not know or recall the history of previous play. Consider the dynamic game played by Allison and Christopher that is described in Fig. 3.18. If we assume that C has imperfect information, he knows when it is his turn to make a choice but does not know (or recall) whether A chose L or R. To indicate ignorance of A's decision, we draw a dashed line between C's decision nodes, as in Fig. 3.20.[36] In essence, this is much like a static game. After all, it does not matter to C whether A moves simultaneously or moved previously. Either way C must make a decision without knowing what A has done. We would solve this game as we would any other static game by identifying all NE. In this case, C has a dominant strategy (l), and the NE is R$-l$. For this reason, static games are sometimes called games of imperfect information.

---

[34] This is not always true in reality. For example, negotiations between firms and unions frequently break down and lead to strikes. Delayed settlements can also result if we relax the assumption of perfect and complete information (Sobel and Takahashi 1983).

[35] The interested reader should see more advanced treatments of game theory to better understand games with incomplete, imperfect, and asymmetric information. These include Gibbons (1992), Watson (2002), Dixit and Skeath (2004), Rasmusen (2007), and Harrington (2009).

[36] In other words, C faces just one big decision node or information set that contains C_1 and C_2, which means that the player does not know what has happened in the past.

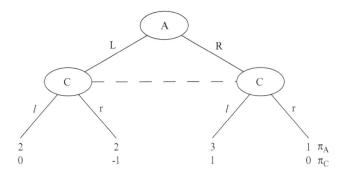

Fig. 3.20 Allison and Christopher game with imperfect competition

Asymmetric information occurs when one player has more information than another. To illustrate, suppose there is asymmetric information in the bank robber game. Consider the extensive form of the game that is described in Fig. 3.17. To make it more realistic, let the loss due to an explosion be $1,000,000 instead of $50. In addition, only the robber knows if the robber is rational or not. Assume that the teller believes that there is a 10% chance that the robber is irrational and will blow up the bank if the teller does not give up the money. What should the teller do in this case? A fully rational teller would calculate the expected payoff from choosing to give versus not give up the money. The expected payoff from giving is –10 (which is a certain event). The expected payoff (or expected value) associated with not giving is $0.9 \cdot (1) + 0.1 \cdot (-1,000,000) = -99,999.1$. In this case, a fully rational teller will clearly give the robber the money in a SPNE.[37] The presence of asymmetric information reverses the outcome.

Static or dynamic games in which players have incomplete information are typically called Bayesian games. Recall that there is incomplete information when one or more players do not know the payoffs of another player. A new poker player in town named Sarah may be either skilled or unskilled, but only Sarah knows this for sure. At the same time, it may be easy for her to find out who are the strong players in town. She knows her ability and the ability and payoff of her opponent, named Jason, but Jason does not know her level of skill and payoff.

In this game, there is asymmetric and incomplete information. With incomplete information, signaling behavior may result. For instance, Sarah may try to signal to Jason that she is an inexperienced and unskilled player by appearing uninformed about the rules of the game. Of course, if Jason is fully rational, he will anticipate that Allison may be sending a signal, and he will need to form a reasonable

---

[37] Another situation where the teller gives up the money right away, even if the robber is rational, is called a trembling-hand equilibrium (Selten 1975). In this case, there is a possibility that the robber will make a mistake and blow up the bank due to a trembling hand that is holding the ignition button to the bomb. If that probability of blowing up the bank is high enough, then the SPNE is for the teller to give up the money immediately.

belief about the probability that Sarah is a skilled player. Similarly, in competition between countries where country 1 cannot tell if country 2 is a hawk or a dove (as in the game in Fig. 3.6), country 2 may try to signal that it is a hawk (by appointing leaders that appear to be tough or irrational). If successful, signaling can give a player a strategic advantage.

3.7 Concluding Remarks

This chapter provides a brief review of game theory topics that will be used throughout the book. For the most part, we have focused on introductory models that assume that all players are fully rational. The additional assumption of perfect and complete information makes it relatively easy to derive NE and SPNE solutions to static and dynamic games.

If our goal is to describe and predict how real players actually play a game, these models are not always successful. Experimental evidence shows that players are more likely to cooperate and reach fair outcomes than simple game theoretic models predict. In some cases this is due to poor experimental design. Nevertheless, more realistic models provide better predictions at the expense of complexity. In the bank robber game, we attain more realistic prediction if we assume asymmetric information about the robber's rationality. We have also seen that cooperation and fairer outcomes are more likely in repeated games or bargaining situations that have no end in sight.

Finally, players may not reach the outcomes that introductory models predict when they are inexperienced or not fully rational. It can be difficult for many of us to identify our best strategy in complex games. For those of us with this problem, studying game theory can help. In addition, people do not always do what is in their long-term best interest. Issues that are associated with cognitive weaknesses are addressed in behavioral economics, which we take up in the next chapter. Again, one of the goals of this book is to incorporate contributions from behavioral economics and game theory (i.e., behavioral game theory) to better understand the behavior of large corporations.

3.8 Summary

1. The purpose of this chapter is to review game theory models in static and dynamic settings. A **game** involves a strategic situation where the payoff of one player depends upon that player's behavior and the behavior of other players in the game. In **static games**, players make decisions (or reveal their decisions) simultaneously. In **dynamic games**, player decisions are made sequentially. The rules of a game identify players, actions, the timing of play, payoffs, and information.

2. A **strategy** defines a player's contingency plan or decision rule that identifies a player's optimal action in every possible circumstance.

3. Regarding Information:

   - There is **complete information** in a game when all players know the payoffs of all the players in the game. Otherwise, there is incomplete information.
   - There is **perfect information** when all players know the history of all previous actions in the game. Otherwise, there is imperfect information.
   - Information is **common knowledge** when it is known by every player in the game and all players know that everyone knows this information.
   - There is **symmetric information** in a game when each player has the same set of information. Otherwise, there is asymmetric information.

4. To develop an optimal strategy when playing a game against another player, you must anticipate how your competitor will behave, how that competitor will anticipate how you will behave, how you will anticipate how that competitor will anticipate how you will behave, ad infinitum. This is a problem of **infinite regress**. Game theory provides tools to solve the infinite regress problem.

5. In introductory game theory, players are fully rational and have perfect and complete information. These assumptions allow us to construct models that give precise predictions that are reasonably accurate when the assumptions of the models are valid.

6. Static games of complete information are generally described in normal form by a **payoff matrix**. A payoff matrix identifies players, actions, and payoffs. Some take the form of a **coordination game** where preplay communication can improve player performance. A classic example is the **prisoners' dilemma**. In a prisoners' dilemma, each player has a dominant strategy that produces a payoff that is lower than if they were to cooperate. Others are **competitive games** in which there is a winner and a loser.

7. There are three types of equilibria in static games:

   - **Dominant-strategy equilibrium**: This occurs when each player has a dominant strategy, a strategy that is optimal regardless of the behavior of competitors.
   - **Iterated-dominant equilibrium**: A strategy is dominated if there is some other strategy that always produces a higher payoff. An iterated-dominant equilibrium is obtained by successively eliminating dominated strategies until each player has only one nondominated action left.
   - **Nash equilibrium (NE)**: In a Nash equilibrium, each player is behaving optimally, given that all other players are behaving optimally. A Nash equilibrium represents a mutual best reply where no player has an incentive to deviate.

8. Nash (1950) proved that every static game of the type discussed in this chapter has at least one NE, perhaps in mixed strategies. A **mixed strategy** is a decision rule that involves randomizing (i.e., assigning probabilities between 0 and 1 to actions). A **pure strategy** is a decision rule that does not involve randomizing.

 9. A **best-reply function** (or correspondence) identifies a player's strategy or best course of action in response to all possible actions of other players.

10. Dynamic games are typically described with a **game tree** that identifies players, actions, the order of play, and the payoffs.

11. Because some NE are based on noncredible threats (i.e., carrying out the threat is never rational), Selten (1965) developed the concept of a **subgame-perfect Nash equilibrium** (SPNE). The SPNE requires that there be a Nash equilibrium at every subgame, or part of the game where a decision is made. This leads to a sequentially rational outcome. **Sequential rationality** means that players behave optimally at every decision node on a game tree. In practice, **backwards induction** is used to identify a SPNE by starting at the bottom and working up the tree to rule out or crop off nonoptimal branches that will never be played by rational players. This process eliminates all NE that are supported by noncredible threats.

12. The experimental evidence shows that players do not always reach a SPNE in an experimental setting. Because it is very hard to replicate a real-world setting in the laboratory, experimental evidence in the social sciences needs to be interpreted with caution. Nevertheless, the evidence shows that introductory game theory models do not provide accurate predictions of player behavior when the assumptions of the model are invalid. Enhancing realism improves model performance. For example, players are likely to behave more rationally with greater experience and are likely to behave more cooperatively in games that are repeated over and over again without an end in sight. In addition, incorporating incomplete, asymmetric, and imperfect information into models when appropriate can lead to more accurate predictions but at the cost of increased complexity.

13. The following is a guide for optimal actions in situations that involve strategy:

    GT Rule 1. Never play a dominated strategy.
    GT Rule 2. If you have a dominant strategy, always play it.
    GT Rule 3. Eliminate dominated strategies and keep eliminating them successively until all dominated strategies are eliminated.
    GT Rule 4. If a dominant-strategy or iterated-dominant equilibrium does not exist, look for a Nash equilibrium where there are mutual best replies and no player has an incentive to deviate.
    GT Rule 5. In a dynamic game, look forward and reason back to obtain the SPNE.

14. Bargaining where players make alternative offers can yield an equal distribution of an economic surplus when players have sufficient time to bargain back and forth.

15. The blending of behavioral economics and game theory produces behavioral game theory, an emerging field that is enhancing the study of industrial organization.

3.9   Review Questions

1. Compare and contrast a dominant-strategy equilibrium with a NE.
2. Consider a static game of complete information with two players (1 and 2).
   Possible actions for player 1 are A, B, C, and D; possible actions for player
   2 are E, F, G, and H. Payoffs are:

   $A - E\ (3,1),$ $A - F\ (2,0),$ $A - G\ (3,1),$ $A - H\ (-2,0)$

   $B - E\ (-2,0),$ $B - F\ (-1,5),$ $B - G\ (-2,0),$ $B - H\ (-1,5)$

   $C - E\ (5,1),$ $C - F\ (5,1),$ $C - G\ (0,0),$ $C - H\ (0,0)$

   $D - E\ (0,0),$ $D - F\ (0,0),$ $D - G\ (1,5),$ $D - H\ (1,5)$

   Note that the first number in parentheses is the payoff for player 1, and the
   second number is the payoff for player 2. Draw the payoff matrix and identify
   the unique iterated-dominant equilibrium for this game.
3. Consider a static game of complete information with two players (1 and 2).
   Player 1's strategic options are up (U) and down (D), and player 2's options are
   left (L) and right (R). Payoffs are: U–L (1, 1), U–R (0, 0), D–L (0, 0), and D–R
   (1, 1). Draw the payoff matrix and identify all pure-strategy NE for this game.
4. Consider the same game as in question 3 above. The only difference is that the
   payoff at D-R is now $(x, 1)$, where $-1 \leq x \leq 1$.

   A. Determine the mixed-strategy NE to this game when $x > 0$.
   B. Determine the mixed-strategy NE to this game when $x < 0$.
   C. When would it make sense to play a mixed-strategy rather than a
      pure-strategy?

5. In a prisoners' dilemma, behavior that is best for the group is not what is best
   for individual players.

   A. Provide an economic example of a prisoners' dilemma.
   B. What is the pure-strategy NE to this game?
   C. Explain why this is called a dilemma.

6. Assume that players 1 and 2 play a dynamic, 3-stage game of perfect and
   complete information. Player 1 moves first, choosing between L and R. Player
   2 moves second, choosing between ℓ and r. In the final stage, player 1 chooses
   between a and b. Their payoffs are as follows:

   $L - \ell - a\ (1,0)$ $L - \ell - b\ (2,1)$ $L - r - a\ (1,3)$ $L - r - b\ (0,1)$

   $R - \ell - a\ (0,0)$ $R - \ell - b\ (2,2)$ $R - r - a\ (1,0)$ $R - r - b\ (2,1)$

Note that the first number in parentheses is the payoff for player 1, and the second number is the payoff for player 2.

A. Describe this game with a game tree.
B. Use backwards induction to identify the unique SPNE to this game.

7. Assume a parent (P) and a child (C) compete in a 3-stage game of perfect and complete information. In the first stage, the parent sets tough (T) or lenient (L) rules for the child. In second period, the child decides whether to mind the rules (M) or not (N). In the third stage, if the child has broken the rules, the parent must decide whether to punish the child (P) or not (X). Their payoffs are as follows.

$$T - M \ (4,4) \quad T - N - P \ (1,-1) \quad T - N - X \ (2,6) \quad L - M \ (4,4)$$
$$L - N - P \ (2,3) \quad L - N - X \ (1,6)$$

The first number in parentheses is the payoff for the parent, and the second number is the payoff for the child:

A. Describe this game with a game tree.
B. Use backwards induction to identify the unique SPNE to this game.
C. How would you change the preferences of the parent (i.e., the parent's payoffs) so that T–M is the SPNE? What type of parent is this compared to the parent with the original payoffs?

8. In the centipede game there are two players (1 and 2) who compete in a dynamic game of perfect and complete information. The stage games work as follows:

A. In the first stage of the game, there is a pot of money worth 10 and player 1 must decide whether to take the money or pass it to player 2. If player 1 takes the money the game is over, with player 1 receiving 10 and player 2 receiving 0. If player 1 passes the money to player 2, the amount increases by 10 (to 20).
B. In the second stage of the game, player 2 can take the money or pass it on. If player 2 takes the money the game is over, with player 1 receiving 0 and player 2 receiving 20. If player 2 passes the money to player 1, the amount increases by 10 (to 30).
C. In the third stage of the game, player 1 can take the money or pass it on. If player 1 takes the money the game is over, with player 1 receiving 30 and player 2 receiving 0. If player 1 passes the money to player 2, the amount increases by 10 (to 40).

This process continues for many periods, say 10.[38]

---

[38] The original centipede game developed by Rosenthal (1991) had 100 periods.

A. Find the SPNE to this game.
B. If the financial increments were 10¢, would you expect experimental subjects to end up at the SPNE? Why or why not?
C. Would your answer to part B change if the financial increments were $10 million instead? Explain.

9. Consider the merger game proposed by Bazerman and Samuelson (1983). The value of a targeted firm (seller) is known to the firm but not to a potential buyer. Before a merger, the value of the firm is uniformly distributed between $0 and $100 (i.e., the average value is $50). Let the premerger value equal V_0. If the buyer purchases the firm, a synergy results which pushes up the value of the target by 50%. The postmerger value equals $V_1 = 1.5\ V_0$. In other words, if the buyer purchases a firm worth $80, the value of the firm increases to $120 after the merger. The timing of play is simple. In the first period, the buyer makes a bid of p. In the second period, the seller accepts if p is greater than or equal to the premerger value of the firm. What is the value of p that maximizes the buyer's expected gain from the merger (i.e., the SPNE offer)?

10. Consider the GM–Ford game in Fig. 3.19, where each firm must decide whether to be a tough (T) or a soft (S) competitor. The only difference is that the payoffs are (1, 1) instead of (0, 0) when both players choose T.

A. Find the NE to this game if it is played only once.
B. Find the SPNE to this game if it is played 10 times.
C. Assume GM and Ford compete in an infinitely repeated game. Devise a trigger strategy that may support cooperation. What value of the discount factor (D) will support cooperation in this case? Explain.

11. Use backwards induction to determine the SPNE to Rubenstein's (1982) bargaining problem when there are four periods and two players, 1 and 2, who bargain over an economic surplus that equals 100 in period I, 75 in period II, 50 in period III, and 25 in period IV.

12. Consider the dollar auction that we discussed in the introduction of this chapter. What is the SPNE strategy to this game?

Chapter 4
Behavioral Economics

In the previous chapters we discussed introductory consumer, producer, and game theory. There, consumers and producers are assumed to be perfectly rational, meaning that they act to achieve a goal given their constraints. In particular, consumers obtain the most beneficial combination of products that they can afford, and firms produce the amount of their product that gives them the highest profit based on consumer demand, technological conditions, and rival behavior.

The introductory models provide a simple and generally useful representation of markets in a complex world. For the most part, these models predict well. Nevertheless, economists know that people do not always behave rationally. At times people suffer from mental errors and biases. For instance, if you flip a coin 10 times and it comes up heads each time, do you think that the next flip will be heads or tails? Some people believe that if you are on a "hot streak" like this one, the next flip will most likely be heads.[1] If you have studied statistics or probability theory, you know that this prediction is wrong—the probability of getting a head on any one flip is 50%. But this type of prediction error turns out to be commonplace.

So what do we do about systematic errors like these? The trick is to know when they matter for making predictions and policy. And when they do matter, how do we modify the introductory models to make them more useful?

The lucky streak mental error is one of many psychological concepts that relate to economics. Behavioral economics uses concepts and evidence from psychology to enhance our understanding of economic decision-making.[2] For example,

---

[1] There are others who believe that after a run of heads, a tails is "due," and that the next flip will likely be tails. In either case, people mispredict the probability of a head on the next flip.

[2] The inclusion of psychological and neuroscientific evidence (discussed below) in the field of economics has been highly controversial (Caplin and Schotter 2008, for example). At one extreme is the argument that psychology and neuroscience do not add anything to, and cannot improve on, economics. At the other extreme, traditional economics is indicted as replete with unexplained anomalies. We take neither extreme position and view behavioral and neuroscientific knowledge as information that is used to augment and extend introductory economic models.

V.J. Tremblay and C.H. Tremblay, *New Perspectives on Industrial Organization*,
Springer Texts in Business and Economics, DOI 10.1007/978-1-4614-3241-8_4,
© Springer Science+Business Media New York 2012

bounded rationality, which is discussed below, is the notion that people behave rationally within the bounds of limited information and mental capacity to deal with complex decisions (Simon 1955). Behavioral economics *is* economics. That is, economists have recognized psychological concepts for centuries.[3]

The new field of neuroeconomics complements and extends the study of behavioral economics. In the past, economists lamented the inability to measure consumer utility. Francis Y. Edgeworth envisioned:

> ... an ideally perfect instrument, a psychophysical machine, continually registering the height of pleasure experienced by an individual. ... From moment to moment the hedonimeter varies; the delicate index now flickering with the flutter of the passions, now steadied by intellectual activity, low sunk whole hours in the neighbourhood of zero, or momentarily springing up towards infinity ...

Today, technical advances in neuroscience, such as functional magnetic resonance imaging (fMRI), make observation of brain activity related to preferences and choices possible.[4] The new study of neuroeconomics combines neuroscience, psychology, and economics. Issues such as the influence of brand names on pleasure centers of the brain can be examined.

In this chapter, we discuss theories and evidence from behavioral economics and neuroeconomics that are most relevant to the study of industrial organization. To set the stage for upcoming chapters, we introduce information about common mental errors that firms can exploit to their advantage. We describe behavioral concepts such as anchoring, framing, overconfidence, endowment effects, and time inconsistency. In addition to illuminating the sources of anomalies, this discussion can help you to avoid mistakes in your own life.

4.1 Why Do We Make Mistakes?

4.1.1 Complexity, Information, and Bounded Rationality

It is difficult to make decisions when information is imperfect or decision-making is highly complex.[5] Buying a home theater system, for example, might involve gathering and processing information on each component and the system as a whole, comparing alternative systems in relation to preferences and needs, and searching for availability and lowest price. People do not usually gather all information available when making

---

[3] See Rabin (1998) and Angner and Loewenstein (2006) for a review of the history of the relationship between economics and psychology.

[4] Neuroscience is the branch of science concerned with the nervous system. The Merriam–Webster Medical Dictionary (2010) defines neuroscience as "a branch (as neurophysiology) of science that deals with the anatomy, physiology, biochemistry, or molecular biology of nerves and nervous tissue and especially their relation to behavior and learning." Neurophysiology is defined as "physiology of the nervous system."

[5] The topic of information is also discussed in Chap. 3.

a particular decision. For the home theater system, most buyers would not actually locate all information about every detailed characteristic on every component and system in existence but would gather information until the added benefits just equaled the added costs of collecting an additional unit of information. Some people will collect more information than others, depending on whether they enjoy learning about home theater systems or enjoy the process, such as talking to salespeople or using the internet. The end choice of a system might not be perfectly rational, in the sense of optimizing under perfect information, but it is optimal given the lack of information. When this occurs, we say that people are boundedly rational.

Bounded rationality is the idea that people are bounded by the limits of their capacity to obtain complete information and to deal with complex issues when they make decisions. In his seminal work on bounded rationality, Simon (1955) stated "the task is to replace the global rationality of economic man with a kind of rational behavior that is compatible with the access to information and the computational capacities that are actually possessed by organisms." An extensive literature on economic decision-making under incomplete information has evolved since that time.

In addition to information and mental capacity considerations, the choice process can be emotional and stressful for some people (McFadden 2006). People may avoid the unpleasantness of decision-making in a number of ways, some of which may be detrimental to their long-term well-being, e.g., procrastination. Common short-cuts include choosing a product out of habit and purchasing products that are popular in one's social network. The former may be suboptimal if market conditions change, and the latter may be suboptimal if an individual's tastes depart from those of the typical network member. The tendency to imitate others in a social network reinforces and spreads the network norm which can generate fads. Firms are motivated to penetrate social networks with their brands early, perhaps through advertising or product placement in movies, for example.

These and other rules of thumb used to simplify decision-making can be applied quickly and easily and are generally effective. Unfortunately, they can occasionally lead to serious errors. The dual systems approach discussed below holds that even when decisions are simple, people may behave irrationally and make mistakes.

4.1.2 Of Two Minds: The Dual Systems Approach

In an article based on his Nobel lecture in Stockholm in 2002, Kahneman (2003) describes a psychological model of two mental processes: "Intuition" and "Reasoning."[6] Intuition governs quick, easy, automatic choices, and can be

---

[6] Other authors characterize dual systems including: automatic versus controlled (Lowenstein et al. 2008), affective versus deliberative (Lowenstein and O'Donoghue 2005), visceral versus cognitive (McFadden 2006), hot versus cold (Bernheim and Rangel, 2004), and simply System 1 and System 2 (Stanovich and West 2000). Camerer et al. (2005) break down mental processes further into four groupings. Controlled processes correspond to Kahneman's reasoning, and automatic processes represent Intuition. Each is further divided into Cognitive and Affective processes to yield controlled-cognitive, controlled-affective, automatic-cognitive and automatic-affective.

vulnerable to emotions. Reasoning involves deliberate and effortful thought. Reasoning takes a lot of energy, while Intuition takes place easily. Intuition is used most of the time and is generally effective. The Reasoning process monitors and can override Intuition, but sometimes the monitoring is lax and errors can occur.

A common example is that of an American man who is visiting Britain. He wants to cross the street. He looks to the left for traffic and seeing none steps into the street, but he is hit by a car coming from the right, as cars must stay on the left hand side of the road in Britain (Camerer 2007, C29). Intuition led him to act spontaneously out of habit, and lax monitoring by Reasoning (i.e., not paying attention) allowed him to be hit.

Unfortunately, we do not have the mental capacity or desire to always concentrate on every simple task that we do all day, every day. Concentration, that is, the deliberate, effortful thought of Reasoning, is costly. Multiple problems considered simultaneously by Reasoning interfere with one another. Intuition serves as a low-cost decision-making process in the face of costly Reasoning power.

McFadden (2006) links the psychological discussion above to information from brain science. The frontal lobe of the cerebrum appears to correspond to Kahneman's Reasoning processes. The frontal lobe is responsible for higher order mental functions. Kahneman's Intuition process relates to the primitive limbic system, which resides at the base of the cerebrum. The limbic system and reward pathways are associated with emotion, pain and pleasure, and survival needs such as hunger, thirst, and sex. Interestingly, these structures are activated by economic trade.

The discussion of the dual systems of the mind above indicates that the weaknesses of Intuition might provide the best inlet for persuasion by others. The primitive brain makes us particularly vulnerable to emotional situations as in provocative advertisements. It is interesting that once a person's attention is captured, he or she will pay attention to all aspects of the product, even those not related to the stimulus (Kahneman 2003). Ads with emotional content, appeal to biological needs, and vivid images are most accessible to the mind. Accessible perceptions and information will carry more weight than warranted based on their importance relative to the person's long-term welfare.

The complexity of the world and quick and sometimes superficial decision-making can lead to mistakes, and people may not end up doing what is best for them. Thoughts that are emotionally loaded, involve sex or other biological needs, are triggered by cues, or are more memorable can distort decision-making. Below we discuss a number of common mistakes and related concepts.

4.2 Salience

Salience is the extent to which something is vivid, striking and memorable. An example of salience involves an eye exam in which an optometrist asks you to look at an eye chart from a distance. The chart has a white background with black letters. If you have had this experience before, what letters do you remember from the chart? For a standard eye chart, the big "E" is the most salient. Today, if you are asked from memory to report on the letters on the chart, you may not remember anything at all besides the E. If you are told ahead of time to memorize the second line (and if your vision is sharp enough to read the second line), with conscious effort (engaging the Reasoning process), you might be able to do so.

In another example, Stone (2012) examines voter ballots of the Associated Press (AP) college football poll, a weekly subjective ranking of the top 25 teams by a group of sportswriters. He is interested in how voters revise their ranks after observing game results. The voters observe information such as whether a team won or lost the game, the margin of victory, and whether the game was played at home or away. Stone claims that win or loss is more salient to the voters than the other information and finds evidence to support his claim.[7]

In economic decision-making, salient features of various options will give them excessive weight unless deliberative thought is employed. A red sports car might be very attractive even though an SUV might better serve a family with five kids and their diaper bags, car seats, tennis rackets, a cello, and backpacks. This is why marketers seek to create vivid and striking ads. Many of the anomalies or mistakes that are discussed below result from excessive salience of a particular option.

4.3 Framing Effects

A common mental error relates to the manner in which information is presented or framed. A classic example of "framing effects" involves the choice of treatment for a serious disease (Tversky and Kahneman 1981). There are 600 lives at stake. Consider two possible treatments, A and B, with outcomes listed below. Would you choose Treatment A or Treatment B?

Treatment A: 200 people will be saved.
Treatment B: A 1/3 chance that 600 people will be saved and a 2/3 chance that no one will be saved.

Now consider a choice between two other treatments, C and D, with outcomes listed below. Would you choose Treatment C or Treatment D?

Treatment C: 400 people will die.
Treatment D: A 1/3 chance that no one will die, and a 2/3 chance that 600 people will die.

---

[7] More specifically, Stone statistically estimates how voters should revise their ranks and finds that voters tend to be unresponsive to less salient information (such as margin of victory, home status) relative to statistical benchmarks. Voters responded appropriately to information about the most salient information about a game result, win or loss information. Technically, Stone evaluates whether voter choices are consistent with estimated Bayesian updating.

In an experiment, a randomly selected group chose between treatments A and B, and a different randomly selected group chose between treatments C and D. Despite the fact that treatment A is equivalent to treatment C, and that B and D are equivalent, 72% of the first group opted for treatment A over B while 78% of the second group opted for D over C. The "people will be saved" phraseology illustrates positive framing and evokes positive emotions, while "people will die" illustrates negative framing and evokes negative emotions.

Companies aware of framing effects will interact with the public by marketing their products through advertising in a more effective way. For instance, liquor companies are using positive framing in their labeling and advertisements when they state "Drink responsibly" rather than "Don't drink and drive."

4.3.1   Framing Effects and False Beliefs

Framing effects and other cognitive errors make people susceptible to false messages disseminated by firms. Glaeser (2004) proposes a model of the demand and supply of false beliefs. On the demand side, there are consumers with cognitive vulnerabilities subject to manipulation by firms. On the supply side, firms who benefit from cultivating false beliefs will supply messages at a cost and receive profits from creating and reinforcing false beliefs.[8] Of course, people may be able to resist false beliefs by thinking logically or gathering more objective information.

The model predicts, not surprisingly, that marketers will promote misinformation to a greater extent when it yields larger returns. Second, according to Glaeser (2004, 410), "Consumers will be more likely to accept false beliefs when those beliefs make them happier." This speaks to the issues of **cognitive dissonance**, **overoptimism**, and **overconfidence** discussed below. Third, false beliefs are spread from consumer to consumer, particularly when one benefits from convincing others as in the case of **fads**. Finally, when consumers are actively engaged in other activities, marketing will have less of an impact on them. If you are driving a race car around a track, you will probably not pay much attention to billboard advertisements. When participating in passive activities, like watching television, people are more vulnerable to the influence of advertising.

4.3.2   Anchoring

Consumer choices are sometimes anchored, or influenced, by irrelevant information conveyed prior to alternative options. Anchoring is a type of context or framing effect. In an experiment conducted by Strack et al. (1988), a group of college

---

[8] Glaeser's paper applies more broadly than to just firms and marketing practices. For instance, political influence is a major theme in his work. This discussion does not include his entire set of implications.

students were first asked how many times they had gone on a date in the past month, and then asked how happy they had been overall in the past month. The correlation between the responses to the two questions was 0.66. A second group of students was asked the questions in reverse order: first, how happy they had been overall in the past month, and then how many times they had gone on a date in the past month. In this case, the correlation between the responses to the two questions was 0.12. We can say that the happiness question was <u>anchored</u> by the dating question for the first group. The emotions evoked by the dating question for some students in the first group biased their evaluation of the second question. Memory is highly subject to emotional content which affected the students' perceptions about their happiness.

4.3.3 Default Effects

Another type of framing effect is the **default effect**, the tendency for people to choose the default option from a set of choices. If you purchase a textbook on the internet, the default for the vendor might be to send you regular e-mail ads in the future. You might be able to "opt out" of receiving e-mails by checking a box at the bottom of the vendor's Web page, often in smaller print. Another vendor might have a default procedure of not sending e-mails in the future, but you can "opt in" by checking a box on the Web page if you would like to receive e-mails. There is often a discrepancy between the fraction of people who end up receiving e-mail ads depending on if there is an "opt out" or "opt in" procedure because of the default effect. We might expect that more people would receive electronic ads in the opt out situation than in the opt in setting (Johnson et al. 2002).

A more serious example is given by Johnson and Goldstein (2003) of organ donation programs in seven European countries. In three of the countries, the default option is enrollment in the organ donation program, and in four, the default is nonenrollment. The average enrollment rate for the three countries with the default of enrollment was 97.4%, while the average enrollment rate for the four countries with the default of nonenrollment was 18%.

Similar striking results have been found in other default effect studies. Choosing the default option is one method of coping with complexity (McFadden 2006). According to Johnson and Goldstein, people might view the default as a recommendation by policymakers or other institutions, might choose the default to avoid the effort of collecting information, and may prefer the status quo due to loss aversion (loss aversion and the status quo are discussed below).[9] Other cases when people revert to the default effect include choice of retirement plans (Madrian and Shea 2001) and insurance policies (Johnson et al. 1993).

---

[9] Another reason for maintaining the status quo is the presence of switching costs.

4.4   If It Makes You Happy

Humans tend to experience positive, sometimes unrealistic, feelings. We might also take action to restore positive feelings when distressed. These tendencies can lead people into poor decisions. Recall Glaeser's claim, "Consumers will be more likely to accept false beliefs when those beliefs make them happier." We consider a few concepts that "make us happy," at least temporarily, below.

4.4.1   Overconfidence

> All the women are strong, all the men are good looking, and all the children are above average.
>
> Garrison Keillor on "Lake Wobegon"

People by nature tend to be overconfident in assessing their abilities. Overconfidence and overoptimism, the unrealistic expectation of positive results in the future, can lead to serious errors such as business failures (see also Chap. 14). A related phenomenon is **over-exuberance**, an excess of enthusiasm for a product. Chapter 15 presents a game theory model where advertising leads to cognitive errors such as over-exuberance.

4.4.2   Confirmation Bias

When a person forms an opinion, new information supporting the opinion becomes more salient, confirming the opinion. Information opposing the opinion is ignored. People also tend to misread evidence in support of their views (Rabin 1998). Confirmation bias is a type of anchoring effect, in which one's opinion is the anchor that carries undue weight. Confirming that one is "right" generates happiness in the short term, but can lead to mistakes in the long run when decisions are being made based on biased information.

Suppose that you decide to vote for a particular candidate for state senator. During the campaign, the media report that the candidate had accepted illegal campaign funds. You might tend to question or dismiss the claims. Now suppose instead that the opposing candidate was accused of accepting illegal funds. Would you be more inclined to believe the accusation and perhaps more inclined to discuss it with others? If so, this is an instance of confirmation bias. Confirmation bias can make people vulnerable to **deception**. It might also delay the spread of information regarding deceptive business practices. (Deception is further discussed in Chaps. 16 and 21).

4.4.3 Cognitive Dissonance

The theory of cognitive dissonance is one of the most important theories in psychology (van Veen et al. 2009). Cognitive dissonance is the distress that people feel when their actions diverge from their beliefs. To relieve the dissonance, people can either change their behavior or change their beliefs. Sometimes, consumers will accept false beliefs because it makes them happier, even though it may lead to mistakes in the long run.

Akerlof and Dickens (1982) describe a number of instances where people display cognitive dissonance. A common situation is in hazardous occupations, where workers deny that they are in any danger. At one workplace, a nuclear power plant, workers were given badges to wear that detected their exposure to radiation. None of the workers wore their badges (except before their mandatory weekly checkups), subconsciously believing or choosing to believe that their health was not at risk. Lack of education did not appear to be an issue, as there were Ph.D.s in the workforce and none wore their badges. As this example shows, there can be serious consequences to cognitive dissonance.[10]

4.5 Choice Under Risk and Uncertainty

When consequences of choices are unknown or uncertain, decision-making becomes even more difficult. In these situations, people often make choices relative to a "reference point." The reference level is often set at the status quo, which in some settings is the consumer's current endowment.

4.5.1 Reference Dependence

Preferences are said to be **reference-dependent** when a change in reference point gives rise to different choices (Kahneman and Tversky 1979).[11] An experiment that involved a group of MBA students illustrates reference-dependent behavior (Ariely et al. 2003). The students were asked to compare the price they were willing to pay for a product with the last 2 digits of their social security number (SSN). The products were cordless trackball, a cordless keyboard, average wine, rare wine, a design book, and Belgian chocolate. When the participants' SSNs were in the lowest fifth of the distribution of SSNs of all of the students, willingness to pay was substantially lower than for students with SSNs in the upper fifth of the distribution. For example, willingness to pay for Belgian chocolate for the lowest quintile was $9.55 compared to $20.64 for the highest quintile.

---

[10] A neuroeconomic study by van Veen et al. (2009) supports the theory of cognitive dissonance.

[11] Reference dependence and loss aversion are modeled by Prospect Theory, also discussed in Kahneman et al. (1991) and Tversky and Kahneman (1992).

4.5.2 Endowment Effects, Loss Aversion, and the Status Quo

People tend to place greater value on what they already own, a phenomenon known as the **endowment effect**. Most people will require a higher price to sell a product that they own, than what they would be willing to pay to buy the same product. A measure of the endowment effect is the difference between the price a person is willing to accept for an item and the price he or she is willing to pay.

Knutson et al. (2008) conducted a behavioral and neuroeconomic study of endowment effects. There were 24 people in the experiment who were asked to buy items, sell items, or choose from a different set of products for cash. The products in the buy and sell conditions were assigned at random from the following: iPod shuffle, 2 gigabyte USB flash drive, noise-canceling headphones, digital camera, and wireless mouse. Individuals were given two of these products at the outset to sell if they liked. The average willingness to sell for the products for the subjects was 65% of retail price, while the willingness to pay averaged only 32% of retail price.[12]

The endowment effect implies that people are prone to make choices consistent with the **status quo**. They also tend to weigh losses relative to a reference point more than comparable gains when making decisions, a phenomenon known as **loss aversion**. Suppose that you were offered the following bet: 50% chance of winning $100 and 50% chance of losing $80. Would you take it? Many people would not take it even though the expected value is $10 because they value the loss (expected value = $40) more heavily than the gain (expected value = $50). In fact, the Knutson et al. study above found that brain activity scans were consistent with loss aversion and reference dependence.

Loss aversion paves the way for brand loyalty (Fox and Poldrack 2009, 152). The trick for a firm is to hook consumers on its brand, making the brand part of the status quo. If not first movers in a market, the challenge is to "reset" the reference point. As will be discussed in Chaps. 14–16, persuasive advertising or systematic errors in consumer decision-making can impact brand loyalty.

4.5.3 Uncertainty and Signals of Quality

When the quality of a product is unknown, consumers might use price or brand name to signal quality. In a study by Plassman et al. (2008), people were given wines that they thought were different and sold at different prices. The subjects reported that the "higher-priced" wine tasted better than the "lower-priced" wine, even though it was all the same wine. The authors performed fMRI scans of the subjects during the wine-price experiment. When "higher-priced" wines were

---

[12] The corresponding neuroscience experiment scanned the brains of the subjects while they were making these decisions. The fMRI scans supported the presence of individual differences in the endowment effect.

consumed, the scans showed increased activity in the pleasure centers of the brain. In other words, people gained pleasure from knowing that a wine was higher priced apart from the taste of the wine itself.

A study using "MIT brew," beer tainted with a few drops of vinegar, sheds light on how knowledge of beer characteristics affects experiences and choices. Lee et al. (2006) found that the percentage of pub patrons preferring the MIT brew to regular beer was lower for those who were informed of the addition of the vinegar before they tasted the beer than for those who were informed after they tasted the beer. That is, disclosure affected the experience of tasting the beer itself. This is consistent with the wine price experiment above, that an indicator that beliefs about product characteristics affects utility apart from the true functional characteristics of the good.

Plassman et al. (2008) suggested that brand names and advertising might signal product quality and generate utility in its own right. If so, how is social welfare affected by marketing tactics that increase the pleasure of consuming a good, *ceteris paribus*? Chapters 15, 16, and 20 address issues of social welfare, brand names, and advertising further.

4.6 Time-Inconsistent Preferences

Some common departures from rationality surround consumer behavior over time.[13] In introductory models, we assume that individuals will maximize a stream of (exponentially) discounted net gains over time, but individuals often do not always behave this way. For instance, dieters plan to eat less now to receive future benefits, but will often succumb to immediate gratification. Addicts shoot up, gamblers bet, and shopaholics spree despite previous plans to quit. Consumers often buy out of habit, although it might be beneficial in terms of lower price or better quality to wait, collect additional information, and switch to another product.[14] The choices that people make over time will depend in part on how they discount future utility, the topic we first address in this section.

4.6.1 Discounting

As we discussed in Chap. 2, people tend to value benefits (or disutility of costs) more when they are received today relative to the future. The decisions that an individual makes over time will depend on how he or she trades off the benefits

---

[13] For a clear, concise summary integrating economic, psychological, and neuroscientific contributions, see Berns et al. (2007).

[14] Purchasing by habit might also be explained by bounded rationality as a way of dealing with imperfect and incomplete information.

from current versus future consumption in each period. A discount function determines the present value of utility (U) received in the future. A commonly used discount function is the exponential

$$PV(U,t) = D^t U, \quad 0 \le D \le 1, \tag{4.1}$$

where t indicates the number of time periods ahead, D is the discount factor, U is the value of a good, and $PV(U, t)$ is the present value of U received in period t. The higher the discount rate, the more weight is placed on future consumption. For example, if $D = 0.80$, the present value of consumption next period is $0.80U$, while if $D = 0.90$, consumption next period is worth $0.90U$ today.

The exponential discount function exhibits time consistency, i.e., the rate at which people trade-off future for current consumption is constant over time. It is also consistent with how future dollars are discounted in finance, as we calculated in Chap. 2. Time consistency means that you would view the value of obtaining a pizza tomorrow versus a pizza today in the same way as you would view the value of obtaining a pizza in 31 days versus a pizza in 30 days.

To illustrate the time consistency of the exponential discount function, consider the values of the function in (4.1) at different points in time. In the current period, $t = 0$, and $PV(U, 0) = D^0 U = U$. If the value of the utility gained from one pizza is 10, the present value of the pizza today is $PV(10, 0) = 10$. Suppose the discount factor $D = 0.90$. Then if $t = 1$, $PV(U, 1) = DU = 0.90U$, the value of the good today when consumed 1 period ahead. For the pizza with $U = 10$, the present value is $PV(10, 1) = 9$. What is the present value of a good consumed in 30 days? At $t = 30$, $PV(U, 30) = D^{30}U = 0.042U$. For the pizza at $U = 10$, $PV(10, 30) = 0.42$. Similarly, for 31 days ahead, $PV(U, 31) = D^{31}U = 0.038U$ or 0.38 for one pizza. In other words, a pizza consumed in 31 days is worth 0.38 today.

How does the trade-off between a good consumed tomorrow versus today compare to the trade-off between a good consumed in 31 days versus 30 days? The present value of a good in period 1 relative to period 0 is $PV(U, 1)/PV(U, 0) = 0.90U/U = 0.90$. The value of a good in period 31 relative to period 30 is $PV(U, 31)/PV(U, 30) = 0.038U/0.042U = 0.90$. In fact, this relationship holds for all comparisons over time with the exponential function: the relative value of two subsequent periods is always D, the discount factor.

In contrast, Strotz (1956) noted that people tend to be more impatient when making immediate choices than when making distant choices. (Impatience is reflected in a lower discount factor.) You might have a strong preference for pizza today versus tomorrow, but you might not care as much about having a pizza in 31 days relative to 30 days. What happens when it becomes day 30? You might care more about pizza on day 30 relative to day 31, than you did on day 0. This is called **time inconsistency**.

The quasi-hyperbolic discount function captures the high rate of time preference in near periods coupled with the lower rate of time preference in distant periods observed in human behavior:

$$PV(U,t) = \begin{cases} U, \ t=0 \\ \beta D^t U, \quad t>0, \ 0<\beta \leq 1, \ 0<D \leq 1 \end{cases}. \tag{4.2}$$

For the quasi-hyperbolic function, the present value of the good in the current period is simply U, while the present value in period 1 is βDU. This implies that the value of the good in period 1 relative to period 0 is $PV(U,1)/PV(U,0)$ $= \beta DU/U = \beta D$, while the value of the good in period 31 relative to period 30 is $PV(U,31)/PV(U,30) = \beta D^{31}U/\beta D^{30}U = D$. If β, $D < 1$, then $\beta D < D$; that is, there is greater discounting in the current period than in future periods.[15] Thus, functions such as the quasi-hyperbolic are capable of capturing time inconsistency, while the exponential function is not.[16]

Time inconsistency and discounting have important implications for issues such as addiction, habit-formation of purchases, procrastination and any decisions where immediate gratification is pitched against long term consequences.

4.6.2 Neuroeconomics and Self Control

Recent research in neuroeconomics posits that there are two interacting brain systems involved in intertemporal choice: one concerned with immediate outcomes and the other concerned with future outcomes. An experiment conducted by McClure et al. (2004a) in which brain scans were performed on people making choices between early monetary rewards and later monetary rewards confirmed this hypothesis. In fact, researchers were able to predict the person's choice (reward now versus reward later) based on the relative activation of the brain areas of the two systems.

In summarizing the neuroeconomic research regarding choices over time, McClure et al. (2004a, 506) state:

> Collectively, these studies suggest that human behavior is often governed by a competition between lower level, automatic processes that may reflect evolutionary adaptations to particular environments, and the more recently evolved, uniquely human capacity for abstract, domain-general reasoning and future planning.

These experiments support the view that discount rates are not constant over time, and uncover the workings of the brain as it aligns with the struggles that humans face between immediate gratification and reasoned foresight.

The implication of this research is that firms can benefit by reducing the cost of first purchase or boosting the temptation of immediate gratification. In Chap. 14,

---

[15] Although the hyperbolic function specifies that $0<\beta \leq 1$, $0<D \leq 1$, in practice, it is usually assumed that $0<\beta<1$, $0<D<1$.

[16] Angeletos et al. (2001). Another discount function that allows for time inconsistency is the hyperbolic: $(\tau) = \frac{1}{(1+\alpha\tau)^{\frac{\gamma}{\alpha}}}$, $\alpha, \gamma > 0$.

we discuss strategies that firms use to do so. As discussed earlier, advertising targeted to primal needs can stimulate immediacy. A model of intertemporal price changes, applicable to addiction and habit formation in purchasing, is presented in Chap. 14.

4.6.3 Impulsivity

One type of "impatience" (high discount rate) is **impulsivity**. Time pressure weakens deliberate monitoring (Kahneman 2003), making way for impulsivity. Home shopping network time limitations and a high pressure sales pitch, for instance, might encourage thoughtless actions. According to Camerer et al. (2005,40) "cognitive overload," such as taxing the prefrontal cortex with multiple tasks, also facilitates impulsivity. In addition, factors furthering impatience include prior exercise of self-control, alcohol, stress, and sleep deprivation.

4.6.4 Addiction and Cues

Decision-making regarding **addictive commodities** is affected by time, risk, complexity of benefit–cost calculation, and biological forces of craving, dependence, and withdrawal. As such, people may be particularly vulnerable to mistakes when it comes to dealing with addictive commodities. For example, Sayette et al. (2008) find that smokers underestimate their desire to smoke when in a "cold" (noncraving) state than when in a "hot" (craving) state.

Hot states can be triggered by **environmental cues** (Bernheim and Rangel 2004). Just as with Pavlov's dog,[17] a continued association of a cue with a consumption good will later lead a person to demand the good when exposed to the cue (Laibson 2001). For instance, if a person usually smokes while gambling, going to a casino may trigger a craving for cigarettes. If someone regularly uses cocaine with friends and later attempts to quit, it may be more difficult to abstain while in their presence. Driving by your favorite bakery might tempt you to buy a treat, and so on. Sometimes while in a "cold" state, people will use precommitment to constrain themselves in the future from succumbing to temptation. A drug addict might check into a drug rehabilitation center. Someone who tends to want to drive home after drinking might arrange for a designated driver or taxi on a night out on the town. A person who is obese might have surgery to limit their capacity to consume food. Another tactic is cue-avoidance, such as taking a route that bypasses your bakery.

---

[17] Pavlov conducted experiments on dogs, in which various stimuli (sound, visual, and tactile) were applied when the dogs were eating food. After the dogs were "conditioned" to expect food with a stimulus, Pavlov found that the stimulus would cause the dogs to salivate even when they did not consume food (http://www.ivanpavlov.com, 2003).

Marketers use cues to entice consumers to purchase their products, such as candy at the checkout counter of stores. Brand names, logos, billboard images, and advertisements can also act as cues to motivate product sales.

4.7   Who Are You? Economics and Identity

In "Economics and Identity," Akerlof and Kranton (2000) incorporate individual identity, or sense of self, into the introductory economic model. They stylize social categories, where each category is governed by its own set of prescriptions for behavior, i.e., how group members are supposed to act. Individuals choose the category to which they belong to a certain extent. In some cases, a social category is assigned, perhaps in accordance with particular characteristics that are difficult or impossible to alter, such as race or gender.

People can experience a loss in utility (i.e., a loss in identity) if they take actions that go against the expected behavior of the group. They also lose utility if someone else in the group violates the prescriptions. As an example, suppose that one social group is men and the other women. If a man wears a dress, he might feel a loss of identity. Other men in his group may also feel a loss in identity, and may lash out against the offender or act in other ways to restore their sense of self.

In addition, social categories and associated acceptable behaviors change over time due to political, economic, and social forces. For example, in the mid-1950s, men did not wear colored shirts, pink shirts in particular. Today, colored shirts are acceptable wear for men (although men's shirts that are pink might be called "salmon"). Advertising campaigns can promote products by tying them to particular social categories or by altering expected behaviors within social groups. The slogan for the deodorant Secret, "Strong Enough for a Man, Made for a Woman," attempts to establish Secret as a prescribed product for those in the social category, women.[18]

Companies can also err in their assessment of the importance of identity to product choice. A case in point is the Coca-Cola company, which initially marketed the diet soda Tab in a hot pink can, but later had to remarket it as Diet Coke in a silver and red can to be saleable to male customers. Perhaps both the diet image and the hot pink image went too far afield of the male identity to make Tab attractive to some men.

The importance of identity in economic decisions indicates that advertising can be effective by creating product images that are desirable to consumers. The framework of Akerlof and Kranton suggests that the image of a product can

---

[18] Interestingly, the chemical composition and patent numbers of Secret and Sure deodorants are identical. http://www.killianadvertising.com/wp16.html. Although Sure Original is a gender-neutral product, the company introduced "Sure for Men" and "Sure for Women" on February 16, 2010 (http://www.suredeodorant.com/), accessed March 4, 2011.

become tied to a social group, that the people within the group will get pleasure from consuming the product due to the reinforcement of their identities, that they will feel pressure from others in the group, and that they will have misgivings for those in the group who use a substitute product. A young woman might drink Corona Light beer, feel happy when her friends drink the same, feel pressure from her friends not to switch to Bud Light, and tease a friend who drinks Bud Light. Would you expect to see students with tattoos, piercings, and spiked hair hanging out with students wearing pearls and cashmere sweaters? Other examples of group identification include college sports teams, fraternities and sororities, unions, occupation, religion, and the military (Akerlof and Kranton 2005).

The Akerlof and Kranton model reflects the psychology literature on personality development, although the language differs from the economic model above. Development of personality, ego, or identity involves internalization of rules of behavior (i.e., values) and identification with people who share the same values. If an individual violates the internalized rules, he or she will experience anxiety, and others in the group will feel anxious. A person can avoid the anxiety by sticking to the rules, or if violated, by acting to restore identity. In the example above, the Bud Light drinker could alleviate discomfort and a "left-out" feeling by conforming and switching to Corona Light.[19]

People often feel strongly about brand names. There is substantive evidence that once a person chooses a brand, he or she is likely to value the brand in and of itself. Blind taste tests on beer (Allison and Uhl 1964), Coke and Pepsi (McClure et al. 2004b), and Perrier (Nevid 1981) show that people will be unable to choose their favorite brand when comparing unidentified servings of their brand with other brands.[20] The brand name appears to be generating utility apart from the product. Perhaps the brand name is reinforcing identity.

Prestige or **snob** effects can also be considered in the context of the identity model. Promotion of prestige products, such as Perrier, might lead a person to buy the product to jump to a "higher" social group or to maintain identity within a prestige-oriented group.

Identity might also shed light on the coexistence of **mass-market** and **niche-market** brands in an industry, as we will discuss in Chap. 13. People who like to belong to a social group will gain utility from identifying with a mass-market brand, such as with **bandwagon effects** as discussed in Chap. 2. In contrast, people who like to set themselves apart from the crowd might gain utility from identifying with a niche-market brand, perhaps due to snob effects or conspicuous consumption.

All in all, the Akerlof and Kranton framework allows us to see how advertising, image, prestige, and brand influences can tap into identity-based preferences and affect consumer choices.

---

[19] For a discussion of the effect of culture and identity on beer demand, see McCluskey and Shreay (2011).

[20] See Chap. 14 for more information about blind taste tests.

4.8 Summary

1. **Behavioral Economics** uses insights from psychology to improve our understanding of how people make economic decisions. **Neuroeconomics** brings neuroscience to economics. Neuroeconomics and behavioral economics can help us understand how the brain works and what neural and psychological variables affect economic choices.
2. A number of mistakes or "anomalies," phenomena not in keeping with introductory economic models, occur systematically in the population. In addition to enriching and extending our knowledge of economic behavior, awareness of typical cognitive mistakes can help us to avoid them.
3. **Bounded rationality** is the idea that people are bounded by the limits of their capacity to obtain complete information and deal with complex issues when they make decisions.
4. The **dual systems** approach explains how departures from rationality can sometimes occur. It identifies a Reasoning process and an Intuition process for making decisions. Reasoning is responsible for deliberate thought, and Intuition is effortless and automatic. Intuition is less costly, used most of the time, and is generally effective, but can make mistakes if Reasoning does not override when necessary.
5. People are more likely to choose options that are **salient**—vivid, striking, and memorable—even though it might not be in their best interest to do so. Options involving emotions or biological needs tend to be more salient.
6. **Framing effects,** such as **anchoring** and **default effects,** occur when people make different choices depending on how their options are presented or framed. Anchoring occurs when a person relies on irrelevant information (the anchor) when making a decision. The default effect occurs because people are more likely to choose the default option from a set of choices. Changing the default option often results in a different choice.
7. People are more likely to absorb misinformation if it makes them happy. **Overconfidence, overoptimism**, and **over-exuberance** can make people happy in the present but lead to errors, such as business failures, in the future. **Confirmation bias** can also cause mistakes: ignoring evidence against one's position while retaining favorable evidence can distort decision-making due to misinformation.
8. When beliefs and actions differ, a person might experience **cognitive dissonance**. To relieve the distress, he or she might achieve consistency by altering actions or altering beliefs.
9. People make choices with respect to a reference point. If the reference point changes and the decision changes, preferences are said to be **reference dependent**.
10. The **endowment effect** arises because people tend to value items that they already own more than they value identical items that they do not own. That is, their willingness to sell a particular good is less than their willingness to buy an identical good. Thus, people often choose the **status quo**, the current state of affairs.

11. People place greater weight on losses than on equivalent gains when they make decisions, i.e., they are **loss averse**.
12. For some people, the rate at which they trade off future for current consumption is not constant over time, that is, preferences are **time inconsistent.** This occurs when people are more impatient (have a higher discount rate) when weighing consumption tomorrow versus today than when weighing consumption in 10 days versus 9 days from now. Loss of **self-control** such as impulsivity, drug usage, and overeating can result from time-inconsistent preferences.
13. The choice to use addictive substances is complex—subject to risk, time, and biological considerations. Environmental **cues** can trigger addictive behaviors such as drinking alcohol, smoking, and gambling.
14. The Akerlof–Kranton model of **identity** holds that people become identified with a social group. When this happens, they gain utility from behaving according to the "rules" of the group, they feel uncomfortable when a group member violates expected behavior, and they may act to restore their sense of self following the violation. Social categories change over time, and advertisers can attempt to tag brand names to rules of acceptable behavior of social groups. Prestige, conspicuous consumption, and bandwagon effects may be associated with a person's identity.

4.9   Review Questions

1. Kahneman (2003, 1469) writes: "people sometimes answer a difficult question by answering an easier one instead." Relate this to the dual systems approach.
2. Give an example of a salient advertisement.
3. In the wine-price experiment, people were given false information about wine prices. Were the people in the wine-price experiment worse off by having a false price belief beforehand? Explain.
4. Give three examples of environmental cues for various self-control problems.
5. Bud and Pat are selling their house. They check http://zillow.com and see that Zillow estimates the value of their house at $500,000, and that is the price that they decide to list. A potential buyer offers $490,000, and they accept the offer. Suppose that instead, Bud and Pat had listed the house price at $400,000. Do you think that the house would have sold for $490,000? What behavioral concept corresponds to the $400,000 value?
6. Your friend, Jed, has a test tomorrow morning. Given how much Jed has studied so far, he thinks that if he studies 3 hr, he will be able to pass the test. Jed's roommate decides to throw a party, and Jed joins the party instead of studying. The next morning before the test, Jed tells himself that he has studied a lot over the term and done well on the previous test, so he should be able to pass the test. Is Jed exhibiting cognitive dissonance or loss aversion? Explain.
7. List three strategies that people use to make choices in complex situations.

8. A casino in Las Vegas boasts on an impressive banner over the slot machines: "We pay 98¢ on the dollar!" One reason why people gamble when the odds are against them is that they enjoy gambling, and the added utility is worth the expected loss. What reason discussed in behavioral economics might also explain why people gamble against the odds?
9. Does procrastination relate to time-inconsistent preferences? Explain.
10. What is meant by "precommitment?" Can you think of an example or examples of precommitment strategies for physical exercise?
11. In the movie "Good Will Hunting," Will is a genius at mathematics but does not want to leave his blue-collar neighborhood, even though he would be better off intellectually and economically if he left and studied advanced mathematics. What can explain his "irrational" behavior?

Part II
Perfect Competition, Monopoly, Product Differentiation, and Market Structure

Chapter 5
Perfect Competition and Market Imperfections*

Competition is a fundamental concept in a market economy. We can think of competition as firm rivalry, where one firm battles to gain a strategic advantage over its competitors. For example, General Motors and Ford have been competing with one another for over a century to produce better cars at lower cost and to create more catchy marketing campaigns. We can also think of competition as a type of market structure. Both concepts are important in industrial organization. In later chapters, we analyze various forms of competitive behavior. In this chapter, we review the market structure of perfect competition.

Before we begin, it is important to distinguish between a market and an industry. A market is a collection of all buyers and sellers, with sellers supplying substitutable goods to the same potential buyers. An industry generally ignores the buyer side of the market, referring to the collection of firms that sell substitutable goods. Market and industry are frequently used interchangeably, but there will be times when it is important to distinguish between them. Practical issues involving how to accurately define a relevant market will be taken up in Chap. 8.

5.1 The Assumptions of Perfect Competition

Although no real-world market is perfectly competitive, the model of perfect competition provides us with a benchmark of market efficiency from which real markets can be judged. In addition, the model is based on a set of assumptions that produces a simple explanation of price and output determination in a free market. In physics, assuming that we live in a perfect vacuum makes the study of how objects fall to earth much easier, even though perfect vacuums do not exist.

---

*This is a review chapter. You can learn more about the basic economic models discussed in the chapter from any introductory or intermediate microeconomics textbook, such as Frank and Bernanke (2008), Mankiw (2011), Bernheim and Whinston (2008), Pindyck and Rubenfield (2009), and Varian (2010). For more advanced treatments, see Nicholson and Snyder (2012) and Mas-Colell et al. (1995).

V.J. Tremblay and C.H. Tremblay, *New Perspectives on Industrial Organization*,
Springer Texts in Business and Economics, DOI 10.1007/978-1-4614-3241-8_5,
© Springer Science+Business Media New York 2012

Similarly, assuming perfect competition simplifies the study of markets. The model is highly reductionist but still provides a viable representation of some real-world markets, especially for agricultural commodities.

The basic demand and supply model derives from a market that is assumed to be perfectly competitive. For a market to be **perfectly competitive**, it must meet the following five conditions:

1. Firms are *profit maximizers.*[1]
2. Firms produce *perfectly homogeneous goods.* That is, there are no real or perceived differences between the products of different firms.
3. There are *many identical firms* in the industry.[2] Extreme models consider the case where the number of firms is close to infinity. In such a market, each firm is so small that its production has no effect on the equilibrium price. Because products are homogeneous and firms are small, firms are said to be price takers. This means that the market price is exogenous (i.e., taken as given) to the firm. A firm is unable to profitably raise its price above the market equilibrium price. The assumption that firms are identical implies that their cost functions are the same.
4. There are *no barriers to entry or exit.* This means that entrepreneurs can enter or exit a market at zero cost.
5. There are *no frictions or other forms of market imperfections.* No frictions means that all buyers and sellers are perfectly informed about market conditions, and transaction costs are zero. In addition, goods are private (not public goods), and there are no externalities. Firms do not impose any benefits or costs on others without compensation.

You can see why this is called "perfect" competition. Each of the assumptions characterizes an extreme or limiting case. Products are not just similar but identical. The number of firms approaches infinity. The cost of entry and exit is zero. And there are no frictions or externalities. In such a market, the price represents the true marginal cost to society of production. One of the goals of the book is to see how market outcomes change when one or more of these assumptions are violated. Before modifying them, we first need to understand the perfectly competitive model.

5.2   Firm Behavior in Perfect Competition

5.2.1   Firm Demand and Revenue Functions

Because a perfectly competitive firm is a price taker, its demand function is a horizontal line at the equilibrium price. The market equilibrium price, p^*, is determined by

---

[1] In Chap. 2 we discuss alternative firm motives.

[2] The model also assumes that there are many buyers. Unless otherwise indicated, we will assume many buyers throughout the book.

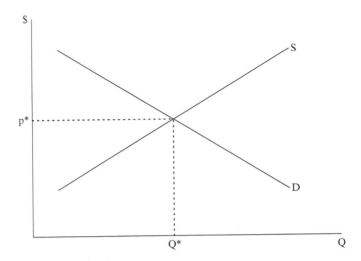

Fig. 5.1 Industry supply and demand

Fig. 5.2 The firm demand curve

industry supply (*S*) and market demand (D) as shown in Fig. 5.1, where Q^* is the
equilibrium level of consumption in the market. If a firm charges a price above p^*, no
consumers will buy from the firm because they can buy all they want at the equilibrium
price. Thus, in perfect competition, a firm cannot charge a price higher than the market
price. A firm will not sell at a price below p^*, because it can sell all that it is capable of
producing at the equilibrium price. To lower price would lower profits unnecessarily.
Under these conditions, firm demand is perfectly or infinitely elastic and represented
by the horizontal line *d* in Fig. 5.2, where *q* is the firm's level of production.

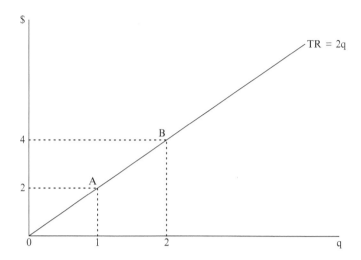

Fig. 5.3 The total revenue function when price $= 2$

Before discussing firm profit, we need to describe **total revenue** (TR) for the perfectly competitive firm. Generally, total revenue is price times quantity, TR $=$ $p(q)q$, where $p(q)$ is inverse demand. Since a perfectly competitive firm will charge the same price regardless of the level of output, the total revenue function for the firm is

$$TR = pq. \tag{5.1}$$

Figure 5.3 shows the total revenue function for a hypothetical firm with a price of \$2, so that TR $= 2q$. For 1 unit of output, TR is \$2 (point A). If $q = 2$, then TR $= 2 \times 2 = \$4$ (point B), and so on. The TR function is a straight line from the origin, and the slope of TR $= 2$ in this example. In general, the TR function for the perfectly competitive firm is a line from the origin with slope equal to p.

Recall from Chap. 2 that **marginal revenue** is the additional revenue the firm receives from a small increase in production, and that the marginal revenue function is the slope of the total revenue function. The equation for marginal revenue is[3]:

$$MR = \frac{\partial TR}{\partial q}. \tag{5.2}$$

Since TR $= pq$ in perfect competition and $p = p^*$,

$$MR = \frac{\partial(p^*q)}{\partial q} = p^*. \tag{5.3}$$

---

[3] Although q is the only variable in this example, we use ∂ instead of d to remind us that there are many other variables that are implicitly assumed to be held fixed.

Marginal revenue for a perfectly competitive firm is the market price because an additional unit of output brings p^* to the firm.

Average revenue is revenue per unit of output. The AR function is

$$AR = \frac{TR}{q}. \tag{5.4}$$

In perfect competition,

$$AR = \frac{p^* q}{q} = p^*. \tag{5.5}$$

Thus, for a perfectly competitive firm,

$$MR = AR = p^*. \tag{5.6}$$

Geometrically, the MR, AR, and firm demand curve coincide. In reference to Fig. 5.2, the MR and AR functions are the same as demand, d.

5.2.2 Profit Maximization

How do firms decide how much output to produce when there is perfect competition? Firms are assumed to choose the amount of output that maximizes profit. Profit is defined as total revenue minus total cost (TC):[4]

$$\pi = TR - TC. \tag{5.7}$$

In general, the profit equation will be concave or hill-shaped, as described in Fig. 5.4. When $q = 0$, no output is produced and profit is 0. From $q = 0$ to $q = q^*$, profit is increasing at a decreasing rate. Profit peaks at q^*, decreases at a decreasing rate until $\pi = 0$ at q', where TR = TC. Beyond q', TC > TR and profit is negative. The firm will produce q^* which generates the highest level of profit. Notice that at the profit-maximizing output level, the slope of the tangent line to the profit equation is zero.

Another way to find q^* is with the use of calculus. To find the output level that maximizes profit, we take the derivative of π with respect to q and set it equal to zero:

$$\frac{\partial \pi}{\partial q} = \frac{\partial TR}{\partial q} - \frac{\partial TC}{\partial q},$$
$$= MR - MC = 0, \tag{5.8}$$

---

[4] Generally, we will consider long-run problems, but at this point, we are abstracting from time.

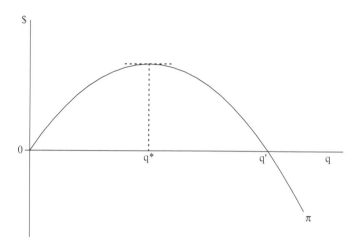

Fig. 5.4 The profit function

where MC is marginal cost ($\partial \text{TC}/\partial q$). Equation (5.8) is called the first-order condition of profit maximization. This equation produces the standard *marginal principle* or *rule of marginalism*: to maximize payoff with respect to activity x (output in this case), the firm must equate the marginal benefit (MR) with the marginal cost (MC) of activity x. This condition indicates that the firm will choose the output level where MR = MC.[5] Given that the market equilibrium price is identical to marginal revenue, the first-order condition for a perfectly competitive firm also implies that

$$p \equiv \text{MR} = \text{MC} \qquad (5.9)$$

at the profit-maximizing level of output.

Referring back to (5.8), consider a simple example where MR = 2 and MC = $2q$.[6] In this case,

$$\frac{\partial \pi}{\partial q} = \text{MR} - \text{MC},$$

$$= 2 - 2q = 0. \qquad (5.10)$$

---

[5] A maximum is assured because the profit equation is concave. If it were convex, this method would identify the output level that would minimize profit. See the Mathematics and Econometrics Appendix at the end of the book for more details.

[6] These functions derive from the following total revenue, total cost, and profit functions: *TR* = $2q$, *TC* = q^2, and $\pi = TR - TC = 2q - q^2$. The TC equation is not the usual representation of a cost equation in perfect competition, as we will see subsequently, but we use it here to provide a simple example.

Solving for the optimal level of output yields:

$$q^* = 1. \tag{5.11}$$

These general methods identify the firm's profit-maximizing output level, whether we are discussing the short run or the long run. As you recall, in the short run some inputs are fixed whereas in the long run all inputs are variable. For the remainder of the chapter and for most of the book, we focus on the long run.

Unfortunately, this discussion of firm behavior is incomplete, as it ignores the firm's **participation constraint**. The participation constraint identifies conditions under which the firm will stay in business versus shut down. That is, there are situations where it is optimal for the firm to produce zero output, even though the first-order condition indicates otherwise. In the example above, the firm is making an economic profit: $\pi^* = 1$, when $q^* = 1$. Thus, the firm has an incentive to stay in business. If, however, profits were negative, the firm would go out of business or shut down in the long run.[7] The long-run participation constraint is that the firm earns nonnegative profits. Thus, to fully understand firm behavior we must analyze both the firm's first-order condition and participation constraint.

5.3 Market Equilibrium and Long-Run Supply

In perfect competition, three conditions will hold when the market is in **long-run equilibrium** (i.e., there is no incentive for change):

- The market will clear. This means that demand equals long-run supply.
- Given profit maximization, the equilibrium price will equal long-run marginal cost, $p^* = MC$.
- Firm (economic) profit will be zero. The free entry/exit assumption assures this zero-profit condition. If profits are positive, firms will enter the market. Entry causes industry supply to increase, equilibrium price to fall, and profits to fall. This process will continue until profits equal zero. Alternatively, if profits are negative, firms will exit the market according to the long-run shutdown condition of profit maximization. This will raise profits and continue until profits equal zero. Profits equal zero when the equilibrium price equals long-run average cost (AC), $p^* = AC$.

This outcome is illustrated in Fig. 5.5, where the left-hand figure identifies firm costs and the right-hand figure identifies market demand (D) and long-run supply (S) conditions. We can summarize these conditions as follows: $D = S$ and $p^* = MC = AC$.

---

[7] In the short run, the firm must pay its fixed costs whether it shuts down or not. In this case, the firm would shut down if its losses from staying in business were less than its fixed cost, which it cannot avoid.

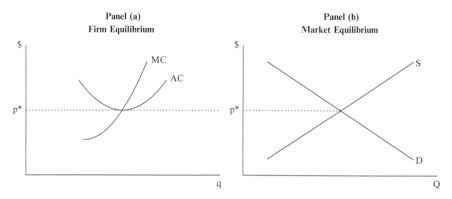

Fig. 5.5 Long-run equilibrium in perfect competition

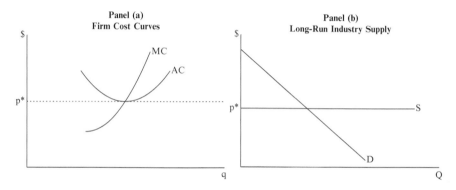

Fig. 5.6 Long-run supply in a constant-cost industry

Because our focus will be primarily on long-run outcomes, it will be useful to review the **long-run industry supply function**.[8] There are three cases, but we will focus only on the two cases that we will use in the book: the constant-cost case and the increasing-cost case.[9]

The **constant-cost** case assumes that the industry is so small that an increase or decrease in industry production (Q) has no effect on input prices, such as the price of labor, capital, and materials. In this case, AC and MC in Fig. 5.5 remain constant as industry production changes. As a result, the long-run equilibrium price is fixed at the minimum AC, and the long-run industry supply curve (S) is a horizontal line at that point, as illustrated in Fig. 5.6. The constant-cost case has an interesting

---

[8] This differs from the short-run supply function. Recall from principles of economics that a firm's short-run supply curve is its marginal cost curve above average variable cost. The short-run industry supply curve is the (horizontal) summation of the marginal cost curves of every firm in the industry. Thus, it reflects the industry's marginal cost of production.

[9] The third is the decreasing-cost case.

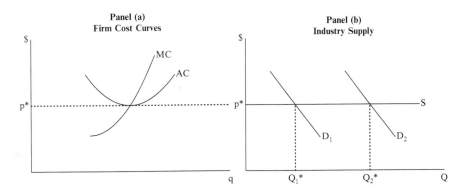

Fig. 5.7 A demand increase in a constant-cost industry

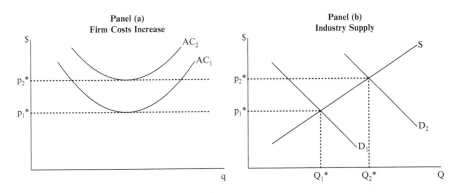

Fig. 5.8 Long-run supply in an increasing-cost industry

feature. The equilibrium price is determined by technology (or the minimum point on AC), while demand determines the equilibrium level of output. Demand has no effect on the long-run equilibrium price. Figure 5.7 illustrates this result for an increase in demand from D_1 to D_2 that causes the equilibrium quantity to change from Q_1^* to Q_2^* but has no effect on p^*.

The **increasing-cost** case produces the traditional long-run supply function that has a positive slope. In this case, an increase in industry production leads to an increase in input prices. This causes the minimum AC point to shift up and p^* to increase as industry production increases. Figure 5.8 shows that when demand increases from D_1 to D_2: (1) equilibrium quantity increases from Q_1^* to Q_2^*, (2) AC rises from AC_1 to AC_2,[10] and (3) the equilibrium price increases from p_1^* to p_2^*. Long-run supply is identified by the equilibrium price and equilibrium output

---

[10] To see the result more clearly, we leave off the MC_1 and MC_2 curves.

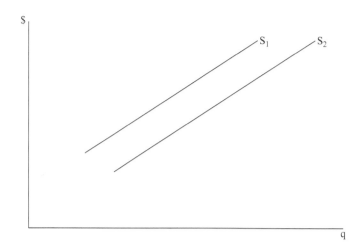

Fig. 5.9 An efficiency-enhancing technological change and firm supply

points. Thus, the long-run supply function has the usual positive slope.[11] Note that long-run supply always reflects the long-run cost of production, because the supply price will equal the minimum AC which equals MC.

Because the long-run supply function depends on the marginal cost of production, supply determinants are the same as cost determinants. That is, long-run industry supply is a function of the price, input prices, and technology. A change in the output price causes a movement along the supply function (in the increasing-cost case). A technological change or an exogenous decrease in the price of one or more inputs causes costs to fall and supply to shift down and to the right, such as in Fig. 5.9, where supply shifts from S_1 to S_2. One way of thinking about this change is that it allows the industry to profitably produce more output at the same price when there are lower production costs. Thus, it represents an increase in supply. The supply curve shifts up and to the left for a decrease in supply.

A useful tool in supply analysis is the **price-elasticity of supply** (ϵ_s), defined as the percentage change in quantity supplied (Q_s) resulting from a percentage change in price. For large changes it is defined as $(\Delta Q_s/Q_s)/(\Delta p/p)$. At times, we are interested in the effect on supply of a small change in price, which requires the use of calculus. In this case,

$$\epsilon_s \equiv \frac{\partial Q_s/Q_s}{\partial p/p} = \frac{\partial Q_s}{\partial p}\frac{p}{Q_s}. \tag{5.12}$$

---

[11] The third case involves decreasing costs. That is, input prices fall as industry production increases. The usual example given to justify this possibility is the presence of economies of scale in the production of a primary input. Scale economies cause the input price to fall with increased production, and the long-run supply function has a negative slope.

The price elasticity conveys the direction and magnitude of change in quantity supplied due to a change in the price. As with the demand curve, the price elasticity of supply can vary along a given supply curve.

The sign of the long-run supply elasticity depends on the cost conditions of the industry. For an increasing-cost industry, supply slopes upwards ($\partial Q_s/\partial p > 0$) and $\epsilon_s > 0$. For a constant-cost industry, supply is horizontal and price supply does not change with output. Thus, $\partial Q_s/\partial p = \infty$ and supply is said to be perfectly or infinitely elastic.[12] If supply is fixed at a particular level of Q, $\partial Q_s/\partial p = 0$ and $\epsilon_s = 0$; supply is perfectly inelastic.[13]

The extent of the long-run response of Q_s to a price change depends on the degree of the impact on input prices. In the case of an increasing-cost industry, if input prices rise substantially as quantity supplied increases, the supply elasticity will be greater than if input prices rise only slightly.

5.4 Comparative Statics

We can perform comparative static analysis on equilibrium models such as demand and supply. **Comparative statics** is the analysis of the change in the endogenous variables of a model that results from a change in an exogenous variable. We call this comparative statics because it involves a comparison of two "static" equilibria, ignoring the process that gets us from one equilibrium to another.

To illustrate, consider a simple demand and supply model in an increasing cost industry as depicted in Fig. 5.10. The market is initially in equilibrium at point A where demand (D_1) equals supply (S). We know that the demand for normal good x will increase with an increase in income, an increase in the price of a substitute, or a decrease in the price of a complement. One or more of these changes will cause demand to shift right from D_1 to D_2. Given sufficient adjustment time, this increase in demand will cause the equilibrium to change from point A to point B, causing an increase in both the equilibrium price (from p_1^* to p_2^*) and equilibrium quantity (from Q_1^* to Q_2^*).

Alternatively, a decrease in the price of an important input or a technological change will cause supply to rise, such as from S_1 to S_2 in Fig. 5.11. The equilibrium will change from point A to point B, causing equilibrium price to fall (from p_1^* to p_2^*) and equilibrium quantity to rise (from Q_1^* to Q_2^*).

We provide a more detailed discussion of comparative static analysis in the Appendix at the end of the book.

---

[12] For a decreasing-cost industry, $\partial Q_s/\partial p < 0$ and $\epsilon_s < 0$.

[13] This would be true, for example, for commodities that are not reproducible, such as van Gogh paintings.

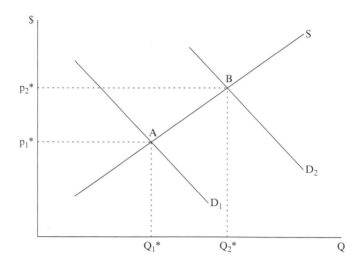

Fig. 5.10 An increase in the demand for good x

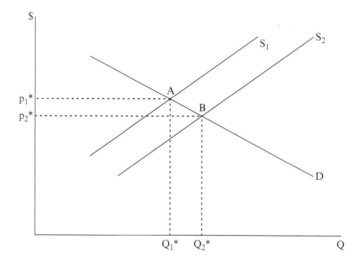

Fig. 5.11 An increase in the supply of good x

5.5 Efficiency and Welfare

In Chap. 1 we saw that desirable market performance requires that four conditions be met. A market outcome must be statically efficient, dynamically efficient, and equitable. When these, along with macro stability, are met in every market, social welfare is maximized. Dynamic efficiency issues will be discussed in Chap. 17, and equity issues will be discussed in Chap. 19. In this section, we are interested in static efficiency.

The concept of **static efficiency** is crucial to the study of welfare economics. Static efficiency is divided into four types. Two apply specifically to the firm:

- **Technical Efficiency**: A firm is technically efficient when it uses the minimum quantity of inputs to produce a given output. In other words, inputs are not being wasted.[14]
- **Economic Efficiency**: A firm is economically efficient when it produces a given output at minimum cost. Inputs are not being wasted and the firm is using the lowest cost combination of inputs to produce a given output.[15] When economically efficient, the firm is producing on (not above) its cost function.

Note that economic efficiency implies technical efficiency, but technical efficiency need not imply economic efficiency. For example, both rickshaw and auto taxies may be technically efficient modes of travel for short distances in large cities. They simply use different combinations of inputs to provide taxi service—an auto taxi uses gas but takes less time (i.e., uses fewer labor hours); a rickshaw uses no gas but takes considerable time. In less developed countries where gas is expensive and wages are low, rickshaw taxies are economically efficient. In developed countries where wages are relatively high, auto taxies are economically efficient.

There are also two types of efficiency at the industry level:

- **Productive Efficiency**: An industry is productively efficient when it produces a given level of output at minimum cost.
- **Allocative Efficiency**: An industry is allocatively efficient when it produces the socially desirable quantity of output. This occurs when the marginal benefit to society of producing another unit of output, reflected in the market price, equals the marginal cost of production.

You might think that if every firm is economically efficient, the industry must be productively efficient, but this is incorrect. For instance, consider a market where the long-run average cost function declines up to where it intersects the market demand function. In this case, a market with many small producers that are economically efficient (i.e., where each firm minimizes its cost of production) does not produce a productively efficient outcome. Industry costs are minimized with just one firm. This represents the natural monopoly case, which we discuss in the next chapter.

Baumol et al. (1982) discuss the formal link between productive efficiency and market structure. They developed the concept of a **cost-minimizing industry structure**, defined as the number of firms that minimizes industry production

---

[14] This means that the firm is operating on its isoquant, where an isoquant represents all minimum combinations of inputs that can just produce a given level of output. For further discussion, see Färe et al. (1985) and Varian (2010).

[15] The economically efficient point occurs where the firm's isoquant is tangent to its isocost function. The isocost function represents all combinations of inputs that generate a given cost. For further discussion, see Färe et al. (1985) and Varian (2010).

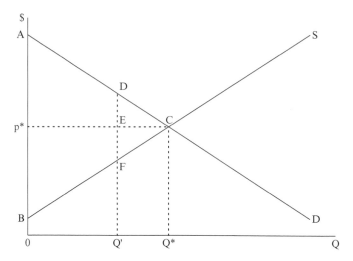

Fig. 5.12 Consumer surplus, producer surplus, and total surplus

costs. By comparing the cost minimizing structure to the actual structure of an industry, we are able to determine whether or not an industry is productively efficient. We will discuss this topic further in Chap. 8.

The reason that the perfectly competitive model is considered a welfare benchmark is that it produces a perfectly efficient outcome in the long run.[16] First, every firm must be economically efficient (and therefore technically efficient) because firms are assumed to be profit maximizers. To maximize profits, the firm must choose the combination of inputs that minimizes its cost of production. Second, the industry is productively efficient in the long run, because every firm produces at the minimum of its long-run average cost function.

Finally, we examine whether the long-run equilibrium in the perfectly competitive model is allocatively efficient by considering the concepts of consumer surplus, producer surplus, and total surplus.[17] Sometimes consumers pay less than they are willing to pay (i.e., the demand price), ending up with a net gain in welfare. **Consumer surplus** (CS) is the net gain that consumers receive from consuming a given quantity of output for a particular price. In other words, it is the difference between what a consumer is willing to pay for a good and what he or she actually pays. Graphically, consumer surplus is the area under the demand curve and above the price line for a given level of output. In Fig. 5.12, when price is p^* and quantity is Q', consumer surplus is area Ap^*ED.

---

[16] Here, we mean that the perfectly competitive model is statically efficient, but it need not be dynamicaly efficient as we will see in later chapters.

[17] This is a partial equilibrium approach, which ignores the effect that a price change in this market will have on other markets. For discussion of these general equilibrium effects, see Bernheim and Whinston (2008), Pindyck and Rubenfield (2009), and Varian (2010).

Just as consumers can receive a surplus, so can producers. Some may be willing to sell their product for less than the market price. **Producer surplus** (PS) is the difference between the price that producers receive for goods sold and the opportunity cost of all inputs used to produce output (i.e., the supply price, which equals marginal cost and is represented by the supply function). Producer surplus for all producers can be depicted graphically as the area under the price line and above the supply curve for a given quantity of output. Returning to Fig. 5.12, this is area p^*BFE at p^* and Q'. [18] Producer surplus represents producer welfare.

Total surplus (TS) is the sum of consumer surplus and producer surplus (TS = CS + PS) and measures total social welfare in this market. Total surplus is the area under the demand curve and above the supply curve, area ABFD at p^* and Q' in Fig. 5.12. Total surplus is the difference between total benefits derived from the good (area under demand curve) and total costs of producing the good (area under supply or marginal cost). Total surplus provides a measure of social efficiency: maximizing TS means achieving the greatest benefits possible given costs in a particular market.

Total surplus is maximized where demand equals supply at p^* and Q^* in Fig. 5.12. Notice that total surplus increases by area DFC when production increases from Q' to Q^*. Producing and consuming one more unit of output beyond Q^* will lower total surplus, however, due to the fact that the added benefit to consumers (reflected by the demand price) is lower than the added cost of producing it (reflected by the supply price, which equals marginal cost). Thus, total surplus is maximized where D = S or where the equilibrium price equals marginal cost. This description is exactly what is meant by allocative efficiency.

The discussion above makes it clear that perfect competition is allocatively efficient. A profit-maximizing firm in a competitive market equates price with marginal cost. In addition, demand equals supply in a competitive equilibrium. If all markets in the economy were perfectly competitive and there were no other market imperfections, then resources would automatically be allocated in an efficient manner without any need for government involvement. This outcome is the basis of Adam Smith's invisible hand theorem that he discussed in *The Wealth of Nations* (1776),

> [An individual] intends only his own gain, and he is in this, as in many other cases, led by an invisible hand to promote an end which was no part of his intention. Nor is it always the worse for the society that it was no part of it. By pursuing his own interest he frequently promotes that of the society more effectually than when he really intends to promote it.

To summarize, a perfectly competitive market is statically efficient, all firms are technically and economically efficient, and the industry is productively and allocatively efficient.

---

[18] When PS is positive, as it is in this example, it is called economic rent. Even when economic profit is zero, firms may earn "economic rent." That is, an entrepreneur may enjoy owning a company so much that he or she is willing to earn only 8% on invested financial capital, even though the normal rate is 10%. If the owner does earn 10%, the 2% above the owner's opportunity cost is rent, not profit. Note that the concept of economic rent is different from the rent you pay on an apartment.

Before discussing market failure, we want to mention that Baumol et al. (1982) have proposed that a "perfectly contestable market" replace perfect competition as our benchmark of social efficiency. Three main assumptions drive the model of perfect contestability: (1) the sunk cost of entry is zero (i.e., there are no barriers to entry or exit), (2) entry is instantaneous, and (3) incumbent firms are slow to adjust price. Under these conditions, the theory implies that the threat of hit-and-run entry of a potential entrant will eliminate economic profits, even in a monopoly market. That is, the equilibrium price will equal average cost (but will be above marginal cost if there are economies of scale). This occurs because a rival enters whenever price exceeds average cost, with the entrant replacing the incumbent firm.

Unfortunately, the model of perfect contestability is deficient on two accounts. First, the assumptions of the model are false. In real markets, incumbents adjust price quickly and entry is slow. Moreover, Stiglitz (1987) showed that even small sunk costs overturn the zero profit result. Thus, hit-and-run entry is implausible. Second, the empirical evidence does not support the implications of the model, as we will discuss in later chapters. We summarize the perfectly contestable market model here because we will see in Chap. 20 that it provided one motivating factor in the deregulation movement of the 1970s and 1980s.

5.6   Market Failure and the Limitations of Perfect Competition

As we saw in the beginning of the chapter, a number of assumptions must hold for a market to be perfectly competitive and, therefore, efficient. When these conditions are not met, free markets generally fail to maximize total surplus. This is called **market failure**. There are four main sources of market failure: monopoly or market power, externalities, public goods, and a lack of information.[19]

Market power is associated with monopoly and imperfectly competitive markets that have too few competitors to guarantee competitive pricing. Specifically, a firm has market power if it has the ability to profitably maintain price above long-run marginal cost. When this happens, too little output is produced from society's perspective and allocative inefficiency results. The subject of market failure due to imperfect competition is the primary focus of this book, although we will refer to the other sources of market failure from time to time. In the next chapter, we discuss models in which strategic interaction is unimportant, the models of monopoly and monopolistic competition. The remainder of the book is devoted primarily to the study of competition in oligopoly markets that have more than one firm but fewer than many firms.

Another type of market failure occurs when goods are public rather than private. Pure **public goods** have two characteristics: nonrivalry in consumption

---

[19] As discussed in Chap. 1, just because markets fail to reach an ideal does not mean that government intervention can improve welfare. We ignore this issue here, but take it up more thoroughly in later chapters.

(one person's use does not diminish the quality or quantity of a good that is available to others) and nonexclusion (the cost of excluding people from using the good is uneconomic). Classic examples include broadcast radio programming, a lighthouse, and national defense. If Desmond listens to a broadcast radio program, you can also. In contrast, a loaf of bread is a private good; if Desmond eats a slice of bread, there are fewer slices available for you. Free markets will undersupply public goods. A private firm that tried to produce a public good would have difficulty earning a profit because (1) it is uneconomic to exclude users once the good is produced and (2) asking people who benefit to pay a share of the cost of producing the good will lead to underreporting given that consumers can receive the benefits whether they pay for it or not. Using a public good without paying for it is called the **free rider problem**. The presence of free riders leads to inadequate funding for public goods, which causes free markets to produce less than the socially optimal quantity of a public good and provides an important motive for government intervention.

An **externality** or spillover occurs when the action of one economic agent (producer or consumer) affects another without compensation. In the case of an external benefit or positive externality, such as a neighbor landscaping his or her front yard, you receive a benefit without having to pay for it. Similar to the public good situation, social benefits exceed private benefits to the neighbor and the act of landscaping will be undersupplied relative to the social optimum. Among producers, externalities are generally negative. The classic example is when a firm pollutes a river, which lowers the quality of drinking water to downstream consumers. This is called an external cost of production. In this case, the marginal cost of production to the firm is less than the marginal cost of production to society, which includes the cost to both the firm and to downstream consumers. Because a profit-maximizing firm will ignore the external cost to others, it will produce too much output and too much pollution from society's perspective. Thus, negative externalities will likely arise in a free market economy, providing a motive for government to impose taxes and regulations to mitigate the effects of externalities.

Externalities relevant to industrial organization can also be associated with consumers. One example is a **network externality**, which arises when one person's demand for a good depends on the number of others who consume the good.[20] Examples of goods and services where positive network externalities are present include cell phone plans, online dating services, and word processing software. If I have a document in one word processing software but you use a different software program, sharing files becomes more costly. By adopting the software package that you use, I benefit you as well as myself. Thus, my decision imposes a positive externality on you. A positive network externality such as this can be thought of as a bandwagon effect, which is discussed in Chap. 2. With a bandwagon effect, one person's demand for the good goes up as more and more consumers purchase it.

---

[20] For a review of the economics of networks, see Shy (2011).

A negative network externality is called a snob effect (see Chap. 2). In this case, the consumer who is a "snob" gets utility from being different from the crowd. Displeasure associated with the snob effect rises as a product becomes more popular. Thus, as the network grows in size, the value of the product declines for this consumer. From a social welfare perspective, network externalities tend to cause free markets to fail to reach the social optimum.

Market failure can also result when agents have **imperfect information** and a limited capacity to make choices in complex situations. If consumers do not know the prices of all suppliers, for example, higher-priced firms will not be driven out of the market and the socially optimal output level will not be produced. If consumers cannot distinguish high from low quality products before purchase, low quality goods (i.e., lemons) may drive high quality goods out of the market. Akerlof (1970) used this idea to explain why there are so few goods used cars available for purchase, which is why it is known as Akerlof's **lemons principle**.[21] Fortunately, the Internet has improved information flows dramatically, helping us to avoid some of these information shortfalls.

Cognitive weaknesses can cause people to fail to accurately assess information and can also lead to nonoptimal outcomes. Producers may manipulate information to their advantage when consumers are subject to framing, anchoring, and default effects, as discussed in Chap. 4. Consider a consumer who is working for a firm that offers three health insurance plans, A, B, or C. Suppose that an insurance company has convinced the firm to offer employees plan A as the default, even though plan B is best for most people. That is, the firm will provide plan A unless the employee overrides the default and chooses B or C. Studies show that people tend to choose the default even though it may not be in their best interest to do so. This creates a social problem because there is oversubscription to the default plan relative to plans B and C. Sellers also face difficulties when information is imperfect, such as identifying high and low quality job applicants or assessing the probability of success upon entering a market. Behavioral factors can also create problems for firms when their managers suffer from **overconfidence** or **over-exuberance**. We will see later in the book that free markets may fail to produce the social optimum when consumer or producer cognitive errors affect economic decisions.

5.7 Summary

1. The **assumptions of perfect competition** are that: firms produce perfectly homogeneous goods; there are many identical, profit-maximizing firms; there are no barriers to entry or exit; and there are no frictions or other forms of market imperfections.
2. The **firm demand** function (d) is horizontal at the market equilibrium price (p^*). Market demand and supply determine p^*.

---

[21] We will see that producers of high quality goods can solve this information problem by offering guarantees or warranties.

3. In perfect competition, the total revenue (TR) function is a ray from the origin with slope $= p$.

4. In perfect competition, $MR = AR = p^* = d$, where MR is marginal revenue and AR is average revenue of the firm.

5. The **profit equation** specifies the relationship between profit and output. The graph of the profit equation is concave or hill-shaped.

6. The output level that maximizes profit corresponds to the peak of the profit equation where the slope of a tangent line to the profit equation is zero. In the long run, this occurs where $MR = MC$. Since $MR = p$, we can also say that profit maximization occurs where $p = MC$ in perfect competition.

7. The firm's long-run **participation constraint** is that profit is nonnegative. If price is less than average cost, the firm is better off by producing nothing at all and exiting the industry.

8. When a perfectly competitive market is in long-run equilibrium, $D = S$ and $p^* = MC = AC$ (i.e., firms earn zero economic profit). The market is in long-run disequilibrium when (economic) profits do not equal zero. When profits are positive, new firms will enter, increasing industry supply and reducing price. Firms will continue to enter until profits are zero ($p^* = AC$). When profits are negative, firms will exit the industry, decreasing supply and raising price. Firms will continue to exit until profits are zero ($p^* = AC$).

9. In a **constant-cost industry**, an increase in industry production does not affect input prices, and long-run industry supply is horizontal. In an **increasing-cost industry**, an increase in industry production pushes input prices up, and long-run industry supply has a positive slope.

10. The (ϵ_s) is the percentage change in quantity supplied resulting from a small percentage change in price, i.e., $\epsilon_s \equiv (\partial Q_s / \partial p)\,(p/Q_s)$.

11. **Comparative statics** is the analysis of the change in the equilibrium value of an endogenous variable of a model that results from a change in an exogenous variable or parameter. It involves a comparison of two "static" equilibria, ignoring the process that gets us from one equilibrium to another.

12. **Static efficiency** is a requirement of social welfare maximization, along with dynamic efficiency, equity, and macroeconomic stability. There are four types of static efficiency, two at the firm level (technical and economic efficiency) and two at the industry level (productive efficiency and allocative efficiency).

   - A firm **is technically efficient** when it uses the minimum quantity of inputs to produce a given output. A firm is **economically efficient** when it produces a given output at minimum cost.
   - An industry is **productively efficient** when it produces a given level of output at minimum cost. An industry is **allocatively efficient** when it produces the socially desirable quantity of output: the level where the marginal benefit to society, as reflected in the price, equals the marginal cost of production.

13. Perfect competition achieves all four types of static efficiency. Profit maximization guarantees economic efficiency (which requires technical efficiency).

Production efficiency occurs because every firm produces at minimum average cost. Allocative efficiency results because price equals marginal cost for all firms.

14. Social efficiency can be measured by **total surplus** which is the sum of consumer surplus and producer surplus. **Consumer surplus** is the difference between what a consumer is willing to pay for a good and the amount he or she actually pays. Graphically, consumer surplus is the area under the demand curve and above the price line. **Producer surplus** is the difference between the price a producer receives for an amount of a good and the marginal cost of production of the good. Graphically, producer surplus is the difference between the price line and the marginal cost curve.

15. Total surplus is the area under the demand curve and above the supply curve. Allocative efficiency is reached when total surplus is maximized. This occurs in perfect competition, because demand equals supply and price equals marginal cost. Total surplus reaches a maximum when demand equals supply and when price equals marginal cost.

16. Because perfect completion is socially efficient, the model of perfect competition serves as a **benchmark** for evaluating the social welfare implications of assumption violations, including alternative market structures.

17. **Market failure** occurs when private markets fail to produce the socially optimal level of output. Price does not equal the true opportunity cost of the resources used. The primary sources of market failure are market power, public goods, externalities, and imperfect information.

18. **Market power** exists when a firm can profitably maintain price above marginal cost, which is more likely in markets with few competitors. Quantity falls short of the social optimum and allocative inefficiency results.

19. Nonexclusion and nonrivalry in consumption are characteristics of **public goods**. Free riders can obtain use of the good without paying for it, and the public good is undersupplied.

20. **Externalities** are present when the actions of one agent affect others without compensation. Goods generating positive externalities are underproduced, while goods generating negative externalities are overproduced from society's perspective.

21. **Network externalities** occur when a person's demand for a good depends on the number of people who are using it. Bandwagon and snob effects are examples of network externalities.

22. **Lack of accurate information** about prices and product quality can lead to nonoptimal prices and output levels. Cognitive weaknesses can cause individuals to fail to accurately assess information and can also lead to non-optimal outcomes. When there are framing, anchoring, and default effects, the demand function will not accurately represent preferences and the socially optimal output levels will not be produced. Overconfidence and over-exuberance can lead to entrepreneurial or managerial errors.

23. If consumers cannot distinguish high from low quality products before purchase, low quality goods may drive high quality goods out of the market. This is called Akerlof's (1970) **lemons principle**.

5.8   Review Questions

1. When a perfectly competitive firm is in long run equilibrium, will its average revenue equal minimum long run average cost? Explain. – Pg 129

2. Consider a good produced in a perfectly competitive market.

   A. Graph the industry supply and market demand curves, where the equilibrium price is $4. Label the axes, curves, price, and quantity.
   B. For the firm, graph the corresponding demand function.
   C. Graph the corresponding total revenue function for the firm and indicate the slope and intercept on the graph.
   D. Graph the firm's average revenue and marginal revenue functions.

3. Consider a perfectly competitive market for a good in a constant-cost industry with market demand function given by $Q_D = 2,500 - 100p$, where Q_D is industry quantity demanded and p is market price. Producers have U-shaped AC curves that reach a minimum average cost at $1 when 100 units of output are produced. In the long run, what will be the equilibrium price, industry level of production, industry profits, and number of firms?

4. State whether each statement is true or false and explain your answer.

   A. "Constant returns to scale" is another term for constant-cost industry.
   B. If economic profits are zero, firms will exit the industry.
   C. If a firm is minimizing costs, it must be maximizing profit.

5. Show graphically the MC, AC, MR, and q^* for a firm that does not meet the long-run participation constraint.

6. Suppose that a firm in a perfectly competitive, constant-cost industry sells 10,000 units at $10 each. The firm's accounting profits are 10% above what would be considered a normal rate of return. Is $10 the long-run equilibrium price? Why or why not?

7. Explain the long-run industry adjustment to a decrease in demand for an increasing-cost industry.

8. In Fig. 5.12, we found that producing less than the competitive level of output yielded less consumer, producer, and total surplus than at the competitive output level, Q^*. What would happen to the level of consumer surplus, producer surplus, and total surplus if the industry produced more than Q^* at a price equal to p^*?

9. Explain why the assumptions of profit maximization, product homogeneity, and free entry are necessary to assure that long-run profit is zero.

10. What is the difference between economic efficiency and productive efficiency?

11. Give an example of a public good, an external benefit, an external cost, and a network externality.

12. Explain how the presence of cognitive weaknesses among consumers, such as susceptibility to environmental cues for tempting or addictive products, can lead to market failure and problems with estimating market failure.

Chapter 6
Monopoly and Monopolistic Competition*

In this chapter, we discuss the market structures of monopoly and monopolistic competition. Unlike perfect competition which has many sellers, a monopoly market has just one seller. In this sense, it is the polar opposite of perfect competition.

Monopolistic competition has qualities of both perfect competition and monopoly. Like perfect competition, it has many sellers. Unlike perfect competition, products are not perfect substitutes. Instead, each firm sells a substitute product that has its own unique set of characteristics, which might differ slightly in quality, style, and color. In this case, products are said to be differentiated. In monopolistic competition, firms sell brands that are unique, giving each firm a monopoly over the sale of its particular brand.

Although monopolistic competition is a form of imperfect competition, each firm is so small that its actions have no affect on rival profits. Thus, it provides the one imperfectly competitive model in which game theory is unimportant. It is not until we discuss oligopoly markets later in the book that game theory becomes invaluable. In each of the models that are discussed in this chapter, firms are assumed to be single product producers. We begin with monopoly.

---

*This is a review chapter. You can learn more detail about the basic models that are found in this chapter from any introductory or intermediate microeconomics textbook, such as Frank and Bernanke (2008), Mankiw (2011), Bernheim and Whinston (2008), Pindyck and Rubenfield (2009), and Varian (2010). For more advanced treatments, see Nicholson and Snyder (2012) and Mas-Colell et al. (1995).

V.J. Tremblay and C.H. Tremblay, *New Perspectives on Industrial Organization*,
Springer Texts in Business and Economics, DOI 10.1007/978-1-4614-3241-8_6,
© Springer Science+Business Media New York 2012

6.1 Monopoly

As just mentioned, an industry with only one seller is called a monopoly. The term "monopoly" can refer to a firm, an industry, or a market structure. The monopoly model is built on the following assumptions:

1. There is only *one firm* in the market. No other firms produce substitute products.
2. *Barriers to entry* are sufficiently high to allow only one firm in the market.
3. The monopolist's demand is the market demand, which has a negative slope. The firm is a *"price maker,"* which means that the firm can raise its price without losing all of its customers.
4. Like perfect competition, the firm is a profit maximizer and there are *no frictions or other forms of market imperfections.*

Monopolies are relatively uncommon in the real world. One reason is that they are illegal under the Sherman Act (1890). Another reason is that when a monopolist earns an economic profit, there is a strong motive for entry. Thus, barriers to entry must be extremely high for there to be just one firm in the industry.

There are three types of barriers to entry. The first is a **natural barrier**, which is due to basic demand and cost conditions. One example occurs when the long-run average cost falls throughout the relevant range of demand. In this case, cost minimization requires a single producer. A market such as this is called a **natural monopoly**. Examples include public utility companies (but they are regulated by government to prohibit excess profits). Another example arises when a firm has sole control of an essential input, such as Alcoa's ownership of all bauxite (aluminum) mines before World War II.

A second type is a **legal barrier to entry**, which is a barrier caused by a government restriction. A patent is one example, which gives an inventor exclusive (monopoly) rights to the production and sale of an invention for 20 years. The purpose of patents is to create property rights for ideas and to stimulate innovation. Without a patent, others can copy an invention and earn profits without incurring the costs of conducting the research necessary to create the invention. A government franchise, which awards selling rights in an area, can also create monopolies. Franchises to taxicab companies in New York City and casino gaming licenses are examples.

Finally, there are **strategic barriers to entry**. Unlike the other types of entry barriers, strategic barriers are endogenous. That is, they involve firm actions that are designed to deter entry. Examples include predatory pricing, where price is set below unit cost, and investments that raise the costs of potential entrants so high that it is too costly to enter the market. We begin with a discussion of an unregulated monopolist and postpone formal discussion of entry barriers until Chap. 8.

6.1.1 Firm Behavior and Market Equilibrium

An unregulated monopolist will want to choose the price and output levels that maximize profit, which are determined simultaneously. For a demand function, a given quantity demanded corresponds to a demand price, and a given price corresponds to a level of quantity demanded. Thus, by determining the optimal output (price), the optimal price (output) can be obtained from the demand function. We will see that maximizing profit with respect to output or price produces the same outcome.

The traditional and simplest approach is to let the firm maximize profit with respect to output. This produces the same optimization principle as with perfect competition—the profit-maximizing level of output occurs where marginal revenue (MR) equals marginal cost (MC). In this chapter and later chapters, we focus on the long run, so MC always refers to the firm's long-run marginal cost. The difference in the profit maximizing level of output between perfect competition and monopoly lies in the nature of the firm demand and MR functions. Since firm demand is industry demand in monopoly, the monopolist's demand is negatively sloped. In contrast, the perfectly competitive firm's demand is a horizontal line, where price (p) is identical to MR and average revenue (AR). That is, $p \equiv AR = MR$ in perfect competition. In monopoly, $p \equiv AR > MR$.[1]

To solve the monopoly problem, we consider a simple example where both demand (D) and total cost functions are linear. The inverse demand takes the following form: $p = a - bq$, where a is the price intercept and b is the slope ($a, b > 0$). This implies that total revenue is $TR \equiv pq = aq - bq^2$. The total cost function is $TC = cq$, where c is long-run marginal and average cost. To assure nonnegative profits, $a > c > 0$. The corresponding marginal functions are $MR = \partial TR/\partial q = a - 2bq$ and $MC = \partial TC/\partial q = c$. Profits ($\pi$) are given by

$$\pi = TR - TC,$$
$$= \left(aq - bq^2\right) - (cq). \tag{6.1}$$

To find the output level that maximizes profit, we take the derivative of π with respect to q and set it equal to zero[2]:

$$\frac{\partial \pi}{\partial q} = \frac{\partial TR}{\partial q} - \frac{\partial TC}{\partial q},$$
$$= MR - MC,$$
$$= (a - 2bq) - c = 0. \tag{6.2}$$

---

[1] In Chap. 2, we saw that $p > MR$ for a downward-sloping demand curve. For a linear demand function, we found that MR and demand have the same y-intercept but that MR is twice as steep as the demand function.

[2] As in the previous chapter, although q is the only variable in this example, we use ∂ instead of d to remind us that there are many other variables that are implicitly assumed to be held fixed.

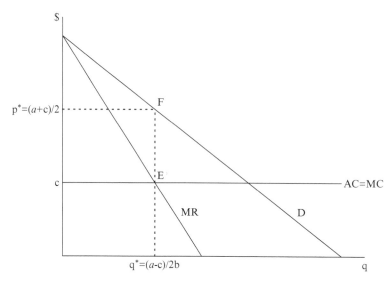

Fig. 6.1 An example of a monopolist's optimal price and quantity

This is the first-order condition of profit maximization, which tells us that the profit maximizing level of output occurs where MR = MC.[3] Solving (6.2) for q yields the profit maximizing level of output, $q^* = (a - c)/2b$. The profit maximizing price (p^*) is determined by substituting q^* into the inverse demand function. Profits are found by substituting p^* and q^* into the profit equation. The optimal values are

$$q^* = \frac{a - c}{2b},$$
$$p^* = \frac{a + c}{2},$$
$$\pi^* = \frac{(a - c)^2}{4b}. \tag{6.3}$$

Figure 6.1 shows demand, marginal revenue, marginal cost, and the profit maximizing price–output pair for the example above. Note that MR = MC at q^*, p^* is the maximum price that will just sell q^* (i.e., the demand price at q^*), and $\pi^* = $ TR − TC.

In this example, the monopolist is earning a positive long-run profit; p^* exceeds average cost at q^*. Firm profit is area p^*cEF in Fig. 6.1. Unlike perfect competition,

---

[3] This produces a maximum because the profit function for each firm is concave. That is, the second-order condition of profit maximization holds, because the second derivative of the profit function is $-2b < 0$.

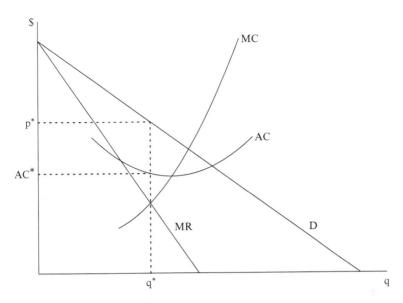

Fig. 6.2 Equilibrium for a monopolist

long-run profit can be positive because entry barriers prevent the entry that would drive profits to zero.[4]

Figure 6.2 provides another example, this time with a U-shaped average cost function. If we optimize with respect to q, the profit maximizing level of output occurs at q^* where MR = MC. The profit maximizing price is the demand price at that level of output, which equals p^*. The firm earns a positive profit, because p^* exceeds the average cost at the profit maximizing level of production (AC*).

To show that the results are the same whether the firm maximizes profit with respect to q or p, we now consider the price problem. In this case, we need to define demand as a function of the choice variable p. To convert the inverse demand to a demand function, we solve demand for q: $q = a/b - (1/b)p$. Thus, the firm's profit equation becomes

$$\pi = \text{TR} - \text{TC},$$
$$= pq - cq,$$
$$= p\left(\frac{a}{b} - \frac{1}{b}p\right) - c\left(\frac{a}{b} - \frac{1}{b}p\right). \tag{6.4}$$

---

[4] Of course, demand and cost conditions could be such that long-run profits are zero. This is precisely the long-run equilibrium in the monopolistically competitive model that we discuss subsequently. In the short run, a monopolist can lose money and stay in business as long as its optimal price is above its short-run variable cost, just as with a competitive firm.

To find the price that maximizes profits, we take the derivative of π with respect to p and set it equal to zero. This is the first-order condition with respect to price:

$$\frac{\partial \pi}{\partial p} = \frac{\partial TR}{\partial p} - \frac{\partial TC}{\partial p},$$
$$= MR_p - MC_p,$$
$$= \left(\frac{a}{b} - \frac{2}{b}p\right) + \frac{c}{b} = 0. \tag{6.5}$$

where MR_p is a different type of marginal revenue, equaling the firm's marginal revenue with respect to a change in p. Similarly, MC_p is the firm's marginal cost with respect to a change in p. Solving (6.5) for p yields the profit maximizing price:

$$p^* = \frac{a + c}{2}. \tag{6.6}$$

The profit maximizing output level is determined by substituting p^* into the demand function above, $q^* = a/b - (1/b)p^* = (a - c)/2b$. These are the same optimal values as before, which demonstrates that the optimal price and output are the same whether the firm optimizes over q or p. Although this is true for monopoly, it is not true in oligopoly markets, as we will see in Chap. 10.

One way to judge the validity of the model is to check to see if the comparative static results are reasonable. In this model, the equilibrium price rises with an increase in demand (parameter a) and an increase in marginal cost (c), and the equilibrium output level rises with demand (an increase in a and a decrease in b) and decreases with marginal cost. These results are consistent with what we would expect to see in reality.

Finally, we can analyze the monopoly problem with general demand and cost functions. Let $p(q)$ represent the firm's inverse demand function. In this case, $TR = p(q) \cdot q$ and the firm's profit equation is $\pi = TR - TC = p(q) \cdot q - TC$. The first-order condition of profit maximization is[5]

$$\frac{\partial \pi}{\partial q} = \frac{\partial TR}{\partial q} - \frac{\partial TC}{\partial q},$$
$$= MR - MC,$$
$$= \left(p + \frac{\partial p}{\partial q}q\right) - MC = 0. \tag{6.7}$$

This and previous examples illustrates the standard marginal principle or rule of marginalism: to maximize profit with respect to activity x (output in this case), the firm must equate the marginal benefit (MR) with the marginal cost (MC) of activity x.

---

[5] This is an application of the product rule, as discussed in the Mathematics and Econometrics Appendix at the end of the book. That is, if $y = wz$ where $w = f(x)$ and $z = g(x)$, then $dy/dx = w$ $(dz/dx) + z(dw/dx)$. The derivative of the product of two functions equals the first function times the derivative of the second function plus the second function times the derivative of the first function. Because $TR = p(q) \cdot q$, $MR = p + (\partial p/\partial q)q$.

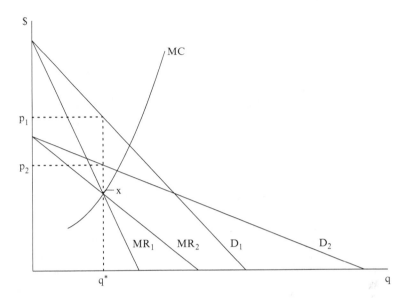

Fig. 6.3 Different prices for the same level of output

6.1.2   No Supply Curve in Monopoly

You might think that a monopolist's marginal cost is its supply function, as is true in perfect competition. We know that in perfect competition there is a single quantity supplied for a given price, but this is not the case with monopoly. There is not a one-to-one correspondence between price and quantity supplied in a monopoly market, implying that a supply function does not exist for a monopoly firm.

Notice that different optimal prices can correspond to the same output level, as in Fig. 6.3. For the demand curve, D_1, and corresponding marginal revenue curve, MR_1, we know that the monopolist will equate MC and MR_1 and produce q^* at p_1. One way to map out a supply function in a perfectly competitive market is to allow demand to shift and identify all optimal points, which maps out the supply function. In the case of monopoly, however, this process does not map out a function. To illustrate, suppose that demand and marginal revenue change so that marginal revenue rotates around a fixed point, x, to produce D_2 and MR_2 in Fig. 6.3. Notice that q^* remains the same but the optimal price decreases to p_2. If we hold costs fixed but change demand functions once again so that x moves up the firm's marginal cost function, we will identify a greater q^* and two new optimal prices. This demonstrates that there is not a unique optimal price for a given optimal level of output. Thus, a supply function does not exist in monopoly. In fact, a supply function only exists in perfect competition.

6.1.3   Allocative Inefficiency

Recall from the previous chapter that for a market to be allocatively efficient, price must equal marginal cost. This is clearly not true in monopoly. As Figs. 6.1 and 6.2 show, $p^* >$ MC. Unlike a competitive firm, a monopolist is a price maker and has the power to raise price above marginal cost, leading to a price that is too high and a production level that is too low from society's perspective. Thus, monopoly is one type of market failure.

The ability of a monopolist to profitably maintain price above marginal cost is called **monopoly power**. An index of exerted monopoly power was developed by Lerner (1934), which is defined as

$$\mathcal{L} \equiv \frac{p - \text{MC}}{p}. \tag{6.8}$$

The Lerner index ranges from 0 to 1. When price equals marginal cost, there is no monopoly power and $\mathcal{L} = 0$. A higher value of $\mathcal{L}$ implies greater monopoly power.[6]

Lerner also showed that this index is related to the price elasticity of demand (η). Recall from Chap. 2 the following relationship between marginal revenue and η:

$$\text{MR} = p\left(1 - \frac{1}{\eta}\right). \tag{6.9}$$

For the profit maximizing monopolist, MR $=$ MC, implying that

$$\text{MC} = p\left(1 - \frac{1}{\eta}\right). \tag{6.10}$$

Rearranging terms gives

$$\mathcal{L} \equiv \frac{p - \text{MC}}{p} = \frac{1}{\eta}. \tag{6.11}$$

Thus, there is an inverse relationship between η and $\mathcal{L}$. Monopoly power increases as demand becomes more inelastic (i.e., as η falls). This is clear from Fig. 6.3, where q^* is the same for D_1 and D_2. At q^*, D_1 is relatively more inelastic than D_2, and the markup of price over marginal cost is greater for D_1 than D_2.

The connection between the Lerner index and the price elasticity of demand tells us something further about monopoly power. Note that even a monopolist faces products that are imperfect substitutes. There may be only one ice cream parlor in a

---

[6] It is also possible for a monopolist to have unexerted monopoly power, where the firm has the ability to raise price but chooses not to for public relations reasons or to avoid an antitrust challenge, for example.

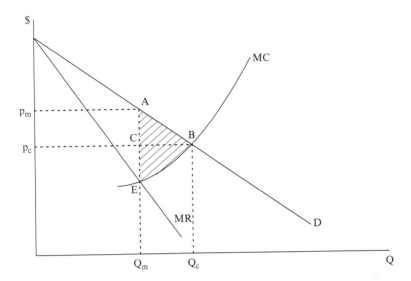

Fig. 6.4 Equilibrium in monopoly and perfect competition and deadweight loss

small town, giving it monopoly status, but a neighboring bakery provides consumers with alternatives to ice cream. With more and more products that become closer and closer substitutes, the firm's demand function becomes more elastic, diminishing monopoly power. Market power falls as the firm faces increased competition from a greater number of substitute goods. As a numerical example, in the highly elastic case, if $\eta = 20$, $\mathcal{L} = 0.05$, whereas if demand is less elastic, $\eta = 2$, $\mathcal{L} = 0.50$, a considerably higher markup of price over marginal cost.

The Lerner index also tells us about the pass-through rate, the increase in price due to a small increase in MC. To demonstrate, we solve (6.11) for price: $p = \text{MC} [\eta/(\eta - 1)]$. For a monopolist, $1 < \eta < \infty$, so that $[\eta/(\eta - 1)] > 1$ and $p > \text{MC}$. If η is constant for a small change in price, a \$1 increase in MC will cause p to rise by more than \$1, indicating that the pass-through rate for a monopolist is greater than 1. Notice that in perfect competition, $\eta \to \infty$, $p = \text{MC}$, and the pass-through rate is 1.

The monopoly solution is inefficient because the optimal price exceeds marginal cost. Consider the monopoly problem in Fig. 6.4. The allocative efficient solution is where price equals marginal cost at the point where MC crosses demand (point B at p_c and Q_c, the perfectly competitive outcome). The monopoly solution is at point A (p_m and $q_m = Q_m$). This shows that the monopolist produces too little output and charges too high a price from society's perspective.

We can get a sense of the magnitude of the efficiency loss by investigating the loss in total (consumer plus producer) surplus due to monopoly. Recall from Chap. 5 that a market is allocatively efficient when total surplus is maximized, which occurs at point B in Fig. 6.4 (i.e., where demand equals supply, which is identical to marginal cost).

By moving from the allocatively efficient point to the monopoly optimum point (A), consumers lose and producers gain. Overall, the decrease in output from Q_c to Q_m causes total surplus to fall by the shaded area AEB, which is called the deadweight loss or efficiency loss due to monopoly. This area measures the dollar value of the welfare loss that is caused by the monopolist producing Q_m instead of Q_c.

6.1.4 X-inefficiency and Rent-Seeking Behavior

To this point, we have assumed that market structure has no effect on firm costs. Profit maximization assures cost minimization and, therefore, economic efficiency. All profit maximizing firms, regardless of market structure, will operate on (not above) their cost function. In reality, managers and workers may not always work as hard as they could and may make mistakes. Regarding behavioral factors, overconfidence can lead to risky investment decisions by managers and risky behavior of workers regarding workplace safety. Other contributing cognitive issues, discussed in Chap. 4, include confirmation bias and cognitive dissonance. Problems such as these cause firm costs to be higher than they would be if the firm were fully efficient.

Cognitive errors and insufficient effort that push up firm costs are less likely to be an issue in competitive markets, because firms with higher costs than their competitors will go out of business in the long run. This is a natural selection argument, where only the fittest (most efficient) institutions survive in the long run (Alchian 1950). Nevertheless, inefficient firms may survive if there is insufficient competition. Thus, inefficiency due to lax work effort and cognitive errors is more likely to occur in a monopoly market. As Hicks (1935, 8) pointed out, "the best of all monopoly profits is the quiet life." Leibenstein (1966) calls this **X-inefficiency**.

X-inefficiency can be viewed as a deadweight loss in the sense that less is produced with no offsetting gain in consumer or producer surplus. Protection from competitive pressure can facilitate X-inefficiency in the public sector and in other industries besides monopolies.

Another type of inefficiency due to monopoly is **rent seeking**, the act of investing resources into nonproductive activities to obtain and maintain monopoly power.[7] This normally takes the form of lobbying efforts and campaign contributions to government officials in exchange for creating and maintaining legal barriers to entry. Tax breaks, subsidies, tariff protection, and licensing laws are common ways of shielding firms from competition. Rent-seeking behavior is socially wasteful, because it is costly and does not lead to an increase in output.

---

[7] These are normally associated with legal activities and exclude rents deriving from corruption and illegal bribes. For further discussion, see Tullock (1967) and Posner (1975).

In fact, when it increases monopoly power, it leads to less production and greater deadweight loss. Thus, the full social cost of monopoly power must include rent seeking expenditures as well as the traditional deadweight loss.[8]

6.1.5 Dynamic Considerations: Addiction and Product Durability

Thus far, we have analyzed monopolistic markets in a static world where decisions, costs, and benefits occur in a single period. In some circumstances, however, it benefits the monopolist to consider more than one period when making a decision. Demand may be interdependent from one period to the next as in the case of addictive commodities. In addition, greater production today may lower costs tomorrow when workers gain from experience or learning by doing. Investment in research and development today may also bring expected benefits in the future. Finally, an increase in product durability affects a consumer's need to replace a good tomorrow. These are examples of dynamic markets where actions in one period affect profits in another period. In this section we introduce two cases where dynamic considerations are important, addiction and product durability.

For addictive commodities like cigarettes or addictive drugs, consuming the good today increases the probability of consuming the good tomorrow. As is dramatized in Hollywood movies, a monopoly dealer will give addictive drugs away for free in the first period, increasing future demand and allowing the dealer to substantially raise price once consumers are addicted. If we were to ignore the dynamic nature of the market, it would look like there is no monopoly power in the first period, because the price is not above MC. Thus, the measurement of monopoly power is a bit more complex in a dynamic market. We discuss this issue in Chap. 12.

In a dynamic market, the firm will want to choose a level of production today that maximizes the sum of profits today and into the future. With two periods, the current period (I) and next period (II), total profit is

$$\Pi = \pi_I + \pi_{II},$$
$$= TR_I - TC_I + \pi_{II}, \tag{6.12}$$

where π_i is profit in period i, I or II, TR_I is total revenue in period I, and TC_I is total cost in period I. The monopolist's first-order condition of profit maximization with respect to production in period I is

---

[8] Rent-seeking expenditures themselves may be viewed as simple transfers from monopolies to politicians. Nevertheless, not all is transferred and rent seeking that effectively increases market power raises the deadweight loss associated with monopoly.

$$\frac{\partial \Pi}{\partial q_{\mathrm{I}}} = \frac{\partial \mathrm{TR}_{\mathrm{I}}}{\partial q_{\mathrm{I}}} - \frac{\partial \mathrm{TC}_{\mathrm{I}}}{\partial q_{\mathrm{I}}} + \frac{\partial \pi_{\mathrm{II}}}{\partial q_{\mathrm{I}}},$$

$$= \mathrm{MR}_{\mathrm{I}} - \mathrm{MC}_{\mathrm{I}} + \frac{\partial \pi_{\mathrm{II}}}{\partial q_{\mathrm{I}}} = 0, \qquad (6.13)$$

where MR_{I} is marginal revenue in period I and MC_{I} is marginal cost in period I. The term $\partial \pi_{\mathrm{II}}/\partial q_{\mathrm{I}}$ represents the effect of a marginal increase in output in period I on profit in period II. Notice that if this were a static problem, $\partial \pi_{\mathrm{II}}/\partial q_{\mathrm{I}} = 0$, and we get the usual condition of profit maximization, $\mathrm{MR}_{\mathrm{I}} = \mathrm{MC}_{\mathrm{I}}$. The market is static because an increase in q_{I} has no effect on future profit.

With an addictive commodity, however, future profits will be positively related to current consumption, i.e., $\partial \pi_{\mathrm{II}}/\partial q_{\mathrm{I}} > 0$. As $\partial \pi_{\mathrm{II}}/\partial q_{\mathrm{I}}$ gets larger, the marginal benefit of increasing production today ($\mathrm{MR}_{\mathrm{I}} + \partial \pi_{\mathrm{II}}/\partial q_{\mathrm{I}}$) goes up, and the firm will produce more output in period I (i.e., charge a lower price in period I), just as in our Hollywood movie example.

The opposite happens in a durable goods market. If a good that is produced in period I is still available to consumers in period II, then an increase in current production and consumption will lower demand tomorrow. In this situation, $\partial \pi_{\mathrm{II}}/\partial q_{\mathrm{I}} < 0$ and the monopolist will produce less of a durable good in period I. Furthermore, the firm will produce less and less in period I as the good becomes more durable. If product durability is under the control of the monopolist, "planned obsolescence"—purposefully designing products that will wear out or become obsolete more quickly—may be a profitable strategy. We take up this topic and formal methods to solve dynamic problems in Chap. 11.

6.1.6   Social Benefits of Monopoly

Although a monopoly is not allocatively efficient, it may be productively efficient. The classic example is the natural monopoly, where industry output is produced at lowest cost by a single firm. Such a market is characterized by substantial scale economies, as depicted in Fig. 6.5. Notice that AC is lowest with one firm producing all industry output. Thus, productive efficiency requires that there be just one firm in a market when there are pronounced scale economies.

Even though an unregulated natural monopoly is productively efficient, it will be allocatively inefficient. Production will take place where $\mathrm{MR} = \mathrm{MC}$, at q^* and p^* in Fig. 6.5. In terms of public policy, a monopoly is required to assure productive efficiency, but price is typically regulated to minimize allocative inefficiency.

To completely eliminate allocative inefficiency, the price would need to be regulated so that it equals marginal cost at the point where it crosses demand (point A in Fig. 6.5). At this price, however, the firm is losing money because $p = \mathrm{MC} < \mathrm{AC}$. Thus, a subsidy would be required to keep the firm in business. To avoid an administratively costly subsidy, in practice price is generally capped so that that firm earns zero profit in the long run. That is, price is set equal to average cost where it crosses demand (at point B in Fig. 6.5). These regulatory issues will be discussed in more detail in Chap. 20.

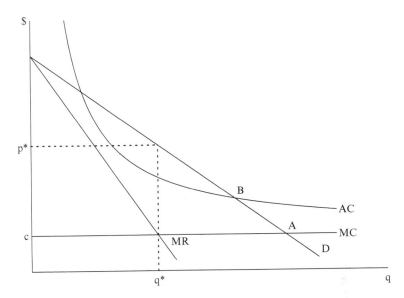

Fig. 6.5 Scale economies and natural monopoly

Finally, monopoly may be more dynamically efficient than other market structures. Schumpeter (1942) hypothesized that large corporations are necessary for dynamic efficiency because they are more likely to invest in the research and development that drives technological change and economic progress. In addition, as we discussed in Chap. 1, Demsetz (1973) argued that many firms gained their monopoly positions by being superior firms. Thus, monopoly profits can be a reward for success, and such rewards encourage effort and innovative activity. We discuss these dynamic issues more fully in Chaps. 17, 19, and 20.

6.2 Monopolistic Competition

Next, we investigate the model of monopolistic competition (Chamberlin 1933). The name derives from the fact that it has features in common with perfect competition and with monopoly. A distinctive aspect of this imperfectly competitive model is that firms are assumed to be so small that strategic interaction is nonexistent. Thus, this model does not require sophisticated game theory tools.

The model of monopolistic competition derives from the following assumptions. Some are similar to perfect competition and others are similar to monopoly:

1. There are *many identical firms* in the industry, and each firm is so small that strategic interaction is zero.
2. Firms produce *differentiated products*. That is, each firm produces a product that performs the same basic function but has slight differences from rival products.

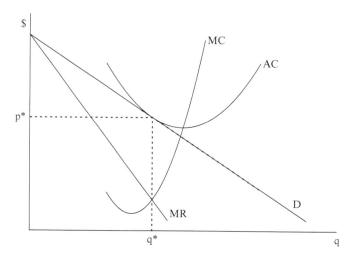

Fig. 6.6 Equilibrium in monopolistic competition

3. There are *no barriers to entry or exit*.
4. Each firm is a profit maximizer, and there are *no frictions or other forms of market imperfections*.
5. There are *economies of scale* in production.

The assumptions of many sellers, no entry barriers, profit maximization, and no market imperfections are identical to those of perfect competition. The key difference is that there is product differentiation.[9] Levi and Lee jeans perform the same function but differ in styling, for example. A differentiated product gives each monopolistically competitive firm a monopoly over the sale of its own brand. Only the Levi Company can sell Levi brand jeans. The importance of the assumption that there are economies of scale will become apparent subsequently.

The long run equilibrium in monopolistic competition has two key features. First, because each firm has a monopoly over the sale of its own brand, firms face negatively sloped demand functions (i.e., they are price makers). We will see that this gives firms monopoly or market power.[10] At the same time, this power is limited by the presence of many close substitutes. Second, free entry ensures that long-run profits are zero, that is, price (p^*) equals long-run average cost (AC). This occurs at the point where demand (D) is tangent to AC, as depicted in Fig. 6.6.

---

[9] In the next chapter, we discuss the different types of product differentiation. At this point, all that matters is that products are different in the eyes of consumers.

[10] Because we are not talking about a true monopoly firm, it may be better to call this market power than monopoly power. Carlton and Perloff (2005, 93) suggest that we define monopoly power as the case where $p^* > MC$ and firm long-run profits are positive and define market power as the case when $p^* > MC$ and long-run profits are zero. However, these terms are generally used interchangeably.

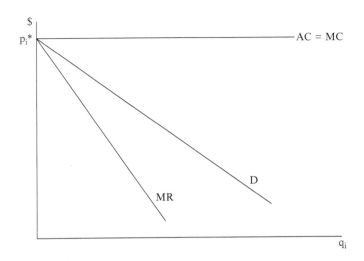

Fig. 6.7 Constant returns to scale and monopolistic competition

Given the presence of scale economies, long-run marginal cost is less than long-run average cost at the optimum. Thus, $p_i^* = AC > MC$; profits are zero even though the firm has monopoly power. For the market to be in equilibrium, these conditions must prevail for every firm.

The welfare implications of this model are complex. On the minus side, the market is allocatively inefficient, because price exceeds marginal cost. Further, production is below efficient scale, as it takes place in the region of economies of scale. Production costs would be lower if there were fewer firms that each produced greater output. With many close substitutes, however, demand is relatively flat. Price will be close to marginal cost, and production will be close to minimum AC.[11] Thus, the social cost of these factors is relatively small. On the plus side, this market structure brings consumers greater product variety than one would find in perfect competition or in monopoly. With fewer firms each producing more output but at lower AC, product variety would diminish. Therefore, it is unlikely that the welfare effect of monopolistic competition is sufficiently negative to warrant a policy response.

The final question we address is: why does the model require economies of scale? It turns out that as scale economies diminish, the market outcome approaches that of perfect competition (Färe et al. 2012). Suppose that there are constant returns to scale. Then AC would be a horizontal line and equal MC. Free entry assures zero profit, $p_i^* = AC$. Thus, $p_i^* = AC = MC$. This produces a corner solution, as depicted in Fig. 6.7, where it is assumed that each firm produces an infinitesimally

---

[11] We exaggerate the steepness of demand (and the markup of price over marginal cost) to make it easier to see the tangency point in the figure.

small amount of output. This demonstrates how the nature of technology can be an important determinant of market power.

In essence, without any economies of scale, each producer becomes identical. For example, if there were no cost savings from the mass production of clothing, we would all shop at a tailor for custom made clothing. In effect, product differentiation is eliminated, as each firm provides the same service of producing custom made clothing. Thus, some degree of scale economies is required for a market to be monopolistically competitive.

6.3 Summary

1. A monopoly exists when there is only one seller in an industry.
2. A monopoly is protected from competition by barriers to entry. There are three types of barriers to entry. A **natural barrier** exists when the presence of scale economies limits the number of competitors that can profitably enter a market. A **legal barrier to entry** is due to a government restriction. A **strategic barrier to entry** is due firm actions that are designed to deter entry.
3. Demand and marginal revenue functions are downward sloping in monopoly because firm demand is industry demand.
4. The monopolist will produce the level of output that maximizes profit where marginal revenue equals marginal cost. Price will be determined along the demand curve at the optimal level of output.
5. In monopoly, price can exceed average cost and economic profit can be sustained in the long run. Unlike perfect competition, new firms cannot enter the market and erode profits because of entry barriers.
6. In equilibrium, $p^* >$ MC, indicating that the monopoly result is **allocative inefficiency**.
7. We cannot specify a supply curve in monopoly as there is no one-to-one correspondence between price and quantity.
8. The **Lerner Index** is the difference between price and marginal cost as a fraction of price. It measures the degree of monopoly power and allocative inefficiency. The Lerner Index is inversely related to the price elasticity of demand. When demand is relatively inelastic, the index is higher indicating that the monopolist has greater power over price.
9. In monopoly, output is lower and price is higher than in perfect competition.
10. Social welfare, as measured by total surplus, is lower under monopoly than under perfect competition. The lost surplus due to monopoly is called the **deadweight loss**.
11. **X-inefficiency** is inefficiency that arises from insulation from competitive pressure on the monopolist and the workers. It leads to higher costs.
12. Resources are also wasted by **rent-seeking**, efforts and monies expended by the firm to protect its monopoly position.

13. Addiction, learning-by-doing, research and development, and product durability lead to **dynamic** problems, where production or investment today can affect profits tomorrow. The firm will maximize profits across periods. When output today positively relates to output tomorrow (e.g., an addictive commodity), the monopolist will produce more today. When output today negatively relates to output tomorrow (e.g., a durable product), the firm will produce less today.

14. A **natural monopoly** arises when industry output is produced at lowest cost by one firm. It is productively efficient but allocatively inefficient.

15. Monopoly may be dynamically efficient if it leads to greater investment in research and development. Monopoly power may serve as an incentive for firms to perform in a superior way.

16. **Monopolistic competition** is characterized by many identical firms that are profit maximizers, product differentiation, free entry and exit, no frictions or other market imperfections, and economies of scale.

17. The assumption of **product differentiation** is that all firms produce goods that serve the same basic function but are slightly different from one another.

18. In long-run equilibrium in monopolistic competition, firm profits are zero but there is allocative inefficiency, i.e., $p^* = AC > MC$. Because each firm's demand is relatively elastic in monopolistically competitive markets, the degree of monopoly power is limited.

6.4   Review Questions

1. Suppose that you are the owner of a metals-producing firm that is an unregulated monopoly. You find that your marginal cost curve can be approximated by a straight line, $MC = 60 + 2q$, where MC is marginal cost (in dollars) and q is output. Inverse demand is $p = 100 - q$, where p is the product price. What is the equation of your MR curve? What are your profit maximizing q and p?

2. A textbook author sells the rights to a book to a publisher, and copyright laws give the publisher a monopoly over the sale of the book. Authors are typically paid a percent of total revenues. If the publisher is a profit maximizer, show that the author will prefer to sell more books than the publisher.

3. Do unregulated monopolists always make positive economic profits? Use a graph to show that a monopolist could earn zero economic profit in the long run.

4. A monopoly producer charges a price of $1 for its product. Assuming that the monopoly is maximizing profits and the absolute value of the price elasticity of demand $\eta = 2$ at that price, calculate the monopolist's MR and MC.

5. Show graphically the deadweight loss associated with monopoly when costs are constant, i.e., $AC = MC = c$. Point out differences in consumer surplus and producer surplus (if any) between the perfectly competitive and monopoly outcomes.

6. Provide an example of rent-seeking behavior and of X-inefficiency.

7. Give an example of how the behavior of managers can lead to X-inefficiency in a firm with monopoly power.

8. Learning-by-doing occurs when workers and management become more productive as they gain experience from producing more output and running the company. When learning-by-doing plays a role in production, what do you expect will be the sign of $\partial \pi_{II}/\partial q_I$? ($q_I$ is the level of production in period I, and π_{II} is profit in period II.) Do you think that the firm should produce more or less of the good in the current period?

9. Suppose that the total cost function in an industry is given by $TC = c \cdot q$. Do you think that there could be a natural monopoly in this industry? Why or why not?

10. Consider an industry with a linear inverse demand, $p = 100 - Q$, and $MC = AC = \$10$. Solve for industry output, price, and profits if the industry is:

   A. Perfectly competitive
   B. Monopolistic

11. This question relates to the Lerner Index, $\mathcal{L}$.

   A. Based on the formula for the Lerner Index in (6.8), how would the value of $\mathcal{L}$ compare for perfect competition versus monopolistic competition? How do you suspect that the value of $\mathcal{L}$ would compare for monopolistic competition versus monopoly?
   B. Based on the relationship between $\mathcal{L}$ and η in (6.11), do you agree with your responses in part (A)? Explain.

12. Consider an established monopoly firm. Explain how the behavioral concept of the endowment effect relates to barriers to entry in the industry.

Chapter 7
Product Differentiation

In our discussion of monopolistic competition in the previous chapter, competing firms produced differentiated products. This occurs when firms sell products that vary slightly from one brand to another. Two loaves of wheat bread may be the same in every way except that one is thin sliced and the other is thick sliced. Although a Mazda Miata and Porsche 911 are both sports cars, they differ in terms of style, power, and fuel economy. This is in contrast to perfectly competitive markets, where products are perfectly homogeneous.

Allowing products to differ blurs what is meant by a market. With perfectly homogeneous goods and perfectly informed consumers, each firm in the market will charge the same price in equilibrium. This is called the law of one price.[1] One could argue that goods of like quality that sell for the same price are in the same market. But prices will not generally be the same for differentiated goods. We might agree that the Honda Civic and Toyota Corolla compete in the same market. They are both small cars that sell for about the same price; the base price is $15,800 for a Civic and is $15,900 for a Corolla.[2] But what about an Acura TSX, a small car that sells for $29,600, or a Porsche 911 that sells for $79,000? Notice that the lines of a market become fuzzy when we introduce product differentiation. In later chapters, we will see that correctly identifying all goods in a market is especially important in antitrust proceedings.

Lancaster (1966) classifies products according to their attributes or characteristics, an approach that distinguishes between products that are in the same market and products that belong to different markets. For example, an apple and a pencil belong to different markets because their characteristics are unrelated. An apple has nutritional value, while a pencil has value as a writing instrument. Alternatively, a traditional pencil and a mechanical pencil are differentiated

---

[1] For a review of the literature and practical concerns with the law of one price, see Lamont and Thaler (2003).

[2] This information is available at http://www.edmunds.com.

V.J. Tremblay and C.H. Tremblay, *New Perspectives on Industrial Organization*,
Springer Texts in Business and Economics, DOI 10.1007/978-1-4614-3241-8_7,
© Springer Science+Business Media New York 2012

products because they are functionally similar (i.e., both are used for writing) but have slightly different characteristics (e.g., a mechanical pencil does not need to be sharpened). We can say that products are differentiated when they perform the same basic function but have slight differences in characteristics.

Chamberlin (1933) distinguished differences between those that are "real" or objective and those that are "fancied" or subjective. Objective characteristics are easy to identify and would include product color, length of warranty, and delivery date. When products differ in objective characteristics, there is **real or objective product differentiation**.

Subjective differences are difficult to quantify, but one way to identify them is as follows. Consider two brands that have the same objective characteristics, but one brand sells for a higher price than the other. If some consumers still buy the more expensive brand, then these brands are subjectively differentiated. If not, then all consumers would buy the cheaper brand. The classic examples are the markets for cola and aspirin. In blind taste tests, consumers cannot generally distinguish one brand of cola from another, yet some buy Pepsi even when Coke is on sale and others buy Coke when Pepsi is on sale. Bayer and generic brands each contain 325 mg of aspirin, yet some consumers buy Bayer even though its price is over twice that of generic aspirin.[3] In these cases, there is **perceived or subjective product differentiation**.

Consumers determine whether or not products are differentiated. For there to be product differentiation, whether objective or subjective, products must perform the same basic function but be different in some way from the perspective of consumers. Although products differ for a variety of reasons, these differences can be classified into four general categories:

1. Physical product differences: Bicycle frames are made with different materials, steel versus carbon fiber, for example. A given style of car comes in a variety of colors. Cell phones can be made with or without Internet connectivity. Fruit can be grown organically or not.
2. Differences in service: Service quality can vary by retail establishment, differing in the number and qualifications of sales staff, length of checkout lines, and return policy restrictions, for example.
3. Differences in geographic location: One grocery store may locate just north and another just south of a college campus. Each store has a location advantage for neighboring students.
4. Differences in product image: Through marketing or other means, firms can create brand images. Returning to the aspirin example above, Bayer has an image of high quality relative to its generic counterparts. In other markets, some producers segment the market by appealing to male versus female consumers or a younger versus an older generation.

---

[3] Of course, they have different packaging and are marketed in different ways. These issues will be discussed in later chapters.

When designing a product, a firm must compare the expected revenues and costs associated with each potential design. Because it is generally expensive to redesign a product from both a technical and marketing perspective, the characteristics of a particular brand are generally fixed for a considerable length of time. Thus, in this chapter, we take product characteristics as given and investigate how different types of product differentiation affect demand and cost conditions. In later chapters, we discuss a firm's product design problem, as well as the private and social optimum level of a product characteristic and a firm's marketing expenditures.

7.1 Types of Product Differentiation

To simplify the discussion, we consider a market with two differentiated products 1 and 2. Although these brands could both be produced by a multiproduct monopolist, we assume two single-product producers. We also limit our discussion to differentiation that is objective. Subjective differentiation involves product image and is normally associated with advertising and other marketing activities, topics that will be taken up in later chapters.

We focus on three types of objective differentiation. In the first, products within a market differ over many different characteristics, and consumers consider most products to be close but not perfect substitutes. In these markets, consumers value variety and purchase many different products. Local restaurants provide one example, where an Italian restaurant may be darkly lit and serve wine and spaghetti, whereas a Mexican restaurant may be brightly decorated and serve beer, tacos, and burritos. Even though most consumers have a favorite style of food, many demand variety and frequent both restaurants due to the diminishing marginal utility associated with consuming the same thing over and over again. We call this **multicharacteristic product differentiation**.

The second type is called **horizontal product differentiation**. In this case, only one characteristic distinguishes products, and consumers disagree over the desirability of this characteristic. An example is two VW Jetta automobiles that are identical in every way except color: one is blue and the other is red. Because some consumers prefer red and others blue, differentiation over the color of a car is said to be horizontal.

The third type is called **vertical product differentiation**, which is also distinguished by a single characteristic. In this case, consumers agree over the preference ordering of the characteristic. The simplest example is product quality. When two brands sell for the same price, all consumers will prefer the brand of higher quality. For example, everyone prefers a Craftsman brand wrench to a Sears brand wrench when priced the same. Both brands are sold by Sears, but Craftsman tools are made from harder steel and have a longer (lifetime) guarantee. Thus, Craftsman tools are undeniably more durable.

7.2   Product Differentiation and Firm Demand

In this section, we discuss how firm demand can be modeled for these three different types of production differentiation.

7.2.1   Multicharacteristic Product Differentiation

With multicharacteristic differentiation, many different characteristics distinguish products 1 and 2, and consumers have a preference for variety. We model firm demands in this case by following Bowley (1924) and Dixit (1979), who assume that demand derives from a utility function of a representative consumer.[4] Their specification produces the following inverse demand system:

$$p_1 = a - q_1 - dq_2, \qquad (7.1)$$

$$p_2 = a - q_2 - dq_1. \qquad (7.2)$$

Notice that the inverse demand functions have a negative slope (both equal -1). Products 1 and 2 are substitutes when d is positive and complements when d is negative.

When they are substitutes, parameter d identifies the degree of substitutability between products. When $d = 1$, they are perfect substitutes or homogeneous goods, and the demand effect of a unit increase in output is the same for products 1 and 2. Thus, one can sum q_1 and q_2 to get total industry output (Q), and demand becomes $p = a - Q$. At the other extreme, $d = 0$ when products 1 and 2 are distinct. In this case, each firm has a monopoly over the sale of its brand, and firm i's demand becomes $p_i = a - q_i$, where $i = 1$ or 2.

Economists define parameter d as an **index of product differentiation** because products 1 and 2 are perfectly homogeneous when $d = 1$ and become more differentiated as $d \rightarrow 0$. Thus, the degree of product differentiation increases as d falls.

7.2.2   Horizontal Product Differentiation

In the model with horizontal differentiation, products differ over a single characteristic, θ, such as the color of a VW Jetta. Consumers are heterogeneous, such that some consumers value the product with a higher amount of θ and others value the product with a lower amount of θ.

One way to think about this is to consider a model of spatial or location competition, where four firms or convenience stores (FM_1, FM_2, FM_3, and FM_4)

---

[4] Thus, it is sometimes called a representative consumer model. Dixit (1979) derives this demand system from the representative consumer's utility function $U(q_1, q_2) = \alpha_1 q_1 + \alpha_2 q_2 - (\beta_1 q_1^2 + \beta_2 q_2^2 + 2\gamma q_1 q_2)/2$. In our specification, we let $a = \alpha_1 = \alpha_2$, $\beta_1 = \beta_2 = 1$, and $d = \gamma$.

Fig. 7.1 Convenience store
location along a circular road

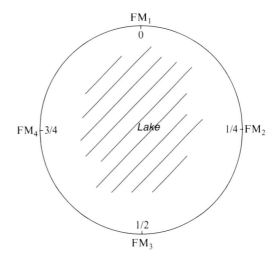

are identical in every way except location. In this case, θ represents store location.
For simplicity, assume that they are located at positions 0, ¼, ½, and ¾ along a
circular road around a lake that is 1 mile long, as in Fig. 7.1. Consumers are located
uniformly along the road. Given a positive transportation cost and the fact that each
store is identical in every way except location, consumers will shop at the nearest
store. Of course, firms may compete in price, and consumers who are nearly equal
distance from two stores will be attracted to the one with lower prices.

This type of differentiation has three interesting features. First, consumers are
heterogeneous in terms of their locations. Second, unlike the case with multicharacteristic product differentiation, consumers will not frequent a variety of stores.
In other words, FM_1 competes with FM_2 for customers along segment 0–¼ and
with F_4 along segment ¾–0, but FM_1 does not compete directly with FM_3.

7.2.2.1   Hotelling's Linear City Model

The simplest way to derive firm demands with horizontal differentiation is to use
Hotelling's (1929) linear city model.[5] In this model, competition occurs along a
linear main street of unit length. There are only two firms, FM_1 and FM_2, with FM_1
located at position 0 and FM_2 located at position 1. N consumers are uniformly
located along main street, and a particular consumer k's location is defined as
$0 \leq \theta_k \leq 1$ (see Fig. 7.2).

If consumer k buys brand i, k's utility equals $U_{ki} = s - p_i - td_{ki}$. Parameter t is
the transportation cost of traveling a unit length, and d_{ki} is the distance that

---

[5] For a discussion of a circular city model as described in Fig. 7.1, see Salop (1979) and Tirole
(1988).

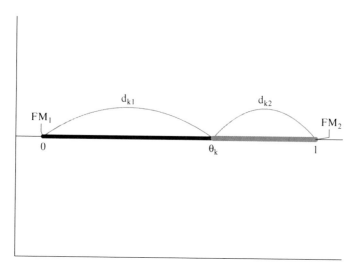

Fig. 7.2 Hotelling's linear main street with two firms: FM_1 and FM_2

consumer k is from FM_i. As seen in Fig. 7.2, $d_{k1} = \theta_k$ and $d_{k2} = 1 - \theta_k$ for consumer k. Parameter s is the surplus enjoyed by the consumer from consuming the brand when the price and distance are 0. Parameter s is the same for both products because they are homogeneous when distance is not an issue. When prices differ and distance is a factor, the consumer will choose the brand that gives the highest utility level, assuming $U_{ki} > 0$. When $U_{ki} < 0$, the consumer does not make a purchase and utility equals zero. Notice that utility increases in s and falls in the price, the transportation cost, and travel distance.

In Fig. 7.3, we illustrate utility for all possible consumers when they buy from FM_1 (U_1) or FM_2 (U_2). When prices are the same, these functions are reflections of each other because s and t are the same regardless of which brand is purchased. The intercepts are $s - p_i$, the slope of U_1 is $-t$, and the slope of U_2 is t. When s is sufficiently high, all consumers receive positive utility from at least one brand or the other. This is true for Allison, for example, who lives at address θ_A and receives U_{A1} units of utility when purchasing from FM_1 and receives U_{A2} units of utility when purchasing from FM_2. Clearly, Allison prefers FM_1 over FM_2.

The marginal consumer (located at $\theta_m = \frac{1}{2}$ in the symmetric case), is indifferent between buying from FM_1 and FM_2. Consumers to the right of θ_m gain greater utility from buying from FM_2, while consumers to the left of θ_m gain greater utility from buying from FM_1. This example describes a **covered market**, a market where no consumer opts out of the market. Toothpaste is a good example, as everyone buys one brand of toothpaste or another. In contrast, the market of motorcycles is uncovered, because some consumers choose not to buy a motorcycle at all.

For a covered market, we can derive firm demand as follows. Consumers are assumed to have **unit demands**. This means that each person consumes 0 or 1 unit

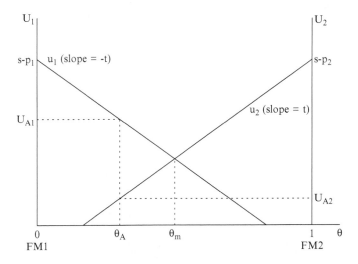

Fig. 7.3 Utility in a Hotelling model with a covered market

of the good or service.[6] For the marginal consumer who is indifferent between buying from FM_1 and FM_2, $U_{m1} = U_{m2}$ or $\theta_m = (t - p_1 + p_2)/(2t)$.[7] Consumers located to the right of θ_m place a higher value on brand 2, and consumers to the left place a higher value on brand 1. Thus, in a market with N consumers, firm demand functions are[8]

$$q_1 = N(\theta_m - 0) = N\left(\frac{t - p_1 + p_2}{2t}\right), \tag{7.3}$$

$$q_2 = N(1 - \theta_m) = N\left(\frac{t + p_1 - p_2}{2t}\right). \tag{7.4}$$

Notice that demand increases in the number of consumers and the price of the rival brand and decreases in its own price.

The model can also be used to analyze horizontal characteristics other than geographic location. Consider the example of breakfast cereal where two brands are similar in every way except sweetness: brand 1 is unsweetened corn flakes, and brand 2 is sugar-coated corn flakes. In this interpretation, θ_k identifies consumer k's

---

[6] In other words, consumers are making discrete purchases, buying 0 or 1 unit at a time. This is common with durable goods, for example, where most consumers buy just one house, automobile, or microwave oven at a time.

[7] This is derived as follows. From above, $d_{m1} = \theta_m$ and $d_{m2} = 1 - \theta_m$. Thus, $U_{m1} = s - p_1 - t d_{m1} = s - p_1 - t\theta_m$ and $U_{m2} = s - p_2 - t(1 - \theta_m)$. Setting $U_{m1} = U_{m2}$ and solving for θ_m leads to the following result: $\theta_m = (t - p_1 + p_2)/(2t)$.

[8] In many applications, N is normalized to 1 for simplicity.

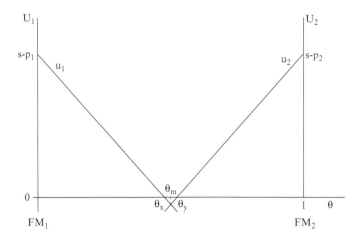

Fig. 7.4 Utility in a Hotelling model with an uncovered market

preference for sweetened cereal, and those located closer to point 1 (brand 2's location) in Fig. 7.3 have more of a sweet tooth. In this case, t equals the added disutility associated with consuming a brand that is 1 unit away from the consumer's ideal brand. For example, when $p_1 = p_2 = 0$, the consumer of type $\theta_k = 1$ has utility equal to $s-t$ from consuming brand 1 and utility equal to s from consuming brand 2 (the ideal brand).

Finally, this model can also characterize a local monopoly. This occurs when s is sufficiently low or t is sufficiently high. In this setting, nearby consumers shop at the store closest to them, but it is uneconomic for the marginal consumer to patronize either store (see Fig. 7.4). High transportation costs isolate consumers and can create an **uncovered market** because consumers located in the θ_y–θ_x neighborhood in Fig. 7.4 will patronize neither store.[9] In this case, the price charged by one firm has no effect on the demand of the other firm, giving each firm a local monopoly.

7.2.2.2 The Circular City Model

Another way to portray horizontal differentiation is with a circular city model that we saw earlier in Fig. 7.1. This model was developed by Salop (1979), who took a linear street and bent it back around itself to form a circle. Other assumptions carry over from the linear city model: consumers are uniformly distributed along the circle, have unit demands, and face a transportation cost equal to t.

---

[9] When this happens, consumers may decide to buy a different good. For example, a substantial increase in the price of cookies will cause some consumers to switch to ice cream, which is called an outside good.

For simplicity, firms are located at equal distances from one another. As we saw before, each firm competes only with its neighbors; for instance, firm 1 competes with firms 2 and 4, but not with firm 3. If firm 1 is located at point 0 and the circle is one unit in circumference, then the distance between firms is $1/n$, where n is the number of firms. The market is assumed to be covered and N is normalized to 1.

Firm demand is derived as follows. A consumer located at point x between firms 1 and 2 would pay a full price of $p_1 + tx$ for good 1 and pay a full price of $p_2 + t(1/n - x)$ for good 2.[10] For the marginal consumer (x_m) who is indifferent between goods 1 and 2, full prices must be the same: $p_1 + tx_m = p_2 + t(1/n - x_m)$. This implies that $x_m = (t/n - p_1 + p_2)/(2t)$, which is firm 1's demand as it competes with firm 2. By the same logic, we can derive firm 1's demand as it competes with firm 4. Thus, total demand is $2x_m$. Because the problem is symmetric, rival prices will be the same in equilibrium (set at p). Thus, the demand for firm i's product is

$$q_i = 2x_m = \frac{t/n - p_i + p}{t}. \tag{7.5}$$

Notice that demand falls in the firm's own price and with the number of competitors and rises with its rivals' price.

7.2.3 Vertical Product Differentiation

In a vertical differentiation model, products differ with respect to a single characteristic z. Recall that all consumers prefer the brand with more z, *ceteris paribus*. Classic examples of vertical characteristics are product quality and durability. When two brands are priced the same and are identical in every way except quality, all consumers prefer the higher quality brand.

Mussa and Rosen (1978) developed a simple way of modeling vertical differentiation. As before, consider a market with two brands, 1 and 2. In this example, we let brand 1 be of higher quality ($z_1 > z_2 > 0$). Each consumer has a unit demand and a different strength of preference for quality.[11] Consumer k's strength of preference is identified by the taste parameter ϕ_k, where $0 < \phi_L \leq \phi_k \leq \phi_H < \infty$ and $\phi_H - \phi_L = 1$. There are N consumers uniformly distributed along the taste interval $\phi_H - \phi_L$.

---

[10] That is, if the distance between firms 1 and 2 is $1/n$, and the distance between firm 1 and consumer x is distance x, then the distance between firm 2 and consumer x is $(1/n - x)$. We use x instead of θ_x to simplify the notation.

[11] For example, the strength of preference for quality could be a positive function of consumer income, with richer consumers having a stronger preference (i.e., willingness and ability to pay) for quality.

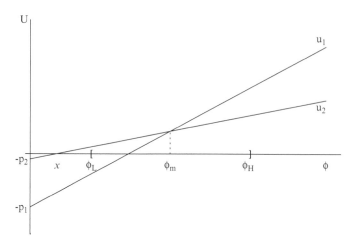

Fig. 7.5 Utility and the marginal consumer in the Mussa–Rosen model

If consumer k buys brand i, k's utility is $U_{ki} = \phi_k z_i - p_i$. When this function is negative, consumer k does not make a purchase and utility is zero. Consumer utility for brands 1 and 2 is described in Fig. 7.5. The slope of each function is the degree of product quality, and because $z_1 > z_2$, U_1 is steeper than U_2. We assume that the marginal consumer (ϕ_m) lies between ϕ_L and ϕ_H, $U(\phi_m) > 0$, with $\phi_H > \phi_L > x$. This guarantees that the market is covered and that demand is positive for both brands.[12]

We derive firm demand in a similar way as in the case of horizontal differentiation. For the marginal consumer, $U_{m1} = U_{m2}$ or $\phi_m = (p_1 - p_2)/z$, where $z \equiv z_1 - z_2$. Consumers with a high preference for quality, located to the right of ϕ_m, receive greater utility from the high quality brand (brand 1). That is, consumers located from ϕ_m to ϕ_H purchase brand 1. Consumers with a low value of quality, located to the left of ϕ_m, receive greater utility from the low quality brand (brand 2). Consumers located from ϕ_L to ϕ_m purchase brand 2. Thus, firm demands are

$$q_1 = N(\phi_H - \phi_m) = N(\phi_H - p_1/z + p_2/z), \tag{7.6}$$

$$q_2 = N(\phi_m - \phi_L) = N(-\phi_L + p_1/z - p_2/z). \tag{7.7}$$

Firm demand increases in the number of consumers and the price of the rival brand and decreases in its own price. A nice feature of the Mussa–Rosen model and of the previous models of horizontal differentiation is that they produce linear demand functions.

---

[12] If $\phi_L < x$, the market would be uncovered because consumers with preferences within the $x-\phi_L$ interval would opt out of the market (i.e., they would buy neither brand 1 nor brand 2).

7.3   Product Differentiation and Firm Costs

When firms produce homogeneous goods and have access to the same technology, it is reasonable to assume that they have the same cost functions. Recall from Chap. 2 that if costs are linear, firm i's total cost equation (TC_i) takes the following form: $TC_i = cq_i + F$, where c is marginal cost and F is fixed (or quasi-fixed) cost. Firms have the same cost functions, because c and F are the same for all firms. In the long run, of course, there are no fixed costs and $F = 0$.

If one firm has a cost advantage over its competitors, it will have lower marginal and/or fixed costs. In this case, $TC_i = c_i q_i + F_i$. If firm 1 has lower costs than firm 2, then $c_1 < c_2$ and/or $F_1 < F_2$. When this occurs, we say that firm 1 has superior cost efficiency.

The presence of product differentiation may be one source of cost asymmetries. This need not always be the case, however, because characteristics that affect demand may have an insignificant effect on costs. For example, some horizontal characteristics have little or no effect on costs. A grocery store on the north side of town is likely to have the same costs as a grocery store on the south side of town (assuming homogeneous land values). A similar argument can be made for like cars of different color, as a blue car is neither more nor less expensive to produce than a red car. Still, some horizontal characteristics do affect costs. One example is sweetened and unsweetened corn flakes, as the added sugar increases costs.

Cost asymmetries are more likely with vertical differentiation, because it is generally more expensive to produce higher quality goods.[13] In this case, $TC_i = c_i q_i + F_i$; because brand 1 is of higher quality, $c_1 > c_2$ and/or $F_1 > F_2$. For instance, if it takes higher quality raw materials to produce brand 1, then $c_1 > c_2$; if it takes a greater investment in more sophisticated equipment to produce brand 1, then $F_1 > F_2$.

7.4   Product Differentiation and the Type of Good

At times, it will be useful to classify products by their dominant characteristics. We have seen in Chap. 6 that product durability is a valuable feature of a good and can affect how it is marketed. We will often distinguish between durable goods and nondurable or convenience goods.

Another meaningful distinction in consumer goods markets is the way in which consumers obtain information about product characteristics. In this regard, a characteristic can be classified into search, experience, and credence categories. To simplify the discussion, consider a good with a single characteristic.[14] With a

---

[13] There are exceptions. In our discussion of damaged goods in Chap. 14, we show that it can be profitable for a multiproduct firm to produce and sell both a high and a low quality brands even though the low quality brand is more expensive to produce than the high quality brand.

[14] Nelson (1970, 1974) identified search and experience goods, and Darby and Karni (1973) identified credence goods.

search good, a consumer can learn all about a product's characteristic before making a purchase. One example is men's jeans, as one can identify color, style, and fit before purchase.

In contrast, the characteristic of an **experience good** cannot be ascertained until after purchase. Most types of fresh fruit are experience goods. One cannot accurately tell the quality of a whole watermelon until one tries it. A **credence good** has the extreme quality that it is uneconomic for consumers to identify the product's characteristic even after purchase. An appendix operation is a credence good, as verification that your appendix was actually removed requires another operation. The same argument applies to many car repairs, such as the replacement of an internal engine part.

7.5   Summary

1. Brands or products are differentiated when they perform the same basic function but differ in the eyes of the consumer in terms of one or more attributes or characteristics. Examples of product characteristics include quality, durability, color, and store location. These are examples of characteristics that are real or objective and characterize **real or objective product differentiation**. Differences between products can also be perceived or subjective and based on product image. In this case, there is **perceived or subjective product differentiation**.

2. When products differ over a variety of characteristics, there is **multicharacteristic differentiation**. In markets such as these, consumers frequently buy a variety of brands. For example, a consumer who most prefers Thai food may occasionally dine at Italian and Mexican restaurants as well as Thai restaurants.

3. For a **horizontal characteristic**, such as grocery store location, consumers disagree over the preference ordering. In this case, consumers prefer the store that is more conveniently located, *ceteris paribus*.

4. For a **vertical characteristic**, such as product quality, all consumers agree on the preference ordering. That is, everyone prefers the high quality brand over the low quality brand when priced the same.

5. A **covered market** is one where everyone buys either one brand or another. The market for toothpaste is an example of a covered market. In contrast, the markets for motorcycles and luxury cars are uncovered. Not everyone likes motorcycles and not all consumers who like luxury cars can afford them.

6. Consumers have **unit demands** if they make discrete purchases, buying 0 or 1 unit of a brand within a market over a given shopping period. Durable goods markets provide an example, as most consumers buy just one car, refrigerator, or dishwasher at a time.

7. The **Hotelling linear city model** and the **circular city model** characterized horizontal differentiation. The **Mussa–Rosen model** characterizes vertical differentiation. All three models produce demand functions that are linear.

8. Whether or not firms have different cost functions in markets with product differentiation depends upon the type and degree of differences among product characteristics. Characteristics that affect demand may have little or no effect on costs. Although costs are likely to be higher for firms that produce higher quality brands, costs need not differ when products vary by color, for example.

9. It is useful to classify consumer goods by the way in which consumers gain information about a product's characteristics. For a **search good**, a consumer can learn all about a product's characteristics before making a purchase. For an **experience good**, consumers cannot ascertain a product's characteristics until after purchase. For a **credence good**, it is uneconomic for consumers to identify a product's characteristic even after purchase.

7.6 Review Questions

1. Provide two real-world examples of markets with multicharacteristic differentiation, horizontal differentiation, and vertical differentiation.

2. Discuss how changes in key parameters affect firm demand when product differentiation is multicharacteristic, horizontal (circular city), and vertical.

3. Discuss how an increase in a rival's decision variable (output or price) affects firm demand in the three demand models discussed in this chapter.

4. Consider the demand system with two firms in (7.1) and (7.2). How would the demand system change if there were three firms instead of two firms?

5. The demand models of this chapter assume that the two goods are (imperfect) substitutes. How would the demand functions change if the two goods were complements?

6. Consider Hotelling's linear city model, but in this case both firms locate outside of town. Assume that FM_1 locates at point 1.5 and FM_2 locates at point 2. Explain why this is now a model of vertical product differentiation.

7. Consider the duopoly market with horizontal differentiation discussed in Sect. 7.2.2.1. Derive each firm's demand function when s is sufficiently low so that the market is uncovered.

8. Assume a market with two firms and vertical differentiation, where firm 1 produces the high quality brand. How would you expect an increase in consumer income to affect the demand for the high versus the low quality brand?

9. (Advanced) In this chapter, we derived demand models when there is multicharacteristic, horizontal, and vertical differentiation. In each case, derive the price elasticity of demand for firm i.

10. Assume a market with two firms and vertical differentiation, where firm 1 produces the high quality brand. If production costs are the same for both firms, show that the cost per unit of quality is lower for the high quality firm.

11. Consider the markets for neckties, canned soup, and automobile engine repair. Classify each as being primarily a search, experience, or credence good. Given the characteristics of these goods and the behavioral issues raised in Chap. 4, in which market would you expect greater deception on the part of producers?

Chapter 8
Market Structure, Industry Concentration, and Barriers to Entry

In economics, we normally classify markets into four market structures: perfect competition, monopoly, monopolistic competition, and oligopoly. In this chapter, we are interested in understanding why real markets are structured so differently. For example, most agricultural commodities approximate competitive markets, as they have many producers of homogeneous or nearly homogeneous goods. In contrast, the market of computer operating systems is nearly monopolized by Microsoft. In 2009, Microsoft Windows had a market share of approximately 92%, while its nearest competitor, Mac, had a market share of just over 5%.

We will see that in many cases market structure is relatively stable over time, although this is not always the case. Technological change can transform industry structure by giving large scale producers a cost advantage and put smaller competitors out of business. This is what happened in the US brewing industry, where the number of traditional brewers declined from 476 in 1945 to about 19 today. The internationalization of the automobile industry led to more foreign cars being sold in the USA. Entry caused the market share of the dominant domestic car companies (General Motors or GM, Ford, and Chrysler) to fall from over 90% in the mid 1950s to approximately 55% in the late 2000s. Thus, we are also interested in understanding how market forces cause market structure to change over time.

How a market is structured can have important welfare implications. We learned in Chaps. 5 and 6 that perfectly competitive markets are allocatively efficient, while monopoly markets are allocatively inefficient. This suggests that static inefficiency rises with less competition, a viewpoint that is consistent with the structure–conduct–performance paradigm discussed in Chap. 1. It is also consistent with the tenor of the Sherman and Clayton Acts, which are designed to support competitive market structures. Although we will see that the hypothesis that an increase in the number of competitors improves welfare is not always correct, understanding the reasons why a market has just a few competitors and why their numbers may change over time will give us a better understanding of the nature of competition in a dynamic world.

V.J. Tremblay and C.H. Tremblay, *New Perspectives on Industrial Organization*,
Springer Texts in Business and Economics, DOI 10.1007/978-1-4614-3241-8_8,
© Springer Science+Business Media New York 2012

8.1 The Delineation of Market Structure

Before discussing the qualities of market structure more generally, we first review the characteristics of the four market structures found in microeconomics textbooks (see Table 8.1). To begin with, profit maximization is assumed throughout. The extreme cases of perfect competition and monopoly were discussed in Chaps. 5 and 6. Recall that in perfect competition there are many producers and goods are homogeneous. Entry and exit are free, and firms are price takers, meaning that the market price is exogenously determined. In a monopoly, entry barriers make it possible for only one firm to enter the market. In this case, the firm is a price maker, meaning that the firm has the power to raise price without losing all of its customers. Although most markets lie between these polar cases, competitive and monopoly models provide us with useful reference points, that is, extremes in market structure that identify lower and upper bounds on the expected equilibrium price in a market.

As we discussed in Chap. 6, monopolistic competition has characteristics of both monopoly and perfect competition. Like perfect competition, entry is free and there are many competitors in the market. A key feature of monopolistic competition is the presence of product differentiation, which gives each firm a monopoly over the sale of its particular brand. Thus, we can think of monopolistic competition as a competitive market with product differentiation or a monopoly market with free entry of closely related goods.

The market structure that has received little attention so far is **oligopoly**. In an oligopoly market, products may or may not be differentiated, and entry barriers are present. The key feature of oligopoly is that only a few firms account for the bulk of industry production. Because strategic interaction is important, with one firm's actions affecting its own profits and the profits of its competitors, game theory is used to develop oligopoly models. The steel and aluminum markets are examples of oligopoly markets with homogeneous goods. The automobile and cell phone industries are examples of differentiated oligopolies.

When asked which of the four market structures are most common in the USA, many students choose monopolistic competition. This response is understandable because most consumer goods markets have many differentiated brands. But typically only a handful of firms produce most brands in a particular market.

Table 8.1 Characteristics of the four main market structures

Market structure	Number of firms	Product type	Entry/exit	Price
Perfect competition	Many	Homogeneous	Free	Exogenous
Monopoly	1	Just 1 Product	B.E.	Endogenous
Monopolistic competition	Many	P.D.	Free	Endogenous
Oligopoly	Few	Homogeneous & P.D.	B.E.	Endogenous

Note: B.E. refers to barriers to entry, and P.D. refers to product differentiation. Exogenous implies that firms have no control over price; endogenous implies that firms have a least some control over price.

These are called multibrand or multiproduct producers, as opposed to the single product producers discussed in most elementary textbooks.

A classic example is the market for breakfast cereal. In most supermarkets you can find over a hundred brands of cereal. Brands are made from a variety of grains (e.g., oats, corn, wheat, bran, and rice), can come in a variety of flavors (e.g., brown sugar, cinnamon, honey, chocolate, strawberry, and peanut butter), and may contain raisins, dried strawberries, dried peaches, or nuts. Yet, the largest five cereal companies produce most of these brands, accounting for 94% of cereal sales in 2008. Although industries such as these appear to be monopolistically competitive, they are actually oligopolies, the most common market structure.

Given that oligopolies are so common, we devote most of our attention to understanding these markets. In this chapter, we begin with a discussion of the concept of industry concentration, which characterizes the extent to which industry production is concentrated in the hands of a few firms in an industry. In Sect. 8.3 we discuss the extent of industry concentration in the USA. In Sect. 8.4 we investigate the main determinants of industry concentration. That is, why do some markets have many firms and others just a few firms? We will also summarize the empirical evidence regarding the causes of high industry concentration. In later chapters, we investigate how equilibrium price and output are determined in oligopoly markets and compare these outcomes with those found in competitive and monopoly markets.

8.2 Industry Concentration

In this section, we summarize the principle methods of measuring industry concentration and discuss their strengths and weaknesses. Because proper measurement requires that a market be correctly defined, we also discuss the issue of market definition.

8.2.1 The Meaning and Measurement of Industry Concentration

A prominent feature of market structure is industry concentration. The number and size distribution of firms within an individual market indicates the extent of concentration.

One way to visualize industry concentration is with a **concentration curve**. A concentration curve plots the cumulative market share of sales that are attributable to the largest through the smallest firms in the industry.[1] To illustrate, consider three hypothetical industries (A, B, and C), which have six, eight, and ten competitors, respectively. Output and market share information for each industry

---

[1] The market share for a particular firm is defined as the firm's sales divided by industry sales, where sales are typically measured by output or by total revenue.

Table 8.2 Firm output, market share, and industry concentration for three hypothetical industries: A, B, and C

Firm	Output (1,000,000 s)			Market share (%)			Squared market share		
	A	B	C	A	B	C	A	B	C
1	4.8	4.8	3.6	40	20	10	1,600	400	100
2	2.4	4.8	3.6	20	20	10	400	400	100
3	1.2	4.8	3.6	10	20	10	100	400	100
4	1.2	4.8	3.6	10	20	10	100	400	100
5	1.2	1.2	3.6	10	5	10	100	25	100
6	1.2	1.2	3.6	10	5	10	100	25	100
7		1.2	3.6		5	10		25	100
8		1.2	3.6		5	10		25	100
9			3.6			10			100
10			3.6			10			100
Industry	12	24	36						

	Industry A	Industry B	Industry C
n	6	8	10
CR_4	80	80	40
HHI (MS_i measured in %)	2,400	1,700	1,000
HHI' (MS_i measured as a decimal)	0.24	0.17	0.10
Numbers Equivalent ($n' = 1/HHI'$)	4.17	5.88	10.0

Note: MS_i is firm i's market share, which can be measured in percent or as a decimal.

is listed in Table 8.2. The concentration curves for these industries are plotted in Fig. 8.1. They reveal two important facts. First, a concentration curve is a straight line when each firm is of equal size, as in industry C. Second, the curve shifts up with fewer competitors and as larger firms gain market share. For instance, industries A and B have fewer firms and higher concentration curves than industry C. In addition, the concentration curve for industry A starts at a higher point than for industry B (and C), because the market share of the largest firm is 40% in industry A and 20% in industry B (10% in industry C). Thus, we can conclude that higher industry concentration is reflected in a higher concentration curve.

Although a concentration curve provides a clear picture of concentration, economists have also tried to create a single index of industry concentration. A single index is useful for empirical work and for addressing antitrust concerns. Ideally, a concentration index should take into account the size distribution of all firms in the industry. It should also increase, implying greater concentration, when the number of firms declines and when a larger firm gains market share from a smaller firm.

Given this criteria, the **number of firms** (n) in an industry is an unsatisfactory index of concentration unless all firms within an industry are of equal size. When this is not the case, two industries with 100 firms would be considered equally concentrated even if one industry had firms of equal size and the other had a large firm with a market share of 95%. A firm such as this is called a **dominant firm** because it typically takes a leadership role in choosing price or output due to its

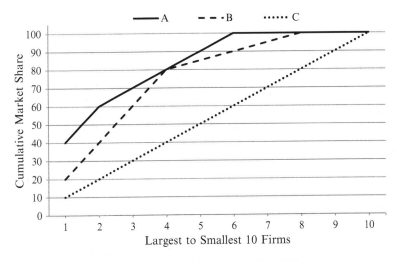

Fig. 8.1 Concentration curves for hypothetical industries A, B, and C

large market share relative to its competitors, which are sometimes called competitive fringe firms. Dominance can result from producing a superior product or producing at lower cost than its competitors. Because the dominant firm in this example has a near monopoly, we would like our index to reflect a higher level of concentration in this case than in the symmetric case where firms are of equal size.

A more commonly used index is the ***k*-firm concentration ratio** (CR_k), defined as the market share of the *k* largest firms in the industry. If we order firms from the largest (firm 1) to the smallest (firm *n*), the *k*-firm concentration ratio is

$$CR_k \equiv \sum_{i=1}^{k} ms_i, \tag{8.1}$$

where ms_i is firm *i*'s market share (which can be measured as a decimal or percent), ms_1 is the market share of the largest firm, ms_2 is the market share of the second largest firm, etc., and ms_k is the market share of the *k*th largest firm. Notice that CR_k approaches 0 as the number of equal sized firms increases and approaches 1 or 100% when the *k* largest firms supply more and more of the industry's output. The four-firm concentration ratio (CR_4) has been used by economists for decades because it is regularly calculated for a variety of industries by the US Census of Manufacturers. Notice that a concentration ratio is represented by a point on a concentration curve. In Fig. 8.1, CR_4 is found by identifying the cumulative market share on the vertical axis associated with firm four on the horizontal axis. For industries A and B it is 80%, and for industry C it is 40%.

The main advantage of a concentration ratio is that it is easy to calculate and understand. Unfortunately, it suffers from three main weaknesses. First, it provides no information about the relative shares of the largest *k* firms. Second, it completely ignores the distribution of sales outside the largest *k* firms. As an example, a merger of firms 7 and 8 in industry B from Table 8.2 will have no effect on CR_4 even though the number of firms has diminished and the distribution of output among firms has changed (i.e., the merged firm becomes the fifth largest firm with a market share of 10%). Third, concentration ratios do not always provide consistent rankings of industry concentration. One can see from Fig. 8.1, for example, where industries A and B are equally concentrated if we use CR_4, but industry A is more concentrated than industry B if we use CR_1, CR_2, CR_3, CR_5, CR_6, or CR_7.

An alternative index of industry concentration is the Herfindahl–Hirschman Index (HHI).[2] Mathematically,

$$HHI \equiv \sum_{i=1}^{n} ms_i^2. \qquad (8.2)$$

When market share is expressed in percent, then HHI approaches 0 in a competitive market and equals 10,000 for a monopoly. To illustrate, based on the squared market share figures in Table 8.2, HHI equals 2,400 for industry A, 1,700 for industry B, and 1,000 for industry C. When market share is expressed as a decimal, HHI ranges from 0 to 1. In this case, HHI equals 0.24 for industry A, 0.17 for industry B, and 0.1 for industry C.

Unlike a concentration ratio, the HHI meets our criteria for a desirable concentration index. In particular, it decreases with the number of firms (n) and increases with the variance in market share (σ^2). When we *measure market share in decimal form*, we can rewrite (8.2) as[3]

$$HHI = n\sigma^2 + 1/n. \qquad (8.3)$$

This demonstrates that HHI increases as the variance in market share increases.

Equation (8.3) also implies that when firms are of equal size, so that $\sigma^2 = 0$, then $HHI = 1/n$. HHI has a value of 1 in a monopoly market and diminishes as n increases and firms remain equal in size. Equation (8.3) can give us a **numbers equivalent**, such that a given value of HHI can be translated into a number of equal sized firms (n'). When market share is measured as a decimal, the numbers equivalent of a given value of HHI is $n' = 1/HHI$. Values of n' are calculated in Table 8.2 for our hypothetical industries. For industry A, n' is 4.17 (i.e., 1/.24),[4] which means that for HHI to equal 0.24, there would need to be 4.17 equal sized firms in the industry. This provides another way of thinking about HHI. Because of

---

[2] For a discussion of the history of this index, see Hirschman (1964).

[3] To see this, note that the variance (σ^2) can be written as $\sigma^2 = [\Sigma ms_i^2/n - (\Sigma ms_i/n)^2]$; market shares sum to 1 (when measured in decimals), so that $\Sigma ms_i = 1$; $HHI = \Sigma ms_i^2$. Thus, $\sigma^2 = HHI/n - 1/n^2$. Solving for HHI gives $HHI = n\sigma^2 + 1/n$. For a discussion of variance, see the Mathematics and Econometrics Appendix at the end of the book.

[4] When market share is measured in decimals, note that HHI is 0.24 or 2,400/10,000. The numbers equivalent is 1/0.24 or 4.17. These are frequented rounded off to the nearest counting number, which would be 4 in this case.

Table 8.3   Industry concentration and market classification in a market with n' equal size firms

n'	$CR_1 = 100 \cdot 1/n'$	CR_4	HHI	HHI$'$	SRS	Merger guidelines
					\multicolumn{2}{c}{Market classification}	
1	100	100	10,000	1.00	T–O	H
2	50.0	100	5,000	0.50	T–O	H
3	33.3	100	3,333	0.33	T–O	H
4	25.0	100	2,500	0.25	T–O	H
5	20.0	80.0	2,000	0.20	T–O	H
5.56	18.0	72.0	**1,800**	0.18	T–O	**H**
6	16.7	66.7	1,667	0.67	T–O	M
6.67	15.0	**60.0**	1,500	0.15	**T–O**	M
7	14.3	57.1	1,429	0.43	O	M
8	12.5	50.0	1,250	0.13	O	M
9	11.1	44.0	1,111	0.11	O	M
10	10.0	**40.0**	**1,000**	0.10	**O**	**M**
11	9.1	36.4	909	0.09	C	Un
20	5.0	20.0	500	0.05	C	Un
100	1.0	4.0	100	0.01	C	Un

Note: Market share is measured in percent for the one-firm concentration ratio (CR_1), the four-firm concentration ratio (CR_4), and the Herfindahl–Hirschman index (HHI). When market share is measured in decimal form: HHI$' = $ HHI/10,000, $n' = 1/$HHI$'$, CR_1 and CR_4 must be divided by 100, and the figures for HHI above must be divided by 10,000.

Regarding market classification. SRS refers to the Scherer and Ross (1990) and Shepherd (1997, 16) market classifications: tight oligopoly (T–O) when CR_4 reaches 60%, oligopoly (O) when CR_4 reaches 40% and is less than 60%, and competitive (C) when CR_4 is less than 40%. These cutoffs are in bold in columns 3 and 6.

Merger Guidelines refers to the Department of Justice and the Federal Trade Commission classification: a market is unconcentrated when HHI is less than 1,000 (Un), moderately concentrated when HHI ranges from 1,000 to less than 1,800 (M), and highly concentrated when HHI is greater than or equal to 1,800 (H). These cutoffs are in bold in columns 4 and 7.

these desirable features, the Department of Justice began using HHI as a measure of industry concentration in 1982 to evaluate potential antitrust violations.[5]

Concentration ratios and HHI are the most commonly used indices of industry concentration, and it is useful to investigate their properties further. When *market share is measured in percent* and all firms are of equal size,

$$CR_4 = \min(100, 400/n)$$

$$HHI = 10,000/n. \tag{8.4}$$

Furthermore, when $n \leq 4$, HHI $= (100 \cdot CR_4)/n$; when $n > 4$, HHI $= 25 \cdot CR_4$. If we *measure market share as a decimal*, then HHI $= CR_1 = 1/n$. To make this more concrete, in Table 8.3 we list several examples for an industry where firms are of equal size and market share is measured in percent.

Experts in the field have identified critical values of concentration indices that distinguish competitive from oligopoly markets. Scherer and Ross (1990, 82) and

---

[5] The obvious drawback with HHI is that it requires sales data on every firm in the industry.

Shepherd (1997, 16) contend that once CR_4 reaches 40%, strategic interaction becomes significant and an industry can be classified as an oligopoly. Once CR_4 reaches 60%, Shepherd classifies it as a tight oligopoly, one where collusion is likely. When enforcing the antimerger laws, the Department of Justice and the Federal Trade Commission use the following delineation:

- An industry is classified as unconcentrated when HHI is less than 1,000.
- An industry is classified as moderately concentrated when HHI ranges from 1,000 to less than 1,800.
- An industry is classified as highly concentrated when HHI is greater than or equal to 1,800.[6]

As Table 8.3 indicates for firms of equal size, CR_4 equals 40% when HHI equals 1,000, and CR_4 equals 72% when HHI equals 1,800. Thus, there is some consistency among experts.

8.2.2 Definition of the Relevant Market

When measuring concentration, a crucial step is to properly define the market. In fact, many antitrust decisions hinge on how broadly or narrowly a market is defined. If defined too broadly, firms will be included that are not true competitors and our concentration index will be biased downwards.

A relevant economic market includes all products that are close substitutes in consumption and production. Defining a market requires that we draw proper product and geographic boundaries. Geographically, markets may be local, regional, national, or international. Typically, this depends on the value of the product, its weight, and shipping costs per mile. A product will ship a longer distance as its unit shipping cost falls and as its value to weight ratio increases.

Several examples illustrate this idea. Diamonds are shipped worldwide, while cement is rarely shipped more than 150 miles. There are thousands of cement suppliers nationally, but only a few firms are true suppliers in any particular region in the country. Thus, if we incorrectly define the cement market as national, our estimate of industry concentration would be biased downwards. In contrast, the automobile market is international in scope, with domestic producers GM, Ford, and Chrysler accounting for about half of US automobile sales. If we ignore foreign competitors, then our estimate of industry concentration will be too high because it will ignore imported cars from Japan, Germany, and other countries.

Correctly defining the product boundary is equally important. If all products were reasonably homogeneous and distinct, product boundaries would be relatively clear: a banana supplier competes with other banana suppliers, and a peanut butter

---

[6] US Department of Justice and the Federal Trade Commission, *Horizontal Merger Guidelines*, April 2, 1992 and April 8, 1997. A comparison of the old with the new structural standard is difficult, because the new 2010 Merger Guidelines have more lenient standards and consider a broader set of factors. For further discussion of the 2010 Guidelines, see Chap. 20.

supplier competes with other peanut butter suppliers. Product boundaries become fuzzy, however, when products are imperfect substitutes.

When discussing product differentiation in Chap. 7, we said that the market includes goods that perform the same basic function, even though there are slight differences among brands (i.e., they have slightly different characteristics). Clearly, different brands of men's athletic shoes should be included in a market, but what about men's shoes and women's shoes? For most consumers, men's and women's shoes are poor substitutes. Another example is salt, where most suppliers produce a homogeneous good. Yet, road salt is not a substitute for table salt.

One way to identify a group of closely substitutable products is to estimate the cross-price elasticity of demand between products. Recall from Chap. 2 that the cross-price elasticity of demand between products i and j (η_{ij}) is defined as the percentage change in the quantity demanded of product i with respect to a small change in the price of good j. More formally, it is given by

$$\eta_{ij} \equiv \frac{\partial q_i}{\partial p_j} \frac{p_j}{q_i}. \tag{8.5}$$

The value of η_{ij} tells us how sharply demand for good i changes in response to an increase in the price of good j. When η_{ij} is large and positive, products i and j are considered close substitutes. We would anticipate a sizable cross-price elasticity for Coke and Pepsi, but what about Coke and Mountain Dew or Coke and orange juice? We would expect that the cross-price elasticity will be higher as we compare Coke to other brands of cola versus all brands of soft drinks or all beverages. Even with accurate estimates of η_{ij}, there is no clear cutoff value that we can use to decide which products belong to a particular market. Some judgment is required.

A more practical approach may be to consider the price movements of a class of like products in a particular geographic region. If prices are similar and move together over time, then products within the class are more likely to be close substitutes. For example, a 2010 Honda Civic Coupe is of similar size to a 2010 Porsche 911, but their price difference ($18,000 versus $79,000) indicates that they are in different markets. If one were to ask Honda dealers who are Civic competitors, they would likely identify a Ford Focus (retailing at $16,000), Subaru Impreza ($17,500), Toyota Corolla ($17,000), and VW Jetta ($18,000), not a 911 Porsche.

When investigating possible antitrust violations regarding horizontal mergers, the Department of Justice and the Federal Trade Commission have their own approach to defining a market.[7] According to their guidelines, a product's competitors include:

- All products to which buyers would switch if a firm raised the price of its product by 5%.
- The products of all potential competitors that would be expected to enter the market within 1 year if all existing firms raised their prices by 5%.

---

[7] US Department of Justice and the Federal Trade Commission, *Horizontal Merger Guidelines*, April 2, 1992 and April 8, 1997.

Although somewhat speculative, this definition acknowledges the importance of potential competition. A year is a short time though, so under this criterion potential competitors would include only those firms that can easily transform existing production capacity from one market to another. For example, it may be relatively quick and easy for a table salt producer to make the conversion to road salt production than for a road salt producer to make the conversion to table salt production.

To summarize, a relevant economic market should include all products that are close substitutes in consumption and production. Delineating a market requires that we draw appropriate geographic and product boundaries and consider all potential entrants.

8.3   The Extent of Industry Concentration in US Markets

In this section we discuss the degree of industry concentration in the USA. We begin by reviewing trends in **aggregate concentration**, the market share of total US sales that are produced by the largest corporations. Next, we list CR_4 and HHI for a sample of well-known industries. Finally, we analyze the trend in concentration for a single industry, the US brewing industry. The results show that aggregate concentration has been relatively stable over time; the level of concentration differs across industries; and concentration can change dramatically over time for an individual industry.

8.3.1   Aggregate Concentration

The leading US corporations have grown to enormous size, and their flagship brands are internationally recognized. In the USA, Wal-Mart was the largest in 2007, with total revenue of \$378 billion. Of the top 5, three are oil companies: Exxon Mobil (number 2), Chevron (3), and ConocoPhillips (5). The fourth is GM. Although some of the largest corporations focus on a single market, most are conglomerates, and their size does not necessarily translate to high concentration in any one industry. Nevertheless, there are concerns that large corporate size generates considerable economic power and political clout.

In spite of this concern, the evidence indicates that aggregate concentration has been fairly constant since the late 1950s. White (2002) investigated this issue by compiling data on the total market share (in terms of value added) for the largest 50 (CR_{50}), 100 (CR_{100}), and 200 (CR_{200}) corporations in the manufacturing sector of the economy. Although aggregate concentration rose between 1947 and 1958, the three measures were remarkably stable from 1958 to 1997 (see Table 8.4). The reader should be aware, however, that the largest US corporations have grown in absolute size as the overall economy has expanded.

Table 8.4 Aggregate concentration of the largest 50, 100, and 200 corporations in the manufacturing sector of the US economy

Year	CR_{50}	CR_{100}	CR_{200}
1947	17	23	30
1958	23	30	38
1963	25	33	41
1967	25	33	42
1970	24	33	43
1977	24	33	44
1982	24	33	43
1987	25	33	43
1992	24	32	42
1997	24	32	40
Mean	23.5	31.5	40.6

Note: Concentration for the manufacturing sector is based on value added (total revenue minus the cost of materials) for the largest 50, 100, and 200 corporations in the USA.
Source: White (2002).

Table 8.5 An example of NAICS subcategories

NAICS Code	Subdivision	Description
31	Sector	Manufacturing
312	Subsector	Beverage and tobacco manufacturing
3121	Industry Group	Beverage manufacturing
312111	Industry	Soft drink manufacturing
312112	Industry	Bottled water manufacturing
312120	Industry	Beer manufacturing
312130	Industry	Wine manufacturing
312140	Industry	Distilled spirits manufacturing

Note: Six-digit codes are used outside the USA.
Source: US Census Bureau, "Concentration Ratios in Manufacturing: 2002," at http://www.census.gov/prod/ec02/ec0231sr1.pdf

8.3.2   Concentration for Selected Industries

One source of concentration data is the US Bureau of the Census. The Census Bureau periodically publishes CR_4 and HHI, based on the North American Industry Classification System (NAICS).[8] The manufacturing and services areas of the economy are split into 20 sectors and are identified by two-digit codes. These are subdivided further into 100 subsectors (identified by three-digit codes), 317 industry groups (four-digit codes), and 1,179 industries (six-digit codes). Table 8.5 provides an example of the NAICS subdivisions for food manufacturing for various

---

[8] This system of classifying industries has been in effect since 1997. Prior to 1997, data were published according to the Standard Industrial Classification (SIC) system.

beverage industries. In terms of product boundary, the six-digit code comes closest to what we would call an economic market, such as soft drink manufacturing (312111) and wine manufacturing (312130).

Table 8.6 lists values of CR_4 and HHI for a set of well-known industries. The data show that concentration varies widely from industry to industry. Concentration for textile mills is very low, while concentration is extremely high in the market for electric light bulbs. The data also reveal a high degree of correlation between these two indices of concentration. In this sample, the correlation coefficient is 97.0%. In other studies for different samples and time periods, the correlation coefficient between CR_4 and HHI ranges from 0.929 to 0.992.[9]

The main drawback with the Census estimates of industry concentration is that they are based on the assumption that markets are national in scope. This geographic boundary is frequently incorrect, however. As discussed above, the market for cement is local, not national; therefore, the true level of industry concentration is higher than those found in Census estimates. Alternatively, the automobile industry in international in scope, and the national Census measures of concentration are too high. As a result, Census estimates of industry concentration must be used with caution.

8.3.3 Changes in Concentration for a Single Industry

Early studies following the structure–conduct–performance tradition maintained that market structure was exogenous and relatively stable over time (Bain 1956, 1959). As Table 8.7 reveals, CR_4 was relatively stable from 1963 through 1997 for petroleum refineries, pharmaceuticals, cement, tires and tubes, and soap and other detergents.[10] Nonetheless, critics of the structure–conduct–performance paradigm contend that market structure can be endogenous and change substantially over time.[11]

The US brewing industry has witnessed extensive changes in concentration since the 1930s. After the end of Prohibition in 1933, the number of independent mass-producing beer companies reached a peak at just over 700 brewers in 1938. These include companies such as Anheuser-Busch, Miller, Coors, and Pabst that brew traditional American lager beer, such as Budweiser, Miller Lite, Coors Light, and Pabst Blue Ribbon. Since then, the number has steadily declined to about 19 independent brewers today.[12]

---

[9] For a review of these studies, see Kwoka (1985), Scherer (1980, 58–59), and Scherer and Ross (1990, 72–73).

[10] A detailed comparison for all industries listed in Table 8.6 is not possible because some industries are defined differently in the NAICS system and the older SIC system.

[11] In particular, see Demsetz (1973), Peltzman (1975), and Sutton (1991). For a review of the literature, see Scherer (1980, Chap. 9) and Martin (2002, Chap. 6).

[12] This excludes microbrewers or specialty brewers that make European style ales and lagers and began entering the market in the mid 1960s. Although the number of specialty brewers exceeds 1,600 today, their combined market share is less than 6% and they generally compete for a different type of customer.

Table 8.6 Concentration indices for selected industries

Industry	CR$_4$	HHI
Textile mills	13.8	94
Sporting and athletic goods	21.4	161
Plastic pipes/fittings	24.8	241
Frozen fruit, juice, and vegetables	34.3	350
Book printing	32.0	364
Meat products	35.0	393
Petroleum refineries	28.5	422
Ice cream and frozen desserts	32.3	445
Iron and steel mills	32.7	445
Pharmaceutical and medicine	32.3	446
Computer and peripheral equipment	37.0	465
Cement	33.5	467
Dolls, toys, and games	40.0	496
Toiletries	38.6	564
Cookies, crackers, and pasta	41.7	602
Computers	40.0	658
Semiconductors	41.7	689
Women's footwear (except athletic)	49.5	795
Soft drinks	47.2	800
Men's and boy's suits and coats	42.0	846
Men's footwear (except athletic)	49.7	857
Telephone equipment	55.3	1,061
Distilleries	60.0	1,076
Aluminum sheet/plate/foil	65.0	1,447
Tires and inner tubes	68.4	1,518
Soap and other detergents	65.6	1,619
Household refrigerators and freezers	81.5	2,025
Automobiles	79.5	2,350
Breakfast cereals	82.9	2,446
Aircraft	84.8	–
Electric light bulbs	88.9	2,849
Motor vehicles and car bodies	87.0	–
Breweries	89.7	–
Cigarettes	98.9	–

Note: CR$_4$ is the four-firm concentration ratio measured in percent, and HHI is the Herfindahl–Hirschman index.
Source: US Census Bureau, "Concentration Ratios in Manufacturing: 2002," at http://www.census.gov/prod/ec02/ec0231sr1.pdf

Table 8.7 A sample of industries for which the four-firm concentration ratio (CR$_4$) is stable over time

Industry	CR$_4$	
	1963	1997
Petroleum refineries	34	29
Pharmaceuticals	22	32
Cement	29	34
Tires and inner tubes	70	68
Soap and other detergent	72	66

Source: US Census Bureau, "Concentration Ratios in Manufacturing," at http://www.census.gov/prod/ec02/ec0231sr1.pdf

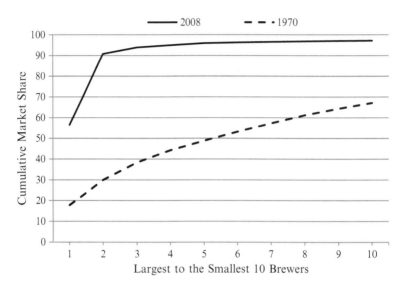

Fig. 8.2 Concentration curves for largest ten brewing companies

One way to see that concentration has increased in brewing is to compare concentration curves over time. Figure 8.2 plots concentration curves for the largest ten brewing companies in 1970 and 2008. Recall that a concentration curve identifies the cumulative market share, in this case based on total domestic beer consumption. Notice that the concentration curve is substantially higher in 2008, reflecting an increased level of industry concentration. It is also more convex in 2008 than in 1970 due to the fact that the largest firms now controlled a much larger share of the market. For example, the cumulative market share of the largest 2 firms (CR_2) was 30% in 1970 and 91% in 2008.[13]

The pattern of rising concentration in brewing can also be seen in Fig. 8.3, which plots CR_4 and HHI from 1947 to 2008. Both series reveal a dramatic and almost continuous increase in concentration.[14] For example, CR_4 rose from 44 to 94% and HHI rose from 7.08 to 43.29 from 1970 to 2008. Consistent with studies using data from other industries, the correlation coefficient between CR_4 and HHI is quite high, at 0.962.

The data in Figs. 8.2 and 8.3 must be interpreted with caution before 1970. CR_4 and HHI are for the nation as a whole, but the market was regional in scope until the

---

[13] In 1970, the two largest firms were the Anheuser-Busch and Miller brewing companies. In 2008, they were Anheuser-Busch and MillerCoors (the combined sales of the Miller and Coors brewing companies which formed a joint venture in 2008).

[14] To compare it to CR_4, HHI is divided by 100 so that it ranges from 0 to 100.

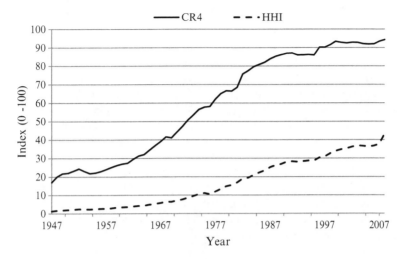

Fig. 8.3 The four-firm concentration ratio and the Herfindahl–Hirschman Index in the US brewing industry, 1947–2008

late 1960s.[15] Given that the market was national by 1970, the Merger Guidelines would classify the brewing industry as unconcentrated before 1974, moderately concentrated from 1974 through 1981 (when HHI rose from 0.1053 to 0.1691), and highly concentrated from 1982 on (with HHI exceeding 0.1800 after 1981).

8.4   The Determinants of Market Structure

We have seen that the level of industry concentration varies across industries and can change considerably over time. In this section, we investigate the main reasons why concentration is high in some industries and low in others.

8.4.1   Gibrat's Law

One of the simplest reasons why industry concentration may increase over time was proposed by Gibrat (1931), who considered the effect of luck on concentration.[16] His analysis assumes an industry that initially had a fixed number of equal sized firms. For our purposes, assume 50 firms, each with a market share of 2%, implying a CR_4 of 8% and an HHI of 200. Over time, firms experience an increase in sales and face the same growth distribution. In this example, the distribution is normal, with a mean

---

[15] For a more complete discussion of the geographic market in brewing, see V. Tremblay and C. Tremblay (2005, Chap. 3).

[16] For an excellent review of the influence of Gibrat's work, see Sutton (1997).

growth rate of 6% and a standard deviation of 16%.[17] This means that firm growth is simply a random event. The key point is that even though the average growth rate is 6%, some firms will be lucky and grow at a faster rate than average, while others will be unlucky and grow at a slower rate. Given these circumstances, Gibrat asked whether or not industry concentration would remain constant over time.

The answer is somewhat surprising. As time goes on, some firms gain market share due to a string of good luck, while persistently unlucky firms lose share. Thus, even though firms start out the same and face the same distribution in growth rates, firm size becomes skewed over time, approaching a lognormal distribution.[18] As a result, the concentration curve shifts upwards, implying higher concentration. This is called Gibrat's Law of Proportionate Effect, or simply **Gibrat's Law**. To illustrate Gibrat's Law, Scherer and Ross (1990, 141–146) ran a simulation of an industry with these characteristics. They found that the distribution of firm size became more skewed over time and that CR_4 rose from period to period, starting out at 8% in period 1 and averaging 54.7% by period 140.

One concern with Gibrat's Law is that it provides no economic rationale for industry concentration; it is simply due to pure chance. There are certainly aspects of business where luck is important. As we will see in Chap. 14, there is an element of luck with advertising. Ex ante, all firms have high expectations for their upcoming advertising campaigns even though only a fraction of them are successful ex post. Thus, lucky firms with successful ad campaigns experience greater growth than their competitors. Nevertheless, advertising agencies would argue that there is more to successful advertising than pure luck.

Consequently, it is highly unlikely that Gibrat's Law is the only explanation for high concentration. After all, industry concentration does not always rise over time. We have already seen in Table 8.7 that concentration has remained relatively constant for petroleum refineries, pharmaceuticals, cement, tires and tubes, and soap and other detergents. In addition, concentration has fallen in some industries. Thus, other forces must also come into play. One example is greater globalization, which can decrease concentration by increasing the number of competitors and reducing the market share of industry leaders, as in the automobile industry. A second example is technological change, which can lower concentration if it favors smaller firms or raise concentration if it favors larger firms.

Another mark against Gibrat's Law is that the prediction that the size distribution will be lognormal does not appear to be true empirically. After reviewing the evidence, Schmalensee (1989, 994) concludes that "all families of distributions so far fail to describe at least some industries well." Thus, the process generating firm size distributions appears to be more complex than that postulated by Gibrat.

Perhaps the strongest piece of evidence to suggest that chance is not the only determinant of concentration is a fairly consistent pattern of industry concentration

---

[17] See the Mathematics and Econometrics Appendix at the end of the book for a review of a normal distribution and a standard deviation.

[18] In a lognormal distribution, the logarithm of firm size is normally distributed.

Table 8.8 The four-firm concentration ratio by country

Industry	Country						
	USA	France	Germany	Italy	Japan	UK	Mean
Processed Meat[a]	19	23	22	11	51	–	25
Bread[a]	25	5	7	4	48	58	25
Sugar confectionary	27	51	39	29	48	38	39
Sugar[a]	46	81	69	72	42	94	67
Canned vegetables[a]	50	40	–	80	–	81	63
Flour[a]	55	29	38	7	67	78	46
Pet food	64	86	93	–	39	83	73
Biscuits	68	62	49	46	49	62	56
Mineral water	–	77	27	55	62	73	59
Soup	75	91	84	–	71	75	79
Beer	81	82	25	55	99	59	67
Salt[a]	82	98	93	80	–	99	90
Breakfast cereal	86	–	–	–	–	79	83
Soft drinks	89	70	57	84	88	48	72
Baby foods	90	88	83	88	–	80	86

Source: Sutton (1991, 106).
[a]Sutton identifies these markets as having relatively homogeneous goods and receiving little advertising support. The remaining are classified as advertising-intensive industries.

across nations (Schmalensee 1989, 992). In their study of six nations,[19] Scherer et al. (1975) found that the markets for cigarettes, bottles, refrigerators, and batteries tended to be highly concentrated in every nation, while the markets for weaving, paints, and shoes tended to be unconcentrated in every nation. In a more recent study, Sutton (1991) finds very similar results (see Table 8.8). This evidence indicates that when industry concentration is high (low) in one nation, it tends to be high (low) in others.

Although luck may be a factor, previous evidence is sufficiently strong to conclude that systematic forces play a dominant role in shaping industry concentration. For this reason, we focus the remainder of our attention on market and strategic rather than random forces that can influence market structure.

8.4.2 Concentration and Barriers to Entry

Fundamentally, entry conditions play a key role in determining industry concentration. Perfectly competitive markets have many producers because the cost of entry and exit is zero. In contrast, barriers to entry insulate a sole firm in a monopoly market from competition. In this section, we discuss in more detail what is meant by a barrier to entry and outline the primary types of barriers that restrict entry and lead to high levels of industry concentration.

---

[19] These are the USA, Canada, the UK, Sweden, France, and Germany.

Economists have defined the concept of a barrier to entry in several different ways.[20] Bain (1959) defines it as a market condition that raises the cost of entering the market to such an extent that incumbent firms earn long-run economic profits. Of course, even a monopoly firm can lose money in the short run and earn zero profit in the long run. Stigler (1968) argues that a barrier to entry exists only if the cost of entry is higher for new entrants than it was for established firms. Finally, von Weizsacker (1980) defines a barrier as a limitation on entry that is socially undesirable.

On the surface, one might think that any constraint on entry is socially undesirable, but this need not be the case. For instance, a patent gives a firm a 20 year monopoly to a new invention, thus eliminating all entry. Yet, this barrier to entry is generally thought to be socially beneficial, because it encourages innovation and dynamic efficiency. Although von Weizsacker's welfare based definition of a barrier to entry is appealing, its main weakness is that it substantially complicates our use of the concept. His perspective does remind us though that if we define a barrier as a cost of entry, then we are ignoring its welfare implication (Martin 2002, 343).

In this book, we take a pragmatic approach, defining a **barrier to entry** to include any limitation on entry that keeps the long-run equilibrium number of firms below the number that would exist in a competitive market. With this definition, there are no barriers to entry in the perfectly competitive and monopolistically competitive models because they both have many competitors. Barriers do exist in a monopoly market with just one firm and in an oligopoly market with just a few competitors. Again, this definition is consistent with what most people mean by entry barrier and is easy to use, but it does not rule out the possibility that a particular barrier is welfare enhancing.

Baumol et al. (1982) show that entry barriers are closely linked to sunk costs, expenditures that cannot be recovered if the firm exits the market. Suppose that you plan to start a new business that requires a $1 billion investment. You apply for a loan, and the first thing that the loan manager asks is what you will put up for collateral. Unless you are extremely wealthy, your answer will depend on your plans for the money. If you are purchasing a factory that will be worth $1 billion if you were to go out of business, then there is no sunk cost associated with the investment and you can use the factory as collateral. If, on the other hand, your investment is speculative, such as hiring scientists to find a cure for the common cold, then most if not all of your investment is a sunk cost. If unsuccessful, the money invested evaporates and is not recoverable. Of these two investment opportunities, which do think would be easier to raise the $1 billion? Obviously, the investment with no sunk cost carries no risk to you or the bank, and financing would be relatively easy to obtain. Accordingly, entry barriers are closely tied to sunk costs.

Another important aspect of entry barriers is that they can be either exogenously or endogenously determined. By exogenous barriers we mean that firms in the industry

---

[20] For examples of different definitions of barriers to entry, see Bain (1956), Stigler (1968), von Weizsacker (1980), and McAfee et al. (2004).

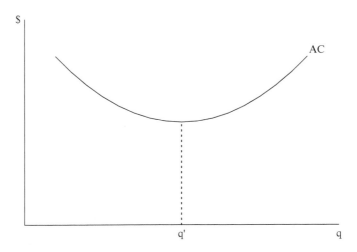

Fig. 8.4 Long-run average cost curve and minimum efficient scale (MES)

have no control over them. Exogenous determinants of entry barriers might derive from basic demand and cost conditions, because demand conditions are determined by consumers and cost conditions are technologically determined.[21] They can also include government regulations that legally restrict entry. Examples include a patent or a government franchise that limits the number of competitors, such as your local cable television company. Barriers that are caused by basic economic conditions are called **natural barriers to entry**. Those that are caused by government restrictions are called **legal barriers to entry**. We postpone discussion of them until Chap. 20.

Barriers that are endogenous are sometimes called **strategic barriers to entry** because they are under the control of firms in the industry and are specifically designed to deter entry. These include a variety of predatory activities that are profitable only because they drive existing competitors out of business or deter potential competitors from entering the market. Examples include predatory pricing, where price is cut below unit cost, and actions that raise rival costs. In the sections below, we illustrate how natural and strategic entry barriers affect industry concentration.

8.4.2.1   Concentration and Natural Barriers to Entry

Natural barriers are determined by market demand and cost conditions. We saw in Chap. 2 that economies of scale exist when the long-run average cost (AC) curve has a negative slope. This is illustrated in Fig. 8.4, where there are economies of scale until output reaches q'. Beyond q', AC has a positive slope, indicating

---

[21] Of course, firms could invest in research and development, which can change technology and lead to an increase or a decrease in scale economies.

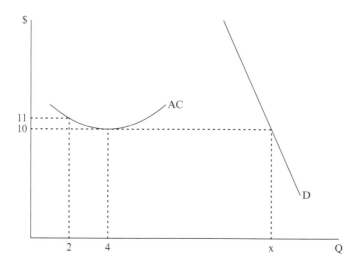

Fig. 8.5   Demand and cost conditions that support a natural oligopoly

diseconomies of scale. Recall from Chap. 2 that the smallest output for which AC is at its minimum, q', is called minimum efficient scale (MES).

One way to see how demand and cost conditions affect entry barriers and concentration is to review the theory of a natural monopoly (discussed in Chap. 6). A natural monopoly occurs when there are substantial scale economies relative to the size of the market (represented by market demand), making it productively inefficient to have more than one firm produce total market output. If there are many firms, each firm can lower its cost by merging with a competitor, a process that will continue to be profitable until there is just one firm left in the market. In this case, demand and cost conditions make it productively efficient and most profitable for a single firm to serve the market.

We can generalize this idea to the case of n firms by considering the demand and cost structure described in Fig. 8.5. Consistent with the notation used previously, AC is long-run average cost and D represents market demand. In this example, MES equals 4 (million units), which corresponds to an average cost of $10. Baumol et al. (1982) define the **cost-minimizing industry structure** as the number of firms in an industry that are needed to produce industry output (x) at minimum cost, which equals x/MES $= n*$.[22] When this occurs, the industry is productively efficient. To demonstrate, when x equals 20, five symmetric firms minimize the total cost of producing $x = 20$ by each producing at MES $= 4$. Thus, the cost-minimizing industry structure is five firms.

In this example, notice that total industry cost is not minimized when the number of firms differs from five. Take the case of ten symmetric firms, each producing two units. In this case, AC $= \$11$, and the total industry cost of producing 20 million

---

[22] Here, we assume that x/MES produces an integer, thus avoiding problems with fractions.

units is $220 million. With five firms, AC = $10, and the total industry cost of producing 20 is only $200 million. Thus, firms have an incentive to merge, as this will lower production costs and raise profits. This example describes a **natural oligopoly**, because demand and cost conditions make it productively efficient and most profitable for there to be just a few firms in the market.

The concept of a cost-minimizing industry structure provides a simple way of showing how scale economies in relation to the size of the market affect industry concentration. That is, when x is small and the cost minimizing number of firms is 1, then the industry is a natural monopoly. If x is very large, then the industry is naturally competitive. At intermediate values of x, we have the natural oligopoly. Thus, when scale economies increase (decrease), causing MES to shift right (left), the cost minimizing number of firms decreases (increases) and concentration rises (falls). When demand increases (decreases), the cost minimizing number of firms increases (decreases) and concentration falls (rises).

8.4.2.2 Concentration and Strategic Barriers to Entry

There has been extensive research on strategic entry deterrence, beginning with the seminal works of Bain (1956), Modigliani (1958), and Sylos-Labini (1962). To illustrate the basic idea, consider a two-stage game with an incumbent firm, a monopolist (M), and a potential entrant (PE). In the first stage, PE must decide whether to enter the market or not. In the second stage, M must decide whether to fight entry or not. Fighting means that M will expand output by lowering price if PE enters the market. This is called a predatory pricing strategy and is designed to maintain or gain a monopoly position. The question is, will M's threat to fight effectively keep PE out of the market?

The extensive form of this game is shown in Fig. 8.6. In this example, if entry does not take place, M's profits are 100. With entry and no price cutting, both firms earn profits of 30. With price cutting, both firms earn profits of 10. For price cutting to be an optimal strategy for M, it must be profitable to fight in the second stage of the game once PE enters the market. You can see from the figure that this is not true, as M's profits are 10 if it fights and 30 if it does not fight. If we assume that information is perfect and complete, PE can look forward and see that M will not fight. As a result, PE will enter because its profits are 30 if it enters (given that M will not fight) and 0 if it does not enter. Thus, the subgame perfect Nash equilibrium (SPNE) to this game is for PE to enter and M not to fight.[23]

---

[23] There are certain market settings where limit pricing can be effective. For example, Milgrom and Roberts (1982) show that limit pricing can effectively block entry when there is incomplete information. In their model, M has either the same or lower costs than PE, but only M knows if it is a low or a high cost producer. They show that if the probability that M is a low cost producer is sufficiently low, then it may be optimal for a high cost M to behave like a low cost M by charging a low price. This action will deter entry of PE.

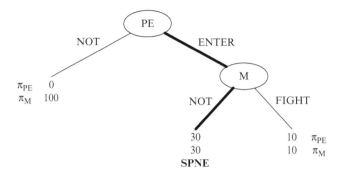

Fig. 8.6 Entry game with a potential entrant (PE) and a monopolist (M)

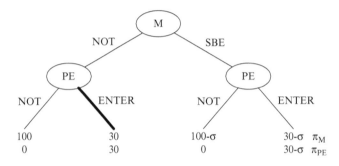

Fig. 8.7 Entry game with a strategic barrier to entry (SBE)

The reason why this strategy does not effectively deter entry is that the threat to fight is merely cheap talk and is not credible, the same problem we found in the bank robber game in Chap. 3. That is, even if M announces before play that it will fight, once PE enters it is not rational to follow through with the threat. It is not a SPNE strategy to fight. For a strategic barrier to be effective, it must be based on a threat that is credible.

One way to make such a threat credible is to formally commit to a course of action before entry takes place. M may commit to an investment that raises the sunk cost of doing business for both M and PE. Examples include investments in advertising or in research and development. That is, if M invests in research and development to improve the quality of its product, PE must do the same to remain competitive. Will an investment that raises the sunk costs of both firms deter entry?

To analyze this problem, we consider the dynamic game described in Fig. 8.7. In the first stage, M either invests in the strategic barrier to entry (SBE) or not. When M invests in the SBE, this raises the cost to both firms by $\sigma > 0$. Notice that

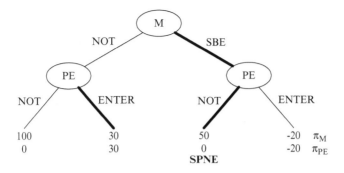

Fig. 8.8 Entry game with a strategic barrier to entry and $\sigma = 50$

M will not invest in SBE if there is no threat of entry, because M earns 100 with no SBE and earns $100 - \sigma$ with SBE. In this example, it clearly pays for PE to enter if M does not invest in the SBE. With the threat of entry, M can successfully deter entry by investing in SBE if $30 < \sigma < 70$. To demonstrate, notice that:

- The SBE fails to deter entry when $\sigma < 30$, because PE's dominant strategy is to enter when $\sigma < 30$. Thus, σ must exceed 30 to deter entry.
- It is unprofitable for M to invest in SBE when $\sigma > 70$. If M does not invest in the SBE, then PE enters and M earns 30. If M invests in SBE and $\sigma > 30$, then PE will not enter and M earns $100 - \sigma$. Thus, it will not be profitable for M to invest in SBE if $\sigma > 70$.
- This implies that M can successfully deter entry by investing in SBE if σ ranges from 30 to 70.

To provide a more specific example, consider the case where $\sigma = 50$, as described in Fig. 8.8. In this example, PE enters with no SBE and does not enter with SBE. M's payoff is 30 with no SBE and 50 with SBE. Thus, the SPNE strategy is for M to invest in SBE and PE to refrain from entry; SBE successfully deters entry and keeps concentration high.

This example shows the inefficiency that can result from a strategic barrier to entry. First, it preserves the monopolist's position, which is allocatively inefficient. Second, M invests in SBE only because it deters entry. As a result, it is socially wasteful because it is costly and serves no purpose other than to insulate the incumbent monopolist from competition.

8.4.3 Sutton's Theory of Sunk Costs and Concentration

According to Sutton (1991, 1999), sunk costs play a key role in determining industry concentration. Sutton uses the following game to illustrate the main idea. Firms compete in two stages or periods:

I. In the first stage, they must decide whether to enter the market, which requires a start-up cost that is a sunk cost.[24]

II. In the second stage, firms compete in output (or price).

There are two possible market settings. In the first, sunk costs are exogenous. This is similar to the case above where natural barriers to entry affect industry concentration. In the second, sunk costs are endogenous, an assumption that leads to considerably different results.

8.4.3.1 Exogenous Sunk Costs and Concentration

To begin, we consider a simple version of Sutton's model with exogenous sunk costs. Suppose that there is a market with n symmetric firms that produce homogeneous goods. To enter the market before competition begins (in stage I), firms must pay a set-up (quasi-fixed) cost ($\sigma > 0$) which is exogenously determined and sunk. Total revenue at the industry level (TR) is defined as n times firm i's total revenue ($p \cdot q_i$), where p is price and q_i is firm i's output. Once competition commences in stage II, a firm's price–cost margin (PCM) is defined as $(p - c)/p$, where c is the marginal cost of production, and firm i's profit is $\pi_i = (p - c)q_i$.

Sutton analyzed this model to determine the effect of sunk costs, market size, and the degree of competition on industry concentration. In the first stage of the game, firms enter the market as long as profits exceed σ. Entry continues until

$$\sigma = (p - c)q_i. \tag{8.6}$$

By multiplying and dividing through by p on the right-hand side of (8.6), we can rewrite this equation as

$$\sigma = \frac{(p - c)}{p}pq_i$$
$$= \text{PCM} \cdot pq_i. \tag{8.7}$$

Recall that TR $= n \cdot pq_i$ and $1/n =$ HHI when firms are symmetric and market share is measured as a decimal. If we multiply both sides of the equality in the second line of (8.7) by n, then it can be rewritten as

$$\frac{1}{n} = \text{HHI} = \frac{\sigma}{\text{PCM} \cdot \text{TR}}. \tag{8.8}$$

---

[24] Sutton (2007, p. 2359) argues that if fixed costs are not sunk, then many of Sutton's conclusions are invalid because it would then be more appropriate to assume that firms play a static rather than a dynamic game. When an investment such as this is made before any output is produced, it is a quasi-fixed cost (see Chap. 2).

Fig. 8.9 The relationship
between concentration
and market size when
sunk costs are exogenous

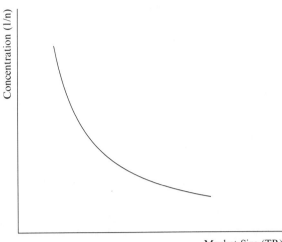

This formulation of the equilibrium has three important implications:

1. Concentration (HHI) increases with sunk costs (σ).
2. An increase in the size of the market (TR) causes concentration to fall.
3. Tougher competition, which decreases profits (PCM), causes concentration to increase.

The first two implications are consistent with those found in our discussion of natural barriers to entry. That is, as start-up costs or MES increases relative to the size of the market (i.e., market demand), concentration increases. The last implication is somewhat surprising: as firm behavior becomes more competitive, moving from monopoly (or collusive) to perfect competition, concentration rises. Sutton calls this the "toughness of competition," and his model implies that tougher competition leads to lower profits, which in turn reduces entry and raises concentration. This is a valuable contribution because it provides one mechanism by which firm behavior affects market structure.

With exogenous sunk costs and intermediate levels of competition, those between cartel and perfect competition, the level of concentration continues to fall as the market expands (see Fig. 8.9).[25] Although this relationship seems natural and appears to hold for many industries, Sutton shows that it does not always hold in markets with differentiated goods where advertising and research and development are significant features of the industry. This observation motivated his work on markets with endogenous sunk costs.

---

[25] Sutton assumed a Cournot model which produces an outcome that lies between cartel and perfect competition. We will discuss the Cournot model in Chap. 10.

8.4.3.2   Endogenous Sunk Costs and Concentration

Sutton's model becomes considerably more complex when sunk costs are endogenous because market structure, firm conduct, and industry performance are now determined simultaneously. The key difference in the endogenous case is that products differ in real or perceived quality, and firms can make sunk cost investments in the first period of the game to improve product quality.[26] Thus, sunk cost investments can cause firms to differ in terms of their competitive fitness. One type of sunk cost investment is research and development, which can enable a firm to gain a real quality advantage over its competitors. Alternatively, a firm may invest in advertising that improves product "image" by informing consumers of the real or perceived quality advantages of the advertised brand.

In this model, an increase in the size of the market is assumed to induce firms to boost their sunk cost investments to enhance the quality of their products.[27] We will see in later chapters that this is generally true for advertising and for research and development, as expenditures in these areas usually rise with sales.

Under these conditions, Sutton's model predicts one strikingly different result from the case of exogenous sunk costs: an increase in the size of the market will not lower industry concentration below some minimum level of concentration. We illustrate this prediction in Fig. 8.10. The intuition behind this result is as follows. As in the case with exogenous sunk costs, an increase in the size of the market raises industry profits which induces entry and puts downward pressure on industry concentration. There is an additional force at work, however, when sunk costs are endogenous. Market growth also induces firms to make investments to improve product quality, which raises sunk costs, lowers profits, and puts upward pressure on concentration. This latter effect keeps concentration from falling below a positive lower bound as the size of the market increases.[28]

---

[26] Recall from Chap. 7 that differentiation can be vertical (e.g., quality differences) or horizontal (e.g., location differences). Because assuming vertical (quality) differentiation produces such dramatically different results, we focus on vertical differentiation here (found in Sutton 1991, Chap. 3). When differentiation is horizontal, Sutton shows that the relationship between concentration and market size is less precise than for the homogeneous goods case found in Fig. 8.9 (see Sutton 1991, pp. 37–42). With horizontal differentiation, acceptable concentration and market size values include the curve and all points to the north and east of the curve in Fig. 8.9. This is called a "bounds approach," because the model provides bounds on the set of outcomes rather than pinning down a precise relationship.

[27] For example, if quality is a normal good, an increase in consumer income could increase sales and the demand for quality, which would induce firms to increase the quality of their products.

[28] In his work on research and development and sunk costs, Sutton (1999, 2007) also argues that concentration can vary, depending upon the type of technological trajectories that are characteristic of an industry. If, for example, goods are relatively homogeneous and firms compete in research and development that is designed to lower production cost (i.e., they follow a single technical trajectory), as in the aircraft industry, then concentration tends to rise over time and remain high. Alternatively, when many submarkets or niche markets exist, as in the flowmeter (i.e., devices that control the flow of gases and liquids through pipes) industry, firms may choose to compete in one or a few submarkets and pursue a proliferation of technical trajectories. This tends to keep concentration from increasing over time.

Fig. 8.10 The relationship between concentration and market size when sunk costs are endogenous

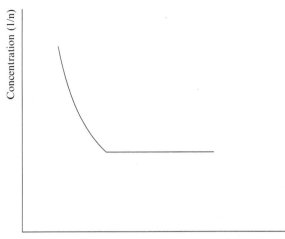

The two predictions illustrated in Figs. 8.8 and 8.9 can be summarized by **Sutton's Limit Theorem**: when sunk costs are exogenous, concentration converges to zero as market size increases; when sunk costs are endogenous, concentration converges to a lower bound that is above zero. The empirical implications of Sutton's work are clear: (1) In industries where sunk costs are exogenous, the level of concentration for a particular industry should be relatively low in large countries and relatively high in small countries. (2) In industries where there are sunk cost investments on such things as advertising and research and development, concentration should be unaffected by the size of the economy. (3) Higher levels of competition produce higher levels of concentration.

8.5 Survey and Empirical Evidence

We have seen previously that the level of industry concentration varies across industries and can change considerably over time. In this section, we summarize the empirical evidence regarding the causes of industry concentration.

Early empirical studies found general support for the hypothesis that demand and cost conditions influence industry concentration. After surveying the evidence, Schmalensee (1989) concludes:

- When concentration in a particular industry is high (low) in one country, it is frequently high (low) in other countries.
- Concentration tends to be positively correlated with MES and capital intensity.
- Outside the USA, mergers are an important cause of high industry concentration.

The reason why mergers have had a lesser effect on US concentration is that antimerger laws are generally more restrictive in the USA. The first two implications are consistent with the hypothesis that natural barriers to entry increase industry concentration. This is not surprising, since MES is likely to be similar across countries.

After reviewing the same evidence, Scherer and Ross (1990, 141) add that "actual concentration in US manufacturing industry appears to be considerably higher than the imperatives of scale economies require." This implies that strategic investments in sunk costs may also play a role, as the work of Sutton and others suggest. Kessides (1990) confirms this viewpoint, finding empirical support for the hypothesis that high sunk costs lead to high levels of industry concentration in a diverse sample of industries.

Smiley (1988) conducted a revealing survey of 293 product managers from major corporations to determine the importance of strategic entry deterrence in the USA. He found that over half indicated that entry deterring activity is as important as other strategic marketing and production decisions. In addition, firms refrained from strategic entry deterring activity when entry was unlikely, entry was inevitable, and when entry deterrence was too costly.

Smiley also tried to identify strategies that are frequently used to limit entry. The survey asked whether a particular entry deterring strategy was common practice in the industry based on a five-point scale, with five meaning frequently and one meaning never. For both new and mature industries, the survey addressed eight potentially important practices that are designed to make entry less attractive:

1. Advertising: Use advertising to create brand loyalty (brand names) and raise sunk costs.
2. Hide profits: Hide excess profits of a particular product from competitors by producing a multitude of products.[29] This applies to mature industries.
3. Brand proliferation: Offer a wide range of brands within an industry to fill all product niches. This applies to mature industries.
4. Research and development (R&D): Invest in R&D to develop new patents and increase sunk costs.
5. Reputation: Develop a reputation for competitiveness, through communication to the media or by past behavior.
6. Learning curve: Expand output today to gain experience and lower future costs. This applies to new industries.
7. Excess capacity: Build an especially large plant to meet all expected future demand.
8. Limit pricing: Choose a sufficiently low price.

The main results of Smiley's study are summarized in Table 8.9. It reports the percent of respondents who indicated that a particular strategy was frequently used in their industry (i.e., had a score of 3 or above). The figures reveal that firms in the real

---

[29] Stigler (1966, 227) puts it this way: "if one can conceal the profitability of his situation, entry will be slower."

Table 8.9 Frequency of strategic entry deterring strategies

	New products	Mature products
Advertising	62%	52%
Hide profits	–	59
Brand proliferation	–	57
R&D patent	56	31
Reputation	27	27
Learning curve	26	–
Excess capacity	22	21
Limit pricing[a]	9	21

[a] These are averages for static limit pricing and dynamic limit pricing.
Source: Smiley (1988).

world use a variety of methods to deter entry. The most prevalent tactics, with scores above 50%, are advertising, hiding profits, brand proliferation, and R&D. Smiley also found that R&D activity is less important in mature industries. Given their importance, much of our attention in upcoming chapters will be devoted to these strategic variables.

Regarding empirical evidence, there is considerable support for Sutton's (1991) theory of market structure. To test his theory, Sutton collected data from twenty food and beverage industries in six countries. These were divided into two groups: those with homogeneous goods and little or no advertising and those with moderate to high levels of advertising.[30] As Table 8.8 indicates, concentration is generally higher for the advertising-intensive group.

Sutton also used regression analysis to determine the effect of market size on concentration for these two groups. The simplest version of the model is presented below:

$$CR_4 = \beta_0 + \beta_1 \ln\left(\frac{TR}{\sigma}\right) + \beta_2 x, \tag{8.9}$$

where the βs are regression parameters, TR is industry sales or total revenue, σ measures start-up costs (i.e., the size of an efficient plant), and x is a vector of other control variables.[31] Sutton's theory predicts that β_1 will be negative for markets with homogeneous goods and 0 for advertising-intensive markets, which is exactly what he found. The regression estimate of β_1 was -0.187 ($t = 3.2$) for homogeneous-goods markets and was -0.02 ($t = 0.63$) for advertising-intensive markets. Thus, endogenous sunk costs associated with advertising appear to substantially diminish the effect of the size of the market on industry concentration.

---

[30] Sutton (1999) also finds support for his theory when research and development expenditures are the primary source of sunk costs.

[31] Control variables include dummy variables for countries and industries; β_2 is a vector of parameters conformable to x. For further discussion, see Sutton (1991, Chaps. 4 and 5).

More recently, Ellickson (2007) analyzed Sutton's model using data from regional US supermarkets. Rather than competing in advertising, Ellickson found that supermarkets competed by offering a greater selection of products. If Sutton's model is correct, an increase in the size of the market should induce firms to build larger stores and offer greater product variety. This in turn would raise sunk costs and keep concentration from falling as the market expands. Ellickson discovered that as individual markets grew, concentration (measured by CR_1, CR_2, CR_4, CR_8, CR_{20}, and HHI) remained virtually unchanged.

Symeonidis (2000, 2001) tested the implication of Sutton's model that greater competition leads to higher industry concentration. He analyzed a natural experiment in the UK in the 1960s when the laws against cartel behavior were strengthened. By reviewing data from a general class of manufacturing industries, he found strong support for Sutton's work. Stiffer laws against cartels resulted in greater price competition, which increased industry concentration by diminishing the number of firms through exit or merger.[32]

Although there is general support for Sutton's work, we should keep one caveat in mind. As Sutton (1991, Chap. 9) points out, sunk costs are not all that matter in the evolution of market structure. History and the idiosyncratic characteristics of an industry may also have influence. One example is when a firm has a first-mover advantage and gains a dominant position, resulting in high levels of concentration. For example, Alcoa gained an early advantage by being the first to acquire aluminum ore deposits in the USA. Similarly, Anheuser-Busch benefitted from locating its first brewery on land with deep caves that could be used to store beer at cool temperatures. This gave the company a strategic advantage before the advent of refrigeration. In any case, the evidence clearly shows that high sunk costs can be an important contributor to high industry concentration.

8.6   Summary

1. Market structure refers to the way in which a market is organized. Markets fall into one of four broad categories: perfect competition, monopoly, monopolistic competition, and oligopoly.

2. An **oligopoly** market consists of just a few competitors in which products are homogeneous or differentiated. The key feature of this market structure is strategic interaction, in that a firm's profits depend on the actions of rival firms as well as its own actions. Thus, game theory is used in oligopoly modeling. Oligopoly is the most common market structure in the US economy.

---

[32] Other studies include Robinson and Chiang (1996) for a sample of US consumer goods industries, Matraves (1999) for the global pharmaceutical industry, Lyons et al. (2001) for a sample of industries in the European Union, and V. Tremblay and C. Tremblay (2005) for the US brewing industry. See Sutton (2007) for a more extensive survey of the empirical evidence.

3. A key element of market structure is industry concentration, which is described by the number and size distribution of firms. Competitive and monopolistically competitive industries have many firms of equal size, and a monopoly has just one firm. There are only a few firms in an oligopoly market, and firms may or may not be symmetric in size.

4. A **concentration curve** provides a visualization of industry concentration. It plots the market share of the largest firm, the two largest firms, the three largest firms, and so on for all firms in the industry. A linear concentration curve implies that firms are of equal size. Fewer firms and a more unequal distribution of firm size shift the curve up and to the left, implying a greater level of industry concentration.

5. It is useful, especially in empirical work, to identify concentration with a single index. Ideally, such an index should increase with the number of firms and with the extent of inequality in the distribution of market shares. We have discussed three indices of industry concentration:

   1. The **number of firms** (n). This is an unsatisfactory index unless firms are symmetric.
   2. The **k-firm concentration ratio** (CR_k), which measures the market share of the largest k firms in the industry. The main advantage of this index is that it is easy to calculate. However, it provides no information about the distribution of market shares among the largest k firms, and it ignores firms outside the largest k firms. Thus, it does not always provide a ranking of industry concentration that is consistent with a concentration curve.
   3. The **Herfindahl–Hirschman index** (HHI), which equals the sum of squared market shares of all firms in the industry. Although the calculation of HHI requires a great deal of data, it has the desirable qualities of increasing with the number of competitors and with the inequality of the distribution of firm sales. When market share is measured as a decimal, $HHI = n\sigma^2 + 1/n$, where σ^2 is the variance of firm market share. This implies that when firms are symmetric (i.e., $\sigma^2 = 0$), $HHI = 1/n$. The relationship that $n = 1/HHI$ is called a **numbers equivalent** because it implies that a given value of HHI can be translated into a number of equal sized firms.

6. A **dominant firm** has a larger market share than its competitors and typically takes a leadership role in choosing price or output. Dominance can result from producing a superior product or from producing at lower cost than competitors.

7. Experts use CR_4 and HHI measures of concentration to distinguish between competitive and oligopoly markets. In terms of CR_4, an industry is classified as oligopolistic once CR_4 reaches 40%. The Department of Justice and the Federal Trade Commission use the following delineation:

   - An industry is classified as unconcentrated when HHI is less than 1,000.
   - An industry is classified as moderately concentrated when HHI ranges from 1,000 to less than 1,800.
   - An industry is classified as highly concentrated when HHI is greater than or equal to 1,800.

8. A critical step in measuring concentration is to properly define the market. The relevant product market includes all products that are close substitutes in consumption and production. Identifying a market also requires the proper definition of the geographic boundary, as markets may be local, regional, national, or international.

9. **Aggregate concentration** is defined as the market share of total US sales that are produced by the largest corporations. Although there are concerns that massive corporate size may provide firms with political and economic power, aggregate concentration has remained relatively stable over the last 50 years.

10. A review of concentration in US industries reveals the following:

    • Concentration varies considerably from industry to industry.
    • Although concentration is relatively stable over time in some industries, it has changed dramatically in others.
    • Across countries, when industry concentration is high (low) in one nation, it tends to be high (low) in other nations.

11. A number of forces cause industry concentration to be high. One is described by **Gibrat's Law**, which says that luck or random shocks to firm growth rates can cause the distribution of firm size to become more skewed, thus raising industry concentration. Traditionally, **barriers to entry** are viewed as the fundamental cause of high concentration. A barrier to entry is defined as any limitation on entry that keeps the long-run equilibrium number of firms below the competitive number. Barriers to entry are classified into three groups: natural barriers, legal barriers, and strategic barriers. **Natural barriers** exist when demand and cost conditions limit the number of firms. **Legal barriers** include government regulations that legally restrict entry. In general, natural and legal barriers are exogenously determined. **Strategic barriers** include all predatory actions of firms that limit entry. These are clearly endogenous barriers to entry.

12. The **cost-minimizing industry structure** is defined as the number of firms needed to produce industry output at minimum cost. When industry cost minimization occurs, the industry is productively efficient. In the case of oligopoly (monopoly), the cost-minimizing industry structure is normally determined by natural barriers to entry. A **natural oligopoly** (monopoly) occurs when the cost-minimizing industry structure is just a few firms (one firm).

13. High sunk costs can be a barrier to entry because a sunk cost represents an expenditure that cannot be recovered when the firm exits the industry.

14. Sutton (1991) developed a model where sunk costs have a critical effect on industry concentration. His model predicts that concentration increases with sunk costs and the vigor of competition. Sutton's model also shows that the effect of sunk costs on industry concentration will be different, depending on whether the sunk costs are exogenous or endogenous. These results are summarized in the **Sutton Limit Theorem**: when sunk costs are exogenous, concentration converges to zero as market size increases; when sunk costs are endogenous, concentration remains above a lower bound when market size increases. Although

sunk costs are important, Sutton also points out that history and the idiosyncratic characteristics of an industry may also influence industry concentration.

15. Survey evidence indicates that the most effective entry deterring strategies are advertising, hiding profits, brand proliferation, and R&D. As one might expect, R&D activity is less prevalent in mature industries.

16. The empirical evidence regarding the main causes of high industry concentration is generally consistent with economic theory. The main conclusions are:

   - In a particular industry, when concentration is high in one country, it is frequently high in other countries, especially in industries with exogenous sunk costs.
   - Concentration tends to be higher in markets with high natural barriers to entry, such as when MES and capital costs are high relative to the size of the market.
   - Mergers are an important source of concentration, especially outside the USA.
   - Concentration tends to be high in markets with high sunk costs and when firms invest in strategic barriers to entry, which generates endogenous sunk costs.

8.7 Review Questions

1. Define industry concentration. Explain how a concentration curve can be used to describe industry concentration. Can a concentration curve be (strictly) convex from below?[33] Explain.

2. Regarding an index of industry concentration.

   A. Describe the characteristics of an ideal index of industry concentration.
   B. Do the three indices of industry concentration described in the book (n, CR_4, and HHI) meet these ideal characteristics?
   C. How is HHI related to n and to CR_4?

3. Explain what is meant by an economic market. How do product and geographic boundaries play a role in your definition? Why is it important to use the correct economic market when constructing an index of industry concentration?

4. Describe what is meant by aggregate concentration. How has aggregate concentration in the USA changed in the last half century? Interpret the mean value of CR_{50} in Table 8.4. Why might high aggregate concentration be a social concern?

5. Table 8.6 shows that HHI is 350 for frozen fruits, juices, and vegetables, 467 for cement, and 2,449 for breakfast cereal. Why is this measure of concentration in the cement market inaccurate? Why do you think that concentration is low for the frozen food industry and high for the breakfast cereal industry?

6. Assume a market where firms produce homogeneous goods and are symmetric (i.e., each firm produces the same amount of output in equilibrium). The long-run

---

[33] A curve is convex when it lies above any tangent line to the curve.

average cost (AC) curve is U-shaped, and total demand is 120 (million units) when price equals minimum long-run average cost.

  A. If minimum efficient scale (MES) is 10, what is the cost-minimizing number of firms (n^*)?
  B. If MES is 11, what is the cost-minimizing number of firms? How will your answer change if AC is relatively flat to the right of MES.

7. Explain how strategic barriers to entry are different from natural barriers to entry. Provide one example of each.

8. Use Sutton's model to explain how concentration is determined when sunk costs are exogenous and when they are endogenous. Use an increase in industry sales or revenues (TR) to explain your answer.

9. Sutton (1991, Chap. 2) developed another model with exogenous sunk costs (σ) where equilibrium profits for firm i are $\pi_i = \text{TR}/n^2 - \sigma$.

  A. Explain how TR, n, and σ affect firm profits.
  B. What will be the equilibrium number of firms in this market?

10. Provide a brief summary of the empirical evidence regarding the main causes of high industry concentration.

Part III
Oligopoly and Market Power

Chapter 9
Cartels

People of the same trade seldom meet together, even for merriment and diversion, but the conversation ends in a conspiracy against the public, or in some contrivance to raise prices.

Adam Smith, The Wealth of Nations (1776)

We have seen in previous chapters how equilibrium price is substantially higher in monopoly than in perfectly competitive markets. In this chapter, we begin to investigate how price and output are determined in oligopoly markets that lie between these polar extremes. There are two types of oligopoly models, those that assume cooperative behavior and those that assume noncooperative behavior. In this chapter, we focus on cooperative settings or cooperative games. In the next two chapters we discuss noncooperative models.

When firms within the same industry cooperate or collude, their goal is to maximize joint or industry profits, the sum of profits from every firm in the industry. Collusion can be explicit or tacit. **Explicit collusion** occurs when firms establish a formal cartel agreement that determines price or production levels. When firms coordinate without explicit communication, contract, or agreement, they are engaging in **tacit collusion**.[1] A group of firms that explicitly collude is called a **cartel**.

Collusion raises firm profits and is socially inefficient. For this reason, collusion is illegal in the USA and in most developed countries, as discussed in Chap. 1. Just because it is illegal does not mean that it does not occur, however. There are plenty of smart managers in search of higher profits who have tried to circumvent the law and collude with competitors. In the early twentieth century, for example, the head of the US Steel Company, Judge Elbert H. Gary, regularly hosted Sunday dinners

---

[1] It is sometimes called conscious parallelism, as firms make strategic moves in concert without being formal members of a cartel. Concert actions do not necessarily imply collusion, however, as competitive firms may behave in unison as well. For further discussion, see Scherer and Ross (1990, Chap. 9).

V.J. Tremblay and C.H. Tremblay, *New Perspectives on Industrial Organization*, Springer Texts in Business and Economics, DOI 10.1007/978-1-4614-3241-8_9, © Springer Science+Business Media New York 2012

with leaders from competing companies to discuss and set steel prices. In the 1950s, General Electric, Westinghouse, and several smaller companies colluded on the price of industrial electronic equipment. From 2000 to 2006, six companies participated in an international conspiracy to fix prices of liquid crystal display (LCD) panels. LCD panels are used in televisions, computer monitors, cell phones, iPods, and other electronic devices. Firms adversely affected include such companies as Apple, Dell, and Motorola (US Department of Justice 2008, 2009).

In the last 30 years, there are numerous examples where airline companies have attempted to collude on price. A dramatic example occurred in 1982 while American Airlines and Braniff Airways were in the midst of fierce price competition. On February 21, 1982, Robert Crandall, president of America, called Howard Putman, president of Braniff, to discuss price. This conversation was taped by Putman and went like this (New York Times, February 24 1983):

Crandall: I think it's dumb as hell for Christ's sake, all right, to sit here and pound the ! @#$%! out of each other and neither one of us making a !@#$%! dime.
Putnam: Well...
Crandall: I mean, you know, !@#$%!, what the hell is the point of it?
Putnam: But if you're going to overlay every route of American's on top of every route that Braniff has—I just can't sit here and allow you to bury us without giving our best effort.
Crandall: Oh sure, but Eastern and Delta do the same thing in Atlanta and have for years.
Putnam: Do you have a suggestion for me?
Crandall: Yes, I have a suggestion for you. Raise your !@#$%! fares 20 percent. I'll raise mine the next morning.
Putnam: Robert, we...
Crandall: You'll make more money, and I will, too.
Putnam: We can't talk about pricing!
Crandall: Oh !@#$%!, Howard. We can talk about any !@#$%! thing we want to talk about.

Although this conversation was not a violation of the Sherman Act because Putman never agreed to the offer, it illustrates how easy it can be to communicate an offer to collude.

If convicted of collusive behavior in the USA, firms are subject to huge fines which have increased steadily over the last decade and a half. Before 1994, the largest corporate fine was $6 million. Since 1996, however, 18 firms have been fined $100 million or more for price-fixing agreements (see Table 9.1). Total antitrust fines have increased by over 400% from 2000 to 2009, reaching $1 billion in 2009. In addition, individuals who violate US antitrust laws are being sent to jail more frequently today. In the 1990s, only 37% of violators were sentenced to jail. This number has risen steadily over the past 10 years, reaching 80% by 2009.[2]

---

[2] These data derive from Hammond (2005, 2010).

Table 9.1 Cartel violators yielding a corporate fine of $100 million or more

Defendant	Year	Product	Country	Fine ($ millions)
F. Hoffmann-La Roche	1999	Vitamins	Switzerland	500
LG Display Co. and LG Display America	2009	LCD panels	Korea	400
Societe Air France and KLM	2008	Air transportation	France/the Netherlands	350
Korean Air Lines	2007	Air transportation	Korea	300
British Airways	2007	Air transportation	UK	300
Samsung Electronics and Semiconductor	2006	DRAM	Korea	300
BASF AG	1999	Vitamins	Germany	225
HI MEI Optoelectronics	2010	LCD panels	Taiwan	220
Hynix Semiconductor	2005	DRAM	Korea	185
Infineon Technologies AG	2004	DRAM	Germany	160
SGL Carbon AG	1999	Graphite electrodes	Germany	135
Mitsubishi	2001	Graphite electrodes	Japan	134
Sharp	2009	LCD panels	Japan	120
Cargolux Airlines	2009	Air transportation	Luxembourg	119
Japan Airlines	2008	Air transportation	Japan	110
UCAR	1998	Graphite electrodes	USA	110
Lan Cargo SA and Aeorlinhas Brasileiras SA	2009	Air transportation	Chile/Brazil	109
Archer Daniels Midland	1996	Lycine and citric acid	USA	100

Source: US Department of Justice, Antitrust Division, http://www.usdoj.gov/atr

In this chapter, we will address four fundamental questions regarding the behavior of firms who form a cartel:

- What motivates firms to form a cartel, in spite of strict antitrust enforcement?
- How do firms make price and output decisions when they are members of a cartel?
- What are the welfare implications of cartels?
- What economic and institutional factors encourage or discourage cartel formation?

Once the economics of a cartel is understood, we will discuss the empirical evidence and provide several case studies of relatively successful cartels.

9.1   Cartel Theory

From the firm's perspective, the main purpose of a cartel is to earn greater profit by behaving cooperatively rather than competitively. If firms within an industry form a **perfect cartel**, all firms work together to maximize joint industry profits. In this section, we discuss how members of a perfect cartel behave and analyze the fundamental problems with establishing and maintaining an effective cartel.

9.1.1   Coordination: Output and Price Determination

When firms within an industry form a cartel, their goal is to maximize joint or industry profits with respect to their choice of price or output levels. To model this idea, we consider a simple oligopoly market with two firms (1 and 2), called a duopoly. Firms produce homogeneous products, and their choice variable is output.[3] Later we will discuss price competition and the effect of product differentiation.

To illustrate, consider a market where both inverse demand and cost functions are linear and take the following familiar form:

$$p = a - bQ, \tag{9.1}$$

$$TC_i = cq_i, \tag{9.2}$$

where p is price, subscript i represents firm 1 or 2, q_i is firm i's output, $Q = q_1 + q_2$, and TC_i is firm i's total cost. For this specification, parameter a is the intercept of inverse demand, $-b$ is the slope of inverse demand, and c is average and marginal cost (which is the same for both firms). Parameters a, b, and c are positive, and $a - c > 0$. Equations (9.1) and (9.2) produce the following profit equation for firm i:

$$\begin{aligned}
\pi_i &= TR_i - TC_i \\
&= pq_i - cq_i = (p - c)q_i \\
&= aq_i - bq_i^2 - bq_iq_j - cq_i, \tag{9.3}
\end{aligned}$$

where TR_i is the total revenue of firm i and subscript j represents firm i's competitor.

The profit-maximizing problem facing the cartel is to choose q_1 and q_2 so as to maximize joint profits. Joint profits (Π) are defined as

$$\begin{aligned}
\Pi &= \pi_1 + \pi_2 = (p - c)(q_1 + q_2) \\
&= \left(aq_1 - bq_1^2 - bq_1q_2 - cq_1\right) + \left(aq_2 - bq_2^2 - bq_2q_1 - cq_2\right). \tag{9.4}
\end{aligned}$$

---

[3] This problem is identical to that of a multiplant monopolist, except that 1 and 2 refer to production plants, not firms, in the multiplant monopoly problem.

The solution to this problem requires that two first-order conditions hold:

$$\frac{\partial \Pi}{\partial q_1} = \frac{\partial \pi_1}{\partial q_1} + \frac{\partial \pi_2}{\partial q_1} = MR_1 - MC_1 + E_1$$
$$= (a - 2bq_1 - bq_2) - c + (-bq_2)$$
$$= a - 2bq_1 - 2bq_2 - c = 0, \qquad (9.5)$$

$$\frac{\partial \Pi}{\partial q_2} = \frac{\partial \pi_1}{\partial q_2} + \frac{\partial \pi_2}{\partial q_2} = E_2 + MR_2 - MC_2$$
$$= (-bq_1) + (a - 2bq_2 - bq_1) - c$$
$$= a - 2bq_1 - 2bq_2 - c = 0, \qquad (9.6)$$

where MR_i is firm i's marginal revenue, MC_i is firm i's marginal cost (c), and E_i is the external effect that an increase in q_i has on firm j's profits ($\partial \pi_j / \partial q_i = -bq_j$). Normally, we would solve these functions simultaneously to identify the optimal values of q_1 and q_2, but this is impossible here, because both first-order conditions are identical ($a - 2bq_1 - 2bq_2 - c = 0$) and cannot be solved for q_1 and q_2. Thus, a cartel faces a **coordination problem**: the output or market shares for each firm are not readily apparent.

Nevertheless, we are able to identify the optimal value of total output (Q^*). Substituting $q_1 = Q^* - q_2$ into the common first-order condition and solving for Q^* gives $Q^* = (a - c)/(2b)$. At this level of output, the cartel price is $p^* = (a + c)/(2)$ and cartel profits are $\Pi^* = (a - c)^2/(4b)$. Notice that this is simply the monopoly solution (see Chap. 6). Thus, firms in a cartel will produce the monopoly level of output, sell at the monopoly price, and earn (as an industry) monopoly profits. This is not surprising, because the goals of a cartel and a monopolist are the same: to maximize industry profits.[4] You can see why firms in relatively competitive markets

---

[4] We can see this by considering a more general model, where the objective is to maximize $\Pi = p(Q) \cdot Q - TC_1 - TC_2$ with respect to q_1 and q_2, where TC_i is firm i's total cost. The first-order conditions are

$$\frac{\partial \Pi}{\partial q_1} = p + \frac{\partial p}{\partial q_1} Q - MC_1 = 0,$$

$$\frac{\partial \Pi}{\partial q_2} = p + \frac{\partial p}{\partial q_2} Q - MC_2 = 0,$$

where MC_i is firm i's marginal cost. These conditions imply that the marginal revenue for the industry must equal marginal cost of production, whether produced by firm 1 or firm 2. Notice how the first-order condition for an individual firm that maximizes its own profit is different from the first equation above. For firm 1, the difference is that the second term within the equal signs in the first equation above would be multiplied by q_1 instead of Q. This means that when firm 1 considers increasing q_1, it pays attention to the effect that this has on the total revenue of the entire industry, rather than just its own total revenue, when it is a member of the cartel. Because $\partial p / \partial q_1$ and $Q > q_1$, the firm's marginal benefit of producing an additional unit of output is less under a cartel. Thus, each firm will produce less output in a cartel setting.

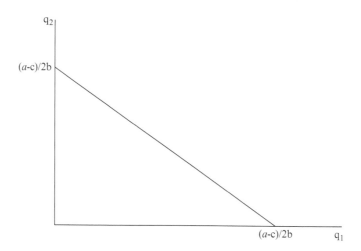

Fig. 9.1 Output combinations that maximize total industry profit in a cartel

would want to form a cartel, as industry profits generally increase as we move from a competitive to a monopoly outcome.

Given that the cartel and monopoly outcomes are the same, many of the insights of monopoly theory carry over to cartel theory. First, the solution will be the same, whether the choice variable is output or price. That is, the cartel solution remains the monopoly solution when firms cooperate on price instead of on output. Second, a cartel transfers wealth from consumers to producers. Third, a cartel outcome is allocatively inefficient and, therefore, socially undesirable. By cutting production below the competitive level, the cartel (or monopoly) price exceeds marginal cost, creating a deadweight or efficiency loss just like in monopoly.

One question still remains: how is output (and therefore profits) distributed among firms? The problem becomes more apparent when we look more closely at the common first-order condition. Solving either (9.5) or (9.6) for q_2 gives $q_2 = Q^* - q_1 = (a - c)/(2b) - q_1$. As depicted in Fig. 9.1, the function is linear, has a slope of -1, and intercepts of $(a - c)/(2b)$. The line identifies all values of q_1 and q_2 that sum to the monopoly level of output, $Q^* = (a - c)/(2b)$. We call this the **output-distribution line**. It indicates that firm 1's cartel level of output ranges from 0 to the monopoly level of output, given that $q_1 = Q^* - q_2$. Thus, the cartel agreement must specify both Q^* (or p^*) and the distribution of output among cartel participants. Once these are identified, the distribution of profits is determined.

We can illustrate the cartel's indeterminacy problem graphically with isoprofit equations. Firm 1's **isoprofit equation** describes all combinations of q_1 and q_2 that represent a constant level of profit, k, for firm 1. Solving firm 1's profit function in

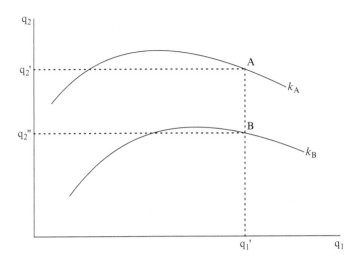

Fig. 9.2 Firm 1's isoprofit curves

(9.3) for q_2 produces its isoprofit equation: $q_2 = \left(aq_1 - cq_1 - bq_1^2 - k\right)/(bq_1).$[5]
Two isoprofit curves are illustrated in Fig. 9.2 for different values of k. Given that
the isoprofit equation is quadratic, each curve is concave to the q_1 axis, with a lower
isoprofit curve implying greater profits for firm 1 (i.e., $k_B > k_A$). The reason for this
is that for a given value of q_1 (e.g., q_1'), firm 1's profits increase as q_2 falls (from
q_2' to q_2''), as indicated by firm 1's profit equation above. Parallel results hold for
firm 2; the only differences are that its isoprofit curve is concave to the q_2 axis and
its profits are higher for isoprofit curves that are closer to the q_2 axis.

Joint profits are maximized when the isoprofit curves of firms 1 and 2 are tangent,
which takes place on the output-distribution line. To illustrate, consider Fig. 9.3
where firm 1 produces q_{1x} (on isoprofit curve π_{1x}) and firm 2 produces q_{2x} (on
isoprofit curve π_{2x}). This is not a cartel outcome because the output pair (q_{1x}, q_{2x}) is
not on the output-distribution line. If both firms cut production equally, each firm
would move to an isoprofit curve that is closer to its output axes. Thus, the profits of
both firms, and therefore industry profits, would rise. Once a tangency is reached at
point y, for example, it is impossible to raise industry profits by adjusting firm output,
and firms are on the output-distribution line. In other words, industry profits reach a
maximum when production takes place on the line and isoprofits are tangent.

Moving from one point to another on the output-distribution line simply
redistributes production and profits between firms. Moving up and to the left raises
firm 2's profits and lowers firm 1's profits. Moving down the line benefits firm 1 at
the expense of firm 2. Taken together, this means that once the optimal distribution

---

[5] This equation maps out a curve that is much like an indifference curve in consumer theory and an
isoquant in production theory. For an isoprofit function, profit is held constant rather than utility
(in an indifference curve) or firm production (in an isoquant). For a review of indifference curves and
isoquants, see Bernheim and Whinston (2008), Pindyck and Rubenfield (2009), or Varian (2010).

E ≡ Move up ↓ L Inc Firm 2 π

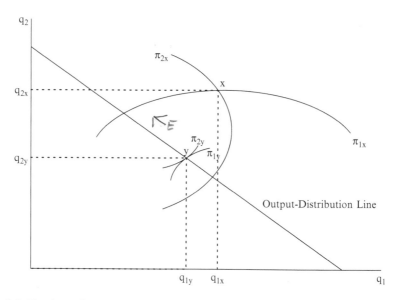

Fig. 9.3 Firm isoprofit curves and cartel output combinations

of output is determined, at q_{1y} and q_{2y} in this example, the distribution of profits is identified by isoprofits π_{1y} and π_{2y}.

9.1.2 The Fundamental Weakness of a Cartel: The Cartel Dilemma

A cartel is attractive to producers in all industries because it guarantees the highest possible profit for the industry (i.e., the monopoly profit). In spite of this fact, Stigler (1964) showed that cartels are surprisingly difficult to maintain in the long run. Although abiding by a cartel agreement produces the best outcome for the group, it is not profit maximizing for an individual firm. In our duopoly example, if firm j produces the cartel level of output, it is profit maximizing for firm i to produce more than the cartel level of output. Thus, firms have an incentive to cheat on the cartel agreement, which may induce firms to expand output and ignite a price war.[6] This is the **cartel dilemma**: what is in the best interest of the cartel is not in the best interest of individual firms.

Because this dilemma is so important, we illustrate it in three ways. First, we use a graph of the output-distribution line and isoprofit curves. Figure 9.4 depicts a symmetric cartel solution at point y, where respective output and isoprofit levels

---

[6] In a price war, each firm has an incentive to undercut the price of its competitor, which can lead to competitive pricing. We discuss the details of price undercutting in the next chapter.

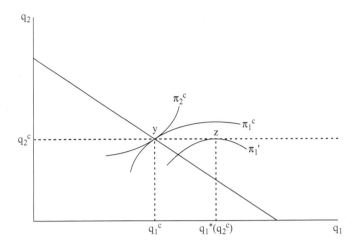

Fig. 9.4 Firm 1's best reply to firm 2's cartel level of output (q_2^c)

are q_1^c, q_2^c, π_1^c, and π_2^c. Notice that when firm 2 produces the cartel output of q_2^c, firm 1's best reply (i.e., its optimal response) is not q_1^c. Instead, firm 1 will choose the level of output that maximizes its profits, given that firm 2 holds output at q_2^c. The given output constraint of firm 2 is shown by the line passing from q_2^c through point y.

Firm 1's best reply to q_2^c is q_1^* (q_2^c), which occurs where firm 1's isoprofit curve is tangent to the constraint line at point z. This increases firm 1's profits (i.e., $\pi_1' > \pi_1^c$) and causes firm 2's profits to decrease. The point is that when firm 2 produces the cartel level of output, firm 1's best reply is to produce more than the cartel level of output. The same argument applies to firm 2. This demonstrates Stigler's point that each firm has an incentive to cheat on the cartel agreement by increasing production.

Another way to illustrate this idea is with a concrete example. Consider our duopoly model above with linear demand and cost functions. For simplicity, assume that $a = 12$, $b = 1$, and $c = 0$. If we consider a symmetric outcome where production is distributed evenly between firms, then the cartel solution is

$$Q^* = 6; \quad q_i^* = \frac{Q^*}{2} = 3; \quad p^* = 6; \quad \pi_i^* = 18. \qquad (9.7)$$

But if firm 1 produces 4 units of output and firm 2 continues to produce 3, then firm 1's profits increase to 20 and firm 2's profits fall to 15. Thus, industry profits fall from 36 to 35.[7] Even though firm 1 does better by boosting production beyond the cartel level, the industry is worse off. This is a classic externality problem.

---

[7] That is, when $q_1 = 4$ and $q_2 = 3$, firm 1's profit equals $(12 - q_1 - q_2)q_1 = 20$ and firm 2's profit equals $(12 - q_1 - q_2)q_2 = 15$.

Fig. 9.5 The cartel dilemma
in a duopoly market

		Firm 2	
		3	4
Firm 1	3	18, 18	15, 20
	4	20, 15	16, 16

An increase in firm 1's production increases its profits even though it also leads to a lower price. This damages firm 2 (i.e., it imposes a negative externality on firm 2), because firm 2's output is fixed at 3. Assuming that firm 1 is concerned with its profits alone, it will ignore the damage it causes firm 2 and will step up production. The same argument applies to firm 2. Thus, a cartel dilemma exists, because each firm wants to push production beyond the cartel level.

The cartel dilemma is fundamentally the same as that of a prisoners' dilemma. These dilemma's occur when what is best for the group is not what is best for each individual player (whether prisoners or firms). The cartel dilemma is described by the payoff matrix in Fig. 9.5. The matrix is based on the example above except that a firm's only choice is to produce 3 units of output (the cartel level) or 4 units. Joint profits are maximized when both firms produce output of 3. Yet, each firm's dominant strategy is to produce 4. For example, if firm 2 produces 3 units, firm 1's best reply is to produce 4 units; if firm 2 produces 4 units, firm 1's best reply is to produce 4 units. Both firms have an incentive to produce more output than they would under a cartel agreement. Notice that the outcome where both firms produce 4 units of output is the dominant-strategy or Nash equilibrium that we discussed in Chap. 3.[8]

The most general way to demonstrate the cartel dilemma is to review the first-order conditions of the cartel's problem in (9.5) and (9.6), which imply that

$$\frac{\partial \pi_i}{\partial q_i} + \frac{\partial \pi_j}{\partial q_i} = 0. \tag{9.8}$$

Because an increase in q_i reduces the demand for j's product, $\partial \pi_j / \partial q_i < 0$. Thus, for the equality in (9.8) to hold, which is required to maximize joint profits, it must

---

[8] In the next chapter, we will see that this is a special type of Nash equilibrium, first investigated by Cournot (1838).

be true that $\partial \pi_i / \partial q_i > 0$ when evaluated at the cartel level of output. This means that when both firms produce the cartel level of output, firm i can increase its profits by producing more output. Just as before, each firm has an incentive to cheat on a cartel arrangement by increasing output.

With product differentiation, the problem is fundamentally the same. Consider the case with multicharacteristic differentiation. Firm i's inverse demand is $p_i = a - b \cdot q_i - d \cdot q_j$, where $d = b$ in the homogeneous goods case and d is less than b but positive when the goods are imperfect substitutes. The rest of the analysis is the same as above. The only difference is that given product differentiation, equilibrium prices, output levels, and profits need not be the same for both firms. In this case, the cartel behaves like a monopolist that produces two differentiated goods, an issue we take up in Chap. 13. In practice, however, differentiation can make it more complicated for firms to coordinate on price.

9.1.3 Other Cartel Weaknesses

Although the cartel dilemma is an important deterrent to cartel success, other factors can also make it difficult to maintain a cartel. One is the degree of antitrust enforcement. Stricter enforcement and penalties for violators reduce the net benefits of forming and sustaining a cartel. Furthermore, cartel members cannot take a company to court for violating an illegal cartel agreement or contract. Illegal contracts are not enforceable and, therefore, cannot be used to overcome the cartel dilemma. Cartel agreements must be struck and enforced in secret, which makes it more difficult to observe cheating and to discipline cheaters. Detecting cheating is especially problematic when there are many firms in the industry, because monitoring and enforcement costs increase with the number of firms (Stigler 1964).

Firm heterogeneity can also be a problem, as it raises the cost of negotiating a cartel agreement. An acceptable output distribution will be more difficult to identify if some firms have lower costs or if technology is changing rapidly. When products are differentiated, they need not sell at the same price, making it more difficult to identify cartel prices.

In addition, the detection of cheaters can be especially difficult in markets where there is considerable demand fluctuation. An increase in production of brand 1 in response to an increase in demand could cause firm 2 to mistakenly believe that firm 1 is cheating. Firm 2 might step up production or start a price war.

Even if all of these problems can be overcome, cartel profits can induce entry of new competitors in markets with low entry barriers. With zero entry barriers, positive economic profits will attract new entrants. Over time, each firm's share of output and monopoly profits will get smaller and smaller as more firms enter, making the cartel unsustainable in the long run.

In summary, collusion is less likely to occur when:

- Cartels are illegal and expected antitrust penalties are steep.[9]
- There are many firms in the market.
- Firms have dissimilar costs and produce differentiated products.
- Demand and cost conditions are unstable.
- Entry barriers are low.

9.2   Strategies That Facilitate Collusion

Cartels will exist when the expected benefits of forming a cartel are at least as high as the cost of establishing and enforcing a cartel agreement. Even though there are obstacles to maintaining a cartel, firms have a tremendous economic incentive to overcome them. Here, we discuss three strategies that firms use to prevent cheating and facilitate a collusive outcome.

9.2.1   Market Division

Perhaps the simplest way to facilitate collusion is to divide the market so that each firm serves a different set of customers or geographic regions. Each firm becomes a monopoly with respect to its own set of customers, eliminating the need to coordinate on price or production levels. Another advantage of this scheme is that firms only need to monitor their own subset of customers, making it easier to detect cheating. In essence, the cartel acts as a price discriminating monopolist, with each firm setting the monopoly price in each submarket. When prices differ among producers, however, resale between different groups of customers must be preventable for this scheme to be successful.

Of the 605 price-fixing cases in the USA from 1910 to 1972, Fraas and Greer (1977) found that 26% involved cartels that divided up markets geographically. A classic example of this occurred from 1928 through 1972 when a two-country cartel called Mercurio Europeo kept the price of mercury at near monopoly levels: suppliers in Spain served the USA and suppliers in Italy served customers in Europe.

---

[9] In this case, firms play a game with antitrust authorities, which may cause them to limit price below the joint profit-maximizing level to avoid antitrust scrutiny.

Fig. 9.6 The cartel dilemma pricing game

		Firm 2	
		p_C	p_L
Firm 1	p_C	20, 20	17, 22
	p_L	22, 17	18, 18

9.2.2 Most-Favored-Customer Clause

One strategy used to diminish the incentive to cheat on a cartel is known as a **most-favored-customer clause**, which is sometimes called a low-price guarantee.[10] The clause guarantees that if a customer purchases a product today and the product is discounted in the next several months, the customer will receive a rebate for the difference in the price. With such a rebate clause in effect, a firm will be less likely to lower its price today because it must pay out rebates to all customers who purchased the product in the last several months. In other words, it substantially lowers the payoff from cutting today's price.

To show how a most-favored-customer clause can facilitate collusion, we analyze a simple duopoly problem where firms 1 and 2 play a static game. Firms can choose to set price equal to the cartel price (p_C) or at a lower, more competitive price (p_L). Payoffs are described in Fig. 9.6. You can see that firms face a classic cartel dilemma in prices. Although joint profits are maximized when both firms set price equal to p_C, each firm's dominant strategy is to cheat on the cartel and choose p_L. Thus, the Nash and dominant-strategy equilibrium is the competitive price pair (p_L, p_L).

Now assume that these firms both implement a most-favored-customer clause. With this clause in place, a firm must send out rebates worth a total of R dollars to previous customers if the firm offers a low price today. Figure 9.7 presents the rebate payoff structure. Notice that the rebate clause reduces the attractiveness of cheating by imposing a penalty on cheaters. In this example, if R is greater than 2, then each

---

[10] This is sometimes called a most-favored-nation clause (Salop 1986).

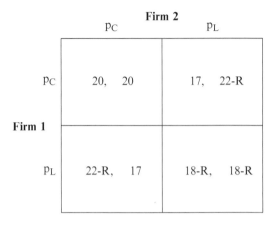

Fig. 9.7 The cartel dilemma
with most-favored-customer
clause

firm's dominant strategy changes from p_L to p_C. The Nash and dominant-strategy equilibrium becomes the cartel outcome. Thus, a simple change in the pricing contract with consumers can support collusion.[11]

9.2.3   Meet-the-Competition Clause

Another strategy that firms use to support collusion is a **meet-the-competition clause**[12] in which a store guarantees to match the low price of any competitor. Such a clause appears to be valuable to you as a consumer, as it seems to guarantee the lowest possible price. Just the opposite may occur, however. One problem is that it encourages customers to monitor prices and report a cheater to rival stores. This alleviates monitoring costs to cartel members, which may help solidify cartel pricing.

A meet-the-competition clause also eliminates any short-run gain from cheating. Continuing with the same duopoly pricing model described above but without a meet-the-competition clause, payoffs are those found in Fig. 9.6. Again, the Nash or dominant-strategy equilibrium is for both firms to cheat on the cartel and set a low price. With a meet-the-competition clause in effect, however, neither firm is able to undercut its competitor, effectively eliminating the price pairs (p_C, p_L) and (p_L, p_C) as possibilities. That is, if firm i cheats by setting price equal to p_L, firm j's price automatically reverts to p_L. Thus, the only possible outcomes are (p_C, p_C) and (p_L, p_L). Given these options, neither firm has an incentive to deviate from the higher cartel price, making the cartel outcome the Nash equilibrium.

---

[11] Chen and Liu (2011) point out that there may be other reasons for implementing a most-favored-customer clause. In their study of electronics retailers, they found that Best Buy introduced such a clause in order to gain market share from its chief competitors.

[12] See Salop (1986) for more detailed discussion.

9.2.4 Trigger Strategy

In most real-world cartels, firms compete time and time again in the marketplace. In a repeated game, firms may develop a strategy that facilitates collusion even though they have no formal contract. Friedman (1971) proposed that firms may use a **trigger strategy** to attain a collusive outcome in an infinitely repeated game. Assuming two firms, a trigger strategy is defined as follows:

- If firm j cooperated in the past, firm i cooperates today.
- If firm j did not cooperate in the past, this triggers a more competitive response from firm i today and forever after.[13]

When applied to price competition, it is called a trigger-price strategy. It turns out that under certain circumstances a trigger strategy can support collusion. That is, it may be in the self-interest of firms to cooperate in every period.

Consider the choices that each firm faces today, at time $t = 0$. To begin, assume that both firms behaved cooperatively in the past and split cartel profits equally, with each firm's share of cartel profits identified as π^C (half the monopoly profits, $\pi^C = \pi^M/2$). A trigger strategy produces the following outcomes:

- If firm i cheats in the current period, it earns π^* today. But from period $t + 1$ on, competition becomes tougher and the firm earns the present value of the stream of profits from a more competitive environment, π^x_{PV}.
- If firm i cooperates in the current period, it earns the present value of the stream of cartel profits today and forever after, π^C_{PV}.

Thus, a trigger strategy will support cooperation if firms earn more from cooperation than from cheating. This occurs when the present value stream of profits from cooperating (π^C_{PV}) exceeds the present value stream of profits from cheating ($\pi^* + \pi^x_{PV}$), or

$$\pi^C_{PV} > \pi^* + \pi^x_{PV}. \tag{9.9}$$

From discussion of the cartel dilemma in the previous section, we know that $\pi^* > \pi^C$. We also know that $\pi^C_{PV} > \pi^x_{PV}$, because cartel profits are higher than profits in a more competitive setting. Thus, the inequality in (9.9) will hold if π^x_{PV} is sufficiently low.

Two forces affect the incentive to cooperate. The net benefit from cooperation increases as cheating triggers a harsher response, which lowers π^x_{PV}. The net benefit also increases as future dollars become more valuable (i.e., the future is less heavily discounted). To see how discounting influences the incentive to cooperate, consider the numerical example for the duopoly pricing game described in Fig. 9.6, where

---

[13] Normally, firm i is assumed to revert to a Nash equilibrium price or output strategy once firm j cheats.

firms can choose the cartel price p_C or to cheat by selling at a low price, p_L. In this case, $\pi^C = 20$, $\pi^* = 22$, and $\pi^x = 18$. At one extreme, if future dollars are not discounted at all (the discount factor, D, equals 1, as discussed in Chap. 2), then the inequality in (9.9) becomes

$$\sum_{t=0}^{\infty} 20_t > 22 + \sum_{t=1}^{\infty} 18_t,$$

$$20 + \sum_{t=1}^{\infty} 20_t - \sum_{t=1}^{\infty} 18_t > 22,$$

$$20 + \sum_{t=1}^{\infty} 2_t > 22. \tag{9.10}$$

This inequality clearly holds, making it optimal for each firm to cooperate. Alternatively, if future dollars do not matter at all (i.e., the discount factor equals 0), then the inequality in (9.9) is

$$20 > 22, \tag{9.11}$$

which does not hold. In this case, it pays to cheat because retaliation tomorrow is of no consequence. Thus, the trigger strategy will support collusion as long as the future is not too heavily discounted (i.e., the discount factor is sufficiently close to 1).

We generalize this result, assuming homogeneous goods and fierce competition in response to cheating that pushes π^x to zero. With homogeneous goods, an incremental decrease in price below p_C causes π^* to be approximately equal to monopoly profit (π^M).[14] With n firms, (9.9) becomes

$$\sum_{t=0}^{\infty} D^t \frac{\pi^M}{n} > \pi^M, \tag{9.12}$$

where D is the discount factor.[15] Notice that the benefits from cooperation, captured by the left-hand side of the inequality in (9.12), increase in D and decrease in n. This is called the **fundamental principle of collusion**: a trigger strategy is more likely to support collusion when there are fewer competitors and future dollars are more highly valued (i.e., D is higher). We will prove this result more formally and identify the cutoff value of the discount factor in Chap. 11.

---

[14] The reason is that with homogeneous goods, all consumers will buy from the low-priced producer. Thus, that firm will sell approximately the monopoly output and its competitors will sell nothing. This is consistent with a Bertrand outcome, which we will discuss in Chap. 10.

[15] Note that when D is less than 1, the left-hand side of the inequality does not sum to infinity.

9.3 Empirical Evidence

In this section, we provide a brief summary of the evidence regarding the economics of cartel activity.[16] The evidence shows that perfect cartels rarely exist in the real world. In most cases, cartels are imperfect because not all firms in the industry are members of the cartel. Thus, the monopoly outcome is rarely achieved. At the same time, the empirical evidence from the USA includes only those cases that were detected by antitrust authorities. The evidence is based on a sample that excludes undetected cartels that may have different characteristics than those of detected cartels. In any case, the available evidence is generally consistent with theory.

First, the evidence shows that collusion leads to considerably higher prices and profits.[17] For example, Griffin (1989) studied 54 international cartels from 1888 to 1984 and found that the average markup of price over marginal cost was 45%. In the graphite electrode market in the USA, Levenstein and Suslow (2004) found that prices rose by over 50% during the cartel period, 1992 to 1997. In his econometric study of auction prices of foreclosed properties in Washington, DC, Kwoka (1997) found that a cartel of real estate buyers suppressed auction prices by 30–45%.[18] After reviewing 200 cartel studies, Connor and Lande (2005) found that cartel activity led to an increase in average median prices by about 32% for international cartels and 18% for domestic cartels. Assuming that a lower price markup reduces the probability of being detected by antitrust authorities, this difference may reflect the fact that US anti-cartel enforcement is generally tougher than in other countries.

The results are less definitive regarding cartel stability. After reviewing 50 cartel cases, Levenstein and Suslow (2004) found that the average duration of a cartel was 5.4 years. Nevertheless, the world's most successful cartel, the DeBeers diamond cartel, has lasted for 100 years. Of course, many attempts to form a cartel fail, as we saw in the introduction between American Airlines and Braniff Airways.

This brings us to the next question: what factors determine cartel success? Consistent with the cartel dilemma, the evidence shows that cheating is a critical cause of cartel failure. In his sample of 29 international cartels, Eckbo (1976) found that 59% ended because of internal conflicts. Although still substantial, lower estimates are found by Griffin (1989), at 33%, and Suslow (2005), at 24%.

The evidence also shows that entry is another factor that undermines cartel success. In a review of 19 case studies, Levenstein and Suslow (2006) found that entry was the most common cause of cartel breakdown. Consistent with this research, Symeonidis (2003) found that collusion is more likely in markets with

---

[16] For more extensive reviews, see Scherer and Ross (1990, Chaps. 6–9), Waldman and Jensen (2006, Chaps. 9 and 10), and Levenstein and Suslow (2006).

[17] The notable exception is the study by Asch and Seneca (1975), which found that colluding firms earned lower profits than noncolluding firms. Their empirical model does not control for industry differences or other important determinants of profitability, however. Another potential concern is that cartels may form in less profitable industries.

[18] For a review of auction theory and a discussion of eBay auctions, see Hasker and Sickles (2010).

Table 9.2 Market conditions facilitating collusion in the markets for lysine, citric acid, and synthetic vitamins A and E in the 1990s

Market condition	Lysine	Citric acid	Vitamins A and E
High entry barriers (sunk costs)	Yes	Yes	Yes
Seller concentration (CR$_4$)			
Global market	>95%	>80%	>95%
US market	>97%	90%	100%
Number of cartel participants	4 or 5	4 or 5	3
Homogeneous products	Perfect	High	High
Annual market growth	10%, steady	8%, steady	2–3%, steady

CR$_4$ is the four-firm concentration ratio.
Source: Connor (2003).

high natural barriers to entry. The erection of strategic barriers, as in merchant shipping cartels (Morton 1997), has also been used to maintain a successful cartel. Finally, Levenstein (1995) argues that attempts to cartelize the salt industry during the nineteenth century failed because of insufficient barriers to entry.

The level of industry concentration also matters. Hay and Kelley (1974) found that cartel duration increased with concentration. Of the 605 US price-fixing cases from 1910 to 1972, Fraas and Greer (1977) found that the median number of firms involved in a cartel was 8. In their review of the evidence, Levenstein and Suslow (2006) found that most cartels involve industries that are relatively concentrated. When this is not the case, industry trade associations or governments played an important role in organizing and supporting a cartel agreement.[19]

Other factors also play a role. In most cases, global cartels involve products that are homogeneous or nearly homogeneous (Hay and Kelley 1974; Connor 2003). In addition, unexpected demand and cost shocks can destabilize a cartel by raising the cost of monitoring a cartel agreement. An unanticipated demand decrease can cause an individual firm to believe that competitors have cheated on a price agreement, which can trigger a price war in a misguided effort to enforce cooperation (Green and Porter 1984).[20] After reviewing the evidence, Levenstein and Suslow (2006, 66) conclude that "demand instability appears to destabilize cartels."

These general findings are consistent with those found by Connor (2003) in his study of successful cartels for lysine, citric acid, and vitamins A and E. His main results are summarized in Table 9.2. Connor's findings confirm that these successful cartels had stiff entry barriers, high levels of concentration (high four-firm concentration ratios and low number of competitors), relatively homogeneous goods, and fairly steady growth rates in demand.

---

[19] Eckbo (1976) also finds that cartel success is more likely when demand is sufficiently inelastic. This implies few close substitutes for the cartelized product and a greater gain in profits when moving from a competitive to a cartel outcome.

[20] Alternatively, Rotemberg and Saloner (1986) argue that price cuts are more likely during boom periods, because the benefit from price cutting is greater during a boom.

9.4   Case Studies of Cartels

Three case studies illuminate the complexity of maintaining a real-world cartel. These examples are designed to show how firms attempt to form price or output agreements and how cheating, entry, and politics can affect cartel success. We consider a classic, historical case, the US steel industry in the early 1900s; the OPEC cartel, established in 1960 and continuing through today; and the international vitamin cartel of the 1990s.

9.4.1   The Steel Industry[21]

One of the most famous examples of collusion occurred in the US steel industry in the early 1900s. This is a case where the ability to collude was enhanced by a major merger in 1901 that substantially bolstered industry concentration. Before that time, the industry was fragmented, consisting of hundreds of small steel producers. Although there were frequent attempts to fix price, cheating was common. To maintain high capacity utilization rates, price competition was frequently cutthroat. Concerned with growing excess capacity, Charles Schwab, president of Carnegie Steel, worked with the leading banker at the time, J. P. Morgan, to consolidate the major US steel companies.

In February of 1901, over ten major steel producers were merged, creating the US Steel Company.[22] This merger substantially raised concentration, as US Steel controlled over 65% of the nation's steel producing capacity. When the new company was formed, an intense debate ensued among the board of directors over its pricing strategy. On the one side was Charles Schwab, who supported former Carnegie Steel's policy of pricing as aggressively as needed to keep mills operating at full capacity. On the other side was Judge Ebert H. Gary, former president of Federal Steel, who wanted to avoid price competition, as it tended to lower profits. Gary's position was ultimately accepted, and he became president of US Steel.

Although it is always difficult to uncover the details of illegal collusive activity, there is general agreement that US Steel cooperated with its competitors through trade associations and private meetings. The most famous of these are called "Gary Dinners," where Judge Gary invited the leaders of competing steel producers to dinner for the purpose of fixing prices at noncompetitive levels during periods of both "stress" and "industrial calm." These meetings continued from 1907 until

---

[21] This discussion borrows from Adams and Mueller (1990) and Scherer (1996).

[22] These include Carnegie Steel, Federal Steel, American Steel and Wire, American Plate, American Steel Hoop, American Bridge Company, and Lake Superior Consolidated Iron Mines.

1911, ending 9 months before an antitrust suit was filed.[23] In this industry, both a merger that substantially raised concentration and Gary's ability to persuade the board of directors of the benefits of cooperation were significant contributors to collusion in the steel industry. Ultimately, enforcement of the antitrust laws led to the demise of cartel behavior.

9.4.2 The OPEC Cartel[24]

Although the Organization of Petroleum Exporting Countries (OPEC) is frequently considered a classic example of a cartel, it does not meet the criteria of a perfect cartel. OPEC is unable to consistently control world oil production. Further, OPEC members have not always pursued purely economic goals. In some cases, both political and economic factors come into play. Thus, at best, OPEC is an imperfect cartel. We summarize OPEC's behavior since its inception, paying particular attention to the causes of the three oil shocks that occurred in 1973–1974, in 1979–1980, and in 2004–2007.

OPEC was established in 1960 when the USA imposed oil quotas that favored imported oil from Canada and Mexico over oil from Venezuela and the Persian Gulf. In response, the minister of Venezuelan Energy and Mining called a meeting in September of 1960 with the major oil producing nations to discuss ways to increase oil prices. OPEC was established at this meeting; founding members were Iran, Iraq, Kuwait, Saudi Arabia, and Venezuela. Since then, several countries have joined OPEC: Qatar (in 1961), Libya (1962), UAE (1967), Algeria (1969), Nigeria (1971), and Angola (2007).[25] In spite of OPEC's efforts, real oil prices did not rise from 1960 through 1972. In fact, real prices (in 2009 dollars) averaged \$23.35 (ranging from \$21.24 to \$24.84) from 1950 to 1959 and averaged \$20.21 (ranging from \$18.84 to \$20.84) from 1960 to 1972.

One reason for its ineffectiveness is that the oil within OPEC nations was extracted and sold by foreign corporations, primarily British Petroleum, Shell, Exxon, Standard Oil of California, Texaco, Gulf Oil, and Mobil. OPEC consists of a group of countries, not producers, making it difficult for OPEC to set price or production quotas. Initially, OPEC countries imposed high excise taxes on oil that was extracted and exported from their countries, but beginning in 1971 each

---

[23] United States v. United States Steel Corporation et al., 251 US 417 (1920). Although this behavior would be considered illegal today, the Supreme Court acquitted US Steel because the government challenged the monopoly status of the company (under Section 2 of the Sherman Act) rather than its collusive behavior (under Section 1). The government could not make a strong enough case that US Steel had monopolized the market because its market share had fallen from 65% to 52% from 1907 to 1915.

[24] This discussion borrows from Scherer (1996), Martin (2005), Mufson (2007), Perry (2007), El-Tablawy (2008), Samuelson (2008), and Jahn (2009).

[25] Ecuador, Gabon, and Indonesia also joined OPEC but later left.

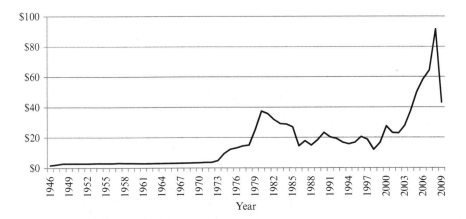

Fig. 9.8 Nominal price of oil in the USA, 1946–2009

country began to nationalize or take over majority ownership of petroleum operations within its borders. Most international oil companies became tenants of their oil operations, receiving a straight fee per barrel for services. Further, OPEC nations gained greater control over oil production.

The first oil shock occurred in 1973. Due to an economic boom of industrial nations, OPEC called a meeting to raise oil prices. Before an agreement was reached, on October 6, 1973 Egypt and Syria invaded the disputed regions that were occupied by Israel, actions that were opposed by many oil importing nations. This opposition led OPEC delegates to agree to a substantial price increase. In addition, Arab OPEC members imposed an oil embargo on shipments to two nations that supported Israel, the USA and the Netherlands. The result was an unprecedented increase in the average (nominal) price of oil per barrel in the USA, rising from $3.60 in 1972 to $9.35 in 1974 (see Fig. 9.8), and an economic recession. The political tension between the West and OPEC countries may be just as important as economic considerations in explaining the oil shock of 1973.

The second oil shock began with the political unrest in Iran at the end of 1978. In response to continued conflict with oil consumers from Western nations, Iranian oil exports ceased for 69 days in early 1979. Unfortunately, Iran accounted for 15% of OPEC oil production in 1978. With insufficient capacity to pick up the slack in the short run, oil prices rose sharply (see Fig. 9.8). In the USA, the average price of oil rose from $15 to $37 per barrel from 1978 to 1980. This embargo triggered another major recession in the USA.

The final oil shock occurred in the 2000s, a period when oil prices rose to record highs (see Fig. 9.8). For example, the nominal price of a barrel of oil rose from about $16 in 1999 to a peak of $147 in July of 2008. There are two main reasons for this steep rise in price. First, the war in Iraq and the political unrest in Nigeria, Iran, and Venezuela caused supply to diminish by an estimated 5% to 8%. Second, a booming world economy and the rapid development of China and India caused world oil demand to increase 13% from 1999 to 2007. In this period, China's demand almost doubled, compared to US demand which grew by 7%. The effect of the world economy on oil prices became even more apparent with the major recession that began in early 2008. By December of 2008 when the recession hit its peak, oil prices declined to just $43 per barrel.

The multitude of factors and events in the market for oil makes it difficult to judge the effectiveness of OPEC in coordinating output and price levels in the world oil market. Although OPEC does not call itself a cartel, it has endeavored to collude. Its Web page indicates that OPEC sets production quotas for member nations and was established to acquire "a major say in the pricing of crude oil on world markets."[26] OPEC has also encouraged non-member nations to coordinate with OPEC in setting production quotas worldwide. If US companies behaved this way, they would be in clear violation of the Sherman Act.

In any case, the evidence indicates that OPEC has not been a perfect cartel. First, coordination is a problem because member nations do not have a single goal. Saudi Arabia and other sparsely populated nations along the Persian Gulf prefer to emphasize the economic interests of OPEC nations (i.e., to act as a profit-maximizing cartel). On the other hand, leaders of other nations have frequently said that OPEC should also be an "active political agent" and pursue the political, frequently anti-American, interests of member nations (Mouawad 2007). This sentiment is consistent with the political motivation of the first two oil shocks.

A second problem that limits OPEC's success is that production costs vary widely among member nations, making coordination more difficult. As an example, oil development and operating costs are less than $2 per barrel for Saudi Arabia but are $7 for Venezuela (*The Economist*, March 6, 1999, 23). Disparate costs can create a difference of opinion concerning how output restrictions should be distributed among member nations.

Third, OPEC nations appear to face a difficult cartel dilemma. One issue is that OPEC controls part but not all of world oil production, ranging from 40 to 41% from 2004 to 2009. Thus, non-OPEC suppliers may encourage production cuts by OPEC nations and then increase their own production. Even among OPEC nations, cheating on production quotas has been a frequent problem, especially in the 1980s when the real price of oil fell dramatically (see Fig. 9.9). Cheating has also been a problem in the last decade. For example, Saudi Arabia was reported to be producing about 5% above its quota in early 2009 (*Petroleum Economist* 2009).

Finally, entry and energy conservation have weakened OPEC's power. Steep oil prices in the early 1980s and in the last decade led to rigorous exploration and the discovery of new oil fields in Alaska, Brazil, Canada, and Russia. New energy conserving technologies have also reduced energy demand. For instance, US per capita oil consumption was 28.5 barrels in 1972 and just 23.4 barrels in 2008.

---

[26] OPEC's stated objective "is to co-ordinate and unify petroleum policies among Member Countries, in order to secure fair and stable prices for petroleum producers; an efficient, economic and regular supply of petroleum to consuming nations; and a fair return on capital to those investing in the industry." Available at http://www.opec.org, accessed May 15, 2010.

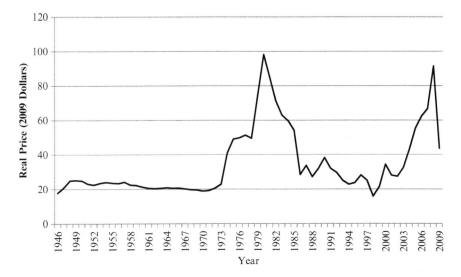

Fig. 9.9 The real price of oil in the USA (2009 dollars), 1946–2009

We can conclude that OPEC is an imperfect cartel that suffers from many of the problems associated with maintaining collusive agreements between independent suppliers. Not only must OPEC deal with coordinating an agreement among countries with different cost structures, address the cartel dilemma, and cope with entry of new suppliers, but it must also operate in the presence of volatile political issues. Given these difficulties, it is not surprising that the real price of oil has fluctuated so dramatically since OPEC gained power in the early 1970s as Fig. 9.9 indicates.

9.4.3   The International Vitamin Cartel[27]

According to a statement from the US Attorney General's office (*Federal News Service* 1999), "the vitamin cartel is the most pervasive and harmful criminal antitrust conspiracy ever uncovered." The vitamin cartel was international in scope, lasted for 10 years, and operated as a near perfect cartel.

The international vitamin cartel was formed in 1989 when F. Hoffmann-La Roche (of Switzerland), BASF (of Germany), and Rhone-Poulenc (now Aventis, of France) met in Switzerland and agreed to raise the prices of vitamins A and E. Soon afterwards, the Japanese chemical company Eisai joined in the price-fixing agreement. By the end of 1991, at least 20 worldwide vitamin producers participated in the conspiracy. Sixteen different vitamin products were involved, which were sold as supplements and added to such products as milk, breakfast cereal, cosmetics, and animal feed.

---

[27] This discussion borrows from the Department of Justice (May 21, 1999), Europa (2001), and Bush et al. (2004).

The cartel was stable and highly successful for three main reasons. First, participants agreed to set prices and allocate volume so that market shares remained stable and revenues were fairly distributed. Second, adherence to cartel agreements were closely monitored and strictly enforced. Participants met quarterly and sometimes monthly to share price and sales information. Finally, entry was thwarted by high entry barriers due to substantial start-up costs and scale economies (Connor and Lande 2006).

The vitamin cartel was exceptionally large in scale. Total affected sales are estimated to be $8.3 billion in the European economic area, $7.4 billion in the USA, and $0.55 billion in Canada. Globally, sales affected by price-fixing agreements are estimated to be $34.3 billion.

The vitamin cartel was able to raise prices and adversely affect consumers throughout the world. After reviewing the evidence, Bush et al. (2004) conclude that the cartel was able to raise average vitamin prices by 20% to 35% in the USA and by 30% to 40% in Canada and Europe. These estimates imply that the dollar value of global injuries were between $9 to $13 billion, with 15% accruing to the USA, 26% to the European economic area, 1% to Canada, and 58% to the rest of the world.

The cartel's only weakness was that collusion is illegal in developed countries. World antitrust authorities were able to crack the cartel by obtaining insider cooperation. Rhone-Poulenc voluntarily reported details of the cartel in exchange for full immunity from the US Department of Justice and the European Commission. Amnesty policies exist in the USA and the European Union, giving immunity to the first company to cooperate with authorities. According to Pate (2004) of the Antitrust Division of the US Department of Justice, "Because cartel activities are hatched and carried out in secret, obtaining the cooperation of insiders is the best and often the only way to crack a cartel." This first to come forward policy adds to cartel instability.

Fines imposed on cartel participants were the highest in history for an antitrust violation. Leading producers and instigators of the cartel received stiff fines in the USA in 1999 and in Europe in 2001. F. Hoffmann-La Roche received fines of $500 million in the USA and $407 million in Europe, BASF received fines of $225 million in the USA and $261 million in Europe, and Eisai received fines of $40 million in the USA and $11.7 million in Europe. Total fines on all cartel participants are estimated to be between $4.4 and $5.6 billion.

Despite the impressive magnitude of the fines, Bush et al. (2004) point out the total fine was considerably less than the estimated gain from cartel activity, of between $9 and $13 billion. Thus, this case raises an important policy concern. Because the probability of being caught is less than 100%, for a fine to be an effective deterrent it must exceed the expected gain in profits that results from cartel activity. In the case of the vitamin cartel, fines should have been well over double their actual amounts.[28] Issues involving the effectiveness of antitrust policy will be taken up in Chap. 20.

---

[28] To illustrate, consider a cartel that increases profits by $10 billion and has a probability of being successfully caught and convicted of 50%. In this case, the expected gain from forming a cartel is $10 billion minus $0.5 \cdot f$, where f is the amount of the fine. For the fine to successfully deter a cartel, the expected gain must be negative. For this to be true, f must exceed $20 billion.

In any case, we can conclude that if it were not for antitrust enforcement, the international vitamin cartel would have continued as a near perfect cartel.

9.5 Summary

1. There are two types of oligopoly models, those that assume cooperation or collusion and those that assume noncooperative behavior. Collusion can be explicit or tacit. **Explicit collusion** occurs when firms make a formal agreement to coordinate on one or more strategic variables. **Tacit collusion** occurs when firms coordinate without a formal agreement.
2. A **cartel** is a group of firms that have made an explicit collusive agreement. In a **perfect cartel**, all firms in the industry are members of the cartel and their goal is to maximize industry profits. This leads to the monopoly price and total output level. Like a monopoly, a cartel outcome is allocatively inefficient.
3. Cartels face a **coordination problem**, because the output levels or market shares of each firm in the cartel are indeterminate. With two firms, the coordination problem is described by the **output-distribution line**, which identifies all combinations of firm output from cartel participants who will produce the total cartel (monopoly) level of output.
4. In a duopoly setting, firm i's **isoprofit equation** describes all possible levels of q_i and q_j that are consistent with a constant level of profit for firm i. The isoprofit curves are tangent at points along the output-distribution line.
5. The **cartel dilemma** is a type of prisoners' dilemma. Action that is most profitable from the cartel's perspective is not what is most profitable from the individual firm's perspective. Individual firms have an incentive to cheat on the cartel agreement by increasing output (or lowering price).
6. Collusion is more likely when the following conditions hold.

   - Cartels are legal or the expected cost of antitrust litigation is low.
   - There are few firms in the market.
   - Firms have similar costs and produce homogeneous goods.
   - Demand and cost conditions are stable.
   - Entry barriers are high.

7. There are several ways firms can facilitate collusion.

   - **Market Division:** The market is divided up so that each firm serves a different set of customers. This avoids direct competition among firms.
   - **Most-Favored-Customer Clause:** If a customer purchases a product today that is discounted in the near future, the customer will receive a rebate for the difference in price. This guarantee reduces a firm's benefit from cutting price.
   - **Meet-the-Competition Clause:** A store will meet the low price of any competitor. This eliminates a firm's benefit from cutting price.

- **Trigger Strategy:** In a duopoly setting, this involves two components: (1) firm i cooperates today if firm j cooperated in the previous period and (2) firm i behaves competitively for an extended period if firm j failed to cooperate in the previous period. The **fundamental principle of collusion** states that a trigger strategy is more likely to support collusion when there are fewer firms and when future profits are not too heavily discounted.

8. The empirical evidence regarding cartels is generally consistent with economic theory. Collusion typically leads to higher prices and profits, but the monopoly outcome is rarely reached because not all firms in the market are cartel members in most real-world cartels. Cheating and the entry of new competitors are prominent causes of cartel failure. Cartels are more successful when concentration is high, products are relatively homogeneous, entry barriers are high, and demand growth is steady.

9. The US steel industry provides an excellent example where company leaders met socially to form price-fixing agreements, as Adam Smith predicted. At best, OPEC is an imperfect cartel because cartel members frequently disagree on economic versus political goals, OPEC nations produce only about 40% of the world supply of oil, and entry and cheating on production quotas have diminished OPEC's economic power to control price. The international vitamin cartel provides an example of the most sophisticated and elaborate conspiracy to fix prices. If it had not been for the antitrust laws in Europe and the USA, it would have continued to this day.

9.6   Review Questions

1. Define collusion and a perfect cartel. Compare and contrast cartel and monopoly outcomes.

2. Assume a duopoly market (firms 1 and 2) with the following inverse market demand: $p = 120 - Q$, where $Q = q_1 + q_2$. Firms face the same costs, and firm i's total cost equation is $TC_i = 20q_i$.

   A. Determine the cartel price and market level of output.
   B. Without additional information about the cartel, explain why you cannot calculate the output and profit levels for each firm.

3. Discuss the efficiency implications of a perfect cartel. Does your answer justify antitrust laws that make collusion illegal?

4. For each pair of industries listed below, which of the two would you expect collusion to be easier to maintain. Explain.

   A. Steel and automobiles.
   B. Cement and wheat.
   C. Fast food and airline service between two cities.

5. Regarding the Cartel Dilemma:

   A. Briefly explain the cartel dilemma.
   B. In the duopoly problem described in question 2 above, calculate the optimal levels of output and profits for each firm if you assume symmetry (i.e., equilibrium output and profits are the same for each firm).
   C. (Advanced) Show that firm 1 will prefer to cheat on the cartel agreement by increasing output.

6. In problem 2 above, assume that firms are able to divide the market in half, so that each firm's inverse demand becomes $p_i = 120 - 2q_i$. Would this be an effective way to facilitate collusion?

7. Office Depot, Office Max, and Staples compete in the office supply market by offering low-price guarantees (i.e., a meet-the-competition clause). Are such guarantees beneficial or harmful to consumers? Explain.

8. Assume that a market consists of three firms (1, 2, and 3) which form a cartel. Firm 3 is a rogue firm that frequently undercuts the price of its competitors. Could such behavior lead to even lower prices than would be found in competitive markets? Explain.

9. Suppose you were looking for an industry in which to form a cartel. Given the empirical evidence, what would be the ideal set of conditions that would maximize the likelihood of cartel success?

10. Provide a behavioral reason why it could be more difficult to establish and maintain an effective cartel among firms in different nations, such as the OPEC cartel, than among firms within a single nation, such as the steel cartel in the USA during the early twentieth century.

Chapter 10
Quantity and Price Competition
in Static Oligopoly Models

We saw in the previous chapter that there are two types of oligopoly models, those that assume cooperative behavior and those that assume noncooperative behavior. In Chaps. 10 and 11, we develop the classic models of oligopoly where firms behave noncooperatively. These models represent the most abstract material that is found in the book. Here you will see how some of the great figures in history have thought about the oligopoly problem.

A fundamental question in industrial organization is the extent to which the number of competitors (n) affects price competition. We have seen that price equals marginal cost (MC) in perfect competition and exceeds marginal cost in a monopoly setting. These equilibrium outcomes are illustrated in Fig. 10.1. Point A identifies the monopoly outcome at the monopoly price (p_M) and $n = 1$. Point B identifies the perfectly competitive outcome where price (p_{PC}) equals marginal cost and $n =$ many. One of our goals is to determine what happens between these two polar extremes when there are only a few competitors. As you might expect, p_M and p_{PC} represent the upper and lower limits on actual prices in most real oligopoly markets. From the previous chapter, we know that a perfect cartel will lead to the monopoly outcome, but what happens if firms behave noncooperatively?

The first formal models of oligopoly were developed by Cournot (1838) and Bertrand (1883). Not only are these models of historical significance, but they also provide the theoretical foundation for more realistic models that will be discussed in applied chapters later in the book. Furthermore, Cournot and Bertrand anticipated the static Nash equilibrium long before game theoretic methods were formally developed. The key difference between the Cournot and Bertrand models is the choice of strategic variable. In Cournot the choice variable is output, and in Bertrand it is price.

These static Cournot and Bertrand models have been extended in two ways. First, in the Cournot–Bertrand model, some firms compete in output (a la Cournot), while others compete in price (a la Bertrand). The second extension allows the

V.J. Tremblay and C.H. Tremblay, *New Perspectives on Industrial Organization*,
Springer Texts in Business and Economics, DOI 10.1007/978-1-4614-3241-8_10,
© Springer Science+Business Media New York 2012

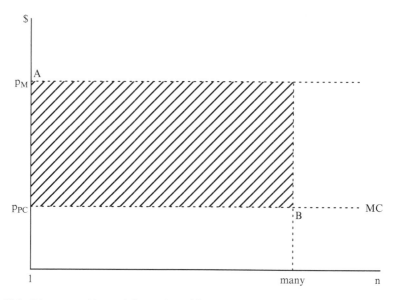

Fig. 10.1 Price competition and the number of firms (n)

choice of strategic variable (output or price) to be endogenously chosen by firms. That is, each firm can choose whether it wants to compete in output or in price. We will see that in contrast to the monopoly case, the choice of strategic variable has a dramatic effect on the equilibrium outcome in an oligopoly setting.

We also consider dynamic versions of these models in Chap. 11. The first is a dynamic version of the Cournot model, where one firm chooses output in the first stage or period and one or more firms choose output in the second stage of the game. This model was first considered by Stackelberg (1934). Other extensions include the dynamic Bertrand model, the dynamic Cournot–Bertrand model, and a model that allows the timing of play to be endogenous. We will see that small changes in the structure of the game concerning the timing of actions and the information possessed by firms, as well as the choice of strategic variable, can profoundly affect market outcomes.

Table 10.1 lists 12 oligopoly models and their key characteristics, labeled M1 through M12. The classic models are Cournot, Bertrand, Dynamic Cournot (or Stackelberg), and Dynamic Bertrand, labeled M1, M2, M5, and M6, respectively. In this chapter, we focus on the static models, M1–M4. In the next chapter, we consider the dynamic models (M5–M8) and cases where the timing of play is endogenous (models M9–M12). We consider the empirical evidence regarding price competition in oligopoly markets in Chap. 12.

Here, discussion begins with a simple market of just two firms that produce homogeneous goods. This minimizes mathematical complexity but still allows us to analyze many of the essential features of firm strategy in the Cournot and Bertrand models. Next, we extend the models to allow for asymmetric costs, more than two firms, and product differentiation. Then, we develop the relatively new

Table 10.1   Twelve Duopoly models: output and price competition in static and dynamic settings

	Timing of actions[b]		
	Static	Dynamic	Endogenous (Early or Late)
Strategic variable[a]			
Output	M1 (Cournot)	M5 (Dynamic-Cournot)[c]	M9
Price	M2 (Bertrand)	M6 (Dynamic-Bertrand)	M10
Output–price	M3 (Cournot–Bertrand)	M7 (Dynamic Cournot–Bertrand)	M11
Endogenous (Output or Price)	M4	M8	M12

[a]Output means that both firms compete in output; Price means that both firms compete in price; Output–price means that one firm competes in output and the other firm competes in price; Endogenous means that firms can choose whether to compete in output or price.
[b]Static means that the game is static (i.e., there is a single stage or period); Dynamic means that the game is dynamic (i.e., there are two stages); Endogenous means that firms choose whether to compete in an early or late period.
[c]The dynamic-Cournot model is also called the Stackelberg model.

Cournot–Bertrand model. Finally, we consider the case where the choice of strategic variable (output versus price) is endogenous and discuss when choice variables are considered strategic substitutes and strategic complements.

10.1   Cournot and Bertrand Models with Homogeneous Products

In this section, we derive the classic models of Cournot (1838) and Bertrand (1883) when products are homogeneous. Because they are prominent in our discussion in later chapters, we formally derive the Nash equilibrium (NE) for each model and describe each result graphically. These are models M1 and M2 in Table 10.1.

10.1.1   The Cournot Model with Two Firms and Symmetric Costs

The first formal model of duopoly was developed by Cournot (1838). He describes a market where there are two springs of water that are owned by different individuals. The owners sell water independently in a given period. Production costs are zero, and demand is negatively sloped. Each owner sets output to maximize its profit at the same moment in time, and the equilibrium price clears the market (p^*).[1] Cournot's goal was to determine the optimal values of firm output, price, and profit. Notice that because the products are homogeneous, $p_1 = p_2 = p^*$ in equilibrium.

---

[1] This assumes an auctioneer who quotes a market price that just clears the market, which is p^*.

For our purposes, we allow costs to be positive and assume linear demand and cost equations. As in previous chapters, inverse demand is $p = a - bQ$ and firm (owner) i's total cost is $TC_i = cq_i$. Recall that p is price and Q is industry output, where Q is the sum of the output from firm 1 (q_1) and firm 2 (q_2). All parameters are positive: a is the price intercept of demand, $-b$ is the slope of inverse demand, and c is the marginal and average cost of production. To assure firm participation, $a > c$. In terms of notation, subscript i identifies firm 1 or 2, and subscript j represents the other firm.

One goal of this chapter is to learn how to describe this economic problem as a game. Recall that to be a game, we must define the players, their choice variables, their payoffs, the timing of play, and the information set. In this chapter, we only consider static games where players have complete information. That is, decisions are made simultaneously and all of the characteristics of the game are common knowledge. In this case, the relevant characteristics are:

1. Players: Firms (owners) 1 and 2.
2. Strategic variable: Firm i chooses nonnegative values of q_i.
3. Payoffs: Firm i's payoffs are profits; $\pi_i(q_i, q_j) = TR_i - TC_i$, where TR_i is firm i's total revenue $(p \cdot q_i)$. In this model, $\pi_i = p \cdot q_i - cq_i = [a - b(q_i + q_j)] \cdot q_i - cq_i = aq_i - bq_i^2 - bq_iq_j - cq_i$.
4. Information is complete.

Note that linear demand and cost functions produce a profit equation that is quadratic, just as in the monopoly model in Chap. 6.[2] The NE solution to this game turns out to be the same as the Cournot solution and has been called the Cournot equilibrium, the Cournot–Nash equilibrium, or the Nash equilibrium in output to a duopoly game. Here, we call it the Cournot equilibrium.

Recall from Chap. 3 that we derive the NE in two steps. The first step is to find each firm's best-reply function, which identifies firm i's profit maximizing output (q_i^{BR}) for all values of q_j. This is simply firm i's first-order condition of profit maximization, where we take the first derivative of the firm's profit and set it to 0. Second, we must derive the output levels that constitute a mutual best reply, where the best-reply functions for both firms simultaneously hold. This identifies NE output levels. In other words, firm i maximizes its profit with respect to q_i, assuming that firm j chooses its NE output level. The first-order conditions for each firm are[3]

$$\frac{\partial \pi_1}{\partial q_1} = \frac{\partial TR_1}{\partial q_1} - \frac{\partial TC_1}{\partial q_1}$$
$$= MR_1 - MC_1$$
$$= (a - 2bq_1 - bq_2) - (c) = 0, \qquad (10.1)$$

---

[2] In fact, firm i's profit equation would be identical to that of a monopolist if $q_j = 0$.

[3] This produces a maximum because the profit equation for each firm is concave. That is, the second-order condition of profit maximization holds, because the second derivative of the profit equation for each firm is $-2b < 0$. For further discussion of second-order conditions, see the Mathematics and Econometrics Appendix at the end of the book.

$$\frac{\partial \pi_2}{\partial q_2} = \frac{\partial TR_2}{\partial q_2} - \frac{\partial TC_2}{\partial q_2}$$
$$= MR_2 - MC_2$$
$$= (a - 2bq_2 - bq_1) - (c) = 0, \tag{10.2}$$

where MR_i is firm i's marginal revenue ($\partial TR_i / \partial q_i$) and MC_i is firm i's marginal cost ($\partial TC_i / \partial q_i$).[4] Again, these first-order conditions identify each firm's best (profit maximizing) reply to its rival's output level. We will illustrate this graphically momentarily.

At the equilibrium, a NE or a mutual best reply means that (10.1) and (10.2) must both be true. To find the Cournot equilibrium output levels, we solve (10.1) and (10.2) simultaneously for output:

$$q_1^* = q_2^* = \frac{a - c}{3b}. \tag{10.3}$$

Substituting these values into the demand function and firm profit equations gives us NE price and profits:

$$p^* = \frac{(a + 2c)}{3}, \tag{10.4}$$

$$\pi_1^* = \pi_2^* = \frac{(a - c)^2}{9b}. \tag{10.5}$$

Equations (10.3)–(10.5) indicate that the Cournot model gives reasonable comparative static predictions, that is, predictions concerning how the equilibrium will change with demand and cost conditions.[5] Just like the monopoly model, output and profit levels go up with a decrease in marginal cost and an increase in demand (i.e., as a increases and b decreases). Price rises with an increase in marginal cost and demand.

An interesting feature of the model is that it produces a symmetric equilibrium, one where output, price, and profits are the same for both firms. This is evident when we inspect the first-order conditions of both firms. Notice that the conditions are interchangeable when we replace subscript 1 with 2 and subscript 2 with 1. This **interchangeability condition** leads to a symmetric outcome where the NE strategies of each firm can be described by a single equation.[6] Symmetry will typically occur when firms have the same cost functions, produce homogeneous goods, and pursue the same goals. But models may be symmetric under other conditions as well, which we will see later in the chapter.

---

[4] We derive firm i's marginal revenue as follows. Firm i's total revenue function is $TR_i = aq_i - bq_i^2 - bq_iq_j$. We obtain the partial derivative of TR_i by taking its derivative and holding rival output (q_j) fixed. Thus, $\partial \pi_i / \partial q_i = a - 2bq_i - bq_j$.

[5] For a discussion of comparative static analysis, see the Mathematics and Econometrics Appendix.

[6] This symmetry condition is sometimes called a level playing field assumption or an exchangeability assumption (Athey and Schmutzler 2001).

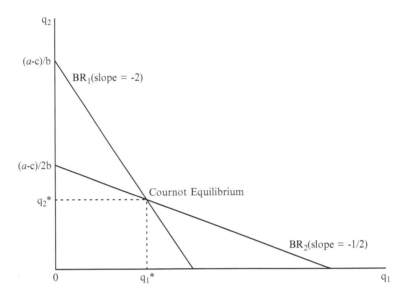

Fig. 10.2 Best-reply functions and the Cournot equilibrium

Now that we have derived the NE for the Cournot model, we want to describe it graphically. One way to do this is to graph the best-reply functions, which are obtained by solving each firm's first-order condition for q_2.[7] From (10.1) and (10.2), the best-reply functions for firm 1 (BR_1) and firm 2 (BR_2) are

$$BR_1 : q_2 = \frac{a - c}{b} - 2q_1, \tag{10.6}$$

$$BR_2 : q_2 = \frac{a - c}{2b} - \frac{1}{2}q_1. \tag{10.7}$$

Notice that these functions are linear and are expressed in slope-intercept form. Both have a negative slope, BR_1 is steeper than BR_2, and BR_1 has a higher intercept than BR_2.[8]

The best-reply functions are graphed in Fig. 10.2, with q_2 on the vertical axis and q_1 on the horizontal axis.[9] The best-reply functions hold simultaneously where they intersect, which identifies the Cournot equilibrium. At this point each firm is maximizing profit, given its belief that its rival is doing the same, a belief that is consistent with actual behavior at the equilibrium. That is, this point represents

---

[7] We solve for q_2 because q_2 will be on the vertical axis and q_1 will be on the horizontal axis in our figures.

[8] That is, the q_2 intercept is $(a–c)/b$ for BR_1 and $(a–c)/(2b)$ for BR_2. The slope is $–2$ for BR_1 and $–\frac{1}{2}$ for BR_2.

[9] As we demonstrate in Appendix 10.A, the equilibrium is stable because BR_1 is steeper than BR_2.

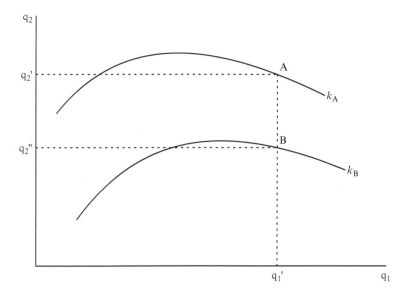

Fig. 10.3 Firm 1's isoprofits

a mutual best reply, and neither firm has an incentive to deviate from it.[10] The diagram can also be used to visualize the comparative static results that output rises with parameter a and falls with parameters b and c.

Another way of depicting the Cournot equilibrium is with isoprofit curves. Recall from the previous chapter that a firm's isoprofit equation maps out all combinations of q_1 and q_2 for a constant level of profit, k. Based on the linear demand and cost functions above, the isoprofit equation for firm i includes all q_1–q_2 pairs of points that satisfy: $\pi_i = k = aq_i - bq_i^2 - bq_iq_j - cq_i$. We obtain firm 1's isoprofit equation by solving for q_2: $q_2 = (aq_1 - cq_1 - bq_1^2 - k)/(bq_1)$, which is a quadratic function. Two isoprofit curves for firm 1 are graphed in Fig. 10.3 for different values of k. Notice that they are concave to the q_1 axis and that firm 1's profits rise as we move to a lower isoprofit curve (i.e., $k_B > k_A$). The reason for this is that for a given value of q_1 (e.g., q_1'), firm 1's profits increase as q_2 falls (from q_2' to q_2''). Parallel results hold for firm 2; the only difference is that its isoprofit curve is concave to the q_2 axis.

Isoprofit curves can be used to identify the cartel outcome and to derive a firm's best-reply function. Consider firm 1's problem when $q_2 = q_2'$, as described in

---

[10] Recall from Chap. 4 that two players have reached a NE when firm i's best reply to s_j^* is s_i^*, for all $i = 1$ or 2 and $j \neq i$. In other words, firm i chooses s_i^* based on the belief that firm j chooses s_j^*. The NE is reached when this belief is correct for both firms. In the Cournot model, this means that (1) when firm 2 chooses q_2^*, firm 1's best reply is q_1^* and (2) when firm 1 chooses q_1^*, firm 2's best reply is q_2^*. Thus, the q_1^*–q_2^* pair is a mutual best reply and neither firm has an incentive to change its level of output.

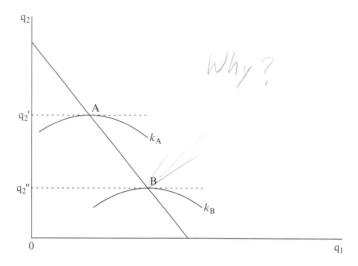

Fig. 10.4 Derivation of firm 1's best-reply function

Fig. 10.4. To obtain firm 1's best reply, firm 1 will choose the level of output that maximizes its profits, given the constraint that $q_2 = q_2'$. This occurs on the lowest possible isoprofit curve, at tangency point A. Notice that this is simply a constrained optimization problem. Similarly, when $q_2 = q_2''$, the tangency point is at B. The locus of these tangency points for all values of q_2 generates firm 1's best-reply function, depicted as the solid line in the figure. The same approach can be used to derive firm 2's best-reply function.

Figure 10.5 describes the Cournot equilibrium with respect to best reply and isoprofit curves. At the equilibrium, it is clear that each firm is maximizing its profit given that its rival is producing at the equilibrium level of output. That is, firm 1's isoprofit curve, π_1^*, is tangent to firm 2's optimal output (dashed) line at q_2^*; similarly, firm 2's isoprofit curve, π_2^*, is tangent to firm 1's output (dashed) line at q_1^*. Thus, this is a NE because it is a mutual best reply and neither firm has an incentive to deviate. However, both firms can earn higher profits if they cut production, which would move them into the shaded, lens-shaped region in Fig. 10.5. As we saw in Chap. 9, the cartel outcome occurs in this region where the isoprofit functions are tangent.

10.1.2   The Cournot Model with Two Firms and Asymmetric Costs

We next consider the Cournot model when there is a dominant firm. A dominant firm has a larger market share than its competitors, which can arise when the firm produces a superior product or produces at lower cost than its competitors.[11]

---

[11] In addition, this firm typically takes a leadership role in choosing output or price, an issue we take up in the next chapter.

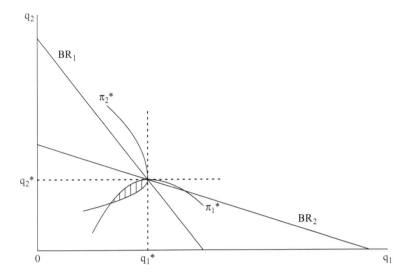

Fig. 10.5 The Cournot equilibrium with best-reply functions and isoprofits

In this section, we consider the case where firm 1 has a cost advantage over firm 2. The only difference from the previous model is that firm i's total cost becomes $TC_i = c_i q_i$, where $c_1 < c_2$. Thus, the firm's profits become $\pi_i = aq_i - bq_i^2 - bq_i q_j - c_i q_i$.

We obtain the NE using the same method as before. We solve the first-order conditions simultaneously for output and plug these optimal values into the demand and profit equations to obtain the Cournot equilibrium. In this case, the first-order conditions are

$$\frac{\partial \pi_1}{\partial q_1} = MR_1 - MC_1$$
$$= (a - 2bq_1 - bq_2) - (c_1) = 0, \tag{10.8}$$

$$\frac{\partial \pi_2}{\partial q_2} = MR_2 - MC_2$$
$$= (a - 2bq_2 - bq_1) - (c_2) = 0. \tag{10.9}$$

Marginal revenue is unchanged, but firm i's marginal cost is now c_i. Cournot values are

$$q_1^* = \frac{a - 2c_1 + c_2}{3b}, \tag{10.10}$$

$$q_2^* = \frac{a + c_1 - 2c_2}{3b}, \tag{10.11}$$

$$p^* = \frac{(a + c_1 + c_2)}{3}, \tag{10.12}$$

$$\pi_1^* = \frac{(a - 2c_1 + c_2)^2}{9b}, \tag{10.13}$$

$$\pi_2^* = \frac{(a + c_1 - 2c_2)^2}{9b}. \tag{10.14}$$

Although firms face different costs, the model is symmetric because the interchangeability condition holds. In other words, we can write firm i's first-order condition as

$$\frac{\partial \pi_i}{\partial q_i} = a - 2bq_i - bq_j - c_i = 0. \tag{10.15}$$

As a result, the NE can be written more compactly as

$$q_i^* = \frac{a - 2c_i + c_j}{3b}, \tag{10.16}$$

$$p^* = \frac{(a + c_i + c_j)}{3}, \tag{10.17}$$

$$\pi_i^* = \frac{(a - 2c_i + c_j)^2}{9b}. \tag{10.18}$$

Note that as c_i approaches c_j (value c), the solution approaches the Cournot equilibrium with symmetric costs found in (10.3)–(10.5). The key insight from studying the asymmetric cost case is that firm i's output and profit levels rise as rival costs increase (see 10.16 and 10.18). Thus, by having lower costs, firm 1 is the superior firm in that $q_1^* > q_2^*$ and $\pi_1^* > \pi_2^*$.

The effect of this cost asymmetry on Cournot output levels can be seen in a graph of best-reply functions. Again, the best-reply functions are derived by solving each firm's first-order conditions for q_2:

$$BR_1 : q_2 = \frac{a - c_1}{b} - 2q_1, \tag{10.19}$$

$$BR_2 : q_2 = \frac{a - c_2}{2b} - \frac{1}{2}q_1. \tag{10.20}$$

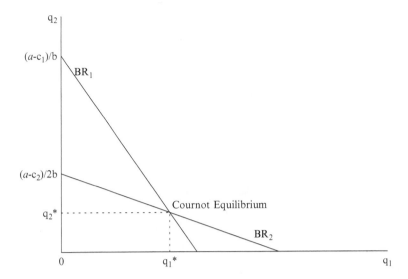

Fig. 10.6 The Cournot equilibrium when firm 1 has lower costs than firm 2

Compared to the symmetric case, the slopes are unchanged but the distance between the q_2 intercepts for the two firms widens. The best replies are plotted in Fig. 10.6 and show that a cost advantage for firm 1 increases the equilibrium value of q_1 and decreases the equilibrium value of q_2.

This model also reveals that if firm 2 has an extreme cost disadvantage compared to firm 1, firm 1 will have a monopoly position. For sufficiently high c_2, the best-reply functions intersect at a negative value of q_2 (see Fig. 10.7). Firm 2 will shut down ($q_2^* = 0$), leaving firm 1 as the sole producer. From (10.19), when $q_2^* = 0$ firm 1's best reply is $q_1^* = (a - c_1)/(2b)$, the monopoly level of output. In this case, the Cournot equilibrium is the same as the monopoly solution that we derived in Chap. 6, with $q_2^* = 0$, $q_1^* = (a - c_1)/(2b)$, $p^* = (a + c_1)/2$, and $\pi_1^* = (a - c_1)^2/(4b)$. This demonstrates that the monopoly outcome is a NE.

10.1.3 The Cournot Model with n Firms and Symmetric Costs

Next we consider the Cournot model with symmetric costs and n firms. Our goal is to see how NE values change as n starts at 1 (monopoly) and approaches infinity (perfect competition). The model is general in that it describes the NE for any market structure from monopoly through perfect competition.

We continue to assume that demand and costs functions are linear. The only difference is that with n firms, $Q = q_1 + q_2 + q_3 + \cdots + q_n$. With these assumptions, the model is symmetric and firm i's profit equation can be written

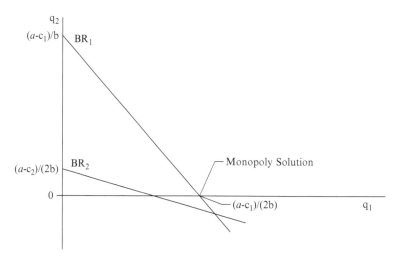

Fig. 10.7 The Cournot equilibrium when firm 2 shuts down, leaving firm 1 in a monopoly position

as $\pi_i = p \cdot q_i - cq_i = [a - b(q_1 + q_2 + q_3 + \cdots + q_n)]q_i - cq_i$. For notational convenience, we can rewrite this as

$$\pi_i = [a - b(q_i + Q_{-i})]q_i - c_i q_i, \tag{10.21}$$

where Q_{-i} is the sum of rival output (i.e., $Q_{-i} = Q - q_i$ or $Q = q_i + Q_{-i}$). The first-order condition for firm i is

$$\frac{\partial \pi_i}{\partial q_i} = MR_i - MC_i$$
$$= (a - 2bq_i - bQ_{-i}) - c = 0. \tag{10.22}$$

Given symmetry, output is the same for each firm and $Q_{-i} = (n - 1)q_i$ in equilibrium.[12] Using this fact and the demand and profit equations above, the Cournot equilibrium with n firms is

$$q_i^* = \frac{a - c}{b(n + 1)}, \tag{10.23}$$

$$p^* = \frac{a}{n + 1} + c\frac{n}{n + 1}, \tag{10.24}$$

---

[12] This is true only in equilibrium. We can set $Q_{-i} = (n-1)q_i$ in the first-order condition because optimal output levels are embedded in it. In other words, it is true that $q_1^* = q_2^* = q_3^* = \ldots = q_n^*$, but it need not be true that $q_1 = q_2 = q_3 = \ldots = q_n$. Thus, we can make this substitution in the first-order condition but not in the profit equation, (10.21).

$$\pi_i^* = \frac{(a-c)^2}{b(n+1)^2},$$ (10.25)

$$Q^* = nq_i^* = \frac{a-c}{b}\frac{n}{n+1}.$$ (10.26)

The Cournot model with n firms produces two substantive implications:

- When $n = 1$, the NE is the monopoly outcome, where $q_i^* = Q^* = (a - c)/(2b)$, $p^* = (a + c)/2$, and $\pi_i^* = (a - c)^2/(4b)$. Thus, the monopoly outcome is a NE when $n = 1$, as in the model in the previous section.
- As n approaches infinity, the NE approaches the perfectly competitive outcome, where $p^* = c$, $\pi_i^* = 0$, and $Q^* = (a - c)/b$.

This demonstrates a key principle in oligopoly theory, the **Cournot Limit Theorem**: the Cournot equilibrium equals the monopoly outcome when n equals 1 and approaches the competitive equilibrium as n approaches infinity.[13]

The Cournot Limit Theorem yields predictable implications regarding the effect of n on allocative efficiency. We illustrate this in Fig. 10.8, where the monopoly outcome is represented by price p_1 and quantity Q_1 and the perfectly competitive outcome by p_∞ and Q_∞. As discussed in Chap. 6, total (consumer plus producer) surplus is maximized in perfect competition and equals area $ap_\infty A_\infty$. For a monopolist, total surplus equals area $ap_\infty EA_1$, implying a deadweight or efficiency loss equal to area $A_1 EA_\infty$. In the Cournot model, the price–quantity pair moves to A_2 with two firms, A_4 with four firms, A_{10} with ten firms, etc. As n approaches infinity, the price–quantity pair approaches A_∞. In other words, competition reduces price and allocative inefficiency: the efficiency loss falls and approaches zero as the number of firms increases from 1 to infinity.

---

[13] We can see this more generally from firm i's first-order condition of profit maximization. Assume that the firm's profit equals $\pi_i = p(Q)q_i - TC(q_i)$, where $p(Q)q_i$ is total revenue and TC (q_i) is total cost. The first-order condition is

$$\frac{\partial \pi_i}{\partial q_i} = p + \frac{\partial p}{\partial q_i}q_i - MC_i = 0,$$

where MC_i is firm i's marginal cost. Given symmetry, $q_i = Q/n$, where Q is industry output. Thus,

$$\frac{\partial \pi_i}{\partial q_i} = p + \frac{\partial p}{\partial q_i}\frac{Q}{n} - MC_i = 0.$$

Notice that if $n = 1$, this is the first-order condition of a monopolist [see Chap. 6, Eq. (6.7)]. Furthermore, as n approaches infinity, Q/n approaches 0 and price approaches marginal cost, the perfectly competitive outcome.

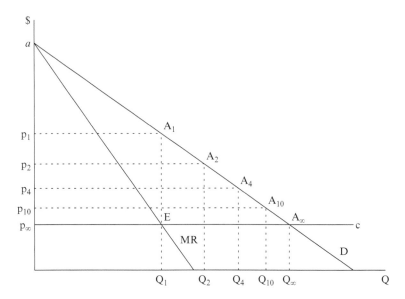

Fig. 10.8 The Cournot equilibrium and the number of competitors

If this implication were always true, there would be little left to say about the effect of market structure on allocative efficiency. Unfortunately, this is not the case, which we will see with the Bertrand model.

10.1.4   The Bertrand Model

The second duopoly model of note was developed by Bertrand (1883) when he reviewed the Cournot model. Bertrand criticized Cournot's assumption that firms compete in output, as Bertrand believed that most real firms set price, not output. In a later review of both Cournot and Bertrand's work, Fisher (1898, 126) reiterated Bertrand's concern, stating that price is a more "natural" choice variable. Recall that for a monopolist, the optimal quantity–price pair is the same whether the firm chooses output or price as the choice variable. We will see that this is not the case in an oligopoly market.

To make it easier to compare and contrast the Cournot and Bertrand models, we use the same demand and cost conditions and begin the discussion by assuming a duopoly setting with symmetric costs and homogeneous goods. Recall that the demand function in the Cournot model is expressed as an inverse demand function, $p = a - bQ$. In the Bertrand model, however, we are interested in the demand function as it has the choice variable on the right-hand side of the demand equation. Solving for output, the demand function is $Q = (a - p)/b$. For this demand function, the quantity intercept is a/b and the slope is $-1/b$.[14] In the Bertrand model, firm i's problem is to maximize $\pi_i(p_i, p_j)$ with respect to p_i instead of q_i. Once firms set prices, consumers determine quantity demanded.

It turns out that the solution to the Bertrand problem is also a NE, which is called a Bertrand equilibrium, a Bertrand–Nash equilibrium, or the NE in prices to a homogeneous goods duopoly game. We simply call it a Bertrand equilibrium. The formal characteristics of this static game are as follows:

1. Players: Firms 1 and 2.
2. Strategic Variable: Firm i chooses a nonnegative value of p_i.
3. Payoffs: Firm i's payoffs are profits: $\pi_i(p_i, p_j) = p_i \cdot q_i - cq_i$.
4. Information is complete.

If the profit equation of each firm were differentiable, we could find the Bertrand equilibrium using the same approach that we used to find the Cournot equilibrium. We would use calculus to identify the first-order conditions with respect to price for each firm and solve them simultaneously to obtain NE prices. Unfortunately, the firm's demand and, therefore, profit equations are discontinuous. Thus, we are unable to differentiate in this case.

Why is there a discontinuity? Consider firm i's demand function. Because the products are homogeneous, consumers will always purchase from the cheapest seller. If prices are the same (i.e., $p \equiv p_i = p_j$), consumers are indifferent between purchasing from firms 1 and 2. In this case, the usual assumption is that half of the consumers purchase from firm 1 and the other half from firm 2. Under these conditions and assuming that prices are less than a, quantity demanded for firm i is

$$q_i = \begin{cases} 0 & \text{if } p_i > p_j \\ \dfrac{a-p}{2b} & \text{if } p_i = p_j \\ \dfrac{a-p_i}{b} & \text{if } p_i < p_j \end{cases} \qquad (10.27)$$

The discontinuity is easy to see in the graph of firm i's demand, $d_i \equiv q_i$, found in Fig. 10.9 for a given $p_j < a$. Demand is 0 when $p_i > p_j$ and equals the market demand, $(a - p_i)/b$ when $p_i < p_j$. By assumption, demand is half the market demand, $(a - p_i)/(2b)$, when $p_i = p_j$. Thus, the firm's demand consists of the grey line segments and the point $(a - p_j)/(2b)$ when $p_i = p_j$.

The discontinuity in demand creates a discontinuity in profits, as seen in Fig. 10.10. Recall that for a monopolist, profits are quadratic for linear demand and cost functions. In this Bertrand duopoly case, firm i has a monopoly position and faces a profit equation that is quadratic when $p_i < p_j$, where $\pi_i = (a - p_i)(p_i - c)/b$. Firm i's profits are 0 when $p_i > p_j$, because firm j now has the monopoly position. When $p_i = p_j$, profits are split evenly between firms, and $\pi_i = (a - p)(p - c)/(2b)$.

---

[14] That is, $dQ/dp = -1/b$, while the slope of the inverse demand function (dp/dQ) is $-b$. In addition, the price intercept equals a.

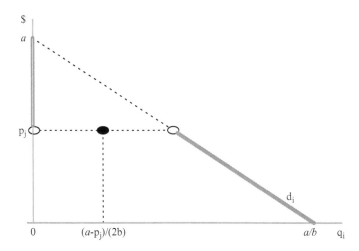

Fig. 10.9 Firm i's demand function in a Bertrand game

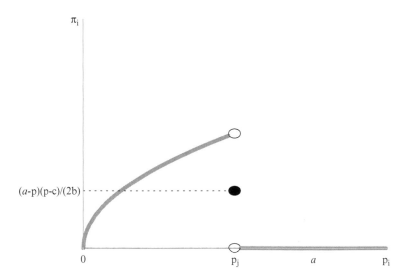

Fig. 10.10 Firm i's profits in a Bertrand game

Even though we cannot differentiate the profit equations, we can use the characteristics of a NE to identify the Bertrand solution. Recall that players will have no incentive to deviate at the NE. In this game, there is a unique NE where $p_i = p_j = c$ for $c < a$. The proof is rather intuitive, and we provide it below.[15]

---

[15] The proof assumes that prices are infinitely divisible.

We need to show that neither player has an incentive to deviate when price equals marginal cost. For this to be a unique equilibrium, we also need to show that there are no other equilibrium outcomes.

Proof Consider all relevant strategic possibilities where p_i and p_j are positive but less than $a > c$.

- $p_i > p_j > c$: This is not a NE because firm i can increase its profits by setting its price between p_j and c.
- $p_i > p_j < c$: This is not a NE because $\pi_j < 0$ and firm j can increase its profits by shutting down.
- $p_i = p_j > c$: This is not a NE because each firm can increase its profit by cutting price below its rival's price and above c.
- $p_i = p_j < c$: This is not a NE because $\pi_i < 0$ and $\pi_j < 0$. Both firms can increase profit by shutting down.
- $p_i = p_j = c$: This is a NE because neither firm can increase profit by raising or lowering price or by shutting down.

The only outcome where neither firm has an incentive to deviate occurs where $p_i = p_j = c$, the unique Bertrand equilibrium to this game. The intuition behind this result is that each firm has an incentive to undercut the price of its rival until price equals marginal cost. This is called **price undercutting** and is normally associated with a price war. Notice that the model produces a perfectly competitive outcome: $p = c$, $\pi_i = 0$, and $Q = (a - c)/b$. Comparative static results are the same as in perfect competition. That is, the equilibrium price increases with marginal cost, and industry production increases with demand and decreases with marginal cost.

The Bertrand solution shows how different the outcome can be in an oligopoly market when we change the strategic variable from output to price. Recall that in the monopoly case the solution is the same whether the firm maximizes profit with respect to output or price, but this is not the case with oligopoly. Although the assumptions of the Bertrand model are identical to the Cournot model except that price is the choice variable instead of output, the outcome is dramatically different. This demonstrates that a firm's strategic choice, as well as its demand and cost conditions, affects the NE in an oligopoly setting.

We next consider the case when $n > 2$. It is easy to verify that the Bertrand model with symmetric costs produces the perfectly competitive result as long as $n > 1$. That is, price undercutting will lead to price competition that is so fierce that only 2 or more firms are necessary to generate a perfectly competitive outcome. This result sharply contrasts with the Cournot outcome where infinitely many competitors are required for a competitive outcome. Because this Bertrand result is so extreme and generally inconsistent with reality, it is called the **Bertrand paradox**.

The analysis so far suggests that neither the Cournot nor the Bertrand model is totally satisfactory. The Cournot model produces the more realistic outcome that price falls with the number of competitors, but the Bertrand model assumes more realistically that firms compete in price rather than output. Nevertheless, the Cournot model may be more realistic than it appears. In the next chapter, we will see that when firms compete in a dynamic game, where the quantities of output are chosen in the first period and prices are chosen in the second period, the NE is Cournot. In defense of the Bertrand model, there are various ways in which firms can avoid the Bertrand paradox.

The Bertrand paradox vanishes when one firm has a competitive cost advantage over its rivals. Returning to the duopoly case, let $c_1 < c_2$. With this cost asymmetry, undercutting produces an outcome where firm 1 charges the highest possible price that is just below c_2.[16] Thus, there will be only one seller in the market, but its price may be below its simple monopoly price. Note that this is different from the Cournot model, where both the high and low cost firms may coexist. An important implication of the Bertrand model with cost asymmetries is that it shows how the presence of a potential entrant can reduce the price charged by a monopolist. Later we will see that product differentiation can also be used to overcome the Bertrand paradox.

10.2   Cournot and Bertrand Models with Differentiated Products

We begin our discussion of differentiated oligopoly with a model that assumes multicharacteristic product differentiation. Recall from Chap. 7 that this occurs when consumers value variety and products differ on a number of characteristics. Later in the chapter we consider models with different types of product differentiation. Our goal is to understand how product differentiation affects equilibrium prices, production, profits, and allocative efficiency. In this chapter, we assume that firms have already chosen product characteristics. Thus, the degree of product differentiation is predetermined. In a later chapter, we will analyze how firms make product design decisions.

To keep things simple, we assume a duopoly market where firms face the same variable costs, although fixed or quasi-fixed costs may differ by firm. Thus, any cost difference between brands is due to a difference in set-up costs, not marginal cost.

10.2.1   The Cournot Model with Multicharacteristic Differentiation

Consider a Cournot duopoly with multiproduct differentiation. From Chap. 7 we saw that the inverse demand functions for each firm are

$$p_1 = a - q_1 - dq_2, \tag{10.28}$$

$$p_2 = a - q_2 - dq_1. \tag{10.29}$$

---

[16] This also assumes that c_2 is less than firm 1's simple monopoly price (p_m).

Recall that parameter d is an index of product differentiation. Products 1 and 2 are homogeneous when $d = 1$; when $d = 0$, the products are unrelated and each firm is a monopolist. Thus, with product differentiation d ranges from 0 to 1, and the degree of product differentiation increases as d gets closer to 0. Firm i's total cost equation is $TC_i = cq_i - F_i$, where F_i is the firm's fixed (or quasi-fixed) cost. Given these demand and cost conditions, firm i's profits are $\pi_i(q_i, q_j) = TR_i - TC_i = (a - q_i - dq_j)q_i - cq_i - F_i = aq_i - q_i^2 - dq_iq_j - cq_i - F_i$.

The profit equation is differentiable, so the Cournot equilibrium can be derived in the same way as in the homogeneous goods case. That is, we obtain the first-order conditions and solve them simultaneously for output. The first-order conditions, which are similar to (10.1) and (10.2), are[17]

$$\frac{\partial \pi_1}{\partial q_1} = MR_1 - MC_1$$

$$= (a - 2q_1 - dq_2) - (c) = 0, \tag{10.30}$$

$$\frac{\partial \pi_2}{\partial q_2} = MR_2 - MC_2$$

$$= (a - 2q_2 - dq_1) - (c) = 0. \tag{10.31}$$

Solving these equations simultaneously for p_1 and p_2 yields the NE output levels. Substituting them into the demand and profit equations above gives their NE values. Notice that the interchangeability condition holds, making for a symmetric Cournot equilibrium:

$$q_i^* = \frac{a - c}{2 + d}, \tag{10.32}$$

$$p_i^* = \frac{(a + c + cd)}{2 + d}, \tag{10.33}$$

$$\pi_i^* = \frac{(a - c)^2}{(2 + d)^2} - F_i. \tag{10.34}$$

We graph the best-reply functions and the Cournot equilibrium in Fig. 10.11, which we will use to compare with the equilibrium in the differentiated Bertrand model.

The main reason for studying the differentiated Cournot model is to determine how product differentiation affects the equilibrium.[18] The key results are:

- The equilibrium converges to the homogeneous Cournot equilibrium as d approaches 1 (i.e., Figs. 10.2 and 10.10 become the same).

---

[17] Notice that the second-order conditions of profit maximization hold, because the second derivative of the profit equation for each firm is $-2 < 0$.

[18] The effects of a change in marginal cost and a change in the demand intercept are the same as in the case with homogeneous goods.

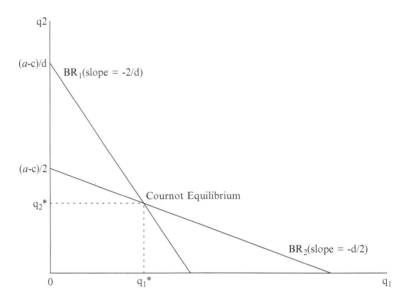

Fig. 10.11 The Cournot equilibrium with product differentiation

- The equilibrium converges to the monopoly equilibrium as d approaches 0. Recall from Chap. 6 that when there is a monopoly firm where $b = 1$, then $Q^* = q_i^* = (a - c)/2$, $p^* = (a + c)/2$ and $\pi_i = (a - c)^2/4 - F_i$.
- Greater product differentiation (i.e., lower d) leads to higher prices and profits.

The effect of product differentiation on price, which is described in (10.33), is exhibited in Fig. 10.12. It illustrates that when the two products are unrelated (i.e., $d = 0$), the equilibrium price (p_i^*) equals the monopoly price, $(a + c)/2$. At the other extreme when the two products are perfect substitutes (i.e., $d = 1$), the equilibrium price equals the homogeneous Cournot price, $(a + 2c)/3$. In between, the price falls with d. The result that greater product differentiation leads to less price competition is called the **principle of product differentiation**.

10.2.2   The Bertrand Model with Multicharacteristic Differentiation

We now want to analyze the Bertrand model with multicharacteristic differentiation. Firms face the same demand structure as in the differentiated Cournot model, (10.28) and (10.29). In the Bertrand model, the demand function is used in place of the inverse demand function. All choice variables (prices) appear on the right-hand side of each equation. Solving the system of inverse demand functions

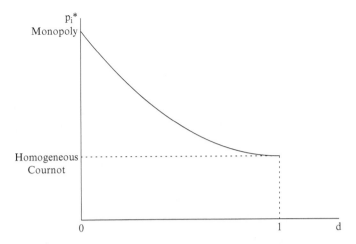

Fig. 10.12 The Cournot equilibrium price for different levels of product differentiation (d)

from the Cournot model simultaneously for q_1 and q_2 yields the following demand system:

$$q_1 = \alpha - \beta p_1 + \delta p_2, \tag{10.35}$$

$$q_2 = \alpha - \beta p_2 + \delta p_1, \tag{10.36}$$

where $\alpha \equiv a(1-d)/x$, $\beta \equiv 1/x$, $\delta \equiv d/x$, and $x \equiv (1-d^2)$.[19] Note that when there is product differentiation, d ranges from 0 to 1 and β exceeds δ. With this demand system, firm i's profits are $\pi_i(p_i, \ p_j) = \mathrm{TR}_i - \mathrm{TC}_i = p_i(\alpha - \beta p_i + \delta p_j) - c (\alpha - \beta p_i + \delta p_j) - F_i$.

In this case, firm i's profit equation is differentiable in p_i, and we can find the NE using the same method as in the Cournot model. First we differentiate each firm's profit equation with respect to its own price to derive the first-order conditions. The first-order conditions are[20]

$$
\begin{aligned}
\frac{\partial \pi_1}{\partial p_1} &= \frac{\partial \mathrm{TR}_1}{\partial p_1} - \frac{\partial \mathrm{TC}_1}{\partial p_1} \\
&= \mathrm{MR}p_1 - \mathrm{MC}p_1 \\
&= (\alpha - 2\beta p_1 + \delta p_2) - (-\beta c) = 0,
\end{aligned}
\tag{10.37}
$$

---

[19] Detailed derivations can be found in Shy (1995, 162–163).

[20] Notice that the second-order conditions of profit maximization hold, because the second derivative of the profit equation for each firm is $-2\beta < 0$, as $\beta > 0$.

$$\frac{\partial \pi_2}{\partial p_2} = \frac{\partial \mathrm{TR}_2}{\partial p_2} - \frac{\partial \mathrm{TC}_2}{\partial p_2}$$
$$= \mathrm{MR}p_2 - \mathrm{MC}p_2$$
$$= (\alpha - 2\beta p_2 + \delta p_1) - (-\beta c) = 0, \tag{10.38}$$

where $\mathrm{MR}p_i$ is firm i's marginal revenue with respect to a change in p_i and $\mathrm{MC}p_i$ is firm i's marginal cost with respect to a change p_i. Second, solving these equations simultaneously for p_1 and p_2 yields the NE prices. Substituting the optimal prices into the demand and profit equations above gives their equilibrium values. Given that the interchangeability condition is met, the Bertrand equilibrium is

$$p_i^* = \frac{\alpha + \beta c}{2\beta - \delta}, \tag{10.39}$$

$$q_i^* = \frac{\beta[\alpha - c(\beta - \delta)]}{2\beta - \delta}, \tag{10.40}$$

$$\pi_i^* = \frac{\beta[\alpha - c(\beta - \delta)]^2}{(2\beta - \delta)^2} - F_i. \tag{10.41}$$

Because this model produces a different outcome from previous models, we describe its best-reply and isoprofit functions. Solving each firm's first-order condition for p_2 gives the best replies

$$\mathrm{BR}_1 : p_2 = -\frac{\alpha + \beta c}{\delta} + \frac{2\beta}{\delta}p_1, \tag{10.42}$$

$$\mathrm{BR}_2 : p_2 = \frac{\alpha + \beta c}{2\beta} + \frac{\delta}{2\beta}p_1. \tag{10.43}$$

The best-reply functions are linear, but unlike the Cournot model they have a positive slope.[21] These functions and their corresponding isoprofit curves are graphed in Fig. 10.13. Bertrand equilibrium prices occur where the best-reply functions intersect. Notice that both firms are better off if they move into the shaded region by raising prices above the NE prices. Thus, the cartel outcome is in this region.

Previously we saw that one way for a firm to avoid the Bertrand paradox is to gain a cost advantage over its competitors. Another way is for firms to differentiate

---

[21] For BR_1, the slope is $2\beta/\delta$ and the p_2 intercept is $-(\alpha + \beta c)/\delta$. For BR_2, the slope is $\delta/2\beta$ and the p_2 intercept is $(\alpha + \beta c)/2\beta$. For the equilibrium to be stable, an issue that we discuss in the Appendix 10.A, BR_1 must be steeper than BR_2 (i.e., $\beta > \delta/2$).

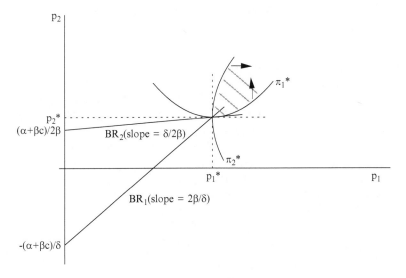

Fig. 10.13 The Bertrand equilibrium with product differentiation

their products. If we rewrite the equilibrium (10.39)–(10.41) in the original parameters a, c, and d,

$$p_i^* = \frac{a + c - ad}{2 - d},\tag{10.44}$$

$$q_i^* = \frac{a - c}{2 + d + d^2},\tag{10.45}$$

$$\pi_i^* = \frac{(a - c)^2(1 - d)}{(2 - d)^2(1 + d)}.\tag{10.46}$$

Recall that the degree of product differentiation increases as d approaches 0. When products are homogeneous ($d = 1$), the model produces the simple Bertrand outcome with price equal to marginal cost (c) and profits equal to zero. It produces the monopoly outcome when the products are unrelated ($d = 0$), again verifying that the monopoly outcome is a NE. Finally, equilibrium prices and profits increase as products become more differentiated (i.e., as $d \to 0$). Thus, this analysis provides further verification of the principle of product differentiation and demonstrates that another way for firms to avoid the Bertrand paradox is to differentiate their products.

10.2.3   The Bertrand Model with Horizontal and Vertical Differentiation

In this section, we consider Bertrand models with horizontal and vertical differentiation. We saw in Chap. 7 that differentiation is horizontal when consumers disagree over their preference ordering of a product's characteristic, as is the case with a red versus a blue VW Jetta. Some consumers prefer the red and others the blue Jetta, *ceteris paribus*. When consumers agree over the preference ordering of a characteristic, we have vertical differentiation. Product quality is an example of a vertical characteristic. These models as well as previous models with product differentiation provide a theoretical framework for later analysis when firms compete in other dimensions, such as product characteristics and advertising.

10.2.3.1   Price Competition in the Linear City Model

Recall that in the Hotelling model discussed in Chap. 7 brands differ in terms of a single characteristic (θ). Consumers have different tastes, with some consumers preferring brands with high levels of θ and others preferring brands with low levels of θ. The Hotelling model is represented by a main street of unit length that starts at 0 and ends at 1. Location is indexed by parameter θ. Consumers live on main street and are uniformly distributed.

In this example, two supermarkets (1 and 2) compete for consumer business, with store 1 located at θ_1 and store 2 located at θ_2, with $0 \leq \theta_1 \leq \frac{1}{2} \leq \theta_2 \leq 1$. Stores 1 and 2 are homogeneous when they both locate at $\frac{1}{2}$ but become increasingly differentiated as they move further and further apart. Suppose store 1 is located at position 0, and store 2 is located at position 1.[22] With positive transportation costs (t), consumers will prefer the store closest to home. As we saw in Chap. 7, these assumptions produce the following linear demand functions:

$$q_1 = \frac{N[t(\theta_2 - \theta_1) - p_1 + p_2]}{2t}, \tag{10.47}$$

$$q_2 = \frac{N[t(\theta_2 - \theta_1) + p_1 - p_2]}{2t}, \tag{10.48}$$

---

[22] To simplify the analysis, we also assume that the market is covered (i.e., no consumer refrains from purchase) and that consumers have unit demands (i.e., each consumer buys just one unit of brand 1 from store 1 or one unit of brand 2 from store 2). To review these concepts, see Chap. 7.

where N is the number of consumers. Note that the model shows that demand increases as stores move further apart. For now, we assume that store location is fixed or predetermined. Firm i's total cost is $\mathrm{TC}_i = cq_i - F_i$, and its profit equation is $\pi_i(p_i, \quad p_j) = \mathrm{TR}_i - \mathrm{TC}_i = p_i\{N[t(\theta_2 - \theta_1) - p_i + p_j]\}/(2t) - c\{N[t(\theta_2 - \theta_1) - p_i + p_j]\}/(2t) - F_i$.

As in the previous model, store i's profit equation is differentiable in p_i, enabling us to derive the NE by differentiation. The first-order conditions are[23]

$$\frac{\partial \pi_1}{\partial p_1} = \mathrm{MR}p_1 - \mathrm{MC}p_1$$
$$= \frac{N[t(\theta_2 - \theta_1) - 2p_1 + p_2]}{2t} - \frac{(-cN)}{2t}$$
$$= \frac{N[t(\theta_2 - \theta_1) - 2p_1 + p_2 + c]}{2t} = 0, \qquad (10.49)$$

$$\frac{\partial \pi_2}{\partial p_2} = \mathrm{MR}p_2 - \mathrm{MC}p_2$$
$$= \frac{N[t(\theta_2 - \theta_1) - 2p_2 + p_1]}{2t} - \frac{(-cN)}{2t}$$
$$= \frac{N[t(\theta_2 - \theta_1) - 2p_2 + p_1 + c]}{2t} = 0. \qquad (10.50)$$

Notice that the interchangeability condition holds. Solving the first-order conditions for prices and substituting them into the demand and profit equations yields the Bertrand equilibrium:

$$p_i^* = c + t(\theta_2 - \theta_1), \qquad (10.51)$$

$$q_i^* = N(\theta_2 - \theta_1)/2, \qquad (10.52)$$

$$\pi_i^* = \frac{Nt(\theta_2 - \theta_1)^2}{2} - F_i. \qquad (10.53)$$

Consistent with the principle of product differentiation, price competition falls and profits rise as stores 1 and 2 move further apart [i.e., as the distance $(\theta_2 - \theta_1)$ increases]. As in the previous model of multicharacteristic differentiation, the linear city model generates positively sloped best-reply functions. Deriving and graphing the best-reply functions is left as an exercise at the end of the chapter.

---

[23] Notice that the second-order conditions of profit maximization hold, because the second derivative of the profit equation for each firm is $-N/t < 0$.

10.2.3.2   Price Competition in the Circular City Model

Next we consider the circular city model of horizontal differentiation where main street is bent around to form a circle (see Chap. 7). The advantage of this model is that it allows us to investigate the NE in a differentiated market with n firms. The model is symmetric, and firm i's demand function is

$$q_i = \frac{t/n - p_i + p}{t},$$

(10.54)

where p represents the price charged by rivals.[24] Firm i's profits are $\pi_i(p_i, p_j) =$ $\mathrm{TR}_i - \mathrm{TC}_i = p_i[(t/n - p_i + p)/t] - c[(t/n - p_i + p)/t] - F_i$.

The profit equation is differentiable in p_i, enabling us to derive the NE by differentiation. The interchangeability condition holds, and the first-order condition for firm i is

$$\begin{aligned}
\frac{\partial \pi_i}{\partial p_i} &= \mathrm{MR}p_i - \mathrm{MC}p_i \\
&= \frac{t/n - 2p_i + p}{t} - \frac{-c}{t} \\
&= \frac{t/n - 2p_i + p + c}{t} = 0
\end{aligned}$$

(10.55)

The firm's best-reply function is $p_i^{\mathrm{BR}} = (t/n + c + p)/2$, which has a positive slope like the other Bertrand models with product differentiation. Because the problem is symmetric, $p_i = p$ in equilibrium. Thus, the Bertrand equilibrium is

$$p_i^* = c + t/n.$$

(10.56)

$$q_i^* = 1/n.$$

(10.57)

$$\pi_i^* = t/n^2 - F_i.$$

(10.58)

In this model, price approaches marginal cost and profits decline as the number of competitors increases. This is the same result as in the Cournot limit theorem. Even though the price equals marginal cost in the homogeneous goods Bertrand model when there are 2 or more firms, the differentiated Bertrand model has similar implications as Cournot regarding the effect of market structure on price competition.

---

[24] In this model, the number of consumers (N) is normalized to 1 for simplicity.

10.2.3.3 The Bertrand Model with Vertical Differentiation

Next, we consider a Bertrand model developed by Choi and Shin (1992), where differentiation is vertical. Firm 1 produces the brand of higher quality or reliability. Recall from Chap. 7 that z_i indexes the quality of brand i, where $z_1 > z_2 > 0$, and the degree of vertical differentiation is $z \equiv z_1 - z_2$. Product quality is assumed to be predetermined. Consumers all prefer the high quality brand but some have a stronger preference for quality than others. A consumer's preference for quality is represented by ϕ, and the diversity of consumer tastes ranges from ϕ_L to ϕ_H, with $\phi_H > \phi_L > 0$ and $\phi_H - \phi_L = 1$.[25]

This model assumes the Mussa and Rosen specification of vertical differentiation, which produces the following linear demand functions:

$$q_1 = \frac{N(z\phi_H - p_1 + p_2)}{z}, \tag{10.59}$$

$$q_2 = \frac{N(-z\phi_L + p_1 - p_2)}{z}. \tag{10.60}$$

Demand for firm i's brand goes up with an increase in the number of consumers, a drop in the firm's own price, and an increase in its rival's price. Costs are assumed to be the same as before. Because $\phi_H \neq -\phi_L$, the problem is not symmetric, and the profit equations for each firm are: $\pi_1(p_1, p_2) = TR_1 - TC_1 = p_1[(z\phi_H - p_1 + p_2)/z] - c[(z\phi_H - p_1 + p_2)/z] - F_1$; $\pi_2(p_1, p_2) = TR_2 - TC_2 = p_2[(-z\phi_L + p_1 - p_2)/z] - c[(-z\phi_L + p_1 - p_2)/z] - F_2$. Profit equations are differentiable, and the first-order conditions are[26]

$$\frac{\partial \pi_1}{\partial p_1} = MRp_1 - MCp_1$$
$$= \frac{N(z\phi_H - 2p_1 + p_2)}{z} - \frac{(-c)}{z}$$
$$= \frac{N(z\phi_H - 2p_1 + p_2 + c)}{z} = 0, \tag{10.61}$$

$$\frac{\partial \pi_2}{\partial p_2} = MRp_2 - MCp_2$$
$$= \frac{N(-z\phi_L - 2p_2 + p_1)}{z} - \frac{(-c)}{z}$$
$$= \frac{N(-z\phi_L - 2p_2 + p_1 + c)}{z} = 0. \tag{10.62}$$

---

[25] Later we will see that another constraint will be important, that is $\phi_H > 2\phi_L > 0$.

[26] The second-order conditions of profit maximization hold, because the second derivative of the profit equation for each firm is $-2/z < 0$.

Solving the first-order conditions for prices and substituting them into the demand and profit equations yields the Bertrand equilibrium when differentiation is vertical:

$$p_1^* = c + \frac{z(2\phi_H - \phi_L)}{3} > p_2^* = c + \frac{z(\phi_H - 2\phi_L)}{3}, \tag{10.63}$$

$$q_1^* = \frac{N(2\phi_H - \phi_L)}{3} > q_2^* = \frac{N(\phi_H - 2\phi_L)}{3}, \tag{10.64}$$

$$\pi_1^* = \frac{Nz(2\phi_H - \phi_L)^2}{9} - F_1 ; \pi_2^* = \frac{Nz(\phi_H - 2\phi_L)^2}{9} - F_2. \tag{10.65}$$

For firm 2 to produce a positive level of output, $\phi_H > 2\phi_L$. Thus, this condition must hold for there to be two firms in the market.

This model of vertical differentiation produces several interesting results. First, the high quality firm sells more output and at a higher price. The high quality firm will also earn greater profit (i.e., have a competitive or a strategic advantage) as long as the difference in fixed costs is not too great. Finally, the principle of differentiation is verified: prices and profits increase as the degree of production differentiation rises (i.e., as z increases).

We also derive and graph the best-reply functions for this model. Recall that we can obtain the best-reply functions by solving each firm's first-order condition with respect to p_2[27]:

$$\mathrm{BR}_1 : p_2 = -(c + z\phi_H) + 2p_1, \tag{10.66}$$

$$\mathrm{BR}_2 : p_2 = \frac{c - z\phi_L}{2} + \frac{1}{2}p_1. \tag{10.67}$$

The best-reply functions are linear and are illustrated in Fig. 10.14. The figure verifies that the high quality producer will charge a higher price than the low quality producer.

10.3   The Cournot–Bertrand Model

One concern with the Cournot and Bertrand models is that they take the strategic variable as given. That is, both firms either compete in output (Cournot) or in price (Bertrand). But why is it not possible for one firm to compete in output and the other in price? After all, Kreps and Scheinkman (1983) argue that it is "witless" to criticize the choice of strategic variable, as it is an empirical question whether or not firms compete in output or in price.

---

[27] For BR$_1$, the slope is 2 and the p_2 intercept is $-(c + z\phi_H)$. For BR$_2$, the slope is 1/2 and the p_2 intercept is $(c - z\phi_L)/2$.

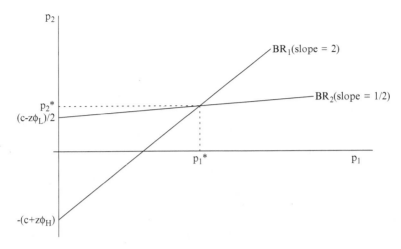

Fig. 10.14 The Bertrand equilibrium with vertical differentiation

Each case is witnessed in the real world. At a farmer's market, Cournot competition is common. Farmers compete in output, choosing how much to bring to market and then allowing price to adjust once there. In contrast, fast food restaurants typically compete in price, as in Bertrand. In addition, a mixture of Cournot and Bertrand behavior is observed in the market for small cars. In each period, Honda and Subaru dealers set quantities and let price adjust to clear the market. On the other hand, Saturn and Scion dealers fill consumer orders at a fixed price.[28] This type of behavior can be described by a Cournot–Bertrand model where one firm competes in output and the other firm competes in price. This corresponds to model M3 in Table 10.1, which was developed by Singh and Vives (1984), C. Tremblay and V. Tremblay (2011a), and V. Tremblay et al. (forthcoming-a).

The assumptions of the Cournot–Bertrand are the same as those of the Cournot and Bertrand models, except that firm 1 competes in output and firm 2 competes in price. This requires that the demand system have the two choice variables $(q_1$ and $p_2)$ on the right-hand side of each demand equation. We use the system of inverse demand functions for the Cournot model found in (10.28) and (10.29), which assumes multicharacteristic differentiation. Solving that system simultaneously for p_1 and q_2 yields the following demand equations:

$$p_1 = (a - ad) - (1 - d^2)q_1 + dp_2, \qquad (10.68)$$

---

[28] Historically, the market for personal computers provides another example of Cournot–Bertrand type behavior. That is, Dell set price and built computers to order, while IBM shipped completed computers to dealers who let price adjust to clear the market. Cournot–Bertrand behavior can also be found in the aerospace connector industry where leading distributors compete in price and smaller distributors compete in output.

$$q_2 = a - p_2 - dq_1. \tag{10.69}$$

Recall that each firm is a monopolist when $d = 0$ and that products are perfectly homogeneous when $d = 1$. In order to simplify the calculations, we set marginal cost equal to zero.[29]

The first thing to note is that the model is naturally asymmetric because firms have different choice variables. This is clear from the firms' profit maximization problems:

$$\max_{q_1} \ \pi_1 = TR_1 - TC_1 = [(a - ad) - (1 - d^2)q_1 + dp_2]q_1 - F_1, \tag{10.70}$$

$$\max_{p_2} \ \pi_2 = TR_2 - TC_2 = p_2(a - p_2 - dq_1) - F_2. \tag{10.71}$$

In this model, firm 1 maximizes profit with respect to output, and firm 2 maximizes profit with respect to price. One can see from the first-order conditions that the interchangeability condition does not hold[30]:

$$\begin{aligned}
\frac{\partial \pi_1}{\partial q_1} &= \frac{\partial TR_1}{\partial q_1} - \frac{\partial TC_1}{\partial q_1} \\
&= MR_1 - MC_1 \\
&= [(a - ad) - 2(1 - d^2)q_1 + dp_2] - (0) = 0,
\end{aligned} \tag{10.72}$$

$$\begin{aligned}
\frac{\partial \pi_2}{\partial p_2} &= \frac{\partial TR_2}{\partial p_2} - \frac{\partial TC_2}{\partial p_2} \\
&= MRp_2 - MCp_2 \\
&= [a - 2p_2 - dq_1] - (0) = 0.
\end{aligned} \tag{10.73}$$

Solving this system of first-order conditions simultaneously gives the NE values of choice variables, q_1 and p_2. This produces what is called the Cournot–Bertrand equilibrium:

$$p_1^* = \frac{a(2 - d - 2d^2 + d^3)}{4 - 3d^2} > p_2^* = \frac{a(2 - d - d^2)}{4 - 3d^2}, \tag{10.74}$$

---

[29] With this assumption, p_i can be thought of as the difference between the price and marginal cost.
[30] Notice that the second-order condition holds for each firm. That is $\partial^2 \pi_1/\partial q_1^2 = -2(1-d^2) < 0$, and $\partial^2 \pi_2/\partial p_2^2 = -2$.

$$q_1^* = \frac{a(2-d)}{4-3d^2} > q_2^* = \frac{a(2-d-d^2)}{4-3d^2}, \tag{10.75}$$

$$\pi_1^* = \frac{a^2(2-d)^2(1-d^2)}{(4-3d^2)^2} - F_1; \quad \pi_2^* = \frac{a^2(2-d-d^2)^2}{(4-3d^2)^2} - F_2. \tag{10.76}$$

The NE in the Cournot–Bertrand model has several interesting properties. First, firm 1 charges a higher price and produces more output. Second, firm 1 earns greater profit as long as the difference in fixed costs is not too great. Third, the degree of product differentiation has a dramatic effect on the equilibrium. As expected, when $d = 0$, firms are not direct competitors and each firm behaves as a monopolist. When products are perfect substitutes ($d = 1$), however, firm 1 produces the competitive output level, price equals marginal cost (which is 0), and firm 2 exits the market.[31] The mere threat of a Bertrand-type competitor that produces a perfectly homogeneous good is enough to assure a competitive equilibrium even when there is only one Cournot-type firm left in the market. In this model, the Bertrand paradox applies even in the monopoly case. This provides a dramatic example where a potential entrant reduces market power. The Cournot–Bertrand equilibrium is also consistent with the principle of product differentiation.

To further analyze the Cournot–Bertrand model, we describe the NE in terms of best-reply and isoprofit diagrams. We obtain the best-reply functions by solving each firm's first-order condition for p_2:

$$\text{BR}_1 : p_2 = \frac{ad-a}{d} + \frac{2(1-d^2)}{d}q_1, \tag{10.77}$$

$$\text{BR}_2 : p_2 = \frac{a}{2} - \frac{d}{2}q_1. \tag{10.78}$$

The best-reply and isoprofit curves are illustrated in Fig. 10.15. The natural asymmetry of the model is evident from the fact that firm 1's best reply has a positive slope and firm 2's best reply has a negative slope.[32] Furthermore, firm 1's profits increase in p_2, and its isoprofit curve is convex to the q_1 axis. In contrast, firm 2's profits decrease in q_1, and its isoprofit curve is concave to the p_2 axis. Finally, notice that both firms are better off if they move into the lens-shaped region where firm 1 reduces production and firm 2 raises price. The cartel outcome would occur in this region. These unique features of best-reply and isoprofit curves occur because the model mixes Cournot and Bertrand strategic choices. Again, even though firms face the same demand and cost conditions, the choice of different strategic variables leads to dramatically different results.

---

[31] This is similar to the outcome of a "contestable market", as discussed in Chap. 5. For further discussion, see C. Tremblay and V. Tremblay (2011a) and C. Tremblay, M. Tremblay, and V. Tremblay (2011).

[32] For BR$_1$, the slope is $2(1-d^2)/d$ and the p_2 intercept is $(ad-a)/d$. For BR$_2$, the slope is $-d/2$ and the p_2 intercept is $a/2$.

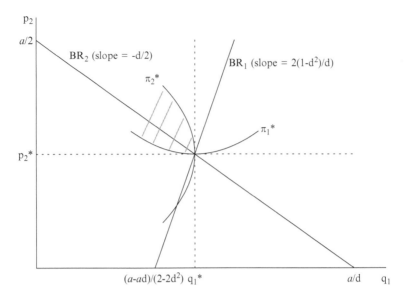

Fig. 10.15 The Cournot–Bertrand equilibrium

10.4   The Choice of Output or Price Competition

We have examined the classic Cournot and Bertrand models in homogeneous and differentiated goods markets and the more recent Cournot–Bertrand model in a differentiated goods market. These models produce several important conclusions:

1. In a market with homogeneous goods, prices and profits are substantially higher in the Cournot model than in the Bertrand model.
2. Although the equilibrium in a monopoly setting is invariant to the choice of strategic variable, output or price, this is not true in an oligopoly setting. The perfectly competitive solution is reached in the Bertrand model when products are homogeneous and there are two or more competitors. In contrast, the Cournot solution approaches the perfectly competitive equilibrium only as n approaches infinity.
3. Competition diminishes with product differentiation in both the Cournot and Bertrand models, and the two models are much more alike in differentiated goods markets.
4. A duopoly model becomes naturally asymmetric when firms compete in different choice variables. In the Cournot–Bertrand model, the firm that chooses to compete in output has a strategic advantage over the firm that chooses to compete in price as long as the Bertrand-type firm does not have a significant cost advantage.

These results raise the following question: If given the option, why would a firm choose to compete in price instead of output? Clearly, when products are homogeneous, output competition is a more profitable strategic choice. Yet, some firms compete in price.

One explanation, provided by Kreps and Scheinkman (1983), involves the nature of technology and the ease with which a firm can adjust output relative to price. They argue that when it is time consuming and costly to change production capacity or output, firms will compete in output and let price adjust to clear the market (as in Cournot). This would be true at a farmers' market, for example, where each farmer brings a fixed supply of produce to the market at a given point in time. Other examples include many heavy manufacturing industries, where it takes a considerable amount of time to produce a product from start to finish. Under these conditions, firms compete in output rather than price.

When price adjustments are relatively more costly than output adjustments, firms set prices and let production adjust to meet demand (as in Bertrand). Most inexpensive restaurants face this situation. Once menus are printed, it is costly to change price in response to short-term demand fluctuations, and a good chef can easily adjust to an increase in demand for pancakes relative to scrambled eggs. Other examples where output can adjust quickly and firms compete in price are the software and banking service industries.[33]

The optimal choice of strategic variable, output or price, can also be influenced by product differentiation and cost asymmetries. These issues are addressed by Singh and Vives (1984), Häckner (2000), and V. Tremblay et al. (forthcoming-a). Singh and Vives (1984) and V. Tremblay et al. (forthcoming-a) consider a duopoly model with multicharacteristic differentiation. A common feature of their work is that the decision to compete in output or price is endogenous. This leads to four possible outcomes:

1. Cournot (C): Both firms choose to compete in output.
2. Bertrand (B): Both firms choose to compete in price.
3. Cournot–Bertrand (CB): Firm 1 chooses to compete in output, and firm 2 chooses to compete in price.
4. Bertrand–Cournot (BC): Firm 1 chooses to compete in price, and firm 2 chooses to compete in output.

This possibility corresponds to model M4 in Table 10.1.

To illustrate their findings, we use a numerical example based on the demand system found in (10.28) and (10.29). Note that this is the demand system for the Cournot model, and it translates to demand system (10.35) and (10.36) in the Bertrand model and demand system (10.68) and (10.69) in the Cournot–Bertrand model. To compare profits in each case, we set $c = 0$, $a = 25$, and $d = 1/2$.

---

[33] Kreps and Scheinkman actually proposed a two-stage game, where each firm makes its decision on the sticky (long run) variable in the first stage and the flexible (short-run) variable adjusts to equilibrium in the second stage. This leads to the same result, however: (1) When output is sticky, firms compete in output, and price adjusts to meet demand, as in Cournot; (2) When price is sticky, firms compete in price, and output adjusts to meet demand, as in Bertrand.

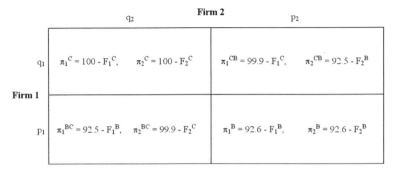

Fig. 10.16 Payoff matrix for the Cournot (C), Bertrand (B), Cournot-Bertrand (CB), and Bertrand-Cournot (BC) outcomes

Figure 10.16 displays the results. Notationally, π_i^C is firm i's profit when both firms compete in output (Cournot), π_i^B is firm i's profits when both firms compete in price (Bertrand), π_i^{CB} is firm i's profits when firm 1 competes in output and firm 2 competes in price (Cournot–Bertrand), and π_i^{BC} is firm i's profits when firm 1 competes in price and firm 2 competes in output (Bertrand–Cournot). When fixed or set-up costs are positive, F_i^C equals fixed costs when firm i competes in output, and F_i^B equals fixed costs when firm i competes in price. As Fig. 10.16 shows, optimal play depends upon our assumptions about fixed costs. If fixed costs are sufficiently low and are the same regardless of the strategic choice (i.e., $F_1^C = F_1^B$ and $F_2^C = F_2^B$), as in the Singh and Vives (1984) model, then both firms are better off competing in output. That is, if firms had the choice, they would always prefer to compete in output because this is the dominant strategy.

The intuition behind this result relates to how the choice of strategic variable affects a firm's price elasticity of demand. When firm j's output is fixed, the slope of firm i's demand function is close to the slope of the market demand function.[34] When firm j's price is fixed, firm i's demand function is relatively more elastic, because firm i can steal sales by undercutting j's price. Thus, firm demand functions are more elastic and equilibrium prices are lower under price competition than under output competition.

Nevertheless, there are three conditions under which price competition is more profitable than output competition. First, as discussed above, it may be prohibitively costly to change price relative to output, causing price competition to be more profitable than output competition. This can occur when fixed costs associated with output competition (F_i^C) are substantially higher than the fixed cost associated with price competition (F_i^B). With output competition, a firm must bring a substantial quantity of output to market, but sales take time and the firm must have a storage facility to hold inventory. A firm that competes in price, however, may fill customer orders only after an order is placed. In the example in Fig. 10.16, if $F_i^C = 10$ and $F_i^B = 0$, then the dominant strategy for both firms is to compete in price (see Fig. 10.17).

---

[34] The slopes of firm and market demand functions converge as the degree of product differentiation diminishes, and the slopes are the same when products are homogeneous.

		Firm 2: q_2	Firm 2: p_2
Firm 1	q_1	$\pi_1^{C} = 100$, $\pi_2^{C} = 90$	$\pi_1^{CB} = 99.9$, $\pi_2^{CB} = 92.5$
	p_1	$\pi_1^{BC} = 92.5$, $\pi_2^{BC} = 89.9$	$\pi_1^{B} = 92.6$, $\pi_2^{B} = 92.6$

Fig. 10.17 Payoff matrix when there are asymmetric costs

Second, Häckner (2000) showed that price dominates output competition when brands are differentiated vertically and this differentiation is sufficiently great. Finally, V. Tremblay et al. (forthcoming-a) showed that in a dynamic setting the follower is just as likely to compete in price as in output, regardless of whether the leader competes in output or price. We take up this issue in the next chapter.

V. Tremblay et al. (forthcoming-b) find that cost asymmetries explain the Cournot–Bertrand behavior in the small car market. They show that Scion dealers compete in price because it has a relatively high cost of competing in output, while Honda dealers compete in output because it has a cost advantage in output competition. If we let Honda be firm 1 and Scion be firm 2 in the example in Fig. 10.16, then this can occur if $F_1{}^{C} = F_1{}^{B} = F_2{}^{B} = 0$ and $F_2{}^{C} = 10$. In this case, Firm 1 will compete in output and firm 2 will compete in price. In all, the choice of strategic variable depends on demand and cost conditions and the degree of asymmetry in the model

10.5 Strategic Substitutes and Strategic Complements

An interesting feature of these simple parametric models is that the best-reply functions exhibit a consistent pattern. When firms compete in output, the best reply functions have a negative slope, and when they compete in price with product differentiation, they have a positive slope.[35] Bulow et al. (1985) discovered these patterns and gave them the following names:

- The strategies of two players are **strategic substitutes** when the best-reply functions have a negative slope.

[35] Although there are exceptions when demand and cost functions are nonlinear, Amir and Grilo (1999) call this the "typical geometry" for the Cournot and Bertrand models. Throughout the book, we assume this typical geometry.

• The strategies of two players are **strategic complements** when the best-reply functions have a positive slope.

So far, we have investigated only best-reply functions for price and output, but these definitions apply to other strategic variables as well (e.g., advertising).

In general, whether a strategic variable between two firms is a strategic substitute or complement hinges on how a change in firm j's strategic variable (s_j) affects the marginal returns of firm i's strategic variable (s_i). More formally, given firm i's profit equation, $\pi_i(s_i, s_j)$, which is assumed to be strictly concave in s_i and twice continuously differentiable, marginal returns are defined as $\partial \pi_i / \partial s_i$.[36] The effect of s_j on firm i's marginal returns is $\partial(\partial \pi_i / \partial s_i)/\partial s_j = \partial^2 \pi_i / \partial s_i \partial s_j \equiv \pi_{ij}$.

It turns out that s_i and s_j are strategic complements when $\pi_{ij} > 0$ and are strategic substitutes when $\pi_{ij} < 0$. A proof is provided in Appendix 10.B.

10.6   Summary

1. An **oligopoly** is characterized by a market with a few firms that compete in a strategic setting. Each firm's profit and best course of action depend on its own action and the actions of its competitors. A **duopoly** is an oligopoly market with two firms.
2. In the **Cournot model**, each firm simultaneously chooses a level of output that maximizes its own profit. The Cournot outcome is a Nash equilibrium (NE) where each firm correctly assumes that its competitors behave optimally. According to the **Cournot Limit Theorem**, as the number of firms in a market changes from 1 to infinity, the Cournot equilibrium changes from monopoly to perfect competition.
3. The **interchangeability condition** means that the first-order conditions of every firm in a model are interchangeable (by reversing firm subscripts). When this condition holds, the model is symmetric.
4. In the **Bertrand model**, each firm simultaneously chooses its price to maximize its own profit. The Bertrand equilibrium is a NE. When products are homogeneous and firms face the same costs, the Bertrand equilibrium price equals marginal cost as long as there are two or more firms in the market. This occurs because of **price undercutting**, where each firm undercuts the price of its rivals until the competitive price is reached. The implication that prices are competitive as long as there are two or more competitors is called the **Bertrand Paradox**. A firm can avoid the Bertrand Paradox if it has a cost advantage over its competitors.

---

[36] This concept is discussed more fully in the Mathematics and Econometrics Appendix.

5. The Bertrand model with homogeneous goods and symmetric costs makes it clear that economic theory cannot prove that market prices will fall as the number of competitors increases beyond two firms.
6. According to the **principle of product differentiation**, price competition diminishes as product differentiation increases. Thus, the Bertrand paradox does not arise when products are differentiated.
7. In the **Cournot–Bertrand model**, firm 1 competes in output and firm 2 competes in price, actions that are made simultaneously. This model produces a naturally asymmetric outcome and gives firm 1 a strategic advantage (i.e., it has higher profits) as long as any difference in costs between firms is sufficiently small.
8. When the choice of strategic variable is endogenous, firms will choose to compete in output as long as there are not substantial cost savings associated with price competition and as long as the degree of vertical product differentiation is not too great.
9. When best-reply functions have a negative slope, as in the Cournot model, the strategic variables between firms are **strategic substitutes**. When best replies have a positive slope, as in the Bertrand model, the strategic variables are **strategic complements**.

10.7   Review Questions

1. (Advanced) Consider a market with two firms (1 and 2) that face a linear inverse demand function $p = a - bQ$, where Q is industry output, q_i is the output of firm i (1 or 2), and $Q = q_1 + q_2$. Costs are also linear, with firm i's total cost equaling $TC_i = cq_i$. In addition, $a > c > 0, b > 0$. Find the Cournot equilibrium output for each firm. How will your answer change if $TC_i = cq_i^2$?
2. Consider a market with two firms (1 and 2) that face a linear demand function $Q = 24 - p$ and a total cost function $TC_i = cq_i, c > 0$. Find the Bertrand equilibrium price. How will your answer change if $c_1 = 10$ and $c_2 = 12$?
3. Explain how an increase in the number of firms affects the equilibrium price and allocative inefficiency in the homogeneous goods Cournot and Bertrand models.
4. Consider the oligopoly problem with n firms in Sect. 10.1.3. Assume that $a = 12, b = 1$, and $c = 0$. Use a graph similar to Fig. 10.8 to identify the NE when n equals 1, 2, 3, and infinity. How does total (consumer plus producer) surplus change as n increases?
5. Explain how a cost advantage or product differentiation can allow firms to avoid the Bertrand paradox.
6. In the Bertrand model with horizontal differentiation, explain how the equilibrium changes as t approaches 0. What does this say about the relationship between t and product differentiation?

7. Derive and graph the best-reply functions in the Bertrand model with horizontal differentiation discussed in Sect. 10.2.3.1. Show how a change in parameters c, t, N, and $(\theta_2 - \theta_1)$ will affect NE prices.

8. Wal-Mart stores typically locate on the edge of a city, even though potential demand may be greatest at the city's center. Assuming a linear city, is this a good location strategy? Explain.

9. In many markets, high quality brands coexist with low quality brands. If all consumers prefer high to low quality goods, *ceteris paribus*, why do some firms choose to supply low quality goods?

10. (Advanced) Consider a market with two firms (1 and 2) where firm 1 competes in output and firm 2 competes in price. Firm 1's inverse demand is $p_1 = 12 - q_1 + p_2$, firm 2's demand is $q_2 = 24 - p_2 - q_1$, $TC_i = cq_i$, $c > 0$. Find the Cournot–Bertrand equilibrium price, output, and profit levels for each firm. How does a change in c affect the equilibrium price, output, and profit?

11. Assume a duopoly market where firms can choose to compete in output or in price. Provide a simple numerical example where it is optimal for both firms to compete in price instead of output.

12. (Advanced) Consider the Cournot and Bertrand models of multicharacteristic differentiation that are discussed in Sect. 10.1. Show that choice variables are strategic substitutes in the Cournot model and are strategic complements in the Bertrand model by evaluating the slope of the best-reply functions or the signs of π_{ij} for each firm in each model.

13. In the Bertrand model in Sect. 10.2.2, discuss what happens to Nash prices when $\beta = \frac{1}{2}$ and $\delta = 1$. Will the model be stable, as described in Appendix 10.A, if $\beta = \frac{1}{2}$ and $\delta = 2$?

14. Assume a duopoly market with two firms, 1 and 2. In case I, firms behave as Cournot competitors, as described in Fig. 10.2. In case II, firms behave as differentiated Bertrand competitors, as described in Fig. 10.13. In case III, firms behave as Cournot–Bertrand competitors, as described in Fig. 10.15. Suppose that the management team of firm 1 is overconfident; they overestimate the demand intercept (a or α in Figs. 10.2, 10.13, and 10.15). Explain how this overconfidence will affect the Nash equilibrium.

Appendix A: Stability of the Cournot and Bertrand Models

Here, we are interested in the stability of the Nash equilibrium (NE) in a Cournot, Bertrand, or Cournot–Bertrand model. According to Mas-Colell (1995: 414), an equilibrium in a static model is stable when the "adjustment process in which the firms take turns myopically playing a best response to each others' current strategies converges to the Nash equilibrium from any strategy pair in a neighborhood of the equilibrium." For a stable NE, the best-reply functions must meet certain regularity conditions.

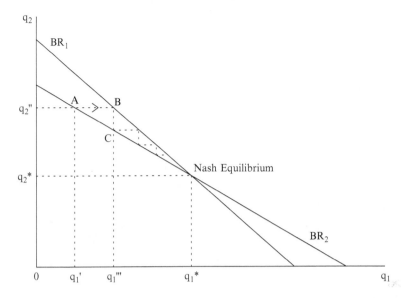

Fig. 10.18 A stable Cournot model

First, we consider the Cournot model developed in Sect. 10.2.1. The Cournot equilibrium is stable when BR_1 is steeper than BR_2, as in Fig. 10.18. To see this, assume that firm 1 chooses a disequilibrium level of output, q_1'. Firm 2's best reply to q_1' is q_2''. When firm 2 chooses q_2'', firm 1's best response is q_1'''. Thus, the adjustment process moves from point A, to B, to C in the graph, a process that continues until the NE is reached. At equilibrium, Firm 1's best reply to q_2^* is q_1^*, and firm 2's best reply to q_1^* is q_2^* (i.e., they are a mutual best reply). The equilibrium is unstable when BR_1 is flatter than BR_2, as illustrated in Fig. 10.19. In this case, when starting at q_1' the adjustment process moves away from the NE.

We now investigate stability of the Cournot equilibrium more generally. In Appendix 10.B, we prove that the slopes of the best-reply functions are $\partial q_1^{BR}/\partial q_2 = -\pi_{12}/\pi_{11}$ for firm 1 and $\partial q_2^{BR}/\partial q_1 = -\pi_{21}/\pi_{22}$ for firm 2. In the graph with q_2 on the vertical axis, the slope of firm 1's best reply is $-\pi_{11}/\pi_{12}$. Thus, stability of the equilibrium in the Cournot model requires that $|-\pi_{11}/\pi_{12}| > |-\pi_{21}/\pi_{22}|$. Because $\pi_{ii} < 0$ and $\pi_{ij} < 0$, we can rewrite the stability condition as $\pi_{11}\pi_{22} - \pi_{12}\pi_{21} > 0$. In the example from Sect. 10.2.1, $\pi_{11} = \pi_{22} = -2$ and $\pi_{12} = \pi_{21} = -d$. Thus, the slope of firm 1's best reply is $-2/d$, the slope of firm 2's best reply is $-d/2$, and the stability condition is $\pi_{11}\pi_{22} - \pi_{12}\pi_{21} = 4 - d^2 > 0$. Thus, the equilibrium is stable when $d < 2$.

Next, we consider the differentiated Bertrand model developed in Sect. 10.2.2. The Bertrand equilibrium is stable when BR_1 is steeper than BR_2, as in Fig. 10.20. If we begin at a disequilibrium point, p_1', firm 2's best reply is p_2''. When firm

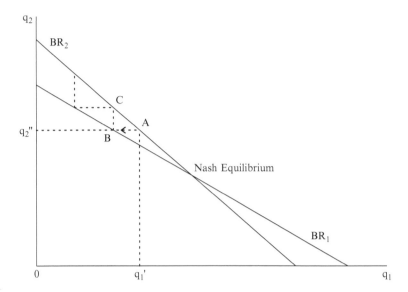

Fig. 10.19 An unstable Cournot model

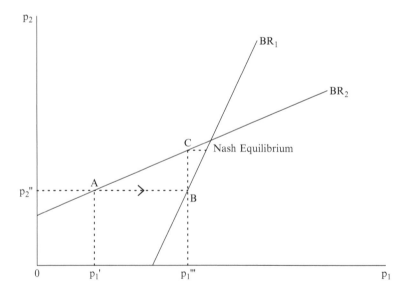

Fig. 10.20 A stable Bertrand model

2 chooses p_2'', firm 1's best response is p_1''', etc. Thus, the adjustment process moves from point A, to B, to C and converges to the NE. This equilibrium is unstable, however, when BR_1 is flatter than BR_2, as in Fig. 10.21. In this case, the adjustment process moves away from the NE.

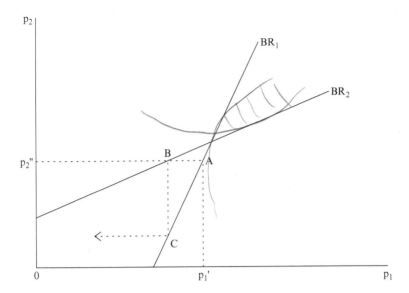

Fig. 10.21 An unstable Bertrand model

In the example from Sect. 10.2.2, $\pi_{11} = \pi_{22} = -2\beta$ and $\pi_{12} = \pi_{21} = \delta$. Thus, the slope of firm 1's best reply is $2\beta/\delta$, the slope of firm 2's best reply is $\delta/2\beta$, and the stability condition is $\pi_{11}\pi_{22} - \pi_{12}\pi_{21} = 4\beta^2 - \delta^2 > 0$. Therefore, Bertrand equilibrium is stable when $\beta > \delta/2$.

Analysis of stability conditions for the Cournot–Bertrand model can be found in V. Tremblay et al. (forthcoming-a).

Appendix B: Strategic Substitutes and Complements and the Slope of the Best-Reply Functions

As discussed in the text, the two strategic variables of firms i and j, s_i and s_j, are strategic complements when $\pi_{ij} > 0$ and are strategic substitutes when $\pi_{ij} < 0$. The proof follows from the first- and second-order conditions of profit maximization and the application of the implicit-function theorem, which is discussed in the Mathematics and Econometrics Appendix at the end of the book. Recall that firm i's best-reply function is derived by solving the firm's first-order condition for s_i, s_i^{BR}, which is the optimal value of s_i given s_j. Even though we are using a general function, embedded in the first-order condition is s_i^{BR}. Thus, we can use the implicit-function theorem to obtain the slope of firm i's best-reply function:

$$\frac{\partial s_i^{BR}}{\partial s_j} = \frac{-\pi_{ij}}{\pi_{ii}}, \tag{10.79}$$

where $\pi_{ii} \equiv \partial^2 \pi_i / \partial s_i^2$, which is negative from our concavity assumption (ensuring that the second-order condition of profit maximization is met). Thus, the sign of $\partial s_i^{BR} / \partial s_j$ equals the sign of π_{ij}. To summarize:

- When $\pi_{ij} < 0$, the best-reply functions have a negative slope and s_i and s_j are strategic substitutes, as in the Cournot model.
- When $\pi_{ij} > 0$, the best-reply functions have a positive slope and s_i and s_j are strategic complements, as in the differentiated Bertrand model.

In the mixed Cournot and Bertrand model developed in Sect. 10.3, $\pi_{12} = d > 0$ and $\pi_{21} = -d < 0$. This verifies that firm 1's best-reply function has a positive slope, and firm 2's best-reply function has a negative slope (Fig. 10.15). It also implies that q_1 and p_2 are strategic complements for the Cournot-type firm and are strategic substitutes for the Bertrand-type firm.

Chapter 11
Dynamic Monopoly and Oligopoly Models

Table 10.1 in the previous chapter identifies 12 classic models of oligopoly. In Chap. 10 we analyzed the static Cournot, Bertrand, and Cournot–Bertrand models. We also investigated the case where firms could choose whether to compete in output (as in Cournot) or price (as in Bertrand). These are labeled models M1–M4 in Table 10.1.

Although static models provide a useful starting point, they are not very realistic because real-world firms compete year after year in most industries. In the automobile industry, for example, General Motors and Ford have been competing against each other on price, product design, and quality for over a century. In this chapter, we develop models where the timing of play is important. As we saw in Chap. 3, these are called dynamic or sequential games.

We begin by analyzing models with just two stages or periods. First, we discuss the classic durable goods monopolist. A surprising point is that even a monopolist can be forced into a game, where the firm competes against itself in different time periods. To behave optimally, it must account for the effect of today's actions on future profits. Next, we investigate the classic two-period duopoly models where firms compete in output and/or price, which are labeled models M5–M12 in Table 10.1. We will see that in some cases the firm that moves first has the strategic advantage, while in others the firm that moves second has the advantage.

Once two-period models are mastered, we consider situations where a specific game, such as Cournot or Bertrand, is repeated many times. We discuss games that are repeated for a finite and an infinite number of periods. As we discussed in Chap. 3, infinitely repeated games are called supergames. In this chapter, our goal will be to identify the subgame perfect Nash equilibrium (SPNE) of each repeated game.

Like Chap. 10, we analyze oligopoly problems from a purely theoretical perspective. These purely theoretical models are designed to help us understand how firms interact strategically. They also provide a modeling framework that will be useful when addressing dynamic issues associated with product design and advertising later in the book. Empirical evidence regarding the price and output behavior of real firms in oligopoly markets will be addressed in Chap. 12, as well as in later chapters.

V.J. Tremblay and C.H. Tremblay, *New Perspectives on Industrial Organization*, Springer Texts in Business and Economics, DOI 10.1007/978-1-4614-3241-8_11, © Springer Science+Business Media New York 2012

11.1 Two-Period Monopoly and Duopoly Models

In this section, we consider noncooperative problems with two periods I and II. The choice variable will be output and/or price. In all models in this chapter, information is perfect and complete. Recall that information is complete when the payoffs and characteristics of the game are common knowledge. Information is perfect when the history of play is common knowledge. In this section we ignore discounting because it has little effect on the outcomes.[1] In contrast, we will see that discounting is consequential when we discuss infinitely repeated games later in the chapter.

11.1.1 The Durable Goods Monopolist

We begin with a durable goods monopolist because it allows us to solve one of the simplest dynamic problems in economics. In Chap. 6, we focused on the case where the monopolist produced a nondurable good, one that has value to consumers only in a single period. Fresh fruits and vegetables are good examples, as they have a short shelf life and their value depreciates to zero very quickly. In this section, the monopolist produces a **durable good**. When a durable good is produced and sold in the first period, it has value to consumers today and in future periods.[2] Examples include automobiles, refrigerators, and computers. These goods provide service value over and over again, unlike nondurable goods such as fruits and vegetables.

As was mentioned in Chap. 6, what makes dynamic problems interesting is that firm sales in the first period affect sales in future periods. For example, a consumer who buys a new car today is unlikely to buy a new car any time soon. Thus, an increase in new car sales today will lead to depressed car sales next period. In effect, new cars sold in the second period compete with used cars that were sold as new cars in the first period.

To illustrate, we consider a two-period (I and II) monopoly problem. Products that are produced in periods I and II are identical. Products that are produced in period I provide consumer value in both periods, but products produced in period II are valuable only in period II. The product has zero value in subsequent periods. Personal computers provide one example, where a substantially faster model that is introduced in period III makes obsolete the previous model that was produced in periods I and II.

To focus on strategic issues, costs are set to zero and demand is linear. Nevertheless, consumer demand is more complicated when a good lasts for more than one period. In this model, consumers' marginal valuation or demand price in the second period is

---

[1] Recall from Chap. 2 that this means that the discount factor (*D*) equals 1. That is, $1 received in 1 year is valued at $1 today.

[2] Because there are only two periods, however, a good that is sold in the second period has value for only a single period.

$p_{II} = a - b(q_I + q_{II})$, where q_t is output in period $t = I$ or II; a and b are positive constants. Notice that the demand price depends on the total supply, $q_I + q_{II}$, because output produced in period I survives and is valuable in period II. As a result, the marginal valuation or demand price in period I is $p_I = (a - bq_I) + [a - b(q_I + q_{II})]$.[3] The period I inverse demand function has two components because consumers who purchase a durable good in period I receive benefits in both periods I and II. The first bracketed term, $a - bq_I$, equals the marginal value in period I to consumers who made purchases in period I; the second term, $a - b(q_I + q_{II})$, equals the marginal valuation that those same consumers receive in period II.

Given that costs are zero in this model, the sum of profits from periods I and II (Π) is

$$\Pi = TR_I + TR_{II} = p_I q_I + p_{II} q_{II}$$
$$= [(a - bq_I) + (a - b(q_I + q_{II}))]q_I + [a - b(q_I + q_{II})]q_{II}, \qquad (11.1)$$

where $TR_t = p_t q_t$, total revenue in period t. The firm's goal is to find the level of output in each period that maximizes profit.

At first glance, you might be tempted to simply differentiate (11.1) with respect to q_I and q_{II} and solve the system of first-order conditions simultaneously to identify the profit-maximizing levels of output in each period. *This turns out to be incorrect.* Let us see why. Differentiating gives the following first-order conditions:

$$\frac{\partial \Pi}{\partial q_I} = \frac{\partial TR_I}{\partial q_I} + \frac{\partial TR_{II}}{\partial q_I} = MR_I + MR_{I-II}$$
$$= [(a - 2bq_I) + (a - 2bq_I - bq_{II})] + (-bq_{II}) = 0, \quad (11.2)$$

$$\frac{\partial \Pi}{\partial q_{II}} = \frac{\partial TR_I}{\partial q_{II}} + \frac{\partial TR_{II}}{\partial q_{II}} = MR_{II-I} + MR_{II}$$
$$= (-bq_I) + (a - bq_I - 2bq_{II}) = 0, \qquad (11.3)$$

where MR_t is the marginal revenue in period t, MR_{I-II} is the effect of a change in q_I on TR_{II}, and MR_{II-I} is the effect of a change in q_{II} on TR_I. Solving these equations simultaneously for output gives the optimal output levels:

$$q_I^* = \frac{a}{2b}; \quad q_{II}^* = 0, \qquad (11.4)$$

and cumulative output, $q_I^* + q_{II}^*$, equals $a/(2b)$, which is the simple static monopoly output when costs are zero. This suggests that the monopolist should produce the simple monopoly level of output in period I and produce zero output in period II.

---

[3] This assumes no discounting, which means that the discount factor (D) equals 1. With discounting, p_I would equal $(a - bq_I) + D[a - b(q_I + q_{II})]$.

The problem with this solution is that once period II arrives, it is not profit maximizing to produce zero output. When $q_I = a/(2b)$, the firm's profit equation in period II is[4]

$$\pi_{II} = \left[a - b\left(\frac{a}{2b} + q_{II}\right)\right]q_{II}. \qquad (11.5)$$

The first-order condition is

$$\frac{\partial \pi_{II}}{\partial q_{II}} = \frac{a}{2} - 2bq_{II} = 0. \qquad (11.6)$$

Solving this for q_{II} gives the profit maximizing output in period II:

$$q_{II}^{**} = \frac{a}{4b}, \qquad (11.7)$$

which exceeds zero. This demonstrates that the approach of maximizing joint profits is **time inconsistent**—it ignores the fact that the firm faces a dynamic problem. In game theoretic terms, it is not sequentially rational for the firm to follow through with zero output in period II. Ignoring this time interdependency means that the firm has failed to understand that it competes with itself in the later period.

To be sequentially rational, the firm must look forward and reason back, enabling it to avoid this time inconsistency problem. The firm will use backwards induction to find the SPNE.[5] This requires that the firm look forward and first identify the optimal output level in period II. The firm would then incorporate this information in forming its optimal decision in period I. Time inconsistency is eliminated because a SPNE requires a NE in every period or subgame. Unlike with the time inconsistent approach, action prescribed in period II under a SPNE will be optimal once period II arrives.

As we saw in Chap. 3, to operationally identify the SPNE we solve the firm's period II problem first. In period II, firm profit is

$$\pi_{II} = [a - b(q_I + q_{II})]q_{II}. \qquad (11.8)$$

The firm's goal is to maximize π_{II} with respect to q_{II}. Solving the resulting first-order condition for q_{II} produces the firm's best-reply function for period II (BR_{II}):[6]

$$BR_{II} : q_{II} = \frac{a - bq_I}{2b}. \qquad (11.9)$$

This is the NE value of q_{II} given q_I.

---

[4] That is, $\pi_{II} = TR_{II}$ given that costs are 0.

[5] As discussed in the Mathematics and Econometrics Appendix at the end of the book, this is an application of dynamic programming.

[6] We derive this by calculating the first-order condition of profit maximization, $\partial \pi_{II}/\partial q_{II} = a - bq_I - 2bq_{II} = 0$. Solving this for q_{II} gives $(a-bq_I)/2b$.

Next, the firm solves its period I problem, given its best-reply function above. The implication is that the firm can look forward to calculate BR_{II} and use this information to behave optimally in period I. Operationally, we substitute (11.9) into (11.1), which gives period I profits as a function of q_I alone. After simplifying, this becomes

$$\pi_I = \frac{a^2 + 4abq_I - 5b^2q_I^2}{4b}. \qquad (11.10)$$

The first-order condition is

$$\frac{\partial \pi_I}{\partial q_I} = \frac{4ab - 10b^2q_I}{4b} = 0. \qquad (11.11)$$

This first-order condition and (11.9) produce the SPNE levels of output in each period:

$$q_I^* = \frac{4a}{10b}; \quad q_{II}^* = \frac{3a}{10b}, \qquad (11.12)$$

and cumulative output $(q_I^* + q_{II}^*)$ equals $0.7a/b$. From these values and the demand functions above, we calculate equilibrium prices $p_I^* = 0.9a$ and $p_{II}^* = 0.3a$. Substituting equilibrium prices and quantities into the profit equation yields $\pi^* = 9a^2/20b$.

Notice that the price falls over time, illustrating that it is profitable for the monopolist to practice a form of **intertemporal price discrimination**. The monopolist charges a high price in the first period, serving only high valuation consumers, and offers a lesser price in the second period, serving consumers with a lower valuation. We will see in Chap. 14 that this is a common pricing pattern for electronics equipment, for example.

One purpose of this exercise is to compare the outcome under different market settings. Notice that if the market were competitive, the equilibrium price would equal 0 in both periods (under the assumption that marginal cost equals 0), and cumulative output would be a/b.[7] If the monopolist's behavior were truly time inconsistent (i.e., it was able to maximize joint profits by choosing q_I and q_{II} simultaneously), cumulative output would be $0.5a/b$ (at prices $p_I^* = a$ and $p_{II}^* = 0.5a$), which is the simple monopoly solution. When the monopolist's behavior is sequentially rational, the SPNE lies between these extremes, with cumulative output equaling $0.7a/b$ and prices equaling $p_I^* = 0.9a$ and $p_{II}^* = 0.3a$.

---

[7] We obtain this by setting $p_I = p_{II} = MC = 0$, where MC is marginal cost, and solving the two inverse demand functions (one for each period) simultaneously for q_I and q_{II}. This produces $q_I = a/b$ and $q_{II} = 0$.

Coase (1972) first recognized the implications of this model. The **Coase conjecture** states that as a monopolist's product becomes more durable (i.e., the number of periods for which the product has value and is priced), the SPNE price converges to the competitive price.[8] The intuition behind this result is that because a durable good that is produced today competes with goods produced tomorrow, the firm competes with itself intertemporally. Greater durability leads to more competition, a lower price, and lower overall profits.

There are several ways in which a firm can avoid the problem associated with the Coase conjecture. The most obvious solution is to lower durability. This appears to be the strategy of many textbook publishers, who require authors to revise their textbooks every 3–4 years to make older editions obsolete. A second solution is for the monopolist to rent or lease the product instead of selling it. This converts a dynamic problem into a static one. Consumers must return the product at the end of each period, which forces them to contract with the firm at the beginning of each period for 1 year's use of the durable good. Firms can then realize simple monopoly profits in each period. IBM used this tactic to market its mainframe computers in the 1960s when it had nearly monopolized the market.

Another way to avoid the Coase problem is for the firm to credibly commit to the monopoly level of production in period I and zero production thereafter. This "limited edition" strategy is used by the Franklin Mint, the world's largest private mint of foreign coins and collectables (e.g., medallions, sculptures, and diecast models). As an example, in 2009 Franklin offered a bronze medal commemorating the presidential inauguration of Barack Obama. Each is individually numbered and includes a guarantee that only 10,000 are minted. Once the last coin was minted, the mold was destroyed. A contract such as this effectively constrains Franklin from increasing production beyond 10,000 in the future, a tactic that increases the firm's overall profit.

11.1.2   The Stackelberg (Dynamic Cournot) Duopoly Model

In 1934, Stackelberg developed the first dynamic model of oligopoly (Stackelberg 1952), which is labeled model M5 in Table 10.1. Stackelberg extended the Cournot model by allowing firms to move sequentially. Known as the Stackelberg model or a dynamic Cournot model, it is also called a Leader–Follower model, because one firm (the leader) chooses output in the first period and the other firm (the follower) chooses output in the second period.

The Stackelberg model is especially relevant for industries that have a dominant or leading firm. In such industries, followers make output decisions only after observing the output level chosen by the dominant firm. General Motors held a dominant position in the US automobile industry in the 1960s, and Anheuser–Busch holds such a position in the US market for regular domestic beer today.

---

[8] For a formal discussion of this conjecture, see Bulow (1982), Gul et al. (1986), and Tirole (1988, Chap. 1).

A simple example will illustrate the main characteristics of the Stackelberg model. For comparison with the Cournot model, we consider a market setting with the same demand and cost structure as in Sect. 10.1.1, where products are homogeneous and firm demand and cost functions are linear. Firm i's total cost function is $\text{TC}_i = cq_i$, and the inverse demand function is $p = a - b(q_i + q_j)$, where subscript i refers to firm 1 or firm 2, and j refers to the other firm. The only difference between the Stackelberg model and the Cournot model is that actions are sequential, with firm 1 choosing output in the first period and firm 2 choosing output in the second period. The relevant characteristics of the game are:

1. Players: Firms 1 and 2.
2. Strategic Variable: Firm i chooses nonnegative values of q_i.
3. Timing: Firm 1 chooses output in the first period (I), and firm 2 chooses output in the second period (II).
4. Payoffs: Firm i's payoffs are profits; $\pi_i(q_i, q_j) = \text{TR}_i - \text{TC}_i = p \cdot q_i - cq_i = [a - b(q_i + q_j)]q_i - cq_i = aq_i - bq_i^2 - bq_iq_j - cq_i$.
5. Information is perfect and complete.

In dynamic models, the timing of play is a fundamental characteristic that must be clearly defined. As we indicated previously, information is perfect and complete in all models in this chapter.

The main goal of this section is to compare and contrast the Cournot and Stackelberg models in terms of output, price, and profits. Specifically, we will investigate whether the first mover or the second mover has a strategic advantage (i.e., earns higher profits).

The game is dynamic and our goal is to find the SPNE. As we discussed above, this is accomplished by using backwards induction. In period II, firm 2's problem is rather simple. Because firm 1 sets output first, firm 2 simply maximizes its profits given q_1. This generates the NE value of q_2 given q_1.

Firm 1's problem is more complex. In period I, for firm 1 to be sequentially rational, it must be able to anticipate firm 2's optimal behavior. We have referred to this as being able to look forward and reason back. Firm 1 will do this by anticipating how firm 2 will respond to different values of q_1. Because information is perfect and complete, firm 1 can calculate the profit maximizing level of q_2 for all values of q_1, which is just firm 2's best-reply function. Firm 1 will then choose its profit maximizing level of output given 2's best-reply function, which is the NE value of q_1 given the correctly anticipated reaction of firm 2.

Operationally, we analyze firm 2's problem first to find its best-reply function. Then we solve firm 1's problem, given firm 2's best-reply function. In the period II subgame, firm 2 calculates its profit maximizing level of output, given q_1. We have calculated firm 2's best reply function in Chap. 10, (10.7), which we reproduce here.

$$\text{BR}_2 : q_2^{\text{BR}} = \frac{a-c}{2b} - \frac{1}{2}q_1. \tag{11.13}$$

Firm 1 is able to calculate firm 2's best-reply function and use it to solve firm 1's problem in the first period.

That is, firm 1 maximizes its profits given q_2^{BR}. Firm 1's profit equation becomes

$$\pi_1 = \left(a - bq_1 - bq_2^{BR} - c\right)q_1$$
$$= \left(\frac{a - bq_1 - c}{2}\right)q_1. \tag{11.14}$$

The first-order condition for firm 1 is

$$\frac{\partial \pi_1}{\partial q_1} = \frac{a - 2bq_1 - c}{2} = 0. \tag{11.15}$$

Solving (11.15) for q_1 gives the SPNE value of firm 1's output. Substituting this value into (11.13) gives the SPNE value for firm 2's output. These values can then be used to determine the SPNE prices and profits from the demand and profit equations:

$$q_1^* = \frac{a - c}{2b} > q_2^* = \frac{a - c}{4b}, \tag{11.16}$$

$$p^* = \frac{a + 3c}{4}, \tag{11.17}$$

$$\pi_1^* = \frac{(a - c)^2}{8b} > \pi_2^* = \frac{(a - c)^2}{16b}. \tag{11.18}$$

Notice that there is a clear first-mover advantage, with the leader earning twice the profit and producing twice the output of the follower. It turns out that it is not always true that the first mover has the advantage, as we will see shortly.

One way to compare the Stackelberg outcome with the Cournot outcome is to subtract Cournot equilibrium values from the Stackelberg values as follows:

$$\Delta q_1 = \frac{a - c}{2b} - \frac{a - c}{3b} > 0,$$
$$\Delta q_2 = \frac{a - c}{4b} - \frac{a - c}{3b} < 0,$$
$$\Delta Q = \left(\frac{a - c}{2b} + \frac{a - c}{4b}\right) - \left(\frac{a - c}{3b} + \frac{a - c}{3b}\right) > 0,$$
$$\Delta p = \frac{a + 3c}{4} - \frac{a + 2c}{3} < 0,$$
$$\Delta \pi_1 = \frac{(a - c)^2}{8b} - \frac{(a - c)^2}{9b} > 0,$$
$$\Delta \pi_2 = \frac{(a - c)^2}{16b} - \frac{(a - c)^2}{9b} < 0. \tag{11.19}$$

When the change in a value is positive, this implies that the Stackelberg value exceeds the Cournot value. For example, because $\Delta q_1 > 0$, Stackelberg output exceeds Cournot output for firm 1. The results above verify that the Stackelberg leader is the dominant firm, producing more output and earning greater profit than both a Cournot competitor and the Stackelberg follower. The Stackelberg follower earns less and produces less than a Cournot competitor. In addition, greater total

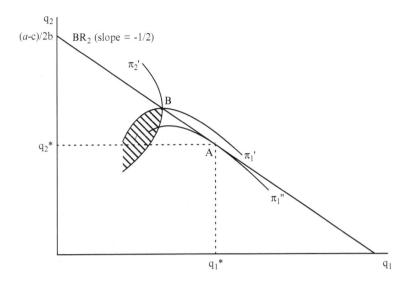

Fig. 11.1 The Stackelberg equilibrium (A) and the static Cournot equilibrium (B)

output (Q) is produced in the Stackelberg model, which results in a lower price than in the Cournot model. Finally, the comparative statics are the same in both models. An increase in marginal cost leads to a higher price and lower output and profit. An increase in demand boosts output, price, and profit.

A graphical depiction of the problem provides another way of thinking about the Stackelberg outcome. We first graph firm 2's best-reply function, (11.13), in Fig. 11.1. Firm 1's goal is to maximize its profit given firm 2's best-reply function (BR_2). In other words, the firm faces a constrained optimization problem. Graphically, this is solved by identifying the lowest isoprofit function given BR_2 (recall that a lower isoprofit function means higher profit for firm 1). This occurs at the tangency point A in the figure. You can see that relative to the Cournot outcome at point B, the leader produces greater output and earns higher profit, while the follower produces less output and earns less profit (i.e., firm 2's isoprofit function is further to the right, implying lower profit). You can also see that moving from point B to point A is not a Pareto move, as point A lies outside the shaded region where both firms would earn a greater profit.

11.1.3   A Dynamic Bertrand Model
with Multicharacteristic Differentiation

It is common for a dominant firm to be the price leader, setting price ahead of its competitors. In this section, we investigate a price leader model that is similar to the model in Sect. 10.2.2. The main difference is that this is a dynamic Bertrand model, with firm 1 setting price in period I and firm 2 setting price in period II. This is labeled model M6 in Table 10.1.

Demand and costs are linear. There is multiproduct differentiation, and we set both price parameters (β and δ) equal to 1 for simplicity, which yields the following demand functions:

$$q_1 = \alpha - p_1 + p_2, \qquad (11.20)$$

$$q_2 = \alpha - p_2 + p_1. \qquad (11.21)$$

Firm i's total cost is $\mathrm{TC}_i = cq_i$. Thus, profits for firm i are $\pi_i(p_i,\ p_j) = \mathrm{TR}_i - \mathrm{TC}_i = p_i(\alpha - p_i + p_j) - c(\alpha - p_i + p_j) = (p_i - c)(\alpha - p_i + p_j)$.

Backwards induction is used to determine the SPNE, solving the period II problem first. In this case, firm 2 maximizes its profits given p_1. From (10.38), we know that the first-order condition is

$$
\begin{aligned}
\frac{\partial \pi_2}{\partial p_2} &= \frac{\partial \mathrm{TR}_2}{\partial p_2} - \frac{\partial \mathrm{TC}_2}{\partial p_2} \\
&= \mathrm{MR}p_2 - \mathrm{MC}p_2 \\
&= \alpha - 2p_2 + p_1 + c = 0,
\end{aligned}
\qquad (11.22)
$$

where $\mathrm{MR}p_2$ is firm 2's marginal revenue with respect to a change in p_2 and $\mathrm{MC}p_2$ is firm 2's marginal cost with respect to a change in p_2. Solving for p_2 yields firm 2's best-reply function,

$$\mathrm{BR}_2: \quad p_2^{\mathrm{BR}} = \frac{\alpha + c}{2} + \frac{1}{2}p_1. \qquad (11.23)$$

Because information is perfect and complete, firm 1 is able to calculate firm 2's best-reply function and use it to maximize profit.

In period I, firm 1 will maximize its profits given p_2^{BR} above. Substituting p_2^{BR} into the firm's profit equation gives

$$
\begin{aligned}
\pi_1 &= \mathrm{TR}_1 - \mathrm{TC}_1 \\
&= p_1(\alpha - p_1 + p_2^{\mathrm{BR}}) - c(\alpha - p_1 + p_2^{\mathrm{BR}}) \\
&= (p_1 - c)[\alpha - p_1 + (\alpha + c + p_1)/2].
\end{aligned}
\qquad (11.24)
$$

The first-order condition is

$$
\begin{aligned}
\frac{\partial \pi_1}{\partial p_1} &= \frac{\partial \mathrm{TR}_1}{\partial p_1} - \frac{\partial \mathrm{TC}_1}{\partial p_1} \\
&= \mathrm{MR}p_1 - \mathrm{MC}p_1 \\
&= \frac{3\alpha + 2c}{2} - p_1 = 0,
\end{aligned}
\qquad (11.25)
$$

where $\mathrm{MR}p_1$ is firm 1's marginal revenue with respect to a change in p_1 and $\mathrm{MC}p_1$ is firm 1's marginal cost with respect to a change in p_1. Solving this equation for p_1 gives firm 1's SPNE price. This, along with demand, cost, profit, and firm 2's best-reply functions, gives the SPNE.

$$p_1^* = \frac{3\alpha + 2c}{2} > p_2^* = \frac{5\alpha + 4c}{4}, \tag{11.26}$$

$$q_1^* = \frac{3\alpha}{4} < q_2^* = \frac{5\alpha}{4}, \tag{11.27}$$

$$\pi_1^* = \frac{9\alpha^2}{8} < \pi_2^* = \frac{25\alpha^2}{16}. \tag{11.28}$$

Unlike the Stackelberg model, the follower or second firm earns greater profit in the dynamic Bertrand game. Thus, there is a second-mover advantage in this model, with the price leader earning lower profits. For the price leader to have a superior position, it must also have lower costs (or produce a better product) than its competitor.

A comparison of the dynamic and static Bertrand outcomes is presented below. Here, we subtract static Bertrand outcomes from dynamic Bertrand outcomes. This yields the following set of results:

$$\Delta q_1 = \frac{3\alpha}{4} - \alpha < 0,$$

$$\Delta q_2 = \frac{5\alpha}{4} - \alpha > 0,$$

$$\Delta Q = \left(\frac{3\alpha}{4} + \frac{5\alpha}{4}\right) - (2\alpha) = 0,$$

$$\Delta p_1 = \frac{3\alpha + 2c}{2} - (\alpha + c) > 0,$$

$$\Delta p_2 = \frac{5\alpha + 4c}{4} - (\alpha + c) > 0,$$

$$\Delta \pi_1 = \frac{9\alpha^2}{8} - \alpha^2 > 0,$$

$$\Delta \pi_2 = \frac{25\alpha^2}{16} - \alpha^2 > 0. \tag{11.29}$$

When the change in a value is positive, this implies that the dynamic Bertrand value exceeds the static Bertrand value. For example, because $\Delta q_1 < 0$, firm 1 produces less output in the dynamic setting than in the static setting. Notice that both firms are better off in a dynamic Bertrand game than in a static Bertrand game (i.e., $\Delta \pi_i > 0$), but each firm wants to be a follower so that the other firm sets the price first.

The intuition behind these results can be seen in the graph of the SPNE, depicted in Fig. 11.2. As before, firm 1 maximizes its profits, subject to firm 2's best-reply function, BR$_2$. In other words, firm 1 moves to the highest isoprofit function possible, which occurs at point A. Point B represents the NE to the static Bertrand game. Clearly, both firms are better off by moving from point B to point A, as they can both move to a higher isoprofit function. Although the second mover earns higher profits, both firms are clearly better off in a dynamic setting, regardless of who moves first.

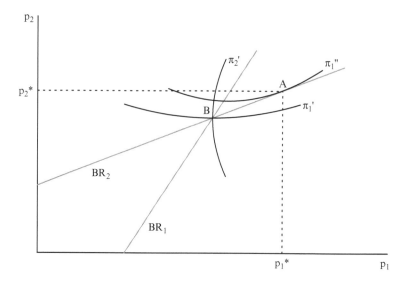

Fig. 11.2 The dynamic Bertrand equilibrium (A) and the static Bertrand equilibrium (B)

11.1.4 A Dynamic Quantity and Price Game Yields a Cournot Outcome

The primary criticism of the Cournot model is that most real firms compete in price rather than output. Yet, Kreps and Scheinkman (1983) support it by showing that the Cournot outcome is a SPNE when firms compete in the following dynamic game. For simplicity, consider a market with two firms (1 and 2) that produce homogeneous goods, where firm i's total cost is $TC_i = cq_i$. The firms simultaneously choose capacity levels in stage I and simultaneously choose prices in stage II. If information is perfect and complete, Kreps and Scheinkman show that the SPNE of this game is the Cournot outcome.[9]

We use backwards induction to derive this result. In stage II, firms simultaneously choose prices. Firms have already built capacities in stage I, equal to $\bar{q}_1$ and $\bar{q}_2$, with capacity assumed to be less than the competitive level of output (where price equals c). Let $\bar{p}$ equal the market price when $\bar{q}_1 + \bar{q}_2$ is produced (which exceeds c). The NE at this stage will be $p_1 = p_2 = \bar{p}$.[10] That is, firms will set their prices in stage II so that they make full use of their productive capacity.

---

[9] This requires that production capacity is less than the competitive level of output and that capacity is costly to change. In addition, the rationing rule that determines which consumers buy from firm 1 and which buy from firm 2 is efficient. This assures that consumer surplus is maximized (Tirole, 1988, p. 213).

[10] This is a unique NE. At $p_1 = p_2 = \bar{p}$, neither firm has an incentive to deviate. At $p_1 = p_2 < \bar{p}$, total demand exceeds total capacity. Firm i could increase profit by raising its price slightly, given the capacity constraint of its competitor. If $p_1 = p_2 > \bar{p}$, each firm has an incentive to undercut the price of its competitor because total demand is less than total capacity. Thus, the only NE is $p_1 = p_2 = \bar{p}$.

Given this fact, the NE output levels (which equal capacity levels) in stage I will be the same as the simple Cournot equilibrium output levels. The reason for this is that firms will set stage II prices so that all that is produced (which equals capacity) in stage I will be sold. This process is similar to that of the static Cournot model, except that the market clearing price is set by an auctioneer in the static Cournot model and by the firms in the dynamic model. Whether prices are set by an auctioneer or by firms, prices are set to clear the market. Thus, equilibrium output (capacity) and price levels will be the same in both models.

The Kreps and Scheinkman result shows that the Cournot model may be more realistic than it first appears. Even though most firms set prices in the real world, this is not inconsistent with a dynamic Cournot model where firms choose capacity in the first period and prices in the second period. To paraphrase Kreps and Scheinkman, quantity precommitment in a Bertrand pricing game yields the Cournot outcome.

11.1.5 A Dynamic Cournot–Bertrand Model with Multicharacteristic Differentiation

V. Tremblay et al. (forthcoming-a) considered a dynamic version of the Cournot–Bertrand model with multicharacteristic differentiation that was discussed in Sect. 10.3, labeled model M7 in Table 10.1. In this model, firm 1 chooses output in the first period, and firm 2 chooses price in the second period. Variable costs are set to zero for simplicity, but fixed (or quasi-fixed) costs (F) vary by firm. As we discussed in Chap. 10, firms are likely to have different fixed costs in this model.

Demand functions derive from those found in (10.28) and (10.29): $p_i = a - q_i - dq_j$, where d is the index of product differentiation. When $d = 0$, each firm is a monopolist; when $d = 1$, products are homogeneous. This specification results in the following demand system, where choice variables (q_1 and p_2) are on the right-hand side of each equation:

$$p_1 = (a - ad) - (1 - d^2)q_1 + dp_2, \tag{11.30}$$

$$q_2 = a - p_2 - dq_1. \tag{11.31}$$

Firm i's profits are $\pi_i(p_i, p_j) = p_i q_i - F_i$.[11]

To identify the SPNE, we use backwards induction as in previous models by solving firm 2's problem first. Firm 2's first-order condition can be found in (10.73). This produces firm 2's best reply, which firm 1 takes as given in the first stage problem when it maximizes its profits. Using the same procedure as in the previous sections leads to the SPNE values:

$$p_1^* = \frac{a(2 - d)}{4} < p_2^* = \frac{a(4 - 2d - d^2)}{4(2 - d^2)}, \tag{11.32}$$

---

[11] Variable costs are set to zero for simplicity.

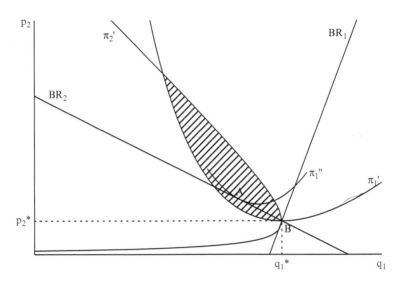

Fig. 11.3 The dynamic Cournot–Bertrand equilibrium (A) and the static Cournot–Bertrand equilibrium (B)

$$q_1^* = \frac{a(2-d)}{4(2-d^2)} > q_2^* = \frac{a(4-2d-d^2)}{4(2-d^2)}, \tag{11.33}$$

$$\pi_1^* = \frac{a^2(2-d)^2}{8(2-d^2)} - F_1; \quad \pi_2^* = \frac{a^2(4-2d-d^2)^2}{16(2-d^2)^2} - F_2. \tag{11.34}$$

Although the Bertrand-type firm charges the higher price, the Cournot-type firm is the dominant firm and has the strategic advantage as long as the difference in fixed costs is not too great.

A detailed comparison of the dynamic and static Cournot–Bertrand outcomes is tedious, but the main implication is easy to see from the graph of best-reply and isoprofit curves in Fig. 11.3. Firm 1 maximizes its profit, subject to firm 2's best-reply function, BR_2, producing the SPNE at point A. Point B represents the NE to the static Cournot–Bertrand game. Because the Pareto (shaded) region covers only firm 2's best-reply function, both firms prefer that the Cournot-type firm moves first.

11.1.6 Endogenous Timing and Choice of Strategic Variable

Whether to compete in the first or second period and to compete in output or price may be dictated by institutional and technological considerations, but what if firms have a choice? In Chap. 10, we found that output competition (Cournot) dominates

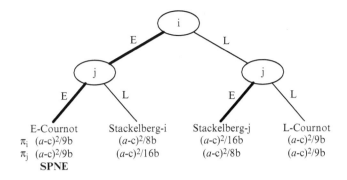

Fig. 11.4 An output game when timing is endogenous

price competition (Bertrand) in a static game as long as differences in costs and vertical differentiation are not too extensive. In this section, we investigate issues involving the strategic timing and choice variable more generally.

First, we consider the case where firms must compete in output but can decide on the timing of play (model M9 in Table 10.1). That is, they have the choice of competing in a static or a dynamic setting. In the output game, the choice is between a Cournot and a Stackelberg-type game. One way to endogenize the timing of play is to allow firms to have the choice of competing in an early period (E) or a later period (L).[12] With two firms, 1 and 2, this leads to four possible outcomes:

- E-Cournot: An early Cournot outcome, where firm 1 chooses output early and firm 2 chooses output early.
- L-Cournot: A late Cournot outcome, where firm 1 chooses output late and firm 2 chooses output late.
- Stackelberg-1: A Stackelberg outcome, where firm 1 is the leader. That is, firm 1 chooses output early and firm 2 chooses output late.
- Stackelberg-2: A Stackelberg outcome, where firm 2 is the leader.

To investigate a model with these possibilities, we assume that products are homogeneous and that inverse demand and cost functions are linear, as in Sect. 10.1.1 (Cournot) and Sect. 11.1.2 (Stackelberg). In this case, the extensive form representation of the game is described in Fig. 11.4. Using backwards induction, you can see that firm j has a dominant strategy: it is always optimal for firm j to produce output early, whether firm i chooses output early or late. Given that j will always choose output early, the optimal strategy for firm i is to choose output early. Thus the SPNE to this game is E-Cournot. If given the choice, both firms will want to avoid being a Stackelberg follower because of the first-mover advantage in the Stackelberg game.

---

[12] This discussion derives from the work of Hamilton and Slutsky (1990), Amir (1995), and Amir and Grilo (1999).

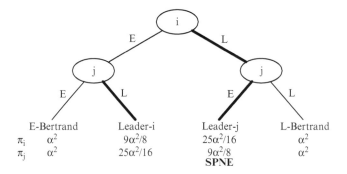

Fig. 11.5 A price game when timing is endogenous

The opposite occurs when firms compete in price instead of output and the timing is endogenous (model M10 in Table 10.1). To see this outcome, consider the models of multiproduct differentiation discussed in Sects. 10.2.2 and 11.1.3, except that $\beta = \delta = 1$ for simplicity. Firms have the choice of competing in price in an early or late period. There are four possible outcomes to this game:

- E-Bertrand: An early Bertrand outcome, where firm 1 chooses price early and firm 2 chooses price early.
- L-Bertrand: A late Bertrand outcome, where firm 1 chooses price late and firm 2 chooses price late.
- Leader-1: A dynamic Bertrand outcome, where firm 1 is the leader. That is, firm 1 chooses price early and firm 2 chooses price late.
- Leader-2: A dynamic Bertrand outcome, where firm 2 is the leader.

The extensive form representation of the game is provided in Fig. 11.5. In this case, firm j does not have a dominant strategy. Instead, firm j will choose L when firm i chooses E and will choose E when firm i chooses L. Given this information, the best option for firm i is to choose L. Thus, the SPNE is Leader-j, where firm i competes in price late and firm j competes in price early. Operationally, this leads to multiple equilibria, as both firms prefer L to E and both prefer dynamic to static play. If firm 1 moves first, firm 1 will choose L and firm 2 will respond E. If firm 2 moves first, firm 2 will choose L and firm 1 will respond E. Both want to choose price L, as long as the other firm chooses price E.

Second, we consider the case where firms must compete in a dynamic setting but have the choice of strategic variable, output or price (model M8 in Table 10.1). Assuming that firm 1 moves first, this leads to four possible outcomes:

- Stackelberg (Dynamic Cournot): Firm 1 competes in output in the first period, and firm 2 competes in output in the second period.
- Dynamic Cournot–Bertrand: Firm 1 competes in output in the first period, and firm 2 competes in price in the second period.

- Dynamic Bertrand–Cournot: Firm 1 competes in price in the first period, and firm 2 competes in output in the second period.
- Dynamic Bertrand: Firm 1 competes in price in the first period, and firm 2 competes in price in the second period.

V. Tremblay et al. (forthcoming-a) investigate this model and find that once firm 1 has made its choice, firm 2's profits are the same whether firm 2 competes in output or in price. Once firm 1 has set its output (or price), firm 2 faces a residual demand function that is devoid of strategic interaction. This is much like a monopolist's problem, where the outcome is invariant to whether the firm optimizes over output or price. Thus, a dynamic mix of strategies (either dynamic Cournot–Bertrand or dynamic Bertrand–Cournot) is just as likely as the Stackelberg or dynamic Bertrand outcome.

Finally, V. Tremblay et al. (forthcoming-a) examine the remaining cases, models M11 and M12 in Table 10.1, where the timing of play is endogenous in the Cournot–Bertrand model and when both the timing of play and the choice of strategic variable can be endogenous decisions of the firm. The analysis is rather tedious, so we do not review it here. The main conclusions are that (1) the SPNE in the Cournot–Bertrand model is for the Cournot-type firm to move first and the Bertrand-type firm to move second and (2) the SPNE in the model where the timing and the choice of strategic variable are endogenous is early Cournot, unless there are substantial demand and/or cost asymmetries.

11.2 Oligopoly Models in Repeated Games

In most industries, firms compete over and over again with their rivals. For the last century GM and Ford have continued to battle for the top spot in the US automobile industry. Coke continues to compete with Pepsi in the market for soft drinks, and Verizon races with AT&T for dominance of the cellular phone market. Period after period, these firms compete in output or price. Recall from Chap. 3 that when a particular game, called a stage game, is played over and over again, it is called a repeated game.

In this section, we review two types of repeated games. The first is a finitely repeated game or a game with a finite number of stages. The second is an infinitely repeated game, called a supergame. In each case, our goal is to identify the SPNE.

11.2.1 Finitely Repeated Duopoly Models

To explore the basic idea, we consider a simple Bertrand model with two firms that produce homogeneous goods. Costs are linear and the same for both firms. In each stage, firms compete by simultaneously setting price. Recall that in this stage game,

the NE is for each firm to set price equal to marginal cost, which produces a zero profit
outcome. The only difference here is that this stage game is repeated three times.

To find the SPNE, we use backwards induction. We saw in Chap. 3 that when a
game is repeated a finite number of times, the SPNE strategy is to play the NE strategy
in every period. This conclusion holds for n firms and for other oligopoly models (e.g.,
Cournot), so analyzing finitely repeated games is rather simple and adds little to our
understanding of oligopoly theory. The SPNE is the NE in every stage game.

One question you might ask is whether there is a strategy that will support a better
outcome for firms in repeated games. For example, a firm might threaten to punish
a competitor for failure to cooperate. This will be ineffective in a finite game,
however. The reason is that in the last period, it pays not to cooperate because
there is no next period in which punishment can be inflicted. Given this lack of
cooperation in the last period, it pays not to cooperate in the second to last period,
and so on. The unraveling of cooperation implies that the Nash equilibrium
(e.g., Cournot or Bertrand) outcome will prevail in every stage of a finitely repeated
game. This need not be true in infinitely repeated games.

11.2.2 Infinitely Repeated Oligopoly Models

Analysis of an infinitely repeated game is somewhat more complicated because the
game goes on forever. With no final period, we are unable to use backwards
induction. One obvious solution is for each firm to repeat its NE strategy in every
period, as this meets the definition of a SPNE. Under certain conditions, however, a
trigger strategy can also make cooperation (i.e., collusion) in every period a SPNE.
Although we have discussed this topic briefly in Chaps. 3 and 9, we discuss it more
formally below for Bertrand and Cournot models.

11.2.2.1 Infinitely Repeated Bertrand Models

To see how collusion in every period is possible, we begin with a Bertrand model
with two symmetric firms that produce homogeneous goods. Firms use a trigger
strategy, which has the following characteristics:

- If firm j chooses to cooperate by charging the monopoly price (p_M) in period
$t - 1$, then firm i charges p_M in period t.
- If firm j cheats by lowering its price below p_M in $t - 1$, the price cut triggers a
harsh or grim response, with firm i charging the NE (Bertrand) price forever.[13]

---

[13] The punishing price need not be as grim or low as the NE price, but this is a common assumption
(Gibbons, 1992).

To decide whether to cheat or not, a firm must compare the net benefits from cooperating with the net benefits from cheating. We will demonstrate that the firm will cooperate as long as the future is not discounted too heavily.

Firm i's payoff from cooperating verses cheating is derived as follows. If firms cooperate, firm i will receive half the monopoly profits $(\pi_M/2)$ in every period. We saw in Chap. 2 that the present value of receiving $\pi_M/2$ in every period out to infinity equals $\pi_M/[2(1 - D)]$, where D is the discount factor. On the other hand, if firm i cheats by slightly lowering its price, it will earn nearly the full monopoly profit today (π_M).[14] This will trigger NE pricing and zero profits forever after. As a result, a trigger strategy will support cooperation if

$$\frac{\pi_M}{2(1 - D)} \geq \pi_M + 0. \tag{11.35}$$

The left-hand side of the inequality in (11.35) is the net benefit from cooperation, and the right-hand side is the net benefit from cheating. This inequality holds as long as $D \geq \frac{1}{2}$, which is highly likely. Recall that if $D \geq \frac{1}{2}$, then a dollar received one year from now is worth at least 50 cents today and the rate of time preference (or interest rate on your investment) is less than or equal to 100%.[15] Thus, as long as these Bertrand competitors do not drastically discount the future, they will cooperate in every period.

The reason for this result is that the punishment imposes such a high cost on those who deviate from cooperation. Deviating does enable the firm to double its profits in the current period, but profits then fall to zero in every period thereafter. As long as firms place a sufficiently high value on future profits, it pays to cooperate. If future profits do not matter at all (i.e., $D = 0$), then it clearly pays to cheat because $\pi_M/2 < \pi_M$.

The problem is only slightly more complicated with n instead of 2 firms. The only change is that firm i's profits from cooperation become π_M/n. In this case, a trigger strategy will support collusion if

$$\frac{\pi_M}{n(1 - D)} \geq \pi_M + 0. \tag{11.36}$$

This condition holds when $D \geq (1 - 1/n)$ or $n \leq 1/(1 - D)$, which implies that firms will cooperate as long as D is sufficiently high and n is sufficiently low. This confirms the fundamental principle of collusion that we discussed in Chap. 9: a trigger strategy is more likely to support collusion when there are fewer competitors and when future dollars are not too heavily discounted. In Fig. 11.6, the shaded region identifies the values of n and D that support collusion. Notice that this is

---

[14] For mathematical convenience, we assume that firm i's profits equal π_M for an infinitesimal price cut.

[15] Recall from Appendix 2.A that the rate of return on your investment, r, is calculated from the equation $D \equiv 1/(1 + r)$ or $r \equiv (1 - D)/D$.

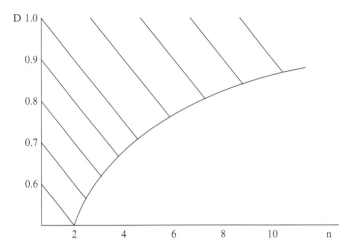

Fig. 11.6 Number of firms (n) and the discount factor (D) that support collusion in a Bertrand model

consistent with Stigler's (1964) theory that collusion is more likely and easier to maintain with fewer firms (see Chap. 9).

11.2.2.2 Infinitely Repeated Cournot Models

Analysis of an infinitely repeated Cournot game is more complicated because NE profits are not zero in the Cournot stage game. We begin by assuming two symmetric firms. As in the Bertrand model, a trigger strategy will support collusion if the net benefits from cooperation are at least as great as the net benefits from cheating. In this case, cooperation means that the firm will produce half of the monopoly output ($q_M/2$), and cheating means that the firm deviates by producing more than half of the monopoly output. To be more precise, cheating today means that firm i will choose the level of output that maximizes profit given that firm j produces the cooperative level of output (i.e., $q_j = q_M/2$).

Formally, the following condition must hold for a trigger strategy to support collusion in this Cournot model:

$$\frac{\pi_M}{2(1-D)} \geq \pi_i^* + \frac{D}{1-D}\pi_i^{NE}. \tag{11.37}$$

In terms of notation:

- $\pi_i^* = \max \pi_i(q_i, q_j = q_M/2)$. In other words, π_i^* is the level of profit that firm i receives when firm j produces the cartel level of output ($q_M/2$) and firm i cheats (optimally) on the cartel agreement. This level of output is defined as q_i^*.
- π_i^{NE} is the profit that firm i receives when both firms produce the Cournot or NE level of output, q_i^{NE}.

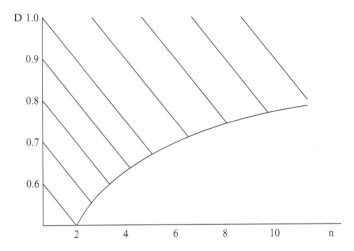

Fig. 11.7 Number of firms (n) and the discount factor (D) that support collusion in a Cournot model

- $[D/(1-D)]\pi_i^{NE}$ is the present value of earning π_i^{NE} forever after.[16]

Rearranging terms in (11.37) yields

$$\frac{\pi_M}{2} \geq (1-D)\pi_i^* + D\pi_i^{NE}. \tag{11.38}$$

From previous discussion, we know that $\pi_i^* > \pi_M/2 > \pi_i^{NE}$. If there is no tomorrow, then $D = 0$ and the inequality in (11.38) does not hold. In this case, the trigger strategy fails to support collusion. If $D = 1$, the inequality clearly holds (because $\pi_M/2 > \pi_i^{NE}$). This means that a trigger strategy will support collusion in an infinitely repeated Cournot game as long as the future is not discounted too heavily (i.e., D is sufficiently close to 1).

Next, we analyze the infinitely repeated Cournot game when there are n firms. We assume that products are homogeneous and that both the inverse demand and cost functions are linear: $p = a - bQ$; $TC_i = cq_i$. As we saw in Chap. 10 Sect. (10.1.3), $\pi_i^{NE} = y/\left[b(n+1)^2\right]$, where $y = (a-c)^2$. The cartel profits for each firm are $\pi_M/n = y/4bn$. When firm i cheats on the cartel agreement, it maximizes profits given that $q_j = q_M/n = (a-c)/2bn$. In this case,

$\pi_i^* = \left[y(n+1)^2\right]/16bn^2$. Substituting these profit values into (11.38) with n instead of 2 firms and solving the inequality for D, yields

$$D \geq \frac{1 + 2n + n^2}{1 + 6n + n^2}. \tag{11.39}$$

The values of n and D that are consistent with this inequality are identified by the shaded region in Fig. 11.7. The principle of collusion is apparent in the figure. As in the Bertrand example above, collusion is more likely with fewer firms and when the future is not discounted too heavily.

In reality, the punishment phase will not last forever. A trigger strategy that imposes a grim response for a finite length of time can still support collusion as long as the punishment cost is severe enough to assure that the inequality in (11.37) holds.

11.3   Strategic Substitutes, Complements, and Entry Barriers

We have seen in Chap. 8 that a firm will invest in a strategic barrier to entry if two conditions are met. First, the investment must be irreversible and sufficiently raise the cost of entry. We modeled this as a dynamic process, where the incumbent makes an irreversible commitment in stage I and the entry decision is made in stage II. Second, the entry deterring investment must be profitable for the incumbent. An example that illustrates this can be found in Sect. 8.4.2.2, Fig. 8.8.

Another way to analyze strategic barriers is to show how they affect best-reply functions in stage II. Consider a two-stage game where a monopoly incumbent (firm 1) must decide whether or not to invest in a research and development (R&D) project in stage I that will lower its marginal cost in stage II.[17] In stage II, firm 2 decides whether or not to enter. If entry takes place, firms compete by simultaneously choosing output (i.e., they play a Cournot game). To find the SPNE, we use backwards induction. In stage II, the NE is described in Fig. 11.8. If firm 1 does not invest in R&D, its best-reply is BR_1, and the Nash equilibrium is point NE. If it makes the investment, its best reply function shifts right to BR_1'.[18] Only if the investment profitably shifts BR_1 so that the new Nash equilibrium is to the right of point y will this be a successful strategic barrier to entry.

In some cases it will be profitable for firm 1 to commit to such investments even though entry still takes place. The firm will then accommodate entry. The profitable strategic choices of firm 1 depend on two factors (1) whether the investment in stage

---

[17] The firm could also invest in a quality improvement, which would have the same effect on the outcome.

[18] That is, a lower marginal cost will cause firm 1 to produce more output for a given q_2.

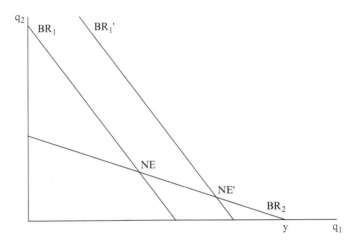

Fig. 11.8 Examples of top dog (BR$_1$ to BR$_1'$) and lean and hungry (BR$_1'$ to BR$_1$) strategies

I leads to tougher or softer competition in stage II and (2) whether the strategic variables in stage II are strategic substitutes or strategic complements. Recall from Chap. 10 that when best-reply functions have a negative slope (as in Cournot), strategic variables are strategic substitutes; when they have a positive slope (as in Bertrand), strategic variables are strategic complements.

Fudenberg and Tirole (1984) investigate this issue as it relates to the incumbent firm's decision to overinvest or underinvest in a strategic variable x in stage I. By overinvestment (underinvestment), they mean that firm 1 invests more (less) in x than if there were no potential entrants. In other words, this overinvestment or underinvestment is due to strategic considerations.[19] Fudenberg and Tirole identify four cases: top dog, lean and hungry, fat cat, and puppy dog strategies.

The "top dog" case arises when firms play a Cournot game in stage II and an investment in x leads to tough competition, as depicted in Fig. 11.8. Investment in x (R&D) in stage I causes firm 1's best-reply function to shift right (from BR$_1$ to BR$_1'$). Because this causes firm 1 to grow in size and take a dominant position in the market, Fudenberg and Tirole call this a top dog strategy. In this case, firm 1 will overinvest in x in order to create a hostile environment for firm 2. Notice that the firm wants to overinvest in x whether it is deterring or accommodating entry.

Second, firm 1's strategy is "lean and hungry" when firms play a Cournot game and profitable investment in x leads to softer competition. In this case, investment in x causes firm 1's best-reply function to shift left (from BR$_1'$ to BR$_1$ in Fig. 11.8), leading to a less dominant position and underinvestment in x. As an example, it may be profitable for firm 1 to enter into another market but diseconomies of scope in

---

[19] To simplify the discussion, we assume that firm 1's investment in x has no direct effect on firm 2's profits. For further discussion, see Fudenberg and Tirole (1984) and Tirole (1988, Chap. 8).

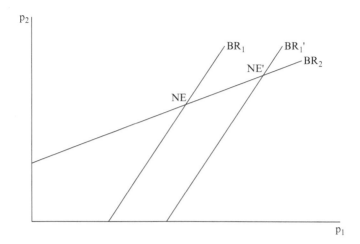

Fig. 11.9 Examples of fat cat (BR_1 to BR_1') and puppy dog (BR_1' to BR_1) strategies

production push up the firm's marginal cost in the original market. Notice that this behavior is not entry deterring.

The next two cases involve Bertrand games, where the best-reply functions have a positive slope. In the third case, firm 1 pursues a "fat cat" strategy, where an increase in x causes firm 1's best-reply function to shift right as in Fig. 11.9. Investment in R&D that enhanced the quality of firm 1's product would result in a rightward shift.[20] The R&D investment softens price competition in stage II, and firm 1 will overinvest in x. By making investments that soften price competition, firm 1 behaves as a nonaggressive fat cat.

Fourth, firm 1's strategy is that of a "puppy dog" when firms play a Bertrand game and profitable investment in x leads to tougher price competition. In this case, investment in x causes firm 1's best-reply function to shift left (from BR_1' to BR_1 in Fig. 11.9), as would happen if R&D led to a reduction in firm 1's marginal cost. To avoid price competition in stage II, firm 1 will want to appear nonaggressive by underinvesting in x.

The Fudenberg and Tirole taxonomy suggests two implications regarding strategic entry deterrence. First, firm 1 will choose a top dog stance if it wants to deter entry. Second, the strategy it chooses to accommodate entry will depend on the slope of the best-reply functions and the effect of x on competition in the final stage of the game.

---

[20] That is, higher quality will cause firm 1 to charge a higher price for a given p_2.

11.4 Summary

1. In many industries, firms compete in a dynamic setting. Rival prices may be set sequentially when a smaller competing firm waits to set its price after a dominant firm sets its price. In addition, even though Cournot-type competitors set output simultaneously, they may repeat this static game year after year. In this case, firms play a repeated Cournot game. When the number of repetitions is finite, this is a finitely repeated game. When the game goes on forever, it is an infinitely repeated game (or supergame).

2. A durable good is a product that consumers value for more than one period. When a monopoly produces a durable good, it competes with itself over time. In the two-period case, the strategy that maximizes joint profits over time is to produce the static monopoly level of output in period I and zero output in period II. This behavior is **time inconsistent** (i.e., sequentially irrational), however, because the firm will desire to produce a positive level of output once period II arrives. To be sequentially rational, the firm must use backwards induction to obtain the SPNE. This leads to greater total output and lower profits than would occur if the firm were able to eliminate production in period II.

3. A durable goods monopolist that charges a high price in period I and a low price in period II is practicing **intertemporal price discrimination**. Consumers with high marginal valuations will purchase in period I, and consumers with low marginal valuations will wait to purchase in period II.

4. The **Coase conjecture** states that as a monopolist's product becomes more durable (i.e., it provides consumer utility over more and more periods), the SPNE price converges to the competitive price. To avoid this problem, the monopolist has an incentive to reduce durability, rent rather than sell the good, and contract with consumers to eliminate production in later periods.

5. The **Stackelberg model** is a dynamic Cournot model, where one firm chooses output in the first period, and the other firm chooses output in the second period. The Stackelberg model results in a first-mover advantage, with higher profits going to the firm that moves first.

6. In a **dynamic Bertrand model**, one firm chooses price in the first period, and the other firm chooses price in the second period. When there is multicharacteristic product differentiation, there is a second-mover advantage, with higher profit going to the firm that moves last.

7. When firms compete in output and have the choice of competing in an early or a later period, both firms will choose to compete in the early period. Thus, static Cournot dominates Stackelberg (dynamic Cournot). If firms compete in price instead of output and have the choice of competing early or late, then the dynamic Bertrand outcome dominates the static Bertrand outcome.

8. Even though most real firms compete in price rather than output, price competition is not inconsistent with the dynamic model where firms choose capacity in the first period and prices in the second period. This capacity–price model produces the simple Cournot outcome.

9. When firms must compete in a dynamic setting and have the choice of competing in output or price, then a dynamic Cournot–Bertrand or dynamic Bertrand–Cournot outcome is just as likely as a Stackelberg or dynamic Bertrand outcome.

10. When the timing and the choice of strategic variable are endogenous, then the static Cournot outcome is a SPNE unless there are substantial demand or cost asymmetries.

11. The SPNE in a finitely repeated game is rather simple: firms choose the NE strategy in each stage or period of the game.

12. In an infinitely repeated game, one possible SPNE strategy is for each firm to choose its NE strategy in each stage. Yet, under certain conditions a trigger strategy can support collusion. With a trigger strategy, a firm will cooperate if rivals have cooperated in the previous period. Noncooperative behavior in the previous period triggers a punishing strategy, which is normally a NE strategy.

13. The fundamental principle of collusion states that a trigger strategy is more likely to support collusion when there are fewer firms and when future profits are not too heavily discounted.

14. In Fudenberg and Tirole's taxonomy of firm strategies:

- An incumbent firm will behave as a top dog (i.e., overinvest in activity x to be big and aggressive) when best-reply functions have a negative slope and the investment in x makes the firm a tougher competitor (e.g., it produces a cost reduction that causes its best-reply to shift right).

- An incumbent firm will behave as a lean and hungry competitor (i.e., underinvest in activity x to be small and unaggressive) when best-reply functions have a negative slope and the investment in x makes the firm a softer competitor.

- An incumbent firm will behave as a fat cat (i.e., overinvest in activity x to soften competition) when best-reply functions have a positive slope and the investment in x makes the firm a softer competitor.

- An incumbent firm will behave as a puppy dog (i.e., underinvest in activity x in order to look nonaggressive) when best-reply functions have a positive slope and the investment in x makes the firm a tougher competitor.

11.5   Review Questions

1. (Advanced) Assume that a durable goods monopolist produces a good that lasts just two periods, I and II. Firm costs are zero, inverse demand in period II is $p_{II} = 12 - (q_I + q_{II})$, and inverse demand in period I is $p_I = (12 - q_I) + [12 - (q_I + q_{II})]$.

   A. Derive the firm's outcome (output, price, and profits for each period) if the firm chooses q_I and q_{II} to simultaneously maximize joint profits. Why is the outcome sequentially irrational?

B. Derive the firm's sequentially rational outcome.

2. Coase's conjecture implies that a durable goods monopolist will have an incentive to lower the durability of its product. Would this necessarily be true if the firm faced one or more competitors? Explain.

3. Assume there are two firms, 1 and 2, that compete in output, products are homogeneous, and the inverse market demand is $p = a - Q$, where $Q = q_1 + q_2$. Assume that production costs are zero for simplicity.

   A. Find the NE (Cournot) price, output, and profits of each firm if this is a static game.
   B. Find the SPNE if this is a dynamic game where firm 1 chooses output first.
   C. Find the cartel equilibrium to this game.
   D. Use a graph of best-reply and isoprofit functions to describe the NE, SPNE, and cartel equilibrium for problems A, B, and C above.
   E. Use a graph of best-reply and isoprofit functions to show that each firm has an incentive to increase its output from the cartel level.

4. (Advanced) Assume three firms (1, 2, and 3) compete in a dynamic game. Firm 1 chooses output in the first period, and firms 2 and 3 simultaneously choose output in the second period. Products are homogeneous, and the inverse market demand function is $p = 144 - Q$, where $Q = q_1 + q_2 + q_3$. Firms face linear cost equations, but firm 1 has a cost advantage over firms 2 and 3: $TC_i = c_i q_i$, $c_1 = 0, 0 < c_2 = c_3 = c < 36$. Find the SPNE (price, output, and profits) for this model. How does this cost asymmetry affect equilibrium values?

5. Assume two firms, 1 and 2, compete in a dynamic Bertrand game. Firm 1 moves first. Products are homogeneous, and the inverse market demand function is $p = a - Q$, where $Q = q_1 + q_2$. Firms face the same linear cost equation: $TC_i = cq_i$. Find the SPNE (price, output, and profits) for this model.

6. (Advanced) Assume two firms, 1 and 2, compete in a dynamic Bertrand game. Firm 1 moves first. Products are differentiated vertically, with firm 1 producing the good of superior quality. Assume the same demand and cost structure as found in Sect. 10.2.3.3 in Chap. 10. Let $N = 1$. Find the SPNE to this game. How does a change in z (the degree of vertical differentiation) and the size of the market (i.e., the distance between ϕ_H and ϕ_L) affect equilibrium price, output, and profit levels?

7. Compare and contrast the Stackelberg duopoly model with the dynamic Bertrand model when there is multicharacteristic product differentiation.

8. Consider the dynamic Cournot–Bertrand model discussed in Sect. 11.1.4, where firm 1 competes in output and firm 2 competes in price. In Fig. 11.3, point B describes the NE when firms move simultaneously, and point A represents the SPNE when firm 1 moves first.

   A. Identify the SPNE on the figure when firm 2 moves first and firm 1 moves second. Call this point C.
   B. Rank firm 1's profits for the three possible equilibria:

1. Firms move simultaneously (point B).
2. Firm 1 moves first (point A).
3. Firm 2 moves first (point C).

   C. Rank firm 2's profits for the three possible equilibria.
   D. Given your answers to parts B and C above, how might firms behave if they can coordinate on the timing of play (but not the level of their choice variables)?

9. Assume two firms, 1 and 2, compete in a dynamic game. Firm 1 competes in output in the first period, and firm 2 has the choice of competing in output or price in the second period. The inverse demand function is $p = a - Q$, and each firm faces the same linear cost equation: $TC_i = cq_i$. Once firm 1 makes its choice, show that firm 2 earns the same level of profit whether it chooses to compete in output or in price.

10. Describe the SPNE in the static Cournot game that is repeated three times.

11. Consider a market with two firms, 1 and 2, that produce homogeneous goods and compete in price.

   A. If firms compete in a static game, find the NE or Bertrand outcome.
   B. Find the SPNE if the static Bertrand game is repeated an infinite number of times.
   C. (Advanced) Consider the same problem as in part B above, except that the present value of future profits reverts to $-\$x$ instead of 0 if a firm cheats on cooperation. Will it take a higher or a lower D to support collusion when punishment is more severe (i.e., $x > 0$)?

12. A monopoly firm produces a durable good that lasts for two periods, I and II. Assume that company managers are myopic, that is, they place too much weight on the current period. Explain how this myopic thinking will affect firm profits in periods I and II. Is the firm better off or worse off (in terms of joint profits) with myopic managers? [To simplify your discussion, you might assume that management gives 0 weight to the future, such that the discount factor (D) equals 0].

Chapter 12
Market Power

In previous chapters, we discussed the static efficiency of markets from a theoretical perspective. We learned that a market is allocatively efficient when total (consumer plus producer) surplus is maximized and price equals marginal cost. A firm is said to have monopoly or market power when it can profitably maintain price above marginal cost. Theory tells us that market power will be present in unregulated monopoly but not perfectly competitive markets. The extent of market power in oligopoly markets will depend on the specific characteristics of the market.

Chapters 9–11 reveal a wide range of predictions regarding oligopoly and market power. Three classic models of oligopoly provide examples:

1. *Cartel model.* Firms that behave cooperatively and form a perfect cartel exert as much market power as a monopolist. Cartels are more likely to be effective when they are legal, in markets with just a few firms, and when future profits are not heavily discounted.
2. *Cournot model.* In the simple Cournot model with n firms, market power diminishes with the number of competitors.
3. *Bertrand model.* In the simple Bertrand model with symmetric firms and homogeneous goods, price equals marginal cost as long as there are two or more competitors in a market.[1]

The extent to which market power is present in the real world is a central policy issue in industrial organization. Market power can substantially harm society and tends to be associated with highly concentrated industries. The main purpose of this chapter is to summarize the empirical evidence regarding this topic. We begin by discussing measurement issues and then review the main determinants of market power.

---

[1] In the simple Cournot–Bertrand model, price equals marginal cost when there are 1 or more firms.

V.J. Tremblay and C.H. Tremblay, *New Perspectives on Industrial Organization*,
Springer Texts in Business and Economics, DOI 10.1007/978-1-4614-3241-8_12,
© Springer Science+Business Media New York 2012

12.1   The Measurement of Market Power

In this section, we describe the most common ways to measure market power. The simplest methods ignore scale economies and assume a static setting. When these conditions do not hold, problems arise. For example, it may be suboptimal or impractical to require that price equal marginal cost when there are substantial economies of scale, as in a natural monopoly or natural oligopoly (see Chap. 8). Moreover, in markets where today's research and development produces lower costs and/or better products tomorrow, it may be socially desirable for price to exceed marginal and average cost today.

Even if scale economies and dynamics are unimportant, data limitations and estimation issues can make it difficult to obtain a precise estimate of exerted market power. In this section, we discuss common measures of static market power and only briefly discuss measurement issues in dynamic markets.[2] Discussion of more complex theoretical and policy issues involving dynamic markets is postponed to later chapters.

12.1.1   The Lerner Index in a Static Setting

As we saw in Chap. 6, the Lerner index provides a precise measure of the degree of allocative inefficiency or monopoly power in a static setting. For a monopolist, recall from Chap. 6 that the Lerner index is defined as $\mathcal{L} = (p - \mathrm{MC})/p = 1/\eta$, where p is price, MC is long-run marginal cost, and η is the absolute value of price elasticity of demand. The Lerner index is frequently referred to as an index of monopoly power. More generally, $\mathcal{L}$ is an index of market power, as it can be used to measure the degree of allocative inefficiency in any market structure. When firm demand is perfectly elastic, as in perfect competition, price equals marginal cost and $\mathcal{L} = 0$. With fewer substitutes, the price elasticity of demand falls and the degree of market power increases. Thus, the Lerner index ranges from 0 to 1, with a higher value indicating greater market power.

It is important to realize that market power depends on technology as well as the price elasticity of demand. To see this point, consider a monopolist that has linear demand and cost functions. Inverse demand is $p = a - q$, and total cost is $\mathrm{TC} = \mathrm{MC} \cdot q$, where q is quantity. In this model, $\mathrm{d}p/\mathrm{d}q = -1$ and the profit maximizing output and price levels are $q^* = (a - \mathrm{MC})/2$ and $p^* = (a + \mathrm{MC})/2$. At the equilibrium,

$$\mathcal{L} = \frac{1}{\eta} = -\frac{\partial p}{\partial q} \frac{q^*}{p^*} = \frac{a - \mathrm{MC}}{a + \mathrm{MC}}. \tag{12.1}$$

---

[2] The threat of government regulation and antitrust enforcement may induce firms to limit their prices below simple profit-maximizing levels, which reduces exerted market power below its potential level. This is an unseen benefit of government regulation and antitrust enforcement.

This equation implies that market power diminishes as marginal cost increases.[3] The reason for this relationship is that when the demand function has a negative slope, the demand elasticity is not a constant; η increases as q^* declines. Thus, an increase in MC lowers q^*, which raises η and lessens market power. Thus, both the nature of demand and technology determine market power.[4]

We can also derive the Lerner index in an oligopoly market with n firms. Consider a general first-order condition for firm i, which is similar to the first-order condition for a monopolist (see Chap. 6):[5]

$$p_i + \theta \frac{\partial p_i}{\partial q_i} q_i - \text{MC} = 0. \tag{12.2}$$

The only difference is that it includes θ, a behavioral parameter of market power, or simply the **behavioral parameter**.[6] We will see subsequently that choosing particular values of θ will produce a first-order condition that is identical to that of a monopolist, a perfectly competitive firm, or an oligopoly firm that competes in a Bertrand- or a Cournot-typesetting as described in Chap. 10. Assuming that firms produce homogeneous goods, $p_i = p$ and $\partial p_i / \partial q_i = \partial p / \partial Q$, where Q is the industry level of output. Under these conditions, (12.2) can be rewritten as

$$\mathcal{L} \equiv \frac{p - \text{MC}}{p} = -\theta \frac{\partial p}{\partial Q} \frac{Q}{p} \frac{q_i}{Q} = \frac{\text{ms}_i \theta}{\eta} = \frac{\theta}{n \cdot \eta}, \tag{12.3}$$

where ms_i is the market share of firm i, which equals $1/n$ because of symmetry.[7] The advantage of this specification is that it describes the Lerner index for a variety of possible cooperative and noncooperative equilibria. For example,

- In a competitive or Bertrand equilibrium with homogeneous goods, $p = \text{MC}$ which implies that $\theta = 0$ and $\mathcal{L} = 0$.Rauchen.
- In the Cournot equilibrium, $\theta = 1$ and $\mathcal{L} = \text{ms}_i / \eta = 1/(n \cdot \eta)$.[8] Notice that when $n = 1$, $\mathcal{L} = 1/\eta$ which is the simple monopoly outcome.

---

[3] That is, $\partial \mathcal{L} / \partial \text{MC} = (-2a)/(a + \text{MC})^2 < 0$.

[4] For further discussion on this topic, see Färe et al. (2012).

[5] This equation is frequently derived from a "conjectural variation" model (Bowley 1924), where θ reflects the firm's conjecture or expectation about the change in industry output (Q) with respect to a change in the firm's own output (q_i). See Bresnahan (1989) for a discussion of the conjectural variation interpretation of this equation. In our representation, θ can be thought of as a reduced form parameter (Schmalensee 1988), where (12.2) is used as a device for describing possible oligopoly outcomes and for estimating market power when the choice variable is output or price (Slade 1995).

[6] Note that the term "behavioral" in this context is distinct from the meaning of the behavioral economics concepts discussed in Chap. 4 and throughout the book.

[7] That is, $\text{ms}_i \equiv q_i / Q = 1/n$ because all firms produce the same level of output in equilibrium.

[8] From (10.1) and (10.2), a Cournot firm's first-order condition is $p + (\partial p / \partial Q) q_i - \text{MC} = 0$. This implies that for (12.2) to hold, θ must equal 1 in the Cournot model.

Table 12.1 Market structure, the behavioral parameter (θ), and the Lerner index ($\mathcal{L}$) of market power

Market structure	θ	$\mathcal{L}$
Perfect competition	0	0
Bertrand oligopoly	0	0
Cournot oligopoly	1	$1/(n \cdot \eta)$
Cartel	n	$1/\eta$
Monopoly	1	$1/\eta$

Note: η is the absolute value of the price elasticity of demand, n is the number of firms, and products are perfectly homogeneous.

- For a monopolist, $\theta = n = 1$ and $\mathcal{L} = 1/\eta$.
- In a perfect cartel, $\theta = n$ and $\mathcal{L} = 1/\eta$.

Given that the market outcome will range from competitive to cartel, $0 \leq \theta \leq n$ and $0 \leq \mathcal{L} \leq 1/\eta$. Thus, we can think of θ as an indicator of the "toughness of competition" found in Sutton's (1991) model of market structure (see Chap. 8). The degree of competition increases as θ decreases. The relationship between θ and $\mathcal{L}$ in different market settings is summarized in Table 12.1. It shows that a higher value of θ implies greater market power.

Equation (12.3) can be modified further to provide a summary of the main forces that influence market power. Recall from Chap. 8 that the Herfindahl–Hirschman index of industry concentration (HHI) equals $1/n$ in a symmetric oligopoly. In this case, the Lerner index becomes

$$\mathcal{L} \equiv \frac{p - \text{MC}}{p} = \frac{\theta \cdot \text{HHI}}{\eta}. \tag{12.4}$$

This simple framework implies that market power increases when:

- Concentration increases (HHI increases)
- Demand becomes less price elastic (η decreases)
- Competition diminishes (θ increases)

Of course, products may not be homogeneous and firms may not be symmetric. When products are differentiated, firms will sell their products at different prices. Even with homogeneous goods, firms may have different costs. Under these conditions, we could calculate the average Lerner index for all firms in the market. One method is to use a weighted average, with market shares used as weights. In this case, the Lerner index becomes

$$\mathcal{L} \equiv \sum_{i=1}^{n} \text{ms}_i \frac{p_i - \text{MC}_i}{p_i}. \tag{12.5}$$

Data limitations frequently make it difficult to estimate a Lerner index in (12.5). First, we need data from every firm in the industry. Second, marginal cost is not observable unless marginal cost equals average cost (i.e., there are constant returns to scale). Thus, economists have developed indirect methods of estimating market power, topics we will take up in Sect. 12.2.

In a similar way, we can derive an index of market power in an input market. For example, a firm that is a single buyer of an input has market power, because it can pay a lower price for the input without completely eliminating the quantity supplied of that input. In other words, the firm is an input price maker, not an input price taker. A firm of this type is called a monopsonist and will gain greater profit by lowering the input price below its perfectly competitive level. Given our interest in output markets and the fact that the derivation is similar to that of the Lerner index, we leave the issue of monopsony power to Appendix 12.A.

12.1.2   The Lerner Index in a Dynamic Setting

As we said previously, it is more difficult to measure market power in a dynamic market. This is an advanced topic, and we do not derive the Lerner index for a dynamic market here. You should be aware, though, that the static Lerner index provides a biased estimate of market power in a dynamic setting. In a dynamic market, production and sales today affects future profits. This can occur for addictive commodities, as greater consumption today leads to more serious addiction and increased demand (and profits) tomorrow. Another example occurs with learning-by-doing, where greater production today leads to learning, more adept workers, and lower costs tomorrow.

How would a dynamic setting affect the measurement of market power? Consider the case of cigarettes. When starting a business it may be profit maximizing to give away cigarettes (i.e., set the price to zero) today to hook new consumers and intensify preexisting addiction. The firm can then hike the price tomorrow, a strategy that can boost overall profit. In essence, market power today is reflected in the firm's ability to raise price tomorrow. Thus, even though price is below marginal cost today, market power is still present because this strategy allows the firm to raise price substantially in the future. Although somewhat more complicated, a similar problem exists when learning-by-doing is present (Pindyck, 1985). These issues are taken up more formally in Appendix 12.B.

12.1.3   Other Measures of Market Power
and Industry Performance

Given the difficulty of measuring the Lerner index, other measures have been proposed to estimate the degree of market power. One such measure is **Tobin's q**, which is defined as the market value of the firm divided by the replacement value of the firm's assets. In a perfectly competitive industry that is in long-run equilibrium, Tobin's q will equal 1 because potential investors will value a firm at its replacement cost. If a firm is expected to earn positive economic profits, Tobin's q will exceed 1 because the firm is now more valuable than its replacement cost.

Other measures of market power are based on profitability. One example is a firm's profit rate or **rate of return** (r), defined as the ratio of the amount earned per dollar invested in the company for a given time period. To illustrate, assume a firm uses three inputs, labor (L), materials (M), and physical capital (K). The owner of the firm invests $p_K K$ in the company, where p_K is the price (or rental rate) of capital. The rate of return on the owner's investment (r) is

$$r \equiv \frac{\mathrm{TR} - T - p_L L - p_M M - \delta p_K K}{p_K K}, \qquad (12.6)$$

where TR is total revenue, T is the tax on profits, p_L is the price of labor, p_M is the price of materials, and δ is the depreciation rate of capital. When long-run economic profits are zero, the owner will earn a normal rate of return, r^*. If $r^* = 10\%$, for instance, the rate the owner could earn from alternative competitive investments is 10%. With positive economic profit, however, r will exceed r^*. Thus, a rate of return above normal implies positive economic profit.

Another profitability measure is the **profit-to-sales ratio**, defined as profit (π) divided by total revenue (sales). That is,

$$\frac{\pi}{\mathrm{TR}} \equiv \frac{\mathrm{TR} - \mathrm{TC}}{\mathrm{TR}}, \qquad (12.7)$$

where TC is total cost. Because it is easy to measure, it is frequently used in the business literature. It is also identical to the Lerner index when the industry is in long-run equilibrium and firms operate in the region of constant returns to scale. In this case, MC equals long-run average cost (AC), and the profit-to-sales ratio becomes

$$\frac{\pi}{\mathrm{TR}} \equiv \frac{p \cdot q - \mathrm{AC} \cdot q}{p \cdot q} = \frac{p - \mathrm{AC}}{p} = \frac{p - \mathrm{MC}}{p}. \qquad (12.8)$$

Although these profitability measures are used in applied studies, they suffer from three main weaknesses when employed to identify market power. First, market power is normally associated with positive long-run economic profit but can exist even though long-run profits are zero. We saw this in the model of monopolistic competition in Chap. 6. Second, most firms are diversified, and it is difficult to identify the portion of revenues, costs, and assets that are associated with a particular product or market. Third, we are interested in economic profits, but only accounting profits are reported by firms.

Accounting profits can be a poor proxy for economic profits. For example, physical capital is typically valued incorrectly at its historical cost rather than at its opportunity cost. In addition, investments that provide future benefits (such as physical capital, advertising and research and development) may be incorrectly treated as a current expense. As Fisher and McGowan (1983) and Fisher (1987) point out, it is nearly impossible to get an accurate estimate of the economically relevant depreciation rate for each of these expenditures. Thus, dynamic effects create measurement problems here too. We conclude that profitability serves as a weak proxy measure of market power and should be used with caution.[9]

More recently, Boone (2008) developed an index of competition that circumvents these accounting problems, the **index of relative profit differences** (RPD). To use RPD to determine the degree of competition, two conditions must hold. First, firms within the same industry must have different levels of efficiency.[10] Second, an increase in competition must punish inefficient firms more harshly than it punishes efficient firms. To illustrate, consider a duopoly case where firms compete in a Cournot-type game and produce homogeneous goods. Firm 1 has lower costs than firm 2. As we saw in Chap. 10, both firms earn positive profits. Now assume that the degree of competition intensifies, with firms now competing in a Bertrand-type game. With an increase in competition, firm 2's profits fall to zero while firm 1's profits remain positive. Firm 2 is harmed relatively more by the increase in competition.

RPD compares the variable profits of different firms. Let $\pi_i^v(E_i, \theta)$ equal firm i's variable profit, which is a function of its efficiency level E_i and the behavioral parameter (θ). Variable profit equals total revenue minus total variable cost. Suppose there are three firms in a market where firm 1 is most efficient and firm 3 is least efficient, such that $E_1 > E_2 > E_3$. Recall that θ ranges from 0 (in homogeneous Bertrand) to n (in a cartel), where the degree of competition increases as θ falls. In this case,

$$\text{RPD} \equiv \frac{\pi_1^v - \pi_3^v}{\pi_2^v - \pi_3^v}. \tag{12.9}$$

Under these conditions, more rigorous competition (i.e., a decrease in θ) will lead to an increase in RPD, $\partial \text{RPD}/\partial \theta < 0$. Thus, if RPD falls over time, we can conclude that market power has diminished.

Boone's index has several desirable qualities. First, variable profit data are readily available for publicly owned firms. Boone (2008, 1255) shows that variable profit is approximately equal to "gross operating profit" found in a company's income statement. Second, using variable profits circumvents the measurement problems associated with accounting profits.[11] Third, data are needed for at least three firms in the industry but are not required for every firm. The only difficulty

---

[9] For a more complete discussion of the problems associated with measuring profitability and the pros and cons of using profitability to measure market power, see Fisher and McGowan (1983), Martin (1984, 2000), Fisher (1987), and Carlton and Perloff (2005). Fisher (1987) takes the strongest position, arguing that because these problems are insurmountable, accounting profit should not be used for empirical research in industrial organization.

[10] This seems reasonable, because in the real world, firms in the same industry are rarely symmetric (unless the market is perfectly competitive, or nearly so).

[11] For example, one does not need to estimate the appropriate depreciation rate of durable assets that is needed to convert accounting profits to economic profits.

is that firms must be ranked in terms of their relative efficiency. Fortunately, Färe et al. (1985, 2008) identify several methods for estimating firm efficiency. A simple alternative is to use average variable cost (i.e., total variable cost divided by output) to measure firm efficiency, where the firm with lower average variable costs is more efficient. Given its advantages, we expect Boone's method to become a common way of determining the extent to which industry competition has changed.

12.2 Estimating Market Power

In this section, we summarize several methods for estimating static market power in a particular industry.[12] Early studies in the structure–conduct–performance tradition used measures of profitability to estimate market power. The weakness of this approach is that price may exceed marginal cost even though profits are zero. More modern approaches make use of information about costs and the price elasticity of demand to estimate market power. The empirical evidence is extensive, and we provide a summary of market power estimates for only a select group of industries.

12.2.1 Estimating Marginal Cost

The most direct method of estimating a Lerner index is to estimate a total cost function and use it to derive marginal cost. Suppose there is a simple production process that employs a single input to produce a single output. For simplicity, assume that the total cost (TC) function that represents this technology is

$$TC = \left(c_0 q + c_1 q^2 + c_2 q^3\right) w, \tag{12.10}$$

where w is the price of the input and c_0, c_1, and c_2 are cost parameters. With appropriate data and the proper estimation technique, parameter values can be estimated with regression analysis. Given these estimates, marginal cost can be calculated as

$$MC \equiv \frac{\partial TC}{\partial q} = \left(c_0 + 2c_1 q + 3c_2 q^2\right) w. \tag{12.11}$$

This estimate of MC can then be applied, along with output price data, to calculate a Lerner index.[13] The main weakness with this approach is that accounting cost data are substituted for economic cost data. Thus, this technique suffers from similar drawbacks as those that use profitability to measure market power.

---

[12] For a review of the extensive literature on the relationship between profitability, concentration, and entry barriers, see Weiss (1974), Schmalensee (1989), Scherer and Ross (1990), Carlton and Perloff (2005), Waldman and Jensen (2006), and Perloff et al. (2007).

[13] Studies that have used this technique include Friedlaender and Spady (1981), Keeler (1983), Wolfram (1999), and Weiher et al. (2002).

12.2.2 The Price Response to a Change in Costs

When it is impossible or impractical to estimate marginal cost, we can still take advantage of average cost data to estimate the degree of competition in a market. If markets are perfectly competitive, any cost hike will be passed on fully to consumers. The pass-through rate equals 1. As we saw in Chap. 6, the pass-through rate will generally not equal 1 for firms with market power. Thus, the extent to which price responds to cost changes can be exploited to assess the extent of market power. Sumner (1981) applied this technique to the US cigarette industry.[14] By comparing tax and price data across states, he rejected the hypothesis that the industry was perfectly competitive.

Hall (1988) compared the change in total revenue with the change in total cost that resulted from demand shocks in 26 manufacturing industries, 1953–1984. Assuming constant returns to scale, he showed that if an increase in demand raises total revenue by the same amount that it raises total cost, the industry is competitive. His evidence rejects the hypothesis that these industries behaved competitively. Applying Hall's method to data from Belgium, Dobbelaere (2004) also found that markets are generally imperfectly competitive.[15]

12.2.3 The New Empirical Industrial Organization Technique

Investigating the effect of a change in the price elasticity of demand on price can also be used to estimate the degree of competition in a market. In a perfectly competitive market, price will be unaffected by a change in elasticity because price always equals marginal cost. On the other hand, when market power is present, the Lerner index indicates that a reduction in the price elasticity of demand will generally lead to a higher price. Thus, whether or not price changes with the demand elasticity is an indicator of market power. Many of the econometric techniques summarized below require a change in the slope or elasticity of demand to identify market power.

One common method that has been used in the past is called the **new empirical industrial organization** (NEIO) approach, to distinguish it from earlier studies of

---

[14] Bulow and Pfleiderer (1983) criticized Sumner's work by showing that the pass-through rate can equal 1 for a monopolist under certain demand conditions. Nevertheless, Sumner's conclusion is confirmed by Sullivan (1985) using a different method.

[15] Panzar and Ross (1987) provide another method that is based on the effect of costs on prices.

the 1960s and 1970s that used profitability to measure market power.[16] Because it has been so widely used, we investigate this technique in some detail.

We demonstrate the main idea by assuming a simple structural model of firm demand and costs.[17] Firms are assumed to compete in a static oligopoly setting with homogeneous goods,[18] and all relevant data are available. Firm i's inverse demand function is

$$p = a + bQ + d_1 Q \cdot y_1 + d_2 y_1 + d_3 y_2, \tag{12.12}$$

where Q is the industry level of output, $b < 0$, and y_1 and y_2 are exogenous variables such as consumer income and the price of a substitute good. We will see that this method of identifying market power requires demand to rotate with y_1. Assume that firm i's marginal cost function takes the following form

$$\text{MC} = c_0 + c_1 w \cdot q_i. \tag{12.13}$$

Returning to the firm's general first-order condition (12.2) and solving for price produces an equation called optimal price equation (supply relation or markup equation)

$$p = \text{MC} - \theta \frac{\partial p}{\partial Q} q_i. \tag{12.14}$$

It indicates that price will depend on marginal cost, the behavioral parameter (which is assumed to be constant), the slope of the inverse demand function, and output. The slope of the inverse demand function in (12.12) is $\partial p / \partial Q = b + d_1 y$. Substituting this partial derivative and the marginal cost function into the supply relation yields

$$
\begin{aligned}
p &= (c_0 + c_1 w q_i) - \theta(b + d_1 y_1) q_i \\
&= c_0 + c_1 w q_i - \theta b q_i - \theta d_1 y_1 q_i.
\end{aligned} \tag{12.15}
$$

We can rewrite this as

$$p = \alpha_0 + \alpha_1 w q_i + \alpha_2 q_i + \alpha_3 y_1 q_i, \tag{12.16}$$

where $\alpha_0 \equiv c_0$, $\alpha_1 \equiv c_1$, $\alpha_2 \equiv -\theta b$, and $\alpha_3 \equiv -\theta d_1$.

---

[16] Early studies include Rosse (1970), Iwata (1974), Gollop and Roberts (1979), Appelbaum (1979, 1982), and Bresnahan (1981). For a review of this approach and its applications, see Bresnahan and Schmalensee (1987), Bresnahan (1989), Slade (1995), and Baker and Bresnahan (2008).

[17] This model is designed to illustrate the main idea and may not be appropriate for a number of reasons, as discussed below.

[18] Although more complex, a similar approach is used to estimate market power when products are differentiated. For example, see Nevo (1998, 2001).

Regression analysis is used to estimate (12.12) and (12.16) jointly as a system of equations. This requires firm level data on p, q_i, Q, y_1, y_2, and w, but not on MC. The regression results produce estimates of the parameters a, b, d_1, d_2, d_3, α_0, α_1, α_2, and α_3. With these estimates, the behavioral parameter is identified if one of the following conditions holds:

- α_2 and b do not equal zero. If α_2 and b are not zero, then $\theta = -\alpha_2/b$.
- α_3 and d_1 do not equal zero. If α_3 and d_1 are not zero, then $\theta = -\alpha_3/d_1$.[19]

This makes it clear why it may be possible to estimate market power when a change in one variable causes demand to rotate ($d_1 \neq 0$). It also begs the question, what variables may cause a change in the slope or elasticity of demand. Porter (1983) found that weather conditions influenced the demand elasticity in his study of market power in the railroad industry. Berry et al. (1995) used product entry and exit as elasticity determining variables.

The NEIO technique can also be used to estimate market power with industry data. In this case, we are estimating the average behavior of firms in the industry. To derive the empirical model, we sum up both sides of (12.14) over all firms.

$$\sum_{i=1}^{n} p_i = \sum_{i=1}^{n} \text{MC}_i - \sum_{i=1}^{n} \theta_i \frac{\partial p}{\partial Q} Q \cdot \text{ms}_i, \tag{12.17}$$

where $q_i = Q \cdot \text{ms}_i$. For homogeneous goods and symmetric firms, $p_i = p_j = p$, $\text{MC}_i = \text{MC}_j = \text{MC}$, and $\theta_i = \theta_j = \theta$ for all firms i and j. Dividing (12.17) by n gives

---

[19] Notice that if both b and d_1 are zero, the demand function is horizontal because the slope is $\partial p/\partial Q = b + d_1 y_1$. For a discussion of identification issues, see Bresnahan (1982) and Lau (1982). To illustrate the NEIO method, Bresnahan (1989) assumed linear demand and cost functions. A linear cost function is not homogeneous of degree 1 in input prices, a property of a true cost function (Varian, 1992). If we were to assume linearity, the marginal cost function becomes

$$\text{MC} = c_0 + c_1 q_i + c_2 w.$$

In this case, substitution produces the following supply relation

$$p = (c_0 + c_1 q_i + c_2 w) - \theta(b + d_1 y) q_i = c_0 + c_2 w + (c_1 - b\theta) q_i - d_1 \theta y q_i.$$

We can rewrite this as

$$p = \alpha_0 + \alpha_1 w + \alpha_2 q_i + \alpha_3 y q_i,$$

where $\alpha_0 \equiv c_0$, $\alpha_1 \equiv c_2$, $\alpha_2 \equiv c_1 - b\theta$, and $\alpha_3 \equiv -d_1 \theta$. In this model, the behavioral parameter is identified if one or both of the following conditions hold:

- $c_1 = 0$, which implies that $\alpha_2 = -b\theta$ or that $\theta = -\alpha_2/b$
- $d_1 \neq 0$, which implies that $\alpha_3 = -d_1 \theta$ or $\theta = -\alpha_3/d_1$

That is, the market power parameter is identified if there are constant returns to scale ($c_1 = 0$) or if y interacts with output in the demand function. However, Perloff and Shen (2012) demonstrate that this specification suffers from a collinearity problem and cannot be accurately estimated.

Table 12.2 Lerner index estimates from selected industries

Study	Industry	Lerner index
Hyde and Perloff (1998)	Retail meat (Australia)	0.00
V. Tremblay and C. Tremblay (2005)	Brewing	0.01
Genesove and Mullin (1998)	Sugar refining (1880–1914)	0.05
Gollop and Roberts (1979)	Coffee roasting (dominant firm)	0.06
Appelbaum (1982)	Textiles	0.07
Slade (1987)	Retail gasoline	0.10
Karp and Perloff (1989)	Rice exports	0.11
Appelbaum (1982)	Electrical machinery	0.20
Porter (1983)	Railroads (with collusion)	0.40
Spiller and Favaro (1984)	Banking (dominant firms)	0.40
Nevo (2001)	Breakfast cereal	0.45
Wolfram (1999)	Electric power (Brittan)	0.48
Suslow (1986)	Aluminum	0.59
Kadiyali (1996)	Photographic film (Kodak and Fuji)	0.65
Appelbaum (1982)	Tobacco	0.67
Taylor and Zona (1997)	Long-distance phone service (AT&T)	0.88

$$p = \text{MC} - \frac{\theta}{n}\frac{\partial p}{\partial Q}Q. \tag{12.18}$$

Thus, given a marginal cost specification we are able to estimate this equation and the market demand function simultaneously, as we did using firm data. With an estimate of θ, assuming it is identified, we can calculate the Lerner index from (12.3).

The NEIO technique has been applied to a variety of industries. The results from several studies are summarized in Table 12.2. Given that these industries have very different structural and institutional characteristics, it is not surprising that their market power estimates vary widely. As one might expect, the results generally indicate that market power in agricultural and food industries is relatively low, while market power is relatively high in manufacturing and service industries.

The main advantage of the NEIO approach is it allows us to obtain an estimate of the Lerner index without a direct measure of marginal cost. One limitation of the NEIO approach is that it tells us the degree of market power but not its cause. Another concern is that the behavioral parameter is assumed to be a continuous variable when the outcome from static games implies that it is a discrete variable.[20] Recall that $\theta = 0$ in a Bertrand game, $\theta = 1$ in a Cournot game, and $\theta = n$ in a monopoly or perfect cartel. We take up these issues in the next section.

---

[20] In a dynamic setting, however, the "folk theorem" indicates that an appropriately defined trigger strategy can support any noncompetitive outcome, implying that θ is continuous and ranges from 0 to n (Friedman 1971). It is called a folk theorem because it was understood by game theorists long before it was published (Gibbons 1992, 89). For further discussion of the strengths and weaknesses of the NEIO approach, see Bresnahan (1989), Slade (1995), Genesove and Mullin (1998), Corts (1999), and Perloff et al. (2007).

12.2.4   The Stochastic Frontier Method of Estimating Market Power

Kumbhakar et al. (2012) developed an alternative method for estimating market power that is based on the stochastic frontier estimation technique. This method is considerably more flexible than the NEIO technique. Not only can it control for technology using a marginal cost function, as is required with the NEIO technique, but it can also control for technology using an input distance function, which requires data on input quantities but not input prices. In some applications, cost data are more difficult to obtain than input data. In addition, market power can be estimated whether there are constant returns or variable returns to scale. Kumbhakar et al. apply their technique to the Norwegian sawmilling industry and find that the markup of price over marginal cost is approximately 8% to 11%.

12.2.5   Estimating Game Theoretic Strategies or Behavior

One weakness with the NEIO and stochastic frontier approaches is that they assume that any type of firm behavior is possible. Another way to approach the market power question is to test to see whether firm behavior is consistent with a specific game. Gasmi and Vuong (1991) and Gasmi et al. (1992) developed an approach based on this idea, which they used to determine which oligopoly model is most consistent with the data: static Nash, Stackelberg, or cartel. Thus, both static and dynamic games are considered. Because the empirical model is rather complex, we describe it in Appendix 12.C.

Gasmi et al. (1992) apply this technique to the market for premium cola, where Coke and Pepsi compete in price and advertising. They use quarterly data, 1968–1986, to estimate demand, cost, and best-reply functions in price and advertising for both Coke and Pepsi. The model that outperformed all others[21] indicates that Coke was a Stackelberg leader in price over the entire sample period, Coke was a Stackelberg leader in advertising from 1968 through 1976, and Coke and Pepsi colluded on advertising from 1977 to 1986.

Gasmi et al. (1992) then estimated the Lerner index for each firm based on the parameter estimates from their best model. Their results are summarized in Table 12.3 and show that market power has increased over time and that Coke has maintained a strategic advantage over Pepsi. Comparing these estimates with those found in Table 12.2, Coke and Pepsi have a level of market power that exceeds that of the banking industry and is similar to that of the electric power and photographic firm industries.

---

[21] This is based on goodness of fit, as determined by the mean square error criterion using a likelihood ratio test as discussed in Greene (2000).

Table 12.3 Lerner index
estimates for Coke and Pepsi

Firm	1968–1976	1977–1986
Coke	0.59	0.64
Pepsi	0.45	0.56

Source: Gasmi et al. (1992)

As with all approaches to estimating market power, this technique has weaknesses. First, like the NEIO approach, it does not tell us the cause of market power. A more important weakness from a practical standpoint is that it requires a great deal of data. With more than two firms, there may not be enough data to estimate parameters accurately without a sufficient number of simplifying assumptions.

12.2.6   Estimating the Overall Efficiency Loss Due to Market Power

How large is the aggregate efficiency loss due to noncompetitive pricing in the US economy as a whole? If inconsequential, market power is not a policy concern and enforcement of our antitrust laws and regulations may be an unnecessary expense (assuming that prices will not rise if antitrust enforcement were abolished). Nonetheless, given the potential importance of this issue, a number of economists have estimated the total deadweight loss due to market power for the US economy as a whole.

In his classic study, Harberger (1954) showed that the deadweight loss (DWL) can be represented by a simple equation. To start, consider a homogeneous goods market with a linear demand function (D) and a technology that exhibits constant returns to scale, implying that long-run marginal cost equals long-run average cost. Market power exists when the equilibrium price (p^*) exceeds long-run marginal cost. This produces a DWL equal to the shaded area ABC in Fig. 12.1, where Q^* is the equilibrium output in the presence of market power, $p_{PC} = MC$ is the perfectly competitive price, and Q_{PC} is the perfectly competitive level of output. Let $\Delta p \equiv (p^* - p_{PC})$ and $\Delta Q \equiv (Q_{PC} - Q^*)$. If we consider small changes, then

$$
\begin{aligned}
\text{DWL} &= \left(\frac{1}{2}\right)\Delta p \cdot \Delta Q \\
&= \left(\frac{1}{2}\right)(\Delta p)^2 \left(\frac{\Delta Q}{\Delta p}\right) \\
&= \left(\frac{1}{2}\right)\left(\frac{p^* - MC}{p^*}\right)^2 \left(\frac{\Delta Q}{\Delta p}\frac{p^*}{Q^*}\right)p^* Q^* \\
&= \left(\frac{1}{2}\right)\left(\frac{p^* Q^* - AC \cdot Q^*}{p^* Q^*}\right)^2 \eta \cdot \text{TR} \\
&= \left(\frac{1}{2}\right)\left(\frac{\text{TR} - \text{TC}}{\text{TR}}\right)^2 \eta \cdot \text{TR} \\
&= \left(\frac{1}{2}\right)x^2 \cdot \eta \cdot \text{TR},
\end{aligned}
\tag{12.19}
$$

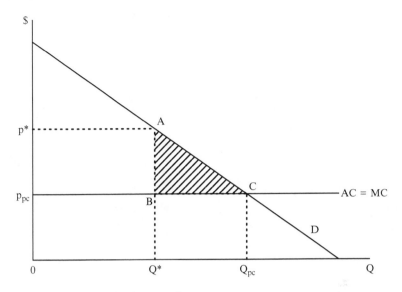

Fig. 12.1 The deadweight loss due to market power

where η is the absolute value of the price elasticity of demand, TR is total industry revenue (or sales), TC is total industry cost, and x is the value of the profit-to-sales ratio for the industry [(TR − TC)/TR]. Because the elasticity of demand is difficult to estimate, Harberger assumed that $\eta = 1$. Given that only accounting data were available, he defined excess profits as profits above average profits for the industries in his sample.

With these assumptions and (12.19), Harberger used data from 73 manufacturing industries for the period 1924–1928 to estimate the aggregate DWL in the US economy. He found that the DWL was less than 0.1% of GNP (gross national product, defined as the dollar value of all goods and services produced in the economy).

If correct, Harberger's estimate suggests that market power was insufficient to warrant much policy concern. As one might expect, this led to a flurry of studies designed to verify or disprove his estimate. Critics claimed that Harberger's measure of economic profit was too low[22] and that η is greater than one, both of

---

[22] Using average profit in manufacturing to identify a normal rate of return produced estimates of economic profit that were too low. A more accurate estimate of normal profit rates can be found in the agricultural and service sectors, as they tend to be more competitive and have lower profit rates than in manufacturing. Harberger defined the economic profit rate as the accounting profit rate in manufacturing minus the average profit rate in manufacturing. Because the average in manufacturing is higher than "normal," his estimate of the economic profit rate is too low.

which biased downward his estimate of DWL.[23] Subsequent studies estimate aggregate DWL in the US economy to range from 0.4% to 6.0% of GNP. After making appropriate corrections for the main problems associated with Harberger's work, Masson and Shaanan (1984) estimated DWL to equal 2.9%. This is almost 30 times Harberger's estimate.

More recent estimates are unavailable, which is unfortunate because increased globalization over the last several decades may have reduced this deadweight loss. Caves and Barton (1990) argue that greater foreign competition leads to greater domestic cost efficiency. Furthermore, Salvo (2011) found that the mere threat of imports reduced domestic market power in his empirical study of the Brazilian cement market.

Other factors, such as rent seeking and X-inefficiency, can push up the social cost of market power. We take up these issues in Chap. 19.

12.3   Determinants of Market Power

Previous sections of the chapter have focused on estimating market power. In this section, we discuss the main causes of market power.

12.3.1   Theory

The most striking determinant of market power is market structure. Predictions from the four traditional models of market structure that we discussed in previous chapters are summarized in Table 12.4. In a perfectly competitive industry, price equals marginal cost because: (1) profit maximization requires that marginal cost equal marginal revenue and (2) price and marginal revenue are identical for

Table 12.4 Model predictions of market power

Market structure	$p - MC$	π_{LR}
Perfect competition	0	0
Monopoly	>0	≥ 0
Monopolistic competition	>0	0
Oligopoly	≥ 0	≥ 0

Note: p is price, MC is marginal cost, and π_{LR} is long-run profit

---

[23] For example, a profit maximizing monopolist will produce in the elastic region of demand (i.e., $\eta > 1$). This is also true in a cartel but need not be true in competitive markets or in oligopoly markets. Consider the n-firm Cournot model described in Chap. 9 where the inverse demand function is $p = a - bQ$ and c is marginal cost. At the Cournot–Nash equilibrium, $\eta = (a + cn)/(an - cn)$ which is less than 1 when $n > a/(a - 2c)$. Thus, $\eta < 1$ when c is sufficiently low and n is sufficiently high.

perfectly competitive firms. In addition, long-run profits (π_{LR}) are zero because of free entry and exit. Recall that zero economic profit implies that entrepreneurs receive a normal rate of return on their financial investments in the firm, giving them no incentive to move resources in or out of the industry. Thus, there is no market power in perfect competition.

In contrast, a monopoly firm has market power and may earn positive profits in the long run. The profit maximizing monopolist produces output where marginal cost equals marginal revenue, but price exceeds marginal revenue and therefore marginal cost since firm (market) demand has a negative slope. In addition, positive profits may persist in the long run because of barriers to entry.[24]

Monopolistic competition has qualities of both competition and monopoly. Like monopoly, price exceeds marginal cost because the firm faces a negatively sloped demand function. Yet, each firm faces considerable competition from products that are close (although not perfect) substitutes. Thus, firm demand is relatively elastic, and the equilibrium price tends to be relatively close to marginal cost. In addition, long-run profits are zero because entry is free, as in perfect competition. One can conclude that a monopolistically competitive firm has little market power and that the absence of long-run economic profit does not preclude the possibility of market power.

The degree of market power in an oligopoly setting is less clear. In a static Cournot model with n firms, the Cournot Limit Theorem states that market power diminishes with more competitors. This theorem suggests that entry barriers that reduce the number of competitors will increase market power, as predicted by the structure–conduct–performance paradigm that we discussed in Chap. 1. This is an intuitively appealing result, but it is not true in other models of oligopoly. In a static Bertrand model with homogeneous goods, for example, market power is zero with two or more competitors. At the other extreme, market power can match that of a monopolist when firms form a perfect cartel. Thus, economic theory demonstrates that there is no simple relationship between market structure and market power. In an oligopoly setting in particular, the degree of market power depends upon the degree of price competition, which in turn depends upon the specifics of the game being played, not just the number of competitors.

From previous discussion, we know that several other factors besides the number of competitors influence price competition in a static oligopoly setting. First, we saw in Chap. 10 that product differentiation tends to dampen price competition. Second, price competition is weaker when firms compete in output (i.e., Cournot) rather than price (i.e., Bertrand). Third, the ability of firms to form an effective and stable cartel will diminish price competition. Cartel viability will depend, in part, on the effectiveness of antitrust laws to limit collusive behavior. Thus, government can have considerable effect on exerted market power.

The degree of price competition also depends on the presence of potential competition. For instance, we saw in Chap. 10 that in the Cournot–Bertrand model with

---

[24] Recall from Chap. 6, however, that even a monopolist may earn zero profit in the long run, depending on demand and cost conditions.

homogeneous goods, a Bertrand-type potential entrant can induce a competitive outcome even in the case of monopoly. Although reality may not be this extreme, the model demonstrates how important potential entry can be to price competition.[25]

Analyzing market power becomes even more complicated in a dynamic setting. We saw in Chap. 11 that firms may make strategic investments today in order to enhance market power in later periods. In markets for addictive commodities, a firm may cut price today, which increases the degree of addiction and enables the firm to charge a higher price tomorrow. In addition, a firm may invest in research and development to lower future marginal cost. These investments can give a firm a strategic advantage, which in turn can increase concentration and profit. Although strategies such as these can boost market power, albeit for different reasons, actions that lower costs and raise firm profits can produce a net benefit to society. These issues will be discussed in Chaps. 14–17.

From this discussion, we can conclude that a number of factors influence market power. To summarize, market power tends to be higher when:

- Entry barriers are present, resulting in high industry concentration.
- There are no potential entrants.
- Products are differentiated.
- Firms compete in output rather than price.
- Firms form an effective cartel.
- Firms make strategic investments today in order to reduce costs and/or raise prices tomorrow.

Because real-world industries vary considerably along these dimensions, it is not surprising that market power varies significantly across industries as we saw in Tables 12.2 and 12.3.

12.3.2 Empirical Evidence

Early empirical studies in the structure–conduct–performance tradition used a cross-section data set from many industries to identify the causes of high industrial profits. Profits were modeled as a function of industry concentration and barriers to entry, with entry barriers typically defined as the capital requirements needed to do business (the value of physical capital divided by total revenue or sales), advertising (advertising expenditures divided by sales), and research and development (research and development expenditures divided by sales).

As we discussed in Chap. 1, this line of research suffers from a number of problems. First, it is difficult to measure economic profit accurately. In addition, many of the variables listed above are endogenous. That is, concentration may affect profits, but high profits can also attract entry and affect concentration.

---

[25] This is similar to the outcome of a "contestable market," as discussed in Chap. 5. For further discussion, see C. Tremblay and V. Tremblay (2011a).

Similarly, advertising may increase barriers to entry and lead to higher profits, but a decline in profits may induce firms to cut advertising spending. The presence of endogeneity makes empirical estimation more difficult.

In spite of these weaknesses, hundreds of empirical studies were conducted during the 1960s through the 1980s to identify the relationship between profits and concentration. In the most reliable studies, adjustments were made to correct for the measurement problem associated with accounting profits. To address the endogeneity problem, by the late 1970s researchers began to estimate systems of equations, such as the following:

$$\pi = a_0 + a_1 CR + a_2 A/S + a_3 K/S + a_4 X_1,$$
$$A/S = b_0 + b_1 \pi + b_2 CR + b_3 X_2,$$
$$CR = d_0 + d_1 \pi + d_2 A/S + d_3 K/S + a_4 X_3, \tag{12.20}$$

where π is a measure of the profit rate of an industry, CR is concentration, A/S is advertising divided by sales, K/S is capital expenditures divided by sales, and the variables X_1–X_3 represented other exogenous variables.

Schmalensee (1989) and Caves (2007) reviewed the evidence and found that these studies produced a number of relationships that hold with some regularity. Schmalensee (1989, 952) concludes that in spite of the weaknesses with this line of research, it "can produce useful stylized facts to guide theory construction and analysis of particular industries." Regarding profits, he concludes that the following stylized facts hold generally:

- The effect of concentration on industry profits is small and statistically weak.
- Individual firm characteristics, such as a relative cost advantage, have a substantial effect on industry profits.
- Advertising spending and capital requirements tend to be positively correlated with industry profits.
- Expenditures on research and development tend to be positively correlated with industry profits when concentration is low, but the relationship may be weak or change sign when concentration is high.
- Regarding firm profits, the effect of concentration is generally negative or insignificant, but the effect of the firm's market share on profits is positive in some industries.

Schmalensee's summary lends credence to studies that focus on individual industries and firms, as the forces that influence profitability tend to be industry and firm specific.[26]

Iwasaki et al. (2008) applied the approach of estimating a system of equations similar to those in (12.20) but for a single industry, the US brewing industry.

---

[26] In imperfectly competitive markets, there is also evidence that unions are able to capture some of the excess profit generated by market power (Domowitz et al. 1988; Dobbelaere 2004).

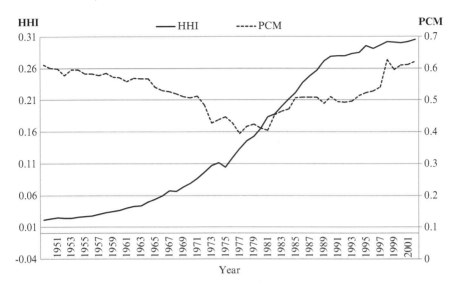

Fig. 12.2 The Herfindahl–Hirschman index (HHI) and the price-cost margin (PCM) for the US brewing industry, 1950–2003

An interesting characteristic of the industry is that industry profits remained low during the 1970s and 1980s in spite of the fact that industry concentration was rising rapidly. These trends can be seen in Fig. 12.2, which plots the Herfindahl–Hirschman index and the price-cost margin (PCM). The Iwasaki et al. empirical results showed that concentration had a significant but small positive effect on profits. The evidence also showed that technological change increased optimal firm size by enlarging the minimum efficient scale needed to take advantage of scale economies in production and advertising.[27] In their race to reach minimum efficient scale, firms engaged in fierce price and advertising competition that took place during the 1970s and 1980s, which explains the low profits during the period. Their study illustrates how the intensity of competition, as well as concentration and barriers to entry, can be an important determinant of industry profits. The so-called "beer wars" are discussed in more detail in Chap. 21.

One needs to be cautious when interpreting profit studies, however, as they need not imply that an increase in concentration is inefficient. As we saw in Chap. 1,

---

[27] The evidence of V. Tremblay and C. Tremblay (2005) and Iwasaki et al. (2008) also shows that brewers were forced into a preemption race in advertising, which caused unsuccessful advertisers to fail. In such a race, Doraszelski and Markovich (2007) show that firms with a string of successful advertising campaigns will replace those with unsuccessful campaigns, a process that leads to a higher level of concentration.

Demsetz (1973) argues that a positive profit–concentration relationship is also consistent with the superior efficiency hypothesis.[28] According to Demsetz, a firm may develop a cost-reducing (or quality improving) innovation that is difficult to imitate. This, in turn, allows the firm to earn higher profits and gain market share and a dominant position in the industry. Thus, a third cause, the superior efficiency of dominant firms, increases profits and fosters high concentration. We take up this dynamic issue more fully in later chapters.

Given Demsetz's argument and the measurement problems associated with profitability, an alternative way to investigate this issue is to look directly at the effect of concentration on price. One approach is intertemporal: determine the effect of entry on prices for a short enough period so that marginal cost is stable. Goolsbee and Syverson (2008) took this approach and found that entry by Southwest Airlines caused airfares to drop by up to 29%. Noether (1988) conducted a similar study in the market for hospital services and found greater price and quality competition with less concentration. The positive price–concentration relationship is further supported by Gilbert (1984), Bailey et al. (1985), and Koller and Weiss (1989) for the banking, airline, and cement industries, respectively. Barton and Sherman (1984) found that a horizontal merger in the microfilm industry led to a significant price increase.

Another approach is intermarket. This requires a comparison of price–concentration pairs in different geographic markets where marginal cost is likely to be the same. Busse and Rysman (2005) provide an excellent example. They analyzed the relationship between price and the number of competitors in the US market for telephone books that contain yellow page advertisements. These markets are local, and generally have one to five competitors selling ad space in books with yellow pages to local businesses. This is nearly an ideal experiment because costs and other factors are likely to be similar across regions; all that differs is the number of competitors. Results showed that one additional competitor caused the median price to fall by 7.2%. Although the evidence that concentration leads to a higher price cannot rule out the superior efficiency hypothesis (i.e., that costs fall as well), it is clearly consistent with the hypothesis that price competition diminishes with concentration.

The Busse and Rysman results provide convincing support for the hypothesis that a reduction in the number of competitors leads to higher prices, *ceteris paribus*. Nevertheless, given that market power can increase when price increases and when marginal cost decreases, appropriate policy analysis will depend on the sources of market power. We will take up this issue further in Chaps. 19 and 20.

Finally, Kwoka and Shumilkina (2010) conduct a case study on the influence of potential competition on airline prices. They investigate the price effect of the 1987 merger between US Air and Piedmont Airlines. In markets with one or more potential

---

[28] Others who have expressed similar views include Brozen (1971) and McGee (1971). Alternatively, Mancke (1974) argued that this strategic advantage can be driven by luck rather than superiority.

competitors,[29] Kwoka and Shumilkina found that the presence of a potential entrant led to significantly lower fares. When a merger eliminated a potential competitor, air fares rose 5 to 6 percent. This provided clear evidence that the presence of a potential competitor can contribute to greater price competition.

12.4   Summary

1. When a firm has the power to profitably maintain price above marginal cost, allocative inefficiency results and the firm is said to have **market power**.
2. The Lerner index in a static setting, defined as $\mathcal{L} \equiv (p - \text{MC})/p$, provides one measure of market power. There is no market power when $\mathcal{L} = 0$. Exerted market power is greater for higher values of $\mathcal{L}$.
3. For homogeneous goods and symmetric firms, the Lerner index for firm i equals $(\text{ms}_i \cdot \theta)/\eta = \theta/(n \cdot \eta) = (\theta \cdot \text{HHI})/\eta$, where ms_i is market share, η is the absolute value of the price elasticity of demand, n is the number of firms, HHI is the Herfindahl–Hirschman index of concentration, and θ is the **behavioral parameter** of market power. The behavioral parameter characterizes a variety of models of cooperative and non-cooperative behaviors. In a Bertrand or competitive setting, $\theta = 0$ and $\mathcal{L} = 0$. In Cournot, $\theta = 1$ and $\mathcal{L} = \text{ms}_i/\eta = 1/(n \cdot \eta) = \text{HHI}/\eta$. In monopoly or a perfect cartel, $\theta = n$ and $\mathcal{L} = 1/\eta$.
4. In a dynamic setting, firm profits are interdependent over time. In this case, market power may still be present even though price equals marginal cost. For example, a firm may price an addictive commodity below marginal cost today substantially boost price above marginal cost tomorrow. The Lerner index in a dynamic setting requires an adjustment factor for the effect that a change in current production has on future profits, as discussed in Appendix 12.B.
5. One measure of market power is **Tobin's q**, which is defined as a firm's market value divided by its replacement value. Market power pushes up the profitability of a firm, which raises its market value above its replacement value. Thus, market power exists when Tobin's q is greater than 1.
6. Because the data are readily available, a measure of accounting **profitability** is sometimes used to identify market power or measure industry performance. Examples include the **rate of return** (the amount earned per dollar invested in the firm) and the **profit-to-sales ratio** (profits divided by total sales). There are two main problems with these measures. First, market power can exist even when long-run profits are zero. Second, accounting profits can be a poor proxy for economic profits.

---

[29] An airline is defined as a potential competitor on a particular route when it serves one or both endpoints of a route but not the route itself.

7. A measure of market competitiveness is the **index of relative profit differences** (RPD). In a market with three firms (1, 2, and 3) where firm 1 is most efficient and firm 3 is least efficient, RPD $= (\pi_1 - \pi_3)/(\pi_2 - \pi_3)$, where π_i is firm i's variable profit. An increase in market competitiveness will lead to an increase in RPD.

8. There are several other ways to estimate market power. First, a cost function could be estimated and used to derive marginal cost and calculate a Lerner estimate (when price data are available). Another example is the **new empirical industrial organization (NEIO)** technique which empirically estimates the behavioral parameter of market power. In addition, Gasmi et al. (1992) developed a technique for identifying firm strategies. Evidence from these and other techniques show that the degree of market power varies considerably from industry to industry and can be high enough to be a policy concern.

9. According to economic theory, many factors influence market power. These include exogenous entry barriers that increase industry concentration, the presence of potential competitors, product differentiation, the choice of strategic variable (output v. price), the ability to maintain an effective cartel, and strategic investments today that affect future costs and competition.

10. There are hundreds of empirical studies that have attempted to determine the main causes of market power. Early studies generally confirm economic theory. In particular, they show that higher concentration leads to higher profits. Some economists question this conclusion, because of various theoretical, methodological, and measurement concerns. For example, the superior efficiency hypothesis, which states that high profits may be due to lower costs rather than higher prices, undermines the conclusion that a positive correlation between concentration and profits is due to collusion. More recent studies that address the criticisms of early work confirm, however, that an increase in concentration does lead to higher prices. These studies also demonstrate that industry-specific characteristics and the presence of a potential competitor can have an important effect on industry performance.

12.5 Review Questions

1. Derive the static Lerner index ($\mathcal{L}$) for a monopoly firm. Explain the properties of $\mathcal{L}$, that is, identify its minimum and maximum values and explain how it changes with the price elasticity of demand.

2. Show that the general first-order condition in (12.2) can be consistent with the first-order condition for a Cournot-type firm and a Bertrand-type firm with homogeneous goods.

3. Explain how a firm can have market power but earn zero economic profits in the long run.

4. Assume that an entrepreneur has invested $1,000 in a company, and this investment will earn a long-run accounting profit of $200 per year. Assume further that a normal profit on such an investment is $100. That is, by earning an accounting profit of $200, the owner earns an economic profit of $100.

   A. Based on accounting profit, what is the owner's rate of return? What is the normal rate of return? Does this company have market power?
   B. If the owner were to sell the company at a competitive auction, at what price would the company be sold? Would the company with a new owner earn positive economic profits? Evaluate.

5. Define Tobin's q and explain why a value greater than 1 indicates the presence of market power.

6. Assume a market with three firms (1, 2, and 3), where firm 1 is most efficient and firm 3 is least efficient. Each firm's variable profit is $\pi_1^v = 6$, $\pi_2^v = 2$, and $\pi_3^v = 1$. A change in market conditions causes variable profits to become $\pi_1^v = 5.5$, $\pi_2^v = 1$, and $\pi_3^v = 0$. Explain how this change has affected the index of relative profit differences. Has this change in market conditions led to an increase or decrease in market competitiveness?

7. Describe two common measures of market power or industry performance. What are their main strengths and weaknesses?

8. Assume a market with two firms, 1 and 2, with multicharacteristic product differentiation. Respective demand and cost functions for firm i are $p_i = a - q_i - dq_j$ and $TC_i = cq_i$.
   Assume that $a = 12$ and $c < 12$.

   A. If $d = 0$, what is the Lerner index?
   B. If $0 < d < 1$ and firms behave as Cournot competitors, what is the Lerner index?
   C. If $d = 1$ (i.e., homogeneous goods) and firms behave as Stackelberg competitors (i.e., firm 1 is the leader and firm 2 is the follower), what is the value of the Lerner index?
   D. If $d = 1$, will market power be greater in the Cournot model or the Stackelberg model?

9. Consider a market where there is an increase in marginal cost.

   A. Assuming linear demand and supply (or cost) functions and a constant cost industry that is perfectly competitive, prove that a unit increase in marginal cost will lead to a unit increase in the long-run equilibrium price.
   B. Assuming a monopoly market with linear demand and cost conditions, prove that a unit increase in marginal cost will cause the equilibrium price to rise by less than one.
   C. Can the difference in the price response to an increase in marginal cost provide a test for monopoly power?

10. Outline the main determinants of market power. Why is it true that an increase in industry concentration need not lead to an increase in market power?
11. If an increase in concentration leads to an increase in economic profit, society need not be worse off. Evaluate.
12. Explain how you could use data from a single industry to demonstrate that concentration does or does not lead to higher prices.
13. (Advanced) Assume that a monopolist produces a single durable good. In this dynamic case, Appendix 12.B shows that the Lerner index equals $\mathcal{L} = (p_t - MC_t + \alpha)/p_t$, where α measures the effect that an increase in durability has on future profits. Without durability, $\alpha = 0$ and $\mathcal{L} = (p_t - MC_t)/p_t$. Explain how an increase in durability affects $\mathcal{L}$.
14. (Advanced) Assume that two firms (1 and 2) compete in the strategic variable, $\mathcal{S}$. Firms are symmetric and face the following profit equation:

$$\pi_i = \mathcal{S}_i - b\mathcal{S}_i^2 + d\mathcal{S}_j\mathcal{S}_i$$

Assume that you have all of the data you need and that firms are either (1) colluding or (2) behaving as static Nash competitors. Show how you would use the Gasmi et al. (1991, 1992) method to empirically test which behavioral assumption is correct (see Appendix 12.C).
15. Suppose that the CEO of a monopoly firm suffers from overconfidence and is interested in empire building over profits. Explain how this will affect market power.

Appendix A: Monopsony Power

As we saw in Sect. 12.1.1, there is a single buyer of an input in a monopsony market. Lack of competition for an input enables the firm to lower the price of the input without completely eliminating supply. Instead of being an input price taker, where the input supply function is perfectly elastic, the firm is an input price maker. Similar to a monopolist that earns greater profit by raising the output price above its competitive level, a monopsonist earns greater profit by lowering the input price below the competitive level.[30]

In this case, the index of input market power for input x is $I_x \equiv (\text{VMP} - w)/\text{VMP}$, where VMP is the value of the marginal product of input x[31] and w is the price of the input. When the input market is perfectly competitive, $w = \text{VMP}$ and the

---

[30] For a more complete discussion of a monopsonist, see Pindyck and Rubenfield (2009, Chap. 10), Varian (2010, Chap. 26), and Nicholson and Snyder (2012, Chap. 16).

[31] The value of the marginal product is defined as the marginal product of the input times the output price, which is the added revenue the firm receives from employing one more unit of the input. For further discussion, see any introductory or intermediate microeconomics textbook, such as Frank and Bernanke (2008), Mankiw (2011), Bernheim and Whinston (2008), Pindyck and Rubenfield (2009), and Varian (2010).

index equals 0. Market power is present when $I_x > 0$. A "bilateral monopoly" exists when there is a monopoly supplier and a monopoly buyer.[32] In this case, Chang and Tremblay (1991) showed that under certain conditions $I_x = (1/\varepsilon_S + 1/\eta)/(1 + 1/\varepsilon_S)$, where ε_S is the price elasticity of supply of input x and η is the absolute value of the price elasticity of demand. In this case, input market power increases as output demand becomes more inelastic (i.e., η falls) and input supply becomes more inelastic (i.e., ε_S falls). Notice that $I_x = 1/\eta$, the Lerner index, when the firm is an input price taker (i.e., the input supply elasticity is infinite).

Azzam (1997) uses an approach that is similar to the NEIO method to estimate the degree of monopsony power in the US beef packing industry. The empirical specification derives from the first-order condition of profit maximization for the beef packing input. He found that higher concentration in beef packing led to greater monopsony power. He also found support for the hypothesis that higher concentration led to greater cost efficiency, with the cost-efficiency effect outweighing the market-power effect.

Appendix B: The Lerner Index in a Dynamic Setting

Here, we formalize our discussion of the measurement of market power in a dynamic market from Sect. 12.1.2. Assume that firm i competes in an oligopoly market where production today affects future profit, as with addictive commodities, learning-by-doing, or a durable good.

Problems such as these can be solved using dynamic programming methods, where the goal of the firm is to choose the level of output in each period that maximizes the present value of the stream of profits now and into the future, V.[33] In essence, this represents the market value of the firm. The firm's problem can be described in period t by a Bellman equation

$$V_t = \max[p_t(Q_t)q_t - \mathrm{TC}_t(q_t) + D \cdot V_{t+1}], \qquad (B.1)$$

where V_t is the value function in period t, D is the discount factor as discussed in Chap. 2, and subscript i is suppressed for notational convenience. The goal is to choose q_t to maximize V_t. The general first-order condition that includes the behavioral parameter θ is

$$\frac{\partial V_t}{\partial q_t} = p_t + \theta \frac{\partial p_t}{\partial Q_t} q_t - \mathrm{MC}_t + \alpha = 0. \qquad (B.2)$$

---

[32] One way to solve the bilateral bargaining problem is to use Rubenstein's (1982) approach, as discussed in Chap. 3.

[33] For a review of dynamic programming techniques, see the Mathematics and Econometrics Appendix at the end of the book.

Note that $\alpha \equiv D \cdot \partial V_{t+1}/\partial q_t$ is an adjustment factor that represents the effect of a change in q_t on the present value of the stream of future profits beginning in period $t + 1$. In a static market with no future effects, $\alpha = 0$ and (B.1) reduces to the first-order condition found in the static model found in (12.2). With addiction and learning-by-doing, this term will be positive. An increase in production today increases future demand with addiction and lowers future costs with learning-by-doing. In a durable goods problem, this term will be negative because an increase in sales today will lower future demand.

The α parameter plays a key role in identifying the degree of market power. After rearranging terms in (B.2), a dynamic Lerner index is defined as

$$\mathcal{L} \equiv \frac{p_t - \mathrm{MC}_t + \alpha}{p_t} = -\theta \frac{\partial p_t}{\partial Q_t} \frac{Q_t}{p_t} \frac{q_t}{Q_t} = \frac{\mathrm{ms}_t \theta}{\eta}. \qquad (B.3)$$

In this case, there is no market power when $\mathcal{L} = 0$, but $\mathcal{L}$ need not equal 0 when price equals marginal cost. In a dynamic setting where $\alpha > 0$, as with addiction, market power is present ($\mathcal{L} > 0$) even when price equals marginal cost.

The issue is even more complicated in a model with learning-by-doing (Pindyck 1985). For example, consider a monopolist whose marginal cost in period t is a negative function of learning and where learning is a positive function of the firm's cumulative past production (ΣQ_{t-1}^{M}). Correctly estimating $\mathcal{L}$ not only requires information on price and α but also requires an estimate of the marginal cost that would result if the industry had been perfectly competitive all along. Note that because cumulative output will be greater under competition (ΣQ_{t-1}^{PC}) than under monopoly, $\mathrm{MC}(\Sigma Q_{t-1}^{M}) > \mathrm{MC}(\Sigma Q_{t-1}^{PC})$. From society's perspective, the correct measure of the Lerner index is

$$\mathcal{L} \equiv \frac{p_t - \mathrm{MC}_t(\Sigma Q_{t-1}^{PC}) + \alpha}{p_t}. \qquad (B.4)$$

Note that only $\mathrm{MC}(\Sigma Q_{t-1}^{M})$ is observable from firm data, however. If $\mathrm{MC}(\Sigma Q_{t-1}^{M})$ is used instead of $\mathrm{MC}(\Sigma Q_{t-1}^{PC})$ to estimate $\mathcal{L}$, this will underestimate the degree of market power. This illustrates how difficult it can be to accurately estimate market power in the presence of learning-by-doing.

Appendix C: Estimating Game Theoretic Strategies

In this appendix, we provide an overview of the Gasmi and Vuong (1991) and Gasmi et al. (1992) method of estimating market power and the particular game being played by firms. Because applying this technique is complicated when there are many strategic possibilities, we illustrate the main idea by considering only nested games of output or price competition and ignore advertising. We consider differentiated Bertrand, Cournot, and cartel games only. The goal is to find a first-order condition that is general enough to nest each of these three possible outcomes. This is different from the NEIO approach, because this technique constrains the market-power parameter to take a discrete value that corresponds to Bertrand, Cournot, or cartel behavior.

We begin with Cournot. Assume that two firms, Coke and Pespi, compete in a static game where the choice variable is output and products are differentiated. Inverse demand, cost, and profit equations are the same as those found in Chap. 10, Sect. 10.2.1:

$$p_i = a - q_i - dq_j,$$

$$TC_i = cq_i,$$

$$\pi_i = TR_i - TC_i = \left(aq_i - q_i^2 - dq_jq_i\right) - cq_i, \qquad (C.1)$$

where subscript i represents Coke or Pepsi and subscript j refers to the other firm. The first-order condition for firm i is

$$\frac{\partial \pi_i}{\partial q_i} = MR_i - MC_i,$$

$$= \left(a - 2q_i - dq_j\right) - (c) = 0, \qquad (C.2)$$

where MR_i is marginal revenue and MC_i is marginal cost.

Next, we consider the case where Coke and Pepsi form an effective cartel. The goal now is to maximize joint profits (Π), which is

$$\Pi = \pi_i + \pi_j$$

$$= \left(aq_i - q_i^2 - dq_jq_i - cq_i\right) + \left(aq_j - q_j^2 - dq_iq_j - cq_j\right). \qquad (C.3)$$

The first-order condition for firm i is

$$\frac{\partial \Pi}{\partial q_i} = \left(a - 2q_i - dq_j - c\right) + \left(dq_j\right)$$

$$= a - c - 2q_i - 2dq_j = 0. \qquad (C.4)$$

In the Bertrand case, recall that we must reorganize demand so that quantity is a function of the choice variables, p_i and p_j. From (10.35) and (10.36), we saw that the demand structure from the Cournot game above produces the following demand function in prices:

$$q_i = \alpha - \beta p_i + \delta p_j, \qquad (C.5)$$

where $\alpha \equiv a(1 - d)/x$, $\beta \equiv 1/x$, $\delta \equiv d/x$, and $x \equiv (1 - d^2)$. This yields the following profit equation for firm i:

$$\pi_i = \text{TR}_i - \text{TC}_i = p_i(\alpha - \beta p_i + \delta p_j) - c(\alpha + \beta p_i - \delta p_j)$$
$$= \alpha p_i - \beta p_i^2 + \delta p_j p_i - \alpha c + \beta p_i c - \delta p_j c. \qquad (C.6)$$

The first-order condition for firm i is

$$\frac{\partial \pi_i}{\partial p_i} = \text{MR}p_i - \text{MC}p_i$$
$$= \alpha - 2\beta p_i + \delta p_j + \beta c = 0. \qquad (C.7)$$

where $\text{MR}p_i$ is firm i's marginal revenue with respect to a change in p_i and $\text{MC}p_i$ is firm i's marginal cost with respect to a change in p_i.

The next step is to solve the first-order conditions in each of the three cases for q_i. This produces firm i's best-reply function in q_i for the Cournot, cartel, and Bertrand cases.[34]

$$\text{Cournot}: q_i = +\frac{a}{2} - \frac{1}{2}c - \frac{d}{2}q_j,$$

$$\text{Cartel}: q_i = +\frac{a}{2} - \frac{1}{2}c - dq_j,$$

$$\text{Bertrand}: q_i = -\frac{\alpha}{2} + \frac{\beta}{2}c - \frac{\delta}{2}p_j. \qquad (C.8)$$

The following equation nests each of these best-reply functions.

$$q_i = \psi_0 + \psi_1 q_j + \psi_2 p_j, \qquad (C.9)$$

where ψ_0 through ψ_2 are parameters that take on different values for each of the three different models. That is,

---

[34] To derive this equation in the Bertrand case, we first solve firm i's demand function for p_i, which we then substitute into the firm's first-order condition (12.27) and solve for q_i.

$$\text{Cournot}: \psi_0 = \frac{a}{2} - \frac{1}{2}c, \quad \psi_1 = -\frac{d}{2}, \quad \psi_2 = 0;$$

$$\text{Cartel}: \psi_0 = \frac{a}{2} - \frac{1}{2}c, \quad \psi_1 = -d, \quad \psi_2 = 0;$$

$$\text{Bertrand}: \psi_0 = -\frac{\alpha}{2} + \frac{\beta}{2}c, \quad \psi_1 = 0, \quad \psi_2 = -\frac{\delta}{2}. \qquad (C.10)$$

The regression model to be estimated includes the system of demand, cost, and best-reply functions for each firm that are found in (C.1) and (C.9). The demand and cost regressions give estimates of parameters a, d, and c which relate directly to the parameters in (C.9). From the estimates of parameters and standard errors, hypothesis tests are conducted to determine which model is most consistent with the data. For example, the data support the Cournot model if the estimates indicate that $\psi_0 = [(a/2) - (1/2)c]$, $\psi_1 = -d/2$, and $\psi_2 = 0$.

Part IV
Other Business Strategies

Chapter 13
Product Design, Multiproduct Production, and Brand Proliferation

One of the most important decisions a firm must make is the style and qualities that its product will possess. Up to this point, we have taken product or brand characteristics as given. The main reason for this is that it can take a considerable amount of time to come up with something innovative, such as a new style of automobile or a more powerful laundry detergent. Nevertheless, when developing a new car a firm must answer a number of design questions—should the company produce an economy or a sports car, should the body style be traditional or cutting-edge, should it have a front-wheel, rear-wheel, or all-wheel drive train.

These are **product design** questions that are driven by demand, technology, and strategic considerations. On the demand side, consumers have different preferences. Many prefer variety and novelty. For these reasons, automobiles come in different colors and color options change over time. In 1957, you could have purchased a Ford Fairlane in coral mist, a color that we do not see today. The 2010 Ford Focus comes in seven colors: black, silver, white, red, metallic, blue, and gray. In spite of these differences, all consumers prefer goods of high quality and durability. As we discussed in Chap. 7, differentiation over a characteristic like car color is horizontal, while differentiation over a characteristic like product quality is vertical.

The nature of technology can also affect a firm's product design decisions. When scale economies are present it may be uneconomic to offer an unlimited amount of variety. Such is the case for automobile manufacturers who limit the number of colors and option packages. In addition, higher quality goods are generally more expensive to produce. Thus, both high and low quality brands may be offered in a given market. High quality goods would command a higher price and serve high valuation consumers, those who are wealthy or have a strong preference for quality. Low quality goods would have a lower price and serve low valuation consumers.

In previous chapters, we focused on firms that produce a single product. But in real markets most firms are multiproduct producers. The portfolio of brands offered by a multiproduct producer is called its **product line**. For example, General Mills offers over 30 brands of breakfast cereal, including Cheerios, Cocoa Puffs, and Lucky Charms. Some firms are multinational conglomerates that produce goods for a variety of different markets. A classic example is General Electric, which produces jet engines, supplies financial services, and owns the NBC television network.

We will see that firms choose product characteristics and breadth of product line in response to consumer preferences and technological constraints. Firms may also make these decisions for strategic reasons. One cell phone company may offer phones with Internet connectivity only because a competitor offers phones with Internet connectivity. Or a firm may broaden its product line in an effort to keep potential entrants out of the market.

In this chapter, we devote our attention to three main issues. First, we analyze a firm's product design decision. In particular, how does a firm decide on a set of product characteristics? Second, we analyze how a firm decides on the composition of its product line. Finally, we are interested in how strategic effects influence a firm's product design and product line decisions.

13.1 Product Design

A considerable amount of effort goes into designing a new product. The firm must identify a set of characteristics that create the highest consumer value for a given cost. This requires the firm to calculate the expected benefits and costs of producing a feasible set of products with different characteristics. To take an example, consider the telephone. Thirty years ago, long before cell phones, telephones were just phones. The main features a manufacturer needed to consider were style and color. Manufacturers offered a single ringtone.

Today, cell phone manufacturers have a much more difficult problem, as there are a myriad of features to consider. As well as style and color, these include:

- Battery type: For example, NiMH batteries have more power but are also heavier than Li-ion batteries.
- Display: These include size, wallpaper options, and whether the screen is backlit.
- Added features: These include a phone directory, custom ringtones, incoming number storage, mute, speed dialing, voice-activated dialing, multiparty calls, speakerphone, clock, calculator, calendar, and games.
- Special features: Many of today's phones include a camera, keyboard for text messaging, wireless Internet connection, Bluetooth, PDA, MP3 player, and GPS receiver.

At one extreme is the Jitterbug, which includes a limited number of features (i.e., phone, voice mail, Bluetooth, and voice dial capability). At the other are the Droid and iPhone, phones that have every possible feature.

For a manufacturer to decide upon a set of cell phone characteristics, it uses standard marginal analysis. In terms of a single characteristic (or set of characteristics), this involves adjusting the quantity of that characteristic until the expected marginal benefit equals marginal cost. We begin our study of product design choice with an investigation of a vertical characteristic.

13.1.1 The Choice of a Vertical Characteristic (Quality)

The firm's problem is to decide on the quality level of its product. As we saw in Chap. 7, quality is a vertical characteristic, as all consumers prefer higher over lower quality goods when priced the same. Freshness of fruits and vegetables is a vertical characteristic, because all consumers prefer fresh over rotten produce. In this section, we address the firm's quality decision. We also want to know whether or not the market produces the socially optimal level of product quality.

13.1.1.1 Quality Choice in Monopoly

To simplify the analysis, consider a monopolist that must decide on the level of quality before selling a particular product to consumers. The firm faces the following linear demand and cost conditions, which are similar to those from Chap. 6. The only difference is that a rise in quality (z) increases demand and costs:

$$p = a - bq + dz, \tag{13.1}$$

$$TC = cq + ez^2, \tag{13.2}$$

where p is price, q is quantity, TC is total cost, and all parameter values (a, b, c, d, and e) are positive constants. The key features of the model are that d measures the effectiveness of quality in raising demand and $2ez$ measures the marginal cost of quality. Notice that an increase in quality causes demand to increase without affecting the slope of demand. To avoid dealing with expectations, the firm is assumed to know its demand and cost equations.

The firm's goal is to maximize profits with respect to q and z, where total revenue is $TR = p \cdot q = aq - bq^2 + dzq$.[1] The firm's profit equation is $\pi = TR - TC = (aq - bq^2 + dzq) - cq - ez^2$. The first-order conditions are

$$\begin{aligned} \frac{\partial \pi}{\partial q} &= \frac{\partial TR}{\partial q} - \frac{\partial TC}{\partial q} \\ &= MR - MC \\ &= (a - 2bq + dz) - (c) = 0, \end{aligned} \tag{13.3}$$

---

[1] Normally, the firm would choose z before making an output decision. For simplicity, we assume a static setting.

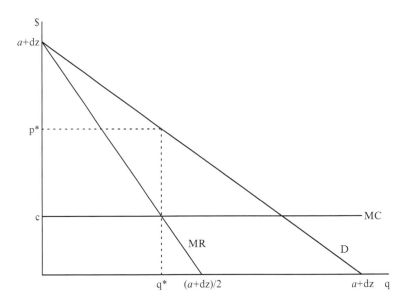

Fig. 13.1 A monopolist's profit-maximizing output and price

$$\frac{\partial \pi}{\partial z} = \frac{\partial \mathrm{TR}}{\partial z} - \frac{\partial \mathrm{TC}}{\partial z}$$
$$= \mathrm{MR}_z - \mathrm{MC}_z$$
$$= (dq) - (2ez) = 0, \tag{13.4}$$

where MR is the marginal revenue with respect to output, MR_z is marginal revenue with respect to quality, MC is marginal cost with respect to output, and MC_z is marginal cost with respect to quality. These equations must be solved simultaneously to obtain the profit-maximizing values of q and z.[2] To gain intuition, though, we begin by analyzing them separately.

Equation (13.3) repeats the standard condition that marginal revenue must equal the marginal cost of production. If we look at the problem graphically, we are able to see how the marginal effectiveness and the marginal cost of quality affect the firm's optimal price–output outcome. We graph the firm's demand, marginal revenue, and marginal cost functions with respect to output in Fig. 13.1. To simplify

---

[2] The second derivatives of the profit equation are $\pi_{qq} = -2b$, $\pi_{qz} = \pi_{zq} = d$, and $\pi_{zz} = -2e$. With this notation, $\pi_{hk} \equiv \partial^2\pi/\partial h\partial k$ for all h and k equal to q and z. For example, $\pi_{qq} \equiv \partial^2\pi/\partial q^2$ and $\pi_{qz} \equiv \partial^2\pi/\partial q\partial z$. Thus, the second-order conditions of profit maximization are met when $4be > d^2$, a condition that must hold for the profit-maximizing level of output and quality to be positive. See the Mathematics and Econometrics Appendix at the end of the book for further discussion of second-order conditions.

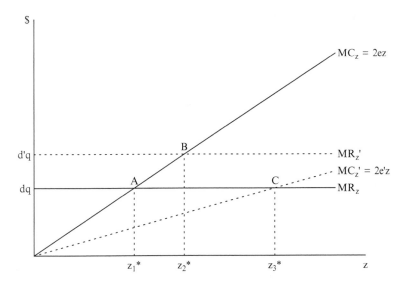

Fig. 13.2 A monopolist's profit-maximizing level of quality (z)

things, we set $b = 1$. The vertical intercept for demand (D) and MR is $(a + dz)$. The horizontal intercept is $(a + dz)/2$ for MR and $(a + dz)$ for D. Optimal output (q^*) occurs where marginal revenue equals marginal cost, and the optimal price (p^*) is the maximum price that will just sell that output level. The main insight of the model is that an increase in the marginal effectiveness of quality (d) causes demand and marginal revenue to increase, which causes the optimum output–price pair to increase.

Equation (13.4) is new and provides another example of the marginal principle. That is, the optimal level of quality occurs where the marginal revenue of quality equals the marginal cost of quality. These marginal functions are pictured in Fig. 13.2. Notice that the marginal revenue of quality is constant at dq, which means that total revenue increases by this amount for a small increase in quality. The marginal cost of quality is $2ez$, which means that total cost goes up by this amount for a small increase in quality. The optimum level of quality (z^*) occurs at point A where $MR_z = MC_z$. This model generates two primary results:

1. The optimal level of quality increases as the marginal effectiveness of quality increases. In the figure, as d increases from d to d', MR_z increases to MR'_z, and the optimum increases from z_1^* to z_2^* (from A and B).
2. The optimal level of quality increases as the marginal cost of quality falls. In the figure, as e decreases from e to e', the marginal cost of quality rotates to MC'_z and the optimum increases from z_1^* to z_3^* (from point A and C).

To obtain the Nash equilibrium values of the strategic variables, we must solve the system of (13.3) and (13.4) simultaneously for q and z. For simplicity, we assume that $b = 1$ and $c = 0$, which gives the following results:[3]

$$q^* = \frac{2ae}{4e - d^2},$$ (13.5)

$$z^* = \frac{ad}{4e - d^2}.$$ (13.6)

Plugging these values into the demand and profit equations produces the firm's optimal price and profit:

$$p^* = \frac{2ae}{4e - d^2},$$ (13.7)

$$\pi^* = \frac{a^2 e}{4e - d^2} z^*.$$ (13.8)

This confirms that the firm will increase quality and earn higher profit as the marginal benefit of quality increases (i.e., d increases) and the marginal cost of quality decreases (e.g., e decreases).[4]

13.1.1.2   Quality Choice in Oligopoly

In an oligopoly setting, strategic effects play a key role in a firm's choice of product quality. To illustrate, we rely on Wauthy's (1996) extension of the model of vertical differentiation that we considered in Chap. 10. The only difference is that here we treat quality as a choice variable instead of being fixed as in Chap. 10. The level of quality of firm i's product, z_i, can range from z_L to z_H, where $0 < z_L < z_H$. Recall that in this model the consumer demand functions for firms 1 and 2 are

$$q_1 = \frac{N(z\phi_H - p_1 + p_2)}{z},$$ (13.9)

$$q_2 = \frac{N(-z\phi_L - p_2 + p_1)}{z},$$ (13.10)

---

[3] When we normalize c to 0, we can interpret the Nash price as the markup of price over marginal cost.
[4] That is, $\partial q^*/\partial e = \partial p^*/\partial e = -(2ad^2)/(4e - d^2)^2 < 0$ and $\partial \pi^*/\partial e = -(a^2 d^2)/(4e - d^2)^2 < 0$.

where $z \equiv z_1 - z_2 > 0$, ϕ_L and ϕ_H are the lower and upper bounds on consumer taste for quality (i.e., $\phi_H > \phi_L > 0$ and $\phi_H - \phi_L = 1$), and N is the number of consumers. For simplicity, we normalize N to 1.

Firms compete in a three stage game. Firm 1 chooses quality in stage I, firm 2 chooses quality in stage II, and they simultaneously choose price in stage III.[5] Our goal is to find the subgame-perfect Nash equilibrium (SPNE) to this game, which is accomplished by using backwards induction.

We saw in Chap. 10 that the Nash equilibrium (NE) to the pricing game that occurs in stage III is

$$p_1^* = c + \frac{z(2\phi_H - \phi_L)}{3} > p_2^* = c + \frac{z(\phi_H - 2\phi_L)}{3}, \tag{13.11}$$

$$q_1^* = \frac{(2\phi_H - \phi_L)}{3} > q_2^* = \frac{(\phi_H - 2\phi_L)}{3}, \tag{13.12}$$

$$\pi_1^* = \frac{z(2\phi_H - \phi_L)^2}{9} - F_1, \quad \pi_2^* = \frac{z(\phi_H - 2\phi_L)^2}{9} - F_2, \tag{13.13}$$

where c is the marginal cost of production and F_i is firm i's fixed (or quasi-fixed) cost. For both firms to participate, $\phi_H > 2\phi_L$. In stage II, firm 2 chooses z_2, given that it can look forward and identify the NE in the final stage of the game. In that case, the firm will maximize profit, (13.13), with respect to z_2. Notice that because $z \equiv z_1 - z_2$, π_2^* declines in z_2. This means that the firm will maximize its profits by choosing the lowest level of quality that is possible: $z_2^* = z_L$.

Finally, we solve the stage I problem. At this stage, firm 1 is assumed to be able to look forward and identify optimal play in the later stages of the game. The solution is obtained by substituting the optimal value of $z_2^* = z_L$ into its profit equation, (13.13), which produces

$$\pi_1^* = \frac{(z_1 - z_L)(2\phi_H - \phi_L)^2}{9} - F_1. \tag{13.14}$$

Notice that firm 1's profits rise with z_1, implying that it will choose the highest level of quality, $z_1^* = z_H$. Thus, the SPNE to this game is

$$p_1^* = c + \frac{z^*(2\phi_H - \phi_L)}{3} > p_2^* = c + \frac{z^*(\phi_H - 2\phi_L)}{3}, \tag{13.15}$$

---

[5] The choice of which firm goes first is irrelevant, as we could have easily let firm 2 move in the first period.

$$q_1^* = \frac{(2\phi_H - \phi_L)}{3} > q_2^* = \frac{(\phi_H - 2\phi_L)}{3}, \tag{13.16}$$

$$z_1^* = z_H > z_2^* = z_L, \tag{13.17}$$

$$\pi_1^* = \frac{z^*(2\phi_H - \phi_L)^2}{9} - F_1; \quad \pi_2^* = \frac{z^*(\phi_H - 2\phi_L)^2}{9} - F_2, \tag{13.18}$$

where $z^* \equiv z_H - z_L$.

This model sheds light on the principle of product differentiation that we discussed in Chap. 10. We saw that an exogenous increase in product differentiation dampened price competition and raised profits. Here, firms have control over quality. If they chose the same level of quality, then equilibrium price would equal marginal cost and profit would equal zero. This is the familiar Bertrand Paradox.

To dampen price competition, in this model firms choose the widest possible gap in quality. This is the **principle of maximum differentiation** and follows from the assumption that consumer tastes are uniformly distributed. If a larger proportion of consumers preferred higher quality, for example, then firm 2 may produce a good that is closer in quality to z_H. Firms will adjust quality in response to consumer preferences.

The model also provides an example of a first-mover advantage/disadvantage. Recall that producing a high quality good is more expensive than producing a low quality good. We can represent this by letting F_1 be greater than F_2. If the difference in fixed costs is sufficiently low, then there is a first-mover advantage because $\pi_1^* > \pi_2^*$. If the timing were endogenous, then both firms would race to be the first to establish a high quality brand. If the difference in fixed costs is sufficiently high, however, then there is a second-mover advantage because $\pi_1^* < \pi_2^*$. In this case, firms would try to delay entry as long as possible.[6] Either way, the model produces an asymmetric outcome, and it is likely that one firm will have a strategic advantage over the other.

13.1.1.3   The Socially Efficient Level of Quality

An important issue is whether or not the market produces the socially optimal level of product quality. Given that firms with market power produce too little output from society's perspective, you might expect them to produce too little quality as well. This need not be the case, however. To illustrate, we consider a simple monopoly problem.[7]

---

[6] Of course, delaying entry may be costly as well. Thus, if the cost of delay is sufficiently lower for firm 2, then firm 1 will be forced to enter first.

[7] For further discussion, see Spence (1975, 1976).

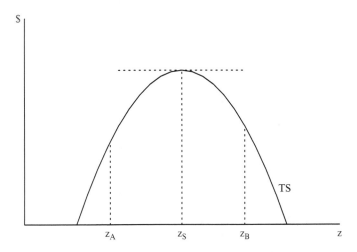

Fig. 13.3 Total (consumer plus producer) surplus with respect to product quality (z)

Assume that the goal of society is to maximize total (consumer plus producer) surplus. The dollar value of consumer surplus (CS) and producer surplus (PS) are functions of price and quality, and the total surplus function (TS) is

$$TS = CS(p, z) + PS(p, z). \tag{13.19}$$

This function is assumed to be strictly concave in z as is illustrated in Fig. 13.3.[8] To maximize TS with respect to z, the first-order condition must equal zero as follows:[9]

$$\frac{\partial TS}{\partial z} = \frac{\partial CS}{\partial z} + \frac{\partial CS}{\partial p}\frac{\partial p}{\partial z} + \frac{\partial PS}{\partial z} + \frac{\partial PS}{\partial p}\frac{\partial p}{\partial z} = 0. \tag{13.20}$$

The social optimum occurs at z_S in the figure.

The TS maximizing condition need not hold in a free market. For a profit-maximizing monopolist, $PS = \pi$ and the firm's first-order conditions of profit maximization imply that $\partial\pi/\partial z = \partial\pi/\partial p = 0$. Thus, for a monopolist, (13.20) becomes

$$\frac{\partial TS}{\partial z} = \frac{\partial CS}{\partial z} + \frac{\partial CS}{\partial p}\frac{\partial p}{\partial z}. \tag{13.21}$$

---

[8] This condition holds for linear demand and cost equations. To illustrate, consider the following inverse demand and total cost functions: $p = 12 - q + z$ and $TC = cq - z^2$, where $c = 0$ for simplicity. In this case, $p^* = q^* = 6 + z/2$; $TS = 54 + 6z - 7z^2/8$, which is strictly concave, with TS reaching a maximum at $z = 3.43$.

[9] This derivative involves the use of the chain rule, which is discussed in the Mathematics and Econometrics Appendix at the end of the book. According to the chain rule, if $y = f(x_1)$ and $x_1 = f(x_2)$, then a change in x_2 causes a change in x_1 which causes y to change. That is, $dy/dx_2 = (dy/dx_1)(dx_1/dx_2)$. In this case, because $CS = CS(p)$ and $p = p(z)$, $\partial CS/\partial z = (\partial CS/\partial p)(\partial p/\partial z)$.

In addition, we know that an increase in price will lower consumer surplus ($\partial CS/\partial p < 0$), and an increase in z will increase consumer surplus ($\partial CS/\partial z > 0$) and increase price ($\partial p/\partial z > 0$). Thus, the sign of (13.21) is indeterminate. That is, the answer depends on the relative magnitude of these effects:

- If an increase in z causes a sufficiently small increase in price, *ceteris paribus*, then $\partial TS/\partial z > 0$ and the monopolist produces too little quality from society's perspective. This corresponds to z_A in Fig. 13.3.
- If an increase in z causes a sufficiently large increase in price, *ceteris paribus*, then $\partial TS/\partial z < 0$ and the monopolist produces too much quality from society's perspective. This corresponds to z_B in Fig. 13.3.

In an oligopoly setting, the analysis is even more complicated because $\partial PS/\partial z$ and $\partial PS/\partial p$ will not generally equal 0. One case is when price falls below the cartel level, such that $\partial PS/\partial p > 0$. Another case is when quality competition results in $\partial PS/\partial z < 0$. This discussion demonstrates that welfare analysis is considerably more complicated for strategic variables other than output (or price), especially for imperfectly competitive markets.

13.1.2 The Choice of a Horizontal Characteristic

A different set of results emerge when differentiation is horizontal instead of vertical. Here we use Hotelling's (1929) model of horizontal differentiation that we discussed in Chap. 7. Recall that consumers are distributed uniformly along a linear Main Street. Consumer k's utility from purchasing from firm i equals $U_{ki} = s - p_i - td_{ki}$, where p_i is the price, t is the transportation cost of traveling a unit length, and d_{ki} is the distance that consumer k is from firm i's location. Parameter s is consumer utility gained from making a unit purchase from a store, assuming a zero price and no transportation costs.[10] In this example, we consider competition among ice cream stores in the summer. Their products are identical, but they can have different locations. Each store must decide on a location along Main Street. Location is a horizontal characteristic, with each consumer preferring the closest store. The natural timing of the game is for firms to choose location in period I and price in period II.

13.1.2.1 The Choice of a Horizontal Characteristic in Monopoly

First, we assume that only one ice cream store enters the market and the firm can locate anywhere along main street. Its location decision is rather simple in this case.

---

[10] In addition, consumers also have unit demands, choosing to buy only a single unit of a brand. A consumer purchases the brand that generates the highest utility, assuming utility is positive. If utility is negative, no purchase is made.

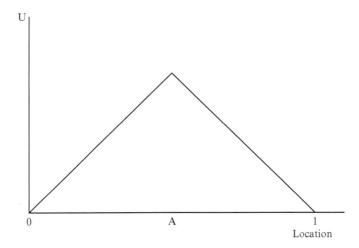

Fig. 13.4 Consumer utility when the monopolist locates at the center of city (A)

To maximize demand, the store will locate at the center of town (point A in Fig. 13.4). The figure depicts the linear utility function described in Chap. 7, which depends on store location. It shows that utility is lower for consumers who live further from the store but that all consumers receive a nonnegative level of utility and make a purchase in this example. Thus, the firm serves all possible customers, and total demand is maximized.[11]

If the firm chose a different location instead, then some consumers may not make a purchase. This is illustrated in Fig. 13.5, where the firm locates at point B and consumers located between x and 1 receive negative utility and will not make a purchase. For these customers, the transportation cost is too high to make a trip to the store worthwhile. Because the firm loses some customers unless it locates at A, the optimal store location is A. Once the store is set up, it will sell ice cream at the monopoly price.

From society's perspective, the goal would be to serve the most customers at the lowest transportation cost. In our example, this occurs at point A. Thus, the monopoly chooses the optimal location, although at a price that exceeds marginal cost. On a mile stretch of beach, for example, this suggests that public restrooms should be located at the middle of the beach to maximize social welfare.

---

[11] This assumes that all consumers are willing to make a purchase when this store location is chosen. If there is an increase in transportation costs, however, then the angle at the top of the triangle in Fig. 13.4 becomes sharper. In this case, the firm serves only customers who are nearby and demand is not diminished by moving slightly left or right from the middle of town.

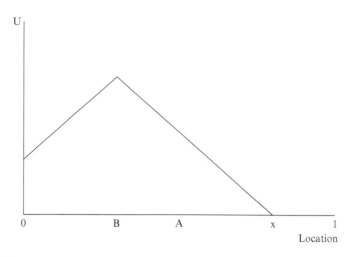

Fig. 13.5 Consumer utility when the monopolist locates to the left of center (B)

13.1.2.2   The Hotelling Model of Horizontal Differentiation and Fixed Prices

Hotelling analyzed a duopoly version of this problem, except that he assumed that output prices were fixed. In this case, we might think of our linear city as a beach of unit length, and along the beach is a paved strand where people can skateboard, bike, jog, and walk. Beach goers spread out so that they are uniformly distributed along the beach. Firms are ice cream vendors on mobile carts, and vendors can costlessly change their locations. The question is, where will the vendors locate?

It turns out that the dominant strategy is for each vendor to locate at the middle of the beach, giving each vendor half of the total sales. What happens if one vendor deviates from this location? Let vendor 1 locate at the center of the strand (FM_1), while vendor 2 locates away from center, say at FM_2 in Fig. 13.6. Because prices are the same, consumers will buy from the closest vendor. Thus, demand for vendor 2's ice cream has two parts:

- All consumers at and to the right of FM_2 will purchase from vendor 2.
- Consumers who are equal distance from FM_1 and FM_2 (at point x) will be indifferent between vendors; as is common practice in economics, we assume that half go to 1 and the other half to 2. All consumers between points x and FM_2 purchase from vendor 2.

Thus, vendor 2's demand is d_2 (distance $1 - x$). Vendor 1's demand equals d_1 (distance $x - 0$). Vendor 2 is worse off at this location. It earns half the market demand when located next to vendor 1 in the middle of the beach but less than half when it moves away from center. Thus, one Nash equilibrium is for both vendors to move to the center of the strand.

The next issue is whether there are other Nash equilibria. To investigate this, let vendor 1 choose a different location from the middle, such as point 0 in Fig. 13.6. In this case, vendor 2 would move just to the right of vendor 1, and few if any

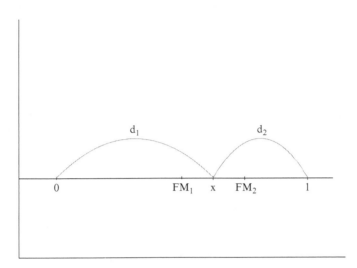

Fig. 13.6 Hotelling's linear model: ice cream vendors along a beach

customers would frequent vendor 1. Thus, vendor 1 would want to move just to the right of vendor 2. This process of movement would continue until they are both in the middle of the strand, which is the only Nash equilibrium.

The implication of Hotelling's model of horizontal differentiation is just the opposite of the vertical differentiation case. The Hotelling model produces minimum differentiation, with each firm choosing the same location. This is called the **principle of minimum differentiation**. There are two ways to overturn this principle. First, if there are more than two firms, they tend to cluster but not all at the same location. We address this issue in a review question. Second, this principle will not hold when firms are allowed to compete in price as well as location. As we will see in the next section, product differentiation dampens price competition but only when firms actually compete in price (i.e., price is not held fixed).

Given that a monopolist will choose a socially optimal location, which is the middle of town, you might think that the market produces the socially optimal locations with two firms as well. This turns out to be incorrect. To minimize consumer travel costs with two vendors, they should locate at 1/4 and 3/4 along the linear city. In this way, the maximum distance any consumer will travel is 1/4. Thus, minimum differentiation in the Hotelling model is not socially optimal when there are two vendors.

13.1.2.3   The Hotelling Model of Horizontal Differentiation When Price Can Vary

Next, we investigate whether or not the principle of minimum differentiation holds when firms are allowed to compete in location in the first stage and in prices in the second stage of the game.

In the linear city model, d'Aspremont et al. (1979) showed that no pure-strategy Nash equilibrium exists when both locations and prices are choice variables. The intuition is as follows. Firms benefit from distancing themselves from one another, because this dampens price competition. At the same time, each firm also wants to inch closer to its competitor to steal its customers. As it turns out, a simple equilibrium does not exist when transportation costs are linear. With quadratic costs, however, d'Aspremont et al. demonstrated that firms will want to maximize their distance apart. That is, the **principle of maximum differentiation** holds, which is just the opposite of Hotelling's result when prices are held constant. This too fails to produce the socially optimal locations (at 1/4 and 3/4).

Economides (1989) verified that the principle of maximum differentiation holds for the circular city model as well, where firms space themselves as far apart as possible. Because firms locate an equal distance apart in a circular city, the market produces the socially desirable amount of differentiation in this case.

Unlike the model with vertical differentiation, models with horizontal differentiation tend to produce a symmetric equilibrium, one where neither firm has a strategic advantage over the other. The assumptions of uniformly distributed tastes and identical firms drive the symmetric result.

13.1.3   Mass-Market and Niche-Market Product Design

Often a firm will develop a product that includes more than a single characteristic. In this case, a product will be designed to serve a particular type or set of consumers. Johnson and Myatt (2006) argued that this typically involves making a decision whether to serve a mass market or a niche market. A **mass-market product design** serves the masses by raising the marginal valuation of a vast number of consumers. In contrast, a **niche-market product design** serves a select group of consumers with idiosyncratic tastes. A niche product raises the marginal valuation of a small targeted group of high valuation consumers.[12]

Work in behavioral economics suggests that the presence of products that have mass- and niche-market appeal within the same market may be driven by the fact that people are exposed to different environments and identify with different groups. Firms will market mass-market goods to people whose identities are tied to social norms and are prone to bandwagon effects. In contrast, firms will develop and market niche-market products to those with distinctive preferences, such as nonconformists and those who are influenced by snob effects.

Johnson and Myatt showed that the choice of design affects the slope of the firm's demand function. A mass-market design will cause demand to rotate

---

[12] Johnson and Myatt point out that this terminology applies to any marketing change. For example, a particular advertising campaign may appeal to the masses or to a niche group of consumers, an issue we take up when we discuss advertising.

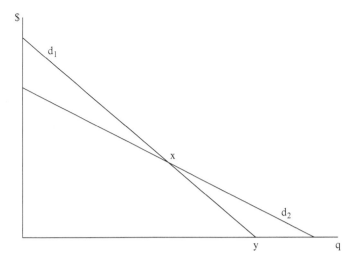

Fig. 13.7 Product design and demand rotation

counterclockwise, from d_1 to d_2 in Fig. 13.7, which produces a positive marginal evaluation for a greater number of consumers (i.e., those located to the right of point y). A niche-market design will cause demand to rotate clockwise, from d_2 to d_1, raising the marginal valuation of a small group of high valuation consumers (i.e., those to the left of point x).

We use the following simple model of inverse demand to incorporate a demand rotation:

$$p = (x + xb) - bq, \qquad (13.22)$$

where x and b are positive constants. Parameter b is the absolute value of the slope of inverse demand, and x is a demand parameter that helps identify the price intercept $(x + xb)$ and the rotation point. Notice that $p = x$ when $q = x$, regardless of the value of b. Thus, as b changes, the demand function rotates around the point $p = q = x$. Johnson and Myatt showed that it is profit maximizing for a monopolist to choose a niche-market design when the equilibrium price–output combination is to the left of point x and will choose a mass-market design when the price–output optimum is to the right of x.[13]

One example where firms design products to serve these different types of consumers is the market for cell phones. Most phones include a camera, clock, calculator, and games. This makes sense because most people (i.e., the masses) value these features. In contrast, the Jitterbug serves a niche market for minimalists

---

[13] Where this equilibrium occurs will depend on demand conditions, cost conditions, and the toughness of competition (i.e., cartel, Cournot, or Bertrand).

who want a phone with a limited number of features that is simple to use. Adding features to a cell phone tends to flatten demand by appealing to more consumers, when limiting features tends to steepen demand. We will use this demand rotation model in later chapters.

13.2 Multiproduct Production

As we have stated previously, most firms are multiproduct producers. Many produce a set of substitute products. As an example, Colgate has over 30 different types of toothpaste, including Colgate Toddler, Kids Pop Star, and Colgate with fluoride, clean mint, whitening, luminous crystals, and mouthwash. Other companies such as Gillette produce complementary products, including razors, razor blades, and shave gel. Then there are conglomerate firms that produce completely unrelated products, like General Electric that produces jet engines and television programming. In this section, we explain why a firm may produce more than one product and analyze the effect that multiproduct production can have on pricing behavior.

13.2.1 Motives for Multiproduct Production

Fundamentally, multiproduct production occurs when it creates some type of synergy. One synergy is that it can reduce the overall risk of doing business. For example, high quality brands sell well in boom periods, and subpremium brands sell well in recessions. Thus, producing both brands tends to even out demand and profit fluctuations over the business cycle, which lowers the cost of raising financial capital.

There may also be synergies in product design, when producing two or more products together leads to either a higher valued product or a lower cost of production. As we discussed in Chap. 2, one reason for this is the presence of economies of scope, which occurs when it costs less to produce goods together than to produce them separately. Products such as these are known as complements in production. In our example of beef and leather hide production, we saw that economies of scope exist because a single firm can produce beef and hides more cheaply than two separate firms, one producing beef and throwing the hides away and the other producing hides and throwing the beef away.

Demand synergies that enhance product value also encourage multiproduct production. Demand synergies may involve products that are complements or substitutes in consumption. Reputation effects can create synergies, whether products are substitutes, complements, or independent goods. Anheuser-Busch's Budweiser brand of beer has a reputation for quality, which made it easier for the company to introduce Bud Light in 1981. Similarly, Eveready's success with flashlights in the early twentieth century facilitated its entry into the market for batteries. Finally, General Electric's success with light bulbs paved the way into unrelated markets such as electronics equipment.[14]

A firm's ability and incentive to broaden its product line may also depend upon its level of success. With imperfect capital markets, it may be cheaper for a successful firm to borrow the financial capital needed to launch a new brand. Alternatively, Aron and Lazear (1990) hypothesize that a failing firm may be more likely to pursue an unconventional strategy because it has so little to lose.[15] That is, when a conventional strategy will lead to almost certain failure, radical action may be the only thing that will give the firm a chance, albeit small, to survive. This is called a **"Hail Mary" strategy**, in reference to the trailing football team that throws long passes at the end of a game, hoping for a miracle touchdown that will win the game. This suggests that marginal firms may be more likely to introduce radically new and different products into the marketplace.

Other multiproduct synergies apply to complementary goods, such as cell phones and batteries. If a cell phone manufacturer develops a longer lasting battery, it not only enhances the value of the battery but also enhances the value of the cell phone. Price spillovers also exist, as a reduction in the price of batteries due to a technological improvement boosts demand for cell phones as well as batteries. Thus, developing and producing them jointly enables a firm to capture these potential spillover effects.

Strategic considerations provide another motive for joint production of substitute goods in oligopoly markets. One case is the merger problem in a differentiated oligopoly market. When two firms compete in output in a static setting, Cournot equilibrium profits rise as the number of competitors falls. If the firms were to merge into a single firm and continue to produce the same portfolio of brands, the new firm would behave as a monopolist, and joint profits would increase. Joint production is clearly superior to separate production from the firm's perspective if it implies less competition, an issue we discuss later in the chapter.

At the same time, the presence of economies of scale limits the benefits of multiproduct production. If there are constant returns to scale, the unit cost of a custom made product would be the same as one that was mass-produced. Consumers could custom order products with characteristics that perfectly match their preferences without paying a price premium. Tailors who make clothing alterations fit this description. In contrast, with declining long-run average costs, broadening a firm's product line of substitute products would lead to lower sales of individual brands and result in higher average costs of production. Thus, the extent of scale economies constrains the degree to which a firm can profitably expand its product line for substitute goods.

---

[14] Of course, if Bud Light, Eveready batteries, and General Electric electronic equipment were of inferior quality, this would harm each company's overall reputation. Thus, they each have an incentive to offer quality goods, something consumers would anticipate.

[15] This strategy is also discussed in McAfee (2002, 135–136).

The evolution of the automobile illustrates these ideas.[16] From 1908 to 1927, the Ford Model T came to dominate the industry. Success was due to Ford's emphasis on improving the efficiency of the assembly line. Ford was able to produce a simple and cheap car for the masses. Scale efficiency was reached by mass producing large quantities of Model Ts that came in one style. Henry Ford's (1922) philosophy is captured in his famous quote: "Any customer can have a car painted any color that he wants so long as it is black." In 1909, a Model T cost less than $900, about half the price of competitor cars, and fell to less than $500 by 1915. In 1908, Ford's US market share was 9.4%, but by 1915 half of all US cars were Model Ts.

Unfortunately, Ford held onto this philosophy too long. As aggregate automobile demand grew over time, scale efficiency became less of an issue. Demand was sufficient to allow most firms to reach minimum efficient scale. In addition, as the country became wealthier there was greater demand for product variety.[17] Finally, economies of scope became increasingly important. General Motors (GM) segmented the market with a variety of different automobiles (e.g., Chevrolet, Buick, and Cadillac), a strategy that enabled GM to overtake Ford in sales by the late 1920s. GM's market segmentation strategy, which soon became the industry norm, is best described by Alfred P. Sloan (1963, 65), president of GM:

> The product policy we proposed is the one for which General Motors has now long been known. We said first the corporation should produce a line of cars in each price area, from the lowest price up to the one for a strictly high-grade quantity-production car, but we would not get into the fancy-price field with small production; second, that the price steps should not be such as to leave wide gaps in the line, and yet should be great enough to keep the number within reason, so that the greatest advantage of quantity production could be secured; and third, that there should be no duplication by the corporation in the price fields or steps.

In other words, GM segmented the market with enough product variety to sever consumer demand and take advantage of economies of scope but still produce enough output of individual brands to take advantage of economies of scale.

To understand a firm's market segmentation problem for substitute goods, we use Hotelling's model of horizontal differentiation. We will extend this model further when we discuss brand proliferation later in the chapter. To begin our analysis, assume there is a monopoly grocery store, and the only characteristic in question is store location on Main Street. Currently, the firm has just one store. This situation is described in Fig. 13.8, which is similar to Fig. 13.4 except that the vertical axis measures consumer surplus (CS) and total surplus (TS) instead of consumer utility. The horizontal axis measures location, and consumers are uniformly distributed between 0 and 1 on this axis. The firm is located at point A.

---

[16] This discussion of the automobile industry borrows from Ford (1922), Sloan (1963), and Norton (2007).

[17] Silberberg (1985) finds that consumer demand for variety appears to be a normal good. Rising income need not imply multiproduct production, as it may simply induce entry of a greater number of single product producers of differentiated goods.

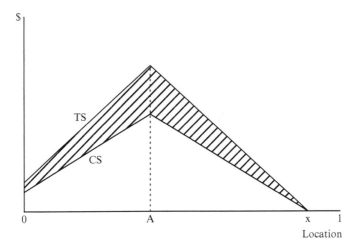

Fig. 13.8 Consumer surplus (CS) and total surplus (TS) for a grocery store at location A

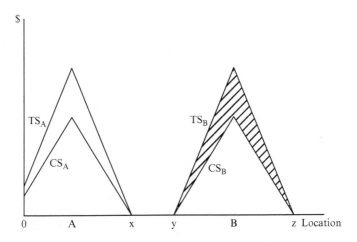

Fig. 13.9 Consumer surplus and total surplus for stores A and B with local monopolies

Producer surplus (PS) equals TS − CS. Firm profit is obtained by adding up the producer surplus from each consumer, which equals the shaded region in the figure. Notice that when the store is located at A, consumers located between 0 and point x receive positive consumer surplus, while consumers located at point x and to the right of point x receive no consumer surplus.

Now consider a monopolist with identical stores at two locations, A and B. There are two possible outcomes. First, if transportation costs are high and stores A and B are sufficiently far apart, then these stores are independent and the firm has a local monopoly at each location. In this case, as shown in Fig. 13.9, consumers located between 0 and x shop at store A, and consumers located between y and z shop at

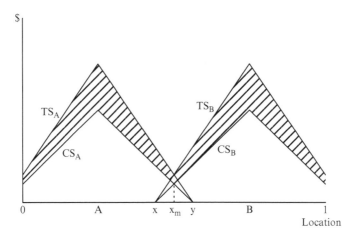

Fig. 13.10 Consumer surplus and total surplus for stores A and B that are competitors

store B. Each store is too far away for consumers between x and y, and these consumers shop at neither store. Thus, the markets are independent because a small change in prices at store A has no effect on demand at store B. Assuming a fixed cost of setting up store B (F_B), the firm will open store B as long as F_B does not exceed gross producer surplus associated with store B (the shaded region in Fig. 13.9).

The second possible location outcome occurs when B is sufficiently close to A, making them interdependent markets. This case is depicted in Fig. 13.10. Consumers to the left of x_m (the marginal consumer) will shop at store A, and those to the right of x_m will shop at store B. Notice that stores A and B compete for consumers located between x and y. That is, if store B (A) goes out of business, these consumers will shop at store A (B). Given a positive fixed cost of setting up store B, the firm will open up this new store only if profits increase. With just one store, profits are the shaded region in Fig. 13.8. With both stores, profits are the shaded regions in Fig. 13.10 minus the set up cost, F_B. Thus, the firm will open store B if it is not too close to store A and if F_B is sufficiently low. We will see later in the chapter that firms may expand their product lines in this way to deter entry.

13.2.2   Multiproduct Production in Monopoly

In this section, we formally investigate the profit-maximizing decision of a multi-product monopolist. The firm produces two brands or products, labeled A and B. The inverse demand function for brand i is general: $p_i(q_A, q_B)$, where subscript i represents product A or B and subscript j represents the other product. Thus, the firm's total revenue is $TR = TR_A + TR_B$, where $TR_A = p_A(q_A, q_B) \cdot q_A$ and $TR_B = p_B(q_A, q_B) \cdot q_B$. We assume that total costs are independent, meaning that there are no economies or diseconomies of scope. This implies that the cost functions for the two brands are separable, such that $TC = TC_A + TC_B$. The firm's profit equation is $\pi = TR - TC = TR_A + TR_B - TC_A - TC_B$.

The firm's goal is to maximize profits with respect to q_A and q_B. The first-order condition with respect to the output of product i is

$$\frac{\partial \pi}{\partial q_i} = \frac{\partial TR_i}{\partial q_i} + \frac{\partial TR_j}{\partial q_i} - \frac{\partial TC_i}{\partial q_i}$$
$$= MR_i + MR_{ji} - MC_i = 0, \tag{13.23}$$

where MR_i is the marginal revenue of brand i, MR_{ji} is the change in TR_j with respect to a change in q_i, and MC_i is the marginal cost of brand i. To identify the optimal output levels, the firm will need to solve this system of equations simultaneously for q_A and q_B. To better understand the economics of this problem we consider two cases: one when demands are independent and the other when they are interdependent.

13.2.2.1 Multiproduct Production with Demand Independence

If products A and B are unrelated, they are neither substitutes nor complements in consumption or production. This would be true for products like sports cars and wooden pencils. From the consumer's perspective, these products are unrelated, neither substitutes nor complements. On the production side, the technologies are separable because they use different inputs and knowledge to produce.

With complete separability, a change in q_i has no effect on brand j's revenues or costs (i.e., $MR_{ji} = 0$). Equation (13.23) becomes

$$\frac{\partial \pi}{\partial q_i} = MR_i - MC_i = 0. \tag{13.24}$$

Notice that this is just the monopolist's first-order condition when the firm produces a single product, as discussed in Chap. 6. With independence, the monopolist can determine the optimal output level of each product by solving each first-order condition separately. Under these conditions, we saw that the Lerner index $(\mathcal{L})$ is

$$\mathcal{L} \equiv \frac{p_i - MC_i}{p_i} = \frac{1}{\eta_i}, \tag{13.25}$$

where η_i is the absolute value of the price elasticity of demand for product i. With complete independence, the firm would act as a separate monopolist with regard to brands A and B.

13.2.2.2   Multiproduct Production with Demand Interdependence

When there is demand interdependence, a change in the output of brand i affects revenues for brand j. If $\partial p_j / \partial q_i < 0$, products i and j are substitutes, as with Bud and Bud Light beer. When two brands are complements, as with Gillette razors and razor blades, $\partial p_j / \partial q_i > 0$.

To understand the implications of (13.23) with interdependence, it is useful to convert it to a Lerner index. With demand interdependence, Tirole (1988, Chap. 1) shows that

$$\mathcal{L}_i \equiv \frac{p_i - \mathrm{MC}_i}{p_i} = \frac{1}{\eta_i} + \alpha, \tag{13.26}$$

where

$$\alpha = \frac{\left(p_j - \mathrm{MC}_j\right) q_j \eta_{ij}}{\mathrm{TR}_j \eta_i}, \tag{13.27}$$

and η_{ij} is the cross-price elasticity of demand for products A and B. Notice that when products are independent, η_{ij} and therefore α equal zero.[18] In this case, the monopolist can determine the price of each product separately. When η_{ij} is not zero, the sign of α equals the sign of η_{ij}. When A and B are substitutes (complements), η_{ij} and α are both positive (negative). Thus, (13.26) has two relevant implications:

1. When products are substitutes ($\alpha > 0$), the firm will charge a higher price than when products are independent. The intuition behind this result is that an increase in the price of brand A raises demand of brand B, a positive externality. When prices are set jointly, this external effect is internalized, which pushes up the price of brand A relative to the case of independence.
2. When products are complements ($\alpha < 0$), the firm will charge a lower price than when products are independent. In this case, an increase in the price of good A lowers demand for good B, a negative externality. When prices are set jointly, this negative external effect is internalized, which lowers the price of product A relative to the case of independence.

To summarize, the price of substitute (complement) brands will be higher (lower) when set jointly than set separately.

When A and B are complements, this effect can be so strong that a firm will sometimes set the price of one good below unit cost. This type of product is called a **loss leader** because even though it is sold at a loss, it generates additional profits from the sale of its complement. The firm loses money on the loss leader, but this

---

[18] That is, a 1% increase in the price of brand j has no effect on the demand for brand i.

practice is profit maximizing overall. A classic example is Gillette's practice of giving away razors (which require the use of Gillette razor blades) to sell more blades.

13.2.2.3   Multiproduct Production in Oligopoly

In an oligopoly market, multiproduct production can also serve as a weapon to gain a strategic advantage over competitors and enhance the firm's market power. One advantage of multiproduct producer is size. According to Edwards (1955), size can give the firm greater financial resources or "deep pockets" (long purse) that can be used to subsidize predatory tactics in a particular market.

Anheuser-Busch, the leading national brewer in the USA, used a predatory tactic when competing with strong regional brewers in the 1960s and 1970s. Some regional brewers sold premium brands of beer, but most sold only sub-premium brands (i.e., those that sold for less than premium prices). In 1957 Anheuser-Busch added a subpremium brand, Busch, to its product line that already included Budweiser, which sold for premium prices.[19] With these two brands, Anheuser-Busch was better able to battle regional brewers by selectively cutting prices of one or both brands and by increasing advertising spending. Rather than take on every region of the country at once, it attacked one region at a time. Although this predatory tactic was expensive, it had less of an impact on Anheuser-Busch's overall profit because of its size.

Although difficult to observe, Edwards (1955) also argues that the degree of multimarket contact among major producers may reduce the rigor of competition. According to Edwards (p. 335), multiproduct producers that compete against one another in a variety of markets

> may come to have recognized spheres of influence and may hesitate to fight local wars vigorously because the prospects of local gain are not worth the risk of general warfare.... A prospect of advantage from vigorous competition in one market may be weighed against the danger of retaliatory forays by the competitor in other markets.

In other words, giant corporations may take a live-and-let-live attitude among themselves. Bernheim and Whinston (1990) address this issue formally, and find that multimarket contact has no effect on market performance when firms and markets are identical and there are constant returns to scale. With asymmetry or product differentiation, however, multimarket contact can facilitate cooperative behavior.

To see how strategic effects can be important in multiproduct oligopoly problems, we adopt a static model developed by Bulow et al. (1985). There are

---

[19] At this time, most brewers marketed a single brand of beer. Anheuser-Busch was the first brewer to segment the market with a subpremium brand (Busch), a premium brand (Budweiser), and a superpremium brand (Michelob). For further discussion of Anheuser-Busch's tactics, see V. Tremblay and C. Tremblay (2005).

two markets, A and B, and two firms, 1 and 2. Firm 1 is a monopolist in market A and competes with firm 2 in market B, where products are homogeneous. The inverse demand function in market A is perfectly elastic for simplicity, with $p_A = 50$, and the demand function in market B is linear, with $p_B = 200 - q_{1B} - q_{2B}$. With this notation, q_{ik} is firm i's output of product k. The total cost functions are $TC_1 = (1/2)(q_{1A} + q_{1B})^2$ and $TC_2 = (1/2)(q_{2B})^2$. Fixed costs are ignored for simplicity.[20] One thing to notice is that TC_1 exhibits diseconomies of scope, because separate production of products A and B is cheaper than joint production.

Firms compete by simultaneously choosing output. Given the demand and cost conditions described above, their profit equations are

$$\pi_1 = TR_1 - TC_1 = p_{1A}q_{1A} + p_{1B}q_{1B} - TC_1$$

$$= [50q_{1A} + (200 - q_{1B} - q_{2B})q_{1B}] - \frac{1}{2}(q_{1A} + q_{1B})^2,$$

$$\pi_2 = TR_2 - TC_2 = p_{2B}q_{2B} - TC_1$$

$$= [(200 - q_{1B} - q_{2B})q_{2B}] - \frac{1}{2}q_{2B}^2. \tag{13.28}$$

Firm 1's goal is to maximize profit with respect to q_{1A} and q_{1B}, and firm 2's goal is to maximize profit with respect to q_{2B}. You might expect that this problem will produce a monopoly outcome in market A and a Cournot outcome in market B. The problem is not that simple, because markets are interconnected. We can see this from the first-order conditions:

$$\frac{\partial \pi_1}{\partial q_{1A}} = MR_{1A} - MC_{1A}$$

$$= (50) - (q_{1A} + q_{1B}) = 0, \tag{13.29}$$

$$\frac{\partial \pi_1}{\partial q_{1B}} = MR_{1B} - MC_{1B}$$

$$= (200 - 2q_{1B} - q_{2B}) - (q_{1A} + q_{1B}) = 0, \tag{13.30}$$

$$\frac{\partial \pi_2}{\partial q_{2B}} = MR_{2B} - MC_{2B}$$

$$= (200 - q_{1B} - 2q_{2B}) - (q_{2B}) = 0, \tag{13.31}$$

where MR_{ik} represents firm i's marginal revenue with respect to product k and MC_{ik} represents firm i's marginal cost with respect to product k. The interdependence is

---

[20] Firms are assumed to have a single production facility. Bulow et al. (1985) assumed that it was too costly for firms to set up multiple plants.

evident from the first-order conditions. Firm i's first-order conditions depend on q_{2B} as well as q_{1A} and q_{1B}.

Given this interdependence, we obtain the Nash equilibrium by solving these three first-order conditions simultaneously. The NE is

$$p_A^* = 50, \ q_{1A}^* = 0,$$

$$p_B^* = 100, \ q_{1B}^* = q_{2B}^* = 50,$$

$$\pi_1^* = \pi_2^* = 3{,}750. \tag{13.32}$$

Notice that it pays firm 1 to refrain from entering market A.

To see how market interactions come into play in this example, suppose that a demand shock pushes up p_A from 50 to 55. In this case, the Nash equilibrium is

$$p_A^* = 55, \ q_{1A}^* = 8,$$

$$p_B^* = 102, \ q_{1B}^* = q_{2B}^* = 47,$$

$$\pi_1^* = \pi_2^* = 3{,}721. \tag{13.33}$$

This leads to the seemingly paradoxical result that a demand increase in the monopoly market actually hurts firm 1. Firm 1 is better off pulling out of market A by finding a way to precommit to staying out of that market. The reason for this is that there are diseconomies of scope with respect to markets A and B. To see this point, consider the case where a third firm, firm 3, operates separately in market A, and firms 1 and 2 compete in market B. When $p_A = 50$, total profit for all three firms is 8,750 (i.e., $\pi_1^* = \pi_2^* = 3{,}750$, and $\pi_3^* = 1{,}250$). When $p_A = 55$, total profit for all three firms is 9,012.5 (i.e., $\pi_1^* = \pi_2^* = 3{,}750$, and $\pi_3^* = 1{,}512.5$). This shows that diseconomies of scope make separate production more profitable than joint production. More importantly, this example demonstrates how multimarket production can influence a monopolist's profits.

13.3   Brand Proliferation

A strategic reason for introducing one or more new brands of substitute goods is to deter entry. That is, an existing firm may flood the market with a variety of differentiated products in order to leave no room for profitable entry by another firm. This is called a brand proliferation strategy or simply **brand proliferation**, a pervasive and powerful practice in business.

The ready-to-eat (RTE) breakfast cereal industry provides an excellent illustration of the basic principles of brand proliferation.[21] Despite relatively low production scale economies, the industry has been highly concentrated and has earned high profits. The minimum efficient firm size is estimated to be between 3% and 5% of market. Yet the market share of each of the largest firms exceeds 15%, and the industry has experienced relatively little entry.

According to the Federal Trade Commission (FTC), a key strategy used to forestall entry in the RTE cereal industry has been brand proliferation. In 1972, a formal complaint was filed against the four largest manufacturers: Kellogg, General Mills, General Foods, and Quaker Oats. The complaint charged that these firms behaved as a shared monopoly and that their "practices of proliferating brands, differentiating similar products, and promoting trademarks through intensive advertising resulted in high barriers to entry into the RTE cereal market."

As every cereal shopper knows, the cereal aisle at any major supermarket is filled with over a hundred different types of breakfast cereal. Although new brands are expensive to launch and many of them fail, existing firms have introduced new brands at an accelerating rate. From 1950 through 1960, 23 new brands were introduced. This number increased to 41 new brands from 1961 to 1970 and to 77 new brands from 2000 to 2010. Brand proliferation such as this makes entry difficult because it not only fills up the product space but also fills up limited shelf space in supermarkets. Although the case was not without merit, charges were dropped because there was insufficient evidence of coordinated behavior.[22]

Motivated by the FTC's position, Schmalensee (1978) developed a model to explain the welfare implications of brand proliferation. According to Schmalensee, three conditions make brand proliferation a profitable strategy. First, products are differentiated horizontally in response to consumer demand for variety. That is, Corn Flakes compete with Wheaties (i.e., wheat flakes) but not with Cocoa Puffs. Second, it can be costly to change the product characteristics of an existing brand. There is no need to tamper with a successful brand, and it would be costly to inform consumers of major changes to an existing brand. Thus, General Mills named its new buckwheat cereal Buc Wheats instead of marketing it under an existing brand name, such Cheerios (which is made from oats). Finally, there are scale economies associated with the production of individual brands. Schmalensee argues that at the beginning of each period a cereal producer must spend a fixed amount on advertising to attract new customers and to reinforce brand awareness among existing customers. Thus, unit cost falls as output increases.[23]

To understand Schmalensee's model, consider a market with brands that are differentiated horizontally, as in Hotelling's linear city model. In this case, we

---

[21] This discussion borrows from Schmalensee (1978), Scherer (1986), and *Federal Trade Commission v. Kellogg* et al., Docket No. 8883, 1982.

[22] For a critical review of this decision, see Scherer and Ross (1990, 465–466).

[23] This is especially true for new brands, as the marketing literature indicates that advertising expenditures for a new brand are typically over four times that of an existing brand (Kolter and Armstrong 1998).

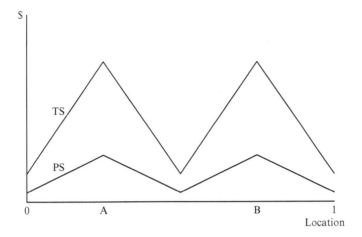

Fig. 13.11 Total surplus and producer surplus for competing brands A and B

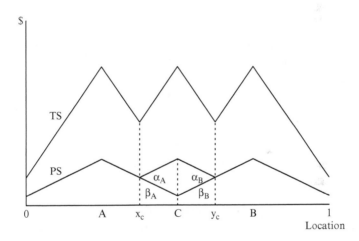

Fig. 13.12 Total surplus and producer surplus for competing brands A, B, and C

assume that a monopoly firm is already producing two brands, A and B, as described in Fig. 13.10. To make the figure more useful for our purposes, we reconfigure it in Fig. 13.11 to plot total surplus (TS) and producer surplus (PS). In this case, CS equals the difference between TS and PS.

The monopolist's problem is to decide whether or not to introduce a new brand, brand C, between brands A and B. Additional brands are assumed to be unprofitable because of the presence of scale economies; sales of each brand fall with an increase in the number of brands, which causes unit costs to rise. In our breakfast cereal example, existing brands could be Cheerios and Cheerios with honey and nuts, while brand C is Cheerios with honey alone. We describe this in Fig. 13.12, where the horizontal characteristic is number of added ingredients. Notice that with brand C, some former A consumers switch to brand C (those between x_C and C) and some former B consumers switch to brand C (those between y_C and C). This transfer of sales from brands A and B to brand C is called **cannibalization**.

The introduction of C causes an increase in monopolist's gross profit, corresponding to area $\alpha_A + \alpha_B$ in Fig. 13.12. It will be profitable to add C if the change in gross profit exceeds the fixed cost of introducing C (i.e., $\alpha_A + \alpha_B > F_C$). However, even if $\alpha_A + \alpha_B < F_C$, the firm may still find it profitable to produce brand C if it successfully deters entry. To illustrate, suppose that an outside firm is considering entry by producing brand C. The entrant's gross profit would increase by area $\alpha_A + \alpha_B + \beta_A + \beta_B$.[24] This includes area $\beta_A + \beta_B$ because the cannibalized profits from brands A and B are transferred from the monopolist to the entrant. So, the entrant will produce brand C if $\alpha_A + \alpha_B + \beta_A + \beta_B > F_C$. We assume this to be the case, and the loss in profit to the monopolist when the entrant produces brand C equals $\beta_A + \beta_B$.

It is this transfer of the monopolist's profit that can make brand proliferation a profitable form of entry deterrence. This is true when the following condition holds: $(\alpha_A + \alpha_B) < F_C < (\alpha_A + \alpha_B + \beta_A + \beta_B)$. As an example, let $\alpha_A = \alpha_B = 10, \beta_A = \beta_B = 8$, and $F_C = 30$. Under these conditions:

- If there is no threat of entry, the monopolist will not introduce brand C because $(\alpha_A + \alpha_B) < F_C$. That is, $(10 + 10) < 30$.
- If the monopolist produces brand C, the potential entrant will not enter and the monopolist loses a profit of 10 (i.e., $F_C - \alpha_A - \alpha_B = 30 - 10 - 10$).
- If the monopolist does not introduce brand C, the potential entrant will introduce it because $F_C < (\alpha_A + \alpha_B + \beta_A + \beta_B)$; $30 < (10 + 10 + 8 + 8)$. In this case, the monopolist loses a profit of 16 (i.e., $-\beta_A - \beta_B = -8 - 8$).

Thus, the monopolist's loss-minimizing strategy is to fill up the product space and crowd out the potential entrant by producing brand C (which costs the firm 10 instead of 16). This is a classic example of a strategic barrier to entry, as discussed in Chap. 8. The monopolist introduces brand C with the sole purpose of keeping the potential competitor out of the market, an activity that is costly and reduces competition (and welfare).

Schmalensee argues that entry deterrence through brand proliferation can also apply to vertically differentiated products.[25] For instance, Sears sells car batteries with warranties that range from 1 to 5 years. Many companies produce both name brand and generic brands of the same product. For example, the Borden Company sells milk in cans with the Borden label and in cans that are unlabeled and sold to retailers for their private label brands. This fills the product space along a vertical characteristic of real or perceived quality, which may also deter entry.

---

[24] This ignores the effect that entry may have on price competition. If competition were to increase, producer surplus would fall and total surplus would rise.

[25] In contrast, Gilbert and Matutes (1993) show that it is more likely in horizontally differentiated markets.

13.4 Empirical Evidence

Anyone who looks for the name of the company that produces the products that they buy knows that multiproduct production is the norm in the business world. A trend towards greater brand proliferation has been occurring for some time. As discussed previously, in the 1920s GM began expanding its product line to serve different price points. Proliferation began to accelerate across all markets by the 1950s, as is evident from the following quote in the Grey Advertising Newsletter, June 1955: "...the stream of new products and new variations of old products which is being forced down the consumer's throat is so swollen that there is great danger of indigestion..." (Alsop 1995).

We can observe this trend by looking at the number of brands produced by the leading US brewing companies. Immediately following the repeal of Prohibition in 1933, most companies entered the market with a single flagship brand of domestic lager beer. These included such brands as Budweiser, Miller, Coors, and Pabst Blue Ribbon. As Table 13.1 shows, the big four beer producers (Anheuser-Busch, Coors, Miller, and Pabst) broadened their product lines by the 1960s and 1970s.[26] Today, only two major beer producers remain. In 2001, Pabst sold all of its production facilities, making it a virtual brewer. Since then, Miller has brewed all of the Pabst brands of beer. In 2008, Miller and Coors united in a joint venture to form MillerCoors. Table 13.2 documents how brand proliferation has become more pronounced for the Anheuser-Busch, Miller, and Coors brewing companies.

Unfortunately, there are few empirical studies on multiproduct production. One reason for this is data limitations. Another is that there are so many theoretical possibilities that it is difficult to distinguish one theory from another. Still, there are a few studies that focus on the causes and economic consequences of brand proliferation.

Table 13.1 Major domestic beer brands of the Anheuser-Busch, Coors, Miller, and Pabst brewing companies

Year	Anheuser-Busch	Coors	Miller	Pabst
1950	2	1	1	1
1960	4	1	1	9
1970	3	1	4	5
1980	5	2	3	10
1990	10	10	9	17
2000	29	14	21	54
2010	55	–	61[a]	33

Sources: V. Tremblay and C. Tremblay (2005) for 1950–2000 and company Web pages for 2010.
[a]This reflects the brands for both Miller and Coors, as the companies united in a joint venture to form MillerCoors in 2008.

---

[26] These numbers only include brands of beer and exclude other products produced by these companies, such as maltalternatives (e.g., Zima), energy drinks, and bottled water.

Table 13.2 Major brands of the Anheuser-Busch, Coors, and Miller brewing companies (1934–2002)

Anheuser-Busch	Coors	Miller
Black and Tan (1996–1998)	Blue Moon (1996–)	1000 Natural (1962–1970)
Budweiser (1934–)	Blue Moon Ale (1996–1999)	Big Sky (1996–1997)
Busch (1957–)	Blue Moon Brown (1996)	Big Sky L (1996–1997)
Bud ML (1972–1973)	Castlemaine (1994–1997)	Buckeye (1973–1975)
Bud L (1983–)	Coors (1934–)	Colders 29 (1994)
Bud Dry (1991–?)	Coors L (1979–)	Gettleman (1962–1975)
Bud Ice (1994–?)	Coors Dry (1992–2000)	Icehouse (1994–)
Bud Ice L (1995–?)	Coors Draft (1986–2000)	Leinenkugel (1991–)
Busch Draft (1996)	Coors Gold (1997–)	Leinenkugel L (1999)
Busch Ice (1996–?)	Coors Ice (1995–1997)	Leinenkugel Dark (1994–1999)
Busch L (1991–)	Coors Ice L (1995–1996)	Leinenkugel ML (1995)
Elephant ML (1992–1996)	Coors Red (1996)	Leinenkugel Special (1995)
Elephant Red (1995–1996)	Herman Joseph (1982–1990)	Magnum ML (1982–)
Elk Ale (1995–1998)	Herman Joseph L (1989–1990)	Meister Brau (1973–2001)
Elk Red (1995–1998)	Keystone (1990–)	Meister Brau L (1994–2001)
Faust (1996–1998)	Keystone L (1990–)	Mickey's ML (2000–)
Hurricane ML (1999–?)	Keystone Dry (1992–2000)	Miller (1934–)
Hurricane Ice (2001–?)	Keystone Ice (1995–)	Miller Lite (1973–)
Killarney's Ale (2001–?)	Keystone Amber (1995–1997)	Miller Ice (1995–)
King Cobra ML (1986–)	George Killians (1982–)	Miller ML (1972–1975)
LA (1985–1990)	Moussy (1992–1995)	Miller Ale (1974–1975)
Michelob (1934–)[a]	Shulers (1994–1995)	Miller Draft (1987–)
Natural L (1978–)	Turbo 1000 ML (1989–1990)	Miller Draft L (1992–)
Natural Ice (1992–1998)	Winterfest (1989–2000)	Miller Dark (1996)
Red Wolf (1995–)	Zima (1994–)	Miller Red (1996)
	Zima Citrus (2001–)	Miller Reserve (1993–1995)
		Miller Reserve Ale (1994–1996)
		Miller Reserve Stout (1995)
		Milwaukee's Best (1973–)
		Milwaukee's Best L (1994–)
		Milwaukee's Best Ice (1995–)
		Old English 800 ML (2000–)
		Red Dog (1995–)
		Southpaw L (1996–)
		Skyy Blue (2002–)
		Henry Weinhard (2000–)[a]
		University Club (1967–1968)

L light, *LA* low alcohol, *ML* malt liquor.
Source: V. Tremblay and C. Tremblay (2005).
[a]The Michelob label has included a variety different styles of beer, including lager, light, bock, black and tan, dark, dry, draft, draft light, honey, and ultra. The Henry Weinhard label has also included many styles of beer.

In an early study, Connor (1981) investigated the motives for new product introductions in the food products industry. He found that the greatest activity occurred in the following industries: nonalcoholic beverages (70 new product introductions in 1977 and 1978), alcoholic beverages (49), pet food (39), and flour mixes and baking ingredients (38). Several hypotheses were tested, two of which are most relevant here. First, brand proliferation increases with market size. This is reasonable, because a larger market has room to support a greater number of products. He also found that brand proliferation rises with industry concentration. Unfortunately, this result is difficult to interpret. Higher levels of concentration may cause brand proliferation, because fewer competitors leave room for a greater number of potential new products. It may also be true that brand proliferation serves as an entry deterrent which causes concentration to rise.

C. Tremblay and V. Tremblay (1996) and V. Tremblay and C. Tremblay (2005) study the causes of brand proliferation in the US brewing industry. Their results show that brand proliferation increases with consumer income, which is not surprising, as Silberberg (1985) finds that demand for variety is a normal good. Brand proliferation that responds to consumer wants in this way certainly raises consumer surplus and is welfare improving. However, V.J. Tremblay and C.H. Tremblay also find that national brewers are more likely than regional brewers to brand proliferate, arguing that this, along with national advertising, was used to force most regional brewers out of business by the mid-1990s. Ultimately, this may have helped raise the market power of survivors. Finally, they found support for the Hail Mary motive for brand proliferation, as it was common for failing firms to introduce new brands within several years of exiting the industry.

Although the evidence is limited, it does suggest that brand proliferation can benefit firms by deterring entry. Schmalensee (1978) and Scherer (1986) make a convincing case that brand proliferation in the breakfast cereal industry forestalled entry and increased profits. Furthermore, Nevo (2001) found that although breakfast cereal prices are below cartel levels, brand proliferation and product differentiation contribute to high prices.

Several other studies find support for the hypothesis that firms brand proliferate to deter entry and gain market power. Putsis (1997) found that brand proliferation led to higher prices in a sample of over 200 food items. In addition, Kadiyali et al. (1998) and Daganska and Jain (2005) found a positive relationship between brand proliferation and prices in the market for yogurt. Daganska and Jain also found that brand proliferation raises production costs, suggesting that it reduces a firm's ability to exploit scale economies. Finally, Smiley's (1988) survey of production managers indicates that one of the most important entry-deterring strategies is brand proliferation.

13.5 Summary

1. One of the first decisions a firm must make involves **product design**—what products to produce and their characteristics. For example, if a firm decides to produce a suitcase, it must also decide on the quality of the components, color, size, etc.

2. When a profit-maximizing firm chooses the level of a particular characteristic, it will equate the marginal revenue with the marginal cost associated with a small change in that characteristic.

3. When oligopoly firms compete in quality and consumers vary in their ability to pay for quality, firms will generally choose to produce products with different levels of quality. This augments the degree of product differentiation, which dampens price competition and illustrates the **principle of product differentiation**.

4. Welfare analysis is considerably more complicated for strategic variables other than price (or output). In terms of product quality, a market is more likely to produce too little (much) quality when an increase in quality produces a sufficiently small (great) increase in price.

5. The **principle of minimum differentiation** means that when firms can choose the degree of product differentiation, they decide to produce homogeneous goods. The **principle of maximum differentiation** means that when firms can choose the degree of product differentiation, they decide on a maximum differentiation.

6. In general, a monopoly firm will choose the socially optimal level of a horizontal characteristic, such as store location. This need not be the case with added competition, as firms may move too far apart from society's perspective to minimize price competition.

7. When the degree of differentiation is endogenous, oligopoly models with horizontal differentiation tend to produce a symmetric equilibrium, while models with vertical differentiation tend to produce an asymmetric equilibrium.

8. A **mass-market product design** appeals to most consumers and causes firm demand to rotate counterclockwise, raising the marginal valuation of a larger number of consumers. A **niche-market product design** appeals to a select group of consumers and causes firm demand to rotate clockwise by elevating the marginal valuation of a small group of high valuation consumers.

9. Most real-world firms are multiproduct producers. For example, General Motors produces different brands of cars and trucks, General Mills produces a variety of different brands of breakfast cereal, and General Electric produces light bulbs and electronics equipment.

10. There are several reasons why firms may choose to produce more than one product:

    • Offering a variety of products can reduce risk by dampening demand fluctuations over the business cycle.

    • Failing firms may be less risk averse and willing to introduce risky new products in a desperate effort to survive. This is called a **Hail Mary strategy**.

    • Producing two or more products can create a synergy in demand. A firm's reputation for quality may make it easier for it to enter a related market. For example, Dole's success as a pineapple supplier made it easier for it to enter

and compete in markets for other types of fruit. For complementary goods such as cell phones and batteries, developing a better battery will increase the demand for cell phones. These external benefits are internalized when a firm produces both cell phones and batteries.
- Producing two or more products may enable a firm to take advantage of economies of scope.
- A firm may offer another brand for strategic reasons.

11. The presence of economies of scale reduces a firm's incentive to produce different brands of substitute goods because producing a greater number of brands reduces sales of each individual brand, which raises average production cost.

12. Optimal pricing for a multiproduct monopolist depends upon the extent to which the products they produce are independent:

- When products are independent, the firm charges the simple monopoly price for each brand.
- When products are substitutes, the firm will charge higher prices than if they were independent products. This is because an increase in the price of one brand generates a positive spillover, as it raises demand for the other brand.
- When products are complements, the firm will charge lower prices than if they were independent products. This is because an increase in the price of one brand generates a negative spillover, as it lowers demand for the other brand. In some cases, the firm may sell one product below cost to increase sales of the other product. Such a good is called a **loss leader**.

13. Multiproduct production may also affect pricing behavior in an oligopoly market. As an example, a large firm is in a better position to use profits from one market to subsidize predatory tactics in another market. In addition, large corporations that compete with each other in many markets may be more likely to take a live-and-let-live attitude among themselves. Although theoretically possible, these hypotheses are difficult to test empirically.

14. **Brand proliferation** occurs when a firm floods the market with a variety of differentiated products in an effort to deter entry. This strategy can be costly, as it is expensive to launch a new brand and it may cannibalize sales of the firm's other substitute brands. Like all strategic barriers to entry, it is also socially inefficient.

15. Although it is difficult to test many of the theories of multiproduct production and brand proliferation, the available empirical evidence is generally consistent with theory:

- In the last 60 years, most firms have expanded their product lines, which is consistent with growing consumer income and the fact that product variety is a normal good.
- Brand proliferation increases with market size and is greater for national producers.
- Failing firms appear to use a Hail Mary strategy, introducing new products in a desperate effort to survive.

- Brand proliferation does appear to hinder entry, a strategy used by the major RTE cereal producers. Survey evidence shows that this is one of the most common strategic barriers to entry. In general, brand proliferation leads to higher prices and higher costs. Thus, the entry deterring motive of brand proliferation is welfare reducing, as it raises costs and enhances market power.

13.6   Review Questions

1. Describe the following economic concepts: product design, multiproduct production, and brand proliferation.
2. Describe how a monopolist goes about deciding on the level of quality of its product. How does this compare to making a decision on the level of a horizontal characteristic?
3. This question relates to monopoly and duopoly markets.

   A. Compare and contrast the equilibrium level of quality (z) offered by a monopoly firm that produces a single product with a duopoly market where each firm chooses a product of different quality, such that $0 < z_L \leq z \leq z_H$ and consumer tastes are uniformly distributed over z_L–z_H. Why might duopoly firms be more likely to choose extreme values of quality compared to the monopolist?

   B. Compare and contrast the equilibrium level of a horizontal characteristic (θ) offered by a monopoly firm that produces a single product with that of a duopoly market. In this market, $\theta_L \leq \theta \leq \theta_H$ and consumer tastes are uniformly distributed over θ_L–θ_H. Under what conditions will it pay duopoly firms to maximize the degree of differentiation?

4. Assume a Hotelling location problem with four firms. The linear city is of unit length. Firms simultaneously choose their locations, but prices are assumed to be fixed. Find their Nash equilibrium locations. (Hint: you will find that all four firms will not choose the same location but that pairs of firms will cluster.)
5. Recall that a mass-market design causes demand to rotate counterclockwise and a niche-market design causes demand to rotate clockwise. Assume that a new product design can cause demand to rotate in three possible ways:

   A. It causes demand to rotate around a point x (as in Fig. 13.7), which occurs in the positive price–quantity quadrant.
   B. It causes demand to rotate around the quantity intercept of demand (i.e., the q-intercept on the horizontal axis remains the same).
   C. It causes demand to rotate around the price intercept of demand (i.e., the p-intercept on the vertical axis remains the same).

   A. On a separate figure, graph each of the three types of demand rotations.
   B. In case (ii), would a mass-market or niche-market design be more profitable?
   C. In case (iii), would a mass-market or niche-market design be more profitable?

6. What cost conditions and/or demand conditions will support multiproduct production?

7. (Advanced) Assume a monopoly firm is considering the production of two brands, 1 and 2. Total cost is $TC = 20q_1 + 20q_2 + \alpha$, where q_i is the output of brand i and α is a constant. The inverse demand for brand i is $p_i = 140 - q_i - dq_j$, where $i \neq j$ and d is a constant.

   A. Determine the firm's optimal output (q_i^*), price (p_i^*), and profit (π^*).
   B. Explain how the value of α affects the firm's profits.
   C. If $\alpha = 0$, how does a change in the degree of product differentiation affect firm profits? Recall that product differentiation increases as d falls.

8. Colgate and Crest each produce over 30 different brands of toothpaste.

   A. When would this form of brand proliferation be socially desirable?
   B. When would it be socially undesirable?
   C. Why do you think Colgate and Crest offer so many brands?

9. Assume that a monopolist is concerned that another firm will enter its market. It is considering a brand proliferation strategy to deter entry. If the monopolist invests in a brand proliferation strategy, this raises its cost and the cost of the potential entrant by $\sigma > 0$. Firms play a two-stage game. In the first stage, the monopolist (M) decides to invest in brand proliferation or not. In the second stage, the potential entrant (PE) decides to enter or not. Payoffs (π) are as follows:

   (i)   With no brand proliferation and no entry, $\pi_M = 36$ and $\pi_{PE} = 0$.
   (ii) With no brand proliferation and entry, $\pi_M = 20$ and $\pi_{PE} = 12$.
   (iii) With brand proliferation and no entry, $\pi_M = 36 - \sigma$ and $\pi_{PE} = 0$.
   (iv) With brand proliferation and entry, $\pi_M = 20 - \sigma$ and $\pi_{PE} = 12 - \sigma$.

   A. Describe this game in extensive form.
   B. Identify the value of σ that will keep PE from entering the market.
   C. Identify the value of σ that will make brand proliferation a profitable strategy for M.
   D. Is this form of brand proliferation socially desirable? Explain.

10. Economy cars are fuel efficient but have low roadside appeal, while sports cars are fast, have cutting edge styling, and come in bright colors. To illustrate, *Car and Driver* magazine gave the Honda Civic, a reliable economy car, an enthusiast rating of 4, and the Lotis Elise, an exotic sports car, a rating of 10.[27] Given the dual systems of the mind that were described in Chap. 4, explain why car manufacturers build sports cars in bright colors with cutting edge body styling compared to economy cars.

---

[27] This was based on a car's driving pleasure, ability to thrill, styling beauty, and ability to impress others (http://www.caranddriver.com, accessed 5 October 2009).

Chapter 14
Price Discrimination and Other Marketing Strategies

A perfectly competitive firm has no need for marketing. Price and firm demand are exogenously determined, making price competition impossible. Expensive advertising campaigns are unprofitable because advertising can have no effect on firm demand. The only thing the firm must decide is how much output to produce and bring to market.

If a firm has some degree of market power, however, it has many more marketing options. We have seen that firms with market power will raise price above marginal cost to transfer some consumer surplus into profit. In this chapter we investigate other methods employed by firms to capture even more consumer surplus.

One tactic is **price discrimination**, which occurs when a firm sells identical goods at different prices. Examples abound. Many movie theaters offer discounts to students and senior citizens. Plastic surgeons charge lower prices to the poor and uninsured. Airlines offer lower fares to those willing to make flight reservations at least two weeks in advance. We will see that under certain circumstances a firm can increase profit by offering more than just one price.

Another common pricing strategy is a **two-part tariff**, where the full price of a good has a variable component and a fixed component. That is, a firm charges consumers a per-unit price plus a fixed fee that does not depend on quantity purchased. For example, warehouse retailers such as Cosco and Sam's Club charge an annual fee plus a separate price for each item purchased. In addition, two-part tariffs are commonly used by nightclubs and amusement parks.

Firms also pursue many nonprice strategies to increase profit. One example is **bundling**. This occurs when two or more related goods are sold together and cannot be purchased separately. If you want to purchase a Honda Civic, for instance, air conditioning is bundled with remote door locks and cruise control, accessories that cannot be purchased individually. Another example is computer software, where word processing and spreadsheet software are typically packaged together.

V.J. Tremblay and C.H. Tremblay, *New Perspectives on Industrial Organization*, Springer Texts in Business and Economics, DOI 10.1007/978-1-4614-3241-8_14, © Springer Science+Business Media New York 2012

These are just a few of the marketing strategies that we will explore in this chapter. Our goal will be to describe them and gain an understanding of the marketing choices of firms. We focus on strategies other than advertising, which is covered in the next two chapters. The evidence will show that there are technological, demand, and strategic reasons why firms pursue a variety of marketing strategies.

It is here and in the chapters to come that behavioral economics has made its greatest contribution to industrial economics. There are many firm strategies that exploit consumer mistakes and cognitive weaknesses which help firms to convert consumer surplus to producer surplus. Without behavioral economics, it would be difficult to motivate and explain the success of many marketing strategies. In the next section, we discuss price discrimination and other pricing strategies. We then turn to nonprice tactics such as bundling, money back guarantees, and 30-day free trials. We explain how firm decisions relate to overconfidence, endowment effects, and other behavioral phenomena. Finally, we will present real world examples and discuss the welfare implications of these various forms of price and nonprice competition.

14.1   Price Discrimination

Price discrimination occurs when a firm charges different prices for different units of output, and the price difference does not reflect a difference in marginal cost.[1] For this to be profitable, the firm must have market power, otherwise the price would be exogenous to the firm. When selling the same product at different prices to different groups of consumers, a firm must also be able to keep consumers from trading among themselves. After all, if a local bakery sold donuts to men for $2 each and to women for 50¢, arbitrage would eliminate the $2 market. Women could make a profit by buying at 50¢ and selling them to men for $1. Men would only purchase donuts from women, thus, destroying the bakery's price discriminatory scheme. It is for this reason that price discrimination is more common in the service sector where resale is impossible or impractical.

A dramatic historical example illustrates how far a company will go to keep markets separate. In the early 1940s a manufacturer of methyl methacrylate plastic, Röhm & Haas, charged $45 a pound to denture manufacturers and 85¢ a pound to other industrial users of this plastic. Because production and shipping costs would be approximately the same whether the plastic is sold to denture manufactures or general industry, this is a clear example of price discrimination. The company had a problem, however, because once this price differential became apparent to denture manufacturers, arbitrage (bootlegging) began to occur. To eliminate this,

---

[1] Formally, price discrimination does not exist for products i and j that are of like quality when $p_i/\mathrm{mc}_i = p_j/\mathrm{mc}_j$, even if $p_i \neq p_j$.

Röhm & Haas considered poisoning the plastic sold for general industrial use, making it unfit for use in dentures. To quote a company memo (Edwards 1944, 19):

A millionth of one percent of arsenic or lead might cause them [the Food and Drug Administration] to confiscate every bootleg unit in the country. There ought to be a trace of something that would make them rear up.

Although Röhm & Haas never followed through with this proposal, it did generate rumors about product safety that may have been sufficient to eliminate arbitrage.

In this section, we will see why a company would go to such great lengths to maintain price discrimination. Three types of price discrimination will be discussed, which are typically called first-degree, second-degree, and third-degree price discrimination.

14.1.1 First-Degree or Perfect Price Discrimination

First-degree or **perfect price discrimination** occurs when a monopolist sells each unit of output at the maximum price that each consumer is willing to pay for it. Recall that this price is called the consumer's demand price or reservation price. Although perfect price discrimination is impractical and not encountered in the real world, the model is rather simple and provides insights into a firm's motivation to price discriminate. It is said to be perfect because we will see that it converts all consumer surplus into firm profit.

To illustrate, consider a monopolist that faces linear demand and cost functions. Inverse market demand is $p = 120 - Q$, where p is the market price, Q is market output, the price intercept is 120 and the slope is -1. Total cost is $TC = 20q$, where q is firm output, which is the same as market output in a monopoly market ($Q = q$). In this case, long-run marginal cost (MC) equals long-run average cost (AC), both equal to 20. Our goal is to compare outcomes when the monopolist charges a single price and when it perfectly price discriminates.

First, we consider the case where the firm charges a single price. Recall that the profit-maximizing level of output (q^*) occurs where marginal revenue (MR $= 120 - 2q$) equals marginal cost (MC $= 20$). The resulting optimal price–output pair is $p^* = 70$ and $q^* = 50$. This outcome is shown in Fig. 14.1, where D is demand. Consumer surplus is 1,250, profit or producer surplus (the shaded region) is 2,500, and total (consumer plus producer) surplus is 3,750.[2] If the market were allocatively efficient, the perfectly competitive outcome would result, where price equals marginal cost (20) and industry output is 100. This outcome maximizes total surplus, with producer surplus equaling 0 and consumer (and total) surplus equaling 5,000.[3]

---

[2] Consumer surplus is $50(120 - 70)/2$, producer surplus is $50(70 - 20)$, and total surplus is consumer surplus plus producer surplus.

[3] In this case, consumer surplus is $100(120 - 20)/2$.

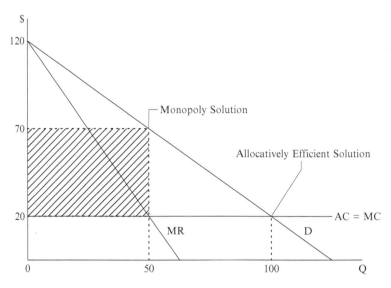

Fig. 14.1 The single-price monopoly solution

With perfect price discrimination, the monopolist charges each consumer his or her demand price. Suppose that each consumer buys just one unit of the good and that consumers are ordered along the quantity axis in Fig. 14.2 from left to right, with those furthest left having the highest valuation of the good. For example, Ann (located at point A) has a demand price of p_A, and Bob (B) has a demand price of p_B. Thus, if the firm sells q' units of output, its total revenue from perfect price discrimination would be the sum of the demand prices for all consumers to the left of q', that is, the shaded region in Fig. 14.2.

Given the demand and cost conditions described in Fig. 14.1, we now want to determine the firm's profit-maximizing output when it perfectly price discriminates. The key thing to notice is that with perfect price discrimination, the firm's demand function is its marginal revenue function. As the firm produces one more unit of output, it earns the demand price for that unit. Prices paid by higher valuation consumers remain the same. Thus, it will be profitable to continue to produce more and more output until marginal revenue, which is now the demand function, equals marginal cost.[4] This outcome is exhibited in Fig. 14.3, where the optimal level of output is 100 and the shaded region identifies firm profits.

---

[4] More formally, the firm's total revenue of producing q' can be described by an integral, which sums up the demand price when q ranges from 0 to q'. Formally, this can be written as $\int_{q=0}^{q'} D(q')dq$. Total cost is $TC(q')$. The firm's problem is to maximize its profit with respect to output, where profit is $\pi = \int D(q)dq - TC(q)$. Because the derivative of $\int D(q)dq$ is $D(q)$, the first-order condition is $D(q) - MC = 0$. That is, the profit-maximizing level of output occurs where $D(q) = MC$.

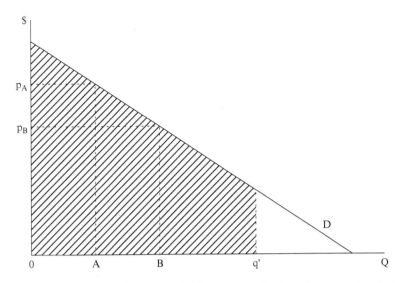

Fig. 14.2 The demand price of Ann (A) and Bob (B) and the firm's total revenue of producing q' with perfect price discrimination

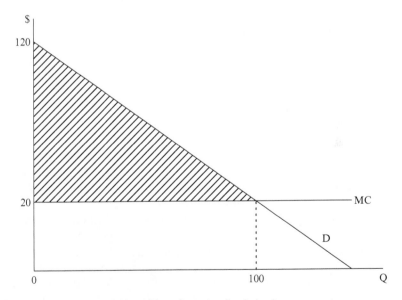

Fig. 14.3 The monopoly solution with perfect price discrimination

Notice that because all surplus goes to the monopolist, it wants to maximize total surplus. Thus, a monopolist that engages in perfect price discrimination will produce the allocatively efficient level of output. This is just like perfect competition, but there is one key difference. With perfect competition, all total surplus goes to consumers; with perfect price discrimination, all total surplus goes to the producer.

Table 14.1 Examples of nonlinear price discrimination

Product	Price	Size (oz)	Price per ounce	Price difference (%)
Kelloggs Frosted Flakes	$5.19	17	$0.305	23
	$5.39	23	$0.234	
Skippy Peanut Butter	$5.19	28	$0.186	11
	$6.59	40	$0.165	
McIlhenny Tabasco	$1.99	2	$0.995	20
Sauce	$3.99	5	$0.798	
Orville Redenbacher	$3.19	10.5	$0.304	34
Microwave Popcorn	$6.99	35	$0.200	
Nabisco Nilla Wafers	$4.29	12	$0.358	32
	$5.88	30	$0.245	

Source: Albertsons Supermarket Web page at https://shop.albertsons.com, accessed May 11, 2010.

By comparing profits with and without perfect price discrimination, you can see that the monopolist has a strong economic incentive to engage in price discrimination. With a single price, profits are 2,500. With perfect price discrimination, profits increase to $5,000. This demonstrates that price discrimination can be an effective strategy of converting consumer surplus into producer surplus.

In reality, we do not observe perfect price discrimination. In a market with many customers, the monopolist will not know every consumer's demand price, and it may be impractical to charge each one a different price even if this information were known with certainty. Nevertheless, the model provides a simple illustration of how price discrimination can increase firm profits and reduce allocative inefficiency, although at the expense of consumer welfare.

14.1.2   Second-Degree or Nonlinear Price Discrimination

With second-degree or **nonlinear price discrimination**, the monopolist charges different prices for different quantities sold, but each consumer faces the same price structure. In other words, each consumer who purchases the same quantity pays the same price. The most common example is quantity or bulk discounting that is found at most supermarkets. Table 14.1 lists several supermarket items where the per-unit price falls when larger quantities are purchased. As an example, suppose that you want to buy nails at your local hardware store. Nails are sold in bulk and are priced at $1 per ounce for the first 10 oz and are priced at 50¢ per ounce thereafter. That is, 10 oz will cost you $10 and 20 oz cost $15 (i.e., $10 for the first 10 oz and $5 for the second 10 oz). You can see why this is sometimes called nonlinear pricing.[5]

---

[5] The price does not remain constant, and this causes a consumer's budget line to be nonlinear. See Varian (2010, 28–29) for further discussion.

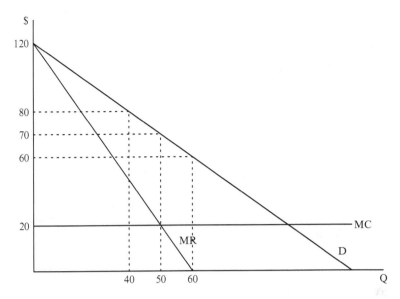

Fig. 14.4 Firm profit with linear and non-linear pricing

Cost asymmetries can cause firms to offer quantity discounts. Shipping costs provide one example, where the per-unit cost of packaging and shipping may be lower on large orders. In addition, firms may use quantity discounts to increase total sales, which lowers long-run average production costs when scale economics are present.

Another motivation for using nonlinear pricing is that it can be a useful, although imperfect, way around the information problem associated with perfect price discrimination. The problem is that if the firm cannot distinguish consumers with high from consumers with low demand prices, the firm can set up a menu of price–quantity options that will induce consumers to choose (or self select) the package that extracts the most surplus from each type of consumer. In our example with nails, nonlinear pricing could increase firm profits (1) if it induces consumers who desire a smaller quantity to pay a higher price than they would have paid with linear pricing and (2) if it causes consumers who desire a larger quantity to purchase sufficiently more than they would have under linear pricing.[6]

The potential for gain in profit from nonlinear pricing can be seen if we return to the example described in Fig. 14.1, which is reproduced in Fig. 14.4. The only difference is that there is now just one consumer in the market, such that the market demand represents that individual's demand. With linear pricing, the price–output pair is $70 and 50 for a profit of $2,500. With nonlinear pricing, assume that the firm chooses a price of $80 when the consumer purchases a quantity of 40 or less.

---

[6] The process of identifying the optimal pricing scheme is rather tedious, so we will not discuss it here. For a more detailed discussion, see Varian (2010, Chap. 25).

Group	Price for a season pass
Adult	$999
Senior:	
65–69	$539
70+	$249
Young adult (19–23)	$439
Teen (13–18)	$319
Youth (6–12)	$189
Child (under 6)	$29

Table 14.2 Examples of segmented price discrimination at the Mt. Bachelor Ski Resort, 2010

Source: https://www.mtbachelor.com, accessed May 12, 2010.

For every unit after 40, the price falls to $60. In this case, the consumer will purchase a total of 60 units for a total expenditure of $4,400. With an average cost of $20, the firm's total cost of producing 60 units is $1,200. Thus, its profits are $3,200 with nonlinear pricing, which is considerably more than it would earn with linear pricing ($2,500). Again, this confirms that there can be strong economic incentives to engage in price discrimination.

14.1.3   Third-Degree or Segmented Price Discrimination

Third-degree or **segmented price discrimination** occurs when a monopolist divides or segments consumers into two or more groups and charges each group a different price. In this case, price discrimination is based on observable customer characteristics. This is the most common form of price discrimination and is found throughout the service sector. For instance, price reductions are frequently offered to women at nightclubs, senior citizens at hotels, and students at amusement parks.

Table 14.2 highlights how elaborate this form of price discrimination is at the Mt. Bachelor Ski Resort in Oregon. Notice that it is based on age, a characteristic that is easily verified, at least for adults. The rates are highest for adults between the ages of 24 and 64 and are lowest for children under the age of 6. One question we wish to address is why the ski resort would choose this price structure.

To see how this form of discrimination can be more profitable than charging a single price, we want to compare firm profits when the monopolist charges a single price with when it price discriminates. To simplify the problem we assume that a monopoly ski resort price discriminates between just two groups: adults (A) and children (C). Adult inverse demand is $p_A = 12 - Q_A$, and child inverse demand is $p_C = 6 - Q_C$, where output (Q) is measured in thousands of adult or children patrons per day. Long-run average cost (AC) and marginal cost (MC) equal 2.

First, we consider the case where the monopolist charges a single price. To see this, we must derive the market demand function, which is adult plus children demand. Geometrically, the market demand (D) is the horizontal sum of adult demand (D_A) and child demand (D_C) in Fig. 14.5. That is, when the price

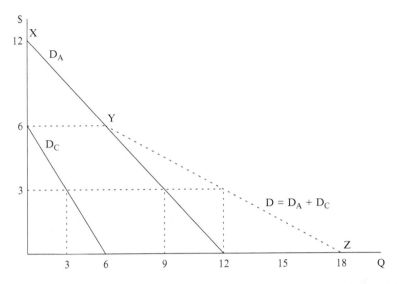

Fig. 14.5 Market demand (D) as the horizontal sum of adult demand (D_A) and child demand (D_C)

exceeds 6, only adults purchase tickets and the market demand corresponds to the adult demand, segment XY. At a lower price, such as 3, the market demand is the sum of child demand (3) and adult demand (6), which is 12. Thus, when the price falls below 6, the market demand corresponds to segment YZ. Formally, the market inverse demand is

$$p = \begin{cases} 12 - Q & \text{for } p \geq 6 \\ 18 - 2Q & \text{for } p < 6 \end{cases}. \tag{14.1}$$

Because demand has a kink, marginal revenue (MR) is disjoint at the output level that corresponds to point Y, as diagrammed in Fig. 14.6. To maximize profit, the monopolist will equate marginal revenue and marginal cost. In this example, however, marginal revenue crosses marginal cost in two places, E_1 and E_2. When this happens, the monopolist must compare the profits for each case and choose the one that earns the most profit (π). At E_1, optimal values are $Q^* = 5$, $p^* = 7$, and $\pi^* = 25$.[7] At E_2, optimal values are $Q^* = 7, p^* = 5.5$, and $\pi^* = 24.5$.[8] Thus, E_1 is the optimum. Notice that only adults will attend the resort at this price.[9]

---

[7] That is, $\pi^* = (p - AC)Q = (7 - 2)5$.

[8] In this case, $\pi^* = (p - AC)Q = (5.5 - 2)7 = 24.5$.

[9] This need not always be the case, however. We will see in a review question at the end of the chapter that some children will enter the resort when marginal cost is sufficiently low.

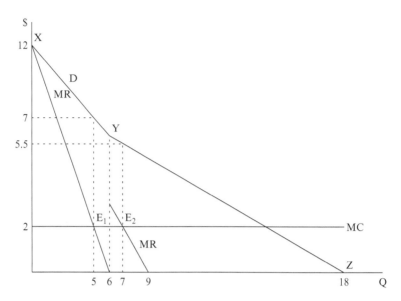

Fig. 14.6 Market demand, marginal revenue and marginal cost

Next, we calculate the outcome when the monopolist price discriminates between adults and children. We assume that the monopolist can keep the markets separate. In this case, the monopolist will treat each group as if they belong to a separate market and set the monopoly price in each.[10] In the adult market, the marginal revenue is $12 - 2q$. Equating marginal revenue with marginal cost (which is 2) gives the profit-maximizing outcome: $q_A^* = 5$, $p_A^* = 7$, and $\pi_A^* = 25$. In the children's market where the marginal revenue is $6 - 2q$, the monopoly outcome is $q_C^* = 2$, $p_C^* = 4$, and $\pi_C^* = 4$. This is illustrated in Fig. 14.7, where the demand and marginal revenue functions for children are reflected over the vertical axis and connected with the diagram of demand and marginal cost functions for adults.

Compared to the case with a single price, price discrimination is better for both consumers and producers. With price discrimination, profits increase from 25 to 29. Consumer surplus for adults remains unchanged because the adult price is unchanged.[11] No children enter the resort when there is a single price of 7. But with price discrimination, the children's price is 4, and 2 children enter the resort, increasing the consumer surplus for children from 0 to 2. Thus, in this example price discrimination raises both producer and consumer surplus.

---

[10] The problem is more complicated when marginal cost is not a constant, because greater sales in one market causes marginal costs to change overall. For further discussion, see Pindyck and Rubenfeld (2009, Chap. 11).

[11] This assumes that the utility of adults is not raised or lowered by having children present.

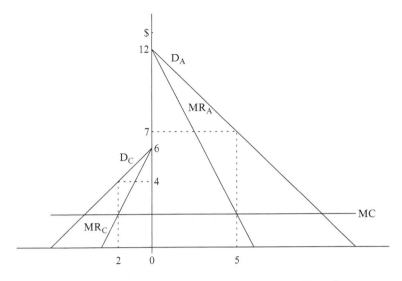

Fig. 14.7 Third-degree price discrimination among adults (A) and children (C)

This still begs the question—why does the ski resort monopolist charge a higher price for adults and a lower price for children? The reason is that the price elasticity of demand is different for these two groups. Given our discussion in Chap. 6, we know that the simple monopoly price increases as demand becomes more inelastic. At the monopoly solution in this example, the price elasticity of demand for adults is 1.4, and the price elasticity of demand for children is 2.[12] Because adults are less responsive to price changes than children, the monopolist charges a higher price for adults.

We can prove this proposition more formally as follows. Assume the following general inverse demand functions for adults and children, respectively: $p_A(q_A)$ and $p_C(q_C)$. The monopolist's profit equation is

$$\pi = TR_A + TR_B - TC$$
$$= p_A(q_A)q_A + p_C(q_C)q_C - TC(q), \qquad (14.2)$$

where TR_i is total revenue in market i (A or C), TC is total cost, and $q = q_A + q_C$. The firm's problem is to maximize profit with respect to q_A and q_C. The first-order conditions of profit maximization are

---

[12] Recall that the price elasticity of demand (η) is the absolute value of the slope of demand ($\partial Q/\partial p$) times the equilibrium price divided by the equilibrium quantity. For both adults and children, $\partial Q/\partial p = -1$. For adults, $p^* = 7$, $Q^* = 5$, and $\eta_A = 1.4$. For children, $p^* = 4$, $Q^* = 2$, and $\eta_C = 2$.

$$\frac{\partial \pi}{\partial q_A} = \frac{\partial TR_A}{\partial q_A} - \frac{\partial TC}{\partial q_A}$$
$$= MR_A - MC$$
$$= \left(p_A + \frac{\partial p_A}{\partial q_A} q_A \right) - \frac{\partial TC(q)}{\partial q_A} = 0, \qquad (14.3)$$

$$\frac{\partial \pi}{\partial q_C} = \frac{\partial TR_C}{\partial q_C} - \frac{\partial TC}{\partial q_C}$$
$$= MR_C - MC$$
$$= \left(p_C + \frac{\partial p_C}{\partial q_C} q_C \right) - \frac{\partial TC(q)}{\partial q_C} = 0, \qquad (14.4)$$

where MR_i is marginal revenue in market i. These are the same first-order conditions we saw in Chap. 6 in the simple monopoly problem. Another fact that we derived in Chap. 2 is that marginal revenue is a function of the absolute value of the price elasticity of demand (η_i) according to the following equation:

$$MR_i = p_i(1 - 1/\eta_i). \qquad (14.5)$$

Given (14.5), we can rewrite the first-order conditions as follows:

$$p_A(1 - 1/\eta_A) = MC(q), \qquad (14.6)$$

$$p_C(1 - 1/\eta_C) = MC(q). \qquad (14.7)$$

Rearranging terms yields the following condition:

$$\frac{p_A}{p_C} = \frac{(1 - 1/\eta_C)}{(1 - 1/\eta_A)}. \qquad (14.8)$$

This implies that if the price elasticity of demand is the same in the A and C markets, then the optimal prices would also be the same. As demand in market A becomes more inelastic (elastic), η_A falls (rises) and p_A rises (falls) relative to p_C. Thus, the firm will charge a higher price in the market with the relatively more inelastic demand function.

Returning to the pricing strategy of the Mt. Bachelor Ski Resort in Table 14.2, the analysis above suggests that senior citizens and those under the age of 24 are more price sensitive than adults. This seems reasonable because adults have relatively high incomes and a high value of time, causing them to be less price sensitive (i.e., have more inelastic demand functions).

A similar argument applies to discount coupons, which let consumers buy products at a reduced price. Coupons normally appear in newspapers, magazines, and over the internet as part of a marketing promotion. Because it takes time and effort to find discount coupons, they appeal to price sensitive consumers who have a higher price elasticity of demand. For example, Narasimhan (1984) found that the average price elasticity is 1.06 for coupon users and 0.81 for nonusers for a sample of 13 supermarket items.[13] Thus, coupons let customers self select into one of two groups, which results in a lower price for the price sensitive group.

To summarize, the discussion in this section indicates that three conditions must hold for segmented price differentiation to be an effective strategy. First, the firm must have market power. Second, the firm must be able to prevent resale. Finally, the price elasticity of demand must differ by consumer group. When these conditions hold, the firm will earn greater profit by charging a higher price to the group that has the lower price elasticity of demand.

14.1.4 The Welfare Effect of Price Discrimination

In terms of efficiency or total (consumer plus producer) surplus, the core principle is that price discrimination can improve efficiency only when it causes total output to increase. With a single price, the monopolist produces too little output to be efficient. Thus, a pricing scheme that induces the firm to increase production moves output in the efficient direction.

We saw that this is exactly what happens with perfect price discrimination. The monopolist finds it profitable to expand output until it produces the allocatively efficient level of production. Thus, total surplus is maximized, just as in perfect competition. Unfortunately, this is accomplished by converting all potential consumer surplus into producer surplus, leaving consumers with zero surplus. Depending on the relative wealth of consumers and monopoly owners, this may not be an equitable outcome (an issue we discuss in Chap. 19).

The welfare implications are less definitive for nonlinear pricing and segmented price discrimination. Consider the case of segmented price differentiation. Clearly profits cannot fall with price discrimination; otherwise the firm would stick with a single price. We showed that a monopolist generally benefits from price discrimination. As we saw in the ski resort example associated with Figs. 14.6 and 14.7, consumers may also benefit from segmented price discrimination. In this example, adults are unaffected by price discrimination but children are priced out of the market without it. Thus, children benefit and both consumer and total surplus increase with price discrimination.[14] However, when it pays the monopolist to serve both groups even without price discrimination, the effect of price discrimination on total surplus depends on the convexity of demand.[15]

---

[13] For a more recent study of the use of coupons in the breakfast cereal industry, see Nevo and Wolfram (2002).

[14] Of course, children could be priced out of the market if costs are sufficiently high.

[15] For a formal discussion, see Schmalensee (1981) and Shih et al. (1988).

14.1.5 Price Discrimination and Strategic Effects

As we discussed in the introduction, rival interaction in oligopoly markets can also influence the degree of price discrimination. In a monopoly market, the degree of price dispersion that results from price discrimination is caused by differences in the price elasticity of demand. In an oligopoly market with price discrimination, strategic effects can also influence the degree of price dispersion.[16] For example, Borenstein and Ross (1994) and Stavins (2001) find that the degree of price discrimination is greater in oligopoly markets than in monopoly markets in the airline industry. Borenstein and Rose found that price dispersion increased by 25% when the number of competitors increased from 1 to 2 airlines. The reason for this is that some flyers are loyal to a particular airline, while others always search for the cheapest seat. As consumer loyalty is more important to firm profits in an oligopoly market, airlines cultivate consumer loyalty by offering frequent flyer programs, for instance, which raises high-end fares. Because consumers who look for the lowest fare are highly price sensitive, lower-end fares generally fall with competition. Thus, price dispersion is higher in oligopoly.

14.2 Other Pricing Strategies

This section presents several other pricing strategies. Although some are a form of price discrimination, we discuss them separately because they have different explanations or features than the simple characterization of price discrimination above.

14.2.1 Intertemporal Pricing Strategies

For many products, firms dramatically change the price of their products over time. There are two important and related reasons for this pricing behavior. As we saw in Chap. 6, firms will raise their prices over time when loyalty (addiction) to a product is positively correlated with the amount of previous consumption. Alternatively, firms may charge different prices at different times as a way of price discriminating among consumers whose characteristics are unknown to the firm. Because these theories produce very similar models, we discuss them together. We also discuss the motivation for peak-load pricing, a policy of charging a high price during different times of the day or different days of the week.

---

[16] In addition, firms may use price discrimination to reduce competition, an issue we take up in Chap. 20.

14.2.1.1   Intertemporal Price Discrimination

When a product is durable and consumer types cannot be observed, one way of inducing consumers to reveal their strength of preference is to use intertemporal price discrimination. Firms separate customers into different groups by setting a high price when a new product is first introduced and then lowering price over time.

Strategic intertemporal pricing behavior succeeds when consumers differ in the value they place on novel and innovative products. This might apply to high fashion goods, for example, where some consumers are willing to pay a high price for the latest styles of clothing while others are not. Personality differences among consumers may also play a role in markets for new gadgets, where some consumers value the bragging rights associated with being the first among their friends to own an iPad, 3-D TV, or fully electric car. Rogers (1962) distinguishes between "early adopters," consumers who place a high value on being the first to own a new product, and "late adopters," those who place a low value on being first. In terms of personality characteristics, early adopters tend to be social, young in age, and interested in scientific innovations. In contrast, late adopters tend to be more traditional, older in age, and have less social interaction.

Intertemporal price discrimination can be successful because early and late adopters differ in their urgency to own (and, therefore, willingness to pay for) a new product. A firm can then price discriminate by charging a high price when product X is first introduced, which serves early adopters who place a high value of buying early. After a sufficient amount of time has elapsed, the price is dropped to meet the demand of late adopters who have a lower valuation of being the first to own X.

Intertemporal price discrimination is especially common among electronics suppliers. One example is Blu-Ray DVD players. When Blu-Ray became the dominant high definition format in early 2008, the price of Blu-Ray players ranged from $400 to $500. Two years later, the price had fallen by over $200.

Perhaps the most extreme example was the Apple iPhone. The original iPhone was introduced in the summer of 2007, with the 4GB model selling for $500 and the 8GB model selling for $600. By September of that year, Apple discontinued the 4GB model and dropped the price of the 8GB model to $400. Thus, some early adopters paid a premium for a consumer durable that became obsolete within three months of purchase. This price drop appears to have been too sudden, as iPhone buyers gained little from being early adopters and many felt cheated. A high level of discontent with Apple's pricing tactics motivated the following song, "Feist 1234 Apple iPod".[17]

---

[17] For further discussion, see Paul (2010). You can see a Mad TV performance of this song on YouTube, http://www.youtube.com, accessed May 23, 2010.

1-2-3-4 went down to the Apple store
Got myself an iPod that I paid 400 dollars for
And just after my purchase was done
those Apple bastards introduced a new one
Oh– oh oh They keep changing the iPod
Oh– oh oh I keep blowing my wad.

2-4-6-8 iPods that are out of date
Sold them on an eBay store
Made a dollar ninety-four
Oh– oh oh They keep changing the iPod
Oh–oh oh Gonna kill someone
I swear to God.

3-4-5-6 hundred bucks I laid down quick
Bought myself an iPhone
They dropped the price and I got poned.
Oh– oh oh They got my money and then
Oh– oh oh They screwed me again
They iScrewed me again.

A-B-C-D Went and bought a plain PC
I know PCs are pretty lame
But at least they'll always stay the same.

PCs: we don't keep changing our product.
We always suck.
And that's something you can count on.

14.2.1.2   Brand Loyalty, Habit, and Addiction

In other circumstances, firms decide to offer an initial low price and then raise the price over time. The initial price is a marketing tactic designed to get the consumer to try a new product, which will lead to greater demand in the future if it creates consumer loyalty, habit, or addiction to the product. Over time, it can also be used to develop a brand name of perceived high quality.

This pricing scheme is especially relevant to addictive commodities, such as heroin and cigarettes, where suppliers have been known to offer free samples to new consumers. Once hooked or addicted, the price rises substantially. Grocery stores use this strategy as well by offering free samples of cookies and other junk foods. Although you may not classify them as addictive, eating cookies or potato chips can be habit forming for many of us. Exercise can also be habit forming, which is why private fitness clubs frequently offer low start-up prices to nonmembers. Finally, many producers of name brand cosmetics and food items give away free samples in an effort to increase consumer goodwill and loyalty to the brand, which can enable the firm to charge higher prices in the future.[18]

---

[18] For a list of companies that offer free samples, see the Shop4Freebies Web site at http://www.shop4freebies.com, accessed July 10, 2011.

14.2.1.3   A Model of Intertemporal Price Changes

To demonstrate why it can be optimal for a firm to charge different prices in different stages or periods, we consider a two-period (I and II) monopoly model of an addictive commodity, a problem we introduced in Chap. 6. Later, we will consider the case of intertemporal price discrimination in markets with early and late adopters.

To simplify things, we assume linear costs and myopic consumers. That is, long-run total cost in period t equals cq_t, where c equals marginal and average cost. Myopic addiction implies that consumers consider the past but not the future.[19] The degree of consumer addiction in period t (AD_t) depends on consumption in the previous period (q_{t-1}). In this case, $AD_t = zq_{t-1}$, where z is an addiction parameter. When z is zero, there is no addiction because the level of previous consumption has no effect on the level of addiction. Addiction is present when z is positive. Notice that AD_t is zero in period I because consumption is zero in period 0, but AD_t is positive in period II if $q_I > 0$. Firm demand in period t is

$$
\begin{aligned}
p_t &= a - bq_t + AD_t \\
    &= a - bq_t + zq_{t-1},
\end{aligned}
\tag{14.9}
$$

where $a > c$.

The firm's goal is to maximize profit (π_t) from periods I and II with respect to q_I and q_{II}. The firm is assumed to be sequentially rational, which means that we use backwards induction to solve this dynamic problem (as discussed in Chaps. 3 and 11). In the last period, the firm's profit equation is $\pi_{II} = TR_{II} - TC_{II} = (a - bq_{II} + zq_I)q_{II} - cq_{II}$. The first-order condition is

$$
\begin{aligned}
\frac{\partial \pi_{II}}{\partial q_{II}} &= \frac{\partial TR_{II}}{\partial q_{II}} - \frac{\partial TC_{II}}{\partial q_{II}} \\
&= MR_{II} - MC_{II} \\
&= (a - 2bq_{II} + zq_I) - c = 0.
\end{aligned}
\tag{14.10}
$$

Solving for q_{II} produces the firm's best-reply function: $q_{II}^{BR} = (a + zq_I - c)/(2b)$. Being sequentially rational means that the firm can look forward, calculate this best reply, and use it to behave optimally in period I. Substituting q_{II}^{BR} into the firm's profit equation in period I produces

---

[19] In the case of rational addiction, as in Becker and Murphy (1988), consumers consider both the past and the future. Behavioral economics suggests that at least some consumers are myopic, however (e.g., Akerlof and Dickens, 1982).

$$\pi_{\mathrm{I}} = TR_{\mathrm{I}} - TC_{\mathrm{I}} + \pi_{\mathrm{II}}\left(q_{\mathrm{II}}^{BR}\right)$$
$$= (a - bq_1)q_1 - cq_1 + \left[(a - bq_{\mathrm{II}}^{BR} + zq_1)q_{\mathrm{II}} - cq_{\mathrm{II}}\right]$$
$$= (a - bq_1 - c)q_1 + \left[(a - c + zq_1)^2/(4b)\right]. \tag{14.11}$$

The first-order condition in this period is

$$\frac{\partial \pi_{\mathrm{I}}}{\partial q_1} = \frac{\partial TR_{\mathrm{I}}}{\partial q_1} - \frac{\partial TR_{\mathrm{I}}}{\partial q_1}$$
$$= MR_{\mathrm{I}} - MC_{\mathrm{I}}$$
$$= (a - 2bq_1 - c) + \left[z(a - c + zq_1)^2/(2b)\right] = 0. \tag{14.12}$$

This condition and q_{II}^{BR} generate the subgame-perfect Nash equilibrium (SPNE) values of output. Our interest is with prices, so we focus on them. Substituting the SPNE values of output into the demand functions above produces the SPNE prices:

$$p_{\mathrm{I}}^* = \frac{b(a + c) - az}{2b - z}, \tag{14.13}$$

$$p_{\mathrm{II}}^* = \frac{b(a + c) - cz}{2b - z}. \tag{14.14}$$

This addiction model produces three interesting results. First, without addiction (i.e., $z = 0$), the monopolist will charge the simple monopoly price in each period, $p_m = (a + c)/2$. Second, with addiction $p_{\mathrm{I}}^* < p_m < p_{\mathrm{II}}^*$. Third, greater addiction (i.e., a greater value of z) produces a lower p_{I}^* and a higher p_{II}^*. This is the pricing behavior we would expect from the supplier of an addictive commodity.

We can also apply this model to the development of brand names, where consumption in the first period leads to brand loyalty in the second period, which enables the firm to raise its price. Over time, this pricing strategy can interact with firm signaling, where the firms use a high price and expensive advertising campaigns to signal to consumers that their product is of high quality. This, in turn, can reinforce brand loyalty.

By redefining z, the model can also explain price discrimination when early adoption is important to consumers. Suppose that the monopolist produces a consumer durable such as an iPad where z is now a measure of the loss in value to early adopters when late adopters purchase an iPad. Because early adopters value being first, z is now negative. That is, consumption by late adopters lowers the utility of early adopters. Because z is negative, (14.13) and (14.14) imply that $p_{\mathrm{I}}^* > p_m > p_2^*$, the reverse of the addiction example. This outcome is consistent with falling prices over time for designer clothing and electronics equipment.

14.2.1.4   Peak-Load Pricing

With peak-load pricing, a firm charges a high price during periods of peak demand and low prices during slack demand. This is a common practice in the market for electricity, which is generally regulated, where the price of electricity is lower at night and during weekends. The purpose of peak-load pricing is to increase efficiency by charging prices that are closer to marginal cost.[20]

Many electricity suppliers have positively sloped marginal cost curves, as some power generators are more efficient than others. When demand is low, they supply energy with their most efficient generators at low marginal cost. As demand increases, less efficient generators must be used and marginal cost rises. Thus, marginal cost is low during periods of low demand and high during periods of high demand. By charging a high price during hours of the day when demand is high and a low price when hours of low demand, consumers are encouraged to use less energy during peak periods and more during slack periods. This is efficient because it lowers the average marginal cost to society of producing a given quantity of electricity.

14.2.2   Damaged Goods and Quality-Dependent Pricing

In some markets, consumers can be segmented by their strength of preference for goods of high quality or prestige. If quality is a normal good, then one would expect the wealthy to be willing and able to pay higher prices for luxury and high quality goods. In addition, as we saw in Chap. 2, some consumers desire to impress their neighbors by purchasing conspicuous goods that signal wealth, high status, and prestige (Veblen 1899; Breit and Elzinga 1974; Bagwell and Bernheim 1996).

In a market where some consumers desire high status goods and others do not, Wolinsky (1987) and Bagwell and Bernheim (1996) showed that a firm may choose to market two brands of like quality, one with a high prestige factor and another with a low prestige factor. The firm may use advertising or other marketing tools to increase the prestige and perceived quality of its name (advertised) brand. The other, generic, brand will receive little if any marketing support. If high status consumers have relatively inelastic demand functions, then firms may be able to extract greater consumer surplus by offering both brands and charging a significantly higher price for the name brand product. Charging a higher price for higher status goods will be reinforced if a higher price is associated with higher real or perceived quality, an issue we will discuss further in Chap. 15.

---

[20] To read more about the theory of peak-load pricing, see Crew et al. (1995).

Deneckere and McAfee (1996) provide a variation on this theme when quality differences are real rather than perceived. In their model, firms market both high and low quality goods and create the low quality good by intentionally damaging a fraction of the high quality good, unbeknownst to consumers. Even though the lower quality (damaged) good is more expensive to produce than the high quality good, this will be the cheapest way to create low and high quality brands if there are substantial scale economies in production. This strategy allows the firm to price discriminate between high-value customers, who choose undamaged goods, and low-value consumers, who choose damaged goods. Denecker and McAfee showed that this behavior can increase both producer and consumer surplus. High-value customers who prefer undamaged goods may pay a lower price when damaged goods are present. In addition, many low-value customers would not purchase the good if only higher priced undamaged goods were offered. Finally, the firm will use this strategy only if it is profitable. Thus, the act of intentionally damaging a good can benefit both the producer and consumers.

The classic example of a damaged good is the 486 computer chip produced by the Intel Corporation. It was first introduced in 1989 and named the 486DX chip. It was faster than previous chips and was the first to have a built-in math coprocessor that could perform complex mathematical calculations. Two years later Intel introduced the 486SX chip, which was designed for lower value consumers as it did not have a math coprocessor. In 1991, Intel priced the 486DX at $588 and the 486SX at $333. What is interesting is that the 486SX is in fact a 486DX with an intentionally damaged math coprocessor. Thus, the less powerful and lower priced 486SX cost more to produce than the 486DX.

This is not an isolated case, as there are many documented examples of damaged goods.[21] We have already discussed the 1940s case of methyl methacrylate plastic, where Röhm & Haas considered adding arsenic to the plastic shipped to industry to keep the markets for industrial and denture use separate. Another example occurred in 1990 when IBM developed a lower priced version of its successful LaserPrinter, the LaserPrinter E. The original and the E versions were identical in every way, except that a computer chip was added to the E version with the sole purpose of slowing its printing speed by 50%. Finally, the Sharp Electronics Company sold two DVD players, with model numbers DVE611 and DV740U. The DVE611 could play both American and European DVDs. The lower priced DV740U version was identical in every way to the DVE611 version, except that it could only play American DVDs. This was accomplished by covering up the button on the remote control that would allow it to play European versions of DVDs.

These examples make it clear that firms will sometimes go to great lengths to differentiate their products, even by intentionally damaging their products to engage in profitable price discrimination. Again, the reason that creating low quality goods by damaging high quality goods is profitable is because the presence of scale economies makes this the cheapest way of creating the low quality good.

---

[21] These examples derive from Deneckere and McAfee (1996), McAfee (2007), and Dixit and Nalebuff (2008).

14.2.3   Two-Part Tariffs

A two-part tariff is another popular pricing scheme used in business. In this case, the firm charges consumers a fixed fee for the right to make a purchase and uniform price for each unit that is purchased. The consumer's total expenditure (TE) would be TE $= f + p \cdot q$, where f is the fixed fee and p is the marginal or per-unit price. With this pricing scheme, the average expenditure or full price, defined as TE$/q = f/q + p$, declines as the consumer buys more of the good.

There are many examples of two-part tariffs in the marketplace. Warehouse stores such as Cosco and Sam's Club require a flat membership fee each year from each customer, as well as a per-unit price for each product. Country clubs typically charge a flat fee for membership and a per-unit fee for each round of golf and each hour on a tennis court. Many nightclubs and amusement parks also charge an entry fee plus a per-unit price.[22]

When considering a two-part tariff, the question is: how will a firm set the entry fee and variable price? To simplify the analysis, assume a monopoly market where the firm's goal is to maximize profit with respect to these two choice variables, f and p. The easiest way to see how this is done is to consider a market with a single consumer whose demand function is described in Fig. 14.8.[23] It is not hard to see that the firm will earn the greatest profit by setting price equal to marginal cost and the fee equal to the remaining consumer surplus.[24] Notice that this leads to the same outcome as that of perfect price discrimination, where the firm produces the allocatively efficient level of output by converting all potential consumer surplus into profit.

The firm's problem becomes more complex, however, when there is more than one consumer and consumers have different preferences. In a market with one low valuation consumer and one high valuation consumer, it becomes optimal to set the fee to capture all consumer surplus from the low-value consumer, assuming the firm wants to serve both customers. This will leave the high-value consumer with some remaining surplus.[25] In this case, it may pay the firm to set the price above marginal cost and adjust the fee accordingly. The optimal p–f pair is found by comparing profits for all feasible p–f combinations.[26]

Cellular phone companies use a more complicated pricing scheme, called a three-part tariff. The monthly contract consists of (1) a fixed fee, (2) free phone minutes up to a set allowance, and (3) a positive per-unit price for usage beyond the allowance.

---

[22] The first to formally address this idea was Oi (1971), who was inspired by the two-part pricing strategy used at Disneyland in the 1960s. Disneyland and Disneyworld only charge a fixed entry fee today, however, perhaps to lower consumer time spent waiting in line.

[23] This discussion also holds for many consumers with identical demand functions.

[24] You can verify this by comparing profits for different prices and fixed fees.

[25] This assumes that fee discrimination is uneconomic (i.e., the firm cannot charge a higher fee to the high-valuation consumer).

[26] For a more detailed discussion, see Oi (1971) and Bernheim and Whinston (2008, Chap. 18).

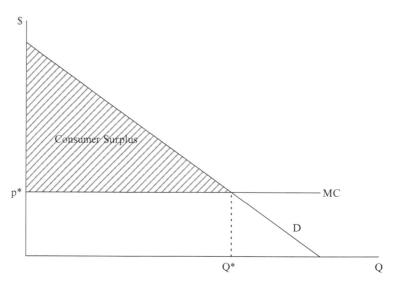

Fig. 14.8 A two-part tariff with a single consumer where the optimal price is p^* and the optimal fee (f) equals consumer surplus

Table 14.3 lists the pricing scheme of major US cell phone companies. For example, the monthly total expenditure (TE) of Sprint's 200 Anytime Minutes Plan is

$$\text{TE} = \begin{cases} \$29.99 & \text{if } m \leq 200 \\ \$29.99 + \$0.45x & \text{if } m > 200 \end{cases}, \tag{14.15}$$

where m is the number of minutes spent on the phone and x is the number of minutes in excess of 200. There is no minute charge when your usage is less or equal to 200.

These complex pricing schemes make it difficult to choose the most cost-effective plan. You need to have a good estimate of the number of minutes you expect to spend on the phone. If you plan to spend no more than 222 min on the phone each month, the Nextel and Sprint 200 Anytime Minutes Plans are lowest cost.[27] If you plan to spend just over 222 min on the phone, you should opt for one of the 450 or 500 Anytime Minutes plans. Of course, quality of service is also important, which may induce you to purchase the Verizon-450 plan over the 450 and 500 min plans of the other suppliers, because in the past Verizon has provided the best service in most regions of the country according to *Consumer Reports*.[28]

---

[27] This will cost \$39.89 (\$29.99 + \$0.45 · 22), whereas all other plans will cost \$39.99.

[28] This information is available at http://www.consumerreports.org, accessed December 22, 2009.

Table 14.3 Three-part tariff pricing for cellular phone contracts for individuals

Company	Fixed monthly fee	Anytime minutes	Per-minute price for additional minutes
AT&T	$39.99	450	45¢
	$59.99	900	40¢
	$69.99	Unlimited	
Nextel	$29.99	200	45¢
	$39.99	450	45¢
	$59.99	900	40¢
	$99.99	Unlimited[a]	
Sprint	$29.99	200	45¢
	$39.99	450	45¢
	$59.99	900	40¢
	$99.99	Unlimited[a]	
T-Mobile	$39.99	500	45¢
	$49.99	1,000	45¢
	$59.99	Unlimited	
Verizon	$39.99	450	45¢
	$59.99	900	40¢
	$89.99	Unlimited	

Note: Anytime minutes refers to the number of phone minutes that can be used before the per-unit price becomes effective within a month's time. For example, the consumer who chooses AT&T's 450 Anytime Minute Plan can make 450 min of phone calls without incurring an additional charge. Each minute beyond 450 min costs the consumer 45¢ per minute.
Source: https://www2.wirefly.com, accessed May 15, 2010.
[a]Includes unlimited text messaging as well as unlimited phone minutes.

14.2.4   A Theory of Sales or a Mixed Strategy in Price

At the retail level, many department stores and supermarkets use temporary price cuts or sales, to increase demand. Each month, Sears puts a different car battery and set of tires on sale. Best Buy sells hundreds of different models and sizes of televisions and puts a different subset of them on sale for a limited time. Many supermarkets run weekly newspaper ads that list food items that will be on sale during the next 6 days.

We have seen that price competition can push price towards marginal cost and cut firm profits. This begs the questions, why would so many firms compete in price in such a haphazard way? The answer has to do with the fact that consumers do not have complete information about prices and have different values of time. For example, Hamermesh and Lee (2007) found that those with greater incomes have greater time pressure, making it more costly for them to search for low priced goods.

Varian (1980) showed how consumer heterogeneity can motivate firms to offer periodic sales. To illustrate, consider a market with two electronics stores, 1 and 2, that compete in price. They each sell a particular model of television set, and have two price options: a regular price (p_R) and a sale price (p_S). To make this concrete, assume

Fig. 14.9 Competition over
a regular price (p_R) and a sale
price (p_S)

that p_R = \$500 and p_S = \$400. In addition, the unit cost for each firm is \$350, giving
it a unit profit of \$150 when sold for \$500 and a unit profit of \$50 when sold at \$400.

On the demand side, let there be just two types of consumers. The first group of
consumers has a high value of time and makes a purchase as long as the price does
not exceed p_R. These buyers are relatively price insensitive, as they do not shop
around for the lowest price. The second group has a low value of time and is price
sensitive. These are consumers who will spend time shopping for the lowest prices
and will only make a purchase when the television set is on sale. In this example,
we assume that there are 80 high-value consumers who show up randomly at each
store. Thus, each store can expect to sell 40 television sets each period to price-
insensitive buyers. There are 100 low-value customers who seek out the lowest
price and make a purchase only when the good is on sale.

This is a game theoretic setting, because each firm's profit depends on its pricing
actions and the actions of its competitor. When both firms choose a regular price,
they each sell 40 television sets to high-value customers and earn a profit of \$6,000
(the profit margin of \$150 × 40 sets). When one firm offers a sale and the other firm
does not, then the low price firm sells a total of 140 sets (40 to high-value consumers
and 100 to low-value consumers) and earns a profit of \$7,000 (the profit margin of
\$50 × 140). If they both have a sale and assuming that low value customers choose a
store randomly, then each store will sell 90 sets (40 to high value consumers and 50
to low-value customers) and earn a profit of \$4,500 (\$50 × 90).

As you can see from the normal form representation of the game in Fig. 14.9,
where profits are measured in thousands, this game has two pure-strategy Nash
equilibria. These are the asymmetric outcomes where one firm is the low priced
seller and the other firm is the high priced seller. Competition between Wal-Mart
and Target discount stores is consistent with this outcome. Wal-Mart has
established itself as the low-price seller, forcing Target to stick with higher prices.[29]

---

[29] According to Naughton (2002), Wal-Mart is the "Everyday Low Price" king among discount
stores.

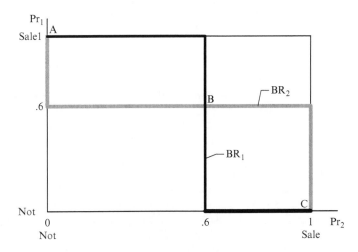

Fig. 14.10 The best-reply equations for two stores that are contemplating a sale price and a regular price

In this section, we are less interested in these pure-strategy outcomes and are more interested in explaining the case where stores vary prices, apparently at random, between regular and sale levels. An outcome such as this is a mixed-strategy Nash equilibrium, where firms choose a sale price with a given probability that exceeds 0 but is less than 1. As we have seen in Chap. 3, we use three steps to find an equilibrium such as this:

1. Firms will compete in probabilities of offering a sale, where $pr_1 \equiv$ probability that firm 1 offers a sale; $pr_2 \equiv$ probability that firm 2 offers a sale.
2. Next, we derive the best-reply equation for firm 1. To do this, we define the firm's expected profit from offering a sale (S) or not a sale (N). The expected profit of firm 1 and strategic choice j (S or N) is $E\pi_{1j}$.

$$E\pi_{1S} = pr_2(6) + (1 - pr_2)(6) = 6,$$

$$E\pi_{1N} = pr_2(7) + (1 - pr_2)(4.5) = 2.5pr_2 + 4.5. \qquad (14.16)$$

This implies that when $pr_2 < 0.6$, $E\pi_{1S} > E\pi_{1N}$ and firm 1 should choose a sale. In other words, firm 1 should choose a sale when firm 2 chooses to offer a sale price with less than a 60% probability. When $pr_2 > 0.6$, $E\pi_{1S} < E\pi_{1N}$ and firm 1 should not choose a sale. When $pr_2 = 0.6$, the expected payoffs are the same so firm 1 is indifferent between a sale and not. This set of strategic options, or firm 1's best response, is plotted as the solid blacked out line in Fig. 14.10 (labeled BR_1).
3. The best reply for firm 2 is calculated in a similar way. Because the problem is symmetric, the analysis is the same as for firm 1. BR_2 is depicted in Fig. 14.10.

All Nash equilibria occur where the best replies intersect, points A, B, and C in Fig. 14.10. We have already identified the pure-strategy Nash equilibria, points A and C, where one firm chooses sale with probability 1 and the other firm chooses sale with probability 0 (the sale and not sale outcome). The mixed-strategy Nash equilibrium occurs at point B, where each firm chooses a sale price with probability 0.6. Notice that this strategy guarantees an expected profit of $6,000 for each firm, the same expected payoff whether it chooses sale or not. This outcome keeps one firm from gaining a competitive advantage over another firm, unlike the Wal-Mart and Target case.

As we saw in Chap. 3, an important feature of this type of game is that it pays each firm to behave unpredictably. In a repeated setting, for example, if firm 2 never offered a sale on Sundays, then firm 1 would always offer a sale on Sundays.[30] This would generate profits of 7 for firm 1 and 6 for firm 2, giving firm 1 the strategic advantage. If firm 2 always chose a sale price on Sunday, firm 2 would have the strategic advantage. One way to avoid giving a strategic advantage to a competitor is to choose a sale price 60% of the time. This guarantees a symmetric outcome and a profit for each firm equal to 6. Sears, Best Buy, and most supermarkets appear to have chosen a defensive strategy such as this.

14.2.5 Price Wars and Wars of Attrition

In Chap. 10, we saw that price competition leads to a competitive outcome when oligopoly firms produce homogeneous goods and play a static game. If firm 1 chooses the monopoly price, a rival can benefit from charging a slightly lower price (price undercutting). Of course, this would lead firm 1 to undercut its rival's price. This process, called a price war, would continue until price equals marginal cost.

In Chap. 11, we saw that the use of a trigger strategy can overturn this outcome when firms play an infinitely repeated game and the value of future dollars is not too heavily discounted. The intuition behind this result is that cheating on a cooperative agreement by undercutting rival prices leads to higher profits today but triggers the punishment of lower prices and profits in the future. With severe enough punishment, cheating is no longer profitable, and firms will cooperate in every period. A price war never occurs.

In reality, of course, cooperative agreements do not last forever, as we saw in Chap. 9. One problem is that price agreements are illegal. Another is that firms do not generally have complete information about rival demand and cost conditions, making it difficult to tell if a price cut is due to cheating or a change in market conditions. For example, Green and Porter (1984) argued that because price cuts are common during a recession, unanticipated economic downturns are more likely to lead to price wars. Alternatively, Rotemberg and Saloner (1986) argued that price

---

[30] A similar argument would apply to consumers. If Sears tires were always on sale on the first week of the month, this information would become common knowledge and consumers would purchase tires only during sale periods.

wars are more likely during periods of unexpected high demand, because the benefits of price undercutting are greatest during a boom period. In any case, there is considerable evidence that temporary price wars do occur.

A classic example occurred in the 1950s when the Anheuser-Busch Brewing Company tried to increase the price of its flagship brand, Budweiser. After a union wage agreement increased the labor costs of all brewers in 1953, Anheuser-Busch raised the price of Budweiser. Although most brewers followed with a price increase of their own, several Midwest brewers (Griesedieck Western, Griesedieck Brothers, and Falstaff) kept their prices constant. In response, Anheuser-Busch punished them by cutting the price of Budweiser by 20%. This punishment phase lasted well over a year, a period when Budweiser's market share in the region more than tripled. Once the punishment phase ended, Anheuser-Busch once again raised the price of Budweiser and rivals responded by matching Anheuser-Busch's price increase.

Anheuser-Busch essentially admitted to these predatory pricing practices during an investigation that the company was violating the Robison-Patman Act (1936). According to the hearing examiner, Anheuser-Busch's price cuts

> were ordered by its president for two admitted reasons: to get business away from its competitors, and to punish them for refusing to increase prices when A.B. [Anheuser-Busch] did so in the fall of 1953. Apparently the lesson was well taught and better learned, because those three St. Louis breweries promptly followed A.B. up with price increases in March 1955….[31]

This is a clear case of noncooperative behavior triggering a price leader to discipline rivals with a substantial price cut.

Although a price war lowers current profits, there are instances when a war is rational. First, as the Anheuser-Busch example implies, it may be necessary to start a price war to discipline a maverick rival and promote greater cooperation in the long run. Second, a firm may be required to fight when a rival starts a price war. Finally, it may be worthwhile to fight if the probability of winning a war that eliminates competitors is high. This case is normally associated with a war of attrition.

In a **generalized war of attrition**, $n = n^* + k$ firms compete in a market that will profitably support only n^* firms in the long run. Thus, if $k > 0$, k firms must exit for the market to reach long-run equilibrium.[32] Firms can be thrust into such a situation, for example, when a technological change increases minimum efficient firm scale. In this setting, each firm can lower its cost by growing in size. The problem is that with a fixed market size, one firm can grow only by stealing customers from another firm. This leads to a dynamic game, where firms battle to survive. To fight such a war, firms will cut price, sometimes below unit cost, and

---

[31] Federal Trade Commission, 277, 281 (1957). For further discussion of this case, see V. Tremblay and C. Tremblay (2005).

[32] For a more complete discussion of a generalized war of attrition, see Bulow and Klemperer (1999).

make other marketing investments in an effort to grow in size and eliminate competitors. The war will continue until $n^* = n$.

The US brewing industry provides one example where a war of attrition has played out.[33] The number of independent beer companies of mass-produced lager, such as Budweiser, Pabst, Miller Lite, and Coors Light, was forced into battle beginning in the 1950s. This is due, at least in part, to changes in technology that made large scale brewing and marketing more profitable. This pushed firms into a war of attrition that caused the number of companies to decline from 476 in 1945 to about 19 firms today. The war not only led to tough price competition but also led to increased advertising spending and brand proliferation, topics that are covered in other chapters. The "beer wars" are discussed in more detail in Chap. 21.

14.3   Other Marketing Strategies

In this section, we show how firms have found clever ways to extract as much consumer surplus from consumers as possible. Based on personal experience and evidence from behavioral economics that we discussed in Chap. 4, we know that consumer behavior is not always fully rational. As a result, we are interested in analyzing how firms exploit the cognitive weaknesses of consumers to their advantage.[34]

14.3.1   Marketing with Framing and Anchoring Effects

We see evidence of this every day in the way in which businesses present their offers to consumers. Because individual decisions can be influenced by irrelevant information and by how various options are presented or framed, businesses present an offer to consumers in a way that is most beneficial to the firm.

---

[33] For a more complete discussion of the war of attrition in brewing, see V. Tremblay and C. Tremblay (2007) and Iwasaki et al. (2008). This discussion ignores the growth in numbers of the microbreweries, as they produce darker lagers and ales that compete with imports more than the light lagers produce by the mass-producing brewers. See V. Tremblay and C. Tremblay (2005) for more discussion of the microbrewery movement.

[34] In these examples, firms do not engage in blatant deception and dishonesty. Instead, their primary goal is to exploit our inherent weaknesses. See Lindsey-Mullikin and Petty (2011) for a list of firm pricing strategies and rewards promises that are more deceptive in nature. Deception and puffing, especially associated with advertising, will be discussed in more detail in later chapters.

For example, behavioral economics shows that people are more receptive to an offer when presented in a positive light. This causes firms to market their brands in the most positive way possible, short of making illegal claims. Marketing divisions at major corporations spend a considerable amount of money to design persuasive packaging and brand slogans. They also invest heavily in advertising campaigns that tout the benefits and downplay (ignore) the weaknesses associated with their product. Consumer aversion to the negative also explains why firms rarely run negative ads that disparage rival brands. With the possible exception of a new entrant, the evidence shows that negative advertisements are generally poorly received by consumers and can hurt the reputation of the entire industry, not just rivals.[35]

Another factor is that many people make decisions based on relative rather than absolute net benefits. For example, assume that you visit a mall and plan to buy a pair of shoes that has a retail price $100 and a new mystery novel that has a retail price of $30. You face two different options:

1. The shoes are not on sale, but the bookstore salesperson informs you that the book you want is on sale for $12 at its other store, which is 15 min away. Would you drive 30 min round trip to buy the book at a 60% discount?
2. The book is not on sale, but the shoe store salesperson informs you that the shoes you want are on sale for $80 at its other store, which is 15 min away. Would you drive 30 min round trip to buy the shoes at a 20% discount?

If you could take advantage of only one of these options, which would you choose? From an objective point of view, these options are identical, as each saves you $20 by driving 30 min.[36] However, most people base their decision on the relative percentage drop in price. Because you save 60% on the book and only 20% on the shoes, some people will say yes to option 1 and no to option 2. This may explain why local retailers advertise a sale to distant locations only when the percentage decrease in price is substantial, regardless of the absolute dollar saving. Given this tendency, the shoe store might frame its offer to distant customers that a 30 min drive will save them $20, enough to cover gas and lunch.

Consumer choice is also influenced by spurious information due to anchoring effects. To illustrate, assume that you want to buy a new laptop computer over the Internet and the seller is considering the use of one of the following options:

1. A laptop with a standard configuration that has 16 GB of memory costs $1,000. To upgrade to 20 GB will cost an additional $200.

---

[35] Another concern is that if firm 1 runs negative ads about firm 2, firm 2 will run negative ads about firm 1, which is bad for the industry as a whole. For further discussion of these issues, see Wilson (1976), McAfee (2002, 114), and del Barrio-Garcia and Luque-Martinez (2003).

[36] For example, would you spend an hour of your time in exchange for a free package of gum, a 100% discount?

2. A laptop with a standard configuration that has 20 GB of memory costs $1,200. To downgrade to 16 GB will save $200.

It turns out that most consumers will choose the default option. That is, when presented with the first offer, most consumers choose the 16 GB memory; when presented with the second offer, most consumers choose the 20 GB memory. Thus, the firm's Web page will market laptops using the default option that is most profitable.

14.3.2   Bundling and Tying Contracts

A strategy used by some multiproduct producers is to tie the sale of one product to the sale of another. A tie-in sale or bundling occurs when a firm requires consumers to buy two or more goods together as a packaged deal. When the only option is the packaged deal, this is called **pure bundling**. When consumers have the option of purchasing items separately or packaged together, this is called **mixed bundling**. A **tying contract** is normally associated a durable good that uses a complementary input that is purchased in variable proportions. For example, a manufacturer of canning machines may require the following contract from a soft drink company: to buy our canning machine, you must also buy our cans for the life of the machine. In this section, our goals are to understand the motivation for these practices and their social implications.

14.3.2.1   Pure Bundling

A famous example of pure bundling occurred in the golden years of the motion picture industry when the major movie studios bundled high and low quality films to local movie theaters.[37] To receive the blockbuster, the theater also had to show the low budget film. Today, many local restaurants offer you a selection of entrées but no choice of vegetables that come with it. Another example is Microsoft's requirement that consumers purchase its word processing (MS-Word) and spreadsheet (Excel) software together in a bundle.

One reason for bundling is that it can be cost effective. For example, automobiles with certain trim levels come with just one type engine. This can lower the cost of production when there are economies of scale, as more consumer options mean smaller scale production of any one trim level of automobile. The same holds true for running shoes, where the upper part of a shoe is sold with a single style of sole. This makes it impossible to mix soles and uppers but lowers the average cost of producing running shoes.

---

[37] For a more complete discussion, see Stigler (1968, Chap. 15).

Table 14.4 Consumer valuation of spreadsheet and word processing programs

| | Consumer valuation | | |
Consumer	Spreadsheet	Word processing	Both
A	100	0	100
B	40	60	100
C	0	100	100

Each consumer's marginal valuation is measured in dollars

Another reason why firms use bundling is to extract surplus from consumers. To illustrate, consider a monopoly firm that sells two goods, 1 and 2, and is contemplating selling them separately or as a bundle. The firm wants to know if bundling is more profitable. It turns out that this is the case when the firm cannot price discriminate and the demand value of the two goods is negatively correlated among consumers. That is, some consumers place a relatively high value on good 1, while others place a relatively high value on good 2.

As a concrete example, consider Microsoft's problem of selling spreadsheet (S) and word processing (WP) software. To simply the calculations, we assume that costs are zero. There are three consumers, A, B, and C, who have different preferences, as described in Table 14.4. The numbers in the table represent each consumer's marginal valuation (or demand price), measured in dollars, of purchasing spreadsheet, word processing, or both software packages. Consumer A places a relatively high value on S, while consumer C places a relatively high value on WP. Consumer B places a medium value on S and WP. However, they each have a value of 100 when S and WP are bundled.

The firm will choose to bundle only if it is more profitable. When marketing S and WP separately, the monopoly firm will choose prices to convert the most consumer surplus to profit (which is total revenue in this case):

- Regarding software: When the price equals 100, the monopolist can sell 1 unit for a profit of 100. When the price is 40, sales are 2 units for a profit of 80. When the price is 0, sales are 3 units but profit is 0. The optimal price of software is 100.[38]
- Regarding word processing: When the price is 100, sales are 1 for a profit of 100. When the price is 60, sales are 2 units for a profit of 120. When the price is 0, sales are 3 for a profit of 0. The optimal price is 60.

Thus, the firm will set the price of software at 100, set the price of word processing at 60, and earn a total profit of 220.

Next, we consider the case of bundling. Now the valuation of the bundled good is 100 for each consumer. Thus, the firm will set a price of 100 for the bundled good. At this price, the firm will sell 3 units for a total profit of 300. Clearly, it pays the firm to offer the bundled good.

---

[38] Note that any other price option will earn the firm less profit. For example, sales are 0 at a price above 100. At a price of 39, 2 units will be sold for a profit of 78.

Table 14.5 Mixed bundling at McDonald's

Entrée	Prices			Savings	
	Individual item	Unbundled	Bundled[a]	Dollars	Percent
Big Mac	$3.55	$6.30	$5.80	$0.50	7.9
Quarter Pounder with Cheese	$3.75	$6.50	$6.00	$0.50	7.7
Grilled Chicken Classic	$4.10	$6.85	$6.35	$0.50	7.3
Chicken McNuggets (ten pieces)	$4.10	$6.85	$6.35	$0.50	7.3
Filet-O-Fish	$3.15	$5.90	$5.40	$0.50	8.5

[a]The bundled price is for a value meal, which includes an entrée, medium fries ($1.75 when purchased separately), and a medium soft drink ($1.00 when purchased separately). Prices are from a McDonald's franchise in Corvallis, OR, summer of 2010

The reason why bundling is so effective at converting consumer surplus to profit is that it eliminates the (negatively correlated) variation in consumer valuations. In this example, bundling allows the firm to charge a price that extracts all possible consumer surplus from every consumer. Although this is the result of the particular numbers chosen in this example, it demonstrates that bundling can increase producer profit.[39]

14.3.2.2   Mixed Bundling

Many firms use mixed bundling by offering consumers the option of buying a bundle or the products individually. This is a common practice at most fast-food restaurants. McDonald's customers have the option of buying a "value meal," such as a Big Mac, medium fries, and a medium drink for $5.80. Purchased separately, they would cost $6.30 (a Big Mac is priced at $3.55, medium fries at $1.75, and a medium drink is at $1.00). Table 14.5 provides a list of several value meal options and shows that the price of a value meal is approximately 7–9% cheaper than the sum of the individual prices when purchased separately.

It is easy to see why a firm may choose a mixed bundling strategy. Consider once again the Microsoft example described in Table 14.4. This time, let the cost of producing an individual spreadsheet or word processing program be $20 each. In this case, if the monopolist were to sell only the bundle, the price would remain the same at $100 but profits would fall to $180 (because total cost is $20 × 6 units). Notice that selling the bundle to consumer C is inefficient because the spreadsheet costs $20 to produce but C receives no value from it. The same problem applies to consumer A and the word processing program. In this case, consumer surplus is 0 and total surplus is $180.

---

[39] For a discussion of additional cases where bundling increases firm profits, besides when consumers have negatively correlated demand functions, see McAfee et al. (1989).

The firm can earn a greater profit and this inefficiency can be eliminated if the firm offers software for sale separately and as a bundle. For example, assume that the firm sells each individual program for $90 and the bundle for $100. In this case, consumer A will purchase the spreadsheet only, which earns $70 in profit; consumer B will purchase the bundle, which earns $60 in profit; consumer C buys the word processing program only, which earns $70 in profit. Total profit is now $200, and the firm is clearly better off with the mixed bundling strategy. This example highlights the fact that pure bundling is more likely for products with very low unit costs.

This example also shows how mixed bundling can be more socially efficient than pure bundling when unit costs are high. With pure bundling, consumer surplus is 0, total profit is $180, and total surplus is $180. With mixed bundling, consumer surplus is $20 ($10 each for consumers A and B), total profit is $200, and total surplus is $220.

14.3.2.3 Tying Contracts

A classic example of a tying arrangement occurred decades ago when IBM leased its computers only to customers who agreed to use IBM computer punch cards.[40] Before scanners and data storage devices were available, data were stored on paper cards and read by mechanical data processing devices. IBM contended that quality control was the reason for this requirement, as faulty cards would cause processing errors. For similar reasons, Xerox tied its copying paper to its copy machines in the 1970s, and McDonald's requires its franchises to purchase all raw food ingredients from accepted McDonald's suppliers.

In addition to quality control, firms may use a tying contract as a means of identifying high-value customers. To illustrate, consider a monopoly supplier of a computer printer that ties the sale of its printer to the sale of the company's ink cartridges. The firm enforces this agreement by threatening to void the warranty for customers who fail to comply. In most cases, the intensity of use distinguishes low from high valuation customers. Under these circumstances, the firm may want to set a competitive price for the printer and a high price for the print cartridge. This increases the number of printers sold and extracts greater rents from high use customers. Much like perfect price discrimination, it also converts more consumer surplus into profit. Thus, tying contracts may promote efficiency but lower consumer surplus.

Because of their exclusionary nature, however, tying contracts may also have anticompetitive effects. In our computer printer example above, there may be several potential suppliers of ink cartridges, but a tying contract makes it impossible for these potential suppliers to successfully enter the market. Thus, the monopolist can use a tying contract to extend its market power in the printer market to the market for ink cartridges. As a result, there may be grounds for making tying contracts illegal, as we will see in Chap. 20.

---

[40] *International Business Machines Corp. v. U.S.*, 298 U.S. 131, 139-140 (1936).

14.3.3 Marketing to Overconfident Consumers

As we discussed in Chap. 4, evidence from behavioral economics shows that most people are overconfident about their abilities relative to the general population.[41] For example, Weinstein (1980) found that most college students are extremely unrealistic about future life events, such as expected income, graduating in the top third of their class, and living past 80 years of age. Svenson (1981) found that 82% of young adults felt that they ranked among the top 30% in terms of driving ability. Camerer (1997) notes that this overconfidence persists even among drivers who have suffered a serious car accident.

Overconfidence can also plague business. Cooper et al. (1988) found that over 80% of business owners assessed the probability of their own success at 70%, even though they thought that less than 40% of like competitors would survive. In reality, most new businesses exit the market rather quickly. In US manufacturing, Dunne et al. (1988) found that 61.5% of entrants exited within 5 years and 79.6% exited within 10 years.

For many people this is more than just a positive outlook, which has its advantages, but more of an unrealistic optimism. This can be a problem if it induces people to engage in risky behavior which increases vulnerability to car accidents, preventable diseases, criminal victimization, and financial ruin. The question we wish to ask here is how do firms take advantage of consumer overconfidence?

Businesses are well aware that some people are excessively overconfident and have used clever sales tactics to exploit them. For example, sales people in the timeshare industry have been known to lure in potential customers by offering gifts and prizes in exchange for sitting through a lengthy, high pressure sales pitch. Overconfident individuals are more likely to accept such an offer and make decisions that they will later regret. In response to numerous complaints, many states now require a cooling-off period. This gives a consumer several days to cancel a timeshare contract without cause. Similar problems exist in the housing market. Shiller (2005) found that many Americans continue to be overconfident that housing prices will rise even in the face of market turmoil. Real estate agents can use this to pressure overconfident consumers to buy homes that need not be good investments.

Grubb (2009) provides strong evidence that consumer overconfidence motivated cell phone companies to adopt the three-part tariff pricing menu that was described in the previous section. To see why, we use a simple version of Grubb's model. There is a monopoly firm that has 0 costs. The firm faces two pricing options: (1) simple linear pricing and (2) a three-part tariff. If we look at each pricing option separately, optimal pricing policies are as follows:

- With linear pricing, the optimal price is $0.11 per min.
- With a three-part tariff, the consumer faces two options, a monthly 500 min plan and a monthly 1,000 min plan. A consumer's total expenditures on the 500 min

---

[41] For a review of the evidence, see Camerer and Lovallo (1999), Rabin and Schrag (1999), Camerer et al. (2005), and Grubb (2009).

Table 14.6 Total expenditures for fictitious cell phone company with a 500 min plan and a 1,000 min plan

| Minutes | Total expenditure | | |
	Linear pricing ($0.11/min)	500 min plan	1,000 min plan
200	$22 (0.11 · 200)	$40	$60
300	$33 (0.11 · 300)	$40	$60
400	$44 (0.11 · 400)	$40	$60
500	$55 (0.11 · 500)	$40	$60
600	$66 (0.11 · 600)	$60 (40 + 0.2 · 100)	$60
700	$77 (0.11 · 700)	$80 (40 + 0.2 · 200)	$60
800	$88 (0.11 · 800)	$100 (40 + 0.2 · 300)	$60
900	$99 (0.11 · 900)	$120 (40 + 0.2 · 400)	$60
1,000	$110 (0.11 · 1,000)	$140 (40 + 0.2 · 500)	$60
1,100	$121 (0.11 · 1,100)	$160 (40 + 0.2 · 500)	$70 (60 + 0.1 · 100)

With this three-part tariff, the cost of the 500 min plan is $40 for the first 500 min and the $0.20 for each additional minute. For the 1,000 min plan, the cost is $60 for the first 1,000 min and $0.10 for each additional minute

plan (TE_{500}) are $40 for the first 500 min and $0.20 for each additional minute. With the 1,000 min plan, total expenditures ($TE_{1,000}$) are $60 for the first 1,000 min and $0.10 for each additional minute. That is,

$$TE_{500} = \begin{cases} \$40 & \text{if } m \leq 500 \\ \$40 + \$0.20x & \text{if } m > 500 \end{cases}, \tag{14.17}$$

$$TE_{1,000} = \begin{cases} \$60 & \text{if } m \leq 1,000 \\ \$60 + \$0.10x & \text{if } m > 1,000 \end{cases},$$

where m is the number of minutes spent on the phone and x is the number of minutes in excess of 500 and 1,000 respectively. To illustrate, several examples are listed in Table 14.6.

Grubb finds that consumer overconfidence in the cell phone market is due to persistent underestimation of the variance in the demand for cell phone minutes.[42] Assume that there is just one consumer who plans to spend 500 min on the phone. Initially, we assume a zero variance. Later we will assume variability in consumer demand.

---

[42] In a *Consumer Reports* (2011a, b) survey, 20% of consumers received an unexpected charge on their cell phone bill.

To determine the firm's optimal pricing strategy, we must compare the firm's profits from each option. We begin with the case where there is zero variance in consumer demand and there is a single consumer who does not suffer from overconfidence:

- With linear pricing the consumer's total expenditure, which is also firm profit (given our 0 cost assumption), is $55 ($0.11 × 500 min).
- With a three-part tariff, the consumer's total expenditure (firm profit) is $40 for the 500 min plan and $60 for the 1,000 min plan.

If given the option, the consumer will choose the 500 min plan. Thus, the firm will earn higher profit with linear pricing, and only a linear pricing scheme will be offered by the firm.

Next, we consider the case where there is variation in consumer minutes but no overconfidence. For example, assume that the consumer knows that there is a 50/50 chance that the minutes used will be either 400 or 600

- With linear pricing, expected total expenditures (profits) are $55 = 0.5 ($0.11 · 400) + 0.5($0.11 · 600).
- With the 500 min plan, expected total expenditures are $50 = 0.5($40) + 0.5 (40 + 0.2 · 100).
- With the 1,000 min plan, expected total expenditures are $60 = 0.5($60) + 0.5 ($60).

Given these options, the consumer will choose the 500 min plan. Thus, linear pricing remains the most profitable and that is the only option the firm will offer.

Finally, we consider the case where the consumer is overconfident in his or her ability to predict the variance in use. In this case, the consumer underestimates the variance, believing that there is a 50/50 chance of using 400 or 600 min when the correct numbers are 300 and 700 min. Because the consumer believes that only 400 or 600 min will be used, the consumer believes that the 500 min plan will cost $50 as before. In reality, with 300–700 min, the following is true:

- With linear pricing, expected total expenditures (profits) are $55 = 0.5 ($0.11 · 300) + 0.5($0.11 · 700).
- With the 500 min plan, expected total expenditures are $60 = 0.5($40) + 0.5 (40 + 0.2 · 100).
- With the 1,000 min plan, expected total expenditures are $60 = 0.5($60) + 0.5 ($60).

The overconfident consumer believes that the 500 min plan is optimal. Because the 500 min plan now earns the firm $60, the firm will prefer the three-part tariff.[43]

---

[43] This begs the question of how firms know that many consumers underestimate their variance of use. Because a considerable amount of money is at stake, cell phone companies hire economists to estimate consumer demand. They have also learned from trial and error.

Similarly, we can motivate the 1,000 min plan with an additional overconfident consumer who expects to use 1,000 min on average.

In this example, consumer overconfidence benefits the producer at the expense of the consumer. In effect, overconfident consumers deceive themselves into choosing a plan that is not in their best interest. Of course, consumers who do not suffer from this flaw will make the correct choice and be better off than those who are overconfident. In any case, concerns with this pricing policy have led the Federal Communications Commission to propose legislation that will require cell phone companies to inform consumers when they approach their monthly limit (*Consumer Reports* 2011a, b).

14.3.4 Thirty-Day Free Trials and the Endowment Effect

Another behavioral issue is buyer's remorse. We have all made a purchase based more on emotion than reason, and such a purchase can lead to buyer's remorse or regret after making a purchase. This can be especially problematic for expensive items such as a computer or an automobile, because the cost of making a poor decision is relatively high. This is certainly bad for business, as thoughtful consumers who fear buyer's remorse may delay purchase or avoid making a major purchase altogether.

Firms have devised a number of techniques to combat this problem, such as exchange programs and guarantees. The 30-day money back guarantee is especially ingenious. First, it alleviates consumer concern with buyer's remorse, which increases current sales. Second, it takes advantage of the endowment effect. Recall from Chap. 4 that individuals who suffer from an endowment effect have a higher value of a good once it is in their possession. This reduces the likelihood that the good will be returned.

As a result, many companies make 30-day offers. A well-known example is the Oreck Corporation, which produces Oreck vacuum cleaners. According to their Web page, here is the Oreck 30-day guarantee offer[44]:

1. Purchase an Oreck.
2. Try it in your own home, on your toughest cleaning problems.
3. If you are not completely satisfied, return the Oreck product for a full refund. We will even pay return shipping costs, so there is no risk to you.

Thirty-day free trials are much more common among software providers, such as Adobe, Microsoft, and Norton. Software is a better candidate for free trials than are hard line goods, because it can be easily disabled after 30 days and a lost sale costs the company very little because there is nothing to return.

---

[44] See http://www.oreck.com/customer-service/30-day-risk-free-trial.cfm, accessed May 27, 2010.

To summarize, this section provides a description of some of the important marketing strategies used by firms with market power. They are designed to convert consumer surplus into producer surplus and frequently exploit our cognitive and emotional weaknesses.

14.4   Summary

1. **Price discrimination** occurs when a firm charges different consumers different prices for the same product and the difference in price does not reflect a difference in marginal cost. For price discrimination to be effective, the firm must have market power and there must be some way to deter arbitrage.
2. With **first-degree or perfect price discrimination**, each consumer is charged his or her demand price, i.e., the maximum price he or she is willing to pay. Because this requires that the firm have complete information about consumer preferences, it is not encountered in the real world. The model is still useful, because it provides insight into how price discrimination converts consumer surplus into producer surplus.
3. A linear pricing policy means that a firm charges consumers the same unit price, regardless of how much is purchased. With **second-degree or nonlinear price discrimination**, different prices are charged for different quantities sold, but each consumer faces the same price schedule. A quantity discount is one example of nonlinear pricing. Such offers get around the information problem associated with perfect price discrimination. That is, compared to linear pricing, a properly defined price menu will cause consumers to self-select into a price–quantity package that extracts more consumer surplus from them. More consumer surplus is converted to producer surplus, but not as effectively as with perfect price discrimination.
4. **Third-degree or segmented price discrimination** occurs when a monopolist segments consumers into groups and charges a different price to each group. There are many examples of this form of price discrimination, where firms discriminate according to age or gender, for example. For it to be profit maximizing for the firm to engage in segmented price discrimination, the price elasticity of demand must differ by group.
5. The welfare implications of price discrimination are not always clear. A perfect price discriminating monopolist produces the competitive level of output and converts all consumer surplus to producer surplus. Thus, this outcome is allocatively efficient but may be inequitable. With both second- and third-degree price discrimination, firm profits cannot decrease. In general, price discrimination can increase or decrease total surplus, depending upon how it affects total consumption.
6. Price discrimination can occur in oligopoly as well as monopoly markets. In fact, the evidence shows that the degree of price dispersion is greater in an oligopoly setting. In the airline industry where price discrimination abounds, for example,

competition lowers the fares for low valuation consumers, while fares remain high for consumers who have greater brand loyalty.
7. There are other pricing strategies that have their own unique features and motivations:

(a) **Damaged Goods and Quality-Dependent Pricing**: Firms may offer a high and a low quality brand of the same basic good, where the quality difference may be real or subjective. When some consumers prefer high status goods, it may be profitable for a firm to market two goods of like quality, one high status good and another low status good. Another strategy used by firms is to produce a single good of high quality and then damage a fraction of them to create a low quality counterpart. Even though the damaged good is more costly to produce, a firm may be able to earn higher profit by selling the damaged good at a discount and the high quality good for a price premium. This is a form of price discrimination that allows the firm to take advantage of economies of scale in production, cheaply create a low quality brand, and extract greater surplus from consumers with different preferences.

(b) **Two-Part Tariffs**: With a two-part tariff, a firm charges consumers a fixed fee plus a unit price. With a single consumer or many consumers with identical tastes, the optimal firm strategy is to set price equal to marginal cost and the fee equal to consumer surplus. This converts all consumer surplus to producer surplus, as with perfect price discrimination. With heterogeneous consumers, the unit price will be higher and the fixed fee lower. This still converts some consumer surplus to producer surplus, but consumer surplus will be positive in this case.

(c) **Mixed Pricing or a Theory of Sales**: At the retail level, firms frequently use sales, temporary price cuts, to increase demand. Over time, prices vacillate from high to low, low to high, etc. This provides an important example of a mixed-strategy, as discussed by Nash (1950), where it pays each player to behave unpredictably. In this case, firms set sale prices in ways that cannot be predicted by consumers or competitors, a strategy that allows firms to charge a higher average price to consumers who do not pay attention to sale information.

(d) **Price Wars and Wars of Attrition**: Undercutting a competitor's price can be beneficial in the short term, as it steals rival customers. In the long run, it can be quite damaging to producers if it leads to a price war that is associated with the Bertrand Paradox (see Chap. 10). When a technological change reduces the efficient number of firms below the actual number of firms, this produces a **war of attrition**. In such a war, each firm will cut price and make other marketing investments in order to gain market share and survive. The war will continue until a sufficient number of firms exit the market, such that the actual number equals the efficient number of firms.

Each of these pricing strategies is designed to convert consumer surplus into producer surplus.

8. Firms with market power compete on a variety of dimensions besides price. These actions are designed to increase profit and exploit the personality weaknesses that many of us have. Important examples include the following:

(a) Framing effects influence the marketing practices and advertising campaigns we see today. Ads typically focus on the positive and communicate discounts in relative rather than absolute savings because this is a more effective way of increasing sales, *ceteris paribus*.

(b) Many multiproduct producers require customers to buy a package of two or more products. When this is the only option, this is called **pure bundling**. When consumers have the choice of buying the bundle or buying products separately, this is called **mixed bundling**. A **tying contract** is normally associated with a durable good, such as a computer printer, that uses a complementary input, such as a printer ink cartridge. With a tying contract, to buy a firm's printer the consumer must agree to buy the firm's printer cartridge.

(c) Many people are overconfident, and firms have found ways to use consumer overconfidence to their advantage. Both the timeshare and real estate markets exploit consumer overconfidence to increase sales. The evidence also shows that cell phone companies offer three-part tariffs because some consumers underestimate the number of minutes or the variance in use of a cell phone.

(d) To avoid potential buyer's remorse, many firms offer liberal exchange programs and money back guarantees. For example, 30-day free trials are particularly common in the computer software industry, given the low marginal cost associated with software production. These programs can be effective at alleviating buyer's remorse given people's propensity to place a higher value on a good in their possession, the endowment effect. Thus, profits increase because fewer goods are returned.

These are just a few of the nonprice strategies that firms with market power use to increase profits. Others will be discussed in the next chapter.

14.5   Review Questions

1. Why is it the case that ski resorts charge a lower lift-ticket price for children than for adults but charge a single price for soft drinks and hamburgers?
2. Assume that a monopoly firm faces a linear inverse demand function and has a positively sloped marginal cost function. If the firm can perfectly price discriminate:

   A. What will be the firm's profit-maximizing pricing strategy and the market level of output?
   B. Identify consumer and producer surplus.
   C. What will be the lowest price that the firm will charge?
   D. Explain why this outcome is allocatively efficient.

3. Why do electric power companies typically practice peak-load pricing? Assuming an unregulated firm, would you expect this practice to improve overall efficiency?

4. Consider the ski resort problem described in Fig. 14.5. If the firm charges a single price but marginal cost is 0, will it still be true that only adults will ski at this price? Explain.

5. Assume that there are two geographic markets (A and B) for maid service. The average and marginal cost of production is 3 in each market, and the inverse demand functions are

$$p_A = 15 - Q_A$$

$$p_B = 12 - Q_B$$

   A. Calculate the optimal (profit-maximizing) prices and output levels if two separate monopolists supply these services to the two geographic markets.

   B. What would be the optimal prices and output levels if a single monopolist supplied maid service to both markets and could successfully price discriminate?

   C. How do your answers in questions A and B compare to the socially optimal price and output levels?

   D. How would your answer to parts A and B change if the marginal cost of production were $2Q_i$, for i equal to market A or B? In part B, assume the firm must use a single production plant.

6. Assume that a monopolist can successfully separate two geographic markets (A and B). The average and marginal cost of production is 3 in both markets, and the inverse demand functions are

$$p_A = 15 - Q_A$$

$$p_B = 15 - 2Q_B$$

   A. What are the optimal (profit-maximizing) prices and output levels if the firm can successfully price discriminate?

   B. Why are the optimal prices the same?

7. Explain why the behavioral weaknesses of consumers may induce firms to give away free samples of addictive commodities (e.g., heroin, cigarettes, and cookies).

8. A monopoly cell phone company is considering two pricing options. The first is linear pricing where the price is $0.20 per minute and consumer total monthly expenditures (TE) are $TE_1 = 0.2 \cdot m$, where m is the number of minutes spent on the phone. The second is a three-part pricing scheme, where total monthly expenditures are

$$TE_2 = \begin{cases} \$30 & \text{if } m \leq 200 \\ \$30 + \$1x & \text{if } m > 200 \end{cases},$$

where x is the number of minutes in excess of 200. Production costs are set to zero for simplicity.

A. Graph the total expenditures equations for each plan.
B. What would be the optimal pricing scheme from the firm's perspective if the average consumer makes 150 min of phone calls each month?
C. What would be the optimal pricing scheme from the firm's perspective if the average consumer makes 250 min of phone calls each month?
D. Explain how the presence of overconfident consumers may affect the firm's pricing decision.

9. A monopoly ski resort has several pricing options.

A. One option is to offer discount coupons to local residents. For this to be profitable, what must be true about the price elasticity of demand for local and distant customers?
B. If the resort is able to perfectly price discriminate, describe the optimum price and output.
C. Under what conditions will a two-part tariff produce the same outcome as the outcome described in problem B for perfect price discrimination?

10. Assume that a monopolist produces two software programs, one to solve math problems (M) and the other to solve statistics problems (S). There are only three consumers (A, B, and C) who are interested in them. Their preferences are as follows:

(i)   Consumer A values M at $50 and S at $30.
(ii) Consumer B values M at $80 and S at $40.
(iii) Consumer C values M at $100 and S at $50.

A. Are demand values among consumers negatively or positively correlated?
B. If the firm's average and marginal cost is 0, will it pay to sell M and S separately or as a pure bundle?
C. How would your answer to part B change if consumer demand values were negatively correlated?

11. Your local supermarket sells cans of soup at a 20% discount on the Tuesday of every week. Explain why this may not be an optimal strategy from the supermarket's perspective in terms of how it is likely to affect consumer behavior and competitor behavior.

12. A price war can be very expensive and cut into firm profits. Identify three strategies from Chap. 9 that might be used to avoid a price war (or tough price competition).

13. Explain how firms with market power can exploit consumers who are overconfident. Would your answer change if all markets were perfectly competitive?

14. Given the endowment effect, many but not all firms offer 30-day free trials of their products. Under what conditions can this be an effective strategy? What types of product characteristics would make this policy impractical?

15. Explain how grocery stores and credit card companies exploit consumer problems with impulsivity.

Chapter 15
Advertising

In consumer goods markets, advertising is almost as important as price competition.[1] Every day firms bombard us with ads on television, radio, newspapers, billboards, and the Internet. A concern raised by critics is the amount of money spent on advertising. In the USA, for example, $280 billion dollars was spent on advertising in 2007. This amounts to about 2% of gross domestic product (GDP), money that could have been spent in other ways. Figure 15.1 plots annual advertising spending as a ratio of GDP from 1919 to 2007. The advertising/GDP ratio fluctuates over time but has hovered around 2% since the end of World War II.[2]

Firms invest their advertising dollars in a variety of media. In 2007, the average firm spent over 40% of its marketing dollars on television advertising and only about 4% on outdoor ads (see Table 15.1). Television advertising has become the dominant medium and has gained share since 1965, primarily at the expense of newspaper and radio advertising. In the last decade, the Internet has become increasingly important. While the share of Internet advertising was less than 1% in 1997, it reached almost 14% in 2009 and is expected to exceed 20% by 2012 according to a leading advertising trade journal, *Advertising Age* (2010).[3]

Investment in advertising varies considerably across industries. Table 15.2 lists the intensity of advertising spending for a sample of industries for 2007. As is common practice in business, we measure advertising intensity as the advertising-to-sales ratio (advertising expenditures divided by total revenue). To put these

---

[1] Although the focus of this chapter is on advertising, the basic theories and models also apply to other marketing activities such as the firm's decision to offer discount coupons and free samples. Much of the discussion in this chapter borrows from Bagwell's (2007) excellent survey on the economics of advertising.

[2] Firms in other countries also spend a great deal of money on advertising. For example, 1.2% of GDP was spent on advertising in Japan in 2005 (*2005 Advertising Expenditures in Japan*).

[3] The data and forecasts derive from *Advertising Age* (http://www.advertisingage.com), Coan (1999) and Bernoff (2009). Coan (1999), and Bernoff (2009) expected Internet ads to reach a 20% share by 2014.

V.J. Tremblay and C.H. Tremblay, *New Perspectives on Industrial Organization*, Springer Texts in Business and Economics, DOI 10.1007/978-1-4614-3241-8_15, © Springer Science+Business Media New York 2012

Fig. 15.1 US advertising expenditures as a percent of GDP: 1919–2007

Table 15.1 US advertising expenditures by major media in 1965 and 2007

Medium	Billions of dollars (percent)		Percentage change in share
	1965	2007	
Television[a]	0.2515 (27.1)	64.43 (43.2)	59.3
Magazines	0.1199 (12.9)	30.33 (20.4)	57.3
Newspapers	0.4457 (48.1)	28.22 (18.9)	−60.6
Internet	0	11.31 (7.6)	−
Radio	0.0917 (1.0)	10.69 (7.2)	−27.5
Outdoor	0.0180 (0.2)	4.02 (2.7)	38.9

Sources: 1965 data from Scherer (1980); 2007 data from *Advertising Age* Web site at http://adage.com/datacenter
[a]In 1965, television advertising includes $0.1237 billion for network, $0.0412 billion for local, and $0.0866 billion for spot television advertising. In 2007, television advertising includes 25.42 for network, 18.02 for cable, 16.82 for local (spot), and 4.17 for syndicated television advertising.

numbers into perspective, Bain (1959) calls advertising "significant" and "substantial" when the intensity of advertising exceeds 5% percent. In general, the leading advertisers include those that market their products to consumers using television and radio advertising. These include liquor, cosmetics, athletic footwear, toys, and soap and detergent. Cigarette producers, once among the leading national advertisers, advertise very little today because government regulations have outlawed cigarette advertising from television and radio since 1971 and from some other media outlets since 1999 (Chaloupka 2007).

Table 15.2 Advertising-to-sales ratios for a sample of US industries, 2007

Industry	Advertising as a percent of sales
Liquor	15.6
Perfume and cosmetics	13.7
Footwear (rubber and plastic)	11.9
Book publishing and printing	11.7
Games and toys	10.7
TV broadcast stations	10.6
Cleaning and polishing preparations	10.4
Food and related products	10.0
Malt beverages (beer)	9.5
Watches and clocks	9.3
Soap and detergent	9.1
Furniture stores	8.5
Jewelry stores	8.5
Motion picture production	8.4
Cable and other pay TV services	7.4
Beverages	7.3
Household audio and video equipment	5.3
Household furniture	5.2
Apparel	5.1
Video rental	4.9
Pharmaceuticals	4.4
Footwear (except rubber)	3.8
Retail stores	3.7
Wine and brandy	3.6
Motor vehicles	2.5
Cigarettes	2.2
Tires	2.1
Paints and varnishes	1.5
Motorcycles and bicycles	1.3
Life insurance	1.2
Grocery stores	0.9
Lumber and wood products	0.6
Cement	0.5
Construction machinery	0.2
Industrial materials	0.1

Source: *Advertising Age* Web site at http://adage.com/datacenter

Advertising intensity not only varies across industries but also across firms within the same industry. One example is the automobile industry. Table 15.3 lists advertising and market share data for the leading automobile companies that supplied cars to the USA in 2007. In general, large car producers spend more on advertising than small car producers. After controlling for size, however, there is still considerable variation in the intensity of advertising spending. In this case, we define advertising intensity as the ratio of advertising to market share. This measures the amount of money a firm spends on advertising for a single market

Table 15.3 Advertising and market share data from the US automobile industry, 2007

Company	Advertising (millions of dollars)	Market share (percent)	Advertising/market share
GM	3,010.1	23.8	126.5
Ford	2,525.2	16.5	153.0
Toyota	1,757.9	17.2	102.2
Chrysler	1,739.4	12.8	135.9
Nissan	1,422.9	6.0	237.2
Honda	1,326.5	9.3	142.6
Hyundai	650.9	4.6	141.5

Sources: *Advertising Age* Web site at http://adage.com/datacenter; Newman (2008).

share percentage point. The data show that Toyota spent about $102 million per market-share percentage point while Nissan spent $237 million. Another way of looking at this is to compare advertising spending per car. In 2007, Honda spent $706 per car while Scion (a Toyota nameplate) spent only $227 per car (V. Tremblay et al. forthcoming-b).

You might ask why the intensity of advertising varies so much and how ad spending affects society overall. In this chapter, we investigate these questions and other facets of the economics of advertising. First, we discuss the main theories of advertising to understand the different types of ads that we see in the marketplace. Next, we discuss the effect of advertising on demand and costs. Once this is understood, we can investigate models of advertising and price competition in different market structures. This will shed light on the benefits and costs of advertising and how strategic factors influence a firm's decision to advertise. Finally, we discuss the relationship between advertising and market structure. We analyze the welfare effect of advertising in the next chapter.

15.1   Theories of Advertising and Product Type

Given that many firms spend a substantial amount of money on advertising each year, firms must expect a substantial increase in demand for advertising to be profitable. This raises a fundamental question regarding the economics of advertising: why do consumers respond to advertising? In this section, we discuss the primary theories designed to explain why advertising works.

15.1.1   Informative Advertising

A prominent theory of advertising is that it provides consumers with useful information about price and product characteristics. There are thousands of goods and services competing for consumer dollars. For breakfast cereal alone, major supermarkets offer hundreds of choices. To complicate matters further, new brands continuously enter the marketplace. Because collecting information on all available products is costly, one theory is that advertising is a market response to consumers' lack of information about price, availability, and product characteristics. For example, advertising can inform consumers that the Chevrolet Volt runs on battery power for up to 50 miles, that the Droid phone allows Internet and GPS connectivity, that all Craftsman hand tools carry a lifetime warranty, and that a new grocery store has just opened for business. Consumers benefit from this form of advertising, as it helps consumers' locate goods that best suit their individual preferences.

Advertising can also play an informative role when it provides a **signal of quality**. In this case, the only information contained in the ad is that the brand is heavily advertised. The idea was developed by Nelson (1970, 1974) and is based on the following logic. First, information is asymmetric—each producer knows the quality level of its brand but consumers cannot identify quality until after purchase. As we saw in Chap. 7, this is called an experience good. Second, we will see shortly that advertising is a sunk cost that cannot be recovered if the firm goes out of business. Third, consumers respond to advertising and make a repeat purchase if the advertised brand is of high quality. In this setting, the high quality producer has an incentive to advertise because consumers will be satisfied with their purchase and become repeat customers. This enables the firm to charge a price premium for quality and recover its investment in advertising. It also allows consumers to identify high quality and low quality brands before purchase. If a low quality firm tries to mimic the high quality firm by investing in advertising, however, consumers will be dissatisfied and will never make a purchase from the low quality producer ever again. Thus, advertising will be unprofitable for the low quality firm. When this occurs, consumers can identify high quality brands by the fact that they are heavily advertised, and the information asymmetry is eliminated.[4]

The key difference between advertising as a signal and purely informative advertising is that the signal only informs consumers that the brand is advertised. No direct information is conveyed about price or product characteristics. Most television ads are like this, as television advertising is expensive and communicates very little information. This is evident with Super Bowl advertising, the most expensive advertising on television. As Fig. 15.2 reveals, the real cost of a 30 s Super Bowl ad was approximately $3 million in 2009, over ten times higher than the real cost of a Super Bowl ad in 1967. This rise in price may reflect the increased importance of advertising's role as a signal of quality, as well as the increased popularity of the Super Bowl.[5] In any case, only major corporations that market leading brands can afford such ads. In 2010, for example, these included Budweiser beer, Audi and Honda automobiles, Bridgestone tires, Coca-Cola, Doritos Chips, and E-trade online investing services.

---

[4] This is called a separating equilibrium. For further discussion of advertising as a signal of quality, see Kihlstrom and Riordan (1984), Milgrom and Roberts (1986), and Fluet and Garella (2002).

[5] For example, the number of viewers more than doubled from 1967 to 2009.

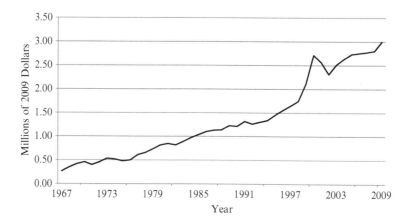

Fig. 15.2 The real price of a 30-s commercial on the Super Bowl, 1967–2009

Medium	Informative (%)	Annoying (%)
Newspapers	59	12
Magazines	48	9
Radio	40	24
Television	38	27

Table 15.4 Percent of advertisements found to be informative and annoying by media

Source: Bauer and Greyser (1968).

The ability of television advertising to provide such an expensive signal may be why many brands indicate on their packages the "As-Seen-On-TV" logo. There is even a web site devoted to these products, AsSeenOnTV.com. The extent to which heavily advertised name brands are truly of higher quality will be discussed later in the chapter.

Television advertising may signal product quality, but we all know that it provides us with very little additional information. An extensive consumer survey by Bauer and Greyser (1968) showed that the most informative ads are found in newspapers, and the least informative ads are found on television (see Table 15.4). This may be one reason why many consumers find television ads so "annoying." Since the 1960s, very little seems to have changed in terms of the information content of advertisements by medium. Television ads still provide very little pure information. In contrast, weekly circulars in newspapers provide consumers with information about the availability of seasonal fruits and vegetables and sale prices on various brands of tires, electronics equipment, clothing, and toiletries. Magazine ads inform consumers that the Chevrolet Volt runs up to 50 miles on battery power and a miles-per-gallon equivalent (MPG-e) of 99 miles (*Consumer Reports* 2011b). In addition, fragrance samples of perfumes can be found in magazine ads.

On the Internet, much of the advertising is informative. A good example is Edmunds.com, a site that provides reviews and price information on new and used cars. It contains advertisements for car insurance and various brands of automobiles. From the firm's perspective, a big advantage of an Internet ad is that people who visit

Edmunds are much more likely to make a car or insurance purchase than the general population. Thus, firms supplying these ads are better able to target potential customers who are less likely to view them as annoying and more likely to view them as informative.

Targeting is a key feature of the advertising networks that are developing on the Internet (Evans, 2009). For example, Google.com has linked hundreds of advertisers to Internet users. Google auctions off a specific keyword to advertisers, and when an Internet user queries that keyword, search results contain ads from high bid advertisers of that keyword. Goldfarb and Tucker (2011) found that Internet advertising such as this is especially important to consumers who are hardest to find through advertising by other media. In any case, as long as it does not inappropriately distort consumer decisions, this form of advertising is socially beneficial because it lowers transaction costs by quickly matching buyers with sellers.

15.1.2 Persuasive Advertising

Clearly not all forms of advertising are informative. Some ads are more persuasive in nature: they change consumer tastes by persuading consumers to buy products that they would not buy otherwise. In addressing this issue, Chamberlin (1933, 119–120) described it as

> "...selling methods which play upon the buyer's susceptibilities, which use against him laws of psychology with which he is unfamiliar and therefore against which he cannot defend himself, which frighten or flatter or disarm him—all of these have nothing to do with his knowledge. They are not informative; they are manipulative. They create a new scheme of wants by rearranging his motives."

Chamberlin's viewpoint is fully consistent with behavioral economics, which shows that many consumers have cognitive weaknesses that can be exploited by the marketing efforts of firms. As DellaVigna (2009, 317) points out, behavioral economics assumes that persuasion leads "to different decisions through the change in [consumer] beliefs that it induces."

Classic examples include cases where consumers suffer from cognitive dissonance and have problems with procrastination, distractibility, or impulsivity.[6] As we saw in Chap. 4, cognitive dissonance is the psychological conflict or turmoil that people feel when their actions are inconsistent with their beliefs. Firms understand that cognitive dissonance can be a problem for unhealthy habits, such as the excess

---

[6] Another theory indicates that persuasive advertising generates subliminal stimulation. This idea arose when James M. Vicary performed an experiment on movie patrons in the 1950s (Brean 1958). Without their knowledge, movie goers were exposed to the words "EAT POPCORN" and "DRINK COCA-COLA," which were flashed on the screen for a fraction of a second in the middle of a film. According to Vicary, this led to 58% increase in popcorn demand and an 18% increase in Coke demand. This result could never be replicated, however, and subsequent research showed that the effectiveness of subliminal advertising is limited (Sheth et al. 1991, 60–62).

consumption of alcohol. A person who abuses alcohol may suffer from dissonance because excessive alcohol consumption is inconsistent with the consumer's concern for health. In response, beer, wine, and liquor ads portray consumers as healthy and energetic individuals, hoping to persuade consumers to ignore the potential health risks associated with alcohol consumption. As Glaeser (2004, 410) points out, "Consumers will be more likely to accept false beliefs when those beliefs make them happier." Of course, reducing alcohol consumption is another way to eliminate dissonance. However, if persuasive advertising causes some consumers to (perhaps temporarily) change their beliefs about the health risks associated with alcohol abuse, alcohol demand will be higher if fewer consumers cut consumption and more individuals are enticed to try alcoholic beverages for the first time.

Procrastination is a perpetual problem for those of us who are trying to lose weight. This can cause individuals who honestly want to lose weight to overeat today, promising to get back on their diet tomorrow. Marketers exploit this weakness in supermarkets, for example, by regularly offering free samples of dessert and snack foods. This may induce some consumers to postpone their diet and purchase just one last box of cookies.

Problems also arise for consumers who tend to be impulsive and are not good with details. These can be especially severe for children and adults who suffer from attention deficit disorders. To exploit these weaknesses, advertisers frequently develop ads that emphasize the positive and downplay the negative. For example, the Federal government requires that alcoholic beverages contain the following warning label:

> GOVERNMENT WARNING: (1) According to the Surgeon General, women should not drink alcoholic beverages during pregnancy because of the risk of birth defects. (2) Consumption of alcoholic beverages impairs your ability to drive a car or operate machinery, and may cause health problems.

Yet, according to the Center for Science in the Public Interest this label is so inconspicuously placed that most consumers of alcohol are unaware of its presence even though such warning labels have been required since 1989.[7] Similarly, print ads for prescription drugs are required to include possible side effects. In such ads, a drug's benefits are touted in large print, while possible side effects are listed in fine print.

15.1.3 Advertising and Subjective Differentiation

The third type of advertising creates product characteristics that are subjective in nature and are a complement to the advertised brand.[8] For example, advertising can have an **image effect** by creating a subjective image that becomes tied to the product. Like real product differentiation, subjective differentiation can have horizontal or vertical qualities.

---

[7] See http://www.cspinet.org.

[8] In fact, Becker and Murphy (1993) call this complementary advertising.

One way for advertising to create subjective vertical differentiation is to help establish a **name brand** that has a reputation for high quality and prestige. This allows name brands to command a price premium. We saw in Chap. 14 that products with real or perceived quality differences can coexist when consumers have different preferences for quality. With subjective differentiation, advertising creates brand names that serve consumers who prefer high status goods, while generic brands serve all other consumers. Rather than changing tastes or signal real quality differences, this form of advertising creates name brands to meet the desires of those who value high prestige goods. Advertising of this type can also enhance Veblen effects among consumers who desire to impress their neighbors by purchasing conspicuous goods that signal wealth, high status, and prestige.

Classic examples can be found in the markets for aspirin and laundry bleach. The nationally advertised name brands in these markets are Bayer aspirin and Clorox bleach. Although their generic counterparts are chemically identical, advertising creates an image of quality that enables them to charge higher prices: the price of Bayer is over 200% higher than unadvertised brands of aspirin, and the price of Clorox is over 10% higher than unadvertised brands of bleach. Name and generic brands of aspirin and of bleach have been in existence for decades, making it clear that some consumers are willing to pay a price premium for advertised name brands, despite the availability of chemically equivalent generic alternatives.

How can advertising cause consumers to believe that the advertised brand is of higher quality when it is not? Recent work by Lee et al. (2006) provides one explanation. They performed blind taste tests on beer and found that consumer evaluation of quality was higher (lower) when consumers were informed that a brand is of high (low) quality before consumption. That is, when consumers believe beforehand that a brand will be good, consumer evaluation of the good increases.[9] This is consistent with Preston's (1996) viewpoint that when advertising puffs up the quality of a brand over and over again, consumers begin to believe it.[10]

Of course, there are other possible reasons for name brands. Klein and Leffler (1981) argue that brand names are a market response to fly-by-night producers that tout quality but sell watered down products. If consumers cannot identify quality before purchase, those who are fooled will do so only once. Fly-by-night firms can survive if it is not too costly to enter a new geographic or product market that has a new set of uninformed customers. By Akerlof's (1970) lemons principle that we discussed in Chapter 5, watered down brands could drive high quality brands out of the market.

---

[9] Similar results are found by Campbell and Goldstein (2010) for beer and by Plassman et al. (2008) for wine.

[10] Adolf Hitler's Propaganda Minister, Joseph Goebbels, understood this, arguing that "if you repeat a lie often enough, people eventually come to believe it."

To avoid the lemons problem, reputable producers could invest in advertising, which is a sunk cost, and offer a money back guarantee. This will eliminate the firm's incentive to water down its product (or allow a high variance in quality),[11] because cheating would lead to high refund costs, eliminate repeat purchases, and make it impossible for the firm to recover its advertising investment. Realizing this, consumers would come to trust well-established brands that are heavily advertised and have money back guarantees. The development of name brands in this setting would be particularly valuable to consumers who want to reduce the risk of purchasing from a fly-by-night company.[12]

Although these examples involve vertical differentiation, advertising can also create subjective horizontal product differentiation. The classic example is the market for premium cola, where Coke and Pepsi are the leading brands. Although there are slight differences in taste, many consumers cannot distinguish Coke from Pepsi in blind taste tests. To avoid the fierce competition associated with the Bertrand paradox, Coke and Pepsi use advertising to create images that become tied to the products and appeal to different segments of the population. Coke ads emphasize traditional values, while Pepsi ads appeal to a younger and more rebellious consumer. This allows consumers to choose the brand that best reflects and promotes their own personal identities (Akerlof and Kranton 2000, 2005); those with traditional values purchase Coke, and those with nontraditional values purchase Pepsi. Although advertising is expensive, Coke and Pepsi benefit from this form of advertising because it creates subjective horizontal differentiation which dampens price competition.

An interesting historical example occurred in the market for cigarettes, where the Marlboro brand and the Virginia Slims brand cultivated very different product images. In the 1960s and 1970s, Marlboro used a cowboy as a spokesperson to promote a rugged male image, while Virginia Slims created an image that would appeal to young professional women. This form of subjective product differentiation was very effective at dampening price competition. Even if both brands are physically identical, very few men would switch to Virginia Slims if Marlboro were to raise its price.

Recent work in neuroscience attempts to determine whether or not consumers truly value product image. In their seminal paper, McClure et al. (2004b) measured consumers' strength of preference for Coke, with and without the Coke label. Using functional magnetic resonance imaging (fMRI), the researchers found that consumers processed their preferences in two separate regions of the prefrontal

---

[11] The variance can be quite pronounced. In a study reported in the *Wellness Letter*, University of California at Berkeley (December 1993), local brands of diet foods had an average of 85% more calories that indicated on their labels. This compared to 25% more for regional brands. Nationally advertised brands had fairly accurate calorie counts.

[12] As one might expect, Klein and Leffler (1981, note 18) found that parents were more likely to purchase a name brand pain reliever for their children than themselves (i.e., the market share of generics was 7% for adult pain relievers and 1% for child pain relievers).

cortex of the brain: the ventromedial region, which is the rational side that evaluates purely sensory information, and the dorsolateral region, which is the emotional side that evaluates image effects associated with the product (McClure et al. 2004, 385). The results confirmed that consumers who drank Coke received greater pleasure or utility when informed that they were drinking Coke than when unaware of the brand of cola they were consuming. Deppe et al. (2005) found similar results for beer and coffee, with consumers receiving greater utility from the emotional side of the brain when they knew they were consuming their favorite brands. These studies demonstrate that both the product and its image are important sources of consumer utility.

Infomercials, long commercials in the format of a television program, make use of this neuroscience research by emphasizing the emotional high some consumers receive from purchasing a product. The typical infomercial does this by identifying a problem you did not realize you had and dramatizes that the advertised brand provides the ultimate solution. According to Lindstrom (2008), this creates a positive emotional response to the product that lasts 5–6 min. For this reason, infomercials frequently make an unbelievable low price offer to those who place a phone order within the next 5 min.

15.1.4 Advertising and the Type of Good

The type of good can influence the way in which it is marketed. A firm typically markets its product quite differently when selling it to consumers versus producers. Firms that sell producer goods to a limited number of loyal buyers may use a sales staff to inform customers about product characteristics, and firms that purchase producer goods may have specialized buyers who are better informed than an average consumer who is making a purchase. Little money is spent on advertising in these markets. Alternatively, firms selling consumer goods to a large number of dispersed consumers may have a relatively small sales staff and spend a great deal on advertising.

We saw in Chap. 7 that we can classify consumer goods by the way in which consumers obtain information about product characteristics. Recall that with a search good, consumers can learn all they need to know about a product before purchase. In contrast, the characteristics of an experience good cannot be determined until after purchase. Finally, it is uneconomic to determine the characteristics of a credence good even after purchase. Examples include men's jeans, a whole watermelon, and an appendix operation, respectively.

These different types of goods tend to be advertised differently. Persuasive advertising that exaggerates quality will be ineffective for search goods, because consumers can identify the level of quality before purchase. This would not be true for experience goods, however, as consumers could be temporarily fooled by advertising that exaggerates the effectiveness of an experience good. Thus, persuasive advertising is more likely with experience goods.

Potential misinformation conveyed by persuasive advertising is most severe with credence goods, as consumers will rarely know when they have been deceived by advertising. For this reason, markets for credence type goods tend to be heavily regulated, where regulations can apply to advertising as well as other business practices. This is an issue we will take up further in Chap. 20.

15.1.5   Implications for Advertising Intensity

The discussion above provides several explanations for the variation in advertising-to-sales ratios found in Table 15.2. First, there should be less advertising for producer goods than consumer goods. This is consistent with the table, as there is very little advertising for producer goods such as lumber, cement, and construction materials and considerable advertising for consumer goods such as liquor, perfume, and toys.

Second, one might expect firms to spend less money on the advertising of search goods. For these types of goods, the informative component remains relevant, but there is little or no room for persuasion. Although it is difficult to identify a good as purely search or purely experience, goods such as household furniture have mostly search characteristics and have relatively low advertising-to-sales ratios. In contrast, items like cosmetics and processed food items have mostly experience characteristics and are heavily advertised.

Finally, a firm's investment in advertising can be high when product image is important. Brand advertising of this type can be found in the markets for perfume, beer, and other beverages. One seeming anomaly is footwear, where athletic shoes (i.e., rubber and plastic footwear) are heavily advertised, while other types of footwear are not. This can be explained by the fact that athletic shoe manufacturers such as Nike invest heavily in image advertising that is targeted to a youthful audience, while ads for dress shoes focus more on information.

These are not the only reasons why the advertising intensity is higher in one industry than another. Other forces that can be important are discussed in subsequent sections of the chapter.

15.2   Advertising, Demand, and Costs

Advertising is costly, and profit-maximizing firms will invest in advertising only if it sufficiently increases firm demand. Two issues are relevant regarding the demand effect of advertising: (1) the extent to which advertising increases the size of the market and (2) whether or not advertising changes the slope of demand. In this section, we discuss the effect of advertising on market demand, firm demand, and firm costs.

15.2.1 Advertising and Market Demand

You may think that when advertising increases firm demand that it will also increase market demand, but this need not be the case. In a new and emerging market, informative advertising is more likely to increase market demand by attracting new customers to the market. Marshall (1890) calls this **constructive advertising** because firm advertising that increases market demand benefits all firms in the market. This form of advertising creates a positive externality.[13] In mature markets, however, advertising may have little effect on market demand because it attracts few if any new customers. When one firm's advertising steals customers from another firm, Marshall calls this **combative advertising**.[14] Thus, it creates a negative externality.

Friedman (1983) partitions advertising into four categories. These are described for an industry with two firms (1 and 2). Typically, demand for firm i's product, q_i, is assumed to be positively influenced by its own advertising, A_i, but may be positively or negatively influenced by rival j's advertising, A_j. With this notation, subscript i identifies firm 1 or 2, and j identifies the other firm:

1. Constructive Advertising: This occurs when an increase in A_j causes q_i to increase (i.e., $\partial q_i / \partial A_j > 0$). In this case, firm advertising increases market demand and may or may not increase the market share of the advertised brand.
2. Perfectly Constructive Advertising: Firm advertising increases rival output ($\partial q_i / \partial A_j > 0$) and increases market demand. In this case, symmetric advertising has no effect on market shares (i.e., $A_i = A_j$ and $\partial q_i / \partial A_j = \partial q_j / \partial A_j > 0$).
3. Combative Advertising: Firm advertising decreases rival output ($\partial q_i / \partial A_j < 0$), may or may not increase market demand, and increases the market share of the advertised brand.
4. Perfectly Combative Advertising: Firm advertising decreases rival output ($\partial q_i / \partial A_j < 0$) and has no effect on market demand. In this case, symmetric advertising has no effect on market shares (i.e., $A_i = A_j$ and $\partial q_i / \partial A_j = \partial q_j / \partial A_j = 0$).

The market for cigarettes is an excellent example that has been both constructive and combative effects. From 1914 to 1940 when the market was taking off, a quote from George Hill, president of the American Tobacco Company, indicates that cigarette advertising was constructive, but not perfectly so:

> The impetus of those great advertising campaigns not only built this for ourselves, but built the cigarette industry as well... Of course, you benefit yourself more than your fellow [competitor] ... but you can help the whole industry if you do a good job." (Tenant 1950, 137)

---

[13] Recall that an externality occurs when one economic agent affects another economic agent without compensation. In this case, firm i's advertising benefits firm j without firm j compensating firm i.

[14] Constructive advertising is sometimes called cooperative advertising, and combative advertising is also known as predatory advertising.

Fig. 15.3 Advertising and a parallel shift in firm demand

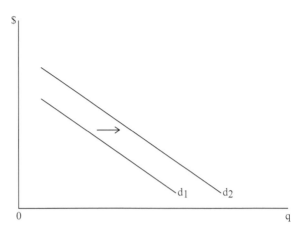

By the 1960s, however, firm advertising had little or no effect on the market demand for cigarettes (Iwasaki and V. Tremblay 2009). Thus, cigarette advertising was initially constructive but became combative once the market matured.

15.2.2   Advertising and Firm Demand

Advertising can shift firm demand in two ways. First, it may cause a parallel shift in demand, as in Fig. 15.3 where firm demand increases from d_1 to d_2. In this case, advertising increases consumers' marginal valuation (or the demand price) by the same amount at each output level.

Advertising can also cause demand to rotate. We illustrate this idea in relation to advertising, using the same demand model as in Chap. 13:

$$p = (x + xb) - bq, \qquad (15.1)$$

where x and b are positive constants. Parameter b is the absolute value of the slope of inverse demand, and x is a demand parameter that helps identify the price intercept $(x + xb)$ and the rotation point. Notice that $p = x$ when $q = x$, regardless of the value of b. Thus, as b changes, the demand function rotates around the point $p = q = x$.[15] Figure 15.4 provides an example where $x = 10$ and b takes on the value 1 in d_1 and ½ in d_2. It shows that demand rotates around the point x, where $p = q = x = 10$, and rotates clockwise (counterclockwise) as b increases (decreases).

Johnson and Myatt (2006) identify two types of advertising that can cause firm demand to rotate.[16] Advertising that rotates demand counterclockwise, from d_1 to

---

[15] Here, we assume that the rotation point lies in the positive p–q quadrant.

[16] Chamberlin (1933) and Aislabie and Tisdell (1988) also address the issue of advertising and demand rotation. For a discussion of how consumer information can cause a nonparallel shift in demand, see Comanor (1985).

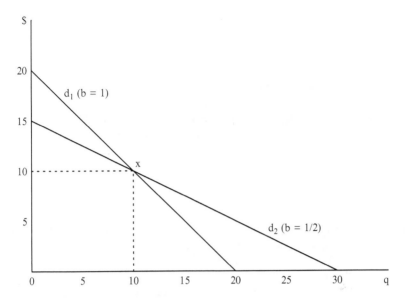

Fig. 15.4 Advertising and demand rotation

d_2 in Fig. 15.4, is called **mass-market advertising**. The name derives from the fact that advertising causes a larger number of consumers to derive a positive marginal valuation from consumption of the good. In contrast, advertising that rotates demand clockwise, from d_2 to d_1 in Fig. 15.4, is called **niche-market advertising** because it raises the marginal valuation of a small group of high valuation consumers (i.e., those to the left of rotation point x in the figure).[17] One example is the market for small cars, where Honda ads appeal to the masses by emphasizing quality and fuel economy, while Scion ads appeal to young males in urban areas who are interested in customizing their cars (V. Tremblay et al., forthcoming-b).

A final issue regarding the demand effect of advertising is that product image or goodwill may depend on past as well as current advertising expenditures. That is, the firm faces a dynamic problem where current advertising affects demand today and in the future. If true, this would give an image advantage to established firms that have advertised their brands for many years. The empirical evidence suggests that the effect of advertising on demand is fleeting, however, as its influence generally depreciates to zero within 1 year.[18]

---

[17] Johnson and Myatt point out that this terminology applies to any marketing change. As we saw in Chap. 13, a change in a product's physical design could appeal to the masses or to a niche group of consumers and rotate demand accordingly.

[18] For reviews of the literature, see Clark (1976), Seldon and Doroodian (1989), Boyd and Seldon (1990), Leone (1995), and Bagwell (2007). In a recent experimental study done at Yahoo, Lewis and Reiley (2009) found that Internet ads generated an increase in sales in excess of 11 times the amount spent on advertising. They also found that the effect of an ad dissipated after several weeks.

15.2.3 The Cost of Advertising

A firm's advertising expenditures or costs equal the price of advertising (p_A) times the number of advertising messages it purchases (A). For example, the quantity of television advertising messages could be measured as the number of ad seconds. As we said, a 30 s Super Bowl ad cost approximately \$3 million. If p_A is constant, then the advertising portion of a firm's total cost function is linear in A.

Generally, production and marketing costs are assumed to be separable.[19] That is, an increase in production costs has no effect on marketing costs, and vice versa. When this is true, a firm's total cost function can be written as

$$\mathrm{TC}(q, A) = C(q) + p_A A. \tag{15.2}$$

The marginal cost of production equals the change in C with respect to q ($\partial C / \partial q$).

Advertising costs need not be linear in A, however. That is, p_A might vary with the level of advertising. Large, established firms may be able to garner an advertising cost advantage over their smaller competitors. There are three main reasons for this. First, they may be able to bargain for a lower price of advertising. Second, large firms can make use of national television advertising, which reaches a given audience at lower cost than local television advertising or advertising in other media. For instance, in 1980 the price of advertising during sporting events was about 43% lower for national than local television ads.[20] Third, there may be increasing returns associated with advertising. This relationship is described by an **advertising response function**, illustrated in Fig. 15.5. It shows that sales increase at an increasing rate at low levels of advertising but eventually increase at a decreasing rate. When increasing returns are present, the average cost of advertising will fall up to a point, called the minimum efficient scale in advertising. Firms that advertise less than this minimum level will have higher unit marketing costs than large scale advertisers.

The empirical evidence in support of the hypothesis that large firms have a substantial marketing cost advantage is not strong, however.[21] For example, Fare et al. (2004) found that a US brewing company would need a market share of approximately 1.6% between 1983 and 1993 to take advantage of all scale economies associated with advertising. During this period, all major brewers had exceeded this size, and the average brewer had a market share of between 5.3 and 6.5%. Given the evidence, we will generally assume that advertising costs are linear and that advertising does not affect future demand.

---

[19] For further discussion of this separability issue, see Iwasaki and V. Tremblay (2009).

[20] For further discussion, see Greer (2002) and V. Tremblay and C. Tremblay (2007).

[21] For reviews of the literature, see Scherer and Ross (1990) and Seldon et al. (2000).

Fig. 15.5 Advertising
response function

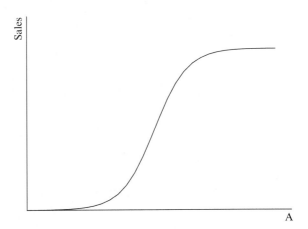

15.3   The Effect of Market Structure on Advertising

Market structure can also influence a firm's decision to advertise. Firms in competitive markets have little incentive to advertise compared to a monopolist. In an oligopoly market, strategic effects can also influence a firm's advertising behavior. In this section, we discuss a firm's costs and benefits of advertising in competitive, monopoly, and oligopoly markets.

15.3.1   Advertising and Perfect Competition

The assumptions of the perfectly competitive model make it unprofitable for a single firm to advertise. In perfect competition, products are perfectly homogeneous, consumers and producers have perfect information, there are many consumers and producers, firms are free to enter or exit the industry, and firm demand is exogenously determined. Under these conditions, it is impossible for persuasive, informative, or other forms of advertising to increase firm demand.

Even if we allow barriers to entry and relax the assumption that consumers are perfectly informed, opening the door to informative advertising, it would still be unprofitable for an individual firm to advertise when there are many firms in the industry. To illustrate, assume that there are n symmetric firms and that $1 worth of advertising increases market demand and industry revenues by $10. This is certainly a good investment for the industry, as industry profits go up by $9. For an individual firm, however, spending $1 on advertising is profitable only if the increase in revenues to the firm ($10/$n$) is greater than or equal to the cost ($1). This is true only if $n \leq 10$. With many firms in a perfectly competitive industry, no individual firm will find it profitable to advertise even with imperfect information. This is a free rider problem because each firm wants another firm to invest in advertising to receive the benefits without incurring the cost.

This situation is a classic coordination problem, as firms acting independently have no incentive to advertise even though they are jointly better with advertising. In our example, if each firm contributes $1/n$ to an industry wide advertising effort, individual firm profits rise by $9/n$ ($10/n - $1/n). That is, firms are better off if they coordinate their marketing efforts.

Coordination or cooperation does happen in many agricultural markets through **commodity checkoff programs**. To avoid the free rider problem, the program imposes a mandatory excise tax on each firm in the industry. The proceeds are then used to finance an advertising campaign that is designed to increase demand by informing consumers of the universal characteristics of the product. A classic example is the "Got Milk" campaign, where a famous celebrity promotes the health benefits of drinking milk. Previous ads have Superman claiming that the calcium in milk helps build bones of steel and Batman claiming that the protein in milk helps build muscle. This is called **generic advertising** because it promotes the general attributes of a product category rather than the characteristics unique to a particular brand.[22]

15.3.2 Advertising and Monopoly

The simplest way to analyze an individual firm's incentive to advertise is to consider a market with just one firm. Two types of effects are possible, static and dynamic. In a static setting, advertising influences current but not future demand. A good example is newspaper advertising that provides consumers with information about a sale at a local supermarket, as this information is accurate for only a short time. It is also possible that advertising affects future as well as current demand, which is likely to occur when advertising enhances product image or goodwill. In this section, we consider a static model of advertising. Because the effect of advertising generally depreciates within 1 year and given the complexity of a dynamic model, we discuss the dynamic case in Appendix 15.A.

In the static model, we assume that the firm's goal is to maximize profit with respect to two choice variables: price and advertising. The firm (and market) demand function is defined as $q(p, A)$, where firm output (q) is the same as market output (Q) in the monopoly case. Demand decreases in price ($\partial q/\partial p < 0$) and increases in advertising at a decreasing rate ($\partial q/\partial A > 0$ and $\partial^2 q/\partial A^2 < 0$).[23]

---

[22] For further discussion of commodity checkoff programs and generic advertising, see Ward (2006), Crespi (2007), and Isariyawongse et al. (2007, 2009).

[23] This last condition assures that the firm's second-order condition of profit maximization is met.

To simplify the discussion, we assume that $p_A = \$1$ so that A equals total advertising expenditures. Thus, the firm's profit equals total revenue (TR) minus total cost (TC), or

$$\pi = \text{TR} - \text{TC}$$
$$= pq(p, A) - [C(q) + A]. \tag{15.3}$$

Because this is a monopoly market, firm output (q) equals market output. The first-order conditions of profit maximization are

$$\frac{\partial \pi}{\partial p} = \frac{\partial \text{TR}}{\partial p} - \frac{\partial \text{TC}}{\partial p}$$
$$= \text{MR}p - \text{MC}p$$
$$= \left(q + p\frac{\partial q}{\partial p} \right) - \left(\frac{\partial C}{\partial q}\frac{\partial q}{\partial p} \right) = 0, \tag{15.4}$$

$$\frac{\partial \pi}{\partial A} = \frac{\partial \text{TR}}{\partial A} - \frac{\partial \text{TC}}{\partial A}$$
$$= \text{MR}_A - \text{MC}_A$$
$$= \left(p\frac{\partial q}{\partial A} \right) - \left(\frac{\partial C}{\partial q}\frac{\partial q}{\partial A} + 1 \right) = 0, \tag{15.5}$$

where MRp is the marginal revenue for a change in price, MCp is the marginal cost for a change in price, MR$_A$ is the marginal benefit or marginal revenue of advertising, and MC$_A$ is the marginal cost of advertising.

Although these equations must be solved simultaneously to obtain the profit-maximizing values of p and A, we will first analyze them separately. From Chap. 6 we saw that the monopoly solution is the same whether the firm maximizes profit over price or output. Thus, (15.4) implies that the Lerner index is $\mathcal{L} \equiv (p - \text{MC})/p = 1/\eta$, where MC is the marginal cost of production ($\partial \text{TC}/\partial q = \partial C/\partial q$) and η is the absolute value of the price elasticity of demand.

Equation (15.5) is new, and its interpretation is our main goal here. Consistent with the marginal principle, the first-order condition implies that the profit maximizing level of advertising is determined by equating the marginal revenue of advertising with the marginal cost of advertising. The marginal revenue is $p(\partial q/\partial A)$, which measures the change in total revenue caused by a small change in advertising. If we think of advertising as a costly input that is used to produce sales, then this term is simply the value of the marginal product of advertising. The last set of terms measures the marginal cost of advertising, which is much like the marginal factor cost of an input.[24] Notice that it has a direct and an indirect effect. The direct effect measures the added cost of increasing A by one unit (which is

---

[24] See Varian (2010) for further discussion of the value of the marginal product and the marginal factor cost for an input.

$p_A = 1$ in this case). The indirect effect captures the influence that advertising has on production costs through the change it causes in output.[25]

We gain further insight into a firm's advertising decision by rearranging (15.5) so that it identifies the firm's advertising-to-sales ratio. From (15.5),

$$1 = \frac{\partial q}{\partial A}(p - MC),$$

$$\frac{A}{pq} = \frac{\partial q}{\partial A}\frac{A}{q}\frac{(p - MC)}{p},$$

$$\frac{A}{pq} = \frac{\eta_A}{\eta}, \tag{15.6}$$

where η_A is the advertising elasticity of demand, which measures the percentage change in quantity demanded resulting from a 1% increase in advertising $[(\partial q/\partial A)(A/q)]$. The last line in (15.6) is called the **Dorfman–Steiner condition** (Dorfman and Steiner 1954). It implies that a firm's advertising-to-sales ratio will be higher when advertising is more effective at increasing demand (i.e., η_A is greater). This provides one possible reason for the variation in advertising intensity among industries found in Table 15.2. For example, consumer demand may be more responsive to perfume and cosmetics advertising than to paint and varnish advertising.

The Dorfman–Steiner condition also implies that advertising will increase as the price elasticity of demand falls. The intuition behind this result can be seen in Fig. 15.6. Marginal cost and the advertising elasticity are assumed to be the same in both cases. The only difference is that the demand function is relatively more inelastic in diagram (a) than in (b). As indicated by the Lerner index, the optimal price will be higher in case (a) where the demand elasticity is lower. Assume that advertising expenditures increase by the same amount in both cases and that this increase causes demand to rise from D_1 to D_2.[26] As the diagrams show, the increase in gross profit generated by advertising, indicted by the shaded regions of each diagram, is greater when the demand function is relatively less elastic (diagram a), *ceteris paribus*. In other words, the benefits of advertising are greater when demand is relatively more inelastic, implying that the firm will advertise more intensively. This result also verifies that when the price elasticity of demand is infinite, as in perfect competition, the firm has no incentive to advertise.

The discussion above reveals a potential link between advertising and market power. An increase in market power, reflected in a higher Lerner index (lower η), leads to a higher advertising-to-sales ratio. The only caveat to keep in mind is that this interpretation of the Dorfman–Steiner condition assumes that price is constant,

---

[25] From the chain rule, which is discussed in the Mathematics and Econometrics Appendix at the end of the book, this equals $(\partial C/\partial q)(\partial q/\partial A)$.

[26] By construction, the quantity intercepts and optimal output levels are the same in both diagrams for D_1 and D_2.

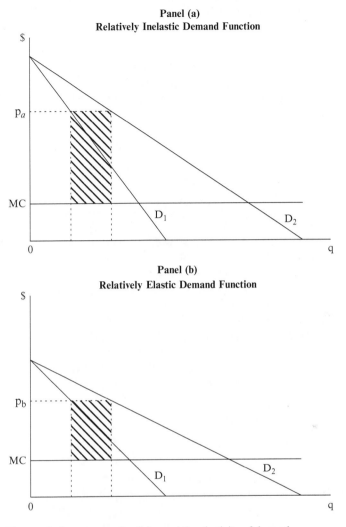

Fig. 15.6 The marginal returns to advertising and the elasticity of demand

an assumption that will not hold when market power increases. For example, a higher Lerner index normally implies a higher price, and a change in advertising generally leads to a change in price. Thus, it is important to remember that both first-order conditions must be solved simultaneously to correctly determine the optimal level of advertising.

In summary, this discussion suggests two conclusions regarding the advertising of a monopolist. First, an increase in the effectiveness of advertising will induce the firm to make a greater investment in advertising. Second, a firm will spend more on advertising as its demand function becomes more inelastic.[27]

---

[27] As we discuss in Appendix 15.A, a firm will also invest more in advertising when it is better able to increase product goodwill today and into the future.

15.3.3 Advertising and Imperfect Competition

It is relatively easy to extend the Dorfman–Steiner condition to an oligopoly market. To illustrate, consider a Cournot model with n symmetric firms that produce homogeneous goods. From Chap. 12, (12.3), we know that the Lerner index in this case equals $(p - \text{MC})/p = 1/(n \cdot \eta)$. Given this fact and (15.6), firm i's advertising-to-sales ratio is

$$\frac{A_i}{p_i q_i} = \frac{\partial q_i}{\partial A_i} \frac{A_i}{q_i} \frac{(p - \text{MC})}{p},$$

$$\frac{A_i}{p_i q_i} = \frac{\eta_A}{n \cdot \eta}. \qquad (15.7)$$

As in the monopoly model, the firm's advertising-to-sales ratio will be higher in markets where advertising has a greater effect on demand (i.e., a higher η_A) and where demand is relatively more inelastic. It also says that advertising intensity increases with a fall in the number of competitors. That is, advertising intensity rises with industry concentration.[28]

In an oligopoly setting, strategic effects can also have an important influence on a firm's advertising decision. In this section, our initial goal is to identify the Nash and cartel levels of advertising in a static setting to show how these equilibria are affected by advertising that is combative versus constructive. Once these concepts are understood, we analyze more formal models where firms compete in a dynamic setting.

To begin, consider a market with two symmetric firms, 1 and 2, that compete by simultaneously choosing advertising. Later in the chapter we consider the more realistic case where firms compete in both advertising and price. Assume that firm i's profit equation is $\pi_i = 100A_i - A_i^2 + bA_iA_j$, where subscript i represents firm 1 or 2, subscript j represents i's competitor. Parameter b, which is assumed to be greater than -1, has an interesting economic interpretation. When b is negative, advertising is combative because firm j's advertising steals customers and lowers firm i's profits; when b is positive, advertising is constructive because firm j's advertising benefits firm i as well as firm j.

Recall that to identify the Nash equilibrium (NE) values of advertising in a problem such as this one, we solve the firms' first-order conditions simultaneously for A_1 and A_2. The first-order condition for firm i is

$$\frac{\partial \pi_i}{\partial A_i} = 100 - 2A_i + bA_j = 0. \qquad (15.8)$$

---

[28] Recall that in this model, the Herfindahl–Hirschman index of industry concentration equals $1/n$.

Because we will subsequently describe the NE in terms of firm best-reply functions (BR), we derive them now. They are obtained by solving each firm's first-order condition for A_2. These are

$$\text{BR}_1 : A_2 = \frac{-100}{b} + \frac{2}{b}A_1, \tag{15.9}$$

$$\text{BR}_2 : A_2 = 50 + \frac{b}{2}A_1. \tag{15.10}$$

Solving them simultaneously for A_1 and A_2 and substituting these values into the profit equations of each firm gives the NE:

$$A_i^* = \frac{100}{2-b}, \quad \pi_i^* = \frac{10,000}{2-b}. \tag{15.11}$$

To understand the effect of combative versus constructive advertising, we compare the equilibrium when $b = -\frac{1}{2}$ (combative) and when $b = \frac{1}{2}$ (constructive). We first consider the <u>combative case</u>, where $b = -\frac{1}{2}$. This produces the following best-reply functions:

$$\text{BR}_1 : A_2 = 200 - 4A_1, \tag{15.12}$$

$$\text{BR}_2 : A_2 = 50 - \frac{1}{4}A_1. \tag{15.13}$$

Firm best-reply and isoprofit functions are shown in Fig. 15.7. As discussed in Chap. 10, the NE occurs where the best-reply functions intersect, which occurs where $A_i^* = 40$. Notice that these functions take on the same mathematical structure as the Cournot model. That is, they have a negative slope, implying that advertising is a strategic substitute, and both firms are better off if they advertise less and move to the shaded region in the figure.

In the case of combative advertising, firms face a **prisoners' dilemma in advertising**. This means that they are collectively better off advertising less than if they behave independently. This is due to the fact that combative advertising generates a negative externality. By ignoring this externality, each firm advertises more than if they were to cooperate. Figure 15.7 makes this apparent, as it shows that the Nash level of advertising at $A_i = 40$ is on a higher isoprofit function (implying lower profit) than the cartel level of advertising at $A_i = 33.3$.[29]

---

[29] This is found by maximizing joint profit with respect to A_1 and A_2 and solving the first-order conditions simultaneously for the optimal values of advertising.

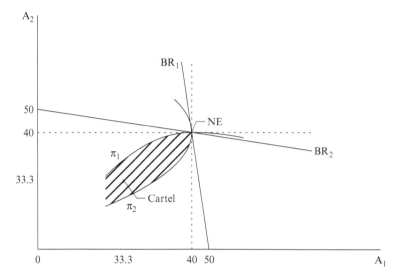

Fig. 15.7 Duopoly with advertising competition (strategic substitutes, $b = -1/2$)

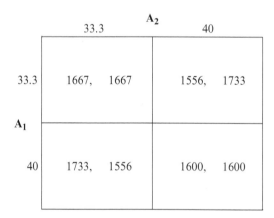

Fig. 15.8 A prisoners' dilemma in advertising

The prisoners' dilemma outcome may be easier to see with a traditional payoff matrix, as in Fig. 15.8. Each firm has only two choices: the Nash level of advertising (40) and the cartel level of advertising (33.3). Notice that each firm has a dominant strategy of 40. This is a prisoners' dilemma type problem because what is good for an individual firm is bad for the group.

Next, we consider the case where <u>advertising is constructive</u> by setting $b = \frac{1}{2}$. In this case, the best replies are

$$BR_1 : A_2 = -200 + 4A_1, \tag{15.14}$$

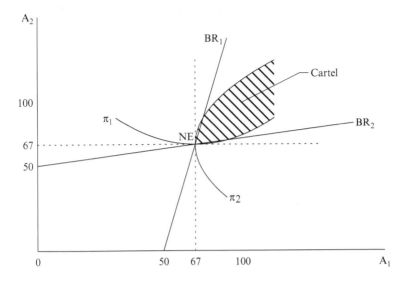

Fig. 15.9 Duopoly with advertising competition (strategic complements, $b = 1/2$)

$$BR_2 : A_2 = 50 + \frac{1}{4}A_1. \tag{15.15}$$

Best-reply and isoprofit functions for this model can be found in Fig. 15.9, which take on the mathematical structure of the differentiated Bertrand model that we discussed in Chap. 10. In this case, industry profits are higher when advertising expenditures exceed NE levels because advertising is constructive (i.e., it generates a positive externality). The best-reply functions have a positive slope, and A_1 and A_2 are strategic complements.

What would cause advertising to be a strategic substitute or complement? Principle factors include the degree of product differentiation, the degree of market maturity, and the extent to which advertising is persuasive or informative. For example, advertising is more likely to be a strategic complement in a new market, when there is little or no product differentiation and when advertising provides consumers with information about the generic characteristics of a commodity. In this setting, advertising would be constructive because one firm's advertising would attract customers to all producers in the market. Thus, firms will advertise less than is best for the industry. In contrast, advertising is more likely to be a strategic substitute and combative when the market is mature and advertising builds subjective differentiation that is tied to a particular brand. In this setting, one firm's advertising draws customers away from its competitors, which can lead to an advertising war.[30] These are features that are common to many oligopoly markets.

---

[30] See Iwasaki et al. (2008) for further discussion.

Although this simple model provides insight into the nature of advertising competition in a duopoly setting, it would be more realistic to assume that firms compete in price (or output) as well as in advertising. In the next sections we investigate models such as these, which are a bit more sophisticated because they are dynamic and allow firms to compete in price and in different types of advertising.

15.3.3.1 Informative Advertising and Search Costs

We begin with a model that is designed to show how informative advertising can affect the market. We assume a duopoly model with multicharacteristic product differentiation as discussed in Chaps. 7 and 10. We simplify the model by setting the demand parameters $\beta = \delta = 1$, which produces the following demand system:

$$q_1 = \alpha - p_1 + p_2, \tag{15.16}$$

$$q_2 = \alpha - p_2 + p_1. \tag{15.17}$$

The fundamental difference between this model and previous models is that consumers also face a unit search cost, s, of obtaining information about product characteristics. When purchasing brand i, consumers pay the full price for brand i (p_{fi}), which equals the market price plus the unit search cost. That is, $p_{fi} = p_i + s_i$ or $p_i = p_{fi} - s_i$.

Advertising plays an informative role in the model, where firm i's advertising is assumed to lower consumer search costs at a decreasing rate. In other words, $s_i = s_i(A_i)$, where $\partial s_i/\partial A_i < 0$ and $\partial^2 s_i/\partial A_i^2 > 0$.[31] Firm i's profit equation is $\pi_i = \text{TR}_i - \text{TC}_i = p_i q_i - c q_i - p_A A_i$, where the marginal cost of production (c) is set to zero for simplicity. Competition occurs in two stages. In the first stage, firms simultaneously choose advertising to lower consumer search costs. In the second stage, firms simultaneously choose price.

Our goal is to find the subgame perfect Nash equilibrium (SPNE) to this game. Recall from Chaps. 3 and 11 that we do this by using backwards induction, finding the NE at the last stage game first. We solved the NE to this final stage in a similar model in Sect. 10.2.2 in Chap. 10[32]:

$$p_i^* = q_i^* = \frac{3\alpha - s_i(A_i) + s_j(A_j)}{3}, \tag{15.18}$$

---

[31] We use a partial derivative because other factors, such as word of mouth information, may also affect search costs and are implicitly assumed to be constant.

[32] Notice that firm participation requires that $3\alpha - s_i + s_j > 0$. In other words, firm i will exit the market if its search costs are too high relative to the search costs of firm j.

$$\pi_i^* = \frac{[3\alpha - s_i(A_i) + s_j(A_j)]^2}{9} - p_A A_i. \tag{15.19}$$

The only difference is that $c = 0$ and NE prices and profits include the term— $s_i(A_i) + s_j(A_j)$. This model implies that prices and profits will be the same when search costs are identical for both firms. If, however, the search costs associated with firm i's product are higher, then firm i will charge a lower price and earn less profit in equilibrium. This implies, for example, that a supermarket that is difficult for consumers to find will charge lower prices to compensate consumers for their higher search cost.

In the first stage of the game, firms are assumed to be sequentially rational. They are able to look forward and identify the NE in the final stage. Each firm then chooses the optimal level of informative advertising based on NE profits in (15.19). Although we will not calculate a specific solution here, the SPNE requires that the following first-order condition holds simultaneously for each firm[33]:

$$\frac{\partial \pi_i^*}{\partial A_i} = MR_{Ai} - MC_{Ai}$$

$$= \left[-\frac{2(3\alpha - s_i + s_j)}{9} \frac{\partial s_i}{\partial A_i} \right] - p_A = 0, \tag{15.20}$$

where the set of terms within the brackets is the marginal revenue of advertising and p_A is the marginal cost of advertising. The marginal revenue is positive because $\partial s_i / \partial A_i < 0$ (i.e., advertising lowers search costs) and given the participation constraint, $(3\alpha - s_i + s_j) > 0$. Thus, both firms will advertise as long as p_A is sufficiently low.[34] If the initial search cost is the same for both firms (i.e., $s_1 = s_2$) and the marginal effectiveness of advertising is the same for both firms (i.e., $|\partial s_1 / \partial A_1| = |\partial s_2 / \partial A_2|$), then each firm will produce the same amount of advertising in equilibrium. If one firm's advertising is more effective at lowering search costs, it will invest more in advertising.

A final implication of the model relates to the effect of advertising on equilibrium prices. Stivers and V. Tremblay (2005) show that in a model such as this, advertising that lowers consumer search costs can raise the market price received by producers and lower the full price paid by consumers. Thus, both consumers and producers may benefit from this form of advertising, an issue that will be taken up in the next chapter.

---

[33] To derive a specific solution, we would need a specific function for $s_i(A_i)$. Because $\partial^2 s_i / \partial A_i^2 > 0$, second-order conditions hold when the participation constraint is met $[(3\alpha - s_i + s_j) > 0]$.

[34] The marginal revenue of advertising must also have a negative slope, which occurs when $\partial^2 s_i / \partial A_i^2$ is sufficiently close to zero.

15.3.3.2 Image Advertising and Horizontal Differentiation

Next, we analyze the effect of image advertising in a simple Hotelling model of horizontal differentiation, as discussed in Chaps. 7 and 10.[35] Recall that in Hotelling's model, two brands, 1 and 2, differ along a single horizontal characteristic (θ). We are interested in advertising that creates subjective differentiation, as in the market for premium cola. In this example, advertising causes one brand to appeal to people who value tradition (Coke) and the other brand to appeal to people with more rebellious personalities (Pepsi). Consumers are uniformly distributed along this characteristic, which ranges from 0 (extremely traditional) to 1 (extremely rebellious). Brand 1 (Coke) is located at θ_1, and brand 2 (Pepsi) is located at θ_2, with $0 \leq \theta_1 \leq \frac{1}{2} \leq \theta_2 \leq 1$. Here, we assume that the only source of differentiation is due to image effects that are created by advertising. Without advertising, brands 1 and 2 are undifferentiated, such that $\theta_1 = \theta_2 = \frac{1}{2}$.

Firms benefit from moving θ_1 and θ_2 away from $\frac{1}{2}$, which they can do with advertising. Firm 1 uses brand advertising to create a traditional image (i.e., move θ_1 toward 0), and firm 2 uses brand advertising to create a more rebellious image (i.e., move θ_2 toward 1). That is, $\partial \theta_1 / \partial A_1 < 0$ and $\partial \theta_2 / \partial A_2 > 0$. As in the previous model, firms compete in two stages by simultaneously choosing advertising in the first stage and simultaneously choosing price in the second stage.

Our goal is to identify SPNE to this game. As we saw in Sect. 10.2.3.1 (Chap. 10), the NE in the final stage game when firms simultaneously compete in price is

$$p_i^* = c + t(\theta_2 - \theta_1), \tag{15.21}$$

$$q_i^* = N(\theta_2 - \theta_1)/2, \tag{15.22}$$

$$\pi_i^* = \frac{Nt(\theta_2 - \theta_1)^2}{2} - p_A A_i, \tag{15.23}$$

where c is marginal production cost, t is the transportation cost or consumer disutility associated with consuming a less than ideal brand, and N is the number of consumers. Notice that when there is no product differentiation (i.e., $\theta_1 = \theta_2$), price equals marginal cost and profits are zero (i.e., the Bertrand paradox when we ignore advertising).

Firms can avoid the Bertrand paradox by investing in brand advertising that changes θ_i in the first stage of the game. In this stage, firms are sequentially rational and use NE values in the final stage to determine optimal behavior in the first stage. Again, we do not calculate a specific solution here, but the SPNE requires that the

---

[35] This model derives from V. Tremblay and Polasky (2002).

following first-order conditions of profit maximization hold simultaneously. The first-order conditions are derived from first-stage profit equations found in (15.23)[36]:

$$\frac{\partial \pi_1^*}{\partial A_1} = MR_{A1} - MC_{A1}$$

$$= \left[-Nt(\theta_2 - \theta_1) \frac{\partial \theta_1}{\partial A_1} \right] - p_A = 0, \qquad (15.24)$$

$$\frac{\partial \pi_2^*}{\partial A_2} = MR_{A2} - MC_{A2}$$

$$= \left[Nt(\theta_2 - \theta_1) \frac{\partial \theta_2}{\partial A_2} \right] - p_A = 0, \qquad (15.25)$$

where the set of terms in the square brackets in each equation is the marginal revenue of advertising for the respective firm and p_A is the marginal cost of advertising. Because $\partial \theta_1/\partial A_1 < 0$ and $\partial \theta_2/\partial A_2 > 0$, the marginal revenue of advertising is positive for both firms,[37] and each firm will advertise as long as p_A is sufficiently low. In this case, both firms will advertise, causing θ_1 to fall below ½ and θ_2 to lie above ½ in equilibrium.

This provides a simple model to explain how firms can invest in advertising to create subjective differentiation along a horizontal dimension. Advertising spreads the distance between θ_1 and θ_2, enabling firms to charge a price above marginal cost and avoid the Bertrand paradox. As long as the marginal effectiveness of advertising is the same for both firms (i.e., $|\partial \theta_1/\partial A_1| = |\partial \theta_2/\partial A_2|$), each firm will choose the same advertising levels. If one firm has an advertising advantage, however, it will invest relatively more in advertising.

15.3.3.3   Behavioral Economics Model 1: Advertising Changes Consumer Beliefs About Product Quality

In this example, we add advertising to the vertical differentiation model discussed in Chaps. 7 and 10. The model is behavioral because advertising changes tastes by persuading consumers to incorrectly believe that the advertised brand is of higher quality. One can also think of this as a model where advertising creates a prestige effect that is desired by some consumers, as in V. Tremblay and Martins-Filho (2001). In this model, recall that the quality of firm i's brand is $z_i > 0$, with

---

[36] To ensure that second-order conditions of profit maximization are met, advertising is assumed to change product image at a decreasing rate. That is, $\partial^2 \theta_1/\partial A_1^2 > 0$ and $\partial^2 \theta_2/\partial A_2^2 < 0$.

[37] Second-order conditions are assumed to hold, which implies that the marginal revenue functions have a negative slope.

$z_1 \geq z_2 > 0$. Every consumer values quality, but some have a stronger preference for quality than others. The diversity of consumer tastes for quality ranges from ϕ_L to ϕ_H, with $\phi_H > \phi_L > 0$. Firms compete in a two-stage game. In stage one, firms compete in persuasive advertising; in stage two, firms compete in price. As in the previous examples, we use backwards induction to obtain the SPNE.

The NE to the second-stage game, where firms compete by simultaneously choosing price, was derived in Sect. 10.2.3.2 (Chap. 10). It is

$$p_1^* = c + \frac{\phi_1(z_1 - z_2)}{3} > p_2^* = c + \frac{\phi_2(z_1 - z_2)}{3}, \tag{15.26}$$

$$q_1^* = \frac{N\phi_1}{3} > q_2^* = \frac{N\phi_2}{3}, \tag{15.27}$$

$$\pi_1^* = \frac{N\phi_1^2(z_1 - z_2)}{9} - p_A A_1, \quad \pi_2^* = \frac{N\phi_2^2(z_1 - z_2)}{9} - p_A A_2, \tag{15.28}$$

where c is marginal production cost, $\phi_1 \equiv 2\phi_H - \phi_L$, and $\phi_2 \equiv \phi_H - 2\phi_L > 0$. Ignoring advertising for the moment, if there is no real quality difference between brands, then price equals marginal cost and profits are zero (ignoring advertising).

To avoid this outcome, a firm may invest in advertising to persuade consumers to incorrectly believe that the advertised brand is of higher quality ($\partial z_i / \partial A_i > 0$). Again, we will not calculate a specific solution to this problem, but the important implications of the model can be seen from the first-order conditions to the stage one problem. Assuming that firms are sequentially rational, they derive from the first-stage profit equations found in (15.28)[38]:

$$\frac{\partial \pi_1^*}{\partial A_1} = MR_{A1} - MC_{A1}$$

$$= \left(\frac{N\phi_1^2}{9} \frac{\partial z_1}{\partial A_1} \right) - p_A = 0, \tag{15.29}$$

$$\frac{\partial \pi_2^*}{\partial A_2} = MR_{A2} - MC_{A2}$$

$$= \left(-\frac{N\phi_2^2}{9} \frac{\partial z_2}{\partial A_2} \right) - p_A < 0. \tag{15.30}$$

The marginal revenue of advertising for each respective firm is in parentheses. This model implies that as long as p_A is sufficiently low, firm 1 will have an incentive to advertise because the marginal revenue of advertising is positive and has a negative

---

[38] Second-order conditions of profit maximization are assumed to hold. This requires that advertising changes perceived quality at a decreasing rate. That is, $\partial^2 z_i / \partial A_i^2 < 0$.

slope (because $\partial^2 z_i/\partial A_i^2 < 0$). The first-order condition for firm 2 is always negative, however. This means that firm 2's optimal level of advertising is zero, and only firm 1 has an incentive to advertise.

The reason for this is that advertising increases perceived quality and firms benefit from increased product differentiation (i.e., increasing $z_1 - z_2$). Firm 1 benefits from increasing z_1, but firm 2's profits fall as z_2 increases. Thus, only firm 1 invests in advertising. This outcome is consistent with the market for aspirin and laundry bleach, where the leading national brands, Bayer and Clorox, advertise heavily and their generic counterparts do not advertise at all. The model implies that advertising causes consumers to believe that the advertised brand is of higher quality, enabling it to sell at a higher price, even though it is of identical quality to the unadvertised brand. By increasing perceived differentiation, this benefits both firms.

15.3.3.4   Behavioral Economics Model 2: Advertising Causes Consumers to Make Mistakes

In this example, we make a slight modification to the previous model. Instead of assuming that advertising changes consumer beliefs about product quality, advertising causes consumers to make mistakes that favor the advertised brand. For example, from behavioral economics we know that advertising could frame information in such a way to induce errors that benefit the advertised brand. Thus, advertising can exacerbate consumer errors.

Recall from Chap. 7 that consumer k's utility function in the vertical differentiation model of Mussa and Rosen (1978) is $U_{ki} = \phi_k z_i - p_i$, which is assumed to represent consumer k's true preferences. If mistakes are possible, then the utility function becomes $U_{ki} = \phi_k z_i - p_i + e_i$, where e_i is an error term assumed to be common to all consumers for simplicity. When $e_i > 0$ (<0), brand i is overvalued (undervalued) by consumers. For example, a rush of over-exuberance would cause e_i to be positive and induce an impulse purchase, something that could not occur if consumers were error free. By modifying the model in Chap. 7 to allow for mistakes such as these, the system of demand functions becomes

$$q_1 = N(\phi_H - p_1/z + p_2/z + e_1/z - e_2/z), \tag{15.31}$$

$$q_2 = N(-\phi_L + p_1/z - p_2/z - e_1/z + e_2/z), \tag{15.32}$$

where $z \equiv z_1 - z_2$. Demand for brand i increases in e_i and decreases in e_j. In this model, advertising plays a role by encouraging over-exuberance (excessive enthusiasm) for the advertised brand ($\partial e_i/\partial A_i > 0$).

All other aspects of the model parallel the previous example. Firms compete in a two-stage game. In stage one, firms compete in advertising that induces consumer mistakes; in stage two, firms compete in price. Again, we use backwards induction

to obtain the SPNE. The NE to the second stage of the game, where firms compete
by simultaneously choosing price, becomes

$$p_1^* = c + \frac{(\phi_1 z + e_1 - e_2)}{3} > p_2^* = c + \frac{(\phi_2 z - e_1 + e_2)}{3}, \tag{15.33}$$

$$q_1^* = \frac{N(\phi_1 z + e_1 - e_2)}{3z} > q_2^* = \frac{N(\phi_2 z - e_1 + e_2)}{3z}, \tag{15.34}$$

$$\pi_2^* = \frac{N(\phi_1 z + e_1 - e_2)^2}{9z} - p_A A_2, \quad \pi_2^* = \frac{N(\phi_2 z - e_1 + e_2)^2}{9z} - p_A A_2, \tag{15.35}$$

where $\phi_1 \equiv 2\phi_H - \phi_L$ and $\phi_2 \equiv \phi_H - 2\phi_L > 0$. As one might expect, firm i is better
off when consumers make an error in favor of its own brand ($e_i > 0$), *ceteris paribus*.

Under certain conditions it is profitable for firms to invest in advertising that
induces consumer mistakes that favor of the advertised brand. This is evident from
the first-order conditions in the advertising stage of the game that derive from the
profit equations in (15.29)[39]:

$$\frac{\partial \pi_1^*}{\partial A_1} = MR_{A1} - MC_{A1}$$

$$= \frac{2N(e_1 - e_2 + \phi_1 z)}{9z} \frac{\partial e_1}{\partial A_1} - p_A = 0, \tag{15.36}$$

$$\frac{\partial \pi_2^*}{\partial A_2} = MR_{A2} - MC_{A2}$$

$$= \frac{2N(e_2 - e_1 + \phi_2 z)}{9z} \frac{\partial e_2}{\partial A_2} - p_A = 0. \tag{15.37}$$

This model produces a different result from the previous behavioral model of
advertising. In this case, if p_A is sufficiently small and ϕ_2 is sufficiently large, then
both firms will have an incentive to advertise because the marginal revenue of
advertising is positive and has a negative slope for both firms. This may be
consistent with ads that claim a product is new and improved, a claim that causes
some consumers to try the product even though there is no noticeable improvement.
Such claims can be made by both high and low quality brands. Nevertheless, like
the previous behavioral model, this model produces an asymmetric outcome. If the
marginal effectiveness of advertising is the same for both firms, the high quality
firm (firm 1) will spend more on advertising than the low quality firm.[40]

---

[39] Second-order conditions of profit maximization are assumed to hold. This requires that advertising increases the error term at a decreasing rate. That is, $\partial^2 e_i / \partial A_i^2 < 0$.

[40] This is because the marginal revenue of advertising is greater for firm 1, given that $\phi_1 > \phi_2$.
Because firm 1 invests more on advertising in equilibrium, e_1 will exceed e_2. Thus, the marginal
revenue of advertising for firm 2 will be negative unless ϕ_2 is sufficiently large. If not, only firm 1
will invest in advertising, as in the previous example.

15.3.4   Summary of Implications and Empirical Evidence

The models discussed in this section indicate that there are multiple factors that affect the degree of advertising intensity. First, the Dorfman–Steiner condition implies that advertising will increase as demand becomes relatively more inelastic. When the price elasticity of demand is infinite, as in perfectly competitive markets, firms have no incentive to advertise unless they form a marketing collective.

The evidence is consistent with this prediction. Consider the market for agricultural commodities. Individual producers of milk, peaches, mushrooms, plums, and grapes compete in relatively competitive markets and do not invest in brand advertising. Instead, they belong to commodity checkoff programs, which supply generic advertising that is designed to promote the general characteristics of the product and benefit all producers in the industry. Supermarkets, which are geographically (horizontally) differentiated, face negatively sloped demand functions, however, and frequently advertise the price and availability of their commodities in weekly newspaper advertisements.

The Dorfman–Steiner condition also implies that firms will advertise more intensively when advertising is more effective at increasing demand (i.e., η_A is greater). After controlling for market power, the evidence from Comanor and Wilson (1974) and Metwally (1975) generally supports this implication. They find that the demand response rates to advertising are high for liquor, drugs, soft drinks, and toothpaste, consumer goods that are intensively advertised. They also find that they are low for tires, motorcycles, and bicycles, products that receive little advertising (see Table 15.5).

Finally, the discussion of oligopoly markets indicates that strategic effects also influence the intensity of advertising. Competition in advertising can become intense when firms face a prisoners' dilemma in advertising, a situation that has plagued many oligopolistic industries. One example is the US brewing industry where firm-level advertising is combative and has little or no effect on total market demand (Nelson 1999; V. Tremblay and C. Tremblay 2005). Advertising is so combative in brewing that it led to what is called an advertising war and explains the high level of advertising intensity found in this industry (see Table 15.2).

There is also strong evidence that US cigarette producers faced a prisoners' dilemma in advertising in the 1960s and 1970s. First, Seldon et al. (1993) found that cigarette advertising is combative. Second, the ban on broadcast (television and radio) advertising in 1971 caused a substantial rise in industry profits (Eckard 1991; Farr et al. 2001). Finally, Iwasaki and V. Tremblay (2009) found that the efficient level of broadcast advertising before the ban was zero. Taken together, it is clear that the unconstrained level of advertising before the ban was excessive from the industry's perspective.

Although advertising is often combative, it can also be constructive. Kwoka (1993) found evidence of constructive advertising in the US auto industry. In addition, Ellison and Ellison (2007) found advertising in the US pharmaceutical industry to be constructive, and Roberts and Samuelson (1988) found that

Table 15.5 Advertising
elasticity of demand

Industry	Advertising elasticity
Clothing—women	0.85
Liquor	0.64
Soft drinks	0.57
Footwear (rubber and plastic)	0.56
Clothing—Men	0.43
Motor vehicles	0.35
Soaps	0.28
Motorcycles and bicycles	0.17
Tires	0.13

Source: Comanor and Wilson (1974, 89–90).

Table 15.6 Advertising and price asymmetries in selected consumer goods markets

MARKET (quantity)	Price	Market share of advertising	Market share of output
Regular Aspirin (100 units)			
Bayer	$4.98	100%	93%
Generic brands	$1.47	0%	7%
Chlorine bleach (gallon)			
Clorox	$0.98	100%	56–72%
Generic Brands	$0.87	0%	28–44%
Lemon Juice (12 oz)			
ReaLemon	$0.62	100%	80%
Generic brands	$0.47	0%	20%
Premium cola (2 L)			
Coke	$1.00	53.5%	53.3%
Pepsi	$1.04	46.5%	46.7%

Sources: V. Tremblay and Polasky (2002) for aspirin, bleach, and cola; *In the Matter of Borden, Inc.*, 92 FTC 669 (1978) for lemon juice.

advertising for new brands of cigarettes in the USA can be constructive.[41] With constructive advertising, individual firms advertise less than is optimal from the industry's perspective.

Another issue of interest in oligopoly markets is the degree to which advertising intensity will be the same across firms within an industry. We saw that advertising intensity is more likely to be asymmetric when firms have different levels of advertising productivity. This result is consistent with the work by Färe et al. (2004), who found that the leading advertiser in the US brewing industry, Anheuser-Busch, had the most efficient marketing campaigns.

We also saw that advertising asymmetry is more likely when advertising promotes perceived vertical differentiation, a form of advertising that leads to advertised (name) and unadvertised (generic) brands. Table 15.6 provides evidence from the aspirin, bleach, and bottled lemon juice markets where name and generic

---

[41] Recall that constructive advertising is more likely for new brands or products, which may account for the different results for the US cigarette industry.

brands coexist. As predicted by the model, more advertising is invested in the brand of higher perceived quality. The market for premium cola provides an example where firms use advertising to create subjective horizontal differentiation, with Coke ads appealing to traditional values and Pepsi ads appealing to a more rebellious consumer. As predicted, the outcome is more symmetric in this case.

In general terms, the discussion earlier in the chapter suggests that the advertising-to-sales ratio should rise with concentration until a near monopoly structure is reached, *ceteris paribus*. Greer (1971) hypothesized a quadratic relationship between advertising intensity and industry concentration, with advertising intensity initially rising and eventually falling as concentration increases. Martin (1979) and Buxton et al. (1984) found evidence to support a quadratic relationship between advertising and concentration in consumer goods industries. Buxton et al. found that the advertising-to-sales ratio reached a maximum when the four-firm concentration ratio reached 64%.[42] More recently, Iwasaki et al. (2008) found significant support for this hypothesis for the US brewing industry, with the advertising-to-sales ratio reaching a maximum when the Herfindahl–Hirschman index (HHI) equals 0.164 (or where the four-firm concentration ratio equals about 67%). Recall from Chap. 8 that the Department of Justice classifies an industry as unconcentrated when HHI is below 0.10, highly concentrated when HHI exceeds 0.18, and moderately concentrated when HHI lies between these two bounds. Thus, advertising intensity in brewing reached a maximum when HHI approached the cutoff for being highly concentrated.

15.4   The Effect of Advertising on Market Structure

In the preceding section we investigated the effect of market structure on advertising intensity. It is also possible that causality runs in the other direction, with advertising influencing market structure. We saw in Chap. 8 that Sutton's (1991) model predicts that higher sunk costs can cause industry concentration to increase. If advertising has a sunk cost component, this is one way in which advertising can affect concentration.

Recall that Sutton's (1991) model made two predictions about the relationship between sunk costs and concentration. First, industry concentration will be higher in markets with high sunk costs. Second, an increase in the size of the market causes concentration to fall when sunk costs are exogenous but will have little effect on concentration when sunk costs are endogenous. Advertising is clearly endogenous, as it is a firm choice variable.

One question that remains is the extent to which advertising expenditures are sunk. The sunk cost portion of an investment is that which cannot be recovered if the firm

---

[42] When all firms are of equal size, the Hirfindahl–Hirschman index equals 0.16 when the four-firm concentration ratio equals 64%.

exits the industry. If advertising enhances the goodwill of a firm, however, then this will be reflected in the market value of the firm. In this case, the goodwill enhancing portion of advertising can be recovered when the firm is sold. The evidence shows that this contribution is small, however. As discussed previously, advertising does not have a long lasting effect on sales. In addition, Thomas (1989), Kwoka (1993), and Landes and Rosenfield (1994) found brand-specific effects such as quality and styling have a much bigger effect on brand loyalty and goodwill than advertising. Thus, most if not all of advertising can be considered a sunk cost.

As we saw in Chap. 8, there is considerable empirical support for Sutton's (1991) theory that high sunk costs due to advertising lead to high levels of concentration. He tests the theory with data from twenty food and beverage industries in six countries by dividing them into two groups: those with homogeneous goods and little or no advertising and those with moderate to high levels of advertising.[43] The results show that concentration is generally higher for the advertising-intensive group. In addition, as market size increases, *ceteris paribus*, concentration falls in the homogeneous-goods group but not for the advertising-intensive group. Thus, endogenous sunk costs associated with advertising appear to cause high levels of concentration.[44]

We should keep one caveat in mind, however. As Sutton (1991, Chap. 9) points out, sunk costs are not all that matter to the evolution of industry structure. History and the idiosyncratic characteristics of an industry may be equally important in explaining industry concentration and the level of advertising rivalry.

The advent of television may have played a key role in the success of national producers after World War II and contributed to rising concentration in many consumer goods industries. In 1950, 9% of households had at least one television set. This number grew dramatically over time, reaching 87% in 1960, 95% in 1970, and 98% in 1980 (the same as today). The advent of television created a tremendous marketing opportunity for large national companies, because television advertising had to be aired nationally in the 1950s and 1960s (Porter 1976). Local and regional ads were unavailable at that time. Thus, small local and regional producers were unable to take advantage of this new marketing media.

Doraszelski and Markovich (2007) showed that a situation such as this can thrust firms into a preemption race in advertising. That is, as firms strive to take advantage of the new marketing opportunity of television, only a small percentage of national

---

[43] The countries are France, Germany, Italy, Japan, the UK, and the USA. The homogeneous-goods group consists of bread, flour, processed meat, salt, sugar, and canned vegetables, which had advertising-to-sales ratios below 1%. The advertising-intensive group includes frozen food, soup, margarine, soft drinks, ready-to-eat breakfast cereal, mineral water, sugar confectionery, chocolate confectionery, roast and ground coffee, biscuits, pet food, baby food, and beer.

[44] Subsequent work provides further support for Sutton's findings. These include studies by Robinson and Chiang (1996) for a sample of US consumer goods industries, Matraves (1999) for the global pharmaceutical industry, Symeonides (2000b) for UK manufacturing, Berry and Waldfogel (2010) for the US newspaper industry, and V. Tremblay and C. Tremblay (2005) for the US brewing industry.

producers are successful given the risky nature of advertising and that smaller producers could not profitably advertise on television. Ads that proved successful helped build such famous national brands as McDonald's restaurants, Budweiser beer, Oreo cookies, Oscar Mayer lunch meats, Levi jeans, and Duracell batteries. With their growing success, concentration increased.

The success of nationally advertised brands is apparent from Table 15.7, which summarizes price information for 29 food categories collected by *Consumer Reports* (2009). In many cases, national brands command a dominant market share in spite of selling at a price premium that averages 40%. The extent to which this price differential is due to advertising or other factors, such as a difference in quality, will be discussed in the next chapter.

Development of the Internet has produced new marketing opportunities that may also affect industry concentration. Beginning in the mid-1990s, a proliferation of Internet firms entered the marketplace. Although many failed at the end of the dot-com bubble (1998–2001), firms such as Amazon.com have become major corporations. Internet marketing opportunities may dampen the advantage of the traditional national brands, as local and regional producers are just as capable as national producers of developing a Web page to promote their product lines. It remains to be seen how the Internet will affect the evolution of industry concentration.

15.5 Summary

1. About 2% of GDP is spent each year on advertising. Because of differences in the marginal benefit of advertising, ad spending varies considerably across industries and across firms within the same industry.
2. There are three main types of advertising: informative, persuasive, and that which creates subjective differentiation. **Informative advertising** provides consumers with information about price, availability, and product character-istics. Advertising can also be used to signal that the heavily advertised brand is of high quality. **Persuasive advertising** enhances brand loyalty by changing consumer tastes in favor of the advertised brand. This can occur by changing consumer beliefs or by inducing consumers to make systematic errors that favor the advertised brand. **Advertising that creates subjective differentiation** builds brand name recognition, frequently by creating a prestige factor or creating a desirable image that becomes associated with the product.
3. The type of good being marketed influences a firm's advertising decision. In general, firms are more likely to use advertising to build subjective differentia-tion when marketing consumer goods than producer goods. Firms tend to use informative advertising to market search goods, goods where product characteristics can be identified before purchase. Firms are more likely to use persuasive advertising on experience goods, goods where product characteristics can be identified only after purchase, and on credence goods,

Table 15.7 National versus store or generic brands in 29 food categories

Category (size) National & store brand	Price		Highest quality		
	National	Store	National	Store	Tie
Oatmeal–raisin cookies (8.6 oz)					
Pepperidge & Archer	$2.98	$2.92		x	
Frozen Lasagna (serving)					
Stouffer & Walmart	1.44	0.88			x
Multigrain Spaghetti (14.5 oz)					
Barella & America's Choice	2.25	1.59			x
Dijon Mustard (serving)					
Grey Poupon & GreenWise	0.05	0.03			x
Barbecue Sauce (24 oz)					
K.C. Masterpiece & Publix	1.92	1.51	x		
Salsa (serving)					
Old El Paso & Kirkland	0.17	0.10		x	
Frozen Broccoli (serving)					
Birds Eye & Whole Foods	0.55	0.38			x
Dried Cranberries (6 oz)					
Ocean Spray & Target	2.41	2.29	x		
Vegetable juice (32 oz)					
V8 & Whole Foods	2.81	2.67	x		
Vanilla extract (1 oz)					
McCormick & Kirkland	3.34	0.35			x
Steak Sauce (10 oz)					
A1 & Whole Foods	3.70	2.84			x
Precooked Bacon (serving)					
Oscar Mayer & Publix	0.85	0.58	x		
Whipped topping (8 oz)					
Cool Whip & Walmart	1.58	0.87		x	
Au Gratin Potatoes (5 oz)					
Betty Crocker & Walmart	1.85	0.92		x	
Frozen Pepperoni Pizza (medium)					
Digiorno & Target	6.20	5.02			x
Frozen Sandwich Steak (serving)					
Steak-umm & A&P	0.70	0.57			x
Raspberry Preserves (serving)					
Polaner & Kroger	0.15	0.12			x
Probiotic Yogurt (16 oz)					
Dannon & Safeway	2.49	2.40			x
Brownie Mix (10 oz box)					
Duncan Hines & Target	1.95	1.32			x
Frozen strawberries (serving)					
Dole & Kirkland	0.86	0.47			x
Granola (serving)					
Quaker & A&P	0.30	0.34	x		
Boxed Chocolates (1 oz)					
Lindt & Kirkland	1.86	0.75			x
Toaster Pastries (14.6 oz)					
Kellogg's & Kroger	2.22	1.42	x		
Average price	1.85	1.32			
Score			26%	17%	57%

Source: Consumer Reports (2009). The quality assessment is based on blind taste tests, with an x indicating that either the national brand was preferred, the store brand was preferred, or they were equally preferred.

goods where it is uneconomic for consumers to identify product characteristics even after purchase.

4. Firm advertising that is **constructive** will increase rival demand and, therefore, market demand. This is more likely to occur when marketing new and pioneering products. Firm advertising that steals customers from rivals is **combative**.

5. A **mass-market advertising** campaign causes firm demand to rotate counter-clockwise, enabling a larger number of consumers to have a positive marginal valuation of the product. **Niche-market advertising** causes firm demand to rotate clockwise by raising the marginal valuation of a small group of high valuation consumers.

6. The **advertising response function** describes the marginal effectiveness of advertising for different levels of advertising expenditures. Beyond some point, advertising will increase total revenue at a decreasing rate, indicating diminishing marginal returns (marginal revenue) to advertising.

7. Because of the free rider problem, individual firms will not advertise in perfectly competitive industries. Instead, they may form a collective to raise funds to support a generic advertising campaign. **Generic advertising** promotes the commodity generally and not a particular brand. This is done in many agricultural markets, such as milk, through **commodity checkoff programs**.

8. The **Dorfman–Steiner condition** indicates that the advertising spending of a monopolist will increase as the marginal effectiveness of advertising increases and as demand becomes more inelastic, *ceteris paribus*. It also suggests that advertising intensity should rise with concentration.

9. In oligopoly markets, strategic effects also influence advertising spending. When advertising is combative, firms face a **prisoners' dilemma in advertising**, and the Nash equilibrium level of advertising will exceed the cartel level of advertising. When advertising is constructive, the Nash level of advertising will be less than the cartel level of advertising.

10. Firm advertising expenditures are more likely to be symmetric when they promote horizontal differentiation and advertising causes consumers to error in favor of the advertised brand. Advertising expenditures are more likely to be asymmetric when they promote vertical differentiation. A firm will invest more in advertising when it has a strategic advantage in advertising.

11. Advertising can be either a strategic complement or a strategic substitute. When advertising is combative, it is more likely to be a strategic substitute and have negatively sloped best-reply functions. When it is constructive, it is more likely to be a strategic complement and have positively sloped best-reply functions. Advertising is more likely to be a strategic complement in a new market, when there is little or no product differentiation and when advertising provides consumers with information about the generic characteristics of a commodity.

12. The empirical evidence supports the fact that some advertising is informative and other advertising is persuasive or image enhancing. The evidence also confirms that:

- There is little advertising in competitive industries, unless a commodity checkoff program is in place.
- Advertising spending tends to be greatest in oligopoly markets.
- Firms invest more in advertising when the marginal effect of advertising on demand is large.
- Advertising competition can be intense when advertising is combative.
- There is greater heterogeneity (homogeneity) in advertising spending within an industry when differentiation is vertical (horizontal).

13. Market structure affects advertising spending, and advertising spending affects market structure. The advertising-to-sales ratio is more likely to be high in oligopoly markets, where advertising is frequently combative. In addition, an increase in advertising spending may raise sunk costs and increase industry concentration.

15.6   Review Questions

1. Discuss the relationships among the following types of advertising: advertising that is a strategic complement, a strategic substitute, constructive, and combative.
2. One way to decompose the effect of advertising is to determine its effect on new versus experienced consumers. Compare and contrast how advertising that is persuasive, informative, and image creating will affect new consumers compared to experienced consumers (those who have purchased each brand or product in the recent past).
3. Consider the markets for neckties, canned soup, and automobile engine repair. Classify each as being primarily a search, experience, or credence good.

   A. In which market would you expect to find the highest advertising intensity (assuming no government regulations)? Explain.
   B. In which market would you expect to find the lowest advertising intensity? Explain.
4. Assume that advertising causes demand to rotate in three possible ways:

   A. Advertising causes demand to rotate around point x, which is located in the positive price–quantity quadrant.
   B. Advertising causes demand to rotate around the quantity intercept of demand. That is, the q-intercept on the horizontal axis remains the same.
   C. Advertising causes demand to rotate around the price intercept of demand. That is, the p-intercept on the vertical axis remains the same.

Graph the three types of demand rotations and explain the type of advertising campaign that would generate them (i.e., whether they imply a mass-market, niche-market, or another type of advertising campaign).

5. Assume that a monopolist faces the following inverse demand function and total cost function, which depend on output (q) and advertising (A):

$$p = a - bq + A^{1/2}, \quad TC = cq + p_A A,$$

where a, b, and c are positive constants and p_A is the price of advertising.

A. Define the firm's total revenue function (TR).
B. Derive the firm's marginal revenue in output ($MR_q = \partial TR/\partial q$) and its marginal revenue in advertising ($MR_A = \partial TR/\partial A$).
C. Derive the firm's marginal cost in output ($MC_q = \partial TC/\partial q$) and its marginal cost in advertising ($MC_A = \partial TC/\partial A$).
D. (Advanced) Determine the optimal level of output (q^*) and advertising (A^*) if the firm's goal is to maximize profit with respect to these two variables. (The problem is easier to solve if you reparameterize the model so that $A^{1/2} = x$ and $A = x^2$. In this case, the monopolist's profit equation becomes $\pi = aq - bq^2 + xq - cq - p_A x^2$.)

6. Assume that two firms (1 and 2) compete in price and advertising. The demand function for firm i is $q_i = a - p_i - bp_j + A_i + dA_j$, where a, b, and d are parameters with a, $b > 0$. What restriction would you place on parameter d to ensure that advertising is (1) constructive, (2) perfectly constructive, (3) combative, and (4) perfectly combative?

7. Assume a duopoly market with firms 1 and 2 that compete by simultaneously choosing advertising. The profit equation for firm i is

$$\pi_i = 120 - 16\frac{A_j}{A_i} - A_i.$$

A. Given that the first-order condition of profit maximization for firm i is

$$\frac{\partial \pi_i}{\partial A_i} = \frac{16A_j}{A_i^2} - 1 = 0,$$

derive and graph the best-reply functions for firms 1 and 2.
B. Determine the Nash equilibrium levels of advertising (A_1^* and A_2^*).
C. (Advanced) How does it compare to the cartel levels of advertising? Is the Nash equilibrium stable?

8. Explain how the price elasticity of demand, the marginal effectiveness of advertising, and strategic considerations affect a firm's decision to advertise.

9. One advantage of Internet advertising is that it can target people who have a high probability of purchasing the advertised product. Explain how the ability of a firm to use targeted advertising will affect a firm's profit-maximizing level of advertising.

10. What characteristics of advertising would increase the likelihood that firms face a prisoners' dilemma in advertising?

11. (Advanced) Assume a duopoly market where firms 1 and 2 compete by simultaneously choosing output and advertising. Inverse demand and total cost functions are $p_i = 12 - (q_1 + q_2) + A_i^{1/2} + dA_j^{1/2}$, $TC_i = A_i$.

   A. Determine the optimal level of advertising and output. (Again, you might reparameterize the model so that $A_i^{1/2} = x_i$ and $A_i = x_i^2$).
   B. Discuss the extent to which advertising is constructive versus combative.

12. Assume that a small resort town has two grocery stores. Store 1 is in the middle of Main Street, and store 2 is on a cross street that is several blocks away from Main Street. Tourists stay in hotels and condos along Main Street.

   A. Which grocery store is likely to have higher consumer search costs, especially for tourists?
   B. Given our discussion of advertising and search costs, which store do you think is more likely to charge lower prices and to spend more on advertising? Explain.

13. (Advanced) In Sect. 15.3.3.4, we developed a model where advertising causes consumers to make mistakes when evaluating an advertised brand. Discuss how the model changes when the error term enters multiplicatively instead of additively so that $U_{ki} = x_k z_i - p_i$, where $x_k = \phi_k + e_i$.

14. Most fast-food commercials use thin, healthy, and athletic actors to promote their brands. For example, basketball stars Dwight Howard and LeBron James appeared in a recent McDonald's commercial. Use contributions from behavioral economics to show why this marketing strategy may be effective.

15. Some consumers have a desire to fit in, as discussed in Chap. 4. Explain why this may induce producers of unhealthy commodities to create an image that appeals to the identity of a certain group. For example, successful rap groups have been used to promote malt liquor (beer with a high alcohol content) to young adults in inner cities.

16. Explain why consumer loss aversion may induce firms to invest in advertising to create brand loyalty and brand names. What does the empirical evidence say about this issue?

Appendix A: A Dynamic Model of Advertising

Consider the dynamic case where a monopolist's advertising affects current and future demand (Nerlove and Arrow 1962). This can occur when advertising enhances a product's long-term image, reputation, or goodwill. Advertising increases demand in current and future periods, although its effect fades over time. To simplify the analysis, we ignore price and focus on the firm's decision to advertise.

The model assumes that the level of product image or goodwill in period t (G_t) depends on advertising expenditures (A) today and in the past. The effect of advertising depreciates, as our memory of an ad fades with time. Demand and total revenue are influenced by advertising through goodwill, which produces a dynamic problem.

To simplify things, assume that there are just two periods, I and II, and ignore discounting.[45] The firm's problem is to maximize the stream of profits with respect to advertising, subject to appropriate constraints. This stream of profits equals

$$\Pi = \pi_I[G_I(A_I)] + \pi_{II}[G_{II}(A_I, A_{II})], \qquad (A.1)$$

where π_t is profit in period t. To obtain the SPNE, we use the same method that we used in Chap. 11.[46] We first solve the stage II problem. This gives us the optimal value of A_{II} and π_{II}, π_{II}^*. Substituting these values into (A.1) produces

$$\Pi = \pi_I[G_I(A_I)] + \pi_{II}^*[G_{II}(A_I)]. \qquad (A.2)$$

Now the firm solves the stage I problem, knowing the solution to the stage II problem. That is, the firm chooses the level of A_I to maximize (A.2). The first-order condition is[47]

$$\frac{\partial \Pi}{\partial A_I} = \frac{d\pi_I}{dG_I}\frac{dG_I}{dA_I} + \frac{d\pi_{II}^*}{dG_{II}}\frac{dG_{II}}{dA_I} = 0. \qquad (A.3)$$

The first set of terms between the equal signs is simply the effect of a change in advertising in period I on profits in period I (indirectly through its effect on G_I). The second set of terms is the effect of a change in advertising in period I on optimal profits in period II (indirectly through its effect on G_{II}). If advertising has no effect on future goodwill, this term would be zero, and we would have a static problem

---

[45] Recall from Chap. 2 that this means that the discount factor (D) equals 1. That is, $1 received in 1 year is valued at $1 today.

[46] More formally, dynamic programming methods should be used to solve this problem, as discussed in the Mathematical and Econometrics Appendix.

[47] This makes use of the chain rule, as discussed in the Mathematical and Econometrics Appendix.

where current advertising only affects current profit. In this case, the normal marginal conditions apply: the firm would equate the marginal revenue of advertising with the marginal cost of advertising in period t. When current advertising increases future goodwill, however, the second set of terms would be positive. This adds to the marginal benefit of advertising and causes the firm to spend more on advertising than if there were no dynamic effects.[48]

This model suggests that when advertising is better able to enhance product goodwill today and into the future, firms will invest more of their resources in advertising. This result provides another possible explanation for the differences in advertising expenditures found among industries in Table 15.2. When advertising promotes a positive long-term image, as in ads for Celine Dion perfume, advertising intensity will be high; when advertising is primarily informative, as are price ads at a local grocery store, advertising intensity will be substantially lower.

---

[48] Of course, if previous advertising builds up considerable goodwill today, this may enable the firm to advertise less today (if it reduces the current marginal benefit of advertising).

Chapter 16
Advertising and Welfare

In the previous chapter, we saw that approximately 2% of GDP is spent on advertising each year. For most of us, it is impossible to escape advertising, as it is found on television and radio, in movie theaters, and on the Internet. Advertising spending is especially prominent in consumer goods industries. The advertising-to-sales ratio exceeds 10% in many consumer goods industries, including liquor, perfume, and cosmetics, but is less than 1% in most producer goods industries, such as cement and industrial materials.

Social critics have debated the merits of advertising for centuries. These are expressed eloquently in the extreme views of Thomas Jefferson and H.G. Wells. In 1819, Jefferson is quoted as saying "Advertisements contain the only truths to be relied on in a newspaper." In 1934, Wells took the opposite viewpoint when he said that "Advertising is legalized lying." Even if all ads were truthful and not socially offensive, many critics would still be concerned that there is too much advertising from society's perspective.[1]

In this chapter, we focus on the effect of advertising on society. As discussed in Chap. 1, welfare analysis is difficult because we want so many things from our political-economic system, and trade offs and value judgments are frequently required. We may all agree that advertisements should be honest and promote socially desirable (not illegal) activities. Yet, distinctions can be subtle, making it difficult to decide which ads cross the line of honesty and acceptability. Efficiency analysis is a cornerstone of economics, and we also want to know if free markets supply too little or too much advertising from an efficiency point of view. Even here, however, we will see that an efficiency analysis is difficult, especially when advertising changes consumer tastes. With these caveats in mind, we take up the welfare issues of advertising in this chapter.

---

[1] See Jackman and Macmillan (1984) for these and other famous advertising quotes. For a review of the social debate regarding advertising, see Bagwell (2007).

V.J. Tremblay and C.H. Tremblay, *New Perspectives on Industrial Organization*,
Springer Texts in Business and Economics, DOI 10.1007/978-1-4614-3241-8_16,
© Springer Science+Business Media New York 2012

16.1   Advertising and Social Responsibility

The most onerous form of advertising makes false and deceptive claims. Such claims are clearly harmful to consumers and are illegal under the Federal Trade Commission (FTC) Act of 1914.[2] According to the FTC, for an ad to be false or deceptive, three conditions must be met. First, the ad must present or omit information that is likely to mislead consumers. A common example is the use of a "bait and switch" tactic where a seller entices customers with an alluring but insincere offer (e.g., a very low price) that the advertiser has no intention of honoring. Once in the store, customers are told that the advertised product is unavailable and are encouraged to buy a higher priced substitute. Another example is when a firm promotes the merits of a product and fails to disclose a known defect to potential customers.

Second, the ad must be viewed as deceptive from the viewpoint of a "reasonable consumer" or the targeted group, such as children and the terminally ill.[3] This concept is a bit fuzzy; several examples illustrate how the reasonable consumer principle is applied. One distinction of interest is the country-of-origin designation. Consider the examples of a Danish pastry and an American car. To advertise a car as domestic, "all significant parts and processes that go into product must be of US origin" ("Complying with the Made in the USA Standard," at http://www.ftc.gov/). In contrast, even though some consumers may believe that a "Danish pastry" sold at a local bakery is made in Denmark, a reasonable consumer would understand that it is a Danish style pastry baked locally. Thus, representing it as a Danish pastry is not illegal.

The FTC also allows ads that are obvious exaggerations or puffing, as they are not taken seriously by ordinary consumers. Such ads frequently use adjectives such as best, perfect, exceptional, original, and wonderful. Every day we are exposed to ads that exaggerate in this way.

> Apple Computers: "The Power to be Your Best"
> BMW: "The Ultimate Driving Machine"
> Coke: "It's the Real Thing"
> Energizer Batteries: "They Keep Going and Going and Going. . ."
> Goodyear: "The Best Tires in the World have Goodyear Written all over Them"
> McDonald's: "I'm Loving It!"
> Minute Rice: "Perfect Rice Every Time"

---

[2] This discussion derives from the Act and Federal Trade Commission documents that clarify its interpretation. These include "FTC Policy Statement on Deception," "Statement of Policy Regarding Comparative Advertising," "FTC Guides Against Deceptive Pricing," "Guides Against Bait Advertising," "The ABCs at the FTC: Marketing and Advertising to Children," and "Complying with the Made in the USA Standard" which are available at http://www.ftc.gov/.

[3] Regarding ads targeted at children, a higher standard is used because of the "limited ability of children to detect exaggerated or untrue statements" ("The ABCs at the FTC: Marketing and Advertising to Children," at http://www.ftc.gov/).

A classic case where the reasonable consumer principle played an important role in litigation involved Listerine mouthwash.[4] Listerine's marketing stated: "Kills germs by millions on contact" and "For general oral hygiene, bad breath, colds, and resulting sore throats." The FTC effectively argued that these statements would mislead the general population into believing that Listerine could prevent a cold and sore throat, and the company had to delete the "colds, and resultant sore throats" phrase.

The third condition that must be met for an ad to be false or deceptive is "materiality." This means that the deceptive information or sales practice must be important enough to have caused consumers to make a different choice in all likelihood. Material information concerns the purpose, safety, efficacy, or cost of the product. If a deceptive statement is immaterial, it is unlikely to affect consumer behavior and is acceptable.

Posner (1973) claims, however, that it is unnecessary to place any restrictions on advertising. His position is based on the argument that most consumers behave according to the principle of *caveat emptor*, which is Latin for "let the buyer beware." In general, consumers will assess product quality before purchase and when they are deceived, consumers will boycott future sales of dishonest firms. Thus, honest firms succeed and dishonest firms fail in the long run. This provides strong motivation for honesty in the marketplace.

Contributions from behavioral economics challenge Posner's viewpoint. For example, Nagler (1993) shows that deception can be profitable because it frequently takes time for a fraudulent claim to become apparent in a world where products have become increasing more complex, and once apparent some consumers are unwilling to admit to themselves and others that they were fooled.[5] In this case, deceptive marketing tactics are more likely to exist and persist.

Two other factors may influence a firm's incentive to engage in false or deceptive advertising. First, a firm that is going out of business will be less interested in its long-run reputation and will be more likely to engage in deceptive tactics. Second, firms that sell experience or credence goods will be more likely to deceive, as consumers will be unable to detect false claims before purchase. This would not be a problem for search goods, however. For example, from 1915 to 1925 the Ford Model T automobile came in just one color, black. The company had no incentive to advertise that it came in multiple colors, because a false claim such as this is readily apparent to consumers before making a purchase. This suggests that deception is more likely for products that are purchased infrequently and for goods with experience/credence characteristics. This is a growing concern in a modern society where products have become increasingly complex. It is for this reason that the sale of products such as these tend to be regulated, a topic that will be discussed in Chap. 20.

---

[4] Warner-Lambert, 86 F.T.C. 1398, 1415 n.4 (1975), aff'd, 562 F.2d 749 (D.C. Cir. 1977), cert denied, 435 U.S. 950 (1978).

[5] In addition, De Long et al. (1990) and De Long et al. (1991) show that markets may behave inefficiently when not all consumers are fully rational.

Another issue of social concern is that advertising can push the boundaries of social acceptability. Historical examples abound. The current premise in advertising is that sex sells, but this has not always been the case. According to Rooney (2010), a hundred years ago most ads were predominately product-centric. It was not until 1911 that the head of J. Walter Thomson Advertising, Helen Lansdowne, developed the first modern advertising campaign that emphasized sex appeal. The ad was for Woodbury soap and featured elegant young women in the company of dashing young men. The headline said, "Skin You Love to Touch."

To attract attention, advertisements sometimes use stereotypes that promote sexism, racism, and ageism. To appeal to a targeted audience, minority groups have been depicted stereotypically and/or derogatorily. Classic examples include ads for Aunt Jemima pancakes in the 1950s, where the spokesperson for the brand is an African-American woman who is depicted as a servant, and 1960s ads for Frito corn chips, where the spokesperson is a Hispanic cartoon character who is depicted as a criminal, "the Frito Bandito."

Sexism also abounds, with some ads depicting women as technically unskilled or as sex objects. One example is a 1953 magazine ad for Del Monte Ketchup, which shows a surprised women holding a ketchup bottle and asking "You mean a woman can open it?" Another is an advertisement for a VW bug that promotes one advantage of owning a bug: Women are prone to hitting things, and if your wife dents a VW fender, "A new one goes on with just ten bolts for $24.95, plus labor" (*Life Magazine*, August 13, 1964, 15).

The brewing industry provides an excellent case study where firms have sometimes skirted the line of good taste in advertisements. Artistic nudes and pinups have been used to market beer in saloons since the late 1880s. An extreme example is the "Nude Beer" brand, marketed by the Eastern Brewing Company in the 1980s, where each can had a sticker that could be peeled off to reveal a picture of a nude woman. Regarding racial insensitivity, the Heileman Brewing Company introduced "Crazy Horse Malt Liquor" in 1992, a name that offended Native American people because Crazy Horse is another name for Tasunke Witko who is a revered defender of the Lakota Sioux people.[6]

Although the examples presented so far are primarily historical, sexist and racist ads continue to this day. Calvin Klein ads for perfume are notorious for being sexually provocative.[7] Since 2005 Paris Hilton has starred in sexually provocative ads for Carl's Jr.'s spicy BBQ burger, claiming that "It's Hot." Both Microsoft and Sony have had to apologize recently for airing racially insensitive ads. In 2006, Sony promoted a new white PSP (portable game system) to complement its black PSP. To market its new white PSP and contrast it with its black version, Sony developed an ad that featured a white, blond women dominating a subordinate

---

[6] For a more complete discussion of the politically incorrect marketing actions of US beer companies, see V. Tremblay and C. Tremblay (2005).

[7] Examples of perfume ads that use sex and romance as selling tools can be reviewed at http://www.fragrantica.com, accessed July 20, 2010.

black women with the caption "PlayStation Portable White is Coming." After public criticism, Sony apologized and discontinued the ads. In 2009, Microsoft featured a white male, a black male, and a white female in an ad in the USA. The same ad was used in some European countries, but the black man's face was removed and replaced with that of a white man. Like Sony, Microsoft quickly pulled the ads after public criticism.

Some claim that ads such as these do not promote or reinforce racism and sexism but simply reflect the social norms of our culture. Racism and sexism are undesirable and the advertising messages described above are of greater social concern if advertising is a contributing factor. We will take up this policy issue in Chap. 20.

16.2   Advertising and Efficiency

Even if advertisements are truthful and free from using undesirable stereotypes, many critics are concerned that there is too much advertising from society's perspective. As we have seen, about 2% of GDP is devoted to advertising each year, money that could be put to other uses. A related issue is the extent to which advertising is persuasive, informative, or image enhancing. There is obviously less concern with advertising that is purely informative.

At least two problems make it especially difficult to analyze the efficiency of advertising. First, Dixit and Norman (1978) point out that when advertising changes consumer tastes, there is no fixed utility function that can be used as a benchmark to make policy comparisons. For purely persuasive advertising that changes tastes in favor of the advertised brand, pre-advertising preferences appropriately reflect a consumer's "true" (unadulterated) preferences. In contrast, for informative advertising that makes a consumer aware of an important and useful product characteristic, post-advertising preferences better represent a consumer's true (unboundedly rational) preferences. When advertising changes tastes, the resulting change in traditional consumer surplus provides an inaccurate measure of the change in consumer welfare.

A second problem associated with evaluating the merits of advertising is that it frequently produces externalities. For example, advertising generates a positive externality when it pays for television and radio broadcasting. It can also produce a negative externality when it increases demand for commodities that themselves have negative externalities associated with them. One example is alcohol advertising, which could lead to greater alcohol consumption, alcohol abuse, and accidents attributable to drunk driving.

16.2.1   Advertising and Efficiency: A Graphical Approach

To illustrate the difficulties associated with identifying the socially efficient level of advertising, we consider a simple monopoly example with no externalities. We set marginal cost of production to zero for simplicity. Advertising is profitable, and to

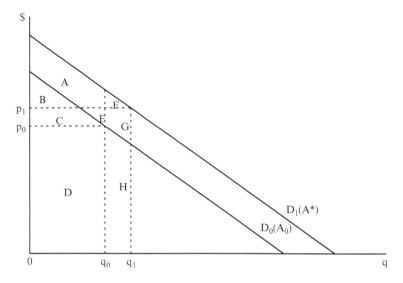

Fig. 16.1 Consumer and producer surplus when advertising equals A_0 and A^* ($A^* > A_0$)

make the effect more apparent, we first consider a discrete change in advertising expenditures from zero (A_0) to the firm's profit-maximizing level (A^*). This produces a parallel increase in demand, as illustrated in Fig. 16.1, and the optimal price and output pairs correspond to p_0–q_0 and p_1–q_1. In this case, advertising is assumed to lead to a higher equilibrium price.[8]

Recall that a market is efficient when it maximizes total (consumer plus producer) surplus. To illustrate the efficiency effect of advertising, we begin with the case where advertising is treated much like a quality improvement (as discussed in Chap. 13), where advertising does not change tastes but produces a product image that society deems beneficial. From Fig. 16.1, an increase in this type of advertising from A_0 to A^* has the following effect on consumer surplus (CS), producer surplus (PS), and total surplus (TS):

- At A_0, $CS_0 = B + C$; $PS_0 = D$; $TS_0 = B + C + D$.
- At A^*, $CS_1 = A + B + F$; $PS_1 = C + D + E + G + H − A^*$; $TS_1 = A + B + C + D + E + F + G + H − A^*$.
- $\Delta TS = TS_1 − TS_0 = CS_1 − CS_0 = A − C + F$.

We derive the change in total surplus as follows. For a profit-maximizing monopolist, the change in producer surplus or profit associated with a small change

---

[8] When advertising rotates demand, the welfare effect of advertising is more complex. You are asked to address this issue in a review question. For further discussion, see Comanor (1985) and V. Tremblay et al. (forthcoming-b).

in advertising equals zero. In other words, at the margin the change in PS (ΔPS) equals zero: $\Delta PS \equiv PS_1 - PS_0 = C + E + G + H - A^* = 0$. This is true whether advertising creates a desirable image, is persuasive, or is informative. Therefore, the change in TS (ΔTS) equals $CS_1 - CS_0 = A - C + F$, which is positive as long as area C is not too large.[9] In this case, total surplus rises with advertising ($\Delta TS > 0$), implying that the firm is supplying too little advertising from society's perspective. The reason for this is that the TS function is strictly concave in advertising,[10] so that the socially optimal level of advertising is reached when $\Delta TS = 0$; the firm undersupplies (oversupplies) advertising from society's perspective when $\Delta TS > 0$ ($\Delta TS < 0$).

Next, we consider the more difficult case where advertising changes consumer tastes. We continue to use Fig. 16.1 to facilitate a comparison with the previous case. When advertising is persuasive and changes tastes, pre-advertising preferences are the accurate benchmark when making welfare comparisons. In this case,

- At A_0, $CS_0 = B + C$; $PS_0 = D$; $TS_0 = B + C + D$.
- At A^*, $CS_1 = B$; $PS_1 = C + D + E + G + H - A^*$; $TS_1 = B + C + D + E + G + H - A^*$.
- $\Delta TS = TS_1 - TS_0 = CS_1 - CS_0 = -C < 0$.

Notice that areas A and F are not part of consumer surplus at the optimal level of advertising, A^*. This is because pre-advertising tastes represent true preferences (i.e., at D_0), and the increase in consumer willingness to pay, represented by areas A and F, is the result of pure persuasion or deception. Thus, they do not count as a true social benefit. Under these conditions, TS falls with advertising, implying that the firm supplies an excessive amount of advertising from society's perspective.

A weaker but similar result holds when informative advertising changes tastes by revealing to consumers that the product is more desirable than they previously believed. In this case, post-advertising preferences are the accurate benchmark, and the following conditions hold:

- At A_0, $CS_0 = A + B + C + E$; $PS_0 = D$; $TS_0 = A + B + C + D + E$.
- At A^*, $CS_1 = A + B + F$; $PS_1 = C + D + E + G + H - A^*$; $TS_1 = A + B + C + D + E + F + G + H - A^*$.
- $\Delta TS = TS_1 - TS_0 = CS_1 - CS_0 = F - C - E$.

Notice that areas A and E are included in consumer surplus at advertising level A_0. This is because post-advertising tastes represent true preferences, which are characterized by demand function D_1. For example, advertising might inform consumers of the health benefits of eating broccoli. Even though a consumer who eats broccoli may not realize the health benefits without advertising, the consumer still

---

[9] Notice that area C will be small if the increase in price is small, an issue that will become apparent shortly.

[10] To illustrate, consider the following inverse demand and total cost functions: $p = 12 - q + A$ and $TC = cq - A^2$, where $c = 0$ for simplicity. In this case, $p^* = q^* = 6 + A/2$. $TS = 54 + 6A - 7A^2/8$, which is strictly concave, and TS reaches a maximum at $A^* = 3.43$.

receives those benefits nevertheless. So, the social gain of consuming q_0 (without advertising) includes area $A + E$. Under these conditions, TS still falls as long as advertising leads to a substantially higher price. When this occurs, the firm will advertise too much from society's perspective. Later in the chapter we will see that informative advertising of a different type can benefit both producers and consumers by lowering consumer search costs, implying that it is undersupplied in the marketplace.

16.2.2   Advertising and Efficiency: A More General Approach Using Calculus

To better understand how the price effect is important when analyzing the efficiency of advertising, we consider a more general model. We assume an oligopoly industry with homogeneous goods where advertising can have external effects. As noted above, there are positive externalities when advertising subsidizes television and radio programming and negative externalities when advertising leads to greater social ills. In this case, the total surplus function (TS) for this industry can be written as

$$\text{TS} = \text{CS}(A,p) + \text{PS}(A,p) + E(A,p), \tag{16.1}$$

where CS is the dollar value of consumer surplus, A is now the industry level of advertising expenditures, PS is producer surplus or industry profit, and E is the dollar value of the externality; $E > 0$ for a positive externality and $E < 0$ for a negative externality. TS is assumed to be strictly concave and twice continuously differentiable. The efficiency effect of advertising is determined by totally differentiating (16.1) with respect to A[11]:

$$\frac{\text{dTS}}{\text{d}A} = \frac{\partial \text{CS}}{\partial A} + \frac{\partial \text{CS}}{\partial p}\frac{\partial p}{\partial A} + \frac{\partial \text{PS}}{\partial A} + \frac{\partial \text{PS}}{\partial p}\frac{\partial p}{\partial A} + \frac{\text{d}E}{\text{d}A}. \tag{16.2}$$

Given that TS is strictly concave, from society's perspective advertising is insufficient when $\text{dTS}/\text{d}A > 0$, is optimal when $\text{dTS}/\text{d}A = 0$, and is excessive when $\text{dTS}/\text{d}A < 0$.

In order to better understand the overall effect of advertising, we consider different market structures and types of advertising. First, we consider a monopoly or cartel setting where there are no externalities and advertising changes tastes, as in Dixit and Norman (1978).[12] In this case,

- $\partial \text{PS}/\partial A = 0$ and $\partial \text{PS}/\partial p = 0$ from the first-order conditions of profit maximization

---

[11] This derivative involves the use of the chain rule, which is discussed in the Mathematics and Econometrics Appendix at the end of the book. According to the chain rule, if $y = f(x_1)$ and $x_1 = f(x_2)$, then a change in x_2 causes a change in x_1 which causes y to change. That is, $\text{d}y/\text{d}x_2 = (\text{d}y/\text{d}x_1)(\text{d}x_1/\text{d}x_2)$. In this case, because $\text{CS} = \text{CS}(p)$ and $p = p(A)$, $\partial \text{CS}/\partial A = (\partial \text{CS}/\partial p)(\partial p/\partial A)$.

[12] For a similar viewpoint, see Braithwaite (1928).

- $dE/dA = 0$ given no externalities
- $\partial CS/\partial A = 0$ given that advertising changes tastes and is, therefore, of no social value

Thus, (16.2) becomes

$$\frac{dTS}{dA} = \frac{\partial CS}{\partial p}\frac{\partial p}{\partial A}. \tag{16.3}$$

Because consumer surplus falls with a price increase ($\partial CS/\partial p < 0$), the sign of dTS/dA is opposite the sign of dp/dA. That is, advertising is excessive when it leads to a higher price, is undersupplied when it leads to a lower price, and is optimal when advertising has no effect on price. When the assumptions of this example hold, (16.3) provides a simple test to determine whether an industry provides too much advertising from society's perspective: advertising is excessive when it leads to a higher price. This explains why Dixit and Norman found that advertising was excessive, as their model assumed that advertising leads to a higher price.

Unfortunately, the problem is more complex when we consider more realistic scenarios. Becker and Murphy (1993) showed that this result does not hold when we add externalities. If advertising generates a positive externality (by paying for television and radio programming), (16.3) becomes

$$\frac{dTS}{dA} = \frac{\partial CS}{\partial p}\frac{\partial p}{\partial A} + \frac{dE}{dA}, \tag{16.4}$$

where dE/dA is positive. In this case, it is clear that advertising is undersupplied if it leads to a lower price. If it leads to a higher price, however, the social welfare implications are not clear.[13]

The problem is complicated further when we assume an oligopolistic industry and the equilibrium is static Nash instead of cartel. In this case, $\partial PS/\partial p > 0$ because the Nash equilibrium price will be less than the cartel or monopoly price. The sign of $\partial PS/\partial A$ will depend on whether advertising is combative or constructive. If combative, we saw in Sect. 15.3.3 that $\partial PS/\partial A < 0$ because the Nash equilibrium level of advertising will be greater than the cartel level of advertising. If constructive, the reverse holds true. Thus, (16.2) becomes

$$\frac{dTS}{dA} = \underbrace{\left(\frac{\partial CS}{\partial p} + \frac{\partial PS}{\partial p}\right)}_{(-)}\underbrace{\frac{\partial p}{\partial A}}_{(?)} + \underbrace{\frac{\partial PS}{\partial A}}_{(?)} + \underbrace{\frac{dE}{dA}}_{(?)}, \tag{16.5}$$

---

[13] Of course, if the externality is negative, then all we can say is that advertising is excessive if it leads to a higher price. If it leads to a lower price, it may or may not be undersupplied.

with the expected signs listed below each term. Taken together, the first two terms in (16.5) will be negative because a higher price leads to a deadweight loss in a market with market power (i.e., it lowers consumer plus producer surplus), *ceteris paribus*. In this case, to argue that advertising is unambiguously excessive when it leads to higher prices, it must also be true that the last two terms on the right-hand side of the equality in (16.5) are not too great. This will certainly occur when advertising is both combative ($\partial PS/\partial A < 0$) and does not produce a positive externality.

Finally, we consider the case where advertising does not change consumer tastes. For example, let advertising create a product image that is valuable to consumers and society, as discussed graphically above, except that advertising need not cause the equilibrium price to increase. Under these conditions, $\partial CS/\partial A > 0$, and

$$\frac{dTS}{dA} = \frac{\partial CS}{\partial A} + \left(\frac{\partial CS}{\partial p} + \frac{\partial PS}{\partial p}\right)\frac{\partial p}{\partial A} + \frac{\partial PS}{\partial A} + \frac{dE}{\partial A} \qquad (16.6)$$
$$\quad\;\; (+) \qquad\qquad (-) \quad\;\; (?) \qquad (?) \quad\;\; (?)$$

Thus, to determine the efficiency effect of advertising requires one to estimate the effect that advertising has on industry price, consumer welfare, industry profits, and externalities. This demonstrates how particular assumptions about the type and influence of advertising affect the efficiency implications of advertising.

16.2.3   Advertising and Efficiency When Advertising Lowers Consumer Search Costs

The sensitivity of the welfare implications of advertising to different assumptions can also be seen when we consider a different type of informative advertising. In this case, consider the Stivers and V. Tremblay (2005) model that we discussed in the previous chapter in which advertising lowers consumer search costs and does not change consumer tastes. They show that the welfare implications are similar in monopoly and oligopoly markets, so we analyze only the monopoly case here. As before, production costs are zero for simplicity.

The basic idea behind the Stivers and V. Tremblay model can be seen in Fig. 16.2. Ignoring advertising for the moment, in the presence of search costs consumer demand is a function of the full price (p_f) and is identified as D_f. Recall from our discussion of this model in the previous chapter that the full price is the market price (p) plus a search cost (s): $p_f = p + s$. Producers only receive the market price, $p = p_f - s$. This means that the firm's effective demand function is D, which is lower than D_f by the amount s.

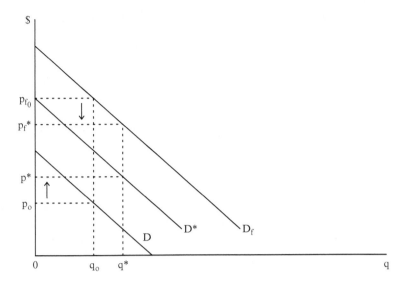

Fig. 16.2 The monopoly outcome when advertising lowers search costs

To understand the welfare effect of advertising, we compare total surplus with and without advertising. With no advertising, the firm's profit-maximizing output is q_0, price is p_0, and full price is p_{f0} in Fig. 16.2. When the firm does invest in advertising, this lowers consumer search costs and raises the firm's effective demand function to D^*. The new optimum values are q^*, p^*, p_f^*. This has three chief effects:

1. Output increases from q_0 to q^*.
2. The consumer price falls from p_{f0} to p_f^*.
3. The producer price increases from p_0 to p^*.

Thus, consumer, producer, and total surplus increase with advertising. This implies that from society's perspective, the market provides too little informative advertising that lowers consumer search costs.[14] This is because the firm will ignore the added benefit that its advertising generates for consumers, as it maximizes only producer surplus.

This may seem like a strange result in a society where advertising is everywhere, but it only applies to advertising that lowers consumer search costs. Government agencies are well aware of the problem. For example, decades ago billboard

---

[14] We can see this more formally by analyzing the effect of advertising on total surplus, $TS = CS(p_f) + PS(A, p)$. Totally differentiating this function with respect to A produces $\frac{dTS}{dA} = \frac{\partial CS}{\partial p_f}\frac{\partial p_f}{\partial s}\frac{ds}{dA} + \frac{\partial PS}{\partial A} + \frac{\partial PS}{\partial p}\frac{\partial p}{\partial A}$. In this setting, $\partial CS/\partial p_f < 0$, $\partial p_f/\partial s = 1$, $ds/dA < 0$. Assuming that advertising does not lower producer surplus, $dTS/dA > 0$. This implies that the firm produces too little advertising from society's perspective.

advertising was the only source of information available to rural interstate travelers regarding upcoming roadside facilities (gas, restaurant, and lodging). Due to the free rider problem, too little information of this kind is provided by the marketplace. In response, the federal government in the USA and Japan post signs on freeways indicating exits with nearby gas, food, and lodging facilities. In addition, many states require gas stations to post their prices so that they are visible from the highway. Finally, some states require restaurants to post their health inspection rating in the front window.[15] These types of regulations suggest that the free market supplies too little advertising that lowers consumer search costs.

In summary, the theoretical literature explains why debate continues regarding the welfare effect of advertising in real markets. The most we can say is that unregulated markets tend to produce too much advertising from society's perspective when advertising is deceptive or changes consumer tastes and does not generate positive externalities. However, advertising that lowers search costs and does not produce negative externalities is likely to be undersupplied. Ultimately, the efficiency effect of advertising is an empirical question that must be studied case by case.

16.2.4   Advertising and Efficiency: Empirical Evidence

We divide our discussion of the empirical evidence into three parts. First, we investigate the extent to which advertising is informative, persuasive, and image enhancing. Then we summarize the evidence on the advertising–price relationship. Finally, we discuss the effect of advertising on externalities.

Survey evidence indicates that most people believe that advertising is more persuasive than informative. In a survey of 2,700 subscribers to the *Harvard Business Review*, 85% believed that advertising "persuades people to buy things they do not need" (Greyser and Reece 1971, 158). After reviewing 20 national surveys from 1930 to 1992, Calfee and Ringold (1994) found that surveys consistently indicate that about 70% of consumers believe that advertising persuades consumers to buy things they do not want. If true, this is a problem because there is greater social concern with advertising that is persuasive.

One hypothesis is that persuasive advertising creates brand loyalty. This is supported by blind taste test studies, which show that advertising induces many consumers to prefer the advertised brand. For example, Allison and Uhl (1964) found that in blind taste tests most consumers cannot distinguish one brand of regular domestic beer from another. Similar to the findings of Lee et al. (2006), they also found that when comparing the same beer in two different bottles, one labeled and the other unlabeled, consumers generally favored the labeled product.

---

[15] Not only does this regulation provide consumers with better information, Jin and Leslie (2003) found that forced disclosure of ratings in the Los Angeles area led to an increase in the hygiene scores by over 5%.

Equivalent results have been reported for wine and soft drinks. As we discussed in Chap. 4, in blind taste tests Plassman et al. (2008) found that subjects gave a higher quality rating to wines that they thought to be of higher price, even though all samples came from the same bottle. Brain scans by McClure et al. (2004a, b) confirm that consumers who are given a Coke receive greater utility when they know that they are drinking Coke than when they are uninformed about the brand of cola that they are drinking. The combined evidence shows that consumers receive utility from both the product and from the product's image that is created by advertising. Unfortunately, these results are consistent with two different points of view: (1) that advertising enhances brand loyalty by persuasive means and (2) that advertising enhances brand loyalty by creating a desirable product image.

Ackerberg (2001) developed a clever way of distinguishing between the informative and other (image, prestige, and persuasive) effects of advertising for a new brand of low calorie yogurt, Yoplait 150. Ackerberg compared the demand effect of advertising on experienced households, those that had purchased the brand previously, with inexperienced households, those that had not purchased the brand before. If advertising is primarily informative, it should influence only inexperienced household demand. If it is primarily persuasive or image enhancing, however, then both experienced and inexperienced households should respond to advertising, as all consumers are influenced by persuasion and all benefit from the enhanced image created by advertising. Ackerberg finds strong empirical support for the hypothesis that advertising for Yoplait 150 increases the demand from inexperienced consumers but not experienced consumers. This supports the informative view of advertising.

The evidence is also consistent with the hypothesis that when advertising lowers consumer search costs, it is undersupplied and requires government intervention. As we discussed in the previous section, society gains when government posts signs with information about service availability at upcoming freeway exits, requires gas stations to post prices on signs that are visible from the highway, and requires restaurants to post health inspection signs in storefront windows.

It is clear from the evidence that advertising can have informative, persuasive, and image-enhancing effects, depending on the market. As discussed above, advertising is more likely to have a persuasive component for experience and credence goods. Informative advertising is more likely to be found in printed materials and for new products. Finally, advertising that creates subjective differentiation is more likely for consumer goods, such as perfume, beer, and soft drinks. One can conclude that the extent to which advertising is beneficial to consumers depends upon the mix of the informative, persuasive, and image-enhancing components of advertising.

A welfare assessment of advertising also requires an analysis of the price effect of advertising. Research on this topic has produced two clear results. First, a complete ban on advertising leads to higher market prices. This line of research began with the seminal study by Benham (1972), who compared the retail price of eyeglasses in states with and without advertising restrictions. Benham found that the price was over twice as high in states that prohibited advertising ($37.48 compared to $17.98). Subsequent studies for prescription drugs, gasoline, toys, optometric services, and legal services confirm that advertising restrictions increase the average price paid by consumers.[16] In a related line of research, Milyo and Waldfogel (1999) found that legalizing price advertising for liquor in Rhode Island led to lower prices on advertised brands. These results are consistent with the informative view of advertising in which advertising promotes price competition.

The second result regarding the advertising–price relationship is that advertised brands are priced higher than their generic or unadvertised counterparts. The data in Table 15.7 confirm this conclusion for a *Consumer Reports* sample of 23 food items. It shows that the average national brand received a 40% price premium over generic store brands. In addition, the empirical results of C. Tremblay and V. Tremblay (1995) and Iwasaki et al. (2008) support the hypothesis that a marginal increase in advertising leads to higher prices in the US brewing and cigarette markets. This evidence is consistent with the persuasive view of advertising.

One concern with this interpretation of the evidence is that advertised brands may command a higher price because they are of higher quality. The evidence does not always support this argument, however. For example, experts at *Consumer Reports* conducted blind taste tests and found that national and store brands for most food items are of like quality. As reported in Table 15.7, for 57% of these food items the experts felt that national and store brands were of similar quality. Only 26% of national brands were viewed as being of higher quality, and 17% of store brands were viewed as being of higher quality. This is consistent with the evidence from the other studies discussed above that used blind taste tests. If price reflects quality, one would also expect national brands to command a higher price premium in the six categories where the national brands were evaluated to be of higher quality than in the four product categories where store brands were evaluated to be of higher quality. Yet, the opposite is true: the price premium for the national brands when they are of higher quality is 19%, and the price premium for national brands when store brands are of higher quality is 37%. Furthermore, Iwasaki et al. (2008) attempt to control for product quality in their regression analysis of the US brewing industry and still found that advertising has a positive effect on price.

Other concerns remain. Even though advertised brands are higher priced than generic brands, the prices of both types might be higher if all advertising were banned, as the work of Benham (1972) and others suggests. It is also possible that a marginal increase in advertising leads to higher prices on average, while a complete ban on advertising also leads to higher prices. If the price effect were all that mattered in our welfare calculation, this would suggest that the market produces too much advertising but that a complete ban is too restrictive from society's perspective.

---

[16] See Bagwell (2007) for a review of this extensive literature.

Table 16.1 The effect of relaxing the broadcast advertising ban on externalities (E), producer surplus (PS), consumer surplus (CS), and total surplus (TS)

Variable	Estimated effect[a]
$\Delta E_{\text{TV-Radio}}$	630
ΔE_{Health}	−1,460
ΔPS	−1,920
ΔCS$_{\text{Persuasion}}$	2,490
ΔCS$_{\text{Information}}$	2,920
ΔCS$_{\text{Image}}$	7,710
ΔTS$_{\text{Persuasion}}$	−250
ΔTS$_{\text{Information}}$	170
ΔTS$_{\text{Image}}$	4,970

[a]Measured in millions of dollars. Total surplus may not add up due to rounding errors.
Source: Farr et al. (2001).

In any case, even if the above factors were understood, a complete welfare analysis would still require us to investigate the effect that advertising has on externalities. Becker and Murphy (1993) point out that advertising produces positive externalities when it helps pay for broadcast television and radio programming. On the other hand, advertising generates negative externalities when it causes consumers to increase consumption of commodities that themselves produce negative externalities. This has been a policy concern in the markets for alcohol and tobacco. Sloan et al. (2004) estimate that cigarette smoking produces $104 billion in annual social costs, $35 billion of which are external to the smoker.[17] For beer, the annual external cost is estimated to be between $18 and $37 billion, which amounts to between $1.74 and $3.49 per six-pack of beer.[18] Thus, negative externalities are substantial in these industries.

Farr et al. (2001) estimated all of these factors when assessing the efficiency of the advertising restrictions in the US cigarette industry. Their welfare estimates are reproduced in Table 16.1. Because cigarette advertising has had elements of information, persuasion, and image creation, they estimated the change in consumer surplus under three different scenarios: advertising is purely persuasive (ΔCS$_{\text{Persuasive}}$), advertising is purely informative (ΔCS$_{\text{Informative}}$), and advertising is purely image enhancing (ΔCS$_{\text{Image}}$). This provides three different estimates of the change in total surplus due to the elimination of advertising restrictions.

The Farr et al. findings are consistent with the implications of this chapter. Estimates from a market model show that the elimination of restrictions on cigarette advertising would lead to a lower average price and an increase in cigarette

---

[17] This is due to the external costs of second-hand smoke and the resulting health care expenditures. According to Levit et al. (1994), 44% of all US health care costs are paid for by the public.

[18] See V. Tremblay and C. Tremblay (2005) for a review of this evidence.

smoking. This generates an estimated \$630 million in positive externalities associated with the subsidy of broadcast television and radio programming ($\Delta E_{\text{TV-Radio}}$) and \$1,460 million in negative externalities associated with increased health problems (ΔE_{Health}). Due to lower prices, producer surplus falls by \$1,920 million (ΔPS). Eliminating all restrictions leads to greater demand and greater consumer surplus (ignoring the adverse health effects) for all three types of advertising. Consistent with our discussion above, the increase in consumer surplus resulting from the increase in advertising is smallest when advertising is purely persuasive and greatest when it is image enhancing. Finally, their evidence shows that eliminating advertising restrictions lowers total surplus by \$250 million if advertising is purely persuasive but increases total surplus otherwise.

Because most cigarette ads had persuasive, informative, and image enhancing effects, we would need to add appropriate weights for them to complete the analysis. Although it is difficult to come up with precise estimates of the appropriate mix, if we use the survey estimate that 70% of advertising is persuasive (Calfee and Ringold 1994) and assume that the remainder is informative, then the change in total surplus is negative, implying that cigarette advertising restrictions are efficient.

16.2.5 *Advertising, Strategic Effects, and Cost Efficiency*

In this section our goal is to characterize a firm's technology when both production and marketing are important to the firm's survival. After all, in many consumer goods industries the success of a new product depends on a successful marketing campaign almost as much as it does on the attractiveness of the product itself.

When both output and advertising are important strategic variables, Färe et al. (2004) argue that a firm's cost function can be decomposed into two parts. The first involves the use of production inputs to manufacture output, and the second involves the use of marketing inputs to sell that output. Assuming that these components are separable,[19] then we can write a firm's total cost function (TC) as

$$\text{TC}(w, q) = \text{TC}_{\text{p}}(w_{\text{p}}, q) + \text{TC}_{\text{A}}(w_{\text{A}}, q), \tag{16.7}$$

where TC_{p} is the total cost of production, TC_{A} is the total cost of marketing or advertising, w is a vector of both production input prices (w_{p}) and advertising input prices (w_{A}), and q is output. To be economically efficient, the firm will want to choose those inputs that minimize the cost of manufacturing output and the cost of advertising. At the firm level, profit maximization guarantees cost minimization.

---

[19] This may be reasonable, given that most manufacturing firms produce and market output at separate locations and the production and marketing divisions are supervised by separate management teams.

At the industry level, however, strategic effects may prevent the industry from producing the productively efficient level of advertising.[20] That is, firms may advertise more than is needed to produce a given level of industry sales. As we saw in Chap. 15, this can occur when advertising is combative, which forces firms into a prisoners' dilemma in advertising. This is productively inefficient because much of each firm's advertising is designed to steal customers from its competitors rather than attract new customers to the industry.[21] As we saw in Chap. 15, the evidence shows that this is the case for the US brewing and cigarette industries. Nelson (1999) and V. Tremblay and C. Tremblay (2005) found that advertising in the brewing industry is combative. In addition, Iwasaki and V. Tremblay (2009) found that before the 1971 ban on television and radio advertising, the productively efficient level of broadcast (television and radio) advertising was zero. This was an era when most of the cigarette marketing dollars were spent on broadcast media. This demonstrates that free markets need not produce the productively efficient level of advertising.

16.3 Summary

1. As a society, we want advertising to be socially responsible and efficient. Responsible advertising is honest and refrains from stereotyping and promoting sexism, racism, and ageism, for example. Not all ads in the USA meet this criterion.
2. Whether free markets produce the socially efficient level of advertising depends upon the effect of advertising on consumer utility, producer surplus, and externalities. Assessing the efficiency effect of advertising both theoretically and empirically is a difficult task, because advertising may generate externalities and can affect prices and consumers in so many different ways.
3. In general, advertising that is deceptive, changes tastes, leads to higher prices, and produces negative externalities will be oversupplied from society's perspective. Advertising that is honest, lowers search costs, and does not produce negative externalities is undersupplied.
4. Advertising bans tend to raise market prices. At the same time, heavily advertised brands tend to be higher priced than generic or unadvertised brands.

---

[20] For a more complete discussion of the effect that marketing externalities can have on a firm's cost efficiency, see Vardanyan and V. Tremblay (2006).

[21] Of course, if advertising is constructive, firms will invest too little in advertising from the industry's perspective. This need not imply that the market produces too little advertising from society's perspective, because it may be persuasive or taste changing, for example.

5. When firms compete in both output (or price) and advertising, a firm's cost function can be decomposed into a manufacturing component and a marketing or advertising component. Even though a firm may use its production and marketing inputs so as to minimize costs, firms will invest too much money in advertising from the industry's perspective when advertising is combative.

16.4   Review Questions

1. Explain why a firm is more likely to use false advertising when it sells experience goods (as opposed to search goods) and plans to exit the industry in the near future. Would you be more or less reluctant to eat at a restaurant that you knew was going out of business in the near future? Explain.
2. Explain the key factors that determine whether or not advertising is excessive from society's perspective.
3. Assume that a monopolist uses informative advertising to change consumer tastes as in Dixit and Norman (1978). In this case, advertising causes demand to rotate in one of two possible ways.

   A. Advertising causes demand to rotate around the quantity intercept of demand. That is, the q-intercept on the horizontal axis remains the same.
   B. Advertising causes demand to rotate around the price intercept of demand. That is, the p-intercept on the vertical axis remains the same.
      Use discrete analysis as in Fig. 16.1 to determine the effect of advertising on efficiency (i.e., total surplus) for each type of demand rotation.

4. Use two behavioral concepts to explain how advertising might change consumer beliefs in ways that benefit the advertiser. If advertising can change beliefs, what are the policy implications? Discuss Ackerberg's (2001) evidence on this issue.
5. Discuss the policy implications of advertising that creates images that are valued by consumers but not by society as a whole.

Chapter 17
Technological Change, Dynamic Efficiency, and Market Structure

To this point, most of our discussion about economic performance has focused on static efficiency and assumed that technology is fixed. Yet economic growth requires that we make investments today to develop better products or new processes that lower the cost of production. Persistent long-run economic growth has led to a continued rise in our standard of living. For example, Elwell (2006) documents that from 1980 to 2004, output per capita grew by about 2.3% per year in Great Britain and by about 2.0% in the USA, Japan, and other major European countries (Germany, France, Italy, and the Netherlands). Although these growth rates may seem inconsequential, a small increase in the growth rate can have a sizable cumulative effect. To illustrate, a 2% growth rate will double the standard of living in approximately 35 years, while a 3% growth rate doubles it in only about 23.5 years.[1]

We can see the effect of growth in our lives by comparing living standards today with a century ago. In 1900, about 40% of Americans could be classified as poor by current standards. About 60% of people lived on farms or in rural areas. The average home did not have electricity, indoor plumbing, or a telephone. Only about 7% of youth completed high school, walking was the most common form of transportation, and average life expectancy was 47 years, about 30 years lower than today.

Even if you were exceptionally wealthy in 1900, your life would still be constrained in many ways compared to today. On the plus side, you could own a large home and employ servants who could cook, clean, and launder cloths. These would be valuable services in an era without the benefit of microwave ovens, vacuum cleaners, dishwashers, and washing machines. However, you would be unable to fly to Europe or own a radio, TV, Blu-Ray player, computer, or

---

[1] The "rule of 72" provides an approximation. That is, if the annual growth rate is x%, then the standard of living will double in approximately $72/x$ years.

V.J. Tremblay and C.H. Tremblay, *New Perspectives on Industrial Organization*,
Springer Texts in Business and Economics, DOI 10.1007/978-1-4614-3241-8_17,
© Springer Science+Business Media New York 2012

cell phone. If you were a woman, you could vote in only four Western states. In addition, entertainment opportunities were very limited. There were few spectator sports, and Vaudeville[2] was the common form of entertainment.

A number of factors contribute to long-run growth in income. First, there must be an adequate infrastructure. This includes legal and other institutions and cultural attitudes that support entrepreneurial activity. Once these are in place, living standards depend on the quantity of physical capital, the level of human capital, and the level of technology. Technology or technical knowledge refers to the entire body of knowledge concerning the methods used to bring inputs together to produce goods and services. Thus, **technological change** occurs when we add to technological knowledge.

You can think of technological knowledge as information that is currently publically available and technological change as new knowledge that is created and will become publically available. Parallel to technological knowledge is human capital, which is defined as a person's level of knowledge (of publically available information); investments in education increase human capital, while investments in research and development (R&D) produce technological change. Each has a positive effect on the other, for the most part, as it takes an educated population to create new knowledge.

Economists have tried to identify the extent to which these factors contribute to economic growth in the USA. Recent evidence[3] indicates that capital accumulation contributed almost 50% to US economic growth, increases in human capital contributed about 20%, and technological change contributed 40% to 50%.[4]

Given the economic importance of technological change, public and private institutions spend a great deal of money each year on R&D. This amount varies considerably across nations, industries, and firms. Figure 17.1 plots R&D spending as a percent of gross domestic product (GDP) for a sample of countries in 2005. In general, the intensity of R&D spending is greater among developed countries. **Patents**, which give an inventor limited ownership of a new idea or method, are observable outcomes of R&D that approximate the extent of technological change. Table 17.1 lists the top ten companies that were awarded patents in the USA in 2009. As you can see, the leaders are from the high tech computer and electronics sectors of the economy. This is consistent with the evidence in Table 17.2, which identifies the most innovative industries in the USA. It shows that the chemical, computer, and electronics industries are highly innovative. In contrast, very few patents have been awarded to companies involved with simple manufacturing such as button making, needle making, typesetting, and book binding.[5]

---

[2] Vaudeville was live theater by circus entertainers, comedians, dancers, and musicians.

[3] For a review of the evidence, see Cohen and Levin (1989), Mankiw et al. (1992), Jorgenson and Stiroh (2000), DeLong et al. (2003), and Elwell (2006).

[4] Percentages exceed 100% because other factors, such as an increase in government regulation and a shorter average work week, have reduced economic growth. Early studies by authors such as Denison (1985) gave an even higher contribution to technological change (at over 60%).

[5] The US Patents and Trademark Office publishes patent information by country, industry, and company at http://www.uspto.gov.

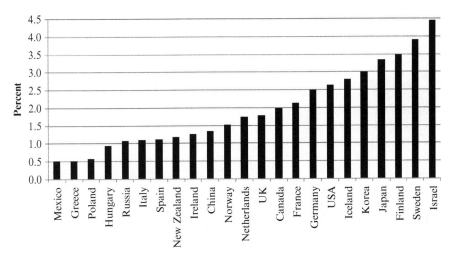

Fig. 17.1 R&D as a percent of gross domestic product by country, 2005

Table 17.1 Top ten patent-receiving firms in the USA, 2009

Company	Number of patents
International Business Machines (IBM)	4,887
Samsung Electronics	3,592
Microsoft	2,901
Cannon	2,200
Panasonic	1,759
Toshiba	1,669
Sony	1,656
Intel	1,534
Seiko-Epson	1,328
Hewlett-Packard	1,269

Source: US Patent and Trademark Office at http://www.uspto.gov

Table 17.2 Top ten patent-receiving industries in the USA, 2009

Industry	Patents granted in 2009	Cumulative patents
Multiplex communications	5,304	42,044
Semiconductor device manufacturing	4,908	68,955
Telecommunications	3,372	34,798
Chemistry: molecular biology and microbiology	2,710	57,381
Image analysis	2,625	26,176
Computer graphics	2,597	32,892
Static information storage and retrieval	2,384	33,891
Pulse and digital communications	2,280	28,005
Radiant energy	2,184	37,441
Electricity: electrical systems and devices	2,122	32,733

Source: US Patent and Trademark Office at http://www.uspto.gov

Because technological change is dynamic in nature and crucial for economic growth, we are just as interested in dynamic efficiency as static efficiency. Static efficiency ignores technological change, while **dynamic efficiency** recognizes that investments in R&D today can be socially desirable if they lead to a better life tomorrow. Dynamic efficiency occurs when there is an optimal amount of technological change from society's perspective.[6] Because one important invention can quickly outstrip the deadweight loss due to market power, maintaining static efficiency period after period need not be dynamically efficient. We will see that it may be socially desirable to give temporary market power to an inventor (which is statically inefficient) to encourage inventive effort (which is dynamically beneficial).

In the sections that follow, we discuss three issues regarding technological change. First, we describe the economics of technological change. Then we analyze a firm's motivation for investing in R&D. We pay particular attention to the connection between market structure and technological change. We will see that technological change can affect market structure, and market structure can affect technological change. A fundamental issue in the field of industrial organization is whether or not one market structure is more dynamically efficient than another. Finally, we discuss the empirical evidence regarding these issues.

17.1   Invention and Technological Change

17.1.1   The Economics of Technological Change

As discussed in the introduction, technological change produces an increase in technological knowledge. This includes the ability to conceive of a completely new product, such as the Internet in the 1980s. It also includes the discovery of new methods to produce existing products of higher quality (at the same cost) or existing products at lower cost (i.e., with fewer inputs).

The electronic calculator provides an excellent example. When first mass marketed in the early 1970s, a simple calculator that could add, subtract, multiply, and divide had a retail price of about $100. Subsequent technological change produced two major advances. First, it led to the development of a cheaper microcoprocessor, enabling simple calculators to sell for less than $5 today. Second, it produced coprocessors that could handle a wider range of calculations. As well as perform simple arithmetic, today's $100 calculator can solve calculus, trigonometric, and financial problems. Many newer calculators also have a memory and can graph a variety of functions.

---

[6] As with most economic problems, this involves tradeoffs because research and development is costly and technological change can have undesirable consequences. For example, new technologies have made mass killing more efficient and have sometimes increased the level of pollution and market power. As we discussed in Chap. 1, equity, fairness, a clean environment, and macrostability are also important to social welfare. In this chapter, we focus on technological change that is beneficial and postpone discussion of these broader concerns to Chaps. 19 and 20.

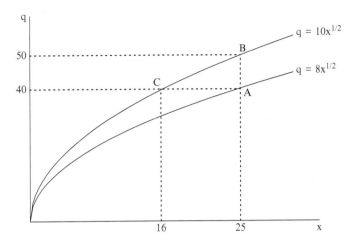

Fig. 17.2 Technological change and the production function, $q(x)$

A technological change enables a firm to produce a given output with fewer inputs, which produces an upward shift in the production function. To illustrate, consider a production function where the quantity of output (q) is a function of a single input (x) and takes the following form: $q = \alpha \cdot x^{1/2}$. Initially, α equals 8, but a technological change that makes x more productive raises α to 10. Figure 17.2 graphs these functions and shows that the production function shifts up and to the left with a technological change. That is, to produce 40 units of output, the firm uses 25 units of x with the old technology and 16 units of x with the new technology. When looking at this as an upward shift of the production function, a technological change enables the firm to produce more output (50 instead of 40) with the same quantity of input x (25).

Another way to see the effects of a technological change is through its influence on a firm's cost function. When a technological change enables a firm to product the same output with fewer inputs, costs fall. An example is provided in Fig. 17.3, where AC represents the long-run average cost function for the old technology and AC' represents it for the new technology. In this case, technological change has no effect on minimum efficient scale (MES). This is a **scale-neutral technological change**. When a technological change causes MES to increase (decrease), it is said to be a **scale-increasing (scale-decreasing) technological change**. An example of a scale-increasing technological change is depicted in Fig. 17.4.

As well as affecting scale, a technological change can affect substitution possibilities between inputs. This becomes apparent by reviewing the effect of a technological change on a firm's isoquants, which is described in Fig. 17.5 for two inputs, labor (L) and capital (K). With the old technology, the firm can produce 100 units of output in an economically efficient manner (i.e., at minimum cost) with 30 units of L and 3 units of K. This occurs where the isoquant ($\bar{q}_{100}$) is tangent to the

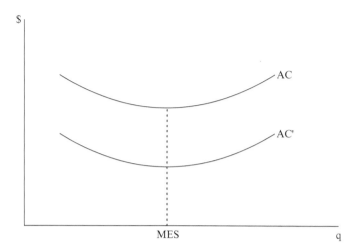

Fig. 17.3 Long-run average cost and a scale-neutral technological change

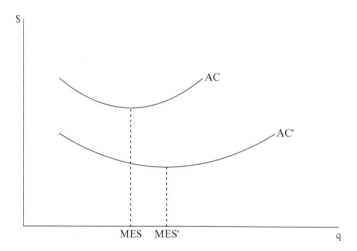

Fig. 17.4 Long-run average cost and a scale-increasing technological change

isocost function ($\bar{C}_{10}$) at point A.[7] With the new technology, the isoquant shifts towards the origin (q'_{100}), and the optimum moves from point A to point B. That is, the firm is able to use less L and K to produce the same units of output. Notice that the optimal labor–capital ratio (L/K) stays the same. With both technologies, the

---

[7] An isoquant maps out the minimum combinations of L and K that will produce a given level of output ($\bar{q}$). An isocost function maps out all combinations of L and K that produce a given total cost ($\bar{C}$). For further discussion, see Varian (2010).

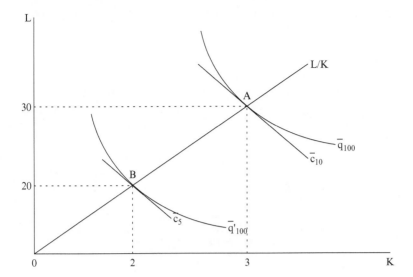

Fig. 17.5 Isoquant and isocost functions for a neutral technological change

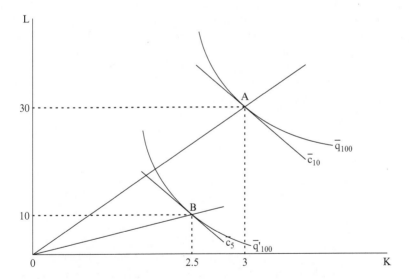

Fig. 17.6 Isoquant and isocost functions for a labor-saving technological change

optimal ratio is 10 units of labor for each unit of capital (i.e., $L/K = 30/3 = 20/2 = 10$). Because the technological change has a neutral effect on the optimal labor–capital ratio, it is called a **neutral technological change**.

There is no guarantee that technological change will be neutral, however. Figure 17.6 illustrates the case of a **labor-saving technological change**. With the old technology, the labor–capital ratio is 10, but with the new technology it is

4 (10/2.5). That is, the new technology now requires only 4 units of labor for each unit of capital. A **capital-saving technological change** occurs when the labor–capital ratio rises with a technological change, making it optimal for the firm to use more labor relative to capital.

If firms have some control over the change in technology through focused R&D efforts, then they can direct technological change in a profit-maximizing direction. For example, in the last half century US automobile producers have developed robots to replace labor on assembly lines. This would have been a rational response to the rise in the price of labor relative to capital in the USA, which may have been anticipated by the automobile industry. The point is that if a firm expects the relative price of an input to rise over time, it pays the firm to cultivate new technologies that would use relatively less of the more expensive input.

17.1.2   A Taxonomy of Research, Invention, and Technological Change

R&D programs can be divided into two types. The first is **basic research**, which involves a theoretical or experimental investigation that is designed to advance scientific knowledge without regard to a specific application. A classic example is the research by physicists on atomic structure before World War II. When first developed, this knowledge was of no apparent value, but after decades of work it led to today's Global Positioning System.[8] The second type is **applied research**, which is designed to create knowledge that has a specific practical purpose. A scientist working on a more effective allergy medicine is conducting applied research.

Basic research has a public quality, as it can benefit a wide range of users simultaneously. As a result, it is typically undertaken by researchers at major universities and research institutes and is funded by government agencies, such as the National Science Foundation, National Institute of Health, and NASA. Applied research is funded by private and public agencies. Data from the National Science Foundation show that R&D spending as a percent of Gross Domestic Product (GDP) reached a peak in 1964 and hovered between 2.2% and 2.8% since 1980 (see Fig. 17.7).[9] Government support for basic research has declined, however, equaling 0.7% of GDP in 1953 and only 0.2% in 2004 (Elwell 2006, 28).

Schumpeter (1934) described three stages of technological change. The first stage is **invention**, the act of creating a new idea or of solving a promising technical possibility. This is the initial research phase of a R&D program. The next is **innovation**, which occurs when an invention is applied for the first time and results in a new product or production process. The final step is **diffusion** (or imitation) in which the final innovation becomes widely used.

---

[8] For further discussion, see the Committee on Science, Engineering, and Public Policy (1999).

[9] The data are available at http://www.nsf.gov/statistics/nsf10314/content.cfm?pub_id=4000&id=1.

Fig. 17.7 US research and development expenditures as a percent of GDP, 1953–2008

Historical examples show that it can take a considerable amount of time to make a viable invention market worthy.[10] One example is the development of the steam engine. Although it was first invented by James Watt in 1765, it needed a considerable amount of work (i.e., time and money) to make it ready for industrial purposes. Not until Matthew Boulton stepped in with financial support was Watt able to complete the final stages of product development, which did not occur until 11 years after its initial invention. Development of photocopying by Xerography suffered similar development problems. It was first invented by Chester Carlson in 1938, but it took 21 years and $20 million before it was made available for commercial use by the Xerox Corporation.

Behavioral economics provides further insight into the rate of diffusion of new technologies. As discussed in Chap. 14, Rogers (1962) theory that personality differences explain the acceptance rates of new products among consumers can also be used to explain the diffusion rate of new technologies among producers. A classic example is the 1928 introduction of hybrid seed corn in Iowa. This new seed was more profitable than traditional seed due to its greater resistance to drought and disease. Nevertheless, it took over 13 years for all farmers in Greene County, IA, to adopt it.

Figure 17.8 shows that the adoption rate of hybrid seed corn among Iowa farmers follows a pattern that is consistent with Rogers' (1962) theory that the diffusion rate

---

[10] See Scherer (1965) and Jewkes et al. (1969).

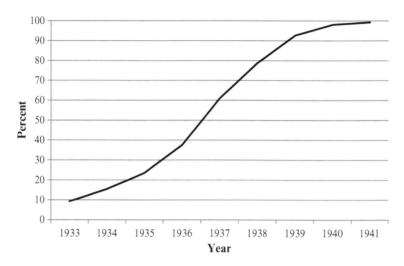

Fig. 17.8 Percent of Iowa farmers who adopted hybrid seed corn, 1933–1941

is based on personality differences among adopters. According to Rogers, a new technology is first accepted by "early adopters," those who place a high value of being first and are opinion leaders within the industry. Then it is adopted by the "early and late majority," which includes individuals who have a certain degree of skepticism about change. Finally, it is put into practice by the "late adopters," those who hold traditional values and are adverse to change.[11] Thus, personality differences among business owners explain why it can take a considerable amount of time for a new technology to become an industry norm, even for a very profitable one like hybrid seed corn.

In real-world examples such as these, it is important to distinguish between invention and innovation. Nevertheless, these terms are used interchangeably in the theoretical literature, a practice we follow in the remainder of the chapter.

17.2 Failure of the Market for Ideas

An important concern with the market for new ideas is that knowledge is a public good, and free markets undersupply public goods from society's perspective. Once created, there is nonrivalry in consumption because everyone can benefit from a new idea and put it to use at the same time.

---

[11] Rogers actually divided individuals into five categories: innovators, early adopters, early majority, late majority, and laggards.

In a completely free market, it will also be impossible (or uneconomic) for you to exclude others from imitating your invention or stealing your ideas. Because an inventor will be unable to recover the benefits others receive from his or her innovation, inventors will have too little incentive to create new ideas from society's perspective. For example, assume that you have an idea for a new type of battery that lasts 10 times longer but costs the same to produce as current batteries. To convince a company that your idea is sound, you must reveal your idea. But once you have done so, the company has no incentive to pay you for it. The public nature of new ideas is a classic form of market failure.

When markets fail in this way, government intervention can improve social welfare. Examples of polices designed to encourage investments in creative endeavors include patents, copyrights, trademarks, and research grants.[12] To stimulate technological change, one option is for government to subsidize R&D. In the USA, corporations are given a 20% tax credit for their R&D expenditures. In addition, the federal government provides grants to support R&D. Of the $398 billion spent on R&D in the USA in 2008, 26% was financed by the federal government. The percent of support from the federal government reached a peak at almost 67% in 1964, but has declined fairly steadily ever since. This undoubtedly has reduced total R&D spending, given Martin and Scott's (1998) finding that government-supported R&D does not crowd out privately funded R&D. Another concern is that this decline in federal support will change the composition of R&D spending, as the federal government is more likely than business to fund basic research.

An important government response to the market failure associated with ideas is a realization that it is fundamentally a property rights problem. That is, if you owned the right to a new idea or creative work, you could then sue for damages if someone stole it. Our founding fathers recognized this property rights problem as it applies to technological change, as Article I, section 8 of the US Constitution states:

> The Congress shall have power ... to promote the progress of science and useful arts, by securing for limited times to authors and inventors the exclusive right to their respective writings and discoveries.

This establishes the foundation for our patent laws, which grant a property right to the inventor of a new idea or method that lasts for a limited amount of time.[13] Property rights such as these encourage innovation, because they facilitate **appropriability** (the ability of an inventor to capture the gains from an invention or new idea) and make inventive activity worthwhile. There can still be diffusion of

---

[12] Given the problem with imitation, Keller (2002) suggests that permitting joint ventures and cooperation in R&D may also increase inventive activity.

[13] This property rights issue also motivates our copyright legislation, which gives creators ownership of their artistic expression, and trademark laws, which protect a company's words or symbols used to identify a firm's particular brand or identity. Because these encourage creativity much like a patent, we focus primarily on patents in this chapter. You can learn more about patent, copyright, and trademark law from the Web page of the US Patent and Trademark Office at http://www.uspto.gov.

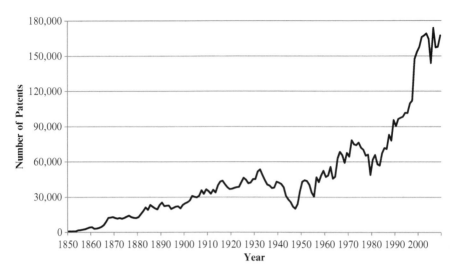

Fig. 17.9 Annual number of patents granted in the USA, 1850–2009

an invention, because clearly defined property rights facilitate the trade of a patented idea or of a licensing agreement that allows others to use the idea for a fee.

The first US patent act was approved by Congress in 1790. In exchange for disclosing the new idea to society, an inventor was granted exclusive ownership of the invention or innovation for 14 years. To receive a patent, the inventor must demonstrate that the invention or innovation is new, useful, and nonobvious.[14] A patent encourages R&D by stopping imitation and giving monopoly ownership to the inventor for a limited period of time. Since 1790, over 7.6 million patents have been awarded in the USA. Patent activity was meager until the middle of the nineteenth century when technological change began to drive the industrial revolution. You can see this from Fig. 17.9, which plots the number of patents granted each year from 1850 to 2009. In 1850, 884 patents were granted, a number that has risen steadily for most of the subsequent period. Several events undoubtedly influenced the trend in patent activity:

- 1861: Patent life was increased from 14 to 17 years, which would increase the value of a patent and encourage R&D.
- 1942–1945: US involvement in World War II diverted funds from R&D and may explain the decline in patent activity during this period.
- 1980–1981: US courts extended patentability to include genetically engineered bacteria in 1980 and software in 1981, which would encourage R&D.

---

[14] For a more complete description of the patent process, see Merges et al. (1997).

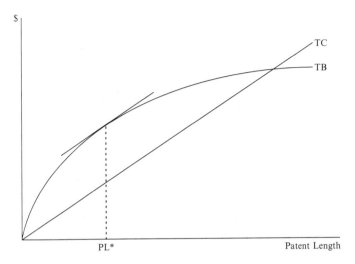

Fig. 17.10 The socially optimal patent length (PL*)

- 1995: To conform to the World Trade Organization's Agreement on intellectual property rights issues, patent life was increased from 17 to 20 years. Again, this would encourage R&D activity.
- 1998: US courts extended patentability to include business practices[15] and financial service products, which would encourage R&D.

A patent's market value increases with patent length, so a longer life should increase the incentive to invest in creative activity, which in turn would lead to greater technological change. This begs the question: why not give an inventor a patent that lasts forever?

To identify the socially optimal patent life, we need to realize that there is a cost–benefit trade-off associated with increasing patent life.[16] On the plus side, a longer life increases the expected returns associated with an innovation, which will encourage R&D activity and promote dynamic efficiency. On the other hand, a patent gives its owner a monopoly over the use of the innovation. The longer the patent life, the greater the static inefficiency associated with the monopoly power that is created by the patent. One would expect the social benefits of a longer patent life to increase at a decreasing rate, assuming diminishing returns. Social costs should rise as well, as a longer life implies greater static inefficiency. To identify the social optimum, consider the example of total benefit (TB) and total cost (TC) functions found in Fig. 17.10. The optimum occurs where the difference between TB and TC is greatest or where the marginal principle holds (i.e., the marginal benefit equals the marginal cost). Patent life (PL) is optimal at PL^* in this example.

---

[15] One example is Amazon.com's one-click method of placing an order on the internet.

[16] For an early discussion of this issue, see Nordhaus (1969).

The obvious problem with this analysis is that the benefits and costs of a longer patent life vary by the type of invention. Those with exceptionally high (low) benefits warrant a longer (shorter) life, while those that produce greater (less) static inefficiency warrant a shorter (longer) life. As a practical matter, it is very difficult and costly to predict these things when an inventor first applies for a patent. Even the inventor, let alone a government agency, would be uncertain of the potential merits of an innovation. Given this uncertainty, a system with a fixed patent life that applies to all innovations may be the best we can do.

17.3   The Effect of Market Structure on Technological Change

In this section, we ignore government involvement and focus on market incentives to invest in R&D that is designed to create profitable new technologies. Although a patent provides ownership for a limited period, it also forces the firm to reveal its new idea for its competitors to see. In some cases, the firm may prefer to keep the new idea a **trade secret** rather than disclose it in a patent application. In fact Levin et al. (1987) and Moser (2005) found that secrecy can be an effective alternative to patent protection in certain industries.

The Coca-Cola Company provides one of the best examples of a successful trade secret. The company has never held a patent for the formula of its Coke brand of cola but has been very effective in protecting it from outsiders. Only a few employees know the formula, and each of them has signed a contract with the company that forbids them from disclosing the formula to others and from opening their own cola company. This strategy has allowed Coca-Cola to conceal its formula for well over a century.

Schumpeter (1942) was the first to emphasize the significance of dynamic efficiency and to analyze the possible connection between market structure and technological change. According to Schumpeter, competition for new technologies is an essential part of capitalism and is more important than price competition. Firms compete to develop new technologies that can be extremely profitable. Through a process that Schumpeter called **creative destruction**, the development of new technologies continually revolutionizes our economy by destroying old ways (i.e., methods, companies, and markets) and creating new ones.

Regarding market structure, Schumpeter went on to say that the statically efficient model of perfect competition "has no title to being set up as a model of ideal efficiency." Instead, large firms in concentrated industries are necessary for dynamic efficiency because they are more likely to invest in the R&D that drives creative destruction through technological change. One possibility is if there are economies of scale in R&D, then large firms will have an innovation advantage.

The presence of market power that is typically associated with large corporations may encourage innovative activity in two ways. First, existing market power gives firms the financial <u>means to invest</u> in R&D. Second, the potential for successful innovation to increase market power gives firms the <u>incentive to invest</u> in R&D.

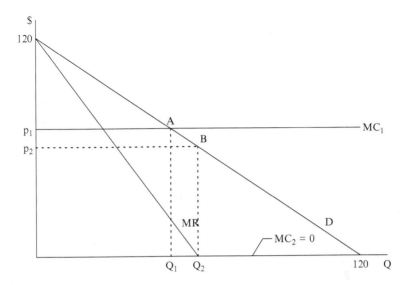

Fig. 17.11 Technological change that transforms an industry from perfect competition (at A) to monopoly (at B)

In the end, this drive to invent leads to better products and processes. Through creative destruction, it also makes the benefits of market power short lived. In Schumpeter's view, large corporations are necessary for progress and are constantly being challenged and replaced by more dynamically efficient competitors who produce better products at lower cost.

To illustrate Schumpeter's point that maintaining static efficiency period after period need not be dynamically efficient, we consider a simple two-period model. Demand and cost conditions are described in Fig. 17.11, where D is demand, MR is marginal revenue, and MC is long-run marginal cost. In period 1, marginal cost is $MC_1 = \$70$, and the market is perfectly competitive. Equilibrium price and quantity are $p_1 = \$70$ and $Q_1 = 50$. Given the lure of monopoly profits, one firm invests in R&D which pays off and lowers its marginal cost to $MC_2 = 0$. This innovation puts all other firms out of business, leaving the inventive firm with a monopoly position, and the optimal price–output pair becomes $p_2 = \$60$ and $Q_2 = 60$. Notice that the market is statically efficient in period 1 (because $p_1 = MC_1 = 70$) but is not statically efficient in period 2 (because $p_2 = 60 > MC_2 = 0$).

This outcome can be dynamically efficient, however, if the cost of R&D is not too high and if the inventive firm would not have undertaken the R&D project without the payback of monopoly profits in period 2. To demonstrate, we compare total surplus in the two alternatives (ignoring discounting):

- Without the innovation, $p_1 = p_2 = MC_1$ in equilibrium. Total surplus is the area under demand and above MC_1 at Q_1 in period 1 (i.e., consumer surplus in period 1) plus the area under demand and above MC_1 at Q_1 in period 2 (i.e., consumer surplus in period 2). This is $2,500 ($1,250 in each period).

- With the innovation (ignoring the cost of R&D for the moment), total surplus is the area under demand and above MC_1 at Q_1 in period 1 ($1,250) plus the area under demand and above MC_2 at Q_2 in period 2 (i.e., consumer plus producer surplus in period 2). This is $6,650 (i.e., total surplus of $1,250 in period 1 plus consumer surplus of $1,800 in period 2 and gross profit of $3,600 in period 2).

As long as the cost of R&D is no greater than the firm's gross profit of $3,600, the firm will invest and the innovation produces a higher total surplus over the two periods. This outcome is dynamically efficient because society is better off with the innovation even though it leads to static inefficiency in period 2. In other words, the benefits of innovation far outstrip the costs of static market power.

Given the importance of Schumpeter's ideas, the purpose of this section is to investigate the link between market structure and innovative activity. We begin by analyzing monopoly, perfect competition, and oligopoly models. We examine the empirical evidence at the end of the chapter. Issues of technological change are clearly dynamic, but to keep things simple we begin by ignoring time.

17.3.1   Monopoly and Technological Change

First, we consider a monopoly market where the firm invests in R&D that produces a new technology. Two cases are analyzed: (1) product innovation where technological change increases product quality; (2) process innovation where technological change lowers production costs.

17.3.1.1   Technological Change that Improves Product Quality

The firm's goal is to maximize profit with respect to price and R&D spending. Investing in R&D is costly and increases demand by improving product quality. Firm (market) demand is defined as $q(p, R\&D)$, where q is quantity demanded and p is price. Demand has a negative slope and increases at a decreasing rate with spending on R&D.[17] Total cost (TC) consists of total production cost, $C(q)$, and spending on research and development, R&D. The firm's profit equation is

$$\pi = TR - TC = pq(p, R\&D) - [C(q) + R\&D], \qquad (17.1)$$

where TR is total revenue.

---

[17] That is, $\partial q / \partial R\&D > 0$ and $\partial^2 q / \partial R\&D^2 < 0$. This last condition assures that the firm's second-order condition of profit maximization is met. To simplify the analysis, we let R&D affect demand or costs directly. That is, its effect on technology (T) is assumed to be 1 (i.e., $\partial T / \partial R\&D = 1$).

To determine the profit-maximizing price and level of R&D, we apply marginal analysis by maximizing profit with respect to p and R&D. Optimal values are obtained by solving these first order conditions simultaneously for p and R&D. It turns out that the first-order conditions are identical to those in the advertising problem in Chap. 15 (Sect. 15.3.2), except that R&D is the choice variable instead of advertising.

Because the advertising and R&D models are so similar, we ignore the first-order condition for price (or assumed that price is fixed) and focus on the firm's R&D problem. The first-order condition with respect to R&D is[18]

$$\frac{\partial \pi}{\partial R\&D} = \frac{\partial TR}{\partial R\&D} - \frac{\partial TC}{\partial R\&D}$$

$$= MR_{R\&D} - MC_{R\&D}$$

$$= \left(p \frac{\partial q}{\partial R\&D}\right) - \left(\frac{\partial C}{\partial q} \frac{\partial q}{\partial R\&D} + 1\right) = 0, \qquad (17.2)$$

where $MR_{R\&D}$ is the marginal revenue associated with R&D and $MC_{R\&D}$ is the marginal cost of R&D. Notice that the marginal principle applies: the optimum is reached where the marginal benefit equals the marginal cost of R&D.

Equation (17.2) has a similar interpretation as the first-order condition for advertising in (15.5). Like advertising, we can think of R&D as a costly input that is designed to increase demand. The marginal benefit, $p(\partial q/\partial R\&D)$, can be thought of as the value of the marginal product of R&D. The marginal cost can be decomposed into two parts. The direct effect measures the added cost of increasing R&D expenditures by one dollar (the +1 with in parentheses). The indirect effect captures the influence that R&D has on the marginal cost of production $[(\partial C/\partial q)(\partial q/\partial R\&D)]$.

Another way of thinking about (17.2) is to rearrange terms so that it identifies the firm's ratio of R&D to total sales (total revenue). This is called the R&D-to-sales ratio. By rearranging terms,[19]

$$1 = \frac{\partial q}{\partial R\&D}(p - MC),$$

$$\frac{R\&D}{p \cdot q} = \frac{R\&D}{q} \frac{\partial q}{\partial R\&D} \frac{(p - MC)}{p},$$

$$\frac{R\&D}{p \cdot q} = \frac{\eta_{R\&D}}{\eta}, \qquad (17.3)$$

---

[18] This derivative involves the use of the chain rule, which is discussed in the Mathematics and Econometrics Appendix at the end of the book. According to the chain rule, if $y = f(x_1)$ and $x_1 = f(x_2)$, then a change in x_2 causes a change in x_1 which causes y to change. That is, $dy/dx_2 = (dy/dx_1)(dx_1/dx_2)$. In this case, because $C = C(q)$ and $q = q(R\&D)$, $\partial C/\partial R\&D = (\partial C/\partial q)(\partial q/\partial R\&D)$.

[19] This derivation is based on the fact that the Lerner index is $\mathcal{L} \equiv (p - MC)/p = 1/\eta$, where MC is the long-run marginal cost of production. Recall from Chaps. 6 and 12 that the Lerner index is derived from the firm's first-order condition of profit maximization.

where η is the absolute value of the price elasticity of demand and $\eta_{R\&D}$ is the R&D elasticity of demand, which measures the percentage change in quantity demanded that is caused by a 1% increase in R&D [i.e., $(\partial q/\partial R\&D)(R\&D/q)$]. This is similar to the Dorfman–Steiner condition of advertising that we discussed in Chap. 15. It implies that:

- A firm's R&D-to-sales ratio will be higher when there is a greater likelihood that R&D will improve product quality and increase demand (i.e., $\eta_{R\&D}$ is greater). In other words, firms will invest more money in R&D when it is expected to produce greater benefits. In cases such as this, R&D is said to have greater **technological opportunity**. Such opportunities for progress will vary by industry.
- R&D spending will be greater the lower the price elasticity of demand.[20] Recall from the Lerner index that a lower η implies greater monopoly power. Thus, (17.3) implies that firms that have greater market power will invest more in R&D. Later in the chapter, we investigate this issue more thoroughly.

17.3.1.2   Technological Change That Lowers Production Costs

Next, we analyze a situation where an investment in R&D lowers the firm's marginal cost of production but has no direct effect on demand. In this case, the firm's total cost is $TC = c(R\&D) \cdot q - R\&D$. In this model, c is the marginal production cost, which falls at a decreasing rate with respect to R&D.[21] The firm's profit equation is

$$\pi = TR - TC = pq(p) - c(R\&D)q - R\&D. \tag{17.4}$$

To determine the profit-maximizing price and level of R&D, we follow the same procedure as before. We maximize profit with respect to p and R&D, and optimal values are obtained by simultaneously solving these first-order conditions for p and R&D. As before, we ignore the price equation so we can focus on R&D. In this model, the first-order condition with respect to R&D is

$$\frac{\partial \pi}{\partial R\&D} = \frac{\partial TR}{\partial R\&D} - \frac{\partial TC}{\partial R\&D}$$
$$= MR_{R\&D} - MC_{R\&D}$$
$$= (0) - \left(\frac{\partial c}{\partial R\&D}q + 1\right) = 0. \tag{17.5}$$

---

[20] This is consistent with Spence (1975), who showed that the gains from improving product quality will be larger as the price elasticity of demand falls. However, Kamien and Schwartz (1970) find that the gains from reducing the cost of production are larger the more elastic is demand.

[21] That is, $\partial c/\partial R\&D < 0$ and $\partial^2 c/\partial R\&D^2 > 0$. This is required for the firm's second-order condition of profit maximization to hold.

In this case, the marginal benefit results from the reduction in marginal cost due to R&D, $\partial c / \partial R\&D < 0$.[22] The model implies that:

- An increase in the effectiveness of R&D to reduce costs (i.e., an increase in the absolute value of $\partial c / \partial R\&D$) raises the marginal benefit of R&D, which causes the firm to increase its R&D spending. When this occurs, there is greater technological opportunity in terms of cost savings.
- The firm will increase its R&D spending as it produces more output. This seems reasonable, as the benefits of R&D increase with greater sales.

Both this model and the model where R&D increases product quality imply that the firm will make greater investments in R&D when it leads to a greater increase in demand or a greater decrease in costs (i.e., there is greater technological opportunity). They also imply that firms are more likely to invest more in R&D as market power and sales increase.[23]

17.3.2   Competition Versus Monopoly

Arrow (1962) is the first to formally model the effect of market structure on innovative activity. He conducted a thought experiment where a single market has either one firm or many (competitive) firms.[24] There is no product differentiation, and firms compete by simultaneously choosing price (i.e., Bertrand). Demand and cost functions are linear. Technological change leads to a decrease in the marginal cost of production. The goal of the model is to determine whether a firm will have greater incentive to invest in innovative activity in a monopoly or a more competitive market setting.

First, we consider the case of monopoly. Figure 17.12 describes the firm's demand, marginal revenue, and marginal cost functions. Marginal cost equals MC before the technological change and is MC$'$ after the change. At MC, the firm's profit-maximizing price–output pair is p and Q_m. At MC$'$, it is p' and Q'_m. This is nondrastic or **minor technological change** because $p' > $ MC. A drastic or **major technological change** occurs when MC falls by so much that $p' < $ MC. At output level Q_m, the firm's total revenue can be defined as the area under the marginal revenue function,[25] and the firm's total production cost can be defined as

---

[22] The second-order condition is met, because $\partial^2 c / \partial R\&D^2 > 0$.

[23] For simplicity, we have ignored the price of conducting research and development. Investment in R&D would also be expected to increase as the price of R&D falls.

[24] Arrow actually compared monopoly with perfect competition (which is the same as the Bertrand outcome when the number of firms exceeds 1). In any case, Arrow's main results are unaffected by assuming any market structure (such as Cournot) that produces an equilibrium level of market output that exceeds the cartel level of market output.

[25] We discuss this fact in Chap. 2.

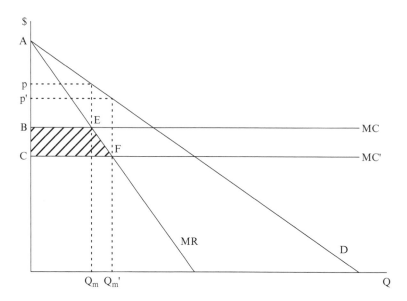

Fig. 17.12 A monopoly firm's incentive to innovate

the area under the marginal cost function as output ranges from 0 to Q_m. Note that monopoly output is considerably less than the socially optimal level of output, which occurs where MC crosses demand. When total revenue and total cost are defined in this way, the firm's total profit under the old technology is area ABE (i.e., total revenue minus total cost). For the new technology, its total gross profit is area ACF (ignoring the cost of R&D). Thus, the technological change causes gross profit to increase by area BCFE.[26] This implies that the firm will invest in R&D as long as it does not cost more than this amount, which we assume to be the case.

  Next, assume that everything is the same except that there are now many firms. One of these firms invests in R&D that leads to the same cost-saving technological change as in the monopoly case. The Bertrand equilibrium for the old technology occurs where price equals marginal cost (MC) at market output level Q_c (the perfectly competitive outcome) described in Fig. 17.13. When a single firm discovers the new technology, its marginal cost falls to MC', but its competitors' marginal cost remains at MC. In this case, the Nash equilibrium occurs where price equals MC − ε, where ε is small. Here, we assume that ε is 0 for simplicity, and the equilibrium output equals Q_c.[27] Profits for the innovative firm are 0 under the old technology and equal area BCHG for the new technology (ignoring R&D costs).

---

[26] If the new technology lasted for many periods, its benefits would equal the present value of the gain in future gross profits. This simply complicates the analysis without providing important new insights.

[27] Alternatively, we could assume that the firm owns the right to the new technology and licenses it out to existing firms for a royalty payment equal to MC − MC'. This produces the same result.

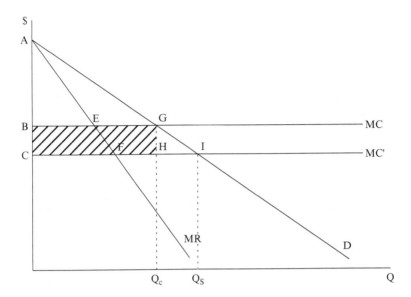

Fig. 17.13 A competitive firm's incentive to innovate

Thus, the new technology causes the innovative firm's gross profits to increase by area BCHG. Because the gain in profit in the competitive case (BCHG) exceeds the gain in profits in the monopoly case (BCFE) and BCFE is assumed to exceed the cost of R&D, the firm in the competitive market will make this investment in R&D.

Arrow's analysis has two important implications. First, because the gain in gross profit due to innovative activity is greater in the competitive market (BCHG) than in the monopoly market (BCFE), the incentive to innovate is greater with more competition. In other words, the monopoly firm is willing to invest up to area BCFE in R&D, while a firm in a more competitive setting is willing to invest up to area BCHG. This is just the opposite of Schumpeter's hypothesis.

The intuition behind Arrow's result is due to the fact that the monopolist restricts output. Thus, the increase in profit per unit (MC − MC′) is applied to a smaller quantity of output in monopoly (Q'_m) than in the competitive case (Q_c). Another issue is that for the monopolist, the new technology replaces the firm's old technology and assets, which is costly to the firm; for a more competitive firm, its new technology primarily replaces the old technology and assets of its competitors. This is a form of creative destruction that is known as the **replacement effect**. Because the replacement effect is greater for the monopolist, a monopolist will have less incentive to innovate.

The second implication of Arrow's analysis is that society values R&D more than the monopolist and the competitive innovator. To see this, recall that the social optimum occurs where price equals marginal cost in each setting (i.e., at Q_c with the old technology and Q_S with the new technology in Fig. 17.13). Thus, the gain in gross profit due to the new technology from society's perspective is area BCIG.

Because area BCIG > BCHG > BCFE, society values the innovation more than the competitive firm, but the competitive firm values it more than the monopolist. Thus, a competitive firm as well as a monopoly firm will underinvest in R&D from society's perspective.

There are at least two reasons to question the conclusion of Arrow's model that competitive firms have greater incentive to innovate. First, firms face a dynamic setting in reality, and over time new processes are more likely to spread quickly to firms within an industry than to firms in unrelated industries. Thus, competitor marginal costs will gradually fall below MC in Fig. 17.13, which reduces the firm's incentive to innovate in a competitive market. If imitation were instantaneous, for example, then MC will fall immediately to MC′, and there will be no incentive for an individual firm in a competitive market to innovate.[28] The point is that imitation discourages R&D. Second, competitive firms do not have excess profits to invest in R&D. If capital markets are imperfect, it may be easier for a monopolist to use internal funds to support R&D than for a competitive firm to raise the same investment dollars from outside sources. Thus, the cost of R&D may be higher for competitive firms.

17.3.3 Monopoly and a Potential Entrant

Another concern with the Arrow model is that it assumes that only one firm invests in R&D, whereas Schumpeter argued that firms actively compete in innovative activity. Gilbert and Newbery (1982) developed a model which is more consistent with Schumpeter because it allows firms to have a choice between investing and not investing in R&D. To focus on the main ideas, we assume just two firms: an incumbent monopolist (M) and a potential entrant (PE). They compete in developing a new process that will lower marginal cost. This innovation is then protected by a patent that cannot be circumvented. They compete in a three stage game. In the first stage, M decides whether or not to invest in R&D. In the second stage, PE decides to enter or not. In the final stage, PE decides whether or not to invest in R&D. A key feature of the model, which has an important effect on the outcome, is that there is no uncertainty regarding the effectiveness of R&D to generate a new innovation.

To make this a concrete example, assume that the inverse demand function is $p = 100 - Q$, where $Q = q_1 + q_2$. Marginal cost equals \$40 before the innovation

---

[28] Even with patents, firms can sometimes circumvent them. Mansfield (1968) found that the time between the introduction of an innovation and when 60% of related products had imitated the innovation ranged from one month for simple production processes to several decades for more complex ones (e.g., steel production). As you might expect, Levin et al. (1987) found that it takes considerably longer to imitate a major new product that has been patented than one that has not been patented.

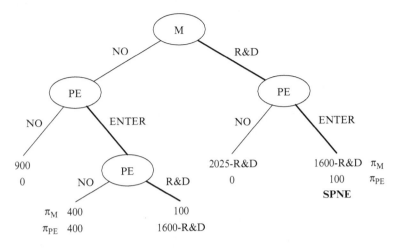

Fig. 17.14 Extensive form of an innovation game with potential entry

and $10 after the innovation. The optimal expenditure on R&D is sufficiently low to ensure that it is a worthwhile investment. In this example, assume that $500 < R&D < $1,200. This makes it profitable for only one firm to invest in R&D. There are five possible outcomes, and profits for each are derived as follows:

- When M chooses not to invest in R&D and

   (1) PE chooses not to enter, M is a simple monopolist and earns a profit of $900. PE's profit is 0.
   (2) PE chooses to enter and not invest in R&D, the outcome is that of a symmetric Cournot game as described in Chap. 10. Each firm earns a profit of $400.
   (3) PE chooses to enter and invest in R&D, the outcome is that of a symmetric Cournot game as described in Chap. 10. M earns $100 and PE earns $1,600 − R&D.

- When M chooses to invest in R&D and

   (4) PE chooses not to enter, M is a simple monopolist and earns a profit of $2,025 − R&D. PE earns 0 profit.
   (5) PE chooses to enter, the outcome is asymmetric Cournot as described in Chap. 10. M earns $1,600 − R&D and PE earns $100.

The extensive form of the game is described in Fig. 17.14.

Recall from Chaps. 3 and 11 that we use backwards induction to solve dynamic games. Notice that if M does not invest in R&D, PE's best reply is to enter and invest in R&D. At this outcome, M earns $100. Alternatively, when M invests in R&D, PE's best reply is to enter. At this outcome, M earns $1,600 − R&D. Thus, the subgame Nash equilibrium is for M to invest in R&D (because R&D < $1,200) and for PE to enter. This outcome is more consistent with Schumpeter because it implies that a monopolist can have a strong incentive to innovate, especially when faced with a potential entrant. Given that R&D is less than $1,200, the net returns to

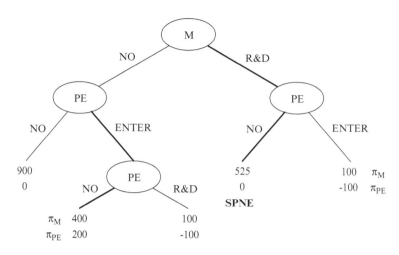

Fig. 17.15 Extensive form of an innovation game with entry costs

R&D for M are quite high (profits of 100 versus profits of more than
$400 = 1,600 - R\&D$). In other words, M has an incentive to preempt PE by
developing a new technology first.

Adding uncertainty regarding the effectiveness of R&D to produce a valuable
innovation can change this result. Lee and Wilde (1980) and Reinganum (1983,
1984, 1985) showed that with uncertainty the potential entrant will enter the market
and spend more on R&D than the incumbent. The reason for this is that the
uncertainty of success induces firms into an R&D race. This speeds up innovation
time, which more quickly lowers the value of the incumbent's old technology and
reduces the incumbent's incentive to invest in R&D. A market with a large
incumbent firm that is less likely to invest in R&D than a potential entrant is
more in keeping with Arrow than with Schumpeter. Nevertheless, industry leaders
are likely to be replaced by entrants in this model, an outcome that is consistent with
Schumpeter's notion of creative destruction.

The Gilbert and Newbery (1982) model can be modified to show how R&D can
serve as a strategic barrier to entry. To illustrate, assume that PE must pay an
additional sunk cost (σ) to enter the market. In this example, $\sigma = 200$ and
R&D = $1,500. This game is described in Fig. 17.15. The monopolist's optimal
strategy is to invest in R&D, which now eliminates entry: the SPNE is for M to
invest in R&D and for PE to not enter. Thus, the monopolist has an even stronger
strategic reason for investing in R&D under this scenario. The motivation for this
result is that the innovation is more profitable to the monopolist because the firm
uses it to preserve its monopoly position, while the potential entrant uses it to enter
the market and become a duopolist. Without that threat, it would not be profitable
for the monopolist to invest in R&D. Thus, R&D serves as a strategic barrier.

Patent races have similar dynamic features. By adding a time dimension to the
patent problem, firms have a choice of when to patent a new product or process.

Faster development of a new technology will be more costly, but it may give a firm a strategic advantage over its competitors. In this setting, firms may be thrust into a **patent race** where each firm races to be the first to obtain a patent.[29] It can also induce an incumbent firm to start early in order to gain a head start in its R&D efforts. An early lead could encourage others to drop out of the race, unless the probability of being able to "leapfrog ahead" of the incumbent is sufficiently high. Races such as these can induce firms to innovate faster than they would prefer if they did not face competition. The rate of innovation may also be faster than is socially optimal. This is consistent with Schumpeter, because these types of races for new technologies are associated with concentrated industries.

17.3.4   Oligopoly and the Incentive to Innovate

Dasgupta and Stiglitz (1980) provided a simple oligopoly model that is consistent with Schumpeter's hypothesis that innovative activity will be greater in more highly concentrated industries. They considered an n firm oligopoly where firms simultaneously choose the level of output and R&D expenditures that lower marginal cost. Firms are symmetric, products are homogeneous, and production costs are linear. Entry is free, so that firm profits will be zero in the long run. In other words, this is a Cournot-type model with R&D and free entry.

Two equilibrium conditions provide a connection between industry concentration and R&D activity. From Chap. 12 (Sect. 12.1.1) we saw the firm's first-order condition of profit-maximization produces the following Lerner index ($\mathcal{L}$) in an oligopoly setting:

$$\mathcal{L} \equiv \frac{p - \text{MC}}{p} = \frac{1}{n \cdot \eta} = \frac{\text{HHI}}{\eta}. \tag{17.6}$$

From symmetry, the Herfindahl–Hirschman index (HHI) equals $1/n$, which is also the market share of each firm when the market is in equilibrium. Given free entry, we also know that long-run equilibrium profits for firm i will be zero. That is,

$$\pi_i = \text{TR} - \text{TC} = p(Q)q_i - [c(\text{R\&D})q_i + \text{R\&D}] = 0, \tag{17.7}$$

where Q is the industry level of output. Aggregating (17.7) over the equilibrium number of firms in the industry (n^*) gives

$$p(Q)Q - c(\text{R\&D})Q - n^* \cdot \text{R\&D} = 0, \tag{17.8}$$

where $n^* \cdot$ R&D is the expenditures on R&D by the industry

---

[29] See Kamien and Schwartz (1982) and Reinganum (1989) for a more complete discussion.

Solving for $n^* \cdot$ R&D and dividing both sides of the equality by $p(Q)Q$ gives

$$\frac{n^* \cdot \text{R\&D}}{p(Q)Q} = \frac{p(Q)Q - c(\text{R\&D})Q}{p(Q)Q} = \frac{p(Q) - c(\text{R\&D})}{p(Q)} = \mathcal{L}. \qquad (17.9)$$

Note that the first term on the left is the ratio of R&D to total revenue at the industry level, the industry R&D-to-sales ratio. Given the definition of the Lerner index in (17.6), this ratio can be written as

$$\frac{n^* \cdot \text{R\&D}}{p(Q)Q} = \frac{\text{HHI}}{\eta}. \qquad (17.10)$$

It says that the R&D-to-sales ratio at the industry level will be greater as the price elasticity of demand falls and as industry concentration (HHI) increases. This is consistent with Schumpeter, as the intensity of R&D spending increases with industry concentration.[30]

17.4   The Effect of Technological Change on Market Structure

Although market structure can affect the degree of technological change, a new technology can also have a dramatic effect on market structure. An entrepreneur who creates a new product may seize a market from existing firms and increase concentration. In addition, a technological change that affects MES will also lead to a change in concentration. For example, Demsetz' (1973) superior efficiency hypothesis indicates that if a superior firm discovers a lower cost technology that increases (decreases) MES, an increase (decrease) in average firm size and industry concentration will follow.

We have also seen that investments that increase sunk costs, such as expenditures on advertising and R&D, can serve as a strategic barrier to entry. As Sutton (1999) points out, however, this relationship can be rather complex for R&D. He argues that the link between R&D and concentration depends upon the nature of the technological change. For example, improved technological opportunities that are vertical in nature (i.e., greater opportunity to raise product quality or lower marginal cost) will lead to greater R&D. They will also cause industry concentration to rise, as a firm that produces a better product at lower cost will take market share away from competitors.[31] Only the best and lowest cost products survive in the long run. This implies that in the vertical case, R&D and concentration will be high (low) when technological opportunities are high (low).

---

[30] This assumes that η is constant, an assumption that may not hold in reality. For further review of the theoretical literature, see Dasgupta (1988) and van Cayseele (1998).

[31] Sutton argues that this is because the degree of substitutability between products is high in the vertical case.

This relationship breaks down when technological opportunities are horizontal in nature, such as when an innovation leads to a new product that is differentiated horizontally. In this case, improved technological opportunities increase R&D but may have a negligible effect on concentration. This is because the degree of substitutability is limited when differentiation is horizontal, and a new product will not generally replace existing products. For example, a firm that develops a new coconut flavored breakfast cereal need not cause other brands such as Cheerios to be squeezed out of the market. Thus, Sutton shows how a third cause, the type of technological opportunity, can influence both R&D spending and industry concentration.

17.5   The Empirical Evidence

Discussion in previous sections indicates that many forces influence R&D expenditures, patent activity, and technological change. These can be organized into three broad categories that are summarized below:

1. **Government incentives:** Given the public nature of information, government uses the patent system and research grants to encourage technological change through investments in R&D.
2. **Private firm incentives:** Economic theory predicts that private firms will be more likely to invest in R&D when they are better able to appropriate the benefits of their innovation. Firms will also be more likely to invest in R&D when there is greater technological opportunity, that is, when such an investment is more likely to successfully lead to a new product, a better quality product, or lower production costs.
3. **The role of market structure:** Economic theory provides no clear link between market structure and technological change. Arrow's model predicts that competitive firms are more likely to invest in R&D. In contrast, Schumpeter's theory predicts that innovative activity is more likely to come from large firms in highly concentrated industries. Finally, causality can flow in the other direction: a technological change may influence market structure.

As discussed in Sect. 17.2, the US government uses a number of methods to encourage R&D activity and create new technological knowledge. Private companies receive a 20% tax credit on their R&D expenditures. The federal government supplies 26% of grant funding in the USA. Finally, the patent system encourages inventive activity by giving an inventor exclusive ownership of an invention or innovation for 20 years (appropriability). In their survey of the evidence, Cohen and Levin (1989) concluded that these government policies have reduced the cost of innovation, especially in agricultural, aircraft, and electronics industries. Mansfield (1968) found that patent protection contributed to technological change in the petroleum, machinery, and metal products industries and was especially important in the pharmaceutical and chemical industries. He estimated that 65% of pharmaceutical inventions and 30% of chemical inventions would not have occurred without patent protection. Finally, Blumenthal et al. (1986) found that university research contributes to technological progress.

It is reasonable to assume that R&D spending follows technological opportunity. After all, a profit-maximizing firm is more likely to make a risky R&D investment when it has a higher probability of success. To test this hypothesis, we need an accurate measure of technological opportunity. Because no such measure exists, most studies use industry dummy variables to control for industry-specific differences in technological opportunity.[32] Consistent with the hypothesis that greater technological opportunity increases R&D spending, these studies find greater R&D spending and patent activity in "high tech" industries that are associated with the scientific or technical fields.[33] These include chemical, computer, and electronics industries, as described in Table 17.2.

Most of the empirical literature on the subject of technological change has focused on Schumpeter's theory that innovative activity increases with firm size and market power or industry concentration. The literature is too vast to summarize here, but those who have surveyed it conclude that the early studies produce evidence that is rather weak and somewhat fragile.[34] This evidence shows that the intensity of R&D spending increases with firm size but only for a limited number of industries, such as chemicals, automobiles, and steel. In addition, many studies find that R&D intensity increases with industry concentration. Compared to other variables such as technological opportunities, however, the overall influence of firm size and concentration on R&D spending is quite small.

It may be too soon to conclude that market structure has little effect on technological change though, as these weak findings may be due to problems associated with estimating a model of technological change. First, there is a measurement problem. Because it is impossible to measure inventive output, most studies use either the intensity of R&D spending or patent counts as a proxy variable. But not all R&D projects are successful, and not all patents are of equal value.[35] Nevertheless, even if inventive output could be accurately measured, it is still difficult to control for the many other factors that influence technological change.

Another concern is that the inventive process may be substantially more complex than Schumpeter's work suggests, making it difficult to accurately capture it in an

---

[32] See, for example, MacLaurin (1954), Scherer (1965), Pakes and Schankerman (1984), Jaffe (1986), Cohen and Levin (1989), Geroski (1990), and Blundell et al. (1999).

[33] An explanation for this is provided by Nelson (1982a), who argues that advances in scientific knowledge increase technological opportunities by lowering the cost of applied research in scientific and technical fields.

[34] For a review of the literature, see Kamien and Schwartz (1982), Cohen and Levin (1989), Geroski (1990), van Cayseele (1988), and Blundell et al. (1999).

[35] The one exception is Gayle (2005), who attempted to control for the relative importance of a patent by using a citation-weighted patent count to measure innovative output. With this measure, Gayle found a stronger positive relationship between patent counts and industry concentration.

empirical model. For example, Henderson (1993) found that large and small firms contribute in different ways to technological progress in the photolithographic alignment equipment industry. She found that larger established firms are more likely to invest in incremental innovation, while small entrants are more likely to invest in radically new inventions. Looking at a series of case studies over time, Jewkes et al. (1969) analyzed the interaction of firms when a small firm comes up with a new invention. They found that in many cases a large firm acquires the smaller inventive firm, as larger firms are better at innovation and at bringing an invention to market. Contrary to both Schumpeter and Arrow, this implies that both small and large firms have an important role to play regarding technological progress.

To further complicate matters, causality between technological change and market structure runs in both directions. As indicated above, the creative destruction of technological change can have a dramatic effect on market structure. However, Sutton (1999) pointed out that this relationship can be complex as well. In Sutton's view, when a technological change is vertical in nature (i.e., it improves product quality or lowers production costs), it causes concentration to rise; when technological change is horizontal (i.e., it creates horizontal product differentiation), it has little effect on industry concentration.

Sutton (1999) and van Cayseele (1998) investigated a number of industries and found general support for Sutton's theory. Industries with products that are more vertically differentiated, have products that are close substitutes, and have high R&D-to-sales ratios are generally highly concentrated. These include digital watches, aircraft engines, glass processing, and photographic film. In industries with horizontal characteristics, such as the market for liquid flow meters, concentration is low even though R&D spending is high.

An alternative way of evaluating the effect of competition on technological change is to investigate the behavior of firms that are involved in patent or R&D races. In a certain world, Gilbert and Newbery (1982) showed that incumbent firms are more likely to invest in R&D than potential entrants. With uncertainty, however, Lee and Wilde (1980) and Reinganum (1983, 1984, 1985) showed that challengers are more likely to invest in R&D. The only test of these competing hypotheses was conducted by Czarnitzki and Kraft (2004), who used data from German corporations. They found strong support for the uncertainty model in which competition contributes to innovation.

Ultimately, we are interested in knowing the extent to which our mixed political-economic system, which provides government support for inventive effort, produces a dynamically efficient outcome. Because it is very difficult to estimate the expected future benefits and costs of our current system and compare them with alternatives, it is not surprising that there are no empirical studies on this subject. The lone study that touches on this topic is by Hughes et al. (2002), who conducted a counterfactual study of the pharmaceutical industry. That is, they estimated the net present value of the benefit to consumers of eliminating all patent protection in this industry. By substantially reducing market power, consumers will be better off today. Consumers would be worst off in the future though, as this policy would reduce the flow of new drugs in the future. Hughes et al. found that for every dollar gain in consumer welfare today, future consumers would lose 3 dollars due to a reduction in innovative activity. Although we might question the accuracy of their estimate, the magnitude of lost future benefits is substantial. Thus, it appears that consumers benefit from patents applied to pharmaceuticals. Of course, this need not be true in other industries, because the amount of lost future benefits would vary by industry.

In summary, technological opportunity and government policies clearly encourage R&D spending and technological change. There is insufficient evidence to know whether or not our current political-economic system is dynamically efficient, however. There is evidence that technological change can dramatically affect market structure, but empirical studies fail to obtain clear results regarding the effect of market structure on technological change. A close inspection of the literature suggests that the process that drives technological change is industry specific. Given this fact and other problems associated with empirical work in this area, historical case studies of technological change may be a fruitful avenue for future research (as suggested by Cohen and Levin 1989).

17.6 Summary

1. **Technological change** occurs when we add to our knowledge about technology. This leads to the creation of new products, the production of better quality products (without an increase in cost), or the invention of a new process (i.e., production of a given output with fewer inputs). Technological change is important because it contributes to economic growth and improves our standard of living.[36]

2. The concept of static efficiency ignores the time dimension that is associated with technological change, where consumption is reduced today in order to invest in research and development (R&D) and create a better life tomorrow. **Dynamic efficiency** is reached when there is a socially optimal amount of technological change. An economy that is statically efficient need not be dynamically efficient. For example, it may be dynamically efficient to allow an inventor to have temporary market power (which is statically inefficient) to encourage inventive effort. The social benefits of a new invention can quickly outstrip the deadweight loss due to market power.

3. A technological change can be scale increasing, decreasing, or neutral. **Scale-neutral technological change** has no effect on minimum efficient scale (MES). **Scale-increasing (-decreasing) technological change** leads to an increase (decrease) in MES.

---

[36] Again, this ignores the possible negative consequences of technological change, an issue that we address in Chaps. 19 and 20.

4. A technological change can affect the cost-minimizing combination of inputs. For example, a **labor-saving technological change** occurs when the cost-minimizing amount of labor falls relative to that of other inputs.

5. There are two types of R&D programs: basic research and applied research. **Basic research** is theoretical or experimental and is designed to create general scientific knowledge. **Applied research** creates knowledge that has a specific practical purpose.

6. The process of technological change can be divided into three stages. **Invention** is the act of conceiving a technical possibility. **Innovation** occurs when an invention is made operational. **Diffusion** (or imitation) occurs when an innovation becomes widely used.

7. Given that ideas are public goods, free markets may produce too few new and useful ideas. This motivates government policies to encourage inventive activity and creative pursuits.

8. Patents, copyrights, trademarks, and research grants are used by the government to encourage inventive activity. A **patent** facilitates **appropriability** of the benefits to the inventor, as it gives an inventor monopoly ownership of an idea or method for a limited length of time. Patent life in the USA is 20 years. A copyright gives creators ownership of their artistic expressions and computer programs. A trademark gives a company protection of a symbol or brand name that is important to the company's identity and reputation. These are designed to give creators and inventors a (sometimes temporary) property right to their inventive and creative works.

9. There are social benefits and costs associated with patents. On the benefit side, they encourage R&D and technological progress. On the cost side, they create static inefficiency by giving an inventor monopoly power. The socially optimal patent life occurs where the social marginal benefits equal the social marginal costs of lengthening patent life. If we had perfect foresight, it would be optimal to have a different patent life for each innovation, with a longer (shorter) life for more (less) valuable innovations. Given uncertainty, a practical solution is to set a single length for all patents.

10. A company can appropriate the benefits of its new products or process by obtaining a patent or by keeping the details of its innovation out of the hands of its competitors (called a **trade secret**). Coca-Cola has kept its formula for Coke a trade secret for over a century.

11. Schumpeter argued that market structure and technological change are closely linked. According to Schumpeter:

    • Capitalist markets are dynamic, as a process of **creative destruction** by which firms create new technologies to replace old technologies (i.e., methods, companies, and markets) is constantly at work.

    • Large firms in concentrated markets are necessary for dynamic efficiency, as they are more likely to invest in R&D that generates technological change. They may benefit from economies of scale in R&D and may have greater means (due to market power) and greater motive to invest in R&D in order to create or preserve market power.

12. A monopolist engages in a **minor (major) technological change** that lowers marginal cost when the equilibrium price with the new technology is above (below) the marginal cost with the old technology.

13. A monopolist is more likely to invest in R&D when:

    • There are greater **technological opportunities**. This occurs when such an investment is more likely to produce greater benefits (i.e., it is better able to increase demand or to lower costs).
    • Demand is more inelastic.
    • The firm produces a greater amount of output.

14. Economic theory provides conflicting predictions regarding the effect of market structure on technological change. Important predictions are listed below:

    • Schumpeter predicts that large firms in concentrated industries are more likely to invent than firms in more competitive markets. This prediction is supported by the Dasgupta and Stiglitz (1980) model.
    • Arrow predicts that the incentive to invent is greater with more competition. This is attributable to the **replacement effect**, which means that an innovation is less valuable to a monopolist because it has more to lose or less to gain from an innovation that replaces its current technology. However, both monopoly and competitive markets underinvest in inventive effort from society's perspective.
    • When a monopoly firm competes with a potential entrant for a new patent, the monopolist will have a stronger incentive to obtain the patent.
    • When firms compete in a **patent race**, where each firm races to be first to obtain a patent, firms may innovate faster than if they were not competitors and faster than is socially optimal.

15. Technological change can also influence market structure. When a change in technology increases (decreases) minimum efficient scale, industry concentration will increase (decrease).

16. Sutton (1999) points out that the relationship between technological change and market structure depends on the type of innovation. According to Sutton:

    • When a technological change is vertical in nature (i.e., it improves product quality or lowers marginal cost), it will cause industry concentration to increase.
    • When technological change is horizontal in nature (i.e., it changes horizontal differentiation or adds a new product that is not a close substitute with competing brands), it will have little if any effect on industry concentration.

17. There are a considerable number of empirical studies on the economics of technological change. A summary of the main results is provided below:

    • The evidence shows that government programs, such as patents and research grants, encourage inventive activity.

- R&D activity follows technological opportunity. Although it is impossible to precisely measure technological opportunity, the evidence shows that the intensity of R&D spending is greater in high tech industries that are associated with scientific and technological fields.
- There is weak and sometimes conflicting support for Schumpeter's view that large firms in concentrated industries are needed to generate technological change. This may be due to data limitations and methodological weaknesses of previous studies, such as the use of R&D spending or patent counts that may be poor proxies for inventive output. In addition, case studies show that the inventive process may be more complex than Schumpeter envisioned. In many cases the inventive process varies by industry, and in some cases small firms invent, while large firms innovate.
- There is also evidence that technological change influences market structure. Although available evidence is limited, there is support for Sutton's (1999) view that the effect of R&D on concentration depends on the type of innovation.
- Given the difficulty of accurately estimating expected future costs and benefits of government and market incentives to promote progress, there is insufficient evidence to know whether or not our current political-economic system is dynamically efficient.

17.7   Review Questions

1. Explain how technological change affects our standard of living. What would the world be like if technological change were to cease? Are there any negative consequences associated with technological change?
2. Compare and contrast the concepts of static and dynamic efficiency.
3. Consider a market with two periods (ignore discounting). Demand is $Q = 120 - p$ in both periods. In period 1, marginal cost (MC_1) is 70, and the market is perfectly competitive. One firm invests in R&D which pays off by lowering its marginal cost to $MC_2 = 20$ in the second period. The marginal cost of all other firms remains at 70.

    A. For each period, determine the equilibrium price (p^*), equilibrium market output (Q^*), consumer surplus (CS), and gross producer surplus (PS).
    B. Is the market statically efficient in each period?
    C. Under what condition(s) will this innovation be dynamically efficient?

4. Explain how the market for ideas may fail without some government involvement.
5. Explain how patents, copyrights, and trademarks may promote technological progress. Why not give creative individuals and firms unlimited ownership of the outcomes of their work?

6. In the USA, corporations are given 20% tax credit for their R&D expenditures. How will this encourage R&D?

7. If over the next decade a firm expects the price of labor to rise substantially compared to the price of capital, would the firm be more likely to invest in R&D that leads to expected labor-saving, capital-saving, or input-neutral technological change? Explain.

8. The Coca-Cola Company has kept its recipe for Coke a trade secret for over a century. Given that a patent lasts for only 20 years, why is it that all firms do not follow Coke and simply keep their new products and processes a secret?

9. Explain what is meant by technological opportunity as it applies to a firm's demand function and its cost function.

10. Schumpeter theorizes that there will be greater inventive activity in concentrated markets, while Arrow argues that there will be greater inventive activity in competitive markets.

   A. Under what set of theoretical conditions is Schumpeter more likely to be correct, and under what set of conditions will Arrow more likely be correct?
   B. Given the summary of the empirical literature, will inventive activity be greater with more or less competition, *ceteris paribus*.

11. In Figs. 17.12 and 17.13 we used a minor technological change to prove Arrow's proposition that competitive firms have greater incentive to innovate than monopoly firms. Prove or disprove Arrow's proposition for a major technological change.

12. Assume a market where the inverse demand is $p = 120 - Q$, p is price, and Q is industry output. Firm i's total cost is $TC_i = cq_i$, where q_i is firm i's output level. A single firm can invest in R&D that leads to a patentable innovation that lowers marginal cost, c. With the old technology $c = 40$, and with the new technology $c = 20$.

   A. Calculate the maximum amount that firm i is willing to invest in R&D to produce this innovation if the innovative firm competes in a

   (i) Monopoly market.
   (ii) Bertrand duopoly.
   (iii) Cournot duopoly.
   Assuming that innovation is profitable, in which market structure will firm i have greater incentive to innovate?

   B. Calculate the maximum amount that society would be willing to pay for this innovation.

13. Explain how the act of creating new technologies and obtaining patents can serve as a strategic barrier to entry.

14. Technological change through creative destruction can have a dramatic effect on market structure.

   A. Explain how technological change can either raise or lower industry concentration.

   B. How will a technological change that increases vertical versus horizontal product differentiation affect industry concentration?

15. What does the empirical evidence suggest regarding the effect of firm size and industry concentration on technological change? What does your answer imply about the dynamically efficient market structure (i.e., perfect competition, oligopoly with a relatively low or high level of concentration, and monopoly)?

16. Will an overconfident management team invest too much or too little in R&D from the firm's perspective? What about from society's perspective?

Chapter 18
Horizontal, Vertical, and Conglomerate Mergers

The immediate and most dramatic way for a company to expand its size and influence market structure is to purchase another company. Historical examples abound. In the late 1800s, Standard Oil Company gained a 90% share of the petroleum market by purchasing more than 120 competitors. In the 1960s, ITT (International Telephone and Telegraph) became a diversified corporation by acquiring 52 domestic and 55 foreign companies, including such well-known businesses as Avis Rent-a-Car, Continental Baking (Wonder Bread), Hartford Insurance, and Sheraton Hotels. By 1968, ITT had become the 11th largest corporation in the USA. The recent financial crisis has forced a number of very large acquisitions. The largest of these occurred in 2008, with Bank of America purchasing Merrill Lynch, a provider of insurance and financial services, for $50 billion and Wells Fargo Bank purchasing Wachovia Bank for $15.1 billion.

In the business and economics literature, these examples are called mergers and acquisitions, which we will typically call mergers.[1] They are said to occur when two or more independent firms come under the control of a single firm. As we discussed in Chap. 2, there are three types of mergers. The first is a horizontal merger, which involves the combination of firms that compete in the same market. Standard Oil's acquisition of a competing oil company constitutes a horizontal merger.

The second type is a vertical merger. This involves the combination of firms that have a buyer–seller relationship. For example, a manufacturer of hardwood desks may purchase one of its input suppliers, such as a hardwood supplier, or one of its distributors. You can think of this as a process where output from various stages of production travel down a stream, with raw input suppliers located furthest upstream and retail distributors located furthest downstream. Thus, when a manufacturer buys

---

[1] Technically, an acquisition happens when one company buys another. Acquisitions are sometimes hostile (i.e., hostile takeovers). This occurs when management of the targeted firm resists being purchased by the acquiring firm. A merger occurs when companies become a single new company. These are sometimes called "mergers of equals," because typically the companies involved are of similar size.

V.J. Tremblay and C.H. Tremblay, *New Perspectives on Industrial Organization*, Springer Texts in Business and Economics, DOI 10.1007/978-1-4614-3241-8_18, © Springer Science+Business Media New York 2012

one of its input suppliers, this is called an **upstream (backward) vertical acquisition**. When a firm buys another firm that purchases its product, this is called a **downstream (forward) vertical acquisition**. Another way of looking at such mergers is that they involve a merger between firms that produce complementary goods.

The third type, a conglomerate merger, captures all mergers that are neither horizontal nor vertical. That is, a conglomerate merger involves firms that produce unrelated products that are neither substitutes nor complements. One example is when ITT, a telephone and telegraph company, purchased Sheraton Hotels. Conglomerate mergers cover a lot of ground and can be divided into two types: pure and impure conglomerate mergers. A **pure conglomerate merger** involves two firms that produce completely unrelated products that compete in separate markets, such as an ice cream parlor that purchases a bicycle shop.

An **impure conglomerate merger** involves firms that compete in markets that are not entirely separate. This can occur when the merging firms produce the same product but in different geographic locations, which is called a **market extension merger**. Another type is a merger between firms that sell "somewhat" related products. This is called a **product extension merger**.[2] For example, a merger between an ice cream parlor and a donut shop could be considered a product extension merger, because ice cream and donuts are imperfect substitutes.[3]

In this chapter, our goal is to provide a brief history of mergers in the USA and discuss why mergers take place.[4] We begin with a general discussion of the main motives for merger. Because the causes and consequences can be quite different for each type, we also discuss the unique motives and empirical evidence for horizontal, vertical, and conglomerate mergers separately.

18.1 A Brief History of US Mergers

Fig. 18.1 plots data from several studies regarding the number of mergers and acquisitions in the USA from 1895 to 2005. It shows that mergers came in waves and that there were four periods of relatively high merger activity.[5] The first wave

---

[2] Notice that product and market extension mergers are related to horizontal mergers, because the firms involved are imperfect competitors in the product extension case and potential competitors in the market extension case. Thus, they can have greater antitrust consequences, as we will see in Chap. 20.

[3] This begs the question of how close is close, a question that is difficult to answer in practice. Certainly, vanilla ice cream and strawberry ice cream are close enough substitutes such that a merger between a supplier of vanilla and a supplier of strawberry ice cream would be considered a horizontal merger. But what about a merger between an ice cream parlor and a bakery? Clearly, judgment calls must be made.

[4] Antitrust implications are discussed in the next chapter.

[5] For a more complete discussion of US merger waves, see Scherer and Ross (1990) and Martin (2007a, b).

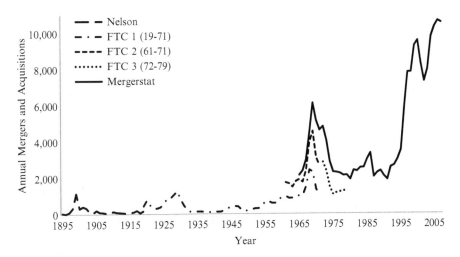

Fig. 18.1   Total number of mergers and acquisitions, 1895–2005

occurred at the end of the nineteenth century. Stigler (1950) called this a period of "merger for monopoly," because these mergers typically involved several firms within the same industry and produced a dominant firm. Of the mergers in this period, Nelson (1959) found that 75% involved at least five firms and 26% involved at least ten firms within the same industry. Many of today's dominant firms gained their positions during this period, including General Electric, Goodyear, Standard Oil (Exxon Mobil today), and US Steel.

The second wave occurred in the 1920s. By the beginning of the twentieth century, strict enforcement of the antitrust laws made it impossible to create a dominant firm by merger. Thus, although most mergers during this period were horizontal, they typically involved small firms. As a result, Stigler (1950) calls this a period of "merger for oligopoly." Besides horizontal mergers, Eis (1969) found that vertical and product-extension mergers also became more common during this wave.

The third wave occurred in the 1960s and marked an era of conglomerate mergers. Passage of the Celler-Kefauver Act of 1950 closed a loophole in the Clayton Act, making it much more difficult for firms to engage in horizontal mergers. This channeled mergers in the conglomerate direction. As a result, approximately 80% of mergers between 1963 and 1972 were conglomerate in nature (Ravenscraft and Scherer 1987).

The fourth wave began in the 1990s and continues to this day. Government policy appears to play a role at the beginning of the wave. In fact, Andrade et al. (2001) call the 1990s the "decade of deregulation," as previously regulated industries accounted for nearly half of the merger activity from 1989 to 1997. Industries and the year of deregulation include: airlines (1978), broadcasting (1984 and 1996), utilities (1992), banking (1994), and telecommunications (1996), and each experienced considerable activity. Although merger activity waned after the terrorist attacks of September 11, 2001, it subsequently picked back up.

Before discussing potential motives for horizontal, vertical, and conglomerate mergers, it is important to put in perspective the merger numbers in Fig. 18.1. They indicate that there has been unparalleled merger activity in the most recent wave. However, the size of the economy is substantially larger today than ever before. If we normalize the number of mergers by real gross national product, the merger wave at the end of the nineteenth century dominates all others (Carlton and Perloff 2005).

18.2   Main Motives for Merger

Mergers occur for a variety of reasons. If firms are profit maximizers, mergers are motivated by purely financial considerations. At any given time, a firm has a number of investment opportunities, one of which is to expand the size of the company. This can be done internally, by building new plant and equipment, or externally, by acquiring another company. Managers who are motivated by profit alone will choose the investment that produces the highest expected profit. A merger will be profitable when it is expected to create some type of synergy, an outcome where the whole exceeds the sum of its parts. This can take the form of a cost synergy, which leads to lower costs, or revenue synergy, which gives the combined company greater market power, for example.

Other factors can influence merger activity. For instance, risk averse managers will pursue safer investments. In addition, research in behavioral economics suggests that managers may have their own psychological motives for mergers. Finally, government policy can influence a firm's merger decision.

In this section, we provide a brief description of the main motives for merger activity. A more detailed discussion will be provided in subsequent sections when a motivation is particularly relevant to horizontal, vertical, or conglomerate mergers. It is important to note that although some motives are more applicable than others, there are typically multiple causes for any given merger. For the most part, we will postpone discussion of antitrust issues until Chap. 20.

18.2.1   Market Power

Perhaps the most obvious potential reason for mergers is to increase market power. After all, if a merger enables the combined firm to raise prices, *ceteris paribus*, it will raise the profit and market value of the firm. This is most natural for horizontal mergers, because they reduce the number of competitors. If firms compete in a Cournot-type game, for example, average firm profit increases with a decrease in the number of competitors. Nevertheless, a vertical merger may also increase market power if it increases entry barriers. Conglomerate mergers are least likely to raise market power, but we will see that under certain circumstances multimarket contact can increase the likelihood of cooperation among firms. Mergers that raise market power are socially undesirable because they increase allocative inefficiency.

18.2.2   Efficiency

Mergers that increase efficiency are socially desirable. There are many ways in which a merger can raise productivity, depending on the type of merger. One example is an industry that has substantial economies of scale, where a horizontal merger between two small firms leads to lower unit costs.

A merger to exploit scale economies represents a static efficiency motive, but dynamic considerations can be just as significant. At any point in time, the relative performance of firms in an industry can vary widely, as superior firms may employ a more effective management team or have access to higher quality raw materials. Over time, firms that fall below an acceptable performance threshold exit the market. Dewey (1961) points out that this can occur through merger as well as bankruptcy. As Dewey (1961, 257) puts it, most mergers "are merely a civilized alternative to bankruptcy or the voluntary liquidation that transfers assets from failing to rising firms."

According to Manne (1965), this line of reasoning motivates the market's way of disciplining inefficient firms through what is called the **market for corporate control**. Ownership shares of public corporations are traded on the stock market. Firms with ineffective managers will experience declining profits, which will cause an observable decline in the market (stock) value of the firm. At some point, the firm will go bankrupt and exit the market. Before this happens, however, a firm with a successful management team may purchase the failing firm and replace its inefficient managers with more efficient ones. According to the market for corporate control hypothesis, this threat of takeover, which can be hostile in nature, will provide sufficient pressure on managers of all corporations to behave efficiently and in the interest of its owners. In Manne's (1965, 113) words:

> The lower the stock price, relative to what it could be with more efficient management, the more attractive the take-over becomes to those who believe they can manage the company more efficiently. And the potential return from the successful take-over and revitalization of a poorly run company can be enormous.

Mergers such as these will be socially efficient, because they eliminate managerial inefficiency.

18.2.3   Other

There are at least three other motives for mergers. First, firms may pursue a merger to reduce risk (i.e., the variance in profits). We will see that this motive can be especially applicable to conglomerate mergers, because a conglomerate merger increases the extent to which a firm is diversified into different markets.

Second, government policy can influence merger activity. We have already seen that many of the mergers in 1990s were motivated by deregulation. Current tax policies can also cause certain types of mergers to be profitable. For example, a vertical merger between a manufacturer and input supplier may allow the firm to charge itself a high-accounting cost or transfer price for internally supplied inputs.

This will reduce the firm's accounting profit and reduce its corporate income (i.e., profit) tax payment. For example, a merger between a firm that earns $100 million with a firm that loses $100 million will eliminate the joint company's profit, enabling it to pay 0 corporate income tax. Moreover, an international merger may allow the joint company to shift profits to subsidiaries in countries with low corporate income tax rates. As an example of divergent tax rates, the average (federal and state) corporate rate is 39.1% in the USA and is 28% in the UK.[6]

The third set of factors that may influence merger activity derive from non-profit-maximizing behavior found in the managerial and behavioral economics literature. As noted in Chap. 2, in very large corporations stockholder ownership is separate from managerial control. From agency theory we know that this creates a *principle–agent problem*, which arises when the principle (owner of a company) and the agent (manager) are separate and have different goals.[7] In other words, agents have a conflict of interest, as it is not in the agent's interest to maximize the welfare of the principle. For large corporations, owners want to maximize profits (or the present value of the stream of present and future profits), while managers are more interested in maximizing their own income. The principle–agent problem can lead to excessive merger activity from the point of view of owners unless manager income is closely tied to corporate profits and the value of the firm.

Furthermore, evidence from behavioral economics shows that some managers are overly optimistic or excessively driven to build corporate empires, which can also lead to excessive merger activity. Because antitrust law effectively constrains large horizontal and vertical mergers, these motives are more common with conglomerate mergers.

With these basic ideas in place, we now discuss how they apply to horizontal, vertical, and conglomerate mergers.

18.3 Horizontal Mergers

Motives for horizontal mergers are the most straightforward, so we discuss them first. In theory, horizontal mergers can reduce both competition and production costs. Because less rigorous competition is socially undesirable and lower costs are socially desirable, the welfare effect of a particular horizontal merger depends on the relative importance of these two effects. In this section, our goal is to unearth these benefits and costs and evaluate the social consequences of horizontal mergers. We begin with a theoretical discussion of the motive for horizontal mergers and conclude by summarizing the empirical evidence.

---

[6] National and state corporate income tax rates are available from the Tax Foundation, http://www.taxfoundation.org/taxdata/show/23034.html.

[7] For early discussions of this problem, see Berle et al. (1932) and Marris (1964). For more recent surveys of the principle–agent problem, see Rees (1985a, b), Eisenhardt (1989), and Shleifer and Vishny (1997).

18.3.1 The Market Power Motive for Mergers

Because a horizontal merger reduces the number of competitors, firms in the same industry may merge to increase market power. Early mergers in our history best reflect this motive. One example is the 1892 merger between Thomson-Houston and Edison General Electric to form the General Electric Company. Regarding the merger, Thomas Edison is quoted as saying, "The consolidation... will do away with a competition that has become so sharp that the product of the factories has been worth little more than ordinary hardware."

In another example, US Steel Corporation became a dominant firm by merging 785 plants in 1901. This gave the company control of about 65% of the steel capacity in the USA. As we discussed in Chap. 9, this merger greatly benefited US Steel by reducing price competition. Before the merger, the combined value of the individual companies was approximately $700 million, and after the merger US Steel was worth approximately $1.4 billion.[8]

The simplest way to illustrate that a horizontal merger can increase market power is to consider a Cournot model with n firms. From the Cournot Limit Theorem, discussed in Sect. 10.1.3, we know that Cournot equilibrium prices and profits increase as the number of competitors decreases. Thus, any horizontal merger will increase the profits of the average firm.[9] Nevertheless, even though the average firm benefits from a horizontal merger, Salant et al. (1983) showed that firms participating in the merger do not necessarily earn greater profit. This is called the **merger paradox**.

To illustrate this idea, consider a Cournot model with n original firms that produce homogeneous goods. Inverse demand is $p = a - bQ$, where p is price, Q is industry output, and firm i's total cost is $TC_i = cq_i$, where q_i is firm i's output, $b > 0$, and $a > c > 0$. From Chap. 10 we saw that firm i's Cournot equilibrium profit (π_i^*) is

$$\pi_i^* = \frac{(a-c)^2}{b(n+1)^2}. \tag{18.1}$$

If m firms engage in a horizontal merger where $2 \leq m \leq n$, this leaves $n - m + 1$ firms in the industry. For example, if three firms merge in a market that originally has six firms, four firms remain ($6 - 3 + 1 = 4$). Thus, if m firms merge, firm i's profits become

$$\pi_{i,m}^* = \frac{(a-c)^2}{b(n-m+2)^2}. \tag{18.2}$$

---

[8] Part of this gain could have been caused by cost efficiencies. For further discussion of this merger, see Scherer and Ross (1990) and Greer (1992).

[9] Of course, not all models give the same prediction. In the homogeneous Bertrand model with symmetric firms, a merger short of monopoly will have no effect on prices and profits.

Because a merger reduces the number of firms, firm i's profits increase as a result of the merger. This is because overall industry output falls with fewer firms in the Cournot model.

For a merger of m firms to be profitable for the combined firm, however, its postmerger profits must be greater than its premerger profits of all m firms. For firms involved in the merger, postmerger profits are $\pi_{i,m}^*$ and premerger profits are m times π_i^*. From (18.1) and (18.2), this means that the following inequality must hold for the merger to be profitable:

$$\frac{(a-c)^2}{b(n-m+2)^2} > \frac{m(a-c)^2}{b(n+1)^2}. \tag{18.3}$$

This condition is met when $(n + 1)^2 > m(n - m + 2)^2$. For this condition to hold, m must be greater than 80% of n.[10] Thus, a horizontal merger generally benefits outside firms more than the merged firm. Notice that this condition does not depend on demand or cost parameters and is, therefore, true for any linear demand and cost equations. The Salant et al. (1983) model suggests that firms are unlikely to pursue horizontal mergers for market power reasons because today's antitrust enforcement would forbid a merger that involved more than 80% of the firms in an industry.[11]

Nonetheless, you would be correct to question this conclusion. A key reason for the merger paradox associated with the Cournot model is symmetry. Firms remain symmetric after the merger, with the merged firm adjusting its equilibrium output level to equal that of its remaining competitors.

The paradox can be overturned if we introduce sufficient asymmetry. For example, if a horizontal merger leaves the merged firm with considerable productive capacity, firms would be asymmetric and the merged firm may behave like a dominant firm or Stackelberg leader, as discussed in Chap. 11. Because the leader earns greater profit than the follower in a Stackelberg (i.e., dynamic Cournot) model, a horizontal merger would be more likely in this case (Daughety 1990). In addition, Creane and Davidson (2004) showed that a horizontal merger can be profitable for the merged firm if it treats its original m firms as independent entities. Finally, Deneckere and Davidson (1985) showed that the merger paradox is overturned in a Bertrand game when there is sufficient product differentiation. In conclusion, the theoretical literature demonstrates that there can be a market power motive for horizontal merger.

---

[10] More precisely, the following condition must hold for a merger to be profitable, $m > n + 1.5\sqrt{5 + 4n}/2$. For example, m must be greater than 80% of n when $n = 5$ firms, 81.5% when $n = 10$, and 91.4% when $n = 100$.

[11] This conclusion would also hold in a Bertrand model where firms compete in price instead of output. In the Bertrand case, as long as $m < n$, the Bertrand price remains at marginal cost. In this model, market power is nonexistent, and a horizontal merger cannot increase market power as long as more than one firm remains.

18.3.2   Efficiency Motive for Horizontal Mergers

Firms may also engage in a horizontal merger if it lowers costs. There are two principle ways that this can happen. First, the market for corporate control applies when an efficiently run firm buys a poorly managed one. As inefficient managers are replaced by a more efficient management team, this can reduce overhead (fixed) costs. It can also cause inputs to be used more efficiently, thus, lowering variable costs. Synergies such as these may be easier to accomplish with a horizontal merger than a vertical or conglomerate merger, because managers in the acquiring firm will have a better understanding of the production and marketing technologies of firms in the same industry.

Second, firms may merge in order to increase their size and take advantage of economies of scale. That is, a single larger firm will have lower unit costs than two smaller firms. There are two types of scale economies, technical and pecuniary economies. **Technical economies** occur when a larger firm can use fewer inputs to produce a unit of output. This produces genuine cost savings to society. **Pecuniary economies** result from a larger firm's ability to bargain for lower input prices, which are normally associated with quantity discounts for raw materials or lower interest rates for financial capital.[12] These savings benefit the larger buyer (firm) at the expense of the seller (input supplier), and, therefore, do not constitute a social gain. Because pecuniary economies involve issues of equity, we focus on technical economies in this chapter.[13]

A horizontal merger that lowers costs can also increase market power, and it is important to compare their relative effects. Williamson (1968) developed a model to address this issue. To illustrate, consider a market with firms that produce homogeneous goods. Demand and cost conditions are described in Fig. 18.2, where D is market demand, MR is marginal revenue, and MC is long-run marginal cost. Before the merger marginal cost equals MC_1 and the market is perfectly competitive. This produces the equilibrium price and market output pair, p_1^* and Q_1^*. Profit or producer surplus is 0 in perfect competition, and total surplus equals consumer surplus, area Ap_1^*B.

Now, consider the effect of a merger on total surplus. After the merger, assume marginal cost falls to MC_2 in Fig. 18.2 and produces a monopoly outcome at Q_2^* and $p_2^* > MC_2$. Notice that two things happen. First, consumer surplus falls to area Ap_2^*H. Second, producer surplus increases from 0 to area p_2^*EFH. Area $p_2^*p_1^*GH$ is transferred from consumers to producers. Total surplus becomes area AEFH. The change in total surplus is $AEFH - Ap_1^*B = p_1EFG - HGB$, which is positive (negative) when the merger is efficient (inefficient). Even though the merger raises price and creates market power, you can see that in this example, it is efficient because it leads to a sufficient reduction in costs (i.e., $MC_1 - MC_2$ or $p_1^* - E$ is sufficiently large).

---

[12] Alternatively, this may occur because the larger firm is more patient in bargaining than the smaller firm, as we discussed in Chap. 3.

[13] We postpone our discussion of equity issues until Chap. 19.

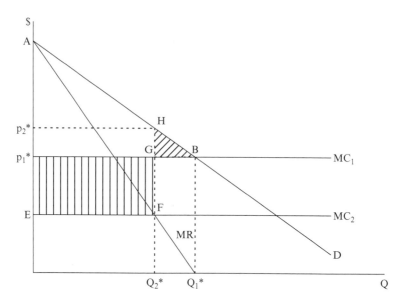

Fig. 18.2 Efficiency and a horizontal merger

To further illustrate this idea, we consider specific functional forms. The inverse market demand is linear, $p = 12 - Q$. Firms face identical costs in each period. Period 1 is pre-merger, and period 2 is post-merger. The total cost equation for each firm in period t is linear, $TC_t = s \cdot c \cdot q_t$, where q_t is firm output in period t and $0 < c < 12$. Parameter $s > 0$ captures the cost savings due to a merger, equaling 1 before the merger and less than 1 after the merger. That is, $MC_1 = c$ and $MC_2 = s \cdot c$. For example, if the merger reduces cost by 10%, s equals 0.9. To provide a concrete answer, let $c = 6$. Before the merger, the market is perfectly competitive, with $p_1^* = Q_1^* = c = 6$. Because long-run profit is 0 in perfect competition, consumer surplus equals total surplus, which is 18.

The post-merger outcome depends upon the number of firms remaining after the merger. Consider the case where a merger involves all firms in the industry, transforming it from perfectly competitive to monopoly. The monopolist's profit equation is total revenue, $TR_2 = (12 - q_2)q_2 = 12q_2 - q_2^2$, minus total cost, $TC_2 = s6q_2$. The equilibrium price is $p_2^* = 3(2 + s)$, and equilibrium market output is $q_2^* = Q_2^* = 3(2 - s)$. Consumer surplus (CS$_2$), profits or producer surplus (PS$_2$), and total surplus (TS$_2$) after the merger are:

$$CS_2 = \frac{(12 - p_2^*)Q_2^*}{2} = \frac{9(2 - s)^2}{2}, \tag{18.4}$$

$$PS_2 = TR_2 - TC_2$$
$$= \left(12q_2^* - q_2^{*2}\right) - \left(6sq_2^*\right) = 9(2 - s)^2, \tag{18.5}$$

$$TS_2 = CS_2 + PS_2 = \frac{27(2-s)^2}{2}, \tag{18.6}$$

Notice that consumer, producer, and total surplus increase with greater cost saving (i.e., as s falls). If a merger does not generate cost savings (i.e., $s = 1$), then $TS_2 = 13.5$, and society is clearly worse off as a result of the merger. If the merger reduces costs by over 15.5% ($s < 0.845$), it will increase total surplus and be socially efficient. Equity may also be a concern, however, as consumers are worse off as a result of a merger that produces a monopoly. The only way in which consumers can be unharmed by the merger is if costs fall by 100% ($s = 0$).

Today, it is illegal for firms to merge and form a monopoly. So, we are more interested in analyzing what happens if the merger creates an oligopoly. The answer to this question depends on the structure of the game that firms play. Consider the case where firms compete in a static pricing game, as described in the Bertrand model of Chap. 10. The total cost function for firms that did not merge would remain the same, $TC_1 = cq_1$, while firms that did merge would see a cost reduction, $TC_2 = s \cdot cq_2$ and $s < 1$. Firms that did not merge would have higher costs, $TC_1 = cq_1$. In the Bertrand equilibrium, the merged firm will set its price just below its rivals' marginal cost of c. This will put rivals out of business but benefit consumers, producers, and society. Of course, rivals might respond with mergers of their own, which would put the Nash price at $s \cdot c$. In this case, all of the gain from lower costs would go to consumers. Producers would earn 0 profits before and after the merger, so all mergers that lower costs in a Bertrand game with homogeneous goods increase consumer and total surplus.

The answer is quite different when firms compete in a Cournot game. We assume that a wave of mergers creates a cost saving but also changes the number of firms from many (competitive) to just a few competitors. Demand and cost functions are the same as in the above example. The Cournot equilibrium was derived in Sect. 10.1.3, except that here marginal cost equals $s \cdot c$.

$$p^* = \frac{12 + scn}{n+1}, \tag{18.7}$$

$$Q^* = nq_i^* = \frac{n(12 - sc)}{n+1}, \tag{18.8}$$

$$PS = n\pi_i^* = \frac{n(12 - sc)^2}{(n+1)^2}, \tag{18.9}$$

$$CS = \frac{(12 - p^*)Q^*}{2} = \frac{n^2(12 - sc)^2}{2(n+1)^2}, \tag{18.10}$$

$$TS = CS + PS = \frac{n^2(12 - sc)^2}{2(n+1)^2}. \tag{18.11}$$

Table 18.1 Cost savings (in percent) needed for a horizontal merger to improve total surplus and consumer surplus

	Costs must fall by more than the following to increase:	
n^*	Total surplus	Consumer surplus
100	0.005%	1.0%
10	0.42%	10.0%
9	0.50%	11.1%
8	0.62%	12.5%
7	0.79%	14.2%
6	1.04%	16.7%
5	1.42%	20.0%
4	2.06%	25.0%
3	3.28%	33.3%
2	6.01%	50.0%
1	15.5%	100.0%

n^* is the number of firms that remain after a merger. Column 2 identifies the minimum cost decrease that is needed for total surplus to increase or remain the same as the result of a merger. Column 3 identifies the minimum cost decrease needed for consumer surplus to increase or remain the same as the result of a merger

In this case, it is unclear whether a wave of mergers benefits society. A merger will lower s, which will put downward pressure on price, but it will also lower n, which puts upward pressure on price.

We use Table 18.1 to explain how s and n affect consumer and total surplus when a cost saving merger changes market structure from perfect competition to Cournot oligopoly. Column 1 lists the equilibrium number of firms that remain after the merger wave, n^*. Column 2 identifies the minimum cost decrease needed for total surplus to increase or remain the same. Column 3 identifies the minimum cost decrease needed for consumer surplus to increase or remain the same. For example, if 100 firms remain after a merger wave, costs must decrease by more than 0.005% for total surplus to increase and by more than 1% for consumer surplus to increase. In this Cournot model, three substantive implications emerge.

1. For a merger wave to be socially efficient, a relatively small cost decrease is required. For example, a merger wave that transforms an industry from perfectly competitive to Cournot with five firms will increase total surplus if costs fall by at least 1.42% (i.e., $s < 0.9858$).
2. For a merger wave to improve consumer surplus, a relatively large cost decrease is required. A merger wave that transforms an industry from perfectly competitive to Cournot with five firms will increase consumer surplus if costs fall by at least 20%.
3. A merger wave increases producer surplus, even if there is no cost saving (i.e., $s = 1$).

The main contribution of Williamson's (1968) work is the so called **Williamson trade-off**: in evaluating the effect of a horizontal merger on economic efficiency, one must compare the loss due to a reduction in competition with the gain due to lower costs. If a merger results in a sufficient reduction in costs relative to the increase in market power, then consumers as well as society can be better off. Society is worse off, however, if horizontal mergers increase market power and have little or no effect on costs.

18.3.3   The Empirical Evidence

Economists have used three methods to analyze the economic effect of horizontal mergers. The first is the event study approach, which was developed by Eckbo (1983), Stillman (1983), and Eckbo and Weir (1985). It is based on the efficient-market hypothesis, which states that markets such as the stock market are informationally efficient (Fama 1965). This means that the price of a company's stock at a point in time reflects all publically available information and, therefore, accurately reflects the true or fundamental value of the firm.

If markets are efficient, one can use stock market data to test the hypothesis that an event like a horizontal merger is motivated by market power or efficiency. Mergers that increase market power will produce higher prices, *ceteris paribus*, which benefits all firms in the industry. This will cause the stock values of all firms to rise, both merging and rival firms alike. Mergers motivated by efficiency alone, however, will make the merging firm a tougher competitor and harm rivals. Thus, the stock value of rival firms will fall. The event study approach implies the following test: a horizontal merger that increases the market value of rival firms implies that the market power effect is dominant; and a horizontal merger that lowers the value of rival firms implies that the efficiency effect is dominant. To use the test, all one needs to do is analyze stock-price reactions of rival firms to a horizontal merger announcement.

Early studies by Eckbo (1983), Stillman (1983), and Eckbo and Wier (1985) rejected the market power motive for merger. That is, horizontal merger announcements did not increase the value of rival firms. More recently, Mullin et al. (1995) and Fee and Thomas (2004) used the event study approach to investigate the effect of horizontal mergers on upstream and downstream markets. These results are mixed: the Mullin et al. evidence suggests that horizontal mergers were anticompetitive; Fee and Thomas found support for the efficiency motive and rejected the market power motive for merger. In most cases, the event study evidence suggests that horizontal mergers are not anticompetitive. If true, this implies that antitrust enforcement has effectively eliminated horizontal mergers that increase market power.

Nevertheless, the event study approach has been criticized for a number of reasons. First, McAfee and Williams (1988) used the event study approach to examine a single horizontal merger, one that was specifically chosen because it was motivated by market power.[14] Yet, their event study results rejected the market

---

[14] It involved the 1979 merger between the Xidex and Kalvar corporations, producers of microfilm. This merger was successfully challenged by the Federal Trade Commission. Barton and Sherman (1984) demonstrated that it led to higher output prices and greater market power.

power hypothesis. McAfee and Williams argued that the main problem with the event study approach is that most acquiring and rival companies are conglomerates that derive only a small percent of their profits from the market affected by the merger. Thus, even if a merger raises market power, it is unlikely to be detected by the event study approach.

Second, Whinston (2007) pointed out that so called "precedent effects" can also be a problem with event studies. That is, a merger may convey other market information that raises the value of rival firms. For example, a merger that improves efficiency may inform the market of the productivity gains associated with mergers in this industry. This would raise the value of all firms in the industry that are likely to engage in similar mergers. In this case, event study results that suggest the presence of market power may be invalid.

The third criticism of the event study approach derives from behavioral economics.[15] Research in behavioral economics shows that some market participants may make systematic errors, which can cause markets to behave inefficiently and refute the efficient-market hypothesis (De Long et al. 1990, 1991). To see how this can invalidate the event study approach, consider the stock value of a hypothetical software company, Macrosoft. The fundamental value of a share of Macrosoft stock is $25 per share. Now imagine that a group of irrational investors become overly pessimistic about Macrosoft's future, which lowers its value to $20. De Long et al. (1990) called these "noise traders". If all investors were rational, they would bid up the price of Macrosoft stock back to $25. With some irrational noise traders, however, the rational investor may avoid Macrosoft stock or sell Macrosoft stock early because they fear that overly pessimistic investors may become even more pessimistic. Thus, the presence of noise traders can keep the price below its true value. Of course, the reverse can happen with overly optimistic investors.

Behavioral criticisms have important implications regarding the effect of a horizontal merger on the stock price of rival firms. There is always some uncertainty regarding the motive of a horizontal merger. Thus, even if a horizontal merger increases market power, the increased uncertainty associated with a merger announcement may cause pessimistic investors to sell. Rational investors correctly anticipate the behavior of pessimistic investors, and this keeps the stock price of rival firms from rising.[16] The point is that market power may exist even though it is undetected by event study evidence.

Given the methodological problems with event studies, economists began to pursue a more direct approach to determine the economic effects of horizontal mergers. Some studies have analyzed the effect that a merger has on output prices. Because of data availability and a proliferation of horizontal mergers, many have focused on the airline and banking industries. Kim and Singal (1993) examined a

---

[15] For a more complete review of behavioral issues as they apply to finance, see Barberis and Thaler (2003, Farmer and Lo (1999), Lo (2004), and Malkiel (2011)).

[16] Dafny (2009) also criticizes the event study approach for failing to correct for endogeneity. With such a correction, he finds that hospital mergers between local competitors lead to higher prices.

large sample involving 14 airline mergers that affected 11,629 routes.[17] They found that horizontal mergers were motivated by both market power and efficiency. Merging firms raised fares an average of 9.4% relative to comparable routes. In mergers involving airlines that use the same airport hub, however, fares declined. This suggests that such mergers were motivated by efficiency considerations (e.g., the merger led to reduced overhead of maintaining the hub).

In US banking, Prager and Hannan (1998) examined the effect on interest rates of horizontal mergers. They separated their sample into substantial mergers and less substantial mergers.[18] They found evidence that both market power and efficiency gains motivated mergers in banking. As you might expect, depositors received lower interest rates after substantial mergers, suggesting that the market power dominated the efficiency effect. For less substantial mergers, efficiency dominated the market power effect. This is consistent with Egger and Hahn's (2010) study of banking mergers in Australia, which found that mergers among smaller banks were more likely to generate cost savings. In Italian banking, Focarelli and Panetta (2003) found that horizontal mergers lowered interest rates received by depositors in the short term but raised them in the long term. This suggests that it takes time to implement changes that improve efficiency.

Ashenfelter and Hosken (2008) examined the price effect of five horizontal mergers that were investigated by the Federal Trade Commission from 1996 to 2003.[19] The authors note that these mergers were not representative but were chosen because they were expected to produce anticompetitive effects and provide an upper bound on the price increase from a horizontal merger. In four of the five mergers, there was a significant but small increase in price, suggesting that efficiency gains were also present. However, cost savings were insufficient to keep prices from rising.

An alternative way of estimating the effect of horizontal mergers is to see how a merger affects the market share of the combined firms. If firms merge to increase market power, we saw in the theoretical section above that this will tend to cause their combined market share to fall. If it increases efficiency, this will cause their combined market share to rise. Gugler and Siebert (2007) used this test to investigate the effect of horizontal mergers in the international semiconductor industry. Their results suggest that mergers generated substantial efficiency gains.

---

[17] Other studies include Borenstein (1990) and Singal (1996).

[18] A substantial merger was defined as one that increases the Herfindahl–Hirschman index (HHI) by at least 200 points. For example, if a market consists of ten equal size firms, they each have a market share of 10%. If two firms merge, this increases HHI by 200 points ($2 \cdot 10 \cdot 10$). That is, before the merger HHI = 1,000 ($10 \cdot 10^2$), and after the merger HHI = 1,200 ($20^2 + 8 \cdot 10^2$). See Chap. 8 for further discussion of HHI.

[19] These were near median size for mergers of the period. Many involved conglomerate firms that also competed in a horizontal market. They include Proctor & Gamble and Tambrands (in 1997, producers of sanitary products), Guinness and Grand Metropolitan (1997, alcoholic beverages), Pennzoil and Quaker State (1998, motor oil), General Mills and Ralcorp (1997, breakfast cereal), and Aurora Foods and Craft's Breakfast Syrup Business (1997, pancake syrup).

When the appropriate data are available, the most effective way to analyze the efficiency effect of horizontal mergers is to estimate a frontier production or cost function before and after the merger. If the merger allows the firm to produce more output with the same inputs or produce the same output at lower cost, the merger is efficient. Using this approach in their study of the US electric power industry, Kwoka and Pollitt (2010) found that horizontal mergers did not improve efficiency.[20]

In summary, there is evidence that horizontal mergers can increase market power and improve efficiency. In some industries, horizontal mergers have reduced output prices, but mergers involving larger firms appear to raise prices. A useful direction for future research would be to conduct additional work on the effect of horizontal mergers on technology, as in Kwoka and Pollitt (2010).

18.4   Vertical Integration, Contracts, and Restrictions

To produce a consumer good and bring it to market involves a number of manufacturing and distribution channels. Raw materials must be harvested and processed. To manufacture steel, ore must be extracted and converted into a useable form, such as sheet metal. At the next stage, sheet metal and other inputs are used to manufacture intermediate goods or physical capital such as heavy machinery and factories. Then, raw materials, physical capital, and labor are brought together to produce a finished product. Finally, a distribution system ships these goods to retail outlets where they are purchased by consumers.[21]

As Coase (1937) pointed out, the vertical relationship between production units can range from complete to separate. When a manufacturer owns all of its distribution outlets and input suppliers (except labor), vertical integration is said to be complete. When each stage of production and distribution is done by separate companies, vertical integration is nonexistent. In some cases, vertical integration is partial. For example, a manufacturer may have a contract with its independent distributors to set a minimum or maximum retail price. It may also restrict its independent distributors by imposing exclusive territories, requiring an exclusive dealing contract, and setting inventory requirements. These are called **vertical restrictions**.

Firms may increase vertical control via internal growth, merger, or vertical restriction. In some cases, a vertically integrated firm may dis-integrate, with a firm selling off one or more input suppliers or distributorships. A vertical merger (or restriction) is costly in terms of negotiating the deal and integrating two corporate cultures into one. Yet, there must be some added benefits for such

---

[20] They used a linear programming technique, called data envelopment analysis. This technique of estimating frontier production and cost functions is discussed in Färe et al. (1985, 2008).

[21] Complementary goods must also be available to consumers. For example, cameras need batteries, and automobiles need gas and oil.

mergers to take place. Our goal is to uncover the motives for vertical relationships and evaluate their social consequences.[22]

Public policy analysis of vertical integration is complex because so many outcomes are possible. In some cases theory predicts that vertical integration improves efficiency, while in others it increases market power. Thus, the welfare implication of a vertical arrangement is an empirical question. Prominent empirical results are discussed within each section below. An overall assessment of the empirical evidence is provided at the end of our discussion of vertical integration. Unfortunately, the available evidence is industry specific, making it difficult to provide a universal policy assessment.

18.4.1 Efficiency Motive for Vertical Mergers and Restrictions

In this section, we discuss socially beneficial reasons for vertical relationships. We will see that these involve reducing costs or eliminating free rider problems.

18.4.1.1 Technological Economies

In some cases, vertical integration is more efficient for purely technical reasons. The classic example is the energy savings of integrating molten steel production with sheet metal production. When separate, the steel producer must mold iron into ingots, let them cool, and ship them to a sheet metal manufacturer. The sheet metal producer must then reheat the iron before converting it to sheet metal. Merging these two operations within one plant eliminates reheating and shipping costs.

According to Stigler (1951), the degree of vertical integration depends on the size of the market and the extent of scale economies at each stage of production and distribution.[23] That is, even though minimum efficient scale in the production of a key input is large, the industry will be vertically integrated if the size of the market is too small to support a specialized input supplier. With sufficient industry growth, however, vertical "disintegration" or separation will take place as the industry becomes large enough to support a specialized firm.

---

[22] Given that the literature is so extensive, we focus on the main benefits and costs. Other possible reasons for vertical integration include a desire to avoid taxes and regulations. For a more complete description, see Waldman and Jensen (2006, Chap. 16), Rey and Tirole (2007), and Pepall (2008, Chaps. 17–19).

[23] This derives from Smith's (1776) insight that the division of labor is limited by the size of the market.

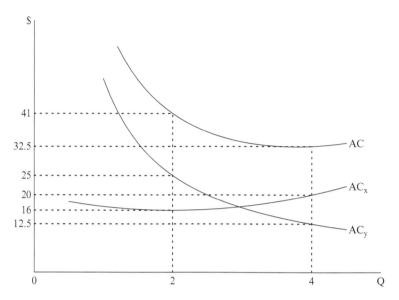

Fig. 18.3 Vertical integration, vertical separation, and efficiency

We illustrate Stigler's idea in Fig. 18.3, which identifies the average cost of production for a monopoly firm (firm 1) in which there are two stages of production (x and y). The average cost at stage x is identified by AC_x, and the average cost of stage y is identified by AC_y. The firm is vertically integrated, and its overall average cost (AC) is the (vertical) sum of AC_x and AC_y. To demonstrate, if the firm's profit maximizing output level is 2 (million units), its average cost is $41 ($AC_x$ = 16 and AC_y = 25). Notice that even though there are substantial scale economies associated with production at stage y, there is insufficient demand to profitably support a separate y producer at output level 2.

Now assume that the size of the market doubles, enabling the market to support two producers that each produce an output level of 2. In this case, if each firm is vertically integrated, each firm's AC = 41 (AC_x = 16 and AC_y = 25). If each firm discontinues their y operation, which is now conducted by a single and separate enterprise, firm y, AC_y falls to 12½. Thus, the average cost of the two x producers falls to 28½ (AC_x = 16 and AC_y = 12½). Vertical disintegration creates a unit cost saving of 12½. Of course, the y producer may charge a price above average cost, which has output cost implications, an issue we take up subsequently. In any case, even if y splits the cost saving and sets the price of y equal to 18.75, firm y and both x producers are better off from this vertical separation.

This theory of vertical integration in an expanding market is consistent with the early development of the automobile industry. At the end of the nineteenth century, car makers such as Ford and Oldsmobile were highly vertically integrated. For example,

Ford was known for fabricating engine pistons from steel pipe. Once demand for automobiles took off in the early twentieth century, however, the presence of input scale economies discouraged vertical integration. In almost every case, car companies were transformed from vertically integrated manufacturers to designers and assemblers of automobiles from parts supplied by other firms.[24]

18.4.1.2   Transaction Costs

Even without scale economies in production, we saw in Chap. 2 that vertical integration can lower transaction costs, the cost of conducting business in the market place. As a firm undertakes more and more of its stages of production and distribution, transaction costs fall. Unfortunately, a growth in firm size generally leads to higher monitoring costs. Thus, a vertical merger can be profitable if it sufficiently lowers transaction costs without substantially raising monitoring costs.

The transaction costs of using a market tend to be high in high-risk markets because this makes it difficult if not impossible to negotiate a contract that addresses every possible contingency. For instance, when there is considerable input supply variability, it will be costly to negotiate all price–quantity possibilities and include them in a contract between a buyer and a supplier. This is especially problematic for a credence good such as a completely assembled automobile engine where it is very difficult for a car manufacturer to determine the long-run durability and quality of an engine that is built by an independent supplier. Consequently, automobile companies assemble their own engines from parts supplied by separate companies that are built to meet certain specifications.

The cost of writing a complete contract is also high when dealing with products that are custom made. Consider an example where firm 1 orders a custom machine from firm 2 at price p', which is paid upon delivery. If firm 1 were to pull out of the contract once the machine is built, the next best alternative is for firm 2 to sell the machine at price p''. With few alternative uses for a custom machine, p'' will be considerably lower than p'. In this situation, firm 1 has an economic incentive to refuse payment when the machine is delivered to renegotiate a price that is closer to p''. If the cost of enforcing the contract is sufficiently high, the best firm 2 can do is renegotiate a price between p' and p''. This is called a **hold-up problem**, which is associated with opportunistic behavior on the part of one of the parties involved with the contract (firm 1 in this case).

A merger provides one solution to the hold-up problem (Alchian and Demsetz 1972; Williamson 1975, 1985; Klein et al. 1978). It internalizes the problem because it gives management the power to keep one division from exploiting

---

[24] For further discussion, see Thomas (1977) and Langlois and Robertson (1989). Langlois and Robertson argue that Ford was later forced to vertically integrate once again due to the rapid success of its Model T and delays in delivery of key inputs.

another. Such a merger would be efficient because it would lower the transaction costs of writing a complete contract and of using the court system, *ceteris paribus*.[25]

According to Klein (1988), hold-up problems motivated General Motors (GM) to buy Fisher Body in 1926. Before that time, Fisher Body manufactured all of the external body parts for GM cars. To stay competitive, GM focused on up-to-date styling that required relatively rapid changes in sheet metal body panels. Because delays in delivery were extremely costly to the success of this strategy, GM was vulnerable to a holdup. In addition, Monteverde and Teece (1982) found that the probability of a vertical relationship increases as the traded product becomes more specialized. In particular, they found an example of quasi-vertical integration in the automobile industry in the 1970s. The supplier retains ownership of the specialized asset, its die casting machine, and rents it out to the automobile manufacturer at an hourly rate.

18.4.1.3 Property Rights

Like transaction cost theory of vertical integration, property right theory emphasizes the importance of incomplete contracts and opportunistic behavior. According to Grossman and Hart (1986) and Hart and Moore (1990), property rights are crucial because ownership bestows power. A merger in which an input supplier buys a manufacturer may result in greater investment in the input division relative to the manufacturing division of the firm. Just the opposite may happen when the manufacturer buys the input supplier. This theory implies that the input supplier will buy the manufacturer when investments of the input supplier are more important than investments of the retailer to the success of the joint venture.

There has been little research on this issue, because the property rights theory is difficult to test. The one exception is Acemoglu et al. (2010), who studied the causes of vertical mergers in the manufacturing sector in the UK. One of their findings was that backward vertical integration is more likely when a manufacturer is more technologically intensive than the input supplier. Although there may be alternative motives for vertical mergers, this result is consistent with the property rights theory.

18.4.1.4 Quality of Service

In many cases, a manufacturer benefits from retailers that provide consumers with presale service. For example, a home theater manufacturer may prefer that its retailers have a knowledgeable sales staff, have a viewing/listening area, and provide free delivery and setup. If the retail sector is competitive, however, price

---

[25] Another solution would be to have the buyer pay in full before production is begun on a custom good. When it is costly to specify all product characteristics, this creates another problem. The seller has an incentive to cut costs by lowering quality.

may be driven so low that an insufficient margin remains to support a knowledgeable sales staff. If a retailer tries to charge a higher price to cover the cost of such a staff, consumers can obtain information from this retailer but buy from the low-priced store that provides little or no service. In this case, the low-priced retailer is free riding off of the information provided by the high-priced retailer. With sufficient price competition, the high-priced retailer would be forced out of business. A free rider problem such as this explains the success of electronics warehouse stores that offer low prices and little or no sales help. Such a situation may produce an outcome that has too little retail service from the point of view of some manufacturers and consumers.

The manufacturer could improve service quality by merging with all of its distributors. This would eliminate free riding, and the firm could set the optimal level of sales effort at each retail outlet. The problem can also be eliminated with vertical restrictions. For example, where such activities are legal the manufacturer could contract for a **resale-price maintenance program** (RPM) with its retailers. This establishes a minimum retail price that sufficiently exceeds marginal cost, eliminating price undercutting and forcing retailers to compete in service quality, thus raising the quality of service. Alternatively, when there are competing manufacturers, one manufacturer may require an **exclusive dealing contract** with its retailers. When such a contract is struck, the retailer cannot distribute brands of competing manufacturers. This assures that a retailer gives sufficient service support to the manufacturer's own product.

Even though these policies provide benefits, there is no guarantee that they are socially beneficial. In a free market, a higher level of service is offered only at a higher price. A profit-maximizing firm will increase the level of service until a marginal increase in quality no longer raises profit. An increase in service quality cannot lower producer surplus. From the consumer's perspective, the higher level of service raises consumer surplus, but the higher price lowers consumer surplus. The net effect on total (consumer plus producer) surplus is ambiguous.[26]

In the market for gasoline in Southern California, for example, Hastings (2004) examined the effect of vertical integration on retail prices. She found that vertical integration led to higher gas prices when branded stations replaced independent gas stations. However, branded stations typically offer a higher level of service than independent stations, making it impossible to tell if the typical consumer benefited or was harmed by vertical integration.

Sass (2005) examined this question for the US beer industry by comparing prices and output levels in states that allow exclusive dealing contracts with states where exclusive dealing contracts are illegal. His regression work shows that exclusive dealing contracts produce three results. First, an exclusive dealing contract by

---

[26] Much like the welfare analysis of advertising that we discussed in Chap. 15, an increase in service quality is more likely to be welfare improving when it leads to a parallel shift in demand and is more likely to lower welfare when it rotates demand clockwise (Scherer 1983; Comanor 1985). For an excellent survey of this literature, see Waldman and Jensen (2006, Chap. 16).

one brewer enabled it to increase sales and charge a higher consumer price. This suggests that distributors provided added services that consumers valued. Second, an exclusive dealing contract by one firm had no effect on the prices of rival brewers. Third, exclusive dealing contracts led to an increase in total beer sales. Taken together and ignoring possible externalities associated with alcohol consumption, these results imply that exclusive dealing contracts in brewing reduced incentive conflicts and increased the welfare of consumers and producers.

18.4.1.5   Double Marginalism

Spengler (1950) developed a model that produced a surprising result regarding the relationship between vertical mergers and market power. He showed that a vertical chain of suppliers (e.g., an input supplier, a manufacturer, and a retailer) where each is a monopolist will be more inefficient than if there were a single monopolist that is completely vertically integrated.[27] This is because at each vertical stage of production, firms charge a price above marginal cost. These margins or markups lead to successively higher marginal costs for downstream producers. In the case of two separate stages of production, this is referred to as the problem of **double marginalism**.[28] We will see that this leads to a higher price and a lower level of output than would occur if all firms merged into a single monopolist that was completely integrated.

To illustrate, we compare outcomes when the input and output markets vary by their degree of competitiveness, which is either perfectly competitive or monopolized by a single firm. To simplify things, consider the wholesale (upstream) market and retail (downstream) market for gasoline, where producers or wholesalers (W) supply gas to service stations or retailers (R). Notice that the wholesaler and the retailer sell the same product, so that there is a one-to-one relationship between the quantity sold by the wholesaler and the quantity sold by the retailer. This is called a fixed-proportions technology. The wholesaler's marginal cost is constant and equal to MC_W. To simplify things, consumer demand is linear and the retailer is assumed to have no additional cost other than the cost of purchasing gas from the wholesaler. The situation is dynamic, with wholesalers making their decisions in the first period and retailers making their decision in the second period.

We begin with the simple case where both the wholesale and retail markets are perfectly competitive, which we call the *competitive–competitive case*. This is illustrated in Fig. 18.4, where the horizontal axis measures the quantity of gasoline supplied by the wholesaler and sold by the retailer. Dynamic effects are unimportant in this case, because price equals marginal cost in competition, leaving no room

---

[27] We will see that the most efficient outcome is when all input and output markets are competitive.

[28] With three stages and a monopolist at each stage, there is triple marginalism.

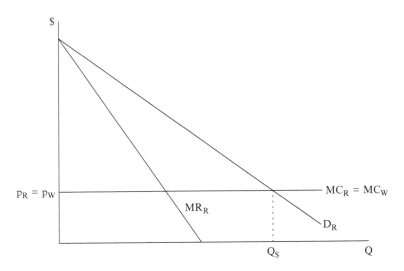

Fig. 18.4 Wholesale and retail equilibrium when both markets are perfectly competitive

for strategic interaction. Nevertheless, we still use backwards induction to illustrate the process of determining the subgame-perfect Nash equilibrium (SPNE).[29] Solving the second stage problem first, the price (p_R) will equal marginal cost (MC_R) in the retail market. Given our assumption that there are no added costs to the retailer, MC_R will be identical to the wholesale price (p_W). Although wholesalers can look forward and reason back in the first stage of the game, this knowledge is inconsequential because the wholesale market is also competitive, p_W equals the marginal cost of the wholesaler (MC_W). In this setting, the equilibrium set of prices is $p_R = MC_R \equiv p_W = MC_W$. This produces the socially efficient level of output, Q_S.

Second, consider the case where the wholesale market is competitive and there is a monopoly retailer, the *competitive–monopoly case*. This is illustrated in Fig. 18.5. Using backwards induction, we solve the second stage problem first. Again, dynamics are unimportant because there is no possibility for strategic interaction between the retailer and wholesalers. Regardless of the expected behavior of the retailer, price will equal marginal cost in the wholesale market, $p_W = MC_W$. The retailer's marginal cost is the wholesale price ($MC_R \equiv p_W$). To maximize profit, the retailer equates its marginal revenue with its marginal cost, which produces the optimum at Q_1 and p_R, where $p_R > p_W = MC_W$. This is the standard monopoly result, which is socially inefficient (i.e., $Q_1 < Q_S$). A vertical merger between all wholesalers and the retailer will have no effect on the market outcome. For the merged firm, the monopoly outcome prevails, with $Q = Q_1$. We call this price–output pair the "simple monopoly" outcome.

---

[29] See Chaps. 3 and 11 for a review of the use of backwards induction to identify the SPNE.

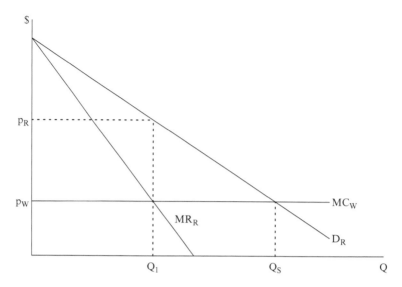

Fig. 18.5 Equilibrium when wholesale market is competitive and there is a monopoly retailer

In the third example, there is a monopoly wholesaler and a competitive retail market, the *monopoly–competitive case*. From the consumer's perspective, the equilibrium output and price levels are the same as in the competitive–monopoly case (p_R and Q_1 in Fig. 18.5). In a review question at the end of the chapter, you are asked to identify the equilibrium wholesale price, retail marginal cost, retail price, and market output level for this case.

The problem of double marginalism occurs when market power exists at both the wholesale and retail levels. To illustrate, we let both the wholesaler and retailer be monopolies, the *monopoly–monopoly case*. Demand and cost conditions are described in Fig. 18.6. To identify the SPNE, we solve the second stage problem first. The retailer is a monopolist and will equate its marginal cost with its marginal revenue (MR_R). At the second stage, the wholesaler correctly anticipates this, knowing that the retailer will choose output where its marginal cost (MC_R), which is the wholesale price (p_w), equals MR_R.

In other words, MR_R is the retailer's best-reply function because for any given p_W, MR_R identifies the retailer's optimal quantity. This means that MR_R is the wholesaler's demand function (D_W). Given that D_W is linear, the wholesaler's marginal revenue function (MR_W) has the same intercept as D_W but is twice as steep (as depicted in Fig. 18.6). Thus, the wholesaler's optimum occurs where $MR_W = MC_W$. This occurs at Q_2, p_R, and p_W, where $p_R > p_W \equiv MC_R > MC_W$. We derive this result more formally in Appendix 18.A.

Notice that the monopoly–monopoly case leads to even greater inefficiency than the simple monopoly case, where the firms are vertically integrated into one firm. The reason for this is that monopoly power at the wholesale level raises the wholesale price, and therefore the marginal cost at the retail level, which in

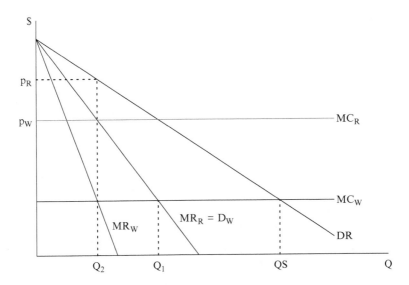

Fig. 18.6 Equilibrium when there is a monopoly wholesaler and a monopoly retailer

turn leads to an even higher price and a greater restriction in output at the retail level. That is, $Q_2 < Q_1 < Q_S$. Although the level of inefficiency will generally be less pronounced in an oligopoly setting, the same general outcome occurs as long as price exceeds marginal cost at each stage of production (i.e., competition is less severe than homogeneous Bertrand). This illustrates what is meant by double marginalism.

In order to gain better insight into this problem, we provide a specific example. Assume inverse demand is $p = 12 - Q$, and marginal cost at the wholesale level equals $MC_W = 2$. For each of the four cases described above, Table 18.2 identifies consumer surplus (CS), producer surplus (PS), total surplus (TS), and the equilibrium prices and output levels for this market. Three primary results emerge:

1. Competition at both stages produces the socially efficient outcome, with TS equaling 50. This is the best outcome for consumers (CS = 50) but the worst for producers (PS = 0).
2. Monopoly at either the wholesale or retail stage of production leads to the simple monopoly outcome (as if they were a single firm), where TS = 37½. This maximizes producer surplus (PS = 25). The wholesaler's profit (π_W) is highest when it is the monopolist, and the retailer's profit (π_R) is highest when it is the monopolist.
3. The least efficient outcome occurs when both the wholesale and retail markets are monopolized by separate firms, with TS equaling 21⅞. Both CS and PS are higher in the monopoly case when there is competition at either the wholesaler or the retailer level. In other words, a market with a monopoly wholesaler and a

Table 18.2 Monopoly power and market equilibria in wholesale (W) and retail (R) markets in competitive (C) versus monopoly (M) settings

Level of competition				
Wholesale market:	Competitive	Competitive	Monopoly	Monopoly
Retail market:	Competitive	Monopoly	Competitive	Monopoly
p_W	2	2	7	7
p_R	2	7	7	9½
Q	10	5	5	2½
π_W	0	0	25	12½
π_R	0	25	0	6¼
PS	0	25	25	18
CS	50	12½	12½	3⅛
TS	50	37½	37½	21⅞

These four cases refer to competition in both the wholesale and retail markets (competitive–competitive); a competitive wholesaler and a monopoly retailer (competitive–monopoly); a monopoly wholesaler and competitive retailer (monopoly–competitive); monopoly at both the wholesale and retail levels (monopoly–monopoly)

Notationally, p_W is the equilibrium wholesale price; p_R is the equilibrium retail price; Q is equilibrium output; π_W is the wholesaler profit; π_R is the retailer profit; PS is producer surplus ($\pi_W + \pi_R$); CS is consumer surplus; TS is total surplus (PS + CS)

monopoly retailer produces less consumer surplus and less producer surplus than markets with more competition at either the wholesale or the retail (or both) stages of production.

This implies that a monopolist has no market power motive to vertically integrate into a competitive stage of production. A merger of this type has no effect on CS, PS, and TS. Nevertheless, a monopoly wholesaler does have an incentive to merge with a monopoly retailer, and vice versa. A merger of this type is socially efficient, because it increases CS, PS, and TS.

This example illustrates the **principle of double marginalism**: vertical integration either increases or has no effect on market efficiency.[30] That is, total surplus is unaffected by a merger between (1) a competitive wholesaler and a competitive retailer, (2) a competitive wholesaler and a monopoly retailer, and (3) a monopoly wholesaler and a competitive retailer. However, a merger between a monopoly wholesaler and a monopoly retailer produces the simple monopoly outcome. This causes output to increase from Q_2 to Q_1 in Fig. 18.6, which benefits both consumers and producers (increasing TS from 21⅞ to 37½ in Table 18.2). Because this theoretical analysis indicates that a vertical merger has either no effect or improves social efficiency, it implies that public policy should not discourage vertical mergers.

---

[30] This is sometimes called the Chicago School critique of early concerns that vertical mergers can enhance market power. As we discussed in Chap. 1, the Chicago School is skeptical that government policy can produce net social benefits. For further discussion, see Posner (1976), Bork (1978), and Riordan (1998).

Caution is warranted, however, as this discussion ignores other possible problems associated with vertical mergers, an issue we will take up in the next section. It is also based on a model that assumes that the retailer does not substitute away from the wholesaler's product when there is a price increase (i.e., there is a fixed-proportions technology). Although this may be true for gasoline, it need not be true for other production processes. For example, when a steel producer raises the price of steel, a producer of exotic motorcycles may substitute aluminum and carbon fiber for steel. Allowing for this substitution possibility, which will occur in a variable-proportions technology, reduces the monopoly power of the steel producer and complicates the analysis, as we will see subsequently.[31]

Vertical restrictions can also be used by the wholesaler to avoid the problem of double marginalism when both the wholesaler and retailer are independent monopolists. First, the wholesaler can impose a price ceiling on the retailer at the simple monopoly retail price. This vertical restriction will generate the monopoly solution and full monopoly profits for the wholesaler, although zero profits for the retailer. In addition, the wholesaler can use a two-part pricing policy, as discussed in Chap. 14.[32] Setting p_W equal to MC_W guarantees the simple monopoly outcome, and charging the retailer a fixed fee that just equals the retailers total profit transfers all monopoly profit to the wholesaler. Finally, the wholesaler could set a sales quota for the retailer, guaranteeing that the simple monopoly outcome is reached (Q_1 in Fig. 18.6).

Mortimer (2007) found that video distributors and video rental stores such as Blockbuster used a two-part pricing policy to solve the double marginalism problem. Market power existed at these stages, although they operated in oligopoly rather than monopoly markets. Prior to 1998, video distributors sold videos at a fixed price of $65–70 per tape to rental stores, creating a double marginalism problem. By 1998, a new contract was widely adopted: videos were sold for $3–8 per tape and rental revenues were shared, with 55% going to video distributors. As the theory predicts, Mortimer found that (1) consumers benefited and (2) upstream and downstream profits increased by about 10%.

---

[31] A variable proportions technology is characterized by a convex isoquant. This implies a certain amount of substitutability between inputs, as with steel and aluminum in automobile production. As the price of steel increases, cost-minimizing manufacturers will substitute aluminum for steel. A fixed-proportion technology implies that inputs are perfect complements and are characterized by right-angled isoquants. This characterizes tires and car chassis. Four tires are used with each chassis, regardless of the relative prices of tires and chassis. For further discussion, see Varian (2010, Chap. 10).

[32] This sometimes takes the form of a franchising fee (Caves and Murphy 1976; Rubin 1978). A franchise contract between a wholesaler and retailer frequently gives the retailer the legal right to sell the wholesaler's product, requires that the wholesaler provide sales training to the retailer, specifies the level of sales effort, and specifies a nonlinear payment contract. Typically, this will include a fixed franchise fee and a split of retail revenues. Contracts such as these are common practice in the fast-food industry, where companies like McDonald's have a franchise contract with retailers for the right to distribute McDonald's food.

18.4.1.6   The Market for Corporate Control

As discussed earlier in the chapter, the market for corporate control is one way of disciplining inefficient management teams and transferring assets from failing to successful firms. Given that our antitrust laws are more strictly enforced for horizontal mergers, vertical and conglomerate mergers would be a likely outlets for this motive for merger. Vertical mergers may be especially appealing to managers, as they may have a better understanding of markets that are vertically related than completely unrelated markets (i.e., conglomerate mergers).

Hortacsu and Syverson (2007) found support for the market for corporate control hypothesis for vertical mergers in the ready-mix concrete industry.[33] Their empirical results showed that large highly efficient producers were more likely to vertically integrate, a process that takes market share from higher-priced and less efficient producers. They also found that vertical integration lowers price, increases production, and has no effect on entry rates. Taken together, the results imply that vertical integration in cement and concrete has been welfare enhancing.

18.4.2   Vertical Relationships and Anticompetitive Effects

We have seen how vertical mergers and vertical restrictions can lower costs and promote economic efficiency. This is not the whole story, as there are situations where vertical mergers and restrictions can increase profit and lower efficiency. We consider these possibilities in this section.

18.4.2.1   Foreclosure

First is the foreclosure argument. Foreclosure occurs when a firm uses its market power in one market to restrict output in another market. With vertical foreclosure, an upstream firm restricts output to a downstream firm or a downstream firm restricts its demand for an upstream firm's product. Such foreclosure is common after a vertical merger, but does it enhance market power? The Supreme Court thought so, as indicated in its ruling in the first antitrust case involving anticompetitive concerns with vertical mergers (*Brown Shoe Co., Inc. v. U.S.*, 370 U.S. 294, 1962)[34]:

> The primary vice of a vertical merger or other arrangement tying a customer to a supplier is that, by foreclosing the competitors of either party from a segment of the market otherwise open to them, the arrangement may act as a "clog on competition,"... which "deprive[s] ... rivals of a fair opportunity to compete."

---

[33] Although often used interchangeably, cement is an input for concrete. Cement is a powered substance made from limestone and clay. Concrete is produced by mixing cement, sand, gravel, and water.

[34] This quote is taken from Stelzer (1976, 133). For further discussion of this case, see Waldman (1986).

Given the problem of double marginalism, which showed that vertical mergers cannot lower total surplus, you might wonder how this can be true.

One way is by increasing entry barriers.[35] To illustrate, consider a market with a monopoly wholesaler (M), two retailers (R_1 and R_2), and a potential entrant into the wholesale market (PE). For entry to be profitable, PE needs at least 2 retailers. Thus, without vertical integration or a vertical restriction, PE will enter. If, however, M buys R_1, then PE can enter at the manufacturing stage only if it adds one of its own retail outputs. This will block entry if it sufficiently raises the cost of entry. Thus, by foreclosing PE's access to R_1, entry is forestalled.

We have discussed strategic behavior like this in Chap. 8, where an incumbent monopolist commits to an investment in a strategic barrier to protect its market power. This problem is described in Fig. 8.7. In this case, however, σ_M is M's sunk cost associated with vertical integration, and σ_{PE} is PE's added sunk costs associated with opening up its own retail store. To simplify things, assume that $\sigma_M = \sigma_{PE} = \sigma$. If $30 < \sigma < 70$, the unique SPNE is for M to vertically integrate and for PE to stay out of the market.[36] As with all strategic barriers, social efficiency diminishes because such barriers are costly and reduce wholesale competition.

Although the evidence is limited, Comanor and Frech (1985) found that GE effectively used exclusive dealing arrangements to forestall entry of Rhodia's silicone sealant in the 1970s. When Rhodia entered the market with a product that sold at a discounted price, GE responded by stopping shipment of GE's sealant to major retailers that had agreed to market Rhodia's product. This discouraged retailers from marketing Rhodia's product and helped GE maintain its dominant market position.

When the wholesale market is oligopolistic, the use of vertical integration or vertical restrictions can raise entry barriers and increase concentration. This in turn can increase the probability of collusion, through the use of a trigger strategy as we discussed in Chaps. 9 and 11. There is also a concern that resale price maintenance agreements may facilitate collusive pricing at the retail level, but there is little evidence that collusion motivates such agreements (Overstreet and Price 1983).

18.4.2.2 Double Marginalism with Variable Proportions

In our discussion of double marginalism we saw that a vertical merger in a market with a monopoly wholesaler and a competitive retail market has no effect on consumer and producer surplus. It turns out that this is only true when retailers use inputs in fixed proportion. For a variable-proportions technology, a vertical merger can reduce total surplus by protecting and enhancing the wholesaler's market power.

---

[35] In addition, Ordover et al. (1990) show that vertical foreclosure can harm competition when products are differentiated.

[36] Given the benefits of learning, a merger is likely to be cheaper than opening up a brand new store, $\sigma_M \leq \sigma_{PE}$. If they are unequal, this will remain a unique SPNE as long as $\sigma_M < 70$ and $\sigma_{PE} > 30$.

With a variable-proportions technology, if a monopoly wholesaler raises its price above marginal cost, competitive retailers are able to mitigate the higher price by substituting away from the monopolist's product. This substitution ability reduces the wholesaler's market power and control over retailers. Moreover, charging a monopoly price still creates an input price distortion which raises retailer costs.

In this case, a vertical merger between the wholesaler and a retailer has two effects. First, by using the marginal cost of the wholesaler as the retailer's opportunity cost of that input, called its transfer price, the retailer can use the least cost combination of inputs. This efficiency effect will lower costs and push down the retail price. Second, it reestablishes the wholesaler's market power because the substitution effect due to charging the retailer a monopoly price is eliminated for the vertically integrated firm. This market power effect will push up the retail price. The net effect on the retail price and total surplus is now ambiguous and depends on demand, cost, and substitution possibilities.[37] Nevertheless, this is a situation where a vertical merger can increase market power.

18.4.2.3 Price Discrimination

Another reason why a firm may prefer to vertically integrate is that when coupled with market power, integration can facilitate third degree price discrimination. Assuming just two groups of consumers, recall from Chap. 14 that a firm will charge a higher price to the group that has a more inelastic demand function. A necessary condition for this to be effective is that the firm must be able to prevent arbitrage. That is, the firm must keep high-price consumers from bypassing the firm and buying directly from low-price consumers. Vertical integration can be an effective way to prevent this type of resale.

To illustrate how this works, assume that an aluminum firm (A) is a monopolist that sells aluminum ingot to groups of manufacturers in competitive markets, B and C. Demand from market B is inelastic relative to demand from market C. Thus, firm A would like to price discriminate by charging a high price in market B and a low price in market C. The problem is that firm A cannot stop arbitrage, where firms in market B buy ingot from firms in market C. The question is whether vertical integration into one of these markets will enable firm A to earn higher profits and avoid the problem with arbitrage.

It turns out that complete integration into either market eliminates arbitrage, but price discrimination becomes more effective when A buys C. The new A–C firm can now charge a higher price in market B because there are no longer any

---

[37] For a more complete discussion, see Vernon and Graham (1971), Schmalensee (1973), Blair and Kaserman (1983), and Salinger (1988).

companies in market C in which to make a purchase. Unfortunately, we are unable to determine the welfare effect of this type of behavior, because price discrimination can increase or decrease total surplus, as we saw in Chap. 14.

Perry (1980) makes an effective argument that this is exactly what Alcoa (Aluminum Company of America) did in the early twentieth century. At that time, Alcoa faced two types of buyers, those who used aluminum to make wire and those who used it to make parts for aircraft. With a greater elasticity of demand for wire, Alcoa integrated downstream into wire production. By eliminating all competing aluminum wire producers, arbitrage became impossible and Alcoa was able to raise the price of aluminum ingot to aircraft manufacturers who had a more inelastic demand for aluminum.

18.4.3 A Summary of the Empirical Evidence

As we have seen throughout the chapter, there is evidence to support some of the theories of vertical integration and vertical restrictions. First, evidence from the US automobile industry is consistent with the technological motivation for vertical integration and separation. That is, vertical integration was high at the industry's inception, but vertical separation became more common with growing market demand. Second, firms do engage in vertical integration to lower transaction costs, especially where there are hold-up problems and quality considerations. Third, evidence from the US brewing industry suggests that exclusive dealing contracts benefit both consumers and producers. Fourth, the evidence shows that the two-part pricing policy of the video rental industry benefits both consumers and producers. Fifth, the evidence regarding vertical mergers between cement and concrete producers is consistent with the market for corporate control hypothesis where successful firms purchase less successful ones. Finally, it does appear that Alcoa vertically integrated to avoid arbitrage and to charge a higher price to consumers with more inelastic demands.

Although there are exceptions, the empirical studies show that efficiency reasons trump anticompetitive motives of vertical integration. In their extensive review of the literature, Lafontaine and Slade (2007, 680) conclude: "...under most circumstances, profit-maximizing vertical-integration decisions are efficient, not just from the firms' but also from the consumers' point of view. Although there are isolated studies that contradict this claim, the vast majority support it." Given the evidence, their policy recommendation is that when "faced with a vertical arrangement, the burden of evidence should be placed on competition [i.e., antitrust] authorities to demonstrate that" a vertical "arrangement is harmful before the practice is attacked."

18.5   Diversification and Conglomerate Mergers

In many cases, firms produce a diversified set of unrelated products. These are conglomerate firms. One example is Procter & Gamble, which produces detergent (Tide), small appliances (Braun), toothpaste (Crest), and paper towels (Bounty). Another example is General Electric, which produces lighting equipment, aircraft engines, appliances, and television entertainment (NBC). General Electric's purchase of the NBC television network in 1986 is an example of a conglomerate merger.

Because conglomerate mergers involve firms that produce unrelated products, you might wonder what motivates them. Are they the result of underlying economic forces, business errors, or historical accident? In this section, we explore the main economic reasons for them. At the end of this section, we also discuss which explanations are best supported by the empirical evidence.

18.5.1   Efficiency Motives for Conglomerate Mergers

One possible motive for a conglomerate merger is efficiency, perhaps due to economies of scope. Recall that economies of scope exist when several products are more efficiently produced by a single firm than by separate firms. In general, this occurs when there are complements in production or marketing.

There are numerous cases where economies of scope play a role in production. Manufacturers of custom motorcycles and of iron fences may both use a water jet machine, which makes precision cuts in aluminum and steel. If each enterprise has sufficient demand to keep a water jet machine operating at half capacity, excess capacity can be eliminated by a merger. This suggests that a merger can be profitable when it involves companies that produce different products but use similar production techniques (Montgomery 1994).

Economies of scope in marketing can also be important. In some cases it may be more efficient to use a single marketing division to market otherwise unrelated products that appeal to the same target audience. This was one of the reasons why Philip Morris, a cigarette company, bought Miller, a beer company, in 1970 (V. Tremblay and C. Tremblay 2005). Even though cigarettes and beer markets are unrelated, the target audience of each is young adults, and executives at Philip Morris felt that their success in marketing cigarettes would spill over to marketing beer.[38] Although reliable profit data are unavailable, the merger did rejuvenate Miller, as its market share rose from 4.13% in 1970 to over 21% in 1980.

---

[38] In 1970, cigarette ads were as common as beer ads are today. Beginning in 1971, the federal government severely limit cigarette advertising, making it illegal to advertise outdoors and on television and radio (Chaloupka 2007; Iwasaki and V. Tremblay 2009).

A second possible efficiency motive for a conglomerate merger is that it may reduce transaction costs. The resulting cost savings is unlikely to be sufficient to motivate many conglomerate mergers, however. Conglomerate firms produce a diverse set of products and are likely to employ a relatively heterogeneous set of workers and managers. Thus, the cost of monitoring a larger and more diverse enterprise will be relatively high.

A final efficiency motive for conglomerate mergers is the market for corporate control hypothesis, where a merger serves as an effective way of transferring managerial control from inefficient to more efficient management teams. This may be more difficult with conglomerate mergers, however, because managerial success in one industry may not translate well to another industry. On the other hand, antimerger laws are more likely to be strictly enforced when firms are in related markets (i.e., in horizontal and vertical mergers). Thus, conglomerate mergers may be a main outlet for the market for corporate control, especially when large firms are involved.

18.5.2   Conglomerate Mergers and Risk Reduction

A potential advantage of a conglomerate merger is that it can reduce the risk of doing business. We borrow an example from Sherman (1974, 104–105) to illustrate the old piece of advice: "Don't put all of your eggs in one basket." Suppose you want to send one dozen eggs to your grandparents who live in the woods. The only means of transportation is via children in your neighborhood who are 5 years old. There is a 50–50 chance that a child making the delivery will break the eggs. What is the best method of delivery if you want to maximize the probability that the eggs will be delivered unbroken?

We can identify the answer by investigating how the probability of failure changes with the number of children used to deliver eggs. By using just one child to make the delivery, the probability that none will arrive safely is 0.5. With two children each carrying six eggs, the probability drops to 0.25 [i.e., $(\frac{1}{2})^2$].[39] With 12 children each carrying one egg, the probability drops to below 0.00025 [i.e., $(\frac{1}{2})^{12}$]. This demonstrates the **principle that diversification reduces risk**. For this principle to hold, the probability of failure must be independent among children (or individual investments). Independence would be violated, for example, if the children held hands and all fell if one fell. In business, independence would mean that the profits of one division would rise or fall independently with the profits of other divisions within the firm, a condition that is more likely to hold for a widely diversified conglomerate firm.

---

[39] That is, four outcomes are possible and each is equally likely to occur: (1) no eggs are broken; (2) all eggs are broken; (3) child 1 breaks the eggs but not child 2; (4) child 2 breaks the eggs but not child 1. Thus, there is a 1 in 4 chance that none of the eggs arrive safely.

18.5.3 Conglomerate Mergers and Anticompetitive Effects

Although conglomerate mergers involve firms in unrelated markets and would have no effect on the concentration level in any one industry, there are cases in which such mergers can increase market power. One way this can happen is if a conglomerate merger eliminates potential competition. We have seen in Chaps. 8 and 10 how the presence of a potential competitor can increase price competition. Thus, competition will diminish when conglomerate mergers eliminate potential competitors. The classic example was when Procter & Gamble (the nation's leading producer of soap and detergent) purchased Clorox (the nation's leading supplier of laundry bleach). The Federal Trade Commission successfully challenged the merger on the grounds that the merger eliminated Procter & Gamble as a potential competitor in the market for bleach.[40]

Second, because conglomerate mergers increase the firm's diversity and size, it may increase the possibility of something called **reciprocity**. For example, assume that firm A supplies inputs to firm B and firm B supplies inputs to firm C. Firm C is a monopsony buyer of firm B's inputs, and several firms besides A provide inputs to firm B. If firms A and C were to merge to form firm A–C, then it can inform firm B that "I will buy from you only if you buy from me." The point is that even though there is no direct link between firms A and C, their merger may increase its bargaining power over firm B.

A conglomerate merger can also increase market power by facilitating collusion. For instance, a firm may be more willing to engage in the punishment phase of a trigger strategy (e.g., a price cut) to discipline an aggressive competitor in one market if it is a conglomerate firm, because it can use profits earned in another market to **cross-subsidize** the cost of punishment. It may also use profits from one market to subsidize aggressive action designed to gain market share and power in another market. It has been argued that Philip Morris used its cigarette profits to cross-subsidize the expensive advertising campaigns of Miller Brewing in the 1970s, a tactic that did substantially increase Miller's market share.[41]

Similarly, Edwards (1955) argued that when conglomerate firms compete with one another in more than one market, they will take a "live and let live" policy. That is, they are more likely to behave cooperatively for fear that noncooperative behavior in one market will trigger punishment in more than just one market in which they compete.[42] This is called the **mutual forbearance hypothesis**.

The best example where the action of a conglomerate firm in one market led to retaliation in another market occurred between Clorox and Procter & Gamble.

---

[40] *Federal Trade Commission v. Procter & Gamble Co.*, (1967). For further discussion of this case, see Waldman (1986).

[41] For further discussion, see *Business Week* (November 8, 1976) and Elzinga (1990).

[42] When information is incomplete and monitoring costs are high, Thomas and Willig (2006) find that firms will be unwilling to link strategies across markets.

In 1988 Clorox entered the detergent market with its Clorox Super Detergent, a market that was the purview of Procter & Gamble. Within a few months, Procter & Gamble not only lowered the price of its detergent but introduced its own brand of bleach. In other words, Clorox's entry led Procter & Gamble to retaliate in both the detergent and bleach markets. This multimarket response caused Clorox to exit the detergent market in 1991.[43]

18.5.4 Managerial Motives for Conglomerate Mergers

We know from previous discussion that in very large corporations, stockholder ownership is separate from managerial control. From agency theory we know that this can create a principle–agent problem, as it may not be in management's interest to maximize the welfare of stockholders.

The most obvious way in which managers can abuse their power is through corporate theft, as occurred at Enron Corporation, Tyco International, and WorldCom in the last decade. At Tyco, the chief executive officer (CEO) was charged with enterprise corruption and falsification of business records to support a lavish life style. Tyco paid for his $30 million New York apartment, including a $6,000 shower curtain and $2 million for his wife's fortieth birthday party, disguising it as a shareholder meeting.[44]

Problems can also arise when manager income is closely tied to sales growth, which is true for many firms according to Mueller (2006). When this occurs, managers may trade-off profits for sales to increase their own income. Because growth is easier to generate by merger than internally and because antitrust laws limit horizontal and vertical merger possibilities, managers may overinvest in conglomerate mergers from the owner's perspective.[45]

Another concern is that managers may make acquisitions that increase the value of the manager to the firm. As an example, a manager of an engineering firm with specific expertise in biology may acquire a biotechnology firm, making it difficult for someone to manage the combined enterprise without a background in both engineering and biology. This can reduce the probability of being replaced and enable the manager to extract higher wages from owners. Shleifer and Vishny (1989) call this "**managerial entrenchment.**"

---

[43] In 1988, Clorox produced laundry bleach, wood stain, restaurant equipment, bottled water, and frozen foods. For further discussion, see Levine (1988), Lappen (1988), Shao (1991), and Hamilton (1997).

[44] For further discussion, see Newton (2006). For a list of *Time Magazine's* top ten corrupt CEOs over the last decade, see http://www.time.com/time/specials/packages/completelist/0,29569,1903155,00. html#ixzz0zSZrWJXl.

[45] See Marris (1964) and Mueller (1969) for further discussion.

Agency theory has focused on designing incentive compatible contracts that induce managers to pursue the interests of owners. As you might expect, such contracts should closely tie manager compensation with the firm's profits and market value. Nevertheless, addressing every contingency in a contract can be prohibitively costly in an uncertain world. It may be quite difficult for an owner to identify the effort and performance of a manager in markets hit by unexpected demand or cost shocks. Such uncertainty creates a difficult problem because the owner is not qualified or adequately informed to make a rational decision regarding corporate decisions and appropriate management compensation in uncertain times, which is why the owner hired the manager in the first place. As a result, managers generally end up with a considerable amount of discretion and salaries that are not closely tied to profits.

Even if the owner and manager are both motivated by profits, they may still have a different preference for risk. Owners or stockholders are likely to be risk neutral because they can diversify their investments (i.e., put their eggs in a variety of baskets). But managers are likely to be more risk averse because they cannot diversify their employment. Thus, managers will prefer to diversify their risk to a greater extent than owners, which may lead to excessive conglomerate merger activity.

18.5.5   Behavioral Economics and Conglomerate Mergers

This discussion would be incomplete without pointing out the influence of personality on conglomerate merger activity. As Flaherty (2011), president of the National Legal and Policy Center, makes clear, the personalities of company presidents have "a tremendous impact on the decisions, direction, mindset, communications tone, and overall persona of their companies. Much more, in fact, than people realize."[46]

For some CEOs, the psychological rewards of managing a large corporation are more meaningful than the pecuniary rewards. After all, it is the conspicuous **empire building** of large corporations that will get a CEO's picture on the cover of a business magazine or an appearance on CNN. In an emerging market, the potential for internal growth may be sufficient to meet a CEOs desire for empire building. In a mature market where growth and investment opportunities are limited, empire building is more likely to come from conglomerate merger.

In addition, a desire for empire building may interact with CEO hubris and lead to an even greater incentive for overinvestment in mergers. We saw in Chap. 14 that overconfidence can be a persistent problem in business. Recall that Cooper et al. (1988) found that over 80% of business owners were overconfident about their likelihood of success. This is not surprising, as psychologists find that individuals

---

[46] PR Newswire, March 10, 2011, available at http://www.highbeam.com/doc/1G1-251110190. html/print, accessed September 20, 2010.

are especially overconfident about the outcome of events they believe to be under their control and in which they are extremely committed.[47] Regarding mergers, a CEO may be overconfident that he or she can turn around a failing firm. Roll (1986) argues that this is much like a winner's curse in auction theory, which leads the acquiring firm to pay too much for the failing firm. It also increases the probability that such a merger will take place.[48]

Note that the empire-building and overconfidence motives for mergers imply different remedies. Both waste company resources on bad acquisitions. However, unlike empire-building CEOs, overconfident CEOs believe that they are behaving in the owner's interest. While an incentive compatible contract can align the goals of owners and a CEO who is prone to empire building, it cannot correct the inefficient behavior of an overconfident CEO.

Throughout history, there are numerous cases of CEOs who have grand aspirations. Here are two notable examples:

- Harold Geneen, CEO of International Telephone and Telegraph Corporation (ITT) from 1959 to 1977, made more than 300 mergers and acquisitions. Although he helped make ITT a conglomerate corporation, many of these mergers proved unprofitable and many of the company holdings were sold off after Geneen's retirement.
- From 1956 to 1981, Charles G. Bluhdorn took Gulf + Western from a small auto parts company to a Fortune 500 company (ranking 61st by 1981). Along the way, he purchased Paramount Pictures, Madison Square Garden, and Simon & Schuster Publishing. In a 1969 interview, he is quoted as saying: "The sky is the limit ... I came to this country without a penny, and built a company with 100,000 employees. This is what America is all about ... to be able to do what I've done is a matter of pride to me and to the country." (*Business Week*, July 5, 1969, p. 34) Subsequent downsizing in the 1980s after Bluhdorn's death suggests that many of these acquisitions were unprofitable.

18.5.6   Empirical Evidence

Assessing the causes and economic consequences of a real-world conglomerate merger is difficult. One problem is that there are many reasons and potential consequences of a conglomerate merger. It will increase profits if it is efficient or it raises market power, but it can lower profits if it is driven by various managerial or behavioral motives. In empirical work, it is generally difficult to control and test

---

[47] For a review of the psychology literature, see Malmendier and Tate (2008).

[48] Bogan and Just (2009) argue that confirmation bias, where individuals attach too much (little) importance on information that confirms (refutes) their beliefs, can also affect a CEO's merger decision. It is unclear whether this will lead to more or less merger activity.

for each of these motives. Another problem is that one can only speculate whether or not the merged firm would have outperformed the separate enterprises had the merger never taken place. Moreover, there are generally no comparator conglomerates by which to judge the merged firm.

In spite of these difficulties, economists have investigated conglomerate mergers in a number of ways. Early studies examined three types of evidence regarding the effect of conglomerate mergers on performance. In the first, event studies examined the effect of a merger announcement on the stock market value of the acquiring and targeted firms. This evidence shows that mergers have a positive net effect on the value of targeted firms, increasing their value from 16 to 30%. In contrast, acquiring firms experienced neutral and sometimes negative returns. The net effect is to increase their joint value. Although this evidence is inconsistent with managerial/ behavioral motives for conglomerate mergers that lead to inefficiency, *ceteris paribus*, we still do not know whether this higher value is due to increased efficiency or market power.[49]

The second type of evidence examines the premerger performance of acquiring and targeted firms. If efficiency drives mergers, then successful firms will buy inefficient or failing firms, as the market for corporate control suggests. After reviewing the evidence, Ravenscraft and Scherer (1987, 74) concluded that "[w]hen would-be acquirers 'fished' among the population of relatively small manufacturing enterprises for noncoercive acquisitions, they tended to haul in mainly specimens with superior records." This does not mean that all such mergers are inefficient, however. For instance, it may be efficient for a successful regional firm to go national if a conglomerate partner can provide distributional or marketing assistance. In addition, more recent work by Lichtenberg (1992) indicates that targeted firms did tend to have inefficient plants and that a merger improved their efficiency over time.

The third type of performance evidence comes from the post-merger data on profitability. Early studies showed that many conglomerate mergers that raised short-run corporate value never translated into higher profits later on. This was especially true during the conglomerate merger wave of the 1960s and early 1970s, when approximately half of the acquisitions were so unsuccessful that the acquired firms or their assets were eventually sold off (Ravenscraft and Scherer 1987). The decline in profits due to a conglomerate merger is consistent with the prevailing wisdom in the finance literature of the existence of a "conglomerate discount," meaning that the shares of conglomerate firms are sold at a relative discount. If true, then conglomerate mergers are inefficient, which supports the managerial and behavioral merger motives.

Firms may have learned from their mistakes of the 1960s and 1970s, as more recent evidence questions the conglomerate discount. Healy et al. (1992) found an increase in post-merger performance for the 50 largest mergers between 1979 and 1984.

---

[49] For a review of the evidence, see Caves (1989), Montgomery (1994), Martin and Sayrak (2003), and Mueller (2006).

An important contribution of their study was to compare the performance of the merged firm with an appropriate set of benchmark firms that have similar characteristics. Healy et al. found that conglomerate mergers actually improved performance, consistent with Graham et al. (2002), Jandik and Makhija (2005), and Villalonga (2004), and that the conglomerate discount disappears when the appropriate benchmark and other controls are taken into account. Overall, it may not be surprising that some conglomerate mergers are profitable and others are not. As Andrade et al. (2001, 119) point out regarding conglomerate mergers, "Ultimately, what the evidence shows is that it is hard to consistently make investment decisions that earn economic rents, which perhaps should not be too surprising in a competitive economy with a fairly efficient capital market."

A more direct way to determine whether a conglomerate merger improves efficiency is to estimate its effect on the firm's overall productivity. Lichtenberg and Siegel (1987) found an increase in plant productivity 3 years after a change in corporate ownership took place during the 1973–1981 period. In their study of US plant level data from 1977 to 1987, McGuckin and Nguyen (1995) found that conglomerate mergers generally improved total factor productivity. These studies are consistent with the efficiency motive for merger. At the same time, Harris and Robinson (2002) found that foreign mergers of U.K. plants led to productivity declines. They attribute the decline to the transition cost of assimilating the plant into a new corporation, something that overconfident managers may overlook. Thus, the limited evidence using this approach suggests that both efficiency and overconfidence may play a role in conglomerate mergers.

The evidence on the market power motive for conglomerate mergers is somewhat inconsistent. Caves (1981) failed to find support for the market power motive for firm diversification. In reviewing the evidence, Montgomery (1994, 175) concluded that it is unlikely that market power "plays a central role in firm diversification." On the other hand, an international comparison on the effect of mergers by Gugler et al. (2003) showed that over 25% of mergers exhibited patterns consistent with the market power motive. Jans and Rosenbaum (1997) provided convincing evidence in support of the mutual forbearance hypothesis. They investigated the performance of regional cement producers and found that price–cost margins in a region rose with multimarket contact among firms in that region.

There is considerable evidence in support of the managerial motives for merger. First, when comparing firms that are owner-controlled versus manager-controlled, Amihud and Lev (1981) found that manager-controlled firms tended to engage in more conglomerate mergers and to be more diversified than owner-controlled firms. This suggests that managers are more interested in sales growth than owners. Second, managers appear to pursue conglomerate mergers in an effort to reduce risk. Marshall et al. (1984) found that acquiring firms tend to purchase targets that have negatively correlated cash flows. In addition, May (1995) found evidence that CEOs tend to make investments in technologies in which they have greater expertise, which is consistent with the managerial entrenchment hypothesis.

Evidence on the behavioral motives for conglomerate mergers is rather limited. We have already discussed examples of CEOs with Napoleonic aspirations, but the only evidence on the effect of CEO overconfidence on conglomerate merger activity comes from Malmendier and Tate (2008). They develop a measure of CEO overconfidence and use it to analyze merger activity in the USA from 1980 to 1994. They find that overconfident CEOs are more likely to make an acquisition and that the market reaction to the merger announcement is substantially more negative than for mergers carried out by nonoverconfident CEOs. Although the evidence is limited, the evidence confirms that a CEO's personality can affect firm behavior.

We are not surprised that the evidence is mixed regarding the motives for conglomerate mergers. After all, conglomerate firms are multifaceted entities. There are many reasons why one firm may buy another, and they are not mutually exclusive. A merger may promote efficiency, increase market power, and serve managerial motives, and each has a different effect on firm performance. Further, the relative importance of these motives is likely to differ among firms, across industries, and over time. This suggests that generalizations are rather difficult and individual case studies may be the only way to fully understand a particular conglomerate merger.

18.6   Summary

1. A firm can rapidly increase its size by merging with another firm. When competitors merge, this is called a **horizontal merger**. A **vertical merger** involves firms that have a buyer–seller relationship. Others are called **conglomerate mergers**.
2. Conglomerate mergers can be pure and impure. Firms involved in a **pure conglomerate merger** produce completely unrelated products that compete in separate markets. An **impure conglomerate merger** involves firms that compete in markets that are not entirely separate. A merger of firms that produce the same product but in different geographic locations is called a **market extension merger**. When firms produce "somewhat" related products, a merger is called a **product extension merger**.
3. There have been four major merger waves in the USA. The first involved predominately horizontal mergers, which occurred at the end of the nineteenth century. The second occurred in the 1920s and involved a greater number of vertical and conglomerate mergers, as well as horizontal mergers between smaller competitors. The third wave of the 1960s involved mostly conglomerate mergers. The final wave has continued since the 1990s and has been influenced by government deregulation.
4. The classic profit motives for mergers are enhanced market power and efficiency. Firms may also merge to reduce risk and in response to changes in government policy. According to the **market for corporate control hypothesis**, mergers may

be an efficient way of disciplining inefficient managers and transferring assets from failing to successful firms.

5. Non-profit-maximizing motives may also influence merger activity. First, when manager compensation is closely tied to company growth, excessive merger activity may result. Second, behavioral theories suggest that some managers are motivated by empire building and suffer from overconfidence. These motives can lead to excessive merger activity.

6. The market power motive is most likely with horizontal mergers. However, the **merger paradox** indicates that merging firms do not necessarily benefit from the resulting increase in market power. In a simple Cournot model, the horizontal merger must involve firms with a combined market share of over 80% for the merger to be profitable for firms involved in the merger. The merger paradox need not hold if the merger produces a Stackelberg leader or if firms compete in a Bertrand-type game with sufficient product differentiation.

7. **Williamson's trade-off** says that when evaluating the social efficiency of a merger, we must compare the resulting efficiency gain with the market power loss. In the Cournot model, it takes a relatively small efficiency gain for a horizontal merger to increase total surplus. It takes a substantially greater efficiency gain for it to increase consumer surplus. Thus, mergers that are socially efficient need not benefit consumers.

8. A vertical merger can improve efficiency when it involves technical economies, lowers transaction costs, and improves product or service quality. It can also eliminate the problem of **double marginalism**, where a chain of monopolies along each stage of vertical suppliers is more *in*efficient than a chain of competitive producers or a monopolist that is completely vertically integrated. The policy implication is captured in the **principle of double marginalism**: vertical integration either increases or has no effect on market efficiency. Caution is warranted, however, as this principle need not always hold.

9. Vertical mergers can increase market power, especially if they lead to foreclosure and enhance the combined firm's ability to price discriminate.

10. In most cases, the empirical evidence shows that vertical mergers promote efficiency and not market power.

11. A conglomerate merger is efficient when it enables the firm to take advantage of economies of scope, reduces transaction costs, and facilitates the transfer of management control from inefficient to efficient management teams.

12. An important way in which a conglomerate merger can increase market power is when it eliminates potential competition, as with a market extension merger. Market power may also be enhanced when a conglomerate merger leads to greater reciprocity, cross subsidization, and coordinated behavior.

13. The separation of owners and managers in large corporations can create a principle–agent problem. This may cause managers to make decisions that are in their interest rather than the interest of owners. Managerial theories of the firm suggest that this can induce a manager to put too high a value on sales growth and to diversify in directions that increase the value of the manager to

the firm (i.e., **managerial entrenchment**). It can also induce managers to over diversify to reduce management's exposure to risk.

14. Behavioral economics suggests that the personality of a company's CEO can influence conglomerate activity. CEOs who are overconfident and interested in **empire building** may overinvest in conglomerate mergers, which is bad for owners. CEOs with a preference for empire building actively pursue different goals from owners, whereas overconfident CEOs believe that they are behaving in the owner's interest. Thus, developing contracts that align the goals of managers and owners will not correct overconfident CEO behavior.

15. Although it is difficult to accurately control for all variables that are likely to influence conglomerate mergers, the available evidence is generally consistent with many of the theories discussed in this chapter. Many, but not all, conglomerate mergers enhance the market value of the firm. Direct productivity studies provide mixed results on a conglomerate merger's ability to lower production costs. Some studies show that conglomerate mergers have increased market power. Finally, there is evidence to support the managerial and behavioral motives for conglomerate mergers. That is, managers with greater discretion and who are overconfident are more likely to engage in conglomerate mergers.

16. In summary, economic theory demonstrates that there are multiple motives for mergers, and they are not mutually exclusive. The empirical evidence provides support for a variety of motives, depending on the type of merger (i.e., horizontal, vertical, and conglomerate), the industry under consideration, and the time period involved. From a policy perspective, this suggests that the causes and economic consequences of mergers should be judged on a case by case basis.

18.7   Review Questions

1. Compare and contrast horizontal, vertical, and conglomerate mergers. What is the difference between a pure and an impure conglomerate merger?

2. Identify the four merger waves in the USA from the late nineteenth century to present. Briefly identify the motives for each of these merger waves.

3. Regarding the market-for-corporate-control hypothesis:

   A. Briefly explain the market-for-corporate-control hypothesis and how it provides an efficiency motive for mergers.

   B. How can the event study method be used to test the market-for-corporate-control hypothesis?

   C. Explain how the market-for-corporate control hypothesis is derived from the efficient-market hypothesis. What are the main weaknesses with the efficient-market hypothesis, and, therefore, the market-for-corporate-control hypothesis?

4. (Advanced) Consider a market with three firms (1, 2, and 3) that produce homogeneous goods. The inverse market demand function is $p = 24 - Q$,

where Q is market output ($q_1 + q_2 + q_3$, with q_i representing firm i's output). The total cost equation for firm i is $TC_i = 12q_i$.

A. Find the Cournot equilibrium price (p^*), output (q_i^*), and profit (π_i^*) levels for each firm.

B. Will it be profitable for firms 1 and 2 to merge and form firm 1–2?

5. Consider a market with three firms (1, 2, and 3) that produce homogeneous goods. The market demand function is $Q = 24 - p$, and firm total cost equations are $TC_1 = 10q_1$, $TC_2 = 10q_2$, and $TC_3 = 12q_3$.

A. Find the Bertrand equilibrium price (p^*), output (q_i^*), and profit (π_i^*) levels for each firm.

B. If firm 1 has the option of acquiring another firm, will it prefer to buy firm 2, buy firm 3, or make no acquisition? Explain.

6. If the primary goal of society is efficiency, explain how the Williamson trade-off is important to antitrust.

7. Explain the difference between an upstream and a downstream vertical merger.

8. You are the CEO of the Macrosoft Corporation and decide to buy a custom motorcycle from US Choppers. The purpose of the motorcycle is to help promote your company, and your only request is that the Macrosoft logo be prominently displayed on the motorcycle.

A. Explain how the hold-up problem applies to this purchase.

B. Who is at greater risk of being held up, you or US Choppers?

C. Identify 2 ways in which to eliminate the hold-up problem.

9. Consider a market much like that which is described in Fig. 18.5. In this problem, there is a monopoly wholesaler and a competitive retailer (the *monopoly–competitive case*).

A. On your own figure, identify the equilibrium wholesale price (p_W), retail marginal cost (MC_R), retail price (p_R), and output level.

B. How does this output level compare to the equilibrium output levels in the competitive–competitive case (Q_S in Fig. 18.4), competitive–monopoly case (Q_1 in Fig. 18.5), and monopoly–monopoly case (Q_2 in Fig. 18.6)?

C. Identify the profits going to the wholesaler and retailer.

10. Consider a market with a monopoly wholesaler and a monopoly retailer. The retailer uses a fixed-proportions technology.

A. Briefly show how double marginalism applies to these vertically related firms.

B. Show how a merger between the manufacturer and the distributor can increase consumer and producer surplus.

C. How could your answer to part B change if the retailer has a variable-proportions technology?

11. Define what is meant by economies of scope. Under what conditions will the presence of economies of scope justify a conglomerate merger from society's perspective?
12. Define the mutual forbearance hypothesis and describe a trigger strategy that would support it.
13. Discuss how the principle–agent problem can explain the tendency of larger corporations to overinvest in conglomerate mergers.
14. The principle–agent problem can induce managers to make acquisitions that are not in the interest of stockholders. Explain how this can lead to "managerial entrenchment."
15. Provide two behavioral motives for conglomerate mergers.

Appendix A: The Economics of Double Marginalism

Here, we formally analyze the economics of double marginalism by considering the problem described in Sect. 18.4.1.5. This is a market for gasoline with a monopoly manufacturer or wholesaler (W) and a monopoly distributor or retailer (R). Gasoline is supplied using a fixed-proportions technology. The total cost of wholesaling is $TC_W = c_W Q$, where c_W is marginal and average cost and Q is output. The retailer pays the wholesale price of gasoline, and there are no added costs to the retailer of doing business. Thus, the retailer's total cost is $TC_R = c_R Q$, where c_R is the retailer's marginal and average cost. Because there are no added costs of retailing, $c_R = p_W$, the wholesale price of gas. The inverse demand at the retail level is linear: $p_R = a - bQ$, where p_R is the retail price.[50] Firms compete in a two-stage game. In the first stage, the wholesaler sets its price. In the second stage, the retailer chooses its output level given the wholesale price of gasoline.

We use backwards induction to identify the SPNE. The problem in the second stage is for the retailer to maximize its profit (π_R), given p_W. The firm's profit equation is

$$\pi_R = TR_R - TC_R$$
$$= p_R Q - c_R Q = (aQ - bQ^2) - c_R Q. \qquad (A.1)$$

Recalling that $c_R = p_W$, the first-order condition of profit maximization is

$$\frac{\partial \pi_R}{\partial Q} = \frac{\partial TR_R}{\partial Q} - \frac{\partial TC_R}{\partial Q}$$
$$= MR_R - MC_R$$
$$= (a - 2bQ) - p_W = 0, \qquad (A.2)$$

---

[50] Given fixed proportions, wholesale and retail output are the same.

where MR_R is the retailer's marginal revenue and MC_R is the retailer's marginal cost. Solving for Q gives the retailer's best-reply function (Q^{BR})

$$Q^{BR} = \frac{a - p_W}{2b}. \tag{A.3}$$

Notice that if the retailer owns the wholesaler or if the wholesale price equals MC_W, then this would be the simple monopoly solution.

Next, we solve the wholesaler's problem. The wholesaler is assumed to be sequentially rational and can look forward and reason back. This enables it to identify the retailer's best-reply and maximize its profits given Q^{BR}. From the wholesaler's perspective, Q^{BR} is the wholesaler's demand. Solving (A.3) for p_W gives the wholesaler's inverse demand: $p_W = a - 2bQ$. Notice that it equals MR_R (from A.2). The wholesaler's profit equation is

$$\begin{aligned}
\pi_W &= TR_W - TC_W \\
&= p_W Q^{BR} - c_W Q^{BR} = (p_W - c_W)Q^{BR} \\
&= (p_W - c_W)\left(\frac{a - p_W}{2b}\right).
\end{aligned} \tag{A.4}$$

The first-order condition with respect to p_W is

$$\begin{aligned}
\frac{\partial \pi_W}{\partial p_W} &= \frac{\partial TR_W}{\partial p_W} - \frac{\partial TC_W}{\partial p_W} \\
&= MR_{p_W} - MC_{p_W} \\
&= \left(\frac{a - 2p_W}{2b}\right) + \left(\frac{c_W}{2b}\right) = 0,
\end{aligned} \tag{A.5}$$

where MR_{p_W} is the wholesaler's marginal revenue with respect to price, and MC_{p_W} is the wholesaler's marginal cost with respect to price. Solving this for p_W gives the profit-maximizing wholesale price. Substituting this value into Q_{BR} and the demand and profit equations gives the other SPNE values:

$$p_R^* = \frac{3a + c_W}{4} > p_W^* = \frac{a - c_W}{2}, \tag{A.6}$$

$$Q^* = \frac{a - c_W}{4b}, \tag{A.7}$$

$$\pi_R^* = \frac{(a - c_W)^2}{16b} < \pi_W^* = \frac{(a - c_W)^2}{8b}, \tag{A.8}$$

$$\pi_R^* + \pi_W^* = \frac{3(a - c_W)^2}{16b}. \tag{A.9}$$

If the firms were to merge, this would produce the simple monopoly solution:

$$p_R^{**} = \frac{a + c_W}{2},$$
(A.10)

$$Q^{**} = \frac{a - c_W}{2b},$$
(A.11)

$$\pi^{**} = \frac{4(a - c_W)^2}{16b}.$$
(A.12)

This demonstrates the principle of double marginalism: compared to a single merged firm, separate wholesale and retail monopolies are (1) less efficient because $Q^{**} > Q^*$; (2) less profitable ($\pi^{**} > \pi_R^* + \pi_W^*$), providing an incentive for vertical merger; (3) bad for consumers, because the retail price is lower and production is greater with the merger. Notice too that this problem is similar to the problem of complementary products that we discussed in Chap. 13.

Part V

Economic Performance and Public Policy

Chapter 19
Efficiency, Equity, and Corporate Responsibility in Imperfect Competition

A crucial objective in industrial organization is to evaluate whether or not imperfectly competitive markets perform well from society's perspective. As discussed in Chap. 1, we focus on three dimensions of market performance: static efficiency, dynamic efficiency, and equity. Up to this point, we have spent most of our time discussing efficiency issues. We now begin this chapter with a review and assessment of what we have learned regarding imperfect competition and different types of inefficiency—market power (i.e., allocative inefficiency), X-inefficiency, rent-seeking behavior, and technological change (i.e., dynamic efficiency).

As members of society, however, we are concerned with more than just efficiency. Most of us do not want to live in a world where individuals and firms behave efficiently but unfairly. Although discussion of social justice, fairness, and morality pushes us into the realm of value judgments and normative issues, current research is underway that addresses economic justice from a positive perspective. The emerging evidence shows that many values are universally shared, such as honesty and fairness, and are important to us in both our social and economic interactions.

Social philosophers have long known that morality is a necessary ingredient of a successful market economy. In the words of Zak (2008, xi), "modern market exchange is inconceivable without moral values." No one will continue to do business with companies that routinely break contracts and make deceptive claims about the quality of their products. Corporate and political corruption will limit market activity and economic growth. Thus, one goal of this chapter is to assess whether or not corporations behave in a socially responsible way.

In this chapter, we first review what we have learned regarding efficiency and then discuss equity and corporate responsibility. This evidence will be used to motivate and guide policy analysis in Chap. 20. There we will investigate the appropriate rules of the game, that is, the socially desirable laws and regulations that are needed to assure socially desirable market performance and firm behavior.

V.J. Tremblay and C.H. Tremblay, *New Perspectives on Industrial Organization*, Springer Texts in Business and Economics, DOI 10.1007/978-1-4614-3241-8_19, © Springer Science+Business Media New York 2012

19.1   Efficiency

As we discussed in Chap. 5, there are four broad concepts of static efficiency: technical, economic, allocative, and productive. A firm is technically efficient when it uses the minimum quantity of inputs to produce a given output. In other words, inputs are not being wasted and the firm is operating on (not above) its isoquant. Economic efficiency means that firms minimize costs—the firm chooses the combination of inputs that produces a given output at minimum cost. When economically efficient, the firm is producing on (not above) its cost function (i.e., its frontier cost function). Economic efficiency requires technical efficiency, but technical efficiency need not imply economic efficiency.[1]

The two other types of efficiency apply to the industry, not the firm. Allocative efficiency is reached when an industry produces the socially desirable quantity of output. This means that resources are allocated among the various uses in a socially efficient manner. If we look at one industry separate from all others, allocative efficiency occurs when price equals marginal cost. Finally, productive efficiency is reached when a given level of industry output is produced at minimum cost for the industry as a whole.[2]

From a theoretical perspective, the perfectly competitive model serves as the benchmark for static efficiency.[3] Goods are private, externalities are nonexistent, and there are no frictions due to a lack of information. Cost minimization is met, because firms are assumed to be profit maximizers. Allocative efficiency is achieved because the equilibrium price equals long-run marginal cost. Productive efficiency is met because all firms produce at minimum long-run average cost. If all markets were like this and there were no other imperfections, the price in each market would reflect the true social cost of producing the last unit of output and resources would be allocated to their most efficient (i.e., highest valued) use.

Of course, these ideals are rarely met in the real world. We do not usually see markets that are "perfectly" competitive. In most markets, market power, externalities, and imperfect information are present to a certain degree. Even if

---

[1] In other words, a firm is technically efficient when operating anywhere on its isoquant and is economically efficient when operating at a point where its isocost function is tangent to its isoquant (Varian, Chap. 20).

[2] Recall that economic efficiency need not imply productive efficiency. In a duopoly market with two economically efficient firms, for example, firm 1 may produce in the region of scale economies and firm 2 in the region of scale diseconomies. This is not productively efficient, because industry costs would be lower if firm 1 were to increase production and firm 2 were to decrease production.

[3] There are imperfectly competitive models that also produce allocatively efficient outcomes, but only under very restrictive conditions. For instance, the Bertrand and Cournot–Bertrand models produce the competitive outcome when products are homogeneous, there are constant returns to scale, and firms are symmetric [see Chap. 10 and C. Tremblay and V. Tremblay (2011a)]. Another example is the perfectly contestable market (Baumol et al., 1982), which assumes that sunk costs of entry are zero and entry is instantaneous (see Chap. 5).

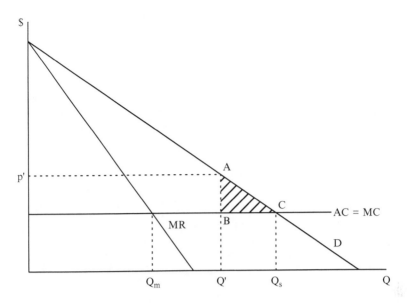

Fig. 19.1 Deadweight (efficiency) loss due to market power

all markets were statically efficient, we saw in Chap. 17 that they may not generate the optimal level of technological change and, therefore, need not be dynamically efficient. When it is socially worthwhile to give up static efficiency today to gain lower costs and better products tomorrow, dynamic efficiency trumps static efficiency. In this section, we review possible inefficiencies associated with imperfectly competitive markets. Policy issues are addressed in the next chapter.

19.1.1 Static Allocative Inefficiency

In most models, static allocative inefficiency is the norm in imperfectly competitive markets. In both monopoly and monopolistically competitive markets, price exceeds marginal cost. In oligopoly models, price exceeds marginal cost except under special conditions in the Bertrand and Cournot–Bertrand models.

The economic consequence of allocative inefficiency is illustrated in Fig. 19.1. It depicts a market demand curve (D) and a marginal revenue curve (MR). Industry costs are linear, so that long-run average cost (AC) equals long-run marginal cost (MC). In this case, the allocatively efficient level of output occurs where price equals marginal cost and output equals Q_S. Monopoly output is at Q_m where MR = MC, but most oligopoly markets with market power produce output that is between Q_m and Q_S. If this occurs at Q', then price (p') exceeds marginal cost and the efficiency loss due to market power equals the shaded area of triangle ABC in Fig. 19.1. Recall that this is called the efficiency or deadweight loss (DWL) due to market power.

We saw in Chap. 12 that a common way of measuring market power is with a Lerner index, defined as $\mathcal{L} = (p - MC)/p$. When $\mathcal{L} = 0$, the market is allocatively efficient; when $\mathcal{L} > 0$, market power exists and the market is allocatively inefficient.

Estimates of the cost of market power for various industries and for the economy as a whole were discussed in Chaps. 9 and 12. Three general conclusions can be gleaned from these results. First, the degree of competition and market power varies widely across industries. In general, market power is relatively low for agricultural commodities and is relatively high in manufacturing and service industries (see Table 12.2). Second, an increase in the number of competitors generally leads to lower prices. As we saw in Chap. 9, cartels are much more likely in concentrated than unconcentrated industries. Finally, the magnitude of the efficiency loss caused by imperfect competition in the overall economy remains uncertain. Estimates range between 0.1% and 6.0% of GNP (gross national product, defined as the dollar value of all goods and services produced in the economy). Perhaps the most reliable estimates were obtained by Masson and Shaanan (1984) who estimated the efficiency loss to be 2.9% of GNP. More recent estimates are unavailable but would likely be lower since more rigorous foreign competition has undoubtedly increased efficiency (Caves and Barton, 1990).

19.1.2   Other Sources of Static Inefficiency

Unfortunately, DWL is not the only type of inefficiency associated with imperfectly competitive markets. Two additional factors can push up the social cost of market power: rent-seeking behavior and X-inefficiency.

Recall from Chap. 6 that rent seeking occurs when firms make investments to obtain and maintain government support for market power. For example, a firm may lobby or bribe government officials to create barriers that reduce foreign competition. Rent seeking is socially wasteful, as it is costly and raises or maintains market power. Thus, the social cost of market power must include the cost of rent seeking along with the traditional DWL.[4] Available evidence suggests that the social cost of rent seeking can be quite high. Posner (1975) estimated that up to 30% of industry revenues are spent on rent seeking in such industries as automobiles, physician services, and oil. In a study of the cellular phone industry, Hazlett and Michaels (1993) found that approximately 50% of monopoly rents were spent on rent-seeking activity.

The presence of X-inefficiency adds further to the social cost of market power. As we discussed in Chap. 6, X-inefficiency exists when production costs are elevated above their cost-minimizing levels. We would expect to see cost minimization in competitive markets, because firms that let their costs creep up will go out of

---

[4] One could view this as a simple transfer from monopolies to politicians. Nevertheless, rent-seeking behavior is costly and may increase market power, which raises the deadweight loss associated with monopoly.

business in the long run. But this natural selection argument requires a sufficient degree of competition. Without it, cost minimization may not be needed for survival. In this setting, utility-maximizing owners/managers may be willing to give up some profit for greater leisure (i.e., less effort). As Hicks (1935, 8) said, "the best of all monopoly profits is the quiet life." Managerial slack such as this causes costs to rise and X-inefficiency to result.

In his extensive review of the literature, Frantz (1997, 146) concluded that the evidence is varied but generally supports the presence of X-inefficiency.[5] One notable example is a study by Aiginger and Pfaffermayr (1997) who estimated the DWL and X-inefficiency due to market power in the European cement and paper industries. They found that the DWL was 2–3% of GDP, which is consistent with the Masson and Shaanan (1984) estimate. The added cost due to X-inefficiency pushes the social cost of market power to about 10%.

One needs to be cautious when evaluating studies such as these, however. A firm may expect to minimize cost ex ante but fail to do so ex post due to unforeseen circumstances.[6] For example, a grocery store may substantially increase its inventory of soft drinks in anticipation of high demand over the 4th of July weekend, but bad weather may reduce demand and leave the store with an excess inventory of soft drinks.[7] This represents bad luck rather than X-inefficiency; X-inefficiency should only include inefficiency due to systematic management error and lack of effort. Bad luck cannot be helped, but systematic cost overruns are a policy concern because they are wasteful and can be avoided.

The appropriate approach would investigate the effect of competition on systematic cost inefficiency. In his summary of the evidence, Frantz (1997) concluded that there is considerable support for the hypothesis that increased competition and openness to international trade lead to less X-inefficiency. Primeaux (1977, 1978) provided a good example of this approach. He estimated firm costs in the US electric utility industry. By comparing costs in markets with a single firm with markets that have two competitors, he was able to determine the effect of competition on costs. He found that unit costs were more than 10% lower in markets served by two firms, *ceteris paribus*. Berger et al. (1993) reviewed a series of studies of the banking industry and concluded that X-inefficiency due to a lack of competition is responsible for a 20–30% increase in costs. Nickell (1996) studied firm efficiency in the UK and found that greater competition led to gains in technical efficiency and productivity growth (a dynamically desirable outcome).

---

[5] Unfortunately, the empirical evidence does not always distinguish between X-inefficiency and other types of inefficiency. For a survey of the evidence on X-inefficiency, see Frantz (1997). For a discussion of the methods used to distinguish among these various types of inefficiency, see Färe et al. (1985, 2008).

[6] For further discussion of inefficiency that has two components, one due to bad luck and the other due to systematic error, see Schmidt (1985–1986) and Greene (2008).

[7] If a firm had perfect foresight and could always correctly anticipate fluctuations in demand, an efficient firm would never have too much or too little inventory or productive capacity.

If these estimates of the cost of allocative inefficiency, rent-seeking behavior, and X-inefficiency are correct, then the market power associated with imperfect competition may be a serious policy concern. At the same time, market power may result from superior efficiency and promote dynamic efficiency.

19.1.3   Dynamic Inefficiency

Recall from previous chapters that analyzing market power in dynamic markets is considerably more complicated than in static markets. As we discussed in Chap. 12, evidence that price equals marginal cost does not necessarily imply an absence of market power in markets where demand or cost functions are connected over time. As an example, cigarette companies have given away free samples to increase the number of (addicted) consumers, which can allow them to raise price and earn higher profits in the future. Similarly, when there is the potential for learning-by-doing, a firm will increase production (lower price) today to lower marginal cost in the future. Firms that set price equal to or less than marginal cost today may be making costly investments to increase market power tomorrow. Thus, special care must be taken when estimating inefficiency in dynamic settings, such as markets where addiction, product durability, and learning-by-doing are prominent features.

Two notable studies control for dynamic effects when analyzing issues of market power. In the first, Jarmin (1994) developed and estimated a dynamic model of learning-by-doing for the US rayon industry from 1911 to 1938. His evidence was consistent with learning but inconsistent with both collusive and perfectly competitive behavior, suggesting that the market was imperfectly competitive. Zulehner (2003) estimated market power in the semiconductor industry from 1974 to 1996, where learning-by-doing was also important. She extended Jarmin's model to allow market power to vary over time. Zulehner's results showed that market power was high until the mid-1980s and remained low thereafter.

The one saving grace of concentrated industries is that they may generate greater innovation. Market power may be necessary for technological change. If so, policy implications shift, because a substantial invention can quickly outstrip the efficiency loss due to static market power. Thus, a policy that maintains static efficiency period after period need not be dynamically efficient. In other words, it may be socially beneficial to tolerate market power today if it produces sufficient technological change tomorrow.

Discussion of technological change and its connection to market structure was presented in Chap. 17. In terms of theory, anything is possible. Arrow's (1962) model predicts that competitive firms are more likely to be innovative than firms in imperfectly competitive markets. Alternatively, Schumpeter's (1942) theory predicts greater innovation from large firms in highly concentrated industries. Finally, causality can also run in the other direction, with technological change affecting market structure. From Demsetz' (1973) superior efficiency hypothesis, superior firms that discover lower cost methods or better products will promote dynamic efficiency even though they cause concentration and profits to rise.

There has been a considerable amount of empirical research on technical change, as discussed in Chap. 17. The main results are summarized as follows. Clearly, technological opportunities[8] and government policies encourage research and development spending and technological change. The literature also suggests that the process that drives technological change is industry specific, which may reflect the fact that technological opportunities vary across industries. Furthermore, there is strong evidence that technological change can dramatically affect market structure, but empirical studies are unclear regarding the effect of market structure on technological change. Finally, the empirical evidence is unable to shed light on the big question—whether or not our current political-economic system is dynamically efficient. Data limitations and the complexity of the forces that shape technological change make it difficult to obtain answers to some of these fundamental questions.

This is not to suggest that technological change does not have negative as well as positive consequences. From Chap. 17, we know that technological change may lower production costs and create new and better products, but it can also raise market power. Furthermore, the process of creative destruction can put some workers out of a job, at least in the short run.[9] New technologies can also produce greater pollution and more powerful weapons of mass destruction, which lowers the physical and psychic health of many of us. As a society, trade-offs must be made. Policies should be designed to encourage the positive and discourage the negative consequences of technological change.

19.2 Equity and Corporate Responsibility

For the greater part of the last two centuries, ethical issues associated with equity (i.e., that which is just, fair, and impartial) were thought to be outside the domain of economics because they involve value judgments and cannot be analyzed scientifically. It was felt that normative issues such as these should be left to religious leaders and social philosophers. In the last two decades, there has been a growing interest among economists in issues of justice.[10] For example, in the 1970s publications reported in *EconLit* on "efficiency" outnumbered publications on "justice" or "fairness" by 16 to 1.[11] By the 1990s, this ratio had fallen to 4.4 to 1.

---

[8] Recall that an increase in technological opportunities means that there are greater expected benefits from investing in research and development.

[9] This can be devastating financially to displaced workers. In the long run, unemployment will be mitigated for the economy as a whole but not necessarily for the individual. And, as John Maynard Keynes said, "we are all dead in the long run."

[10] This discussion of economics and social justice borrows from a survey by Konow (2003) and from Zak (2008).

[11] *EconLit* is the American Economic Association's search engine for publications in economics.

A new line of research is emerging that looks at economic equity or justice from a positive perspective.[12] At issue is whether there is a universal theory of justice on which all or most of us can agree. Evidence regarding this question derives from survey and experimental evidence where subjects are asked to identify fair outcomes to a set of vignettes or hypothetical situations. To illustrate, consider the following hypothetical proposed by Konow (2003, 1197):

> Mike and Bill are identical twins who were reared in an identical family and educational environment. They are the same in terms of physical and mental abilities, but Mike is more industrious than Bill. For that reason, after they begin their careers Mike ends up earning more than Bill. Please indicate whether you view such a difference in their earnings as: Fair or Unfair.

This question addresses attitudes about effort and earnings. In his survey of 150 individuals, Konow found that 99% felt that a difference in salary was fair. Answers to similar types of questions indicate that people feel that it is equitable to give greater reward to those who contribute greater effort, *ceteris paribus*.

Research in this area is leading to a unifying theory of distributive justice that incorporates three competing elements: needs, just deserts, and efficiency. In terms of distributive justice, the "needs principle" requires that more is provided to those who have greater needs, *ceteris paribus*. For instance, if a child from a poor family that is without health insurance needs a life saving operation, justice requires that the child receive the operation. This principle provides for the least well off members of society. The "just-deserts principle" requires that greater compensation be given to those who put forth greater effort, *ceteris paribus*.[13] Finally, the "efficiency principle" advocates maximizing total surplus or wealth.

Unfortunately, there are trade-offs among needs, just deserts, and efficiency. In his classic work on the efficiency-equality trade-off, Okun (1975) argued that placing greater emphasis on equality comes at the expense of those who put forth greater effort.[14] Placing greater emphasis on equality can cause the economic pie to grow more slowly and lower dynamic efficiency. This is certainly true if we ignore other dimensions to equity and take it to simply mean an equal division of income and wealth. A more complete theory of equity or social justice calls for a multicriterion approach, which requires that we identify socially acceptable weights

---

[12] Recall from Chap. 1 that positive economics refers to the study of "what is" as opposed to normative economics which is the study of "what ought to be".

[13] One can think of the needs and just-deserts principles as being elements for the "golden rule"— do unto others as you would have them do unto you. According to Flew (1979), the golden rule has roots in a wide range of cultures and religions. For example, Jesus (Matthew 7:12) is quoted as saying, "always treat others as you would like them to treat you." The needs principle is consistent with Karl Marx (1875) who wrote "from each according to his ability, to each according to his needs," which was first proclaimed by Louis Blanc, a utopian socialist (Capaldi 2004). This is also consistent with St. Paul (Acts 2: 44–45) who wrote that "the faithful all lived together... and shared out the proceeds according to what each one needed."

[14] Okun (1975, 120) said that "the conflict between equality and economic efficiency is inescapable." For a less pessimistic view of this trade-off, see Blank (2002).

for needs, just deserts, and efficiency. Unfortunately, surveys and experimental evidence suggest that such weights vary depending on the particulars of the context that is associated with the issue in question.[15] Nevertheless, this line of research is noteworthy for identifying the elements that people view as important to justice and fairness.

Equity is essential to a market economy because exchange and a stable political-economic system cannot flourish in an unjust society.[16] Trade is not possible without sufficient trust and honesty. Businesses that behave unfairly will perish in the long run as customers patronize more trustworthy competitors. Corrupt governments face citizen revolt. The French Revolution at the end of the eighteenth century provides one example. Before the Revolution, harsh economic conditions placed undue strain on the lower classes, with people experiencing bread shortages and a severely regressive tax system that favored the rich, nobility, and clergy. This coupled with an indifferent French monarchy led the people to kill the King, eliminated the monarchy, and establish a new legal system. Even animals are known to rebel and discontinue cooperation with their group if treated inequitably (Brosan 2008).

Next, we address two issues that pertain to justice and fairness in imperfectly competitive markets. First, we discuss issues of corporate responsibility. Second, we are interested in determining the effect of market power on the distribution of income and wealth.

19.2.1   Corporate Social Responsibility

A concern raised by critics of free markets is that by focusing primarily on the bottom line, corporations will behave in a socially irresponsible way. One example derives from the "Hail Mary" strategy used by failing firms that we discussed in Chap. 13. According to Aron and Lazear (1990), a failing firm may pursue an unconventional and potentially socially undesirable strategy in a desperate effort to survive.

V. Tremblay and C. Tremblay (2005, 2007) document numerous cases where brewing companies have used sexually provocative ads in an attempt to save a failing brand. Examples include the "Nude Beer" brand of the Eastern Brewing Company in the 1980s, where each can contained the picture of a nude woman who is concealed by a scratch-off covering. In 2005, the Pabst Brewing Company used a "Swedish Bikini Team" (consisting of women in blond wigs and bikinis) to market their Old Milwaukee brand. In 2002–2003, the Miller Brewing Company

---

[15] Attitudes about justice are dependent on how a problem is framed and whether an outcome is reached by just means.

[16] Of course, virtuous behavior can be a good thing in and of itself. Socrates said that his virtuous behavior was ultimately self-interested, as it was "for the good of his soul" (Solomon, 2008, 24).

introduced its so-called cat-fight ads to promote its Miller Lite brand. These ads featured two young women arguing over whether Miller Lite is "less filling" or "great tasting," an argument that ends with them in a fight ripping off each other's clothes in a water fountain. Rance Crain (2003), editor-in-chief of *Advertising Age*, called the Miller ads "blatant sexism and exploitation of the female body."

Many consumer advocates argue that if left unchecked, some firms will use unfair business practices and even risk injury to consumers as long as it is profitable to do so. This viewpoint is reflected in the titles of the early critiques of business behavior in the 1970s when the consumer movement began. For example, Ralph Nader's (1973) book on corporate responsibility and contains such chapters as "Selling Death" (on cigarette advertising) and "The Burned Children" (on flammable clothing).[17]

There are numerous examples of corporate callousness throughout US history. A particularly shocking example is the case of the Ford Pinto. In 1977 critics alleged that the Pinto had a poorly designed gas tank, which increased the risk that a rear end collision would cause a deadly fire. A controversy ensued when internal corporate documents became public, revealing that Ford knew of the problem and decided that it was not cost effective to fix it. It was felt that the $11 cost of the repair was not worth the monetary value of the lives it would save. A company memo titled "Fatalities Associated with Crash-Induced Fuel Leakages and Fires" stated that the total cost of the repair was about $137.5 million but the estimated value of saved lives was only $49.53 million.[18] Once this information surfaced, public outcry led the National Highway Traffic Safety Administration to pressure Ford to recall the Pinto in 1978.

Alarming levels of fraud in the financial sector (along with ineffective government regulations and bad decisions by home buyers) precipitated the recession of 2008–2009. As an example, in 2007 managers at Bear Stearns deceived investors by painting a sunny picture of the future of their hedge funds and concealing the fact that the funds were down 18%. At the same time, top managers at Bear Sterns were pulling their own money out of the funds, leading to the arrest of two fund managers, eventual losses of $1.6 billion, and the demise of Bear Stearns.[19]

---

[17] For a more recent critique of business behavior, see Friedrichs (1996) and Mitchell (2001). The following Web page provides a list of dozens of consumer organizations: http://www.infoplease. com/ipa/A0002120.html, accessed July 12, 2011.

[18] For a complete account, see Birsch and Fielder (1994). The cost of fixing the problem was 12.5 million vehicles times $11, equaling $137 million. The expected benefit of fixing the problem was 180 saved lives valued at $200,000 each plus 180 saved burn injuries valued at $67,000 each plus 2,100 saved cars valued at $700 each, equaling $49.53 million. The value of a life was estimated to be $200,000 in 1970 by the National Highway Traffic Safety Administration. The US Department of Transportation estimated the value of a life to be $3 million in 2004 (Ashenfelter 2006).

[19] Bear Stearns was purchased by JPMorgan Chase in spring of 2008. For further discussion, see Thomas (2008) and *The Economist* (November 14, 2009).

Another type of fraud involves deceptive claims by manufacturers regarding product effectiveness. Recent examples of false claims that were investigated by the Federal Trade Commission (FTC) include the following:

- From 2003 to 2004, Window Rock Enterprises claimed that its CortSlim tablets cause users to lose up to 4–10 pounds a week and lose weight specifically in the stomach and thighs. The ads were particularly insidious because the company used infomercials designed to look like independent television programs.[20]
- From 2005 to 2009, POM Wonderful claimed that its POM Wonderful 100% Pomegranate Juice and its POMx supplements prevented or treated heart disease and prostate cancer.[21]
- In 2009, Dutchman Enterprises claimed that its Hydro-Assist Fuel Cell would double fuel mileage. One magazine ad claimed that it boosted a 2007 Honda Civic's mileage from 35 to 85 miles per gallon.[22]

Such statements are patently false, which is why the FTC successfully forced these companies to cease and desist making these dishonest claims.[23]

As we saw in Chap. 16, deception such as this is frequently associated with advertising. Although the concept of truth may seem black and white, the concept of false and deceptive advertising is not quite as clear. For an ad to be a violation of the law, it must clearly mislead a "reasonable" consumer. Ads that are obvious exaggerations or "puffing" are acceptable from a legal standpoint. This applies to claims that are not easily measurable and that use adjectives such as best, perfect, exceptional, original, and wonderful. As we discussed in Chap. 16, examples include: Apple Computers, "The Power to be Your Best"; Coke, "It's the Real Thing"; and Minute Rice, "Perfect Rice Every Time."

Another example of a deceptive tactic is something called "reference price advertising" (Lindsey-Mullikin and Petty, 2011). This is where a retailer advertises a sale price for its product that is substantially below a reference price, typically the "manufacturer's suggested list price," which is much higher than the price charged at most stores. Thus, consumers are deceived into believing that the deal is a better bargain than it really is. Reference price advertising can discourage consumer search for lower priced outlets and lead to higher prices overall.

---

[20] For a more complete review of this case, see http://www.ftc.gov/opa/2004/10/windowrock.shtm.

[21] For a more complete review of this case, see http://www.ftc.gov/opa/2010/11/pom.shtm.

[22] For a more complete review of this case, see http://www.ftc.gov/opa/2009/02/dutchman.shtm.

[23] This is a common remedy. In extreme cases, the FTC has ordered a company to spend 25% of its previous year's ad budget on corrective advertising, which corrects the misinformation created by the false claim. In *ITT Continental Baking Co.*, 79 FTC 248 (1971), the ITT Continental Baking Company marketed its Profile brand of bread as a diet bread. Although each slice of Profile was lower in calories than a slice of most other brands of bread, this is because it was sliced thinner. As a result of this deception, the FTC required ITT Continental Baking to use corrective ads to inform consumers that Profile is not a diet bread. See Pitofsky (1977) for further discussion and additional examples. These issues will be discussed more fully in Chap. 20.

When firm actions of this nature cross the line of social responsibility, the primary source of market failure is imperfect and incomplete information. It would be uneconomic for firms to use deceptive or false claims if consumers had full information about the products they purchase. Even with incomplete information, such problems would not occur for search goods, because consumers can determine whether or not a claim is false before purchase. Information problems are more problematic for experience and credence goods where not all product characteristics are apparent before purchase. This is a growing concern in a modern society where products have become increasingly complex. For this reason, deceptive and fraudulent actions that are "materially damaging" to consumers are illegal, an issue that we discuss in some detail in Chap. 20.

In spite of these examples, not all corporations behave irresponsibly. After all, life is full of risks, and it may not be cost effective from society's perspective to make all products perfectly safe. In addition, firms that value consumer loyalty and future sales have an economic incentive to behave in a socially responsible manner. That is, socially beneficial behavior today builds up a corporation's reputation, which enhances long-run profits. This motivates successful firms to supply consumers with quality products at competitive prices. Of course, there may be owners of firms who behave responsibly out of a sense that it is simply the "right thing to do." Thus, ethical behavior can survive in a marketplace when firms care about repeat sales and when there are generally accepted moral values.

Hafner and Deutsch (2005) document corporate donations made to victims of Hurricane Katrina. Wal-Mart donated $17 million, as well as 100 truckloads of goods, to the Gulf Coast. Amgen, a biotechnology company, donated $2.5 million to help cover medical costs. General Electric donated a portable power plant. Even companies that did not do business in the south and would not benefit directly from donating have contributed funds to disaster victims.

It is clear from this discussion that both socially desirable and undesirable behaviors are observed in the marketplace. The important policy question is what factors encourage desirable behavior and discourage undesirable behavior. One way to think about this is to consider the firm's problem from a game theoretic perspective. A firm that plans to be in business for many years will value its reputation. Such a firm will behave in a socially responsible manner today because it values repeat customers and future sales. Firms that are more likely to behave irresponsibly are those with managers who are myopic and place little value on the future. These would include the fly-by-night companies that we discussed in Chap. 15. We can also expect to see more irresponsible behavior in markets where it takes time for consumers to learn about firm deception. This would be more likely in markets with credence goods, goods that are complex, and goods that are purchased infrequently. The Ford Pinto fits this description. It is policy issues such as these that we discuss in the next chapter.

19.2.2 Market Power and the Distribution of Income and Wealth

Previous research suggests that one element of distributive justice is the principle of just deserts in which those who put forth greater effort and make greater investments in the future receive greater compensation. But what about income and wealth that derive from market power or pure luck?[24]

Many of the richest Americans received their wealth from inheritance. Being born into the right family is one way to end up rich. For instance, five of the richest 136 Americans in 2010 inherited their wealth from Sam Walton of Wal-Mart.[25] Canterbery and Nosari (1985) report that inheritance accounts for a large share of the wealth among the richest 400 Americans.

Another concern is that some of the richest Americans derived their wealth from market power.[26] After all, the wealthy are more likely to benefit from the profits associated with market power than the poor. For example, Bill Gates was the wealthiest American in 2010, with a net worth of $54 billion. Most of this wealth derived from profits earned by Microsoft, a near monopoly seller of computer operating system software. Although a portion of his success is due to innovative genius and hard work, Gates himself admits that his success is partially due to luck (Manes and Andrews, 2002). We discuss Microsoft in more detail in Chap. 21.

We might consider the distribution of income and wealth an issue of social concern for two reasons. The first is based on the growing trend towards greater inequality in income and wealth in the USA and on the egalitarian principle, which advocates the elimination of economic inequality among individuals.

The second reason why distributional issues may be of social concern is that rewards that derive from luck and static market power are not consistent with what most people consider to be fair. Such rewards cannot be fully justified by the three criteria that are emerging from the unifying theory of distributive justice. That is, there is no need-based rationalization for such rewards. Neither are these rewards entirely attributable to greater effort. Thus, allowing individuals to gain from market power and to pass along an inheritance to others may not be needed to encourage hard work and improve static efficiency.[27] On the other hand, individual gains from market power that promote dynamic efficiency may be justified. Regarding luck, experimental work by Johansson-Stenman and Konow (2009) indicates that most people believe that it is fair to redistribute from lucky to unlucky

---

[24] Buchanan (1986) identifies four determinants of income and wealth: effort, choice, luck, and birth.

[25] For a list of the richest 400 Americans in 2010, see *Forbes*, October 11, 2010 at http://www.forbes.com/wealth/forbes-400/list?page=1, accessed July 23, 2011.

[26] Siegfried et al. (1995) and Hazlett and Siegfried (1997) estimate that market power is responsible for about a third of the greatest fortunes in Australia, Great Britain, New Zealand, and the USA.

[27] Alternatively, one could argue that individuals may work hard to provide their children with an inheritance and should be free to do so in a society that values liberty.

risk takers. At the same time, most people also believe that the socially productive risk taker should receive a larger share of the economic pie.

Two common indices that are used to describe income and wealth inequality are the concentration ratio and the Gini coefficient. In this context, a concentration ratio measures the total income (or wealth) held by various income groups. The Gini coefficient derives from the Lorenz curve and equals 0 when there is perfect equality and equals 1 when there is maximum inequality.[28] Since the late 1960s, both measures indicate a trend towards greater concentration of income and wealth in the USA. The Gini coefficient of household income rose from 0.40 to 0.47 from 1967 to 2008 (Smeeding and Thompson, 2010). From 1989 to 2007, the concentration of income earned by the richest 10% of the population rose from 67.2% to 71.2% (Kennickell, 2009). Concentration of wealth is even more pronounced, with a Gini coefficient of 0.79 in 1989 and 0.81 in 2007 (Kennickell, 2009).[29]

There has been considerable speculation about the reasons why the rich have benefitted more than the poor from economic growth in the last several decades. Possible explanations include the fact that the rich are better able to afford a college education, technological change and free trade have benefitted white collar relative to blue collar workers, and changes in corporate tax laws have benefitted the wealthy relative to others. Another issue is whether market power benefits the wealthy more than the poor.

The little evidence that exists on this subject suggests that the wealthy benefit most from market power. Regarding income, Powell (1987) discovered that the middle class spent a larger share of their income than the rich and the poor on goods and services from high concentration industries. In addition, she found that most of the profits attributable to market power went to the wealthiest Americans.[30] Her analysis indicates that if concentration in highly concentrated manufacturing industries were reduced to unconcentrated levels (i.e., four-firm concentration ratios were no more than 40% and the Herfindahl–Hirschman index was no more than 1,000, as discussed in Chap. 8), the wealthiest sixth of the population would suffer a net loss in income of 1.45%. Everyone else would receive an average gain in income of between 0.3% and 0.7%.

Comanor and Smiley (1975) address a more daunting question—to what extent have monopoly (or oligopoly) profits earned from 1890 to 1962 contributed to the disparity of wealth in the USA? To answer this question, they assume: (1) the

---

[28] The Lorenz curve is a graph of the cumulative distribution function of income (wealth), with the vertical axis representing the cumulative share of people's income (wealth) and the horizontal axis representing the cumulative share of people, who are ordered from lowest to highest income (wealth) levels. With an equal distribution of income (wealth), the Lorenz curve is a 45° line. With an unequal distribution, the Lorenz curve falls below the 45° line. The Gini coefficient is defined as the area between the 45° line and the Lorenz curve divided by the area under the 45° line. For a more complete discussion of the Lorenz curve and Gini coefficient, see Wolff (2009).

[29] For further discussion, see Wolff (2009) and Smeeding and Thompson (2010).

[30] Similarly, Creedy and Dixon (1998) found that low-income households paid a larger share of the welfare loss due to monopoly power in Australia.

transfer from consumers to monopoly producers was proportional to current wealth; (2) monopoly profits were 2% of gross national product; (3) monopoly profits were distributed in proportion to current wealth; and (4) the average life of market power in a given market was 10 to 40 years.[31] Their estimates indicate that eliminating monopoly profits would have benefited the poor relative to the rich. The richest 2.4% of the population would have experienced a reduction in wealth, falling from 40% to 32% of US wealth. The poorest 60% of the population would have experienced a gain in wealth, increasing from 8% to 13% of US wealth. More recently, Siegfried et al. (1995) found similar results, although they also showed that market power is responsible for only about a third of the greatest fortunes in Australia, Great Britain, and the USA.[32]

We should keep three caveats in mind when assessing the evidence regarding market power and the distribution of income and wealth. First, increased globalization has made the economy more competitive over the last several decades, so that there may be declining gains from market power to distribute. Second, some may feel that it is inappropriate to redistribute money from the rich to the poor in a society that values freedom. Individuals who work hard to accumulate money for their children should be allowed to do so.[33] Third, a redistributive policy may negatively impact dynamic efficiency. Hopefully, renewed interest in equity issues within the profession will revive this area of research in industrial organization.

19.3 Summary

1. In this book, we focus on three dimensions of economic performance: static efficiency, dynamic efficiency, and equity. The main goal of this chapter is to assess whether or not imperfectly competitive markets meet these performance standards.
2. There are four concepts of static economic efficiency. The first two apply to the firm, and the second two apply to the industry. The first is technical efficiency, which is reached when a firm uses the fewest inputs to produce a given output. The second is economic efficiency, which is reached when a firm combines

---

[31] These assumptions are designed to minimize the benefit that the wealthy receive from monopoly profits. Thus, the transfer of wealth due to market power to the wealthy is biased downwards.

[32] Hazlett and Siegfried (1997) find similar results for New Zealand.

[33] Another concern with inheritance taxes is that they apply to financial wealth and not inherited genes from parents. If it is fair to tax away all inheritance that is financial, it would also be fair to tax away inherited genetic gifts from parents. For example, Payton Manning and Eli Manning are successful quarterbacks in the NFL primarily because their father is Archie Manning, a former NFL quarterback. To tax away financial inheritance and not genetic inheritance would be unfair to financial inheritance recipients.

inputs to minimize the cost of producing a given output. The third type is allocative efficiency, which is met when an industry produces the socially desirable level of output. This occurs when production takes place where price equals marginal cost. Finally, productive efficiency is reached when industry output is produced at lowest cost.

3. The model that serves as a benchmark for static allocative efficiency is perfect competition. Most, but not all, models suggest that allocative inefficiency will exist in imperfectly competitive markets.

4. The empirical evidence discussed in Chap. 12 confirms that price exceeds marginal cost in many imperfectly competitive markets, particularly in markets with few competitors. The evidence seems to suggest that the cost of allocative inefficiency for the economy as a whole is less than 3% of gross domestic product.

5. Rent-seeking behavior can also be a problem in imperfectly competitive markets. This occurs when a firm lobbies government to gain or maintain its market power. A few studies tackled the difficult problem of estimating the cost of rent seeking and found that it can be substantial.

6. The presence of X-inefficiency adds further to the social cost of market power. X-inefficiency occurs when a firm fails to minimize its costs. The theory suggests that sufficient competition is required for cost minimization, implying that X-inefficiency is more likely in monopoly and oligopoly markets. There is evidence that X-inefficiency results from inadequate competition.

7. The empirical evidence suggests that the social cost of rent-seeking activity and X-inefficiency may be a policy concern over and above allocative inefficiency alone.

8. Dynamic efficiency is considerably more complex than static efficiency. In a dynamic market where addiction or learning-by-doing is present, the equality of price and marginal cost does not imply allocative efficiency. At the same time, high concentration may be associated with greater innovative activity and, therefore, dynamic efficiency. Further research is needed to determine the extent to which our political-economic system is dynamically efficient.

9. New research indicates that most people agree that distributive justice and equity depend upon three competing elements: need, just deserts, and efficiency. That is, the pie should be divided in a way that gives more to those with greater need, that gives more to those who contribute more, and that promotes efficiency.

10. Ideally, firms should behave in a responsible manner. Marketing campaigns should reflect social norms, and sellers should not defraud their customers. The evidence shows that firms have not always behaved responsibly. Nevertheless, firms have contributed large sums of money to charitable causes, even companies that would not benefit directly from these gifts. We are more likely to observe responsible behavior from companies that care about their reputations and in markets where deception is readily apparent to consumers.

11. The evidence shows that many of the richest Americans obtained their wealth from inheritance and that the wealthy have received a greater share of profits that

derive from market power. Some might view these as ill-gotten gains that should be taxed and redistributed, while others may feel that this is inappropriate in a free society. After all, if parents want to give their hard-earned wealth to their children, why should they not be allowed to do so? These are serious equity issues that may grow in importance if the wealth gap between rich and poor continues to widen in the USA.

19.4 Review Questions

1. Briefly describe the four concepts of static efficiency that are used in this book: technical efficiency, economic efficiency, allocative efficiency, and productive efficiency.
2. Distinguish between static and dynamic efficiency. Explain why it is more difficult to estimate allocative inefficiency in a dynamic market than a static market.
3. Explain how the intensity of competition affects X-inefficiency.
4. Explain the relationship between market power and rent-seeking behavior.
5. Describe the efficiency–equity trade-off. Why might equity diminish when a society places greater emphasis on efficiency, and vice versa?
6. The evidence shows that private firms do not always behave in a socially responsible manner.

   A. Under what conditions will a profit-maximizing firm be less likely to behave responsibly?
   B. What are the policy implications of your answer to part A above? In other words, what should be the rules of the game in business?

7. Monopoly profits tend to benefit the rich relative to the rest of society. One solution would be to tax away all excess economic profits and redistribute the proceeds in a more equitable manner. Although this may promote equity, why might it be dynamically inefficient?

Chapter 20
Antitrust Law and Regulation

Laws and regulations touch nearly every aspect of our lives. Most states require children to wear a helmet when riding a bicycle.[1] The US Department of Agriculture requires that your "cheese pizza" contain no more than 11% of a cheese substitute. Food containing more than one ingredient can be labeled "organic" only if at least 95% of its contents are organic.[2] Your power company cannot raise its rates without regulatory approval.

To live safe and prosperous lives, we need the state or government to define the rules of the game and establish institutions that promote socially desirable outcomes using socially acceptable means. We also need a court system to settle disputes. Government involvement is minor in a free market and pronounced in a regulated market or for a publicly owned firm. We have seen that when an ideal set of conditions are met, free markets are efficient.[3] Markets fail, however, when public goods, externalities, uncertainty, and market power are present. When this happens, government intervention can improve social welfare. Interventions include laws, which define illegal individual and business activities, and regulations, which give a government agency control over firm behavior.

From a normative perspective, we want government policies to promote the interests of society, which is called the **public-interest theory** of law and regulation. There are two major concerns with this view of government. First, the evidence shows that our political representatives do not always pursue the goals of society at large. Politicians have their own agendas, such as getting reelected, and respond to the interests of their constituents and the lobbying efforts of special

---

[1] For a detailed list of helmet laws by state, see the Web page of the Bicycle Helmet Safety Institute at http://www.bhsi.org/mandator.htm.

[2] This means that it must be produced without chemical fertilizers, insecticides, chemical herbicides, or given growth hormones or antibiotics. For a discussion of US Department of Agriculture (USDA) regulations, see http://www.fsis.usda.gov and http://usda-fda.com.

[3] Although we focus primarily on efficiency issues in this chapter, as discussed in Chaps. 1 and 19 both equity and efficiency are important to society.

V.J. Tremblay and C.H. Tremblay, *New Perspectives on Industrial Organization*,
Springer Texts in Business and Economics, DOI 10.1007/978-1-4614-3241-8_20,
© Springer Science+Business Media New York 2012

interest groups. Lobbying by large corporations is especially common, because they frequently have much at stake when a government policy is enacted or rescinded. Based on these concerns, the **interest-group theory** was developed, which states that government officials respond in a self-interested way to the demand for new laws and regulations that derive from individual firms, voters, and interest groups. When policy is driven by special interest groups, "government failure" may result.

The second concern with the public-interest approach is that it ignores the cost of government. When a particular market failure costs society $1 billion but the most effective government policy to correct it costs $1.1 billion, government action is not socially worthwhile. In this case the market outcome, although imperfect, is the most desirable outcome possible. As a result, proper policy analysis requires a comparative institution approach (Demsetz 1969).[4] That is, we should compare a real market outcome with a real alternative that takes into account all benefits and costs of government intervention. We would then enact the government policy that produces the greatest net gain for society.

Proper policy analysis requires that we follow three steps. First, we should evaluate the effect of the policy on static efficiency. Second, we should evaluate the expected long run effect of the policy on dynamic efficiency. This would include all possible gains or losses from product and process innovations. Finally, we should estimate the cost of implementing and enforcing the policy. If efficiency is the only criterion, then the policy should be implemented only when (static plus dynamic) efficiency gains outweigh the cost of the policy. Existing policies that fail this test should be rescinded. In practice, this is a difficult task given that we are talking about expected future benefits and costs of a government policy. As a result, we will frequently consider the expected benefits of a policy and ignore the cost of government (i.e., we consider steps one and two but ignore step three). We can think of this as the beginning of a more complete analysis of a policy that identifies necessary conditions to make a policy worthwhile.

The range of topics involving legal and regulatory policies is too broad to cover in a single chapter. In fact, we could devote a whole book to each topic. As a result, we focus on just four main themes. First, we briefly discuss law and economics, outlining several philosophical underpinnings of the law, evaluating the relative efficiency of the common and civil law systems, and identifying factors that influence the evolution of a legal system. Second, we describe the major US antitrust laws and review major court cases that have helped shape their evolution regarding monopoly, collusion, and mergers. Third, we discuss the economics of regulation/deregulation, focusing on the regulation of a firm's primary strategic variables: price, output, and advertising. These issues are associated with market power due

---

[4] Comparing market outcomes with and without a government policy that ignores the cost of government is called the "nirvana" approach to public policy analysis by Demsetz (1969). Noll (1989a, b) argued that ideally (1) a corrective policy is enacted only when genuine market failure exists and after an optimal policy is identified; (2) the policy is rescinded once it is no longer socially beneficial.

to imperfect competition, a fundamental concern in industrial organization. We also consider behavioral tendencies and regulatory issues in relation to product safety.[5] Finally, we briefly discuss social regulations, those that address issues related to the environment and consumer welfare.

20.1 An Introduction to Law and Economics

The disciplines of law and economics are more closely linked than you might think. Laws that regulate corporations can affect market supply by changing firm behavior and the cost of doing business, and laws affecting consumers can influence market demand. Poor business performance can lead to new legislation designed to correct market imperfections. The great recession or financial crisis of 2008–2009 provides one example, where excessive risk taking in the financial sector led to stiffer government regulations regarding lending. We begin this chapter with a brief discussion of the field of law and economics.[6]

20.1.1 The Philosophy of Law[7]

Every country has a legal system that consists of a set of rules that influence market outcomes and govern the behavior of individuals and (public and private) institutions. A legal system has three important characteristics. First, it is a social phenomenon. Laws are unnecessary if you live alone on an island. With more and more people, social interaction occurs, some of which will be undesirable. Typically, this leads a community to establish laws that protect individuals and their property from harm. Second, law is authoritative. That is, a law establishes rules that are taken seriously because sanctions ensure that they are obeyed.

The third characteristic of law is that it serves a particular aim. We can think of this from a positive or a normative perspective. For centuries, social philosophers have debated the appropriate goal of law. For example, **natural law** theorists view the law from a normative perspective. They argue that law should be a rational standard, should promote the common good, and should be created by those who care for the community.[8] This assumes an absolute moral standard in which

---

[5] When discussing public policy, we restrict our attention to issues involving antitrust and regulation. We do not discuss "industrial policy," which is aimed toward supporting domestic firms in one or more key sectors of the economy to gain a strategic advantage over foreign competitors.

[6] For those interested in further discussion of law and economics, see Cooter and Ulen (2012) and Harrison and Theeuwes (2008).

[7] Discussion in this section derives from Wacks (2006), Murphy (2007), Cooter and Ulen (2012), and Harrison and Theeuwes (2008).

[8] These include Aquinas (1225–1274), Rousseau (1712–1778), and Finnis (1949-).

to guide and judge the law. It is paternalistic and can lead to morals legislation. Christian natural law theorists such as Aquinas (1225–1274), a Catholic theologian, argued that human law should conform to God's divine law. Secular natural-law theorists argue that certain actions are intrinsically wrong, even if not originating from God.

Alternatively, **legal positivists** take a more relativist position, arguing that the law derives from social norms. Bentham (1748–1832) thought that an appeal to an absolute moral standard is invalid because it is nothing more than private opinion. Societies with different histories and cultures are likely to have different laws and legal systems, each of which is equally valid. Kelsen (1881–1973), an extreme positivist, argued that ultimate authority resides with the state. His legal order is built on a hierarchical set of norms, with each norm drawing its validity from a higher norm. The ultimate norm, the *Grundnorm*, is taken to be a given or universally accepted fact, such as a country's constitution. Once a state constitution is established, this philosophy gives the state monopoly lawmaking power.

In contrast, **political liberalism** defends the rights of the individual over the rights of the state. John Stuart Mill's *On Liberty* (1859) best illustrates this viewpoint. In it he expresses concern with a state's monopoly control of the law, arguing that state intervention should be constrained by what is now called Mill's Principle (or the harm principle): each individual has the right to act as he or she wants, as long as this action does not directly harm others. This substantially limits the role of the state to achieve the common good, as it implies that the only acceptable laws that limit individual freedom are those that protect others.

Mill also had concerns with democracy, because the majority could limit the rights of the minority.[9] This concern provides further support for placing a high value on individual freedom. It also motivates a political system that has checks and balances designed to limit the power of any one branch of government.

There are abundant examples of government abuse of power throughout history. Under Hitler in Nazi Germany, the government killed an estimated 6 million Jews and 5 million other "undesirables" (i.e., Gypsies, political opponents of Nazism, etc.). Records show that in the American South, more than 2,500 African-Americans, including 50 women, were lynched between 1889 and 1918 (Wacks 2006, 57). By order of President Roosevelt, US citizens of Japanese descent were placed in internment (i.e., concentration) camps from 1942 to 1945 during World War II. Japanese-American citizens not only lost their liberty but lost much of their property as well (Higgs 1978). These violations of basic human rights raise the classic question, "who should monitor the monitors" in a society?

Mill is not the only one to voice concern with the state's inability to enact socially desirable laws. For example, the Marxist view is that the law is enacted to benefit those with economic and political power. Moreover, legal realists express

---

[9] Horowitz (2009) argued that a similar problem exists on college campuses. He is concerned that the majority of college professors are liberal, which makes it difficult to hire conservatives and leads to a lack of intellectual diversity.

concern with both the law and its enforcement, especially when applied to women, minorities, and the poor. We will see that those in power can shape the evolution of government regulation of business. Thus, studying laws (and regulations) from a normative and a positive perspective can be useful.

20.1.2 Arrow's Impossibility Theorem

When choosing among a set of policies (laws or regulations), you might ask whether there is a rule we can use to make such decisions and maximize social welfare. Kenneth Arrow (1951) addressed this issue. His goal was to identify a social welfare function that can be used to make such decisions. According to Arrow, it should meet the following conditions:

- The social welfare function should satisfy the same general properties as a utility function. That is, it should be complete, transitive, and monotonic.[10]
- If everyone prefers alternative x (a basket of goods or a particular legal option) to alternative y, the social welfare function should rank x ahead of y.
- The social rank of x and y should not depend on the social rank of another alternative z. This is called the independence of irrelevant alternatives assumption.
- The social welfare function should not reflect the preference of just one member of society (i.e., a dictator) but should reflect the preferences of all members of society.

What Arrow was able to prove is that no such function exists. In addition, a function that meets the first three requirements must be dictatorial. This is called **Arrow's Impossibility Theorem** or the Dictator Theorem.[11]

The theorem explains why no political system is perfect and why social decisions are made by a political process that has been rather messy throughout history. Simple voting rules fail to meet all of the conditions above. Thus, democracies need not produce socially optimal results. In theory, a benevolent dictator could produce a social optimal outcome, but because power corrupts, dictators are rarely benevolent. Thus, the best we can expect is a system that allows for an open dialogue about the merits of a policy, gives limited power to voters, politicians, and the courts in making and enforcing policy, and enables policies to be rescinded when they are no longer socially desirable.

---

[10] When considering two alternatives x and y (e.g., different baskets of goods or different legal options), preferences are complete when they clearly identify whether x is preferred to y, y is preferred to x, or that x and y are equally valued. When we add a third alternative (z), preferences are transitive when the following condition holds: if x is preferred to y and y is preferred to z, then x is preferred to z. Monotonicity implies welfare does not decline with the increase of a good.

[11] For an excellent summary of welfare economics and of Arrow's Impossibility Theorem, see Varian (2010, Chap. 33).

20.1.3   Legal Systems and the Evolution of the Law

In the western world, two main systems are used to make social decisions and establish laws, the common law and civil law systems. The **common law system** derives from England where disputes were originally decided by a king's court and were based on social norms, decrees from the king, and previous decisions (judicial precedent). This system gives the court a certain degree of discretion and the power to change law through the establishment of a new precedent. The set of such decisions is called "the common law" because it is said to derive from the common norms of the people. Today, the legal systems of countries that were colonized by England are based on the common law tradition, including the USA, Australia, Canada, Ireland, New Zealand, and parts of Africa and Asia.

Civil law, sometimes called Roman law, derives from the Corpus Juris Civilis ("The Body of Civil Law"). It was compiled in 528–534 AD by order of the Emperor of the Eastern Roman Empire, Justinian I, and included a collection of fundamental works on Roman and other law. The main characteristic of this system of law is that decisions over disputes are based on a comprehensive set of statutes and codes (i.e., rules), leaving less room for judicial discretion. This tradition spread to most of continental Europe through France. With the French Revolution at the end of the eighteenth century, revolutionaries thought that judges as well as the king were corrupt. Thus, the people killed the king, ousted his judges, and destroyed the common laws of France. In its place, France adopted a system of civil law which set up well defined codes and gave judges little discretionary power. Conquests by Napoleon and later French colonization spread this system to much of Europe, Central and South America, and parts of Asia.[12]

This demonstrates how historical events influence a country's legal system, but other forces are also important. Early authors used efficiency arguments to explain the evolutionary path of a legal system.[13] In its simplest form, the **evolution to efficient laws hypothesis** says that (1) a legal system will be established once the benefits exceed the costs of doing so and (2) specific laws, regulations, and government institutions are selected and evolve in ways that produce more efficient outcomes.

Coase's (1960) theorem provides one mechanism by which laws may evolve for efficiency reasons. It implies that if transaction costs are zero and property rights are well defined, lobbying by affected parties will cause legislators to adopt efficient laws and regulations, eliminating market failure. With market frictions, however, the evolution to efficient laws can take time. The evolutionary process may occur as follows. Once a law is established, affected parties are more likely to challenge it in

---

[12] We do not want to over generalize, however. As Cooter and Ulen (2012) pointed out, US states have adopted a set of codes for commercial business (the Uniform Commercial Code), which is in keeping with civil law. In addition, La Porta et al. (2008) pointed out that French courts have gained greater discretion over time.

[13] For example, see Demsetz (1967), Alchian and Demsetz (1972), Priest (1977), Rubin (1977), and Posner (1980). For a summary of this argument, see Harrison and Theeuwes (2008).

court if it turns out to be inefficient. The potential gains are greater from overturning a law that is inefficient. In addition, most violations of efficient laws are settled out of court. Thus, judges are more likely to rule and set a new precedent in a case involving an inefficient law. Even if only half of all judges support a more efficient ruling, the law will eventually evolve through a series of court precedents in an efficient direction.

Alchian and Demsetz (1973) provided an example in support of this theory, regarding the development of (private property) land laws in thirteenth century England. Before that time, much of the grazing land for sheep was a common property resource.[14] Initially, this was an efficient system because the population was low and only a few sheep grazed on the land. Thus, the grass grew faster than the existing sheep could consume it. With a rising population, more sheep were put on the land. This ultimately made grass scarce and created a negative externality: the more grass that my sheep consume the less grass for your sheep, a cost I will ignore if I am a profit maximizer. This led to overgrazing and an inefficient use of grazing land. One way to deal with the externality is to create private property rights by converting public lands into private property. With this right, each owner can exclude others by putting up a fence, thus eliminating the externality. According to Alchian and Demsetz, this is what happened in thirteenth century England during the "enclosure movement" when the benefits began to exceed the costs of defining and enforcing private land rights.

Although this theory appears to explain why private land laws developed in England, it does not explain why the common law system and the civil law system have existed for so long and continue to this day. If one is more efficient than the other, it should eventually become the dominant legal system.

A number of scholars suggest that the evolution of a legal system is driven by forces other than efficiency alone. Stigler (1971) proposed that government officials respond to the lobbying efforts of special interest groups which pressure for (demand) new laws and regulations that benefit these groups. Thus, legislation is driven by the power and influence of these special interest groups. This is similar in some ways to the viewpoints of Marxists and legal theorists.

Roe (1996) argued that historical accidents and specific circumstances play an important role in shaping a legal system. For instance, initial conditions associated with the French Revolution explain why France suddenly favored a system that emphasized rules over government/court discretion. Given different starting points, it is not surprising that the British and French systems took different evolutionary paths. Efficiency may still be relevant, however, and one would expect one country to change to another legal system if it is clearly the efficient thing to do. If switching costs are sufficiently high though, neither country will switch. In other words, different starting conditions and high switching costs preserve the status quo, allowing both systems to coexist even if one is more efficient than the other. Thus, history matters, especially when the cost of change is high.

---

[14] Recall that this means that everyone could use the land, and no one could be excluded from use.

An emerging literature evaluates the relative efficiency of different legal systems, **legal origins theory**. Research shows that the historical origin of a legal system can affect the way a country relies on rules versus discretion in dealing with social and economic issues. This in turn influences economic regulation and performance.[15] La Porta et al. (2008) surveyed the evidence and found that there are different strengths and weaknesses associated with the common law and civil law systems.[16] Their survey shows the following distinguishing characteristics:

- Although judges in both the common and civil law systems are limited by the rules of law, judges have greater discretion in the common law system. Thus, the common law system is somewhat more flexible than the civil law system.
- In response to market failure, common law systems tend to add regulations that buttress markets. Civil law systems are more likely to restrict markets.
- The common law system provides better contract enforcement and better protection to stockholders and creditors, giving greater security to contracts and private property.[17]

These differences suggest that a common law system is more consistent with market-focused capitalism, while a civil law system is more consistent with state-centered capitalism (or socialism).

Which system will be more efficient in the real world? Is court discretion or fixed rules better from society's perspective? The main advantage of the strict rules approach is that it provides better clarity, which reduces uncertainty and the transactions costs of reaching a legal decision. The trade-off is that it can lead to serious errors when change is warranted. The reverse is true with a discretionary legal system. It promises fewer errors by allowing the courts to review the extenuating circumstances of a case, but it comes at the cost of greater uncertainty and higher transaction costs.[18]

Thus, each legal system has its advantages and disadvantages. Generally, when the political-economic environment is stable, fixed rules associated with a civil law system will be more efficient. In a more dynamic setting, discretion is valuable because it enables judges to shape the law in response to new circumstances and social problems.[19] This suggests that a civil law system will be more efficient in a

---

[15] The literature is too extensive to list here. For a review of the evidence, see Dam (2006), La Porta et al. (2008), and Roe and Siegel (2009).

[16] Not all agree with the simple interpretation and with La Porta et al.'s argument that the common law system is more flexible than the civil law system today. For alternative viewpoints, see Dam (2006), Fairfax (2009), and Roe and Siegel (2009).

[17] Glaeser and Shleifer (2002, 1194) concluded that "[o]n just about any measure, common law countries are more financially developed than civil law countries."

[18] For further discussion of these trade-offs as they relate to antitrust enforcement, see Beckner and Salop (1999) and Baker and Bresnahan (2008).

[19] For example, Heart (1994) argued that discretion is especially valuable in the "penumbra," or grey areas of the law, where a judge may use the entire body of legal knowledge to make a decision and set a precedent.

stable world, and a common law system will be more efficient in a dynamic setting. From an equity perspective and assuming an uncorrupt court system, a certain degree of discretion may be worthwhile if each case involving issues of fairness has a unique set of circumstances. Such a system is said to allow an individual to "throw oneself at the mercy of the court."

Empirical evidence regarding the relative efficiency of these legal systems is just emerging. The evidence reported by La Porta et al. (2008) indicates that countries with common law systems are associated with better economic outcomes in terms of economic growth, unemployment, and education. If these results hold up to continued scientific scrutiny, the common law system would appear to be better at promoting efficiency; sufficiently high switching costs may explain why both systems continue to survive, which is consistent with Roe's (1996) viewpoint.

Without perfect foresight, it is difficult to say which legal system will be best in the future. A change in the economic environment could make the civil law system more efficient. Civil law countries may anticipate greater stability in the future, making it unwise to switch. In addition, in an uncertain world, there may be less risk to the world economy with a diverse set of legal systems.

Nevertheless, the legal origins theory has important implications for the type and extent of market intervention we would expect to see in countries that have a common law system like the USA. For example, when a change increases the benefits of deregulation, one would expect that the USA would be more likely to deregulate than a country under a civil law system. One would also expect to see considerable change in the enforcement of US antitrust law over time. These are issues we take up in subsequent sections.

Before leaving this topic, we want to emphasize that the empirical evidence regarding the legal origins theory is preliminary. It is difficult to test the theory, because it is hard to control for all of the political, social, and economic forces at work. Further, the relative efficiency of common versus civil law systems may vary over time with changing economic circumstances. This is an issue that future scholars will need to address.

In any case, government response to the financial crisis of 2008–2009 provides some insights into the validity of the legal origins theory. Fairfax (2009) argued that the US response was legislative and executive rather than judicial, which is more in keeping with a civil law system. However, this may simply imply that a legislative response is appropriate, regardless of the legal system, when dealing with a crisis. In any case, Fairfax showed that the response was designed to shore up (banking and automobile) markets rather than nationalize them, which is in keeping with legal origins theory.

20.2 Antitrust Law

A review of US antitrust cases allows us to see how one set of laws has evolved over time. In principle, antitrust legislation is designed to promote competition and limit the negative effect of market power. Typically, the legislature establishes rather general antitrust principles, and the courts are expected to fill in the gaps. Court precedents modify the law, causing it to evolve toward efficiency in many cases. In this section, we summarize major legislation and court precedents that help to define antitrust enforcement today.

20.2.1 Antitrust Legislation

Public interest in antitrust legislation began in the late nineteenth century when railroads opened up new markets in the west, large-scale corporations began to flourish, and the formation of business "trusts" became common. A trust is another word for a cartel, which consists of a group of firms in a single industry that come together to increase profits through collusion. In response to the growing power of these emerging trusts and larger corporations, the antitrust laws were enacted.

As we saw in Chap. 1, the first law was the **Sherman Act (1890)**, as amended in 1975. The Sherman Act has two important provisions:

Section 1: "Every contract, combination in the form of trust or otherwise, or conspiracy, in restraint of trade or commerce among several states, or with foreign nations, is declared to be illegal."

Section 2: "Every person who shall monopolize, or attempt to monopolize, or combine or conspire with any other person or persons, to monopolize any part of the trade or commerce. . .shall be deemed guilty of a felony."

Section 1 is relatively straightforward and is taken to mean that any cartel agreement that reduces competition is illegal. However, Section 2 fails to provide a precise meaning to the words "conspiracy" and "monopolize," leaving final interpretation to the courts. In addition, enforcement was limited because Congress provided the Department of Justice (DOJ) with no additional funding in 1890 to enforce this new law.

It did not take long before concerns were raised that the Sherman Act failed to challenge various kinds of unreasonable business practices. This led to passage of the Clayton Act and the Federal Trade Commission Act in 1914. There are three key sections in the **Clayton Act (1914)**.

Section 2 makes price discrimination illegal where the effect may be "to substantially lessen competition or tend to create a monopoly." The provision does allow for price differences that reflect differences in costs and to meet the low price of a competitor.[20]

Section 3 makes market restrictions such as exclusive-dealing contracts and tying contracts illegal where the effect is "to substantially lessen competition or tend to create a monopoly."

---

[20] The Robinson-Patman Act (1936) amended Section 2 and gave greater protection to small retailers who were battling the growing chain-store movement in the USA.

Section 7 makes mergers illegal where the effect may be "to substantially lessen competition or tend to create a monopoly."

The original Section 7 had a loophole that allowed mergers by asset acquisition, but the loophole was later eliminated in the **Celler–Kefauver Act (1950)**.

The **Federal Trade Commission Act (1914)** set up a commission of 5 members who were appointed by the President, each to a 7-year term. They, along with members of DOJ, were charged with interpreting and enforcing the antitrust laws. The Act also contained an important provision (Section 5), which states that "the Commission is hereby empowered and directed to prevent persons, partnerships, or corporations...from using unfair methods of competition in commerce." This gives the Federal Trade Commission (FTC) a broad mandate, because it can apply to almost any business activity. The intent of the Act was to bring together a group of experts to address policy issues related to antitrust and business behavior.

20.2.2   Enforcement Procedure and Remedies

In most cases, the antitrust process begins with an investigation by either the FTC or the Antitrust Division of the DOJ. A DOJ case proceeds through the federal court system, from the lower (District and Circuit) courts to the Supreme Court. A decision is rendered by a District Court, but a ruling can be appealed to one of 11 Circuit Courts. Once a Circuit Court makes a ruling, an appeal can be made to the Supreme Court. Cases can also be investigated by the FTC. In general, the case is heard by an administrative law judge who then makes a ruling. The decision can then be appealed to the Circuit Court and the Supreme Court if desired. Finally, private parties that are damaged by violations of the antitrust laws can file suit. Of the three, private suits are the most common, accounting for 94.7% of all antitrust suits in 2009.[21]

When a firm loses an antitrust case, several penalties and remedies are possible. The four main remedies are:

1. **Treble damages**: A plaintiff that can prove harm due to a violation of an antitrust law receives three times the value of damages incurred (plus court costs and legal fees). This provision is designed to encourage private enforcement of the law and discourage antitrust violations.

2. **Fines and jail**: Fines have increased significantly since the Sherman Act was enacted. The original Act set a maximum fine of $5,000 per violation. According to the Antitrust Criminal Penalty Enhancement and Reform Act (2004), the maximum fine per violation is now $100 million for corporations and $1 million for individuals; the maximum jail time for an individual is 10 years per violation.

---

[21] This information is obtained from Andrew E. Ebere, "Private Antitrust Cases Decreased in 2009," Princeton Economics Group, available at http://econgroup.com/peg_news_view.asp?newid=40&pageno=1, accessed October 13, 2010.

3. **Injunctions**: An injunction forbids some specific future business behavior without penalizing the defendant for past behavior. For example, after attempting to merge with a small brewery in Florida in 1960, the Anheuser-Busch Brewing Company was ordered to refrain from purchasing another brewery for 5 years (*U.S. v. Anheuser-Busch*, 1960).
4. **Structural changes**: This is the most dramatic antitrust weapon, as it can be used to split guilty firms into 2 or more independent units. Because it is so difficult to carry out successfully in practice, this remedy is rarely used today.[22]

20.2.3   Important Antitrust Cases and Precedents

With well over a century of enforcement, there are too many antitrust cases to summarize here.[23] Instead, we discuss the most influential cases, those that give you a feel for the ebb and flow of antitrust enforcement and for current antitrust enforcement. Consistent with Roe (1996) and Stigler (1971), historical events and political forces appear to have shaped current enforcement of the law. We will see that political trends and social norms have played a role, especially during the Great Depression when many workers lost their jobs and support waned for free market capitalism.

In the last 40 years, court decisions have been influenced by economic analysis of antitrust enforcement. Beginning in the 1960s, the "Chicago School" began to make headway in its criticism of US antitrust enforcement. Recall from Chap. 1 that the Chicago School represents a philosophy that tends to favor market over government solutions to economic problems. Government policy is thought to be costly to administer and can produce unexpected and socially undesirable consequences, making market failure the lesser of two evils (Wright 2009). Critics of antitrust enforcement include Williamson (1968) and Demsetz (1973, 1974), who identified previously ignored benefits associated with mergers and high levels of concentration. Another concern, expressed by Hayek (1945), is that free markets react more quickly than government to information about changing demand and technological conditions. Finally, Stigler (1971) and Peltzman (1976) questioned the motives of government agencies, arguing that government officials are more likely to promote their own interests than the interest of society.[24]

---

[22] For example, Elzinga (1969) investigated 39 cases involving divesture and found that only 25% were successful.

[23] Reviews of important antitrust cases, including those discussed in this chapter, can be found in Asch (1983), Waldman (1986), Breit and Elzinga (1989), Scherer and Ross (1990), Posner (2001), Hovenkamp (2008), Sherman (2008), Blair and Kaserman (2009), and Kwoka and White (2009).

[24] This new Chicago critique is clearly expressed by Milton Friedman, a leader of the Chicago School, who said: "Because we all believed in competition 50 years ago, we are generally in favor of antitrust.... We've gradually come to the conclusion that, on the whole, it does more harm than good. [Antitrust laws] tend to become prey to the special interests." This quote is taken from an interview for the *Wall Street Journal* by Sieb (1998).

At times, early antitrust enforcement responded to the demands of populists who favored protection of small business. The Chicago School opposed this goal because it could lead to an inefficient outcome, arguing instead that antitrust policy "should" be guided by economic efficiency alone. Over time, this position began to be taken seriously, which led to more permissive enforcement and a greater emphasis on efficiency.

In addition, studies conducted by economists outside and within the Chicago school have shown that narrowing the scope of antitrust enforcement can be socially beneficial. According to Kwoka and White (2009, 1–5) and Crane (2009), this narrower focus has led to a substantial reduction in challenges related to vertical mergers, price discrimination, and conglomerate mergers. The financial crisis of 2008–2009 appears to be changing this focus, leading to greater scrutiny of free markets, especially in the financial sector of the economy. Even before the crisis, a recent series of papers in Pitofsky (2008) presented evidence that the Chicago School "overshot the mark" in the area of antitrust.[25]

Our focus in this section will be on the antitrust cases that have had the greatest effect on the economy, those that involve monopolization, collusion, and mergers. Cases against collusive behavior are reasonably clear and distinct. We will see that monopoly and merger concerns are more difficult to identify: the law does not clearly define what is meant by monopoly, and future consequences of a merger are difficult to predict. We will also see how enforcement has changed over time.

20.2.3.1 Monopolization

Antitrust cases involving monopolization are some of the most dramatic in history, because they involve the largest corporations that have the most to lose from an antitrust conviction. Initial antitrust enforcement proved difficult, given that Section 2 of the Sherman Act failed to define what is meant by the terms "monopolize" and "attempt to monopolize."

The first lawsuit of importance was *Standard Oil of New Jersey v. U.S.* (1911), undoubtedly the most famous antitrust case in history. Standard Oil was owned by the Rockefeller brothers, who grew the company's market share to 90% by the late 1800s. This was accomplished by purchasing more than 120 competitors, foreclosing competitor access to its pipelines and allegedly using localized price cuts[26] to drive some of its toughest rivals out of the market. The Supreme Court ruled against Standard Oil, ordering it to be broken up into such oil companies as Exxon (Standard Oil of New Jersey), Mobil (Standard Oil of New York), Chevron

---

[25] Furthermore, Posner (2009), a Chicago economist and legal scholar, argued uncharacteristically that the recent crisis is due to insufficient government involvement in financial markets. See Wright (2009) for an alternative viewpoint.

[26] However, McGee (1958) argued that Standard Oil did not gain market share through predatory pricing tactics.

(Standard Oil of California), Amoco (Standard Oil of Indiana), and BP America (acquirer of Standard Oil of Ohio).

The significance of this case stems from the Supreme Court's articulation of the **rule of reason** in the restraint of trade. Speaking for the Court, Chief Justice White said:

> If the criterion for judging the legality of a restraint…is the direct or indirect effect of the acts involved, then of course the rule of reason becomes the guide.[27]

Regarding monopolization, the rule of reason came to mean two things: (1) being a monopolist need not be a violation; (2) the firm also had to behave unreasonably. This gives the courts considerable discretion in deciding a case, because the court must evaluate the direct and indirect effect of a firm's action and because reasonable people can disagree about what is unreasonable. In contrast, an action that is a **per se** violation is illegal regardless of the reasonableness or unreasonableness of its social consequences.[28] Thus, there is no legal defense of an action that is a per se violation.

For the next 30 years, subsequent court cases reinforced the rule of reason. Seminal cases include *U.S. v. American Tobacco (1911)*, which led to the breakup of the so called Tobacco Trust, *U.S. v. American Can Co. (1916)* in which American Can won because it did not behave unreasonably, and *U.S. v. United States Steel Company (1920)*. In the US Steel case, the company had gained a 65% market share through horizontal merger, but rather than using tough price competition to drive rivals out of business, US Steel set high prices, which eventually led to new entry and a loss in market share to its competition. Consistent with the rule of reason, US Steel won the case because it had not exercised its market power to harm competition. In the words of the Court:

> …the law does not make mere size an offense or the existence of unexpected power an offense. It … requires overt acts…[29]

Pressure to temper the rule of reason began during the Great Depression of the 1930s. With high unemployment and waning trust in free markets, President Roosevelt favored greater government involvement in business. This led to the appointment of judges who were more supportive of interventionist policies. Roosevelt also appointed Thurman Arnold to head the Antitrust Division of the DOJ in order to revitalize antitrust enforcement.

These events set the stage for the Alcoa case in which Alcoa was charged in 1937 with monopolizing the aluminum ingot market (*U.S. v. Aluminum Company of America*, 1945). By some accounts, Alcoa had market power but had not behaved

---

[27] Quote taken from Breit and Elzinga (1989, 138).

[28] These are sometimes called "bright-line rules," because behavior is per se illegal when it crosses a clear and distinct line.

[29] Quote taken from Breit and Elzinga (1989, 145).

unreasonably, as defined by the rule of reason.[30] It initially gained control of the aluminum market because it held important patents. Further, Alcoa was able to take advantage of economies of scale. The only behavioral concern was the accusation that Alcoa built capacity ahead of demand, making entry more risky. To the Supreme Court, this was sufficient to rule against Alcoa.[31] The Alcoa decision was consistent with two later rulings involving the tobacco industry (*American Tobacco Co. et al. v. U.S.*, 1946) and the motion picture industry (*U.S. v. Griffith Amusement Co.*, 1948). Although these cases did not make monopolization illegal per se, they certainly invigorated antitrust enforcement.

Influence of the Alcoa precedent continued through the mid-1970s. There were no notable decisions in the 1950s and 1960s, but greater scrutiny of industry began in 1965 when the DOJ strengthened its economics staff. Subsequent DOJ studies motivated two important monopolization complaints, one against IBM and the other against AT&T. In 1969, the DOJ filed suit against IBM, claiming that the company had used unfair business practices to monopolize the computer industry. Unlike previous cases, IBM vigorously fought the government's accusations, resulting in an extremely long and expensive trial.[32] Competition in the computer industry substantially increased by the early 1980s, and the Department withdrew its complaint in 1982 because the case no longer had merit.

In 1974 the Department filed suit against AT&T for monopolizing the telecommunications industry. At that time, AT&T owned 22 local telephone companies (providers of local telephone service), Bell Long Lines Division (provider of long distance telephone service), Western Electric (a telephone equipment producer), and Bell Labs (its research division). The Department's complaint charged that AT&T had harmed competition by making purchases exclusively from Western Electric and by excluding access of competing long-distance telephone suppliers to AT&T's telephone network. The complaint recommended that AT&T retain its 22 local telephone companies and divest its other holdings. A milder penalty was imposed when the case was settled out of court in 1982.

---

[30] An important issue was the definition of the market for aluminum. As in all antitrust cases, a first step in determining whether or not a firm has a monopoly position is to correctly define the market. In practice, this is a difficult task, and the courts have sometimes chosen a broad definition and in others a narrow definition of the market. In the Alcoa case, the company's market share was 90% of US ingot production but only 33% of ingot and scrap aluminum production (not including aluminum retained for its own use). Thus, the company argued in favor of a broad definition and the government argued in favor of a narrow definition of the market. The courts chose a narrow definition, which implied that Alcoa had market power. See Scherer and Ross (1990) for further discussion of this issue and its effect on antitrust rulings.

[31] Alcoa was not broken up though. A final remedy was postponed until 1950 when aluminum plants built by the government during World War II and operated by Alcoa were sold at public auction. Alcoa was barred from bidding, and winning bidders formed two new competitors, Reynolds Aluminum and Kaiser Aluminum.

[32] For a detailed discussion of this case, see Fisher et al. (1983).

AT&T agreed to divest of its 22 local telephone companies, just the opposite of what the Department had originally requested.[33]

In the 1970s, new economic analysis began to influence antitrust enforcement. This was a time when a number of economists raised concerns with the social desirability of government regulation and antitrust enforcement. We have already discussed Stigler's (1971) position that government agencies will not pursue the interests of society. Regarding antitrust, Demsetz (1973) superior efficiency hypothesis provides an argument against strict antitrust enforcement.[34] According to Demsetz (1973, 3), many firms gain monopoly power by developing better products or lower cost methods of production. "To destroy such power [through antitrust enforcement] ... may very well remove the incentive for progress." In other words, penalizing a successful firm for monopolizing a market will reduce the firm's incentive to innovate and promote dynamic efficiency. This position appears to be understood by the courts. In *Berkey Photo Inc. v. Eastman Kodak Co.* (1979, 81), the Court said:

> It is the possibility of success in the marketplace, attributable to superior performance, that provides the incentives on which the proper functioning of our competitive economy rests.

The growing support for a more pro-business position is also reflected in President Reagan's appointment of William Baxter to head the Antitrust Division of the DOJ (January 1981 to December 1983). Baxter thought that antitrust laws should promote economic efficiency, a belief that undoubtedly influenced the resolution of the IBM and AT&T cases. His views also motivated a major revision of the 1968 Merger Guidelines that put greater emphasis on efficiency, an issue we will take up later in the chapter.

The final case of interest involves the monopolization of the market for PC operating systems by Microsoft Windows. Not only did the case receive a great deal of national attention, it highlighted a trend toward settling antitrust cases out of court. The suit was filed by the DOJ in 1998 when Windows had a market share in excess of 90%. There were concerns that Microsoft used predatory tactics to drive its competitors out of the market. For example, Microsoft bundled Windows with its Internet browser, Internet Explorer, thus giving Internet Explorer away for free. This put competing browser companies such as Netscape at a tremendous marketing disadvantage. On the other hand, it greatly benefited consumers. An important issue in the case was the presence of network externalities, which thrust Microsoft into a winner-take-all situation, where only the most dynamically efficient firm is likely to survive in the long run.

The courts initially decided to break up the company into two parts, one that produced Windows and the other that produced all other software. Microsoft challenged the decision, and at the end of 2001 the DOJ and Microsoft reached

---

[33] This led to the creation of seven regional phone companies, or "baby bells": NYNEX, Bell Atlantic, Bell South, Ameritech, Southwestern Bell, US West, and Pacific Telesis.

[34] For similar views, see Brozen (1971) and McGee (1971).

an agreement that required Microsoft to refrain from its anticompetitive marketing practices and to reveal much of its computer code to competing software developers. The Microsoft example illustrates what a difficult task it is to assess antitrust cases. On the one hand, Microsoft gained market power by being innovative and providing society with a superior product. On the other hand, once Microsoft had gained power its behavior hurt its competitors. Thus, the final decision may have been the most reasonable one. The company remained intact, which promoted the incentive for progress, but Microsoft's anticompetitive behavior was stopped.[35]

20.2.3.2 Collusion

One of the greatest achievements of the US antitrust laws has been to reduce cartel activity. We learned in Chap. 9 that collusion involves agreements to raise price or restrict output. These agreements increase market power and are therefore economically inefficient. Because collusive agreements are unreasonable from society's perspective, they are generally considered illegal per se today.

Two cases helped establish the doctrine against price-fixing and output restrictions. The first is *Addison Pipe and Steel Co. v. U.S.* (1899). This involved six producers of iron pipe that set up a bid-rigging scheme. The companies divided the market so that each had a regional monopoly. For example, firm 1 would be designated the low bidder in region 1. When bidding on a contract in region 1, other firms would submit fraudulently high bids. This would enable firm 1 to bid a higher price and still be guaranteed the contract. Rather than claim innocence, the companies argued that their behavior was reasonable because it was intended to avoid ruinous price competition. The Court did not accept this argument, however, and although it did not make this a clear per se violation, it made it clear that price-fixing behavior is unreasonable.

The per se doctrine was made transparent in *U.S. v. Trenton Potteries Co.* (1927). This case involved 23 companies from the vitreous pottery industry (makers of bathtubs, sinks, and toilets) that met and agreed to set minimum list prices. The defendants were convicted in district court but won their appeal in circuit court. The reversal was due to the fact that the judge had incorrectly instructed the jury that it could return a guilty verdict without considering the reasonableness of the pricing agreement. The case was then taken to the Supreme Court to evaluate whether the judge's instructions were appropriate. The Court ruled against the defendants, arguing that price fixing is prohibited by the Sherman Act, "despite the reasonableness of the particular prices agreed upon." This is a per se ruling, as it makes price fixing illegal regardless of the circumstances.

---

[35] For a review of the potential costs and benefits of breaking up Microsoft, see Elzinga et al. (2001). For a more detailed account of Microsoft's success and run-ins with antitrust authorities, see the Microsoft case study in Chap. 21.

Nevertheless, the dire economic circumstances of the Great Depression appear to have been sufficient to cause the Court to waiver on its view of price-fixing behavior. The US coal industry was under tremendous stress at the time, with substantial excess capacity, frequent industry losses, and persistent company bankruptcies. In response, 137 companies in the Appalachian region of the country formed Appalachian Coals Inc. as a selling agency for the group. Its sole purpose was to obtain the "best prices" possible for the 137 firms. Based on the Trenton Potteries decision, the government challenged the combination and won the case in 1932. It was overturned by the Supreme Court, however (*Appalachian Coals Inc., v. U.S.*, 1933).

Writing for the 8–1 majority, Judge Hughes argued that an "essential standard of reasonableness" was applied to Appalachian Coals because of the unusual circumstances at the time. Judge Hughes wrote that during the Great Depression:

> [t]he interests of producers and consumers are linked. When industry is grievously hurt, when producing concerns fail, when unemployment mounts . . . the wells of commerce go dry. So far as actual purposes are concerned, the conclusion of the court . . . was amply supported that defendants were engaged in a fair and open endeavor to aid the industry in a measurable recovery from its plight. . . .[36]

This decision is consistent with Roe's (1996) position that historical events and not just efficiency considerations drive court precedents. It also demonstrates how judges in a common law system have sufficient power to modify the law based on a broader set of societal norms and circumstances.

Once the impact of the Great Depression dissipated, the Court quickly reverted back and made collusive behavior illegal per se. In particular, the government won an important price-fixing case involving the oil refining industry (*U.S. v. Socony-Vacuum Oil Co.*, 1940) and a market segmentation case involving the supermarket industry (*U.S. v. Topco Associates Inc.*, 1972). Thus, the Appalachian Coals case was an aberration that had no long-term effect on cartel enforcement.

Although the legal status of collusive agreements concerning price and output are clear, they are per se illegal, enforcement is still a problem. The main difficulty, at least in more recent cases, is that the evidence is usually circumstantial. Because cartels are illegal, agreements are unwritten and kept secret. But without direct evidence of a contract, how can we be sure that a cartel agreement really exists? At times, courts have inferred guilt based on facts short of clear evidence of a conspiracy.

One piece of damaging evidence is when firms within the same industry behave in an identical way. After all, firms in an effective cartel will change their prices (or output levels) in unison and use identical marketing tactics (i.e., have identical agreements with retailers and offer the same financing options and delivery schedules to customers). When there is no proof of a conspiracy but firms behave in unison, their behavior is called **conscious parallelism** (or tacit collusion) by

---

[36] Quote taken from Waldman (1986, 139).

the courts and a unilateral anticompetitive effect in the Horizontal Merger Guidelines (US Department of Justice and the Federal Trade Commission, 1992, 1997, 2010).[37]

Although there will be conscious parallelism in an effective cartel, parallel behavior can occur for innocent reasons as well. In the homogeneous goods Cournot model discussed in Chap. 10, we saw that firm behavior is symmetric. That is, firms will charge the same price, produce the same output level, and respond identically to changes in demand and cost conditions. Asch (1983, 225) calls this "innocent parallelism," which is not illegal. For example, in *Theatre Enterprises Inc., v. Paramount Film Distributing Corp et al.* (1954), the Supreme Court ruled:

> ... this court has never held that proof of parallel business behavior conclusively established agreement or ... that such behavior itself constitutes a Sherman Act offense. Circumstantial evidence of consciously parallel behavior may have made inroads ..., but "conscious parallelism" has not yet read conspiracy out of the Sherman Act entirely.[38]

Without direct evidence of a conspiracy, the courts appear to follow a rule of reason, where a guilty verdict requires evidence of conscious parallelism plus additional damaging evidence. This could include circumstantial evidence of an agreement or of actions that discourage price cutting. For instance, in the 1960s General Electric (GE) and Westinghouse engaged in parallel pricing behavior for their new electric turbines. In 1963, GE announced a set of prices and a price-protection agreement (i.e., a most-favored-customer clause), which guaranteed that if a customer purchases a product today and the product is discounted in the next 6 months, the customer will receive a rebate for the difference in the price. GE also eliminated the possibility of secret price cuts by opening up its books for public inspection. Within days of this policy, Westinghouse followed suit with an identical pricing policy.

There was no question that GE and Westinghouse behaved in a parallel fashion, but further evidence was needed to pursue a conspiracy conviction. One thing to remember is that a most-favored-customer clause can reduce the incentive for firms to cheat on a cartel agreement (see Chap. 9). What sealed the deal was that the DOJ uncovered company documents indicating that the price-protection agreement was intended to stabilize prices. Given the evidence, GE and Westinghouse agreed to a consent decree in 1976 (*U.S. v. General Electric Co. Civil No. 28, 228 E.D. Pennsylvania*, December 1976). Among other things, the consent decree prohibited them from using a price-protection plan and from making their pricing history public.

Before we proceed further, it is important to realize that not all forms of collusion are illegal or harmful to society. One case involved members of the Chicago Board of Trade who competed with each other in the buying and selling of grain contracts. Concern was raised with an agreement among members that any

---

[37] The Guidelines are available at http://www.justice.gov/atr/public/guidelines/hmg.htm#22.

[38] Quote taken from Waldman (1986, 152).

trade after the Board had closed must be transacted at the closing price of that day. The Board argued that the agreement encouraged that transactions only take place during regular business hours. This not only made it easier for the Board to collect and disseminate market information to buyers and sellers, but it also helped avoid a free rider problem. To compensate the Board for providing this service, it charged a small fee on each transaction. But traders could avoid the fee by trading after hours. Fixing the price on late traders imposed a cost on them and discouraged free riding. In this price-fixing case, the Court ruled in favor of the Board because the agreement "merely regulates" and promotes the efficient operation of the market (*Board of Trade of the City of Chicago v. U.S.*, 1918).

Trade associations can also facilitate cooperative behavior that is socially desirable and legal. A trade association is an organization of firms in the same industry with the goal of promoting industry interests. A trade association may collect and disseminate information about demand and technological conditions, an activity that promotes economic efficiency. It can also try to influence public policy in directions favorable to the industry. Antitrust concerns arise when a trade association is used to establish and police price-fixing agreements. Previous court cases indicate that the collection and dissemination of information, even price information, is generally permitted. However, attempts by a trade association to force adherence to a price or to restrict price-cutting behavior are illegal.[39]

Historically, sports and higher education are two markets where the application of antitrust has been both intricate and lax. In professional sports, there are many antitrust exemptions given by the Courts and Congress.[40] This began with *Federal Baseball Club v. National League* (1922), when the Supreme Court ruled that the Sherman Act did not apply to major league baseball. Although the exemption was intended to apply to professional baseball alone, and some of baseball's exemptions were reversed by the Curt Flood Act of 1968, the Supreme Court ruling led to a series of court cases that gave professional sports preferential treatment compared to other businesses when it comes to antitrust enforcement.

According to Fort (2007), the special antitrust status of professional sports is due to the fact that team cooperation is needed for the efficient operation of a sports league. Both fans and team owners benefit from an efficiently operated league, which requires cooperation on establishing the rules of the game, scheduling, and policies that assure competitive balance. Because there are social benefits from certain forms of cooperation and there is an idyllic image associated with

---

[39] In *Sugar Institute, Inc. v. United States* (1936), the Sugar Institute was found guilty of violating Section 1 of the Sherman Act because of the steps it took to eliminate price cutting, whereas in *Tag Manufacturers Institute v. Federal Trade Commission* (1949), the Tag Manufacturers Institute (of business tags) was found innocent of price fixing. Even though members were required to report prices, they were encouraged to set prices independently. Thus, the Institute collected market information but did not facilitate price fixing.

[40] For a complete list of antitrust exemptions that apply to many different industries, see von Kalinowski (1982).

professional sports, the Courts and Congress have also allowed teams to cooperate in ways that enhance their market power. For example, teams exploit their monopsony power by limiting a player's right to switch teams. They exploit their monopoly power by limiting the number of teams that can participate in a league. In essence, Congress and the Courts have allowed sports leagues to erect legal entry barriers.

A legal justification for such barriers stems from court decisions that treat the sports league, not an individual team, as a "single entity."[41] When this precedent holds, teams within a league are allowed to cooperate on both the actions needed for the efficient operation of a league and on actions that preserve and enhance the value of the league. The courts have allowed a league (i.e., the cartel) to limit entry of new teams into the league and player rights to switch teams. The single entity argument was effectively used by the National Hockey League to prevent the San Francisco Seals from moving to Vancouver (*San Francisco Seals, Ltd., v. National Hockey League*, 1974). Furthermore, Congress passed the Sports Broadcasting Act in 1961, giving sports leagues the right to negotiate TV contracts for all teams in the league. Clearly, these actions would be antitrust violations in any other industry.[42]

The evolution of antitrust precedents in sports makes it clear that if the law evolves in efficient directions at all, it does so very slowly. Consistent with Roe's (1996) position, *Federal Baseball Club v. National League* (1922) led the evolution of sports law down a different path than other industries. Considerable antitrust immunity led to collusive behavior that increased market power as well as efficient league operation. Although players have gained limited free agency rights since the 1950s, Johnson (1979) and Fort (2007) argued that the political power of owners has enabled leagues to preserve the status quo and their favored antitrust status. This is consistent with the interest-group theory. It remains to be seen whether this special treatment will deteriorate in the future.

Like owners of professional sports teams, presidents at MIT and the elite Ivy League schools have also argued for special antitrust treatment.[43] This issue came to a head in 1989 when the DOJ began a price-fixing investigation of these universities, called the "Ivy League Overlap Group." For 35 years, members of the Overlap Group had agreed to award scholarships based solely on need and used a common financial-aid formula to ensure that a student who applied to any of these schools received a uniform financial aid offer from each school. In essence, they colluded to prevent scholarship competition for the brightest students.

---

[41] For a review of court precedents on the decision to view a league as a "single entity", see Lehn and Sykuta (1997).

[42] For a discussion of similar antitrust issues involving college athletics, see *NCAA v. University of Oklahoma*, 1984.

[43] For a more detailed discussion of this case, see LaFraniere (1991) and Austin (2006). The Ivy League schools are Brown University, Columbia University, Cornell University, Dartmouth College, Harvard University, Princeton University, the University of Pennsylvania, and Yale University.

The Overlap Group gave two reasons for its behavior. First, members argued that because they were nonprofit institutions, their actions should not be viewed as per se illegal. This sentiment was aptly put by a spokesperson for Dartmouth College, "Schools like ours should not be seen as competitors in the same way that toaster manufacturers are."[44] Second, the purpose of their agreement was to meet an important social goal: to fairly distribute scholarship funds to students with the greatest need for financial aid. Thus, they argued that based on a rule of reason, the action of the Overlap Group was not an antitrust violation.

The DOJ disagreed, however, arguing that the Overlap Group agreement illegally eliminated competition for students. According to Attorney General Thornburgh, "The revered stature of these institutions does not insulate them from the requirements of the antitrust laws." As a result, the members from the Ivy League agreed to a consent decree that prohibited future price fixing. MIT took the case to court, but eventually agreed to a similar consent decree in 1993. Although not all cooperative behavior among nonprofit organizations is per se illegal, the behavior of these institutions was viewed as unreasonable. Unfortunately, this remedy has not translated to higher average financial aid awards to students (Carlton et al. 1995; Hoxby 2000).

One mechanism that antitrust authorities use to identify collusion is to promise antitrust immunity to the first firm to come forward and report the illegal activity to antitrust authorities. According to Pate (2004) of the Antitrust Division of the US Department of Justice, "Because cartel activities are hatched and carried out in secret, obtaining the cooperation of insiders is the best and often the only way to crack a cartel." As we discussed in Chap. 9, this first to come forward policy is what brought down the international vitamin cartel in the 1990s.

20.2.3.3 Mergers

We saw in Chap. 18 that mergers can have both desirable and undesirable effects. Society benefits from mergers that lower costs, but mergers that raise market power are socially undesirable. The government uses a rule of reason when evaluating the legality of a merger. Because the market power effects of vertical and conglomerate mergers are generally small, we focus on antitrust issues involving horizontal mergers.

The original antitrust laws were not very effective at preventing potentially anticompetitive mergers. Section 2 of the Sherman Act (1890) could be used to stop a merger, but only if it led to the monopolization of a market. To remedy this limitation, the Clayton Act was enacted in 1914, but this legislation was flawed because it banned only those anticompetitive mergers that involved stock acquisitions. In *Thatcher Manufacturing Company v. Federal Trade Commission* (1926), the Supreme Court

---

[44] LaFraniere (1991, A3).

ruled that the Clayton Act did not apply when one firm purchased the assets of a competitor. This loophole made the Clayton Act ineffective at stopping the merger wave of the 1920s, the so-called merger for oligopoly wave that we discussed in Chap. 18. To close the loophole, Congress passed the Celler–Kefauver Act in 1950, which launched a relatively strict, perhaps too strict, antimerger enforcement campaign.

The first major case under the new law was *U.S. v. Bethlehem Steel Corp.* (1958), which involved a merger between Bethlehem Steel and Youngstown Steel. At the time of the merger, Bethlehem was the second largest steel producer in the USA, with a market share of 15.4%. Youngstown was the sixth largest producer, with a market share of 4.7%. Industry concentration was high; the four-firm concentration ratio of 60%.

Two issues were relevant in the Bethlehem-Youngstown case. First, Bethlehem-Youngstown defended the merger by claiming that they operated in separate geographic markets. Bethlehem operated primarily on the east and west coasts, while Youngstown operated primarily in the center of the nation. The district court rejected this defense, defining the market as national in scope. Second, the firms argued that the merger would be pro-competitive, because the combined firm would be a more formidable competitor with the industry leader, US Steel. This argument was also rejected. In the opinion of Judge Weinfeld, "[T]he argument does not hold up as a matter of law. If the merger offends the statute in any relevant market then good motives and even demonstrable benefits are irrelevant and afford no defense."[45] As a result, the decision went against Bethlehem and Youngstown. A significant aspect of the decision was the court's reliance on market share and industry concentration data, which is consistent with the Structure–Conduct–Performance approach to industrial organization that gained acceptance at the time.

The Bethlehem–Youngstown steel precedent was solidified by *Brown Shoe Co. v. U.S.* (1962). The case involved a merger between Brown Shoe and Kinney Shoe. The companies were each vertically integrated, with each producing shoes and owning retail outlets. Brown's main activity was production, while Kenney's was primarily retailing. In addition, both the production and retail markets for shoes were highly competitive. Brown and Kenney had low market shares in production and in retailing. Thus, the merger would have little effect on competition at either stage of production. In spite of these facts, the Supreme Court ruled against the merger. The Court's argument, called the "incipiency doctrine," was that even in competitive markets horizontal mergers should be banned to prevent an increase in concentration. The doctrine virtually says that horizontal mergers are per se illegal.

One concern with antimerger enforcement was that the courts did not always behave consistently in defining a geographic market. In the Bethlehem–Youngstown case, a broad definition was used. In *U.S. v. Philadelphia National Bank* (1964), however, the court defined the relevant market as a single city when evaluating the legality of a merger between Philadelphia National Bank and Girard Trust.

---

[45] Quote taken from Waldman (1986, 91).

Similarly, the court defined the market as a single city in the merger between Von's and Shopping Bag supermarkets (*U.S. v. Von's Grocery Co.*, 1966). Finally, in *U.S. v. Pabst Brewing Co.* (1966), the courts defined the relevant market to be a single state. The case involved a merger between the Pabst and Blatz brewing companies; the market share of the combined company was 4.5% at the national level and was 24% in the state of Wisconsin. In each case, the courts ruled against the mergers.

The courts have also failed to use a consistent definition of the product market. In the Bethlehem–Youngstown case, the market was defined narrowly to include finished steel products. In contrast, in the proposed merger between the Continental Can Company and the Hazel-Atlas Glass Company, the court used a broad definition, arguing that cans and bottles are sufficiently close substitutes to be included in the same market (*U.S. v. Continental Can Co.*, 1964).

From an economic standpoint, the courts have erred when defining a market, a notion that was clearly understood by some judges. In the dissenting opinion in the Von's and Shopping Bag case, Judge Stewart wrote, "The sole consistency that I can find is that in litigation under Section 7, the Government always wins."[46] Scherer and Ross (1990, 177) suggested that these decisions represent the

> ... consistent willingness to accept market definitions that resolve intrinsic uncertainties on the side of preventing mergers with possible anticompetitive effects. This in turn may have been no more than faithful stewardship to the will of Congress.

In any case, many economists and representatives from the business community were concerned that this inconsistency created too much uncertainty regarding what was legal and illegal. In the civil law tradition, Stigler (1955, 182) argued that the government should establish clear "bright lines" that "would serve the double purpose of giving the business community some advanced knowledge of public policy toward mergers and of achieving the important goals of the legislature."[47] This viewpoint was also expressed in a *Fortune* magazine editorial (February 1965, 228), which said that the business community does not want to "make present laws less restrictive on mergers ... [but] would simply codify them in such a way that businessmen know what they can and can't do."

In response, the DOJ established a set of "Merger Guidelines" in 1968.[48] The Merger Guidelines reduced uncertainty and were designed to be consistent with court precedents and the economic understanding of markets at the time. The key standards are summarized in Table 20.1. They show that enforcement will be tougher on mergers between firms in highly concentrated industries, where the four-firm concentration ratio (CR_4) exceeds 75%. The Merger Guidelines also provide some discretion. A stricter standard applies in markets where concentration

---

[46] Quote taken from Scherer and Ross (1990, 177).

[47] Similarly, Bok (1960, 299) argued that "there is much to be said for a simple standard which can at least be fairly and inexpensively administered in a fashion that is understandable to the businessman contemplating merger."

[48] The 1968 Guidelines are available at http://www.justice.gov/atr/hmerger/11247.htm.

Table 20.1 Summary of the 1968 Horizontal Merger Guidelines

1. Once a market is defined, the following "structural standard" is applied.

   A. Where the four-firm concentration ratio is 75% or more, the market is defined as <u>highly concentrated</u> and the government "will ordinarily challenge" mergers between firms with the following market shares:

Acquiring firm	Acquired firm
4%	4% or more
10%	2% or more
15% or more	1% or more

   B. Where the four-firm concentration ratio is less than 75%, the government "will ordinarily challenge" mergers between firms with the following market shares:

Acquiring firm	Acquired firm
5%	5% or more
10%	4% or more
15%	3% or more
20%	2% or more
25%	1% or more

2. The Guidelines also list several "exceptional circumstances or additional factors" that may require a departure from the structural standard above. The Guidelines state:

   A. The structural standards may be ignored for *industries being significantly transformed* (by technological change, for example), since market boundaries may be uncertain.

   B. A stricter standard will be applied to markets where there is a *significant trend toward concentration*.

   C. The government will not allow the acquisition of an *important* (disturbing, disruptive, or unusually competitive) *rival* in the market.

   D. The government will allow the acquisition of a failing firm if the *failing firm* does not have a reasonable prospect for survival and there are no other buyers that would better promote competition.

   E. An *efficiency defense* will be accepted but only in exceptional circumstances.

   F. A more lenient standard will be applied for *market extension mergers* (i.e., firms selling similar products in different regions of the country).

Source: US Department of Justice, *Merger Guidelines*, Washington, DC, May 30, 1968, available at http://www.justice.gov/atr/hmerger/11247.htm

is rising, and a more lenient standard applies when one of the firms is clearly failing. An efficiency defense is possible, but only in exceptional circumstances.

The consideration of an efficiency defense was an important turning point in antimerger enforcement. The law and previous court precedents did not allow for an efficiency defense. For example, in *Federal Trade Commission v. Procter and Gamble Company* (1967), the court held that "Possible economies cannot be used as a defense to illegality."[49] Yet, recall from Chap. 18 that Williamson (1968) showed that the social gain from a relatively small cost reduction can offset the social cost of increased market power from a horizontal merger. Thus, it makes economic sense to consider the efficiency gain generated by a merger.

---

[49] Quote taken from Breit and Elzinga (1989, 170).

The last important piece of antimerger legislation enacted in this era is the Hart–Scott–Rodino Act (1976). It required firms of a minimum size to notify the DOJ and the FTC of their intention to merge.[50] The government then has 30 days to collect and study the evidence before making a decision whether or not the merger is an antitrust concern. When a merger is formally opposed, the government can seek an injunction to temporarily stop the merger or the case can go to trial. Today, in most cases the government works with the firms involved to reach a negotiated settlement. Advanced notification led to a dramatic drop in antimerger litigation, as Hart–Scott–Rodino effectively made the DOJ and the FTC antimerger regulators (Beuttenmuller 1979; Johnson and Smith 1987).[51]

There are many examples where firms interested in a merger have worked with the government to find a way to purge the socially undesirable aspects of the merger. One was the proposed merger between the Miller Brewing Company and the Stroh Brewing Company in 1999. To gain approval from the DOJ, a portion of Stroh's brands and assets were sold to the Pabst Brewing Company and to the Yuengling Brewing Company.[52] Given the high cost of a trial, this regulatory approach has improved the efficiency of antimerger enforcement. Since 1976 no major merger case has worked its way to the Supreme Court.

This is not to say that all cases avoid a legal challenge. For example, the DOJ formally challenged the 2003 merger between the Oracle Corporation and PeopleSoft Inc. These were companies that supply specialized software to businesses.[53] The case hinged on the definitions of the market and of appropriate potential entrants. The government identified the market to be national in scope and used a product definition that implied a market with three dominant firms: Oracle, PeopleSoft, and SAP American. Thus, the merger would convert the market from a triopoly to a duopoly. Oracle's defense was that the market was much broader: it was international and included a number of potential competitors, such as Microsoft. In 2004, a California district court judge, Judge Walker, accepted the broader definition of the market and found in favor of the merger, a decision that was not appealed by the DOJ.

The Merger Guidelines have been revised several times since 1968. The first set of revisions occurred in 1982 and 1984. A substantive change in the revisions was that they gave even greater weight to the efficiency defense.[54] According to the 1984 Guidelines (at 26,834):

---

[50] Additional information on this premerger notification program can be found at http://www.ftc.gov/bc/hsr/index.shtm.

[51] Given the high cost of a trial, this is socially desirable as long as government enforcement is consistent with the law and court precedent. The National Association of Attorneys General Antitrust Enforcement (1993) questioned the desirability of giving so much power to the DOJ and the FTC, claiming that they put too much weight on efficiency and too little weight on consumer welfare and the incipiency precedent.

[52] For further detail of this complex agreement, see V. Tremblay and C. Tremblay (2005).

[53] For a more complete discussion of this case, see McAfee et al. (2009).

[54] The main difference between the 1982 and 1984 Merger Guidelines is that the 1984 Merger Guidelines clarify the efficiency defense.

Table 20.2   Summary of the Horizontal Merger Guidelines, 1982 and 1984

1. The 1982 and 1984 Merger Guidelines continue to use a structural standard but replace the four-firm concentration ratio with the Herfindahl–Hirschman Index (HHI) to measure industry concentration.

   A. A market is defined as highly concentrated when HHI is above 1,800. A merger that increases HHI by 100 points or more will likely be challenged. A merger that increases HHI from 50 to 100 points will be investigated.

   B. A market is defined as moderately concentrated when HHI ranges from 1,000 to 1,800. A merger will be investigated when HHI increases by 100 points or more.

   C. A market is defined as unconcentrated when HHI is less than 1,000. A merger in an unconcentrated market is unlikely to be challenged.

2. The 1982 and 1984 Merger Guidelines propose a "5% test" to define a market. That is, if a hypothetical firm increases its price by 5%, the market is defined to include all existing competitors that consumers would turn to within one year and all new competitors that would enter the market within one year if all existing firms increased their prices by 5%.

3. Like the 1968 Guidelines, the 1982 and 1984 Merger Guidelines consider other factors, such as the rate of technological change, the rate of industry growth, and the ease of entry. They also provide for a failing firm and an efficiency defense.

4. The 1984 Guidelines revise the 1982 Guidelines by clarifying and strengthening the efficiency defense. The 1984 Guidelines state (p. 26, 834): "The primary benefit of mergers to the economy is their efficiency-enhancing potential, which can increase the competitiveness of firms and result in lower prices to consumers. ... [T]he Guidelines will allow firms to achieve available efficiencies through mergers without interference from the Department [of Justice]."

Source: US Department of Justice, *Merger Guidelines*, Washington, DC, June 30, 1982, available at http://www.justice.gov/atr/hmerger/11248.htm, and June 29, 1984, available at http://www.justice.gov/atr/hmerger/11249.htm

"The primary benefit of mergers to the economy is their efficiency-enhancing potential, which can increase the competitiveness of firms and result in lower prices to consumers. ... [T]he Guidelines will allow firms to achieve available efficiencies through mergers without interference from the Department."

The main details of the 1982–1984 revisions of the Merger Guidelines are presented in Table 20.2.[55] Besides giving greater weight to the efficiency defense, there are two additional differences of substance between the 1968 Guidelines and the revisions. First, in the revisions the Herfindahl–Hirschman Index (HHI) replaces CR_4 as a measure of industry concentration, reflecting the realization that HHI may be a better measure of concentration (as discussed in Chap. 8). In the revision, industries are categorized into three groups rather than two:

- Unconcentrated, which occurs when HHI < 1,000.
- Moderately concentrated, which occurs when $1,000 \leq$ HHI $\leq 1,800$.
- Highly concentrated, which occurs when HHI > 1,800.

---

[55] The 1982 Guidelines are available at http://www.justice.gov/atr/hmerger/11248.htm; the 1984 Guidelines are available at http://www.justice.gov/atr/hmerger/11249.htm.

Table 20.3 Summary of the Horizontal Merger Guidelines, 1992 and 1997

1. The 1992 and 1997 Merger Guidelines use the same structural standard as the 1982 and 1984 Guidelines.
2. The 1992 and 1997 Guidelines define a market using the rule of a "small but significant and nontransitory" increase in price (SSNIP). Like the 1982 and 1984 Guidelines, this will be a 5% increase in price in most cases. If a hypothetical firm increases its price by 5%, the market is defined to include all existing competitors that consumers would turn to for supplies within one year. The 1992 and 1997 Guidelines also offer a more detailed discussion on how entry conditions will be considered when defining the market.
3. The 1992 and 1997 Guidelines elaborate on how a merger may diminish competition and how the government will evaluate the potential harm that may result from a merger.
4. Like the 1982 and 1984 Guidelines, the 1992 and 1997 Guidelines provide for an efficiency defense and a failing firm defense.
5. The 1997 Guidelines revise the 1992 Guidelines regarding the efficiency defense. The revision makes clear that efficiency gains can be an important justification for a merger but more clearly defines what evidence is necessary to substantiate such a defense.

Source: US Department of Justice and the Federal Trade Commission, *Horizontal Merger Guidelines*, Washington, DC, April 2, 1992 and April 8, 1997, available at http://www.justice. gov/atr/public/guidelines/hmg.htm#22

As indicated in Table 20.2, a merger that increases HHI by 100 points or more will likely be challenged in a highly concentrated industry and will be investigated further in a moderately concentrated industry.[56] A challenge is unlikely in an unconcentrated industry. To compare these breaks with corresponding values of CR_4, note that if firms are of equal size, then $CR_4 = 40\%$ when HHI $= 1,000$, $CR_4 = 72\%$ when HHI $= 1,800$, and $CR_4 = 75\%$ when HHI $= 1,875$.

The second key difference between the 1968 Guidelines and the revisions is that the newer Guidelines provide a more precise definition of the market, an improvement over previous case law and the 1968 Guidelines. The newer Guidelines used the so-called "five-percent test" to identify a market. That is, a firm's competitors include (1) all firms that buyers would switch to if the firm raised its price by 5% and (2) all potential competitors that would be expected to enter the market within one year if all existing firms raised their prices by 5%.

The next set of changes occurred in 1992 and 1997 when the DOJ and the FTC worked together to make minor revisions to the Guidelines.[57] They both use the same structural standard as the 1982–1984 Guidelines (see Table 20.3), but the 1992 and 1997 Guidelines further refine the definition of a market and elaborate on how entry conditions will be considered. The only differences between the 1992

---

[56] Recall from Chap. 18 that when firms 1 and 2 are in the same industry and have respective market shares of ms_1 and ms_2, their merger will cause HHI to increase by $2 \cdot ms_1 \cdot ms_2$. For example, consider a market with 4 firms, 1 through 4, that have the following market shares in percent: $ms_1 = 5$, $ms_2 = 20$, $ms_3 = 40$, and $ms_4 = 45$. If firms 1 and 2 merge, this increases HHI by 100 points $(2 \cdot 5 \cdot 10)$. That is, before the merger HHI $= 3,750 = 5^2 + 10^2 + 40^2 + 45^2$, and after the merger HHI $= 3,850 = 15^2 + 40^2 + 45^2$.

[57] The 1992 and 1997 Guidelines are available at http://www.justice.gov/atr/hmerger/11251.htm.

Table 20.4 Summary of the Horizontal Merger Guidelines, 2010

1. The 2010 Merger Guidelines use a new structural standard and classify markets differently.

  A. A. A market is defined as <u>highly concentrated</u> when HHI is above 2,500. A merger that increases HHI by between 100 and 200 points will be investigated. A merger that raises HHI by more than 200 points will likely be challenged.
  B. A market is defined as <u>moderately concentrated</u> when HHI ranges from 1,500 to 2,500. A merger that increases HHI by 100 points or more will be investigated.
  C. A market is defined as <u>unconcentrated</u> when HHI is below 1,500. A merger in an unconcentrated market is unlikely to be challenged.
  D. A merger involving an increase in HHI by less than 100 points is unlikely to be challenged.

2. The 2010 Guidelines is considerably more nuanced than previous Guidelines. The 2010 Guidelines place less weight on the possible link between market share and economic performance. Instead, it assesses something called "upward pricing pressure" or whether the merger is likely to lead to an increase in prices of the merged firms' products. This avoids the need to define the market and serves as a simple screening device. In addition, greater attention is given to nonprice effects, including innovation and entry conditions.

Source: US Department of Justice and the Federal Trade Commission, *Horizontal Merger Guidelines*, Washington, DC, August 9, 2010, available at http://www.justice.gov/atr/public/guidelines/hmg-2010

and 1997 Guidelines is that the latter include a more detailed description of the evidence required to justify an efficiency defense.

A more substantial revision was made in 2010.[58] As seen in Table 20.4, the 2010 Merger Guidelines have a more lenient structural standard and place less weight on the possible link between market share and economic performance. They also consider a broader set of factors when assessing the competitive effects of a merger (Farrell et al. 2010). A new screening device is whether or not a proposed merger is likely to generate net upward pricing pressure (UPP). A merger that reduces competition will put upward pressure on price, but a merger that increases efficiency will put downward pressure on price. When the net effect is an expected price increase, a merger is likely to be challenged.[59] The UPP criterion avoids the need to define the market and identify market shares and concentration, which is especially difficult in markets with product differentiation.

As expected with a common law system, the Guidelines and antimerger enforcement have changed considerably over time. Baker and Shapiro (2007) argued that enforcement fluctuated cyclically with the political climate of the country, being too leniently enforced during the 1980s and 2000s when Ronald Reagan and George W. Bush were presidents. Alternatively, Kovacic (2009) argued that a review of the history of antimerger enforcement over the last 50 years reveals a more rational

---

[58] The 2010 Guidelines are available at http://www.justice.gov/atr/public/guidelines/hmg-2010.html.
[59] For a discussion of the methods of measuring UPP, see Farrell and Shapiro (2010). For further discussion, see Schmalensee (2009), Carlton (2010), Epstein and Rubinfield (2010), and Willig (2011).

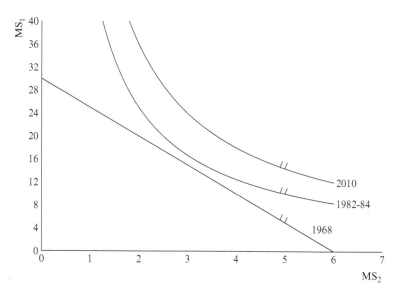

Fig. 20.1 The antimerger constraint in 1968, 1982–1984, and 2010 for a highly concentrated industry

evolution of law enforcement, one that is in keeping with the evolution to efficient laws hypothesis. That is, the Merger Guidelines and court precedents steadily progressed to produce more efficient outcomes. We take up these issues next.

It is clear that the Guidelines have become progressively more lenient since 1968. Figure 20.1 plots the antimerger constraints that would apply for highly concentrated industries under the structural standards of the 1968, 1982–1984, and 2010 Merger Guidelines.[60] The vertical and horizontal axes identify the market shares of two firms that are considering a horizontal merger, and the area above a curve identifies the pairs of market shares that would likely be challenged under each set of Merger Guidelines. For example, if a buyer's market share is 28% and a seller's market share is 1%, the merger would be challenged under the 1968 Guidelines but not under the 1982–1984 and 2010 Guidelines. A merger between firms with respective market shares of 28% and 2% would be challenged under the 1968 and 1982–1984 Guidelines but not under the 2010 Guidelines. Finally, a merger between firms with respective market shares of 28% and 3% would be challenged under all three Guidelines. Other changes also appear to have relaxed antimerger enforcement. For instance, Fisher and Lande (1983, 1,683) argued that

---

[60] The 2010 structural standard for a highly concentrated industry is that HHI cannot increase by more than 200 points. However, because the cutoff for a highly concentrated industry differs (is 1,800 in the 1982–1984 Guidelines and 2,500 in the 2010 Guidelines), the 2010 constraint is reduced by 38.9% for consistency. This implies that a merger would be challenged in 2010 if HHI increases by more than 144 points, $200 \cdot (1{,}800/2{,}500)$.

the 5% test in the 1982 Guidelines yields a broader market definition and "probably loosened merger enforcement standards far more than the change due to the different numerical [structural] standards."

As mentioned previously, some experts contend that the more lenient 1982–1984 Merger Guidelines are the result of President Reagan's appointment of William Baxter to head the Antitrust Division of the DOJ in 1981.[61] The evidence suggests, however, that this trend began in the middle 1970s with the appointment of more conservative Supreme Court justices. For example, the Supreme Court allowed a merger between General Dynamics and Material Service Corporation, principal rivals in the coal industry (*U.S. v. General Dynamics Corporation*, 1974). According to Waldman (1986, 99), "[t]he General Dynamics decision signaled that a more conservative Supreme Court would no longer automatically side with the government in all section 7 cases [of the Clayton Act]. . .." In any case, even though the new Merger Guidelines were more lenient, the government opposed several horizontal mergers during the Reagan administration. These include proposed mergers between Jones & Laughlin Steel and Republic Steel, between Mobil Oil and Marathon Oil, and between the Schlitz and Heileman brewing companies.

Baker and Shapiro (2007) argued that antimerger enforcement was too lenient during President Bush's administration. A striking example is DOJ approval of the Whirlpool and Maytag merger in 2006. Nevertheless, the Clinton administration allowed a similar merger between Boeing and McDonnell Douglas in the aircraft industry (Kovacic 2009).

One reason for the evolutionary drift in antimerger enforcement has been the emerging evidence that there can be substantial net benefits to a horizontal merger. As we have discussed, Williamson (1968) found that a merger that produces a small cost reduction can be socially beneficial even when it increases market power. In addition, Demsetz (1973, 1974) showed that more efficient firms tend to grow in size and that stifling this growth will reduce the incentive for progress. Finally, Bork (1978) and Landes and Posner (1981) spread these ideas to legal scholars. Ultimately, contributions from the new learning led the antitrust authorities to deemphasize the simple structural approach to antitrust that was associated with the Structure–Conduct–Performance paradigm and place greater emphasis on the potential benefits of a merger.

Ghosal (2007) tested for the influence of the short-run political climate and the long-run trend toward milder antimerger enforcement in the USA from 1958 to 2002. He found little support for the hypothesis that there are fewer merger challenges when there was a Republican president in office.[62] However, he did find that there was a general weakening of antimerger enforcement over time, which is consistent with the evolution of the Merger Guidelines.

---

[61] For example, see Meadows (1981), Adams and Brock (1988), Krattenmaker and Pitofsky (1988), and Baker and Shapiro (2007).

[62] Although there is no support for the political cycle using merger cases, Ghosal (2007) did find support for the political cycle when the sample includes all civil cases.

Table 20.5 Antimerger enforcement and major horizontal mergers in the US Brewing

Year	Buyer	Seller	MS_B	MS_S	CR_4	HHI	ΔHHI	Successfully challenged
1957	Lucky	Fisher	2.02	0.11	24.0	272	0.4	Yes
1958	A-B	American	8.20	0.22	25.1	293	3.6	Yes
1958	Pabst	Blatz	2.99	2.00	25.1	293	12	Yes
1961	Schlitz	Burgermeister	6.42	0.81	27.4	359	10	Yes
1964	Schlitz	Lucky	8.30	1.77	32.0	432	29	Yes
1965	Falstaff	Narr.	6.23	0.76	34.5	487	9.5	
1965	Rheingold	Ruppert	4.17	0.79	34.5	487	6.6	
1965	Pittsburgh	Duquesne	0.88	0.68	34.5	487	1.2	Yes
1972	Heileman	Associated	2.73	1.89	50.8	857	10	
1978	Pabst	Carling	9.29	2.01	65.2	1,345	37	Yes
1982	Heileman	Pabst	8.11	6.87	75.8	1,909	111	Yes
1982	Heileman	Schlitz	8.11	7.98	75.8	1,909	129	Yes
1982	Stroh	Schlitz	3.41	7.98	75.8	1,909	54	
1989	Coors	Stroh	9.65	10.0	86.5	2,707	194	Yes
1999	Miller	Stroh	21.1	7.48	93.4	3,093	316	Yes
2008	Miller	Coors	21.3	12.9	94.4	4,329	549	

A-B represents Anheuser-Busch, and Narr. represents Narragansett. A firm's market share is for the closest year for which data are available. A successful challenge means that the case was successfully challenged in the courts or that the merger was abandoned due to antitrust concerns
Source: V. Tremblay and C. Tremblay (1988, 2005) and *Beer Industry Update* (2009)

Another approach is to investigate the drift in antitrust enforcement in a single industry over time. We choose the US brewing industry because rising concentration motivated close scrutiny of the industry and because some of the earliest court cases based on the Celler–Kefauver Act involved mergers in brewing.[63] Table 20.5 lists the major mergers that were investigated by the DOJ. It identifies the important characteristics of the merger, including the firms involved, the market share of the buyer (MS_B), the market share of the seller (MS_S), the four-firm concentration ratio (CR_4), the Herfindahl–Hirschman index (HHI), the change in HHI (ΔHHI), and whether the merger was successfully challenged by the government.

Evaluating these mergers based on structural standards alone, you can see that the antimerger laws have become much more lenient over time. None of the mergers before 1980 violate the simple structural standards of the 1982–1984 and the 2010 Guidelines. One reason for this tough stance is that industry concentration was rising rapidly.[64] For example, from 1950 to 1980, HHI (CR_4) rose steadily from 132 to 1,549 (22–66%). Another reason was that the incipiency doctrine was in effect, at least through the 1960s, and the courts took a tough stance against

---

[63] For a more complete discussion of antitrust enforcement in brewing, see Elzinga and Swisher (2005, 2011), V. Tremblay (1993), and V. Tremblay and C. Tremblay (2005).

[64] Another factor that complicated the analysis is that the beer market was regional in scope until the 1970s.

horizontal mergers to stem the tide of rising concentration. The mergers involving Heileman, Pabst, and Schlitz in 1982 that were successfully challenged would be viewed as acceptable today.

The recent case involving the Miller and Coors brewing companies involves a joint venture between the second and third largest beer companies in the USA. Based on the structural standard, it would be unacceptable, even according to the 2010 Guidelines. Nonetheless, the joint venture was approved because of the continued internationalization of the industry and the expected efficiency gains due to reduced transportation and marketing costs (Fillion 2008; C. Tremblay and V. Tremblay 2011b). Thus, additional factors come into play when scrutinizing a horizontal combination.

Evidence from brewing industry mergers demonstrates two things. First, antimerger enforcement has become more lenient over time. Early mergers that were successfully stopped would have been allowed today, and a merger allowed today would be successfully challenged in the past. Second, current enforcement puts less emphasis on the structural standard (i.e., measures of market share and concentration) and greater emphasis on other factors in deciding whether or not to challenge a horizontal merger.

In summary, it seems clear that the antimerger laws were too strict during the 1950s and 1960s. The revisions of the Merger Guidelines are in keeping with the hypothesis that (antimerger) laws evolve to improve efficiency. The 1968 Guidelines provided the business community with a more transparent structural standard. The 1982–1984 revisions added a more precise definition of the market and allow for an efficiency defense. Although there is some evidence that enforcement is influenced by the political climate of the country, the 1968 Merger Guidelines and the 1982–1984 revisions appear to be consistent with the evolution to efficient laws hypothesis. They deter the most damaging mergers and direct the DOJ and FTC to investigate mergers that are most likely to have negative social effects. The requirement that firms must notify the government of intent to merge has resulted in many cases being resolved by negotiation, avoiding the high social cost of going to court. The 2010 Guidelines relax further the antimerger constraint but also give greater weight to other factors. It remains to be seen whether or not the 2010 Guidelines are an improvement over the past.

20.2.3.4 Antitrust Assessment

It is clear from our discussion that antitrust enforcement has not remained constant. Court decisions have been influenced by politics and dramatic economic events. The most striking trend is that enforcement has become less restrictive since the inception of the antitrust laws, a trend that is supported by both theory and evidence. Theoretical research over the last several decades demonstrates that mergers and high concentration may bestow greater economic benefits than previously thought, especially in dynamic markets where technological change and international competition are common.

Although data are limited, the empirical evidence confirms that antitrust enforcement has not been cost effective, except in collusion and major merger cases. In their review of the evidence, Crandall and Winston (2003, 24) concluded that until better evidence becomes available, "[T]he Federal Trade Commission and the Department of Justice should focus on the most significant and egregious violations, such as blatant price fixing and merger-to-monopoly and treat most other apparent threats to competition with benign neglect." Although this assessment may undervalue potentially important benefits, such as the deterrent effect of antitrust enforcement that is difficult if not impossible to measure, it suggests that strict, broad-based antitrust enforcement may not be socially desirable. It also appears that the trend toward more lenient enforcement is consistent with the evolution to efficient laws hypothesis. It does not appear that further relaxation of the antitrust enforcement is warranted, however.

20.3   Regulation and Deregulation

The government enacts regulations and establishes regulatory agencies to promote a number of social goals. Some protect public safety. For example, the Food and Drug Administration of the Department of Health and Human Services regulates food safety and drug safety and effectiveness. The Occupational Safety and Health Administration of the Department of Labor is responsible for the safety and health of workers. After the 9-11 terrorist attack in 2001, the Transportation Security Administration of the Department of Homeland Security was established to improve airport security. Other agencies are set up to protect the environment, such as the Environmental Protection Agency and the Department of the Interior.

Some agencies and regulations address economic issues associated with particular industries. Regarding the banking industry, the financial crisis of 2008–2009 spawned new legislation that expanded the powers of the Federal Reserve, the Department of the Treasury, and the Federal Deposit Insurance Corporation (FDIC). One contributing factor to the crisis was that the FDIC insured most bank deposits against bank failure but failed to adequately monitor the riskiness of bank loans. Federal insurance and little oversight created a moral hazard problem, causing banks to accept too many risky loans.[65] This increased their probability of failure. The impact of loan defaults for particular banks extended further because banks form a financial network; a financial network is a public good that provides liquidity which serves as a lubricant to the overall economy. In this case, the failure of several large banks generates a negative externality. Once the recession began, a substantial number of borrowers began to default on their loans (primarily because the housing bubble burst) and banks began to fail. This diminished financial liquidity

---

[65] Moral hazard is the tendency of firms and consumers to exert less effort and diligence when their investments are insured against loss, damage, or theft.

(lubrication) in the economy, which contributed further to the recession. That is, individuals and companies could no longer obtain loans which further constrained demand for consumer and producer goods. To avoid this problem in the future, new legislation limits home buyers and banks from taking excessive risk and forces banks to set aside greater financial reserves to cover potential losses.[66]

There are several different types of regulations. In this section, we discuss price/output regulation that is designed to address market failure due to market power. Joskow and Rose (1989) called this "economic regulation." This is distinct from "social regulation," which is designed to protect the environment and the safety of consumers and workers, a topic we take up later in the chapter.

20.3.1   The Role of Industry Regulation

The US Constitution gives Congress the power to "regulate commerce . . . among the several states." Yet, government regulation of business did not begin until the late nineteenth century when technological change gave a cost advantage to large enterprises and increased their market power. This was especially problematic in the railroad industry, where price discrimination was common. Farmers in sparsely populated areas called for government intervention because many faced monopoly railroad providers and high prices. In addition, even though the railroads formed a cartel in the 1880s, many consumers and producers were more concerned about price instability, as this was a period when frequent price wars destroyed cartel pricing (Porter 1983).[67] In response, the Interstate Commerce Act (1887) was passed, which established the Interstate Commerce Commission to regulate railroad rates.[68]

A pivotal step in the evolution of government regulation was the landmark case of *Munn v. Illinois* (1877). This case involved a dispute over the right of the state of Illinois to set prices charged by grain elevators and warehouses. The court ruled that states have the right to regulate the prices of private firms when it promoted the "common good." This precedent was strengthened by the Supreme Court ruling in

---

[66] These agencies were also given greater power to oversee or regulate consumer loans, bank executive bonuses, and the percent of their investments in derivatives and hedge funds. The Federal Reserve Bank is also given the power to break up excessively large financial institutions. For additional discussion, see Davidson et al. (2010), Gordon (2010), and Paletta and Hitt (2010).

[67] Recall that cartels were legal until 1890. Porter found that railroad companies used a trigger strategy to support collusion. Given the cost of detecting cheating, collusion occasionally broke down, resulting in a temporary punishment phase of tougher competition. In addition, railroads have very high fixed costs, causing them to compete in price during periods of low demand to reduce excess capacity and help cover these costs. Thus, prices were unstable.

[68] This was amended by the Motor Carrier Act of 1935 to regulate bus lines, trucking, and common carriers.

Nebbia v. New York (1934), a case that revolved around New York's right to regulate
the price of milk. The majority opinion in the case indicated that ". . . a state is free to
adopt whatever economic policy may reasonably be deemed to promote the public
welfare, and to enforce that policy by legislation adapted to its purpose."

Since then, much of the regulation of business has involved industries with
demand and cost characteristics that render perfect competition impossible. On the
cost side, the presence of substantial scale economies gives a cost advantage to a
larger producer. This is common with public utilities, such as a water, sewer, or
power company, where there are scale economies in distribution. On the demand
side, the presence of network externalities, where consumer value increases with the
number of users, gives a revenue advantage to larger producers. Traditional (i.e.,
land line) telephone service provides one example, where each consumer benefits
from having more and more people connected to a company's phone network. In the
extreme, these conditions make a monopoly structure the most productively efficient
but also the most allocatively inefficient. This is called a natural monopoly.

Government regulation is a common response to this form of market failure. Ideally,
we want a regulatory agency to promote the interests of society, which is consistent
with the public-interest theory of regulation. As prescribed by the Supreme Court in
Nebbia v. New York (1934), this is both a legal and a desirable goal of regulation.

Although the primary aim of this section is to identify regulatory policies that
improve social efficiency, there is evidence to show that regulators do not always act
in this way. In fact, much of the empirical evidence shows that regulation has been
pro-business.[69] This led to the **capture theory of regulation** which argues that
regulation serves the industry either because it is set up in response to the industry's
demand for regulation (that creates legal barriers to entry) or because regulators
come to be controlled by the industry over time (Bernstein 1955). This theory
appears to explain transportation and public utility regulation. The airline industry
provided an ideal experiment, because airfare regulation applied to interstate but not
intrastate travel. A comparison of airline rates for flights of comparable distances
within the state of California and across state lines revealed that regulation led to
considerably higher fares. For example, in the mid-1970s Pacific Southwest Airlines
(PSA) offered service within California at about half the price of interstate flights
offered by airlines that were subject to regulation (Breyer 1982). Nevertheless, the
capture theory does not explain all forms of regulation: social regulation has
generally lowered industry profits.

The failure of the public-interest and capture theories to fully explain regulatory
behavior led economists to seek a better theory. The most prominent is the interest-
group theory, discussed at the beginning of the chapter, which emphasizes political
and economic causes of regulation.[70] Developed by Stigler (1971), Posner (1974),

---

[69] Since the seminal work by Stigler and Friedland (1962), there have been hundreds of studies on
the economic effect of government regulation. For a review of the evidence, see Jordon (1972),
Joskow and Rose (1989), Winston (1993, 1998), and Viscusi et al. (2005).

[70] See Noll (1989a, b) for a review of the political causes of regulation.

Peltzman (1976), and Becker (1983, 1985), the theory consists of three important parts. First, government has the power to control the supply of regulation, which transfers wealth among members of society. Second, the behavior of government officials is driven by a desire to remain in office. In other words, their goal is to maximize their political support or political capital. Third, business and other interest groups demand legislation which favors their interests. The end result is that regulation need not be efficient. It will favor interest groups that are more influential, are better organized, and have more to gain from a particular piece of legislation. *Ceteris paribus*, legislation will favor groups (1) with more political power, (2) with fewer numbers, because a smaller group is easier to organize, and (3) that have much at stake.[71]

How these political forces play out depends on the relative importance of these factors but also on the structure of the market. Producers in competitive industries have more to gain from regulation that raises price and limits entry, while consumers have more to gain from the regulation of monopolies. Thus, we would expect to see more regulation at the extremes of market structure, competitive and monopoly markets. Nevertheless, in many markets there are more consumers than producers, and an individual firm typically has much to gain from regulation compared to an individual consumer. When this happens, regulation will be established to favor producers and at the expense of consumers and may reduce total surplus.

Although the interest-group theory is an important advancement, it is still incomplete and not always consistent with the evidence. For one, it ignores the role of the courts. For instance, deregulation of the airline and telecommunications industries in the 1970s and 1980s did not have the support of Congress but moved forward because of judiciary approval (Ladha 1990). In addition, deregulation of trucking in 1980 appears to be inconsistent with the interest-group theory. The industry and its unions were earning large rents from regulation, and consumers of trucking services had not gained political power during the time of deregulation. Thus, the motives for regulation and deregulation are not fully understood.

With this caveat in mind, we proceed by using what Demsetz (1969) called the nirvana approach to public policy. That is, we identify regulatory solutions to problems of market failure, ignoring the cost of government. In the case of a natural monopoly, for example, this means that our goal is to identify a policy that reduces the deadweight loss due to monopoly power, ignoring the direct cost of regulation. We will, however, briefly discuss the unintended side effects of regulation and the benefits of deregulation later in the chapter. The nirvana approach serves as a useful starting point for policy analysis by identifying potentially desirable solutions to a particular problem. Again, a complete analysis would require a comparison of all benefits and costs of alternative regulatory options.

---

[71] In other words, individual consumers and voters have little influence on the political process. As Noll (1989, 1263) notes, "The central problem of a citizen in dealing with government is powerlessness."

20.3.2 Natural Monopoly Regulation

A valid argument for the economic regulation of an industry is the presence of a natural monopoly, which exhibits large-scale economies relative to the size of the market. Such a situation is illustrated in Fig. 20.2, where D is demand, MR is marginal revenue, AC is long-run average cost, and MC is long-run marginal cost. As we saw in Chap. 6, a natural monopoly exists when it is productively efficient for there to be just one producer in the industry.[72] That is, a single firm produces at lower unit cost than two or more firms in an industry. Unfortunately, a single producer will set the monopoly price, which is allocatively inefficient. That is, a profit maximizing monopolist will produce where marginal revenue equals marginal cost, at output (q^*) and price (p^*) in the figure. This creates a deadweight loss equal to area AEC. There is a clear trade-off, because fewer firms improve productive efficiency but lower allocative efficiency, making it a prime candidate for government regulation.

What regulation would be optimal? Assuming a single output producer, allocative efficiency requires that price equal marginal cost. Thus, one solution is for the regulatory authority to use a **marginal-cost pricing rule**. This sets price equal to marginal cost (p_{MC}) and requires the firm to supply all that is demanded at that price (q_{MC}). Notice that with this rule the firm is losing money because the price is below its average cost of production at q_{MC}. The firm will either exit the market or it will need to be subsidized. It is certainly undesirable for the firm to exit the market. In addition, to finance the subsidy requires government taxation in the form of a sales tax on other goods or an added income tax on consumers or firms. Thus even though marginal-cost pricing produces an ideal or first-best solution from society's perspective, it is not considered a viable solution to the natural monopoly problem.[73]

A more practical solution is to regulate the price so as to maximize total surplus (or minimized the deadweight loss due to monopoly) subject to the constraint that profits are not negative. This is called **Ramsey pricing** (Ramsey 1927). For a single product producer as in Fig. 20.2, Ramsey pricing implies setting price equal to average cost at the point where it crosses the demand function (p_{AC}) and requiring

---

[72] This does not mean that there must be economies of scale throughout the entire region of market demand. It simply means that industry costs are minimized when there is just one producer. When this occurs, the cost function is said to be subadditive (Baumon 1977; Braeutigam 1989; Viscusi et al. 2005, 404–408).

[73] Along similar lines, Robinson (1933) proposed the following solution. Much like a Piguovian tax (Pigou 1920), the regulatory authority provides the monopolist with a per-unit subsidy sufficient to induce the firm to produce the socially optimal level of output. This eliminates the deadweight loss. To prevent the monopolist from profiting from the subsidy, the regulatory authority imposes a lump-sum tax that is sufficient to reduce the firm's profit to zero. The drawback with such a policy is that it requires knowledge of the appropriate subsidy and tax. An alternative solution would be for the firm to engage in perfect price discrimination. This too would eliminate all deadweight loss but would favor the producer over the consumer (Braeutigam 1989).

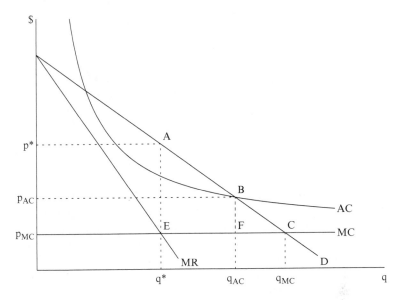

Fig. 20.2 Natural monopoly and price regulation

the firm to produce all that is demanded at that price (q_{AC}).[74] This is an **average-cost pricing rule**, which is a second-best solution. Although some deadweight loss still remains (equal to area BFC), it avoids the need to subsidize the firm.

Second-best pricing is more complicated when the firm is a multiproduct producer. When the firm produces a variety of products or markets a single product in a variety of locations, the Ramsey pricing rule for product i becomes,

$$\frac{p_i - MC_i}{p_i} = \frac{k}{\eta_i},\qquad(20.1)$$

where η_i is the absolute value of the price elasticity of demand for product i and k is a positive constant that ranges from 0 to 1.[75] Note that setting $k = 1$ produces the unregulated monopoly solution, and setting $k = 0$ eliminates all deadweight loss due to monopoly (i.e., $p_i = MC_i$). A Ramsey pricing rule requires that the monopoly markup over marginal cost in each market be scaled down by k until profits are zero.

The Ramsey pricing rule has been used for many years in the railroad industry, where it is called "value of service" pricing. It is common for rail rates per pound to be relatively low for products with elastic demand functions (i.e., high η_i), such as

---

[74] Demsetz (1968) showed that this outcome could also be reached if there was competitive bidding to serve the market, with the winner being the firm that offered to serve the market at lowest price. Sufficient competition would then drive the winning bid to average cost.

[75] We derive this rule in Appendix 20.A.

gravel and potatoes, compared to products with more inelastic demand functions, such as liquor and electronics equipment. The main weakness with using this approach to regulate prices is that it requires estimates of the price elasticity of demand for every product.

Another method that has been commonly used in public utilities is to regulate the firm's rate of return. For a firm that produces m products, this approach is based on the following accounting equation:

$$\sum_{i=1}^{m} p_i q_i = \text{OE} + r \cdot B, \qquad (20.2)$$

where OE is the firm's operating expenses, B is the value of the firm's investment capital (i.e., its base), and r identifies the firm's rate of return on its investment. Given OE and B, under **rate-of-return regulation** the regulatory agency or commission decides on the rate of return on the firm's investment and on a set of output prices so that the equality in (20.2) holds. Assuming that the regulatory agency acts in the interest of society, it will choose a "fair" rate of return, one which earns the firm zero economic profit. In the 1980s, for example, the Federal Communications Commission (FCC) identified a fair rate of return at $r = 12.2\%$ (Viscusi et al. 2005).

Once r is chosen, rate hearings are held between representatives of the firm and the regulatory commission to decide on prices. Assuming a single product producer, the price will be set so that the firm earns a fair rate of return (zero economic profit), which is identical to the Ramsey price. For a multiproduct producer, there are a variety of price combinations that satisfy (20.2), not all of which are consistent with Ramsey pricing.

Rate-of-return regulation creates serious incentive problems because it is basically a cost-plus form of regulation. With a guaranteed rate of return, X-inefficiency may result as there is little incentive for the firm to minimize costs. If the firm behaves irresponsibly, resulting in a cost increase, the right-hand side will exceed the left-hand side of (20.2). To avoid a fall in the firm's realized rate of return, the firm can simply make a request to increase price(s). Of course the regulatory commission can deny the increase if it believes that the firm's request is motivated by X-inefficiency. However, most requests to increase prices are approved.

Another way of looking at this issue is to realize that rate-of-return regulation is designed to encourage the firm to reduce its profits by increasing its output (i.e., lower its profit by choosing a higher level of output and lower price). This is socially desirable because it reduces deadweight loss. But the firm can also reduce its profit by wasting inputs, assuming it can get away with it. Averch and Johnson (1962) showed that not only does the firm have little incentive to minimize its use of inputs but rate-of-return regulation also encourages it to use too much capital relative to other inputs. This overcapitalization result is called the **Averch–Johnson effect**.[76] Although there is limited evidence that there has been overcapitalization in the

---

[76] For a more complete discussion, see Takayama (1969) and Sherman (1992).

electric utility industry, there is general agreement that rate-of-return regulation tends to increase costs.[77] For this reason, regulators in the USA have been moving away from this form of regulation.

Some economists recommended deregulation while others looked for better ways to regulate. Regulatory refinements began with Littlechild (1983) and Sappington (1983). These are called **incentive regulations**, which identify policies that reduce deadweight loss and encourage the regulated firm to minimize cost (increase innovation and improve quality). Here, we focus on the most popular type of incentive regulation, price cap regulation.[78]

Price-cap regulation requires that the regulatory commission set a maximum price, which is recalibrated on periodic intervals, usually several years, according to a specific formula. The price-cap formula is based on the expected inflation rate and the expected cost reduction due to technological change in the industry during the period. By severing the link between prices and costs, the firm can now keep any profit gained from a cost reduction. Thus, it has an incentive to minimize costs.[79]

The main difficulty with price-cap regulation is determining the expected cost reduction for the regulatory period. Setting the cost reduction factor too high will put undue financial stress on the firm. Setting it too low creates excessive deadweight loss. What is generally done is to look at historic productivity growth plus an adjustment factor based on current and expected future circumstances.

In March 1989, the FTC approved the right of states to replace rate-of-return regulation with price-cap regulation in the telecommunications industry. Table 20.6 shows that price-cap regulation has come to replace rate-of-return regulation over time. Although change has been gradual, it is consistent with the evolution to efficient laws hypothesis discussed previously, because incentive regulation is more efficient than rate-of-return regulation.

20.3.3 Economic Deregulation

A deregulation movement began in the late 1970s and continues to have a dramatic effect on the US economy. Legislation to deregulate began in the transportation sector, which included airlines (Air Cargo Deregulation Act, 1977, and Airline Deregulation Act, 1978), trucking (Motor Carrier Act, 1980), and railroads

---

[77] To review the evidence, see Stevenson (1982), Jones and Biases (1983), Joskow and Rose (1989), Winston (1993, 1998), and Viscusi et al. (2005).

[78] A number of types of incentive regulations have been proposed, with some being more practical than others. For a review of the literature, see Vogelsang (2002), Viscusi et al. (2005), and Sherman (2008).

[79] This idea derives from Baumol (1967), who observed that a regulatory lag (i.e., the lag between the time in which a regulated price can change) creates an incentive for the firm to minimize its costs. During the period between regulatory meetings, any cost reduction leads to higher profits which will persist until the next regulatory meeting.

Table 20.6 Number of US
states using different
regulations in the
telecommunications industry

Year	Rate-of-return regulation	Price-cap regulation	Other
1985	50	0	0
1990	23	1	26
1995	18	9	23
2000	7	40	3

Source: Sappington (2002)

(Staggers Act, 1980). The movement soon carried over to banking, cable TV, natural gas, oil, radio, and telecommunications. Viscusi et al. (2005) provided a summary, identifying over 40 pieces of deregulation legislation from 1971 to 2000. Moreover, the percent of GDP produced by fully regulated industries fell from 17% in 1977 to just 6.6% by 1988.[80] Whinston (1993, 1263) called this "one of the most important experiments in economic policy of our time."

Several reasons are given for the deregulation movement in the USA. According to political scientists Derthick and Quirk (1985, 36), economic deregulation "would never have occurred" if not for the convincing criticism of regulation by academic economists. Theoretically, the capture and interest-group theories of regulation questioned whether a regulatory commission could promote the interest of society. In addition, contestable market theory, which was developed in the 1970s, showed that there will be no market power in a natural monopoly when sunk costs are zero (Baumol et al. 1982). This is a dubious assumption, but the contestable market model provided additional impetus for deregulation (see Chap. 5). As discussed previously, the empirical evidence shows that regulation often promoted the welfare of industry or special interest groups over society. Noll (1989a) added that another motive for deregulation was a change in the political climate of the country, as it was becoming more supportive of free enterprise. The deregulation movement actually started with President Carter, a Democrat, and continued with President Reagan, a Republican.

In any case, the general effect has been positive. Winston (1993, 1998) reviewed the evidence in transportation, communications, finance, and energy. Table 20.7 provides a summary of his findings, listing the degree of public support for a particular type of deregulation and the benefits to consumers and producers.[81] It indicates that there was considerable public support for deregulation of the airline and telecommunications industries, consistent with evidence that the annual gain to

---

[80] It is important to realize, however, that although there was a general trend toward deregulation, government restrictions on business persisted to varying degrees throughout the economy. Not only did antitrust enforcement continue, but there has also been a trend toward increased social regulation of health, safety, and the environment (Gruenspecht and Lave 1989). In addition, Gattuso (2010) reported that the Obama administration has increased government regulation and red tape dramatically in response to the 2008–2009 financial crisis.

[81] These estimates ignore the additional benefit that would occur if unregulated markets were to behave optimally.

Table 20.7 Public support and annual welfare effects of deregulation (billions of 1990 dollars)

Industry	Consumers	Producers	Total	Public support for deregulation
Airlines	(8.8, 14.0)	4.9	(13.7, 19.7)	69%
Railroads	(7.2, 9.7)	3.2	(10.4, 12.9)	n.a.
Trucking	15.4	−4.8	10.6	n.a.
Telecommunications	(0.73, 1.6)	0	(0.73, 1.6)	52%
Cable television	(3.7, 1.3)	0	(0.37, 1.3)	47%
Brokerage	0.14	−0.14	0	n.a.
Total	(32.6, 43.0)	3.2	(35.8, 46.2)	

Note that the numbers in parentheses indicate a range of estimates, and n.a. means not available. Public support for deregulation is in response to the question: has deregulation generally worked in or against the public's interest?
Source: See Winston (1993). In addition, Winston (1998) found that regulation caused operating costs in banking to decline by 8% and operating and maintenance costs in the transmission and distribution of natural gas to decline by 35%

society has been large, at least $36–$46 billion. This translates to a 7–9% improvement in productivity in these areas of the economy.[82] The success of deregulation in the USA led to a deregulation movement in Japan and among some members of the European Union. As Noll (1989b) cautioned, however, the case for deregulation is industry and regulation specific. The evidence should not be taken to mean that society gains from all forms of deregulation and for every industry. A prime example is the excessive deregulation of the financial sector, which began in the 1990s and contributed to the financial crisis of 2008–2009.

In any case, given evidence of the social gains in certain sectors of the economy, you might ask why deregulation in these industries did not occur sooner. One reason is that many academic economists did not become convinced of the benefits of deregulation until the 1960s. It may have taken additional time for policymakers to become sufficiently persuaded that the benefits outweighed the costs of deregulation. Under the public-interest theory of regulation, Noll (1989a, 1260) pointed out that deregulation will occur when it becomes apparent that "the costs of regulation exceed . . . the cost of repealing it plus the costs of the remaining market failure." In addition, Joskow and Rose (1989) noted that regulatory systems respond slowly to new economic and political environments.

Unfortunately, we are unable to determine conclusively whether the deregulation movement in the USA favors the public-interest over the special-interest theory of regulation/deregulation. Given lags in awareness of the substantial gains from deregulation, the deregulation movement is consistent with the public-interest theory. However, Peltzman (1989) argued that the evidence is not inconsistent with the special-interest theory either. First, consumers clearly benefitted from deregulation, and consumers became better organized in the 1970s under such consumer advocates as Ralph Nader. Second, many, although not all, producers

---

[82] According to Noll (1989a, b) and Winston (1993), the evidence also shows that labor generally benefited from deregulation.

benefited from deregulation; Peltzman argued that many industry leaders began to realize that regulation had become excessively burdensome. Thus, there was diminished interest group support and, therefore, political support for regulation.

We can draw two final conclusions from the US deregulation movement. First, the success of deregulation shows that society's interests were well served by economists' recommendation to eliminate certain types of regulation. Second, the movement clearly improved economic efficiency, which is consistent with the evolution to efficient laws hypothesis.

20.4 Social Regulation

Most of our attention has been devoted to issues of static and dynamic efficiency. However, as we discussed in previous chapters, issues of fairness and concerns with the environment are also important social goals. For example, a technological change can lead to greater wealth but also to higher levels of pollution and an increased risk of war. As a society, we must make trade-offs between economic growth and regulations that address a broader range of social concerns. In this section, we limit our discussion to regulations that are designed to curb firm behavior that is detrimental to consumers, issues that are most relevant to the field of industrial organization.[83]

Evidence from behavioral economics shows that consumers do not always make decisions that are in their long-run best interest. We have seen that some consumers make systematic errors, are influenced by context and inertia, and have self-control problems. One of the main goals of this book has been to show how rational firms exploit these weaknesses. This opens the door to policies or social regulations that are designed to help consumers make better decisions. It is in the area of consumer policy that behavioral economics has been most valuable.

A serious weakness of the Sherman and Clayton acts was that they failed to address unfair business practices that can harm consumers. We saw in Chap. 19 that some firms have made false claims and engaged in fraud, actions that clearly harm consumers. To correct this policy shortcoming, the Federal Trade Commission Act (1914, as amended by the Wheeler–Lea Act in 1938) was enacted, making it illegal for a firm to engage in fraud, deception, and unfair business practices. In addition, the consumer movement, which gained steam in the 1960s (Nader 1973), led to increased legislation to protect consumers.

In this section, we review examples where firms have used unfair practices to exploit consumers and describe various public policy responses. We begin by addressing issues that are directly related to consumer protection. Next, we address social concerns with deception and advertising.

---

[83] For a more complete discussion of the economics of social regulations, see Asch (1988), Gruenspecht and Lave (1989), Greer (1992), Viscusi et al. (2005), and Sherman (2008).

20.4.1 Pricing and Packaging Behavior

An early concern with firm behavior was pricing policies designed to confuse the customer. Friedman's (1966) study clearly illustrates the problem. In 1965, he asked 33 college students to pick out the most economical packages of 20 grocery store items. To get a feel for how difficult it was to be a cost-minimizing shopper in the early 1960s, you need to realize that consumers might face the following set of prices for boxes of detergent: 25 jumbo ounces for $0.53, 1 pound for $0.59, or 28½ full ounces for $0.57. In spite of their above average education, the average student in Friedman's study had difficulty identifying the lowest price option and spent 9.1% more than they should have spent. This is not surprising given the use of weight and volume for the same commodity, the use of fractions to measure quantities, and no clear definition of the adjectives "jumbo" and "full." By making it so costly to find the lowest priced item, firms are exploiting people's bounded rationality to benefit themselves at the expense of consumers.

These labeling tactics led to the passage of the **Fair Packaging and Labeling Act (1966)**.[84] It requires that the net quantity be clearly labeled and expressed in a unit of measure that is appropriate for the product. In addition, many states have unit-pricing laws, which require supermarkets to indicate not only the price of a packaged good but also the price per unit of weight or volume.[85] For example, at a local store a 16 ounce box of Captain Crunch breakfast cereal sold for $6.29 and a 13.5 ounce box of Special K sold for $4.39. The different container sizes make it difficult to tell which is cheaper per ounce. Unit-pricing laws require stores to also list the price per ounce, which is $0.393 for Captain Crunch and $0.325 for Special K. If cost is the only consideration, Special K is the better buy.

Similar concerns led to the **Truth in Lending Act (1968)**, which promotes the informed use of consumer credit. To minimize cognitive errors, it requires lenders to disclose the terms of a loan and to define the cost of a loan as an annual percentage rate (APR). Thus, a lender cannot offer you a loan for an interest rate of 1.5% per month, hoping that you will not realize that it is a very high rate of interest on a yearly basis, an APR of over 16%.

20.4.2 Behavioral Economics and Credit Cards

Bar-Gill (2004) used evidence from behavioral economics to make a case for greater regulation of the credit card industry. Bar-Gill argued that the abuse of credit cards gets many people into financial trouble because of a variety of cognitive

---

[84] In addition, since 1994 the Food and Drug Administration has required firms to list basic food facts on their labels. The Nutrition Labeling and Education Act (1990) extended labeling requirements to dietary supplements.

[85] To see the details of state laws, see http://ts.nist.gov/WeightsAndMeasures/pricinglaws_guide.cfm.

weaknesses. Many consumers have imperfect self-control, leading to excessive borrowing. This abuse is compounded for those who behave in a time-inconsistent manner or are prone to overestimate their willpower in the future (i.e., they consequently underestimate their future borrowing). Another problem is that some people simply forget to pay their bills on time, causing them to incur late fees and interest charges.

To exploit these weaknesses, credit card companies have devised a number of strategies. They offer unsolicited cards to high risk consumers with annual fees, reward programs, and low initial interest rates. They also levy expensive late charges and high interest rates once the promotional period expires. Thus, forgetful consumers pay high late charges, and consumers with self-control problems pay much higher interest rates than they would with a traditional bank loan.

Concern that credit card issuers exploit the most vulnerable consumers coupled with the financial crisis of 2008–2009 led to the passage of the **Credit Card Act (2009)**.[86] Provisions of the Act include:

- Requiring greater transparency in terms of interest rates and late charges.
- Reducing spending rewards and requiring higher up-front charges and annual fees.
- Giving consumers clearer due dates and more time to pay their monthly bill before incurring a late fee.
- Substantially limiting credit cards for consumers under 21 years of age.

These provisions address many of the concerns with the credit card industry that are raised by behavioral economists.[87]

20.4.3 Behavioral Economics and Libertarian Paternalism: Framing and Inertia

When searching for a policy solution to the behavioral weaknesses of consumers, we must remember that there can be a trade-off with paternalistic protection. Both protection and liberty are valuable, but greater protection generally means less freedom. Thus, social philosophers continually debate where policy lines should be drawn. For example, Mill's Principle implies that laws that limit individual freedom should be

---

[86] For a more complete discussion, see the White House Fact Sheet, *Reforms to Protect American Credit Card Holders*, available at http://www.whitehouse.gov/the_press_office/Fact-Sheet-Reforms-to-Protect-American-Credit-Card-Holders/.

[87] For a discussion of concerns with the behavioral policy approach, see Wright (2007), Werden et al. (2010), and Salinger (2010). Wright argues that paternalism will reduce learning and the incentive to behave rationally, which makes for less effective consumers in the long run.

enacted only to protect harm to others, not to protect us from ourselves. This principle is based on the belief that individuals know better than the state what is best for them. At the same time, evidence from behavioral economics suggests that too much freedom can be harmful.

In response to these concerns, Thaler and Sunstein (2003, 2008) made a strong case for paternalism that corrects behavioral errors while minimally constraining freedom. They call this "libertarian paternalism." To illustrate, they consider the problem that every elementary school administrator (or manager of a large corporation) faces: how food should be arranged in the cafeteria. School officials might face the following options:

1. Place fruit first and dessert last on the cafeteria line.
2. Randomly arrange food along the cafeteria line.
3. Place dessert first and fruit last on the cafeteria line.

If people were fully rational, their choices would not be affected by how food items are placed. However, behavioral economics shows that framing effects do matter; we choose more fruit and less dessert under option 1. Given the obesity problem in the USA, the first option is best for students and society in the long term. A decision to choose option 1 is paternalistic, because it is designed to influence student behavior in a way that makes them better off. Moreover, it is a form of libertarian paternalism because it does not coerce anyone to do anything. Students are free to buy as much dessert as they want under each option. Thus, Thaler and Sunstein argued that not even a libertarian like Mill would object to this type of paternalistic policy.

A high stakes example involves employee choice of a pension plan. When employees become eligible to participate in a 401k pension plan, companies may offer one of two different default options: (1) Employees are not automatically enrolled in the plan. To participate, they must fill out a form to enroll. (2) Employees are automatically enrolled in the plan. If they do not want to be a part of the plan, they must fill out a form to opt out. Given problems with procrastination and inertia, most people stay with what is automatically set up for them. Madrian and Shea (2001) found that enrollments in 401k plans were 49–86% higher for option 2 than option 1. This research and the work by Thaler and others led to the **Pension Protection Act (2006)**, which encourages companies to set up pension plans using defaults that are better for employees.[88]

The behavioral approach also justifies laws that require a cooling-off period before certain contracts or purchases can be finalized. Such rules are based on the idea that a consumer who makes a purchase in an emotionally hot state would not do so in cooler or more rational state. For example, people who are shopping for a

---

[88] Thaler and Sunstein (2008) argued that this approach applies to all consumer decisions that are complex. For example, they advocate that if senior citizens are required to enroll for a drug benefit program, they should be given a limited number of options and the default should be a sensible one.

new car and are susceptible to a forceful sales pitch may end up making a purchase that they later regret. Knowing this tendency, a shopper may decide to bring along a knowledgeable friend who can dampen the emotional heat generated by the salesperson. One cannot use this strategy when a door-to-door salesperson comes to your home unannounced, however. These behavioral issues are addressed by cooling-off laws, which give consumers three days to cancel a purchase that was made in your home or when you purchase real estate, insurance, or a security.[89]

20.4.4 Behavioral Economics and Asymmetric Paternalism: Selectively Limiting Choices

To address different policy concerns that are relevant to behavioral economics, Camerer et al. (2003) proposed something called "asymmetric paternalism." A policy that is asymmetrically paternalistic constrains uninformed or cognitively challenged consumers from making mistakes without constraining the choices of rational and informed individuals. Classic examples include laws that constrain the consumption opportunities of children but not adults. Because children are cognitively developing and are frequently uniformed, it is illegal for children to buy alcohol and cigarettes. Similarly, to legally drive a car you must be of a certain age and pass both a written and a driving test.

As Camerer et al. (2003) and Thaler and Sunstein (2003, 2008) pointed out, however, paternalistic policies are always problematic. Restrictions that go beyond libertarian paternalism raise the question of where to draw the line and who should draw it. Mill would be more worried about protecting us from the state than from ourselves. Even if we could trust the state with this task, we would still need to ask whether the benefits exceed the costs of government involvement.

There is particular concern with asymmetric paternalism, because it treats people differently and opens the door for the majority or the state to levy unacceptable restrictions on certain groups. For example, in the nineteenth century married women were deemed incapable of entering into contracts on their own (Camerer et al. 2003, 1213). For over a century, various rationales were used to justify unfair and asymmetric treatment of African-Americans. During World War II, the law was changed to take away the freedom and property of American citizens of Japanese descent. Of course, such restrictions are inconsistent with our view of asymmetric paternalism today. Nevertheless, fairness considerations require careful scrutiny of any asymmetric treatment of individuals.

---

[89] For further discussion, see the FTC's statement on the cooling-off rule at http://www.ftc.gov/bcp/edu/pubs/consumer/products/pro03.shtm.

20.5 Social Concerns with Advertising

As we discussed in previous chapters, the welfare effect of advertising hinges on a number of factors. Advertising that is honest and informative is beneficial to consumers and helps markets perform more efficiently, while that which is dishonest, deceptive, or offensive is harmful to consumers and society. Moreover, advertising that encourages unhealthy behavior, such as smoking, excessive alcohol consumption, and poor dietary habits, is undesirable. These varying benefits and costs make policy analysis of advertising rather difficult. Another facet of advertising is that it is a form of communication, and as such, any restriction on advertising raises the issue of freedom of speech. In this section, we begin by reviewing what we learned about social concerns with advertising, and then we discuss advertising regulations.

20.5.1 Advertising and Social Responsibility

In Chap. 4, we learned how advertisements that are salient, particularly those with emotional content and appeal to biological needs, would be most effective at generating sales. Unfortunately, such ads may be socially offensive. In many consumer goods industries, firms use romance and sexually provocative ads to increase sales. We saw in Chap. 16 that the 1911 advertising for Woodbury soap featured a young woman in the company of several handsome youngmen with the caption, "Skin You Love to Touch." In addition, recent Calvin Klein perfume ads and Paris Hilton's ads for Carl's Jr. have been sexually charged.

To attract the attention of a targeted audience, we saw in Chaps. 16 and 19 that some ads use stereotypes that promote sexism, racism, and ageism. In the 1950s, the spokesperson for Aunt Jemima pancakes was an African-American woman who was depicted as a servant. In the 1960s, the spokesperson for Frito corn chips was the "Frito Bandito," a Hispanic cartoon character depicted as a criminal. In 1992, the Heileman Brewing Company introduced "Crazy Horse Malt Liquor," a name that offended Native American people because Crazy Horse is another name for Tasunke Witko who is a revered defender of the Lakota Sioux people.[90] In 2006, Sony introduced a white version of its PSP game system to complement its black version with an ad that featured a blond white woman dominating a subordinate African-American woman with the caption "PlayStation Portable White is Coming."

---

[90] For a more complete discussion of the politically incorrect marketing actions of US beer companies, see V. Tremblay and C. Tremblay (2005, 2007).

Supporters of advertising claim that these ads simply reflect the cultural norms in our society and do not promote or reinforce racism and sexism. Nevertheless, such ads remain a policy concern if they are contributing factors.

Advertising is also a social concern when it is false and deceptive. In Chap. 19, we presented many examples where firms have used deceptive business practices to exploit consumers. These included false claims about the effectiveness of diet pills and devices to boost the gas mileage of your car. In most of these cases, it is uneconomic for consumers to obtain complete information about product characteristics before purchase.

But even in case of false claims, Posner (1973) argued that no government involvement is necessary. His position is based on the argument that competition among firms and the response by rational consumers will deter firms from behaving deceptively. That is, profit maximizing firms will consider the fact that fully rational consumers will boycott dishonest firms, an especially effective form of discipline when repeat purchase is common. If the future is sufficiently important, a firm will want to treat its customers fairly. Although it may be profitable today to water down quality (because it lowers current costs) or make false claims (because it raises current demand), it will reduce repeat purchases, which lowers demand and profits tomorrow. As a result, reputable firms will not cheat their customers. Instead, they will develop quality name brands and guarantee their products in response to these information problems.[91] Thus, honest firms succeed and dishonest firms fail in the long run.

However reasonable Posner's argument sounds, there are two counterarguments to his position. First, a firm that is planning to go out of business or that cares little about the future will benefit financially from cheating customers. As we discussed in Chap. 14, consumers are not always able to avoid fly-by-night companies, because such companies can be difficult to identify.

The second counterargument to Posner's position derives from behavioral economics evidence. Even when the future matters to firms, confirmation bias may cause a sufficient number of consumers to ignore negative outcomes, which can delay the dissemination of information about deceptive business behavior. Nagler (1993) showed that businesses offering bad deals can survive because it frequently takes time for deception to become apparent, and once apparent some consumers are psychologically unwilling to admit to themselves and others that they were deceived. In this case, accurate information about deceptive marketing tactics may not be spread throughout the market, allowing deception to persist for a considerable period of time. Furthermore, Salop and Stiglitz (1977) demonstrated that firms offering bad deals can survive in markets with informed and uninformed consumers as long as there is a continuous supply of uniformed consumers.

Much of the discussion about deception involves a firm's use of advertising. Clearly, ads that make false and deceptive claims benefit the firm at the expense of consumers in the short run. This is why the Federal Trade Commission Act (1914,

---

[91] For the remainder of the chapter, we will discuss problems associated with information and advertising. For those interested in issues of product safety, see Asch (1988).

as amended by the Wheeler-Lea Act in 1938) makes fraudulent, unfair, and deceptive ads illegal. Unfortunately, defining what is false and deceptive can be tricky. As we saw in Chap. 16, three conditions must be met for an ad to be deemed false and deceptive from a legal standpoint. First, it must present or omit information that is likely to mislead consumers.[92] One example is the "bait and switch" tactic where a seller entices customers to a store with a low price offer that the firm has no intention of honoring. Once in the store, customers are told that the advertised product is sold out and are persuaded to buy a higher priced substitute. Another example is when a firm fails to disclose to consumers a product defect that is known to the seller.

Second, the ad must be viewed as deceptive from the viewpoint of a targeted group or "reasonable consumer."[93] As we discussed in Chap. 16, this concept is a bit nebulous. For example, it can be very difficult for a reasonable consumer to identify a domestic car, because not every part in a domestic car derives from the USA. To avoid deception, the FTC requires that to market a car as domestic, all "significant parts and processes" must be of US origin ("Complying with the Made in the USA Standard," at http://www.ftc.gov/). On the other hand, a reasonable consumer is expected to realize that a French pastry is simply a French style pastry that is made locally. Thus, marketing it as a French pastry is not illegal. The evidence from behavioral economics raises the concern that consumers who fall below the reasonable consumer standard may be deceived, however.

A reasonable consumer is expected to see through ads that use puffing as a marketing ploy. As we saw in Chap. 19, this applies to claims that are not easily measurable and frequently use adjectives such as best, perfect, exceptional, original, and wonderful. A classic puff is Minute Rice's claim of "Perfect Rice Every Time." The reasonable consumer principle played a prominent role in deciding the case involving Listerine mouthwash, which was said to "Kills germs by millions on contact" and "For general oral hygiene, bad breath, colds, and resulting sore throats." The FTC effectively argued that these statements would mislead a reasonable consumer into believing that Listerine could prevent colds and sore throats, and the "colds, and resultant sore throats" phrase had to be removed from all marketing materials.

The last condition that must be met for an ad to be viewed as false and deceptive is "materiality." Information regarding the purpose, safety, and price of a product would be considered material. If a deceptive claim is not expected to cause consumers to make a different choice, then it is considered immaterial and would not be challenged by the FTC.

---

[92] Failure to disclose relevant information can be just as misleading as providing false information. For example, if a used car salesperson knew that a car needed new brakes within the next month and failed to disclose this information to a buyer, this would be considered deceptive.

[93] Targeted groups could include the terminally ill or children. Regarding ads targeted at children, a higher standard is used because of the "limited ability of children to detect exaggerated or untrue statements" ("The ABCs at the FTC: Marketing and Advertising to Children," at http://www.ftc. gov/).

20.5.2   Advertising Bans and Regulations

In spite of these concerns, the legislature and the courts are reluctant to vigorously regulate advertising given First Amendment protection of freedom of speech.[94] In an early decision in *Valentine v. Chrestensen* (1942), the Supreme Court ruled that certain classes of speech could be exempt from First Amendment protection and added commercial speech to the list that already included obscene, libelous, and insulting (i.e., fighting words) speech. A clear interpretation of the protection of commercial speech did not occur until 1980 with the decision in *Central Hudson Gas v. Public Service Commission* (1980). In essence, the precedent set by this case made government regulation of advertising or commercial speech permissible when (1) advertising is misleading, (2) there is substantial gain from the regulation, (3) the regulation directly advances the interests of society, and (4) the regulation is not more extensive than is necessary. Given this relatively high standard, there are few government regulations on advertising.

The few that have been imposed involve products that generate negative externalities, particularly alcohol and tobacco products that are addictive. In markets such as these, the government generally imposes excise taxes and advertising restrictions to reduce consumption and mitigate the resulting externalities.[95] Restrictions on alcohol ads have not been supported by the Supreme Court, however. For example, the Supreme Court overruled the Federal Alcohol Administration Act of 1935 [section 5(e)(2)], which prohibited beer labels from displaying alcohol content (V. Tremblay and C. Tremblay 2005). Similarly, in 1996 the Supreme Court overturned a 1956 Rhode Island law that made it illegal to advertise the price of alcoholic beverages (Milyo and Waldfogel, 1999). In both cases, the Court based its ruling on the fact that such laws were "more extensive than necessary" and that the goal of reducing consumption could be reached more directly through higher taxes.

The most extensive set of advertising restrictions have been imposed on the US cigarette industry. Convincing medical research linking cigarette smoking to various health risks became apparent by the early 1950s. As continued research confirmed these negative health effects, the federal government instituted a number of policies that were designed to reduce cigarette demand. We discuss these in detail in Chap. 21 and focus on advertising restrictions here.

Given public concern that cigarette companies used advertising to attract underage smokers and used public relations efforts to confound consumers about the health risks of smoking, two pieces of legislation were enacted to reduce cigarette demand. First, the Federal Communication Commission required television networks to air one antismoking ad for every three prosmoking ads by cigarette companies, effective July 1967 through 1970, under what is called the "fairness

---

[94] For a more complete discussion of regulatory issues involving advertising, see Pitofsky (1977).

[95] Unfortunately, the evidence shows that higher taxes lead to higher prices and less alcohol consumption but not less alcohol abuse (V. Tremblay and C. Tremblay 2005; Cooper and Wright, 2010).

doctrine." Second, Congress passed the Public Health Cigarette Smoking Act (1970), which banned all (prosmoking and antismoking) advertising from television and radio, effective January 1, 1971.[96]

Unfortunately, the broadcast advertising ban proved ineffective. First, it did not significantly reduce the market demand for cigarettes. Second, it had the unintended consequence of increasing industry profits (Eckard 1991; Farr et al. 2001; Iwasaki and V. Tremblay 2009). This evidence is consistent with combative-type advertising and explains why the industry did not oppose the ban (Hamilton 1972; Pollay 1994).

The history of marketing regulations in the cigarette industry provides a dramatic example of both market and government failure. On the one hand, cigarette companies failed to behave responsibly when marketing their product. On the other hand, the government enacted marketing restrictions that proved ineffective at reducing cigarette demand. In fact, the evidence shows that the broadcast advertising ban benefitted the industry more than the public at large (Farr et al. 2001). At the same time, this is not to say that all government policies have been ineffective. The evidence shows that higher taxes and clean indoor air laws have reduced cigarette demand without redistributing wealth from consumers to cigarette producers (Keeler et al. 1993; Evans and Farrelly 1998; Farr et al. 2001).

20.6 Summary

1. From a normative perspective, laws and regulations ought to promote the interests of society. This is consistent with the **public-interest theory**. Unfortunately, not all laws and regulations meet this high standard. As a result, they set up laws and regulations in response to their constituents, consisting of the public, firms, and special interest groups. This can lead to a form of government failure.
2. When a market fails to produce an ideal outcome, laws and regulations may increase social welfare. However, appropriate public policy requires a comparison of the market outcome with a real alternative outcome, one that takes into account the cost of implementing a government fix and the possibility of government failure.
3. A legal system has three important characteristics: it is a social phenomenon, it is authoritative, and it serves a particular goal or aim.

---

[96] In addition, the Master Settlement Agreement of 1998 between the tobacco industry and most state governments prohibited most outdoor and transit advertising and the use of cartoon characters in cigarette ads (Chaloupka 2007). In 2009, Congress passed the Family Smoking Prevention and Tobacco Control Act, which required that warning labels cover the top 50% of the front and back panels of the package. See Curfman et al. (2009) for a discussion of the law. The complete transcript can be found at http://www.govtrack.us/congress/bill.xpd?bill=h111-1256.

4. **Arrow's Impossibility Theorem** states that a social welfare function (or rule) that meets certain regularity requirements and is nondictatorial does not exist. This implies that simple voting rules will not lead to socially optimal solutions. Dictatorships fail because dictators are rarely benevolent. Thus, a decision process that allows for an open dialogue and has sufficient checks and balances is perhaps the best we can do.

5. There are two main systems of law, the **common law** and the **civil law** systems. In general, a common law system gives judges more discretion than does a civil law system. This suggests that the common law system would be more efficient in a dynamic setting. The empirical evidence typically shows that countries with common law systems have better economic outcomes than civil law systems, at least in the recent past.

6. There are several forces that help shape our legal system. According to the **evolution to efficient laws hypothesis**, laws will evolve to produce more efficient outcomes. Stigler (1971) and others have proposed that laws are influenced by special interest groups. Roe (1996) added that historical events and circumstances play an important role. When faced with a problem that requires a legal remedy, differing circumstances may cause a different law to be implemented, and the law may not evolve toward efficiency if switching costs are sufficiently high.

7. In principle, antitrust laws are designed to promote competition and limit the negative effect of market power. Key legislation includes:

   • **The Sherman Act** (1890), which makes collusion (Section 1) and monopolization (Section 2) illegal.
   • **The Clayton Act** (1914, as amended by the Celler–Kefauver Act of 1950) makes price discrimination (Section 2), exclusive dealing and tying contracts (Section 3), and mergers (Section 7) illegal when the effect is to reduce competition or create a monopoly.
   • **The Federal Trade Commission Act** (1914, as amended by the Wheeler–Lea Act of 1938) created the Federal Trade Commission to enforce the antitrust laws. The Act also made it illegal for firms to engage in fraud, deception, and unfair business practices.

8. In practice, both the Department of Justice and the Federal Trade Commission pursue antitrust cases. Antitrust violations can result in fines, jail time for managers, injunctions, and the breakup of the firm.

9. Some business practices are always illegal and are said to be **per se illegal**. For others, a **rule of reason** applies, because they are illegal only under certain circumstances.

10. Regarding the monopolization of a market, the courts have generally followed a rule of reason. That is, to be guilty of Section 2 of the Sherman Act, a firm must have a sufficiently large market share and be guilty of behaving unreasonably toward its competitors. Conviction can have dire consequences, as it can result in the breakup of the firm. Prominent examples include the breakup of Standard Oil of New Jersey, American Tobacco, and AT&T.

11. Unless cooperation promotes the efficient operation of a market, collusion is per se illegal under Section 1 of the Sherman Act. But by their nature collusive agreements are kept secret, making it difficult for government agencies and the courts to be sure that a cartel agreement actually exists. Without direct evidence of a conspiracy, the courts follow a rule of reason. That is, a guilty verdict requires there to be parallel behavior, called **conscious parallelism**, plus additional evidence such as market segmentation.

12. A loophole made the original antimerger laws ineffective at preventing anticompetitive mergers. The Celler–Kefauver Act (1950) closed the loophole, and the courts began to take a tough stand against horizontal mergers. A problem in implementing the Act was that the courts frequently used inconsistent definitions of geographic and product markets. Given concern among economists and within the business community that the law was unclear, the Department of Justice developed a set of **Merger Guidelines** in 1968 that identified which mergers would likely be challenged by the Department of Justice. The Guidelines have been revised in 1982–1984, 1992–1997, and 2010. Revisions allow for an efficiency defense and provide a clearer definition of a market.

13. A review of the history of antitrust court cases reveals three observations:

    1. The courts have modified the law to address the particular circumstances of the times, such as weighing equity and the welfare of labor more heavily during the Great Depression. This is what one would expect in a common law system.
    2. Economics research has influenced the application of the antitrust laws. For example, the work by Williamson (1968) influenced the decision to consider a static efficiency defense when evaluating mergers. Demsetz's (1973) superior efficiency hypothesis, which says that a firm may gain monopoly power from innovative activity as well as from anticompetitive firm behavior, led to greater consideration of dynamic efficiency issues.
    3. Enforcement of the antitrust laws has changed considerably over time. In response to economic arguments and empirical evidence, the courts have generally placed greater emphasis on efficiency since the antitrust laws were instituted. The one exception is in the sports industry, which has had an antitrust exemption. At best, there is weak evidence that enforcement is influenced by the political-economic views of the president.

14. There are two types of business regulations. The first is social regulation, which is designed to protect the environment and the safety of consumers and workers. The second is economic regulation, which addresses problems of market failure. In this chapter, we focus on the economic regulation of a firm's price, output, and advertising decisions and social regulation involving unfair business practices.

15. There are three theories of regulation. The first is the **public-interest theory of regulation** in which a regulatory agency or commission chooses the best policy to serve society. The second is the **capture theory of regulation**, which proposes that the regulatory commission serves the interests of the industry it is supposed to be regulating. Finally, there is the **interest-group theory of regulation**, which posits that the regulatory commission behaves in its own self

interest and responds to those groups that have the most power over the commission. The evidence shows that the capture theory best explains railroad and public utility regulation and that special interest groups have considerable power in our political system. These theories are incomplete because they ignore the role of the courts and poorly explain the social regulation movement.

16. In a natural monopoly, the presence of substantial scale economies means that a monopoly structure is required for productive efficiency. If unregulated, the firm will set the monopoly price, which produces allocative inefficiency. As a result, these firms are generally regulated. Common regulatory schemes are the following:

   • The first-best solution is to regulate the price at marginal cost and require the firm to produce all that is demanded at that price. This is called a **marginal-cost pricing rule**. It is an impractical solution, because the firm earns negative profits. Either the firm will go out of business or will need to be subsidized.

   • It is more common for the regulatory commission to set price equal to average cost. The **average-cost pricing rule** minimizes the deadweight loss associated with monopoly, given no subsidy to the firm. When the firm produces a single product, this is consistent with **Ramsey Pricing**. With Ramsey Pricing for a multiproduct monopoly, the Lerner index will be proportional (but not equal) to one divided by the price elasticity of demand.

   • Another regulatory solution is **rate-of-return regulation**, such that the firm's prices are regulated so that the firm earns zero economic profit or a normal rate of return.

   • The main problem with these pricing rules is that they create serious incentive problems. That is, if prices are set to just cover costs, the firm does not have an incentive to minimize costs. This observation led economists to develop new policies, called **incentive regulation**. The most common example is **price-cap regulation**, where the regulatory commission sets the maximum price, which remains unchanged for a particular period of time and is based on a formula that depends on expected changes in inflation and productivity. Because this formula is not a function of costs, the firm can retain any gains resulting from a cost reduction. Thus, the firm has an incentive to innovate and minimize its costs.

17. The deregulation movement began in the 1970s. According to Derthick and Quirk (1985), motivation for the movement came from the research of academic economists which pointed out the merits of deregulation. Economic deregulation resulted in dramatic efficiency gains in such industries as airlines, railroads, trucking, telecommunications, and cable television. Thus, the deregulation movement is consistent with the evolution to efficient laws/regulations hypothesis.

18. To protect consumers, the Federal Trade Commission Act (1914, as amended by the Wheeler-Lea Act in 1938) makes fraud, deception, and unfair business practices illegal. In addition, the **Fair Packaging and Labeling Act (1966)**, requires that packages be labeled in a way that makes it easier for consumers to make unit price comparisons across brands.

19. Contributions from behavioral economics have led to new regulations to protect consumers, such as (1) the **Pension Protection Act (2006)**, which encourages companies to set up retirement pension plans and use defaults that are better for employees and (2) the **Credit Card Act (2009)**, which provides greater protection to credit card users who tend to make behavioral errors.

20. Thaler and Sunstein (2003, 2008) made a strong case for a type of paternalism that corrects behavioral errors while minimally constraining liberty. They call this "libertarian paternalism." One example is a policy that requires employers to make enrollment in its pension plan the default and requires employees to formally indicate if they opt out of the pension plan. This will lead more employees to enroll in the plan. It is paternalistic because it is designed to influence behavior in a way that makes individuals better off. Yet, it preserves liberty because it does not limit individual choice.

21. There are many cases where free markets fail to provide socially beneficial advertising. Firms may push the boundaries of social responsibility by using derogatory stereotypes to appeal to a target audience. In addition, they may use false and deceptive ads to fool customers and gain an advantage over their competitors, at least in the short run. The FTC serves as the watchdog of the advertising practices to ensure that they are honest and fair.

22. Because advertising is a form of speech and freedom of speech is highly valued, the government can restrict advertising only if the restriction is clearly beneficial to society and is not more limiting than necessary. One regulation that was allowed is the broadcast advertising ban on cigarettes, which was intended to reduce smoking and improve public health. Unfortunately, the ban has been ineffective at reducing the market demand for cigarettes and actually raised industry profits by facilitating coordination in advertising. This is one example where government policy produced unintended consequences.

20.7 Review Questions

1. Appropriate policy analysis requires one to analyze when markets fail and when government fails to generate socially desirable outcomes.

   A. Briefly describe what is meant by market failure and by government failure.
   B. Briefly describe what Demsetz (1969) meant by the nirvana approach and the comparative institutional approach to public policy analysis. Why do we frequently use the nirvana approach as a starting point when discussing the merits of an economic policy?
   C. In general, do you think it would be socially more costly to correct a government policy that places too many restrictions on a market than a policy that places too few? Explain.

2. Briefly describe the public-interest, interest-group, and capture theories of law and regulation.

3. Regarding the philosophy of law:

   A. Identify the three characteristics of a legal system.
   B. Compare and contrast the concepts of natural law and legal positivism.
   C. Briefly describe John Stuart Mill's concerns with government power and democracy.

4. Regarding the common law and civil law systems:

   A. Describe the key features of the common law and civil law systems. What are the prominent strengths and weaknesses of each system?
   B. What are the primary forces that cause laws to evolve and change over time?
   C. According to research on legal origins theory, which system has been more efficient?
   D. Discuss the main ways in which a dictatorial legal system would differ from common and civil law systems. Would you expect a dictatorial system to be more or less efficient and socially desirable than common and civil law systems (Arrow 1951; Sen 1970)? Explain.

5. In antitrust law, firm behavior can be evaluated according to a *rule of reason* or it can be considered *per se illegal*. Explain.

6. Regarding the Sherman Act:

   A. Section 1 makes collusion illegal. Is this socially desirable? Are there any conditions where collusion is socially desirable? Explain.
   B. Section 2 makes it illegal for a firm to attempt to monopolize a market. Is this socially desirable? Are there any conditions where such an attempt is socially desirable? Explain.

7. Explain how Section 7 of the Clayton Act (as amended by the Celler–Kefauver Act) can prevent market power.

8. In principle, the antitrust laws are designed to promote competition and improve market efficiency. Given the work by Williamson (1968) and Demsetz (1973), explain why these laws may fail to promote dynamic efficiency.

9. Regarding the evolution of the antitrust laws:

   A. Briefly discuss how the application of the antitrust laws has evolved over time in relation to long-term trends and political cycles.
   B. Does the evolution of the Merger Guidelines tell us anything about the long-term trend in antimerger enforcement? Explain.
   C. Are your answers above consistent with the evolution to efficient laws hypothesis? Explain.

10. One reason for the economic regulation of industry is to address the unique economic problems associated with a natural monopoly.

    A. Briefly explain what is meant by a natural monopoly.
    B. How is a natural monopoly efficient in one way but inefficient in another?

C. Discuss two ways in which a regulatory commission could eliminate the inefficiency associated with a natural monopoly.

D. Do your answers in part C meet the incentive regulation criteria? Explain.

11. Regarding deregulation:

A. Explain what is meant by economic deregulation.

B. Much of the empirical evidence shows that deregulation has improved efficiency. How is this possible?

12. Regarding behavioral economics and social regulation:

A. How has research in behavioral economics contributed to new and better social regulations?

B. By definition, social regulations limit individual freedom and are paternalistic. Explain how a policy that is consistent with libertarian paternalism minimizes limits on freedom.

13. Posner (1973) argued that unfair business practices will not be a problem in the long run, because rational consumers will quit buying products from firms that behave irresponsibly. Provide two reasons why Posner may be wrong.

14. Regarding advertising bans:

A. Assume the government imposes an advertising ban on a monopoly firm. How will this affect firm costs? Would your answer be the same if the government imposed a ban on the firm's use of labor? Explain.

B. Assume the government imposes an advertising ban on an industry with two firms. Use a payoff matrix to show how this can facilitate coordination and higher profits for firms. In this case, is advertising likely to be a strategic complement or substitute?

C. Assume the government imposes a marketing ban on an industry with two firms. Use a payoff matrix to show how this can lower firm profits. In this case, is advertising likely to be a strategic complement or substitute?

D. Given the evidence from behavioral economics, in what types of markets will it be most likely that advertising restrictions are socially beneficial?

Appendix A: The Ramsey Pricing Rule

The derivation of the Ramsey (1927) pricing rule makes use of constrained optimization techniques (Simon and Blume 1994). Consider a single product monopolist. The social goal is to maximize total surplus, defined as the area under the inverse demand function $[p(q)]$ minus total cost (TC) or $p(q)dq - TC(q)$, subject to the constraint that total revenue $[p(q) \cdot q]$ equals total cost. To solve this constrained optimization problem, we first define the Lagrangian function: $\mathcal{L} = \int p(q)dq - TC(q) + \lambda[p(q)q - TC(q)]$, where λ is the Lagrange multiplier. The first-order conditions are

$$\frac{\partial \mathcal{L}}{\partial q} = p - MC + \lambda\left[p + \frac{\partial p}{\partial q}q - MC\right] = 0, \tag{A.1}$$

$$\frac{\partial \mathcal{L}}{\partial \lambda} = p(q) \cdot q - TC(q) = 0 \text{ or that } p = \frac{TC}{q} \equiv AC. \tag{A.2}$$

The second equation implies that price must equal average cost, TC/q, which guarantees zero profit. The first equation can be rearranged as follows:

$$\frac{p - MC}{p} = -\lambda\left[p\left(1 + \frac{\partial p}{\partial q}\frac{q}{p}\right) - MC\right]/p,$$

$$\frac{p - MC}{p} = -\lambda\left[p\left(1 - \frac{1}{\eta}\right) - MC\right]/p,$$

$$\frac{p - MC}{p}(1 + \lambda) = \lambda\left(\frac{1}{\eta}\right),$$

$$\frac{p - MC}{p} = \frac{\lambda}{1 + \lambda}\left(\frac{1}{\eta}\right) = \frac{k}{\eta}, \tag{A.3}$$

where $k \equiv \lambda/(1 + \lambda)$. Note that if the profit constraint is not binding, $k = \lambda = 0$, and price equals marginal cost. Otherwise, λ and k are positive and price exceeds marginal cost.

For a detailed mathematical derivation of the Ramsey pricing rule for a multi-product monopolist, see Brown and Silbey (1986) and Braeutigam (1989).

Chapter 21
Industry and Firm Studies

In this chapter we use case studies to identify patterns of behavior that highlight what we have learned from studying industrial organization. We begin with an investigation of three US industries: brewing, cigarettes, and college sports. Rather than provide a comprehensive study of them, we focus on the most important forces that have shaped each industry and/or have influenced public policy. This will allow us to show how industrial organization theory is relevant and can help us understand reality.

One weakness with traditional industry studies is that they frequently fail to account for idiosyncratic firm effects. From game theory we know that superior firms behave differently than their competitors and that their behavior can transform industry structure. In addition, from behavioral economics we know that company strategy can be shaped by the unique personalities of company presidents. To highlight these forces, we study three US firms: Schlitz, Microsoft, and General Motors.

21.1 Industry Studies

21.1.1 The US Brewing Industry[1]

Brewing is an interesting industry for at least two reasons. First, it is representative of a traditional consumer goods industry in that firm success depends on a winning marketing campaign and on efficient production. As we saw in Chap. 15, the advertising-to-sales ratio is over 9% in brewing. Advertising has had an important effect on the evolution of brewing, as well as other consumer goods industries. Thus, understanding advertising in brewing provides insights that carry over to a variety of consumer industries.

---

[1] For more comprehensive analysis of the industry, see Elzinga (1990, 2009) and V. Tremblay and C. Tremblay (2005, 2007).

V.J. Tremblay and C.H. Tremblay, *New Perspectives on Industrial Organization*,
Springer Texts in Business and Economics, DOI 10.1007/978-1-4614-3241-8_21,
© Springer Science+Business Media New York 2012

The second interesting feature of the brewing industry is that it has undergone dramatic structural change in the last 70 years. The traditional macro or mass producing beer companies have declined dramatically in number since World War II. In 1945 there were 476 macrobrewers, a number that has fallen steadily to about 19 firms today. As we saw in Fig. 8.3, this led to continued increases in the four-firm concentration ratio and the Herfindahl–Hirschman index. Recall that the macros produce large quantities of light American lager to take advantage of economies of scale. Today, the macros include the Anheuser-Busch, MillerCoors, and Pabst brewing companies that produce such brands as Budweiser, Coors Light, Miller Lite, and Pabst Blue Ribbon.

Structural change also resulted from the entry of a new type of brewer, the microbrewery. A microbrewery is a relatively small brewer that produces darker beers and ales, which are more in the European tradition. Although microbreweries are too small to take advantage of scale economies, they are better able to serve the differing tastes of their local markets. Micros began on the west coast in the 1970s and have grown steadily ever since, reaching over 1,700 firms today. Still, the microbrewery share of domestic beer consumption remains small, at less than 6%. For this reason, we focus on the causes of structural change among the macrobrewers.[2]

Of the many forces that explain the tremendous rise in concentration in brewing, two are most prominent. The first is the increased marketing opportunities created by the advent of television. Recall from Chap. 15 that the percent of households with a television set grew from 9% in 1950 to 95% in 1970 (see column 2 of Table 21.1). This gave a tremendous marketing advantage to the larger brewers and thrust the industry into a preemption race in television advertising. That is, firms fought to gain a strategic advantage in television marketing. Because television ads could air nationally and not regionally during the 1950s and 1960s, television advertising was cost effective for national brewers alone. Thus, they were the winners of the race. The national brewers invested heavily in advertising during this period, pushing advertising per barrel to record levels (see Fig. 21.1). As is evident from column 3 of Table 21.1, this enabled the national brewers to gain market share from 1950 through 1970.[3] George (2009, 2011) found that these gains came at the expense of local and regional brewers, many of whom were forced out of business.

The second reason for the dramatic increase in concentration was technological change that increased minimum efficient scale (MES). New technologies led to increased automation of brewing facilities and faster canning/bottling lines, all of

---

[2] We also ignore imports, which have gained market share since the 1970s as well. For further discussion of the import and microsectors, see V. Tremblay and C. Tremblay (2005) and C. Tremblay and V. Tremblay (2011b). For a discussion of the international beer market, see Adams (2006, 2011) and Swinner (2011).

[3] During this period, the national brewers were the Anheuser-Busch, Schlitz, Miller, and Pabst brewing companies.

Table 21.1 TV households and the characteristics of the US brewing industry

Year	Households with a TV (%)	Market share of national brewers (%)	MES in brewing Output	MES in brewing Market share (%)	n^*	n	k
1950	9	16	0.1	0.1	840	350	0
1960	87	21	1.0	1.5	87	175	88
1970	95	45	8.0	6.0	16	82	66
1980	98	59	16.0	9.0	11	40	29
1990	98	79	16.0	8.0	12	29	17
2000	98	89	23.0	14.0	8	24	16
2009	98	93	23.0	14.0	8	19	11

Notes: MES output measures minimum efficient scale, measured in millions of (31 gal) barrels. MES market share represents the market share needed to reach minimum efficient scale. n^* is the cost-minimizing industry structure (i.e., the number of firms that the industry can support if all firms produce at minimum efficient scale). n is the number of macrobrewers. $k = n^* - n$ when $(n - n^*) > 0$, and k equals 0 otherwise. Number discrepancies are due to rounding errors.
Sources: Steinberg (1980), the *Statistical Abstract of the United States*, V. Tremblay et al. (2005), and V. Tremblay and C. Tremblay (2005).

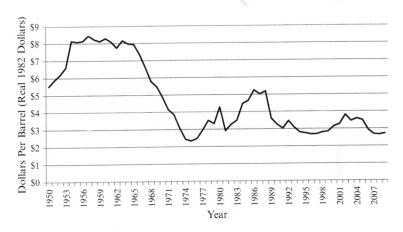

Fig. 21.1 Advertising per barrel for the US Brewing Industry, 1950–2009

which led to lower costs for larger brewing operations. Estimates of MES in terms of output (in millions of barrels) and market share (in %) are listed in columns 4 and 5 of Table 21.1 for various years. The figures imply that a brewer would need a market share of about 0.1% in 1950 to reach MES, a number that rose to about 14% by 2000.[4] The rise in MES led to further increases in market share of the national brewers. Note that this means that the cost-minimizing industry structure (n^*) would

---

[4] Domestic beer sales of the macro brewers were about one million barrels in 1950 and about 180 million barrels in 2009.

have been about 840 firms in 1950 and only about 8 firms by 2000.[5] The data show that the actual number of firms exceeded the cost-minimizing numbers by 1960.

These two forces gave a strategic advantage to larger brewers and thrust the industry into a war of attrition. Recall from Chap. 14 that a war of attrition exists when $n = n^* + k$ firms compete in a market that will profitably support only n^* firms in the long run. When $k > 0$, k firms must exit for the industry to reach equilibrium. The value of k was extremely high in the 1960s and 1970s (see Table 21.1), which led to what has been called the "beer wars." During the wars there were escalating advertising spending in the 1950s and 1960s and intense price competition from the 1970s through the 1990s. As discussed in Chap. 13, since the late 1970s the leading brewers also used a brand proliferation strategy to gain market share.

The battles that were fought during the beer wars are clearly portrayed in *Newsweek* (September 4, 1978, 60):

> After generations of stuffy, family-dominated management, when brewers competed against each other with camaraderie and forbearance, they are now frankly at war. Marketing and advertising, not the art of brewing, are the weapons. Brewers both large and small are racing to locate new consumers and invent new products to suit their taste. Two giants of the industry, Anheuser-Busch of St. Louis and Miller Brewing Company of Milwaukee, are the main contenders.

This description is remarkably accurate, as Anheuser-Busch and MillerCoors have emerged as the dominate survivors of the war.

Continued strife kept market power low and put all but the largest brewers under financial pressure. This explains the low Lerner index in brewing that we reported in Table 12.2. During these battles, the most inefficient firms exited the industry, many by merging with other more successful brewers. During the heat of battle, some made a gallant effort to become national brewers. From the 1960s through the 1990s, the Falstaff, Heileman, and Stroh brewing companies made unsuccessful attempts to go national and are no longer in business today. Two of the smaller national brewers also suffered during these battles. Due to ineffective marketing efforts, Pabst was forced to become a regional brewer in the 1980s, and Schlitz, once a dominant national brewer, exited the market in 1981. We discuss the problems at Schlitz later in the chapter. The Coors Brewing Company was the only macrobrewer to reach national status in the post World War II era, which it accomplished in 1991.

In the last decade, the final stages of consolidation have taken place. In 2002, Miller was purchased by South African Breweries, an international brewing conglomerate, to form SABMiller. In 2008, Coors and SABMiller established a joint venture called MillerCoors, which enabled them to benefit from a larger distribution system. In 2001, Pabst became a marketing entity when the company shut down all of its production facilities and contracted with Miller to produce all of Pabst's beer.[6] Finally, in 2008 Anheuser–Busch was purchased by Belgium's InBev, another

---

[5] This is the number of firms that are needed to produce total market demand when each firm produces at MES. That is, $n^* = Q/MES$, as discussed in Chap. 8.

[6] There is continued speculation that MillerCoors will purchase Pabst.

international brewing conglomerate, to form Anheuser–Busch InBev. With these changes, the macrosector of the brewing industry has evolved into a global industry, much like many other consumer goods industries today.

21.1.2 The US Cigarette Industry[7]

Like brewing, the US cigarette industry has many of the characteristics that are found in other imperfectly competitive consumer goods industries. Products are differentiated and entry barriers are high, due primarily to scale economies in production and the sunk costs associated with marketing expenditures. As a result, industry concentration has remained high for decades. In 2005, the top two firms, Philip Morris and Reynolds American, had a combined market share of over 80%.

Three features distinguish the cigarette industry from other consumer goods industries. First, cigarette smoking is highly addictive. As a result, a wealth-maximizing firm will pay attention to dynamic effects when making marketing decisions. We know from Chap. 12 that just because price is equal to (or below) marginal cost today does not mean that market power is nonexistent in a market for addictive commodities. Second, tobacco use produces adverse health consequences. Smoking can harm the health of smokers and nonsmokers who are exposed to second-hand smoke. Finally, the character of company presidents from the early 1950s set a course that was designed to deceive consumers about the health risks of smoking. This behavior and the health consequences of smoking ultimately led to harsh policy sanctions against the industry.

The addictive nature of smoking influences how cigarettes are marketed to consumers. Although government restrictions limit cigarette advertising expenditures today, cigarettes have been among the most heavily marketed products in the USA. In 2006, the leading cigarette companies spent $12.5 billion on advertising and other promotional activities.[8] Cigarette companies understand the implications of behavioral economics regarding addictive commodities, as they develop marketing tactics that exploit the cognitive weaknesses of consumers to their advantage. For example, most people start smoking in their teens, a period when we are most likely to be overconfident and ignore the future cost of risky behavior. The evidence shows that young people underestimate the risk of becoming addicted to smoking, and most adult smokers regret having ever taken up smoking (Fong et al. 2004). Given these facts, cigarette companies offer discount coupons and sale prices on brands that are most preferred by young smokers.

---

[7] For more comprehensive analysis of the industry, see Sloan et al. (2004), Chaloupka (2007), and Hay (2009).

[8] These include magazine, point of sale, direct mail advertising, discount coupons, and promotional funding given to retailers.

Premium brands that are preferred by adults who are already hooked, such as Parliament and Winston, are rarely discounted.[9]

Greater awareness of the health concerns with tobacco products has driven public policy for the past half century. Convincing medical research linking cigarette smoking to lung cancer became apparent in the early 1950s. As continued research in the 1950s and 1960s confirmed the negative health effects of smoking, the US Surgeon General issued a report in 1964 which concluded that cigarette smoking causes lung cancer. Subsequent studies confirmed that cigarette smoking is addictive and contributes to a myriad of diseases. According to the Centers for Disease Control and Prevention, nearly one in five deaths in the USA is attributable to smoking.[10]

As the evidence began to mount, political opposition to cigarette smoking escalated and a number of antismoking policies were implemented. These include health warnings on cigarette packages, higher federal and state excise taxes, and more restrictive clean-indoor air laws, which make it illegal to smoke in public (and many private) buildings. Given the loss of loved ones and the greater cost of caring for those who are in poor health because of smoking, in the 1990s many individuals and state governments began to sue cigarette companies for restitution. To avoid continued litigation, by 1998 the leading cigarette producers reached a global settlement with every state, the Master Settlement Agreement (MSA). In exchange for immunity from future lawsuits, the industry agreed to pay state governments a total amount of $206 billion over a 25-year period.[11] Each year, a firm's share of the payment is based on current sales, much like an excise tax. The MSA pushed up cigarette prices by about 45%, which in turn caused per capita consumption to fall by 8%.[12]

Some of the most severe restrictions on advertising in US history have been imposed on the cigarette industry. To appease critics who objected to ads that appeal to children, beginning in 1963 the industry adopted a series of voluntary advertising restrictions. They (1) required that ads use actors who were at least 25 years of age, (2) eliminated ads that appeal to children, and (3) eliminated ads that use the testimonials of athletes. According to Pollay (1994), the voluntary restrictions created an appearance of social responsibility but led to no noticeable change in cigarette advertising.[13] Senator Robert Kennedy (1967) clearly expressed this sentiment:

---

[9] Note that this is a form of price discrimination where a low price is offered to potential consumers who have relatively elastic demand functions and a high price is offered to addicted consumers.

[10] According to the Centers for Disease Control and Prevention, smoking contributes to heart disease and strokes, as well as various types of cancers. This information is available at http://www.cdc.gov/tobacco/data_statistics/fact_sheets/health_effects/effects_cig_smoking/.

[11] It also included other marketing restrictions, such as a ban on outdoor advertising, ads that used cartoon characters, and the sponsorship of sporting events.

[12] See Chaloupka (2007) for a review of the evidence.

[13] Although self-regulation of advertising is common in most industries, Pitofsky (1977) argues that it is generally ineffective. For a review of concerns with voluntary advertising guidelines in the US brewing industry, see V. Tremblay and C. Tremblay (2005).

> If we were starting fresh, I would say the first line of action would be industry self-regulation of [cigarette] advertising. But we have witnessed a charade of purported self-regulation for some years. The codes of self-regulation have been largely ineffective, and I see little hope of change.[14]

Given the lack of an effective voluntary response from industry, two pieces of legislation were enacted to reduce cigarette demand. First, the Federal Communication Commission required television networks to air one antismoking ad for every 3 prosmoking ads by the cigarette companies, effective July 1967 through 1970, under what is called the "Fairness Doctrine Act." Second, Congress passed the Public Health Cigarette Smoking Act (1970), which banned all (pro- and antismoking) advertising from television and radio, effective January 1, 1971.[15]

Unfortunately, these pieces of legislation produced economic consequences that were inconsistent with their intent. First, the bulk of the evidence shows that advertising and therefore the ban on broadcast advertising has little if any effect on the market demand for cigarettes. The evidence shows that cigarette advertising since the 1950s has been combative, with the advertising of one firm stealing customers from rivals but having little effect on market demand. Second, the ban on broadcast advertising had the unintended consequence of benefiting cigarette companies. In 1970, over $300 million was spent on cigarette advertising, which was $60 million more than was spent in 1971. Iwasaki and V. Tremblay (2009) estimate that the privately optimum level of broadcast advertising in the cigarette industry was zero. This implies that broadcast advertising was purely combative and that the ban improved marketing efficiency in the industry. Consistent with this result is the work by Eckard (1991) and Farr et al. (2001) who found that the ban led to higher industry profits. These results explain why the industry did not oppose the ban (Hamilton 1972; Pollay 1994).

This begs the question, if the ban increased industry profits, why did the cigarette companies fail to eliminate broadcast advertising without government help? The reason is that when advertising is combative, firms are forced into a prisoners' dilemma in advertising (see Chap. 15). To review this idea, consider two cigarette companies (1 and 2) that face the payoff matrix in Fig. 21.2. Notice that if firms were able to cooperate that they would choose to ban advertising and each earn 18. Without a way to effectively enforce cooperation, however, the dominant (Nash) equilibrium strategy for both firms is to advertise, earning each firm 16. This example illustrates how government regulation that bans advertising can unintentionally benefit industry and how difficult it can be to anticipate the social consequences of government regulation.

---

[14] Robert Kennedy, "Proceedings of the First World Conference on Smoking and Health," New York, American Cancer Society, 1967, 3–13, as quoted in Saloojee and Dagli (2000, 7).

[15] In addition, the Master Settlement Agreement of 1998 between the tobacco industry and most state governments prohibited most outdoor and transit advertising and the use of cartoon characters in cigarette ads (Chaloupka 2007). In 2009, Congress passed the Family Smoking Prevention and Tobacco Control Act, which required that warning labels cover the top 50% of the front and back panels of the package. See Curfman et al. (2009) for a discussion of the law. The complete transcript can be found at http://www.govtrack.us/congress/bill.xpd?bill=h111-1256.

Fig. 21.2 Cigarette industry advertising game

		2	
		Ban	Advertise
1	Ban	18, 18	14, 20
	Advertise	20, 14	16, 16

A prominent policy issue involving the cigarette industry is deception. For decades the industry tried to deceive the public about the health risks of smoking. The blatant disregard for public health and the apparent view that firms would not be penalized may be rooted in the hubris of the leaders of the top cigarette companies. From behavioral economics, we can think of this as a form of overconfidence.

Corporate deception began in 1953 when the presidents of the leading companies met to address the "health problem" created by the scientific evidence linking cigarette smoking to cancer. The outcome of those meetings led to a public relations effort to protect the image of the industry, which began with the publication of a letter to the public titled "A Frank Statement to Cigarette Smokers." The letter was signed by leaders from the cigarette and tobacco industries and appeared in over 400 newspapers across the country, January 4, 1954.[16] The letter made the following points:

- The cigarette and tobacco industries are concerned with the welfare of their consumers.
- There is no proof that cigarette smoking causes cancer, and the authors do not believe that cigarettes are injurious to health.
- The cigarette and tobacco industries will establish the Tobacco Industry Research Committee (later called the Council for Tobacco Research) and provide funding for research on the link between tobacco and health.

The ethical turning point came when the industry's own research in the 1950s began to confirm that smoking causes various types of cancer. Instead of admitting the truth, the industry decided to conceal this information from the public. Once this path was chosen, the industry stuck with it for 50 years. Even by as late as 1994, executives from the 7 largest tobacco companies swore in congressional testimony

---

[16] This is available at http://www.tobacco.neu.edu/box/BOEKENBox/Boeken%20Evidence%20PDF/0363.pdf, accessed August 24, 2011.

that they did not believe that nicotine is addictive, testimony that they knew to be clearly false given internal company documents that were released in later litigation. Perhaps the momentum to sustain such deception was driven by an industry culture that required new company leaders to share the values and hubris of those they replaced. Thus, those who applied for jobs and were selected into corporate positions with cigarette companies would have different ethical values than those who selected into more socially beneficial industries.

In 2006, this deceptive behavior finally caught up with the industry when the US government successfully prosecuted the leading cigarette companies for violating the Racketeer Influenced and Corrupt Organization Act (RICO 1970). The government charged that the major companies worked together to engage in a lengthy and unlawful conspiracy to deceive the public about the health risks of smoking. The court held that industry defendants:

- Knowingly and falsely denied (1) that smoking and second-hand smoke cause disease and (2) that nicotine is addictive
- Promoted low tar/light cigarettes as less harmful when they knew this was false
- Intentionally designed their marketing to attract young smokers
- Concealed and destroyed scientific evidence that demonstrated the health risks of smoking

In the words of Judge Kessler, "In short, Defendants have marketed and sold their lethal product with zeal, with deception, with single-minded focus on their financial success, and without regard for the human tragedy or social cost that success exacted."[17] The court ordered that the defendants stop these deceptive activities, make corrective statements to the public on television and retail displays, and disclose their disaggregated marketing data to the government.

This example teaches two lessons. First, it shows how company deception can be successful (at least for an extended period of time) when the public is imperfectly informed. Second, it suggests that a legal remedy to market failure can take decades when very large corporations (and profits) are involved.

21.1.3   The Economics of College Sports[18]

Although college athletics has become big business, many of our policies assume that it is not a business at all. The Football Bowl Subdivision (Division I-A) earned revenues in excess of $5 billion in 2009. Conference realignment and growing

---

[17] *United States* et al. *v. Philip Morris* et al., United States District Court for the District of Columbia, 2006, p. 4, available at http://www.tobacco.neu.edu/litigation/cases/DOJ/20060817KESSLEROPI NIONAMENDED.pdf, accessed August 25, 2011.

[18] For more comprehensive analysis of the economics of college sports, see Fort (2007), Kahn (2007), Lazaroff (2007), and Fizel and Bennett (2009). Data are available from the NCAA web site at http://www.ncaapublications.com/productdownloads/RE2008.pdf, accessed August 19, 2011.

demand for college sports entertainment are enabling conferences to earn greater income than ever before. For example, the PAC-10 earned less than $60 million in 2010 from media rights. In 2011, it added the University of Colorado and the University of Utah to the conference and signed a 12-year television contract with ESPN and Fox that is worth $225 million per year.

Growing revenues have led to increased competition for top coaches and athletes, especially in the revenue earning sports of football and basketball.[19] Coaches salaries have risen sharply: in 2010, each of the top 10 highest paid college football coaches earned more than $2.9 million a year, which exceeded the salary of the highest paid university president.[20] The highest paid coach in 2010 was Nick Saban of the University of Alabama, who earned almost $6 million, compared to Alabama's president, Robert Witt, who earned less than $700,000.

A successful team also depends on a college's ability to recruit top athletes. Yet, this has not led to higher salaries for players. The problem is that the maximum monetary rewards for players are set by the National Collegiate Athletic Association (NCAA). If such wage ceilings were set in professional sports, they would be a restraint of trade and a violation of the Sherman Act. Thus, the main goal of this case study is to describe the NCAA and analyze why such pay caps are legal in college sports.

In response to a number of serious injuries and deaths in college football, the NCAA was created in the early 1900s at the urging of President Theodore Roosevelt. The NCAA established rule changes that reduced the degree of violence in football. It also encouraged cooperation more generally. First, it led to the standardization of the rules of athletic competitions. Second, it established rules of player eligibility and acceptable forms of competition for athletic talent. In the early twentieth century, some college athletes were not students at all and would play for the highest paying college team. The NCAA soon required that college athletes be full-time students and amateurs, not professionals. Until the 1950s, compliance was voluntary and recruiting violations were common. To facilitate cooperation, membership in the NCAA required that an institution play against schools that abided by NCAA rules. It also established a Compliance Committee that could impose penalties on violators and terminate an institution's NCAA membership for violations of the rules.

The third type of cooperation encouraged by the NCAA has more direct antitrust implications. It involves cartel activity that is designed to directly improve the profits of member colleges and universities. These include limiting the number of members in the lucrative Football Bowl Subdivision and setting the number of games that would be broadcast on television, thus eliminating an institution's right to negotiate independently with television stations. The NCAA has also acted as a cartel on the input side of the market by putting a cap on compensation to athletes and attempting to set income limits for assistant coaches. Of course, competition is

---

[19] In the Football Bowl Subdivision, football and basketball generate approximately 60% of athletic department revenues.

[20] See *USA Today*, "Football Bowl Subdivision Coaches for 2010," at http://www.usatoday.com/sports/college/football/2010-coaches-contracts-table.htm.

difficult to constrain, and these regulations caused colleges to compete with more and more lavish stadiums, training facilities, and locker rooms.

The courts have taken a dichotomous approach to the enforcement of the antitrust laws in college sports. As with professional sports, the courts allow cooperation on scheduling and the development of rules that promote fair play and competitive balance among amateur athletic teams. They have also supported NCAA rules that promote a spirit of amateurism, giving the NCAA the legal right to impose input restrictions, such as limits on player compensation, player mobility, and the number of scholarship players on a team. By limiting costs, such restrictions clearly benefit NCAA members, but this gain comes at the expense of the athletes. Justification for the court's position stems from the fact that the antitrust laws apply to commercial or business endeavors. From the court's viewpoint, college players are students, not professional athletes, and an athletic contest on a college campus is part of an educational program, which is not a business activity. In other words, student-athletes are not employed in a commercial labor market and are, therefore, not protected by antitrust laws.

Although the NCAA is able to set cartel restrictions that lower student-athlete compensation, the courts have not given the NCAA complete cartel power. In *NCAA v. Board of Regents* (468, U.S. 85, 1984), the NCAA claimed that its control of football television broadcasts was designed to maintain competitive balance. This argument was rejected by the Supreme Court, a ruling that gave broadcast rights to individual schools in 1984. Similarly, the courts ruled against the NCAA when it tried to place a limit on the wages of entry-level assistant coaches, based on the competitive balance defense. In this case, the courts held that the coaches were engaged in a legitimate trade or business and that such a restriction was an antitrust violation (*Law v. NCAA*, 134F.3d 1010, 10th Circuit, 1998).

It is difficult to justify the NCAA's control over compensation to students for their athletic services. College football and basketball programs generate considerable revenue for their schools,[21] and caps on athlete compensation serve to transfer wealth from athletes to the NCAA, schools, and athletic departments. Clearly there is a market for athletic talent, which is why there are so many recruiting scandals and illegal payments to star athletes.[22] As Lazaroff (2007, 370–371) points out, the

---

[21] Although NCAA figures indicate that the median athletic program ran a deficit in 2009, Kahn (2007) and Fizel and Bennett (2009) point out that these figures do not represent an economic loss. Accounting methods used by athletic departments overestimate costs and omit the marketing benefits of a successful sports program. NCAA data are available at http://www.ncaapublications. com/productdownloads/REV_EXP_2010.pdf.

[22] For example, Reggie Bush received illegal compensation while playing football at USC. After an NCAA investigation, Bush was forced to relinquish his 2005 Heisman Trophy, and USC was stripped of its 2004 national championship. Similarly, at Ohio State University five football players were suspended for rules violations in the first half of the 2011 football season. This scandal also caused head coach, Jim Tressel, to resign. Finally, in his survey of professional football players, Sack (1991) found that 31% admitted to receiving illegal side payments while playing college football. For further discussion, see ESPN reports at http://sports.espn.go.com/espn/commentary/news/story?page=bryant/100922 and http://sports.espn.go.com/ncf/columns/story?columnist=schlabach_mark&id=6195223, accessed August 26, 2011.

NCAA's position is "inconsistent with economic reality and sound policy" because it fosters a system that economically exploits student athletes. "Federal courts should apply the Sherman Act to the NCAA's amateurism rules . . . ."

21.2   Firm Studies

21.2.1   The Schlitz Brewing Company[23]

We can gain a deeper understanding of business strategy by investigating the behavior of failing as well as successful firms. We begin with Schlitz, as it illustrates how production and marketing mistakes can destroy a successful firm. Schlitz is the last brewer to hold the number one spot in brewing before the Anheuser-Busch Brewing Company took it over in 1957. Schlitz remained the number two brewer until it was overtaken by the Miller Brewing Company in 1977. Studying this case may seem like an exercise in ancient business history, but the reasons for Schlitz's demise are as relevant today as they were in the 1970s.

Problems started in the early 1970s when Schlitz made a management decision to implement a new brewing technique to improve the bottom line. This technique cut costs by reducing aging time by 16%. In response, competitors claimed that Schlitz was selling "green beer," cheap beer that was inadequately aged. This was the beginning of set of actions that tarnished the image of the Schlitz brand. The second problem was that Schlitz was the only major brewer without a successful light beer, the fastest growing segment of the beer market in the 1970s. Schlitz had introduced its version of light beer in late 1975, but it was much less successful than its competitors, Miller Lite and Coors Light.

Perhaps the most devastating blow came when longtime company president, Robert Uihlein died unexpectedly in late 1976. With no one ready to take his place, a battle for control of the company ensued, which was eventually won by Eugene Peters, the company's head accountant. With little understanding and appreciation of marketing, Peters dropped the company's previously successful advertising theme that emphasized product quality in favor of more aggressive advertising messages. One example, dubbed the "drink Schlitz or I'll kill you" campaign, featured a boxer who threatened an off camera spokesperson who suggested that the boxer switch from Schlitz to another brand of beer. These ads further tarnished the Schlitz image and were quickly pulled off the air.

Increased stress during the beer wars also played a role in Schlitz's demise. This was exacerbated in 1970 when Philip Morris, a cigarette company, bought Miller and injected considerable marketing money into Miller. An advertising war ensued beginning in the mid-1970s between Miller and Anheuser-Busch, putting

---

[23] For a more complete discussion, see V. Tremblay and C. Tremblay (2005) and Goldfarb (2007).

considerable pressure on Schiltz (see Fig. 21.1).[24] The cumulative effects of these mistakes and outside pressures caused Schlitz's market share of domestic beer to fall from 15.86% in 1976 to 11.84% in 1978.

As is common with a failing firm like Schlitz, the company resorted to a number of Hail Mary or unconventional strategies. As we saw in Chap. 13, a failing firm may be more willing to try something new when a conventional strategy will lead to almost certain failure. In this case, radical action may be the only thing that will give the firm a chance, albeit small, to survive. In the case of Schlitz, new advertisements in the late 1970s used its new company president, Frank Sellinger, as the spokesman for the Schlitz brand, a tactic that is rarely used in brewing. In the final stages of decline, Schlitz chose another uncommon strategy of resorting to blind taste test commercials that aired live during the professional football playoffs and Super Bowl XV (1980–1981). In spite of these efforts, the company's market share continued to decline, reaching just 7.98% before it was purchased by the Stroh Brewing Company at the end of 1981.

Errors at Schlitz are estimated to have reduced the value of the Schlitz brand by 91% from 1974 to 1982 (Aaker 1991). The lesson to be learned is that a firm's long-term success depends upon the reputation of its brands. Firms that sacrifice quality for short-run gain will not survive in the long run. In the words of Ted Rosenak, former advertising manager at Schlitz [*Advertising Age* (April 20, 1981, 52)], "In the beer business, if a company loses its resources and money, but retains its reputation, it can always be rebuilt. But if it loses its reputation, no amount of money and resources will bring it back."

21.2.2 Microsoft[25]

The Microsoft Corporation is a successful and dominant firm in the high tech sector of the economy. In 2010, it was the 38th largest US corporation, with annual sales in excess of $62 billion. With a profit to sales ratio of 30.0%, it ranks second among the leading 100 US corporations, just behind Coca-Cola at 33.6%. What makes Microsoft so interesting is that both luck and superior innovative activity contributed to Microsoft's success. In addition, strategic actions that proved successful in the 1980s when Microsoft was small led to trouble with antitrust authorities in the 1990s as Microsoft gained prominence. Thus, the main purpose of this firm study is to discuss the sources of Microsoft's early success and its later antitrust problems.

---

[24] Goldfarb (2007) found support for the hypothesis that Schlitz actions to cut corners in production and marketing were a rational response to stiff competition from Anheuser-Busch and Miller.

[25] For more complete discussion, see Elzinga et al. (2001), Gilbert and Katz (2001), Baye (2002), Blaxill and Eckardt (2009), and "Microsoft and Yahoo Seal Web Deal," BBC News at http://news.bbc.co.uk/2/hi/business/8174763.stm, accessed August 7, 2011.

Microsoft was started in 1975 by Bill Gates and Paul Allen, and its early success is attributed to good fortune. In 1980, IBM sought an independent company to develop an operating system for its new personal computer. IBM first approached Digital Research, but when negotiations broke down, IBM eventually awarded the contract to Microsoft. Without a viable operating system of its own, Microsoft purchased DOS (Disk Operating System) from Seattle Computer Products. Microsoft modified DOS to meet IBM's needs and marketed it as MS-DOS. Had Digital Research accepted the contract or had IBM gone directly to Seattle Computer Products for DOS, it is very unlikely that Microsoft would be the dominant firm that it is today.

In any case, the company's continued success through the 1980s and 1990s is attributable to three factors. First, as is common with most thriving new companies, success is due to the drive and focus on winning of those who founded the company. At Microsoft, this was Bill Gates, the company's long-time chief executive officer.[26] Second, Microsoft was able to continue to develop and improve the DOS system, which is marketed today as Microsoft Windows. Finally, Microsoft has been able to compete effectively against all new rivals. As a result, Microsoft supplied over 90% of the operating systems for Intel-based personal computers by the early 1990s.

Microsoft's large size and business tactics that were designed to thwart competition eventually caused problems with antitrust authorities. To improve sales of Microsoft's Word (a word processing program) and Excel (a spreadsheet program) in the early 1990s, Microsoft manipulated the application programming interfaces (APIs) of its Windows upgrades to deteriorate the performance of competing software packages (e.g., WordPerfect, Lotus 1–2–3, and Quatto Pro). At the same time, Microsoft negotiated contracts with original equipment manufacturers (OEMs such as Dell and Hewlett-Packard) which discouraged the OEMs from installing software that competed with Microsoft Word and Excel. In essence, Microsoft leveraged control of its operating system software to gain a strategic advantage in other software markets.

Microsoft's most formidable threat in the 1990s was Netscape's Navigator, an Internet browser that was a direct competitor with Microsoft's Internet Explorer (IE). In January of 1997, the market share of monthly browser usage was nearly 80% for Navigator and about 20% for IE.[27] Netscape was a particularly serious threat and not just because of its size. Netscape's browser was a distribution platform for the Java language that could have evolved into an operating system to compete with Windows. To address this threat to Microsoft's core business, Microsoft used its "embrace, extend, and extinguish" strategy.[28] This meant that

---

[26] Paul Allen played a diminished role at Microsoft after his bout with cancer in 1982.

[27] Monthly browser market share data are available at http://www.justice.gov/atr/cases/exhibits/5.pdf, accessed August 7, 2011.

[28] According to government documents, Microsoft vice president Paul Maritz used this phrase in 1995 when discussing the company's way of dealing with competitors. These documents are available at http://www.justice.gov/atr/cases/f2600/2613.htm, accessed August 7, 2011.

Microsoft upgraded its newer versions of Windows to embrace the Internet by extending its application programming to favor IE over Navigator. Next, it bundled Windows 98 with IE, thus giving IE away for free. This clearly benefitted consumers at the expense of competing browser companies. Finally, OEMs that purchased and installed Windows were prohibited from uninstalling IE. These tactics were very effective: IE reached a market share of over 50% by the end of 1998, Navigator was virtually eliminated by 2002, and IE continues to be the dominant Internet browser today.

Tying IE to Windows and other anticompetitive agreements led to a series of legal problems for Microsoft. The Federal Trade Commission began an initial investigation in 1990, which led to a consent decree in 1994. Along with other marketing restrictions, the FTC banned Microsoft from bundling Windows with other Microsoft products. However, it still allowed Microsoft to continue to innovate new features into the Windows operating system. When Microsoft bundled IE with Windows 98, the Department of Justice brought an antitrust suit against Microsoft in May 1998, alleging that the company used predatory tactics to monopolize the market for computer operating systems and Internet browsers.[29]

Several issues are crucial to understanding the antitrust implications of the case. First, Microsoft's behavior enabled it to gain market power, earn high profits, and be deemed a monopoly from a legal standpoint. Thus, the market was statically inefficient. Second, it is clear that Microsoft is an innovative company that earned market power by developing better consumer products. In other words, Microsoft promoted dynamic efficiency. The final issue of importance is that there are substantial network externalities in the operating system and browser markets. In a market where consumers gain from having just one supplier, firms compete in a winner-take-all contest, with the contest winner being the superior firm. These market features make it rather difficult to judge the case and determine an appropriate remedy.

As one might expect, the government focused on the fact that Microsoft had market power, while Microsoft made the argument that its market power resulted from innovation and superior efficiency. For example, Microsoft claimed that the integration of Windows 98 and IE produced a superior product and that IE was simply a new feature of Windows 98. Microsoft claimed that to separate them would diminish the overall performance of the integrated product.[30] Whether this is true or not, Judge Jackson ruled in favor of the government in November of 1999, claiming that Microsoft violated the Sherman Act by monopolizing the market and using anticompetitive means to maintain its market dominance. In April of 2000, the judge decided that Microsoft would be divided into two separate companies: one to produce the operating system and the other to produce other types of software.

---

[29] Court documents in *US v. Microsoft* (1998–2007) are available at http://www.justice.gov/atr/cases/ms_index.htm.

[30] Another interesting feature of the case is that Richard Schmalensee served as expert witness for Microsoft, and his dissertation advisor, Franklin Fisher, was the expert witness for the Department of Justice.

Subsequently, the case was appealed, and in November of 2001 the Department of Justice and Microsoft reached a settlement out of court. The company remained intact but was required to refrain from using anticompetitive business practices in the future. In particular, Microsoft was required to share its API with third-party companies and refrain from making contracts with OEMs that put other software companies at a strategic disadvantage. What is most interesting is that the settlement did not require Microsoft to unbundle Windows and IE and did not prevent it from tying Windows to other software in the future.

The final decision may have been in the best interest of society. Microsoft had gained a dominant position through innovation, not from the more common means of mergers and acquisitions. The presence of network externalities forced the company to be innovative or fail, and innovate it did. The agreement does not penalize the company for contributing to dynamic efficiency but does penalize behavior that is designed to preserve its static market power. An event study by Bittlingmayer and Hazlett (2000) suggests that strict antitrust enforcement against Microsoft would have been detrimental to society overall. This suggests that social interests were served by curtailing Microsoft's anticompetitive behavior, while preserving the company's long-run incentive to innovate.[31]

Over the last decade, Microsoft has continued to develop Windows, but demand growth for operating system software has diminished as the computer industry matures. In response, Microsoft has expanded into complementary markets. One is the market for Internet searches, which is dominated by Google. In June of 2009, Microsoft launched its own search engine, which it calls Bing. A month later, Microsoft made an agreement to power the search engine of Yahoo, second behind Google. The Yahoo Web page now says "Powered by Bing." This agreement gives Bing the scale necessary to compete with Google.

Bing has used several strategies to gain share from Google. First, Bing was introduced with a huge advertising campaign, with ad spending reaching nearly $100 million during its June 2009 launch. In comparison, Google's total ad spending in 2008 was $25 million (Kleessen 2009). In addition, Microsoft frequently used untraditional methods to market Bing. For example, Microsoft donated $2,500 to the Gulf of America Charity Fund each time Stephen Colbert said the word "Bing" during an episode of his television show, The Colbert Report, raising $150,000.[32] Second, Bing offers a rewards program for users, which can be redeemed for gift cards from companies such as Amazon and charitable donations to charities such as the Kids in Need Foundation. Finally, Bing competes with Google on a number for fronts besides its search engine, including Bing dictionary, entertainment (e.g., movie reviews), events, news, maps, and Wolfram Alpha

---

[31] In 2004, the European Union also brought an antitrust suit against Microsoft. This resulted in a $613 million fine.

[32] This show aired June 7, 2010 and can be seen at http://www.colbertnation.com/the-colbert-report-videos/311926/June-07-2010/charity-begins-at-11-30.

(provides answers to math questions). From September 2010 to March 2011, Google's share of Internet searches fell from 73% to 64%, while Bing's (with Yahoo) share rose from 24% to 30%.

Most recent growth has come from Microsoft's acquisition of Skype, a company that provides visual Internet telephone service. With Skype, Microsoft can provide Internet telephone service into everything from Windows, Bing, and its Xbox entertainment system. This acquisition is consistent with the company's long-run strategy of embracing new technologies and extending its reach into all areas of computer software and the Internet. According to Cheng (2011), buying Skype will enable Microsoft to remain competitive with technology rivals Google and Apple in the years to come. Acquiring innovative related technologies makes sense in industries where technological change is rapid. For Microsoft to remain successful, it must be prepared to address the creative destruction that a new technology may bring.

21.2.3 General Motors[33]

The General Motors (GM) story has elements of both success and failure. The company rose to dominance from 1920 through the early 1970s and was the world's largest car maker from 1931 until 2008 when Toyota took over the top spot. GM's domestic market share reached over 50% in the 1960s, but it has steadily declined to only about 20% today. If it were not for a federal government bailout, the company may have gone out of business in 2008. The purpose of this case study is to analyze the reasons for GM's rise and fall from dominance and to assess the economics of the government bailout.

As we discussed in Chap. 13, GM's early success is attributable to the acumen of the company's president, Alfred P. Sloan. Sloan was able to boost profits and gain market share by segmenting the market and improving efficiency. In contrast with Ford that produced a single car (the Model T) at low cost, in the 1920s GM began offering a variety of cars to attract consumers with different tastes and levels of income. Chevrolet served low income consumers, Cadillac served luxury car buyers, and Buick served the middle class. In addition, Chevrolet and Pontiac began offering high power engines to serve consumer demand for acceleration and speed. This not only broadened the consumer base for GM automobiles but also kept the GM divisions from competing with one another. Efficient production was assured by allowing cars from different divisions to share components that exhibited economies of scale in production, such as frames, brake systems, and engine components. This strategy was adopted well ahead of its competitors and gave GM a competitive advantage that persisted for decades.

---

[33] For more complete discussion, see Norton (2007), Brock (2009), Horton (2010), and Ikenson (2011).

Another factor that contributed to success was insulation from foreign competition following World War II. With much of the production facilities of Europe and Japan destroyed by war, US automobile and other major manufacturers flourished. In time though, lack of competition made the big three (GM, Ford, and Chrysler) soft, causing them to invest too little in product and quality innovation. Once foreign competitors recovered from war, they began producing quality cars that were exported to the USA. In 1955, imports accounted for less than 1% of car sales in the USA, a number that increased to 6% in 1965 and 28% in 1980.

A contributing factor to the growing success of imports was the 1973 oil shock which caused the price of crude oil to rise by 160% from early 1973 to 1974 (see Chap. 9). This induced consumers to switch to more fuel efficient cars. At the time, GM and the other domestic companies were focused on the production of larger cars with very poor fuel economy. Thus, the only fuel efficient option available to consumers was to switch to imports.

Another factor was product reliability. Many foreign cars, especially those originating from Japan, were of superior quality to cars produced in the USA. As the reputation for producing reliable cars increased, more and more consumers began to switch to foreign brands. A quality gap persists to this day and has continued to erode the market share of the big three. For example, *Consumer Reports* indicates that domestic automobiles represent only 12% of the 50 most reliable cars and 44% of the 41 least reliable cars from the 2010 model year.[34] In contrast, cars built by Japanese companies represent 70% of the most reliable cars and only 12% of the least reliable cars.[35]

One of GM's fundamental weaknesses was its unwillingness to diversify into small car and hybrid car production. Through the mid-1980s, foreign firms served the small car market, while US companies focused on large cars, SUVs, and trucks.[36] By the late 1980s, Japanese companies began to diversify into larger cars, luxury cars, and trucks, giving them a complete product mix. Yet, GM refused to compete head to head with Japanese companies in the small car market. In the early 2000s, Brock (2005, 101) speculated that GM earned as much as 90% of its profits from SUV and truck sales. This was a profitable strategy in the 1990s when oil prices were low but not since oil prices began their steep rise in 2003.

A contributing factor to GM's inability to compete with foreign companies in the last decade is its growing "legacy costs." In place of higher wages, chief executive officers (CEO's) of decades past gave union auto workers greater health care and

---

[34] This information is available at http://www.consumerreports.org.

[35] All of the least reliable Japanese cars are produced by Nissan, of which Renault of France owns a 44% share.

[36] White (1971) argued that the reason why the big three refrained from producing small cars was that the presence of scale economies in production and a belief that demand for small cars was limited made small car production unprofitable. This was not a problem for foreign producers, however, because they were already producing small cars at efficient scale for their home countries. All they needed to overcome was the cost of shipping their cars to the USA.

other benefits once they retired. This strategy benefited the company in the 1980s and 1990s because it postponed payouts into the future, which is hurting profits today now that these workers are beginning to retire. It is estimated that GM plants have a full labor cost (all wages and benefits) of $73 an hour, while Toyota plants in the USA have a full labor cost of only $48 per hour.[37] Clearly, these legacy costs put GM at a strategic disadvantage compared to Toyota.

The combined effect of these factors explains why GM lost more than $80 billion from 2004 through 2009.[38] If it had not been for the financial bailout by the federal government, it is unlikely that GM (and Chrysler) would be in business today. To address the economic consequences of the great recession, Congress established the Troubled Asset Relief Program (TARP) to provide funds to shore up the financial sector. Because every market depends on the financial sector of the economy, its health is critical to the wellbeing of the overall economy. As a result, most of the bailout money was used to save some of the country's largest banks and financial institutions, based on the argument that these companies are too large to fail from society's perspective.

This argument was also used to justify the bailout of GM, which received almost $50 billion to help the company restructure and stay in business.[39] The Center for Automotive Research estimated that three million jobs were at stake if the big three automobile makers were to fail (Ikenson 2011), based on the argument that failure of the big three would cause a domino effect by causing bankruptcies to many of the auto input suppliers as well.

With the bailout came considerable restructuring at GM. In exchange for the $50 billion in bailout money, the government owned 60.8% of GM and gained considerable power to influence the direction of restructuring. The first step was for the government to replace GM's CEO and a large portion of the GM board of directors. In addition, the government required GM to produce more environmentally friendly and fuel efficient cars (Horton 2010). Restructuring led to a reduction in excess capacity, the elimination of several brands, and the introduction of new and more fuel efficient cars. GM discontinued the Pontiac brand in 2009 and the Saturn and Hummer brands in 2010.[40] Hummers represented the epitome of the American gas guzzler, with a 14–18 miles-per-gal rating. The Chevrolet Volt was introduced in 2011, a car that runs on battery power for up to 50 miles and earns a 93 miles-per-gal equivalent (MPG-e).

The bailout successfully saved GM and benefitted both auto workers and stockholders, at least in the short term. The company earned a profit in 2010, and its first quarter earnings in 2011 were the highest in 10 years. Given the large

---

[37] These estimates are found in William P. Hoar, "Uncle Sam Grabs the Wheel," *The New American*, available at http://www.highbeam.com/doc/1G1-193452520.html/.

[38] See Associated Press Online, "Earnings Preview: General Motors Co.," at http://www.highbeam.com/doc/1A1-14035cfa9a814ef28fec7538f3b0e94a.html.

[39] Chrysler, the only other auto company given bailout money, received about $30 billion.

[40] In 2004, GM also shut down its Oldsmobile brand.

number of voters who were immediately affected by the bailout, it is not surprising that it received considerable political support from both the Bush and Obama administrations.

In the long term, however, Ikenson (2011) argued that it is not clear that society benefitted from the bailout. First, consumers may have been harmed, because the bailout saved dynamically inefficient firms. Had GM failed, assets would have been transferred to more efficient auto producers, such as Ford, Toyota, Honda, and Subaru. By rewarding failing at the expense of successful firms, the bailout discouraged long-run innovation. Second, the long-run employment effect of the bailout would have been rather small. With the exit of GM, demand for cars produced by other firms would have increased, most of which would have been produced in the USA. In 2009, for example, almost 84% of Hondas sold in the USA were produced in North America. Finally, the bailout is costly to taxpayers, as it is estimated that 20% of the bailout money in the automobile industry will never be repaid to the government.[41]

21.3 Term Paper Topics on Industries and Firms

1. Choose a real-world industry from Chap. 8 that has experienced considerable change in market structure. Document this change and explain its main causes.
2. Choose a real-word cartel other than OPEC and explain the successes and failures of the cartel. In this particular cartel, what are the principle forces that make cooperation difficult?
3. Find a real-world industry in which Cournot–Bertrand behavior is observed (other than the market for small cars, Chaps. 10 and 11). Document this behavior and explain why some firms compete in output and others in price.
4. Choose two real-world oligopoly industries, one where market power is low and another where market power is high. Document and explain these differences.
5. Choose a real-world industry in which firms compete by regularly changing their product characteristics (i.e., in product differentiation and/or product design). Document this behavior and explain why it is common in this industry.
6. In many consumer goods markets, it is common for advertised brands to coexist with unadvertised brands. As we saw in Chaps. 15 and 16, advertised brands generally command the higher price. Choose a real-world market where this is true, and document the price difference between advertised and unadvertised

---

[41] It is estimated that GM's bailout cost the taxpayer $27 billion. But, Ikenson (2011) points out that this estimate ignores many indirect costs. These include a $12–$14 billion in tax breaks, $25 billion from the Energy Department to underwrite research on green technologies, and the $7,500 tax credit that consumers receive on the purchase of each Volt.

brands. Discuss whether the price difference is due to a difference in quality or some other factor. How does advertising play a role in this price–quality issue?

7. In some industries, advertising is combative while in others it is constructive. Discuss the theoretical reasons why advertising may be combative versus constructive. Choose a real-world industry where firms compete in advertising and discuss whether advertising is combative or constructive.

8. Choose a real-world industry in which government has imposed a marketing restriction. Explain the restriction. Discuss the (1) government motives, (2) economic consequences, and (3) social welfare implications of the restriction.

9. Technological change continues to improve the efficiency of the Internet, and this change has had a dramatic impact on the newspaper and newsmagazine industries. Discuss these changes and their social desirability.

10. Choose a real-world industry that is highly concentrated and discuss the extent to which X-inefficiency is present. If it is present, why? If not, why not?

11. In professional sports, leagues are given permission to cooperate in some areas but not others. Document this fact for one professional sport and explain which forms of cooperation are socially desirable and which are socially harmful.

12. College football stars are paid a nominal salary (generally tuition, room, and board), which is far below what they would earn if they turned pro. Is this policy fair given the amount of money major universities earn from football programs? Is such a policy socially desirable if we think of these stars as students first? As athletes first?

13. Choose a real-world firm that has experienced unusual success or failure. Document this and explain the exogenous, strategic, and government forces that explain the firm's performance.

14. Both Standard Oil (*Standard Oil of New Jersey v. US*, 1911) and Microsoft (*US v. Microsoft*, 1998–2007) were found guilty of monopolizing their respective markets. Compare and contrast these two cases and explain why it would be appropriate to break up Standard Oil but not Microsoft.

15. Discuss the social pros and cons of the government bailout of GM and Chrysler. On balance, was the bailout socially desirable?

16. In Chap. 20, we discussed various reasons for government regulation that were motivated by evidence from behavioral economics. Discuss one particular regulation that is motivated by behavioral economic evidence and explain the social benefits and costs of the regulation.

Appendix A: A Review of Mathematics and Econometrics

This appendix summarizes the main math and statistics tools that are used in the book. Mathematics is required for model building, and both mathematics and statistics are needed to analyze real world data. The emphasis is on intuition and application rather than formal technique.

A.1 Mathematics Review

Much of what we study in industrial organization involves concepts that are quantifiable, such as revenues, costs, and profits. This makes industrial organization amenable to mathematical analysis. The advantage of mathematics is that it provides a systematic framework or language for analyzing quantitative relationships. It is a complement to economics, as it makes it easier to analyze complex economic systems. According to Weintraub (2002), the use of mathematics in economics is the most important development in the field of economics in the twentieth century.[1] The disadvantage is that mathematics is a difficult subject for most of us. In spite of its difficulty, we have found that knowledge of several math concepts makes the study of industrial organization much easier.

The purpose of this part of the appendix is to review the key math concepts that we use in the book. A number of Web sites offer mathematical resources, including http://mathworld.wolfram.com/ and http://planetmath.org.

---

[1] This is not to say that you should be obsessed with technique over substance; mathematical models, however elegant, are not an end unto themselves but are developed to help us understand the real world (Hodgson 2009).

V.J. Tremblay and C.H. Tremblay, *New Perspectives on Industrial Organization*,
Springer Texts in Business and Economics, DOI 10.1007/978-1-4614-3241-8,
© Springer Science+Business Media New York 2012

A.1.1 Functions

In economic modeling, we will be interested in using a mathematical **function** to describe the relationship between variables. Consider the case with just two variables x and y, where the value of y depends on the value of x. In general form, we write this as $y = f(x)$ or $y = y(x)$, and it is read: y is a function of x. To be a true function, there must be just one value of y for each value of x.[2] By convention, y is called the **dependent variable** and x is called the **independent variable**, meaning that its value is exogenously or independently determined. Variables are assumed to be real numbers, with context determining more restrictive bounds on a variable. For example, quantities of outputs cannot be negative.

Functions can also be described with a specific functional form. One example is $y = bx$, where b is a constant and is called a parameter or coefficient. The function becomes even more specific when b takes on the value of a real number. For instance when $b = 4$, $y = 4x$. This tells us that in the case of $x = 2$, $y = 8$. It is sometimes useful to express a function in implicit form, which is written $f(y, x) = 0$. For example, $y = 2x^2$ is an explicit form of the function, and $y - 2x^2 = 0$ is the corresponding **implicit function**. These can be rather complicated, making it difficult to solve for y. One example is $y^2 - y^4 + x^2 - 12 = 0$.

For the most part, we will consider explicit functions that are smooth and continuous. A **continuous function** has no breaks or jumps, and a **smooth function** has no kinks or sharp corners. When a function is always increasing or decreasing in x, it is said to be **monotonic**. A positive monotonic function always increases in x, and a negative monotonic function always decreases in x.

There will be times when it is useful to consider the inverse of a function. The inverse is derived by solving the function $y = y(x)$ for x so that $x = x(y)$.[3] As an example, if $y = bx$, then the inverse function is $x = y/b$. This is an important concept when we discuss demand theory, for example, because it will sometimes be convenient to use the inverse demand function. The inverse of a function is not always a function itself. When a function is monotonic, its inverse is also a function and it is called an **inverse function**. That is, there is a unique value of x for each value of y.

In most cases, dependent variables in economics depend on more than one independent variable. In the case of 3 independent variables (x_1, x_2, and x_3), we write the function $y = f(x_1, x_2, x_3)$. A specific example is the following: $y = 2x_1^2 + 3x_2 - 4x_3$. In this case, the value of y depends on the values of all three independent variables. When y depends on $k > 1$ independent variables, it is sometimes convenient to write it as $y = f(\underline{x})$, where $\underline{x}$ represents the vectors $x_1, x_2, x_3, \ldots, x_k$.

---

[2] When y can take on more than one value for a given x, this is a correspondence and not a function. The inequality $y \leq x$ provides one example of a correspondence. In most cases, we will deal with functions.

[3] This is sometimes written as $y^{-1}(x)$ or $f^{-1}(x)$, where the -1 is an inverse indicator and not an exponent.

A.1.2 Graphing

A **graph** provides a picture that describes the behavior of a function. Although three-dimensional graphs are used in economics, most of our graphs will be described in two dimensions, x and y. In mathematics, the dependent variable (y) is depicted on the vertical axis, and the independent variable (x) is on the horizontal axis.[4]

Almost all of the functions that we use and graph will be polynomial functions.[5] When y is a function of a single variable, the general form of a polynomial function is

$$y = a_0 + a_1 x + a_2 x^2 + a_3 x^3 + \cdots + a_k x^k, \tag{A.1}$$

where $a_0, a_1, a_3, \ldots, a_k$ are parameters. The highest power, which is k in this case, is called the degree of the polynomial function. Examples of subclasses of polynomials are listed below:

$$\text{Constant function } (k = 0) : y = a_0, \tag{A.2}$$

$$\text{Linear function } (k = 1)^6 : y = a_0 + a_1 x,$$

$$\text{Quadratic function } (k = 2) : y = a_0 + a_1 x + a_2 x^2,$$

$$\text{Cubic function } (k = 3) : y = a_0 + a_1 x + a_2 x^2 + a_3 x^3.$$

Specific examples are provided in the following figures. Figure A.1 graphs the linear function, $y = 4$. Notice that it represents a straight line and that the value of y does not depend on x. Figure A.2 describes the linear function $y = 12 - 2x$, and Fig. A.3 depicts the quadratic function $y = 12x - x^2$.

We will make extensive use of linear and quadratic functions, so it is important to understand their properties. Linear functions are commonly written in slope–intercept form as $y = a - bx$. Parameter a is the y-intercept, which identifies where the line crosses the y-axis (or the value of y when $x = 0$). In essence, it identifies the line's location. Parameter b is the slope of the line, which tells us two things: (1) whether the line increases or decreases when we increase x and (2) the magnitude of the incline or decline. With $b > 0$, the line slopes up and to the right (i.e., y increases with x), and when $b < 0$, the line slopes down to the right (i.e., y decreases with x). In

---

[4] Keep in mind, however, that this is sometimes reversed in economics. For example, with a demand function the quantity demanded (Q_D) is a function of price (p), $Q_D(p)$, but Q_D is on the horizontal axis and p is on the vertical axis.

[5] Polynomial means multiterm.

[6] Technically, this is called an affine function if $a_0 \neq 0$. To be a linear function in mathematics, a_0 must equal zero. We will ignore this distinction.

Fig. A.1 Graph of $y = 4$

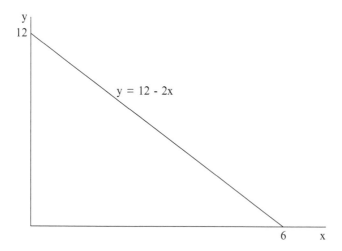

Fig. A.2 Graph of $y = 12 - 2x$

the example in Fig. A.2, 12 is the y-intercept and -2 is the slope. We can interpret the slope of a line as the change in y that results when we increase x by 1 unit. In this case, y decreases by 2 units when we increase x by 1 unit.

Because linear functions are so easy to understand and graph, we will use them whenever possible. By this we mean that we will assume that a function is linear whenever this is a reasonable approximation of reality. For instance, it is common to assume linear demand and supply functions.

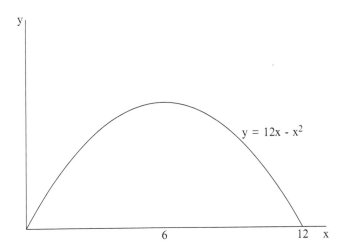

Fig. A.3 Graph of $y = 12x - x^2$

There are some cases where linearity is inappropriate. For example, firm profits normally rise, reach a peak, and then fall as the firm produces more and more output. This relationship is best described by a quadratic function, as in Fig. A.3. There are four features of this function to notice. First, it initially increases at a decreasing rate. That is, y increases with x but the increase in y becomes smaller and smaller as x increases. Second, when the function reaches a maximum, the slope of a tangent line to the curve equals zero.[7] Third, beyond the maximum, the function declines at an increasing rate. That is, the magnitude of the decrease in y gets larger as x increases. Finally, when $y = 0$, x takes on two values. An example of a quadratic function with these properties is $y = ax - bx^2$, where $a, b > 0$. In this case, we can rewrite it as $y = x(a - bx)$. Note that $y = 0$ when x takes on two values: $x = 0$ and $x = a/b$. For the equation in Fig. A.3, this occurs where $x = 0$ and 12.

A.1.3 Derivatives of Functions with One Independent Variable

In economics, we frequently investigate how a dependent variable changes with a change in an independent variable. For the function $y = f(x)$, the change in y that results from a change in x is defined as

$$\frac{\Delta y}{\Delta x} = \frac{f(x + \Delta x) - f(x)}{\Delta x}, \tag{A.3}$$

where Δ is the symbol for change. Note that $f(x + \Delta x)$ is the value of y when x changes by the value Δx, and $f(x)$ is the original value of y. Thus, $f(x + \Delta x) - f(x)$ is

---

[7] A line is tangent to a curve where the line touches the curve at just one point.

the change in y, Δy. This becomes the **derivative** of the function as Δx approaches 0. In this case, the change in y resulting from an infinitesimally small increase in x is written as dy/dx.

We begin by calculating the derivative of a linear function, which is relatively easy. First, we calculate the change in y (Δy) due to an increase in x (Δx) as the change in x goes to 0. Let $\Delta y = y_2 - y_1$, where $y_1 = a + bx$ and $y_2 = a + b(x + \Delta x)$. Substitution produces

$$\begin{aligned}
\Delta y &= y_2 - y_1 \\
&= [a + b(x + \Delta x)] - (a + bx) \\
&= (a + bx) + b\Delta x - (a + bx) \\
&= b\Delta x.
\end{aligned} \tag{A.4}$$

Dividing both sides of the equality by Δx yields

$$\frac{\Delta y}{\Delta x} = b. \tag{A.5}$$

Because $\Delta y/\Delta x = b$ does not depend on the value of x, we need not consider what happens when Δx approaches 0 in this case, $\Delta y/\Delta x = dy/dx = b$. This says that a unit increase in x causes y to increase by b (the slope of the line). The derivative of a linear function is a constant and equals the slope of the line.

Next, consider the quadratic function $y = a_0 + a_1 x + a_2 x^2$. Let $y_1 = a_0 + a_1 x + a_2 x^2$ and $y_2 = a_0 + a_1(x + \Delta x) + a_2(x + \Delta x)^2$. Thus,

$$\begin{aligned}
\Delta y &= y_2 - y_1 \\
&= \left[a_0 + a_1(x + \Delta x) + a_2(x + \Delta x)^2\right] - (a_0 + a_1 x + a_2 x^2) \\
&= [a_0 + a_1(x + \Delta x) + a_2(x^2 + 2x\Delta x + (\Delta x)^2)] - (a_0 + a_1 x + a_2 x^2) \\
&= (a_0 + a_1 x + a_2 x^2) + (a_1\Delta x + a_2 2x\Delta x + a_2(\Delta x)^2 - (a_0 + a_1 x + a_2 x^2) \\
&= a_1\Delta x + a_2 2x\Delta x + a_2(\Delta x)^2.
\end{aligned} \tag{A.6}$$

Dividing both sides of the equality by Δx yields

$$\frac{\Delta y}{\Delta x} = a_1 + 2a_2 x + a_2\Delta x. \tag{A.7}$$

Because $a_2\Delta x$ vanishes in the limit as Δx approaches 0, $dy/dx = a_1 + 2a_2 x$. Notice that this is a linear function. That is, the derivative of a quadratic function is linear. In the example in Fig. A.3 where $y = 12x - x^2$, $dy/dx = 12 - 2x$.

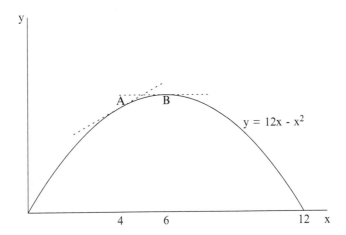

Fig. A.4 Graph of $y = 12x - x^2$ and tangent lines at $x = 4$ and $x = 6$

For a function that is nonlinear, the derivative can be interpreted as the slope of the tangent to the curve for a particular value of x. This is illustrated in Fig. A.4, for the quadratic function $y = 12x - x^2$ and $dy/dx = 12 - 2x$. For example, when $x = 4$, the slope of the tangent equals 4, the value of dy/dx at point A. Notice that when $x = 6$, the slope of the tangent equals 0 (point B). This will be true when a function reaches a maximum, as in this case, or a minimum.

There are several rules of differentiation that are used in the book. These are listed below:

1. For $y = a$, where a is a constant, $dy/dx = 0$. That is, the derivative of a constant is 0.
2. If $y = az$, where $z = f(x)$, then $dy/dx = a(dz/dx)$. The derivative of the product of a constant (a) and a differentiable function [$z = f(x)$] is the constant times the derivative of the function.
3. If $y = x^k$, then $dy/dx = kx^{k-1}$. The derivative of a variable raised to the kth power is k times the $k{-}1$ power of the variable.
4. If $y = f(x) + g(x)$, then $dy/dx = df/dx + dg/dx$. The derivative of the sum of differentiable functions is the sum of their derivatives.
5. If $y = wz$ where $w = f(x)$ and $z = g(x)$, then $dy/dx = w(dz/dx) + z(dw/dx)$. The derivative of the product of two functions equals the first function times the derivative of the second function plus the second function times the derivative of the first function.[8]

In some cases, we will consider the indirect effect that a change in x will have on a function. Consider the situation where $y = f(z)$ and $z = g(x)$. In this case, a

---

[8] This can be used to derive the quotient rule. That is, if $y = z/v$, where $w = 1/v$, $v = f(x)$, and $z = g(x)$, then $\frac{dy}{dx} = \frac{v(dz/dx) - z(dv/dx)}{v^2}$.

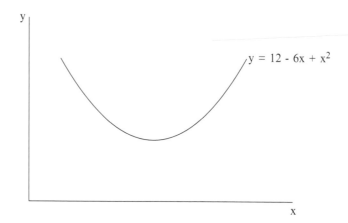

Fig. A.5 Graph of $y = 12 - 6x + x^2$

change in x will affect y indirectly through its effect on z. In other words, the following chain of events will occur: $\Delta x \rightarrow \Delta z \rightarrow \Delta y$, where the symbol $\rightarrow$ means "implies that." In this case,

$$\frac{dy}{dx} = \frac{dy}{dz} \cdot \frac{dz}{dx}. \tag{A.8}$$

This is called the **chain rule of differentiation.**

Finally, we are interested in finding the **second derivative** of a function, that is, the derivative of the derivative of a function. The second derivative is $d(dy/dx)/dx$ and is denoted as d^2y/dx^2.[9] For example, consider the quadratic function $y = a_0 + a_1x + a_2x_2^2$. In this case,

$$\text{First derivative}: \quad \frac{dy}{dx} = a_1 + 2a_2x,$$

$$\text{Second derivative}: \quad \frac{d^2y}{dx^2} = 2a_2. \tag{A.9}$$

The second derivative tells us how the slope of a tangent line to the curve changes as we increase x. This informs us of the curvature of the function. When the second derivative is negative, the function is concave from below, as in Fig. A.4. This means that the curve bends down and towards the x-axis. When the second derivative is positive, the function is convex from below, as in Fig. A.5.

When curvature is needed, we will focus on functions that are either strictly concave or strictly convex and have either a unique maximum or minimum.

---

[9] Similarly, we obtain the third derivative of a function by differentiating it three times. This is written as d^3y/dx^3.

Functions such as these have no linear segments. A function is **strictly concave** if the tangent line to every point on the curve lies everywhere above the function. It is **strictly convex** if the tangent line to every point on the curve lies everywhere below the function.[10]

Most of the functions that we will encounter in the book will have a derivative for every real value of x. If $y = f(x)$ has a derivative for every value of x over a particular interval of x (e.g., $0 \leq x \leq 10$), then $f(x)$ is **differentiable** over that interval.[11] If the resulting derivative is continuous for every x over that interval, then $f(x)$ is continuously differentiable or C^1 over that interval. If the second derivative is continuous for every x over that interval, then $f(x)$ is twice continuously differentiable or C^2. If the third derivative is continuous for every x over that interval, then $f(x)$ is thrice continuously differentiable or C^3.

A.1.4   Derivatives of Functions with More than One Independent Variable

Next, we are interested in taking derivatives of functions that have more than one independent variable. This is called **partial differentiation**. We can write $y = y(x_1, x_2)$, which means that y is a function of both x_1 and x_2. We derive a partial derivative of the function by holding one of the x's constant. For example, we could compute the derivative of y with respect to x_1, holding x_2 constant. To distinguish it from a derivative of a function with a single variable, the partial derivative is denoted by $\partial y / \partial x_1$.

To understand the idea of a partial derivative, consider the function $y = a + b_1 x_1^2 + b_2 x_2$. We derive $\partial y / \partial x_1$ by assuming that x_2 is a constant. In effect, this makes the constant of the equation equal to $a' = (a + b_2 x_2)$, so that $y = a' + b_1 x_1^2$. We know from our discussion above that a constant has no effect on the rate of change of the function. The calculation of the partial derivative follows directly from what we have done above. The equation is a simple quadratic equation in one variable, x_1, and $\partial y / \partial x_1 = 2b_1 x_1$.

Similarly, we can calculate the partial derivative of y with respect to x_2. If we hold x_1 constant, then $y = a'' + b_2 x_2$ where $a'' = (a + b_1 x_1^2)$. This is a linear function, and $\partial y / \partial x_2 = b_2$. The partial derivative provides a classic example of the *ceteris paribus* assumption that is frequently used in economics, as it shows how a change in one variable affects y when all other variables are assumed to be fixed.

---

[10] For more formal definitions, see Chiang (1984, 241–244), Simon and Blume (1994, 43–46), Carter (2001), Baldani et al. (2005, 29–31), and Chiang and Wainwright (2005, 229–231).

[11] This can also be written as $x \in [0, 10]$, where $\in$ reads "is an element of"; x is an element of the set of real numbers that ranges from 0 to 10. That is, the following statements are equivalent: $a \leq x \leq b$ and $x \in [a, b]$. In addition, when $a < x \leq b$, this can be written as $x \in (a, b]$; if $a \leq x < b$, then $x \in [a, b)$; if $a < x < b$, then $x \in (a, b)$.

A.1.5   Solving Systems of Equations

Many problems in economics involve the solution to a system of equations. In the simple demand and supply model, the equilibrium price and output occurs where the demand and supply functions intersect. At that point, both the demand and supply functions hold simultaneously. Thus, it is important to know how to formally solve such systems.

To illustrate, we consider a system with just two linear equations: $y_1 = a_1 + b_1 x$ and $y_2 = a_2 + b_2 x$, where a_1, a_2, b_1, and b_2 are parameters. The solution occurs where the graphs of these two functions intersect. This occurs where $y_1 = y_2$, denoted by x^*, y^*. To find the solution, we set $y_1 = y_2$ and solve for x as follows.

$$a_1 + b_1 x = a_2 + b_2 x, \tag{A.10}$$

$$x^* = \frac{a_2 - a_1}{b_1 - b_2}.$$

Substituting x^* into either of the original equations produces y^*:

$$y^* = y(x^*) = \frac{a_2 b_1 - a_1 b_2}{b_1 - b_2}. \tag{A.11}$$

Notice that for a solution to exist, $b_1 \neq b_2$. When $b_1 = b_2$, the functions have the same slopes and are parallel lines. Thus, they will never intersect. We will see that solving systems such as these will enable us to perform comparative static analysis. That is, with the solution to the system we can determine how the parameters of the model affect x^* and y^*.

To make this more concrete, consider a simple demand and supply model. Demand is $Q_D = 20 - 2p$, and supply is $Q_S = 3p$, where Q_D is quantity demanded, Q_S is quantity supplied, and p is the price. In equilibrium, demand equals supply ($Q_D = Q_S$), and the solution to this system is

$$20 - 2p = 3p, \tag{A.12}$$

$$p^* = 4, \quad \text{and} \quad Q^* = Q_D = Q_S = 12.$$

The solution to this problem, along with the demand (D) supply (S) functions, is illustrated in Fig. A.6.

The same procedure is used to solve nonlinear systems. The only difference is that the algebra becomes more tedious. Consider the following system: $y_1 = c + bx$ and $y_2 = -ax^2$. In this case, setting $y_1 = y_2$ produces the following equation: $ax^2 + bx + c = 0$. This is a quadratic function, and the solution is derived from the quadratic formula

$$x^* = \frac{-b \pm \sqrt{b^2 - 4ac}}{2a}. \tag{A.13}$$

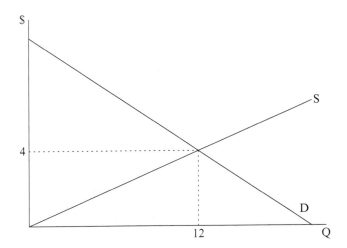

Fig. A.6 Demand and supply model

Notice that this gives two values for x, one for the positive and the other for the negative square root term. This explains why we assume linear approximations of our functions whenever possible.

A.1.6   Optimization

An important role of derivatives in economics is that they enable us to find optimum (i.e., maximum or minimum) values of a function. Examples include finding the output that maximizes firm profit and the combination of inputs that minimize firm costs. In the examples used in the book, functions will be either strictly concave or strictly convex and have a unique optimum. For convenience, when we assume that a function is concave (convex), we mean that it is strictly concave (convex).

The function $y = f(x)$ achieves a maximum at x^* when the following conditions hold. These are referred to as first- and second-order conditions:

$$\text{First-order condition :} \quad \frac{dy}{dx} = 0, \tag{A.14}$$

$$\text{Second-order condition :} \quad \frac{d^2y}{dx^2} < 0. \tag{A.15}$$

The first-order condition indicates that the slope of the tangent to the curve equals zero at x^* and identifies either a maximum or a minimum. The second-order condition indicates that the function is concave. Both conditions together imply that the function reaches a maximum at x^*.

The only change in the case of a minimum is that the function is convex instead of concave. Thus, the conditions that must hold for a minimum are

$$\text{First-order condition}: \quad \frac{dy}{dx} = 0, \tag{A.16}$$

$$\text{Second-order condition}: \quad \frac{d^2y}{dx^2} > 0. \tag{A.17}$$

When both of these conditions hold, the function reaches a minimum at x^*.

You can see that if we know from prior information whether a function is concave or convex, we do not need to check the second-order condition. When convex, the function reaches a minimum when $dy/dx = 0$. When concave, the function reaches a maximum when $dy/dx = 0$. The equations described in Figs. A.4 and A.5 provide two examples. In Fig. A.4, $y = 12x - x^2$. In this case, when $dy/dx = 12 - 2x = 0$, $x^* = 6$. This is a maximum because the function is concave (i.e., $d^2y/dx^2 = -2 < 0$). In Fig. A.5, $y = 12 - 6x + x^2$. Here, $dy/dx = -6 + 2x$, and $x^* = 3$. This is a minimum because the function is convex (i.e., $d^2y/dx^2 = 2 > 0$).

Optimization problems are slightly more complex when there are two or more independent variables.[12] Assume that $y = f(x_1, x_2)$. For an optimum, the following first-order conditions must hold:

$$\text{First-order conditions}: \quad \frac{\partial y}{\partial x_1} = 0 \quad \text{and} \quad \frac{\partial y}{\partial x_2} = 0. \tag{A.18}$$

The second-order conditions determine whether or not the critical values (x_1^*, x_2^*) identify a maximum or a minimum.

Second-order conditions for a Maximum:

$$\frac{\partial^2 y}{\partial x_1^2} < 0, \quad \frac{\partial^2 y}{\partial x_1^2}\frac{\partial^2 y}{\partial x_2^2} - \left(\frac{\partial^2 y}{\partial x_1 \partial x_2}\right)^2 > 0, \tag{A.19}$$

Second-Order Conditions for a Minimum:

$$\frac{d^2 y}{dx_1^2} > 0; \quad \frac{\partial^2 y}{\partial x_1^2}\frac{\partial^2 y}{\partial x_2^2} - \left(\frac{\partial^2 y}{\partial x_1 \partial x_2}\right)^2 > 0. \tag{A.20}$$

The second-order conditions are more complicated because we are now talking about three-dimensional functions. Geometrically, a maximum represents the top of a dome and a minimum represents the bottom of a bowl. These second-order

---

[12] For a more formal discussion, see Simon and Blume (1994, Chap. 17), Baldani et al. (2005, Chap. 7), or Chiang and Wainwright (2005, Chap. 11).

conditions rule out such things as a saddle point, where the function is convex in one direction (e.g., the north–south direction) and is concave in another direction (e.g., the east–west direction). The critical value of a saddle point will meet the first-order conditions even though it represents neither a maximum of a dome nor the minimum of a bowl.

To illustrate this optimization technique, consider the following example. Our goal is to examine the following function for a maximum or a minimum: $y = 2 + 3x_1 - x_1^2 - x_1 x_2 + 3x_2 - x_2^2$. The first-order conditions are

$$\frac{\partial y}{\partial x_1} = 3 - 2x_1 - x_2 = 0 \quad \text{and} \quad \frac{\partial y}{\partial x_2} = -x_1 + 3 - 2x_2 = 0. \qquad \text{(A.21)}$$

We obtain the critical values by solving the system of first-order conditions simultaneously for x_1 and x_2. The result is $x_1^* = 1$, $x_2^* = 1$. The second derivatives are[13]

$$\frac{\partial^2 y}{\partial x_1^2} = -2; \quad \frac{\partial^2 y}{\partial x_1 \partial x_2} = -1,$$

$$\frac{\partial^2 y}{\partial x_2^2} = -2; \quad \frac{\partial^2 y}{\partial x_2 \partial x_1} = -1. \qquad \text{(A.22)}$$

In this case, the second-order conditions imply a maximum:

$$\frac{\partial^2 y}{\partial x_1^2} = -2 < 0, \quad \frac{\partial^2 y}{\partial x_1^2} \frac{\partial^2 y}{\partial x_2^2} - \left(\frac{\partial^2 y}{\partial x_1 \partial x_2}\right)^2 = 3 > 0. \qquad \text{(A.23)}$$

Thus, a maximum is reached at $x_1^* = 1, x_2^* = 1$, and $y^*(x_1^*, x_2^*) = 5$.

A.1.7 Dynamic Programming[14]

Dynamic programming is a method for solving dynamic or sequential decision problems that occur over time. These are problems where you must choose an optimal action at each stage or time period $0, 1, 2, \ldots, T$. The problem at each stage is called a subproblem. In most cases, T is a finite number, but it is allowed to approach infinity in infinitely repeated games.

---

[13] In general, $\partial^2 y / \partial x_1^2 \neq \partial^2 y / \partial x_2^2$. By Young's theorem $\partial^2 y / (\partial x_1 \partial x_2)$ will always equal $\partial^2 y / (\partial x_2 \partial x_1)$. For further discussion, see Simon and Blume (1994, 330), Baldani et al. (2005, 124), or Chiang and Wainright (2005, 296).

[14] For a complete discussion of dynamic programming methods, see Novshek (1993, Chap. 11).

The solution to dynamic problems is based on the Bellman principle of optimality: given whatever has been done in previous periods, actions in remaining periods must be optimal. This suggests that an efficient way to solve dynamic problems is to work backwards through each subproblem. This is called backwards induction. It means that we first solve for the optimal action in period T. Given that, we next solve the optimal action in period $T - 1$, then $T - 2$, etc.

Backwards induction is analogous to the approach used to solve a childhood maze, where you must find the path through a maze from a starting point to a finish point. Most children learn that the fastest (most efficient) way to solve the problem is to start at the finish and work backwards.

To illustrate this concept, consider the following problem. Your goal is to choose the value of x_t in each period $t (= 0, 1, 2, \ldots, T)$ that maximizes the stream of payoffs (Π) over this time horizon. The objective function is

$$\Pi = \sum_{t=0}^{T} D^t f(x_t), \tag{A.24}$$

where D is the discount factor (see Chap. 2). In the last period (T), this is a simple static problem in which the optimal value of x_T is the solution to the first-order condition: $d\Pi/dx_T = D^T \cdot df/dx_T = 0.$[15] The optimal value of the choice variable is labeled x_T^*, and the optimal value of the objective function at T is $V_T = D^T \cdot f(x_T^*)$, which is called the value function at period T.

Next, we solve the subproblem in period $T - 1$. In this case, the objective function becomes $f(x_{T-1}) + V_T$. We then derive the optimal value of x_{T-1}. We continue this process until we have found the optimal value of x at period 0. Once this is done, we have identified $x_0^*, x_1^*, x_2^*, \ldots, x_T^*$ and $f(x_0^*), f(x_1^*), f(x_2^*), \ldots, f(x_T^*)$.

In economics, it is frequently useful to analyze the problem in period $t < T$. At this time period, the problem satisfies the Bellman equation

$$V_t = \max[f(x_t) + V_{t+1}], \tag{A.25}$$

where V_t is the value function in period t. In this case, the first-order condition is

$$\frac{\partial V_t}{\partial x_t} = \frac{\partial f(x_t)}{\partial x_t} + \frac{\partial V_{t+1}}{\partial x_t} = 0. \tag{A.26}$$

Note that $\partial V_{t+1}/\partial x_t$ represents the effect of a change in x_t on the present value of the stream of future payoffs. This demonstrates that to behave optimally in a dynamic setting, you must optimally trade off the effect that a change in x_t has on today's payoffs [$f(x_t)$] versus future payoffs (V_{t+1}).

The approach of backwards induction will be used in dynamic games to identify their subgame–perfect Nash equilibria (see Chap. 3).

---

[15] This assumes that $f(x_t)$ is a purely concave function.

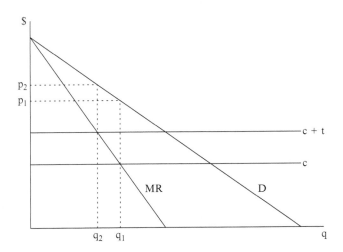

Fig. A.7 Monopoly model with excise tax (t)

A.1.8   Comparative Static Analysis

Economic models provide us with a better understanding of the real world by predicting how a change in a policy, exogenous factor, or parameter affects a particular aspect of the economy. Making such a prediction is called comparative static analysis. The most elementary approach involves the use of graphs. One example is the demand and supply model, which can be used to predict how an increase in demand will affect equilibrium price and output levels. Three other methods involve greater mathematical sophistication. We call these the brute-force method, implicit-function theorem method, and monotone method.

To illustrate these methods, we investigate the effect of an excise or per-unit tax (t) on a monopolist's profit-maximizing level of output (q). The graphical approach is illustrated in Fig. A.7. It describes the firm's demand function (D), marginal revenue (MR), marginal cost (MC), and the marginal cost plus the tax ($c + t$). This assumes a constant marginal cost of production (c). Without the tax, a profit-maximizing monopolist will produce where $MR = c$ at output q_1, which it sells at price p_1. With the tax, the firm will produce where $MR = c + t$, which corresponds to q_2 and p_2. This demonstrates that an increase in the tax will reduce the firm's profit-maximizing level of output. The limitation of this approach is that it cannot tell us the magnitude of the change.

This limitation is overcome by the brute-force method when we have more specific information about demand and cost conditions. Continuing with the excise tax example, assume that a profit-maximizing monopolist faces linear demand and cost functions. Let the firm's inverse demand be $p = a - bq$, where a and b are positive constants. The firm's total revenue (TR) is pq and its total cost function (TC) is

$TC = cq + tq$. Thus, the firm's profit equals $\pi(q, t) = TR - TC = (a - bq - c - t)q$. To ensure that profits are non-negative in equilibrium, $a > c + t$.

With specific functional forms, comparative static results can be derived directly from the solution to the monopoly problem. The firm's first- and second-order conditions of profit maximization are[16]

$$\frac{\partial \pi}{\partial q} = a - c - t - 2bq = 0,$$
$$\frac{\partial^2 \pi}{\partial q^2} = -2b < 0. \tag{A.27}$$

The sign of the second-order condition indicates that the profit function is concave and that the first-order condition identifies a maximum and not a minimum. Solving the first-order condition for q gives its profit-maximizing level (q^*):

$$q^* = \frac{a - c - t}{2b}. \tag{A.28}$$

From this equation we can see that an increase in t will cause the firm's profit-maximizing level of output to fall (i.e., $\partial q^*/\partial t = -1/(2b) < 0$). For a discrete increase in t from t_1 to t_2, the change in q^* is $(t_1 - t_2)/(2b) < 0$. When demand and cost functions can be expressed explicitly, both the sign and magnitude of change can be obtained and nothing is gained from using other comparative static methods.

Unfortunately, the brute-force method cannot be used when specific functional forms are unknown and are replaced by general ones. In this case, q^* cannot be derived explicitly. For example, assume that the firm faces general inverse-demand function $p = p(q)$ that has a negative slope, is differentiable, and is not too convex.[17] The firm's total cost function is also general and given by $TC = C(q) + tq$. Both the firm's total cost and marginal cost ($\partial C/\partial q$) functions are assumed to be differentiable and increasing in q. In this case, the profit equation, $\pi(q, t) = p(q)q - C(q) - tq$, is concave (i.e., $d^2\pi/dq^2 < 0$). The firm's first-order condition is

$$\frac{\partial \pi}{\partial q} = p + \frac{\partial p}{\partial q}q - \frac{\partial C}{\partial q} - t = 0. \tag{A.29}$$

The optimal value of q cannot be derived explicitly, making it impossible to use the brute-force method to determine the effect of a change in t on q^*.

Nevertheless, the implicit-function theorem can be used to determine the sign (but not the magnitude) of $\partial q^*/\partial t$. Even though q^* cannot be derived explicitly, it is

---

[16] We use a partial derivative to remind us that a firm typically has other decision variables to consider, which are assumed to be fixed.

[17] For the second-order condition of profit maximization to hold, the demand function cannot be too convex (i.e., $\partial^2 p/\partial q^2$ is sufficiently small). This produces a concave profit equation.

embedded in the first-order condition. As a result, derivatives of the first-order conditions with respect to t and q tell us something about the change in q^*. Under certain regularity conditions, the implicit-function theorem implies that[18]

$$\frac{\partial q^*}{\partial t} = -\frac{\partial^2 \pi / \partial q \partial t}{\partial^2 \pi / \partial q^2}. \tag{A.30}$$

Note that the numerator on the right-hand side of the equality above equals -1. The denominator is negative from the second-order condition of profit maximization. Thus, an increase in the tax will decrease q^*. This demonstrates that with the implicit-function theorem, differentiability and concavity of the objective function are required to perform comparative static analysis.

The primary limitations of the implicit-function method are that it cannot be used when functions are not differentiable, the objective function is not concave, or a change in the policy variable is discrete rather than continuous.[19] To perform comparative static analysis under these conditions, we can use Edlin and Shannon's (1998) (strict) monotonicity theorem.[20] The theorem states that if there are **increasing marginal returns** to a policy variable (x), then an increase in x will lead to an increase in the optimal level of the decision variable of an objective function.

The intuition behind this theorem comes from the concept of increasing marginal returns. In the case of our monopolist, marginal returns are defined as the change in profit that results from a change in output, $\Delta \pi / \Delta q$. There are increasing marginal returns when $\Delta \pi / \Delta q$ is increasing in x. If we assume continuity and consider a small change in x, marginal returns equals $\partial \pi / \partial q$ and there are increasing marginal returns if $\partial(\partial \pi / \partial q)\partial x = \partial^2 \pi / (\partial q \partial x) > 0$. When this condition holds, an increase in x causes q^* to increase because the marginal benefit of increasing q has increased. To use the theorem, all we need to do is check to see if the function exhibits increasing marginal returns with respect to the policy variable or parameter in question.

We return to our monopoly tax example to illustrate this method. For there to be increasing marginal returns in x, we must define x to equal $-t$ (i.e., x is a subsidy). Thus, a reduction in t causes an increase in x. The firm's profit is $\pi = \text{TR} - \text{TC}$, where TR is total revenue, $\text{TC} = C(q) - xq$. First, consider the case of a continuous profit function where we change x by an infinitely small amount. Here, marginal returns are $\partial \pi / \partial q = \text{MR} - \partial C / \partial q + x$, where MR is marginal revenue and $\partial C / \partial q$ is the marginal production cost. In this case, there are increasing marginal returns because $\partial^2 \pi / \partial q \partial x = 1 > 0$. Thus, by the monotonicity theorem an increase in x (i.e., a reduction in the per-unit tax) causes the firm's profit-maximizing level of output to increase.

---

[18] For a more formal discussion, see Simon and Blume (1994, Chap. 15), Baldani et al. (2005, Chap. 5), or Chiang and Wainwright (2005, Chap. 8).

[19] We will see that this is a common occurrence in policy analysis. For example, advertising restrictions can completely ban certain forms of advertising, and excise taxes have been known to double.

[20] For a survey of this and other comparative static techniques, see C. Tremblay and V. Tremblay (2010).

Analysis of a discrete change is more tedious but similar to the discussion above. Now, assume a discrete increase in x from x_1 to x_2. In this case, marginal returns are discrete as well, equaling

$$\frac{\partial \pi(x_2)}{\partial q} - \frac{\partial \pi(x_1)}{\partial q} = \left(\frac{\partial TR}{\partial q} - \frac{\partial TC(x_2)}{\partial q} \right) - \left(\frac{\partial TR}{\partial q} - \frac{\partial TC(x_1)}{\partial q} \right). \qquad (A.31)$$

This simplifies to the following

$$\frac{\partial \pi(x_2)}{\partial q} - \frac{\partial \pi(x_1)}{\partial q} = -\frac{\partial TC(x_2)}{\partial q} + \frac{\partial TC(x_1)}{\partial q}. \qquad (A.32)$$

Equation (A.32) equals $x_2 - x_1 > 0$ in our example. Because marginal returns rise as we increase x, the profit function exhibits increasing marginal returns with respect to x. Thus, a discrete increase in x will cause the firm to increase its profit-maximizing level of output.

These examples illustrate how easy it is to use the monotonicity theorem. It also demonstrates that the differentiability and concavity assumptions needed to use the implicit-function theorem are not necessary to perform comparative static analysis.

A.1.9   Convex, Closed, and Bounded Sets[21]

In game theory, we will assume that the strategy set of all players in a game meets certain regularity conditions. By a set, we simply mean a collection of elements. In game theory, this would include all possible strategies of the players. It may contain finitely many or infinitely many elements. Strategic possibilities for a baseball pitcher are finite and may include a fastball, curveball, and a slider. An example of a set with infinitely many elements would include the elements on and within a circle (i.e., all points on the edge and inside the circle).

When discussing strategic sets, regularity normally applies to sets that are closed, convex, and bounded. A set is **closed** if it contains all of its boundary points. A set is **convex** if all of the points of a line connecting any two points on the boundary of the set are a part of the set. This would be true of the set of points on and within a triangle or circle.[22] A set is **strictly convex** if all of the points (other than the endpoint) lie inside the boundary. This would be true of the circle but not the triangle. Finally, a set is **bounded** when the distance between any two points in the set is less than infinity. In other words, the boundary is finite. When a set is closed and bounded, it is said to be **compact**.

---

[21] Discussion of these more advanced topics can be found in Simon and Blume (1994).

[22] Do not confuse a convex function from a convex set. An upward bending parabola is a convex function (from below) but is not a convex set. A circle that contains all of its boundary and interior points is a convex set, but it is not a function at all.

These concepts are important when discussing the set of all possible mixed strategies in game theory. Because a mixed strategy is a probability, it ranges from 0 to 1 for each player. With two players, the strategy set is a square that contains all points on and inside the boundary, as described in Fig. 3.10. A set such as this is closed, convex, and bounded. It is not a strictly convex set.

The math tools discussed in this section are sufficient for understanding the math used in the book. We now turn to econometrics tools.

A.2   Regression Analysis

Econometrics is the study of the measurement of economic relationships. It can be thought of as statistics as applied to economics. Econometrics encompasses estimation, hypothesis testing, and prediction. A primary tool of econometrics is regression analysis, widely used in economics and in other fields. In this section, we discuss simple regression (involving just two variables), then hypothesis testing, multiple regression (more than two variables), prediction, and finally evaluating regression estimates. Before we embark on regression techniques, we briefly describe uniform, normal, and t-distributions.

A.2.1   Probability Distributions

At times in the text, we refer to probability distributions such as the uniform distribution and the normal distribution. An example of a **uniform distribution** involves the experiment of rolling a six-sided die. The outcome of the roll, the number of dots on the face of the die, is a **random variable**. A variable is considered random if it takes on values by chance. The roll of the die has six possible outcomes: 1, 2, 3, 4, 5, 6. Each outcome is equally likely and will occur with probability 1/6. The probability distribution for the roll of the die, graphed in Fig. A.8, maps each possible value to the probability that the value will occur. This distribution is defined as $f(x) = 1/6$ for $x = 1, 2, 3, 4, 5, 6$ and is a discrete uniform distribution. A **discrete variable** has a countable number of values, in contrast to a continuous variable, which has an infinite number of values. A discrete **probability distribution** indicates the probabilities associated with each possible value of a discrete random variable. A probability distribution is also known as a probability density function.

The continuous uniform density function is specified over a range of values, such as a to b, and is given by $f(x) = 1/(b - a)$ within the interval a to b and 0 outside the interval. (See Fig. A.9) The equation for $f(x)$ tells us that for values between a and b, outcomes are equally likely. The mean (average) of the continuous uniform density is: $(\mu) = (a + b)/2$ as might be expected. In the text, we assume that variables such as consumer tastes or location of consumers have uniform distributions. We might assume that consumer tastes for sweetness are evenly distributed along an interval

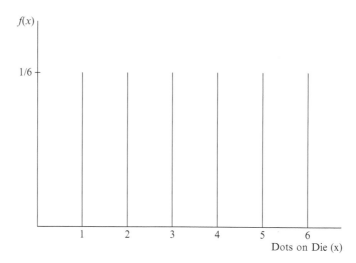

Fig. A.8 The probability distribution for a roll of the die

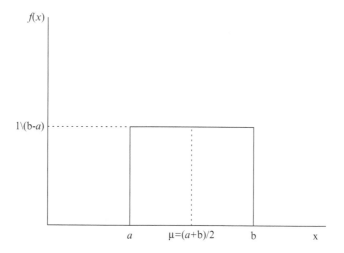

Fig. A.9 A continuous uniform distribution

for cereal sweetness or that consumers are located evenly along a strip of land. We can make assumptions in theoretical models regarding the distributions of various variables as in these cases, but we can also use distributional assumptions for hypothesis testing on sample data.

Perhaps the most commonly used distribution is the normal (or Gaussian) distribution. Shown in Fig. A.10, the **normal distribution** is bell shaped, symmetric, and peaks at its mean value. Because the normal distribution is symmetric, the mean and

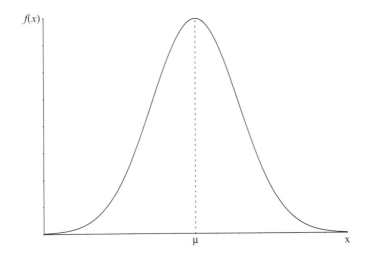

$f(x)$

μ

x

Fig. A.10 The normal distribution

the median (middle value of ordered values) are the same. The shape of the normal distribution also depends on its variance, a measure of dispersion or spread of the distribution. Two normal distributions appear in Fig. A.11. Although they each have the same mean value, the distribution marked $f(x)'$ has a lower variance than the distribution marked $f(x)''$.[23]

IQ test scores are an example of a normally distributed variable.[24] IQ stands for Intelligence Quotient, and the IQ test score is based on the performance of an individual on a set of intelligence tests. Fig. A.12 shows the distribution of IQ scores. The mean IQ score (within an age group) is 100 and the standard deviation (the square root of the variance) is 15. About 68.2% of the population score between 85 and 115, 95.4% score between 70 and 130, and 99.7% score between 55 and 145. In fact, in general the probability that a normally distributed random variable lies within one standard deviation from the mean is 68.2%, within two standard deviations of the mean is 95.4%, and within three standard deviations of the mean is 99.7%.

The popularity of the normal distribution arises from both theoretical and empirical evidence. Mathematically, it can be shown that many other probability distributions approach the normal distribution as the sample becomes very large. In practice, this means that the normal distribution can serve as a fair representation of many distributions in large samples (but not all distributions). Further, empirical studies have shown again and again that distributions of observed data approximate

---

[23] In the figure, the mean of each distribution is 0, the variance of $f(x)'$ is 1, and the variance of $f(x)''$ is 0.25.

[24] This discussion is not meant as an endorsement of the use of IQ scores, but just serves as a statistical (not psychometric) example.

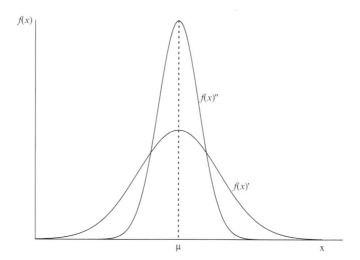

Fig. A.11 Normal distributions with alternative variances

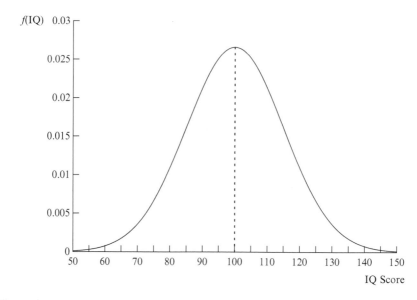

Fig. A.12 Distribution of IQ scores

the normal distribution. Examples include weights of dogs and tomatoes, length of thumbs, and leaves on trees.[25] When the mean of a normal distribution is zero and the variance is 1, the distribution is said to be a standard normal distribution.

---

[25] Studenmund (2006, Chap. 16 by Gary Smith).

Use of the normal distribution requires knowledge of the true variance. In applications that use a sample of data, the variance is unknown and must be estimated. In this case, we use the *t*-distribution, also known as the Student *t*-distribution. The *t*-distribution is bell shaped and symmetric like the normal, but has a lower peak, wider spread, and more area in the tails. The shape of the *t*-distribution changes as the sample size changes. When the sample size becomes very large, the *t*-distribution approaches the normal distribution. William Sealy Gosset developed the Student *t*-distribution and small sample hypothesis testing techniques. As a chemist at the Guinness brewery in Ireland, Gosset conducted *t* tests to check for consistent quality across batches of Guinness beer. Guinness required that Gosset use a different name to publish his results. Gosset chose "Student" and hence the term Student *t*-distribution (Pearson 1990). Below we discuss the application of *t* tests to regression coefficients, but first we lay out the basics of simple regression.

A.2.2   Simple Regression

We are often interested in asking questions of the form "how does x affect y" such as how does advertising affect profits or how does industry concentration affect prices? Of interest is the sign of an effect, for example, does advertising increase or decrease profits, and the magnitude, how much does advertising increase or decrease profits?

A model such as $y = \beta_0 + \beta_1 x$ could give us an answer to the question of how x affects y: the effect of x on y is simply $dy/dx = \beta_1$. Unfortunately, we usually do not know the value of β_1 and cannot always obtain it using theory. In these circumstances, we often turn to data to find an estimate of β_1.

Regression analysis is a statistical tool that is commonly used to estimate economic relationships. A simple **regression equation** is given by

$$y = \beta_0 + \beta_1 x + u, \tag{A.33}$$

where y is the **dependent variable**, x is the **independent variable**, β_0 and β_1 are true values of the **parameters** to be estimated, and u is an **error term**. Another name for x is a regressor or explanatory variable; β_0 and β_1 are also known as coefficients. The sum, $\beta_0 + \beta_1 x$, on the right-hand side of (A.2.1) represents the average value of y for a particular value of x, and the error term represents how y for a particular observation (e.g., firm, industry, consumer) deviates from the average.

As a simple example, suppose that we want to find out how advertising (A) affects profit (π). We collect data on profits and advertising from firms in the aerospace industry (at a point in time) to estimate the following regression equation[26]:

$$\pi = \beta_0 + \beta_1 A + u.$$

---

[26] This model is highly stylized and is assumed here to accurately represent reality.

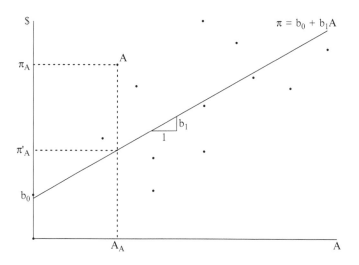

Fig. A.13 A regression line

Figure A.13 shows a scatter plot of hypothetical firm data on advertising expenditures and profit. Point A represents Accel Connector Company which spent A_A on advertising last year and earned B_A in profit. Each of the other points on the graph represents a particular firm's advertising and profit combination. To find out how advertising affects profits on average, we can fit a line to the data and estimate the **regression line**: $\pi = b_0 + b_1 A$. The terms b_0 and b_1 are estimates of the true parameters β_0 and β_1, respectively, and the points on the line are estimates of average profit. In the figure, the estimated slope parameter b_1 is positive, indicating that greater advertising is expected to raise profit, $d\pi/dA = b_1 > 0$. Profit is expected to increase by b_1 dollars when advertising expenditures increase incrementally. If the average firm did not invest in advertising, then $A = 0$ and estimated profit would be b_0.

Notice that for Accel, profit at point A, π_A, is higher than the corresponding profit level on the regression line, for the advertising level A_A. The distance, $\pi_A - \pi_A N$, is the estimated error term or residual for Accel, u_A. The positive value of u_A means that Accel fared better than average for the firms in the sample, perhaps due to greater efficiency or managerial talent. Firms lying below the regression line have negative errors and performed worse than average.

Regression analysis allows us to estimate the parameters of the model. Many of the empirical studies that we review in the book use a type of least squares estimation technique (i.e., ordinary least squares, two-stage least squares, three-stage least squares) to estimate regression models, and we assume that the appropriate estimation technique has been used. Least squares techniques are designed to estimate parameter values so that the sum of squared errors (where the error equals the distance from an observation to the regression line) is minimized.[27]

---

[27] For a more detailed discussion, see any econometrics text, for example, Studenmund (2006) or Wooldridge (2009).

Returning to our example, suppose that we use data on 245 firms and obtain the following estimated regression:

$$\pi = 110,200 + 1.40A, \qquad\qquad\qquad (A.34)$$

where both π are A are measured in dollars. The slope parameter, $b_1 = 1.40$, indicates that a \$1 increase in advertising expenditures is expected to generate a \$1.40 increase in profit. If you think of these values in terms of \$1,000s, a \$1,000 increase in advertising is expected to increase profit by \$1,400. We can also use these estimates to make predictions. For instance, if a firm is considering investing \$10,000 in advertising, the expected profit would be $\pi = 110,200$ $+1.4(10,000) = 124,200$.

A.2.3   Hypothesis Testing

Regression results are frequently presented with corresponding standard errors or t-ratios. In the following example, the values in parentheses are t-ratios:

$$\pi = 110,200 + 1.40A \qquad\qquad\qquad (A.35)$$
$$(1.30)\quad\ (2.35)$$

The purpose of a **t-ratio** is to check for the **statistical significance** of a parameter estimate. Our sample gives us only an estimate. How sure are we that the estimated parameter from our sample, $b_1 = 1.40$, represents the true parameter for the population? It is possible that the true population slope parameter is zero, even though our estimate of b_1 is not zero.

We can test the hypothesis, $\beta_1 = 0$ (known as the null hypothesis, H_0) against the alternative hypothesis (H_1), $\beta_1 \neq 0$.[28] The null hypothesis, in this case, means that advertising does not affect profits in the population, and the alternative means that advertising does affect profits. We can use a t-ratio to conduct this hypothesis test.

A t-ratio is the estimated coefficient divided by its standard error, $t_1 = b_1/$ $[se(b_1)]$, where the subscript 1 indicates that the t-ratio corresponds to the slope coefficient.[29] The standard error of b_1 is a measure of the variability of b_1 and is always nonnegative. If b_1 is close to zero, the t-ratio is also close to zero, and the more likely that the true population parameter is zero. When the value of t is far from zero, the chance that the population value of β_1 is zero is lower. At some point,

---

[28] We do not present the cases where the alternative hypothesis is an inequality ($\beta_1 > 0$ or $\beta_1 < 0$) but focus on the more common $\beta_1 \neq 0$.

[29] In the discussion here, we will address null hypotheses of the form $b_1 = 0$, i.e., we will be testing if coefficient estimates are significantly different from zero. If the null is $b_1 = c$, where c is a constant, the numerator of the t-ratio becomes ($\beta_1 - c$).

the t-ratio is large enough that we are willing to take the chance of rejecting the hypothesis that β_1 is zero, even though there is a small chance that it is really is zero. When that chance is 5%, we say that the parameter estimate is statistically significant at the 5% level of significance.[30] How do we determine if the value of t for the sample is large enough to meet the 5% significance level? The threshold value, the "critical value of t" (t_c), is 1.96 in large samples.[31] If our estimated t-ratio exceeds t_c, we reject the hypothesis that b_1 is zero and conclude that b_1 is significantly different from zero. In the profit-advertising example, the estimated t-ratio on A, $t = 2.35$, exceeds $t_c = 1.96$. We could state the conclusion of this hypothesis test in a number of different ways, such as we reject the null hypothesis at the 5% significance level, the advertising parameter estimate is significantly different from zero; advertising significantly affects profit, and advertising is a significant determinant of profit.

A.2.4   Multiple Regression

Usually in economics, there is more than one factor affecting the dependent variable. As an example, a demand function would depend on income, prices of substitute and complementary goods, and population as well as price. In that case, a simple regression model, where there is only one independent variable, is not sufficient. In a multiple regression model, there are many independent variables (x_k)

$$y = \beta_0 + \beta_1 x_1 + \beta_2 x_2 + \beta_3 x_3 + \cdots + \beta_K x_K + u, \qquad (A.36)$$

where the β terms are the parameters, and $k = 1, 2, 3, \ldots, K$ indexes the independent variables or regressors. The impact of an individual regressor, say x_1, on y is $\partial y / \partial x_1 = \beta_1$. Notice that β_1 is the *partial* derivative of y with respect to x_1. As we discussed above, this means that all of the other variables are held constant. The regression equation then can give us the effect of x on y, *ceteris paribus*. This is a powerful tool as it parallels our theoretical models, and it also is a way of simulating a controlled experiment. Regression analysis is used widely within and outside of economics.

---

[30] In economics, the 5% level of significance (also called the 95% level of confidence) is commonly used in hypothesis testing. Significance levels of 1% and 10% are often indicated in the results as well.

[31] More than 120 observations is roughly large enough to use 1.96. For fewer observations, a t-table, available in econometrics textbooks, or http://en.wikipedia.org/wiki/T-table#Table_of_selected_values, can be consulted for critical values, or look for any discussion of significance levels by the author.

Returning to the profit-advertising example, suppose that we include the number of products sold by the firm (PRODS) as a regressor. The model for estimation becomes

$$\pi = \beta_0 + \beta_1 A + \beta_2 \text{PRODS} + u.$$

The estimated model is

$$\pi = 106,240 + 1.80A + 1,020\text{PRODS} \qquad R^2 = 0.76 \qquad \text{(A.37)}$$
$$ {\scriptstyle (1.76)} \qquad {\scriptstyle (2.24)} \qquad\quad {\scriptstyle (3.01)}$$

The parameter estimate on advertising, $\partial \pi / \partial A = b_1 = 1.80$, indicates that profit is expected to increase by \$1.80 for a \$1 increase in advertising, holding number of products constant. Producing one more product is expected to increase profits by \$1,020, holding advertising constant ($\partial \pi / \partial \text{PRODS} = b_2 = 1,020$). The parameter estimate on advertising is significantly different from zero at 5% ($t = 2.24 > 1.96$), as is the parameter estimate on number of products ($t = 3.01 > 1.96$).

A.2.5 Fit and Prediction

The term R^2 listed in the regression results indicates how well the model fits the data. R^2 measures the variation in the dependent variable that is explained by the regression model. In our example, $R^2 = 0.76$ means that 76% of the variation in profits is explained by the model. R^2 ranges from 0 to 1, with 0 indicating that the model explains no variation and 1 indicating that the model explains all of the variation in y (π in this case). We need to be careful in putting too much weight on the value of R^2. Time series models (based on data observed over time) tend to have far greater R^2 values than cross-section models (based on data for a particular group at a given point in time). This does not mean that time series models are "better"— more reliable—than cross section models at explaining economic behavior. It is the totality of information about the model that causes one to gain or lose faith in the estimates (see Sect. A.2.5 below)

Prediction in the multiple regression model is similar to prediction in the simple regression model. If we are interested in knowing the level of profits when the firm produces four products, without changing the level of advertising, we substitute in the mean level of advertising for A and substitute 4 in for PRODS. Suppose that the mean level of advertising is \$8,000. The prediction equation is

$$\pi = 108,240 + 1.80(8,000) + 1,020(4)$$
$$\pi = 126,720.$$

In other words, with four products, we expect a firm's profit to be \$126,720. We can also allow more than one variable to change in making predictions if we like, setting A and PRODS equal to whatever values we choose.

A.2.6   *Evaluating Regression Estimates*

Regression estimates are estimates, not truth, and some estimates are better than others. In evaluating estimates you might consider the following: is the model based on theory/established knowledge? Does it contain all, or at least most, relevant variables? Are the data reliable? Are the signs and values of the regressors reasonable? Have the values been interpreted appropriately? The answers to these questions will help you to assess what estimates to weigh more heavily as you learn about industrial organization. Taking a course in econometrics will make this a much easier task.

A.3   Summary

1. A **function** describes the relationship between variables. With just two variables x and y, where y is a function of x, y is called the **dependent variable** and x is called the **independent variable**. Formally, to be a function there must be just one value of y for each value of x.
2. In most cases, we will consider the explicit description of a function, which is written as $y = f(x)$ or $y = y(x)$. When a function is expressed as $f(y, x) = 0$, it is an **implicit function**.
3. A **continuous function** has no breaks or jumps, and a **smooth function** has no kinks or sharp corners. When a function is always increasing or decreasing in x, it is said to be **monotonic**. A positive monotonic function always increases in x, and a negative monotonic function is always decreasing in x. The **inverse of the function** $y = y(x)$ is obtained by solving the function for x, $x = x(y)$.
4. A function is **strictly concave** if the tangent line to every point on the curve lies everywhere above the function. It is **strictly concave** if the tangent line to every point on the curve lies everywhere below the function.[32]
5. In many cases, we will consider functions with more than one independent variable, such as $y = f(x_1, x_2, x_3)$. This can be written more compactly as $y = f(\underline{x})$, where $\underline{x}$ represents the vector: x_1, x_2, x_3.
6. Most of the functions that we use in the book are linear function or quadratic function.

$$\text{Linear function } (k = 1): \quad y = a_0 + a_1 x,$$

$$\text{Quadratic function } (k = 2): \quad y = a_0 + a_1 x + a_2 x^2,$$

---

[32] For more formal definitions, see Chiang (1984, 241–244), Simon and Blume (1994, 43–46), Carter (2001), Baldani et al. (2005, 29–31), and Chiang and Wainwright (2005, 229–231).

where $a_0, a_1, a_3, \ldots, a_k$ are parameters. Our focus will be on two specific types of polynomial functions.

7. A **graph** provides a picture that describes the behavior of a function. In most cases, we will consider two-dimensional figures.

8. A **derivative** is the change in the dependent variable with respect to an infinitely small change in an independent variable. For functions with just one variable, $y = f(x)$, the derivative is denoted dy/dx. For functions of more than one variable, this is identified as $\partial y/\partial x$ and is called a partial derivative. The **partial derivative** indicates the change in y due to an infinitely small change in x, holding all other independent variables constant. Thus, it is a formal way of describing what is meant by the *ceteris paribus* assumption.

9. The indirect effect that a change in x will have on a function can be taken into account using the chain rule of differentiation. When $y = f(z)$ and $z = g(x)$, then $\dfrac{dy}{dx} = \dfrac{dy}{dz} \cdot \dfrac{dz}{dx}$. This is called the **chain rule of differentiation**.

10. If $y = f(x)$ has a derivative for every value of x over a particular interval of x (e.g., $0 \le x \le 10$), then $f(x)$ is **differentiable** over that interval. If the resulting derivative is continuous for every x over that interval, then $f(x)$ is continuously differentiable or C^1.

11. In many economic applications, we need to solve a system of simultaneous equations. This means that the all equations hold simultaneously. Graphically, this occurs where the functions intersect.

12. For a strictly concave or convex function with one independent variable, the optimum of the function occurs where the first derivative equals zero ($dy/dx = 0$). It is a maximum if the function is concave ($d^2y/dx^2 < 0$). It is a minimum if the function is convex ($d^2y/dx^2 > 0$).

13. **Dynamic programming** is a method for solving dynamic problems. The most effective method for solving a dynamic programming problem is to use backwards induction, which means that we begin by solving the last period problem first, then the next to the last period problem, and so on until all stage period problems are solved.

14. **Comparative static analysis** is used to predict how a change in a policy or exogenous factor affects the optimum or equilibrium value of a model. At the elementary level, this is accomplished with graphs. Other methods that use more sophisticated mathematics include the (1) brute-force method, (2) implicit-function theorem method, and (3) monotone method.

15. A set is a collection of elements, which may be finite or infinite. A set is **closed** if it contains all of its boundary points. A set is **convex** if all of the points of line connecting any two points on the boundary of the set are a part of the set. A set is **strictly convex** if all of the points (other than the endpoint) lie inside the boundary. A set is **bounded** when the distance between any two points in the set is less than infinity. In other words, the boundary is finite. When a set is closed and bounded, it is said to be **compact**.

16. A random variable, such as the outcome of the roll of a die, is a variable that takes on values by chance.

17. A probability distribution shows all possible values of a random variable matched to the corresponding probability that each value will occur.
18. Examples of probability distributions are the uniform, normal, and t-distributions. The values of a uniform distribution are equally likely to occur. If we assume that consumers are located evenly along a strand of beach, we are assuming that their location is uniformly distributed. The normal distribution applies to a wide range of phenomena and is used extensively. The normal distribution is bell shaped, symmetric, and peaks at its mean value. We use the t-distribution for hypothesis testing. When the sample size becomes very large, the t-distribution approaches the normal distribution.
19. An example of a **regression equation** is $y = \beta_0 + \beta_1 x + u$, where y is the dependent variable, x is the independent variable, β_0 and β_1 are parameters, and u is an error term. The **error term**, u, is the difference between the actual value of y and the predicted value of y. **Regression analysis** is a statistical tool used to estimate relationships among economic variables, such as how x affects y.
20. The estimated **regression line** is $y = b_0 + b_1 x$ where b_0 is the estimated intercept and b_1 is the estimated slope. b_1 is the estimated effect of x on y.
21. To test for the **statistical significance** of b_1, we compare the **t-ratio** for b_1 to the critical value of t, $t_c = 1.96$, for large samples. If $t_1 > 1.96$, b_1 is significantly different from zero at the 5% level of significance.
22. A **multiple regression** has many independent variables: $y = \beta_0 + \beta_1 x_1 + \beta_2 x_2 + \beta_3 x_3 + \cdots + \beta_K x_K + u$, where $K =$ number of regressors.
23. When there are two independent variables, the estimated regression is given by $y = b_0 + b_1 x_1 + b_2 x_2$: The estimated impact of x_1 on y, holding x_2 constant, is $b_1 = \partial y / \partial x_1$. The estimated impact of x_2 on y, holding x_1 constant, is $b_2 = \partial y / \partial x_2$.
24. R^2 measures the variation in the dependent variable that is explained by the regression model. It ranges from 0 to 1, with higher values indicating a better fit.
25. In the simple regression model, we can predict y at a particular value of x by substituting the desired value of x into the estimated equation. If the x of interest is 10 for example, we simply plug it in for x: $y = b_0 + b_1(10)$.
26. In the multiple regression model, we can predict y for a chosen value of x_1, say 10, and hold x_2 constant at its mean value, $\bar{x}_2$: $y = b_0 + b_1(10) + b_2 \bar{x}_2$. We can also make predictions at specific values of x_1 and x_2.

A.4   Review Questions

1. Determine the first and second derivatives (dy/dx and d^2y/dx^2) for the following functions.

    A. $y = 1 - 5x$
    B. $y = 10 - 2x + x^2$

C. $y = 2x^{1/2}$

D. $y - 2 + 5x^4 = 0$

2. Assuming that $y = 24x - 3x^2$, graph:

A. y

B. y/x

C. dy/dx

3. Assuming that $y = 50 + 60x - 12x^2 + x^3$, graph:

A. y

B. y/x

C. dy/dx

4. Consider the following function: $y = \sqrt{x^2}$.

A. Graph this function for $-10 < x < 10$

B. Is this a continuous function for $-10 < x < 10$ (i.e. can you draw the function without lifting your pencil)?

C. Is this function differentiable for $x = 0$?

5. Use the chain rule to calculate dy/dx if $y = v^2$ and $v = 1 + 2x$.

6. Derive the partial derivatives ($\partial y/\partial x$ and $\partial y/\partial z$) for the following functions.

A. $y = 10 - x + 4x^2 + z^3$.

B. $y = x^2 + xz + z^4$.

7. Find the values of x and y that solve the following systems of equations.

A. $y_1 = 36 - 3x$ and $y_2 = 12 + x$

B. $y_1 = 12 - x$ and $y_2 = x$.

8. Assume a demand and supply model where the inverse demand is $p_D = 90 - Q^2$ and the inverse supply is $p_S = Q$, where p_D is the demand price, p_S is the supply price, and Q is quantity. Determine the equilibrium values of p and Q (p^* and Q^*).

9. Determine the value of x where y reaches a maximum for each of the following questions.

A. $y = 12 + 36x - 2x^2$

B. $y = 100 + ax - bx^2$ (a and b are positive constants)

C. How do you know that these are convex or concave functions?

10. Assume that a monopoly firm receives a per-unit subsidy of s. The firm's profit equation is $\pi = 24q - q^2 + sq$, where π is profit and q is output.

A. Graph the firm's profit function when $s = 0$ and when $s = 10$. Now determine the firm's profit-maximizing level of output for these values of s.

B. Use the brute-force method, the implicit-function theorem, and the monotone comparative static method to determine how an increase in s will affect the firm's profit-maximizing level of output.

11. Consider the following regression equation for an inverse demand function for a consumer:, $p = \beta_1 + \beta_2\, q + u$, where p = price, q = quantity demanded, and u is an error term.

   A. Interpret the meaning of β_2 in words.
   B. What sign do you expect to find on the estimate of β_2? Explain.

12. On two separate graphs, draw a regression line for the general equation, $y = b_0 + b_1\, x$, and for (A.34). Indicate the slope and intercept on each graph.

13. Suppose that the firm is interested in knowing how much profit it will make if it produces five products and spends \$9,000 on advertising. Provide a prediction based on (A.2.4).

14. Consider the following regression results. Absolute values of the t-ratios are in parentheses.

$$y = 10.2 + 16.40x_1 - 4x_2 \qquad N = 1,000$$
$$(0.54) \quad (3.56) \quad (1.98) \quad R^2 = 0.68$$

   A. What is the meaning of the coefficient estimate on x_2?
   B. Which of the coefficient estimates are significantly different from zero at the 5% level of significance?
   C. What is the meaning of the value of R^2?

Appendix B: Answers to Review Questions

Listed below are short answers to review questions and problems. Basic definitions can be found in the summary section of each chapter.

Chapter 2   Demand, Technology, and Theory of the Firm

1. We expect that an increase in consumers will shift demand to the right, as shown in Fig. RQ.2.1.
2. For the snob effect, purchases are made to stand apart from the crowd, whereas conspicuous consumption implies making expensive purchases to impress others.
3. A drop in the price of a substitute good would lower the demand for good 1. Graphically it would shift the demand curve for good 1 down and to the left, as illustrated in Fig. RQ.2.3.
4. The good is normal.
5. Regarding income elasticity:

   A. This implies that a change in income has no effect on quantity demanded.
   B. Neither normal nor inferior. The good is income-neutral.

6. Regarding cross-price elasticity:

   A. An increase in price of good y by 1% will lower the demand for good x by 0.5%.
   B. The brands are complements.

7. Regarding TR, MR, and the price elasticity of demand:

   A. $TR = pQ = (a - 2bQ)Q$; $MR = a - 4bQ$.
   B. See Fig. RQ.2.7.
   C. $MR = 0$ when $\eta = 1$.
   D. The maximum value of $TR = a^2/8b$ occurs when $MR = 0$ and $\eta = 1$.

V.J. Tremblay and C.H. Tremblay, *New Perspectives on Industrial Organization*,
Springer Texts in Business and Economics, DOI 10.1007/978-1-4614-3241-8,
© Springer Science+Business Media New York 2012

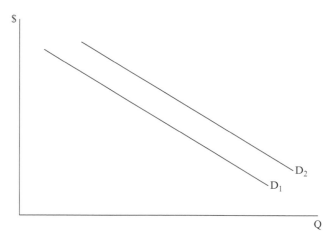

Fig. RQ.2.1 An increase in number of consumers and market demand

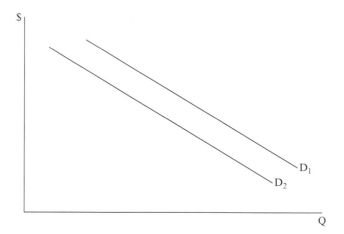

Fig. RQ.2.3 A decrease in demand when the price of a substitute good falls

8. Tattoo demand:

   A. The functional demand for tattoos did not change over either period.
   B. The demand for tattoos is not influenced by a speculative motive. Band-wagon effects likely have the greatest impact. It is possible that the snob effect was at work for people who were tattooed when tattoos were not popular. Conspicuous consumption may be at work for people who obtain particularly elaborate tattoos from exclusive tattoo parlors. (See http://mag. rankmytattoos.com/tattoo-pricing-guidelines.html for a discussion of

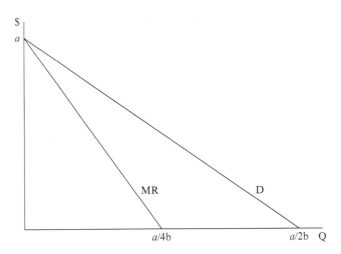

Fig. RQ.2.7 An example of demand and marginal revenue curves

famous tattoo artists and clients, including a report of a $150,000 tattoo that was inked aboard a private jet in midair.)

9. The correct answers are filled in below.

Q	Total cost	Average cost	Marginal cost
0	70	–	–
1	200	200	130
2	320	160	120
3	459.9	153.3	139.9

10. It will lower long-run average and marginal cost.
11. It will lower the transaction costs of the firm and decrease optimal firm size. In Fig. 2.9, the C_{MKT} curve would shift down, which would move the minimum point of the TC curve to the left.
12. The firm that sells low cost dresses is more likely to use the market. The transaction cost of interacting with the market is higher for the designer dress firm, where each dress is unique. Communication per dress would be considerably lower for inexpensive dresses, which are mass produced in large quantities. As a result, the firm selling designer dresses is more likely to vertically integrate.
13. Generally, a firm will grow if it increases profit or if it increases the utility of the manager. A firm might grow horizontally to take advantage of scale economies or to gain or increase market power. Vertical integration can be advantageous when the transaction costs of doing business with input suppliers are high. A firm may benefit from conglomerate growth when there are economies of scope.

Chapter 3   Game Theory and Information

1. Consider the case with two players. A Nash equilibrium is a mutual best reply: player i is doing what is best for him or her, given that player j has chosen an optimal strategy. A dominant strategy is best for player i, regardless of any action taken by player j.
2. C, E with payoffs (5, 1).
3. U, L (1, 1); D, R (1, 1).
4. Let pr_1 be the probability that player 1 plays U and pr_2 be the probability that player 2 plays L.

   A. For $x > 0$, $pr_1 = \frac{1}{2}$ and $pr_2 = x/(1 + x)$.
   B. For $x < 0$, player 1 has a dominant strategy of U. Thus, player 2 will choose L.
   C. When no dominant strategy exists.

5. Prisoners' dilemma:

   A. The cartel problem.
   B. To confess.
   C. Both are better off by cooperating (not confess), but the dominant strategy is to confess.

6. For parts A and B, see Fig. RQ.3.6A.
7. For parts A and B, see Fig. RQ.3.7A.
   For part C, change T–N–P from $(1, -1)$ to $(2 + a, -1)$ where $a > 0$ and change L–N–P from (2, 3) to (1–b, 3) where $b > 0$. In words, the parent places greater value on punishment.
8. Centipede game:

   A. The SPNE for player 1 is to keep 10 in the first period.
   B. Equity matters for many people, and players are more likely to cooperate when the stakes are low.
   C. When the stakes are very high, player 1 may be less likely to risk losing $10 million, so may keep it in the first stage.

9. The seller will accept the offer if $p \geq V_0$. This means that all firms valued from 0 to p will accept, and the expected value of firms that accept $E[V_0] = p/2$ (given the uniform distribution of values). For the buyer, $V_1 = 1.5 \cdot E[V_0] = (1.5p)/2 = 0.75p$. Making a purchase is a good investment if $V_1 - p > 0 \rightarrow 0.75p - p > 0$, which is untrue. Thus, SPNE is for the potential buyer to decline to make an offer.
10. GM–Ford game:

    A. (T, T)
    B. Play (T, T) in every period.
    C. In an infinitely repeated game, a trigger strategy will support cooperation if $\frac{5}{1-D} \geq 10 + \frac{D}{1-D}$. The last term is the present value of the payoff stream if the firm cheats in the current period (i.e., a payoff of 1 in every period, instead of 0 in the problem in Fig. 3.19). Because this payoff starts in the next period, it

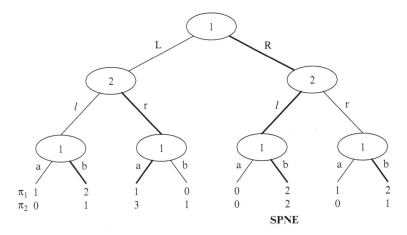

Fig. RQ.3.6A A dynamic 3-stage game

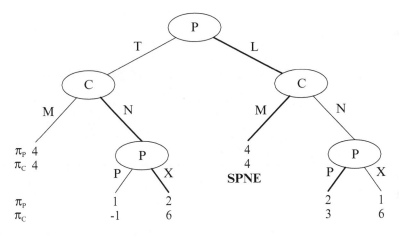

Fig. RQ.3.7A The parent–child 3-stage dynamic game

must be discounted by D. This inequality will hold, implying that cooperation is profitable, as long as $D \geq 5/9$. This type of problem is covered in more detail in Chap. 9.

11. Assume that offers are accepted under indifference. If the game reaches:

Stage IV, player 2 offers (0, 25) and the game is over
Stage III, player 1 offers (25, 25), which would induce player 2 to accept
Stage II, player 2 offers (25, 50), which would induce player 1 to accept
Stage I, player 1 offers (50, 50), which would induce player 2 to accept

Thus, the SPNE is for player 1 to offer (50, 50) in stage I and for player 2 to accept.

12. This is a slippery slope, and the best strategy is not to make a bid.

Chapter 4   Behavioral Economics

1. In the dual systems approach, Intuition is the automatic and relatively quick and easy mental process used most of the time to make decisions. People may make the easy decision automatically rather than engage the effortful Reasoning process to address the difficult question.

2. Examples of salient commercials: Budweiser frogs; Most Interesting Man; Geiko Gecko; E-Trade Baby.

3. On the one hand, they receive more pleasure (higher utility) from consuming what they believe to be a more expensive wine. On the other hand, some people will receive lower utility when they find out that they were tricked—they may feel foolish or they may resent being deceived on ethical grounds. Overall, we cannot say if the people are worse off. It may vary by individual as well.

4. Examples of environmental cues include going to a bar with friends for an alcoholic, passing by a coffee bar for a caffeine addict, and spotting a lottery machine at the grocery store for a gambling addict.

5. It is not likely that the house would have sold for $490,000 if they had listed the house at $400,000. Buyers would view $400,000 as the starting price for bidding and would probably not go as high as $90,000 over the list price unless there was a bidding war. The $400,000 serves as a reference point, and this example illustrates the concept of reference dependence: the selling price is dependent on the reference (the asking price).

6. Cognitive dissonance: Jed's actions diverged from his original beliefs.

7. Three examples of strategies include: choosing the default, maintaining the status quo (e.g., buying by habit), and following what your friends do.

8. Overconfidence (or overoptimism, overexuberance).

9. Yes, both have greater discounting of utility in the current period than in future periods. With procrastination, utility is negatively related to the behavior or task that is being put off to the future, so that utility today depends on avoiding the task. You might have a strong preference for putting the task off to tomorrow (i.e., avoiding the task today versus tomorrow), but you might not care as much about avoiding it in 7 days versus 6.

10. Precommitment is setting up strategies to avoid giving in to temptation in the future. Precommitment tactics for physical exercise include hiring a personal trainer, joining an athletic club, promising a friend to work out on a regular basis, and signing up for an exercise class.

11. Will's identity was tied to his neighborhood and friends, where the group members are supposed to act like blue-collar workers, not Harvard professors. He would experience a loss in identity (and utility) by leaving the neighborhood.

Chapter 5   Perfect Competition

1. Yes. In perfect competition, $AR = p$. In equilibrium, $p = $ minimum AC. Therefore, $AR = $ minimum AC in equilibrium in perfect competition.
2. See Figs. RQ.5.2A–RQ.5.2D.
3. $p^* = $ min AC $= \$1$. $Q = 2{,}500 - 100(1) = 2{,}400$. Number of firms $= 2{,}400/100 = 24$. Firm $\pi = TR - TC = q (p - AC) = 100 (0 - 0) = 0$.
4. True or false questions:

   A. False. Constant returns to scale refers to constant long-run average costs when firm output increases, while a constant-cost industry refers to constant input prices as the industry expands.
   B. False. If economic profits are zero, firms are earning a normal rate of return and as much as they could elsewhere.
   C. False. Profits depend on revenues as well as costs.

5. See Fig. RQ.5.5.
6. No. Better than average accounting profits will draw firms into the industry. Supply in the industry will increase, reducing prices and profits. Entry will continue until economic profits are zero.
7. A decrease in output demand will reduce the demand for inputs in the industry, which in turn will lower average and marginal cost. A new equilibrium will occur where the new minimum AC = price. Long-run supply will have a positive slope.
8. Consumer surplus is the area between D and the price line. In this case, price exceeds D, indicating that consumer surplus would be negative for this added level of production. Similarly, producer surplus is negative for this added level of production, because S (which represents marginal cost) lies above the price line. TS, therefore, would fall.

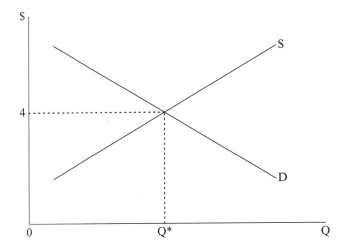

Fig. RQ.5.2A Industry supply and demand

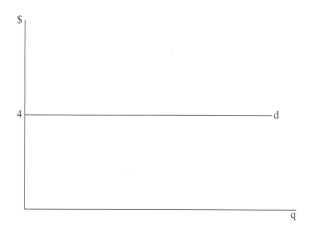

Fig. RQ.5.2B The firm's demand curve

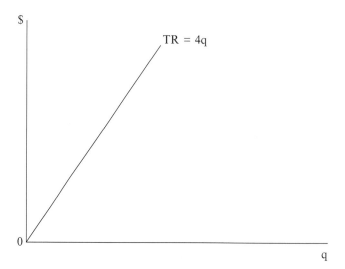

Fig. RQ.5.2C Total revenue function

9. If firms are not profit maximizers, they might not enter a market that has excess profits, industry supply will not expand, and economic profits will not be eliminated. If firms produce goods that are not homogeneous, a firm could raise its price, and some consumers would not switch to another product. Thus, the firm would not be a price taker, and we will see in the next chapter that price will exceed marginal cost in equilibrium. With barriers to entry, firms cannot enter in response to positive economic profits. Thus, profits need not equal zero in the long run.

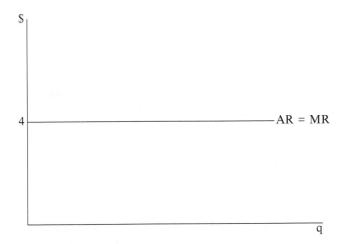

Fig. RQ.5.2D Marginal revenue function

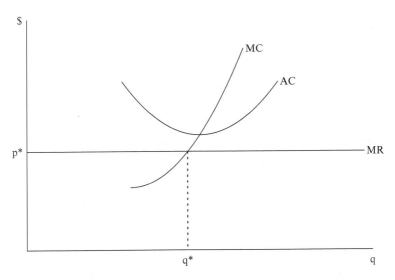

Fig. RQ.5.5 MR, MC, and AC for a firm not meeting the participation constraint

10. Economic efficiency refers to producing a given level of output at minimum cost for the firm, whereas productive efficiency refers to producing a given level of output at minimum cost for the industry.
11. Examples of a public good: dam, police and fire protection; external benefit: neighbor's landscaped front yard; external cost: airport noise, second-hand smoke, drunk driving; a network externality: Facebook.

12. If firms are able to successfully induce consumers to buy more of a good or service than is in their "true" best interest, then a competitive market will produce more output than is socially beneficial. In this case, the demand function we observed in the marketplace is not the demand function that should be used in policy analysis. Thus, our estimates of consumer (and, therefore, total) surplus are inaccurate, which can lead to incorrect policy analysis.

Chapter 6 Monopoly

1. $MR = 100 - 2q$; it has the same intercept but is twice as steep as demand. $q^* = 10$ and $p^* = 90$.
2. The author's income is maximized when the number of books sold (q^A) maximizes total revenue, which occurs where marginal revenue is 0 (see Chap. 2, or note that to maximize TR, take the derivative and set it equal to zero: $\partial TR/\partial q = MR = 0$). The profit-maximizing level of output (q^*) occurs where $MR = MC > 0$. Because MR has a negative slope, MC crosses MR to the left of where $MR = 0$. Thus, $q^* < q^A$ (see Figs. 6.1 and 6.2).
3. No, costs may be high relative to demand. In Fig. 6.2, MC and AC are low enough so that the firm can earn positive economic profits given the demand for the product. If MC and AC are high enough, the firm can earn zero profit. Graphically, a monopolist with zero economic profit might appear like the monopolistically competitive firm in Fig. 6.6.
4. $MR = \$0.50$ and since the firm is maximizing profit, $MC = MR$ equals $\$0.50$.
5. In Fig. RQ.6.5, the deadweight loss is the area BCE. At the allocatively efficient level of output (at Q_c and p_c), consumer surplus equals area Ap_cE and producer surplus is 0. Total surplus equals consumer surplus. At the monopoly outcome $(q_m = Q_m, p_m)$, consumer surplus is reduced to area Ap_mB, producer surplus increases to area p_mp_cCB, and total surplus equals area Ap_cCB. Thus, consumers lose, producers gain, and society loses. The social loss is the deadweight loss, area BCE.
6. X-inefficiency: persistent tardiness by workers and management. Rent-seeking: playing golf with one's senator to gain perks for the company.
7. One example is the manager who is more interested in prestige and growth than profits and engages in unprofitable mergers. In addition, without the pressure of competition, the boundedly rational manager may put in too little time collecting information before making a corporate decision.
8. The sign would be positive—experience today should increase profits tomorrow. The firm will produce more today.
9. No. AC is constant; there is no unit cost advantage to firm size.
10. Perfect competition versus monopoly:

    A. $Q_c^* = 90$, $p_c^* = 10$, $\pi_c^* = 0$.
    B. $Q_m^* = 45$, $p_m^* = 55$, $\pi_m^* = 2{,}025$.

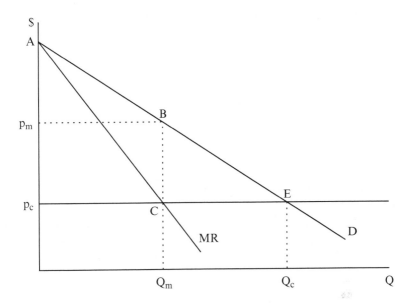

Fig. RQ.6.5 Deadweight loss due to monopoly under constant costs

11. Lerner index: In perfect competition $\mathcal{L} = 0$, because $p = MC$. In monopolistic competition, $\mathcal{L} > 0$, because $p > MC$. Because the product produced by a monopolistically competitive firm will have many close substitutes and the product of a monopolist will have no close substitutes, demand will be relatively more inelastic for a monopolist. Thus, $\mathcal{L}$ will be higher for a monopoly firm.

12. The endowment effect says that consumers place a greater value on a good once it is owned. If previous purchase creates a sense of ownership, then the endowment effect may create brand loyalty and make it difficult for a new entrant to get consumers to try a new brand. This makes entry more difficult.

Chapter 7   Product Differentiation

1. Multicharacteristic: automobiles, TV dinners

   Horizontal: rare versus well-done steak, loose versus tight fitting jeans
   Vertical: first-class versus coach airline seats, small versus large storage space on a memory stick

2. Multi-characteristic: an increase in the intercept increases demand; an increase in the degree of product differentiation (a decrease in d) increases demand.

   Horizontal: an increase in the number of consumers will increase demand; an increase in transportation costs has an indeterminate effect on demand.
   Vertical: an increase in the number of consumers will increase demand; an increase in the size of the market ($\phi_H - \phi_L$) increases demand.

3. For multicharacteristic differentiation, an increases in q_j decreases firm i's demand $(\partial p_i/\partial q_j < 0)$. For horizontal and vertical differentiation, an increase in p_j increases firm i's demand $(\partial q_i/\partial p_j > 0)$.

4. For firm i where subscripts j and k refer to firm i's rivals: $p_i = a - q_i - d_j q_j - d_k q_k$. In this case, d_j represents the degree of product differentiation with respect to firm j's product and d_k represents the degree of product differentiation with respect to firm k's product.

5. For multicharacteristic differentiation, an increase in q_j decreases firm i's demand $(d < 0)$. For horizontal and vertical differentiation, an increase in p_j decreases, instead of increases, firm i's demand.

6. If prices are the same, all consumers will shop at the closest firm, FM_1. For FM_2 to survive, it must charge lower prices. By definition, this is a model of vertical differentiation.

7. Now, each firm becomes a monopolist, which occurs when the marginal consumer receives negative utility from purchasing either brand. Firm 1's demand becomes N times the $\theta_x (< \theta_m)$, as in Fig. 7.4. In this case, $q_1 = N(s - p_1)/t$. Similarly for firm 2.

8. An increase in income will generally cause consumers to have a stronger preference for quality. This will increase both ϕ_L and ϕ_H, which will increase demand for the high quality brand and decrease demand for the low-quality brand (see Fig. 7.5).

9. The price elasticity of demand (η) equals $-(\partial q_i/\partial p_i)(p_i/q_i)$. For multiproduct differentiation, $\eta_i = p_i/q_i$, where p_i is the firm's inverse demand $(a - q_i - dq_j)$. In the Hotelling model, $\eta_i = [N/(2t)](p_i/q_i)$, where q_i is the firm's demand. For vertical differentiation, $\eta_i = (N/z)(p_i/q_i)$, where q_i is the firm's demand.

10. If $c_1 = c_2 > 0$ and $z_1 > z_2 > 0$, then $c_1/z_1 < c_2/z_2$.

11. A necktie is a search good, canned soup is an experience good, and automobile engine repair is a credence good. Deception would be impossible for a search good, which is defined as a good in which consumers can identify all relevant product characteristics before purchase. Deception is most likely for engine repair, where it is uneconomic to check the mechanic's work.

Chapter 8   Market Structure, Industry Concentration, and Barriers to Entry

1. Industry concentration describes the number and size distribution of firms. Higher concentration is reflected in a higher concentration curve. A concentration curve cannot be strictly convex from below. It is linear when each firm has the same market share. As the distribution of market shares becomes more unequal, the concentration curve becomes more concave.

2. Concentration indices:

A. An ideal index of concentration should take into account the size distribution of all firms in the industry and should increase as the number of firms declines and as larger firms gain market share from smaller firms.

B. CR_4 and n do not meet these criteria. CR_4 does not account for the market share of all but the four largest firms, and n ignores the size distribution of firms.

C. These relationships depend on how market share is measured (decimal or percent) and whether or not firms are of equal size.

- When market share is measured in decimal form, $HHI = n\sigma^2 + 1/n$. When all firms are of equal size (i.e., the variance in market share equals zero, $\sigma^2 = 0$), $HHI = 1/n = CR_1$.
- When market share is measured in percent and all firms are of equal size, $CR_4 = \min(100, 400/n)$. When $n \leq 4$, $HHI = (100 \cdot CR_4)/n$. When $n > 4$, $HHI = 25 \cdot CR_4$.

3. An economic market includes all products that are close substitutes and producers that compete for consumers, which may include firms that are located locally, regionally, nationally, or internationally. If we construct a concentration index based on a market that is too narrowly (broadly) defined, the index will be biased upward (downward).

4. Aggregate concentration is measured by the percent of US sales accruing to the largest US corporations. From 1947 to 1997, the largest 50 US corporations controlled an average of 23.5% of sales (ranging from 17% to 25%). The main concern with high aggregate concentration is that it may bestow greater economic and political power to a handful of large corporations. This may lead to greater collusion among firms and political pressure to erect legal barriers to entry.

5. The cement market is local rather than national in scope, due to high shipping costs. Hence, a national measure of HHI will be biased downward. It is likely that concentration is higher for breakfast cereal than for frozen vegetables because there are higher sunk costs in breakfast cereal manufacturing.

6. Regarding the cost-minimizing number of firms (n^*):

A. $n^* = 12$ symmetric firms.

B. If AC and firms are symmetric, $n^* = 11$. If AC is sufficiently flat to the right of MES and firms are symmetric, then $n^* = 10$ with each firm producing 12.

7. Strategic barriers are endogenous to the firm, while natural barriers are exogenous to the firm. Advertising is an example of a strategic barrier, and economies of scale (relative to the size of demand) is a natural barrier.

8. In Sutton's model, $HHI = \sigma/(PCM \cdot S)$, where σ equals sunk costs, PCM is the price–cost margin, and S is total industry sales (total revenue). When sunk costs are exogenous, an increase in S causes HHI to fall. When sunk costs are endogenous, an increase in S has a direct and an indirect effect. The direct effect is to lower HHI. The indirect effect is to raise HHI. That is, an increase in S causes

the existing firms to make greater strategic investments in sunk costs, which raises HHI. Thus, an increase in S is less likely to lower HHI when sunk costs are endogenous.

9. Equilibrium number of firms in Sutton's model:

   A. Firm profits increase with S and decrease with n and σ.
   B. The equilibrium number of firms is the positive root of $\sqrt{S/(\pi_i + \sigma)}$.

10. Concentration tends to be higher in markets with high natural barriers to entry. This occurs when MES and capital costs are high relative to the size of the market. Mergers are an important source of concentration, especially outside the USA. Concentration tends to be high in markets where firms invest in strategic barriers to entry, which generate endogenous sunk costs.

Chapter 9   Cartels

1. Collusion occurs when firms coordinate their strategic decisions. A perfect cartel involves all firms in the industry and leads to behavior that maximizes joint profits. This leads to the same output as that of a monopolist.

2. Solution to the cartel problem:

   A. The industry level of output, Q^*, is 50 and the price, p^*, is 70.
   B. The first-order conditions of profit maximization do not tell us how Q^* is divided between the two firms. The output-distribution line (as in Fig. 9.1) shows the possible combinations of output for the two firms that can sum to Q^*, but not where the firms will locate along the line.

3. A perfect cartel, just like a monopoly, is allocatively inefficient. Thus, antitrust laws that make collusion illegal will improve efficiency as long as the cost of antitrust enforcement is not too great.

4. Industries with greater collusion:

   A. Collusion would be easier in the steel than the automobile industry because products are more homogeneous.
   B. Collusion would be easier in the cement than in the wheat industry because there are fewer competitors.
   C. Collusion would be easier in airline service between two cities because there is greater homogeneity and fewer competitors than in the fast-food industry.

5. The cartel dilemma:

   A. With the cartel dilemma, actions that are best for individual firms are not what are best for the group as a whole.
   B. If firms behave symmetrically, then each firm will produce an output level of 25 when faced with demand and cost conditions in question 2.

C. Firm 1's best reply is $q_1^{BR} = 50 - \frac{1}{2}q_2$. If firm 2 produces the cartel level of output ($q_2 = 25$), firm 1's best reply is $q_1 = 37.5$. Thus, firm 1 will want to produce more than the cartel level of output. The same argument holds for firm 2.

6. Yes. By dividing up the market, each firm becomes a monopolist.
7. Harmful, because guarantees such as these reduce firm incentives to lower prices and reduce consumer incentives to search for lower prices. This leads to higher prices.
8. Because firm 3 is a rogue firm, firms 1 and 2 may use a trigger strategy to punish firm 3 for failing to cooperate. This could cause price to fall temporarily below marginal cost if it leads to greater cooperation in the future. Punishment that produces negative profits would be temporary because a strategy that earns negative profits in every period could never be a subgame-perfect Nash equilibrium strategy.
9. The ideal set of conditions would be an industry with few firms, homogeneous goods, symmetric firms, stable demand and cost conditions, and high entry barriers. You would also look for a situation where it would be difficult for the antitrust authorities to detect cartel activity.
10. Identity that is tied to one's home country may generate negative attitudes and actions towards those outside the social group—in this case, other nations. This would add to the cost of coordination.

Chapter 10   Quantity and Price Competition in Static Oligopoly

1. As derived in the text, when $TC_i = cq_i$, $q_i^* = (a - c)/(3b + 2c)$. When $TC_i = cq_i^2$, $q_i^* = a/(3b + 2c)$.
2. The Bertrand equilibrium price would be $p^* = c$, where c is marginal cost. When $c_1 = 10$ and $c_2 = 12$ and the monopoly price for firm 1 is less than 12, then $p^* = 12 - \varepsilon$, where ε is infinitesimally small. Otherwise, firm 1 will set the monopoly price.
3. For Cournot, see Fig. 10.8. For Bertrand, price equals the monopoly price when $n = 1$, and price equals marginal cost when $n \geq 2$.
4. Figure RQ.10.4 shows the Nash equilibria for $n = 1$ (point A), $n = 2$ (point B), $n = 3$ (point C), and $n = \infty$ (point E). In this model, the Nash equilibrium is $Q^* = 12n/(n + 1)$ and $p^* = 12/(n + 1)$. As $n \to \infty$, the market approaches that of perfect competition: $Q_{pc} = 12$ and $p_{pc} = 0$. In this case, the deadweight loss (DWL) equals $(p^* - p_{pc})(Q_{pc} - Q^*)/2 = 72/(1 + n)^2$. Thus, the DWL falls as n increases and approaches 0 as $n \to \infty$.
5. A firm with lower costs can set its price just below the unit cost of its competitor, enabling it to earn an economic profit. Product differentiation gives a firm a monopoly of the sale of its brand. This enables the firm to earn economic profits (i.e., the principle of product differentiation).

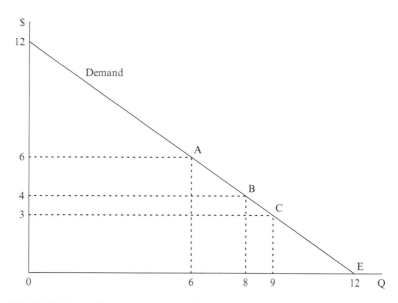

Fig. RQ.10.4 Nash equilibria as the number of firms changes

6. When $t = 0$, product differentiation vanishes because there is no cost to traveling to near or far locations. In this case, when $t = 0$, p_i^* equals marginal cost and $\pi_i^* = 0$ (i.e., the Bertrand paradox holds once again).

7. The best replies are BR$_1$: $p_2 = 2p_1 - t(\theta_2 - \theta_1) - c$ and BR$_2$: $p_2 = (p_1 + t(\theta_2 - \theta_1) + c)/2$. BR$_1$ has a p_2 intercept of $-t(\theta_2 - \theta_1) - c$ and a slope of 2; BR$_2$ has a p_2 intercept of $[t(\theta_2 - \theta_1) + c]/2$ and a slope of ½. The Nash equilibrium price is $p_i^* = c + t(\theta_2 - \theta_1)$. p_i^* increases in c, t, and the distance between stores $(\theta_2 - \theta_1)$.

8. Locating at the edge of town may reduce price competition. Land prices may also be lower, which reduces Wal-Mart's costs.

9. Low quality brands may be produced at lower cost, which enables them to have a lower price. If an incumbent firm offers only a high quality brand, there may be a sufficient number of consumers who prefer a low-priced brand of lesser quality.

10. The Cournot–Bertrand equilibrium is

$$p_1^* = \frac{4(12 + c)}{5} > p_2^* = \frac{3(12 + c)}{5},$$

$$q_1^* = \frac{48 - c}{5} > q_2^* = \frac{2(18 - c)}{5},$$

$$\pi_1^* = \frac{(48 - c)^2}{25} > \pi_2^* = \frac{4(18 - c)^2}{25}.$$

To assure that both firms participate, marginal cost (c) must be less than 18. An increase in c causes prices to increase and the output and profits of both firms to fall.

11. See Fig. 10.17, where the fixed cost of competing in output (F_i^C) is 10 and the fixed cost of competing in price (F_i^B) is zero.

12. From Appendix 10.A, the sign of the slope of a firm's best reply equals $\pi_{ij} = \partial^2 \pi_i / \partial s_i \partial s_j$, where s_i is firm i's strategic variable (output or price) and s_j is firm j's strategic variable (output or price). In the Cournot model, the best-reply functions have a negative slope ($\pi_{ij} < 0$); in the Bertrand model the best-reply functions have a positive slope ($\pi_{ij} > 0$). By definition, strategic variables across firms are strategic substitutes when $\pi_{ij} < 0$ and are strategic complements when $\pi_{ij} > 0$. Thus, q_1 and q_2 are strategic substitutes in the Cournot model, and p_1 and p_2 are strategic complements in the Bertrand model. In the duopoly models with multicharacteristic differentiation of Sect. 10.2, $\pi_{ij} = -b < 0$ in the Cournot model and $\pi_{ij} = \delta > 0$ in the Bertrand model.

13. When $\beta = \frac{1}{2}$ and $\delta = 1$, the slopes of the best-reply functions for each firm equal 1. Thus, they are parallel and a Nash equilibrium does not exist. When $\beta = \frac{1}{2}$ and $\delta = 2$, the model is unstable, as described in Appendix 10.A.

14. In each case, this will cause firm 1 to expect its best-reply function to be further away from the origin (although the slope will remain the same). In the Cournot model, this causes q_1^* to increase and q_2^* to decrease. In the Bertrand model, this causes p_i^* to increase. In the Cournot-Bertrand model, this causes q_1^* to increase and p_2^* to decrease.

Chapter 11   Dynamic Monopoly and Oligopoly Models

1. Dynamic monopoly:

   A. If the firm maximizes the simple sum of profits, then $q_I^* = 6$, $q_{II}^* = 0$, $p_I^* = 12$, $p_{II}^* = 6$, and $\pi^* = 72$. This is sequentially irrational, because once period II arrives, it is no longer profit maximizing to produce $q_{II} = 0$. Once period II arrives and given that $q_I^* = 6$, the firm's profit equals $6q_{II} - q_{II}^2$. The first-order condition is $6 - 2q_{II} = 0$, implying that the optimal $q_{II} = 3 > 0$.

   B. We use backwards induction to obtain the sequentially rational solution: $q_I^* = 4.8$, $q_{II}^* = 3.6$, $p_I^* = 10.6$, $p_{II}^* = 3.6$, and $\pi^* = 64.8$.

2. Competition will invalidate the Coase conjecture if firms compete in durability and this can lead to a durability race.

3. Static and dynamic duopoly with output competition:

   A. The Cournot outcome is $q_1^* = q_2^* = p^* = a/3$ and $\pi^* = a^2/9$.

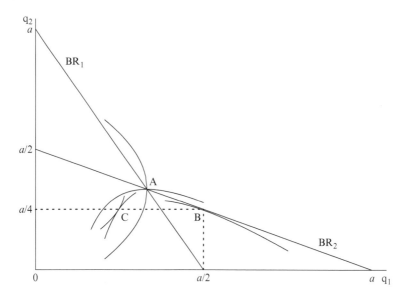

Fig. RQ.11.3D Nash (A), Stackelberg (B), and Cartel (C) Equilibria

B. The dynamic Cournot (Stackelberg) outcome is $q_1^* = a/2$, $q_2^* = a/4$, $p^* = a/4$, $\pi_1^* = a^2/8$, and $\pi_2^* = a^2/16$.

C. Assuming symmetry, the cartel outcome is $q_1^* = q_2^* = a/4$, $p^* = a/2$, and $\pi_1^* = \pi_2^* = a^2/8$.

D. See Fig. RQ.11.3D.

E. See Figs. 9.4 and 11.1.

4. The SPNE values are:

$$p^* = \frac{72 + c}{3},$$

$$q_1^* = 72 + c > q_2^* = q_3^* = \frac{72 - 2c}{3},$$

$$\pi_1^* = \frac{(72 + c)^2}{3} > \pi_2^* = \pi_2^* = \frac{4(36 - c)^2}{9}.$$

Firm 1's cost advantage enables it to produce more output and earn higher profits than its higher cost competitors.

5. The Bertrand paradox still holds with price equal to marginal cost and profits equal to zero.

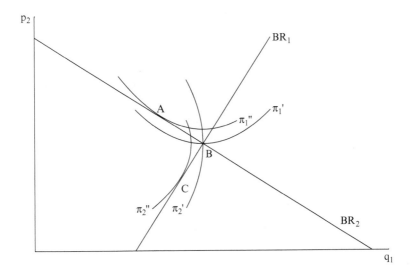

Fig. RQ.11.8A The Cournot-Bertrand SPNE when Firm 2 moves first (Point C)

6. The SPNE values are

$$p_1^* = c + \frac{z(\phi_H - \phi_L)}{2} > p_2^* = c + \frac{z(2\phi_H - 3\phi_L)}{4},$$

$$q_1^* = \frac{2\phi_H - \phi_L}{4} > q_2^* = \frac{2\phi_H - 3\phi_L}{4},$$

$$\pi_1^* = \frac{z(2\phi_H - \phi_L)^2}{8} > \pi_2^* = \frac{z(2\phi_H - 3\phi_L)^2}{16}.$$

Prices, output, and profits increase with an increase in the degree of vertical differentiation and as the size of the market grows.

7. The results are asymmetric in both. The main difference is that it pays to move first in the Stackelberg model (first-mover advantage), while it pays to move second in the dynamic Bertrand model (second-mover advantage).

8. Cournot–Bertrand model:

A. In Fig. RQ.11.8A, point C is where firm 2's isoprofit function is tangent to firm 1's best-reply function, which is below point B.

B. $\pi_1(A) > \pi_1(B) > \pi_1(C)$.

C. $\pi_2(A) > \pi_2(C) > \pi_2(B)$.

D. They both prefer point A and will coordinate so that firm 1 moves first and firm 2 moves second.

9. Once firm 1 chooses an action, this leaves firm 2 with a residual demand curve, which reflects the market demand that remains after firm 1's action. Thus, in period II, firm 2 faces a monopoly problem. As we showed in Chap. 6, the monopoly outcome and profits are the same whether the firm chooses output or price as its strategic variable.

10. The SPNE is for firms to repeat the Cournot outcome in each subgame.

11. Repeated Bertrand game:

   A. p^* equals marginal cost (MC).
   B. If the discount factor (D) is greater that ½, then the trigger strategy discussed in the book will support cooperation in every period. Otherwise, firms will set $p^* = $ MC in every period.
   C. In this case, (11.35) becomes

$$\frac{\pi_M}{2(1-D)} \geq \pi_M - \frac{D}{(1-D)}x,$$

where the last term on the right-hand side of the inequality is the present value of profits when the firm cheats today and is paid $-x$ from the next period on. Firms will cooperate when this inequality holds or when

$$D \geq \frac{1}{2} \cdot \frac{\pi_M}{\pi_M + x}.$$

This shows that when $x = 0$, D must be greater than or equal to ½. As x increases (i.e., a greater penalty from cheating), a lower D supports collusion. This means that even more impatient firms will cooperate.

12. If the firm ignores the future, in period I it will produce the simple monopoly output and earn profits of $\pi_I^* = a^2/(4b)$. In period II, it will then earn profits of $\pi_{II}^* = a^2/(16b)$. This derives directly from the text, Sect. 11.1.1. Thus, $\pi_I^* + \pi_{II}^* = (5a^2)/(16b) = 0.3125a^2$, considerably below the SPNE profits that we derived in the text, which were $(9a^2)/(20b) = 0.45a^2$. Myopic behavior lowers profits.

Chapter 12   Market Power

1. The Lerner index derives from the monopolist's first-order condition of profit maximization (see Chap. 6): $\partial\pi/\partial q = p + (\partial p/\partial q)q - \text{MC} = 0$. By rearranging terms, this becomes

$$\mathcal{L} \equiv \frac{p - \text{MC}}{p} = -\frac{\partial p}{\partial q}\frac{p}{q} = \frac{1}{\eta},$$

where η is the price elasticity of demand. When $p = $ MC, $\mathcal{L} = 0$. As MC $\to 0$, $\mathcal{L} \to 1$. Thus, an increase in $\mathcal{L}$ implies greater market power. As the firm's demand function becomes more inelastic (i.e., η falls), market power increases.

2. Equation (12.2) is

$$p_i + \theta \frac{\partial p_i}{\partial q_i} q_i - \text{MC} = 0.$$

The first-order condition for a Bertrand-type firm is $p_i - \text{MC} = 0$. This is consistent with (12.2) when $\theta = 0$. The first-order condition for a Cournot-type firm is $p_i + (\partial p_i / \partial q_i) q_i - \text{MC} = 0$. This is consistent with (12.2) when $\theta = 1$.

3. The classic example is the long-run equilibrium in a monopolistically competitive market (see Chap. 6). In that case, the firm's demand is not perfectly elastic, so that $p > $ MC. In addition, free entry drives long-run profits to zero.

4. Market power and abnormal returns:

   A. The owner's rate of return on accounting profits is 20% ($200/$1,000). A normal rate of return is 10% ($100/$1,000). Because the firm is able to earn economic profits (a normal rate of return) in the long run, there must be sufficient barriers to entry to ensure market power.

   B. At a competitive auction, the price of the firm would be bid up to $2,000, so that the new owner would just earn a normal rate of return ($200/$2,000). Thus, only the original owner benefits from the firm's market power.

5. Tobin's q equals the market value of the firm divided by its replacement value. In a perfectly competitive market, Tobin's $q = 1$. In general, market power will raise the value of the firm so that Tobin's $q > 0$.

6. The index of relative profit differences (RPD) is

$$\text{RPD} \equiv \frac{\pi_1^v - \pi_3^v}{\pi_2^v - \pi_3^v}.$$

In this case, the change in market conditions causes RPD to increase from 5 to 5.5. Thus, the event caused the degree of market competitiveness to increase.

7. See the text.

8. Product differentiation and market power:

   A. When $d = 0$, each firm is a monopolist and $q^* = (12 - c)/2$ and $p^* = (12 + c)/2$. In this case, $\mathcal{L} = (12 - c)/(12 + c)$.

   B. When $0 < d < 1$, $\mathcal{L} = (12 - c)/(12 + c + cd)$. This implies that market power increases with product differentiation (a decrease in d).

   C. From Chap. 11 (Sect. 1.1.2), the equilibrium price in the Stackelberg model is $p* = (12 + 3c)/4$. Thus, $\mathcal{L} = (12 - c)/(12 + 3c)$.

   D. With homogeneous goods, there is greater market power in the Cournot model than the Stackelberg model.

9. The price effect of a unit increase in marginal cost.

   A. In perfect competition, the equilibrium price (p^*) equals minimum long-run average cost, which is equal to long-run marginal cost. If marginal cost increases by 1, minimum long-run average cost increases by 1. Thus, p^* increases by 1.
   B. From Chap. 6, we know that $p^* = (a + c)/2$. Thus, $\mathrm{d}p^*/\mathrm{d}c = \frac{1}{2}$.
   C. Yes, because it implies that equilibrium prices will be less responsive to cost increases in monopoly than in competitive industries.

10. The main determinants of market power are outlined in Sect. 12.3.1. An increase in concentration need not lead to an increase in market power because prices may be relatively competitive until concentration reaches a critically high level.
11. As the superiority hypothesis indicates, innovation that lowers costs will increase market power and may lead to higher concentration. This innovative activity may increase total (consumer plus producer) surplus.
12. One could collect data on price, marginal cost determinants (e.g., output, input prices, and technology), and output and use it to estimate a supply relation, as described in Sect. 12.2.2. Quite generally, the supply relation takes the following form $p = <\mathrm{MC}> + \lambda q$, where p is price, q is output, and $<\mathrm{MC}>$ is a marginal cost function. Market power is present if $\lambda > 0$.
13. An increase in durability means that greater production today leads to lower demand tomorrow. Thus, future prices and profits fall with product durability (i.e., $\alpha < 0$). This means that an estimate of $\mathcal{L}$ will be too high if α is ignored.
14. This test is based on the fact that the first-order conditions for Nash behavior and for collusive behavior are different. In a Nash equilibrium, firm i's first-order condition is

$$\frac{\partial \pi_i}{\partial s_i} = 1 - 2bs_i + ds_j = 0.$$

With a cartel, the goal is to maximize joint profits ($\pi = \pi_i + \pi_j$). In this case, the first-order condition for firm i is

$$\frac{\partial \pi}{\partial s_i} = 1 - 2bs_i + 2ds_j = 0.$$

Assume we are able to accurately estimate the following general regression equation:

$$s_i = \psi_0 + \psi_1 s_j.$$

Notice that this equation nests the first-order conditions above, where

$$\text{Nash}: \psi_0 = \frac{1}{2b}, \ \psi_1 = \frac{d}{2b};$$

$$\text{Cartel}: \psi_0 = \frac{1}{2b}, \psi_1 = \frac{d}{b}.$$

The data support Nash behavior if parameter estimates indicate that $\psi_1 = d/2b$, and they support cartel behavior if $\psi_1 = d/b$.

15. If this translates to an increase in output beyond that which is profit maximizing, then market power will fall, at least in the current period.

Chapter 13   Product Design, Multiproduct Production, and Brand Proliferation

1. Product design is the process that a firm goes through to determine the specific characteristics of its products. Multiproduct production means that a firm produces more than one brand or product. Brand proliferation is a strategy that is used by firms to flood the market with a variety of differentiated products to deter entry.

2. Like other firm decisions, the monopolist chooses the level of quality that will maximize its profits, which is another application of marginal analysis. From the firm's first-order condition of profit maximization, this involves equating the marginal benefits with the marginal costs of increasing quality by an infinitesimally small amount. The same principle applies to HPD.

3. Product differentiation in monopoly and duopoly markets:

   A. A monopoly firm will choose the profit-maximizing level of quality, ignoring any strategic considerations. In general, this will lead the firm to produce an average level of quality. In a duopoly setting, firms can avoid the Bertrand paradox (i.e., tough price competition) by differentiating their products, with one firm choosing a high level of quality and the other firm choosing a low level of quality. In the model discussed in the chapter, firms chose maximum differentiation (i.e., the principle of maximum differentiation applies).

   B. Assuming the linear city model, the monopolist will tend to locate in the middle of town. The duopoly problem is more complex. In the Hotelling specification where prices are assumed to be fixed, firms locate in the middle of town, just as in the monopoly case. If, however, firms compete in location and in price, firms locate at the opposite ends of town (i.e., the principle of maximum differentiation applies).

4. At the Nash equilibrium, no firm has an incentive to change location. This occurs where two firms locate (side by side) at ¼ and the other two firms locate (side by side) at ¾, where each firm serves ¼ of all consumers.

5. Demand rotation:

   A. See Fig. 13.7 for case (i), Fig. RQ.13.5A(ii) for case (ii), and Fig. RQ.13.5A (iii) for case (iii).

   B. Niche market.

   C. Mass market.

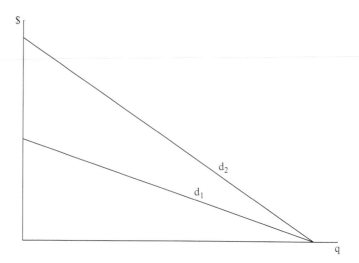

Fig. RQ.13.5A (ii) Demand rotation around the quantity intercept

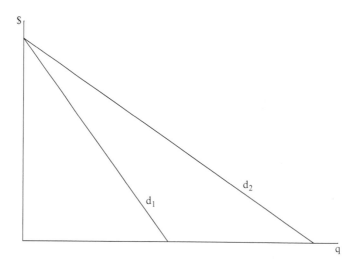

Fig. RQ.13.5A (iii) Demand rotation around the price intercept

6. See the chapter summary.
7. Multiproduct monopolist:

    A. Optimal values are $q_i^* = 60/(1 + d)$, $p_i^* = 80$, and $\pi^* = (7{,}200 - \alpha - \alpha d)/(1 + d)$.

    B. Parameter α captures the degree of economies of scope. If $\alpha < 0$, there are economies of scope; if $\alpha > 0$, there are diseconomies of scope. $\partial \pi / \partial \alpha < 0$, implying that profits rise with an increase in the degree of economies of scope (decrease in α).

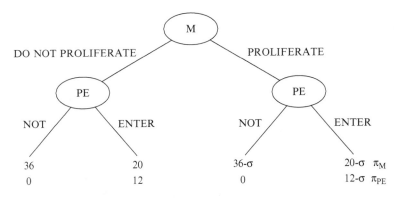

Fig. RQ.13.9A Brand proliferation and entry deterrence

    C. With $\alpha = 0$, $\pi^* = 7{,}200/(1 + d)$. $\partial\pi/\partial d < 0$, implying that profits rise with the degree of product differentiation (a decrease in d).

8. Brand proliferation by Colgate and Crest:

    A. This will be socially desirable if (1) consumer preference for variety is high, (2) the cost of multiproduct production is low, and (3) it does not discourage entry.

    B. When the opposite is true.

    C. To deter entry.

9. Brand proliferation and entry deterrence:

    A. See Fig. RQ.13.9A.

    B. $\sigma > 12$.

    C. $12 < \sigma < 16$.

    D. No, because it is costly and increases market power.

10. Sports cars are relatively impractical—they seat only two passengers, have a small trunk, and get poor fuel economy. The salience of "hot" styling and bright colors (such as Ferrari yellow and red) can induce the intuitive side to act impulsively and favor the sports car (especially if money is no object). The reasoning side might overrule in favor of the practical.

Chapter 14   Price Discrimination and Other Market Strategies

1. Resorts do not allow adults to use children passes but children can easily resell soft drinks and hamburgers.

2. Price discrimination:

    A. The firm will charge the demand price for each quantity sold until q^* is reached in Fig. RQ.14.2A.

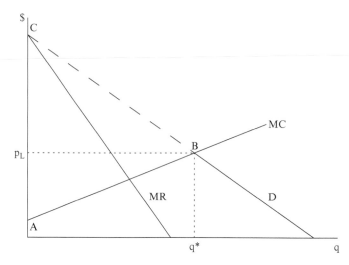

Fig. RQ.14.2A Perfect price discrimination

    B. Consumer surplus $= 0$ and producer surplus $=$ area CAB.
    C. p_L
    D. Because total surplus is maximized (deadweight loss is minimized) when production takes place where $MC = D$.

3. To cut their mean marginal cost over time. This will be efficient if it lowers production costs and causes total output to increase.
4. No. In this case, the profit-maximizing price is 3 (i.e., $MR = MC = 0$ at $Q = 9$), and both adults and children have a positive demand at this price.
5. Price discriminating monopolist

    A. $Q_A^* = 6$, $p_A^* = 9$, $\pi_A^* = 36$, $Q_B^* = 4.5$, $p_B^* = 7.5$, $\pi_B^* = 20.25$.
    B. The same outcome, with total profit (π^*) equal to 56.25.
    C. The social optimum occurs where price equals marginal cost, which is 3. The optimal output level would be 21 ($Q_A^* = 12$, $Q_B^* = 9$).
    D. In this case, the separate monopoly solution is: $Q_A^* = 3.75$, $p_A^* = 11.25$, $\pi_A^* = 28.125$, $Q_B^* = 3$, $p_B^* = 9$, $\pi_B^* = 18$, $\pi^* = 46.125$. With a single price-discriminating monopolist that has a total cost equal to $(Q_A + Q_B)^2$, the solution is: $Q_A^* = 3$, $p_A^* = 12$, $Q_B^* = 1.5$, $p_B^* = 10.5$, $\pi^* = 31.5$. In this case, separate monopolies earn greater profit than a joint monopolist.

6. Price discriminating monopolist with the same price elasticity of demand in each market.

    A. $Q_A^* = 6$, $p_A^* = 9$, $Q_B^* = 3$, $p_B^* = 9$.
    B. Prices are the same because the price elasticity of demand at the equilibrium values of price and quantity is the same, at 3/2.

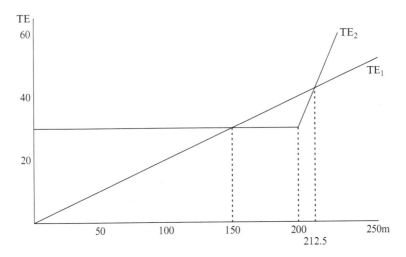

Fig. RQ.14.8A Cell phone pricing

7. People who are overconfident are more likely to try the product if the price is low enough, because they overestimate their willpower and underestimate the addictiveness of the product.
8. Three-part tariff:

   A. See Fig. RQ.14.8A.
   B. Profits are the same under either scheme.
   C. The second scheme earns greater profit.
   D. Overconfidence can make it profitable for the firm to offer a three-part pricing scheme. Consider a consumer, Eddie, who believes that he will use 200 min every month but in fact uses 100 min one month and 300 min the next. If given the option, Eddie would choose three-part tariff pricing, as he would expect $TE_1 = \$40$ and $TE_2 = \$30$. In reality, with the three-part tariff Eddie's average payment would be $TE_2 = \$80$ (i.e., \$30 one month and \$130 the next month). In this case, the firm would offer the three-part tariff and earn higher profit.

9. Monopoly ski resort:

   A. Local residents must have more price elastic demand functions than distant residents.
   B. The maximum price (i.e., the demand price) will be charged for each unit sold. Quantity sold will occur where marginal cost crosses the demand function.
   C. When there is just one consumer or all consumers have the same preferences.

10. Monopoly software problem:

   A. Positively correlated.

B. Separate pricing is optimal given the positive correlation among consumer demand.

C. With a negative correlation, bundling becomes profitable, as in the example associated with Fig. 14.4.

11. Consumers will eventually learn of this pricing policy and will shop primarily on Tuesdays. Competitors will adopt this pricing strategy, eliminating the firm's pricing advantage.

12. (1) Most-favored-customer clause, (2) Meet-the-competition clause, and (3) trigger strategy.

13. Producers may offer consumers gifts if they sit through a high pressure sales pitch. Those who are overconfident in the ability to resist such sales pressure are more likely to accept the offer and succumb to the sales pressure. The three-part tariff of cell phone companies may exploit those who underestimate the variance in their monthly minutes. Sufficient competition may induce competitors to inform consumers of this tactic and reduce a firm's goodwill. This will lower the benefit of using such tactics and reduce the probability of their occurrence.

14. This strategy will be more effective when buyer's remorse is pronounced and will be less likely for nondurable goods and when shipping costs are high (assuming the firm pays for return shipping). To avoid the hold-up problem, special ordered items generally cannot be returned unless they are defective.

15. At checkout counters, grocery stores place tempting items that we do not plan to buy and would not buy if our preferences were time consistent. These include candy and snack foods. To exploit consumer impulsivity to buy things they may not be able to afford, credit card companies offer unsolicited cards to high-risk consumers and offer low initial interest rates and reward programs for using the credit card.

Chapter 15   Advertising

1. The advertising expenditures of rivals are strategic complements (substitutes) when the advertising of one firm causes rival advertising to increase (decrease). This implies that the best-reply function of each firm has a positive (negative) slope. Advertising is constructive (combative) when one firm's advertising increases (decreases) its rival's demand. Combative advertising tends to be a strategic complement, and constructive advertising tends to be a strategic substitute.

2. New consumers will respond to informative advertising. Experienced consumers are unlikely to respond to informative advertising, as they are already aware of the product's characteristics. Both new and experienced consumers are likely to respond to persuasive and image-enhancing advertising.

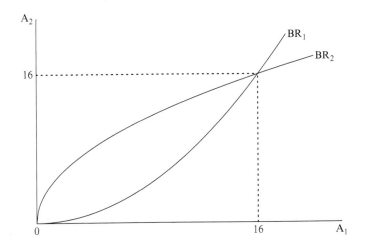

Fig. RQ.15.7A Best reply functions for a Duopoly competing in Advertising

3. A necktie is a search good, canned soup is an experience good, and engine repair is a credence good. With no government regulation, advertising for engine repair will be highest and advertising for neckties the lowest.
4. Case 1 is graphed in Fig. 15.4. The other two cases are shown in Fig. RQ.13.5A (ii) and Fig. RQ.13.5A (iii). In the first case, mass-market advertising will make demand flatter, and niche-market advertising will make demand steeper. In the second case, a firm will use niche-market advertising to make demand steeper. In the third case, a firm will use mass-market advertising to make demand flatter.
5. Monopoly output and advertising problem:

   A. $TR = aq - bq^2 + A^{1/2}q$.
   B. $MR_q = a - 2bq + A^{1/2}$, $MR_A = \frac{1}{2}A^{-1/2}q$.
   C. $MC_q = c$, $MC_A = p_A$.
   D. $q^* = \frac{2p_A(a-c)}{4p_A-1}$; $x^* = \frac{a-c}{4p_A-1}$, where $x = A^{1/2}$ and $A = x^2$.

6. (1) Constructive: $d > 0$; (2) perfectly constructive: $d = 1$; (3) combative: $d < 0$; (4) perfectly combative: $d = -1$.
7. Advertising duopoly:

   A. BR_1: $A_2 = A_1^2/16$; BR_2: $A_2 = 4\sqrt{A_1}$. See Fig. RQ.15.7A.
   B. $A_i^* = 16$.
   C. The cartel level of advertising is difficult to derive analytically. However, because advertising is a strategic complement in this case, the cartel level will be above the Nash equilibrium level of advertising.

8. From the Dorfman–Steiner condition, a firm will make a greater investment in advertising as the price elasticity of demand falls and as the marginal effectiveness of advertising increases. Strategic considerations are also important in

that rivals will make greater investments in advertising when advertising is combative rather than constructive.

9. The ability to target an ad increases the marginal effectiveness of advertising. This causes the firm to make a greater investment in advertising.

10. Combative advertising will produce a prisoners' dilemma in advertising because one firm's combative advertising produces a negative externality on its competitor.

11. Duopoly model in output and advertising:

   A. Nash equilibrium values are
   $$q_i^* = \tfrac{24}{5-d}, \ x_i^* = \tfrac{12}{5-d},$$
   where $A_i^* = \sqrt{x_i^*}$

   B. Advertising is constructive when $d > 0$ and is combative when $d < 0$. In this model, each firm advertises more as advertising becomes more constructive.

12. Store location and advertising:

   A. If tourists drive primarily on main street, they will have a harder time locating store 2.

   B. To attract sufficient customers, store 2 will charge lower prices and spend more on advertising that informs consumers of its location.

13. This leads to a similar outcome as found in Sect. 15.3.3.4. The main difference is that the effect of the error term for firm i is magnified by z_i. Thus, because $z_1 > z_2$, firm 1 will have an even greater incentive to advertise than in the example in Sect. 15.3.3.4.

14. First, behavioral economics shows that framing effects, how information is presented, can affect behavior. Second, people who suffer from cognitive dissonance and confirmation bias may gain utility from commercials that support their belief that eating fast food is not unhealthy. As Glaeser (2004) says, "Consumers will be more likely to accept false beliefs when those beliefs make them happier." Thus, framing their commercials in this way may reduce the cognitive dissonance of this unhealthy habit by confirming our desired belief that we can eat fast food and remain thin, healthy, and athletic.

15. Firms may cultivate a product image that appeals to a certain group of consumers, hoping to tie the product to the identity of the group. This will increase the likelihood that members will purchase the good and cause them to look down on those who do not consume it.

16. If a firm can use advertising to create brand loyalty, then loss aversion will lock consumers into the brand and enable the firm to increase price. The empirical evidence shows that advertising does not have a long lasting effect on sales. In addition, Thomas (1989), Kwoka (1993), and Landes and Rosenfield (1994) find brand-specific effects such as quality and styling have a much bigger effect on brand loyalty and goodwill than advertising.

Chapter 16   Advertising and Welfare

1. For experience goods, a false claim cannot be verified until after a purchase is made. Thus, false statements can successfully increase firm demand in the short run. If a firm is going out of business, it will care little about its reputation and is more likely to lower the quality of its experience goods. Thus, you should avoid a restaurant that is going out of business in the near future.

2. The level of advertising in a particular market will tend to be excessive when it is deceptive, changes tastes, leads to higher prices, and produces negative externalities. Advertising that is honest, lowers search costs, and does not produce negative externalities is undersupplied.

3. Let $D_0(A_0)$ be a demand curve when there is no advertising, $D_1(A^*)$ be a demand curve at the profit-maximizing level of advertising, and marginal production cost be zero. Note that when advertising changes tastes and is informative, the true or benchmark demand curve is $D_1(A^*)$.

   A. Figure RQ.16.3A depicts the case where demand rotates around the quantity intercept from $D_0(A_0)$ to $D_1(A^*)$ and the optimal price-quantity pair is p_0-q_0. The measures of social welfare are:

   - At A_0, $CS_0 = A + B + C + E$; $PS_0 = D$; $TS_0 = A + B + C + D + E$.
   - At A^*, $CS_1 = A + B + F$; $PS_1 = C + D + E + G + H - A^*$; $TS_1 = A + B + C + D + E + F + G + H - A^*$.
   - $\Delta TS = TS_1 - TS_0 = F - C - E$.

   $\Delta TS = \Delta CS$ because $\Delta PS = 0$ at the profit-maximizing level of advertising. (The advertising-profit function is hill shaped. If the firm is maximizing profits at A^*—the peak of the function—marginal changes will be zero). The impact of advertising on efficiency is positive if $F > C + E$ and is negative if $F < C + E$, which is difficult to tell in this particular graph.

   B. Figure RQ.16.3B shows the case where advertising induces a rotation of demand around the vertical axis. At the new optimum, p_1-q_1, the change in total surplus is also $\Delta TS = F - C - E$; $F > C + E$ indicates that advertising increases social welfare and $F < C + E$ indicates a decrease in social welfare.

4. Advertisers may send messages that are particularly salient that can change beliefs to favor the product. They can also take advantage of consumer cognitive dissonance by changing beliefs in ways that make consumers happier and induce them to buy the advertised brand. If advertising could substantially change beliefs, society might gain from placing restrictions on business and political advertising (assuming a sufficiently low cost of regulation). However, Ackerberg found support for the hypothesis that advertising for Yoplait 150 yogurt increases the demand from inexperienced consumers but not experienced consumers, which is more consistent with the informative view than the persuasive view of advertising.

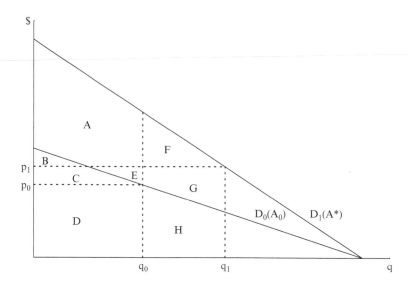

Fig. RQ.16.3A Demand rotation around the quantity intercept and social welfare

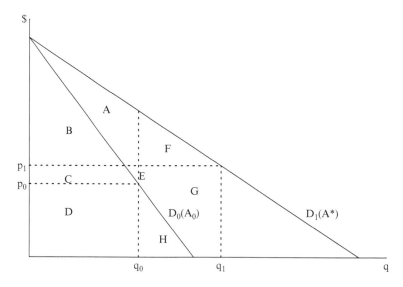

Fig. RQ.16.3B Demand rotation around the price intercept and social welfare

5. This is a difficult question to answer, as it requires us to make a value judgment concerning who knows what is best for an individual, the individual or the majority in a society. If you believe that the individual knows what is best, no policy remedy is needed. If not, then some restriction on image advertising may be in order. We take up this issue further in Chap. 20.

Chapter 17   Technological Change, Dynamic Efficiency, and Market Structure

1. A technological change increases our standard of living by creating new products, increasing the quality of existing products, and lowering production costs (and prices). Without technological change, there would be no economic growth (per capita). There can be negative effects as well, such as increased pollution and the creation of weapons of mass destruction.
2. See the chapter summary.
3. Cost innovation:

   A. Period 1: $p^* = MC_1 = 70$, $Q^* = 50$, CS $= 1{,}250$, and PS $= 0$.
      Period 2: $p^* = 69.99$, $Q^* = 50.01$, CS $= 1{,}250.5$, and PS $= 2{,}499.99$.
   B. No. In period 2, price exceeds marginal cost.
   C. It will be dynamically efficient as long as the cost of R&D does not exceed the gain in gross total (consumer plus producer) surplus, which is 3,750.5.

4. Given the public good quality of an idea, it can be easily stolen if the government does not provide inventors property rights for their ideas.
5. By giving them ownership, they are able to earn money from their creative activity. This encourages creative effort. This also creates monopoly power, which is allocatively inefficient. This trade-off suggests that ownership should not last forever.
6. This lowers the marginal cost of R&D activity, which encourages R&D.
7. With rising labor costs, the firm can earn greater profits if it can use less of this input. Thus, it will pay to invest in R&D that is designed to reduce the employment of labor, assuming technological opportunities are the same for each input.
8. Some secrets are easier to keep than others. In Coke's case, only a few employees know the formula, and all of them have signed a contract that requires that they keep the formula a secret.
9. See the chapter summary.
10. Inventive activity in monopoly and perfect competition:

    A. Schumpeter is more likely to be correct when there are economies of scale and scope related to R&D activity, imitation of a new product or process is swift, the replacement effect is small, and when R&D activity successfully limits entry. Arrow is more likely to be correct when the reverse holds.
    B. There are no definitive conclusions given estimation problems. Nevertheless, the evidence shows that the number of competitors has a small but positive effect on R&D spending.

11. A monopolist can have greater incentive to innovate when there is a major technological change. This is illustrated in Fig. RQ.17.11A for a monopoly and RQ.17.11B for a firm in perfect competition, where a technological change lowers marginal cost from MC to MC'. For a monopoly firm, the gain in profit

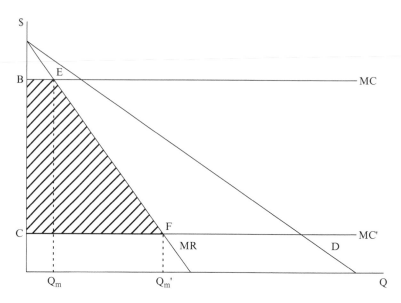

Fig. RQ.17.11A Major technological change in monopoly

from innovation (ignoring the cost of R&D) equals area BCFE. In a competitive market, the gain to a single firm from innovation equals area BCHG. (The equilibrium price after the technological change will actually be slightly less than MC, but we assume that it equals MC to make the graph simple.) In this example, the monopolist has greater incentive from innovation since area BCFE > BCHG. Arrow's proposition does not hold.

12. Market structure and the incentive to innovate:

   A. The maximum amount a firm will be willing to pay for R&D that lowers marginal cost from 40 to 20 is

      (1) 900 in a monopoly market.
      (2) 1,600 in a Bertrand duopoly.
      (3) 888.9 in a Cournot duopoly.

      A Bertrand duopolist has the greatest incentive to innovate.

   B. The maximum amount society is willing to pay for R&D is 1,800.

13. This can occur if it sufficiently raises the sunk cost of entry, as in Fig. 17.15.

14. Technological change and market structure:

   A. A technological change that increases (decreases) MES will lead to a higher (lower) level of industry concentration.

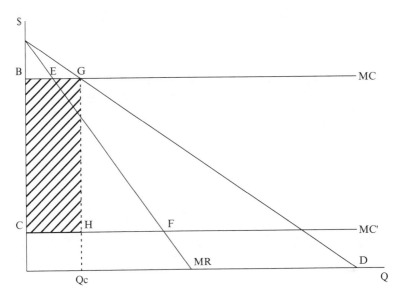

Fig. RQ.17.11B Major technological change in perfect competition

  B. A technological change that increases vertical differentiation tends to increase concentration, while that which increases horizontal differentiation tends to have little effect on concentration.

15. The empirical evidence is insufficiently clear to draw definitive conclusions. It appears that market structure is of minor importance and that the results are case specific. There is not an optimal market structure that applies to every industry.
16. If managers are overly optimistic about the benefits of investing in R&D, too much will be invested from the firm's perspective. From society's perspective, the answer depends on a number of factors. For example, in Arrow's model, free markets invest too little in R&D, so overconfidence may be welfare improving. However, R&D that is driven by patent races can be excessive from society's perspective. In this case, overconfidence would be welfare reducing.

Chapter 18   Horizontal, Vertical, and Conglomerate Mergers

1. See the chapter summary.
2. See the chapter summary.
3. Regarding the market-for-corporate-control hypothesis:

  A. See the chapter summary.
  B. This method evaluates the effect that a merger announcement has on the market value of firms in the industry. If a merger increases market power, the announcement of a merger will increase the value of competing firms. If

a merger increases the efficiency of the merging firms, it will lower the value of competing firms.

C. The efficient-market hypothesis states that markets such as the stock market are informationally efficient, which means that the price of a company's stock at a point in time reflects all publically available information and, therefore, accurately reflects the fundamental value of the firm. Thus, a merger announcement that increases efficiency (market power) will drive down (up) the market value of competing firms. There are a number of weaknesses with this method. For example, a merger may convey more than just information about market power or efficiency. In addition, behavioral economics research suggests that markets may not always be informationally efficient.

4. A merger in a Cournot triopoly:

   A. $q_i^* = 3$, $p^* = 15$, and $\pi_i^* = 9$.
   B. No, with the merger there are just two firms, 1–2 and 3. In this case, $\pi_{1-2}^* = 16$ which is less than the sum of their profits in the market with three firms, which is 18; although firm 3 is better off, with profits increasing from 9 to 16.

5. A merger in a Bertrand triopoly:

   A. $p_1^* = p_2^* = 10$, $q_1^* = q_2^* = 7$, $q_3^* = 0$, $\pi_1^* = \pi_2^* = \pi_3^* = 0$.
   B. It will prefer to buy firm 2. This will allow it to charge a price just below the unit cost of firm 3 (at 11.99, set to 12 for simplicity) and earn a positive profit. In this case, $p_1^* = 12$, $q_{1-2}^* = 12$, $q_3^* = 0$, $\pi_{1-2}^* = 24$, and $\pi_3^* = 0$.

6. It says that a merger that raises market power will increase total (consumer plus producer) surplus as long as it leads to a sufficient reduction in costs. Thus, a trade-off exists when a merger raises market power but lowers production costs.

7. See the chapter summary.

8. Custom motorcycle problem:

   A. Because the custom motorcycle is of lesser value to everyone but Macrosoft, Macrosoft could renegotiate for a lower price once the motorcycle is manufactured.
   B. US Choppers.
   C. A merger and payment before fabrication begins.

9. Monopoly wholesaler and competitive retailer (monopoly–competitive case):

   A. See Fig. RQ.18.9A.
   B. This output level (Q^*) is the same as the output level in the competitive––monopoly case (Q_1). In reference to Fig. 18.6, this is greater than the output level in the monopoly-monopoly case (Q_2) and less than the output level in the competitive–competitive case (Q_S).

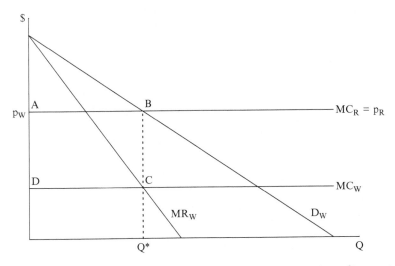

Fig. RQ.18.9A Equilibrium wholesale price, retail marginal cost, retail price, and output in the monopoly-competitive case

    C. Profits to the retailer are 0 and profits to the wholesaler equal area ABCD (or p_WBCD).

10. Monopoly wholesaler and monopoly retailer (monopoly–monopoly case):

    A. This is displayed in Fig. 18.6, where the price is marked up above marginal cost twice, once by the wholesaler and once by the retailer.

    B. The merger produces the outcome found in Fig. 18.5. Because this maximizes joint profits, producer surplus increases. Because it leads to greater output that is closer to Q_S in Fig. 18.6, consumer surplus increases.

    C. With variable-proportions technology, the retailer will substitute away from the wholesaler's product as the wholesaler raises price due to market power. This leads to an economically inefficient use of inputs due to higher costs for the retailer and reduces the market power of the wholesaler. A merger will reestablish the wholesaler's market power, which puts upward pressure on the retail price. It also produces greater cost efficiency for the retailer, which puts downward pressure on the retail price. Thus, the net effect of the merger is uncertain.

11. Assuming two unrelated outputs, q_1 and q_2, a cost function exhibits economies of scope when the total cost of joint production [$TC(q_1, q_2)$] is cheaper than the total cost of separate production [$TC(q_1) + TC(q_2)$]. That is, when $TC(q_1, q_2) < TC(q_1) + TC(q_2)$. Conglomerate mergers are justified if they lead to sufficiently lower costs.

12. The mutual forbearance hypothesis states that when conglomerate firms compete with one another in more than one market, they will take a "live and let live" policy. They are more likely to behave cooperatively for fear that noncooperative behavior in one market will trigger punishment in more than just one market in which they compete.
13. See the chapter summary.
14. This is a legal issue because managers who make acquisitions that are not in the interest of stockholders are violating the spirit of their contracts. The principle–agent problem can lead a manager to make acquisitions that increase the value of a manager to the firm. For example, a manager of a drug company who has a degree in engineering may acquire an artificial heart manufacturer, making it difficult to find someone else who has expertise in both fields to manage the combined firm.
15. See the chapter summary.

Chapter 19   Efficiency, Equity, and Corporate Responsibility in Imperfect Competition

1. See the chapter summary.
2. See the chapter summary for a discussion of static and dynamic efficiency. It is difficult to estimate allocative inefficiency in a dynamic market because evidence that price equals marginal cost need not imply that market power does not exist. For example, cigarette companies give away cigarettes today to increase demand and price tomorrow. In this case, market power is manifest in higher future prices.
3. See the chapter summary.
4. Rent-seeking behavior occurs when a firm lobbies government to change the economic environment to increase firm profit. This may take the form of a legal barrier, which increases market power.
5. The efficiency–equity trade-off states that placing greater emphasis on equity may discourage effort and innovation, which diminishes efficiency. Similarly, putting greater emphasis on efficiency may lead to a wider distribution of income and wealth, an outcome that is viewed as inequitable by some social philosophers.
6. Private firms and social responsibility:

   A. Irresponsible behavior is more likely from firms that produce experience and credence goods, that are on the brink of failure, and that care little about their corporate reputations.
   B. Policy should penalize dishonest and deceptive behavior, and policy officials should pay particular attention to industries of experience and credence goods and to firms that produce negative externalities, have poor reputations, or are on the brink of failure.

7. If R&D leads to temporary monopoly power and economic profits, then taxing it away would reduce the incentive to innovate and be dynamically inefficient.

Chapter 20   Antitrust Law and Regulation

1. Market and government failure:

   A. Market failure exists when a free market fails to produce a socially optimal outcome. This is normally associated with market power, externalities, public goods, and risk and uncertainty. Government failure occurs when laws and government activities fail to produce a socially desirable outcome. This can occur when a policy is excessively expensive or produces unintended consequences.

   B. The nirvana approach to public policy means that we identify policy solutions to problems of market failure but ignore the cost of government. The comparative institution approach to policy analysis means that we compare the net social benefits of a real-market outcome with a real alternative that takes into account all benefits and costs of government intervention. We would then enact a government policy only when it produces a net gain to society. The nirvana approach provides a useful starting point for policy analysis.

   C. In many cases, it is easier to institute a new law than eliminate an existing law. Thus, new laws should be implemented only after careful study and consideration of all potential costs, benefits, and unintended consequences.

2. See the chapter summary.
3. Regarding the philosophy of law:

   A. See the chapter summary.

   B. Natural law theorists tend to be paternalistic and absolutist, believing that laws should provide a rational standard that promotes the common good. Legal positivists are more relativistic, arguing that laws derive from the norms that evolve in a particular society.

   C. Mill promoted the concept of political liberalism, which expresses concerns with the monopoly power of the state. He argued that state action should be constrained by the so-called Mill's Principle: each individual has the right to act as he or she wants, as long as this action does not directly harm others.

4. Regarding the common law and civil law systems:

   A. See the chapter summary.

   B. See the chapter summary.

   C. At least in the recent past, countries with common law systems have experienced superior economic outcomes.

   D. A dictatorial system would establish one person to make all legal and political decisions. Arrow (1951) demonstrates that a political system with a benevolent dictator can produce the most socially desirable outcome. Unfortunately, most dictators suffer from the same moral and cognitive weaknesses as the rest of us and need not be benevolent. As the old adage goes, power corrupts.

5. Actions that are socially undesirable regardless of context are per se illegal (i.e., always illegal). When firm action is beneficial or harmful depending on the circumstances, the courts use a rule of reason when deciding legality.

6. Regarding the Sherman Act:

   A. In general, collusion benefits firms at the expense of society overall. There are exceptions, however. Cooperation among equity traders regarding trading rules can improve the efficiency of the market. Similarly, cooperation among professional sports teams in defining the rules of the game and setting up team schedules can maximize fan enjoyment and owner profits.

   B. In most cases, eliminating market power is socially desirable. Important exceptions include a natural monopoly and the case where market power derives from superior efficiency or inventiveness.

7. The purpose of Sect. 7 of the amended Clayton Act is to stop mergers that lead to high concentration. If successful, this can prevent market power from increasing.

8. Williamson's work suggests that a merger that increases market power need not be socially inefficient as long as it also leads to a sufficient reduction in costs. Demsetz argues that innovative activity can be socially efficient even though it also leads to greater market power. Thus, static efficiency need not imply dynamic efficiency.

9. Regarding the evolution of the antitrust laws:

   A. The trend is that enforcement has become less restrictive since the inception of the antitrust laws. It has also been alleged that enforcement has fluctuated with the political climate, being too lenient when republican presidents were in office. There is some support for the political cycle, at least when evaluating all civil cases.

   B. The evidence suggests that the antimerger laws were too strict during the 1950s and 1960s. The revisions of the merger guidelines are in keeping with the hypothesis that (antimerger) laws evolve to improve efficiency. Today's enforcement places less emphasis on the structural standard (i.e., measures of market share and concentration) and greater emphasis on efficiency and other factors in deciding whether or not to challenge a horizontal merger.

   C. Although extreme economic conditions and the political climate have influenced enforcement, there has been a general long-term trend towards less restrictive antitrust enforcement. The evidence shows that this has promoted efficiency and is consistent with the evolution to efficient laws hypothesis.

10. See the chapter summary.
11. Regarding deregulation:

A. Economic deregulation means that laws and regulatory agency restrictions are changed to give greater freedom to individuals and private companies.

B. Deregulation promotes efficiency when an existing regulation does not promote the public interest (i.e., it results from capture or special-interest motives) and when an existing regulation imposes excessively high costs on industry. Of course, there are costs as well as benefits to deregulation.

12. See the chapter summary.

13. Posner's argument fails when a firm cares little about the future. It also fails when there is a continuous flow of uniformed consumers or when consumers are slow to learn of and respond to a firm's irresponsible behavior.

14. Regarding advertising bans:

A. For a nonstrategic inputs like labor, a ban on the use of labor will force the firm to replace labor with other inputs (e.g., robots), which will raise the firm's costs of production. In oligopoly markets, coordination effects can come into play for a strategic input like advertising, When advertising is purely combative (i.e., steals customers from rival firms and attracts no new consumers to the market), an advertising ban will lower firm costs.

B. See Fig. 21.2. When the Nash level exceeds the cartel level of a strategic variable, as in this case, it is a strategic complement.

C. In the payoff matrix in Fig. 21.2, switch "Ban" with "Advertise" for both firms. When the Nash level is less than the cartel level of a strategic variable, as in this case, it is a strategic substitute.

D. In markets where bounded rationality, cognitive dissonance, confirmation bias, and consumer impulsivity are most likely to be a problem. Examples include markets for credence goods (i.e., medical procedures), addictive commodities (cigarettes and alcoholic beverages), and fast food.

Mathematics and Econometrics Review Appendix

1. The first and second derivatives are:

A. $dy/dx = -5$, $d^2y/dx^2 = 0$.
B. $dy/dx = -2 + 2x$, $d^2y/dx^2 = 2$.
C. $dy/dx = x^{-1/2}$, $d^2y/dx^2 = -.5x^{-3/2}$.
D. $dy/dx = -20x^3$, $d^2y/dx^2 = -60x^2$.

2. Graphing functions of a quadratic function:

A. See Fig. RQ.A.2A.
B. $f(x) = 24 - 3x$. See Fig. RQ.A.2B.
C. $dy/dx = 24 - 6x$. See Fig. RQ.A.2C.

742

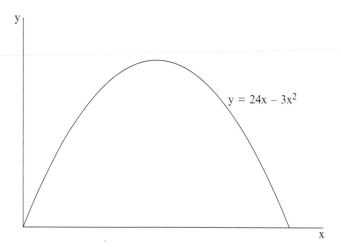

Fig. RQ.A.2A Graph of $y = 24x - 3x^2$

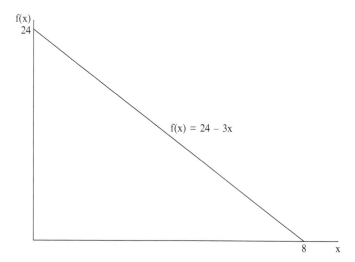

Fig. RQ.A.2B Graph of $f(x) = 24 - 3x$

3. Graphing functions of a cubic function:

    A. See Fig. RQ.A.3A.
    B. See Fig. RQ.A.3B.
    C. See Fig. RQ.A.3C.

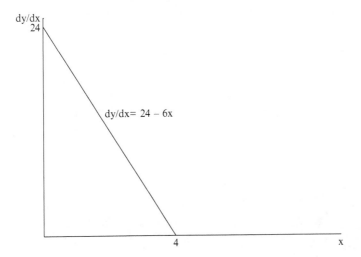

Fig. RQ.A.2C Graph of $dy/dx = 24 - 6x$

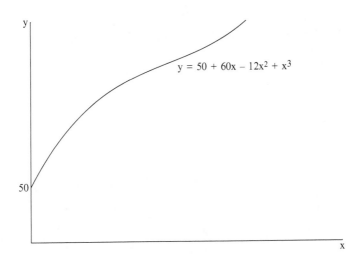

Fig. RQ.A.3A Graph of $y = 50 + 60x - 12x^2 + x^3$

4. For the function, $y = \sqrt{x^2}$:

   A. See Fig. RQ.A.4A.
   B. Yes.
   C. No.

5. $dy/dx = 4v$.

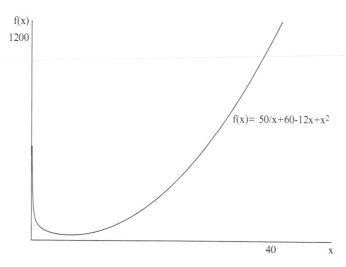

Fig. RQ.A.3B   Graph of $f(x) = 50/x + 60 - 12x + x^2$

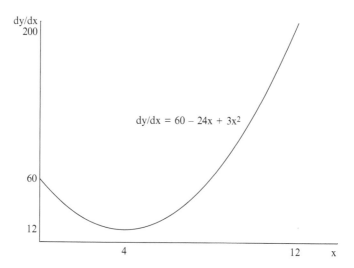

Fig. RQ.A.3C   Graph of $dy/dx = 60 - 24x + 3x^2$

6. The partial derivatives are:

   A. $\partial y/\partial x = -1 + 8x, \quad \partial y/\partial z = 3z^2$.
   B. $\partial y/\partial x = 2x + z, \quad \partial y/\partial z = 4z^3 + x$.

7. Solutions to the systems of equations:

   A. $y_1 = -3y_2 + 72, \quad y_2 = -y_1/3 + 24$.
   B. $y_1 = 12 - y_2, \quad y_2 = 12 - y_1$.

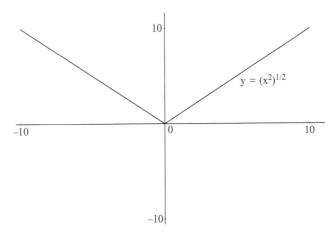

Fig. RQ.A.4A Graph of $y = (x^2)^{1/2}$ for $-10 < 0 < 10$

8. $Q^* = 9, p^* = 9$.
9. The maxima for the functions are:

   A. $x = 9$.
   B. $x = a/2b$.
   C. These equations are convex because their second derivatives are negative,
   $$\frac{d^2 y}{dx^2} < 0.$$

10. The impact of a subsidy on profits:

   A. See Fig. RQ.A.10A. $q^*(s = 0) = 12$, $q^*(s = 10) = 17$.
   B. An increase in s will increase the firm's profit-maximizing quantity.

11. Based on the inverse demand function:

   A. β_2 is the amount that price changes when quantity increases by 1 unit.
   B. Negative, because of the law of demand, i.e., price and quantity are inversely related.

12. See Figs. RQ.A.12A and RQ.A.12B.
13. From (A.37), $\pi = 106,240 + 1.80A + 1,020PRODS$. Predicted profits are $\pi = 106,240 + 1.80(9,000) + 1,020(5) = 127,540$.
14. According to the regression results:

   A. The x_2 coefficient estimate of -4 indicates that a 1-unit increase in x_2 results in an estimated 4 unit decrease in y, holding x_1 constant.
   B. The coefficient estimates on x_1 and x_2 are significantly different from zero at the 5% level of significance.

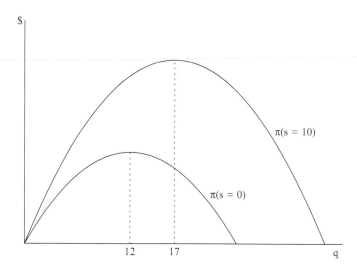

Fig. RQ.A.10A Profit function with subsidies of 0 and 10

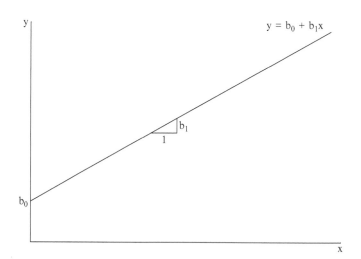

Fig. RQ.A.12A Regression line

C. $R^2 = 0.68$ implies that the model explains 68% of the variation in y.

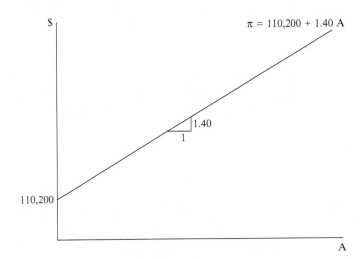

Fig. RQ.A.12B Plot of advertising-profit equation

Appendix C

Notation

English Letters

In general, lower case letters are used as parameters and upper case letters are used as variables. In addition, the following notation is used consistently throughout the book.

a	A is the quantity of advertising expenditure or messages
b	B is the value of a firm's investment capital (i.e., its base)
c	Marginal cost
d	d is firm or individual consumer demand, D is market demand, D is the discount factor
e	e is consumer error, E the dollar value of an externality
f	Fee
g	G is product goodwill
i	Subscript used to represent agent (individual or firm) i
j	Subscript used to represent an agent (individual or firm) other than agent i
k	K is the quantity of capital (which usually includes raw materials)
l	L is the quantity of labor
m	m is money income, M is the quantity of raw materials
n	n is the number of firms; n' is the numbers equivalent number of firms; n^* is the equilibrium number of firms or the number of firms that will minimize industry costs (i.e., the cost-minimizing industry structure); N is the number of consumers
p	Price
q	q is firm production, Q is market output or monopoly production
r	Annual rate of return on an investment
s	s is a parameter that can represent consumer tastes, consumer search costs, or the efficiency gain in marginal cost from a merger, S is industry supply
t	t represents consumer tastes, T represents technology
u	U is consumer utility
v	V is the market value of a firm
w	Input price
x	Quantity of an input (e.g., labor, capital, materials) or a general variable

(continued)

V.J. Tremblay and C.H. Tremblay, *New Perspectives on Industrial Organization*, Springer Texts in Business and Economics, DOI 10.1007/978-1-4614-3241-8,

y	A general variable
z	The level of product quality or an addiction parameter
AC	Long-run average cost
AD	Level of consumer addiction
AR	Average revenue
CS	Consumer surplus
DOJ	Department of Justice
DWL	Deadweight loss
FTC	Federal Trade Commission
MC	Long-run marginal cost
MR	Marginal revenue
ms	Market share
OE	A firm's operating expenses
PS	Producer surplus
TC	Long-run total cost
TR	Total revenue (price times quantity sold)
TS	Total surplus
$\mathcal{S}$	Strategy
$\mathcal{L}$	Lerner index

Greek Letters

Greek letters are also used as parameters and to abbreviate key terms in economics.

A	α	alpha	
B	β	beta	
Γ	γ	gamma	
Δ	δ	delta	δ is the depreciation rate of capital, Δ means change
E	ϵ	epsilon	ϵ is the price elasticity of demand ($\eta = -\epsilon$), ϵ_S is the price elasticity of supply
Z	ζ	zeta	
H	η	eta	η is the price elasticity of demand (measured as a positive number), η_m is the income elasticity of demand, η_{ij} is the cross-price elasticity of demand between products i and j
Θ	θ	theta	θ is a horizontal product differentiation characteristic
I	ι	iota	
K	κ	kappa	
Λ	λ	lambda	λ is the Lagrange multiplier that is used in constrained optimization problems
M	μ	mu	
N	ν	nu	
Ξ	ξ	xi	
O	o	omicron	
Π	π	pi	π is firm profit, Π is joint profit (as in a cartel or dynamic setting)
P	ρ	rho	
Σ	σ	sigma	σ is the cost of a strategic barrier to entry
T	τ	tau	
Y	υ	upsilon	
Φ	ϕ	phi	ϕ is a vertical product differentiation characteristic
X	χ	chi	
Ψ	ψ	psi	
Ω	ω	omega	

Mathematics Notation

The following is a list of mathematical notations that is used throughout the book.

$=$	Equal
$\equiv$	Equal by definition (identically equal)
∞	Infinity
$\in$	Is an element of
ε	An arbitrarily small positive number
$[a, b]$	A closed interval of real numbers that ranges from a to b, including the endpoints a and b
(a, b)	An open interval of real numbers that ranges from a to b, excluding endpoints a and b
$x \in [a, b)$	This means that $a \leq x < b$
Δ	Change
d	Derivative (representing an infinitesimally small change) of a function with one independent variable
∂	Partial derivative of a function with more than one independent variable
$\frac{dy}{dx}$	The first derivative of the function $y = f(x)$
$\frac{d^2y}{dx^2}$	The second derivative of the function $y = f(x)$
$\sum_{i=1}^{n} x_i$	Is the summation operator and equals $x_1 + x_2 + x_3 + \ldots + x_n$
I	Stage I of a game (the first stage)
II	Stage II of a game (following stage I)
III	Stage III of a game (following stage II)

References

Aaker DA (1991) Managing brand equity: capitalizing on the value of a name brand. Free Press, New York

Acemoglu D, Aghion P, Griffith R, Zilibotti F (2010) Vertical integration and technology: theory and evidence. J Eur Econ Assoc 8(5):989–1033

Ackerberg D (2001) Empirically distinguishing informative and prestige effects of advertising. Rand J Econ 32:316–333, Summer

Adams W, Brock JW (1988) Reaganomics and the transmogrification of merger policy. Antitrust Bulletin 33(2):309–359

Adams W, Mueller H (1990) The steel industry. In: Adams W (ed) The structure of American industry. MacMillan, New York

Adams WJ (2006) Beer in Germany and the United States. J Econ Perspect 20(1):185–202

Adams WJ (2011) Determinants of the concentration in Beer markets in Germany and the United States: 1950–2005. In: Swinnen JFM (ed) The economics of beer. Oxford University Press, New York, pp 227–246

Aiginger K, Mueller DC, Weiss C (1998) Objectives, topics, and methods in industrial organization during the nineties: results from a survey. Int J Ind Organ 16(1):799–830

Aiginger K, Pfaffermayr M (1997) Looking at the cost side of monopoly. J Ind Econ 45 (3):245–267

Aislabie CJ, Tisdell CA (1988) Profit maximization and marketing strategies: demand rotation and social influences. Manag Dec Econ 9(1):77–82

Akerlof GA (1970) The market of 'Lemons': quality uncertainty and the market mechanism. Quart J Econ 84(3):488–500

Akerlof GA (1991) Procrastination and obedience. Am Econ Rev 81(2):1–19

Akerlof GA, Dickens WT (1982) The economic consequences of cognitive dissonance. Am Econ Rev 72(3):307–319

Akerlof GA, Kranton RE (2000) Economics and identity. Quart J Econ 115(3):715–753

Akerlof GA, Kranton RE (2005) Identity and the economics of organizations. J Econ Perspect 19 (1):9–32

Alchian AA (1950) Uncertainty, evolution, and economic theory. J Polit Econ 58(3):211–221

Alchian AA, Demsetz H (1972) Production, information costs, and economic organziation. Am Econ Rev 62:777–795

Allison RI, Uhl KP (1964) Influence of beer brand identification on taste perception. J Market Res 1(3):36–39

Alsop R (April 24, 1995) What year is this? Wall Street J, New York, R5

Altman M (2006) Handbook of contemporary economics: foundations and developments. M.E. Sharpe, Armonk, NY

Amihud Y, Lev B (1981) Risk reduction as a managerial motive for conglomerate mergers. Bell J Econ 12(2):605–617

Amir R (1995) Endogenous timing in two-player games: a counterexample. Games Econ Behav 9(2):234–237

Amir R, Grilo I (1999) Stackelberg versus Cournot equilibrium. Game Econ Behav 26:1–21

Amir R, Isabel Grilo (1999) Stackelberg versus Cournot equilibrium. Games Econ Behav 26(1):1–21

Andrade G, Mitchell M, Stafford E (2001) New evidence and perspectives on mergers. J Econ Perspect 15(2):103–120

Angeletos G-M, Laibson D, Repetto A, Tobacman J, Weinberg S (2001) The hyperbolic consumption model: calibration, simulation, and empirical evaluation. J Econ Perspect 15 (3):47–68

Angner E, Loewenstein G (2006) "Behavioral Economics," working paper, Carnegie Mellon, November 2006, to appear in Elsevier's Handbook of the Philosophy of Science, Vol. 5

Appelbaum E (1979) Testing price-taking behavior. J Econometrics 9(3):283–299

Appelbaum E (1982) The estimation of the degree of oligopoly power. J Econometrics 19(2–3):287–299

Ariely D (2008) Predictably irrational: the hidden forces that shape decisions. Harper-Collins, New York

Ariely D, Loewenstein G, Prelec D (2003) 'Coherent Arbitrariness': Stable demand curves without stable preferences. Quart J Econ 118:73–105

Aron DJ, Lazear EP (1990) The introduction of new products. Am Econ Rev 80(2):421–426

Aronson E (1999) The social animal. Worth Publishers, New York

Arrow KJ (1951) Individual values and social choice. Wiley, New York (2nd edition, 1963)

Arrow KJ (1962) The economic implications of learning by doing. Rev Econ Stud 29(3):155–173

Arya A, Mittendorf B, Sappington DEM (2008) Outsourcing, vertical integration, and price v. quantity competition. Int J Ind Organ 26(1):1–16

Asch P (1983) Industrial organization and antitrust policy. Wiley, New York

Asch P (1988) Consumer safety regulation: putting a price on life and limb. New York, Oxford University Press

Orley A (2006) Measuring the value of a statistical life: problems and prospects. National Bureau of Economic Research, Working Paper 11916, January 2006

Asch P, Seneca JJ (1975) Characteristics of collusive firms. J Ind Econ 23(3):223–237

Ashenfelter O (2006) Measuring the value of a statistical life: problems and prospects. Econ J 116 (510):C10–C23

Ashenfelter O, Hosken D (2008) The effect of mergers on consumer prices: evidence from five selected case studies. National Bureau of Economic Research, Working Paper 13859, March 2008

Ashenfelter O, Sullivan D (1987) Nonparametric tests of market structure: an application to the cigarette industry. J Ind Econ 35(4):483–498

Athey S, Schmutzler A (2001) Investment and market dominance. Rand J Econ 32(1):1–26

Austin A (2006) Ivy league price-fixing: conflict from the intersection of education and commerce. St John's J Legal Comment 21(1):1–52

Averch H, Johnson LL (1962) Behavior of the firm under regulatory constraint. Am Econ Rev 52(5):1052–1069

Azzam AM (1997) Measuring market power and cost-efficiency effect of industrial concentration. J Ind Econ 45(4):377–386

Bagwell K (2007) The economic analysis of advertising. In: Armstrong M, Porter RH (eds) Handbook of industrial organization, vol 3. North-Holland, New York, pp 1701–1844

Bagwell LS, Bernheim BD (1996) Veblen effects in a theory of conspicuous consumption. Am Econ Rev 86(3):349–373

Bailey EE, Graham DR, Kaplan DP (1985) Deregulating the airlines. MIT Press, Cambridge

Bain JS (1956) Barriers to new competition: their character and consequences in manufacturing industries. Harvard University Press, Cambridge, MA

Bain JS (1959) Industrial organization. Wiley, New York

Baker J (2003) The case for antitrust enforcement. J Econ Perspect 17:27–50

Baker J, Bresnahan T (2008) Economic evidence in antitrust: defining markets and measuring market power. In: Buccirossi P (ed) The economics of antitrust law. MIT Press, Cambridge, MA

Baker JB, Shapiro C (2007) Reinvigorating horizontal merger enforcement. Reg-Markets Center. Working Paper No. 07-12. Available at SSRN: http://ssrn.com/abstract=1089198

Baldani J, Bradfield J, Turner RW (2005) Mathematical economics. Thomson South-Western

Baldwin BA, Meese GB (1979) Social behavior in pigs studied by means of operant conditioning. Anim Behav 27:947–957

Bar-Gill O (2004) Seduction by plastic. Northwestern University Law Review. 1395–1411

Barberis N, Thaler R (2003) A survey of behavioral finance. In: Constantinides GM, Harris M, Stulz R (eds) Handbook of the economics of finance. Elsevier

Barton DM, Sherman R (1984) The price and profit effects of horizontal merger: a case study. J Ind Econ 33:165–177

Bauer RA, Greyser SA (1968) Advertising in America: the consumer view. Harvard University Press, Boston

Baumol WJ (1967) Reasonable rules for rate regulation: plausible policies for an imperfect world. In: Phillips A, Williamson OE (eds) Prices: issues in theory, practice, and public policy. University of Pennsylvania Press, Philadelphia

Baumol WJ (1977) On the proper cost test for natural monopoly in a multiproduct industry. Am Econ Rev 67:809–822

Baumol WJ, Panzar JC, Willig R (1982) Contestable markets and the theory of industry structure. Harcort Brace Javonovich, Inc., New York

Baye MR (2002) Managerial economics and business strategy. McGraw-Hill/Irwin, New York

Bazerman MH, Samuelson WF (1983) I won the auction but don't want the prize. J Conflict Resolution 27:618–634

Beath J, Katsoulacos Y (1991) The economic theory of product differentiation. Cambridge University Press, Cambridge

Becker G (1983) A theory of competition among pressure groups for political influence. Quart J Econ 98:371–400

Becker G (1985) Public policies, pressure groups, and deadweight costs. J Public Econ 28(3):329–347

Becker GS, Murphy KM (1988) A theory of rational addiction. J Polit Econ 96(4):675–700

Becker G, Murphy K (1993) A simple theory of advertising as a good or bad. Quart J Econ 108:941–964

Beckner CF III, Salop SC (1999) Decision theory and antitrust rules. Antitrust Law J 67:41–75

Bellant D (2004) Edward Chamberlin: monopolistic competition and Pareto optimality. J Bus Econ Res 2(4):17–26

Benham L (1972) The effect of advertising on the price of eyeglasses. J Law Econ 15(2):337–352

Berg J, Dickhaut J, McCabe K (1995) Trust, reciprocity, and social history. Games Econ Behav 10:122–142

Berger AN, Hunter WC, Timme SG (1993) The efficiency of financial institutions: a review and preview of research past, present and future. J Bank Finance 17:221–249

Berle AA, Means GC (1932) The modern corporation and private property. Macmillan Publishing Co., New York

Bernheim B (2004) Douglas and Antonio Rangel, "Addiction and cue-triggered decision processes, Am Econ Rev 94(5):1558–1590

Bernheim BD, Whinston MD (1990) Multimarket contact and collusive behavior. Rand J Econ 21(1):1–26

Bernheim BD, Rangel A (2004) Addiction and cue-triggered decision processes. Am Econ Rev 94(5):1558–1590

Bernheim B, Michael D (2008) Microeconomics. McGraw-Hill Iwrin, Boston

Bernheim BD, Whinston MD (2008) Microeconomics. McGraw-Hill/Irwin, Columbus

Bernoff J (2009) Advertising will change forever. Advertising Age, July 20

Berns GS, Laibson D, Loewenstein G (2007) Intertemporal choice – toward an integrative framework. Trends Cogn Sci 11(11):482–488

Bernstein MH (1955) Regulating business by independent commission. Princeton University Press, Princeton, NJ

Berry ST (1992) Estimation of a model of entry in the airline industry. Econometrica 60(4):889–918

Berry ST, Levinsohn J, Pakes A (1995) Automobile prices in market equilibrium. Econometrica 63(4):841–890

Berry ST, Waldfogel J (2010) Product quality and market size. J Ind Econ 58(1):1–31

Bertrand J (1883) Review of Théorie Mathématique de la Richesse Sociale and Recherches sur les Principles Mathématique de la Théorie des Richesses. Journal des Savants 68:499–508

Bertrand M, Mullainathan S (2003) Enjoying the quiet life? Corporate governance and managerial preferences. J Polit Econ 111(5):1043–1075

Beuttenmuller RW (1979) The goal of the new premerger notification requirements: preliminary relief against anticompetitive mergers. Duke Law Rev 249(1):249–285

Bikhchandani S, Friedman D, Welch I (1992) A theory of fads, fashion, custom, and cultural change as information cascades. J Polit Econ 100(5):992–1026

Birsch D, Fielder JH (1994) The Ford Pinto: a study in applied ethics, business, and technology. State University of New York Press

Bittlingmayer G, Hazlett TW (2000) DOS *Kapital*: has antitrust action against Microsoft created value in the computer industry? J Fin Econ 55:329–357

Blair RD, Kaserman DL (1983) Law and economics of vertical integration and control. Academic, New York

Blair RD, Kaserman DL (2009) Antitrust economics. Oxford University Press, New York

Blank RM (2002) Can equity and efficiency complement each other? Labour Econ 9(4):451–468

Blaxill M, Eckardt R (2009) The invisible edge: taking your strategy to the next level using intellectual property, Portfolio Press

Blumenthal D, Epstein S, Maxwell J (1986) Commercializing university research. N Engl J Med 314:1621–1626

Blundell R, Griffith R, Van Reenen J (1999) Market share, market value and innovation in a panel of British manufacturing firms. Rev Econ Stud 66:529–554

Bogan V, Just D (2009) What drives merger decision making behavior? Don't seek, don't find, and don't change your mind. J Econ Behav Organ 72(3):930–943

Bok DC (1960) Section 7 of the Clayton Act and the merging of law and economics. Harv Law Rev 74(2):226–355

Boland L (1979) A critique of Friedman's critics. J Econ Lit 17(2):503–522

Bolton GE, Katok E (1995) An experimental test for gender differences in beneficent behavior. Econ Lett 48:287–292

Boone J (2008) A new way to measure competition. Econ J 118:1245–1261

Borenstein S (1992) The evolution of US airline competition. J Econ Perspect 6(2):45–73

Borenstein S, Ross NL (1994) Competition and price dispersion in the U.S. airline industry. J Polit Econ 104(4):653–683

Bork RH (1978) The antitrust paradox: a policy at war with itself. Basic Books, New York

Bowley AL (1924) Mathematical groundwork of economics: an introductory treatise. Oxford University Press, Oxford

Boyd R, Seldon BJ (1990) The fleeting effect of advertising: empirical evidence from a case study. Econ Lett 34:375–379

Braeutigam RR (1989) Optimal policies for natural monopoly. In: Schmalensee R, Willig RD (eds) Handbook of industrial organization, vol II. North-Holland, New York, pp 1289–1346

Braithwaite D (1928) The economic effects of advertisements. Econ J 38(149):16–37

Brean H (1958) Hidden sell technique is almost here: new subliminal gimmicks now offer blood, skulls, and popcorn to movie fans. Life 44:102–114

Breit W, Elzinga KG (1974) Product differentiation and institutionalism: new shadows on old terrain. J Econ Iss 5(4):813–826

Breit W, Elzinga KG (1989) The antitrust casebook: milestones in economic regulation. Dryden, Chicago

Bresnahan TF (1981) Departures from marginal cost pricing in the American automobile industry: estimates for 1977–1978. J Econometrics 17(2):201–227

Bresnahan TF (1982) The oligopoly solution concept is identified. Econ Lett 10(1–2):87–92

Bresnahan TF (1987) Competition and collusion in the American automobile oligopoly: the 1955 price war. J Ind Econ 35(4):457–482

Bresnahan TF (1989) Empirical studies with market power. In: Schmalensee R, Willig RD (eds) Handbook of industrial organization, vol II. North-Holland, New York, pp 1011–1057

Bresnahan TF, Schmalensee R (1987) The empirical renaissance in industrial economics: an overview. J Ind Econ 35(4):371–378

Breyer S (1982) Regulation and its reform. Harvard University Press, Cambridge, MA

Brock JW (2005) The automobile industry. In: Adams W, Brock J (eds) The structure of American industry. Pearson Prentice Hall, Upper Saddle River, NJ, pp 96–118

Brock JW (2009) The automobile industry. In: Brock J (ed) The structure of American industry. Pearson Prentice Hall, Upper Saddle River, NJ, pp 155–182

Brosan SF (2008) Fairness and other-regarding preferences in nonhuman primates. In: Zak PJ (ed) Moral markets: the critical role of values in the economy. Princeton University Press, Princeton, pp 77–104

Brown SJ, Silbey DS (1986) The theory of public utility pricing. Cambridge University Press, New York, NY

Brown SJ, Sibley DS (1986) The theory of public utility pricing. Cambridge University Press, New York

Brozen Y (1971) Concentration and structural and market disequilibria. Antitrust Bull 16:244–248

Bruni L, Porta PL (2007) Handbook on the economics of happiness. Edward Elgar Press, Cheltenham, UK

Bulow J (1982) Durable goods monopolists. J Polit Econ 15:314–332

Bulow J, Klemperer P (1999) The generalized war of attrition. Am Econ Rev 89:439–468

Bulow J, Pfleiderer P (1983) A note on the effect of cost changes on prices. J Polit Econ 95(1):182–185

Bulow JI, Geanakoplos JD, Klemperer PD (1985) Multimarket oligopoly: strategic substitutes and complements. J Polit Econ 93(3):488–511

Burns M (1986) Predatory pricing and the acquisition costs of competitors. J Polit Econ 94:266–296

Bush D, et al. (2004) How to block cartel formation and price-fixing. AEI-Brookings Joint Center for Regulatory Studies, April 2004

Business Week (1969) Some glitter is gone at Gulf and Western. July 5, 1969, p. 34–38.

Business Week (1976) Turmoil among the brewers: Miller's fast growth upsets the beer industry. November 8, 1976, 58

Busse M, Rysman M (2005) Competition and price discrimination in yellow pages advertising. Rand J Econ 36(2):378–390

Buxton AJ, Davies SW, Lyons BR (1984) Concentration and advertising in consumer and producer markets. J Ind Econ 32(4):451–464

Calfee JE, Ringold DJ (1994) The 70% majority: enduring consumer beliefs about advertising. J Public Policy Mark 13(2):228–238

Camerer C (1997) Progress in behavioral game theory. J Econ Perspect 11:167–188

Camerer CF (2007) Neuroeconomics: using neuroscience to make economic predictions. Econ J 117:C26–C42

Camerer C, Issacharoff S, Loewenstein G, O'Donoghue T, Rabin M (2003) Regulation for conservatives: behavioral economics and the case for 'Asymmetric Paternalism'. University of Pennsylvania Law Review 151(3):1211–1254

Camerer C, Loewenstein G, Prelec D (2005) Neuroeconomics: how neuroscience can inform economics. J Econ Lit 43:9–64

Camerer C, Lovallo D (1999) Overconfidence and excess entry: an experimental approach. Am Econ Rev 89(1):306–318

Camerer C, Malmendier U (2007) Behavioral economics of organizations. In: Diamond PA, Vartiainen H (eds) Behavioral economics and its applications. Princeton University Press, Oxford

Campbell S, Goldstein R (2010) The beer trials. Fearless critic media, New York

Canterbury ER, Nosari EJ (1985) The Forbes four hundred: the determinants of super-wealth. Southern Econ J 51:1073–1982

Canterbery ER, Joe Nosari E (1985) The Forbes four hundred: the determinants of super-wealth. South Econ J 51(4):1073–1083

Capaldi N (2004) John Stewart Mill: a biography. Cambridge University Press, Cambridge

Capaldi N, Stewart J (2004) John Stewart Mill: a biography. Cambridge University Press, Cambridge, UK

Caplin A, Schotter A (eds) (2008) The foundations of positive and normative economics. Oxford University Press, Oxford

Carlton DW (1979) Contracts, price rigidity, and market equilibrium. J Polit Econ 87(5):1034–1062

Carlton DW (1986) The rigidity of prices. Am Econ Rev 76(4):637–658

Carlton DW (2010) Revising the horizontal merger guidelines. J Competition Law Econ 6(3):617–652

Carlton DW, Bamberger GE, Epstein RJ (1995) Antitrust and higher education: was there a conspiracy to restrict financial aid? Rand J Econ 26(Spring):131–147

Carlton DW, Perloff JM (2005) Modern industrial organization. Person, Addison, Wesley, Boston

Carter M (2001) Foundations of mathematical economics. MIT Press, Cambridge, MA

Caves RE (1981) Diversification and seller concentration: evidence from changes, 1963–1972. Rev Econ Stat 63(2):289–293

Caves RE (1989) Mergers, takeovers, and economic efficiency: foresight and hindsight. Int J Ind Organ 7(1):151–173

Caves RE (2007) In praise of the old I.O. Int J Ind Organ 25:1–12

Caves RE, Barton D (1990) Efficiency in U.S. manufacturing industries. MIT Press, Cambridge, MA

Caves RE, Murphy WF (1976) Franchising: firms, markets, and intangible assets. Southern Econ J 42:572–586

Chaloupka FJ (2007) Cigarettes: old firms facing new challenges. In: Tremblay VJ, Tremblay CH (eds) Industry and firm studies. M.E. Sharpe, Amonk, NY, pp 80–118

Chamberlin E (1933) The theory of monopolistic competition. Harvard University Press, Cambridge

Chang Y-M, Tremblay VJ (1991) Oligopsony/oligopoly power and factor market performance. Manag Decis Econ 12(5):405–409

Chen J, Liu Q (2011) The effect of most-favored customer clauses on prices. J Ind Econ 59(3):343–371

Cheng R (2011) 2nd update: Microsoft agrees to buy Skype for $8.5 billion, Wall Street Journal, May 10, 2011

Chiang AC (1984) Fundamental methods of mathematical economics. McGraw Hill, New York

Chiang AC, Wainwright K (2005) Fundamental methods of mathematical economics. McGraw Hill, New York

Choi CJ, Shin HS (1992) A comment on a model of vertical product differentiation. J Ind Econ 40:229–231

Ciminillo JA (2005) Scion's TV ads focus on youthful attitude. Automotive News, April 25, 2005, 28

Clark CE (1927) Effective regulation of public utilities. J Polit Econ 35(4):543–555

Coan RJ (1999) U.S. Ad growth hits 7.5% in 98 to outpace GDP. Advertising Age, May 17, 1999

Coase R (1937) The nature of the firm. Economica 4:386–405

Coase R (1960) The problem of social cost. J Law Econ 3:1–44

Coase R (1972) Durable goods monopolists. J Law Econ 15(1):143–150

Cohen WM, Levin RC (1989) Empirical studies of innovation and market structure. In: Schmalensee R, Willig R (eds) Handbook of industrial organization, Vol. 2. Elsevier, pp 1059–1107

Comanor WS (1985) Vertical price-fixing, vertical market restrictions, and the new antitrust policy. Harv Law Rev 98(5):983–1002

Comanor WS, Wilson TA (1974) Advertising and market power. Harvard University Press, Cambridge

Comanor WS, Smiley RH (1975) Monopoly and the distribution of wealth. Q J Econ 89(2):177–194

Comanor WS, Frech HE III (1985) The competitive effects of vertical agreements. Am Econ Rev 75:539–546

Committee on Science, Engineering, and Public Policy (1999) Evaluating Federal Programs: Research and the Government Performance and Results Act, National Academy of Sciences, National Academy of Engineering, and Institute of Medicine

Connor JM (1981) Food product proliferation: a market structure analysis. Am J Agric Econ 63:607–617

Connor JM (2003) Private international cartels: effectiveness, welfare, and anticartel enforcement. Working paper, Social Science Research Network, 2003, http://papers.ssrn.com/sol3/papers.cfm?abstract_id=611909

Connor JM, Lande RH (2005) How high do cartels raise prices? Implications for optimal cartel fines. Tulane Law Rev 80(513):1–55

Connor JM, Lande RH (2006) The great global vitamins conspiracy: sanctions and deterrence. Working paper, Purdue University, February 24, 2006

Connor JM, Lande RH (2006) The size of cartel overcharges: implications for US and EU fining policies. Antitrust Bull 51(4):983–1022

Consumer Reports (2009) It pays to buy store brands. October 2009, 16–20

Consumer Reports (2011a) Stop phone-bill shock. August 2011, 6

Consumer Reports (2011b) Chevrolet Volt. October 2011, 58–60

Cooper JC (2010) State regulation of alcohol distribution: the effects of post & hold laws on consumption and social harm. Federal Trade Commission, Working Paper No. 304, August 2010

Cooper JC, Wright JD (2010) State regulation of alcohol distribution: the effects of post & hold laws on consumption and social harms. FTC Bureau of Economics, Working Paper

Cooper AC, Woo CY, Dunkelberg WC (1988) Entrepreneurs' perceived chances for success. J Bus Venturing 3(2):97–108

Cooter R, Ulen T (2011) Law and Economics. Prentice Hall, Upper Saddle River

Cooter R, Ulen T (2012) Law and economics. Addison-Wesley, Boston

Corts KS (1999) Conduct parameters and measurement of market power. J Econometrics 88(2):227–250

Cournot A (1838) Researches into the mathematical principles of the theory of wealth. L. Hachette, Paris

Cournot Augustin (1988) Recherches sur les Principles Mathématique de la Théorie des Richesses. Paris, 1838. English translation reprinted in Andrew F. Daughety, Cournot Oligopoly: Characterizations and Applications. New York: Cambridge University Press

Cowling K, Cable J, McGuiness T (1975) Advertising and economic behavior. Macmillan, London

Crain R (2003) Can Miller beer survive the mess it's in? Advertising age, May 2, 2003

Crandall R, Winston C (2003) Does antitrust policy improve consumer welfare? Assessing the evidence. J Econ Perspect 17:2–26

Crane DA (2009) Chicago, Post-Chicago, and Neo-Chicago. University of Chicago Law Review 76:1911–1933

Creedy J, Dixon R (1998) The relative burden of monopoly on households with different incomes. Economica 65:285–293

Crespi JM (2007) Generic advertising and product differentiation revisited. J Agric Food Ind Organ 5:691–701, Article 3

Crew MA, Fernando CS, Kleindorfer PR (1995) The theory of peak-load pricing: a survey. J Regul Econ 8:215–248

Creane A, Davidson C (2004) Multidivisional firms, internal competition and the merger paradox. Can J Econ 37(4):951–977

Curfman GD, Morrissey S, Drazen JM (2009) Tobacco, public health, and the FDA. New Engl J Med 23:402–403

Czarnitzki D, Kraft K (2004) An empirical test of the asymmetric models on innovative activity: who invests more into R&D the incumbent or the challenger? J Econ Behav Organ 54(2): 153–173

d'Aspremont CJ, Gabszewicz J, Thisse JF (1979) On Hotelling's "stability in competition". Econometrica 47(5):1145–1150

Dafny L (2009) Estimation and identification of merger effects: an application to hospital mergers. J Law Econ 52:523–550

Daganska M, Jain D (2005) Product line length as a competitive tool. J Econ Manage Strat 14:1–28

Dam K (2006) The law – growth nexus: The rule of law and economic development. Brookings Institution Press

Darby MR, Karni E (1973) Free competition and the optimal amount of fraud. J Law Econ 16(1): 67–88

Darby MR, Kapur S (1973) Free competition and the optimal amount of fraud. J Law Econ 16(1):67–88

Dasgupta P (1988) Patents, priority and imitation, or the economics of races and waiting games. Economic J 98:66–80

Dasgupta P, Stiglitz S (1980) Industrial structure and the nature of innovative activity. Econ J 90(358):266–293

Daughety AF (1990) Beneficial concentration. Am Econ Rev 80(5):1231–1237

David P (1985) Clio and the economics of QWERTY. Am Econ Rev 75(2):332–337

Davidson P, Wiseman P, Waggoner J (2010) Will new financial regulations prevent future meltdowns? USA Today, June 28, 2010

Del Barrio-Garcia S, Luque-Martinez T (2003) Modeling consumer response to differing levels of comparative advertising. Eur J Market 37:256–274

DellaVigna S (2009) Psychology and economics: evidence from the field. J Econ Lit 97(2):315–372

De Long Bradford J, Shleifer A, Summers LH, Waldman RJ (1990) Noise trader risk in financial markets. J Pol Econ 98:703–738DeLong BJ, Goldin KL (2003) Sustaining U.S. economic growth. In: Aaron H et al (eds) Agenda for the nation. Washington, D.C, The Brookings Institution, pp 17–60

De Long JB, Shleifer A, Summers LH, Waldman RJ (1991) The survival of noise traders in financial markets. J Bus 64(1):1–19

Demsetz H (1967) Towards a theory of property rights. Am Econ Rev 57(2):347–359

Demsetz H (1968) Why regulate utilities? J Law Econ 11(1):55–65

Demsetz H (1969) Information and efficiency: another view. J Law Econ 12:1–22

Demsetz H (1973) Industry structure, market rivalry, and public policy. J Law Econ 16(1):1–9

Demsetz H (1974) Two systems of belief about monopoly. In: Goldschmidt H, Michael Mann H, Fred Weston J (eds) Industrial concentration: the new learning. Little Brown, Boston, pp 164–183

Deneckere R, Davidson C (1985) Incentives to form coalitions with Bertrand competition. RAND J Econ 16(4):473–486

Deneckere R, McAfee RP (1996) Damaged goods. J Econ Manage Strat 5(2):149–174

Denison EF (1985) Trends in American economic growth 1929-82. The Brookings Institution, Washington, DC

Deppe M, Schwindt W, Kugel H, PlaBann H, Kenning P (2005) Nonlinear responses within the medical prefrontal cortex reveal when specific implicit information influences economic decision making. J Neuroimag 15(2):171–82

Department of Justice (1999) Hoffmann-La Roche and BASF agree to pay record criminal fines for participating in international vitamin cartel. news release, May 21, 1999

De Roover R (1951) "Monopoly prior to Adam Smith: a revision. Quart J Econ 56(4):492–524

Derthick M, Quirk PJ (1985) The politics of deregulation. The Brookings Institution Press, Washington DC

Dewey D (1961) Mergers and cartels: some reservations about policy. Am Econ Rev 51(2):255–262

Dixit A (1979) A model of duopoly suggesting a theory of entry. Bell J Econ 10(1):20–32

Dixit A (1986) Comparative statics for oligopoly. Int Econ Rev 27(1):107–122

Dixit A, Nalebuff BJ (1991) Thinking strategically: the competitive edge in business, politics, and everyday life. W.W. Norton, New York

Dixit A, Nalebuff BJ (2008) The art of strategy: a game theorist's guide to success in business and life. W. W. Norton, New York

Dixit A, Norman V (1978) Advertising and welfare. Bell J Econ 19(1):1–17

Dixit A, Skeath S (2004) Games of strategy. W. W. Norton & Co., New York

Dobbelaere S (2004) Estimation of price-cost margins and union bargaining power for Belgian manufacturing. Int J Ind Organ 22(10):1381–1398

Domowitz I, Glenn Hubbard R, Petersen BC (1988) Market structures and cyclical fluctuations in U.S. manufacturing. Rev Econ Stat 70(1):55–66

Doraszelski U, Markovich S (2007) Advertising dynamics and competitive advantage. Rand J Econ 38(3):557–592

Dorfman R, Steiner PO (1954) Optimal advertising and optimal quality. Am Econ Rev 44(5):826–836

Draganska M, Dipak J (2005) Product line length as a competitive tool. J Econ Manag Strat 14(1): 1–28

Dunne T, Roberts MJ, Samuelson L (1988) Patterns of firm entry and exit in US manufacturing industries. RAND J Econ 19(4):495–515

Durbin D-A (2008) Toyota will start making hybrid Prius in US. USA Today, July 11, 2008

Eckard EW Jr (1991) Competition and the cigarette TV advertising ban. Econ Inq 29:119–133

Eckbo PL (1976) The future of world oil. Ballinger, Cambridge, Ma

Eckbo BE (1983) Horizontal mergers, collusion, and stockholder wealth. J Financ Econ 11:241–273

Eckbo BE, Wier P (1985) Antimerger policy under the Hart-Scott-Rodino Act: a reexamination of the market power hypothesis. J Law Econ 28:119–149

Economides N (1989) Symmetric equilibrium existence and optimality in differentiated product markets. J Econ Theory 47(1):178–194

The Economist (2009) Subcrime: white-collar trials. November 14, 2009

Edwards CD (1944) Economic and political aspects of international cartels, U.S. Senate, Subcommittee on War Mobilization of the Committee on Military Affairs, 78th Congress, Second Session

Edwards CD (1955) Conglomerate bigness as a source of power. In: Business Concentration and Price Policy. Princeton University Press

Egger P, Hahn FR (2010) Endogenous bank mergers and their impact on banking performance: some evidence from Austria. Int J Ind Organ 28(2):155–166

Eisenhardt K (1989) Agency theory: an assessment and review. Acad Manage Rev 14(1):57–74

Eis C (1969) The 1919-1930 merger movement in American industry. J Law Econ 12:280–284

Edlin AS, Shannon C (1998) Strict monotonicity in comparative statics. J Econ Theory 81(1): 201–219

Einav L, Nevo A (2006) Empirical models of imperfect competition: a discussion. In: Blundell R, Newley WK, Persson T (eds) Advances in economics and econometrics: theory and applications, vol II. Cambridge University Press, Cambridge, England, pp 86–96

Ellickson PB (2007) Does Sutton apply to supermarkets? Rand J Econ 38(1):43–59

Ellison G (2006) Bounded rationality and industrial organization. In: Blundell R, Newey WK, Persson T (eds) Advances in economics and econometrics: theory and applications. Cambridge University Press, Cambridge, England, pp 142–174

Ellison G, Ellison SF (2007) Strategic entry deterrence and the behavior of pharmaceutical incumbents prior to patent expiration. National Bureau of Economic Research, 13069

El-Tablawy T (2008) OPEC divisions again on display heading to Algeria. AP Worldstream, December 14, 2008

Elwell CK (2006) Long-term growth of the U.S. economy: significance, determinants, and policy. Congressional Research Service, Library of Congress

Elzinga KG (1969) The antimerger law: pyrrhic victories? J Law Econ 12:43–73

Elzinga KG (1973) The restructuring of the U.S. brewing industry. Ind Organ Rev 1(2):101–114

Elzinga KG (1990) The beer industry. In: Adams W (ed) The structure of American industry. MacMillan Publishing Co., New York

Elzinga KG (2009) The beer industry. In: Brock J (ed) The structure of American industry. Pearson Prentice Hall, Upper Saddle River, NJ

Elzinga KG, Evans DS, Nichols AL (2001) United States v. Microsoft: remedy or malady. 9 Geo. Mason L. Rev. 633, 651

Elzinga KG, Swisher AW (2005) The Supreme Court and beer mergers: from Pabst/Blatz to the DOJ-FTC merger guidelines. J Ind Organ 26(3):245–267

Elzinga KG, Swisher AW (2011) Development in US merger policy: the beer industry as lens. In: Swinnen JFM (ed) The economics of beer. Oxford University Press, New York, pp 196–212

Epstein RJ, DL Rubinfield (2010) Understanding UPP. Berkeley Electron J Theor Econ 10(1)

Europa (2001) Commission imposes fines on vitamin cartels. Press Release, November 21, 2001. Europa is the official website of the European Union, available at http://europa.eu.

Evans DS (2009) The online advertising industry: economics, evolution, and privacy. J Econ Perspect 23(3):37–60

Evans WN, Farrelly MC (1998) The compensating behavior of smokers: taxes, tar, and nicotine. Rand J Econ 29(3):578–595

Fairfax LM (2009) The legal origins theory in crisis. Brigham Young University Law Rev, 1571–1618

Fama EF (1965) The behavior of stock market prices. J Bus 38:34–105

Fama E, Jensen M (1983) Agency problems and residual claims. J Law Econ 26:327–349

Färe R, Grosskopf S, Seldon BJ, Tremblay VJ (2004) Advertising efficiency and the choice of media mix: a case of beer. Int J Ind Organ 22(4):503–522

Färe R, Grosskopf S, Tremblay VJ (2012) Market Power and Technology. Review of Industrial Organization 40(2):139–146

Färe R, Grosskopf S, Knox Lovell CA (1985) The measurement of efficiency of production. Springer, New York

Färe R, Grosskopf S, Knox Lovell CA (2008) Production frontiers. Cambridge University Press, Cambridge, England

Färe R, Grosskopf S, Seldon BJ, Tremblay VJ (2004) Advertising efficiency and the choice of media mix: a case of beer. Int J Ind Organ 22(4):503–522

Farmer D, Lo A (1999) Frontiers of finance: evolution and efficient markets. Proc Natl Acad Sci USA 96:9991–9992

Farr S, Tremblay Carol Horton, Tremblay Victor J (2001) The welfare effect of advertising restrictions in the U.S. Cigarette industry. Rev Ind Organ 18(2):147–160

Farrell J, Pappalardo JK, Shelanski H (2010) Economics at the FTC: mergers, dominant-firm conduct, and consumer behavior. Rev Ind Organ 37:263–277

Farrell J, Shapiro C (2010) Antitrust evaluation of horizontal mergers: an economic alternative to market definition. Berkeley Electron J Theor Econ 10(1)

Federal News Service (1999) Press Conference with Attorney General Janet Reno and Joel Klein, Assistant Attorney General, Antitrust Division May 20, 1999

Federal Trade Commission v. Procter & Gamble Co., 386 U.S. 568 (1967)

Fee CE, Thomas S (2004) Sources of gains in horizontal mergers: evidence from customer, supplier, and rival firms. J Financial Econ 74(3):423–460

Fillion R (2008) MillerCoors execs face difficult to-do list cutting jobs among tasks for joint outfit. Rocky Mountain News, Denver, June 28, 2008

Fisher AA, Lande RH (1983) Efficiency considerations in merger enforcement. California Law Rev 71(6):1582–1696

Fisher FM, McGowan JJ (1983) On the misuse of accounting rates of return to infer monopoly profits. Am Econ Rev 73:82–97

Fisher FM (1987) On the misuse of the profits-sales ratio to infer monopoly power. RAND J Econ 18:384–396

Fisher FM, McGowan JJ, Greenwood J (1983) Folded, spindled, and mutilated: economic analysis and US v IBM. MIT Press, Cambridge

Fisher I (1898) Cournot and mathematical economics. Quart J Econ 12(2):119–138

Fizel JL, Bennett RW (2009) The college sports industry. In: Brock J (ed) The structure of American industry. Pearson Prentice Hall, Upper Saddle River, NJ

Flaherty P (March 10, 2011) Experts available to discuss turmoil at General Motors. Bloomberg. Available at http://www.bloomberg.com, accessed May 9, 2012

Flew A (1979) Philosophy: an introduction. Hodder and Stoughton, London

Fluet C, Garella P (2002) Advertising and prices as signals of quality in a regime of price rivalry. Int J Ind Organ 20:907–930

Focarelli D, Panetta F (2003) Are mergers beneficial to consumers? Evidence from the market for bank deposits. Am Econ Rev 93(4):1152–1172

Fonda D, Philadelphia D, Szczesny JR (2003) Baby you can drive my car. Time 30:46–48

Fong GT, Hammond D, Laux FL, Zanna MP, Cummings KM, Borland R, Ross H (2004) The near-universal experience of regret among smokers in four countries: findings from the International Tobacco Control Policy Evaluation Survey. Nicotine Tob Res 6(3):S341–S351

Ford H, Crowther S (1922) My life and work. Garden City Publishing, New York

Ford H, in collaboration with Crowther S (1922) My life and work. Doubleday, Page and Company, Garden City, NY

Fort R (2007) The sports industry and antitrust. In: Tremblay VJ, Tremblay CH (eds) Industry and firm studies. Armonk, NY, M.E. Sharpe, pp 245–266

Fox CR, Poldrack RA (2009) Prospect theory and the brain. In: Glimcher PW et al (eds) Neuroeconomics: decision making and the brain. Elsevier, Amsterdam, p 152

Fraas AG, Greer DF (1977) Market structure and price collusion: an empirical analysis. J Ind Econ 26(1):21–44

Frank RH (2000) Microeconomics and behavior, 4th edn. Irwin McGraw-Hill, Boston

Frank RH (2007) The economic naturalist: in search of explanations for everyday enigmas. Basic Books, New York

Frank RH, Bernanke BS (2008) Principles of microeconomics. Irwin Publishing, Boston

Frantz RS (1997) X-efficiency, theory, evidence, and applications. Kluwer, Boston

Frederick CB III, Salop SC (1999) Decision theory and antitrust rules. Antitrust Law J 67:41–76

Friedlaender AF, Spady RH (1981) Freight transport regulation. MIT Press, Cambridge

Friedman JW (1971) A noncooperative equilibrium for supergames. Rev Econ Stud 28(1):1–12

Friedman M (1953) The methodology of positive economics. In: Essays in positive economics. Chicago: University of Chicago Press, pp 3–43

Friedman JW (1983) Advertising and oligopolistic equilibrium. Bell J Econ 14(2):464–473

Friedrichs DO (1996) Trusted criminals: white collar crime in contemporary society. Wadsworth, New York

Fudenberg D, Tirole J (1984) The fat cat effect, the puppy dog ploy, and the lean and hungry look. Am Econ Rev 74(2):361–368

Fudenberg D, Tirole J (1987) Understanding rent dissipation: on the use of game theory in industrial organization. Am Econ Rev 77(2):176–183

Garfield B (2003) Toyota finds attractive effort to push the plug-ugly scion. Advertising Age, August 4, 2003

Gasmi F, Laffont JJ, Vuong Q (1992) Econometric analysis of collusive behavior in a soft-drink market. J Econ Manag Strat 1(2):277–311

Gasmi F, Vuong Q (1991) An econometric analysis of some duopolistic games in prices and advertising. In: Rhodes G, Fromby T (eds) Advances in econometrics: econometric methods and Models for industrial organization. JIA Press, 225–254

Gattuso JL (2010) Red tape rising: Obama's torrent of new regulation. Wall Street Journal, October 29, 2010

Gayle PG (2005) New empirical evidence on the relationship between market concentration and innovation. Working Paper, Department of Economics, Kansas State University

Genesove D, Mullin WP (1998) Testing static oligopoly models: conduct and cost in the sugar industry, 1890–1914. Rand J Econ 29(2):355–377

George LM (2009) National television and the market for local products: the case of beer. J Ind Econ 57(1):85–111

George LM (2011) The growth of television and the decline of local beer. In: Swinnen JFM (ed) The economics of beer. Oxford University Press, New York, pp 213–226

Geroski P (1990) Innovation, technological opportunity, and market structure. Oxford Econ Pap 42:586–602

Ghosal V (2007) Economics, politics, and merger control. In: Choi JP (ed) Recent developments in antitrust: theory and evidence. MIT Press, Cambridge, MA, pp 123–151

Gibbons R (1992) Game theory for applied economists. Princeton University Press, Princeton, NJ

Gibrat R (1931) Les inégalités économiques. Librairie du Recueil, Sirey, Paris, 1931

Gilbert RA (1984) Bank market structure and competition: a survey. J Money Credit Banking 16:617–645

Gilbert RJ, Matutes C (1993) Product line rivalry with brand differentiation. J Ind Econ 41:223–240

Gilbert RJ, Newbery DM (1982) Preemptive patenting and the persistence of monopoly. Am Econ Rev 72:514–526

Gilbert RJ, Katz ML (2001) An economist's guide to U.S. v. Microsoft. J Econ Perspect 15(2):25–44

Glaeser EL (2004) Psychology and the market. Am Econ Rev 94(2):408–413

Glaeser EL, Shleifer A (2002) Legal origins. Quart J Econ 117(4):1193–1229

Glimcher PW, Camerer CF, Fehr E, Poldrack RA (eds) (2009) Neuroeconomics: decision making and the brain. Elsevier, Amsterdam

Goldfarb A (2007) Schlitz: why the Schlitz hit the fan. In: Tremblay VJ, Tremblay CH (eds) Industry and firm studies. Armonk, NY, M.E. Sharpe, pp 293–320

Goldfarb A, Tucker C (2011) Search engine advertising: channel substitution when pricing ads to context. Manag Sci 57(3):458–470

Goldfarb RS, Ratner J (2008) 'Theory' and 'Models': terminology through the looking glass. Economic Watch 5(1):91–107

Goldschmidt HJ, Michael Mann H, Weston JF (eds) (1974) Industrial concentration: the new learning. Little Brown and Company, Boston

Gollop FM, Roberts MJ (1979) Firm Interdependence in oligopolistic markets. J Econometrics 10(3):313–331

Goolsbee A, Syverson C (2008) How do incumbents respond to the threat of entry? Evidence from major airlines. Quart J Econ 78(1):1611–1633

Gordon M (2010) Bernanke, others working together on overhaul. Washington Post, September 30, 2010

Graham JR, Lemmon ML, Wolf JG (2002) Does corporate diversification destroy value? J Finance 42(2):695–720

Green EJ, Porter RH (1984) Noncooperative collusion under imperfect price information. Econometrica 52(1):87–100

Greene WH (2000) Econometric analysis. Prentice Hall, Upper Saddle River, NJ

Greene WH (2008) The econometric approach to efficiency analysis. In: Fried HO, Lovell CAK, Schmidt SS (eds) The measurement of productive efficiency and productivity growth. Oxford University Press, Oxford

Greer DF (1971) Product differentiation and concentration in the brewing industry. J Ind Econ 19:201–219

Greer DF (1992) Industrial organization and public policy. MacMillan, New York

Greer DF (2002) Beer: causes of structural change. In: Duetsch LL (ed) Industry studies. M.E. Sharpe, Armonk, NY

Grether ET (1970) Industrial organization: past history and future problems. Am Econ Rev 60 (2):83–89

Greyser SA, Reece BB (1971) Businessmen look hard at advertising. Harv Bus Rev 49, May–June 1971, 18–26 and 157–165

Griffin JM (1989) Previous cartel experience: any lessons for OPEC? In: Klein LR, Marquez J (eds) Economics in theory and practice: an eclectic approach. Kluwer Academic, Dordrecht, pp 179–206

Grossman GM, Shapiro C (1984) Informative advertising with differentiated products. Rev Econ Stud 51:63–81

Grossman SJ, Hart O (1986) The costs and benefits of ownership: a theory of vertical and lateral integration. J Polit Econ 94(4):691–719

Grubb MD (2009) Selling to overconfident consumers. Am Econ Rev 99(5):1770–1807

Gruenspecht HK, Lave LB (1989) The economics of health, safety, and the environmental regulation. In: Schmalensee R, Willig RD (eds) Handbook of industrial organization, vol II. North-Holland, New York, pp 1507–1550

Gugler K, Mueller DC, Burcin Yurtoglu B, Zulehner C (2003) The effects of mergers: an international comparison. Int J Ind Organ 21(5):625–653

Gugler K, Siebert R (2007) Market power versus efficiency effects of mergers and research joint ventures: evidence from the semiconductor industry. Rev Econ Stat 89(4):645–659

Gul F, Sonnenschein H, Wilson R (1986) Foundations of dynamic monopoly and the Coase conjecture. J Econ Theory 39:155–190

Guth W, Schmittberger R, Schwarze B (1982) An experimental analysis of ultimatum bargaining. J Econ Behav Organ 3:367–388

Häckner J (2000) A note on price and quantity competition in differentiated oligopolies. J Econ Theory 93(2):233–239

Hafner K, Deutsch CH (2005) Storm and crisis: the helping hands; when good will is also good business. New York Times, September 14, 2005

Hall RE (1988) The relation between price and marginal cost in U.S. industry. J Polit Econ 96(5):921–947

Hamermesh DS, Lee J (2007) Stressed out on four continents: time crunch or Yuppie Kvetch? Rev Econ Stat 89(2):374–383

Hamilton JL (1972) The demand for cigarettes: advertising, the health scare, and the Cigarette Advertising Ban. Rev Econ Stat 54(4):401–411

Hamilton J (1997) Brighter days for Clorox. Business Week, June 16, 1997, 62 and 65

Hamilton J, Slutsky S (1990) Endogenous timing in duopoly games: stackelberg or Cournot equilibria. Games Econ Behav 2(1):29–46

Hammond SD (2005) Criminal enforcement program. Department of Justice, November 16, 2005, at http://www.justice.gov/atr

Hammond SD (2010) The evolution of criminal antitrust enforcement over the last two decades. Department of Justice, February 25, 2010, at http://www.justice.gov/atr/public/speeches/255515.htm

Harberger A (1954) Monopoly and resource allocation. Am Econ Rev 44(2):77–87

Hart O, Moore J (1990) Property rights and the nature of the firm. J Polit Econ 98(6):1119–1158

Harrington JE Jr (2009) Games, strategies, and decision making. Worth Publishers, New York

Harris R, Robinson C (2002) The effect of foreign acquisitions on total factor productivity: plant-level evidence from U.K. manufacturing, 1987–1992. Rev Econ Stat 84(3):562–568

Harrison JL, Theeuwes J (2008) Law and economics. W. W. Norton, New York

Harsanyi J (1967) Games with incomplete information played by 'Bayesian' players, I: the basic model. Manag Sci 14(3):159–182

Hasker K, Sickles RC (2010) eBay in economic literature: analysis of an auction marketplace. Rev Ind Organ 37(1):3–42

Hasker K, Sickles RC (1968a) Games with incomplete information played by 'Bayesian' players, II: Bayesian equilibrium points. Manag Sci 14(5):320–334

Hasker K, Sickles RC (1968b) Games with incomplete information played by 'Bayesian' players, III: the basic probability distribution of the game. Manag Sci 14(7):486–502

Hastings JS (2004) Vertical relationships and competition in retail gasoline markets: empirical evidence from contract changes in Southern California. Am Econ Rev 94(1):317–328

Hay DA, Morris DJ (1991) Industrial economics and organization: theory and evidence. Oxford University Press, Oxford

Hay GA (2009) The cigarette industry. In: Brock J (ed) The structure of American industry. Pearson Prentice Hall, Upper Saddle River, NJ

Hay GA, Kelley D (1974) An empirical survey of price fixing conspiracies. J Law Econ 17(13):13–38

Von Hayek F (1945) The use of knowledge in our society. Am Econ Rev 45(4):519–530

Hazlett TW, Michaels RJ (1993) The cost of rent-seeking: evidence from cellular telephone license lotteries. Southern Econ J 59(3):425–435

Hazlett T, Siegfried J (1997) How did the wealthiest New Zealanders get so rich? New Zealand Economic Papers 31(1):35–47

Healy PM, Palepu KG, Ruback RS (1992) Does corporate performance improve after mergers? J Financ Econ 31(2):135–175

Heart HLA (1994) The concept of the law. Clarendon, Oxford, U.K

Henderson R (1993) Underinvestment and incompetence as responses to radical innovation: evidence from the photolithographic alignment equipment industry. RAND J Econ 24(2):248–270

Henrich J, Boyd R, Bowles S, Camerer C, Fehr E, Gintis H, McElreath R (2001) In search of Homo Economicus: behavioral experiments in 15 small-scale societies. Am Econ Rev 91(2):73–78

Hicks J (1935) Annual survey of economic theory: the theory of monopoly. Econometrica 3(1):1–20

Higgs R (1978) Landless by law: Japanese immigrants in California agriculture to 1941. J Econ Hist 38(1):205–225

Hirschhorn N (2001) Tobacco industry documents: what they are, what they tell us, and how to search them. World Health Organization

Hirschman AO (1964) The paternity of an index. Am Econ Rev 54(50):761

Hirshleifer J, Glazer A (1992) Price theory and applications. Prentice-Hall, Englewood Cliffs, NJ

Hodgson GM (2009) The great crash of 2008 and the reform of economics. Cambridge J Econ 33(6):1205–1221

Holmstrom B, Kaplan SN (1980) Corporate governance and merger activity in the United States: making sense of the 1980s and 1990s. J Econ Perspect 15(2):121–144, Spring

Horowitz D (2009) Indoctrination U: the left's war against academic freedom. Encounter Books

Hortacsu A, Syverson C (2007) Cementing relationships: vertical integration, foreclosure, productivity, and prices. J Polit Econ 115(2):250–301

Horton BJ (2010) The TARP Bailout of GM: a legal, historical, and literary critique. Texas Rev Law Polit 14:216–275

Hotelling H (1929) Stability in competition. Econ J 39:41–57

Isariyawongse K, Kudo Y, Tremblay VJ (2007) Generic advertising in markets with product differentiation. J Agr Food Ind Organ 5(6)

Hovenkamp H (2008) The antitrust enterprise: principles and execution. Harvard University Press, Cambridge, MA

Hoxby CM (2000) Benevolent Colluders? The effects of antitrust action on college financial aid and tuition. National Bureau of Economic Research, Working Paper No. 7754

Hughes JW, Moore MJ, Snyder EA (2002) 'Napstering' pharmaceuticals: access, innovation, and consumer welfare. National Bureau of Economic Research, Working Paper Number 9229, September 2002

Hyde CE, Perloff JM (1998) Multimarket market power estimation: the Australian retail meat sector. Appl Econ 30(9):1169–1176

Ikenson DJ (2011) Lasting implications of the general motors bailout. June 22, 2011, Available at http://www.Cato.org

Iwasaki N, Seldon BJ, Tremblay VJ (2008) Brewing wars of attrition for profit and concentration. Rev Ind Organ 33:263–279

Iwasaki N, Tremblay CH, Tremblay VJ (2006) Advertising restrictions and cigarette smoking: evidence from myopic and rational addiction models. Contemp Econ Pol 24(3):370–381

Iwasaki N, Tremblay VJ (2009) The effect of marketing regulations on efficiency: LeChatelier versus coordination effects. J Prod Anal 32(1):41–54

Iwata G (1974) Measurement of conjectural variations in oligopoly. Econometrica 42(5):947–966

Jensen MC, Meckling WH (1976) Theory of the firm, managerial behavior, agency costs, and ownership structure. J Fin Econ 3:305–360

Jackman M, Macmillan T (1984) Book of business and economic quotations. Macmillan, New York

Jaffe AB (1986) Technological opportunity and spillovers of R&D: evidence from firms' patents, profits and market value. Am Econ Rev 76(5):984–1001

Jahn G (2009) OPEC oil keeps output steady. AP Worldstream, May 28, 2009

Jandik T, Makhija AK (2005) Can diversification create value? Evidence from the electric utility industry. Fin Manag 34(1):61–93

Jans I, Rosenbaum DI (1997) Multimarket contact and pricing: evidence from the U.S. cement industry. Int J Ind Organ 15(3):391–412

Jans I, Rosenbaum DI (1997) Multimarket contact and pricing: evidence from the U.S. cement industry. Int J Ind Organ 15(3):391–412

Jarmin RS (1994) Learning by doing and competition in the early rayon industry. Rand J Econ 25(3):441–543, Autumn

Jewkes J, Sawers D, Stillerman R (1969) The sources of invention. Norton, New York

Jin GZ, Leslie P (2003) The effects of disclosure regulation: evidence from restaurants. Quart J Econ 118(2):409–451

Jiraporn P, Kim YS, Davidson WN, Singh M (2006) Corporate governance, shareholder rights, and firm diversification: an empirical analysis. J Bank Fin 30(3):947–963

Johnson AT (1979) Congress and professional sports: 1951–1978. Ann Am Acad Polit Soc Sci 445(1):102–115

Johnson EJ, Bellman S, Lohse GL (2002) Defaults, framing and privacy: why opting in-opting out. Market Lett 13(1):5–15

Johnson EJ, Goldstein D (2003) Do defaults save lives? Science 302(5649):1338–1339

Johnson EJ, Hershey J, Meszaros J, Kunreuther H (1993) Framing, probability distortions, and insurance decisions. J Risk Uncertain 7:35–51

Johansson-Stenman O, Konow J (2009) Fairness concerns in environmental economics – do they really matter and if so how? Department of Economics, Loyola-Marymount University, Los Angeles, CA, Working Paper, October 2009

Johnson JP, Myatt DP (2006) On the simple economics of advertising, marketing, and product design. Am Econ Rev 96(3):756–784

Johnson RL, Smith DD (1987) Antitrust division merger procedures and policy, 1968–1984. Antitrust Bull 32(4):967–988, Winter

Jones F (1983) Input biases under rate-of-return regulation. Garland, New York

Jordon WA (1972) Producer protection, prior market structure and the effects of government regulation. J Law Econ 5:151–176

Jorgenson DW, Stiroh KJ (2000) U.S. economic growth at the industry level. Am Econ Rev 90 (2):161–167

Joskow PL, Rose NL (1989) The effects of economic regulation. In: Schmalensee R, Willig RD (eds) Handbook of industrial organization, vol II. North-Holland, New York, pp 1449–1506

Kadiyali V (1996) Entry, its deterrence, and its accommodation: a study of the U.S. photographic film industry. Rand J Econ 27(3):452–478, Autumn

Kadiyali V, Vilcassim N, Chintagunta P (1998) Product line extensions and competitive market interactions: an empirical analysis. J Econometrics 89:339–363

Kahn LM (2007) Cartel behavior and amateurism in college sports. J Econ Perspect 21(1):209–226, Winter

Kahneman D, Knetsch J, Thaler R (1986) Fairness and the assumptions of economics. In: Hogarth RM, Reder MW (eds) Rational choice. University of Chicago Press, Chicago, pp 101–116

Kahneman D (2003) Maps of rationality: psychology for behavioral economics. Am Econ Rev 93(5):1449–1475

Kahneman D, Tversky A (1979) Prospect theory: an analysis of decisions under risk. Econometrica 47(2):263–291

Kamien MI, Schwartz NL (1970) Market structure, elasticity of demand and incentive to invent. J Law Econ 13(1):241–252

Kamien MI, Schwartz NL (1982) Market structure and innovation. Cambridge University Press, Cambridge

Karni E, Schmeidler D (1990) Fixed preferences and changing tastes. Am Econ Rev 80(2): 262–267

Karp LS, Perloff JM (1989) Oligopoly in the rice export market. Rev Econ Stat 71(3):462–470

Katz ML, Rosen HS (1994) Microeconomics. Irwin, Burr Ridge, IL

Keeler TE (1983) Railroads, freight, and public policy. Brookings Institution, Washington, DC

Keeler TE, Teh-Wei H, Barnett PG, Manning WG (1993) Taxation, regulation, and addiction: a demand function for cigarettes based on time-series evidence. J Health Econ 12(1):1–18

Keller KL (2002) Branding and brand equity. In: Weitz B, Wensley R (eds) Handbook of Marketing. Sage Publications, London, UK, pp 151–178

Keillor GK, "News from Lake Wobegon," A Prairie Home Companion radio show, Minnesota Public Radio, ongoing

Kennedy R (1967) Proceedings of the first world conference on smoking and health. American Cancer Society, New York, pp 4–13

Kennickell AB (2009) Ponds and streams: wealth and income in the U.S., 1989–2007. Finance and economics discussion series. Federal Reserve Board, Washington, DC

Kessides IN (1990) Market concentration, contestability, and sunk costs. Rev Econ Stat 72(4): 614–622

Kihlstrom R, Riordan M (1984) Advertising as a signal. J Polit Econ 92:427–450

Kim EH, Singal V (1993) Mergers and market power: evidence from the airline industry. Am Econ Rev 83(3):549–569

Kleessen A (2009) Microsoft aims big guns at Google, Ask consumers to rethink search. Advertising Age, May 25, 2009

Klein B (1988) Vertical integration as organizational ownership: the fisher body – General motors relationship revisited. J Law Econ Organ 4:199–213

Klein B, Crawford R, Alchian A (1978) Vertical integration, appropriable rents, and the competitive contracting process. J Law Econ 21:297–326

Klein B, Leffler K (1981) The role of market forces in assuring contractual performance. J Polit Econ 89(4):615–641

Knutson B, Wimmer GE, Rick S, Hollon NG, Prelec D, Loewenstein G (2008) Neural antecedents of the endowment effect. Neuron 58:814–822

Koller RH, Weiss LW (1989) Price levels and seller concentration: the case of Portland cement. In: Weiss LW (ed) Concentration and price. MIT Press, Cambridge

Kolter P, Armstrong G (1998) Marketing, an introduction. Prentice Hall, Upper Saddle River, NJ

Konow J (2003) Which is the fairest one of all? A positive analysis of justice theories. J Econ Lit 61:1188–1239

Kovacic WE (2009) Assessing the quality of competition policy: the case of horizontal merger enforcement. Compet Pol Int 5:129–150

Krattenmaker TG, Pitofsky R (1988) Antitrust merger policy and the Reagan administration. Antitrust Bull 33(2):211–232

Kreps DM, Scheinkman JA (1983) Quantity precommitment and Bertrand competition yield Cournot outcomes. Bell J Econ 14(2):326–337

Kreps D, Jose S (1983) Quantity precommitment and Bertrand competition yield Cournot outcomes. Bell J Econ 14(2):326–337

Kumbhakar S, Baardsen S, Lien G (2012) A new method for estimating market power with an application to Norwegian sawmilling. Rev Ind Organ 40(2):109–129

Kwoka JE Jr (1984) Advertising and the price and quality of optometric services. Am Econ Rev 74:211–216

Kwoka JE Jr (1985) The Herfindahl Index in theory and practice. Antitrust Bull 30:915–947

Kwoka JE Jr (1993) The sales and competitive effects of styling and advertising practices in the U.S. auto industry. Rev Econ Stat 75:649–656

Kwoka JE Jr (1997) The price effect of bidding conspiracies: evidence from real estate knockouts. Antitrust Bull 42(503):503–516

Kwoka JE Jr., Pollitt M (2010) Do Mergers Improve Efficiency? Evidence from Restructuring the US Electric Power Sector. Int J Ind Organ 28(6):645–656

Kwoka JE Jr, White LJ (2009) Antitrust revolution: economics, competition, and policy. Oxford University Press, New York

Kwoka JE Jr, Shumilkina E (2008) The price effect of eliminating potential competition: evidence from an airline merger. J Ind Econ 58(2):767–793

Kwoka J, Shumilkina E (2010) The price effect of eliminating potential competition: evidence from an airline merger. J Ind Econ 58(4):767–793

Ladha KK (1990) The pivotal role of the judiciary in the deregulation battle between the executive and legislature. Washington University, Washington

LaFraniere S (1991) Ivy league schools agree to halt collaboration on financial aid. The Washington Post, May 23, 1991.

Lafontaine F, Slade M (2007) Vertical integration and firm boundaries: the evidence. J Econ Lit 45:629–685

Laibson D (2001) A cue-theory of consumption. Quart J Econ 116(1):81–119

Lamont OA, Thaler RH (2003) Anomalies: the law of one price in financial markets. J Econ Perspect 17(4):191–202, Fall

Lancaster KJ (1966) A new approach to consumer theory. J Polit Econ 74:132–157

Landes EM, Rosenfield AM (1994) The durability of advertising revisited. J Ind Econ 42:263–274

Landes W, Posner R (1981) Market power in antitrust cases. Harv Law Rev 94:937–996

Langlois RN, Robertson PL (1989) Explaining vertical integration: lessons from the American automobile industry. J Econ Hist 49(2):361–375

La Porta R, Lopez-de-Silanes F, Shleifer A (2008) The economic consequences of legal origins. J Econ Lit 46(2):285–332

Lappen AA (1988) Battling for a bleachhead. Forbes, November 28, 1988, 138

Lau LJ (1982) On identifying the degree of competitiveness from industry price and output data. Econ Lett 10(1–2):93–99

Lazaroff DE (2007) The NCAA in its second century: defender of amateurism or antitrust recidivist. Oregon Law Rev 86(2):329–371

Leamer EE (1996) Questions, theory, and data. In: Medema SG, Samuels WJ (eds) Foundations of research in economics: how do economists do economics? Edward Edgar, Cheltenham, UK

Leamer EE (2007) Linking the theory with the data: that is the core problem in international economics. Handbook of Econometrics, Chapter 67

Lee L, Frederick S, Ariely D (2006) Try it, you'll like it: the influence of expectations, consumption, and revelation on preferences for beer. Psychol Sci 17:1054–1058

Lee T, Wilde LL (1980) Market structure and innovation: a reformulation. Quart J Econ 94(2):429–436

Lehn K, Sykuta M (1997) Antitrust and franchise relocation in professional sports: an economic analysis of the Raiders case. Antitrust Bull 42:541–563, Fall

Leibenstein H (1950) Bandwagon, snob, and Veblen effects in the theory of consumers' demand. Q J Econ 64(2):183–207

Leibenstein H (1966) Allocative Inefficiency v. X-Inefficiency. Am Econ Rev 56(3):392–415

Leijonhufvud A (1997) Models and theories. J Econ Method 4(2):193–197

Leone RP (1995) Generalizing what is known about temporal aggregation and advertising carryover. Market Sci 14:141–150

Lerner AP (1934) The concept of monopoly and the measurement of monopoly power. Rev Econ Stud 1:157–175

Levenstein MC (1995) Mass production conquers the pool: firm organization and the nature of competition in the nineteenth century. J Econ Hist 55(3):575–611

Levenstein MC, Suslow VY (2004) Contemporary international cartels and developing countries: economic effects and implications for competition policy. Antitrust Law J 71(3):801–852

Levenstein MC, Suslow VY (2006) What determines cartel success? J Econ Lit 44:43–95

Levine JB (1988) Clorox makes a daring move in the laundry room. Business Week, May 2, 1988, 36

Levin RC, Klevorick AK, Nelson RR, Winter SG (1987) Appropriating the returns from industrial research and development. Brookings Pap Econ Act 3:783–820

Levinson JC (2007) Guerrilla Marketing. Mariner Books

Levit KR et al (1994) A national health expenditures. Health Care Fin Rev 16(1):247–294

Levitt SD, Dubner SJ (2009) SuperFreakonomics: global cooling, patriotic prostitutes, and why suicide bombers should buy life insurance. HarperCollins, New York

Levitt SD, List J (2007) What do laboratory experiments measuring social preferences reveal about the real world? J Econ Perspect 21(2):153–174

Lewis R, Reiley D (2009) Retail advertising works! Measuring the effects of advertising on sales via a controlled experiment on Yahoo! MIT Working Paper, January 2009

Lichtenberg FR (1987) The effect of government funding on private industrial research and development: a re-assessment. J Ind Econ 36:97–104

Lichtenberg FR (1992) Corporate takeovers and productivity. MIT Press, Cambridge, MA

Lichtenberg FR, Siegel D (1987) Productivity and changes in ownership of manufacturing plants. Brookings Pap Econ Act 3:643–683

Liebowitz S, Margolis SE (1990) The fable of the keys. J Law Econ 33(1):1–26

Lindsey-Mullikin J, Petty RD (2006) Marketing tactics discouraging price search: deception and competition. J Bus Res 64(1):67–73

Lindsey-Mullikin J, Petty RD (2011) Marketing tactics discouraging price search: deception and competition. J Bus Res 64(1):67–73

Lindstrom M (2008) Buyology: truth and lies about why we buy, Broadway Business.

List J (2007) On the interpretation of giving in dictator games. J Polit Econ 115(3):482–492

Littlechild SC (1983) Regulation of British telecommunications' profitability, report to the secretary of state. Department of Industry: Her Majesty's Stationary Office, London

Lo A (2004) The adaptive markets hypothesis: market efficiency from an evolutionary perspective. J Portfolio Manage 30:15–29

Lowenstein G, O'Donoghue T (2005) Animal spirits: affective and deliberative processes in economic behavior. Working paper, Cornell University

Lowenstein G, Rick S, Cohen JD (2008) Neuroeconomics. Annu Rev Psychol 59:647–672

Lyons B, Matraves C, Moffat P (2001) Industrial concentration and market integration in the European Union. Economica 68(269):1–26

Maclaurin WR (1954) Technological progress in some American industries. Am Econ Rev 44(2): 178–189

Madrian BC, Shea D (2001) The power of suggestion: Inertia 401(k) participation and savings behavior. Quart J Econ 116(4):1149–1187

Malkiel B (2011) The efficient-market hypothesis and the financial crisis. Princeton University, Department of Economics

Mankiw NG, Romer D, Weil DN (1992) A contribution to the empirics of economic growth. Q J Econ 107(2):407–437

Malmendier U, Tate G (2008) Who makes acquisitions? CEO overconfidence and market reaction. J Fin Econ 89:20–43

Mancke RB (1974) Causes of interfirm profitability differences: a new interpretation of the evidence. Quart J Econ 88:181–193

Manes S, Andrews P (2002) Gates: how Microsoft's mogul reinvented an industry and made himself the richest man in America. Touchstone, New York

Mankiw GN (2011) Principles of microeconomics. South-Western College Publishing, Cincinnati, OH

Manne HG (1965) Mergers and the market for corporate control. J Polit Econ 73:110–120

Mansfield E (1968) Industrial research and technological innovation: an econometric analysis. W.W. Norton and Co., New York

Marris R (1964) The economic theory of managerial capitalism. The Free Press, Glencoe, IL

Marshall A (1890) Principles of economics. Macmillan, London

Marshall WJ, Yawitz JB, Greenberg E (1984) Incentives for diversification and the structure of conglomerate firms. Southern Econ J 51(1):1–23

Martin S (2002) Advanced industrial economics, 2nd edn. Blackwell Publishers, Malden, Massachusetts

Martin JD, Sayrak A (2003) Corporate diversification and shareholder value: a survey of recent literature. J Corp Fin 9(1):37–57

Martin S (1979) Advertising, concentration, and profitability: the simultaneity problem. Bell J Econ 10:639–647

Martin S (1984) The misuse of accounting rates of return: comment. Am Econ Rev 74:501–506

Martin S (2000) The theory of contestable markets. Department of Economics, Purdue University, Available at http://www.krannert.purdue.edu/faculty/smartin/aie2/contestbk.pdf

Martin S (2002) Advanced industrial organization. Blackwell, Malden MA

Martin S (2005) Petroleum. In: Adams W, Brock JW (eds) The structure of American industry. Pearson Prentice Hall, Upper Saddle River, NJ

Martin S (2007a) Mergers: an overview. Working paper. Department of Economics, Purdue University, IN, USA

Martin S (2007b) Remembrance of things past: antitrust, ideology, and the development of industrial economics. In: Stennek J (ed) The political economy of antitrust. Emerald Group Publishing Limited, England, pp 25–57

Martin S, Scott JT (1998) Market failure and the design of innovative policy. OECD, February 1998, 1–79

Marx K (1875) Critique of the Gotha Program, 1875, retrieved from Part I of http://www.marxists.org/archive/marx/works/1875/gotha/index.htm, April 27, 2011

Mas-Colell A, Whinston MD, Green J (1995) Microeconomic theory. Oxford University Press, New York

Mason ES (1939) Price and production policies of large-scale enterprise. Am Econ Rev 29(1):61–74

Masson RT, Shaanan J (1984) Social costs of oligopoly and the value of competition. Econ J 94(375):520–535

Matraves C (1999) Market structure, R&D and advertising in the pharmaceutical industry. J Ind Econ 47(2):169–194

May DO (1995) Do managerial motives influence firm risk reduction strategies? J Fin 50(4):1291–1309

McAfee RP (2002) Competitive solutions: the strategist's toolkit. Princeton University Press, Princeton

McAfee RP (2007) "Pricing damaged goods," Economics: the open access, Open-Assessment E-Journal, 1, 2007. http://www.economics-ejournal.org/economics/journalarticles/2007-1

McAfee RP, McMillan J, Whinston MA (1989) Multi-product monopoly, commodity bundling, and correlation of values. Quart J Econ 103:371–383

McAfee RP, Mialon HM, Williams MA (2004) What is a barrier to entry. Am Econ Rev 94(2):461–465

McAfee RP, Sibley DS, Williams MA (2009) Oracle's acquisition of PeopleSoft: U.S. v. Oracle (2004). In: Kwoka, JE Jr, LJ White (eds) Antitrust revolution: economics, competition, and policy. New York: Oxford University Press, pp 67–88

McAfee RP, Williams MA (1988) Can event studies detect anticompetitive mergers? Econ Lett 28:199–203

McClure SM, Ericson KM, Laibson DI, Loewenstein G, Cohen JD (2007) Time discounting for primary rewards. J Neurosci 27(21):5796–5804

McClure SM, Laibson DI, Loewenstein G, Cohen JD (2004a) Separate neural systems value immediate and delayed monetary rewards. Science 306:503–507

McClure SM, Li J, Tomlin D, Cypert KS, Montague LM, Montague PR (2004b) Neural correlates of behavioral preference for culturally familiar drinks. Neuron 44(2):379–387

McCluskey JJ, Shreay S (2011) Culture and beer preferences. In: Swinnen JFM (ed) The economics of beer. Oxford University Press, New York, pp 161–170

McFadden D (2006) Free markets and fettered consumers. Am Econ Rev 96(1):5–29

McGee JS (1958) Predatory price cutting: the standard oil (N.J.) case. J Law Econ 1:137–169

McGee JS (1971) In defense of industrial concentration. Praeger, New York

Mcguckin RH, Nguyen SV (1995) On productivity and plant ownership change: new evidence from the longitudinal research database. Rand J Econ 26(2):257–276

McManus JC (1975) The costs of alternative economic organization. Can J Econ 8(3):334–350

Meadows E (1981) Bold departures in antitrust. Fortune, October 5, 1981, 180–188

Means GC (1935a) Industrial prices and their relative inflexibility. US Senate Document 13, 74th Congress, 1st Session, Washington DC

Means GC (1935b) Price inflexibility and the requirements of a stabilizing monetary policy. J Am Stat Assoc 30:401–413

Metwally MM (1975) Advertising and competitive behavior of selected Australian firms. Rev Econ Stat 47:417–427

Milgrom P, Roberts J (1982) Limit pricing and entry under incomplete information: an equilibrium analysis. Econometrica 50:443–459

Milgrom P, Roberts J (1986) Price and advertising as signals of product quality. J Polit Econ 94:796–821

Milgrom P, Shannon C (1994) Monotone comparative statics. Econometrica 62(1):157–180

Mitchell LE (2001) Corporate irresponsibility. Yale University Press, New Haven, CT

Milyo J, Waldfogel J (1999) The effect of price advertising on prices: evidence in the wake of 44 Liquormart. Am Econ Rev 89(5):1081–1096

Modigliani F (1958) New developments on the oligopoly front. J Polit Econ 66(2):215–232

Monteverde K, Teece DJ (1982) Appropriable rents and quasi-vertical integration. J Law Econ 25:403–418

Montgomery CA (1994) Corporate diversification. J Econ Perspect 8(3):163–178

Morgon MS (2002) Symposium on Marshall's tendencies: how models help economists know. Econ Phil 18:5–16

Morrissee B (2007) Scion web strategy takes a stealth approach. Adweek 2(2):12

Mortimer JH (2007) Vertical contracts in the video rental industry. Rev Econ Stud 75(1):165–199

Morton FS (1997) Entry and predation: British shipping cartels 1879–1929. J Econ Manage Strat 6(4):679–724

Moser P (2005) How do patent laws influence innovation? Evidence from nineteenth-century worlds fairs. Am Econ Rev 95(4):1214–1236

Mouawad J (2007) At OPEC Summit, signs of a dysfunctional family. International Harold Tribune, Highbeam Research at http:///www.highbeam.com

Mueller DC (1969) A theory of conglomerate mergers. Quart J Econ 83(4):643–659

Mueller DC (2006) Corporate governance and economic performance. Int Rev Appl Econ 20(5):623–643

Mullin GL, Mullin JC, Mullin WP (1995) The competitive effects of mergers: stock market evidence from the U.S. steel dissolution suit. RAND J Econ 26(2):314–330

Mulholland JP (2007) Behavioral economics and the federal trade commission. Federal Trade Commission, December 12, 2007

Mufson S (2007) Uncertainty hovers over OPEC summit: Cartel contends with politics, prices and its future. The Washington Post, November 16, 2007

Mussa M, Rosen R (1978) Monopoly and product quality. J Econ Theory 18(2):301–317

Nader R (1973) Consumer and corporate accountability. Harcourt Brace Jovanovich, New York

Nagel E (1963) Assumptions in economic theory. Am Econ Rev 52:211–219

Nagler MG (1993) Rather bait than switch: deceptive advertising with bounded consumer rationality. J Public Econ 51:359–378

Narasimhan C (1984) A price discrimination theory of coupons. Market Sci, Spring 1984

Nasar S (1998) A beautiful mind. Simon and Schuster, New York

Nash J (1950) Equilibrium points in n-Person games. Proc Natl Acad Sci 36:48–49

National Association of Attorneys General Antitrust Enforcement (1993) Horizontal merger guidelines of the national association of Attorneys general. The Association, Washington, D.C., March 30, 1993

Naughton K (January 28, 2002) Crisis at Kmart. Newsweek

Murphy MC (2007) Philosophy of law. Blackwell, Malden, MA

Nelson RR (1959) The simple economics of basic scientific research. J Polit Econ 67(3):297–306

Nelson JP (1999) Broadcast advertising and U.S. demand for alcoholic beverages. Southern Econ J 65(4):774–790

Nelson JP (2005) Beer advertising and marketing update: structure, conduct, and social costs. Rev Ind Organ 26(3):269–306

Nelson JP, Young DJ (2001) Do advertising bans work? An international comparison. Int J Advertising 20(3):273–296

Nelson P (1970) Information and consumer behavior. J Polit Econ 78:311–329

Nelson P (1974) Advertising as information. J Polit Econ 82:729–754

Nerlove M, Arrow KJ (1962) Optimal advertising policy under dynamic conditions. Economica 29(114):129–142

Nevid JS (1981) Effects of brand labeling on ratings of product quality. Percept Motor Skills 53:379–387

Nevo A (1998) Identification of the oligopoly solution concept in a differentiated-products industry. Econ Lett 59(3):391–395

Nevo A (2001) Measuring market power in the ready-to-eat cereal industry. Econometrica 69:307–342

Nevo A, Whinston MD (2010) Taking the dogma out of econometrics: structural modeling and credible inference. J Econ Perspect 24(2):69–81

Nevo A, Wolfram C (2002) Prices and coupons for breakfast cereal. Rand J Econ 33:319–339

Newman R (2008) How Toyota could become the U.S. sales champ. U.S. News and World Report

New York Times (1983) Blunt talk on the phone. February 23, 1983, Section D, p. 4

Newton LH (2006) Permission to steal: revealing the roots of corporate scandal, Blackwell Publishing

Nickell SJ (1996) Competition and corporate performance. J Polit Econ 104(4):724–746

Nicholson W, Snyder C (2012) Microeconomic theory: basic principles and extensions. South-Western, OH, USA

Noether M (1988) Competition among hospitals. J Health Econ 7:259–284

Noll RG (1989a) Economic perspectives on the politics of regulation. In: Schmalensee R, Willig RD (eds) Handbook of industrial organization, vol II. North-Holland, New York, pp 1253–1287

Noll RG (1989) The economic theory of regulation after a decade: comments. Brookings Papers on Economic Activity: Microeconomics, 48–58

Nordhaus WD (1969) Inventions, growth, and welfare: a theoretical treatment of technological change. MIT Press, Cambridge, MA

Norton SW (2007) General motors: lost dominance. In: Tremblay VJ, Tremblay CH (eds) Industry and firm studies. Amonk, NY, M.E. Sharpe, pp 269–292

Novshek W (1993) Mathematics for economists. Academic, New York

Okun A (1975) Equality and efficiency: the big trade-off. The Brookings Institution, Washington, DC

Oi W (1971) A Disneyland dilemma: two-part tariffs for a Mickey Mouse monopoly. Quart J Econ 85:77–96

Ordover JA, Saloner G, Salop SC (1990) Equilibrium vertical foreclosure. Am Econ Rev 80(1):127–142

Overstreet TR (1983) Resale price maintenance: economic theories and empirical evidence, Washington D.C.: FTC Bureau of Economics Staff Report

Pakes A, Shankerman M (1984) An exploration into the determinants of R&D intensity. In: Griliches Z (ed) R&D, patents, and productivity. University of Chicago Press, Chicago and London, pp 209–232

Paletta D, Hitt G (2010) House vote sends finance overhaul to senate. Wall Street Journal. July 1, 2010

Palmeri C, Elgin B, Kerwin K (2003) Toyota's Scion: dude, here's your car. Business Week, June 9, 2003

Panzar JC, Rosse JN (1987) Testing for 'monopoly' equilibrium. J Ind Econ 35(4):443–456

Pate RH (2004) International anti-cartel enforcement. Antitrust Division of the U.S. Department of Justice, November 21, 2004

Paul I (2010) Five ways early adopters have been screwed. PCWorld, February 9, 2010, at http://www.pcworld.com/article/188889/five_ways_early_adopters_have_been_screwed.html, accessed May 23, 2010

Pearson ES (1990) 'Student:' a statistical biography of William Sealy Gosset. Oxford University Press, Oxford

Peltzman S (1975) The effects of automobile safety regulation. J Polit Econ 83:677–725

Peltzman S (1976) Toward a more general theory of regulation. J Law Econ, April 1976, 211–240.

Peltzman S (1989) The economic theory of regulation after a decade of deregulation. Brookings Papers on Economic Activity. Microeconomics 1989:1–59

Pepall L, Richards D, Norman G (2008) Industrial organization: contemporary theory and empirical applications. Blackwell Publishing, Malden, MA

Perloff JM, Karp LS, Golan A (2007) Estimating market power and strategies. Cambridge University Press, New York

Perloff JM, Shen EZ (2012) Collinearity in linear structural models of market power. Rev Ind Organ. 40(2):131–138

Perry MK (1980) Forward integration by Alcoa: 1888–1930. J Ind Econ 29(1):37–53

Perry MK (1989) Vertical integration: determinants and effects. In: Schmalensee R, Willig RD (eds) Handbook of industrial organization, volume 1, 183–255

Perry W (2007) OPEC struggles to maintain control. Middle East Economic Digest, November 23, 2007

Phillips A, Stevenson RE (1974) The historical development of industrial organization. Hist Polit Econ 1974, 324–342

Pigou AC (1920) The economics of welfare. MacMillan, London

Pindyck RS (1985) The measurement of monopoly power in dynamic markets. J Law Econ 28(1):193–222

Pindyck RS, Rubenfield DL (2009) Microeconomics. Pearson Prentice Hall, Upper Saddle River, NJ

Pitofsky R (1977) Beyond Nader: consumer protection and the regulation of advertising. Harv Law Rev 90(4):661–701

Pitofsky R (ed) (2008) How the Chicago school overshot the mark. Oxford University Press, New York

Plassman H, O'Doherty J, Shiva B, Ragel A (2008) Marketing actions can modulate neural representations of experienced pleasantness. Proc Natl Acad Sci 105(3):1050–1054

Plott CR (2007) An updated review of industrial organization: applications of experimental economics. In: Armstrong M, Porter R (eds) Handbook of industrial organization, vol 3. Elsevier North Holland, Boston

Pollay RW (1994) Promises, promises: self-regulation of US cigarette broadcast advertising in the 1960s. Tob Control 3:134–144

Porter ME (1976) Interbrand choice, media mix, and market performance. Am Econ Rev 66(2):398–406

Porter RH (1994) Recent developments in empirical industrial organization. J Econ Edu 25:149–161

Porter RH (1983) A study of cartel stability: the joint executive committee, 1880–1886. Bell J Econ 14:301–314

Posner RA (1970) A statistical study of antitrust enforcement. J Law Econ 13(2):365–419

Posner RA (1973) Regulation and advertising by the FTC. American Enterprise Institute, Washington DC

Posner RA (1974) Advertising as an impediment to competition: dialogue. In: Goldschmid HJ, Mann HM, Weston JF (eds) Industrial concentration: the new learning. Little, Brown, Boston, pp 156–161

Posner RA (1974) Theories of economic regulation. Bell J Econ, Autumn 1974, 335–358.

Posner RA (1975) The social cost of monopoly and regulation. J Polit Econ 83:807–827

Posner RA (1979) The Chicago School of antitrust analysis. Univ Penn Law Rev 127:925–952

Posner RA (2001) Antitrust law. University of Chicago Press, Chicago

Posner RA (2009) The failure of capitalism: the crisis of 08 and the descent into depression. Harvard University Press, Cambridge, MA

Poundstone W (1992) Prisoner's dilemma. Doubleday Books, New York

Powell I (1987) The effect of reductions in concentration on income distribution. Rev Econ Stat 69(1):75–82

Prager RA, Hannan TH (1998) Do substantial horizontal mergers generate significant price effects? Evidence from the banking industry. J Ind Econ 46(4):433–452

Preston IL (1996) The Great American blowup: puffery in advertising and selling. The University of Wisconsin Press, Madison, WI

Priest GL (1977) The common law process and the selection of efficient rules. J Legal Stud 6(1):65–82

Putsis WP Jr (1997) An empirical study of the effect of brand proliferation on private label – national brand pricing behavior. Rev Ind Organ 12:355–371

Rabin M (1998) Psychology and economics. J Econ Lit 36:11–46

Rabin M, Schrag JL (1999) First impressions matter: a model of confirmatory bias. Quart J Econ 114(1):37–82

Ramsey F (1927) A contribution to the theory of taxation. Econ J 37:47–61

Randall L (2011) How science can lead the way: what we lose when we put faith over logic. Time, October 3, 2011, 20

Rasmusen E (2007) Games and Information: an introduction to game theory. Blackwell, Oxford, UK

Ravenscraft DJ, Scherer FM (1987) Mergers, sell-offs, and economic efficiency. Brookings Institution, Washington DC

Rey P, Tirole J (2007) A primer on foreclosure. In: volume III (ed) Handbook of Industrial Organization. Armstrong M, Porter R, North-Holland, Amsterdam, pp 2145–2220

Rechtin M (2006) Scion's dilemma: be hip – but avoid the mainstream. Automotive News, May 22, 2006, 432-46

Rees R (1985a) The theory of principle and agent, Part I. Bull Econ Res 37(1):3–26

Rees R (1985b) The theory of principle and agent, Part II. Bull Econ Res 37(2):75–97

Reinganum JF (1983) Uncertain innovation and the persistence of monopoly. Am Econ Rev 73:741–748

Reinganum JF (1984) Practical implications of game theoretic models of R&D. Am Econ Rev 74:61–66

Reinganum JF (1985) Innovation and industry evolution. Quart J Econ 100(1):81–99

Reinganum JF (1989) The timing of innovation: research, development, and diffusion. In: Richard S, Willig RD (eds) Handbook of industrial organization. North-Holland, Amsterdam, pp 849–905

Reder MW (1982) Chicago Economics: permanence and change. J Econ Lit 20(1):1–38

Rick S, Loewenstein G (2008) Intangibility in intertemporal choice. Phil Transact Roy Soc B 363:3813–3824

Riordan MH (1998) Anticompetitive vertical integration by a dominant firm. Am Econ Rev 88:1232–1248

Ripley WZ (1907) Industrial concentration as shown by the Census. Quart J Econ 21(4):651–658

Ripley WZ (ed) (1916) Trusts, pools and corporations, Rev Edn Ginn, Boston

Roberts MJ, Samuelson L (1988) An empirical analysis of dynamic, nonprice competition in an oligopolistic industry. Rand J Econ 19(2):200–220

Robinson J (1933) The economics of imperfect competition. Macmillan, London

Robinson WT, Chiang J (1996) Are Sutton's predictions robust?: empirical insights into advertising, R&D, and concentration. J Ind Econ 44(4):389–408

Roe MJ (1996) Chaos and evolution in law and economics. Harv Law Rev 109(3):641–668

Roe MJ, Siegel JI (2009) Finance and politics: a review essay based on Kenneth Dam's analysis of legal traditions in the law – growth Nexus. J Econ Lit 47(3):781–800

Roll R (1986) The hubris hypothesis of corporate takeovers. J Bus 59(2, Part 1):197–216

Rogers EM (1962) Diffusion of innovations. Free Press, Glencoe

Rooney J (2010) A look back at 10 ideas that changed the marketing world. Advertising Age, February 15, 2010, 14.

Rosenthal RW (1991) Games of perfect information, predatory pricing, and the chain-store paradox. J Econ Theory 25:92–100

Rosse JN (1970) Estimating cost function parameters without using cost data: illustrated methodology. Econometrica 38(2):256–275

Rotemberg JJ, Saloner G (1986) A supergame-theoretic model of price wars during booms. Am Econ Rev 76(3):390–407

Roth AE, Prasnikar V, Okuno-Fujiwara M, Zamir S (1991) Bargaining and market behavior in Jerusalem, Ljubljana, Pittsburgh, and Tokyo: an experimental study. Am Econ Rev 81(5): 1068–1095

Rubin PH (1977) Why is the common law efficient? J Legal Stud 6(1):51–63

Rubin PH (1978) The theory of the firm and the structure of the franchise contract. J Law Econ 21:223–233

Rubinstein A (1982) Perfect equilibrium in a bargaining model. Econometrica 50:97–109

Sack AL (1991) The underground economy of college football. Sociol Sport J 8(1):1–15

Salant SW, Switzer S, Reynolds RJ (1983) Losses from horizontal merger: the effects of an exogenous change in industry structure on Cournot-Nash equilibrium. Quart J Econ 98(2):185–213

Salinger MA (1988) Vertical mergers and market foreclosure. Quart J Econ 103:345–356

Salinger MA (2010) Behavioral economics, consumer protection, and antitrust. Competition Policy International, Spring 2010

Saloojee Y, Dagli E (2000) Tobacco industry tactics for resisting public policy on health. Bull World Health Organ 78(7):1–12

Salop S (1979) Monopolistic competition with outside goods. Bell J Econ 10:141–156

Salop S, Stiglitz J (1977) Bargains and ripoffs: a model of monopolistically competitive price dispersion. Rev Econ Stud 44(3):493–510

Salop S (1986) Practices that (credibly) facilitate oligopoly coordination. In: Stiglitz J, Mathewson GF (eds) New developments in the analysis of market structure. MIT Press, Cambridge, MA

Salvo A (2011) Inferring market power under the threat of entry: the case of the Brazilian cement industry. Rand J Econ 41(2):326–350

Samuelson L (1997) Evolutionary games and equilibrium selection. MIT Press, Cambridge, MA

Samuelson RJ (2008) OPEC's triumph: acting like a true cartel – with America's help. The Washington Post, March 12, 2008

Santos L (2010) A Monkey economy as irrational as ours. TEDGlobal 2010, http://www.ted.com/talks/lang/eng/laurie_santos.html, accessed March 4, 2011

Sappington DEM (1983) Optimal regulation of a multiproduct monopoly with unknown technological capabilities. Bell J Econ 14(2):453–463

Sappington DEM (2002) Price Regulation. In: Cave ME, Majemdar SK, Vogelsang I (eds) Handbook of telecommunications. Vol. 1, Structure, regulation, and competition. Elsevier, Amsterdam:

Sass TR (2005) The competitive effects of exclusive dealing: evidence from the U.S. beer industry. Int J Ind Organ 23:203–225

Sayette MA, Loewenstein G, Griffin KM, Black JJ (2008) Exploring the cold-to-hot empathy gap in smokers. Psychol Sci 19(9):926–932

Schelling TC (1960) The strategy of conflict. Harvard University Press, Cambridge, MA

Scherer FM (1965) Invention and innovation in the Watt-Boulton steam-engine venture. Technol Cult 6:165–187

Scherer FM (1979) The welfare economics of product variety: an application to the ready-to-eat cereals industry. J Ind Econ 28:113–134

Scherer FM (1980) Industrial market structure and economic performance. Rand McNally, Chicago

Scherer FM (1986) The breakfast cereal industry. In: Adams W (ed) The structure of American industry. MacMillan, New York

Scherer FM (1996) Industry structure, strategy, and public policy. Harper Collins College Publishers, New York

Scherer FM, Beckenstein A, Kaufer E, Murphy RD (1975) The economics of multi-plant operation: an international comparisons study. Harvard University Press, Cambridge

Scherer FM, Ross D (1990) Industrial market structure and economic performance. Houghton Mifflin Co., Boston

Schmalensee R (1973) A note on the theory of vertical integration. J Polit Econ 81(2):442–449

Schmalensee R (1978) Entry deterrence in the ready-to-eat breakfast cereal industry. Bell J Econ 9:305–327

Schmalensee R (1979) On the use of economic models in antitrust: the ReaLemon case. University of Pennsylvania Law Review 127:994–1050

Schmalensee R (1981) Output and welfare implications of monopolistic third-degree price discrimination. Am Econ Rev 71:242–247

Schmalensee R (1988) Industrial economics: an overview. Econ J 98(392):643–681

Schmalensee R (1989) Inter-industry studies of structure and performance. In: Schmalensee R, Willig RD (eds) Handbook of industrial organization, vol II. North-Holland, New York, pp 951–1009

Schmalensee R (2009) Should new merger guidelines give UPP market definition? Competition Policy International, December 2009, at http://www.competitionpolicyinternational.com

Schmidt P (1985–1986) Frontier production functions. Econ Rev 4: 289–328

Schumpeter JA (1934) The theory of economic development: an inquiry into profits, capital, interest, and the business cycle. Harvard University Press, Cambridge

Schumpeter JA (1942) Capitalism, socialism, and democracy. Harper and Row, New York

Schumpeter JA (1954) History of economic analysis. Oxford University Press, Oxford

Scherer FM (1980) Industrial market structure and economic performance, 2nd edn. Rand McNally, Chicago

Scherer FM (1983) The economics of vertical restraints. Antitrust Law J 52:687–707

Schwartz M (1986) The nature and scope of contestability theory. Oxford Econ Pap 38:37–57

Scott MF (1997) Entry and predation: british shipping cartels 1879–1929. J Econ Manage Strat 6(4):679–724

Seib G (1998) Antitrust suits expand and libertarians ask, who's the bad guy? Wall Street J, Classroom Edition, 1998, at http://info.wsj.com/classroom/archive/wsjce.98nov.politics.html

Seldon BJ, Banerjee S, Boyd RG (1993) Advertising conjectures and the nature of advertising competition in an oligopoly. Manag Decis Econ 14:489–498

Seldon BJ, Doroodian K (1989) A simultaneous model of cigarette advertising: effects of demand and industry response to public policy. Rev Econ Stat 71:673–677

Seldon BJ, Jewell RT, O'Brien DM (2000) Media substitution and economies of scale in advertising. Int J Ind Organ 18(8):1153–1180

Selten R (1965) Spieltheoretische behandlung eines oligopolmodells mit nachfragetragheit. Zeitschrift fuer die gesampte Staatswissenschaft 121(301–329):667–689

Selten R (1965) Spieltheoretische Behandlung eines Oligopolymodells mit Nachfragetragheit. Zeitschrift fur die gesamte Staatswissenschaft 121:667–689

Selten R (1975) Reexamination of the perfectness concept for equilibrium points in extensive games. Int J Game Theory 4(1):25–55

Sen A (1970) The impossibility of a paretian liberal. J Polit Econ 78(1):152–157

Shao M (1991) A bright idea that Clorox wishes it never had. Business Week, June 24, 1991, 118–119

Shapiro C (1980) Advertising and welfare: comment. Bell J Econ 11(2):49–52

Shelanski HA, Sidak JG (2001) Antitrust divestiture in network industries. University of Chicago Law Rev 68(1):1–93

Shepherd WG (1997) The economics of industrial organization: analysis, markets, policies, 4th edn. Prentice Hall, Upper Saddle River, N.J

Shepherd WG (1984) 'Contestabilty' versus competition. Am Econ Rev 74:572–587

Sherman R (1974) The economics of industry. Little Brown, Boston

Sherman R (1992) Capital waste in the rate-of-return regulated firm. J Regul Econ 4:197–204

Sherman R (2008) Market regulation. Pearson Addison-Wesley, Boston

Sheth JN, Newman BI, Gross BL (1991) Consumption values and market choices: theory and applications. Thompson South-Western

Shih J, Mai C, Liu J (1988) A general analysis of the output effect under third-degree price discrimination. Econ J 98:149–158

Shiller RJ (2005) Irrational exuberance. Princeton University Press, Princeton

Shleifer A, Vishny RW (1989) Management entrenchment: the case of manager-specific investments. J Fin Econ 25:123–139

Shleifer A, Vishny RW (1997) A survey of corporate governance. J Fin 52(2):737–783

Shubik M (1971) The dollar auction game: a paradox in noncooperative behavior and excalation. J Conflict Resolut 15(1):109–111

Shubik M (1980) Structure and behavior. Harvard University Press, Cambridge

Shubik M (1982) Game theory for social sciences. MIT Press, Cambridge, MA

Shughart WF II (1990) The organization of industry. BPI Irwin, Boston

Shy O (1995) Industrial organization: theory and applications. MIT Press, Cambridge, MA

Shy O (2011) A short survey of network economics. Rev Ind Organ 38(2):119–149

Siegfried J, Blitz RC, Round DK (1995) The limited role of market power in generating great fortunes in Great Britain, the United States, and Australia. J Ind Econ 43(3):277–286

Silberberg E (1985) Nutrition and the demand for tastes. J Polit Econ 93(5):881–900

Simon CP, Blume L (1994) Mathematical economics. W.W. Norton, New York

Simon HA (1955) A behavioral model of rational choice. Quart J Econ 69(1):99–118

Singal V (1996) Airline mergers and multimarket contact. Manag Decis Econ 17(6):559–574

Singh N, Vives X (1984) Price and quantity competition in a differentiated duopoly. Rand J Econ 15(4):546–554

Slade ME (1987) Interfirm Rivalry in a Repeated Game: An Empirical Test of Tacit Collusion. J Ind Econ 35(4):499–516

Slade M (1995) Empirical games: the oligopoly case. Can J Econ 28:368–402

Sloan AP (1963) My years with General Motors. Doubleday, New York

Sloan FA, Ostermann J, Picone G, Conover C, Taylor DH (2004) The price of smoking. MIT Press, Cambridge MA

Smeeding TM, Thompson JP (2010) Recent trends in the distribution of income: labor, wealth and more complete measures of well being. Political Economy Research Institute, University of Massachusetts, Amherst

Smiley R (1988) Empirical evidence on strategic entry deterrence. Int J Ind Organ 6:167–180

Smith A (1776) An inquiry into the nature and causes of the wealth of nations

Sobel J, Takahashi I (1983) A multistage model of bargaining. Rev Econ Stud 50(3):411–426

Solomon RC (2008) Free enterprise, sympathy, and virtue. In: Zak PJ (ed) Moral markets: the critical role of values in the economy. Princeton University Press, Princeton

Spence AM (1975) Monopoly: quality and regulation. Bell J Econ 6:417–429

Spence AM (1976) Product differentiation and welfare. Am Econ Rev 66:407–414

Spengler JJ (1950) Vertical integration and antitrust policy. J Polit Econ 58:347–352

Spiller PT, Favaro E (1984) The effects of entry regulation on oligopolistic interaction: the Uruguayan Banking Sector. RAND J Econ 15(2):244–254

von Stackelberg H (1934) Marktform und Gleichgewicht. Julius Springer, Vienna

Stanovich KE, West RF (2000) Individual differences in reasoning: implications for the rationality debate? Behav Brain Sci 23(5):645–665

Stavins J (2001) Price discrimination in the airline market: the effect of market concentration. Rev Econ Stat 83(1)

Steinberg CS (1980) TV facts. Facts on File, Inc., New York

Stelzer IM (1976) Selected antitrust cases. Richard D, Irwin, Homewood

Stevenson R (1982) X-efficiency and interfirm rivalry: evidence in the electric utility industry. Land Econ 58:52–66

Stigler GJ (1949) Monopolistic competition in retrospect. In: five lectures in economic problems. Longmans, Green, and Co., London, pp 12–24, reprinted in GJ Stigler (1968) The organization of industry. Richard D. Irwin, Inc., Homewood, IL

Stigler GJ (1950) Monopoly and oligopoly by merger. Am Econ Rev 40(2):23–34

Stigler GJ (1951) The division of labor is limited by the extent of the market. J Polit Econ 59(3): 185–193

Stigler GJ (1955) Mergers and preventive antitrust policy. Univ Penn Law Rev 104(2):176–184

Stigler GJ (1964) A theory of oligopoly. J Polit Econ 72(1):44

Stigler GJ (1966) The theory of price. Macmillan, New York

Stigler GJ (1968) The organization of industry. Richard D. Irwin, Homewood, IL

Stigler GJ (1971) The theory of economic regulation. Bell J Econ Manage Strat 2(1):3–21

Stigler GJ, Kindahl JK (1973) Industrial prices, as administered by Dr. Means. Am Econ Rev 63(4):717–721

Stigler GJ (1976) The Xistence of X-efficiency. Am Econ Rev 66(1):213–216

Stigler GJ, Becker GS (1977) De Gustibus Non Est Disputandum. Am Econ Rev 67(2):76–90

Stigler GJ, Friedland C (1962) What can regulators regulate: the case of electricity. J Law Econ 5:1–16

Stiglitz J (1987) Technological change, sunk costs, and competition. Brookings Pap Econ Act 1987(3):883–937

Stillman R (1983) Examining antitrust policy towards horizontal mergers. J Financ Econ 11:225–240

Stone DF (2012) Testing Bayesian Updating with the AP Top 25. Economic Inquiry forthcoming.

Stivers A, Tremblay VJ (2005) Advertising search costs, and welfare. Inform Econ Pol 17(3): 317–333

Strack F, Martin L, Schwarz N (1988) Priming and communication: social determinants of information úse in judgments of life satisfaction. Eur J Soc Psychol 18(5):429–442

Strotz RH (1956) Myopia and inconsistency in dynamic utility maximization. Rev Econ Stud 23:165–180

Studenmund AH (2005) Using econometrics, 5th edn. Addison Wesley, Boston

Sullivan DA (1985) Testing hypotheses about firm behavior in the cigarette industry. J Polit Econ 93(3):586–598

Sumner DA (1981) Measurement of monopoly behavior: an application to the cigarette industry. J Polit Econ 89:1010–1019

Suslow VY (1986) Estimating monopoly behavior with competitive recycling: an application to Alcoa. Rand J Econ 17(3):389–403

Suslow VY (2005) Cartel contract duration: empirical evidence from inter-war international cartels. Ind Corp Change 14(5):705–744

Sutton J (1991) Sunk costs and market structure. MIT Press, Cambridge

Sutton J (1997) Gibrat's Legacy. Journal of Economic Literature 35(1):40–59

Sutton J (1999) Technology and market structure. MIT Press, Cambridge

Sutton J (2002) Marshall's tendencies: how models help economists know. MIT Press, Cambridge, MA

Sutton J (2007) Market structure: theory and evidence. In: Armstrong M, Porter R (eds) Handbook of industrial organization, vol 3. Elsevier North Holland, Boston

Svenson O (1981) Are we all less risky and more skillful than our fellow drivers? Acta Psychol 47:143–148

Sweeting A (2010) The effects of mergers on product positioning: evidence from the music radio industry. Rand J Econ 41(2):372–397

Swinnen JFM (ed) (2011) The economics of beer. Oxford University Press, New York

Sylos-Labini P (1962) Oligopoly and technological progress. Harvard University Press, Cambridge

Symeonidis G (2000) Price competition and market structure: the impact of restrictive practices legislation on concentration in the U.K. J Ind Econ 48(1):1–26

Symeonidis G (2000) Price competition and market structure: the impact of cartel policy on concentration in the UK. J Ind Econ 48(1):1–26

Symeonidis G (2001) The effects of competition: cartel policy and the evolution of strategy and structure in British industry. MIT Press, Cambridge

Symeonidis G (2003) In which industries is collusion more likely? Evidence from the UK. J Ind Econ 51(1):45–74

Takayama A (1969) Behavior of the firm under regulatory constraint. Am Econ Rev 59:255–260

Taylor WE, Zona JD (1997) An analysis of the state of competition in long-distance telephone markets. J Regul Econ 11(3):227–255

Tennant RB (1950) The American cigarette industry. Yale University Press, New Haven

Thaler RH, Sunstein CR (2003) Libetarian paternalism. Am Econ Rev 93(2):175–179

Thaler RH, Sunstein CR (2008) Nudge: improving decisions about health, wealth, and happiness. Yale University Press, New Haven

Thomas CJ, Willig RD (2006) The risk of contagion from multimarket contact. Int J Ind Organ 24(6):1157–1184

Thomas LG (1989) Advertising in consumer good industries: durability, economies of scale, and heterogeneity. J Law Econ 32:164–194

Thomas L Jr. (2008) FBI arrests 2 former Bear Sterns hedge fund managers. New York Times, June 16, 2008

Thomas RP (1977) An analysis of the pattern of growth of the automobile industry, 1895–1929. Arno Press, New York

Tirole J (1988) The theory of industrial organization. MIT Press, Cambridge, MA

Tremblay VJ, Tremblay CH (1988) The determinants of horizontal acquisitions: evidence from the U.S. brewing industry. J Ind Econ 37(1):21–45

Tremblay CH, Tremblay VJ (1995a) Advertising, price, and welfare: evidence from the U.S. brewing industry. Southern Econ J 62(2):367–381

Tremblay CH, Tremblay VJ (1995b) Firm success, national status, and product line diversification: an empirical examination. Rev Ind Organ 11(6):771–789

Tremblay CH, Tremblay VJ (1996) Firm success, national status, and product line diversification: an empirical examination. Rev Ind Organ 11(6):771–789

Tremblay CH, Tremblay VJ (2010) The neglect of monotone comparative statics methods. J Econ Edu 41(2):177–193

Tremblay CH, Tremblay VJ (2011a) The Cournot-Bertrand Model and the degree of product differentiation. Econ Lett 111(3):233–235

Tremblay CH, Tremblay VJ (2011b) Recent economic developments in the import and craft segments of the U.S. brewing industry. In: Swinnen JFM (ed) The economics of beer. Oxford University Press, New York, pp 141–160

Tremblay CH, Tremblay MJ, Tremblay VJ (2011) A general Cournot-Bertrand model with homogeneous goods. Theor Econ Lett 2:38–40

Tremblay VJ (1993) Consistency between the law and its enforcement: the case of mergers. Antitrust Bull 38(2):327–348

Tremblay VJ, Iwasaki N, Tremblay CH (2005) The dynamics of industry concentration for U.S. micro and macro brewers. Rev Ind Organ 26(3):307–324

Tremblay VJ, Filho CM (2001) A model of vertical differentiation, brand loyalty, and persuasive advertising. In: Baye M, Nelson J (eds) Advances in applied microeconomics: advertising and differentiated products, vol 10. JAI Press, New York, pp 221–238

Tremblay VJ, Polasky S (2002) Advertising with subjective horizontal and vertical product differentiation. Rev Ind Organ 20(3):253–265

Tremblay VJ, Tremblay CH (1988) The determinants of horizontal acquisitions: evidence from the U.S. brewing industry. J Ind Econ 37(1):21–45

Tremblay VJ, Tremblay CH (2005) The U.S. brewing industry: data and economic analysis. MIT Press, Cambridge

Tremblay VJ, Tremblay CH (2007) Brewing: games firms play. In: Tremblay CH, Tremblay VJ (eds) Industry and firm studies. ME Sharpe, Armonk, NY

Tremblay VJ, Tremblay CH, Isariyawongse K (forthcoming) Endogenous timing and strategic choice: the Cournot-Bertrand model. Bull Econ Res

Tremblay VJ, Tremblay CH, Isariyawongse K (forthcoming) Cournot and Bertrand competition when advertising rotates demand: the case of Honda and Scion. Int J Econ Bus

Tullock G (1967) The welfare costs of tariffs, monopolies, and theft. Western Econ J 5(3):224–232

Tversky A, Kahneman D (1992) Advances in prospect theory: cumulative representation of uncertainty. J Risk Uncertainty 5(4):297–323

Tversky A, Kahneman D (1981) The framing of decisions and the psychology of choice. Science 211:453–458

Tversky A, Kahneman D (1991) Loss aversion and riskless choice. Quart J Econ 106(4):1039–1061

US Department of Justice (1968) Merger Guidelines. Available at http://www.justice.gov/atr/public/guidelines

US Department of Justice (1982) Merger Guidelines. Available at http://www.justice.gov/atr/public/guidelines

US Department of Justice (1984) Merger Guidelines. Available at http://www.justice.gov/atr/public/guidelines

US Department of Justice and the Federal Trade Commission (1992) Merger Guidelines. Available at http://www.justice.gov/atr/public/guidelines

US Department of Justice and the Federal Trade Commission (1997) Merger Guidelines. Available at http://www.justice.gov/atr/public/guidelines

U.S. Department of Justice (2008) LG, Sharp, Chunghwa agree to plead guilty, pay total of $585 million in fines for participating in LCD price-fixing conspiracies. November 12, 2008, www. usdoj.gov

U.S. Department of Justice (2009) Taiwan LCD producer agrees to plead guilty and pay $220 million fine for participating in LCD price-fixing conspiracy. December 9, 2009, www.usdoj.gov

US Department of Justice and the Federal Trade Commission (2010) Merger Guidelines. Available at http://www.justice.gov/atr/public/guidelines

Van Cayseele PJG (1998) Market structure and innovation: a survey of the last twenty years. De Economist 146(3):391–417

Van Cayseele PJG (1998) Market structure and innovation: a survey of the last twenty years. De Economist 146(3):391–417

Van Overtveldt J (2007) The Chicago school: how the University of Chicago assembled the thinkers who revolutionized economics and business. Chicago, The B2 Book

Van Veen V, Krug MK, Schooler JW, Carter CS (2009) Neural activity predicts attitude change in cognitive dissonance. Nat Neurosci 12:1469–1475

Vincent VV, Krug MK, Schooler JW, Carter CS (2009) Neural activity predicts attitude change in cognitive dissonance. Nat Neurosci 12(1):1469–1475

Vardanyan M, Tremblay VJ (2006) The measurement of marketing efficiency in the presence of spillovers: theory and evidence. Manag Decis Econ 27(5):319–331

Varian HR (1974) Equity, envy, and efficiency. J Econ Theor 9:63–91

Varian HR (1980) A model of sales. Am Econ Rev 70:651–659

Varian HR (1992) Microeconomic analysis. W.W. Norton, New York

Varian HR (1997) How to build an economic model in your spare time. Am Economist 41(2):3–10

Varian HR (2010) Intermediate microeconomics: a modern approach. W.W. Norton, New York

Veblen T (1899) The theory of the leisure class. Macmillan

Vernon JM, Graham DA (1971) Profitability of monopolization by vertical integration. J Polit Econ 79(5):924–925

Villalonga B (2004) Does diversification cause the 'diversity discount'? Fin Manag 33(2):5–27

Viscusi WK, Harrington JE, Vernon JM (2005) Economics of regulation and antitrust. MIT Press, Cambridge, MA

Vives X, Pricing O (1999) Old ideas and new tools. MIT Press, Cambridge, MA

Vogelsang I (2002) Incentive regulation and competition in public utility markets: a 20-year perspective. J Regul Econ 22(1):5–27

Von Kalinowski J (1982) Antitrust laws and trade regulation. Mathew Bender and Co, New York

Von Stackelberg H (1952) The theory of the market economy. Oxford University Press, Oxford, England

von Weizsacker CC (1980) A welfare analysis of barriers to entry. Bell J Econ 11(2):399–420

Wacks R (2006) Philosophy of law: a very short introduction. Oxford University Press, New York

Waldman DE (1986) The economics of antitrust: cases and analysis. Little, Brown, and Company, Boston

Waldman DE, Jensen EJ (2006) Industrial organization: theory and practice. Person Addison-Wesley, Boston

Waldman Don E, Ruffer R (2007) Microsoft: who is Microsoft today? In: Tremblay VJ, Tremblay CH (eds) Industry and firm studies. M.E. Sharpe, Armonk, NY

Ward RW (2006) Commodity checkoff programs and generic advertising. Choices 21:55–60

Watson J (2002) Strategy: an introduction to game theory. W.W. Norton & Co., New York

Wauthy X (1996) Quality choice in models of vertical differentiation. J Ind Econ 44(3):345–353

Weiher JC, Sickles RC, Perloff JM (2002) Market power in the U.S. airline industry. In: Slottje DJ (ed) Economic issues in measuring market power: contributions to economic analysis, vol 255. Elsevier, Amsterdam

Weinstein ND (1980) Unrealistic optimism about future life events. J Pers Soc Psychol 39(5): 806–820

Weintraub ER (2002) How economics became a mathematical science. Duke University Press, Durham, NC

Weiss LW (1974) The concentration-profits relationship and antitrust. In: Goldschmidt HJ, Mann HM, Weston JF (eds) Industrial concentration: the new learning. Little Brown and Company, Boston, pp 184–245

Welch D (2007) Scion's street credentials. Business Week, April 27, 2007, 11

Werden GJ, Froeb L, Shor M (2010) Behavioral antitrust and merger control. Vanderbilt University Law School, Working Paper Number 10–14, May 2010

Winston C (1993) Economic deregulation: days of reckoning for microeconomists. J Econ Lit 31(3):1263–1289

Winston C (1998) U.S. industry adjustment to economic deregulation. J Econ Perspect 12(3):89–110

Whinston MD (2007) Antitrust policy toward horizontal mergers. In: Armstrong M, Porter RH (eds) Handbook of industrial organization, vol 3. Elsevier North-Holland, Boston, pp 2369–2440

White LJ (1971) The US automobile industry since 1945. Harvard University Press, Cambridge, MA

White LJ (2002) Trends in aggregate concentration in the United States. J Econ Perspect 16(4):137–160

Williamson OE (1968) Economies as an antitrust defense: the welfare trade-offs. Am Econ Rev 58(1):18–36

Williamson OE (1975) Markets and heirachies: analysis and antitrust implications: a study in the economics of internal organization. The Free Press, New York

Williamson OE (1985) The economic institutions of capitalism: firms, markets, and relational contracting. The Free Press, New York

Willig R (2011) Unilateral competitive effects of mergers: upward pricing pressure, product quality, and other extensions. Rev Ind Organ 39(1–2):19–38

Wilson EB (1952) An introduction to scientific research. McGraw-Hill

Wilson RD (1976) An empirical evaluation of comparative advertising messages. Adv Consum Res 3:53–57

Wolff EN (2009) Poverty and income distribution. Wiley-Blackwell, Malden, MA

Wolfram CD (1999) Measuring market power in the British electricity spot market. Am Econ Rev 89(4):805–826

Wolinsky A (1987) Brand names and price discrimination. J Ind Econ 35(3):255–268

Wooldridge J (2009) Introductory econometrics: a modern approach, 4th edn. South-Western College Publishing, Cincinnati, OH

Wootton B (1938) Lament for economics. George, Allen, and Unwin, London

Wright JD (2007) Behavioral law and economics, paternalism, and consumer contracts: an empirical investigation. New York University Journal of law and Liberty, 470–511

Wright JD (2009) Overshot the Mark? A simple explanation of the Chicago School's influence on antitrust. Competition Policy International, March 31, 2009

Zak PJ (ed) (2008) Moral markets: the critical role of values in the economy. Princeton University Press, Princeton

Zanchettin P (2006) Differentiated duopoly with asymmetric costs. J Econ Manag Strat 15(4):999–1015

Zulehner C (2003) Testing dynamic oligopolistic interaction. Int J Ind Organ 21(10):1527–1556

Index

V.J. Tremblay and C.H. Tremblay, *New Perspectives on Industrial Organization*,
Springer Texts in Business and Economics, DOI 10.1007/978-1-4614-3241-8,
© Springer Science+Business Media New York 2012

Experience good, 173–175, 427, 433, 434, 459,
   712, 729, 731
Explicit collusion, 213, 237
Extensive form representative of a game, 298
Externalities
   and advertising, 471, 474, 475, 478, 480,
      482, 484, 731
   and cartels, 474
Eyeglasses, 479

F

F. Hoffmann-La Roche, 215, 235, 236
Fabio, P., 535
Fads, 36, 103, 106
Failing firm defense, 614
Fair Packaging and Labeling Act (1966),
   631, 642
Fair rate of return, 626
Fairfax, L.M., 594, 595
False advertising *See* Advertising
Fame, E., 658
Färe, R., 438
Farr, S., 455, 481, 639, 653
Farrell, J., 615
Farrelly, M.C., 639
Fat cat strategy, 306
Federal Alcohol Administration Act
   (1935), 638
Federal Baseball Club v. National League
   (1922), 606, 607
Federal Communication Commission, 638
Federal Deposit Insurance Corporation
   (FDIC), 620
Federal News Service, 235
Federal Trade Commission
   act (1914), 15, 596, 597, 630, 636, 640,
      642, 661
   and antitrust enforcement, 620
   and unfair business practices, 630, 640
Federal Trade Commission Act (1914), 15,
   596, 597, 630, 636, 640, 642, 661
Federal Trade Commission v. Kellogg et al.
   (1982), 368
*Federal Trade Commission v. Procter and
   Gamble Company* (1967), 611
Fee, C.E., 533
Fehr, E.,
Fernando, C.S., 397
Fielder, J.H., 578
Fillion, R., 619
Finitely repeated game, 88, 89, 300,
   307, 308

Firm
   boundaries, 43, 46–48
   demand, 25–51
   goals or motives, 43–46
   ownership, 45
   size, 7, 8, 47, 183
   theory of the firm, 25–51
First to file policy, 236, 608
First-degree price discrimination, 381–384, 416
First-mover advantage, 290, 297, 307, 350, 719
Fisher, A.A., 616
Fisher, F.M., 316, 317
Fisher, I., 6, 254
Fixed-proportion technology *See* Technology
Fizel, J.L., 655, 657
Fluet, C., 427
Focal point, 61, 62, 79
Focarelli, D., 535
Folk theorem, 322
Fonda, D.,
Food and Drug Administration (FDA), 16,
   620, 631
Ford, 49, 80, 87–90, 100, 123, 177, 184, 185,
   283, 299, 343, 360, 469, 538, 539,
   578, 580, 663, 664, 666, 704
Ford, H., 360
Foreclosure, 548–549
Fort, R., 606, 607, 655
Fox, C.R., 110
Fraas, A.G., 230
Framing effects
   and advertising, 106
   and libertarian paternalism, 632–634
Franchise, government, 146, 195
Frank, R.H., 27, 44, 61, 123, 145, 335, 661
Frantz, R.S., 573
Frech, H.E.III, 549
Frederick, S., 111
Free entry, 129, 143, 158, 159, 327, 509, 721
Free rider problem, 139, 440, 461, 478,
   541, 606
Free trials, 415–416, 418, 421
Friedlaender, A.F., 318
Friedland, C., 622
Friedman, D., 30
Friedman, J.W., 90, 227, 322
Friedman, M., 12
Friedrichs, D.O., 578
Froeb, L., 632
Fudenberg, D., 12, 305
Functional demand, 35, 36, 49, 52, 702
Fundamental principle of collusion, 228, 238,
   301, 308

P

Pabst Brewing, 371, 577, 610, 612, 648

Pakes, A., 321, 512

Paletta, D., 621

Palmeri, C.,

Panasonic, 487

Panzar, J.C., 43, 135, 138, 194, 196, 319, 570, 628

Pappalardo, J.K., 615

Paramount Pictures, 557

Pareto optimality, 61

Pareto-coordination game, 61, 62, 64, 75, 76

Participation constraint, 129, 141, 449, 709

Partnership, 15, 43, 50, 597

Pate, R.H., 236, 608

Patent(s)
    disclosure, 111, 478
    and incentives, 497, 516
    race, 508, 509, 513, 516, 735
    versus trade secret, 498, 515, 518

Patent and Trademark Office, 486, 487, 495

Patent race, 508, 509, 516, 735

Paul, I., 393

Payoff matrix, 60–65, 67, 69, 71, 77, 96, 98, 222, 274, 275, 446, 645, 653, 741

PCM *See* Price–cost margin (PCM)

Peak-load pricing, 392, 397, 419

Pecuniary economies, 529

Peltzman, S., 188, 598, 623, 629, 630

Pension Protection Act (2006), 633, 643

Pepsi, 21, 29, 116, 164, 185, 299, 323, 324, 338, 432, 450, 456, 457

Per se violation, 600, 603

Perceived or subjective product differentiation, 164, 174

Perfect cartel, 216, 229, 232, 234, 235, 237, 241, 311, 314, 322, 327, 332, 714

Perfect competition
    and advertisingv, 439–440,
    assumptions, 123–124, 140, 158
    and welfare, 134–138,

Perfect information, 58, 79–87, 91, 93, 96, 103, 439

Perfect price discrimination, 381–385, 391, 399, 411, 416, 417, 420, 624, 726

Perloff, J.M., 9, 158, 317, 318, 321, 322, 524

Perry, M.K., 551

Perry, W., 232

Persuasive advertising, 110, 429–430, 433, 434, 452, 459, 471, 478, 481, 728

Peters, E., 658

Peterson, B.C., 329

Petty, R.D., 406, 579

Pfaffermayr, M., 573

Pfleiderer, P., 319

Pharmaceutical industry *See* Drug industry

Philadelphia, D.,

Philip Morris, 552, 554, 651, 658

Phillips, A., 7

Philosophy of law, 589–591, 644, 739

Picone, G., 481, 651

Pigou, A.C., 624

Pindyck, R.S., 27, 28, 37, 44, 61, 123, 136, 145, 219, 315, 335, 337, 388

Pitofsky, R., 9, 10, 579, 599, 617, 638, 652

PlaBann, H., 431

Planned obsolescence *See* Obsolescence, planned

Plassman, H., 110, 111, 431, 479

Plott, C.R., 13

Polasky, S., 450, 456

Poldrack, R.A., 110

Political liberalism, 590, 739

Pollay, R.W., 639, 652, 653

Pollitt, M., 536

Pontiac, 663, 665

Porter, M.E., 458

Porter, R.H., 230, 321, 322, 404, 621

Posner, R., 617

Poundstone, W.,

Prager, R.A., 535

Prasnikar, V., 86

Predatory pricing, 146, 195, 197, 405, 599

Preemption race, 330, 458, 648

Prelec, D., 103, 109, 110, 114, 412

Present value, 44, 45, 53–54, 89, 112, 113, 227, 301, 303, 310, 336, 337, 504, 513, 526, 682, 704, 720

Prestige effect, 116

Preston, I.L., 431

Price(s)
    and advertising, 478, 480
    limit, 197, 204, 205, 224
    market structure and, 178–180, 185, 195, 197, 200, 206
    non-linear (*see* Price discrimination)
    predatory (*see* Predatory pricing)
    ramsey (*see* Ramsey pricing)
    transfer, 525, 550
    trigger, 227, 230, 301

Price cap regulation, 627, 628, 642

Price discounts *See* Discounts

Price discrimination
    and antitrust, 596, 599, 621, 624, 640
    and arbitrage, 48, 51, 380–381, 550
    First degree (perfect), 381–384, 416

Printed by Publishers' Graphics LLC
SO20130228.19.18.9